Frommer's®
Australia

My Australia

by Lee Mylne
photo captions by Lee Mylne & Marc Llewellyn

HOW TO SUM UP AUSTRALIA IN JUST A FEW WORDS? IMPOSSIBLE. How to nominate a favorite place? Equally difficult. The only thing I can say with certainty is that preconceptions of this vast continent and the people who call it home are sure to be challenged once you get here.

Australians are a mixed bunch; for more than two hundred years, people have come from all over the world to settle here. I'm one of those people and although I may have lived in and visited more places than most native Australians, I still find something new and surprising every time I travel in this country. If I had to choose, Melbourne—with its European style, unpredictable weather and rattling green trams—is my pick (sorry, Sydney). But my other love is the dusty red earth of the Outback. It's harsh and bright, and unlike any other place. Everyone should experience the brooding, mystical presence of Uluru (Ayers Rock) at least once.

Whatever you're looking for—beaches, rainforest, desert, mountains, smart cities, quiet country towns, or outdoor adventure, you'll find it somewhere in Australia.

The pictures in the following pages showcase this diverse, unique country at its best.

I'm always bowled over when I see the **SYDNEY OPERA HOUSE (left)** with the Harbour Bridge behind it. It must be one of the most impressive sights in the world. This particular view is taken from Mrs. Macquarie's Chair, in the Royal Botanic Gardens.

When the sun is shining (and it almost always is here), the colors of the **GREAT BARRIER REEF (above)** are beyond belief. Snorkelers on the day cruise boats may feel crowded in their commercial reef enclosures, but divers can get away from it all and commune with the deep . . . reef sharks, turtles, rays and a myriad of tiny vivid fish. It's no wonder the boats take hundreds of people each day and they all come back longing for more.

© Jack Sullivan/Alamy

CLIMBING AYERS ROCK (left) is frowned upon by the Aboriginal guardians of Uluru (its Aboriginal name), but tourists do it every day. It's easy to see why local Aborigines refer to these intruders as *minga*—or little ants. Watching the sun go down on **ULURU (right)**, is one of the most magical experiences I've had in Australia. The colors turn from pink, to orange, to purple and red—it's like one giant rocky sunset in itself. They've come a long way from a basement in Kuranda in 1987, and there's no looking back for the **TJAPUKAI DANCERS (below)**. Now a much slicker, sophisticated show, the Tjapukai Aboriginal Cultural Park on the outskirts of Cairns is more theme park than theater, but still one of the best opportunities many visitors will have to meet and talk to Aborigines in Queensland. No, you've not been abducted by aliens. You're in northern Australia, where the land is an ocher moonscape and the insects are building towers. Litchfield National Park, a day trip from Darwin, is home to these amazing **TERMITE MOUNDS (below right)**. Spookily, they are all aligned with each other and on a north-south axis.

© Dave Levitt/Lonely Planet Images

© Pete Turner/Getty Images

© Gisela Damm/eStock Photo

© Glen Allison/AGE Fotostock

Walk on this side of the Brisbane River for the best views of the city. Once derelict, the land under Kangaroo Point cliffs is now one of my favorite Brisbane parks. Walk from South Bank Parklands to the Story Bridge, and you'll find sculptures like these **RED GYMNASTS (above)**, families picnicking, bikes whizzing by . . . and watch out for those inline skaters!

The annual **SYDNEY GAY AND LESBIAN MARDI GRAS (right)** is a huge event and I've lost count of the times I've stood on milk crates to watch the procession swing by. It's all color and sequins, and fun for all the family.

Opposite page: © Jeff Yates/Lonely Planet Images

© Greg Elms/Lonely Planet Images

A day out at cricket—with a rulebook in hand—is one of the quintessential Aussie experiences. The sound of leather against willow, the roar of the crowd as a ball's hit for six, the sun beating down on the **MELBOURNE CRICKET GROUND (MCG).** They also play Australian Rules football here before packed houses.

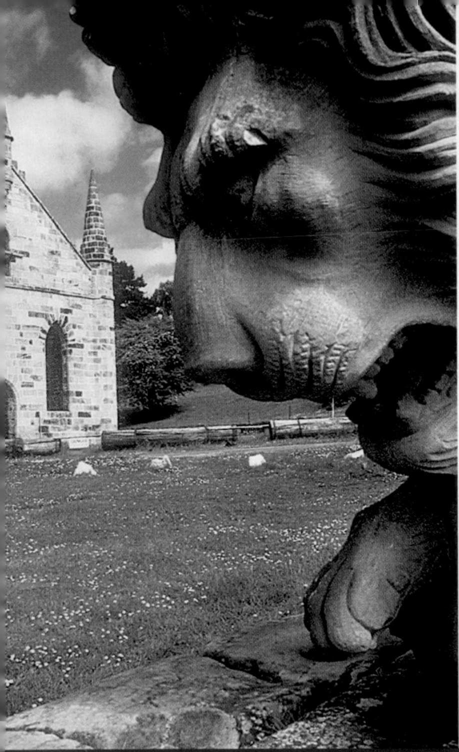

© Sean Davey/Australian Picture Library/Corbis

Tasmania's so beautiful that you might never know it once hosted one of the harshest penal colonies in the old British Empire. I'm always struck by **PORT ARTHUR**'s **(left)** peacefulness when I visit, despite the horrors that the convicts endured. **KANGAROO ISLAND (below),** in South Australia, is my favorite place to spot native animals. It's not all seals and koalas though, as these weather-shaped rocks attest. Aboriginal **ROCK ART (right)** is a reminder of how ancient this culture is. Aboriginal legends and Creation stories are told in these simple outlines, so if you can take a guide who can explain the meanings, do so. Because it is so stunning in its beauty and its wildlife, I fell in love with **HERON ISLAND (below right)** more than a decade ago. It is one of my favorite places in the world for its laid-back style, away-from-the-world on the edge of the Continental shelf. The gently sighing, weeping turtles lay their eggs starting in November and in February their tiny hatchlings scuttle across the sand to start a life that will eventually—if they survive—bring them home again.

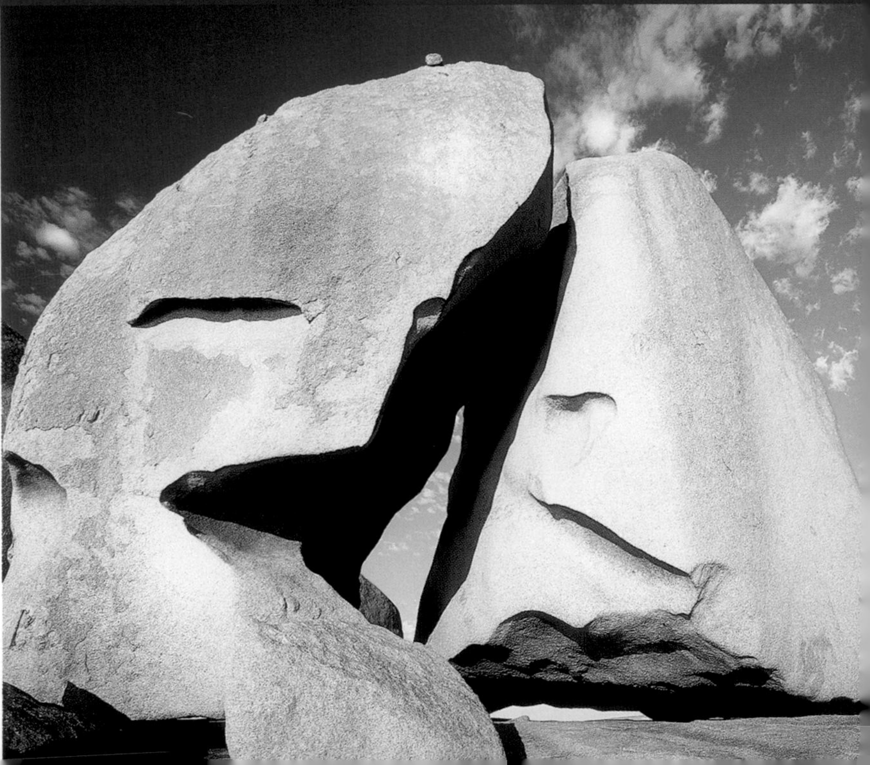

© Richard I'Anson/Lonely Planet Images

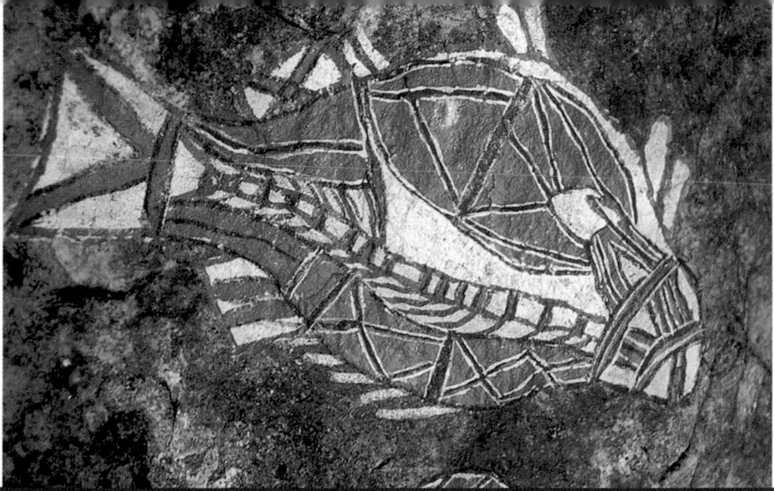

© Charles & Josette Lenars/Corbis

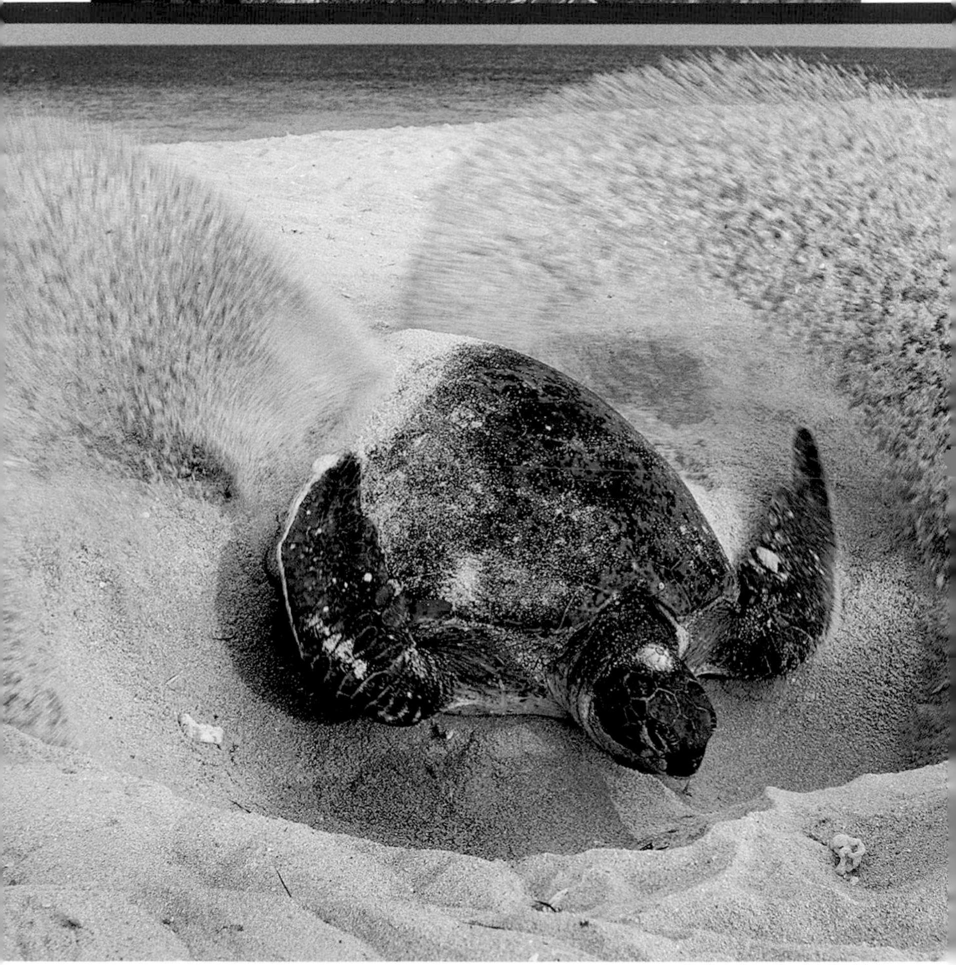

© Cousteau Society/Getty Images

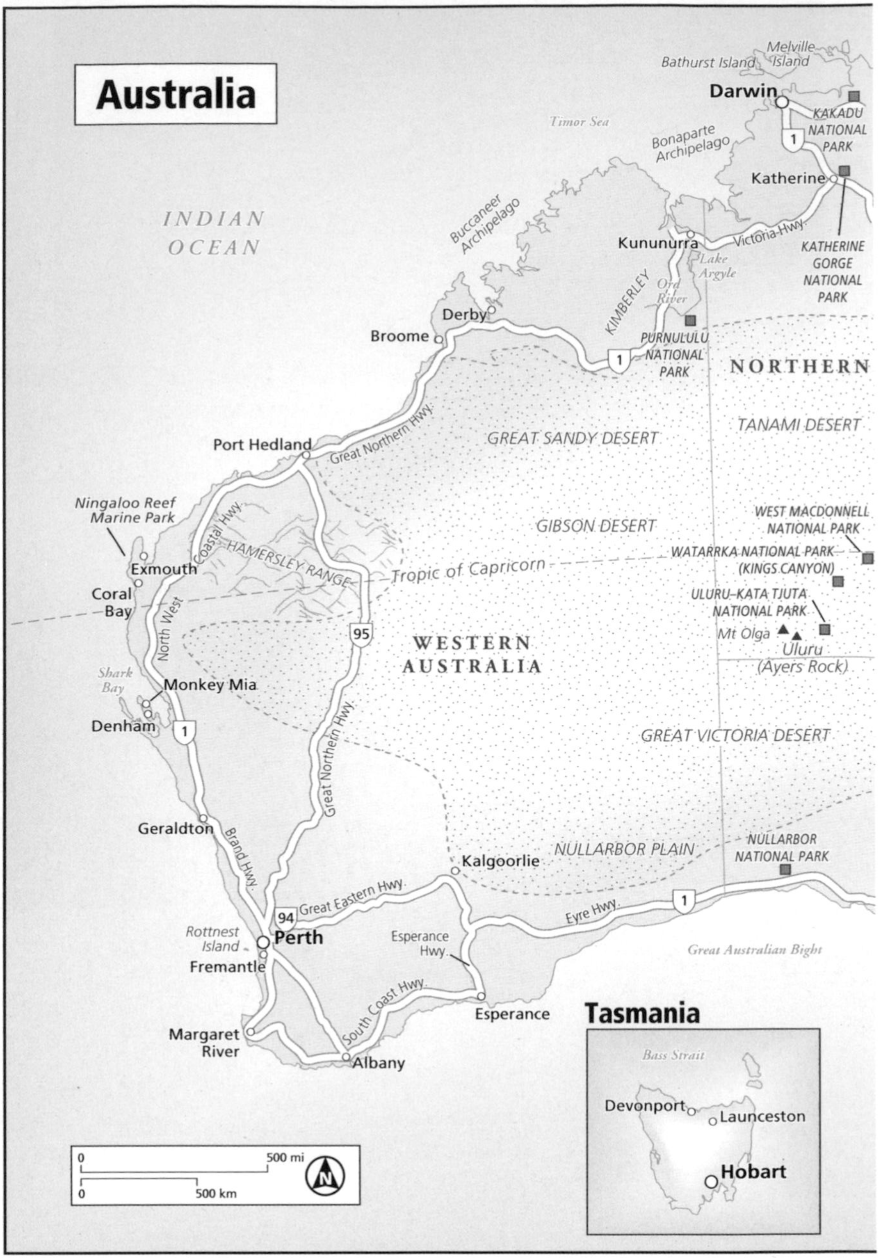
Australia
Melville Island
Bathurst Island
Darwin
Timor Sea
KAKADU NATIONAL PARK
Bonaparte Archipelago
Katherine
INDIAN OCEAN
Buccaneer Archipelago
Kununurra
Victoria Hwy.
KATHERINE GORGE NATIONAL PARK
Lake Argyle
Ord River
KIMBERLEY
Derby
Broome
PURNULULU NATIONAL PARK
NORTHERN
TANAMI DESERT
GREAT SANDY DESERT
Port Hedland
Great Northern Hwy.
Ningaloo Reef Marine Park
Coastal Hwy.
GIBSON DESERT
WEST MACDONNELL NATIONAL PARK
HAMERSLEY RANGE
WATARRKA NATIONAL PARK (KINGS CANYON)
Exmouth
Tropic of Capricorn
Coral Bay
ULURU–KATA TJUTA NATIONAL PARK
North West
Mt Olga
Uluru (Ayers Rock)
WESTERN AUSTRALIA
Shark Bay
Monkey Mia
Denham
GREAT VICTORIA DESERT
Great Northern Hwy.
Geraldton
Brand Hwy.
NULLARBOR PLAIN
NULLARBOR NATIONAL PARK
Kalgoorlie
Great Eastern Hwy.
Eyre Hwy.
Rottnest Island
Perth
Fremantle
Esperance Hwy.
Great Australian Bight
South Coast Hwy.
Esperance
Margaret River
Albany
Tasmania
Bass Strait
Devonport
Launceston
Hobart
0
500 mi
0
500 km
N

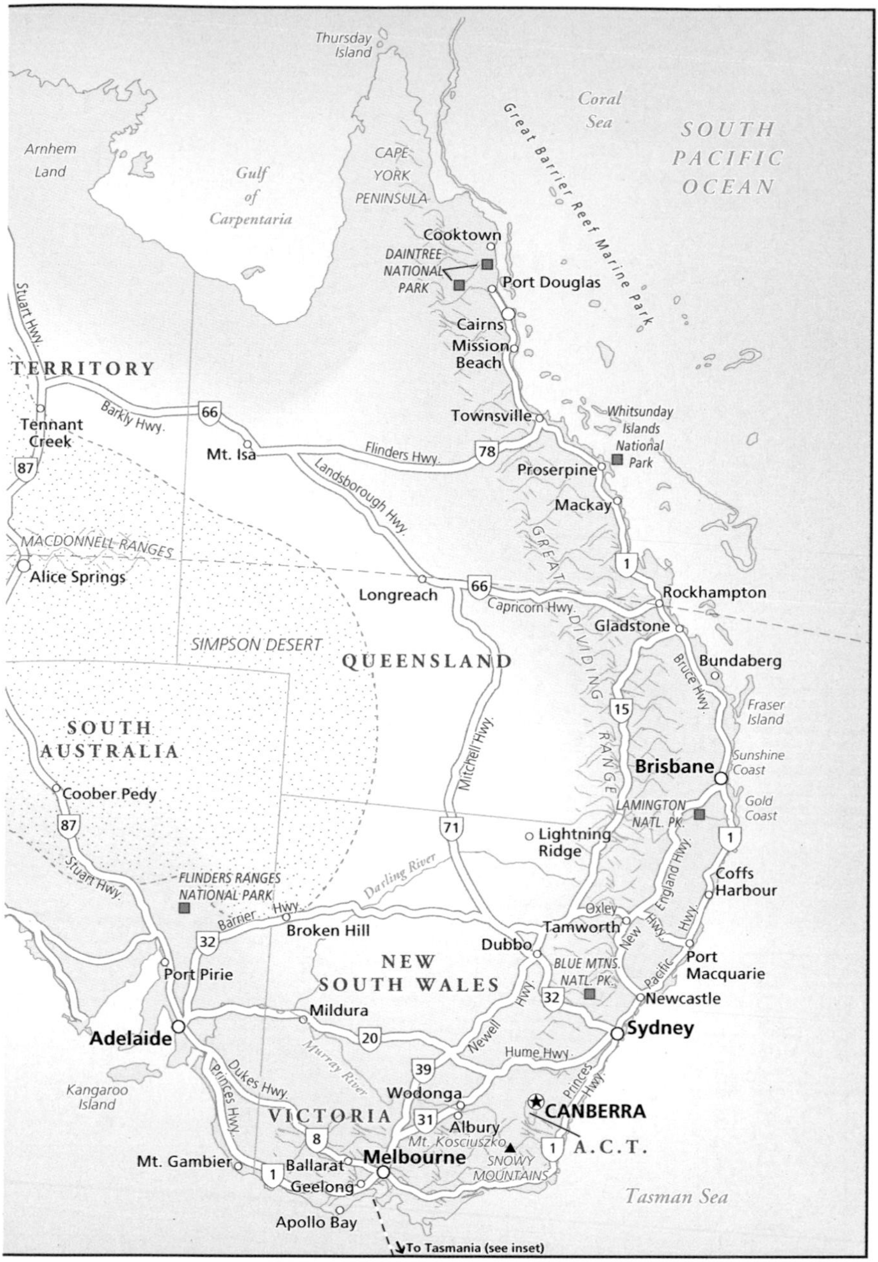
Thursday Island
Coral Sea
SOUTH PACIFIC OCEAN
Great Barrier Reef Marine Park
Arnhem Land
Gulf of Carpentaria
CAPE YORK PENINSULA
Cooktown
DAINTREE NATIONAL PARK
Port Douglas
Cairns
Mission Beach
TERRITORY
Stuart Hwy.
Tennant Creek
87
Barkly Hwy.
66
Mt. Isa
Flinders Hwy.
78
Townsville
Whitsunday Islands National Park
Proserpine
Landsborough Hwy.
Mackay
MACDONNELL RANGES
Alice Springs
GREAT DIVIDING RANGE
1
Longreach
66
Capricorn Hwy.
Rockhampton
Gladstone
SIMPSON DESERT
QUEENSLAND
Bundaberg
Bruce Hwy.
15
Fraser Island
SOUTH AUSTRALIA
Mitchell Hwy.
Brisbane
Sunshine Coast
Coober Pedy
LAMINGTON NATL. PK.
Gold Coast
87
71
Lightning Ridge
1
Stuart Hwy.
Darling River
FLINDERS RANGES NATIONAL PARK
England Hwy.
Coffs Harbour
Barrier Hwy.
Broken Hill
Oxley
Tamworth
New Hwy.
Hwy.
32
Dubbo
Port Pirie
NEW SOUTH WALES
BLUE MTNS. NATL. PK.
Pacific
Port Macquarie
Newell Hwy.
32
Newcastle
Mildura
Adelaide
20
Sydney
Murray River
Hume Hwy.
Dukes Hwy.
39
Princes Hwy.
Kangaroo Island
Princes Hwy.
Wodonga
CANBERRA
VICTORIA
31
Albury
8
Mt. Kosciuszko
1
A.C.T.
Mt. Gambier
1
Ballarat
Melbourne
SNOWY MOUNTAINS
Geelong
Tasman Sea
Apollo Bay
To Tasmania (see inset)

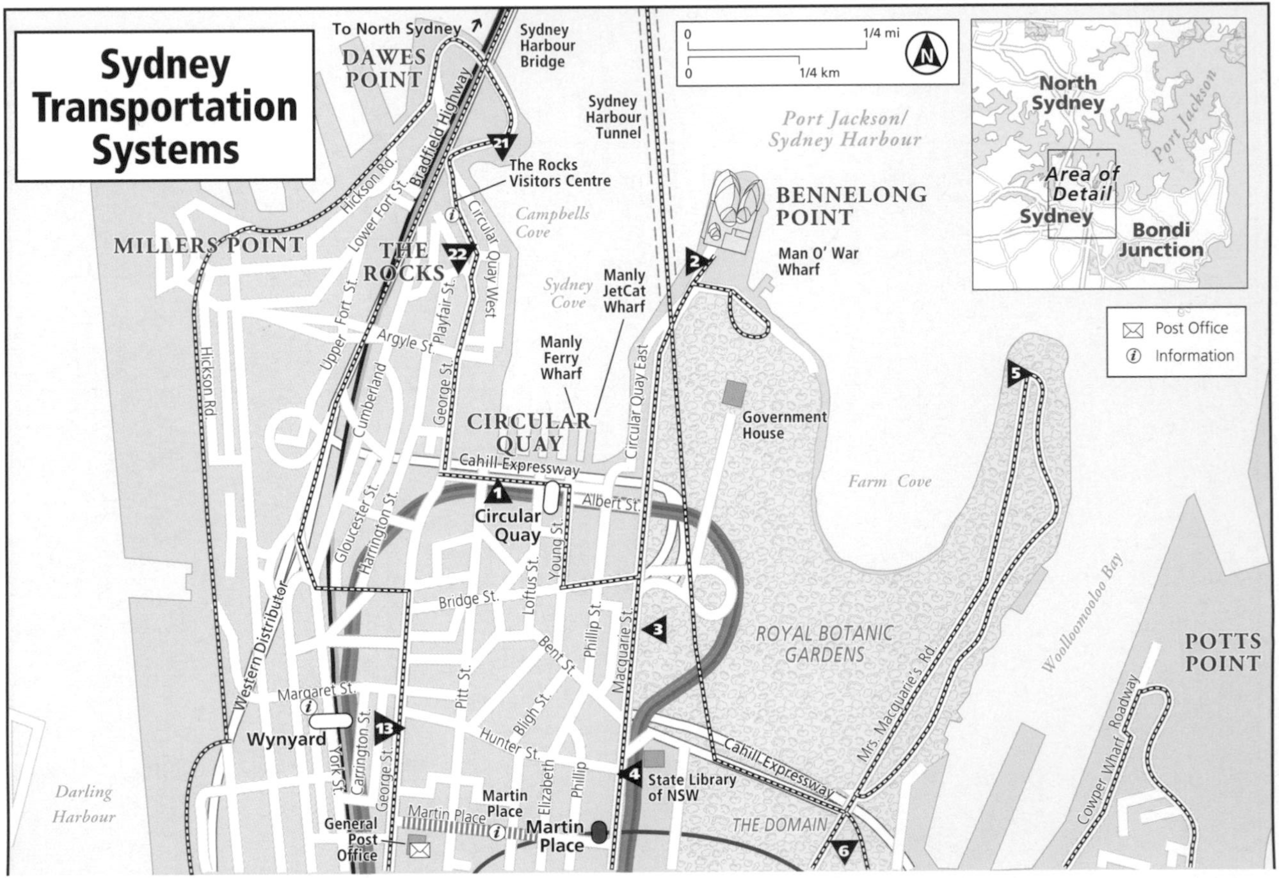
Sydney Transportation Systems
To North Sydney
Sydney Harbour Bridge
Sydney Harbour Tunnel
DAWES POINT
MILLERS POINT
THE ROCKS
The Rocks Visitors Centre
Campbells Cove
Sydney Cove
Manly JetCat Wharf
Manly Ferry Wharf
CIRCULAR QUAY
Circular Quay
Port Jackson/ Sydney Harbour
BENNELONG POINT
Man O' War Wharf
Government House
Farm Cove
ROYAL BOTANIC GARDENS
THE DOMAIN
Woolloomooloo Bay
POTTS POINT
State Library of NSW
Martin Place
General Post Office
Wynyard
Darling Harbour
Hickson Rd.
Lower Fort St.
Upper Fort St.
Bradfield Highway
Argyle St.
Playfair St.
Circular Quay West
George St.
Cumberland
Gloucester St.
Harrington St.
Cahill-Expressway
Albert St.
Young St.
Loftus St.
Bridge St.
Phillip St.
Macquarie St.
Circular Quay East
Bent St.
Bligh St.
Hunter St.
Pitt St.
Elizabeth
Phillip
Margaret St.
Carrington St.
York St.
Western Distributor
Mrs. Macquarie's Rd.
Cowper Wharf Roadway
Cahill Expressway
0
1/4 mi
1/4 km
N
North Sydney
Port Jackson
Area of Detail
Sydney
Bondi Junction
Post Office
Information
1
2
3
4
5
6
13
21
22

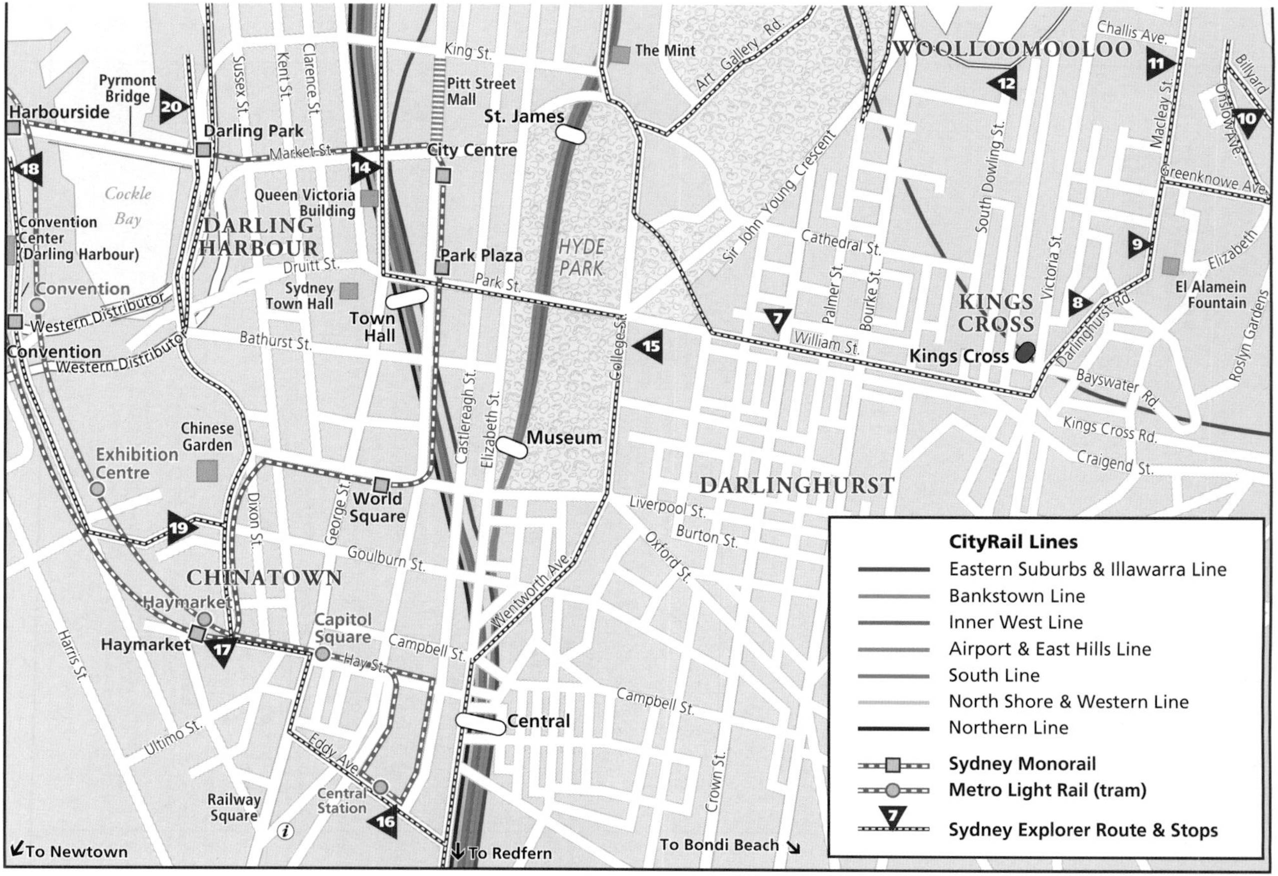

WOOLLOOMOOLOO
KINGS CROSS
DARLING HARBOUR
HYDE PARK
DARLINGHURST
CHINATOWN
Challis Ave.
Billyard
Onslow Ave.
Macleay St.
Greenknowe Ave.
Elizabeth
El Alamein Fountain
Roslyn Gardens
Darlinghurst Rd.
Bayswater Rd.
Kings Cross Rd.
Craigend St.
Victoria St.
South Dowling St.
Kings Cross
Cathedral St.
Palmer St.
Bourke St.
William St.
Sir John Young Crescent
Art Gallery Rd.
The Mint
King St.
Pitt Street Mall
St. James
City Centre
Park Plaza
Park St.
College St.
Museum
Elizabeth St.
Castlereagh St.
Liverpool St.
Burton St.
Oxford St.
Crown St.
Campbell St.
Wentworth Ave.
Central
Town Hall
Sydney Town Hall
Queen Victoria Building
Druitt St.
Bathurst St.
World Square
George St.
Goulburn St.
Dixon St.
Capitol Square
Hay St.
Eddy Ave.
Central Station
Railway Square
Ultimo St.
Harris St.
Haymarket
Chinese Garden
Exhibition Centre
Convention
Western Distributor
Convention Center (Darling Harbour)
Cockle Bay
Harbourside
Pymont Bridge
Darling Park
Market St.
Sussex St.
Kent St.
Clarence St.
To Newtown
To Redfern
To Bondi Beach
CityRail Lines
Eastern Suburbs & Illawarra Line
Bankstown Line
Inner West Line
Airport & East Hills Line
South Line
North Shore & Western Line
Northern Line
Sydney Monorail
Metro Light Rail (tram)
Sydney Explorer Route & Stops

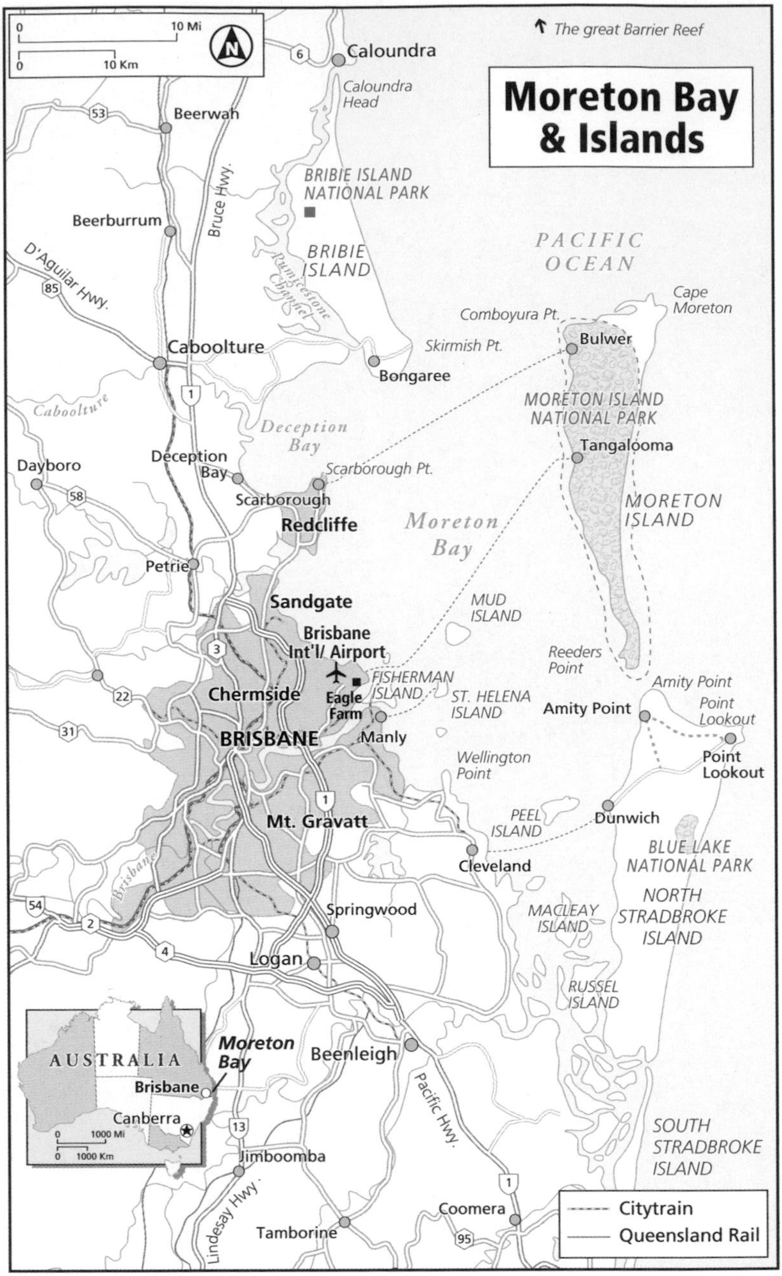

Moreton Bay & Islands
0
10 Mi
0
10 Km
The great Barrier Reef
Caloundra
Caloundra Head
Beerwah
BRIBIE ISLAND NATIONAL PARK
Bruce Hwy.
Beerburrum
D'Aguilar Hwy.
BRIBIE ISLAND
Pumicestone Channel
PACIFIC OCEAN
Cape Moreton
Comboyura Pt.
Bulwer
Skirmish Pt.
Caboolture
Bongaree
Caboolture
MORETON ISLAND NATIONAL PARK
Deception Bay
Tangalooma
Dayboro
Deception Bay
Scarborough Pt.
Scarborough
Redcliffe
Moreton Bay
MORETON ISLAND
Petrie
Sandgate
MUD ISLAND
Brisbane Int'l/ Airport
Reeders Point
Chermside
Eagle Farm
FISHERMAN ISLAND
ST. HELENA ISLAND
Amity Point
Amity Point
Point Lookout
Point Lookout
BRISBANE
Manly
Wellington Point
Mt. Gravatt
PEEL ISLAND
Dunwich
Cleveland
BLUE LAKE NATIONAL PARK
Brisbane
NORTH STRADBROKE ISLAND
MACLEAY ISLAND
Springwood
Logan
RUSSEL ISLAND
AUSTRALIA
Moreton Bay
Beenleigh
Brisbane
Canberra
0 1000 Mi
0 1000 Km
Pacific Hwy.
SOUTH STRADBROKE ISLAND
Jimboomba
Lindesay Hwy.
Coomera
Tamborine
Citytrain
Queensland Rail

The Great Barrier Reef
Submerged Reefs
0 100 mi
0 100 km
N
Great Barrier Reef
AUSTRALIA
Sydney
Canberra
0 1000 Mi
0 1000 Km
Torres Strait
Cape York
Weipa
Lizard Is.
Coral Sea
PACIFIC OCEAN
GREAT BARRIER REEF MARINE PARK
Cooktown
Daintree Natonial Park
Green Is.
Port Douglas
Cairns
Fitzroy Is.
Mission Beach
Tully
Dunk Is.
Bedarra Is.
Cardwell
Orpheus Is.
1
Magnetic Is.
Townsville
Ayr
Charters Towers
Airlie Beach
Proserpine
Whitsunday Islands
Flinders Hwy.
78
GREAT DIVIDING RANGE
Mackay
Bruce Hwy.
Yeppoon
Great Keppel Is.
Tropic of Capricorn
Longreach
Rockhampton
Landsborough Hwy.
66
Heron Is.
Gladstone
Lady Elliot Is.
QUEENSLAND
Bundaberg
Fraser Is.
Hervey Bay
Maryborough
Noosa
Sunshine Coast
Charleville
54
Caloundra
71
Dalby
Brisbane
Ipswich
Toowoomba
Gold Coast
Surfers Paradise
Lamington Natonial Park
Coolangatta

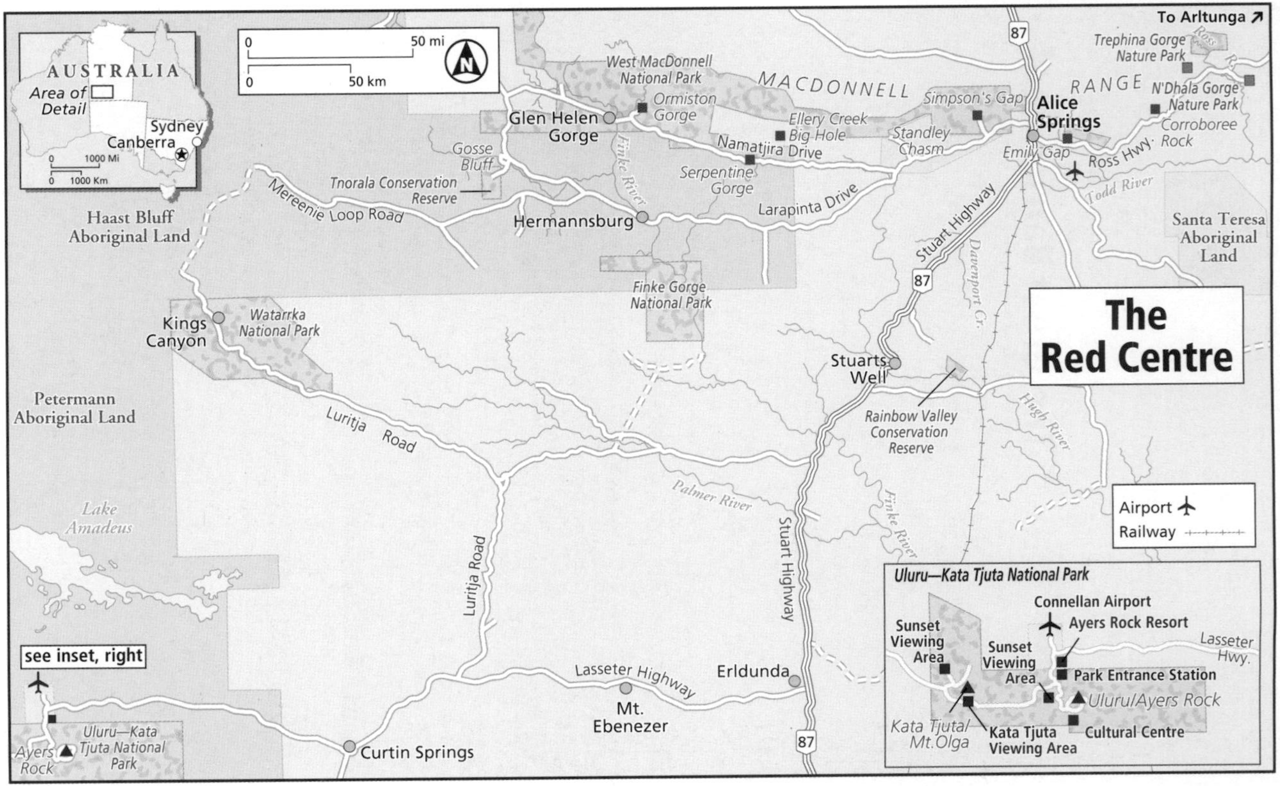

The Red Centre
To Arltunga
AUSTRALIA
Area of Detail
Sydney
Canberra
0 1000 Mi
0 1000 Km
0 50 mi
0 50 km
N
Airport
Railway
West MacDonnell National Park
MACDONNELL RANGE
Glen Helen Gorge
Ormiston Gorge
Ellery Creek Big Hole
Namatjira Drive
Simpson's Gap
Standley Chasm
Alice Springs
Emily Gap
Ross Hwy.
Todd River
Corroboree Rock
N'Dhala Gorge Nature Park
Trephina Gorge Nature Park
Ross R.
Santa Teresa Aboriginal Land
Gosse Bluff
Tnorala Conservation Reserve
Finke River
Serpentine Gorge
Larapinta Drive
Hermannsburg
Mereenie Loop Road
Haast Bluff Aboriginal Land
Stuart Highway
87
Davenport Cr.
Finke Gorge National Park
Kings Canyon
Watarrka National Park
Stuarts Well
Rainbow Valley Conservation Reserve
Hugh River
Petermann Aboriginal Land
Luritja Road
Palmer River
Lake Amadeus
see inset, right
Uluru—Kata Tjuta National Park
Ayers Rock
Lasseter Highway
Erldunda
Mt. Ebenezer
Curtin Springs
Uluru—Kata Tjuta National Park
Connellan Airport
Ayers Rock Resort
Lasseter Hwy.
Sunset Viewing Area
Sunset Viewing Area
Park Entrance Station
Uluru/Ayers Rock
Kata Tjuta/Mt.Olga
Kata Tjuta Viewing Area
Cultural Centre

Frommer's®

Australia 2008

by Ron Crittall, Marc Llewellyn
& Lee Mylne

Here's what the critics say about Frommer's:

"A major publishing challenge for any travel guide is keeping it up to date, and when travelers pick up one on a destination as big as Australia, they want to know that what the writers are giving them is accurate . . . Australian-based writers, including Brisbane-based Lee Mylne, are on the ball."

—*Courier Mail*

"Detailed, accurate, and easy-to-read information for all price ranges."

—*Glamour Magazine*

"Hotel information is close to encyclopedic."

—*Des Moines Sunday Register*

"Frommer's Guides have a way of giving you a real feel for a place."

—*Knight Ridder Newspapers*

BICENTENNIAL 1807 WILEY 2007 BICENTENNIAL

Wiley Publishing, Inc.

Published by:

Wiley Publishing, Inc.

111 River St.
Hoboken, NJ 07030-5774

ISBN 978-0-470-16536-2

Editor: Kathleen Warnock
Production Editor: Eric T. Schroeder
Cartographer: Andrew Murphy
Photo Editor: Richard Fox
Anniversary Logo Design: Richard Pacifico
Production by Wiley Indianapolis Composition Services

Front cover photo: Mungo National Park: "The Walls of China"
Back cover photo: Close-up of a koala.

For information on our other products and services or to obtain technical support, please contact our Customer Care Department within the U.S. at 800/762-2974, outside the U.S. at 317/572-3993 or fax 317/572-4002.

Wiley also publishes its books in a variety of electronic formats. Some content that appears in print may not be available in electronic formats.

Manufactured in the United States of America

5 4 3 2 1

Contents

3 Suggested Itineraries 88

by Ron Crittall, Marc Llewellyn & Lee Mylne

4 Sydney 102

by Marc Llewellyn

5 New South Wales 197

by Marc Llewellyn

6 Brisbane 249

by Lee Mylne

7 Queensland & the Great Barrier Reef 279

by Lee Mylne

8 The Red Centre 392

by Marc Llewellyn

9 The Top End 423

by Lee Mylne

10 Perth & Western Australia 452

by Ron Crittall

11 Adelaide & South Australia 532

by Marc Llewellyn

12 Melbourne 577

by Lee Mylne

13 Victoria 624

by Lee Mylne

14 Canberra 646

by Marc Llewellyn

15 Tasmania 662

by Marc Llewellyn

Appendix: Australia in Depth 694

by Marc Llewellyn

Index 703

List of Maps

An Invitation to the Reader

In researching this book, we discovered many wonderful places—hotels, restaurants, shops, and more. We're sure you'll find others. Please tell us about them, so we can share the information with your fellow travelers in upcoming editions. If you were disappointed with a recommendation, we'd love to know that, too. Please write to:

Frommer's Australia 2008
Wiley Publishing, Inc. • 111 River St. • Hoboken, NJ 07030-5774

An Additional Note

Please be advised that travel information is subject to change at any time—and this is especially true of prices. We therefore suggest that you write or call ahead for confirmation when making your travel plans. The authors, editors, and publisher cannot be held responsible for the experiences of readers while traveling. Your safety is important to us, however, so we encourage you to stay alert and be aware of your surroundings. Keep a close eye on cameras, purses, and wallets, all favorite targets of thieves and pickpockets.

About the Authors

Ron Crittall was on a long slow loop around the world when he arrived in Perth for a possible two-year stay. 35 years on he knows there's nowhere better to live. A travel writer for 15 years, he loves traveling round, and writing about, the vast expanse of Western Australia. He is the author of *Walking Perth.*

Sydney resident **Marc Llewellyn** is one of Australia's premier travel writers and the winner of several writing awards. He is the President of the Australian Society of Travel Writers. He's written two travelogues, *Riders to the Midnight Sun,* which tells of his journey from the Ukrainian Black Sea to the Russian Arctic on a cheap bicycle. His latest manuscript, with the working title *Islands of the Winds,* tells the story of a year working as a peasant farmer and shrimp fisherman on an island off Sicily. He is the co-author of the forthcoming first edition of *Australia For Dummies.*

Lee Mylne is Melbourne based but writes for a range of consumer and travel trade publications around Australia. Born and raised in New Zealand, she has worked in newspapers, magazines, and radio and traveled widely before she started to make a living out of it. She has lived in Australia since 1986 and is a Life Member and past president of the Australian Society of Travel Writers. Her other books include *Frommer's Portable Australia's Great Barrier Reef* and the forthcoming first edition of *Australia For Dummies.*

Frommer's Star Ratings, Icons & Abbreviations

Every hotel, restaurant, and attraction listing in this guide has been ranked for quality, value, service, amenities, and special features using a **star-rating system.** In country, state, and regional guides, we also rate towns and regions to help you narrow down your choices and budget your time accordingly. Hotels and restaurants are rated on a scale of zero (recommended) to three stars (exceptional). Attractions, shopping, nightlife, towns, and regions are rated according to the following scale: zero stars (recommended), one star (highly recommended), two stars (very highly recommended), and three stars (must-see).

In addition to the star-rating system, we also use **seven feature icons** that point you to the great deals, in-the-know advice, and unique experiences that separate travelers from tourists. Throughout the book, look for:

Finds	Special finds—those places only insiders know about
Fun Fact	Fun facts—details that make travelers more informed and their trips more fun
Kids	Best bets for kids and advice for the whole family
Moments	Special moments—those experiences that memories are made of
Overrated	Places or experiences not worth your time or money
Tips	Insider tips—great ways to save time and money
Value	Great values—where to get the best deals

The following **abbreviations** are used for credit cards:

AE	American Express	DISC	Discover	V	Visa
DC	Diners Club	MC	MasterCard		

Frommers.com

Now that you have this guidebook, to help you plan a great trip, visit our website at **www.frommers.com** for additional travel information on more than 3,600 destinations. We update features regularly, to give you instant access to the most current trip-planning information available. At Frommers.com, you'll find scoops on the best airfares, lodging rates, and car rental bargains. You can even book your travel online through our reliable travel booking partners. Other popular features include:

- Online updates of our most popular guidebooks
- Vacation sweepstakes and contest giveaways
- Newsletters highlighting the hottest travel trends
- Online travel message boards with featured travel discussions

What's New in Australia

The land Down Under continues to change in exciting ways. Travelers have new possibilities for getting to and around the country, and a greater choice of things to do once they are here. You'll find more detail in the specific chapters.

PLANNING YOUR TRIP/GETTING AROUND The past year has once again seen a number of changes in the Australian skies.

Domestic airlines **Virgin Blue** (© **13 67 89** in Australia, or 07/3295 2296; www.virginblue.com.au) and Qantas subsidiary **Jetstar** (© **13 15 38** in Australia; www.jetstar.com.au) are about to face increased competition with the arrival of Singapore-based **Tiger Airways** (www.tigerairways.com) which plans to launch domestic routes by 2008. In mid-2007, Tiger Airways began flights from Singapore to Perth and Darwin, and has announced that its Australian headquarters will be in Melbourne. At press time, few details were available, but we predict that you *will* see price wars driving down the costs of flights.

Jetstar has also entered the international market, challenging Virgin's **Pacific Blue** on the trans-Tasman route to New Zealand as well as launching flights to a number of other destinations including Honolulu.

Pacific Blue (© **13 16 45** in Australia; www.flypacificblue.com) now services a growing number of Australian cities from Auckland, Wellington, and Christchurch in New Zealand, and flies to a few Pacific islands, including Tonga, Samoa, and the Cook Islands.

For those who prefer their travel at ground level, **Great Southern Railway**'s ***Overland*** train has been refurbished and re-launched, with greater levels of comfort for its thrice-weekly daylight service between Adelaide and Melbourne. Rail travelers can also take advantage of two new rail passes from Queensland's **Traveltrain Holidays** (© **1300/131 722** in Australia, or 07/3235 1133; www.traveltrain.com.au), the Wanderer and Stopover rail passes. The **Wanderer** and **Stopover** passes provide greater flexibility for traveling the route between Brisbane and Cairns.

International visitors traveling solo and looking to meet Australians can make use of the new Sydney-based online service **Trip Mates** (www.tripmates.com.au), which will match you up with a traveling companion.

SYDNEY The year 2007 was the 75th Anniversary of the Sydney Harbour Bridge. While you've been able to clamber all over it for years now, why not try the new **Discovery Climb** experience offered by BridgeClimb (www.bridgeclimb.com). Traversing the suspension arch, you climb through the Bridge via stairs and catwalks, and wind your way through a tangle of hatchways and steel girders high above the traffic. You can even see the location where the arch was joined for the first time. Then you climb between the arches to the summit, 134m (439 ft.) above the water.

Tips **Butt Out Down Under . . .**

Smokers traveling to Australia will find greater restrictions on where they can light up. Smoking is banned or heavily restricted in most public places, such as museums, cinemas, theaters, and airports. A total ban on smoking now applies in pubs and clubs in Queensland, Western Australia, Tasmania, Victoria, the ACT, and New South Wales, with South Australia following in 2008. Only in the Northern Territory can you still light up in some areas of pubs.

The big addition to Darling Harbour is **Sydney Wildlife World** (**© 02/9333 9288;** www.sydneywildlifeworld.com.au which is next to the fabulous Sydney Aquarium. While it's not on a par with Taronga Zoo, it does showcase some interesting reptiles and insects, some smaller marsupials (as well as some that prefer to wander around at night), a few birds, and some rare wallabies. It's worth investing in a new attractions pass, which allows you discounted entry here, as well as Sydney Tower and Sydney Aquarium.

For an Aboriginal perspective on Sydney Harbour take a boat cruise on the ***Deerubbun,*** an Aboriginal-owned-and-operated vessel that sails on Sydney's famous waterway. Two-hour cruises follow the harbor around Circular Quay and beyond. Your guide outlines the history of the area, from an Aboriginal viewpoint. They recount stories and Aboriginal place names, uncover traditional fishing methods and food-gathering techniques, and point out rock carvings and old Aboriginal settlements. As part of the cruise, the boat pulls up at Clark Island in the middle of the harbor, where Aboriginal dancers put on a song-and-dance show with the famous Sydney Harbour Bridge behind. (For information, call **© 02/9699 3491;** www.tribalwarrior.org.)

Another new cruise well worth doing is a half-day exploring Port Hacking, with **Cronulla Cruises** (**© 02/9544 1400;** www.cronullacruises.com.au). This company uses a flat-bottomed "pontoon" boat that allows for great views of some of Sydney's waterside homes, as well as a look at the fringes of the Royal National Park. The cruise leaves from Cronulla, the beachside suburb in Sydney's south.

QUEENSLAND Accommodations Claiming to be the world's tallest residential building, Surfers Paradise tower **Q1** (**© 1300/792 008** in Australia, or 07/5630 4500; www.Q1.com.au) offers the best views in town—and that's really saying something. Q1 peaks at 323m (1,058 ft.) and is also home to the Q1 Observation Deck (see "Attractions," below). Each apartment-style hotel room has a luxury kitchen, dining and lounge area, and is given a daily miniservice. There's also an in-house cinema in the tower.

Fitzroy Island Resort (www.fitzroyisland.com.au), which closed in early 2006 for a A$10-million-plus (US$8-million/UK£4-million) redevelopment, had not reopened by press time. The renovation will take it upmarket, with the addition of 48 new two-bedroom apartments, a spa, bar and restaurant, dive shop, general store, conference rooms and other amenities.

Attractions The Gold Coast's newest, tallest building, Q1 (see "Accommodations," above) is a gleaming steel-and-glass tower, inspired by the Sydney 2000 Olympic torch. A super-fast elevator takes 43 seconds to reach the **Q1 Observation Deck** (**© 07/5630 4700;** www.Q1observationdeck.com.au), 230m (754 ft.) above the ground on levels 77 and 78. From there, you can gaze down on all the Gold Coast has to offer, with

360-degree views. Head up there before sunset, for a cocktail in the Skybar.

Dreamworld's new water park, **White-Water World** (© **1800/073 300** in Australia, or 07/5588 1111; www.whitewaterworld.com.au) is a A$60-million (US$48-million/UK£24-million), startlingly colorful addition to the Pacific Highway, between Brisbane and the Gold Coast. The new park has some of the most modern water slides and thrill rides in the world, and is themed around Australian surf culture. The Super Tubes HydroCoaster is a "roller coaster on water" and is one of only two in the world; the Blue Ringed Octopus (BRO) is the world's only eight-lane Octopus Racer—you get the idea? For families, there's Nickelodeon's Pipeline Plunge, a playground for kids aged 5 to 12.

BRISBANE The new **Queensland Gallery of Modern Art** has opened at South Bank next door to its sister, the **Queensland Art Gallery** (© **07/3840 7303;** www.qag.qld.gov.au), providing more space for the state's collections of modern and contemporary Australian, indigenous Australian, Asian, and Pacific art. The complex also includes the **Australian Cinémathèque,** which it presents retrospective and thematic film programs, as well as a gallery dedicated to screen-related exhibitions.

MELBOURNE If you suffer from vertigo, Melbourne's newest attraction is not for you. **Eureka Skydeck 88** (© **03/9685 0188;** www.eurekatower.com.au) is the highest public vantage point in the Southern Hemisphere, giving a 360-degree view of the city below from 285m (935 ft.) above ground in the Eureka Tower at Southbank. You can also—if you are brave—ride in a huge moving glass cube called The Edge, which moves horizontally from inside the walls of Skydeck 88, carrying 12 passengers out over the tower's east side.

Aboriginal elder Carolyn Briggs has opened an Indigenous Australian cuisine restaurant, **Tjanabi @ Fed Square** (© **03/9662 2155;** www.tjanabi.com.au), offering a menu which uses native produce including plants, fruits, and berries, matched with Australian game and fresh steaks from regional Victoria. There's a casual bistro and a bar serving Victorian wines and boutique beers, and the walls are hung with contemporary Aboriginal artworks. Tjanabi also offers guided walking tours of indigenous Melbourne, followed by dinner.

TOP END **Skycity Darwin** (© **1800/891 118** in Australia, or 08/8943 8888; www.skycitydarwin.com.au) will gain a new outdoor restaurant and bar in 2008, as well as expanded dining facilities to further increase the entertainment options on offer.

New luxury safari camp **Bamurru Plains** (© **1300/790 561** in Australia, or 02/9231 2923; www.bamurruplains.com) is set on a working buffalo station, about 3 hours drive from Darwin near Kakadu National Park. The nine permanent tents have timber floors, fine linens on the beds, and high-pressure showers in the bathroom but no phone or TV. Meals, served at the main lodge, feature crocodile, emu, and other local delicacies.

TASMANIA Five of Tasmania's key convict sites are to be included in a nomination for World Heritage Listing. They include the Port Arthur Historic Site and the Cascade Female Factory in South Hobart. The World Heritage List contains natural and cultural sites that demonstrate outstanding and continuing importance on a global scale with the objective to ensure that they are protected for future generations. There are 15 Australian sites already inscribed on the World Heritage List including the Tasmanian Wilderness and the Great Barrier Reef.

1

The Best of Australia

by Ron Crittall, Marc Llewellyn & Lee Mylne

Maybe we're biased because we live here, but Australia has a lot of bests—world bests, that is. It has some of the best natural scenery, the weirdest wildlife, the most brilliant scuba diving and snorkeling, the best beaches (shut up, California), the oldest rainforest (110 million years and counting), the oldest human civilization (some archaeologists say 40,000 years, some say 120,000; whatever—it's old), the best wines (come see what we mean), the best weather (give or take the odd Wet season in the north), the most innovative East-meets-West-meets-someplace-else cuisine—all bathed in sunlight that brings everything up in Technicolor.

"Best" means different things to different people, but scarcely a visitor lands on these shores without having the Great Barrier Reef at the top of the "Things to See" list. So they should, because it really is a glorious natural masterpiece. Also high on most folks' lists is Ayers Rock. This monolith must have some kind of magnet inside it designed to attract planeloads of tourists. We're not saying the Rock isn't special, but we think the vast Australian desert all around it is even more so. The third attraction on most visitors' lists is Sydney, the Emerald City that glitters in the antipodean sunshine on—here we go with the "bests" again—the best harbor, spanned by the best bridge in the world (yes it is, San Francisco).

But as planes zoom overhead delivering visitors to the big three attractions, Aussies in charming country towns, on far-flung beaches, on rustic sheep stations, in rainforest villages, and in mountain lodges shake their heads and say sadly, "They don't know what they're missin'." Well, that's the aim of this chapter—to show you what you're missin'. Read on, and consider taking the road less traveled.

1 The Top Travel Experiences

- **Hitting the Rails on the *Indian Pacific* Train:** This 3-day journey across the Outback regularly makes it onto travel magazines' "Top Rail Journeys in the World" lists. The desert scenery ain't all that magnificent—it's the unspoiled, empty vastness that passengers appreciate. It includes the longest straight stretch of track in the world, 478km (296 miles) across the treeless Nullarbor Plain. Start in Sydney and end in Perth, or vice versa, or just do a section. See "Getting Around Australia" in chapter 2.
- **Experiencing Sydney** (NSW): Sydney is more than just the magnificent Harbour Bridge and Opera House. No other city has beaches in such abundance, and few have such a magnificently scenic harbor. Our advice is to board a ferry, walk from one side of the bridge to the other, and try to spend a week here, because you're going to need it. See chapter 4, "Sydney."

Tips A Note on Abbreviations

In the listings below, NSW stands for New South Wales, QLD for Queensland, NT for the Northern Territory, WA for Western Australia, SA for South Australia, VIC for Victoria, TAS for Tasmania, and ACT for the Australian Capital Territory.

- **Seeing the Great Barrier Reef** (QLD): It's a glorious 2,000km-long (1,240-mile) underwater coral fairyland with electric colors and bizarre fish life—and it comes complete with warm water and year-round sunshine. This is what you came to Australia to see. When you're not snorkeling over coral and giant clams almost as big as you, scuba diving, calling at tropical towns, or lying on deserted island beaches, you'll be trying out the sun lounges or enjoying the first-rate food. See chapter 7, "Queensland & the Great Barrier Reef."
- **Exploring the Wet Tropics Rainforest** (QLD): Folks who come from skyscraper cities like Manhattan and Los Angeles can't get over the moisture-dripping ferns, the neon-blue butterflies, and the primeval peace of this World Heritage rainforest stretching north, south, and west from Cairns. Hike it, four-wheel-drive it, or glide over the treetops in the Skyrail gondola. See "Cairns" in chapter 7.
- **Bareboat Sailing in the Whitsundays** (QLD): Bareboat means unskippered—that's right, even if you think port is an after-dinner drink, you can charter a yacht, pay for a day's instruction from a skipper, and then take over the helm yourself and explore these 74 island gems. It's easy. Anchor in deserted bays, snorkel over dazzling reefs, fish for coral trout, and feel the wind in your sails. See "The Whitsunday Coast & Islands" in chapter 7.
- **Exploring Kata Tjuta (the Olgas) & Uluru (Ayers Rock)** (NT): Just why everyone comes thousands of miles to see the big red stone of Ayers Rock is a mystery, and that's why they come—because the Rock is a mystery. Just 50km (31 miles) from Ayers Rock are the round red heads of the Olgas, a second rock formation more significant to Aborigines and more intriguing to many visitors. See "Uluru–Kata Tjuta National Park (Ayers Rock/The Olgas)" in chapter 8.
- **Taking an Aboriginal Culture Tour** (Alice Springs, NT): Eating female wasps, contemplating a hill as a giant resting caterpillar, and imagining that the stars are your grandmother smiling down at you will give you a new perspective on Aboriginal culture. See what we mean on a half-day tour from the Aboriginal Art & Culture Centre. See p. 399.
- **Discovering the Kimberley** (WA): Australia's last frontier, the Kimberley is a romantic cocktail of South Sea pearls, red mountain ranges, aqua seas, deadly crocodiles, Aboriginal rock art, and million-acre farms in a never-ending wilderness. Cross it by four-wheel-drive, stay in safari tents on a cattle ranch, swim under waterfalls, ride a camel along the beach in Broome, and more. See chapter 9, "The Top End."
- **Rolling in Wildflowers** (WA): Imagine Texas three times over and covered in wildflowers. That's what much of Western Australia looks like every spring, from around August

Australia

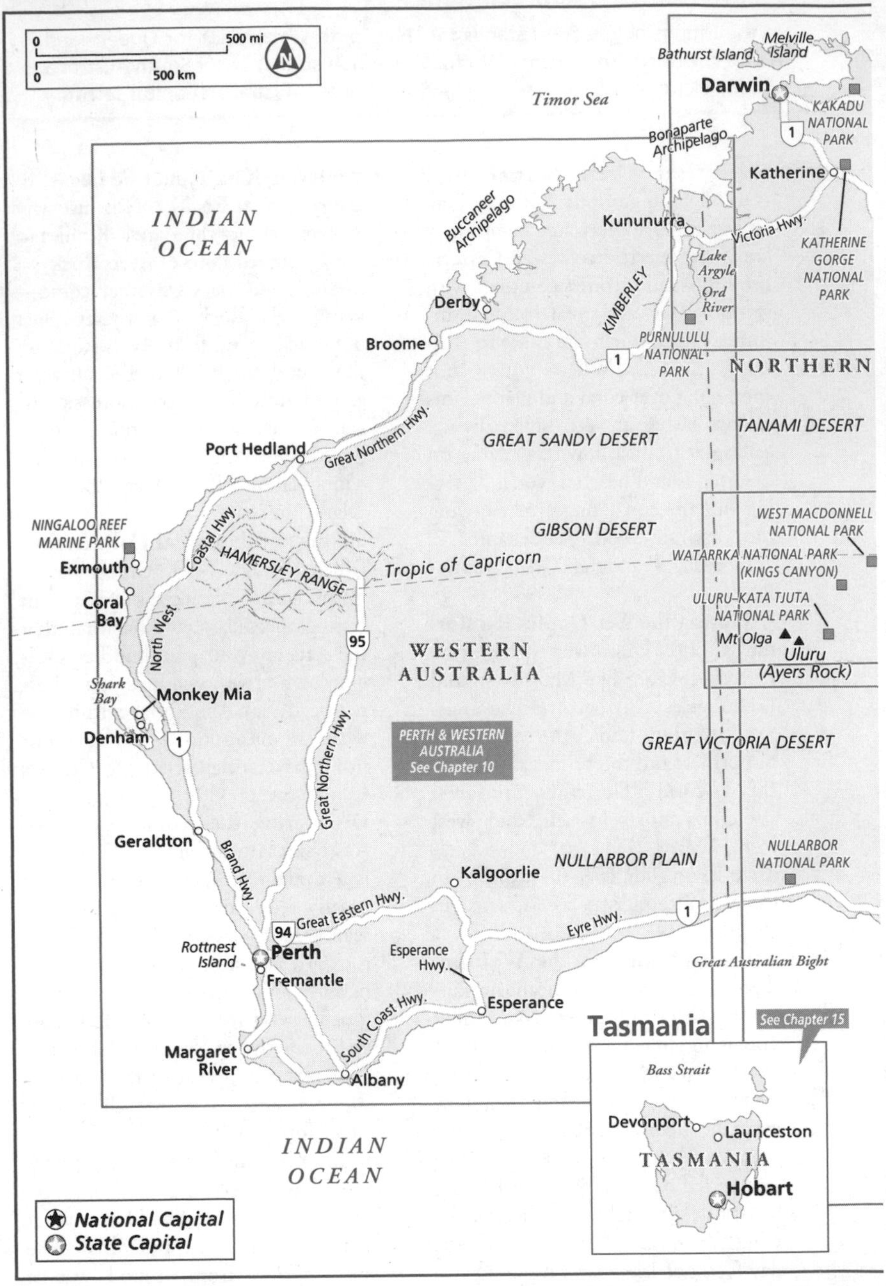
0
500 mi
0
500 km
N
Timor Sea
Melville Island
Bathurst Island
Darwin
KAKADU NATIONAL PARK
1
Bonaparte Archipelago
Katherine
KATHERINE GORGE NATIONAL PARK
INDIAN OCEAN
Buccaneer Archipelago
Kununurra
Victoria Hwy.
Lake Argyle
Ord River
KIMBERLEY
Derby
Broome
PURNULULU NATIONAL PARK
NORTHERN
TANAMI DESERT
GREAT SANDY DESERT
Port Hedland
Great Northern Hwy.
NINGALOO REEF MARINE PARK
Exmouth
Coastal Hwy.
HAMERSLEY RANGE
GIBSON DESERT
Tropic of Capricorn
WEST MACDONNELL NATIONAL PARK
WATARRKA NATIONAL PARK (KINGS CANYON)
ULURU–KATA TJUTA NATIONAL PARK
Mt Olga
Uluru (Ayers Rock)
Coral Bay
North West
95
WESTERN AUSTRALIA
Shark Bay
Monkey Mia
Denham
1
PERTH & WESTERN AUSTRALIA See Chapter 10
GREAT VICTORIA DESERT
Great Northern Hwy.
Geraldton
Brand Hwy.
NULLARBOR PLAIN
NULLARBOR NATIONAL PARK
Kalgoorlie
Great Eastern Hwy.
94
1
Eyre Hwy.
Rottnest Island
Perth
Fremantle
Esperance Hwy.
Great Australian Bight
Esperance
South Coast Hwy.
Tasmania
See Chapter 15
Margaret River
Albany
Bass Strait
Devonport
Launceston
TASMANIA
Hobart
INDIAN OCEAN
National Capital
State Capital

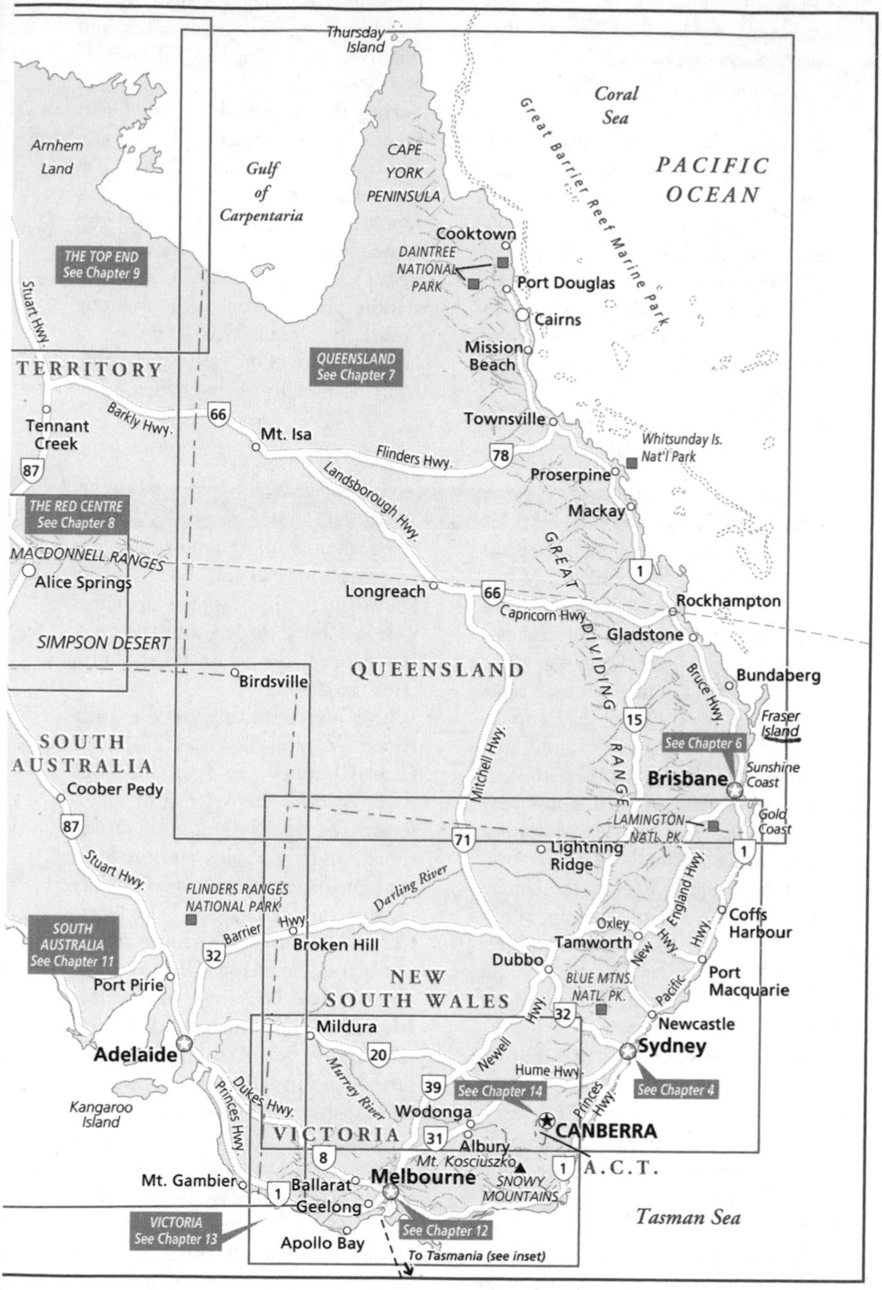
Thursday Island
Coral Sea
Great Barrier Reef Marine Park
PACIFIC OCEAN
Arnhem Land
Gulf of Carpentaria
CAPE YORK PENINSULA
Cooktown
DAINTREE NATIONAL PARK
Port Douglas
Cairns
THE TOP END See Chapter 9
Stuart Hwy.
Mission Beach
TERRITORY
QUEENSLAND See Chapter 7
Tennant Creek
Barkly Hwy.
66
Mt. Isa
Townsville
Whitsunday Is. Nat'l Park
Flinders Hwy.
78
87
Proserpine
Landsborough Hwy.
Mackay
THE RED CENTRE See Chapter 8
MACDONNELL RANGES
Alice Springs
GREAT DIVIDING RANGE
1
Longreach
66
Rockhampton
Capricorn Hwy.
Gladstone
SIMPSON DESERT
Birdsville
QUEENSLAND
Bruce Hwy.
Bundaberg
15
Fraser Island
SOUTH AUSTRALIA
See Chapter 6
Mitchell Hwy.
Brisbane
Sunshine Coast
Coober Pedy
87
LAMINGTON NATL. PK.
Gold Coast
71
Lightning Ridge
1
Stuart Hwy.
Darling River
New England Hwy.
FLINDERS RANGES NATIONAL PARK
Coffs Harbour
SOUTH AUSTRALIA See Chapter 11
Barrier Hwy
Broken Hill
Oxley Hwy.
Tamworth
New
Pacific Hwy.
32
Dubbo
Port Macquarie
Port Pirie
NEW SOUTH WALES
BLUE MTNS. NATL. PK.
Newell Hwy.
32
Newcastle
Mildura
Adelaide
20
Sydney
Hume Hwy.
Murray River
Dukes Hwy.
Princes Hwy.
39
See Chapter 14
See Chapter 4
Kangaroo Island
Wodonga
Princes Hwy.
CANBERRA
VICTORIA
31
Albury
8
Mt. Kosciuszko
1
A.C.T.
Mt. Gambier
1
Ballarat
Melbourne
SNOWY MOUNTAINS
Geelong
Tasman Sea
VICTORIA See Chapter 13
See Chapter 12
Apollo Bay
To Tasmania (see inset)

through October, when pink, mauve, red, white, yellow, and blue wildflowers bloom. Aussies flock here for this spectacle, so book ahead. See the box "Tiptoeing through the Wildflowers" in chapter 10.

- **Drinking in the Barossa Valley** (SA): One of Australia's four largest wine-producing areas, this German-speaking region less than an hour's drive from Adelaide is also the prettiest. Adelaide's restaurants happen to be some of the country's best, too, so test out your wine purchases with the city's terrific food. See "Side Trips from Adelaide" in chapter 11.
- **Getting Dusty in the Desert** (SA): Head inland from Adelaide to the Outback to visit remote pubs and settlements, the craggy ridges of the Flinders Ranges, dry salt lakes, and deserts. See chapter 11, "Adelaide & South Australia."
- **Seeing the Sights along the Great Ocean Road** (VIC): This 106km (66-mile) coastal road carries you past wild and stunning beaches, forests, and dramatic cliff-top scenery—including the Twelve Apostles, a scattering of pillars of red rock standing in isolation in the foaming Southern Ocean. See "The Great Ocean Road: One of the World's Most Scenic Drives" in chapter 13.

2 The Best Outdoor Adventures

- **Sea Kayaking:** Kayaking is a great way to explore Queensland's Whitsunday Islands as well as Dunk Island off Mission Beach in Queensland. **Rivergods (© 08/9259 0749;** www.rivergods.com.au) in Perth even takes you on a sea-kayaking day trip to snorkel with wild sea lions and watch penguins feeding. This Western Australian company also runs multiday expeditions past whales, dolphins, and sharks in Shark Bay, and over coral at Ningaloo Reef on the Northwest Cape. For details on the Whitsunday Islands and Dunk Island, see chapter 7. For information about Perth and Western Australia, see chapter 10.
- **Horse Trekking in the Snowy Mountains** (NSW): Ride the ranges like the man from Snowy River, staying in bush lodges or camping beneath the stars. See "In the Footsteps of the Man from Snowy River" in chapter 5.
- **Abseiling (Rappelling) in the Blue Mountains** (NSW): Careering backward down a cliff face with the smell of eucalyptus in your nostrils is not everyone's idea of fun, but you sure know you're alive. Several operators welcome both novices and the more experienced. See "The Blue Mountains" in chapter 5.
- **White-Water Rafting on the Tully River** (Mission Beach, QLD): The Class III to IV rapids of the Tully River swoosh between lush, rainforested banks. The guides are professional, and the rapids are just hairy enough to be fun. It's a good choice for first-time rafters. See "The North Coast: Mission Beach, Townsville & the Islands" in chapter 7.
- **Four-Wheel-Driving on Fraser Island** (QLD): Burning down 75-mile Beach in a 4×4 on the biggest sand island in the world is liberating, if not great for the environment. Paradoxically, the island is ecologically important and popular with nature lovers. Hike its eucalyptus forests and rainforests, swim its clear lakes, and fish off the beach. See "Fraser Island: Ecoadventures & Four-Wheel-Drive Fun" in chapter 7.

- **Game Fishing:** Battle a black marlin off Cairns and you might snare the world record; that's how big they get down there. Marlin and other game catches run around much of the Australian coastline—Exmouth on the Northwest Cape in Western Australia (see chapter 10), and Broome and Darwin in the Top End (see chapter 9) are two other hot spots.
- **Canoeing the Top End** (NT): Paddling between the sun-drenched ocher walls of Katherine Gorge sharpens the senses, especially when a (harmless) freshwater crocodile pops up! **Gecko Canoeing (© 1800/634 319** in Australia, or 08/8972 2224; www.geckocanoeing.com.au) will take you downriver to the rarely explored Flora and Daly River systems to visit Aboriginal communities, shower under waterfalls, hike virgin bushland, and camp in swags on the banks. See "Katherine" in chapter 9.
- **Surfing in Margaret River** (WA): A 90-minute surf lesson with four-time Western Australia surf champ Josh Palmateer is a great introduction to the sport—if only to hear Josh's Aussie accent! In July and August, Josh shifts his classes to Cable Beach in Broome. See chapter 10.
- **Skiing in the Victorian Alps** (VIC): Skiing in Australia? Sure. When you've had enough coral and sand, you can hit the slopes in Victoria. Where else can you swish down the mountain between gum trees? See "The High Country" in chapter 13.

3 The Best Places to View Wildlife

- **Pebbly Beach** (NSW): The eastern gray kangaroos that inhabit Murramarang National Park, 20 minutes south of Ulladulla on the south coast of New South Wales, tend to congregate along this beach and the adjoining dunes. See "South of Sydney along the Princes Highway" in chapter 5.
- **Montague Island** (Narooma, NSW): This little island just offshore from the seaside town of Narooma, on the south coast, is a haven for nesting seabirds, but the water around it is home to the main attractions. Dolphins are common; fairy penguins, too. In whale-watching season, you're sure to spot southern right and humpback whales. See "South of Sydney along the Princes Highway" in chapter 5.
- **Jervis Bay** (NSW): This is probably the closest place to Sydney where you're certain to see kangaroos in the wild—and where you can pet them, too. The national park here is home to hundreds of bird species, including black cockatoos, as well as plenty of possums. See "South of Sydney along the Princes Highway" in chapter 5.
- **Lone Pine Koala Sanctuary** (Brisbane, QLD): Cuddle a koala (and have your photo taken doing it) at this park, the world's first and largest koala sanctuary. Apart from some 130 koalas, lots of other Aussie wildlife—including wombats, Tasmanian devils, 'roos (which you can hand-feed), and colorful parakeets—are on show. See p. 263.
- **Hervey Bay** (QLD): The warm waters off Hervey Bay, and in particular the lovely Platypus Bay, on the Queensland coast, are where the humpback whales come each year between June and October in increasing numbers to give birth. The long journey from Antarctica brings them up the coast to frolic with their young for several months before making the

return trip. Hervey Bay's many cruises can bring you closer to these gentle giants than you'll ever come elsewhere. See "Fraser Island: Ecoadventures & Four-Wheel-Drive Fun" in chapter 7.

- **Australian Butterfly Sanctuary** (Kuranda, near Cairns, QLD): Walk through the biggest butterfly "aviary" in Australia and see some of Australia's most gorgeous butterflies, including the electric-blue Ulysses. See many species of butterfly feed, lay eggs, and mate, and inspect caterpillars and pupae. Wearing pink, red, or white encourages the butterflies to land on you. See p. 303.
- **Wait-a-While Rainforest Tours** (QLD): Head into the World Heritage–listed Wet Tropics Rainforest behind Cairns or Port Douglas with this ecotour operator to spotlight possums, lizards, pythons, even a platypus, so shy that most Aussies have never seen one in the wild. About once a month, a group will spot the rare, bizarre Lumholtz's tree kangaroo. See "Cairns" in chapter 7.
- **Heron Island** (off Gladstone, QLD): There's wonderful wildlife on this "jewel in the reef" any time of year, but the best time to visit is November to March, when the life cycle of giant green loggerhead and hawksbill turtles is in full swing. From November to January, the turtles come ashore to lay their eggs. From late January to March, the hatchlings emerge and head for the water. You can see it all by strolling down to the beach, or join a university researcher to get the full story. See "The Capricorn Coast & the Southern Reef Islands" in chapter 7. Mon Repos Turtle Rookery, near Bundaberg in Queensland (see "Up Close & Personal with a Turtle," p. 359) and the Northwest Cape in Western Australia (see "The Coral Coast: Where the Outback Meets the Sea" in chapter 10) are two other good turtle-watching sites.
- **Currumbin Wildlife Sanctuary** (The Gold Coast, QLD): Tens of thousands of unbelievably pretty red, blue, green, and yellow rainbow lorikeets have been screeching into this park for generations to be hand-fed by delighted visitors every morning and afternoon. The sanctuary has 'roos and other Australian animals, too, but the birds steal the show. See p. 381.
- **Kakadu National Park** (NT): One-third of Australia's bird species live in Kakadu; so do lots of saltwater crocs. A cruise on the Yellow Water Billabong, and aboard the Original Jumping Crocodiles cruise en route to the park, are some of the best ways to see them in the wild. See "Kakadu National Park" in chapter 9.
- **The Northwest Cape** (WA): For the thrill of a lifetime, go snorkeling with a whale shark. No one knows where they come from, but these mysterious monsters (up to 18m/60 ft. long) surface in the Outback waters off Western Australia every year from March to early June. A mini-industry takes snorkelers out to swim alongside the sharks as they feed (on plankton, not snorkelers). See "The Coral Coast: Where the Outback Meets the Sea" in chapter 10.
- **Tangalooma** (QLD), **Bunbury** (WA) **& Monkey Mia** (WA): In several places, you can see, hand-feed, or swim with wild dolphins. At Bunbury, south of Perth, you can swim with them or join cruises to see them (they come right up to the boat). If you want an almost guaranteed dolphin sighting, head to Tangalooma Wild Dolphin Resort on Moreton Island, off Brisbane, where you can hand-feed them, or to Monkey Mia

on the lonely Outback coast, where they cruise past your legs. Even better is a cruise on the *Shotover* catamaran to see some of the area's 10,000 dugongs (manatees), plus turtles, sea snakes, sharks—and more. See chapters 6 and 10.

- **Kangaroo Island** (SA): You're sure to see more native animals here—including koalas, wallabies, birds, echidnas, reptiles, seals, and sea lions—than anywhere else in the country, apart from a wildlife park. Another plus: The distances between major points of interest are not great, so you won't spend half the day just getting from place to place. See "Kangaroo Island" in chapter 11.

4 The Best Places to Experience the Outback

- **Broken Hill** (NSW): There's no better place to experience real Outback life than in Broken Hill. There's the city itself, with its thriving art scene and the Royal Flying Doctor service; a historic ghost town on its outskirts; a national park with Aboriginal wall paintings; an opal mining town nearby; and plenty of kangaroos, emus, and giant wedge-tailed eagles. See "Outback New South Wales" in chapter 5.
- **Lightning Ridge** (NSW): This opal-mining town is as rough-and-ready as the stones the miners pull out of the ground. Meet amazing characters, share in the eccentricity of the place, and visit opal-rush areas with mole-hill scenery made by the old sun-bleached mine tailings. See "Outback New South Wales" in chapter 5.
- **Uluru–Kata Tjuta National Park** (Ayers Rock, NT): Sure, Ayers Rock will enthrall you with its eerie beauty, but the nearby Olgas are more soothing, more interesting, and taller than the Rock, so make the time to wander through them, too. Hike the Rock's base, burn around it on a Harley-Davidson, saunter up to it on a camel, climb it if you must. Don't go home until you've felt the powerful heartbeat of the desert. See "Uluru–Kata Tjuta National Park (Ayers Rock/The Olgas)" in chapter 8.
- **The MacDonnell Ranges** (NT): The Aborigines say these red rocky hills were formed by the Aboriginal "Caterpillar Dreaming" that wriggled from the earth here. To the west of Alice Springs are dramatic gorges, idyllic (and bloody cold) water holes, and cute wallabies. To the east are Aboriginal rock carvings and the Ross River Homestead, where you can crack a cattle whip, throw a boomerang, feast on damper and billy tea, and ride a horse or camel in the bush. See "Road Trips from Alice Springs" in chapter 8.
- **Kings Canyon** (NT): Anyone who saw the cult flick *The Adventures of Priscilla, Queen of the Desert* will remember the scene in which the transvestites climb a soaring orange cliff and survey the desert floor. That was Kings Canyon, about 320km (198 miles) from Alice Springs in one direction, with Ayers Rock in the other. Trek the dramatic rim or take the easier shady route along the bottom. Don't forget your lipstick, guys. See "Kings Canyon" in chapter 8.
- **The Northwest Cape** (WA): This treeless moonscape of red anthills, spiky spinifex, and blazing heat seems to go on forever, so it's all the more amazing to find a beautiful coral reef offshore. Drive the rugged hills in a four-wheel-drive vehicle, dodging kangaroos on the way; swim with giant manta rays; snorkel right off the beach; scuba dive coral outcroppings; and laze on blindingly white beaches.

This is where the Outback meets the sea. See "The Coral Coast: Where the Outback Meets the Sea" in chapter 10.

- **Coober Pedy** (SA): It may be hot and dusty, but you'll get a true taste of the Outback when you tag along with the local mail carrier as he makes his rounds to the area's remote cattle stations (ranches). It's a 12-hour, 600km (372-mile) journey along sun-baked dirt roads. See "Outback South Australia" in chapter 11.

5 The Best Beaches

- **Palm Beach** (Sydney): At the end of a string of beaches stretching north from Sydney, Palm Beach is long and white, with good surfing and a golf course. See chapter 4, "Sydney."
- **Hyams Beach** (Jervis Bay, NSW): This beach in off-the-beaten-path Jervis Bay is said to be the whitest in the world. You need to wear sunblock if you decide to stroll along it, because the reflection from the sun, even on a cloudy day, can give you a nasty sunburn. The beach squeaks as you walk. See "South of Sydney along the Princes Highway" in chapter 5.
- **Four Mile Beach** (Port Douglas, QLD): The sea is turquoise, the sun is warm, the palms sway, and the low-rise hotels starting to line this country beach can't spoil the feeling that it is a million miles from anywhere. But isn't there always a serpent in paradise? In this case the "serpents" are north Queensland's seasonal, potentially deadly marine stingers. Come from June through September to avoid them, or confine your swimming to the stinger net the rest of the year. See "Port Douglas, Daintree & the Cape Tribulation Area" in chapter 7.
- **Mission Beach** (QLD): Azure water, islands dotting the horizon, and white sand edged by vine forests make this beach a real winner. The bonus is that hardly anyone comes here. Cassowaries (giant emulike birds) hide in the rainforest, and the tiny town of Mission Beach makes itself invisible behind the leaves. Visit from June through September to avoid marine stingers. See "The North Coast: Mission Beach, Townsville & the Islands" in chapter 7.
- **Whitehaven Beach** (Whitsunday Island, QLD): It's not a surf beach, but this 6km (3¾-mile) stretch of white silica sand on uninhabited Whitsunday Island is pristine and peaceful. Bring a book, curl up under the rainforest lining its edge, and fantasize that the cruise boat is going to leave without you. See "The Whitsunday Coast & Islands" in chapter 7.
- **Surfers Paradise Beach** (Gold Coast, QLD): Actually, all 35 of the beaches on the 30km (19-mile) Gold Coast strip in south Queensland are worthy of inclusion here. Every one has sand so clean it squeaks, great surf, and fresh breezes—ignore the tacky high-rises. Surfers will like Burleigh Heads. See "The Gold Coast" in chapter 7.
- **Cable Beach** (Broome, WA): Is it the South Sea pearls pulled out of the Indian Ocean, the camels loping along the sand, the sunsets, the surf, or the red earth meeting the green sea that gives this beach its exotic appeal? Maybe it's the 26km (16 miles) of white sand. The only time to swim here is June through September, when deadly marine stingers aren't around. See "The Kimberley: A Far-Flung Wilderness" in chapter 10.
- **Cottesloe Beach** (Perth, WA): Perth has 19 great beaches, but this petite crescent is the prettiest. After you've checked out the scene, join the fashionable set for brunch in the Indiana

Tea House, a mock-Edwardian bathhouse fronting the sea. Surfers head to Scarborough and Trigg. See chapter 10, "Perth & Western Australia."

6 The Best Diving & Snorkeling Sites

- **Port Douglas** (QLD): Among the fabulous dive sites off Port Douglas, north of Cairns, are Split-Bommie, with its delicate fan corals and schools of fusiliers; Barracuda Pass, with its coral gardens and giant clams; and the swim-through coral spires of the Cathedrals. Snorkelers can glide over the coral and reef fish life of Agincourt Reef. See "Port Douglas, Daintree & the Cape Tribulation Area" in chapter 7.
- **Lizard Island** (QLD): Snorkel over 150-year-old giant clams—as well as gorgeous underwater coral—in the Clam Garden, off this exclusive resort island northeast of Cairns. Nearby is the famous Cod Hole, where divers can hand-feed giant potato cod. See p. 310.
- **Cairns** (QLD): Moore, Norman, Hardy, Saxon, and Arlington reefs and Michaelmas and Upolu cays—all about 90 minutes off Cairns—offer great snorkeling and endless dive sites. Explore on a day trip from Cairns or join a live-aboard adventure. See "Cairns" in chapter 7.
- **Coral Sea** (QLD): In this sea east of the Great Barrier Reef off north Queensland, you'll see sharks feeding at Predator's Playground; 1,000m (3,280-ft.) drop-offs in the Abyss; reefs covering hundreds of square miles; and tropical species not found on the Great Barrier Reef. This is not a day-trip destination; many dive operators run multiday trips on live-aboard vessels. Visibility is excellent—up to 100m (328 ft.). See "The North Coast: Mission Beach, Townsville & the Islands" in chapter 7.
- ***Yongala* wreck** (QLD): Sunk by a cyclone in 1911, the 120m (394-ft.) SS *Yongala* lies in the Coral Sea off Townsville. Schools of trevally, kingfish, barracuda, and batfish surround the wreckage; giant Queensland grouper live under the bow, lionfish hide under the stern, turtles graze on the hull, and hard and soft corals make their home on it. It's too far for a day trip; live-aboard trips run from Townsville and Cairns. See "The North Coast: Mission Beach, Townsville & the Islands" in chapter 7.
- **The Whitsunday Islands** (QLD): As well as Blue Pearl Bay, these 74 breathtaking islands offer countless dive sites both among the islands and on the Outer Great Barrier Reef, 90 minutes away. Bait Reef on the Outer Reef is popular for its drop-offs. Snorkelers can explore not just the Outer Reef, but also patch reefs among the islands and rarely visited fringing reefs around many islands. See "The Whitsunday Coast & Islands" in chapter 7.
- **Heron Island** (QLD): Easily the number-one snorkel and dive site in Australia. If you stayed in the water for a week, you couldn't snorkel all the acres of coral stretching from shore. Take your pick of 22 dive sites: the Coral Cascades, with football trout and anemones; the Blue Pools, favored by octopus, turtles, and sharks; Heron Bommie, with its rays, eels, and Spanish dancers; and more. Absolute magic. See "The Capricorn Coast & the Southern Reef Islands" in chapter 7.
- **Lady Elliot Island** (QLD): Gorgeous coral lagoons, perfect for snorkeling, line this coral cay island off the town of Bundaberg. Boats take you farther out to snorkel above

manta rays, plate coral, and big fish. Divers can swim through the blowhole, 16m (52 ft.) down, and see gorgonian fans, soft and hard corals, sharks, barracudas, and reef fish. See "The Capricorn Coast & the Southern Reef Islands" in chapter 7.

- **Rottnest Island** (WA): Just 19km (12 miles) off Perth, this former prison island has excellent snorkeling and more than 100 dive sites. Wrecks, limestone overhangs, and myriad fish will keep divers entertained. There are no cars, so snorkelers should rent a bike and snorkel gear, buy a visitor-center map of suggested snorkel trails, and head off to find their own private coral garden. The sunken grotto of Fishhook Bay is great for fish life. See "Side Trips from Perth" in chapter 10.
- **Ningaloo Reef** (WA): A well-kept secret is how we'd describe Australia's second great barrier reef, stretching 260km (161 miles) along the Northwest Cape halfway up Western Australia. Coral starts right on shore, not 90 minutes out to sea as at the Great Barrier Reef. You can snorkel or dive with manta rays, and dive to see sharks, angelfish, turtles, eels, grouper, potato cod, and much more. Snorkel with whale sharks up to 18m (59 ft.) long from March to early June. See "The Coral Coast: Where the Outback Meets the Sea" in chapter 10.

7 The Best Places to Bushwalk (Hike)

- **Blue Mountains** (NSW): Many bushwalks in the Blue Mountains National Park offer awesome views of valleys, waterfalls, cliffs, and forest. All are easy to reach from Sydney. See "The Blue Mountains" in chapter 5.
- **Whitsunday Islands** (QLD): Most people think of snorkeling and watersports when they come to these subtropical national-park islands clad in dense rainforest and bush, but every resort island we recommend has hiking trails. Some are flat, some hilly. Wallabies and butterflies are common sights. South Molle has the best network of trails and 360-degree island views from its peak. See "The Whitsunday Coast & Islands" in chapter 7.
- **Lamington National Park** (QLD): Few other national parks in Australia have such a well-marked network of trails (160km/99 miles in all) as this one, just 90 minutes from the Gold Coast. Revel in dense subtropical rainforest, marvel at mossy 2,000-year-old Antarctic beech trees, delight in the prolific wallabies and birds, and soak up the cool mountain air. See "The Gold Coast Hinterland: Back to Nature" in chapter 7.
- **Larapinta Trail** (The Red Centre, NT): You can start from Alice Springs and walk the entire 250km (155-mile) semidesert trail, which winds through the stark crimson McDonnell Ranges. You don't have to walk the entire length—plenty of day-length and multiday sections are possible. This one's for the cooler months only (Apr–Oct). See "Alice Springs" in chapter 8.
- **Kakadu National Park** (NT): Whether a wetlands stroll or an overnight hike in virgin bushland, you can find it in this World Heritage–listed park. You'll see red cliffs, cycads, waterfalls, lily-filled lagoons hiding man-eating crocodiles, what sometimes looks like Australia's entire bird population, and Aboriginal rock art. See "Kakadu National Park" in chapter 9.
- **Cape-to-Cape** (WA): Rugged sea cliffs, a china-blue sea, eucalyptus

forest, white beaches, and coastal heath are what you will find as you hike between Cape Naturaliste and Cape Leeuwin, in the southwest corner of Western Australia. In season, you'll see whales and wildflowers. See "Margaret River & the Southwest: Wine Tasting among the Forests" in chapter 10.

- **Freycinet National Park** (TAS): The trek to Wine Glass Bay passes pink-granite outcrops, with views over an ocean sliced by a crescent of icy sand. It's prehistorically beautiful. See "Freycinet National Park" in chapter 15.
- **Cradle Mountain & Lake St. Clair National Park** (TAS): The 80km (50-mile) Overland Track is the best hike in Australia. The trek, from Cradle Mountain to Lake St. Clair, takes 5 to 10 days, depending on your fitness level. Shorter walks, some lasting just half an hour, are also accessible. See "Cradle Mountain & Lake St. Clair National Park" in chapter 15.
- **The Great Ocean Walk** (VIC): This 91km (56-mile) trail from Apollo Bay to Glenample Homestead (near the Twelve Apostles) on Victoria's Great Ocean Road is designed so walkers can "step on–step off" at a number of places, completing short walks of around 2 hours, or day or overnight hikes. And the views are to die for. See "Great Ocean Walk" in chapter 13.

8 The Best Places to Learn about Aboriginal Culture

- **Umbarra Aboriginal Cultural Centre** (Wallaga Lake, near Narooma, NSW): This center offers boomerang- and spear-throwing instruction, painting with natural ochers, discussions on Aboriginal culture, and guided walking tours of Aboriginal sacred sites. See p. 238.
- **Tjapukai Aboriginal Cultural Park** (Cairns, QLD): This multimillion-dollar center showcases the history of the Tjapukai people—their Dreamtime creation history and their often-harrowing experiences since the white man arrived—using a film, superb theatrical work, and a dance performance. Its Aboriginal art and crafts gift shop is one of the country's best. See p. 298.
- **Aboriginal Art & Culture Centre** (Alice Springs, NT): You'll taste bush food, see a dance, throw boomerangs and spears, and learn about Aboriginal family values in one half-day tour of this Aborigine-owned center in Alice Springs. Be sure to hang around for the 1-hour didgeridoo lesson at the end. See p. 399.
- **Anangu Tours** (Ayers Rock, NT): The Anangu are the owners of Ayers Rock or, in their native tongue, Uluru. Join them for walks around the Rock as you learn about the poisonous "snake men" who fought battles here, pick bush food off the trees, throw spears, visit rock paintings, and watch the sun set over the monolith. Their Cultural Centre near the base of the Rock has displays about the Aboriginal Dreamtime. See "Uluru–Kata Tjuta National Park (Ayers Rock/The Olgas)" in chapter 8.
- **Manyallaluk—The Dreaming Place** (Katherine, NT): This Aboriginal community welcomes visitors and teaches them to paint, weave, throw boomerangs, and perform other tasks of daily life. A low-key day and the chance to chat one-on-one with Aboriginal people in their bush home. See "Katherine" in chapter 9.
- **Mangarrayi People** (Katherine, NT): Mike Keighley of **Far Out**

Adventures (✆ **0427/152 288;** www.farout.com.au) takes tours to beautiful Elsey Station (a ranch) near Katherine, where you visit with the children of the local Mangarrayi people. Sample bush tucker, learn a little bush medicine, and swim in a natural "spa-pool" in the Roper River. See "Katherine" in chapter 9.

- **Tandanya Aboriginal Cultural Institute** (Adelaide, SA): This is a great place to experience life through Aboriginal eyes. You might catch one of the dances or other performances, and you'll have plenty of other opportunities to find out more about Aboriginal culture. See p. 548.

9 The Best of Small-Town Australia

- **Central Tilba** (NSW): Just inland from Narooma on the south coast, this historic hamlet is one of the cutest you'll see, complete with blacksmiths and leatherwork outlets. The ABC Cheese Factory offers free tastings, and you can spend hours browsing antiques stalls or admiring the period buildings. See "South of Sydney along the Princes Highway" in chapter 5.
- **Broken Hill** (NSW): Known for its silver mines, the quirky town of Broken Hill has more pubs per capita than just about anywhere else. It's the home of the School of the Air—a "classroom" that transmits lessons by radio to communities spread over thousands of miles of Outback. Here you'll also find the Palace Hotel, made famous in *The Adventures of Priscilla, Queen of the Desert,* as well as plenty of colonial mansions and heritage homes. See "Outback New South Wales" in chapter 5.
- **Port Douglas** (QLD): What happens when Sydneysiders and Melbournians discover a one-street fishing village in tropical north Queensland? Come to Port Douglas and find out. A strip of groovy restaurants and a championship golf course have not diminished "Port's" old-fashioned air. Four Mile Beach is at the end of the street, and boats depart daily for the Great Barrier Reef. See "Port Douglas, Daintree & the Cape Tribulation Area" in chapter 7.
- **Mission Beach** (QLD): You'd never know this tidy village existed (it's hidden in lush rainforest off the highway) if you weren't well-informed. Aussies know it's here, but few bother to patronize its dazzling beach, offshore islands, and rainforest trails, so you'll have the place to yourself. There's great white-water rafting on the nearby Tully River, too. See "The North Coast: Mission Beach, Townsville & the Islands" in chapter 7.
- **Broome** (WA): This romantic pearling port on the far-flung Kimberley coast on the Indian Ocean blends Aussie corrugated-iron architecture with red pagoda roofs left by Chinese pearl divers. The town fuses a sophisticated international ambience with Outback attitude. Play on Cable Beach (see "The Best Beaches," earlier in this chapter) and stay at glamorous Cable Beach Club Resort. This is the place to add to your South Sea pearl collection. See "The Kimberley: A Far-Flung Wilderness" in chapter 10.
- **Kalgoorlie** (WA): This is it, the iconic Australian country town. Vibrant Kalgoorlie sits on what used to be the richest square mile of gold-bearing earth ever. It still pumps around 2,000 ounces *a day* out of the ground. Have a beer in one of the

gracious 19th-century pubs, peer into the world's biggest open-cut gold mine, and wander the ghost-town streets of its sister town, Coolgardie. See "The Goldfields" in chapter 10.

- **Hahndorf** (SA): A group of Lutheran settlers founded this German-style town in the Adelaide Hills in the 1830s. You'll love the churches, the wool factory and crafts shops, and the delicious German food at the local cafes, restaurants, and bakeries. See "Side Trips from Adelaide" in chapter 11.
- **Coober Pedy** (SA): For an Outback experience that's fair-dinkum (genuine), few places are as weird and wonderful as this opal-mining town in the middle of nowhere. Visit mines, see wacky museums, and stay in a hotel underground—not all that unusual, considering that the locals live like moles anyway. See "Outback South Australia" in chapter 11.
- **Launceston** (TAS): Tasmania's second city is not much larger than your average European or American small town, but it's packed with Victorian and Georgian architecture and remnants of Australia's convict past. Spend a few days and discover the scenery; splurge a little on a stay in a historic hotel. See "Launceston" in chapter 15.

10 The Best Museums

- **Australian National Maritime Museum** (Sydney, NSW): The best things about this museum are the ships and submarines often docked in the harbor out front. You can climb aboard and experience what it's like to be a sailor. Inside are some fascinating displays relating to Australia's dependence on the oceans. See p. 165.
- **Alice Springs Telegraph Station Historical Reserve** (NT): It's not called a museum, but that's what this restored telegraph-repeater station out in the picturesque hills by a spring—Alice Springs—really is. From the hot biscuits turned out of the wood-fired oven to the old telegraph equipment, this 1870s settlement is as real as history can get. See p. 400.
- **Australian Aviation Heritage Centre** (Darwin, NT): The pride of this hangar is a B-52 bomber on permanent loan from the U.S. But there's loads more, and not just planes, engines, and other aviation paraphernalia—there are stories, jokes, and anecdotes associated with the exhibits that will appeal even if you don't have avgas (aviation fuel) running in your veins. See "Darwin" in chapter 9.
- **Warradjan Aboriginal Cultural Centre** (NT): "Memorable and moving" were the words used by one reader to describe her visit to this small, stylish museum in Kakadu National Park. Learn about Dreamtime myths and daily life of Aboriginal people in Kakadu. See "Kakadu National Park" in chapter 9.
- **Western Australian Maritime Museum** and the adjacent **Shipwreck Galleries** (Perth, WA): Housed in the historic port precinct of Fremantle, Perth, this museum tells tales of the harsh Western Australian coastline since the Dutch first bumped into it and abandoned it as useless in the 1600s. Anyone who ever dreamed of finding a shipwreck laden with pieces of eight will relish the displays of treasure recovered from the deep. See p. 481.
- **New Norcia Museum and Art Gallery** (New Norcia, WA): This tiny museum in the Spanish Benedictine

monastery town of New Norcia holds a mind-boggling collection of European Renaissance art. The museum has all kinds of memorabilia: the monks' manuscripts, clothing, instruments, and gifts from Queen Isabella of Spain. See "New Norcia: A Touch of Spain in Australia" in chapter 10.

- **The Migration Museum** (Adelaide, SA): This museum gives visitors insight into the people who came to Australia, how and where they settled, and how many suffered getting here. Don't expect a lot of musty displays—this museum is full of hands-on activities. See p. 547.
- **Australian War Memorial** (Canberra, ACT): Given its name, you might think this museum is a bleak place, but you'd be wrong. It gives important insight into the Anzac (Australian and New Zealand Army Corps) spirit, including an exhibit on the tragic battle of Gallipoli. There's also a pretty good art collection. See p. 656.
- **National Museum of Australia** (ACT): Using state-of-the-art technology and hands-on exhibits, Australia's newest and most impressive museum concentrates on Australian society and its history since 1788, the interaction of people with the Australian environment, and Aboriginal and Torres Strait Islander cultures and histories. See p. 658.

11 The Best Luxury Accommodations

- **Park Hyatt Sydney** (NSW; ✆ **800/633-7313** in the U.S. and Canada, or 02/9241 1234 in Australia): You'll have to book well in advance to snag a room at Sydney's best-situated property, at the edge of the city's historic Rocks district. Many rooms have fabulous views across the harbor to the Sydney Opera House. See p. 126.
- **The Sebel Reef House & Spa Palm Cove** (Cairns, QLD; ✆ **1800/079 052** in Australia, or 07/4055 3633): Everyone who stays here says the same thing: "It feels like home." Airy rooms look into tropical gardens, waterfalls cascade into the pools, mosquito nets drape over the beds, and you could swear pith-helmeted colonial officers will be back any minute to finish their gin-and-tonics in the Brigadier Bar. Idyllic Palm Cove Beach is just across the road. See p. 308.
- **Lizard Island** (off Cairns, QLD; ✆ **1300/134 044** in Australia, or 02/8296 8010): Lizard Island has long been popular with Americans for its game fishing, wonderful coral and diving, smart food, and simple upscale lodge accommodations. See p. 310.
- **Bedarra Island** (off Mission Beach, QLD; ✆ **1300/134 044** in Australia, or 02/8296 8010): Presidents and princesses in need of a little time out come to this small rainforest island ringed by beaches. The timber villas are cozy, and the discreet staff assures privacy. Best of all, though, is the extravagant 24-hour open bar. See p. 329.
- **Orpheus Island Resort** (off Townsville or Cairns, QLD; ✆ **07/4777 7377** in Australia): Beloved of film stars and others who relish privacy, this resort has simple, attractive rooms; good food; a marvelous sense of seclusion; and a beautiful location in the curve of a palm-lined bay. The only way in is by seaplane. See p. 337.
- **Hayman** (Whitsunday Islands, QLD; ✆ **1800/075 175** in Australia, or Leading Hotels of the World, 800/745-8883 in the U.S. and Canada,

0800/1010-1111 in the U.K. and Ireland, or 0800/44 1016 in New Zealand): On Hayman Island in the Whitsundays, this is Australia's most glamorous resort. It has classy rooms, excellent restaurants, a staff that's keen to please, a superb hexagonal swimming pool, and a fleet of charter boats waiting to spirit you off to the Reef or your own deserted isle. See p. 348.

- **Longitude 131** (Uluru/Ayers Rock, Red Centre, NT; ✆ **08/8957 7888**): A newcomer to the Ayers Rock resort scene, Longitude 131 is an African-style luxury safari camp set in the sand dunes, with great views of Uluru (Ayers Rock). It's very exclusive and very expensive, but you experience the Outback in style. See p. 420.
- **El Questro Homestead** (The Kimberley, WA; ✆ **1300/134 044**): Charming country decor spiced up with Indonesian antiques, good cooking, and a dramatic gorge location make this glamorous homestead on a million-acre cattle station popular with jet-setters. Cruise wild gorges, heli-fish for barramundi, and hike to Aboriginal rock art while you're here. See p. 522.
- **Cable Beach Club Resort Broome** (Broome, WA; ✆ **1800/199 099** n Australia, or 08/9192 0400): Chinatown meets the Outback at this elegant corrugated-iron-and-pagoda-studded resort lying low along glorious Cable Beach in the romantic pearling port of Broome. Three to-die-for suites are decorated with superb Asian antiques and paintings by luminaries of the Australian art world. See p. 528.
- **The Como Melbourne** (Melbourne, VIC; ✆ **1800/033 400** in Australia, or 03/9825 2222): Great service, nice rooms, and free plastic ducks make this one of our favorite top-flight Australian hotels. See p. 592.
- **Hyatt Hotel Canberra** (Canberra, ACT; ✆ **800/233-1234** in the U.S. and Canada, or 02/6270 1234): Visiting heads of state and pop stars make this their residence when staying in Canberra. It's a 2-minute drive from the central shopping district, and a stone's throw from Lake Burley Griffin and the Parliamentary Triangle. See p. 651.

12 The Best Moderately Priced Accommodations

- **Hotel George Williams** (Brisbane, QLD; ✆ **1800/064 858** in Australia, or 07/3308 0700): It's hard to believe that this trendy, clean, and bright hotel is a Y. This is what an affordable hotel should be like, with helpful staff, a pleasant, inexpensive restaurant, and the kind of services you'd expect to be paying more for. See p. 259.
- **The Reef Retreat** (Cairns, QLD; ✆ **07/4059 1744**): It's not often you find so much decorating taste—wooden blinds, teak furniture, and colorful upholstery—at a price you want to pay, but that's what you get at the apartments in trendy Palm Cove, one of Cairns's most desirable beachfront suburbs. There's a pool on the lovely landscaped grounds, but the beach is just a block away. See p. 309.
- **Archipelago Studio Apartments** (Port Douglas, QLD; ✆ **07/4099 5387**): They may be tiny, but these pretty apartments have a homey atmosphere and are seconds from Four Mile Beach. Some units have sea views. The solicitous proprietor is a font of advice on things to see and do. See p. 319.

- **Miss Maud Swedish Hotel** (Perth, WA; ✆ **1800/998 022** in Australia): Staying here is like staying at Grandma's—just as she's finished a major redecoration job. You're right in the heart of Perth, and the friendly staff and huge buffet breakfasts (included in the room rate) complete the picture. See p. 466.
- **North Adelaide Heritage Group** (Adelaide, SA; ✆ **08/8272 1355**): These accommodations consist of 18 fabulous properties in North Adelaide and Eastwood. The former Friendly Meeting Chapel Hall resembles a small church stocked with Victorian antiques. Another memorable place is the George Lowe Esq. Apartment, done in the style of a 19th-century gentleman's bachelor pad. See p. 543.
- **York Mansions** (Launceston, TAS; ✆ **03/6334 2933**): If you feel that where you stay is as important to your visit as what you see, then don't miss on a night or two here. This National Trust–classified building has five spacious apartments, each with a distinct character. It's like living the high life in the Victorian age. See p. 685.

13 The Best Alternative Accommodations

- **Underground Motel** (White Cliffs, NSW; ✆ **1800/021 154** in Australia, or 08/8091 6677): All but two of this motel's rooms are underground. Rooms are reached by a maze of spacious tunnels dug out of the rock beneath this opal-mining town. See p. 246.
- **South Long Island Nature Lodge** (The Whitsunday Islands, QLD; ✆ **07/4946 9777**): You'll be one of only a maximum of 14 guests staying in the 10 comfy and recently refurbished beachfront cabins at this island ecoretreat. Sea kayak, snorkel, swim, hike rainforest trails, dine with other guests outside under the Milky Way, and take sailing trips—every day if you like—on the lodge's own yacht. Considering you'll only shell out for wine and maybe a seaplane trip to the Reef, this is a great value for its exclusivity. See p. 349.
- **Kingfisher Bay Resort** (Fraser Island, QLD; ✆ **1800/072 555** in Australia, or 07/4120 3333): If it weren't for the ranger station and natural-history videos in the lobby, the wildlife walks, the guided four-wheel-drive safaris, and the other ecoactivities, you'd hardly know that this comfortable, modern hotel is an ecoresort. See p. 366.
- **Binna Burra Mountain Lodge** (✆ **1800/074 260** in Australia, or 07/5533 3622) **& O'Reilly's Rainforest Guesthouse** (✆ **1800/688 722** in Australia, or 07/5502 4911), both in the Gold Coast Hinterland, QLD: Tucked almost 1,000m (3,280 ft.) up on rainforested ridges, these cozy retreats offer fresh mountain air, activities, and instant access to the hiking trails of Lamington National Park. At O'Reilly's you can hand-feed brilliantly colored rainforest birds every morning. See p. 390.
- **Emma Gorge Resort** (The Kimberley, WA; ✆ **1300/134 044** in Australia, or 08/9169 1777: At this spick-and-span little safari camp on the 400,000-hectare (1-million-acre) El Questro cattle station, guests stay in cute tents with wooden floors and electric lights, eat at a rustic gourmet restaurant, and join in the many hikes, bird-watching tours, river cruises, and more. See p. 523.
- **Prairie Hotel** (Flinders Ranges, SA; ✆ **08/8648 4844**): This remarkable

tin-roofed, stone-walled Outback pub in the Flinders Ranges has quaint rooms, a great bar out front where you can meet the locals, and some of the best food in Australia. See p. 571.

- **Freycinet Lodge** (Freycinet National Park, Coles Bay, TAS; ✆ **1800 420 155** or 03/6225 7000: These eco-friendly bush cabins are right next to one of the nation's best walking trails. The ocean views from the magnificent restaurant and the surrounding balconies are spectacular. See p. 681.
- **Cradle Mountain Lodge** (Cradle Mountain, TAS; ✆ **13 24 69** in Australia, or 03/6492 1303): Just minutes from your comfortable cabin are 1,500-year-old trees, moss forests, craggy mountain ridges, limpid pools and lakes, and hordes of scampering marsupials. See p. 689.

14 The Best Bed & Breakfasts & Guesthouses

- **The Russell** (The Rocks, Sydney; ✆ **02/9241 3543**): This B&B, wonderfully positioned in the city's old quarter, is the coziest place to stay in Sydney. It has creaky floorboards, a ramshackle feel, brightly painted corridors, and rooms with immense character. See p. 128.
- **Echoes Hotel & Restaurant, Blue Mountains** (Katoomba, NSW; ✆ **02/4782 1966**): Echoes is right on the edge of a dramatic drop into the Jamison Valley. The views from the balconies are breathtaking. See p. 204.
- **Barrington Guest House** (Barrington Tops National Park, The Hunter, NSW; ✆ **02/4995 3212**): Nestled in a valley just outside the Barrington Tops National Park, this charming guesthouse and luxury cabin property offers magnificent rainforest walks, plenty of native animals, and excellent activities, such as horseback riding through the bush. See p. 217.
- **Ulladulla Guest House** (Ulladulla, NSW; ✆ **02/4455 1796**): Works of art on the walls, fabulous food, and a lagoonlike pool among the palm trees—all this and lovely rooms, with hosts who can't do enough for you. See p. 235.
- **Cotterville** (Melbourne, VIC; ✆ **1300/301 630** in Australia, or 03/9826 9105): A beautifully and lovingly restored terrace house with elegant courtyard gardens, where you will be surrounded with art and music, and entertained by gregarious hosts and their friendly dogs. A home away from home in every sense. See p. 592.
- **Lilybank Bed & Breakfast** (Cairns, QLD; ✆ **07/4055 1123**): This rambling 1890s homestead used to be the Cairns mayor's residence. Today, owners Pat and Mike Woolford welcome guests to its comfy rooms, wide verandas, and blooming gardens. You can also stay in the renovated gardener's cottage. See p. 307.
- **Marae** (near Port Douglas, QLD; ✆ **07/4098 4900**): Lush bushland full of butterflies and birds is the setting for this gorgeous contemporary Queenslander house with hip rooms and an outdoor plunge pool. Owners John and Pam Burden promise a warm welcome and a wonderful breakfast. See p. 320.
- **Hansons Swan Valley** (near Perth, WA; ✆ **08/9296 3366**): Goodbye faded lace, hello Art Deco—here is a B&B with cutting-edge style for young sophisticates. Jon and Selina Hanson have created a stylish retreat nestled among the Swan Valley vineyards, an easy drive from Perth. See p. 491.

- **Heritage Trail Lodge** (Margaret River, WA; ✆ **08/9757 9595**): How many B&Bs do you know that provide a double Jacuzzi in every room? These salmon-pink cabins abut tall karri forest where parrots flit. 'Roos hop into the parking lot on occasion, and the fabulous Margaret River wineries surround you. See p. 501.
- **Collingrove Homestead** (Angaston, the Barossa Valley, SA; ✆ **08/8564 2061**): This country house, built in 1856, has an air of colonial manor farm living, with hunting trophies, rifles, and oil paintings festooning the walls, and plenty of oak paneling and antiques scattered about. See p. 555.

15 The Best Restaurants

- **Rockpool** (Sydney, NSW; ✆ **02/9252 1888**): With the chefs on view and designer chairs to sit on, Rockpool is a consistent favorite, not least for its fabulous, inventive food. See p. 145.
- **Mezzaluna** (Sydney, NSW; ✆ **02/9357 1988**): Come here for exquisite food, flawless service, and a great view across the city's western skyline. The main dining room opens onto an all-weather terrace kept warm in winter by giant, overhead fan heaters. Don't miss it. See p. 152.
- **Quay** (Sydney, NSW; ✆ **02/9251 5600**): Sydney's best seafood restaurant offers perhaps the loveliest view in town. Gaze through the large windows toward the Opera House, the city skyline, the North Shore suburbs, and the Harbour Bridge. See p. 144.
- **Tetsuya's** (Sydney, NSW; ✆ **02/9267 2900**): Chef Tetsuya Wakuda is arguably Sydney's most famous chef, and his nouveau Japanese creations are imaginative enough to guarantee that this hip eatery is a constant number one in Australia, and in 2007, the restaurant ranked no. 5 in the world! See p. 149.
- **e'cco bistro** (Brisbane, QLD; ✆ **07/3831 8344**): Simple food, elegantly done, has won this small but elegant bistro a stack of awards, and you'll soon see why. Not least among its titles is Australia's top restaurant award, the Remy Martin Cognac/Gourmet Traveller Restaurant of the Year. Booking ahead is essential. See p. 260.
- **Donovans** (Melbourne, VIC; ✆ **03/9534 8221**): A glass in hand while the sun goes down over St. Kilda beach, watched from the veranda at Donovans, is a perfect way to end the day. This 1920s bathing pavilion has been transformed into a welcoming beach-house-style restaurant complete with views across the sand and a seafood-rich menu. See p. 599.
- **Fraser's** (Perth, WA; ✆ **08/9481 7100**): The city center and Swan River sparkling in the sunshine seem so close that you can almost reach out and touch them from the terrace of this parkland restaurant. Come here for sensationally good Modern Australian food turned out with flair and flavor; seafood is a specialty. See p. 469.
- **Newtown House** (Vasse, near Margaret River, WA; ✆ **08/9755 4485**): Chef Stephen Reagan makes intelligent, flavorsome food that beautifully partners with premium Margaret River wines. Stay in his homestead B&B overnight and explore the wineries the next day. See p. 502.
- **Prairie Hotel** (Flinders Ranges, SA; ✆ **08/8648 4844**): Chef Darren ("Bart") Brooks serves high-class cuisine in the middle of nowhere. His

"feral" food, such as kangaroo tail soup and a mixed grill of emu sausages, camel steak, and kangaroo, is remarkable. See p. 571.

- **Flower Drum** (Melbourne, VIC; ✆ **03/9662 3655**): Praise pours in for this upscale eatery serving Cantonese food. The food is exquisite and the service impeccable. See p. 594.
- **Courgette** (Canberra, ACT; ✆ **02/6247 4042**): A plush dining room with large windows overlooking a pebbled garden. French-influenced with a marvelous seven-course degustation menu. See p. 654.

16 The Best Reasonably Priced Restaurants

- **Phillip's Foote** (Sydney, NSW; ✆ **02/9241 1485**): In the heart of the historic neighborhood known as The Rocks, this barbecue restaurant serves fish, meat, and poultry. Pick your own protein and throw it on the "barbie" in the courtyard behind a historic pub. See p. 146.
- **Green Papaya** (East Brisbane, QLD; ✆ **07/3217 3599**): Flavorful North Vietnamese cuisine in a cheerful setting—a simple formula that draws enthusiastic crowds. If you need advice as you contemplate the menu, the helpful staff will offer as much guidance as you need. New owners promise the same standard of service regulars are used to—and have retained the same chef. See p. 262.
- **Salsa Bar & Grill** (Port Douglas, QLD; ✆ **07/4099 4922**): The animated atmosphere and attractive surroundings set the scene for an excellent dining experience. Appetizers and main courses run the gamut from simple fare to sophisticated tropical creations; desserts are fantastic. See p. 322.
- **Zouí Alto** (Townsville, QLD; ✆ **07/4721 4700**): The reasonable prices belie the quality of the Modern Australian food at this 14th-floor establishment. The husband-and-wife team of Mark and Eleni Edwards (he's the chef) presides over one of the best restaurants in the country. See p. 334.
- **Season** (Sunshine Coast, QLD; ✆ **07/5447 3747**): A great location right on the beach, a chef who made a name for himself in Sydney, and flavorful Modern Australian cuisine combine to make Season one of the area's most popular restaurants. See p. 375.
- **Red Ochre Grill** (Alice Springs, NT; ✆ **08/8952 9614**: "Gourmet bush tucker" might sound like a contradiction, but this restaurant (part of an upscale chain) pulls it off. The kitchen combines native ingredients and international techniques to exceptionally good effect. See p. 408.
- **Hansons** (Henley Brook, WA; ✆ **08/9296 3366**): In the wine country just outside Perth, Hansons serves Modern Australian dishes indoors and outdoors. The elegant restaurant is part of Hansons Swan Valley, a sleek, contemporary B&B. See p. 491.
- **Bamboo House** (Melbourne, VIC; ✆ **03/9662 1565**): A favorite with both local businesspeople and the Chinese community, Bamboo House offers superb service as well as excellent Cantonese and northern Chinese cuisine. Top choices on the extensive menu include duck in plum sauce, chicken with shallot sauce, and the signature Szechuan smoked duck. See p. 596.
- **Mures Upper Deck** (Hobart, TAS; ✆ **03/6231 2121**): Views of the water make a perfect backdrop for

ultrafresh seafood and scrumptious desserts. The menu relies heavily on the catch that comes in on the restaurant's own fishing boat. Lower Deck, in the same complex, is a reasonably priced self-service family restaurant. See p. 675.

- **Spirit House** (Sunshine Coast, QLD; © **07/5446 8994**): Winding jungle paths lead to tables set around a lagoon, illuminated at night by torches and discreet lighting. The flavors from the kitchen are mainly Thai but with other Asian influences, and there's nowhere else quite like this in Queensland for atmosphere and terrific food. See p. 375.

2

Planning Your Trip to Australia

by Lee Mylne

1 The Regions in Brief

About 84% of Australia's 20 million people huddle in cities around the coast covering a mere 1% of this vast continent. The reason is simple: Much of Australia is harsh Outback country, characterized by savanna land, spectacular rocky outcrops, shifting deserts, and dry salt lakes. In these parts of the country, the soil is poor and the rainfall scarce, and some rivers don't even make it to the ocean. The roads that traverse the interior are sometimes barely distinguishable, and most people choose air travel or stick to the coastal fringe.

In spectacular contrast, on the coast—particularly in the east, where most people live—Nature's bounty has almost overdone it. Here, Australia is blessed with one of the greatest natural attractions in the world: the Great Barrier Reef. There are also rainforests in Queensland, alpine scenery in Tasmania, wildflowers in Western Australia, rolling wine country in South Australia, a great coastal drive in Victoria, bird-filled wetlands in the Northern Territory, and countless sand beaches more or less everywhere.

Australia consists of six states—New South Wales (NSW), Queensland (QLD), Victoria (VIC), South Australia (SA), Western Australia (WA), and Tasmania (TAS)—and two internal territories, the Australian Capital Territory (ACT) and the Northern Territory (NT). The national capital is Canberra, in the ACT.

See the map on p. 6 or the map on the inside back cover to visualize the regions described here.

NEW SOUTH WALES Australia's most populated state is also the most visited by tourists. They come to see Sydney—and who can blame them? It's one of the most glamorous and beautiful cities in the world, with dozens of harbor and ocean beaches in and around it, and a mixture of bushland and city development around Sydney Harbour. Sydney is also a good base for day trips or overnight excursions inland, especially to the scenic Blue Mountains and the wineries of the Hunter Valley.

Farther afield, a string of quaint beachside towns stretches down the southern coast to Victoria. Along the north coast are remnant areas of rainforest and a more tropical air in the laid-back hangout of Byron Bay.

The inland is dry and sparsely forested. Highlights include the mining town of Broken Hill (known for wildlife, art galleries, and Aboriginal influences), and Outback opal-mining towns White Cliffs and Lightning Ridge, which exist in a wacky underground world of their own.

QUEENSLAND Without a doubt, the biggest draw for visitors to Queensland is the Great Barrier Reef. Ogling the tropical fish, sea creatures, and rainbow-hued corals is a holiday highlight for most people. The Reef stretches more than 2,000km (1,240 miles) along Queensland's coast, as far south as Bundaberg, 384km (238 miles) north of Brisbane, the state capital. Alluring island resorts dot the coast; while most are expensive, we've found a few that won't break the bank.

Queensland is also known for its white-sand beaches. Many of the best are on the Gold Coast in the state's south (about an hour's drive from Brisbane), and the Sunshine Coast (a 2-hr. drive north of Brisbane). Cairns and Port Douglas in the north have their fair share of beaches, too, but be warned: Swimming in their waters can be *very* hazardous to your health. Deadly box jellyfish, or "stingers," halt all ocean swimming at beaches in the northern third of the country from October through May. In Queensland, stingers may be found in all coastal waters north of Gladstone. Most patrolled beaches in these areas have "stinger nets," which aim to keep the little blighters out, but the thimble-size Irakandji jellyfish is small enough to sneak through the mesh, and its sting can be fatal. All patrolled beaches have warning signs, and the lifeguards do regular net drags to see if there are any in the water. If they find any, they promptly close the beach. But to be absolutely sure, at this time of year you should stick to the waterfront lagoons at Airlie Beach and Cairns, or to your hotel pool. The jellyfish are mainly found in coastal waters and do not interfere with Great Barrier Reef activities like snorkeling or diving, which are out of the habitat of marine stingers.

Island swimming is mostly stinger-free, but be careful and take advice from the lifeguards before plunging into that inviting water.

One of the most appealing of Queensland's destinations is the aquatic playground made up of the 74 Whitsunday Islands in the Great Barrier Reef Marine Park. These mostly uninhabited islands are a paradise for kayaking, snorkeling, diving, fishing, hiking, watersports, birding, and bareboat sailing.

Another big attraction is the lush 110-million-year-old Daintree Rainforest, just north of Port Douglas.

Brisbane has Australia's largest koala sanctuary (you can cuddle one if you like), and you can hand-feed wild dolphins on a day trip across Brisbane's Moreton Bay. In the Gold Coast hinterland is Lamington National Park, a rainforested mountain region great for hiking and spotting wildlife.

THE RED CENTRE The eerie silence of Uluru, also known as Ayers Rock, is what draws everyone to the sprawling ocher sands of the Red Centre, the heart of the Northern Territory. Many visitors make the delightful discovery that the lesser-known nearby domes of Kata Tjuta, or "the Olgas," are even more spectacular (if that's possible). A half-day's drive from the Rock brings you to Kings Canyon, an awesomely lovely desert gorge popular with hikers. If you visit the Red Centre, try to spend at least a few days in Alice Springs. This laid-back Outback town has

---

***Tips* Size Does Matter**

When planning your trip, keep in mind that Australia is as big as western Europe and about the same size as the 48 contiguous U.S. states. Melbourne and Brisbane are a long day's drive from Sydney, and driving from Sydney to Perth takes the better part of a week.

The Drought Continues

Australia has been experiencing a severe drought since 1992. In 2007, the dry spell was officially classified as the worst on record. Most state capitals have been trying to cope with severe water restrictions for years, as lakes dry up and the population grows due to increased immigration. Some major reservoirs are so depleted of water that emergency water procedures have been put in place. One of Australia's largest water supplies, Lake Eucumbene, in the Snowy Mountains of NSW, is so low that the remains of the town of Old Adaminaby have been exposed. The town has been submerged deep under water since 1957, during the construction of Australia's biggest hydroelectric project.

In 2007, Australians saw trees die and important wetlands for breeding birds dry up or become polluted by salt and other contaminants. A desalination plant designed to turn to turn sea water into fresh, was being seriously considered in Sydney. Irrigators along the enormous Murray–Darling river system faced having their water supplies cut off. Fruit and vegetable prices rose, and there was talk of a milk shortage. Some farmers committed suicide, and the threat of bush fires was ever present. Grape harvests were poor, leading to a drop in wine production. And so it went on . . . and on.

Australian environmentalists point to the increasing frequency and severity of drought-causing El Niño weather patterns, blamed on global warming. Australia is among the world's biggest per-capita energy consumers, and produces more carbon dioxide emissions per capita than anywhere else in the world. Deforestation is still a major problem. In 2007, Australia, along with the U.S, were the only two industrialized nations refusing to ratify the 1997 Kyoto protocol.

the best Aboriginal arts-and-crafts shopping in Australia, Aboriginal tours, a world-class desert wildlife park, stunning scenery, hikes through the stark MacDonnell Ranges, an Outback ranch to stay at, and even camel rides along a dry riverbed.

THE TOP END The northwest reaches of the country (from the rocky red ranges of the Kimberley in Western Australia to the northern third of the Northern Territory) encompass what Aussies eloquently dub "the Top End." This is Crocodile Dundee territory, a remote, vast, semidesert region where the cattle probably outnumber the people. In this book, we have concentrated on the Northern Territory section of the "Top End." (The Kimberley appears in the Western Australia chapter.)

Near the tropical city of Darwin, the territory's capital, is Kakadu National Park, where you can cruise past crocodiles on inland billabongs (ponds), bird-watch, and visit ancient Aboriginal rock-art sites. Closer to Darwin is Litchfield National Park, where you can take a dip in fern-fringed swimming holes surrounded by red cliffs—stuff straight from Eden. You can cruise the waterways of Katherine Gorge, a few hours' drive south of Darwin, or explore them by canoe. Near Katherine you can canoe rarely explored, croc-infested inland rivers and learn to make your own didgeridoo (a large wooden traditional Aboriginal musical instrument).

WESTERN AUSTRALIA Distance and high airfares work against Western Australia's tourism industry, which is a shame, because this is one of Australia's most wild and beautiful regions. The seas teem with whales in season, and thrill-seekers can swim alongside gigantic but gentle whale sharks on the Northwest Cape every fall (Mar–June). This cape is home to one of Australia's best-kept secrets, a second barrier reef called Ningaloo Marine Park, which runs for 260km (161 miles). It's one of the few reefs in the world to grow on a western coast. You can snorkel with manta rays here or try the fantastic diving. Just 19km (12 miles) off Perth, snorkelers can gaze at corals and fish on Rottnest Island, and in Shark Bay at Monkey Mia, tourists can greet wild dolphins (or is it the other way around?).

In the southwest "hook" of the continent lies the Margaret River wine region. Wild forests, thundering surf, dramatic cliffs, rich bird life, and wild 'roos make it one of the country's most attractive wine regions. The state's capital, Perth, has surf beaches and a restored 19th-century port with a fun atmosphere and some great museums. One or 2 hours' drive from the city brings you to some cute towns, like the Spanish Benedictine monastery town of New Norcia. Inland, the state is mostly wheat fields and desert, but if you have the inclination, head 600km (372 miles) east of Perth to the gold-mining town of Kalgoorlie, where you'll find the world's largest open-cast gold mine. With its gracious old pubs lining the wide bustling streets, it's what an Aussie country town should look like.

In the Kimberley, you can visit the ancient Geikie and Windjana gorges, farms where the world's best South Sea pearls grow, and the charming (in a corrugated-iron sort of way) beachside frontier town of Broome. This tract of the country is so little populated and so underexplored that most Aussies never contemplate coming here. Getting around is expensive, because the region is so vast. Near Kununurra, on the eastern edge of the Kimberley, is a 400,000-hectare (1-million-acre) cattle station, El Questro, where you can camp in safari tents (or stay in an upmarket—read: "expensive"—homestead). From Kununurra you can fly over or hike into the beehive-shaped rock formation of the Bungle Bungles, cruise on the bird-rich, croc-infested Ord River, and tour the Argyle Diamond Mine, the world's biggest.

SOUTH AUSTRALIA Stretched between Western Australia and Victoria is the nation's breadbasket, South Australia. The capital, Adelaide, is a stately place known for its conservatism, parks, and churches. It makes an ideal base for exploring Australia's illustrious wine region, the Barossa Valley. Big labels like Penfolds, Seppelts, and Wolf Blass are here, but take time to sniff out the many smaller, though no less outstanding, vineyards. And it's less than an hour from the city!

Bring your binoculars to the massive water-bird sanctuary, the Coorong. Stay in an underground hotel in the offbeat opal-mining town of Coober Pedy (it's too hot aboveground), or order a 'roo-burger at the historic Prairie Hotel in the craggy, ancient lands of the Flinders Ranges in the South Australian Outback.

The greatest of South Australia's attractions—apart from wine, of course—is Kangaroo Island, the best place in Australia to see native animals. In a day you can spot wallabies, kangaroos, koalas, oodles of birds (from black swans to kookaburras), echidnas, and penguins. The beach teems with sea lions.

VICTORIA Australia's second-largest city, Melbourne, is the capital of Victoria. Melbourne is more stately and "Old World" than Sydney, and offers an exciting

Fun Fact **Where to Cuddle a Koala**

Koalas might look soft and cuddly, but the reality is a bit different. They are wild animals with sharp claws, and you should treat them with caution. Koalas in the wild are not safe to approach—even if you could reach them. Most of your encounters with them will be at a distance, looking on as they rest high in the branches of a tree, or in a wildlife park where "controlled cuddling" is allowed. Cuddling is allowed only in Queensland, South Australia, and Western Australia. In Victoria, New South Wales, and Tasmania, holding a koala is not allowed, but in some places you can pose beside one and have your photo taken. There are no koalas in the Northern Territory.

For more on koalas and where to see them in their natural habitat, contact the **Australian Koala Foundation (AKF)** (**✆ 1800 4KOALA** or 07/3229 7233; www.savethekoala.com) or drop into their office at 40 Charlotte St., Brisbane.

mix of ethnicities and the country's best fashion shopping. Nearby Phillip Island is famous for its Penguin Parade, during which hundreds of tiny penguins dash up the beach to their burrows at dusk. The historic gold-mining city of Ballarat is not far away. Victoria is also the site of one of Australia's great road trips, the Great Ocean Road. It stretches for 106km (66 miles) along the southern coast, where the eroded rock towers named the Twelve Apostles stand tall in the sea. Then there's the inland "high country," the stamping ground of the title character in Banjo Paterson's 1890 poem "The Man from Snowy River."

AUSTRALIAN CAPITAL TERRITORY (ACT) Surrounded entirely by New South Wales is the Australian Capital Territory. The ACT is made up of bushland and the nation's capital, Canberra, a planned city similar in architectural concept to Washington, D.C. Many Australians consider the capital boring, but Canberra will surprise you. It has some of the country's best museums and great restaurants, so don't automatically exclude it from your itinerary.

TASMANIA Last stop before Antarctica is the island state of Tasmania. Visit the Apple Isle for its beautiful national parks, stretches of alpine wilderness and gloomy forests, fruit and lavender farms, the world's best trout fishing, and an exquisitely slow pace of life rarely experienced anywhere else. If you're up to it, you could tackle the Overland Track, an 85km (53-mile) hiking trail between Cradle Mountain and Lake St. Clair that passes through highland moors, dense rainforests, and several mountains. A more leisurely option is a visit to the picturesque stone ruins of Port Arthur, Australia's version of Devil's Island, where thousands of convicts brought in to settle the new British colony were imprisoned and died. All of Tasmania is spectacular, but you haven't seen anything until you've experienced Freycinet National Park, with its pink granite outcrops set against an emerald-green sea.

2 Visitor Information & Maps

Tourism Australia is the best source of information on traveling Down Under. Its website, **www.australia.com**, has more than 10,000 pages of listings of tour operators, hotels, car-rental companies, special travel outfitters, holidays, maps,

Australia: Pre-Departure Checklist

- Are there any **special requirements** for your destination? Special visas, passports, or IDs? Detailed road maps? Bug repellents? Do you have your passport (and have you made sure it's current)?
- Did you check to see if any travel advisories have been issued by the U.S. State Department (http://travel.state.gov) regarding your destination?
- Do you have the address and phone number of your country's embassy or consulate with you?
- Did you find out your daily ATM withdrawal limit?
- Do you have your credit card PINs? If you have a five- or six-digit PIN, did you obtain a four-digit number from your bank? Australian ATMs operate with four-digit PINs, so make sure you get one before you leave.
- To check in at a kiosk with an e-ticket, do you have the credit card you bought your ticket with or a frequent-flier card?
- If you purchased traveler's checks, have you recorded the check numbers, and stored the documentation separately from the checks?
- Did you bring ID cards that could entitle you to discounts, such as AAA and AARP cards, student IDs, and the like?
- Did you leave a copy of your itinerary with someone at home?
- Do you need to book any theater, restaurant, or travel reservations in advance?

distance charts, suggested itineraries, and much more. The site provides information tailored to travelers from your country of origin, including packages and deals. Tourism Australia certifies a handpicked group of 133 "Aussie specialist" travel agents throughout North America, and you can search online by zip code or state to find one near you. By signing up for the free e-newsletter, you will receive updates on hot deals, events, and the like on a regular basis. You can also order brochures online. Tourism Australia operates a website only, no telephone lines. Other good sources are the websites of Australia's state tourism marketing offices. They are:

- **Australian Capital Tourism:** www.visitcanberra.com.au
- **Northern Territory Tourist Commission:** www.travelnt.com
- **South Australian Tourism Commission:** www.southaustralia.com
- **Tourism New South Wales:** www.visitnsw.com.au or www.sydneyaustralia.com
- **Tourism Queensland:** www.queenslandholidays.com.au
- **Tourism Tasmania:** www.discovertasmania.com
- **Tourism Victoria:** www.visitvictoria.com
- **Western Australian Tourism Commission:** www.westernaustralia.com

To read a few blogs about Australia (and other places) take a look at:

- www.gridskipper.com
- www.salon.com/wanderlust
- www.travelblog.com
- www.travelblog.org
- www.worldhum.com
- www.writtenroad.com

Two of the biggest map publishers in Australia are **HEMA Maps** (© **07/3340 0000;** www.hemamaps.com.au) and

Universal Publishers (© **1800/021 987** in Australia, or 02/9857 3700; www.universalpress-online.com). Both publish an extensive range of national, state, regional, and city maps. HEMA has a North American office (© **317/257-4362;** www.hemamaps.com) and maps are sold in the United States through **Barnes & Noble** (www.bn.com) and **Map Link** (© **800/962-1394;** www.maplink.com). HEMA maps are also distributed in Canada, by **ITMB,** or International Travel Maps and Books (© **604/879-3621;** www.itmb.com), and in the U.K. by **Blackwell** (© **01865/792 792;** www.blackwell.co.uk). Universal is also sold through Map Link (© **800/962-1394;** www.maplink.com) in the U.S.

3 Entry Requirements

PASSPORTS

For information on how to get a passport, go to "Passports" in the "Fast Facts: Australia" section, later in this chapter—the websites listed provide downloadable passport applications as well as the current fees for processing passport applications. Don't forget that children entering Australia on their parent's passport still need their own visa. For an up-to-date, country-by-country listing of passport requirements around the world, go to the "Foreign Entry Requirement" Web page of the U.S. State Department at **http://travel.state.gov**.

VISAS

Along with a current passport valid for the duration of your stay, the Australian government requires a visa from visitors of every nation, except New Zealand, to be issued before you arrive. If you are a short-term visitor or business traveler, the process is easy and can be done in a few minutes on the Internet, using the Australian government's **Electronic Travel Authority (ETA).** This is an electronic visa that takes the place of a stamp in your passport.

Tourists should apply for a **Visitor ETA.** The visa itself is free, though there is a service charge for getting it via the Internet, and permits unlimited visits to Australia of up to 3 months each within a 1-year period. Tourists may not work in Australia, so if you are visiting for business, you have two choices: Apply for a **Short Validity Business ETA,** which covers a single visit of 3 months within a 1-year period, or pay A$70 (US$56/UK£28) to apply for a **Long Validity Business visa,** which entitles you to as many 3-month stays in Australia as you like for the life of your passport but cannot be done online.

You can apply for an ETA yourself, or have your travel agent or airline do it when you book your plane ticket. (This service may incur an additional fee from the airline or travel agent.) To apply online, visit **www.eta.immi.gov.au**; the A$20 (US$16/UK£8) charge is payable by credit card (Amex, Diners Club, MasterCard, or Visa). Assuming you do not have a criminal conviction and are in good health, your ETA should be approved quickly. You can also apply for the visa at Australian embassies, high commissions, and consulates (see below for their locations). Children traveling on their parent's passport must have their own ETA.

Fees mentioned in this section are in Australian dollars; the exact amount charged by the Australian embassy, consulate, or high commission in your country will depend on the foreign currency exchange rate.

If your travel agent or airline is not connected to the ETA system, you will need to apply for a visa the old-fashioned way—by taking or mailing your passport, a completed visa application form, and the appropriate payment to your nearest Australian embassy or consulate.

In the United States, Canada, the United Kingdom, Ireland, and many other countries, most agents and airlines are ETA-compatible. You will also need to go the old-fashioned route if you are someone other than a tourist or a business traveler—for example, a student studying in Australia; a businessperson staying longer than 3 months; a long-term resident; an athlete going for a competition; a member of the media on assignment; a performer; or a member of a social group or cultural exchange. If you fall into one of these categories, you will need to apply for a **Temporary Residence visa.** Non-ETA visa application fees for other kinds of travelers vary, from free to thousands of dollars. Contact the Australian embassy, consulate, or high commission to check the forms of payment they accept.

Apply for non-ETA visas at Australian embassies, consulates, and high commissions. In the United States, apply to the Australian Embassy, 1601 Massachusetts Ave. NW, Washington, DC 20036 (© **888/990-8888** toll-free or 202/797-3000; immigration.washington@dfat.gov.au). The website of the Australian Embassy in North America is www.austemb.org.

In Canada, contact the Australian High Commission, 50 O'Connor St., No. 710, Ottawa, ON K1P 6L2 (© **613/236-0841;** www.canada.embassy.gov.au).

In the United Kingdom and Ireland, contact the Australian High Commission, Australia House, The Strand, London WC2B 4LA (© **020/7379 4334** for 24-hr. recorded information, or you can speak to an operator between 9am and 4pm weekdays; www.australia.org.uk). There is counter service only by appointment at the High Commission in London, and you should obtain an application form for a non-ETA visa by post or over the Internet at the Australian Department of Immigration and Multicultural Affairs website (www.immi.gov.au). This site also has a good explanation of the ETA system. Allow at least a month for processing of non-ETA visas.

British and Irish citizens aged from 18 to 30 may qualify for a working holiday visa which allows them to stay and work in Australia for a year (with conditions) and costs A$185 (US$148/UK£74).

MEDICAL REQUIREMENTS

For information on medical requirements and recommendations, see "Health," p. 46.

CUSTOMS

For information on what you can bring into and take out of Australia, go to **"Customs"** in the **"Fast Facts: Australia"** section of this chapter.

4 When to Go

When it is winter in the Northern Hemisphere, Australia is basking in the Southern Hemisphere's summer, and vice versa. Midwinter in Australia is July and August, and the hottest months are November through March. Remember, unlike in the Northern Hemisphere, the farther south you go in Australia, the colder it gets.

THE TRAVEL SEASONS

Airfares to Australia offered by U.S. airlines are lowest from mid-April to late August—the best time to visit the Red Centre, the Top End, and the Great Barrier Reef.

HIGH SEASON The peak travel season in the most popular parts of Australia

> *Tips* **Steer Clear of the Vacation Rush**
>
> Try to avoid Australia from Boxing Day (Dec 26) to the end of January, when Aussies take their summer vacations. In popular seaside holiday spots, hotel rooms and airline seats get scarce as hen's teeth, and it's a rare airline or hotel that will discount full rates by even a dollar.

is the Aussie winter. In much of the country—Queensland from around Townsville and northward, all of the Top End and the Red Centre, and most of Western Australia—the most pleasant time to travel is April through September, when daytime temperatures are 66° to 88°F (19°–31°C) and it rarely rains. June, July, and August are the busiest months in these parts; you'll need to book accommodations and tours well in advance, and you will pay higher rates then, too.

On the other hand, Australia's summer is a nice time to visit the southern states—New South Wales, Victoria, South Australia, Western Australia from Perth to the south, and Tasmania. Even in winter, temperatures rarely dip below freezing, and snow falls only in parts of Tasmania, in the ski fields of Victoria, and in the Snowy Mountains of southern New South Wales.

The best months to visit Australia, I think, are September and October, when it's often still warm enough to hit the beach in the southern states, it's cool enough to tour Uluru (Ayers Rock), and the humidity and rains have not come to Cairns and the Top End (although it will be very hot by Oct). And the wildflowers are in full bloom in Western Australia.

LOW SEASON October through March (summer) it is just too hot, too humid, too wet—or all three—to tour the Red Centre, the Top End, and anywhere in Western Australia except Perth and the southwest. The Top End, the Kimberley, and North Queensland, including Cairns, suffer an intensely hot, humid Wet season from November or December through March or April. In the Top End and Kimberley, this is preceded by an even stickier "build-up" in October and November. Some attractions and tour companies close, floodwaters render others off-limits, and hotels drop their rates, often dramatically. So if you decide to travel in these areas at this time—and lots of people do—be prepared to take the heat, the inconvenience of floods, and, in tropical coastal areas, the slight chance of encountering cyclones.

HOLIDAYS

In addition to the period from December 26 to the end of January, when Aussies take their summer vacations, the 4 days at Easter (from Good Friday to Easter Monday) and all school holidays are very busy, so book ahead. The school year in Australia is broken into four semesters, with 2-week holidays around Easter, the last week of June and the first week of July, and the last week of September and the first week of October. Some states break at slightly different dates. There's a 6-week summer (Christmas) vacation from mid-December to the end of January.

Almost everything shuts down on Good Friday, Christmas Day, and Boxing Day (Dec 26), and much is closed January 1, Easter Sunday, and Easter Monday. Most establishments close until 1pm, if not all day, on Anzac Day (Apr 25), a World War I commemorative day.

Among the major public holidays are: New Year's Day (Jan 1); Australia Day (Jan 26); Labour Day (second Mon in Mar, WA); Eight Hours Day (first Mon in Mar, TAS); Labour Day (second Mon in Mar, VIC); Canberra Day (third Mon in Mar, ACT); Good Friday; Easter Sunday; Easter Monday; Anzac Day (Apr 25); May Day (first Mon in May, NT); Labour Day (first Mon in May, QLD); Adelaide Cup (third Mon in May, SA); Foundation Day (first Mon in June, WA); Queen's Birthday (second Mon in June, except WA); Royal National Show Day (second or third Wed in Aug, QLD); Queen's Birthday (Mon in late Sept/early Oct, WA); Labour Day (first Mon in Oct, NSW and SA); Melbourne Cup Day (first Tues in Nov, Melbourne); Christmas (Dec 25); and Boxing Day (Dec 26). If December 26 falls on a weekend, the following Monday is a holiday.

AUSTRALIA CALENDAR OF EVENTS

January

Sydney Festival. Highlights of Sydney's visual and performing arts festival are free jazz or classical music concerts held outdoors on 2 Saturday nights near the Royal Botanic Gardens. (Take a picnic and arrive by 4pm to get a place.) Call © **02/8248 6500** or go to www.sydneyfestival.org.au. January 5 to January 26, 2008.

Hyundai Hopman Cup, Perth. Tennis greats from the world's nine top tennis nations battle it out in a 7-day mixed-doubles competition. For tickets, contact Ticketek (© **132 849** in Australia; www.ticketek.com), or check www.hopmancup.com.au. December 29, 2007, to January 4, 2008.

Tamworth Country Music Festival, Tamworth (459km/285 miles northwest of Sydney), New South Wales. It may look like an Akubra Hat Convention, but this gathering of rural folk and city folk who would like to be rural folk is Australia's biggest country music festival. The Tamworth Visitor Information Centre (© **02/6767 5300;** www.tamworth.nsw.gov.au) takes bookings. January 18 to January 27, 2008.

Australia Day. Australia's answer to Fourth of July marks the landing of the First Fleet of convicts at Sydney Cove in 1788. Every town puts on some kind of celebration; in Sydney, there are ferry races and Tall Ships on the harbor, food and wine stalls in Hyde Park, open days at museums and other attractions, and fireworks in the evening. January 26.

March

Sydney Gay & Lesbian Mardi Gras. A month of events, culminating in a spectacular parade of costumed dancers and decorated floats, watched by several hundred thousand onlookers, followed by a giant warehouse party (by invitation only). Contact Sydney Gay & Lesbian Mardi Gras (© **02/9568 8600;** www.mardigras.org.au). The parade is scheduled for March 1, 2008.

Australian Formula One Grand Prix, Melbourne. The first Grand Prix of the year on the international FIA Formula One World Championship circuit is battled out on one of its fastest circuits, in Melbourne. For tickets, contact Ticketek (© **132 849** in Australia) or order online at http://cars.grandprix.com.au. Four days in the first or second week of March.

Australian Surf Life Saving Championships, Scarborough Beach, Perth, Western Australia. Traditionally held at Queensland's Gold Coast, this event has moved across the country until 2009. It sees up to 8,000 bronzed Aussie and international men and women swim, ski paddle, sprint relay, pilot rescue boats, parade past admiring crowds, and resuscitate "drowning" swimmers in front of around 10,000 spectators. Contact Surf Life Saving Australia (✆ **02/9300 4000;** www.slsa.com.au). Four or 5 days in mid to late March.

June

Sydney Film Festival. World and Australian premieres of Aussie and international movies take place in the State Theatre and other venues. Contact the Sydney Film Festival (✆ **02/9318 0999;** www.sydneyfilmfestival.org). Two weeks from first or second Friday in June.

August

***Sun-Herald* City to Surf,** Sydney. Fifty thousand Sydneysiders pound the pavement (or walk or wheelchair it) in this 14km (8¾-mile) "fun run" from the city to Bondi Beach, which has been run for the past 35 years. For entry details, visit http://city2surf.sunherald.com.au (from June onward) or call ✆ **1800/555 514** in Australia. If slots are available, you can enter the day of the race. The fee is A$30 (US$24/UK£12). Second Sunday in August.

September

Floriade, Canberra. A million tulips, daffodils, hyacinths, and other blooms carpet the banks of Canberra's Lake Burley Griffin in stunning themed flower-bed designs at this celebration, which features performing arts and other entertainment. Contact Canberra & Region Visitors Centre (✆ **1300/554 114** in Australia; www.visitcanberra.com.au). For more detail on Floriade, check out the website, www.floriadeaustralia.com. September 13 to October 12, 2008.

Henley-on-Todd Regatta, Alice Springs. Sounds sophisticated, doesn't it? It's actually a harum-scarum race down the dry bed of the Todd River in homemade "boats" made from anything you care to name—an old four-wheel-drive chassis, say, or beer cans lashed together. The only rule is the vessel has to look *vaguely* like a boat. Contact the organizers at ✆ **08/8952 6796** or www.henleyontodd.com.au. September 6, 2008.

October

Lexmark Indy 300 Carnival, Surfers Paradise, Queensland. The world's best Indy-car drivers race a street circuit around Surfers Paradise on the glitzy Gold Coast, as part of the international FedEx Championship champ car motor-sport series. Contact Ticketek (✆ **1300/303 103** in Australia; www.ticketek.com), or check the event's website (www.indy.com.au). Four days in mid- or late October.

November

Melbourne Cup, Flemington racecourse. They say the whole nation stops to watch this horse race. That's about right. If you're not actually at the A$3.5-million (US$2.8-million/UK£1.4-million) race, you're glued to the TV—or, well, you're probably not an Australian. Women wear hats to the office, files on desks all over the country make way for a late chicken and champagne lunch, and don't even think about flagging a cab at the 3:20pm race time. For tickets, contact Ticketmaster (✆ **1300/136 122** in Australia; www.ticketmaster.com.au); for information, visit www.vrc.net.au. First Tuesday in November.

December

Sydney-to-Hobart Yacht Race. Find a cliff-top spot near the Heads to watch the glorious show of spinnakers as 100 or so yachts leave Sydney Harbour for this grueling world-class event. The organizer is the Sydney-based Cruising Yacht Club of Australia (✆ **02/8292 7800;** www.cyca.com.au). Starts December 26.

New Year's Eve. Watching the Sydney Harbour Bridge light up with fireworks is a treat. The main show is at 9pm, not midnight, so young kids don't miss out. Pack a picnic and snag a Harbour-side spot by 4pm, or even earlier at the best vantage point—Mrs. Macquarie's Chair in the Royal Botanic Gardens.

5 Getting There

BY PLANE

Australia is a long, long haul from anywhere except New Zealand. Sydney is a nearly 15-hour nonstop flight from Los Angeles, longer if you come via Honolulu. From the East Coast, add 5½ hours. If you're coming from the States via Auckland, add transit time in New Zealand plus another 3 hours for the Auckland-Sydney leg. If you are coming from the United Kingdom, brace yourself for a flight of 12 hours, more or less, from London to Asia; then possibly a long day in transit, because flights to Australia have a habit of arriving in Asia early in the morning and departing around midnight; and finally the 8- to 9-hour flight to Australia.

Sydney (SYD), Cairns (CNS), Melbourne (MEL), Brisbane (BNE), Adelaide (ADL), Darwin (DRW), and Perth (PER) are all international gateways, but most airlines fly only into Sydney. A few fly to Melbourne and Brisbane.

THE MAJOR CARRIERS

Here are toll-free reservations numbers and websites for the major international airlines serving Australia. The "13" prefix in Australia means that the number incurs the same cost as a local call from anywhere in the country.

Tips Getting through the Airport

- Arrive at the airport at least 2 hours before an international flight. You can check the average wait times at your airport by going to the TSA **Security Checkpoint Wait Times** site (waittime/tsa.dhs.gov).
- Know what you can carry on and what you can't. For the latest updates on items you are prohibited to bring in carry-on luggage, go to **www.tsa.gov/travelers/airtravel.**
- Beat the ticket-counter lines by using the self-service electronic ticket kiosks at the airport or even printing out your boarding pass at home from the airline website. Using curbside check-in is also a smart way to avoid lines.
- Help speed up security before you're screened. Remove jackets, shoes, belt buckles, heavy jewelry, and watches and place them either in your carry-on luggage or the security bins provided. Place keys, coins, cellphones, and pagers in a security bin. If you have metallic body parts, carry a note from your doctor. When possible, keep packing liquids in checked baggage.
- Use a TSA-approved lock for your checked luggage. Look for Travel Sentry certified locks at luggage or travel shops and Brookstone stores (or online at www.brookstone.com).

Tips Don't Stow It—Ship It

Though pricey, it's sometimes worthwhile to travel luggage-free, particularly if you're toting sports equipment, meetings materials, or baby equipment. Specialists in door-to-door luggage delivery include **Virtual Bellhop** (www.virtualbellhop.com); **SkyCap International** (www.skycapinternational.com); **Luggage Express** (www.usxpluggageexpress.com); and **Sports Express** (www.sportsexpress.com).

CARRIERS FLYING FROM NORTH AMERICA

- **Air Canada** (✆ **888/247-2262** in the U.S. and Canada, 02/8248 5757 in Sydney, or 1300/655 767 from elsewhere in Australia; www.aircanada.com).
- **Air New Zealand** (✆ **800/262-1234** in the U.S., 310/615-1111 in the Los Angeles area, 800/663-5494 in Canada, or 13 24 76 in Australia; www.airnewzealand.com).
- **Qantas** (✆ **800/227-4500** in the U.S. and Canada, or 13 13 13 in Australia; www.qantas.com.au).
- **United Airlines** (✆ **800/538-2929** in the U.S. and Canada, or 13 17 77 in Australia; www.united.com or www.united.ca).

CARRIERS FLYING FROM THE UNITED KINGDOM

- **British Airways** (✆ **0870/850 9850** in the U.K., 1890/626 747 in Ireland, or 1300/767 177 in Australia; www.britishairways.com).
- **Cathay Pacific** (✆ **020/8834 8888** in the U.K., or 13 17 47 in Australia; www.cathaypacific.com).
- **Malaysia Airlines** (✆ **0870/607 9090** in the U.K. and Ireland, or 13 26 27 in Australia; www.malaysiaairlines.com).
- **Qantas** (✆ **0845/774 7767** in the U.K., or 13 13 13 in Australia; www.qantas.com.au).
- **Singapore Airlines** (✆ **0844/800 2380** in the U.K., or 13 10 11 in Australia; www.singaporeair.com/uk).
- **Thai Airways International** (✆ **0870/6060 911** in the U.K., or 1300/651 960 in Australia; www.thaiair.com).

FLYING FOR LESS: TIPS FOR GETTING THE BEST AIRFARE

- Passengers who can book their ticket either **long in advance or at the last minute,** or who **fly midweek** or **at less-trafficked hours** may pay a fraction of the full fare. If your schedule is flexible, say so, and ask if you can secure a cheaper fare by changing your flight plans.
- Search **the Internet** for cheap fares. The most popular online travel agencies are **Travelocity.com** (www.travelocity.co.uk); **Expedia.com** (www.expedia.co.uk and www.expedia.ca); and **Orbitz.com**. In the U.K., go to **Travelsupermarket** (✆ **0845/345-5708;** www.travelsupermarket.com), a flight search engine that offers flight comparisons for the budget airlines whose seats often end up in bucket-shop sales. Other websites for booking airline tickets online include **Cheapflights.com**, **SmarterTravel.com**, **Priceline.com**, and **Opodo** (www.opodo.co.uk). Meta search sites (which find and then direct you to airline and hotel websites for booking) include **Sidestep.com** and **Kayak.com**—the latter includes fares for budget carriers like Jet Blue and Spirit as well as the major airlines. **Site59.com** is a great source for last-minute flights

and getaways. In addition, most **airlines** offer online-only fares that even their phone agents know nothing about. British travelers should check **Flights International** (✆ **0800/0187050;** www.flights-international.com) for deals on flights all over the world.

- Keep an eye on local newspapers for **promotional specials** or **fare wars,** when airlines lower prices on their most popular routes.
- Try to book a ticket **in its country of origin.** For instance, if you're planning a one-way flight from Sydney to Auckland, an Australia-based travel agent such as Flight Centre (✆ **133 133** in Australia or 07/3011 7830, 24 hr. a day; www.flightcentre.com.au) will probably have the lowest fares. For multi-leg trips, book in the country of the first leg; for example, book Melbourne–Auckland–Los Angeles in Australia.
- Travel agents specializing in cheap fares include **Austravel** (✆ **0870/166 2020** in the U.K.; www.austravel.net); **Downunder Direct,** a division of Swain Australia (✆ **800/642-6224** in the U.S. and Canada; www.downunderdirect.com); and **Goway** (✆ **800/387-8850** in the U.S. and Canada; www.goway.com).
- **Consolidators,** also known as bucket shops, are wholesale brokers in the airline-ticket game. Consolidators buy deeply discounted tickets ("distressed" inventories of unsold seats) from airlines and sell them to online ticket agencies, travel agents, tour operators, corporations, and, to a lesser degree, the general public. Consolidators advertise in Sunday newspaper travel sections (often in small ads with tiny type), both in the U.S. and the U.K. They can be great sources for cheap international tickets. On the downside, bucket shop tickets are often rigged with restrictions, such as stiff cancellation penalties (as high as 50%–75% of the ticket price). And keep in mind that most of what you see advertised is of limited availability. Several reliable consolidators are worldwide and

---

Tips Coping with Jet Lag

Jet lag is a pitfall of traveling across time zones. If you're flying north-south and you feel sluggish when you touch down, your symptoms will be the result of dehydration and the general stress of air travel. When you travel east-west or vice versa, however, your body becomes thoroughly confused about what time it is, and everything from your digestive system to your brain is knocked for a loop. Traveling east, say from Chicago to Paris, is more difficult on your internal clock than traveling west, say from London to Atlanta, because most peoples' bodies are more inclined to stay up late than fall asleep early.

Here are some tips for combating jet lag:

- **Reset your watch** to your destination time before you board the plane.
- **Drink lots of water** before, during, and after your flight. Avoid alcohol.
- **Exercise and sleep well** for a few days before your trip.
- If you have trouble sleeping on planes, **fly eastward on morning flights.**
- **Daylight** is the key to resetting your body clock. At the website for **Outside In** (www.bodyclock.com), you can get a customized plan of when to seek and avoid light.

Tips for Digital Travel Photography

- **Take along a spare camera—or two.** Even if you've been anointed the "official" photographer of your travel group, encourage others in your party to carry their own cameras and provide fresh perspectives—and backup. Your photographic "second unit" may include you in a few shots so you're not the invisible person of the trip.
- **Stock up on digital film cards.** At home, it's easy to copy pictures from your memory cards to your computer as they fill up. During your travels, cards seem to fill up more quickly. Take along enough digital film for your entire trip or, at a minimum, enough for at least a few days' of shooting. At intervals, you can copy images to CDs. Many camera stores and souvenir shops offer this service, and a growing number of mass merchandisers have walk-up kiosks you can use to make prints or create CDs while you travel.
- **Share and share alike.** There's no need to wait until you get home to share your photos. You can upload a gallery's worth to an online photo sharing service. Just find an Internet cafe where the computers have card readers, or connect your camera to the computer with a cable. You can find online photo sharing services that cost little or nothing at **www.clickherefree.com**. You can also use America Online's Your Pictures service, or other sites that give you free or low-cost photo sharing: Kodak's EasyShare gallery (**www.kodak.com**), Snapfish (**www.snapfish.com**), or Shutterfly (**www.shutterfly.com**).
- **Add voice annotations to your photos.** Many digital cameras allow you to add voice annotations to your shots after they're taken. These serve as excellent reminders and documentation. One castle or cathedral may look like another after a long tour; your voice notes will help you distinguish them.
- **Experiment!** Travel is a great time to try out new techniques. Take photos at night, resting your camera on a handy wall or other support as your self-timer trips the shutter for a long exposure. Try close-ups of flowers, crafts, wildlife, or maybe the exotic cuisine you're about to consume. Discover action photography—shoot the countryside from trains, buses, or cars. With a digital camera, you can experiment and then erase your mistakes.

—*From* Travel Photography Digital Field Guide, *1st Edition (John Wiley & Sons, 2006)*

available online. **STA Travel** (www.statravel.com) has been the world's leading consolidator for students since purchasing Council Travel, but their fares are competitive for travelers of all ages. **Flights.com** (✆ **800/TRAV-800;** www.flights.com) has excellent fares worldwide, particularly to Europe. They also have "local" websites in 12 countries. **FlyCheap** (✆ **800/FLY-CHEAP;** www.1800flycheap.com) has especially good fares to sunny destinations. **Air Tickets**

Flying with Film & Video

Never pack film—exposed or unexposed—in checked bags, because the new, more powerful scanners in U.S. airports can fog film. The film you carry with you can be damaged by scanners as well. X-ray damage is cumulative; the faster the film, and the more times you put it through a scanner, the more likely the damage. Film under 800 ASA is usually safe for up to five scans. If you're taking your film through additional scans, U.S. regulations permit you to demand hand inspections. In international airports, you're at the mercy of airport officials. On international flights, store your film in transparent baggies, so you can remove it easily before you go through scanners. Keep in mind that airports are not the only places where your camera may be scanned: Highly trafficked attractions are X-raying visitors' bags with increasing frequency.

Most photo supply stores sell pouches designed to block damaging X-rays. The pouches fit both film and loaded cameras. They should protect your film in checked baggage, but also may raise alarms and result in a hand inspection.

You'll have little to worry about if you are traveling with **digital cameras.** Unlike film, which is sensitive to light, the digital camera and storage cards are not affected by airport X-rays, according to Nikon.

Carry-on scanners will not damage **videotape** in cameras, but the magnetic fields emitted by the walk-through security gateways and hand-held inspection wands will. Always place your loaded camcorder on the screening conveyor belt or have it hand-inspected. Be sure your batteries are charged, as you may be required to turn the device on to ensure that it's what it appears to be.

Direct (✆ **800/778-3447;** www.airticketsdirect.com) is based in Montreal and leverages the currently weak Canadian dollar for low fares; they also book trips to places that U.S. travel agents won't touch, such as Cuba.

- Join **frequent-flier clubs.** Frequent-flier membership doesn't cost a cent, but it does entitle you to free tickets or upgrades when you amass the airline's required number of frequent-flier points. You don't even have to fly to earn points; **frequent-flier credit cards** can earn you thousands of miles for doing your everyday shopping. But keep in mind that award seats are limited, seats on popular routes are hard to snag, and more and more major airlines are cutting their expiration periods for mileage points—so check your airline's frequent-flier program so you don't lose your miles before you use them. ***Inside tip:*** Award seats are offered almost a year in advance, but seats also open up at the last minute, so if your travel plans are flexible, you may strike gold. To play the frequent-flier game to your best advantage, consult the community bulletin boards on **FlyerTalk** (www.flyertalk.com) or go to Randy Petersen's **Inside Flyer** (www.insideflyer.com). Petersen and friends review all the programs in detail and post regular updates on changes in policies and trends.

LONG-HAUL FLIGHTS: HOW TO STAY COMFORTABLE

- Your choice of airline and airplane will definitely affect your leg room. Find more details about U.S. airlines at **www.seatguru.com**. For international airlines, the research firm Skytrax has posted a list of average seat pitches at **www.airlinequality.com**.
- Emergency exit seats and bulkhead seats typically have the most legroom. Emergency exit seats are usually left unassigned until the day of a flight (to ensure that someone able-bodied fills the seats); it's worth getting to the ticket counter early to snag one for a long flight. Many passengers find that bulkhead seating (the row facing the wall at the front of the cabin) offers more legroom, but keep in mind that bulkhead seats have no storage space on the floor in front of you.
- To have two seats for yourself in a three-seat row, try for an aisle seat in a center section toward the back of coach. If you're traveling with a companion, book an aisle and a window seat. Middle seats are usually booked last, so chances are good you'll end up with three seats to yourselves. And if a third passenger is assigned the middle seat, he or she will probably be more than happy to trade for a window or an aisle.
- Ask about entertainment options. Many airlines offer seatback video systems where you get to choose your movies or play video games—but only on some of their planes. (Boeing 777s are your best bet.)
- To sleep, avoid the last row of any section or the row in front of an emergency exit, as these seats are the least likely to recline. Avoid seats near highly trafficked toilet areas. Avoid seats in the back of many jets—these can be narrower than those in the rest of coach. Or reserve a window seat so you can rest your head and avoid being bumped in the aisle.
- Get up, walk around, and stretch every 60 to 90 minutes to keep your blood flowing. This helps avoid **deep vein thrombosis,** or "economy-class syndrome." See the box "Avoiding 'Economy-Class Syndrome,'" p. 46.
- Drink water before, during, and after your flight to combat the lack of humidity in airplane cabins. Avoid alcohol, which will dehydrate you.
- If you're flying with kids, don't forget to carry on toys, books, pacifiers, and snacks and chewing gum to help them relieve ear pressure buildup during ascent and descent.

6 General Travel Resources

MONEY & COSTS

It's always advisable to bring money in a variety of forms on a vacation: a mix of cash, credit cards, and traveler's checks. You should also exchange enough petty cash to cover airport incidentals, tipping, and transportation to your hotel before you leave home, or withdraw money upon arrival at an airport ATM.

In many international destinations, ATMs offer the best exchange rates. Avoid exchanging money at commercial exchange bureaus and hotels, which often have the highest transaction fees.

CURRENCY

The Australian dollar is divided into 100¢. Coins are 5¢, 10¢, 20¢, and 50¢ pieces (silver) and $1 and $2 pieces (gold). Prices often end in a variant of 1¢ and 2¢ (for example, 78¢ or $2.71), a relic from the days before 1-cent and

2-cent pieces were phased out. Prices are rounded to the nearest 5¢—so 77¢ rounds down to 75¢, and 78¢ rounds up to 80¢. Bank notes come in denominations of $5, $10, $20, $50, and $100.

The Universal Currency Converter (www.xe.com/ucc) will give you up-to-the-minute conversions for your dollar or pound in dozens of countries.

For American and European travelers, Australia is quite affordable. Over the past few years, the Australian dollar has fluctuated but seems to have steadied at around A$1.25 = US$1 in the past year or so, and this is the rate we have used throughout this book. Most travelers will find money matters relatively easy in Australia, but beware the small town where traveler's checks may not be readily accepted. We've also included price conversions to British pounds.

You should consider changing a small amount of money into Australian currency before you leave, (though don't expect the exchange rate to be ideal), so you can avoid lines at airport ATMs (automated teller machines). You can exchange money at your local American Express or Thomas Cook office or your bank. If you're far away from a bank with currency-exchange services, **American Express** offers traveler's checks and foreign currency, though with a $15 order fee and additional shipping costs, at www.americanexpress.com or ✆ **800/807-6233.**

ATMs

The easiest and best way to get cash away from home is from an ATM (automated teller machine), sometimes referred to as a "cash machine" or a "cashpoint." The **Cirrus** (✆ **800/424-7787;** www.mastercard.com) and **PLUS** (✆ **800/843-7587;** www.visa.com) networks span the globe. Go to your bank card's website to find ATM locations at your destination. Be sure you know your daily withdrawal limit before you depart. Australian ATMs use a four-digit code, so check with your bank and make sure you change yours before you leave home. ***Note:*** Many banks impose a fee every time you use a card at another bank's ATM, and that fee can be higher for international transactions (up to $5 or more) than for domestic ones (where they're rarely more than $2). In addition, the bank from which you withdraw cash may charge its own fee. For international withdrawal fees, ask your bank.

CREDIT CARDS

Credit cards are another safe way to carry money. They also provide a convenient record of all your expenses, and they generally offer relatively good exchange rates. You can withdraw cash advances from your credit cards at banks or ATMs but high fees make credit card cash advances a pricey way to get cash. Keep in mind that you'll pay interest from the moment of your withdrawal, even if you pay your monthly bills on time. Also, note that many banks now assess a 1%-to-3% "transaction fee" on **all** charges you incur abroad (whether you're using the local currency or your native currency).

Visa and MasterCard are universally accepted in Australia; American Express and Diners Club are less common, and Discover is not used. Always carry a little cash, because many merchants will not

---

Tips **Going with the Gold**

Australia has $1 and $2 coins which are a dull bronze but generally known as "gold." It's common for attractions or charities to request "gold coin" contributions as an entry fee. (So keep some handy!)

The Australian Dollar, the U.S. Dollar & the British Pound

For U.S. Readers The rate of exchange used to calculate the dollar values given in this book was US$1 = approximately A$1.25 (or A$1 = US80¢).

For British Readers The rate of exchange used to calculate the pound values in the accompanying table was £1 = A$2.45 (or A$1 = 40p).

Note: International exchange rates for the Australian dollar can fluctuate markedly. Check the latest rate when you plan your trip. The table below, and all the prices in this book, should be used only as a guide.

A$	US$	UK£	A$	US$	UK£
0.25	0.20	0.10	30.00	24.00	12.00
0.50	0.40	0.20	35.00	28.00	14.00
1.00	0.80	0.40	40.00	32.00	16.00
2.00	1.60	0.80	45.00	36.00	18.00
3.00	2.40	1.20	50.00	40.00	20.00
4.00	3.20	1.60	55.00	44.00	22.00
5.00	4.00	2.00	60.00	48.00	24.00
6.00	4.80	2.40	65.00	52.00	26.00
7.00	5.60	2.80	70.00	56.00	28.00
8.00	6.40	3.20	75.00	60.00	30.00
9.00	7.20	3.60	80.00	64.00	32.00
10.00	8.00	4.00	85.00	68.00	34.00
15.00	12.00	6.00	90.00	72.00	36.00
20.00	16.00	8.00	95.00	76.00	38.00
25.00	20.00	10.00	100.00	80.00	40.00

take cards for purchases under A$15 (US$12/UK£6) or so.

TRAVELER'S CHECKS

You can buy traveler's checks at most banks. They are offered in denominations of $20, $50, $100, $500, and sometimes $1,000. Generally, you'll pay a service charge ranging from 1% to 4%.

The most popular traveler's checks are offered by **American Express** (© **800/807-6233,** or 800/221-7282 for card holders—this number accepts collect calls, offers service in several foreign languages, and exempts Amex gold and platinum cardholders from the 1% fee); **Visa** (© **800/732-1322**)—AAA members can obtain Visa checks for a $9.95 fee (for checks up to $1,500) at most AAA offices or by calling © **866/339-3378;** and **MasterCard** (© **800/223-9920**).

However, be warned that traveler's checks are not as widely accepted in Australia as in many other countries. If you do opt for them, get them in Australian dollars. Checks in U.S. dollars are accepted at banks, big hotels, currency exchanges, and some shops in major tourist regions, but smaller shops, restaurants, and other businesses will have no idea what the exchange rate is when you present a U.S. check. Another advantage of Australian-dollar checks is that the two largest Aussie banks, ANZ and Westpac, cash them free; it will cost you around

A$5 to A$11 (US$4–US$8.80/UK£2–UK£4.40) to cash checks denominated in foreign currency at most Australian banks.

Be sure to keep a record of the traveler's checks serial numbers separate from your checks in the event that they are stolen or lost. You'll get a refund faster if you know the numbers.

American Express, Thomas Cook, Visa, and **MasterCard** offer **foreign currency traveler's checks,** useful if you're traveling to just one country; they're accepted at locations where dollar checks may not be.

Another option is the new prepaid traveler's check cards, reloadable cards that work much like debit cards but aren't linked to your checking account. The **American Express Travelers Cheque Card,** for example, requires a minimum deposit, sets a maximum balance, and has a one-time issuance fee of $15. You can withdraw money from an ATM (for a fee of $2.50 per transaction, not including bank fees), and the funds can be purchased in dollars, euros, or pounds. If you lose the card, your available funds will be refunded within 24 hours.

TRAVEL INSURANCE

The cost of travel insurance varies widely, depending on the destination, the cost and length of your trip, your age and health, and the type of trip you're taking, but expect to pay between 5% and 8% of the vacation itself. You can get estimates from various providers through **InsureMyTrip.com**. Enter your trip cost and dates, your age, and other information, for prices from more than a dozen companies.

U.K. citizens and their families who make more than one trip abroad per year may find an annual travel insurance policy works out cheaper. Check **www.moneysupermarket.com**, which compares prices across a wide range of providers for single- and multi-trip policies.

Most big travel agents offer their own insurance and will probably try to sell you their package when you book a holiday. Think before you sign. **Britain's Consumers' Association** recommends that you insist on seeing the policy and reading the fine print before buying travel insurance. **The Association of British Insurers** (✆ **020/7600-3333;** www.abi.org.uk) gives advice by phone and publishes *Holiday Insurance,* a free guide to policy provisions and prices. You might also shop around for better deals: Try **Columbus Direct** (✆ **0870/033-9988;** www.columbusdirect.net).

TRIP-CANCELLATION INSURANCE

Trip-cancellation insurance will help retrieve your money if you have to back out of a trip or depart early, or if your travel supplier goes bankrupt. Trip cancellation traditionally covers such events as sickness, natural disasters, and State Department advisories. The latest news in trip-cancellation insurance is the availability of **expanded hurricane coverage** and the **"any-reason"** cancellation coverage—which costs more but covers cancellations made for any reason. You won't get back 100% of your prepaid trip cost, but you'll be refunded a substantial portion. **TravelSafe** (✆ **888/885-7233;** www.travelsafe.com) offers both types of coverage. Expedia also offers any-reason cancellation coverage for its air-hotel packages.

For details, contact one of the following recommended insurers: **Access America** (✆ 866/807-3982; www.accessamerica.com); **Travel Guard International** (✆ 800/826-4919; www.travelguard.com); **Travel Insured International** (✆ 800/243-3174; www.travelinsured.com); and **Travelex Insurance Services** (✆ 888/457-4602; www.travelex-insurance.com).

Travel in the Age of Bankruptcy

Airlines go bankrupt, so protect yourself by **buying your tickets with a credit card.** The Fair Credit Billing Act guarantees that you can get your money back from the credit card company if a travel supplier goes under (and if you request the refund within 60 days of the bankruptcy). **Travel insurance** can also help, but make sure it covers against "carrier default" for your specific travel provider. And be aware that if a U.S. airline goes bust mid-trip, a 2001 federal law requires other carriers to take you to your destination (albeit on a space-available basis) for a fee of no more than $25, provided you rebook within 60 days of the cancellation.

MEDICAL INSURANCE

For travel overseas, most U.S. health plans (including Medicare and Medicaid) do not provide coverage, and the ones that do often require you to pay for services upfront and reimburse you only after you return home.

As a safety net, you may want to buy travel medical insurance, particularly if you're traveling to a remote or high-risk area where emergency evacuation might be necessary.

Australia's immense distances mean you can sometimes be a long way from a hospital or a doctor. Make sure your policy covers medical evacuation by helicopter or Australia's Royal Flying Doctor Service airlift. (You might well need this if you become sick or injured in the Outback.)

Australia has a reciprocal medical-care agreement with Great Britain and a limited agreement with Ireland and New Zealand. It covers travelers for medical expenses for immediately necessary treatment in a public hospital (but not evacuation to your home country, ambulances, funerals, and dental care) by Australia's national health system, called Medicare, which is similar to the program by the same name in the United States. It's crucial to buy insurance, though, because medical care in Australia is expensive, and the national healthcare system typically covers only 85%, sometimes less, of treatment; you will not be covered for treatment in a private hospital; and evacuation insurance is a must. Most foreign students must take out the Australian government's Overseas Student Health Cover as a condition of entry.

If you require additional medical insurance, try **MEDEX Assistance** (© 410/453-6300; www.medexassist.com) or **Travel Assistance International** (© **800/821-2828;** www.travelassistance.com; for general information on services, call the company's **Worldwide Assistance Services, Inc.,** at © **800/777-8710**).

Canadians should check with their provincial health plan offices or call **Health Canada** (© **866/225-0709;** www.hc-sc.gc.ca) to find out the extent of their coverage and what documentation and receipts they must take home in case they are treated overseas.

LOST-LUGGAGE INSURANCE

On international flights (including U.S. portions of international trips), baggage coverage is limited to approximately $9.07 per pound, up to approximately $635 per checked bag. If you plan to check items more valuable than what's covered by the standard liability, see if your homeowner's policy covers your valuables, get baggage insurance as part of your comprehensive travel-insurance package, or buy Travel Guard's "BagTrak" product.

If your luggage is lost, immediately file a lost-luggage claim at the airport, detailing the luggage contents. Most airlines require that you report delayed, damaged, or lost baggage within 4 hours of arrival. The airlines are required to deliver luggage, once found, directly to your house or destination free of charge.

HEALTH

STAYING HEALTHY

You don't have to worry much about health issues on a trip to Australia. Hygiene standards are high, hospitals are modern, and doctors and dentists are well qualified. Because of the continent's size, you can sometimes be a long way from a hospital or a doctor, but help is never far away, thanks to the Royal Flying Doctor Service. However, standard medical travel insurance may be advisable (see the previous section).

GENERAL AVAILABILITY OF HEALTHCARE

Before you go: No vaccinations are needed to enter Australia unless you have been in a yellow fever danger zone—that is, South America or Africa—in the past 6 days.

Australian pharmacists may only fill prescriptions written by Australian doctors, so carry enough medication with you for your trip. Doctors are listed under "M," for "Medical Practitioners," in the Yellow Pages, and most large towns and cities have 24-hour clinics. Failing that, go to the local emergency room.

Contact the **International Association for Medical Assistance to Travelers (IAMAT)** (✆ **716/754-4883** or, in Canada, 416/652-0137; www.iamat.org) for tips on travel and health concerns in the countries you're visiting. The United States **Centers for Disease Control and Prevention** (✆ **800/311-3435;** www.cdc.gov) provides up-to-date information on health hazards by region or country and offers tips on food safety.

Travel Health Online (www.tripprep.com), sponsored by a consortium of travel medicine practitioners, may also offer helpful advice on traveling abroad. You can find listings of reliable medical clinics overseas at the **International Society of Travel Medicine** (www.istm.org).

COMMON AILMENTS

BUGS, BITES & OTHER WILDLIFE CONCERNS Snake and spider bites may not be as common as the hair-raising stories you will hear would suggest, but it pays to be wary. Australia's two deadly spiders are the large hairy funnel web and the tiny red-back, which has a distinctive red slash on its back. Snakes are common throughout Australia. You are most likely to see one if you are in the bush or hiking. If you are bitten, keep calm; moving

Avoiding "Economy-Class Syndrome"

Deep vein thrombosis, or as it's known in the world of flying, "economy-class syndrome," is a blood clot that develops in a deep vein. It's a potentially deadly condition that can be caused by sitting in cramped conditions—such as an airplane cabin—for too long. During a flight (especially a long-haul flight), get up, walk around, and stretch your legs every 60 to 90 minutes to keep your blood flowing. Other preventative measures include frequent flexing of the legs while sitting, drinking lots of water, and avoiding alcohol and sleeping pills. If you have a history of deep vein thrombosis, heart disease, or another condition that puts you at high risk, some experts recommend wearing compression stockings or taking anticoagulants when you fly; always ask your physician about the best course for you. Symptoms of deep vein thrombosis include leg pain or swelling, or even shortness of breath.

Healthy Travels to You

The following government websites offer up-to-date health-related travel advice.

- **Australia:** www.dfat.gov.au/travel
- **Canada:** www.hc-sc.gc.ca/index_e.html
- **U.K.:** www.dh.gov.uk/en/Policyandguidance/Healthadvicefortravellers/index.htm
- **U.S.:** www.cdc.gov/travel

as little as possible may save your life. Demobilize the limb and wrap that whole section of the limb tightly (but not tight enough to restrict blood flow) with a wide cloth or bandage (not a narrow tourniquet). Then head to the nearest hospital, where antivenin should be available.

If you go bushwalking (hiking through the bush), check your whole body for ticks, which are common. If you find one, dab it with methylated spirits or some other noxious chemical. Wait for a while, and then gently pull the tick out with tweezers, carefully ensuring that you don't leave its head buried inside the wound.

Many Aussie marine creatures are deadly. Avoid stingrays, stonefish (which look like stones, so don't walk on underwater "rocks"), lionfish, and puffer fish. Never touch a blue-ringed octopus (it has blue circles all over its body) or a cone shell (a large shellfish shaped like a blunt cone). Marine stingers, or box jellyfish, inhabit the coastal waters of the northern third of the country in summer. Their sting is very painful and can cause heart failure and death. If you are stung, pour vinegar over the affected site immediately—local authorities leave bottles of vinegar on the beach specifically for this purpose. On beaches in Sydney and other areas, you might come across "blue bottles" (which are sometimes also called "stingers" but are not the same as the jellyfish that plague swimmers and divers in the waters farther north). These long-tentacled blue jellyfish (also known as Portuguese men-of-war) inflict a generally harmless but painful sting that can last for hours. Sometimes you'll see warning signs on patrolled beaches. The best remedy if you are stung is to rinse the area liberally in seawater or fresh water to remove any tentacles stuck to the skin. For intense pain, apply heat or cold, whichever feels better. If you experience breathing difficulties or disorientation following a jellyfish sting, seek medical attention immediately.

There are two types of crocodiles in Australia: the freshwater crocodile, which grows to almost 3m (10 ft.), and the highly dangerous estuarine (or saltwater) crocodile, which reaches 5 to 7m (17–23 ft.). Freshwater crocs are considered harmless; unfortunately, estuarine crocs aren't. They are called "saltwater" crocs but live mostly in freshwater rivers, wetlands, gorges, and billabongs (ponds). They are very dangerous, move at lightning speed, and can remain unseen even an inch beneath the water; few people survive an attack. *Never* swim in, or stand near the bank of, any river, swamp, or pool in the northern third of Australia, unless you know for certain it's croc-free, and don't swim at beaches near stream or river mouths.

SUN/ELEMENTS/EXTREME WEATHER EXPOSURE Australians have the world's highest death rate from skin cancer because of the country's intense sunlight. Limit your exposure to the sun, especially during the first few days of your trip, and from 11am to 3pm in summer and 10am to 2pm in winter. Remember that UV rays reflected off walls, water, and the ground can burn you even when you're not in direct sunlight. Use a broad-spectrum sunscreen with a high protection factor (SPF 30 or higher).

Wear a broad-brimmed hat that covers the back of your neck, ears, and face (a baseball cap won't do it), and a long-sleeved shirt. Remember that children need more protection than adults do. Don't even think about traveling without sunglasses, or you'll spend your entire vacation squinting against Australia's "diamond light."

Cyclones occasionally affect tropical areas such as Darwin and Queensland's coastal regions, from about Gladstone north, during January and February, but serious damage is relatively rare.

WHAT TO DO IF YOU GET SICK AWAY FROM HOME

Australian pharmacists may only fill prescriptions written by Australian doctors, so carry enough medication with you for your trip. Doctors are listed under "M," for "Medical Practitioners," in the Yellow Pages, and most large towns and cities have 24-hour clinics. Failing that, go to the local hospital's emergency room.

We list **hospitals** and **emergency numbers** under "Fast Facts," in each chapter.

For travel abroad, you may have to pay all medical costs upfront and be reimbursed later. Medicare and Medicaid do not provide coverage for medical costs outside the U.S. Before leaving home, find out what medical services your health insurance covers. To protect yourself, consider buying medical travel insurance (see "Medical Insurance," under "Travel Insurance," above).

Very few health insurance plans pay for medical evacuation back to the U.S. (which can cost $10,000 and up). A number of companies offer medical evacuation services anywhere in the world. If you're ever hospitalized more than 150 miles from home, **MedjetAssist** (© **800/527-7478;** www.medjetassistance.com) will pick you up and fly you to the hospital of your choice virtually anywhere in the world in a medically equipped and staffed aircraft 24 hours day, 7 days a week. Annual memberships are $225 individual, $350 family; you can also purchase short-term memberships.

If you suffer from a chronic illness, consult your doctor before your departure. Pack **prescription medications** in your carry-on luggage, and in their original containers, with pharmacy labels—otherwise they won't make it through airport security. Carry the generic name of prescription medicines, in case a local pharmacist is unfamiliar with the brand name.

SAFETY

STAYING SAFE

Driving probably poses one of the greatest risks to visitors to Australia. Australians drive on the left, something that North American and European visitors often have difficulty remembering. Drivers and passengers, including taxi passengers, must wear a seat belt at all times, by law. Avoid driving between dusk and dawn in country areas, because this is when kangaroos are most active, and a collision with a 'roo is something to be avoided at all costs. Road trains—as many as three big truck carriages linked together, which can be up to 54m (177 ft.) long—are another danger, particularly in the Outback. ***Warning:*** If you break down or get lost, never leave your vehicle. Most people who get lost do so in Outback spots, and those who wander off to look for help or water usually die in the attempt. If it happens to you, stay with your car. See "By Car" in the "Getting Around Australia," section, p. 64.

7 Specialized Travel Resources

TRAVELERS WITH DISABILITIES

Most disabilities shouldn't stop anyone from traveling. There are more options and resources than ever before. Most hotels, major stores, attractions, and public restrooms in Australia have wheelchair access. Many smaller lodges and even B&Bs are starting to cater to guests with disabilities, and some diving companies cater to scuba divers with disabilities. National parks make an effort to include wheelchair-friendly pathways. Taxi companies in bigger cities can usually supply a cab equipped for wheelchairs.

TTY facilities are still limited largely to government services. For information on all kinds of facilities and services (not just travel-related organizations) for people with disabilities, contact **National Information Communication Awareness Network,** P.O. Box 407, Curtin, ACT 2605 (✆ **1800/806 769** voice and TTY in Australia, or 02/6285 3713; www.nican.com.au). This free service can put you in touch with accessible accommodations and attractions throughout Australia, as well as with travel agents and tour operators who understand your needs.

Organizations that offer a vast range of resources and assistance to disabled travelers include **MossRehab** (✆ **800/CALL-MOSS;** www.mossresourcenet.org); the **American Foundation for the Blind (AFB)** (✆ **800/232-5463;** www.afb.org); and **SATH** (Society for Accessible Travel & Hospitality) (✆ **212/447-7284;** www.sath.org). **AirAmbulanceCard.com** is now partnered with SATH and allows you to preselect top-notch hospitals in case of an emergency.

Access-Able Travel Source (✆ **303/232-2979;** www.access-able.com) offers a comprehensive database on travel agents from around the world with experience in accessible travel; destination-specific access information; and links to such resources as service animals, equipment rentals, and access guides.

Many travel agencies offer customized tours and itineraries for travelers with disabilities. Among them are **Flying Wheels Travel** (✆ **507/451-5005;** www.flyingwheelstravel.com) and **Accessible Journeys** (✆ **800/846-4537** or 610/521-0339; www.disabilitytravel.com).

Flying with Disability (www.flying-with-disability.org) is a comprehensive information source on airplane travel. **Avis Rent a Car** (✆ **888/879-4273**) has an "Avis Access" program that offers services for customers with special travel needs. These include specially outfitted vehicles with swivel seats, spinner knobs, and hand controls; mobility scooter rentals; and accessible bus service. Be sure to reserve well in advance.

Also check out the quarterly magazine ***Emerging Horizons*** (www.emerginghorizons.com), available by subscription ($16.95 year U.S.; $21.95 outside U.S.).

The "Accessible Travel" link at **Mobility-Advisor.com** (www.mobility-advisor.com) offers a variety of travel resources to disabled persons.

British travelers should contact **Holiday Care** (✆ **0845-124-9971** in the U.K. only; www.holidaycare.org.uk) to access a wide range of travel information and resources for those with disabilities and seniors.

GAY & LESBIAN TRAVELERS

Sydney is one of the most gay-friendly cities in the world, and across most of Australia, the gay community has a high profile and lots of support services. There are plenty of gay and lesbian bars, and most Saturday nights see a privately operated gay dance party taking place in an inner-city warehouse somewhere. The cafes and pubs of Oxford Street in Darlinghurst, a short cab ride or long stroll from Sydney's downtown area, are the liveliest gay spots. The annual Sydney Gay & Lesbian Mardi Gras, culminating in a huge street parade and party in late February or early March, is a high point on the city's calendar.

In rural areas of Australia, you may still encounter a little conservative resistance to gays and lesbians, but Australians everywhere are generally tolerant. Noosa, on Queensland's Sunshine Coast, is a favored destination for revelers after Mardi Gras, and a couple of resorts in north Queensland cater to gay and lesbian travelers. One of the best known is **Turtle Cove Resort & Spa** (© **1300/727 979** in Australia, or 07/4059 1800; www.turtlecove.com.au), on a private beach between Cairns and Port Douglas.

Some services you may find useful are the **Gay & Lesbian Counselling Service of NSW** (© **02/8594 9500** for the administration office), which runs a national hot line (© **1800/184 527** in Australia, or 02/8594 9596) from 7:30 to 10pm daily. Its website, www.glccs.org.au, has contact information for each state. In Sydney, the **Albion Street Centre** (© **02/9332 9600** for administration, or 02/9332 9700 for the information line) is an AIDS clinic and information service.

The International Gay and Lesbian Travel Association (IGLTA) (© **800/448-8550** or 954/776-2626; www.iglta.org) is the trade association for the gay and lesbian travel industry, and offers an online directory of gay- and lesbian-friendly travel businesses and tour operators. **Gay & Lesbian Tourism Australia** (www.galta.com.au) has listings of businesses in each state.

Many agencies offer tours and travel itineraries specifically for gay and lesbian travelers. **Above and Beyond Tours** (© **800/397-2681;** www.abovebeyondtours.com) are gay Australia tour specialists. San Francisco–based **Now, Voyager** (© **800/255-6951;** www.nowvoyager.com) offers worldwide trips and cruises, and **Olivia** (© **800/631-6277;** www.olivia.com) offers lesbian cruises and resort vacations.

Gay.com Travel (© **800/929-2268** or 415/644-8044; www.gay.com/travel or www.outandabout.com), is an excellent online successor to the popular ***Out & About*** print magazine. It provides regularly updated information about gay-owned, gay-oriented, and gay-friendly lodging, dining, sightseeing, nightlife, and shopping establishments in every important destination worldwide. British travelers should click on the "Travel" link at **www.uk.gay.com** for advice and gay-friendly trip ideas.

The Canadian website **GayTraveler** (**gaytraveler.ca**) offers ideas and advice for gay travel all over the world.

The following travel guides are available at many bookstores, or you can order them from any online bookseller: ***Spartacus International Gay Guide, 35th Edition*** (Bruno Gmünder Verlag; www.spartacusworld.com/gayguide) and the ***Damron*** guides (www.damron.com), with separate, annual books for gay men and lesbians.

SENIOR TRAVEL

Seniors—often called "pensioners" in Australia—from other countries don't always qualify for the discounted entry prices to tours, attractions, and events that Australian seniors enjoy, but mostly they do. Always inquire about discounts when booking hotels, flights, and train or bus tickets. The best ID to bring is something that shows your date of birth or that marks you as an "official" senior, like a membership card from AARP.

Members of **AARP,** 601 E St. NW, Washington, DC 20049 (© **888/687-2277;** www.aarp.org), get discounts on hotels, airfares, and car rentals. AARP offers members a range of benefits, including *AARP: The Magazine* and a newsletter. Anyone over 50 can join.

Many reliable agencies and organizations target the 50-plus market.

Elderhostel (**© 800/454-5768;** www.elderhostel.org) arranges worldwide study programs for those aged 55 and over.

Recommended publications offering travel resources and discounts for seniors include the quarterly magazine ***Travel 50 & Beyond*** (www.travel50andbeyond.com) and the bestselling paperback ***Unbelievably Good Deals and Great Adventures That You Absolutely Can't Get Unless You're Over 50 2005–2006, 16th Edition*** (McGraw-Hill), by Joann Rattner Heilman.

In Australia, pick up a copy of ***Get Up & Go,*** the only national travel magazine for the over-50s and the official Seniors Card travel magazine (www.getupandgo.com.au). It's a glossy quarterly, available at most newsdealers for A$4.95 (US$3.95/UK£2), and has an extensive section called Destination Australia, which covers a region in each state/territory in every issue.

FAMILY TRAVEL

Australians travel widely with their own kids, so facilities for families, including family passes to attractions, are common.

A great accommodations option for families is Australia's huge stock of serviced or unserviced apartments (with or without daily maid service). Often less expensive than a hotel room, they offer a living room, a kitchen, a bathroom or two, and the privacy of a separate bedroom for adults. "Tips on Accommodations," later in this chapter, has details on the major apartment chains. Most Australian hotels will arrange babysitting given a day's notice.

International airlines and domestic airlines in Australia charge 75% of the adult fare for kids under 12. Most charge 10% for infants under 2 not occupying a seat. Australian transport companies, attractions, and tour operators typically charge half price for kids under 12 or 14 years.

Many Australian resorts have "kids' clubs" with extensive programs designed for under-12s and, in some cases, teenagers. The French-owned Accor chain of hotels and resorts, which is Australia's largest chain, has kids' clubs, kids' menus designed by a nutritionist (and not just the same boring fodder you get everywhere else), and other family-friendly facilities including family rooms. Other resorts, such as Hamilton Island, have "kids stay, eat, and play free" offers, particularly during holiday periods. Many hotels will offer connecting units or "family rooms." Ask when booking.

Don't forget that children entering Australia on their parent's passport still need their own visa. See "Entry Requirements," earlier in this chapter.

Rascals in Paradise (**© 415/921-7000;** www.rascalsinparadise.com) sells family vacation packages to Australia.

To locate accommodations, restaurants, and attractions that are particularly kid-friendly, refer to the "Kids" icon throughout this guide.

Recommended family travel websites include **Family Travel Forum** (www.familytravelforum.com), a comprehensive site that offers customized trip planning; **Family Travel Network** (www.familytravelnetwork.com), an online magazine providing travel tips; and **TravelWithYourKids.com** (www.travelwithyourkids.com), a comprehensive site written by parents for parents offering sound advice for long-distance and international travel with children. Australian travel magazine ***Holidays with Kids*** has a comprehensive website listing great options for family travel in Australia, www.holidayswithkids.com.au.

WOMEN TRAVELERS

Check out the award-winning website **Journeywoman** (www.journeywoman.com), a "real life" women's travel-information network where you can sign up for a free e-mail newsletter and get advice on everything from etiquette and dress to safety. The travel guide ***Safety and Security for Women Who Travel*** by Sheila

Swan and Peter Laufer (Travelers' Tales Guides), offering common-sense tips on safe travel, was updated in 2004.

STUDENT TRAVEL

The **International Student Travel Confederation (ISTC)** (www.istc.org) was formed in 1949 to make travel around the world more affordable for students. Check out its website for comprehensive travel services information and details on how to get an **International Student Identity Card (ISIC),** which qualifies students for substantial savings on rail passes, plane tickets, entrance fees, and more. It also provides students with basic health and life insurance and a 24-hour helpline. The card is valid for a maximum of 18 months. You can apply for the card online or in person at **STA Travel** (✆ **800/781-4040** in North America; www.statravel.com), the biggest student travel agency in the world; check out the website to locate STA Travel offices worldwide. If you're no longer a student but are still under 26, you can get an **International Youth Travel Card (IYTC)** from the same people, which entitles you to some discounts. **Travel CUTS** (✆ **800/592-2887;** www.travelcuts.com) offers similar services for both Canadians and U.S. residents. Irish students may prefer to turn to **USIT** (✆ **01/602-1904;** www.usit.ie), an Ireland-based specialist in student, youth, and independent travel.

SINGLE TRAVELERS

On package vacations, single travelers are often hit with a "single supplement" to the base price. To avoid it, you can agree to room with other single travelers or find a compatible roommate before you go, from one of the many roommate-locator agencies.

Australian online travel-companion service **Trip Mates** (www.tripmates.com.au) is a free service which can help you match yourself up with an Aussie wanting to travel he same route as you, or take the same package tour. **Travel Buddies Singles Travel Club** (✆ **800/998-9099;** www.travelbuddiesworldwide.com), based in Canada, runs small, intimate, single-friendly group trips and will match you with a roommate free of charge. **TravelChums** (✆ **212/787-2621;** www.travelchums.com) is an Internet-only travel-companion matching service with elements of an online personals-type site, hosted by the respected New York–based Shaw Guides travel service.

Many reputable tour companies offer singles-only trips. **Backroads** (✆ **800/462-2848;** www.backroads.com) offers "Singles + Solos" active-travel trips to destinations worldwide, including to Australia and New Zealand.

For more information, check out Eleanor Berman's classic ***Traveling Solo: Advice and Ideas for More Than 250 Great Vacations, 5th Edition*** (Globe Pequot), updated in 2005.

VEGETARIAN TRAVEL

Travelers will find it easy to find good vegetarian restaurants—and veggie options on restaurant menus—in Australia. **Happy Cow's Vegetarian Guide to Restaurants & Health Food Stores** (www.happycow.net) has a restaurant guide with more than 6,000 restaurants in 100 countries. **VegDining.com** also lists vegetarian restaurants (with profiles) around the world.

8 Sustainable Tourism/Ecotourism

Each time you take a flight or drive a car CO_2 is released into the atmosphere. You can help neutralize this danger to our planet through "carbon offsetting"—paying someone to reduce your CO_2 emissions by the same amount you've added. Carbon offsets can be purchased in the U.S. from companies such as

Carbonfund.org (www.carbonfund.org) and **TerraPass** (www.terrapass.org), and from **Climate Care** (www.climatecare.org) in the U.K.

Although one could argue that any vacation that includes an airplane flight can't be truly "green," you can go on holiday and still contribute positively to the environment. You can offset carbon emissions from your flight in other ways. Choose forward-looking companies that embrace responsible development practices, helping preserve destinations for the future by working alongside local people. An increasing number of sustainable tourism initiatives can help you plan a family trip and leave as small a "footprint" as possible on the places you visit.

In Australia, the national body which sets guidelines and standards for ecotourism is **Ecotourism Australia** (✆ **07/3229 5550**; www.ecotourism.org.au). When planning your holiday in Australia, look out for tourism operators who have their tour, attraction, or accommodations accredited under the Eco Certification Program. Also look for nature and ecotour guides who have credentials through the EcoGuide Australia Certification Program. **Savannah Guides** (✆ **08/8985 3890**; www.savannah-guides.com.au) is a network of professional tour guides, mostly in north Queensland, the Northern Territory, and Western Australia's Kimberley region, who have an in-depth knowledge of the natural and cultural assets of the tropical savannas of northern Australia. Savannah Guides sites and stations feature nature and/or culture based interpretive activities, and all Savannah Guides promote ecologically sustainable tourism principles, encourage the protection and conservation of natural and cultural resources, and are committed to conservation values.

Responsible Travel (www.responsibletravel.com) contains a great source of sustainable travel ideas run by a spokesperson for responsible tourism in the travel industry. **Sustainable Travel International** (www.sustainabletravelinternational.org) promotes responsible tourism practices and issues an annual Green Gear & Gift Guide.

You can find ecofriendly travel tips, statistics, and touring companies and associations—listed by destination under "Travel Choice"—at the TIES website,

Tips It's Easy Being Green

We can all help conserve fuel and energy when we travel. Here are a few simple ways you can help preserve your favorite destinations:

- Whenever possible, choose nonstop flights; they generally require less fuel than those that must stop and take off again.
- If renting a car is necessary on your vacation, ask the rental agent for the most fuel-efficient one available. Not only will you use less gas, you'll save money at the tank.
- At hotels, request that your sheets and towels not be changed daily. You'll save water and energy by not washing them as often, and you'll prolong the life of the towels, too. (Most Australian hotels have programs like this in place.)
- Turn off the lights and air conditioner (or heater) when you leave your hotel room.

Frommers.com: The Complete Travel Resource

It should go without saying, but we highly recommend **Frommers.com,** voted Best Travel Site by *PC Magazine.* We think you'll find our expert advice and tips; independent reviews of hotels, restaurants, attractions, and preferred shopping and nightlife venues; vacation giveaways; and an online booking tool indispensable before, during, and after your travels. We publish the complete contents of over 128 travel guides in our **Destinations** section covering nearly 3,600 places worldwide to help you plan your trip. Each weekday, we publish original articles reporting on **Deals and News** via our free **Frommers.com Newsletter** to help you save time and money and travel smarter. We're betting you'll find our new **Events** listings (http://events.frommers.com) an invaluable resource; it's an up-to-the-minute roster of what's happening in cities everywhere—including concerts, festivals, lectures, and more. We've also added weekly **Podcasts, interactive maps,** and hundreds of new images across the site. Check out our **Travel Talk** area featuring **Message Boards** where you can join in conversations with thousands of fellow Frommer's travelers and post your trip report once you return.

www.ecotourism.org. Also check out **Conservation International** (www.conservation.org)—which, with *National Geographic Traveler,* annually presents **World Legacy Awards** (www.wlaward.org) to those travel tour operators, businesses, organizations, and places that have made a significant contribution to sustainable tourism. **Ecotravel.com** is part online magazine and part ecodirectory that lets you search for touring companies in several categories (water-based, land-based, spiritually oriented, and so on).

In the U.K., **Tourism Concern** (www.tourismconcern.org.uk) works to reduce social and environmental problems connected to tourism and find ways of improving tourism so that local benefits are increased.

The **Association of Independent Tour Operators (AITO)** (www.aito.co.uk) is a group of interesting specialist operators leading the field in making holidays sustainable.

For information about the ethics of swimming with dolphins and other outdoor activities, visit the **Whale and Dolphin Conservation Society** (www.wdcs.org) and **Tread Lightly** (www.treadlightly.org).

9 Staying Connected

TELEPHONES

To call Australia:

1. Dial the international access code: 011 from the U.S.; 00 from the U.K., Ireland, or New Zealand.
2. Dial the country code 61.
3. Dial the city code (drop the 0 from any area code given in this book) and then the number.

To make international calls: To make international calls from Australia, first dial 0011 and then the country code (U.S. or Canada 1, U.K. 44, Ireland 353, New Zealand 64). Next you dial the area code and number. For example, if you wanted to call the British Embassy in Washington, D.C., you would dial 0011-202-588-7800. You may want to

than $100 for a
ling card. Local
0¢ per minute,
ming calls are

tele-
m)

ill
s a
able

12455
inside Aus-
umbers to all

tination
www.

most
ave
ess

ance: If you need
making a call, dial
ying to make an inter-
1234 if you want to call
Australia.

within Australia: Each Aus-
state has a different area code: (02)
New South Wales and the ACT, (07)
or Queensland, (03) for Victoria and
Tasmania, (08) for South Australia, the
Northern Territory, and Western Australia. You must dial the appropriate code
if calling outside the state you are in;
however, you also need to use the code if
you are calling outside the city you are in.
For example if you are in Sydney, where
the code is (02) and you want to call
another New South Wales town, you still
dial (02) before the number.

Toll-free numbers: Numbers beginning with 1800 within Australia are toll-
free, but calling a 1-800 number in the
United States from Australia country is
not toll-free. In fact, it costs the same as
an overseas call.

Other numbers: Numbers starting
with 13 or 1300 in Australia are charged
at the local fee of A25¢ (US20¢/UK£10)
anywhere in Australia. Numbers beginning with 1900 (or 1901 or 1902 and so
on) are pay-for-service lines, and you will
be charged as much as A$5 (US$4/UK£2)
a minute.

Pay phones: The primary telecommu-
nications network in Australia is **Telstra**
(www.telstra.com). Telstra pay phones are
found in most city streets, shopping centers, transport terminals, post offices, and
along highways—even in some of the
most remote areas of Australia. To find
the nearest one to you, call © **1800/011
433** or look online at www.telstra.com.
au/payphoneservices/index.htm. The cost
of a local call from a pay phone is A50¢
(US40¢/UK20p), either in coins or by
using a phone card. Some phones only
take prepaid phone cards, which can be
purchased from newsdealers and other
retailers in denominations of A$5, A$10,
and A$20, and are good for local,
national, and international calls. There
are no access numbers—you just insert
the card and dial. Credit phones take
most major credit cards. As well as pay
phones in the usual booths, you may find
some inside convenience stores and the
like, called "blue phones" or "gold
phones."

CELLPHONES

The three letters that define much of the
world's wireless capabilities are **GSM**
(Global System for Mobile Communications), a big, seamless network that makes
for easy cross-border cellphone use
throughout Europe and dozens of other
countries worldwide. In the U.S., T-
Mobile, AT&T Wireless, and Cingular
use this quasi-universal system; in
Canada, Microcell and some Rogers customers are GSM, and all Europeans and
most Australians use GSM. GSM phones
function with a removable plastic SIM
card, encoded with your phone number
and account information.

If your cellphone is on a GSM system,
and you have a world-capable multiband
phone such as many Sony Ericsson,
Motorola, or Samsung models, you can
make and receive calls across civilized areas
around much of the globe. Just call your
wireless operator and ask for "international
roaming" to be activated on your account.
Unfortunately, per-minute charges can be

high—usually $1 to $1.50 in western Europe and up to $5 in places like Russia and Indonesia.

For many, **renting** a phone is a good idea. While you can rent a phone from any number of overseas sites, including kiosks at airports and at car-rental agencies, we suggest renting the phone before you leave home. North Americans can rent one before leaving home from **InTouch USA** (✆ **800/872-7626;** www.intouchglobal.com) or **RoadPost** (✆ **888/290-1606** or 905/272-5665; www.roadpost.com). InTouch will also, for free, advise you on whether your existing phone will work overseas; simply call ✆ **703/222-7161** between 9am and 4pm EST, or go to **http://intouchglobal.com/travel.htm**.

In Australia, mobile phone company **Vodafone** (✆ **1300/365 360;** www.vodarent.com.au) has outlets at Brisbane, Cairns, and Melbourne international airports, and at Sydney and Perth international and domestic airports and a store in Southport on the Gold Coast. They cost A$5 (US$4/UK£2) to A$8 (US$6.40/UK£3.20) a day, plus call charges and insurance, depending on the kind of phone and coverage you want. You can rent a SIM card for A$1 (US80¢/UK40p) a day or A$15 (US$12/UK£6) a month.

In Australia—reputed to have one of the world's highest per-capita rates of ownership of "mobile" telephones, as they are known here—the cell network is digital, not analog. Calls to or from a mobile telephone are generally more expensive than calls to or from a fixed telephone. The price varies depending on the telephone company, the time of day, the distance between caller and recipient, and the telephone's pricing plan.

Buying a phone can be economically attractive, as many nations have cheap prepaid phone systems. Once you arrive at your destination, stop by a local cellphone shop and get the cheapest package; you'll probably pay les
phone and a starter ca
calls may be as low as 1
and in many countries inc
free.

INTERNET/E-MAIL

WITHOUT YOUR OWN COMPUTER

To find cybercafes in your de
check **www.cybercaptive.com** an
cybercafe.com.

Aside from formal cybercafes,
youth hostels and **public libraries**
Internet access. Avoid **hotel busi**
centers unless you're willing to pay ex
bitant rates.

Cybercafes (called Internet cafes i
Australia) can be found almost everywhere. In major tourist cities like Cairns and Darwin, there are whole streets full of them.

Most major airports have **Internet kiosks** that provide basic Web access for a per-minute fee that's usually higher than cybercafe prices. Check out copy shops like **Kinko's** (http://fedex.kinkos.com), which offers computer stations with fully loaded software (as well as Wi-Fi). They have stores in Sydney and Melbourne.

WITH YOUR OWN COMPUTER

More and more hotels, resorts, airports, cafes, and retailers are going **Wi-Fi** (wireless fidelity), becoming "hotspots" that offer free high-speed Wi-Fi access or charge a small fee for usage. Most laptops sold today have built-in wireless capability. To find public Wi-Fi hotspots at your destination, go to **www.jiwire.com**; its Hotspot Finder holds the world's largest directory of public wireless hot spots.

For dial-up access, most business-class hotels throughout Australia offer dataports for laptop modems, and some of them offer free high-speed Internet access.

Wherever you go, bring a **connection kit** of the right power and phone adapters,

Online Traveler's Toolbox

Veteran travelers usually carry some essential items to make their trips easier. Following is a selection of handy online tools to bookmark and use.

- **Airplane Food** (www.airlinemeals.net)
- **Airplane Seating** (www.seatguru.com and www.airlinequality.com)
- **Maps** (www.mapquest.com)
- **Subway Navigator** (www.subwaynavigator.com)
- **Time and Date** (www.timeanddate.com)
- **Travel Warnings** (http://travel.state.gov, www.fco.gov.uk/travel, www.voyage.gc.ca, or www.dfat.gov.au/consular/advice)
- **Universal Currency Converter** (www.xe.com/ucc)
- **Visa ATM Locator** (www.visa.com), **MasterCard ATM Locator** (www.mastercard.com)
- **Weather** (www.intellicast.com and www.weather.com)

a spare phone cord, and a spare Ethernet network cable—or find out whether your hotel supplies them to guests.

Australia's electricity supply is 240 volts, 50 Hz. North Americans and Europeans will need to buy a converter before they leave home, because Australian stores usually only stock converters for Aussie appliances to fit American and European outlets.

10 Packages for the Independent Traveler

Package tours are simply a way to buy the airfare, accommodations, and other elements of your trip (such as car rentals, airport transfers, and sometimes even activities) at the same time and often at discounted prices.

One good source of package deals is the airlines themselves. Most major airlines offer air/land packages, including **American Airlines Vacations** (© 800/321-2121; www.aavacations.com), **Delta Vacations** (© 800/654-6559; www.deltavacations.com), **Continental Airlines Vacations** (© 800/301-3800; www.covacations.com), and **United Vacations** (© 888/854-3899; www.unitedvacations.com). Several big **online travel agencies**—Expedia, Travelocity, Orbitz, Site59, and Lastminute.com—also do a brisk business in packages.

Austravel (© 0870/166-2020 in the U.K.; www.austravel.net) offers independent packages Down Under. The following companies offer both independent and escorted tours: **ATS Tours** (© 888/781-5170 in the U.S. and Canada; www.atstours.com); **Collette Vacations** (© 800/340-5158 in the U.S., 800/468-5955 in Canada, or 0800/0921-888 in the U.K.; www.collettevacations.com); **Goway** (© 800/387-8850 in the U.S. and Canada; www.goway.com); **Maupintour** (© 800/255-4266 in the U.S. and Canada; www.maupintour.com); **Qantas Vacations** (© 800/348-8145 in the U.S., or 800/348-8137 in Canada; www.qantasvacations.com); **Swain Tours** (© 800/22-SWAIN in the U.S. and Canada; www.swaintours.com); Swain's budget-travel division, **Downunder Direct** (© 800/642-6224 in the U.S. and Canada; www.downunderdirect.com); and **United Vacations** (© 888/854-3899 in the U.S. and Canada;

Tips Ask Before You Go

Before you invest in a package deal or an escorted tour:

- Always ask about the **cancellation policy.** Can you get your money back? Is there a deposit required?
- Ask about the **accommodations choices and prices** for each. Then look up the hotels' reviews in a Frommer's guide and check their rates online for your specific dates of travel. Also find out what types of rooms are offered.
- Request a complete **schedule.** (Escorted tours only.)
- Ask about the **size** and demographics of the group. (Escorted tours only.)
- Discuss what is included in the **price** (transportation, meals, tips, airport transfers, and so on). (Escorted tours only.)
- Finally, look for **hidden expenses.** Ask whether airport departure fees and taxes, for example, are included in the total cost—they rarely are.

www.unitedvacations.com). Swain Tours is operated and largely staffed by Aussies, and has an office in Sydney, as does Goway.

Travel packages are also listed in the travel section of your local Sunday newspaper. Or check ads in national travel magazines such as *Arthur Frommer's Budget Travel Magazine*, *Travel +Leisure*, *National Geographic Traveler*, and *Condé Nast Traveler.*

11 Escorted General-Interest Tours

Escorted tours are structured group tours, with a group leader. The price usually includes everything from airfare to hotels, meals, tours, admission costs, and local transportation.

Connections Adventures (call Australian Pacific Touring © **800/290-8687** in the U.S.; Goway © **800/387-8850** in Canada; © **020/8946 4536** in the United Kingdom; © **0800/278 687** in New Zealand; or © **1800/077 251** or 02/8252 5300 in Australia; www.connections adventures.com), and **Contiki** (© **888/CONTIKI** in the U.S. and Canada; 09/300 1601 in New Zealand; 1300/188 635 or 02/9511 2200 in Australia; www.contiki.com) specialize in escorted tours for 18- to 35-year-olds. These trips attract a lot of Australians, too, so they are a good way to meet locals. **Premier Vacations** (© **800/321-6720** in the U.S. and Canada; www.premierdownunder.com) is another reliable escorted tour operator.

Despite the fact that escorted tours require big deposits and predetermine hotels, restaurants, and itineraries, many people derive security and peace of mind from the structure they offer. Escorted tours—whether they're navigated by bus, motorcoach, train, or boat—let travelers sit back and enjoy the trip without having to drive or worry about details. They take you to the maximum number of sights in the minimum amount of time with the least amount of hassle. They're particularly convenient for people with limited mobility and they can be a great way to make new friends.

On the downside, you'll have little opportunity for serendipitous interactions with locals. The tours can be jam-packed with activities, leaving little room for individual sightseeing, whim, or adventure—plus they often focus on the heavily touristed sites, so you miss out on many a lesser-known gem.

12 The Active Traveler

Australia's wide-open spaces and great weather cry out to even the most dedicated lazybones. Most operators and outfitters listed below specialize in adventure vacations for small groups. Meals, accommodations, equipment rental, and guides are usually included in their packages, though international airfares are not. Where you end up spending the night varies depending on the package you select—on a sea-kayaking trip, you almost always camp on the beach; on a hiking expedition you may stay at a wilderness lodge; and on a biking trip you often stop over at B&B-style lodgings. More information on the outdoor activities discussed below appears in the relevant regional chapters.

SCUBA DIVING

Diving Down Under is one of the best travel experiences in the world. There are good dive sites all around the coastline, not just on the Great Barrier Reef. A second barrier reef in Ningaloo Reef Marine Park stretches 260km (161 miles) off the coast of Western Australia. (See chapter 10 or Exmouth Diving Centre's website at www.exmouthdiving.com.au for a good description of dive sites there.) Not all the good sites are on coral. In Tasmania, for instance, you can dive kelp beds popular with seals, and in South Australia you can cage-dive with great white sharks. For a rundown on the country's outstanding dive areas, see "The Best Diving & Snorkeling Sites" in chapter 1.

Wherever you find coral in Australia, you'll find dive companies offering learn-to-dive courses, day trips, and, in some cases, extended journeys on live-aboard vessels. Most international dive certificates, including PADI, NAUI, SSI, and BSAC, are recognized. It's easy to rent gear and wet suits wherever you go, or you can bring your own.

Beginners' courses are known as "open-water certification" and usually require 2 days of theory in a pool at the dive company's premises, followed by 2 or 3 days on a live-aboard boat where you make between four and nine dives, including a night dive if you opt for the 5-day course. Open-water certification courses range from an intensive 3 to 5 days, for which you can expect to pay about A$350 to A$600 (US$280–US$480/UK£140–UK£240). A 5-day course is seen as the best. When comparing the value offered by dive schools, keep in mind that if the practical section of your course does not take place on a live-aboard boat, you will have to budget for accommodations and meals. Most operators offer courses right up to instructor level. If you're pressed for time, a PADI Referral course might suit you. It allows you to do your theory work at home, do a few hours of pool work at a PADI dive center in your home country, and then spend 2 or 3 days in the Australian ocean doing your qualifying dives.

Remember to allow time in your itinerary for a medical exam in Australia (see the next paragraph), and expect the dive instructor to grill you on your theory again before you hit the water.

If you're already a certified diver, remember to bring your "C" card and log book. If you're going to do a dive course, you'll need a medical certificate from an Australian doctor that meets Australian standard AS4005.1, stating that you are fit for scuba diving. (An all-purpose physical is not enough.) Virtually all dive schools will arrange the medical exam for you; expect to pay around A$50 (US$40/UK£20) for it. Remember, you

Tips **Peak Time on the Reef**

August through January is peak visibility time on the Great Barrier Reef, but the marine life will amaze you any time of year.

must complete your last dive 24 hours before you fly in an aircraft. This catches a lot of people off guard when they are preparing to fly to their next destination the day after a visit to the Reef. You won't be able to helicopter off the Reef back to the mainland, either. Check to see if your travel insurance covers diving. **The Divers Alert Network** (✆ **800/446-2671;** www.diversalertnetwork.org) sells diving insurance and has diving and nondiving medical emergency hot lines, and an information line for dive-related medical questions.

If you've never been diving and don't plan to become qualified, you can see what all the fuss is about on an "introductory" dive that lets you dive in the company of an instructor on a one-time basis, with a briefing beforehand. Most dive operators on the Great Barrier Reef and other dive locations offer introductory dives.

See "Exploring the Great Barrier Reef" in chapter 7 for more information.

For information on dive regions and operators, try the state tourism marketing boards' websites (see "Visitor Information & Maps," earlier in this chapter). **Tourism Queensland's** website (**www.queensland holidays.com.au**) has information on most dive operators working the Great Barrier Reef. If you know where you want to dive, you may obtain an even more detailed list of operators by bypassing the big tourism boards and contacting the local tourist office for a list of local dive operators. **Dive Queensland** (the Queensland Dive Tourism Association; ✆ **07/4051 1510;** fax 07/4051 1519; www.divequeensland.com.au) requires its member operators to abide by a code of ethics. Its website has a list of members and the services they offer. It includes a few in other states, too. Another good source is **Diversion Dive Travel** (✆ **1800/607 913** in Australia, or 07/4039 0200; www.diversionoz.com), a Cairns-based travel agent that specializes in dive holidays on the Great Barrier Reef, as well as in other good dive spots in Australia. It books day trips and extended diving excursions on a choice of live-aboard vessels, as well as dive courses, island resorts with diving, accommodations, and nondiving tours. It also sells diving insurance. Its proprietors are both dive instructors, and one of them is trained as a handicapped diving instructor for divers with disabilities.

BUSHWALKING (HIKING)

With so much unique scenery and many rare animals and plants, it's not surprising that Australia is full of national parks crisscrossed with hiking trails. You're never far from a park with a bushwalk, whether it's an easy stroll, or a 6-day odyssey on the Cape-to-Cape trail in Western Australia.

A good Australian bushwalking website is **www.bushwalking.org.au**. The best place to get information about bushwalking is the National Parks & Wildlife Service, or its equivalent in each state; sources include:

- **Environmental Protection Agency** (QLD Parks & Wildlife Service; ✆ **07/3227 8185;** www.epa.qld.gov.au).
- **NSW National Parks & Wildlife Service** (www.nationalparks.nsw.gov.au). It has a visitor information center at Cadmans Cottage, 110 George St., The Rocks, Sydney (✆ **02/9247 5033**).

- **Parks & Wildlife Commission of the Northern Territory** (✆ **08/8999 4555;** www.nt.gov.au/nreta/parks). The Northern Territory Tourist Commission (see "Exploring the Red Centre," in chapter 8) is the official source of information on parks and wildlife matters.
- **Parks Victoria** (✆ **13 19 63;** www.parkweb.vic.gov.au).
- **South Australian Department for Environment and Heritage** (✆ **08/8204 9010;** www.environment.sa.gov.au).
- **Tasmania Parks and Wildlife Service** (✆ **1300/368 550** in Australia, or 03/6233 8011; www.dpiwe.tas.gov.au).
- **Western Australian Department of Environment and Conservation** (✆ **08/9334 0333;** www.naturebase.net).

Some parks charge an entry fee, often ranging from A$6 to A$18 (US$4.80–US$14/UK£2.40–UK£7.20).

MORE ACTIVE VACATIONS FROM A TO Z

ABSEILING Rappelling is another name for this sport that involves backing down vertical cliff faces on a rope and harness. The rugged, beautiful Blue Mountains near Sydney are Australia's abseiling capital. In the Margaret River region in Western Australia, you can do it as mighty breakers crash on the cliffs below. You can even do it in the heart of Brisbane on riverside cliffs.

BIKING Much of Australia's countryside is flat and ideal for cycling, as Aussies call biking, but consider the heat and vast distances before setting out. There are plenty of biking trails. The rainforest hills behind Cairns hosted the world mountain-biking championships in 1996, and Sydney's Blue Mountains have good mountain-biking trails. On Rottnest Island off Perth, it's the only mode of transport from one coral-filled bay to the next. All major towns and most resort centers rent regular bikes and mountain bikes.

Remote Outback Cycle Tours (✆ **08/9279 6969;** www.cycletours.com.au) takes novice and expert riders, young and old, on extended tours across the country. The distances are vast, but the trip combines cycling with four-wheel-drive travel. Itineraries include the Red Centre, the historic Oodnadatta Track cattle-driving route from Alice Springs to Adelaide via the underground opal-mining town of Coober Pedy in South Australia, and from Adelaide to Perth across the Nullarbor Plain desert and through the pretty Margaret River wine region in southern Western Australia.

BIRD-WATCHING Australia's unique geography as an island continent means it has species you won't see anywhere else. It is probably best known for its brilliant parrots, but you will see species from the wetlands, savanna, mulga scrub, desert, oceans, dense bushland, rainforest, mangroves, rivers, and other habitats. More than half of the country's species have been spotted in the Daintree Rainforest area in north Queensland, and one-third live in wetlands-rich Kakadu National Park in the Top End. The Coorong in South Australia and Broome in the Top End are home to marvelous waterfowl populations.

To get in touch with birding clubs all over Australia, contact **Birds Australia** (✆ **1300/730 075** in Australia, or 03/9347 0757; www.birdsaustralia.com.au).

Kirrama Wildlife Tours (✆ **07/4065 5181;** www.kirrama.com.au) operates birding expeditions to remote regions in northern Australia from a base in north Queensland. Broome-based ornithologist George Swann of **Kimberley Birdwatching, Wildlife & Natural History Tours**

Fun Fact **Something Different: Camel Trekking**

Camels Down Under? You bet. Australia has one of the world's largest camel populations, and even exports racing camels to the Middle East. Camels were imported to negotiate waterless deserts in the 1900s but were later set free. They are now a popular way to trek the country. Short rambles of an hour or two in Alice Springs and at Uluru (Ayers Rock) are a novel way to see the Outback, or you can join extended camel treks through Outback deserts offered by a number of operators. Several companies in Broome lead guided rides along beautiful Cable Beach.

(© **08/9192 1246;** www.kimberleybirdwatching.com.au) leads extended birding trips throughout the Kimberley and the Northern Territory. Fine Feather Tours (© **07/4094 1199;** www.finefeathertours.com.au), based near Port Douglas near the Daintree Rainforest, operates bird-watching day trips and afternoon river cruises.

CANOEING & SEA KAYAKING Katherine Gorge in the Northern Territory offers some spectacular flat canoeing. You'll find delightful canoeing on the bird-rich Ord River in the Top End. Katherine Gorge and the Ord are full of generally harmless freshwater crocodiles, but *never* canoe in saltwater-crocodile territory. White-water canoeing can be found in Barrington Tops National Park north of Sydney.

A growing number of operators all around the coastline rent kayaks and lead guided expeditions. Popular spots are the Whitsunday Islands in north Queensland, the cold southern seas around Tasmania, and Byron Bay, where you can take a 3-hour "dolphin kayaking" trip to see wild dolphins (and whales June–Oct) and "kayak-surf" the waves.

Rivergods (© **08/9259 0749;** www.rivergods.com.au) conducts multiday sea-kayaking, canoeing, and white-water-rafting adventures throughout Western Australia's pristine ocean and rivers, in which whales, sharks, dugongs (manatees), sea snakes, turtles, and dolphins abound. The company also runs a "sea kayak with wild seals" day outing from Perth. **Gecko Canoeing** (© **1800/634 319** in Australia, or 08/8972 2224; www.geckocanoeing.com.au) leads canoeing trips of 1 to 7 days from Katherine along remote Top End rivers between April and September.

CAVING Australia doesn't have a lot of caves, but the ones it has are spectacular. The best spots are in the Blue Mountains west of Sydney and the Margaret River region in southwest Western Australia. For tourists who want to see caves and stay clean and safe (as opposed to spelunkers), the best caves are the spectacular Jenolan Caves in the Blue Mountains, a honeycomb of caverns bursting with intricate stalactites and stalagmites, and the 350 limestone caves in Margaret River, of which five are open to the public. Two are "adventure caves," which any novice caver (as opposed to an experienced spelunker) can explore on a 2- or 3-hour tour. You can also go caving at Olssen's Capricorn Caverns, near Rockhampton, in Central Queensland.

FISHING Reef, game, deep sea, beach, estuary, and river fishing—Australia's massive coastline lets you do it all. Drop a line for coral trout on the Great Barrier Reef; go for the world-record black marlin off Cairns; hook a fighting "barra" (barramundi) in the Northern Territory or the Kimberley; or cast for trout in Tasmania's highland lakes. Charter boats will take you out for the day from most towns all around the coast.

GOLFING Australians are almost as passionate about golf as they are about football and cricket—after all, Greg Norman started life as an Aussie! Queensland has the lion's share of the stunning resort courses, such as the Sheraton Mirage in Port Douglas, Laguna Quays Resort near the Whitsundays, and the Hyatt Regency Sanctuary Cove Resort on the Gold Coast. The Gold Coast has more than 40 courses. One of the world's best desert courses is at Alice Springs.

Most courses rent clubs for around A$30 (US$24/UK£12). Greens fees start at around A$20 (US$16/UK£8) for 18 holes but average A$65 (US$52/UK£26) or more on a championship course. **Koala Golf** (© **1300/301 686** in Australia, or 02/9746 6646; www.koalagolf.com) offers escorted day trips and package tours to excellent golf courses in major cities and holiday areas around Australia.

HORSEBACK RIDING Horsebackriding operators are everywhere in Australia. A particularly pleasant vacation is a multiday riding and camping trek in "The Man from Snowy River" country, the Snowy Mountains in New South Wales.

SAILING The 74 islands of the Whitsundays in Queensland are an out-of-this-world backdrop for sailing. And you don't have be an expert—the Whitsunday region is Australia's "bareboating" capital. Bareboating means you can charter an unskippered yacht and sail yourself. Even those without a scrap of experience can do it, although it's best to have someone on board who knows aft from fore. Perth and Sydney are mad about sailing; experienced sailors can head to the nearest yacht club to offer themselves as crew, especially during summer twilight races. The clubs are often short of sailors, and most will welcome out-of-towners.

SURFING You'll have no trouble finding a good surf beach along the Australian coast. Perth and Sydney are blessed with loads right in the city. Other popular spots include the Gold and Sunshine coasts in Queensland, the legendary Southern Ocean swells along Victoria's southern coast, and magnificent sets off Margaret River in Western Australia. Don't take your board much north of the Sunshine Coast—the Great Barrier Reef puts a stop to the swell from there all the way to the northern tip of Queensland. Loads of companies rent surf gear. Beginner lessons are offered at many surf beaches. Remember, surf only at patrolled beaches, and never surf alone.

WHITE-WATER RAFTING The best rapids are the Class V torrents on the Nymboida and Gwydir rivers behind Coffs Harbour in New South Wales. More Class V rapids await you on the Johnstone River in north Queensland, where access is by helicopter. Loads of tourists who have never held a paddle hurtle down the Class III to IV Tully River or the gentler Class II to III Barron River on a day trip from Cairns. The Snowy River National Park in Victoria and the Franklin River in the wilds of Tasmania are other popular spots. See also "Canoeing & Sea Kayaking," above.

AUSTRALIA-BASED OUTFITTERS & OPERATORS

Auswalk (© **03/5356 4971;** www.auswalk.com.au) offers self-guided or escorted/accommodated walking tours through picturesque parts of Australia such as the Great Ocean Road in Victoria, Lamington National Park Island in Queensland, the Red Centre, and the Blue Mountains in New South Wales.

Tasmanian Expeditions (© **03/6339 3999;** www.tas-ex.com) conducts day trips and extended expeditions featuring hiking, cycling, rafting, abseiling, canoeing, sea kayaking, and rock-climbing throughout Tasmania's national parks and unspoiled rural areas.

World Expeditions (© **415/989-2212** in the U.S., 613/241 2700 in Canada, 020/8545-9030 in the U.K., 09/368 4161 in New Zealand, or 02/8270 8400 or 1300/720 000 in Australia; www.worldexpeditions.com.au) runs expeditions in many parts of Australia. Destinations include places less traveled, such as Hinchinbrook Island in the Great Barrier Reef Marine Park, and the long-distance Bibbulmun Track in Western Australia's southwest. Some trips incorporate other pursuits, like rafting, sailing, or biking.

U.S.-BASED OUTFITTERS & OPERATORS

The **Great Outdoor Recreation Pages (GORP)** site (**http://gorp.away.com**) not only has links to adventure-tour operators to Australia, but also contains articles, sells books and maps, and has links to heaps of sites on Australia with an action slant.

Outer Edge Expeditions (© **800/322-5235** or 517/552-5300; www.outer-edge.com) and **The World Outdoors** (© **800/488-8483** or 303/413-0938; www.theworldoutdoors.com) both offer ecologically minded multisport diving, hiking, mountain-biking, canoeing, and kayaking packages to the Great Barrier Reef and North Queensland rainforest.

13 Getting Around Australia

Lesson number one: You won't be able to see Uluru (Ayers Rock) from your Sydney hotel room window. It's 2,841km (1,761 miles) away. Possibly the biggest mistake tourists make Down Under (apart from getting horribly sunburned) is failing to comprehend the distances between popular locations. One of the urban legends that grew up around the 2000 Olympics was the tale of the tourist who asked where in Sydney Harbour he could catch the boat to the Great Barrier Reef. That's a mere 2,800km (1,736 miles) north. Don't try to cram too much into your trip.

Traveling overland may make sense in Europe or North America, but in Australia flying is the best way between most points. People who go by train, bus, or car are often disappointed at Australia's flat vistas of desert, wheat fields, and gum trees—the same landscape can go on for days. A good compromise is to take to the air for long trips and save the land travel for short hops of a few hours. Try not to backtrack, which eats up valuable time and money.

BY PLANE

Australia is a big country with a small population to support its air routes. Airfares are high.

Most domestic air travel is operated by **Qantas** (© **800/227-4500** in the U.S. and Canada, 0845/7747 767 in the U.K. or 208/600 4300 in London, 1/407 3278 in Ireland, 09/357 8900 in Auckland, 0800/808 767 in New Zealand, or 13 13 13 in Australia; www.qantas.com.au) or **Virgin Blue** (© **13 67 89** in Australia, or 07/3295 2296; www.virginblue.com.au), its sibling company **Pacific Blue** (© **13 16 45** in Australia, or 07/3295 2284; **0800 67 0000** in New Zealand; www.virginblue.com.au), or Qantas-owned newcomer **Jetstar** (© **13 15 38** in Australia, or 03/8341 4901; **0800 800 995** in New Zealand; www.jetstar.com.au).

Regional Express (© **13 17 13** in Australia; www.regionalexpress.com.au) serves regional New South Wales, South Australia, Victoria, and northern Tasmania.

Between them, Virgin Blue, Qantas and its subsidiaries QantasLink and Jetstar service every capital city, as well as most major regional towns on the east coast, Tasmania, and places like Broom in Western Australia. Melbourne has two airports: the main international and domestic terminals at Tullamarine, and Avalon Airport, about 50km (31 miles) from the city, which is used by Jetstar. Make sure you check which one your flight leaves from before you book. Competition is hot, so it's likely that all airlines will have added to their route networks by the time you read this.

Low-cost Asian carrier **Tiger Airways** (www.tigerairways.com), already flying into Darwin and Perth from Singapore, will have launched its first Australian domestic flights before you arrive.

Australia's air network is not as well developed as that of North America or Europe, so don't assume there is a direct flight to your chosen destination, or that there is a flight every hour or even every day. ***Note:*** All flights in Australia are nonsmoking.

FARES FOR INTERNATIONAL TRAVELERS Qantas typically offers international travelers a discount of around 30% off the full fares that Australians pay for domestic flights bought within Australia. To qualify, quote your passport number and international ticket number when reserving. Don't assume the fare for international travelers is the best deal, though—the latest deal in the market that day (or even better, perhaps, a package deal with accommodations thrown in) may be cheaper still.

AIR PASSES If you are visiting from the U.S. and plan on whipping around to more than one city, purchasing a Qantas **Aussie AirPass** is much cheaper than buying regular fares. The pass is good for travel on certain flights between Los Angeles, San Francisco, or Honolulu and Sydney, Melbourne, or Brisbane, and also gives you up to another three destinations within Australia (or more for an extra US$100 each).

The AirPass price starts from US$1,099 to US$1,599 depending on the season, and is for economy-class travel only. Prices also vary according to which "zone" you are traveling to. Zone 1 covers travel to Sydney, Canberra, Melbourne, Brisbane, the Gold Coast, Adelaide, Hobart, and Launceston. Zone 2, which costs an extra US$200, will take you to Cairns, Townsville, Hamilton Island, Rockhampton, Mackay, Gladstone, Alice Springs, Ayers Rock (Uluru), and Darwin. Zone 3, costing an extra US$400 or US$500, will get you as far as Perth, Broome, and Hayman Island.

If you are starting your trip in the U.S. from somewhere other than Los Angeles or Honolulu, special fares are available—but only from San Jose, San Diego, Seattle, Portland, Las Vegas, Dallas, Denver, St. Louis, Chicago, New York (JFK and Newark), Washington, D.C., Miami, and Boston. Check with Qantas (© **800/227 4603;** www.qantas.com) for details.

The AirPass is also only available on certain flights but you can pay a US$300 surcharge to travel on other flights and still get an AirPass.

The Aussie AirPass has a minimum stay of 7 days and a maximum of 21 days from your first trans-Atlantic flight.

You must buy the pass before you arrive in Australia. Residents of England, New Zealand and Australia cannot purchase this pass.

AERIAL TOURS The great thing about aerial touring is that it allows you to whiz around the vast Australian continent to see many highlights, and you get to skip all the featureless countryside that typically separates Australia's most fascinating bits. Much of the landscape (such as the weird Bungle Bungles formations in the Kimberley) is best seen from the air, anyhow. **Aircruising Australia** ★★ (© **1800/252 053** in Australia, or 02/9693 2233; 0800/445 700 in New Zealand; www.aircruising.com.au) operates upscale aerial tours of 8 to 12 days in a private aircraft, usually a 38-passenger Dash 8, which is nimble enough to "flight-see" as low as 300m (1,000 ft.). One factor you may regard as a plus is that the company mainly markets within Australia, so your fellow passengers are likely to be Aussies. Perhaps because the tours are expensive for Australians, most passengers are over 55. Those who have taken these tours recommend them, saying they are extremely well organized, with lots of time for the land-based sightseeing, some free time, and a maximum 2 hours in the air most days. Accommodations are usually the best available, and the itineraries include "fun extras." Fares in 2007 ranged from A$8,949 to A$12,695 (US$7,159–US$10,156/£3,575–£5,048) per person sharing a double or twin room.

You may not think of Antarctica as part of your Australian vacation, but **Antarctica Sightseeing Flights** (✆ **1800/633 449** in Australia, or 03/9725 8555; www.antarcticaflights.com.au) offers once-in-a-lifetime visits to the icy continent. The 12-hour journey offers spectacular viewing over the frozen beauty of Antarctica—a truly memorable experience that comes at a high price for a day trip. Flights are seasonal (Nov–Feb) and include a New Year's Eve flight. Most leave from Sydney or Melbourne, with connections from Brisbane, Canberra, and Adelaide. The tours have been running for 13 years, operated by Croydon Travel with chartered Qantas jumbo jets carrying 350 passengers. You reach the Antarctic coastline after about 4 hours flying and spend the next 4 hours above some of the world's most pristine and spectacular territory. Below are magnificent glaciers, mountain ranges, soaring coastal cliffs, and ice floes. There's no problem viewing all this, despite the fact that you might not have a window seat—everyone moves around and takes turns, and a rotating seating system works well. In 2007/2008, fares ranged from A$999 (US$799/UK£400) in an economy center seat to A$5,499 (US$4,399/UK£2,199) in first class—but this is unlike any other flight you've been on.

BY TRAIN

Australia's trains are clean, comfortable, and safe, and for the most part service standards and facilities are perfectly adequate. The rail network in Australia links Perth to Adelaide, and continues on to Melbourne and north to Canberra, Sydney, Brisbane, and right up the coast to Cairns. There's also a line from Adelaide to Alice Springs and Darwin. Some rural towns, such as Broken Hill, also have rail service. Trains generally cost more than buses but are still reasonably priced. The exceptions are two trains promoted as "experiences" rather than a mere mode of transport—the *Indian Pacific* and the *Ghan* (described below)—that can be frightfully expensive.

Most long-distance trains have sleepers with big windows, air-conditioning, electric outlets, wardrobes, sinks, and fresh sheets and blankets. First-class sleepers have en-suite (attached private) bathrooms, and fares often include meals. Second-class sleepers use shared shower facilities, and meals are not included. Some second-class sleepers are private cabins; on other trains you share with strangers. Single cabins are usually of broom-closet dimensions but surprisingly comfy, with their own toilet and basin. The food ranges from mediocre to pretty good. Smoking is usually banned, or allowed only in the club cars or special "smoking rooms."

Different entities manage Australia's rail routes. They are the private enterprise **Great Southern Railway** (✆ **13 21 47** in Australia, or 08/8213 4592; www.gsr.com.au), which runs the *Indian Pacific,* the *Overland,* and the *Ghan,* and these government bodies: **Traveltrain,** the long-distance train division of Queensland Rail (© **1300/131 722** in Australia, or 07/3235 1133; www.traveltrain.com.au), which handles rail within that state; **Countrylink** (© **13 22 32** in Australia; www.countrylink.info), which manages travel within New South Wales and from Sydney to Canberra, Melbourne, and Brisbane; and the **Public Transport Authority,** or PTA (© **1300/662 205** in Western Australia, or 08/9326 2600; www.transwa.wa.gov.au), which operates trains in Western Australia.

Outside Australia, the umbrella organization **Rail Australia** (www.railaustralia.com.au) handles inquiries and makes reservations for all long-distance trains, with the exception of PTA routes, through its overseas agents: **ATS Tours** (© **800/423-2880**) in the U.S.; **Goway** (© **800/387-8850**) in Canada; **International Rail** (© **0870/751-5000**) in the U.K.; and **Tranz Scenic** (© **0800/808 900** or 03/339 3809) in New Zealand.

Great Southern Railway's ***Indian Pacific*** ★★ is a glamorous train linking Sydney, Broken Hill, Adelaide, Kalgoorlie, and Perth in a 3-day Outback run twice a week. Slightly less posh but still comfortable, the ***Ghan*** (named after Afghani camel trainers who traveled the Outback in the 19th c.) travels between Adelaide and Darwin twice a week via Alice Springs, with connections from Sydney and Perth on the *Indian Pacific* and from Melbourne on Great Southern Railway's third train, the ***Overland.*** The *Overland* was refurbished and relaunched in mid-2007, to provide greater levels of comfort. It travels in daylight between Adelaide and Melbourne three times a week. All three trains offer a choice of economy seats and second- or first-class sleepers.

Countrylink runs daily trains from Sydney to Melbourne, Canberra, and Brisbane, and to a number of New South Wales country towns.

Queensland Rail's Traveltrain operates two trains on the Brisbane-Cairns route: The ***Sunlander*** runs twice a week from Brisbane to Cairns, offering a choice of the premium, all-inclusive Queenslander Class; single-, double-, or triple-berth sleepers; or economy seats. Two services also run as far as Townsville on this route without Queenslander Class. The high-speed **Tilt Train** operates two weekly trips on the same route in less time—by about 8 hours—with business-class-style seating. Tilt Trains also serve Rockhampton daily (except Sat) from Brisbane. Traveltrain also operates trains to Outback towns. All Traveltrain and most Countrylink long-distance trains stop at most towns en route, so they're useful for exploring the eastern states.

PACKAGES Great Southern Railway, Countrylink, and Queensland Rail Traveltrain (see above) offer rail packages that include accommodations and sightseeing.

RAIL PASSES Rail passes are available from Rail Australia (see above) at its overseas agents. Passes are not valid for first-class travel, but upgrades are available.

The national **Austrail Flexipass** is good for economy seats and second-class sleepers on all long-distance trains (except PTA service in Western Australia) and is even good for suburban city train networks. It allows you to travel for 15 or 22 days, consecutive or not, within a 6-month period. Prices are A$862 (US$690/UK£345) for a 15-day Flexipass to A$1,210 (US$968/UK£484) for a 22-day Flexipass. This pass, and the **Great Southern Railway pass,** must be bought before you arrive in Australia and are available only to holders of non-Australian passports.

Queensland's Traveltrain Holidays (© **1300/131 722** in Australia, or 07/3235 1133; www.traveltrain.com.au), has the new Wanderer and Stopover rail passes. The **Wanderer** pass costs A$266 (US$213/UK£106) and provides 6 months of unlimited one-way travel in economy seating on Queensland's coastal trains, with departures from Brisbane or Cairns. Pass holders also receive up to 50% discounts for return journeys on any of the Queensland's Outback rail services. The **Stopover** fare lets travelers choose to stop up to four times (including their final stop) in 4 weeks when traveling on the Tilt Train. Prices vary depending on the number of stops.

BY BUS

Bus travel in Australia is a big step up from the low-rent affair it can be in the United States. Terminals are centrally located and well lit, the buses—called "coaches" Down Under—are clean and air-conditioned, you sit in adjustable seats, videos play on board, and the drivers are polite and sometimes even point out places of interest along the way. Some buses have restrooms. Unlike Australia's train service, the extensive bus network will take you almost everywhere. Buses are all nonsmoking.

Australia has one national coach operator: **Greyhound Australia** (**© 13 14 99** in Australia, or 07/4690 9950; www.greyhound.com.au; no relation to Greyhound in the U.S.). The company does not operate within Tasmania, which is serviced by **Redline Coaches** (**© 1300/360 000** in Australia; www.redlinecoaches.com.au). In addition to point-to-point services, Greyhound Australia also offers a limited range of tours at popular locations on its networks, including Uluru, Kakadu, Monkey Mia in Western Australia, and the Great Ocean Road in Victoria.

Note: Fares and some passes are considerably cheaper for students, backpacker cardholders, and Hostelling International/YHA members.

BUS PASSES Bus passes are a great value. There are several kinds—day passes (for between 3 and 30 days), preset itinerary passes, and kilometer passes. Look into the one that suits you best. Note that even with a pass, you may still need to book the next leg of your trip 12 or 24 hours ahead as a condition of the pass; during school vacation periods, which are always busy, booking as much as 7 days ahead may be smart.

If you know where you are going and are willing to obey a "no backtracking" rule, consider Greyhound Australia's **Aussie Explorer** predetermined itinerary pass. These passes allow unlimited stops in a generous time frame on a preset one-way route (you are permitted to travel the route in either direction). There is a huge range of itineraries to choose from. As an example, the **Aussie Reef and Rock** pass takes in Alice Springs, Katherine, Darwin, Mount Isa, Cairns, and the whole east coast down to Sydney. The pass is valid for 6 months and costs A$1,293 (US$1,034/UK£517) from Sydney, including tours to Uluru (Ayers Rock), Kakadu National Park, and Kings Canyon. You don't have to start in Sydney; you can start at any point along any of the pass routes, in which case the pass may be cheaper. In the case of the Reef and Rock pass, that means you could start farther up the track, at Brisbane (in which case the pass costs A$1,176/US$941/UK£470) or Cairns (from where the pass costs A$943/US$754/UK£377). The **All Australian Pass** costs A$2,827 (US$2,262/UK£1,131) and is valid for a year.

The **Aussie Kilometre Pass** allows unlimited stops in any direction within the mileage you buy. Passes are available in increments of 1,000km (620 miles). Prices range from A$360 (US$288/UK£144) for 2,000km (1,240 miles)—enough to get you from Cairns to Brisbane—to A$2,597 (US$2,078/UK£1,039) for a whopping 20,000km (6,200 miles).

SAMPLE TRAVEL TIMES & BUS FARES

Here are sample bus fares and travel times, to give you an idea of what you're getting yourself into as you step aboard. All fares and travel times are one-way.

Route	Travel Time (Approx.)	Fare
Broome-Darwin	27 hr.	A$367 (US$294/UK£147)
Sydney-Brisbane	17 hr.	A$121 (US$97/UK£48)
Cairns-Brisbane	29 hr.	A$243 (US$194/UK£97)

BY CAR

Australia's roads sometimes leave a bit to be desired. The taxes of 19 million people get spread pretty thin when it comes to maintaining roads across a continent. Most highways are two-lane affairs with the occasional rut and pothole, often no outside line markings, and sometimes no shoulders to speak of.

When you are poring over the map of Australia, remember that what looks like a road may be an unsealed (unpaved) track suitable for four-wheel-drive vehicles only. Many roads in the Top End are passable only in the Dry season (about Apr–Nov). If you plan long-distance driving, get a road map (see below for sources) that marks paved and unpaved roads.

You cannot drive across the middle of the country (except along the north-south Stuart Hwy. linking Adelaide and Darwin) because most of it is desert. In most places you must travel around the edge on Highway 1. The map inside the back cover of this book marks the major highways.

You can use your current driver's license or an international driver's permit in every state of Australia. By law, you must carry your license with you when driving. The minimum driving age is 16 or 17, depending on which state you visit, but some car-rental companies require you to be 21, or sometimes 26, if you want to rent a four-wheel-drive vehicle.

CAR RENTALS

Think twice about renting a car in tourist hot spots such as Cairns. In these areas most tour operators pick you up and drop you back at your hotel door, so having a car may not be worth the expense.

The "big four" car-rental companies all have networks across Australia:

- **Avis** (© **13 63 33** in Australia, www.avis.com.au; 800/230-4898 in the U.S. and Canada, www.avis.com; 8445/81 81 81 in the U.K., www.avis.co.uk; 214/281 111 in Ireland; 0800/655 111 in New Zealand, www.avis.co.nz).
- **Budget** (© **1300/362 848** in Australia, www.budget.com.au; 800/472-3325 in the U.S., www.budget.com; 800/268-8900 in Canada, www.budget.ca; 8701-565656 in the U.K., www.budget-uk.com; 090/6627-711 in Ireland, www.budget-ireland.com; 0800/283 438 in New Zealand, www.budget.co.nz).
- **Hertz** (© **13 30 39** in Australia, www.hertz.com.au; 800/654-3001 in the U.S. and Canada, www.hertz.com; or 800/263-0678 in French in Canada, www.hertz.ca; 0870/844 844 in the U.K., www.hertz.co.uk; 0800/654 321 in New Zealand, www.hertz.co.nz).
- **Thrifty** (© **1300/367 227** in Australia, www.thrifty.com.au; 800/847-4389 in the U.S. and Canada, www.thrifty.com; 01494/751-540 in the U.K., www.thrifty.co.uk; 1800/515-800 in Ireland, www.thrifty.ie; 0800/73 7070 in New Zealand, www.thrifty.co.nz).

Two other large companies with offices around Australia are:

- **Europcar** (✆ **1300/13 13 90** in Australia or 03/9330 6160, www.europcar.com.au; 877/940-6900 in the U.S. and Canada, www.europcar.com; 0870/607-5000 in the U.K., www.europcar.co.uk; 1/614-2800 in Ireland, www.europcar.ie; 0800/800 115 in New Zealand, www.europcar.co.nz). Europcar has the third-largest fleet in Australia.
- **Red Spot Car Rentals** (✆ **1300/668 810** in Australia, or 02/8303 2222; www.redspotrentals.com.au). It has depots in Sydney, Melbourne, Brisbane, Perth, Cairns, the Gold Coast, Hobart, and Launceston.

SAMPLE DRIVING DISTANCES & TIMES

Here are a few sample road distances between popular points and the minimum time it takes to drive between them.

Route	Distance	Approx. Driving Time
Cairns-Sydney	2,495km (1,547 miles)	29 hr. (allow 4–5 days)
Sydney-Melbourne	873km (541 miles)	15 hr. (allow 1–2 days)
Sydney-Perth	4,131km (2,561 miles)	51 hr. (allow 6–7 days)
Adelaide-Darwin	3,024km (1,875 miles)	31 hr. (allow 4–6 days)
Perth-Darwin	4,163km (2,581 miles)	49 hr. (allow 6–8 days)

A small sedan for zipping around a city or touring a wine region will cost about A$45 to A$80 (US$36–US$64/UK£18–UK£32) a day. A feistier vehicle with enough grunt to get you from state to state will cost around A$70 to A$100 (US$56–US$80/UK£28–UK£40) a day. Rentals of a week or longer usually reduce the price by A$5 (US$4/UK£2) a day or so.

A regular car will get you to most places in this book, but because the country has many unpaved roads, it can make sense to rent a four-wheel-drive vehicle. All the major car-rental companies rent them. They are more expensive than a regular car, but you can get them for as little as A$75 (US$60/UK£30) per day if you shop around, cheaper for rentals of a week or longer.

The rates quoted here are only a guide. Many smaller local companies—and the big guys, too—offer competitive specials, especially in tourist areas with distinct off seasons. Advance purchase rates, usually 7 to 21 days, can offer significant savings.

INSURANCE Insurance for loss of, or damage to, the car, and third-party property insurance are usually included, but read the agreement carefully, because the fine print contains information the front-desk staff may not tell you. For example, damage to the car body may be covered, but not damage to the windshield or tires, or damage caused by water or driving too close to a bushfire.

The deductible, known as "excess" in Australia, on insurance may be as high as A$2,000 (US$1,600/UK£800) for regular cars and up to A$5,500 (US$4,400/UK£2,200) on four-wheel-drives and motor homes. You can reduce it, or avoid it altogether, by paying a premium of between about A$20 to A$50 (US$16–US$40/UK£8–UK£20) per day on a car or four-wheel-drive, and around A$25 to A$50 (US$20–US$40/UK£10–UK£20) per day on a motor home. The amount of the excess reduction premium depends on the vehicle type and the extent of reduction you choose. Your rental company may bundle personal accident insurance and baggage insurance into this

Tips **Insurance Alert**

Damage to a rental car caused by an animal (hitting a kangaroo, for instance) is not covered by car-rental companies' insurance policies. Nor is driving on an unpaved road—and Australia has a lot of those.

premium. And again, check the conditions; some excess reduction payments do not reduce excesses on single-vehicle accidents, for example.

ONE-WAY RENTALS Australia's distances often make one-way rentals a necessity, for which car-rental companies can charge a hefty penalty amounting to hundreds of dollars. A one-way fee usually applies to motor-home renters, too—usually around A$200 to A$220 (US$160–US$176/UK£80–UK£88), more for remote outback areas such as Broome and Alice Springs. And there's a 7-day rental minimum.

MOTOR HOMES Motor homes (Aussies call them camper vans) are popular in Australia. Generally smaller than the RVs in the United States, they come in two-, three-, four-, or six-berth versions, and usually have everything you need, such as a minifridge/freezer (icebox in the smaller versions), microwave, gas stove, cooking and cleaning utensils, linens, and touring information including maps and campground guides. All have showers and toilets, except some two-berthers. Most have air-conditioned driver's cabins, but not all have air-conditioned living quarters, a necessity in most parts of the country from November through March. Four-wheel-drive campers are available, but they tend to be small, and some lack hot water, toilet, shower, and air-conditioning. Minimum driver age for motor homes is usually 21.

Australia's biggest national motor-home-rental companies are **Apollo Motorhome Holidays** (✆ **1800/777 779** in Australia, or 07/3265 9200; www.apollocamper.com.au), **Britz Campervan Rentals** (✆ **1800/331 454** in Australia, or 03/8379 8890; www.britz.com), and **Maui** (✆ **1300/363 800** in Australia, or 03/8379 8891; www.maui.com.au).

For a two-berth motor home with shower and toilet, Britz's rates range from around A$55 to A$170 (US$44–US$136/UK£22–UK£68) per day, over a 5- to 20-day rental period. For a four-berth with shower and toilet over the same period, you are looking at A$125 to A$250 (US$100–US$200/UK£50–UK£100) per day. Rates vary with the seasons. May and June are the slowest months; December and January are the busiest. It's sometimes possible to get better rates by booking in your home country before departure. Renting for longer than 3 weeks knocks a few dollars off the daily rate. Most companies will demand a minimum 4- or 5-day rental. Give the company your itinerary before booking, because some routes, such as the ferry across to Tasmania—or, in the case of a four-wheel-drive motor home, the Gibb River Road in the Kimberley—may need the company's permission.

Companies may not permit you to drive their two-wheel-drive motor home on unpaved roads, although they may make an exception for relatively short unsealed access roads to recognized campgrounds. Check with them first.

Frustratingly, most local councils take a dim view of "free camping," the practice of pulling over by the roadside to camp for the night. Instead, you will likely have to stay in a campground.

ON THE ROAD

GAS The price of petrol (gasoline) will probably elicit a cry of dismay from Americans and a whoop of delight from Brits. Prices go up and down, but at press time you were looking at around A$1.25 (UK50p) a liter (or US$3.80 per U.S. gallon) for unleaded petrol in Sydney, and A$1.35 (UK55p) a liter (or US$4.10 per U.S. gallon), or more, in the Outback. One U.S. gallon equals 3.78 liters. Most rental cars take unleaded gas, and motor homes run on diesel, which at press time was averaging around the same price as unleaded petrol.

DRIVING RULES Australians drive on the left, which means you give way to the right. Left turns on a red light are not permitted unless a sign says so.

Roundabouts (traffic circles) are common at intersections; approach these slowly enough to stop if you have to, and give way to all traffic on the roundabout. Flash your indicator as you leave the roundabout (even if you're going straight, because technically that's a left turn).

The only strange driving rule is Melbourne's requirement that drivers turn right from the left lane at certain intersections in the city center. This allows the city's trams to carry on uninterrupted in the right lane. Pull into the left lane opposite the street you are turning into, and make the turn when the traffic light in the street you are turning into becomes green. These intersections are signposted.

The maximum permitted blood alcohol level when driving is .05%, which equals approximately two 200-milliliter (6.6-oz.) drinks in the first hour for men, one for women, and one drink per hour for both sexes after that. The police set up random breath-testing units (RBTs) in cunningly disguised and unlikely places all the time, so getting caught is easy. You will face a court appearance if you do.

The speed limit is 50kmph (31 mph) or 60kmph (37 mph) in urban areas, 100kmph (62 mph) in most country areas, and sometimes 110kmph (68 mph) on freeways. In the Northern Territory, the speed limit is set at 130kmph (81 mph) on the Stuart, Arnhem, Barkly, and Victoria highways, while rural roads are designated 110kmph (68 mph) speed limits unless otherwise signposted. But be warned: The Territory has a high road death toll. Speed-limit signs are black numbers circled in red on a white background.

Drivers and passengers, including taxi passengers, must wear a seat belt at all times when the vehicle is moving forward, if the car is equipped with a belt. Young children are required to sit in the rear seat in a child-safety seat or harness; car-rental companies will rent these to you, but be sure to book them. Tell the taxi company you have a child when you book a cab so that it can send a car with the right restraints.

MAPS The maps published by the state automobile clubs listed below in "Auto Clubs" will likely be free if you are a member of an affiliated auto club in your home country. None will mail them to you overseas; pick them up on arrival. Remember to bring your auto-club membership card to qualify for discounts or free maps.

Two of the biggest map publishers in Australia are **HEMA Maps** (✆ **07/3340 0000;** www.hemamaps.com.au) and **Universal Publishers** (✆ **1800/021 987** in Australia, or 02/9857 3700; www.universalpress-online.com). Both publish an extensive range of national, state, regional, and city maps. HEMA has a strong list of regional maps ("Gold Coast and Region" and "The Red Centre" are just a few), while Universal produces a complete range of street directories by city, region, or state under the "UBD" and "Gregory's" labels. HEMA produces four-wheel-drive and motorbike road atlases and many regional four-wheel-drive maps—good if you plan to go off the trails—an atlas of Australia's national parks, and maps to Kakadu and Lamington national parks.

Both companies produce a range of national road atlases. Universal's UBD *Complete Motoring Atlas of Australia* helpfully publishes street maps of small regional towns in each state. Australia is so big that a national atlas is good for overall trip planning and long-distance or interstate journeys, but sometimes of limited use on day trips or short journeys, because it is not detailed enough. You may find it worthwhile to purchase a map to the local area—say, a "Cairns to Cooktown" map if you want to explore Cairns, Kuranda, Port Douglas, and other towns within an hour or two of Cairns.

In Australia, auto clubs (see below), bigger newsdealers, and bookstores are your best sources for maps. Gas stations stock a limited range relating to their location, and visitor information centers sometimes stock a range of maps to the area and the whole state.

ROAD SIGNS Australians navigate by road name, not road number. The easiest way to get where you're going is to familiarize yourself with the major towns along your route and follow the signs toward them.

AUTO CLUBS Every state and territory in Australia has its own auto club. Your auto association back home probably has a reciprocal agreement with Australian clubs, which may entitle you to free maps, accommodations guides, and emergency roadside assistance. Don't forget to bring your membership card.

Even if you're not a member, the clubs are a good source of advice on local traffic regulations, touring advice, road conditions, traveling in remote areas, and any other motoring questions you may have. They sell maps, accommodations guides, and camping guides to nonmembers at reasonable prices. They share a website: **www.aaa.asn.au**. You can drop into numerous regional offices as well as the head office locations listed here.

- **New South Wales & ACT: National Roads and Motorists' Association (NRMA),** 388 George St., Sydney, NSW 2000 (© **13 11 22** in New South Wales, or 02/8741 6000).
- **Victoria: Royal Automobile Club of Victoria (RACV),** 550 Princes Hwy., Noble Park, VIC 3174 (© **13 13 29** in Australia, or 03/9790 2211). A more convenient city office is at 438 Little Collins St., Melbourne.
- **Queensland: Royal Automobile Club of Queensland (RACQ),** 300 St. Pauls Terrace, Fortitude Valley, QLD 4006 (© **13 19 05** in Australia, or 07/3361 2444). A more convenient city office is in the General Post Office (GPO) building, 261 Queen St., Brisbane (© **07/3872 8465**).
- **Western Australia: Royal Automobile Club of WA (RACWA),** 228 Adelaide Terrace, Perth, WA 6000 (© **13 17 03** or 08/9436 4444).
- **South Australia: Royal Automobile Association of South Australia (RAA),** 55 Hindmarsh Sq., Adelaide, SA 5000 (© **08/8202 4600**).
- **Northern Territory: Automobile Association of the Northern Territory (AANT),** 79–81 Smith St., Darwin, NT 0800 (© **08/8981 3837**).
- **Tasmania: Royal Automobile Club of Tasmania (RACT),** corner of Murray and Patrick streets, Hobart, TAS 7000 (© **13 27 22** in Tasmania, or 03/6232 6300).

ROAD CONDITIONS & SAFETY

Here are some common motoring dangers and ways to avoid them:

FATIGUE Fatigue is a killer on Australia's roads. The rule is to take a 20-minute break every 2 hours, even if you don't feel tired. In some states, "driver reviver" stations operate on major roads during holiday periods. They serve free tea, coffee, and cookies, and are often at roadside picnic areas that have restrooms.

KANGAROOS & OTHER WILDLIFE It's a sad fact, but kangaroos are a road hazard. Avoid driving in country areas between dusk and dawn, when 'roos are most active. If you hit one, always stop and check its pouch for live joeys (baby kangaroos), because females usually have one in the pouch. Wrap the joey tightly in a towel or old sweater, don't feed or overhandle it, and take it to a vet in the nearest town or call one of the following wildlife care groups: **Wildlife Information & Rescue Service (WIRES)** in New South Wales (© 02/8977 3333); **Wildlife Victoria** (© 0500/540 000 or 03/9663 9211); **Wildlife Rescue** in Queensland (© 0418/792 598); **RSPCA Wildlife** in the ACT (© 02/6287 8100 or 0413/495 031); **Wildcare** in Western Australia (© 08/9474 9055); **Wildlife Rescue** in the Northern Territory (© 0409/090 849); **Fauna Rescue of S.A.** in South Australia (© 08/8289 0896); or **Wildcare** in Tasmania (© 03/6233 2852). Most vets will treat native wildlife for free.

Some highways run through unfenced stations (ranches), where sheep and cattle pose a threat. Cattle like to rest on the warm bitumen road at night, so put your lights on high to spot them. If an animal does loom up, slow down—but never swerve, or you may roll. If you have to, hit it. Tell ranchers within 24 hours if you have hit their livestock.

Car-rental companies will not insure for animal damage to the car, which should give you an inkling of how common an occurrence this is.

ROAD TRAINS Road trains consist of as many as three big truck carriages linked together to make a "train" up to 54m (177 ft.) long. If you're in front of one, give the driver plenty of warning when you brake, because the trains need a lot of distance to slow down. Allow at least 1 clear kilometer (over ½ mile) before you pass one, but don't expect the driver to make it easy—"truckies" are notorious for their lack of concern for motorists.

UNPAVED ROADS Many country roads are unsealed (unpaved). They are usually bone-dry, which makes them more slippery than they look, so travel at a moderate speed—35kmph (22 mph) is not too cautious, and anything over 60kmph (37 mph) is dangerous. Don't overcorrect if you veer to one side. Keep well behind any vehicles, because the dust they throw up can block your vision.

FLOODS Floods are common in the Top End and north of Cairns from November or December through March or April (the Wet season). Never cross a flooded road unless you are sure of its depth. Crocodiles may be in the water, so do not wade in to test it! Fast-flowing water is dangerous, even if it's very shallow. When in doubt, stay where you are and wait for the water to drop; most flash floods subside in 24 hours. Check the road conditions ahead at least once a day in the Wet season.

RUNNING OUT OF GAS Gas stations (also called "roadhouses" in rural areas) can be few and far between in the Outback, so fill up at every opportunity.

WHAT IF YOUR VEHICLE BREAKS DOWN?

Warning: If you break down or get lost, never leave your vehicle. Many a motorist—often an Aussie who should have known better—has died wandering off on a crazy quest for help or water, knowing full well that neither is to be found for maybe hundreds of miles. Most people who get lost do so in Outback spots; if that happens to you, conserve your body moisture by doing as little as possible and staying in the shade of your car. Put out distress signals in patterns of three—three yells, three columns of smoke, and so on. The traditional Outback call for help is "Coo-*ee,*" with the accent on the "ee" and yodeled in a high pitch; the sound travels a surprisingly long way.

The state auto clubs listed above provide free breakdown emergency assistance to members of many affiliated automobile associations around the world.

EMERGENCY ASSISTANCE

The emergency breakdown assistance telephone number for every Australian auto club is ✆ **13 11 11** from anywhere in Australia. It is billed as a local call. If you are not a member of an auto club at home that has a reciprocal agreement with the Australian clubs, you'll have to join the Australian club on the spot before the club will tow or repair your car. This usually costs only around A$80 (US$64/UK£32), not a big price to pay when you're stranded—although in the Outback, the charge may be considerably higher. Most car-rental companies also have emergency assistance numbers.

TIPS FOR FOUR-WHEEL DRIVERS

Always keep to the four-wheel-drive track. Going off-road causes soil erosion, a significant environmental problem in Australia. Leave gates as you found them. Obtain permission from the owners before venturing onto private station (ranch) roads. On an extended trip or in remote areas, carry 5 liters (1⅓ gal.) of drinking water per person per day (dehydration occurs fast in the Australian heat); enough food to last 3 or 4 days more than you think you will need; a first-aid kit; spare fuel; a jack and two spare tires; spare fan belts, radiator hoses, and air-conditioner hoses; a tow rope; and a good map that marks all gas stations. In seriously remote areas outside the scope of this book, carry a high-frequency and CB radio. (A cellphone may not work in the Outback.) Advise a friend, your hotel manager, the local tourist bureau, or a police station of your route and your expected time of return or arrival at your destination.

14 Tips on Accommodations

Accommodations properties in Australia carry star ratings given by AAA Tourism, which has been awarding ratings since the 1950s. This independent assessment is based on facilities, amenities, maintenance, and cleanliness. Ratings run from one to five stars. Stars are featured in AAA Tourism guides, and recent research shows 70% of travelers use the star ratings when choosing their accommodations (these star ratings are noted below using asterisks). The rating scheme covers over 18,000 accommodations throughout every state and territory.

* Offers a basic standard of accommodations, simply furnished, with a resident manager.

** Similar standard to one star but offers more comfort and value with additional features. These are well-maintained properties offering an average standard of accommodations with average furnishings, bedding, and floor coverings.

*** Well appointed, with a comfortable standard of accommodations, and above-average furnishings and floor coverings.

**** Exceptionally well-appointed establishments with high-quality furnishings, a high degree of comfort, high standard of presentation, and guest services.

***** International standard establishments offering superior appointments, furnishings, and decor, with an extensive range of first-class guest services. Reception, room service, and housekeeping available 18 hours a day, with restaurant/bistro facilities available 7 nights a week. A number and variety of room styles, suites, or both are available. Choice of dining facilities, 24-hour room service, housekeeping, and valet parking. Porter and concierge service available, as well as a dedicated business center and conference facilities.

Note: All accommodations listed in this book have private bathrooms unless otherwise noted.

HOTELS It's a rare hotel room that does not have reverse-cycle air-conditioning for heating and cooling, a telephone, a color TV, a clock radio, a minifridge (if not a minibar), an iron and ironing board, and self-serve coffee and tea. Private bathrooms are standard, although they often have only a shower, not a tub.

The largest hotel group in Australia is the French chain Accor, which has more than 100 properties (that's about 15,000 rooms) under its Sofitel, Novotel, Mercure, All Seasons, Ibis, and Formule 1 brands. Many other international chains, such as Marriott, Sheraton, and Hilton, have properties in Australia.

SERVICED APARTMENTS Serviced apartments are favored by many Aussie families and business travelers. You get a fully furnished apartment with one, two, or three bedrooms, a living room, a kitchen or kitchenette, a laundry, and often two bathrooms—in other words, all the facilities of a hotel suite and more, often for less than the cost of a four-star hotel room. (Not every apartment kitchen has a dishwasher, so check if that's important to you.) A nice two-bedroom apartment can cost anywhere from around A$170 to A$720 (US$136–US$576/UK£218–UK£288) a night, depending on your location and the season. Australia's apartment inventory is enormous and ranges from clean and comfortable, if a little dated, to luxurious. Most apartments can be rented for 1 night, especially in cities, but in popular vacation spots, some proprietors will insist on a minimum 3-night stay, or even a week in high season.

Medina Serviced Apartments (© **1300/633 462** in Australia, or 02/9356 1000; www.medinaapartments.com.au) has a chain of midrange to upscale properties in Sydney, Melbourne, Brisbane, Canberra, Adelaide, and Perth (and a new property to open in Darwin in 2008). Australia's biggest apartment chain, with more than 100 properties, is **Quest Serviced Apartments** (© **1800/334 033** in Australia, or 03/9645 8357, 0800/944 400 in New Zealand; www.questapartments.com.au). It has apartments in every state and territory.

MOTELS & MOTOR INNS Australia's plentiful motels are neat and clean, if often a little dated. You can count on them to provide air-conditioning, a telephone, a color TV, a clock radio, a minifridge or minibar, and self-serve tea and coffee. Most have only showers, not bathtubs. Some have restaurants attached, and many have swimming pools. Motor inns offer a greater range of facilities and a generally higher standard of rooms than motels. Rates average A$80 to A$120 (US$64–US$96/UK£32–UK£48) double.

BED & BREAKFAST INNS B&Bs are cheap and plentiful in Australia. It is easy to find charming rooms for under A$100 (US$80/UK£40) for a double. Bathroom facilities are often shared, although more properties now offer private, if not always en-suite (attached), bathrooms.

Travel agents rarely list B&Bs because the establishments are not big enough to pay a commission, so they can be hard to find. A good source is ***The Australian Bed & Breakfast Book*** (www.bbbook.com.au), which lists more than 400 B&Bs across Australia. Although the B&Bs pay to be in the book, they have to

Tips Meet the People Down Under

If you want to see an Australian Rules football game in the company of a knowledgeable local in Melbourne or swim at Bondi Beach with a Sydneysider, contact **Friends Overseas—Australia** (**© 718/261-0534;** www.friendsoverseas.org). This program is designed to match visitors with friendly Aussies of like age and interests, so you can spend time with them. The membership fee is US$25.

meet standards set by the editors. The entire book is posted on the website, and in Australia, it's widely available in bookshops and newsdealers, or you can order it direct (**© 02/6658 5701**) for A$20 (US$16/UK£8) plus A$15 (US$12/UK£6) for overseas air-express postage.

What Next? Productions (**© 0438/600 696** mobile phone; www.beautifulaccommodation.com) publishes a series of *Beautiful Accommodation* color guides listing around 500 exquisite properties in every state and territory, many in charming country areas. The properties listed are more upscale than most, roughly in the A$150-to-A$300 (US$120–US$240/UK£60–UK£120) range. Each book sells for A$30 (US$24/UK£12) in Australian bookstores and can be ordered online.

Another good website is that of **Bed & Breakfast and Farmstay Australia** (www.australianbedandbreakfast.com.au)which has links to all state B&B organizations.

PUBS Aussie pubs are really made for drinking, not spending the night, but many offer rooms upstairs, usually with shared bathroom facilities. Because most pubs are decades old, the rooms may be either old-fashioned or just plain old. Pub accommodations are dying out in the cities but still common in the country. Australians are rowdy drinkers, so sleeping over the bar can be hellishly noisy, but the pub's saving grace is incredibly low rates. Most charge per person, not per room, and you will rarely pay more than A$50 (US$40/UK£20) per person a night.

FARMSTAYS The Aussie answer to the dude ranch is a farmstay. Australian farmstays are rarely as well set up for tourists as the dude ranch Billy Crystal's character visited in *City Slickers.* Most are farms first, tourist operations second, so you may have to find your own fun and know how to take care of yourself, at least to a degree.

Accommodations on farms can be anything from a basic bunkhouse (ask if it's air-conditioned, because most farms are in very hot areas) to rustically luxurious digs. Do some research on your farm—a lot of activities are seasonal, some farmers will not allow you to get involved in dangerous work, not all will offer horseback riding, and *farm* means different things in different parts of Australia. If you like green fields and dairy cows, Victoria may be the place for you. If checking fences on a dusty 500,000-hectare (1.2-million-acre) Outback station (ranch) sounds wildly romantic, head to Western Australia, Queensland, or the Northern Territory.

The website of **Bed & Breakfast and Farmstay Australia** (www.australianbedandbreakfast.com.au) has links to all state farmstay organizations.

Another good contact is **Accommodation Getaways Victoria** (**© 1300/132 358** in Australia, or 03/9431 5417; www.agv.net.au). **Bed & Breakfast and Farmstay NT** (www.bed-and-breakfast.au.com) lists about 20 Northern Territory properties in Darwin, the Top End, and the Red Centre.

Rates vary, but you will find many properties charging under A$200 (US$160/UK£80) for a double, which sometimes includes breakfast. Meals are often available as an optional extra.

SURFING FOR HOTELS

In addition to the online travel booking sites **Travelocity, Expedia, Orbitz, Priceline,** and **Hotwire,** you can book hotels through **Hotels.com; Quikbook** (www.quikbook.com); and **Travelaxe** (www.travelaxe.net).

HotelChatter.com is a daily webzine offering smart coverage and critiques of hotels worldwide. Go to **TripAdvisor.com** or **HotelShark.com** for helpful independent consumer reviews of hotels and resort properties.

It's a good idea to **get a confirmation number** and **make a printout** of any online booking transaction.

SAVING ON YOUR HOTEL ROOM

The **rack rate** is the maximum rate that a hotel charges for a room. Hardly anybody pays this price, however, except in high season or on holidays. To lower the cost of your room:

- **Ask about special rates or other discounts.** You may qualify for corporate, student, military, senior, frequent flier, or other discounts.
- **Dial direct.** When booking a room in a chain hotel, you'll often get a better deal by calling the individual hotel's reservation desk rather than the chain's main number.
- **Book online.** Many hotels offer Internet-only discounts, or supply rooms to Priceline, Hotwire, or Expedia at rates much lower than the ones you can get over the phone.
- **Remember the law of supply and demand.** You can save big on hotel rooms by traveling in a destination's off season or shoulder seasons, when rates typically drop, even at luxury properties.
- **Look into group or long-stay discounts.** If you come as part of a large group, you should be able to negotiate a bargain rate. Likewise, if you're planning a long stay (at least 5 days), you might qualify for a discount. As a general rule, expect 1 night free after a 7-night stay.
- **Sidestep excess surcharges and hidden costs.** Many hotels have adopted the unpleasant practice of surprising their guests with opaque surcharges. When you book a room, ask what is included in the room rate, and what is extra. Avoid dialing direct from hotel phones, which can have exorbitant rates. And don't be tempted by the room's minibar offerings: Most hotels charge through the nose for water, soda, and snacks. Finally, ask about local taxes and service charges, which can increase the cost of a room by 15% or more.
- Consider the pros and cons of **all-inclusive** resorts and hotels. The term "all-inclusive" means different things at different hotels. Many all-inclusive hotels include three meals daily, sports equipment, spa entry, and other amenities; others may include most alcoholic drinks. In general, you'll save money going the "all-inclusive" way—as long as you use the facilities provided. The downside is that your choices are limited and you're stuck eating and playing in one place for the duration of your vacation.
- **Book an efficiency.** A room with a kitchenette allows you to shop for groceries and cook your own meals. This is a big money saver, especially for families on long stays.
- **Consider enrolling in hotel chains' "frequent-stay" programs,** which are upping the ante to win the loyalty of repeat customers. Frequent guests can accumulate points or credits to earn free hotel nights, airline miles, in-room amenities, merchandise,

Swap Your House?

House-swapping is becoming a more popular and viable means of travel; you stay in their place, they stay in yours, and you both get an authentic and personal view of the area, the opposite of the escapist retreat that many hotels offer. Try **HomeLink International** (Homelink.org), the largest and oldest home-swapping organization, founded in 1952, with over 11,000 listings worldwide ($75 for a yearly membership). There is a branch of HomeLink in Australia. Others with lots of Australian properties to choose from are **HomeforExchange.com** ($55 for 6 months membership), **InterVac.com** ($95 for 1 year), and the U.K.-based **Home Base Holidays** (www.homebase-hols.com), where you can browse the listings free, but it costs UK£29 for a year to view the contact details or to list your own home.

tickets to concerts and events, discounts on sporting facilities—and even credit toward stock in the participating hotel, in the case of the Jameson Inn hotel group. Perks are awarded not only by many chain hotels and motels (Hilton HHonors, Marriott Rewards, Wyndham ByRequest, to name a few), but individual inns and B&Bs. Many chain hotels partner with other hotel chains, car-rental firms, airlines, and credit card companies to give consumers additional incentive to do repeat business.

LANDING THE BEST ROOM

Somebody has to get the best room in the house. It might as well be you. You can start by joining the hotel's frequent-guest program, which may make you eligible for upgrades. A hotel-branded credit card usually gives its owner "silver" or "gold" status in frequent-guest programs for free. Always ask about a corner room. They're often larger and quieter, with more windows and light, and they often cost the same as standard rooms. When you make your reservation, ask if the hotel is renovating; if it is, request a room away from the construction. Ask about nonsmoking rooms and rooms with views. Be sure to request your choice of twin, queen- or king-size beds. If you're a light sleeper, ask for a quiet room away from vending or ice machines, elevators, restaurants, bars, and discos. Ask for a room that has been recently renovated or refurbished.

If you aren't happy with your room when you arrive, ask for another one. Most lodgings will be willing to accommodate you.

In resort areas, particularly in warm climates, ask the following questions before you book a room:

- What's the view like? Cost-conscious travelers may be willing to pay less for a back room facing the parking lot, especially if they don't plan to spend much time in their room.
- Does the room have air-conditioning or ceiling fans? Do the windows open? If they do, and the nighttime entertainment takes place alfresco, you may want to find out when showtime is over.
- What's included in the price? Your room may be moderately priced, but if you're charged for beach chairs, towels, sports equipment, and other amenities, you could end up spending more than you bargained for.
- How far is the room from the beach and other amenities? If it's far, is there transportation to and from the beach, and is it free?

15 Tips on Dining

Australia's multicultural population is to thank for the fantastic cuisine which has developed over the past few decades. The food here is fresh and the chefs are innovative. Whether it is seasonal produce from local growers or seafood straight from the ocean, you'll find your taste buds rewarded more often than not. Once a land of British-style "meat and three veg," Australia is now a place where you can get top-class food in any cuisine—Italian, Greek, Vietnamese, and other immigrants have seen to that.

The fusion of flavors and styles has melded into what's now commonly referred to as "Contemporary" or "Modern Australian"—a distinctive cuisine blending the spices of the East with the flavors of the West.

Make sure you take time to check out the many "farmer's markets" in major cities, where fresh produce from the surrounding countryside is brought in for sale direct to consumers. It might mean getting up early, but it will be worth it.

Tipping is not essential in Australia, but it is usual to leave something. In a casual place it's enough to round the bill up to the nearest A$10 (US$8/UK£4) or so, and in a good restaurant it is usual to tip around 10% to 15%.

With the maturing of Australian palates came the need for good wines to go with the food. Winemaking has come a long way since the first grape vines were brought to Australia on the First Fleet in 1788. These days, more than 550 major companies and small winemakers produce wine commercially in Australia. Vintages from Down Under consistently beat competitors from other wine-producing nations in major international shows. The demand for Australian wine overseas has increased so dramatically in the past few years that domestic prices have risen, and new vineyards are being planted at a frantic pace.

Australian wines are generally named after the grape varieties from which they are made. Of the white wines, big favorites include the fruity chardonnay and Riesling varieties, the "herbaceous" or "grassy" sauvignon blanc, and the dry semillon. Of the reds, the dry cabernet sauvignon, the fruity merlot, the burgundy-type pinot noir, and the big and bold Shiraz come out tops.

But there's nothing an Aussie likes better on a hot day than a cold "tinnie" or can of beer. Barbecues would not be the same without a case of tinnies, or "stubbies" (small bottles). In hotter climes, you may be offered a polystyrene container or "stubby holder" in which to place your beer to keep it cool.

Among the most popular Aussie beers are Victoria Bitter (known as "VB"), XXXX (pronounced "four ex"), Fosters, and various brews produced by the Tooheys company. All are popular in cans, bottles, or on tap (draft). Another popular choice is Cascade, a German-style beer that you'll usually find only in a bottle. It's light in color, strong in taste, and made from Tasmanian water straight off a mountain. If you want to get plastered, try Coopers—it's rather cloudy in looks, very strong, and can cause a terrific hangover. Most Australian beers range from 4.8% to 5.2% alcohol.

In New South Wales, bars serve beer by the glass in a "schooner" or a smaller "midi"—though in a few places it's also served in British measurements, by pints and half pints. In Victoria you should ask for a "pot," or the less copious "glass." In South Australia a schooner is the size of a NSW midi, and in Western Australia a midi is the same size as a New South Wales midi, but a glass about half its size is called a "pony." Confused? The easiest way is to point out the size you want.

Alcohol is only sold to those 18 years old or over.

Fun Fact Witchetty Grubs, Lilli-Pillies & Other Good Eats

In the past decade or so, Europeans have woken up to the variety and tastes of "bush tucker," as native Aussie food is tagged. Now it's all the rage in the most fashionable restaurants where wattle seed, lemon myrtle, or some other native taste has a place in one or two dishes on the menu. Below is a list of those foods you may encounter in trendy restaurants:

Bush Tucker	**Explanation**
Bunya nut	Crunchy nut of the bunya pine, about the size of macadamias.
Bush tomato	Dry, small darkish fruit more like raisins in look and taste.
Cranberry (native)	Small berry that tastes a bit like an apple.
Illawarra plums	Dark berry with a rich, strong, tangy taste.
Kakadu plum	Wonderfully sharp tangy green fruit that boasts the highest recorded vitamin C level of any food.
Kangaroo	A red meat with a strong gamey flavor. Tender when correctly prepared, tough when not. Excellent smoked.
Lemon aspen	Citrusy, light yellow fruit with a sharp tangy flavor.
Lemon myrtle	Gum leaves with a fresh lemony tang; often used to flavor white meat.
Lilli-pillies	Delicious juicy, sweet pink berry; also called a riberry.
Macadamia nut	Sweet white nut. Macadamias come from Australia, not Hawaii as most of us think.
Quandong	A tart, tangy native peach.
Rosella	Spiky red petals of a flower with a rich berry flavor; traditionally used by Europeans to make rosella jam.
Wattle seed	Roasted ground acacia seeds that taste a little like bitter coffee; commonly used by Europeans in pasta or desserts.
Wild lime	Smaller and more sour than regular lime; good in salads.

One ingredient you will *not* see on menus is **witchetty grubs;** most people are too squeamish to eat these fat, slimy white critters. They live in the soil or in dead tree trunks and are a common protein source for Aboriginals. You eat them alive, not cooked. If you are offered one in the Outback, either freak out (as most locals would do) or enjoy its pleasantly nutty taste as a reward for your bravery!

FAST FACTS: Australia

American Express For all travel-related customer inquiries regarding any American Express service, including reporting a lost card, call ✆ **1300/132 639** in Australia or 02/9271 8664. To report lost or stolen traveler's checks, call ✆ **1800/688 022.**

Area Codes Each state has a different area code: **02** for New South Wales and the ACT, **07** for Queensland, **03** for Victoria and Tasmania, **08** for South Australia, the Northern Territory, and Western Australia. You must dial the appropriate code if calling outside the state you are in; however, you also need to use the code if you are calling outside the city you are in. For example if you are in Sydney, where the code is 02 and you want to call another New South Wales town, you still dial 02 before the number. See "Staying Connected," p. 54.

ATM Networks See "Money & Costs," p. 41.

Business Hours Banks are open Monday through Thursday from 9:30am to 4pm, Friday 9:30am to 5pm. General business hours are Monday through Friday from 8:30am to 5:30pm. Shopping hours are usually 8:30am to 5:30pm weekdays and 9am to 4 or 5pm on Saturday. Many shops close on Sunday, although major department stores and shops in tourist precincts are open 7 days.

Customs **What You Can Bring Into Australia** The duty-free allowance in Australia is A$900 (US$720/UK£360) or, for those under 18, A$450 (US$360/UK£180). Anyone over 18 can bring in up to 250 cigarettes or 250 grams of cigars or other tobacco products, 2.25 liters (41 fluid oz.) of alcohol, and "dutiable goods" to the value of A$900 (US$720/UK£360), or A$450 (US$360/UK£180) if you are under 18. "Dutiable goods" are luxury items such as perfume, watches, jewelry, furs, plus gifts of any kind. Keep this in mind if you intend to bring presents for family and friends in Australia; gifts given to you also count toward the dutiable limit. Personal goods that you're taking with you are usually exempt from duty, but if you are returning with valuable goods that you already own, file form B263. Customs officers do not collect duty of less than A$50 (US$40/UK£20) as long as you declared the goods in the first place.

A helpful brochure, available from Australian consulates or Customs offices, as well as online, is *Know Before You Go.* For more information, contact the Customs Information and Support Centre (✆ **1300/363 263** in Australia, or 02/6275 6666) or check out www.customs.gov.au.

You need not declare cash in any currency, and other currency instruments, such as traveler's checks, under a value of A$10,000 (US$8,000/UK£4,000).

Australia is a signatory to the Convention on International Trade in Endangered Species (CITES), which restricts or bans the import of products made from protected wildlife. Examples of the restricted items are coral, giant clam, wild cats, monkey, zebra, crocodile or alligator, bear, some types of caviar, American ginseng, and orchid products. Banned items include ivory, tortoise (marine turtle) shell, rhinoceros or tiger products, and sturgeon caviar. Bear this in mind if you stop in other countries en route to Australia where souvenirs made from items like these may be sold. Australian authorities may seize these items.

Because Australia is an island, it is free of many agricultural and livestock diseases. To keep it that way, strict quarantine applies to importing plants, animals, and their products, including food. "Sniffer" dogs at airports detect these products (as well as drugs). Some items may be confiscated, and others may be held over for you to take with you when you leave the country. Amnesty trash bins are available before you reach the immigration counters in airport arrivals halls for items such as fruit. Don't be alarmed if, just before landing, the flight attendants spray the aircraft cabin (with products approved by the World Health Organization) to kill potentially disease-bearing insects. For more information on what is and is not allowed, contact the nearest Australian embassy or consulate, or Australia's Department of Agriculture, Fisheries, and Forestry, which runs the Australian Quarantine and Inspection Service (✆ **02/6272 3933; www.affa.gov.au**). Its website has a list of restricted or banned foods, animal and plant products, and other items.

What You Can Take Home from Australia

U.S. Citizens: For specifics on what you can bring back and the corresponding fees, download the invaluable free pamphlet *Know Before You Go* online at **www.cbp.gov** (click on "Travel," and then click on "Know Before You Go! Online Brochure"). Or contact the **U.S. Customs & Border Protection (CBP),** 1300 Pennsylvania Ave., NW, Washington, DC 20229 (✆ **877/287-8667**), and request the pamphlet.

Canadian Citizens: For a clear summary of Canadian rules, write for the booklet *I Declare,* issued by the **Canada Border Services Agency** (✆ **800/461-9999** in Canada, or 204/983-3500; **www.cbsa-asfc.gc.ca**).

U.K. Citizens: For information, contact **HM Customs & Excise** at ✆ **0845/010-9000** (from outside the U.K., 020/8929-0152), or consult their website at **www.hmce.gov.uk**.

New Zealand Citizens: Most questions are answered in a free pamphlet available at New Zealand consulates and Customs offices: *New Zealand Customs Guide for Travellers, Notice no. 4.* For more information, contact **New Zealand Customs,** The Customhouse, 17–21 Whitmore St., Box 2218, Wellington (✆ **04/473-6099** or 0800/428-786; **www.customs.govt.nz**).

Drugstores These are called "chemist shops" or "pharmacies." Australian pharmacists are permitted to fill only prescriptions written by Australian doctors. In major cities there are usually a number of late-night or 24-hour pharmacies, often attached to medical clinics.

Electricity The current is 240 volts AC, 50 hertz. Sockets take two or three flat, not rounded, prongs. North Americans and Europeans will need to buy a converter before they leave home (don't wait until you get to Australia, because Australian stores are likely to stock only converters for Aussie appliances to fit American and European outlets). Some large hotels have 110V outlets for electric shavers (or dual voltage), and some will lend converters, but don't count on it in smaller, less expensive hotels, motels, or B&Bs. Power does not start automatically when you plug in an appliance; you need to flick the switch beside the socket to the "on" position.

Embassies & Consulates Most diplomatic posts are in Canberra: **British High Commission,** Commonwealth Avenue, Canberra, ACT 2601 (✆ 02/6270 6666); **Embassy of Ireland,** 20 Arkana St., Yarralumla, ACT 2600 (✆ 02/6273 3022); **High Commission of Canada,** Commonwealth Avenue, Yarralumla, ACT 2600 (✆ 02/6270 4000); **New Zealand High Commission,** Commonwealth Avenue, Canberra, ACT 2601 (✆ 02/6270 4211); and the **United States Embassy,** 21 Moonah Place, Yarralumla, ACT 2600 (✆ 02/6214 5600). Embassies or consulates with posts in state capitals are listed in "Fast Facts" in the relevant state chapters of this book.

Emergencies Dial ✆ **000** anywhere in Australia for police, ambulance, or the fire department. This is a free call from public and private telephones and needs no coins. The TTY emergency number is ✆ **106.**

Holidays Major public holidays—where almost everything shuts down—are New Year's Day, Good Friday, Easter Sunday and Easter Monday, Christmas Day, and Boxing Day (Dec 26). On Anzac Day (Apr 25), a war veterans' commemorative day, most shops and all government departments are closed, but some tourist attractions reopen at around 1pm. Australia Day is a national public holiday on January 26.

For more information on holidays, see "Australia Calendar of Events," earlier in this chapter.

Internet Access Internet access is available just about everywhere, including some of the smallest Outback towns, which generally have at least one cybercafe, coin-operated machines, or both. Coin-op terminals are also available at larger airports. Major tourist towns such as Darwin and Cairns sometimes have whole streets full of cybercafes. See "Online Traveler's Toolbox" (p. 57).

Liquor Laws Hours vary from pub to pub, but most are open daily from around 10am or noon, to 10pm or midnight. The minimum drinking age is 18. Random breath tests to catch drunk drivers are common, and drunk-driving laws are strictly enforced. Getting caught drunk behind the wheel will mean a court appearance, not just a fine. The maximum permitted blood alcohol level is .05%. Alcohol is sold in liquor stores, in the "bottle shops" attached to every pub, and in some states in supermarkets.

Lost & Found Be sure to tell all of your credit card companies the minute you discover your wallet has been lost or stolen and file a report at the nearest police precinct. Your credit card company or insurer may require a police report number or record of the loss. Most credit card companies have an emergency toll-free number to call if your card is lost or stolen; they may be able to wire you a cash advance immediately or deliver an emergency credit card in a day or two.

In Australia, call toll-free: **American Express** (✆ **1300/132 639**), **MasterCard** (✆ **1800/120 113**), and **Visa** (✆ **1800/450 346**).

If you need emergency cash over the weekend when all banks and American Express offices are closed, you can have money wired to you via **Western Union** (✆ **800/325-6000;** www.westernunion.com).

Mail A postcard costs A$1.25 (US$1/UK50p) to send anywhere in the world. A card will take up to 6 working days to reach the U.S.

Measurements Australia uses the metric system.

Newspapers & Magazines The national daily newspaper is *The Australian,* which publishes an expanded edition with a color magazine on Saturday. Most capital cities have their own daily papers, usually a tabloid and a broadsheet. The Australian current-affairs magazine, *The Bulletin with Newsweek,* is published weekly, and there is an Australian edition of *Time.*

Passports Allow plenty of time before your trip to apply for a passport; processing normally takes 3 weeks but can take longer during busy periods (especially spring). And keep in mind that if you need a passport in a hurry, you'll pay a higher processing fee.

For Residents of Canada: Passport applications are available at travel agencies or from the central **Passport Office,** Department of Foreign Affairs and International Trade, Ottawa, ON K1A 0G3 (✆ **800/567-6868;** www.ppt.gc.ca).

For Residents of Ireland: You can apply for a 10-year passport at the **Passport Office,** Setanta Centre, Molesworth Street, Dublin 2 (✆ **01/671-1633;** www.irlgov.ie/iveagh). Those under age 18 and over 65 must apply for a 3-year passport. You can also apply at 1A South Mall, Cork (✆ **021/272-525**) or at most main post offices.

For Residents of New Zealand: You can pick up a passport application at any New Zealand Passports Office or download it from their website. Contact the **Passports Office** at ✆ **0800/225-050** in New Zealand or 04/474-8100, or log on to www.passports.govt.nz.

For Residents of the United Kingdom: To pick up an application for a 10-year passport (5-year passport for children under 16), visit your nearest passport office, major post office, travel agency or contact the **United Kingdom Passport Service** at ✆ **0870/521-0410** or search its website at www.ukpa.gov.uk.

For Residents of the United States: Whether you're applying in person or by mail, you can download applications from the U.S. State Department website at **http://travel.state.gov**. To find your regional passport office, either check the U.S. State Department website or call the **National Passport Information Center** toll-free number (✆ **877/487-2778**) for automated information.

Police Dial ✆ **000** anywhere in Australia. This is a free call from public and private telephones and requires no coins.

Restrooms Restrooms are easy to find—and free—in most Australian cities and towns. If you are driving, most towns have restrooms on the main street (although the cleanliness may vary wildly). In some remote areas, toilets are "composting," meaning there is no flush, just a drop into a pit beneath you.

Smoking Smoking in most public areas, such as museums, cinemas, and theaters, is restricted or banned. Smoking in restaurants may be limited—Western Australia and New South Wales ban it altogether, and in many other states, restaurants have smoking and nonsmoking sections. Pubs and clubs, for a long time the last bastion for smokers, are heading for total bans across the country. South Australia will introduce these bans in 2008, joining Queensland, Tasmania, Western Australia, Victoria, the ACT, and New South Wales. Only in the Northern Territory can you still light up in some parts of a pub. Australian aircraft on all routes are completely nonsmoking, as are all airport buildings.

Taxes Australia applies a 10% Goods and Services Tax (GST) on most products and services. Your international airline tickets to Australia are not taxed, nor are domestic airline tickets for travel within Australia *if you bought them outside Australia.* If you buy Australian airline tickets once you arrive in Australia, you will pay GST on them.

Through the **Tourist Refund Scheme** (TRS), Australians and international visitors can claim a refund of the GST (and of a 14.5% wine tax called Wine Equalisation Tax, or WET) paid on a purchase of more than A$300 (US$240/UK£120) from a single outlet, within the last 30 days before you leave. More than one item may be included in that A$300. For example, you can claim the GST you paid on 10 T-shirts each worth A$30 (US$24/UK£12), as long as they were bought from a single store. Do this as you leave by presenting your receipt or "tax invoice" to the Australian Customs Service's TRS booths, in the International Terminal departure areas at most airports. If you buy several things on different days from one store, which together add up to A$300 or more, you must ask the store to total all purchases on one tax invoice (or receipt)—now there's a nice piece of bureaucracy to remember Australia by! Pack the items in your carry-on baggage, because you must show them to Customs. You can use the goods before you leave Australia and still claim the refund, but you cannot claim a refund on things you have consumed (film you use, say, or food). You cannot claim a refund on alcohol other than wine. Allow an extra 15 minutes to stand in line at the airport and get your refund.

You can also claim a refund if you leave Australia as a cruise passenger from Circular Quay or Darling Harbour in Sydney, Brisbane, Cairns, Darwin, Hobart, or Fremantle (Perth). If your cruise departs from elsewhere in Australia, or if you are flying out from an airport other than Sydney, Melbourne, Brisbane, Adelaide, Cairns, Perth, Darwin, or the Gold Coast, telephone the **Australian Customs Service** (✆ **1300/363 263** in Australia, or 02/6275 6666) to see if you can still claim the refund.

Items bought in duty-free stores will not be charged GST. Nor will items you export—such as an Aboriginal painting that you buy in a gallery in Alice Springs and have shipped straight to your home outside Australia.

Basic groceries are not GST-taxed, but restaurant meals are.

Other taxes include departure tax of A$38 (US$30/UK£15) for every passenger 12 years and over, included in the price of your airline ticket when you buy it in your home country; landing and departure taxes at some airports, also included in the price of your ticket; and "reef tax," officially dubbed the Environmental Management Charge, of A$5 (US$4/UK£2) for every person over the age of 4 every time he or she enters the Great Barrier Reef Marine Park. (This charge goes toward park upkeep.)

Time Zone Eastern Standard Time (EST, sometimes also written as AEST) covers Queensland, New South Wales, the Australian Capital Territory, Victoria, and Tasmania. Central Standard Time (CST) is used in the Northern Territory and South Australia, and Western Standard Time (WST) is the standard in Western Australia. When it's noon in New South Wales, the ACT, Victoria, Queensland, and Tasmania, it's 11:30am in South Australia and the Northern Territory, and 10am in Western Australia. All states except Queensland, the Northern Territory, and Western Australia observe daylight saving time, usually from the first Sunday in October to the first Sunday in April. However, not all states switch over to daylight saving on the same day or in the same week.

The east coast of Australia is GMT (Greenwich Mean Time) plus 10 hours. When it is noon on the east coast, it is 2am in London that morning, and 6pm in Los Angeles and 9pm in New York the previous night. These times are based on standard time, so allow for daylight saving in the Australian summer, or in the country you are calling. New Zealand is 2 hours ahead of the east coast of Australia, except during daylight saving, when it is 3 hours ahead of Queensland.

Tipping Tipping is not expected in Australia. It is usual to tip around 5% or round up to the nearest A$10 for a substantial meal in a family restaurant. Some passengers round up to the nearest dollar in a cab, but it's okay to insist on every bit of change back. Tipping bellboys and porters is sometimes done, but no one tips bar staff, barbers, or hairdressers.

Water Water is fine to drink everywhere. In the Outback, the taps may carry warm brackish water from underground, called "bore water," for showers and laundry, while drinking water is collected in rainwater tanks.

3

Suggested Itineraries

by Ron Crittall, Marc Llewellyn & Lee Mylne

Australia's size and its distance from Northern Hemisphere destinations are the two most daunting things about planning a visit. It's a long way to come for just a week, but if that's all you can spare, you still want to see as much as possible. While our inclination is to immerse ourselves in one spot, we're aware that not everyone wants to do that. Seeing as much as you can is often a priority.

Australia is a complex and fascinating place, merging ancient Aboriginal culture with modern life. You'll learn a lot in a week or two but will have just scraped the surface of this vast nation.

If you're a first-time visitor, with only 1 or 2 weeks, you may find these two itineraries most helpful: **Australia in 1 Week** or **Australia in 2 Weeks.** These itineraries can be shifted around to suit your needs; you could substitute the Cairns section of Australia in 1 Week for the Uluru/Red Centre suggestions in Australia in 2 Weeks, flying from Sydney to Uluru.

If you've been to Australia before, or have already visited our major icons—Sydney, the Great Barrier Reef, or Uluru (Ayers Rock)—you might want to focus on another aspect of the country. You may even want to head out West to see the lesser-known, but very rewarding, parts of the country. If you're bringing your family with you, our Australia for Kids itinerary may give you some ideas to keep the young ones occupied (at the same time entertaining their parents).

You might also review our "Best of" chapter to see what experiences or sights have special appeal to you, and adjust the itineraries to suit your own interests.

Getting around this vast continent, where the major attractions are thousands of miles apart, is daunting and time-consuming. **Flying** is the only way to cover long distances efficiently, but unfortunately it can also be expensive. Remember to allow flying time in your itineraries and don't try to pack too much in on the days you fly—even domestic flights can be around 3 hours, and can be draining. See "Getting Around Australia" in chapter 2 for information about air passes and getting the best rate on Australia's domestic carriers.

Our best advice is to take a tip from Australians: If the pace gets too hectic, just chill out and reorder your sightseeing priorities. Take time to meet the locals and ask their advice on what you should see as well.

1 Australia in 1 Week

Impossible! Australia is so vast that in 1 week, only a small corner of it—perhaps one city or a few of the natural wonders—will be all you get in such a short time. It will be memorable, nevertheless, and careful planning will maximize your time and allow you to see some of the major sights.

Use the following itinerary to make the most out of a week in Australia, but make sure you don't exhaust yourself trying to cram everything in. Australians are a laid-back lot, generally, and in some places the pace is relaxed. And that's just the way to enjoy it. One week provides barely enough time to see the best of Sydney, which for most people is the entry point to Australia. Your first view of the **Sydney Harbour Bridge** and the **Opera House** may well be from the air as your plane comes in. It's a spectacular introduction to a great city.

If you have only a week and want to head farther afield, there are two main choices, depending on your interests. The **Great Barrier Reef** is a "must" for divers, but don't forget that you must allow time either side of your reef trip for flying. There are no such problems with Australia's other icon, **Uluru (Ayers Rock),** in the heart of the **Red Centre.** This triangle, of course, is something of a cliché, but still gives you a complete Australian experience. Realistically, you will have to choose between the Reef and the Rock, or choose not to scuba dive while you are in Queensland.

Days 1 & 2: Arrive in Sydney ★★★

Check into your hotel and spend whatever time you have after arrival recovering from almost-guaranteed jet lag. If you arrive in the morning and have a full day ahead of you, try to stay up and hit the nearest cafe for a shot of caffeine to keep you going. Head to **Circular Quay** and from there get a fantastic view of **Sydney Harbour Bridge,** before strolling to the **Sydney Opera House** and soaking up some history at **The Rocks.** If you have time, you can take the ferry from Circular Quay to Manly beach to round off a fairly easy day with fish and chips, then head to bed for some much-needed sleep.

Start **Day 2** with a ride to the top of the Sydney Tower to experience Sydney's newest and highest open-air attraction, **Skywalk,** a breathtaking 260m (853 ft.) above Sydney. Harnessed onto a moving, glass-floored viewing platform that extends out over the edge of the tower, you can view of all Sydney landmarks including the Sydney Harbour Bridge, Sydney Opera House, Sydney Harbour, and all the way to the Blue Mountains. And it's not actually as scary as it sounds. Sydney Tower has several attractions, including **OzTrek**—a simulator ride the kids will love. For an introduction to Australia's wildlife, head to Taronga Zoo or the Sydney Aquarium. If you enjoy museums, put the Australia Museum, the Australian National Maritime Museum at Darling Harbour, and the interactive Powerhouse Museum on your list for the day. For an insight into Sydney's beginnings as a convict settlement, visit the Hyde Park Barracks Museum, a convict-built prison. Finish off your day with a twilight (or later at weekends) **BridgeClimb** ★ or take the kids to **Luna Park,** a small and fairly traditional amusement park that's at its best at night. For information about all these attractions, see chapter 4.

Day 3: A day trip to the Blue Mountains ★★★

Take the train from Central Station to Katoomba for a day, exploring the beauty of the Blue Mountains, 2 hours from Sydney. Once there, jump on the Blue Mountains Explorer Bus, which allows you to hop on and off wherever you please. There are also many day-tour operators running to the Blue Mountains from Sydney. Whichever mode of transport you use, don't miss the spectacular Three Sisters rock formations, best viewed from Echo Point Road at Katoomba.

The adventurous might prefer to take a tour from Katoomba to the **Jenolan Caves,** about a 90-minute drive southwest. Nine caves are open for exploration, and you can take canyoning tours of between

Suggested Australia Itineraries

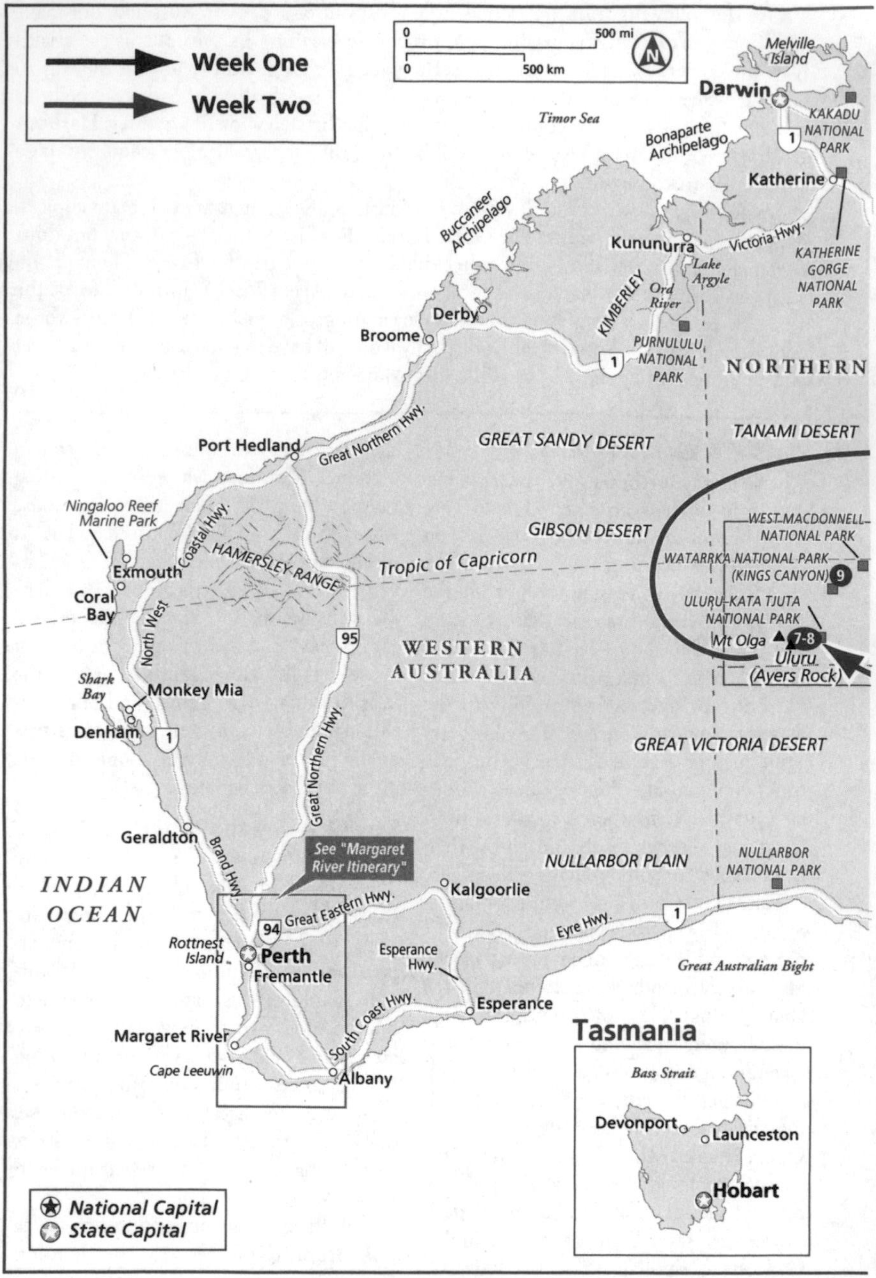

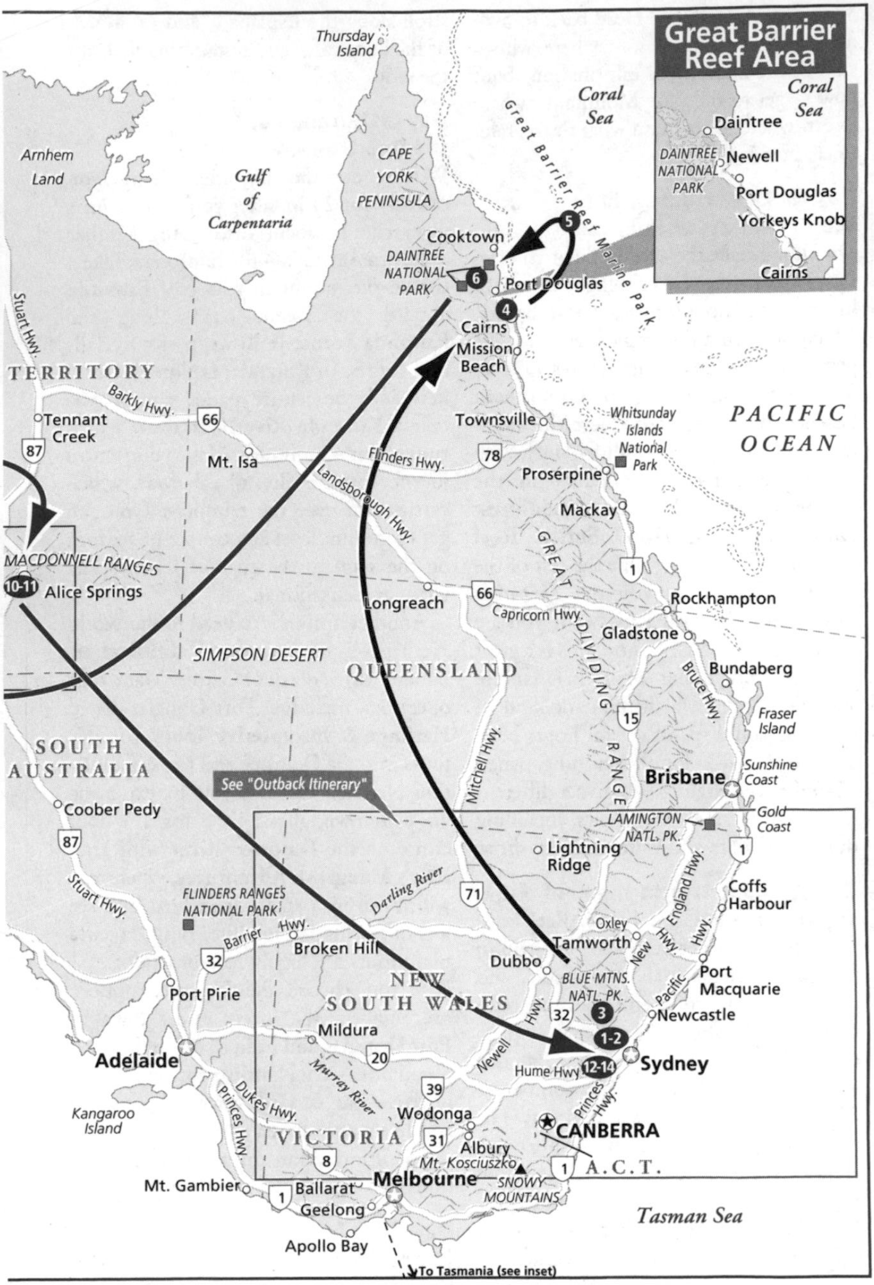

Great Barrier Reef Area
Coral Sea
Daintree
DAINTREE NATIONAL PARK
Newell
Port Douglas
Yorkeys Knob
Cairns
Thursday Island
Coral Sea
Great Barrier Reef Marine Park
Arnhem Land
Gulf of Carpentaria
CAPE YORK PENINSULA
Cooktown
DAINTREE NATIONAL PARK
Port Douglas
Cairns
Mission Beach
Stuart Hwy.
TERRITORY
Barkly Hwy.
Tennant Creek
Mt. Isa
Flinders Hwy.
Townsville
Whitsunday Islands National Park
PACIFIC OCEAN
Landsborough Hwy.
Proserpine
Mackay
GREAT DIVIDING RANGE
MACDONNELL RANGES
Alice Springs
Longreach
Capricorn Hwy.
Rockhampton
Gladstone
SIMPSON DESERT
QUEENSLAND
Bundaberg
Bruce Hwy.
Fraser Island
SOUTH AUSTRALIA
Mitchell Hwy.
Brisbane
Sunshine Coast
See "Outback Itinerary"
Coober Pedy
LAMINGTON NATL. PK.
Gold Coast
Lightning Ridge
Stuart Hwy.
FLINDERS RANGES NATIONAL PARK
Darling River
New England Hwy.
Coffs Harbour
Barrier Hwy.
Broken Hill
Oxley
Tamworth
Dubbo
Port Macquarie
Port Pirie
NEW SOUTH WALES
BLUE MTNS. NATL. PK.
Pacific Hwy.
Newcastle
Mildura
Newell Hwy.
Adelaide
Hume Hwy.
Sydney
Murray River
Princes Hwy.
Dukes Hwy.
Kangaroo Island
Wodonga
VICTORIA
Albury
CANBERRA
Mt. Kosciuszko
A.C.T.
Mt. Gambier
Ballarat
Melbourne
SNOWY MOUNTAINS
Geelong
Tasman Sea
Apollo Bay
To Tasmania (see inset)

3 hours and a full day. Head back to Sydney and have dinner somewhere with a view of the harbor. For information about how to get to the Blue Mountains, where to eat, where to stay, and what to see, refer to chapter 5.

Day 4: Cairns, gateway to the Great Barrier Reef

On **Day 4,** take the earliest flight you can from Sydney to Cairns—flight time is 3 hours—and check into a hotel in the city, which on such a tight schedule will make getting to the major attractions quicker and easier than staying on the northern beaches, out of town. Explore the city a little and to see some wildlife—including a massive saltwater crocodile—in the bizarre setting of the **Cairns Rainforest Dome,** atop the **Hotel Sofitel Reef Casino.** You will have time the rest of the day to head out to visit the **Tjapukai Aboriginal Cultural Park** ★. If you are not going to the Red Centre, this is a great place to learn about Aboriginal culture and life, albeit in a theme-park kind of way. You could spend several hours here, or save the visit for the evening, when **Tjapukai by Night** tours give a different look at traditional ceremonies, including dinner and a fire-and-water outdoor show.

Day 5: A day trip to the Reef ★★★

Day trips to the Great Barrier Reef leave from the Reef Fleet Terminal. The trip to the outer reef takes about 2 hours, and once there you will spend your day on a pontoon with about 300 people. Experienced divers may prefer to take a day trip with one of the dive charter companies who take smaller groups and visit two or three reefs. The pontoons of the big operators also offer the chance to take a scenic flight—a truly spectacular experience. Divers must spend another 24 hours in Cairns before flying. If you are content to snorkel, ride the glass-bottom boats, and soak up the sun, you will be able to fly the next day. After returning to Cairns, take a stroll along the Esplanade and eat at one of the busy cafes and restaurants that line the strip.

Day 6: Kuranda or the Daintree ★★

Waiting out the day after diving (you can't fly for 24 hr. after you've been on a dive) can be spent discovering another aspect to Australia—the rainforest. Take a trip to the mountain village of **Kuranda** aboard the steam train along the **Kuranda Scenic Railway,** past waterfalls and gorges. In Kuranda, explore the markets and the nature parks, and maybe take a **Kuranda Riverboat Tour,** which runs about 45 minutes. Make your return journey on the **Skyrail** cableway, which carries you over the rainforest (you can get to ground level at a couple of stations on the way) to the edge of Cairns. The views are sensational.

Another option is to head to the World Heritage–listed **Daintree Rainforest** ★, 2 hours' drive north of Cairns. Many tour operators, including Port Douglas–based **Heritage & Interpretive Tours,** run day tours into the Daintree and Cape Tribulation National Parks. If you are exploring on your own, make time for a 1-hour cruise on the **Daintree River** with **Dan Irby's Mangrove Adventures,** where you will travel in a small open boat and see lots of fascinating wildlife. Both day and night tours are highly recommended.

If you choose the Daintree option, overnight in the lovely resort town of **Port Douglas** and head to one of its great restaurants—try **Nautilus** for fine dining or **Salsa Bar & Grill** for a more relaxed and lively atmosphere.

For information on all these destinations, see chapter 7.

Day 7: Cairns to Sydney

Drive back to Cairns in the morning, and head to the airport for your flight to Sydney. Unless you have a flight directly out of Cairns, you will spend most of your last day in Australia returning to Sydney. With the time you have left in Sydney, treat yourself to dinner at a restaurant overlooking the harbor, with its bridge and Opera House illuminated. It's a sight you'll carry home with you.

2 Australia in 2 Weeks

With 2 weeks, your visit to Australia will be much more relaxed and you will get a greater sense of the diversity of Australia, its landscape, and its people. You will get to see all three icons—Sydney, the Great Barrier Reef, and Uluru—in more depth, and maybe even have time to go outside those areas, especially if you limit your icons to two instead of three.

Days 1 through 6: Follow itineraries as outlined above

Day 7: Cairns to Uluru

On **Day 7,** leave Cairns as early as you can (this will probably mean spending the night in Cairns rather than Port Douglas). Your flight to Ayers Rock Airport will take around 3 hours, sometimes more, depending on the type of aircraft you are on. Make sure you book a direct flight, and not one that goes via Sydney! Try to get a window seat for the spectacular views as you fly over the Outback.

If you take the early flight, you can be in **Uluru** by around 9am, which gives you the whole day to take in the enormity of this fabulous monolith. Take the shuttle from Ayers Rock Resort (which is the only place to stay, but offers many accommodations choices) to the Rock. If you decide to **climb** Uluru (remembering that the Aboriginal traditional owners would prefer you didn't), make sure you don't do it at the hottest time of day. A climb will take you between 2 and 4 hours, depending on your fitness. An alternative is to join **Anangu Tours** for a walk around it; one of the best is the late-afternoon Kuniya walk, which concludes with watching sunset over Uluru—an unforgettable sight. Spend some time in the impressive and interesting **Uluru–Kata Tjuta Cultural Centre** near the base of Uluru. And after doing all that in a day, you'll be ready for a quiet dinner at whatever hotel you've chosen.

Day 8: Exploring Uluru ★★★

Sunrise is one of the magic times at Uluru, so make the effort to get up early on Day 8. This is also a great time to do the 9.6km (6-mile) Base Walk circumnavigating Uluru, which takes 2 to 3 hours. There are a range of other ways to experience Uluru, including camel rides, Harley-Davidson tours, and helicopter joy-flights, but walking up close to the Rock beats them all, in my opinion.

You will also have time today to head to **Kata Tjuta** (also called The Olgas) where you will see there is much more to the Red Centre than just one Rock. Kata Tjuta is about 48km (30 miles) west of Uluru, but plenty of tours go there if you do not have your own wheels.

End your day in the desert with the **Sounds of Silence** dinner, run by Ayers Rock Resort. Sip champagne as the sun sets over Uluru, to the eerie music of the didgeridoo, then tuck into kangaroo, barramundi, and other native foods. But it's not the food you're here for—it's the silence and the stars. A short stargazing session with an astronomer ends a memorable evening.

Day 9: Uluru to Kings Canyon

Hire a 4WD and tackle the long Outback drive from Uluru to Alice Springs, stopping for a night at **Kings Canyon.** It is 306km (190 miles) from Uluru to Kings Canyon (also known as **Watarrka National Park**), which offers another unbeatable look at Outback Australia.

You can spend the afternoon walking up the side of the canyon and around the rim. It is very steep and will take you around 4 hours. A gentler walk is the short and shady canyon floor walk. Stay overnight at Kings Canyon Resort.

Day ⑩: Kings Canyon to Alice Springs

Get an early start for Alice Springs, and take the unpaved but interesting Mereenie Loop Road, which will take you through the Glen Helen Gorge or the historic Hermannsburg mission settlement. Whichever road you take, the scenery is like nowhere else in Australia. You will probably spend most of the day driving to Alice, making a few stops along the way.

On arrival check into a hotel and head out to one of the local restaurants, several of which offer sophisticated versions of "bush tucker" including kangaroo, emu, and crocodile dishes.

Day ⑪: Alice Springs

If you can stand another early start, take a **dawn balloon flight** over the desert, usually followed by a champagne breakfast. If you don't head back to bed immediately for a few hours catch-up sleep, there are plenty of attractions to discover, including the **Alice Springs Desert Park** for a look at some unusual Australian creatures, the **School of the Air,** and the **Royal Flying Doctor Service** base. In the afternoon, take a half-day tour with an Aboriginal guide at the **Aboriginal Art & Culture Centre.** Alternatively, visit the **Alice Springs Telegraph Station Historical Reserve** set in an oasis just outside town for a look at early settler life. Finish the day with a **sunset camel ride** down the dry Todd River bed and have dinner at the camel farm.

For information on all these attractions and destinations in the Red Centre, see chapter 8.

Day ⑫: Alice Springs to Sydney

Direct flights from Alice Springs to Sydney leave in the early afternoon, so you have all morning to explore more of the town and perhaps buy some Aboriginal art (this is one of the best places to get it).

On arrival in Sydney after an almost 3-hour flight, book into your hotel and spend the night discovering some of the city's nightlife.

Day ⑬: A day at Bondi Beach

For sands of a different kind from those you've experienced in recent days, take the bus to Sydney's most famous beach, **Bondi,** and spend it lazing on the sand or—in summer, at least—taking a dip in the surf. Take the Bondi Explorer bus from Circular Quay, which gives you a choice of harborside bays and coastal beaches, or take the train to Bondi Junction and then a bus to the beach. The scenic cliff-top walk to **Bronte Beach** is worth doing, or you can continue farther to **Coogee.**

Day ⑭: Sydney

Your final day in Australia can be spent on last-minute shopping and seeing those Sydney sights that you haven't had time for so far. Cap it all off with a slap-up seafood dinner somewhere with a fantastic view of the Harbour Bridge.

3 Australia for Families (Starting in Sydney)

Australia is an unbelievable destination for kids—and not just for the kangaroos and koalas that almost every child (and parent!) is desperate to see. Our suggestion is to explore Sydney for 2 days with family in tow, then head up to the beautiful Blue Mountains on a day trip to ride the cable car and the world's steepest railway. The climax comes with a few days exploring the Barrier Reef and the rainforest around Port Douglas.

Days ❶ & ❷: Sydney

First off, head to Circular Quay to see the Sydney Opera House. A tour inside might be a bit much for younger kids, but you can walk around a fair bit of it and take the obligatory photos of Australia's most famous landmark. To stretch your legs, head from here into the Royal Botanic Gardens to spot long-beaked ibises wandering around the grass and hundreds of fruit bats squabbling among the treetops in the jungle section in the middle of the gardens.

Walk back past the Opera House and the ferries to The Rocks, where you can take a quick stroll through the historic streets, stopping off for a look at some of the trendy shops, or The Rocks Market on Saturdays.

There are plenty of places to eat lunch, but a filling prospect is pasta or ravioli or the likes at **Rossini** (p. 143), opposite the ferry terminals, where you can sit outside and watch the world go by. Portions are large, so you might want to split a meal between younger kids.

After lunch take a ferry to **Taronga Zoo** (p. 169), where a cable car takes you up the hill to the main entrance. All the kids' favorites are here, from kangaroos and koalas to platypuses, located in a nocturnal house. A farmyard section edges onto a playground of sorts with lots of water features to give your kids a sprinkle on a hot day.

On **Day 2** head to the city center for an elevator ride up to the top of **Sydney Tower** (p. 167), where you can look right across Sydney as far as the Blue Mountains in the distance. Entry includes admission to Skytour, which features a darkened storytelling room where the kids can learn a little about Australian legends and Aborigines, and there's also a thrilling simulator ride that takes you on adventures throughout Australia.

It's a short walk from here to Darling Harbour, where you can cap off the morning with a visit to **Sydney Aquarium** (p. 166). The sharks are huge here, and they swim right above your head, but the real attraction is the Barrier Reef section, where tens of thousands of colorful fish swim by in huge tanks to the sound of classical music.

Eat lunch at one of the many cheap eateries on the other side of the bridge before taking the monorail back to Town Hall or taking another ferry from near the Aquarium back to Circular Quay.

If it's a hot day, or you just want to go to the beach, you have two main choices: From Circular Quay you can take a half-hour ferry ride, or a 15-minute high-speed JetCat to Manly. Here you can laze the afternoon away, and can even rent a surfboard, body board, or in-line skates. Or, take a CityRail train from Town Hall to Bondi, then a bus to Bondi Beach, where you can reward your efforts with ice cream or a late-afternoon pizza from Pompei's, on the main drag.

Day ❸: The Blue Mountains

You could easily spend a couple more days with the kids having fun in Sydney, but you shouldn't miss a trip the mountains. Several companies run tour buses to the area, stopping off at an animal park along the way. The best one to visit is **Featherdale** (p. 168), where you can get up close to more kangaroos, koalas, and Tasmanian devils. The tour will also stop at **Scenic World** (p. 203), where you can take the short ride on the Scenic Railway. It's very steep, so hold on tight. At the bottom you'll find yourselves among an ancient tree fern forest—it's truly remarkable. A short walk takes you to the **Skyway,** a cable car that travels 300m (984 ft.) above the Jamison Valley.

Elsewhere in the mountains there are fabulous views across craggy bluffs and deep bowls of gum trees. It's a long day, so pack plenty of snacks and a few favorite toys.

Days 4, 5 & 6: The Reef & the Rainforest

Now it's time to head north, up the Tropics. You'll need to fly, of course, otherwise it would take you several days to drive up the coast. Most people base themselves in Port Douglas rather than Cairns, because the beach is huge and uncrowded and some of the best trips originate from here.

After the flight, relax on the beach, but remember to swim inside the nets off the sand; the "stingers" (box jellyfish) around here can cause life-threatening stings, especially where kids are concerned.

The next day, it's time to visit the Reef. Thankfully, once on the Reef itself, the dangerous jellyfish are very uncommon. Cruise boats take around 90 minutes to get from Port Douglas to the outer Reef, but once there you are in for some amazing snorkeling. Expect to see numerous species of corals and fish, and even an occasional turtle. A good seafood lunch is generally served on board so you won't go hungry!

On **Day 6,** it's time for a real jungle experience. Tours leave Port Douglas daily for the Daintree National Park and the Cape Tribulation Rainforests. Usually included in the tour is a boat trip among the local crocodiles, a stroll along an isolated beach, and, of course, walks in the rainforest, where you emerge into a dripping world of palms, strangler figs, staghorns, pythons, frogs, and electric-blue butterflies.

Day 7: Fly back to Sydney

If you have time, take the kids by ferry to Luna Park, just across from Circular Quay, or walk there across the Harbour Bridge. The fun park is small, with a few rides suitable for younger kids, but it does boast a magnificent view across to the Harbour Bridge and Opera House, which look glorious after the sun's gone down.

4 An Outback Odyssey: Driving from Sydney to Melbourne

When Sydneysiders get tired of the city they often dream of "going bush." If they could, they'd head west into the setting sun and out into the Outback. Not many local city slickers ever get to realize their dream, but you can do it for them on this 7-day Outback odyssey from Sydney to Melbourne.

Day 1: The Blue Mountains

Armed with your road map, leave Sydney via Parramatta Road, by the M4 motorway and the Great Western Highway. Two hours should see you safely in the cool of the Blue Mountains. Drive into the little town of Katoomba, where you could stop for a quick coffee break or early lunch at the historic **Paragon Café** (p. 206) before taking a short spin to see the incredible views across to the Three Sisters rock formation from Echo Point. From here, follow the signs to Scenic World, where you can take the world's steepest railway into an enchanting world of tree ferns—it will take just a couple of minutes to get down. Take the cable car up and continue on your journey.

Keep following the Great Western Highway as it heads west for 39km (24 miles), through Blackheath, Mount Victoria, and Hartley, and then downhill toward the old mining town of Lithgow. The most famous attraction around here is the **Zig Zag Railway** ★★, a former coal route that crosses the valleys on impressive viaducts and winds around the eucalyptus-covered hills. A steam train runs the 18km (11-mile) back-and-forth route on Wednesdays, Saturdays, Sundays, and school holidays, and a diesel train does the route on other days. It costs A$20 (US$16) for adults round-trip and

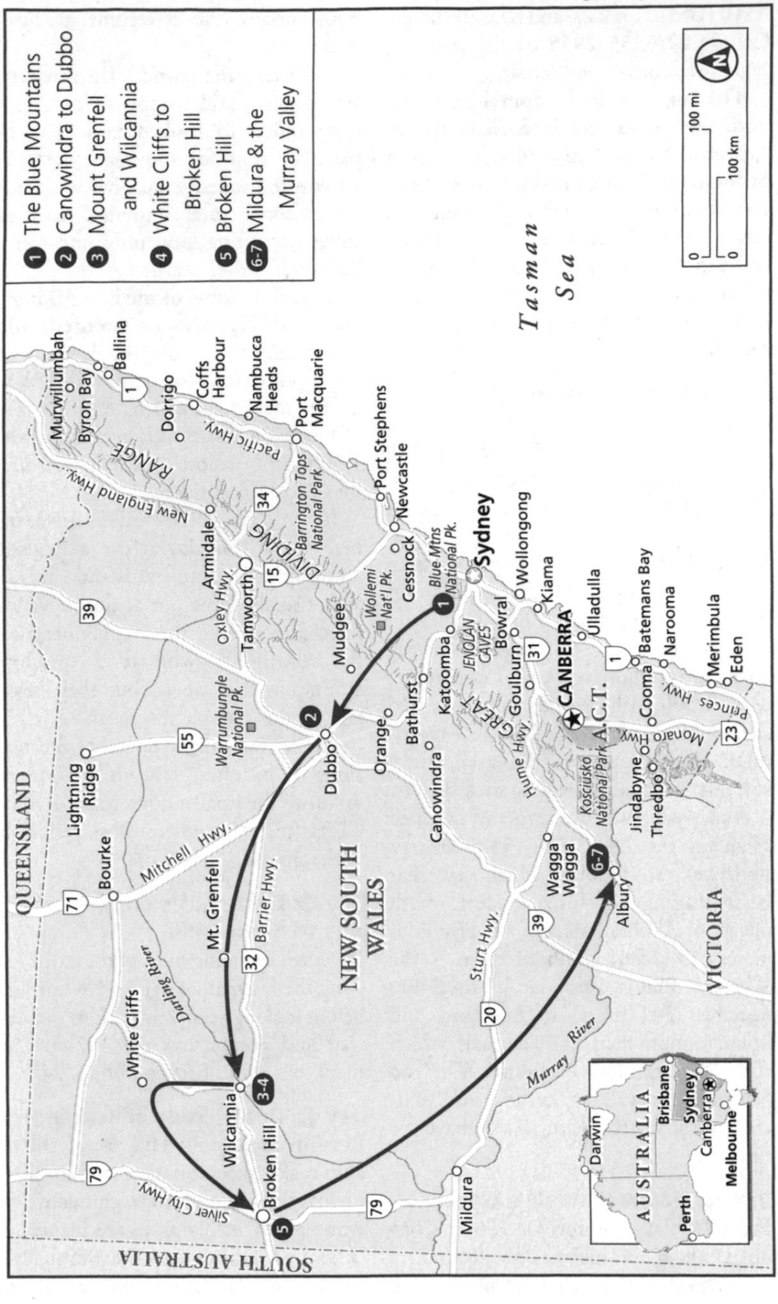
1 The Blue Mountains
2 Canowindra to Dubbo
3 Mount Grenfell and Wilcannia
4 White Cliffs to Broken Hill
5 Broken Hill
6-7 Mildura & the Murray Valley
0
100 mi
0
100 km
N
Tasman Sea
QUEENSLAND
NEW SOUTH WALES
SOUTH AUSTRALIA
VICTORIA
A.C.T.
CANBERRA
Sydney
Murwillumbah
Byron Bay
Ballina
Dorrigo
Coffs Harbour
Nambucca Heads
Port Macquarie
Pacific Hwy.
RANGE
New England Hwy.
Armidale
Port Stephens
Newcastle
Barrington Tops National Park
DIVIDING
Tamworth
Oxley Hwy.
Cessnock
Blue Mtns National Pk.
Wollemi Nat'l Pk.
Mudgee
Katoomba
JENOLAN CAVES
Bowral
Wollongong
Kiama
Goulburn
GREAT
Ulladulla
Batemans Bay
Narooma
Merimbula
Eden
Cooma
Princes Hwy.
Monaro Hwy.
Jindabyne
Thredbo
Kosciusko National Park
Hume Hwy.
Wagga Wagga
Albury
Bathurst
Orange
Canowindra
Dubbo
Warrumbungle National Pk.
Lightning Ridge
Bourke
Mitchell Hwy.
Mt. Grenfell
Barrier Hwy.
Sturt Hwy.
Darling River
White Cliffs
Wilcannia
Broken Hill
Silver City Hwy.
Murray River
Mildura
AUSTRALIA
Darwin
Perth
Brisbane
Sydney
Canberra
Melbourne
1
15
23
31
34
39
55
71
32
20
79

A$10 (US$8) for kids, and takes 1½ hours. Call ✆ **02/6355 2955** or visit www.zigzagrailway.com.au for details.

The highway leads from here down onto the plains and into **Bathurst** ★, approximately 200km (124 miles) west of Sydney, and 5km (3 miles) west of Lithgow. Bathurst, which was proclaimed a city in 1815, is the oldest inland settlement in Australia. Its 19th-century architecture is beautifully preserved, and makes for pleasant wandering. Stay here for the night.

Day ❷: Canowindra to Dubbo

It's a 56km (34-mile) drive along the Mitchell Highway from Bathurst to Orange. Highly recommended is a 58km (36-mile) sidetrack down through a landscape of spare trees and orange soil to **Canowindra,** to visit the Age of Fishes Museum (www.ageoffishes.org.au). A chance discovery in 1955 near here revealed an extensive fossil bed dating back 360 million years, and containing over 3,500 fish, some with armored shells, lungs, and huge jaws like crocodiles. The fish are well displayed, many still in their muddy-looking rock shelves.

Make your way back to the Mitchell Highway for the 150km (93-mile) trek northwest to Dubbo, which has that beginning-of-the-Outback feel, with plenty of Akubra hats around. Five kilometers (3 miles) south of town is the **Western Plains Zoo,** set in over 300 hectares (741 acres) of bushland and home to more than 1,000 animals, which roam large outdoor enclosures. The zoo has paths for walking, cycling, and vehicles, and is worth visiting if you have the time.

Day ❸: Mount Grenfell & Wilcannia

From Dubbo continue for 166km (103 miles) along the highway to Nyngan, a small township on the edge of the true Outback where you can while away a short time in the local museum or spot birds among the rivergums at Rotary Park.

From here the Barrier Highway scoots across dusty arid red plains for 597km (370 miles) to Broken Hill. The best place to stop for the night is Cobar, 133km (83 miles) from Nyngan. There's an excellent rural museum here, and some fascinating local pubs and historic buildings.

You'll find some of the best Aboriginal art in NSW at **Mount Grenfell,** 40km (25 miles) farther along the Barrier Highway from Cobar—a signpost directs you off the main road and it's another 32km (19 miles) to three rock overhangs where 1,300 richly colored stencils and drawings cover the surfaces.

It's a 265km (164-mile) drive from here to **Wilcannia,** across a landscape scuttling with giant lizards and emus (the 'roos usually come out at dusk). Wilcannia can seem a bit threatening because of the Aborigines who tend to cluster around in the streets, but they love to talk, so don't worry too much.

From Wilcannia you can veer north along a bitumen road for 97km (60 miles) to the opal-mining town of **White Cliffs** (p. 245), where most people live underground.

Day ❹: White Cliffs on the way to Broken Hill

It's worth spending most of the day discovering the fascinating sights of White Cliffs before making your way back to the highway and completing the 197km (122-mile) journey to Broken Hill (p. 242).

Day ❺: Opal mining in Broken Hill

Rest up in **Broken Hill** ★ for the day, and make sure you take a tour of the town with a local tour company; you won't regret it. Sights to see include the School of the Air and the Royal Flying Doctor Service base, as well as popping out to Silverton (p. 244).

Days ❻ & ❼: Down to Mildura & the Murray Valley

A long, 295km (183-mile) drive takes you south along the Silver City Highway to Mildura, where you can stop for lunch. It's another 544km (337 miles) from here to Melbourne, but there are good highways much of the way. A good stopover for the night is Echuca (p. 636), 210km (130 miles) north of Melbourne, reached by the Murray Valley Highway, where you can spend the morning on a paddle steamer on the Murray River.

5 A Few Days in Margaret River, WA

Getting to see more of Australia than its most famous icons and the east-coast beaches is not always easy. But if you have the time, there are many wonderful places to discover off the beaten track, which will give another dimension to your image and memories of Australia. Here, we suggest a few days in the Margaret River region, just a few hours' drive south of the Western Australia capital, Perth. You can add it on to the end of a week or so in the east, or change it with the latter part of the 1- or 2-week itineraries above.

Note that each year from August to mid-November, the southern half of Western Australia is blessed with a carpet of 12,000 species of white, yellow, mauve, pink, red, and blue **wildflowers** ★. Wildflower shows and festivals in country towns throughout the state accompany the annual blossoming. September and October are the peak months.

Starting from the pleasant, sunny city of Perth, you can tailor your trek to take in some great beaches and surfing, winery tours, excellent food and wine, and the chance to see kangaroos, whales, and dolphins.

Fly to Perth from any of the other destinations above; for specific information on getting there from the other capitals or overseas (if you choose to start in the west and head east), see chapter 10, "Perth & Western Australia."

Day ❶: Welcome to Perth

The capital of Western Australia, **Perth** ★, has a superb climate, a great setting on the Swan River, a fabulous outdoor life of biking and beaches, excellent restaurants, and a beautiful historic port, Fremantle. If you'd like to spend a day or so recovering from jet lag as well as getting to know the city, you can overnight here before taking off on your exploration of WA. A relaxing way to spend the day is at the port of **Fremantle** ★, about 19km (12 miles) southwest of Perth's CBD at the mouth of the Swan River.

"Freo" is a bustling district of 150 National Trust buildings, alfresco cafes, museums, galleries, pubs, markets, and shops in a masterfully preserved historical atmosphere. It's still a working port, so you will see container ships and fishing boats unloading, and yachts gliding in and out of the harbor. It's a favorite destination for Perth's population every weekend, resulting in a wonderful hubbub of shoppers, merchants, cappuccino drinkers, tourists, and fishermen. You can enjoy the parade as you knock back a beer or two on the veranda of a gorgeous old pub.

Day ❷: Perth to Margaret River

A leisurely 4-hour drive southwest from Perth will put you on the edge of the vineyards of Margaret River, one of Australia's finest and most scenic wine regions. En route, stop off at the town of Bunbury, where you may be lucky enough to see the **wild dolphins,** which regularly come in to "play" with visitors.

Margaret River Itinerary

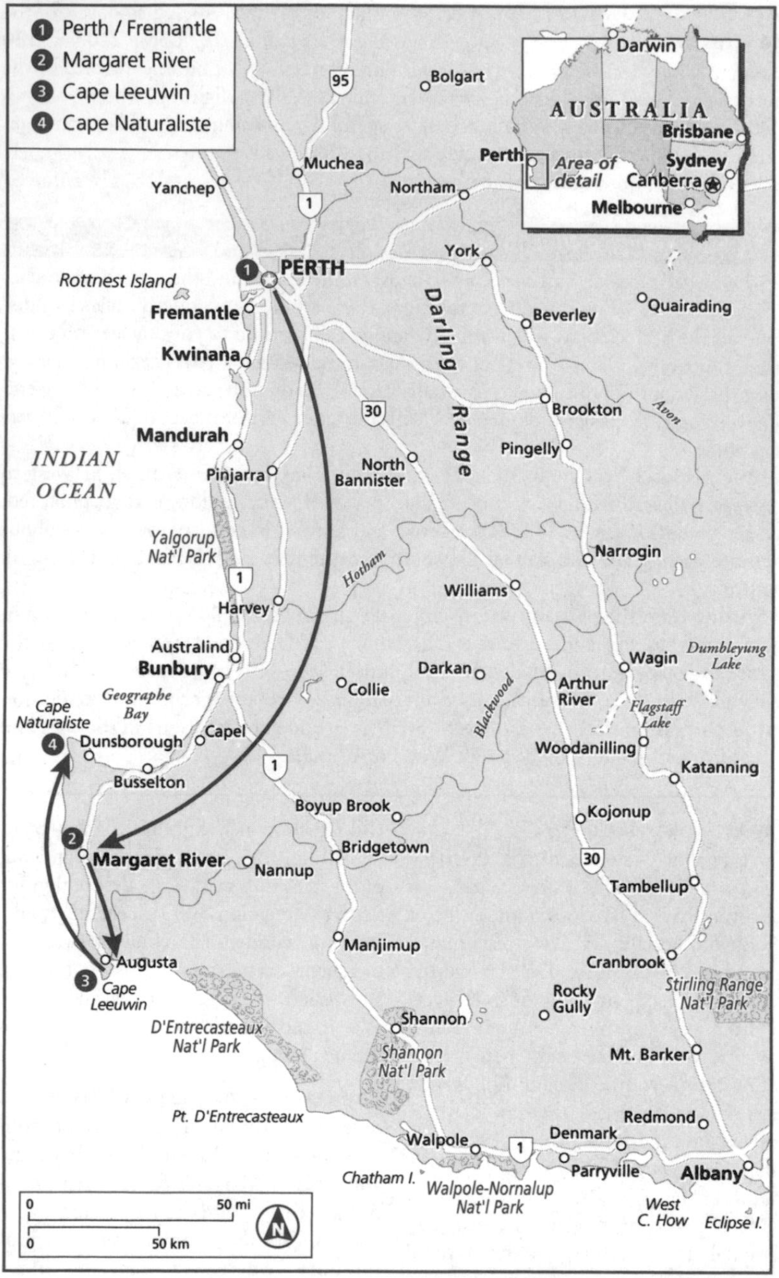

The area is really compact, so you can make your base at any of the numerous boutique lodges or B&Bs. You can then readily take your choice from around 80 wineries, as well as numerous art and craft galleries and the many gourmet produce outlets. Eat out at one of the excellent local restaurants—perhaps try one of the local specialties, marron (a freshwater crustacean), or venison, with a bottle of Margaret River wine.

Day ❸: South to Cape Leeuwin

Spend the day traveling the winding country roads of the southwest "hook" of Western Australia. Prevelly, west of Margaret River, has some of Australia's best surfing. Follow Caves Road south from here to Augusta and the historic lighthouse at **Cape Leeuwin,** where the Indian and Southern oceans meet. Augusta is one of the best places in the south to see migrating whales (both humpback and southern right) in season—with tours available. Your trip will take you through stands of massive karri and jarrah trees. Don't miss Boranup Drive, a scenic detour that cuts through a magnificent karri forest. For the adventurous, there is a maze of caves, some of which are open to the public. Have lunch at one of the winery restaurants or picnic in their lovely gardens. Wind your way back to your accommodations, with the car stocked with some newly favorite wines to drink or take home, as well as local cheeses, olive oil, and perhaps some craft work. Remember to designate a driver before setting out if you are planning to taste several wines; Australia's drunk-driving laws are strictly enforced and carry heavy penalties.

Day ❹: North to Cape Naturaliste & Perth

The area north of Margaret River town has the biggest concentration of wineries including some of Australia's big names, as well as the **Margaret River Chocolate Company.** Caves Road runs north from here heading for Dunsborough and Cape Naturaliste. Don't hurry along the tree-lined country roads and take time to explore some of the local galleries and enjoy the scenery. At Yallingup, you will swing northeast for Dunsborough, where—between September and November—you can do more whale-watching. Another stop on your way back to Perth should be at the seaside town of Busselton, where a visit to the underwater observatory on at the end of the longest timber jetty in the Southern Hemisphere is well worthwhile.

Information about getting to, getting around, where to stay, and where to eat in Western Australia can be found in chapter 10.

4

Sydney

by Marc Llewellyn

Sunny, sexy, and sophisticated, Sydney (pop. 4.1 million) basks in its worldwide recognition as the shining star of the Southern Hemisphere. The "Emerald City" is one of the most attractive on earth. Some people compare it to San Francisco—it certainly has that relaxed feel—but the gateway to Australia is very much its own unique city.

First, of course, there's the Sydney Opera House, one of the most recognized buildings in the world. This white-sailed construction on Sydney Cove, designed by Jørn Utzon, is the pride of the city—but there's far more on offer.

You can walk across that other great icon, the Sydney Harbour Bridge. Those with a daredevil spirit can join a Bridge-Climb Sydney tour across catwalks and ladders to the top of the main arch for 360-degree views across the Opera House and the ferries and boats far below.

Sydney is one of the biggest cities in the world—but fortunately most of the interesting things are concentrated in a relatively compact area around one of the finest urban harbors in the world.

There's so much to do in Sydney that you could easily spend a week here and still find yourself crashing into bed at night exhausted by trying to see all the main attractions.

Sydney's greatest summer experience is on the beaches—and with over 20 strung along the city's oceanfront and dozens more around the harbor, you'll be spoiled for choice. The most famous is Bondi, a strip of golden sand legendary for its Speedo-clad Lifesavers and surfboard riders. From here a "must do" is the 3.2km (2-mile) coastal path that leads off across the cliff tops, via Tamarama Beach (dubbed "Glamourama" for its chic sun worshipers), to Bronte Beach, where you can cool down in the crashing waves.

Another beach favorite is Manly, a 30-minute ferry trip from Circular Quay. Pick up some fish and chips and head for the main beach, flanked by a row of giant pines that chatter with hundreds of colorful lorikeets at dusk.

The best time to return is in the early evening, when the lights of the skyscrapers around Circular Quay streak like rainbows across the water of the harbor, and the sails of the Opera House and the girders of the Harbour Bridge are lit up—it's magical.

History is enshrined in its many museums and art galleries, while modern Sydney comes alive in the more recent developments around Darling Harbour and the restaurant and entertainment area nearby at Cockle Bay and King Street Wharf. At Darling Harbour you'll find the world-class Sydney Aquarium. You can also start your gourmet tour of Sydney's Contemporary cooking style, which encompasses the best of freshness with spices from Asia and flavors from the Mediterranean.

Add to this the side trips to the gorges and cliffs of the Blue Mountains, the wineries of the Hunter Valley, and the dolphin- and whale-watching around

Port Stephens (see "Port Stephens: Dolphin- & Whale-Watching" in chapter 5), and you'll see why Sydney gets so much praise.

The frugal traveler will find that, compared to many other major international cities, Sydney offers good value. Food and public transport are cheap, and attractions are generally not prohibitively expensive. (Senior and student prices are almost always available with ID.) The price of a hotel room is far cheaper than in other major population centers such as New York and London.

1 Orientation

ARRIVING

BY PLANE **Sydney International Airport** is 8km (5 miles) from the city center. Free shuttle buses link the international and domestic terminals. In both terminals, you'll find luggage carts, wheelchairs, a post office (open Mon–Fri 9am–5pm), mailboxes, currency exchange, duty-free shops (including one before you go through Customs on arrival, selling alcohol and perfume), restaurants, bars, stores, showers, luggage lockers, a Baggage Held Service for larger items, ATMs, and tourist information desks. You can rent mobile phones in the international terminal. There is also a Sydney Visitors Centre bookings desk (✆ **02/9667 6050**) offering cheap deals on hotels (see "Where to Stay," later in this chapter), as well as car rental, phone cards, and maps and brochures. Here you can also buy the SydneyPass (see section 2, "Getting Around"). The airport is efficient, has extremely strict quarantine procedures—you must declare all food—and is completely nonsmoking. On arrival, pick up a copy of *Sydney The Official Guide,* from the rack just before passport control, which contains tear-out discount tickets for some of Sydney's major attractions. Luggage trolleys are free to use in the international arrival terminal but cost A$4 (US$3/UK£1.50) outside departure terminals (you'll need coins). ***Tip:*** Duty-free alcohol and perfumes are available on arrival in Sydney from an international flight. You can take two bottles of standard alcohol through Customs without declaring them.

GETTING INTO TOWN The **Airport Link** connects the international and domestic airports to the city stations of Central, Museum, St. James, Circular Quay, Wynyard, and Town Hall. You'll need to change trains for other Sydney stations. Unfortunately, the line has no dedicated luggage areas and, because it's on a scheduled route into the city from the suburbs, it gets very crowded during rush hours (approximately 7–9am and 4–6:30pm). If you have lots of luggage and you're traveling into the city at these times, it's probably best to take an airport bus (below) or a taxi. Otherwise walk to the end of the platform, and there should be more room onboard.

Tips **Tourist Refund Scheme**

Visitors to Australia are entitled to claim any Goods and Services Tax (GST) on purchases over A$300 (US$240/UK£140) per store. The GST component is 10% of the sale price. Do this at the refund booth located past Customs. After doing the paperwork—you need to have the goods and receipt with you, not in your checked luggage—you will receive your refund by check on the spot. You can convert this to cash at any foreign exchange booth at Sydney Airport.

Tips Taxi Savvy

Especially in busy periods, taxi queues can be long, and drivers may try to cash in by insisting you share a cab with other passengers in line at the airport. Here's the scam: After dropping off the other passengers, the cabdriver will attempt to charge you the full price of the journey, despite the fact that the other passengers paid for their sections. You certainly won't save any money sharing a cab if this happens, and your journey will be a long one. If you are first in line in the taxi stand, the law states that you can refuse to share the cab. Taxi drivers obviously like a tip, but there is no requirement to do so. If you've had good service then 10% extra on top of the fare is enough.

There are elevators at the Airport Link stations and some at the city train stations (but the crowds and lack of staff and signs mean you'll probably end up lugging it all up loads of steps anyway). The train takes 10 minutes to reach the Central Railway Station and continues to Circular Quay. Trains leave every 15 minutes or so and cost A$13 (US$10/UK£5) one-way for adults and A$8.80 (US$7/UK£4.40) for children. Round-trip tickets are only available if you really hate Sydney and want to return to the airport on the same day. Ask at the ticket office about group tickets, and Family Fare tickets which allow a second child, or more, to travel for free with an adult. (The first child pays the standard child fare.)

Sydney Airporter coaches operate to the city center from bus stops outside the terminals every 15 minutes. This service will drop you off (and pick you up) at hotels in the city, Kings Cross, and Darling Harbour. Pickups from hotels require at least 3 hours advance notice (© **02/9666 9988;** www.kst.com.au). You can book online. Tickets cost A$10 (US$8/UK£5) one-way and A$17 (US$14/UK£7) round-trip from the International Terminal and A$12 (US$9.60/UK£6) one-way and A$20 (US$16/UK££8) round-trip from the Domestic Terminal. The return portion can be used any time in the future.

Both short-term and long-term parking are available at both terminals. An example is a 4-day stay at the Domestic terminal, which costs A$79 (US$63/UK£39).

A **taxi** from the airport to the city center costs about A$30 (US$24/UK£12) total. In 2006 a A$2 (US$1.60/UK55p) surcharge was added to taxi fares from the airport. An expressway, the Eastern Distributor, is the fastest way to reach the city from the airport. There's a A$4.50 (US$3.60/UK£1.80) toll from the airport to the city (the taxi driver pays the toll and adds the cost to your fare), but there is no toll to the airport. A 10% credit card charge applies. The flag-fall rate is A$2.90 (US$2.30/UK£1.15) and a booking fee (not necessary at the airport) is A$1.50 (US$1.20/UK60p).

BY TRAIN **Central Station** (© **13 15 00** for CityRail, or 13 22 32 for Countrylink interstate trains) is the main city and interstate train station. It's at the top of George Street in downtown Sydney. All interstate trains depart from here, and it's a major CityRail hub. Many city buses leave from neighboring Railway Square for places like Town Hall and Circular Quay.

BY BUS **Greyhound** coaches operate from the **Sydney Coach Terminal** (© **02/9212 1500**), on the corner of Eddy Avenue and Pitt Street, bordering Central Station.

BY CRUISE SHIP Cruise ships dock at the **Overseas Passenger Terminal** in The Rocks, opposite the Sydney Opera House, or in Darling Harbour if The Rocks facility is already occupied.

BY CAR Drivers enter Sydney from the north on the Pacific Highway, from the south on the M5 and Princes Highway, and from the west on the Great Western Highway.

VISITOR INFORMATION

The Sydney Visitor Centre at The Rocks, First Floor, The Rocks Centre, Corner of Argyle and Playfair streets, The Rocks (✆ **02/9240 8788;** www.sydneyvisitor centre.com), is a good place to pick up maps, brochures, YHA cards, and general tourist information about Sydney as well as towns in New South Wales; it also sells books, T-shirts, DVDs, postcards, and the like. The office is open daily from 9am to 5pm. There's also the **Sydney Visitors Centre—Darling Harbour,** 33 Wheat Rd., Darling Harbour, near the IMAX Theatre. It's open from 9:30am to 5:30pm daily. In Manly, find the **Manly Visitors Information Centre** (✆ **02/9976 1430**), at Manly Wharf (where the ferries come in). It's open Monday to Friday from 9am to 5pm, and on weekends between 10am and 4pm.

Also in The Rocks is the **National Parks & Wildlife Centre,** in Cadmans Cottage (a little sandstone building, built in 1816, which is set back from the water in front of The Rocks), 110 George St. (✆ **02/9247 5033**). This place has lots of national park information and runs boat tours to some of the islands in Sydney Harbour. It's open Monday to Friday 9:30am to 4:30pm, Saturday and Sunday 10am to 4:30pm.

Elsewhere, there are **City Host information kiosks,** at Martin Place (between Elizabeth and Castlereagh sts.), on George Street (adjacent to Sydney Town Hall), and at Circular Quay (corner of Pitt and Alfred sts.). They provide maps, brochures, and advice and are open daily from 9am to 5pm. There's also a Visitor Centre at the International Terminal. If you want to inquire about destinations and holidays in Sydney or the rest of New South Wales, call **Tourism New South Wales**'s help line (✆ **13 20 77** in Australia).

Electronic information on cinema, theater, exhibitions, and other events is available through **Talking Guides** (✆ **13 16 20** in Australia). You'll need a code number for each topic, which you can find on page three of the A-K section of the *Sydney Yellow Pages.* The service costs the same as a local call.

A good website is **CitySearch Sydney** (www.sydney.citysearch.com.au), for events, entertainment, dining, and shopping.

CITY LAYOUT

Sydney is one of the largest cities in the world by area, covering more than 1,730 sq. km (675 sq. miles) from the sea to the foothills of the Blue Mountains. Thankfully, the city center is compact. The jewel in Sydney's crown is its harbor, which empties into the South Pacific Ocean through headlands known as North Head and South Head. On the southern side of the harbor are the high-rises of the city center; the Sydney Opera House; a string of beaches, including Bondi; and the inner-city suburbs. The Sydney Harbour Bridge and a tunnel connect the city center to the high-rises of the North Sydney business district and the affluent northern suburbs and ocean beaches beyond.

MAIN ARTERIES & STREETS The city's main thoroughfare, **George Street,** runs up from **Circular Quay** (pronounced "Key"), past Wynyard CityRail station and

Town Hall, to Central Station. A whole host of streets run parallel to George, including Pitt, Elizabeth, and Macquarie streets. **Macquarie Street** runs up from the Sydney Opera House, past the Royal Botanic Gardens and Hyde Park. **Martin Place** is a pedestrian thoroughfare that stretches from Macquarie to George streets. It's about halfway between Circular Quay and Town Hall—in the heart of the city center. The easy-to-spot Sydney Tower (also known as Centrepoint Tower), facing onto pedestrian-only **Pitt Street Mall** on Pitt Street, is the main city-center landmark. Next to Circular Quay and across from the Opera House is **The Rocks,** a cluster of small streets that was once part of a larger slum and is now a tourist attraction. Roads meet at **Town Hall** from Kings Cross in one direction and Darling Harbour in the other. From Circular Quay to The Rocks it's a 5- to 10-minute stroll, to Wynyard about 10 minutes, and to Town Hall about 20 minutes. From Town Hall to the near side of Darling Harbour it's about a 10-minute walk.

NEIGHBORHOODS IN BRIEF

South of the Harbour

Circular Quay This transport hub for ferries, buses, and CityRail trains is tucked between the Harbour Bridge and the Sydney Opera House. The Quay, as it's called, is a good spot for a stroll, and its outdoor restaurants and street performers are popular. The Rocks, the Royal Botanic Gardens, the Contemporary Art Museum, and the start of the main shopping area (centered on Pitt and George sts.) are a short walk away. To get there by public transit, take a CityRail train, ferry, or city bus to Circular Quay.

The Rocks This small historic area, a short stroll west of Circular Quay, is packed with colonial stone buildings, intriguing back streets, boutiques, pubs, tourist stores, and top-notch restaurants and hotels. It's the most exclusive place to stay in the city because of its beauty and its proximity to the Opera House and harbor. Shops are geared toward Sydney's yuppies and wealthy tourists—don't expect bargains. On weekends a portion of George Street is blocked off for The Rocks Market, with stalls selling souvenirs and crafts. To reach the area on public transport, take any bus for Circular Quay or The Rocks (on George St.) or a CityRail train or ferry to Circular Quay.

Town Hall In the heart of the city, this area is home to the main department stores and two Sydney landmarks, the Town Hall and a historic shopping mall called the Queen Victoria Building (QVB). In this area are Sydney Tower and the boutique-style chain stores of Pitt Street Mall. Farther up George Street are movie houses, the entrance to Sydney's Spanish district (around Liverpool St.), and the city's Chinatown. To reach the area by public transit, take any bus from Circular Quay on George Street, or a CityRail train to the Town Hall stop.

Darling Harbour Designed as a tourist precinct, Darling Harbour features Sydney's main convention, exhibition, and entertainment centers; a waterfront promenade; the Sydney Aquarium; the Panasonic IMAX Theatre; the Australian Maritime Museum; the Powerhouse Museum; Star City (Sydney's casino); a food court; and plenty of shops. Nearby are the funky restaurants of Cockle Bay and King Street Wharf. To reach Darling Harbour by public transport, take a ferry from Circular Quay (Wharf 5), the monorail from Town Hall, or the light rail (tram) from Central Station. It's a short walk from Town Hall.

Kings Cross & the Suburbs Beyond "The Cross," as it's known, is the city's red-light district—though it's also home to some of Sydney's best-known nightclubs and restaurants. The area has plenty of backpacker hostels, a few bars, and some upscale hotels. The main drag, Darlinghurst Road, is short but crammed with strip joints, prostitutes, addicts, drunks, and such. Also here are cheap e-mail centers that offer discount overseas phone rates. There's a heavy police presence, but do take care. Beyond the strip clubs and glitter, the suburbs of Elizabeth Bay, Double Bay, and Rose Bay hug the waterfront. To reach the area on public transport, take a CityRail train to Kings Cross. From the next stop, Edgecliff, it's a short walk to Double Bay and a longer one to Rose Bay along the coast.

Paddington/Oxford Street This inner-city suburb, centered on trendy Oxford Street, is known for its expensive terrace houses, off-the-wall boutiques and bookshops, and restaurants, pubs, and nightclubs. It's also the heart of Sydney's large gay community and has a liberal scattering of gay bars and dance spots. To reach the area by public transport, take bus no. 380 or 382 from Circular Quay (on Elizabeth St.); no. 378 from Railway Square, Central Station; or no. 380 or 382 from Bondi Junction. The lower end of Oxford Street is a short walk from Museum CityRail Station (take the Liverpool St. exit).

Darlinghurst Between grungy Kings Cross and upscale Oxford Street, this extroverted, grimy terraced suburb is home to some of Sydney's best cafes. It's probably not wise to wander around at night. Take the CityRail train to Kings Cross and head right from the exit.

Central The congested, polluted crossroads around Central Station, the city's main train station, has little to recommend it. Buses run from here to Circular Quay, and it's a 20-minute walk to Town Hall. The Sydney Central YHA (youth hostel) is here.

Newtown This popular student area centers on car-clogged King Street, which is lined with alternative shops, bookstores, and ethnic restaurants. People-watching is the thing to do—see how many belly-button rings, violently colored hairdos, and Celtic arm tattoos you can spot. To reach the area on public transport, take a CityRail train to Newtown Station.

Glebe Young professionals and students come to this inner-city suburb for the cafes, restaurants, pubs, and shops along the main thoroughfare, Glebe Point Road. All this, plus a location 15 minutes from the city and 30 minutes from Circular Quay, makes it a good place for budget-conscious travelers. To reach Glebe, take bus no. 431, 433, or 434 from Millers Point, The Rocks (on George St.), or bus no. 459 behind Town Hall.

Bondi & the Southern Beaches Some of Sydney's most glamorous surf beaches—Bondi, Bronte, and Coogee—lie along the South Pacific coast southeast of the city center. Bondi has a wide sweep of beach (crowded in summer), some interesting restaurants and bars, plenty of attitude, and beautiful bodies—and no CityRail station. To reach Bondi by public transport, ride bus no. 380 to Bondi Beach from Circular Quay—it takes up to an hour—or (a quicker alternative) a CityRail train to Bondi Junction to connect with the same buses. The new bus no. 333 takes around 40 minutes from Circular Quay to Bondi Beach. It has limited

Sydney at a Glance

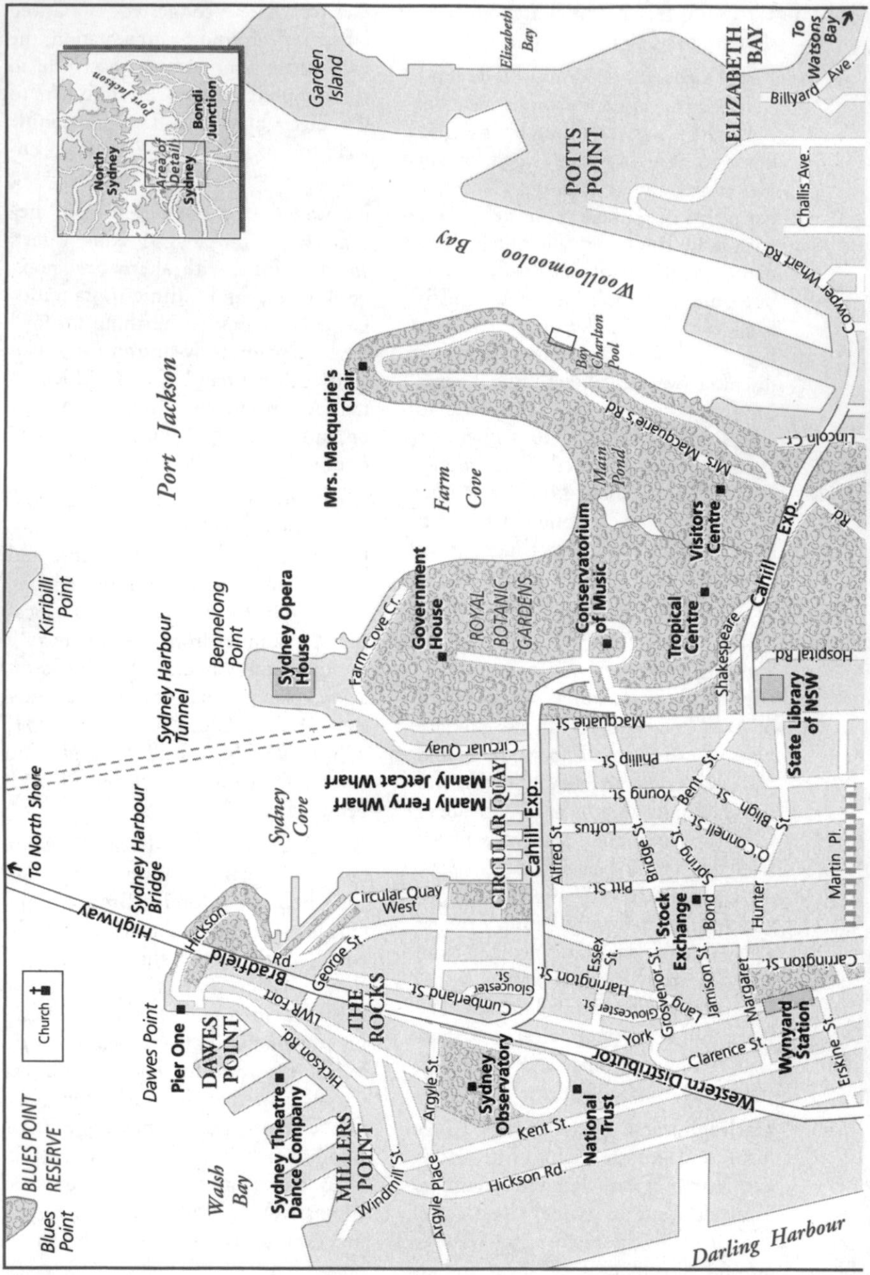

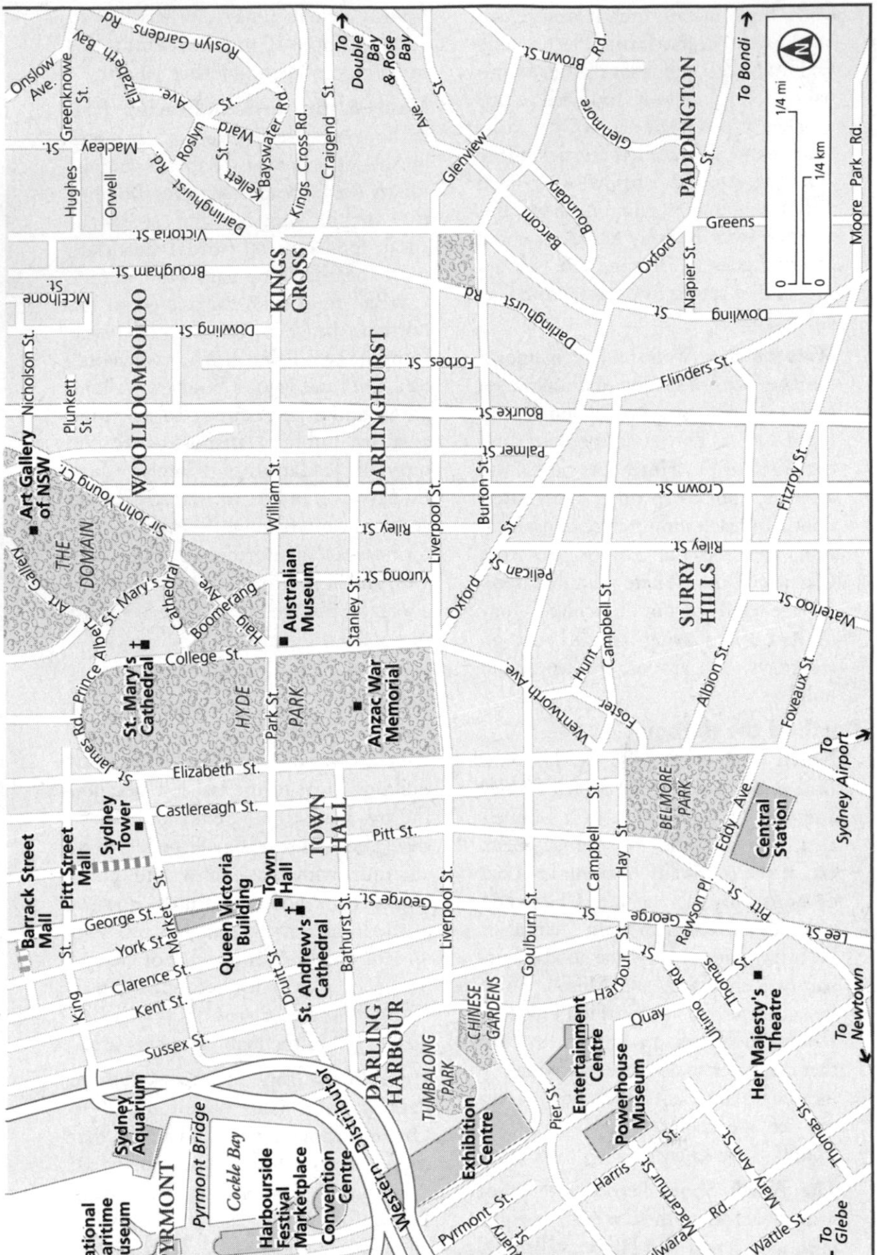

National Maritime Museum
PYRMONT
Pyrmont Bridge
Cockle Bay
Sydney Aquarium
Harbourside Festival Marketplace
Convention Centre
Western Distributor
Exhibition Centre
TUMBALONG PARK
DARLING HARBOUR
CHINESE GARDENS
Powerhouse Museum
Entertainment Centre
Her Majesty's Theatre
Barrack Street Mall
Pitt Street Mall
Sydney Tower
Queen Victoria Building
Town Hall
St. Andrew's Cathedral
TOWN HALL
St. Mary's Cathedral
HYDE PARK
Anzac War Memorial
Australian Museum
THE DOMAIN
Art Gallery of NSW
WOOLLOOMOOLOO
KINGS CROSS
DARLINGHURST
SURRY HILLS
PADDINGTON
BELMORE PARK
Central Station
To Double Bay & Rose Bay
To Bondi
To Sydney Airport
To Newtown
To Glebe
Onslow Ave.
Greenknowe St.
Elizabeth Bay Rd.
Roslyn Gardens Rd.
Macleay St.
Hughes
Orwell
Roslyn Ave.
Ward St.
Kellett St.
Darlinghurst Rd.
Bayswater Rd.
Kings Cross Rd.
Craigend St.
Victoria St.
Broughham St.
McElhone St.
Nicholson St.
Plunkett St.
Dowling St.
Sir John Young Cr.
Art Gallery Rd.
Prince Albert Rd.
St. Mary's Rd.
Cathedral St.
Boomerang St.
Haig Ave.
College St.
William St.
Stanley St.
Yurong St.
Riley St.
Liverpool St.
Burton St.
Forbes St.
Bourke St.
Palmer St.
Crown St.
Glenview St.
Glenmore Rd.
Brown St.
Barcom Ave.
Boundary St.
Oxford St.
Greens Rd.
Moore Park Rd.
Napier St.
Flinders St.
Fitzroy St.
Pelican St.
Campbell St.
Hunt St.
Foster St.
Wentworth Ave.
Albion St.
Waterloo St.
Foveaux St.
St. James Rd.
Elizabeth St.
Castlereagh St.
Pitt St.
George St.
Park St.
Market St.
York St.
Clarence St.
Kent St.
Sussex St.
King St.
Druitt St.
Bathurst St.
Goulburn St.
Hay St.
Eddy Ave.
Rawson Pl.
Lee St.
Harbour St.
Ultimo Rd.
Thomas St.
Quay St.
Pier St.
Harris St.
Pyrmont St.
Quarry St.
Macarthur St.
Mary Ann St.
Bulwara Rd.
Wattle St.
0 1/4 mi
0 1/4 km

stops, but you can catch it from Elizabeth Street near Martin Place, along Oxford Street, and from the bus terminal at Bondi Junction. You need to buy a ticket at a newsdealer or 7/11 store beforehand. A Travelten bus ticket (See "Getting Around," below) is a good option if you are staying in Bondi. Bus no. 378 from Railway Square, Central Station, goes to Bronte, and bus no. 373 or 374 travels to Coogee from Circular Quay.

Watsons Bay Watsons Bay is known for The Gap—a section of dramatic sea cliffs—as well as several good restaurants, such as Doyles on the Beach and the Watsons Bay Hotel beer garden. It's a terrific spot to spend a sunny afternoon. To reach it on public transportation, take bus no. 324 or 325 from Circular Quay. There's limited ferry service daily from Circular Quay (Wharf 2), starting at 10:15am on weekdays, 9:15am on weekends and holidays.

North of the Harbour

North Sydney Across the Harbour Bridge, the high-rises of North Sydney attest to its prominence as a business area. There's little for tourists here, except the possibility of being knocked over on a busy thoroughfare. Chatswood (take a CityRail train from Central or Wynyard station) has some good suburban-type shopping, and Milsons Point has a decent pub, the Kirribilli Hotel, as well as Luna Park, an amusement park that continues to do battle with wealthy locals who complain it's too noisy—you can see the giant smiling clown face from Circular Quay.

The North Shore Ferries and buses provide access to these wealthy neighborhoods across the Harbour Bridge. Gorgeous Balmoral Beach, Taronga Zoo, and upscale boutiques are the attractions in Mosman. Take a ferry from Circular Quay (Wharf 2) to Taronga Zoo—10 minutes—and a bus to Balmoral Beach (another 10 min.).

Manly & the Northern Beaches Half an hour away by ferry, or 15 minutes by the faster JetCat, Manly is famous for its ocean beach—it gives Bondi a run for its money—and scores of cheap food outlets. Farther north are more beaches popular with surfers. CityRail train lines do not go to the northern beaches. The farthest beach from the city, Palm Beach, has magnificent surf and lagoon beaches, walking paths, and a golf course. To reach the area by public transport, take the ferry or JetCat from Circular Quay (Wharves 2 and 3) to Manly. Change at Manly interchange (transfer point) for buses to the northern beaches, nos. 148 and 154 through 159. You can also take bus no. L90 from Wynyard station.

West of the City Center

Balmain West of the city center, a short ferry ride from Circular Quay, Balmain was once Sydney's main shipbuilding area. In the last few decades, the area has become trendy and expensive. The suburb has a village feel to it, abounds with restaurants and pubs, and stages a popular Saturday market at the local church. Take bus no. 441, 442, or 432 from Town Hall or George Street, or a ferry from Circular Quay (Wharf 5), and then a short bus ride up the hill to the main shopping area.

Homebush Bay Sydney Olympic Park was the main site of the 2000 Olympic games. You'll find Telstra Stadium (once named Stadium Australia), the Aquatic Center, and Homebush Bay Information Centre, parklands, and a water-bird reserve. To reach the area by public transport, take a CityRail train from Circular Quay to the Olympic Park station.

2 Getting Around

BY PUBLIC TRANSPORTATION

State Transit operates the city's buses and the ferry network, CityRail runs the urban and suburban trains, and Sydney Ferries runs the public passenger ferries. Some private bus lines operate buses in the outer suburbs. In addition, a monorail connects the city center to Darling Harbour, and a light rail (tram) line runs between Central Station and Wentworth Park in Pyrmont.

MONEY-SAVING TRANSIT PASSES Several passes are available for visitors who will be using public transportation frequently. All work out to be much cheaper than buying individual tickets.

The **SydneyPass** includes unlimited travel on Sydney Explorer coaches, Bondi & Bay Explorer coaches, three Sydney Harbour cruises, the JetCat to Manly, the high-speed RiverCat to Parramatta (linking the city center to this important heritage and business center along a historic waterway), Sydney buses, Sydney Ferries, and CityRail trains (within the "Red TravelPass" travel zone, which includes the entire city center, as well as to Bondi Junction). The SydneyPass costs A$110 (US$88/UK£44) for adults and A$55 (US$44/UK£22) for children for 3 days of travel over a 7-day period; A$145 (US$116/UK£58) for adults and A$70 (US$56/UK£28) for children for 5 days over a 7-day period; and A$165 (US$132/UK£66) for adults and A$80 (US$64/UK£32) for children for 7 consecutive days. Family fares are also available. Buy tickets at the information desk at the airport, at the TransitShop at Circular Quay (near McDonald's), from the Sydney Ferries ticket offices at Circular Quay, and from Explorer bus drivers.

A **Weekly Travel Pass** allows unlimited travel on buses, trains, and ferries. There are six different passes (each a different color) depending on the distance you need to travel. The passes visitors most commonly use are the Red Pass and the Green Pass. The Red Pass costs A$33 (US$26/UK£13) for adults and A$17 (US$13/UK£7.50) for kids and covers all transportation within the city center and near surroundings. This pass will get you aboard inner harbor ferries, for example, but not the ferry to Manly. The Green Pass, which costs A$41 (US$33/UK£17) for adults and A$21 (US$16/UK£8) for kids, will take you to more distant destinations, including Manly (aboard the ferry but not the JetCat before 7pm). You can buy either pass at newsdealers or bus, train, and ferry ticket outlets.

The **Day Tripper** ticket gives you unlimited bus, train, and ferry travel for 1 day. Tickets cost A$15 (US$12/UK£6) for adults and A$7.70 (US$6/UK£3) for children. The pass is available at all bus, train, and ferry ticket outlets.

The **City Hopper** allows unlimited all day CityRail travel around 11 stations within the city area. They include: Central, Martin Place, Museum, Town Hall, St.

Tips **Transit Information**

For bus, ferry, and train timetable information, call **Infoline** (© **13 15 00** in Australia) daily from 6am to 10pm. Otherwise check the website for Sydney buses and ferries (www.sydneybuses.nsw.gov.au) or CityRail (www.cityrail.info). Pick up a **Sydney Transport Map** (a guide to train, bus, and ferry services) at any rail, bus, or ferry office.

Sydney Public Transit Systems

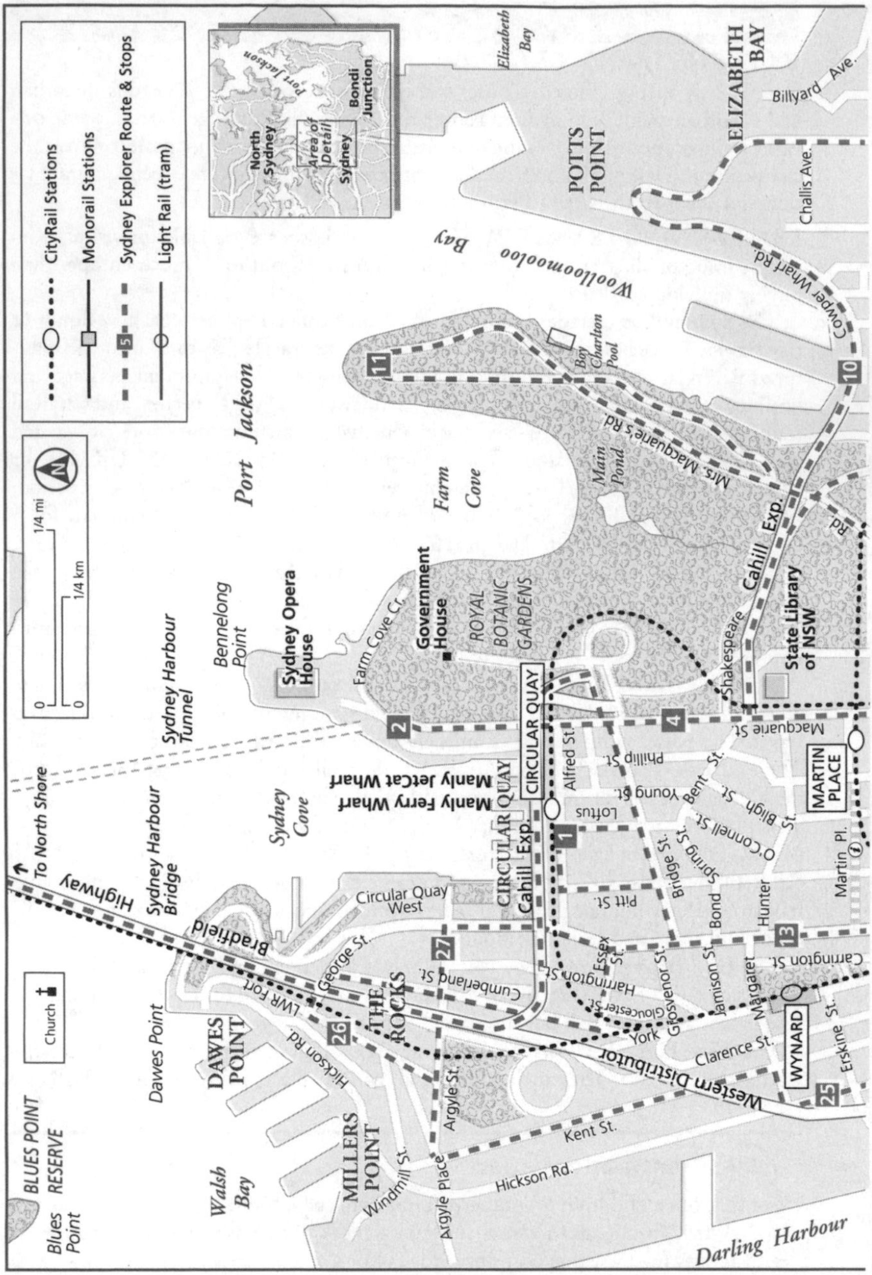

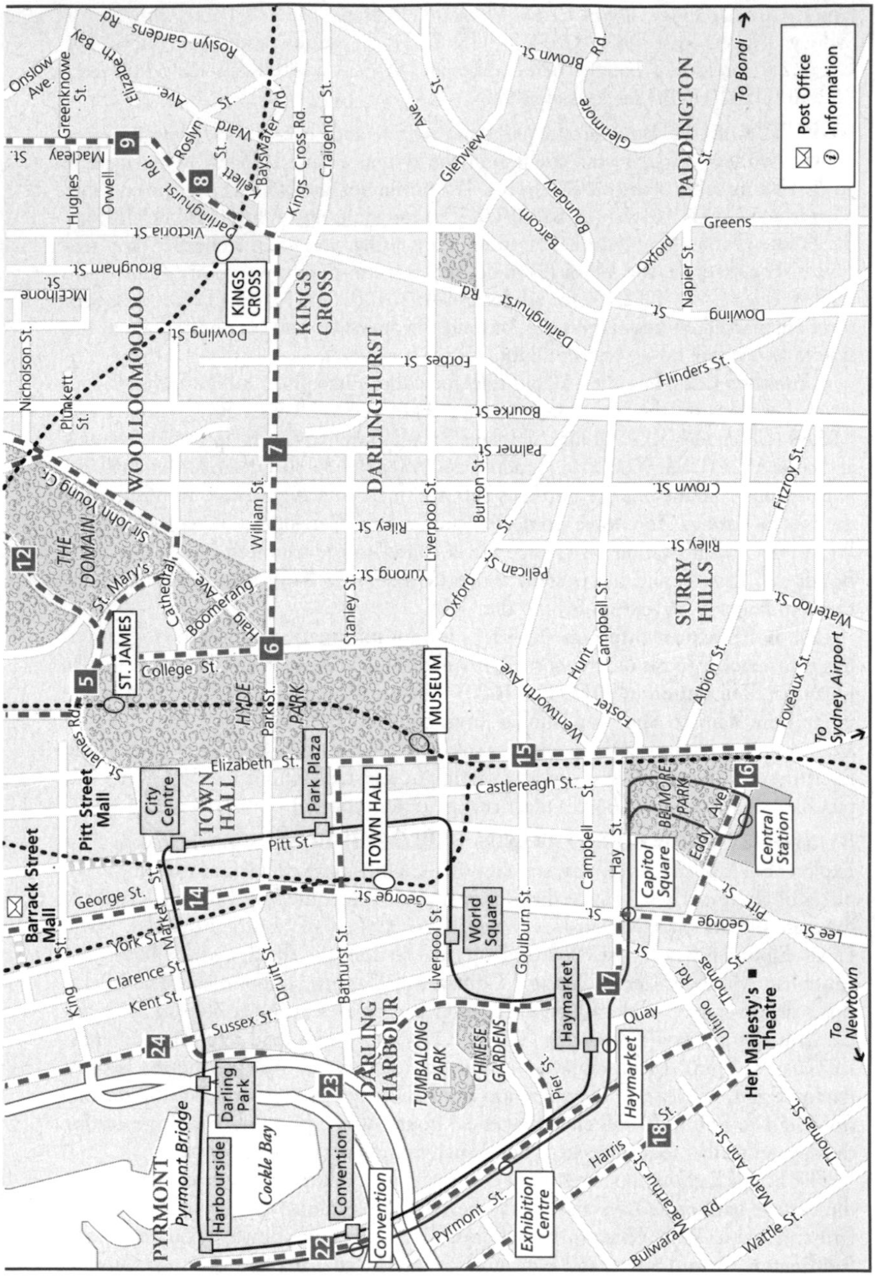

Post Office
Information
To Bondi
PADDINGTON
KINGS CROSS
DARLINGHURST
WOOLLOOMOOLOO
THE DOMAIN
HYDE PARK
SURRY HILLS
TOWN HALL
DARLING HARBOUR
PYRMONT
Cockle Bay
Pyrmont Bridge
TUMBALONG PARK
CHINESE GARDENS
BELMORE PARK
Central Station
Capitol Square
Haymarket
World Square
Park Plaza
City Centre
Pitt Street Mall
Barrack Street Mall
ST. JAMES
MUSEUM
Harbourside
Darling Park
Convention
Exhibition Centre
Her Majesty's Theatre
To Sydney Airport
To Newtown
William St.
Oxford St.
Elizabeth St.
Castlereagh St.
Pitt St.
George St.
York St.
Clarence St.
Kent St.
Sussex St.
Market St.
King St.
Liverpool St.
Bathurst St.
Park St.
College St.
Goulburn St.
Campbell St.
Hay St.
Druitt St.
Wentworth Ave.
Foveaux St.
Albion St.
Riley St.
Crown St.
Bourke St.
Flinders St.
Dowling St.
Darlinghurst Rd.
Victoria St.
Kings Cross Rd.
Bayswater Rd.
Macleay St.
Nicholson St.
Harris St.
Pyrmont St.
Ultimo Rd.
Wattle St.
Thomas St.
Lee St.
Eddy Ave.

James, Circular Quay, Kings Cross, Wynyard, Redfern, Milsons Point, and North Sydney. Tickets cost A$7 (US$5.50/UK£2.75) for adults and A$3 (US$2.50/UK£1.25) for kids if bought before 9am and A$5 (US$4/UK£2) for adults and A$2.50 (US$2/UK£1) for kids after 9am.

BY PUBLIC BUS Buses are frequent and reliable and cover a wide area of metropolitan Sydney—though you might find the system a little difficult to navigate if you're visiting some of the outer suburbs. The minimum fare (which covers most short hops in the city) is A$1.70 (US$1.40/UK75p) for adults and A80¢ (US65¢/UK35p) for children for a 4km (2½-mile) "section." The farther you go, the cheaper each section is. For example, the 44km (27-mile) trip to Palm Beach, way past Manly, costs A$5.40 (US$4.30/UK£2.15) for adults and A$2.70 (US$2.15/UK£1) for kids. Sections are marked on bus-stand signs, but most Sydneysiders are as confused about the system as you will be—when in doubt, ask the bus driver.

A **Travelten ticket** bus offers 10 bus rides for a discounted price. A Blue Travelten covers two sections on the bus route and costs A$14 (US$11/UK£5.50) for adults and A$6.80 (US$5.40/UK£2.70) for children; a Brown Travelten covers up to nine sections and costs A$23 (US$19/UK£10) for adults and A$12 (US$9.30/UK£4.50) for children.

Most buses bound for the northern suburbs, including night buses to Manly and the bus to Taronga Zoo, leave from Wynyard Park on Carrington Street, behind the Wynyard CityRail station on George Street. Buses to the southern beaches, such as Bondi and Bronte, and the western and eastern suburbs leave from Circular Quay. Buses to Balmain leave from behind the QVB.

Call the **Transport Info Line** (✆ **13 15 00**) for information, or ask the staff at the bus information kiosk on the corner of Alfred and Loftus streets, behind Circular Quay CityRail station (✆ **02/9219 1680**). The kiosk is open Monday through Saturday from 8am to 8pm and Sunday from 8am to 6pm. Buses run from 4am to around midnight during the week, less frequently on weekends and holidays. Some night buses to outer suburbs run after midnight and throughout the night. You can purchase single tickets onboard; exact change is not required.

BY SYDNEY EXPLORER & BONDI EXPLORER BUSES Bright red Sydney Explorer buses operate every day, traveling a 28km (18-mile) circuit and stopping at 27 places of interest. These include the Sydney Opera House, the Royal Botanic Gardens, the State Library, Mrs. Macquarie's Chair, the Art Gallery of New South Wales, Kings Cross, Elizabeth Bay House, Wynyard CityRail station, the QVB, Sydney Tower, the Australian Museum, Central Station, Chinatown, Darling Harbour, and The Rocks. Buses depart from Circular Quay at 18-minute intervals starting at 8:40am, with the last "round-trip" service departing Circular Quay at 5:20pm (and returning to Circular Quay at 7pm). Board anywhere along the route where you see the red Sydney Explorer sign, and leave at any attraction along the way. If you want to stay on the bus from start to finish, the full circuit takes 1½ hours. When planning your itinerary for the day, remember that some attractions, such as museums, close at 5pm.

The Bondi Explorer operates every day, traveling a 30km (19-mile) circuit around the eastern harborside bays and coastal beaches. Stops along the way include Kings Cross, Double Bay, Watsons Bay, Bondi Beach, Bronte Beach, Coogee Beach, Paddington, Oxford Street, and Martin Place. The bus departs from Circular Quay at 25-minute intervals starting at 9:15am, with the last "round-trip" service departing Circular Quay at 4:20pm (and returning to Circular Quay at 5:55pm). Board anywhere along the route where you see the Bondi & Bay Explorer sign, and get off at

Value Special Attraction Passes

Sydney Ferries have teamed up with Taronga Zoo and Sydney Aquarium to provide two discount passes. The **Zoo Pass** includes return ferry trips from Circular Quay to Taronga Zoo, a trip on the Aerial Safari cable car to the top of the zoo, and a bus trip back to the ferry if you somehow end up back up at the top (which is unlikely, because generally you start at the top of the hill and work your way down). It costs A$39 (US$31/UK£20) for adults and A$21 (US$17/UK£13) for kids aged 4 to 15. A family ticket costs A$37 (US$30/UK£15) for the first adult, A$32 (US$26/UK£13) for a second adult, A$20 (US$16/UK£8) for the first child and A$12 (US$9.60/UK£4.80) for each additional child.

The **Aquarium Pass** includes return ferry travel from Circular Quay to the Sydney Aquarium and also entry. It costs A$33 (US$26/UK£13) for adults, A$17 (US$14/UK£7.50) for kids, and A$81 (US$65/UK£37) for a family of two adults and two kids. Buy tickets at Circular Quay.

any attraction along the way. If you wish to stay on board from start to finish without making any stops, the entire circuit takes 1½ hours.

Tickets entitle you to free travel on regular "blue and white" Sydney Buses within the same zones covered by your explorer tickets until midnight. You also get discounts on some attractions, such as a 15% discount on tickets to Sydney Aquarium.

Combined 1-day tickets for both buses cost A$39 (US$31/UK£15) for adults, A$18 (US$14/UK£7) for children 4 to 16, and A$97 (US$77/UK£39) for a family. Buy tickets onboard the bus. You can also buy a 2-day ticket costing A$68 (US$54/UK£28) for adults, A$34 (US$27/UK£13) for children, and A$170 (US$136/UK£68) for a family. The second-day portion must be used within 8 days.

BY FERRY & JETCAT The best way to get a taste of a city that revolves around its harbor is to jump aboard a ferry. The main ferry terminal is at Circular Quay. Machines at each wharf dispense tickets. (There are also change machines.) For ferry information, call © **13 15 00** or visit the ferry information office opposite Wharf 4. Timetables are available for all routes.

One-way journeys within the inner harbor (virtually everywhere except Manly and Parramatta) cost A$5.20 (US$4/UK£2.60) for adults and A$2.60 (US$2/UK£1) for children aged 4 to 15. Kids under 4 travel free.

The **Travelten ferry ticket** costs A$34 (US$27/UK£13) for adults and A$17 (US$14/UK£7) for kids and is good for 10 trips within the inner harbor (this excludes Manly). Buy Travelten tickets at newsdealers, bus depots, or the Circular Quay ferry terminal. Tickets are transferable, so if two or more people travel together, you can use the same ticket.

The ferry to Manly takes 30 minutes and costs A$6.40 (US$5/UK£2.50) for adults and A$3.20 (US$2.50/UK£1.75) for children. It leaves from Wharf 3. The rapid Jet-Cat service to Manly takes 15 minutes and costs A$8.20 (US$4/UK£2) for both adults and children. A Manly Ferry Ten ticket (allowing 10 journeys) costs A$48 (US$38/UK£19) for adults and A$24 (US$19/UK£10) for kids, and a weekly JetCat ticket costs A$68 (US$54/UK£27) per person. After 7pm all trips to and from Manly are by JetCat at ferry prices. Ferries run from 6am to midnight.

BY CITYRAIL Sydney's publicly owned train system is a good news/bad news way to get around. The good news is that it can be a cheap and efficient way to see the city, the bad news is that the system is limited; many tourist areas—including Manly, Bondi Beach, and Darling Harbour—are not connected to the network. In the last few years, it's become even more problematic. While trains tend to run regularly, the idea of some sort of timetable has gone out of the window in the last few years when safety issues relating to a crash forced the state government to institute strict medical tests on its train drivers. The result, compounded with decades of underinvestment, meant drastic cuts to services—particularly on weekends.

Though a new timetable was introduced in late 2005, this should be viewed as a basic guide only. Single tickets within the city center cost A$2.40 (US$1.90/UK£1.20) for adults and A$1.20 (US95¢/UK45p) for children. Return (two-way) tickets cost A$4.80 (US$3.80/UK£1.70) for adults and A$2.40 (US$1.90/UK90p) for children for travel starting before 9am, and A$3.40 (US$2.70/UK£1.30) for adults and A$2.40 (US$1.90/UK£1) for children after 9am. To Bondi Junction from Circular Quay it costs A$2.80 (US$2.20/UK£1.10) for adults and A$1.40 (US$1.15/UK55p) for kids one-way, and return tickets cost A$5.60 (US$4.50/UK£2.75) for adults and A$2.80 (US$2.25/UK£1.10) for kids for travel starting before 9am and A$4 (US$3.20/UK£1.60) for adults and A$2.50 (US$2/UK£1) for kids for travel after 9am.

Prices regularly increase. Information is available from **Infoline** (✆ **13 15 00** in Australia).

BY COUNTRYLINK Comfortable and efficient **Countrylink** trains out of Central Station link the city with the far suburbs and beyond. For reservations, call ✆ **13 22 32** in Australia between 6:30am and 10pm, or visit the **Countrylink Travel Center** (✆ **02/9224 2742;** www.countrylink.info), Station Concourse, Wynyard CityRail station, for brochures and bookings.

BY METRO MONORAIL The metro monorail, with its single overhead line, is seen by many as a blight and by others as a futuristic addition to the city. The monorail connects the central business district to Darling Harbour—though it's only a 15-minute walk from Town Hall. The system operates Monday through Thursday from 7am to 10pm, Friday and Saturday from 7am to midnight, and Sunday from 8am to 10pm. Tickets are A$4.50 (US$3.60/UK£1.80), free for children under 5. An all-day monorail pass costs A$9 (US$7.20/UK£4.50). The trip from the city center to Darling Harbour takes around 12 minutes. Look for the gray overhead line and the plastic tubelike structures that are the stations. Call **Metro Monorail** (✆ **02/8584 5288;** www.metrolightrail.com.au) for more information.

BY METRO LIGHT RAIL A system of trams runs on a route that traverses a 3.6km (2¼-mile) track between Central Station and Wentworth Park in Pyrmont. It provides good access to Chinatown, Paddy's Markets, Darling Harbour, the Star City casino, and the Sydney Fish Markets. The trams run every 10 minutes. The one-way fare is A$3 to A$4 (US$2.40–US$3.20/UK£1.20–UK£1.60) for adults and A$1.80 to A$3 (US$1.40–US$2.40/UK75p–UK£1.20) for children 4 to 15, depending on distance. Two-way tickets are also available. A day pass costs A$8.40 (US$6.70/UK£3.30) for adults, A$6.50 (US$5.20/UK£2.60) for children, and A$20 (US$16/UK£8) for a family of five. Contact **Metro Light Rail** (✆ **02/8584 5288;** www.metrolightrail.com.au) for details.

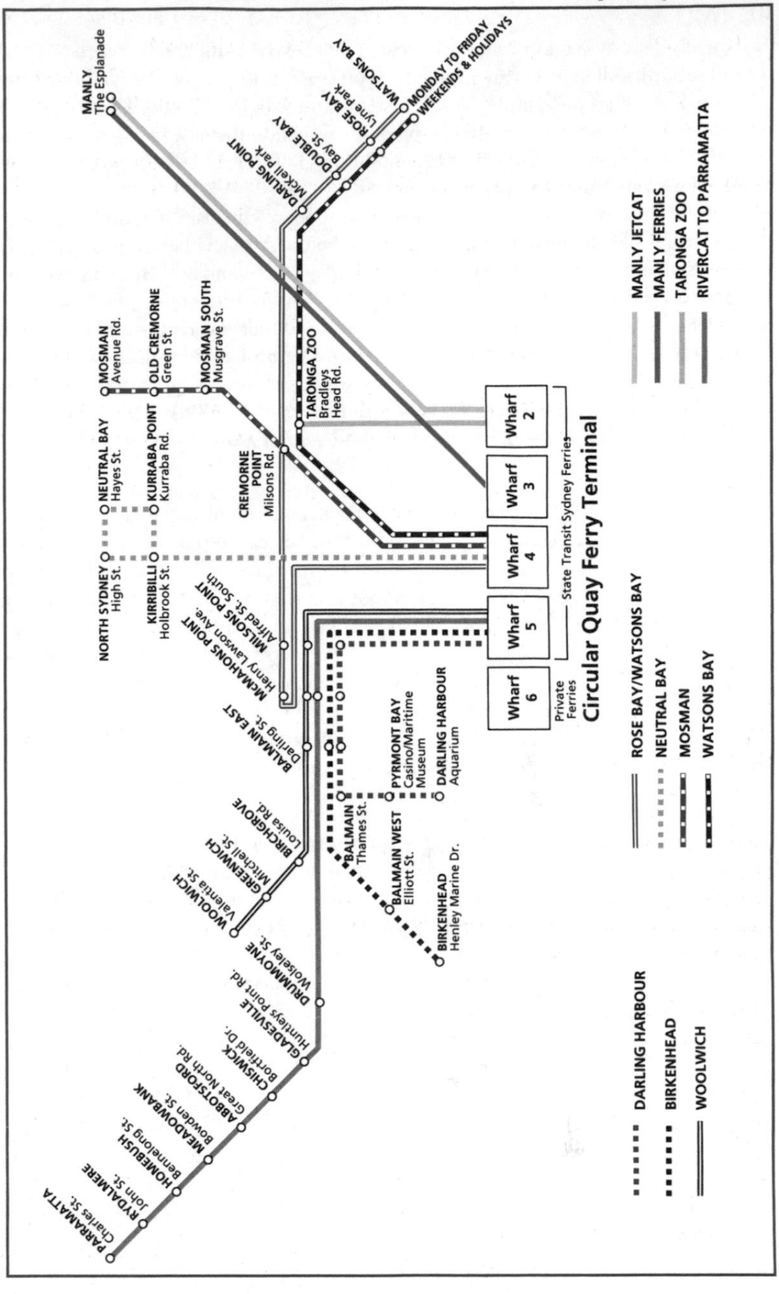
MANLY
The Esplanade
WATSONS BAY
ROSE BAY
Lyne Park
DOUBLE BAY
Bay St.
DARLING POINT
McKell Park
MONDAY TO FRIDAY
WEEKENDS & HOLIDAYS
MOSMAN
Avenue Rd.
OLD CREMORNE
Green St.
MOSMAN SOUTH
Musgrave St.
TARONGA ZOO
Bradleys
Head Rd.
NEUTRAL BAY
Hayes St.
KURRABA POINT
Kurraba Rd.
CREMORNE
POINT
Milsons Rd.
NORTH SYDNEY
High St.
KIRRIBILLI
Holbrook St.
MILSONS POINT
Alfred St. South
McMAHONS POINT
Henry Lawson Ave.
BALMAIN EAST
Darling St.
BIRCHGROVE
Louisa Rd.
GREENWICH
Mitchell St.
WOOLWICH
Valentia St.
DRUMMOYNE
Wolseley St.
GLADESVILLE
Huntleys Point Rd.
CHISWICK
Bortfield Dr.
ABBOTSFORD
Great North Rd.
MEADOWBANK
Bowden St.
HOMEBUSH
Bennelong St.
RYDALMERE
John St.
PARRAMATTA
Charles St.
BALMAIN
Thames St.
BALMAIN WEST
Elliott St.
BIRKENHEAD
Henley Marine Dr.
PYRMONT BAY
Casino/Maritime
Museum
DARLING HARBOUR
Aquarium
Wharf 2
Wharf 3
Wharf 4
Wharf 5
Wharf 6
Private
Ferries
State Transit Sydney Ferries
Circular Quay Ferry Terminal
MANLY JETCAT
MANLY FERRIES
TARONGA ZOO
RIVERCAT TO PARRAMATTA
ROSE BAY/WATSONS BAY
NEUTRAL BAY
MOSMAN
WATSONS BAY
DARLING HARBOUR
BIRKENHEAD
WOOLWICH

BY TAXI

Taxis are a relatively economical way to get around. Several companies serve the city center and suburbs. All journeys are metered. If you cross either way on the Harbour Bridge or through the Harbour Tunnel, it will cost an extra A$3 (US$2.40/UK£1.20)—a rip-off considering there's only an official toll on the way into the city. If you take the Eastern Distributor from the airport, it's A$4.50 (US$3.60/UK£1.80). An extra 10% will be added to your fare if you pay by credit card.

Taxis line up at stands in the city, such as those opposite Circular Quay and Central Station. They are also frequently found in front of hotels. A yellow light on top of the cab means it's vacant. Cabs can be hard to get on Friday and Saturday nights and between 2 and 3pm every day, when cabbies are changing shifts after 12 hours on the road. Some people prefer to sit up front, but it's certainly not considered rude if you don't. Passengers must wear seat belts in the front and back seats. The **Taxi Complaints Hotline** (© **1800/648 478** in Australia) deals with problem taxi drivers. Taxis are licensed to carry four people.

The main cab companies are **Taxis Combined** (© 13 33 00); **RSL Taxis** (© 02/9581 1111); **Legion Cabs** (© 13 14 51); and **Premier Cabs** (© 13 10 17).

BY WATER TAXI

Water taxis operate 24 hours a day and are a quick, convenient way to get to waterfront restaurants, harbor attractions, and some suburbs. They can also be chartered for private cruises. Fares for a direct transfer are based on an initial flag-fall for the hire of the vessel, then a charge per person traveling. On most transfers, the more people that are traveling, the lower the fare per person. The typical fare for a group of six people would be A$10 to A$15 (US$8–US$12/UK£4–UK£6) per person for an inner harbor jaunt. Sometimes you can combine with other people if you ring up well in advance. The main operators are **Water Taxis Combined** (© 02/9555 8888; www.watertaxis.com.au); **Beach Hopper** (© 0412 400 990 mobile; www.watertaxi.net.au); and **Yellow Water Taxis** (© 02/9299 0199; www.yellowwatertaxis.com).

BY CAR

Traffic restrictions, parking, and congestion can make getting around by car frustrating, but if you plan to visit some of the outer suburbs or take excursions elsewhere in New South Wales, then renting a car will give you more flexibility. The **National Roads and Motorists' Association (NRMA)** is the New South Wales auto club; for emergency breakdown service, call © **13 11 11.**

Car-rental agencies in Sydney include **Avis,** 214 William St., Kings Cross (© 1800/225 553); **Budget,** 93 William St., Kings Cross (© 13 27 27 in Australia, or 02/9339 8888); **Hertz,** corner of William and Riley streets, Kings Cross (© 13 30 39 in Australia); and **Thrifty,** 75 William St., Kings Cross (© 02/9380 5399). Avis, Budget, Hertz, and Thrifty also have desks at the airport. Rates average about A$60 (US$48/UK£24) per day for a small car. One of the best-value operations is **Bayswater Car Rentals,** 180 William St., Kings Cross (© 02/9360 3622; www.bayswatercarrental.com.au), which has small cars for around A$40 (US$32/UK£16) a day with everything included.

You can rent a motor home (called a "camper van" by some Aussies) from **Britz Campervans,** 653 Gardeners Rd., Mascot, NSW 2020 (© **1800/331 454** in Australia, or 02/9667 0402; www.britz.com). Plan to pay about A$105 (US$84/UK£42) a day for a two-person van in winter and around A$145 (US$116/UK£58) in summer. You can drop off your van at most state capitals and in Cairns, a convenience that costs an extra A$200 (US$160/UK£80).

CLOSED
due to
accidental demolition
WEGEN BISSIGEN
EICHHÖRNCHEN GESCHLOSSEN
CERRADO
CABRAS
Κλειστό
Μετεωρίτες
POOL CLOSED
プールも
閉鎖中
ELECTRIC EELS
FERMÉ POUR
RAISON
DE GRÈVE
DES BONNES
Hotel
closed for
facelifting
FECHADO!
POR CAUSA DE
ATAQUES DOS CROCODILOS

I don't speak
sign language.

FAST FACTS: Sydney

American Express The main Amex office is at Level 3, 130 Pitt St., near Martin Place (✆ **02/9236 4200**). It cashes traveler's checks and acts as a travel-booking service. It's open Monday through Friday from 8:30am to 5pm and Saturday from 9am to noon. Another foreign exchange office is on the walkway leading up to the Sydney Opera House (✆ **02/9251 1970**). If you've lost your traveler's checks, go to the head office, 175 Liverpool St. (✆ **02/9271 1111**). It's a locked security building so you'll need to call ahead.

Babysitters **Dial an Angel** (✆ **02/9416 7511** or 02/9362 4225) is a well-regarded babysitting service.

Business Hours General office and banking hours are Monday through Friday from 9am to 5pm. Many banks, especially in the city center, are open from around 9:30am to 12:30pm on Saturday. Shopping hours are usually from 8:30am to 5:30pm daily (9am–5pm Sat), and most stores stay open until 9pm on Thursday. Most city-center stores are open from around 10am to 4pm on Sunday.

Currency Exchange Most major bank branches offer currency exchange services. Small foreign-currency exchange offices are clustered at the airport and around Circular Quay and Kings Cross. **Thomas Cook** has offices at the airport; at 175 Pitt St. (✆ **02/9231 2877**), open Monday through Friday from 6:45am to 5:15pm and Saturday from 10am to 2pm; and on the lower ground floor of the QVB (✆ **02/9264 1133**), open Monday through Friday from 9am to 6pm (until 9pm Fri), Saturday from 9am to 6pm, and Sunday from 11am to 5pm.

Dentist A well-respected office in the city is **City Dental Practice,** Level 2, 229 Macquarie St., near Martin Place (✆ **02/9221 3300**). For dental problems after-hours, call **Dental Emergency Information** (✆ **02/9369 7050**).

Doctor The **Park Medical Centre,** Shop 4, 27 Park St. (✆ **02/9264 4488**), in the city center near Town Hall, is open Monday through Friday from 8am to 6pm; consultations cost A$40 (US$32/UK£16) for 15 minutes. (***Note:*** If you plan to take a dive course in Australia, get your medical exam done here. It costs A$70/US$56/UK£28, about the cheapest in Australia.) The **Kings Cross Travellers' Clinic,** Suite 1, 13 Springfield Ave., Kings Cross, just off Darlinghurst Road (✆ **1300/369 359** in Australia, or 02/9358 3066), is great for travel medicines and emergency contraception pills, among other things. Hotel visits in the Kings Cross area cost A$80 (US$64/UK£32); consultations cost A$40 (US$32/UK£16). The **Travellers' Medical & Vaccination Centre,** Level 7, 428 George St., in the city center (✆ **02/9221 7133**), stocks and administers travel-related vaccinations and medications.

Embassies & Consulates All foreign embassies are based in Canberra. You'll find the following consulates in Sydney: **United Kingdom,** Level 16, Gateway Building, 1 Macquarie Place, Circular Quay (✆ **02/9247 7521**); **New Zealand,** 55 Hunter St. (✆ **02/9223 0144**); **United States,** Level 59, MLC Centre, 19–29 Martin Place (✆ **02/9373 9200**); and **Canada,** Level 5, 111 Harrington St., The Rocks (✆ **02/9364 3000**).

Emergencies Dial ✆ **000** to call police, the fire service, or an ambulance. Call the **Emergency Prescription Service** (✆ **02/9235 0333**) for emergency drug prescriptions, and the NRMA for car breakdowns (✆ **13 11 11**).

Eyeglass Repair **Perfect Vision,** Shop C22A, in the Sydney Tower, 100 Market St. (✆ **02/9221 1010**), is open Monday through Friday from 9am to 6pm (until 9pm Thurs) and Saturday from 9am to 5pm. It's the best place to replace lost contact lenses; bring your prescription.

Holidays See "When to Go" in chapter 2. New South Wales also observes Labour Day on the first Monday in October.

Hospitals Make your way to **Sydney Hospital,** Macquarie Street, at the top end of Martin Place (✆ **02/9382 7111** for emergencies). **St. Vincent's Hospital** is at Victoria and Burton streets in Darlinghurst, near Kings Cross (✆ **02/9339 1111**).

Hot Lines Call the **Poisons Information Center** (✆ **13 11 26**); the **Gay and Lesbian Counselling Line** (✆ **02/9207 2800**; (5:30pm–10:30pm daily); the **Rape Crisis Center** (✆ **02/9819 6565**); or the **Crisis Center** (✆ **02/9358 6577**).

Internet Access Several Internet and e-mail centers are scattered around Kings Cross, Bondi, and Manly.

Lost Property There is no general lost property bureau in Sydney. Contact the nearest police station if you think you've lost something. For items lost on trains, contact the **Lost Property Office,** 494 Pitt St., near Central Railway Station (✆ **02/9379 3000**). The office is open Monday through Friday from 8:30am to 4:30pm. For items left behind on planes or at the airport, go to the Federal Airport Corporation's administration office on the top floor of the International Terminal at Sydney International Airport (✆ **02/9667 9583**). For stuff left behind on buses or ferries, call ✆ **02/9245 5777.** Each taxi company has its own lost property office.

Luggage Storage You can leave your bags at the International Terminal at the airport. The storage room charges around A$8 (US$6.40/UK£3.20) per bag for up to 6 hours and A$11 (US$9/UK£4.50) for up to 24 hours. The room is open from 4:30am to the last flight of the day. Call ✆ **02/9667 0926** for information. Otherwise, leave luggage at the cloakroom at Central Station, near the front of the main building (✆ **02/9219 4395**). Storage at the rail station costs A$5 (US$4/UK£2) per article per day. The **Travelers Contact Point,** seventh floor, 428 George St., above the Dymocks bookstore (✆ **02/9221 8744**), stores luggage for A$15 (US$12/UK£6) per piece per month. It also operates a general delivery service; has Internet access, a travel agency, and a jobs board; and ships items to the U.K. and Ireland.

Newspapers The *Sydney Morning Herald* is considered one of the world's best newspapers—by its management, at least—and is available throughout metropolitan Sydney. The equally prestigious *Australian* is available nationwide. The metropolitan *Daily Telegraph* is a more casual read and publishes a couple of editions a day. The *International Herald Tribune, USA Today,* the British *Guardian Weekly,* and other U.K. newspapers can be found at Circular Quay newspaper stands and most newsdealers.

Pharmacies (Chemist Shops) Most suburbs have pharmacies that are open late. For after-hours referral, contact the **Emergency Prescription Service** (✆ **02/9235 0333**).

Police In an emergency, dial ✆ **000.** Make nonemergency police inquiries through the Sydney Police Centre (✆ **02/9281 0000**).

Post Office The General Post Office (GPO) is at 130 Pitt St., not far from Martin Place (✆ **13 13 18** in Australia). It's open Monday through Friday from 8:30am to 5:30pm and Saturday from 10am to 2pm. General-delivery letters can be sent c/o Poste Restante, G.P.O., Sydney, NSW 2000, Australia (✆ **02/9244 3733**), and collected at 310 George St., on the third floor of the Hunter Connection shopping center. It's open Monday through Friday from 8:15am to 5:30pm. For directions to the nearest post office, call ✆ **1800/043 300.**

Restrooms These can be found in the QVB (second floor), at most department stores, at Central Station and Circular Quay, near the escalators by the Sydney Aquarium, and in the Harbourside Festival Marketplace in Darling Harbour.

Safety Sydney is an extremely safe city, but as anywhere else, it's good to keep your wits about you and your wallet hidden. If you wear a money belt, keep it under your shirt. Be wary in Kings Cross and Redfern at all hours and around Central Station and the cinema strip on George Street near Town Hall station in the evening—the latter is a hangout for local gangs, though they're usually busy holding each other up for their sneakers. Other places of concern are the back lanes of Darlinghurst, around the naval base at Woolloomooloo, and along the Bondi restaurant strip when beet-root red, drunken tourists spill out after midnight. Several people have reported thieves at the airport on occasion. If traveling by train at night, travel in the carriages next to the guard's van, marked with a blue light on the outside.

Taxes Australia imposes a 10% Goods and Services Tax (GST) on most goods sold in Australia and most services. The GST applies to most travel-related goods and services, including transport, hotels, tours, and restaurants. By law, the tax has to be included in the advertised price of the product, though it doesn't have to be displayed independently of the pretax price. See the box "Tourist Refund Scheme," p. 103.

Taxis See "Getting Around," earlier in this chapter.

Telephones Sydney's public phone boxes take coins, and many also accept credit cards and A$10 (US$8/UK£4) phone cards available from newsdealers. Local calls cost A40¢ (US25¢/UK£.15).

Transit Information Call the **Infoline** (✆ **13 15 00** in Australia) daily from 6am to 10pm.

Useful Telephone Numbers For news, dial ✆ **1199;** for the time, ✆ **1194;** for Sydney entertainment, ✆ **11 688;** for directory assistance, ✆ **12 455;** for Travelers Aid Society, ✆ **02/9211 2469.**

Weather For the local forecast, call ✆ **1196.**

3 Where to Stay

Although it's unlikely you'll find the city's hotels completely booked if you turn up looking for a bed for the night, it's probably wise to reserve rooms in advance.

DECIDING WHERE TO STAY The best location for lodging in Sydney is in The Rocks and around Circular Quay—a short stroll from the Sydney Opera House, the Harbour Bridge, the Royal Botanic Gardens, and the ferry terminals.

Hotels around Darling Harbour offer good access to the local facilities, including museums, the Sydney Aquarium, and the Star City casino. Most Darling Harbour hotels are a 10- to 15-minute walk, or a short monorail or light rail trip, from Town Hall and the central shopping district in and around Sydney Tower and Pitt Street Mall.

Another way to hunt for discounted hotel rooms is through an independent hotel search site. The two most popular are **www.lastminute.com.au** and **www.wotif.com**. Lastminute allows you to check prices of various room categories at least a month in advance. Wotif allows you to search for a room up to 14 days in the future. Hotels also provide both sites with special deals for rooms for the next couple of days.

More hotels are grouped around Kings Cross, Sydney's red-light district. Some of the hotels here are among the city's best, and you'll also find a range of cheaper lodgings, including several backpacker hostels. Kings Cross can be unnerving at any time, but especially on Friday and Saturday nights when the area's strip joints and nightclubs are jumping. Staying here does have its advantages: You get a real inner-city feel, and it's close to excellent restaurants and cafes around the Kings Cross, Darlinghurst, and Oxford Street areas.

Glebe, with its ethnic restaurants, is another inner-city suburb popular with tourists. It's well served by local buses.

If you want to stay near the beach, check out the options in Manly and Bondi, though you should consider their distance from the city center and the lack of CityRail trains to these areas. A taxi to Manly from the city will cost around A$37 (US$29/UK£15) and to Bondi around A$28 (US$22/UK£11).

MAKING A DEAL The prices given below for very expensive and expensive hotels are mostly the **rack rates,** the recommended retail price, which guests can pay at the busiest periods if they book at short notice or walk in off the street. Always ask about discounts, package deals, and any other special offerings when booking a hotel, especially if you are traveling in winter when hotels are less likely to be full. Ask about weekend discounts, corporate rates, and family plans.

Booking direct through a hotel's website can also yield savings. For instance, a search of the website for Accor, a company that manages 31 quality hotels in and

---

Value Last-Minute Room Deals

If you turn up in town without a reservation, you should definitely use the Sydney Visitors Centre bookings desk (**© 02/9667 6050**), in the arrivals hall of the airport's International Terminal. It negotiates deals with many of Sydney's hotels (but not hostels) and offers exceptional discounts on rooms that haven't been filled that day. You can save up to 50%. The desk is open from 6am to the last flight of the day. It also offers discounts on tours (to the Blue Mountains, for example) and cheap tickets for flights within Australia.

---

around Sydney, shows that you could save up to 50% of the rack rate. A double room at the four-star Mercure Hotel Sydney on Broadway, for example, can cost A$157 (US$125/UK£62), including breakfast. The rack rate is A$220 (US$176/UK£88) a night. A night at the four-star All Seasons Premier Menzies Hotel, near Wynyard, costs A$148 (US$118/UK£60) for a double room, including breakfast. The rack rate is A$300 (US$240/UK£120). On the Accor website (**www.accorhotels.com.au**), you can check rates months in advance.

Serviced apartments are also well worth considering because you can save a bundle by cooking your own meals; many also have free laundry facilities. We list a couple of choices below. Almost all hotels offer nonsmoking rooms; inquire when you make a reservation if it's important to you. Most moderately priced to very expensive rooms will have tea- and coffee-making facilities and an iron. Like hotels elsewhere, some of Sydney's lodgings are in on the increasing trend to rip off guests with pay-per-view movie channels (around A$16/US$13/UK£6.40 per movie), rather than to provide full access to a range of free cable TV channels.

By the way, coffeemakers as such are rare in Australian hotels, and where listed below they generally refer to tea- and coffee-making facilities (such as tea bags, instant coffee, small plastic milk cartons, and a kettle).

The price categories used are as follows: Very Expensive, A$300 (US$240/UK£120) and up; Expensive, A$200 to A$300 (US$160–US$240/UK£80–UK£120); Moderate, A$100 to A$200 (US$80–US$160/UK£40–UK£80); Inexpensive, below A$100 (US$80/UK£40). Prices are for a double. In Australia, a "double" room means you get one double, queen-size, or king-size bed in a room.

THE ROCKS/CIRCULAR QUAY

VERY EXPENSIVE

Four Seasons Hotel Sydney ★★ The Four Seasons features impressive views of Sydney Harbour and the Opera House and is perfectly positioned close to the historic Rocks district and the Sydney Opera House. The rooms are elegantly decorated, with marble bathrooms and plenty of mahogany, and though neither a modern nor a historic hotel—a bit of a 1970s block from the outside—it still has a nice charm about it. The staff is helpful and efficient, the outdoor pool is the largest in any hotel in Sydney, the spa is one of the city's best, and the restaurant, **Cables,** is a high-standard eatery, too. If you are traveling with kids then little touches, like a gingerbread man with your child's name iced across its chest, make it all the more welcoming.

199 George St., The Rocks, Sydney, NSW 2000. ✆ **02/9238 0000.** Fax 02/9251 2851. www.fourseasons.com/sydney. 531 units. A$350 (US$280/UK£140) city view double; A$395 (US$316/UK£158) Opera House view double; A$470 (US$376/UK£188) full harbor view double; A$530–A$1,050 (US$424–US$840/UK£212–UK£420) suite. Children under 14 stay free in parent's room. AE, MC, V. Parking A$27 (US$21/UK£10). Bus, train, ferry: Circular Quay. **Amenities:** Restaurant; bar; outdoor pool; health club; spa; sauna; concierge; business center; 24-hr. room service; babysitting; laundry service; dry cleaning. *In room:* A/C, TV w/pay movies, Wi-Fi minibar, hair dryer, safe.

Observatory Hotel ★★★ This exclusive hotel, a 10-minute walk uphill from The Rocks and 15 minutes from Circular Quay, is a turn-of-the-20th-century beauty competing for top-hotel-in-Sydney honors. It's fitted with antiques, objets d'art, and the finest carpets, wallpapers, and draperies. Plus, it's renowned for its personalized service. Rooms are plush and quiet, with huge bathrooms. Some rooms have city views; others look out over the harbor. The pool here is one of the best in Sydney: Note the Southern Hemisphere constellations on the roof. The day spa is one of the most exclusive in

Where to Stay in Central Sydney

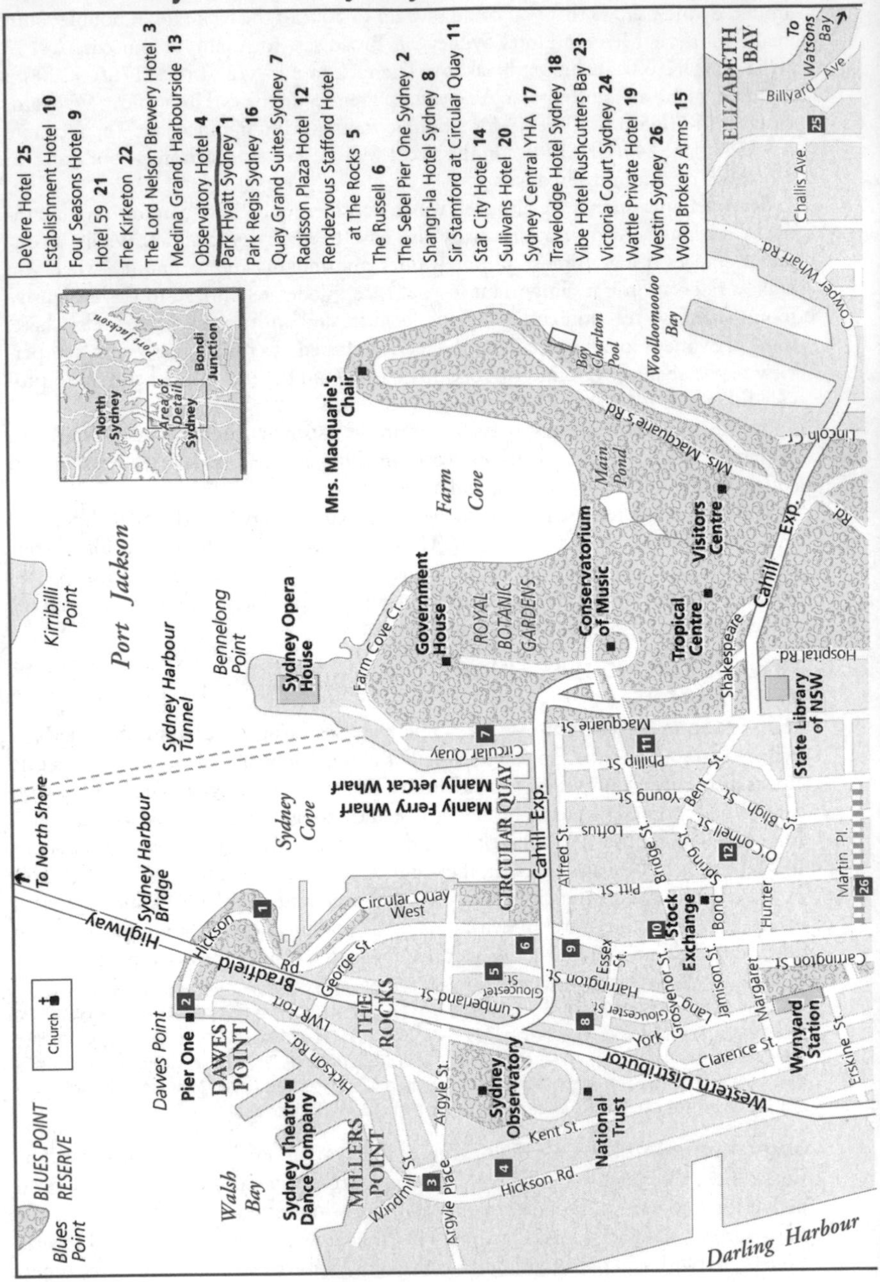
DeVere Hotel 25
Establishment Hotel 10
Four Seasons Hotel 9
Hotel 59 21
The Kirketon 22
The Lord Nelson Brewery Hotel 3
Medina Grand, Harbourside 13
Observatory Hotel 4
Park Hyatt Sydney 1
Park Regis Sydney 16
Quay Grand Suites Sydney 7
Radisson Plaza Hotel 12
Rendezvous Stafford Hotel at The Rocks 5
The Russell 6
The Sebel Pier One Sydney 2
Shangri-la Hotel Sydney 8
Sir Stamford at Circular Quay 11
Star City Hotel 14
Sullivans Hotel 20
Sydney Central YHA 17
Travelodge Hotel Sydney 18
Vibe Hotel Rushcutters Bay 23
Victoria Court Sydney 24
Wattle Private Hotel 19
Westin Sydney 26
Wool Brokers Arms 15
North Sydney
Area of Detail
Sydney
Bondi Junction
Port Jackson
Church
Blues Point
BLUES POINT RESERVE
Kirribilli Point
To North Shore
Sydney Harbour Bridge
Sydney Harbour Tunnel
Bennelong Point
Sydney Opera House
Walsh Bay
Dawes Point
DAWES POINT
Pier One
MILLERS POINT
Sydney Theatre Dance Company
THE ROCKS
Sydney Cove
Manly Ferry Wharf
Manly JetCat Wharf
CIRCULAR QUAY
Circular Quay West
Government House
ROYAL BOTANIC GARDENS
Farm Cove
Mrs. Macquarie's Chair
Conservatorium of Music
Main Pond
Tropical Centre
Visitors Centre
Bay Charlton Pool
Woolloomooloo Bay
ELIZABETH BAY
To Watsons Bay
Sydney Observatory
National Trust
Stock Exchange
State Library of NSW
Wynyard Station
Darling Harbour
Bradfield Highway
Western Distributor
Cahill Exp.
Hickson Rd.
Kent St.
Argyle St.
Argyle Place
Windmill St.
George St.
Cumberland St.
Gloucester St.
Harrington St.
Essex St.
York St.
Clarence St.
Erskine St.
Margaret St.
Jamison St.
Grosvenor St.
Lang
Carrington St.
Hunter
Bond
Martin Pl.
Pitt St.
Bridge St.
Alfred St.
Loftus
Young St.
Phillip St.
Macquarie St.
Spring St.
O'Connell St.
Bligh St.
Bent St.
Hospital Rd.
Shakespeare
Farm Cove Cr.
Mrs. Macquarie's Rd.
Lincoln Cr.
Cowper Wharf Rd.
Challis Ave.
Billyard Ave.

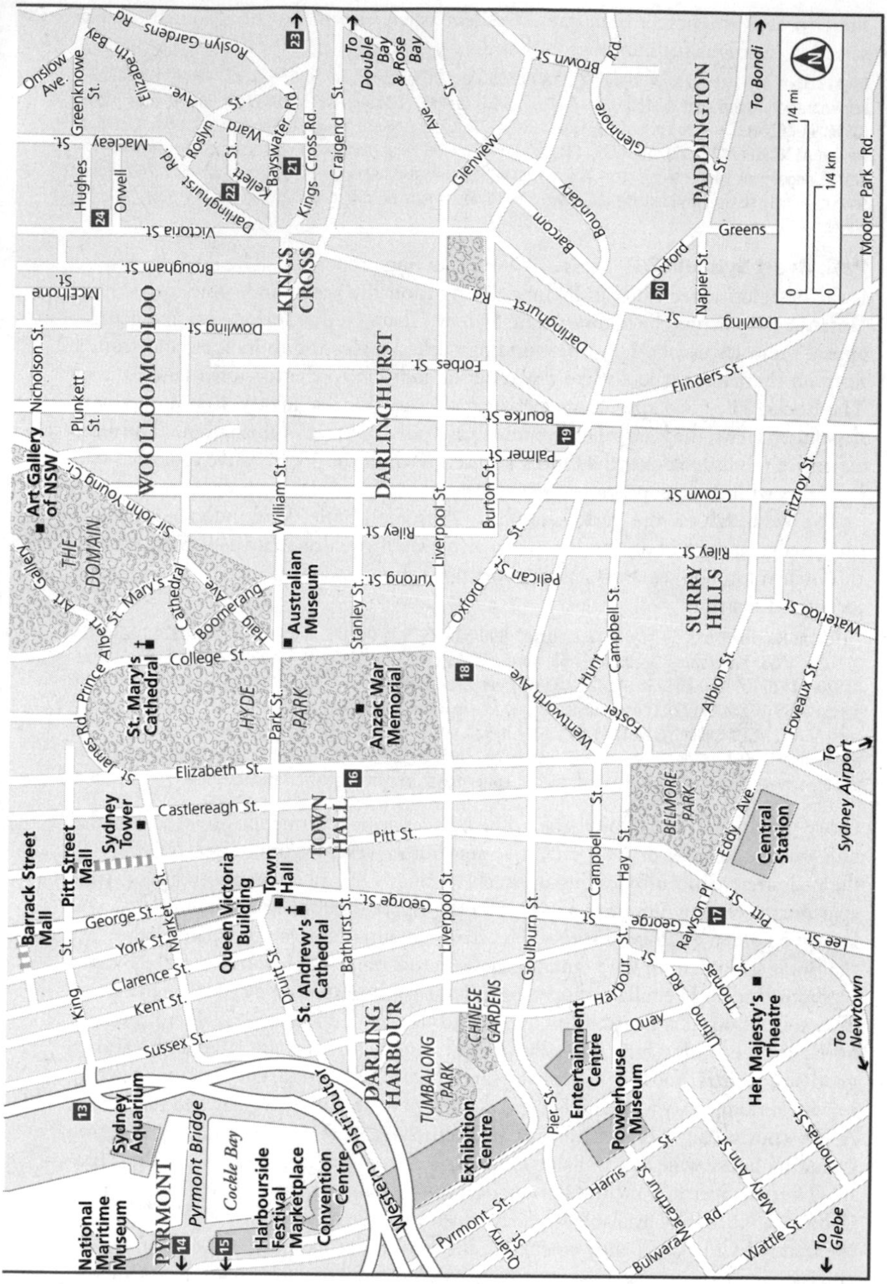

National Maritime Museum
PYRMONT
Pyrmont Bridge
Cockle Bay
Harbourside Festival Marketplace
Convention Centre
Sydney Aquarium
Western Distributor
DARLING HARBOUR
TUMBALONG PARK
CHINESE GARDENS
Exhibition Centre
Entertainment Centre
Powerhouse Museum
Her Majesty's Theatre
Barrack Street Mall
Pitt Street Mall
Sydney Tower
Queen Victoria Building
Town Hall
St. Andrew's Cathedral
TOWN HALL
HYDE PARK
St. Mary's Cathedral
Anzac War Memorial
Australian Museum
THE DOMAIN
Art Gallery of NSW
WOOLLOOMOOLOO
KINGS CROSS
DARLINGHURST
SURRY HILLS
BELMORE PARK
Central Station
PADDINGTON
To Double Bay & Rose Bay
To Bondi
To Sydney Airport
To Newtown
To Glebe
Onslow Ave.
Greenknowe St.
Elizabeth Bay Rd.
Roslyn Gardens
Macleay St.
Hughes St.
Orwell St.
Roslyn St.
Ward Ave.
Darlinghurst Rd.
Kellett St.
Bayswater Rd.
Kings Cross Rd.
Craigend St.
Victoria St.
Brougham St.
McElhone St.
Dowling St.
Nicholson St.
Plunkett St.
Sir John Young Cr.
Art Gallery Rd.
Prince Albert Rd.
St. Mary's Rd.
Cathedral St.
Boomerang St.
Haig Ave.
College St.
William St.
Stanley St.
Yurong St.
Riley St.
Liverpool St.
Burton St.
Forbes St.
Palmer St.
Bourke St.
Crown St.
Oxford St.
Pelican St.
Glenview St.
Brown St.
Glenmore Rd.
Barcom Ave.
Boundary St.
Greens Rd.
Napier St.
Flinders St.
Fitzroy St.
Moore Park Rd.
Campbell St.
Hunt St.
Foster St.
Wentworth Ave.
Albion St.
Waterloo St.
Foveaux St.
St. James Rd.
Elizabeth St.
Castlereagh St.
Pitt St.
George St.
Park St.
Bathurst St.
Goulburn St.
Hay St.
Eddy Ave.
Rawson Pl.
Lee St.
Thomas St.
Harbour St.
Ultimo Rd.
Quay St.
Pier St.
Harris St.
Macarthur St.
Mary Ann St.
Wattle St.
Bulwara Rd.
Pyrmont St.
Quarry St.
King St.
York St.
Market St.
Clarence St.
Kent St.
Sussex St.
Druitt St.
1/4 mi
1/4 km
0
0
N

the city, as is the hotel's restaurant, **Galileo,** where superb Japanese/French food is served in luxurious surroundings with a clubby feel.

89–113 Kent St., Sydney, NSW 2000. ✆ **1800/806 245** in Australia, or 02/9256 2222. Fax 02/9256 2233. www.observatoryhotel.com.au. 100 units. A$415–A$450 (US$332–US$360/UK£165–UK£180) double; from A$510 (US$408/UK£204) suite. Extra person A$66 (US$53/UK£26). Children under 14 stay free in parent's room. AE, MC, V. Parking A$30 (US$24/UK£12). Bus: 339, 431, or 433 to Millers Point. **Amenities:** Restaurant; bar; chemical-free heated indoor pool; floodlit tennis court; health club w/flotation tank; sauna; concierge; business center; 24-hr. room service; laundry service; dry cleaning. *In room:* A/C, TV w/pay movies, VCR, dataport, minibar, hair dryer, safe, CD player.

Park Hyatt Sydney ★★ This artistically curving property on The Rocks foreshore is the best-positioned hotel in Sydney. It's right on the water, and some rooms have fantastic views across the harbor to the Sydney Opera House. Its location and general appeal mean it's usually full. The building itself is a pleasure to look at, and from a ferry on the harbor it looks like a wonderful addition to the toy-town landscape of The Rocks. The good-size rooms incorporate every possible luxury. Room rates here depend on views; the least expensive units have only glimpses of the harbor. (The most expensive rooms look over the Opera House.) Each of the 33 executive suites has two balconies with a telescope.

The **Verandah on the Park** restaurant offers good buffet food indoors or outside on the edge of the harbor, and is worth a visit even if you don't stay here. Visit the Little Kitchen for high tea, the Club Bar for cognacs and a Cuban, and the Harbour Bar for a good martini.

7 Hickson Rd., The Rocks, Sydney, NSW 2000. ✆ **800/633-7313** in the U.S. and Canada, or 02/9241 1234. Fax 02/9256 1555. www.sydney.hyatt.com. 158 units. A$650–A$700 (US$520–US$560/UK£260–UK£280) double; A$820–A$920 (US$656–US$736/UK£328–UK£368) executive studio; from A$1,000 (US$800/UK£400) suite. Extra person A$55 (US$44/UK£22). Children under 18 stay free in parent's room. Ask about weekend discounts and packages. AE, DC, MC, V. Parking A$22 (US$17/UK£13). CityRail, bus, or ferry: Circular Quay. **Amenities:** 2 restaurants; bar and lounge; heated outdoor pool; health club and spa; concierge; business center; 24-hr. room service; babysitting; laundry service. *In room:* A/C, TV, dataport, minibar, coffeemaker, hair dryer, iron/ironing board, safe.

Quay Grand Suites Sydney ★★ The best serviced-apartment complexes, like this one, can outdo superior AAA-rated five-star hotels—even in price. This building, on the pedestrian concourse leading up to the Sydney Opera House, also houses private apartments costing upwards of A$750,000 (US$600,000/UK£300,000)—so you know you are in exclusive territory. The spacious, ultramodern apartments either face the Botanic Gardens or have fantastic views across the ferry terminals and the Sydney Harbour Bridge. The fully equipped units have balconies so you can admire the views. The noises from the CityRail station (including train announcements) and the ferry horns are captivating but can easily be shut out. Bathrooms are large and feature a good-size Jacuzzi. You might want to eat at the hotel's **Quadrant** restaurant, which serves Contemporary food and has spectacular views to Circular Quay and the harbor. A two-course daily "Lunch Special" here costs A$59 (US$47/UK£23) per person including house wine. It's available on weekdays from noon until 2pm. A "Pre-Theatre Dinner Special" includes a main course and a glass of wine for A$35 (US$28/UK£14). It's available Monday to Saturday from 5:30 to 7:30pm. The bar is the trendy ECQ. The Dendy cinema, in the same strip, has good art-house movies.

61 Macquarie St., E. Circular Quay, Sydney, NSW 2000. ✆ **1800/091 954** in Australia, or 02/9256 4000. Fax 02/9256 4040. www.mirvachotels.com.au. A$335–A$507 (US$268–US$405/UK£134–UK£202) 1-bedroom apt. Extra person A$35 (US$28/UK£14). Ask about weekend packages and long-term discounts. AE, DC, MC, V. Valet parking A$20 (US$16/UK£8). CityRail, bus, or ferry: Circular Quay. **Amenities:** Restaurant; bar; small health club; concierge; 24-hr.

room service; massage; babysitting; laundry service; dry cleaning; nonsmoking rooms. *In room:* A/C, TV w/pay movies, dataport, kitchen, minibar, coffeemaker, hair dryer, iron/ironing board, washing machine, dryer.

Shangri-la Hotel Sydney ★★ For a room with a view, you're not going to do better than this ultramodern landmark hotel with a touch of Asian flair. It's just a 5-minute walk from Circular Quay. Try to book a room on the 20th floor or above: From here Sydney and its harbor is laid out at your feet, with ferries buzzing around below you like bathtub toys. All rooms are contemporarily furnished and rely on the views perhaps more than the decor to impress. The top five room floors, from level 29 to 34, have use of the Horizon Club lounge. This supplies breakfast and evening canapés. The trendy **Café Mix** on level 1 serves breakfasts and has a good lunch and dinner buffet with contemporary and Asian-style meals (including Japanese). Also here is The Rocks Tepenyaki restaurant, which serves good Japanese cuisine. The stylish **Altitude** restaurant and **Blue Horizon Bar** (both on the 36th floor), have panoramic harbor views. The associated historic Harts Pub, at street level, offers a lunchtime Aussie barbecue in the beer garden Tuesdays to Fridays.

176 Cumberland St., The Rocks, Sydney, NSW 2000. ✆ **1800/801 088** in Australia, or 02/9250 6000. Fax 02/9250 6250. www.shangri-la.com. 563 units. A$450–A$500 (US$360–US$400/UK£180–UK£200) double; A$750 (US$600/UK£300) corner room; A$550–A$4,900 (US$440–US$3,920/UK£220–UK£2,000) suite. Extra person A$60 (US$48/UK£24). Children stay free in parent's room. Ask about packages. AE, DC, MC, V. Parking A$21 (US$17/UK£8). CityRail or ferry: Circular Quay. **Amenities:** 2 restaurants; lounge; 2 bars; heated indoor pool; exercise room; Jacuzzi; sauna; concierge; business center; salon; 24-hr. room service; babysitting; laundry service; currency exchange; early-arrivals/late-departures lounge. *In room:* A/C, TV w/pay movies, dataport, minibar, hair dryer, iron/ironing board, safe.

Sir Stamford at Circular Quay ★★ From the moment the doorman doffs his top hat to you, you enter the world of aristocracy, complete with the slight scent of cigar smoke and aged brandy in the air. This hotel has a prime location, just a short walk from Circular Quay and the Opera House, and just across the road from the Royal Botanic Gardens. Rooms are exceptionally large and luxurious, with good-size marble bathrooms—though, to be honest, it may be time for a refurbishment. Most rooms have a small balcony. The rooms on the east side of the hotel have the best views across the Botanic Gardens. Most rooms are accessible to wheelchairs.

93 Macquarie St., Sydney, NSW 2000. ✆ **1300/301 391** in Australia, or 02/9252 4600. Fax 02/9252 4286. www.stamford.com.au. 105 units. A$540 (US$432/UK£215) double; A$580 (US$464/UK£232) deluxe harbor-view double; A$705–A$3,000 (US$564–US$2,400/UK£280–UK£1,200) Sir Stamford presidential suite. AE, DC, MC, V. Parking A$40 (US$32/UK£16). CityRail, bus, or ferry: Circular Quay. **Amenities:** Restaurant; bar; solar-heated outdoor pool; exercise room; sauna; concierge; business center; 24-hr. room service; babysitting; laundry service; currency exchange. *In room:* A/C, TV w/pay movies, fax, dataport, minibar, hair dryer, iron/ironing board, safe.

EXPENSIVE

Rendezvous Stafford Hotel at The Rocks The Stafford offers some of the best-positioned serviced apartments in Sydney, right in the heart of The Rocks, very close to the harbor and Circular Quay, and a short stroll from the central business district. The property consists of modern apartments in a six-story building (the best units, for their harbor and Opera House views, are on the top three floors) and seven two-story terrace houses dating from 1870 to 1895. The Stafford is highly recommended for its location, spacious rooms, and varying kitchen facilities. Studio rooms are the least expensive and come with a choice of a queen-size bed or two single beds, a shower over a tub, a microwave, toaster, and refrigerator.

75 Harrington St., The Rocks, Sydney, NSW 2000. ✆ **02/9251 6711.** Fax 02/9251 3458. www.rendezvoushotels.com. 61 units. A$235–A$275 (US$188–US$220/UK£94–UK£110) studio double; A$280 (US$225/UK£112) 1-bedroom apt;

A$320 (US$256/UK£128) executive 1-bedroom apt; A$295 (US$236/UK£118) terrace house; A$370 (US$295/UK£150) 1-bedroom penthouse. Extra person A$15 (US$12/UK£6). Children under 12 stay free in parent's room. Ask about weekly discounts. AE, DC, MC, V. Parking A$15 (US$12/UK£6). CityRail or ferry: Circular Quay. **Amenities:** Small outdoor pool; exercise room; Jacuzzi; sauna; tour desk; car-rental desk; business center; limited room service; babysitting; laundry service; dry cleaning. *In room:* A/C, TV, dataport, kitchen, minibar, coffeemaker, hair dryer, iron/ironing board.

The Russell ★★ *Finds* This is the coziest place to stay in The Rocks, and perhaps in all of Sydney. It's more than 100 years old, and it shows its age wonderfully in the creaks of the floorboards and the ramshackle feel of the brightly painted corridors. Every room is different in style, size, and shape; all come with a queen-size bed, and most have cable TV. (Others can have a TV moved in if requested.) All rooms have immense character, including a series of rooms added on in 1990 above the Fortune of War Hotel next door. There are no harbor views, but from some rooms you can see the tops of the ferry terminals at Circular Quay. Guests have the use of a sitting room, a living room with magazines and books, and a rooftop garden. The apartment is a large, open-plan unit with a king-size bed and small kitchen; it's suitable for three people (there's a double sofa bed). It overlooks Circular Quay.

143A George St., The Rocks, Sydney, NSW 2000. © **02/9241 3543.** Fax 02/9252 1652. www.therussell.com.au. 29 units, 19 with bathroom. A$140–A$195 (US$112–US$156/UK£62–UK£78) double without bathroom; A$235–A$270 (US$188–US$216/UK£94–UK£108) double with bathroom; A$280 (US$224/UK£112) suite or apt. Extra person A$30 (US$24/UK£12). Rates include continental breakfast. AE, DC, MC, V. No parking available. CityRail or ferry: Circular Quay. **Amenities:** Restaurant; lounge. *In room:* TV, coffeemaker, iron/ironing board.

The Sebel Pier One Sydney ★ *Finds* A premier waterfront hotel, The Sebel is in the historic Woolloomooloo Wharf complex and has been painstakingly renovated, leaving as much of the original structure intact as possible. It's a wonderfully intoxicating blend of old wooden beams and tasteful modern art. The only drawback to staying in one of the tastefully appointed waterfront rooms is that the harbor views—through windows that run all the way to the polished wooden floorboards—could make you want to stay in for the rest of the day. Or perhaps the cocktail bar, one of the trendiest in town, is more your scene.

11 Hickson Rd., Walsh Bay, Sydney, NSW 2000. © **1800/780 485** in Australia. Fax 02/8298 9777. www.mirvachotels.com.au. 160 units. A$235 (US$188/UK£94) double; A$290 (US$232/UK£116) waterfront room. Rates include breakfast. AE, DC, MC, V. CityRail or ferry: Circular Quay. Bus: George St. **Amenities:** Restaurant; bar; gym; Jacuzzi; outdoor terrace. *In room:* A/C, TV, dataport, minibar, hair dryer, iron/ironing board, safe.

MODERATE

The Lord Nelson Brewery Hotel Sydney's oldest pub was established in 1841 after serving as a private residence since its construction in 1836. It's an attractive, three-story sandstone building with a busy pub on the ground floor, a good brasserie on the second, and hotel accommodations on the third. The rooms are compact and simple, but spacious enough to swing your bags around without hitting the walls. From its creaky floorboards and bedroom walls made from convict-hewn sandstone blocks, to the narrow corridors, the wood fire, and the homemade beer in the bar, The Lord Nelson positively wallows in colonial atmosphere.

At the corner of Kent and Argyle sts., The Rocks, Sydney, NSW 2000. © **02/9251 4044.** Fax 02/9251 1532. www.lordnelsonbrewery.com. 9 units, 8 with bathroom. A$120 (US$96/UK£48) double without bathroom; A$180 (US$144/UK£72) double with bathroom. Extra person A$30 (US$24/UK£12). Rates include continental breakfast. AE, DC, MC, V. No parking available. CityRail or ferry: Circular Quay. **Amenities:** 2 restaurants; bar. *In room:* TV, fax, coffeemaker, hair dryer, iron/ironing board.

CITY CENTER

VERY EXPENSIVE

Establishment Hotel ★★★ Sydney's coolest hotel offers sleek modernist rooms in two styles: one with beautifully restored warehouse ceilings, japan black floorboards, and flashes of strong color, and the other more tranquil in color and softer in feel. All rooms come with generous-size marble or bluestone bathrooms. If you are a superstar with a taste for the cutting-edge of fashion then this is where you'd choose to stay. In the same building you'll find one of Sydney's best restaurants, **est.,** and the small but gorgeous **Sushi E.** Also here are a couple of trendy bars, and the popular Tank nightclub. The building is a historic Sydney landmark, but the feel is "now" rather than then.

5 Bridge Lane (off George St., near Wynyard CityRail Station), Sydney, NSW 2000. ✆ **02/9240 3110.** Fax 02/9240 3101. www.merivale.com. A$350 (US$280/UK£140) Junior Room; A$415 (US$332/UK£166) Establishment Room; A$970–A$1,150 (US$776–US$920/UK£388–UK£460) penthouse. AE, DC, MC, V. Parking A$35 (US$28/UK£14). CityRail: Wynyard. **Amenities:** 2 restaurants; 2 bars; gym; concierge; 24-hr. room service; nightclub. *In room:* A/C, TV, dataport, minibar, coffeemaker, hair dryer, iron/ironing board, safe, CD/DVD.

Radisson Plaza Hotel Sydney ★★ Right in the heart of the city in a gorgeous heritage building, the Radisson Plaza Hotel Sydney has chic rooms, with muted chocolate tones and sensual fabrics. Each guest room features an en-suite bathroom with marble vanity, separate shower, and extra-deep European-style bathtub. Premier Rooms feature a king-size, queen-size, or two double beds; Atrium Rooms overlook the light well, which is open to the sky. Deluxe Rooms are located on the 11th and 12th floors of the hotel and feature full-length glass doors which open onto a Juliet-style balcony. Studio Spa Suites are larger and open plan, while One Bedroom Spa Suites have a separate living area, and balcony. All in all, it's a modern-style business/leisure hotel with a very nice feel.

27 O'Connell St., Sydney, NSW 2000. ✆ **800/333-3333** in the U.S., 1800 333 333 in Australia, or 02/8214 0000. Fax 02/8214 1000. www.radisson.com/sydneyau_plaza. 362 units. A$300 (US$240/UK£120) Premier and Atrium rooms; A$330 (US$264/UK£132) Deluxe Room; A$394 (US$315/UK£157) suite; A$430 (US$344/UK£174) 1 bedroom. AE, DC, MC, V. Parking A$35 (US$28/UK£14). CityRail: Wynyard. **Amenities:** Restaurant; bar; heated indoor lap pool; gym; sauna; concierge; business center; 24-hr. room service; massage; babysitting; laundry service; currency exchange. *In room:* A/C, TV, dataport, minibar, coffeemaker, hair dryer, iron/ironing board, safe.

Sydney Harbour Marriott ★ One of two Marriotts in town, this well-located property is a quick stroll to Circular Quay and The Rocks by foot. A third of the rooms have views over the harbor, with the Deluxe BridgeView rooms and the Deluxe Opera View rooms having the pick of the vantage points. The semi-indoor/outdoor pool is reasonable, the contemporary rooms are a fair size and always nice and bright, and each room features an large work desk area and a safe for your laptop. The historic Customs House Bar down below has a nice courtyard for an outside drinkie.

30 Pitt St. (corner of Alfred St.), Sydney, NSW 2000. ✆ **800 251 259** in Australia, 02/9259 7000. Fax 02/9251 1122. www.marriott.com.au. 550 units. A$550–$850 (US$440–$680/UK£220–340) always check for online specials/packages, which can reduce rates considerably) double. AE, DC, MC, V. rack rates. Parking A$35CityRail: Circular Quay. **Amenities:** Restaurant; bar; pool; gym; concierge; 24-hr. room service. *In room:* A/C, TV, dataport, minibar, coffeemaker, hair dryer, iron/ironing board, safe.

Westin Sydney ★ One of Sydney's most celebrated AAA-rated five-star hotels, the Westin is in the center of the city, in the Martin Place pedestrian mall. Integrated into a former post office from the 19th century, the Westin's charm is modern and classic all at once. The large rooms have comfortable beds and floor-to-ceiling windows. The hotel is home to several bars, restaurants, and clothing shops. Just steps from the central shopping streets and the QVB, and a 10- to 15-minute walk to both the Sydney Opera House and Darling Harbour, the hotel features an impressive seven-story atrium, a wonderful two-level health club, and an exclusive day spa.

1 Martin Place, Sydney, NSW 2000. ✆ **800/WESTIN-1** in the U.S., or 02/8223 1111. Fax 02/8223 1222. www.westin.com.au. 416 units. A$286 (US$229/UK£115) double. AE, DC, MC, V. Parking A$25 (US$20/UK£10). CityRail: Martin Place. **Amenities:** Cafe; bar; day spa; massage; babysitting; laundry service; currency exchange. *In room:* A/C, TV, dataport, minibar, coffeemaker, hair dryer, iron/ironing board, safe.

EXPENSIVE

Park Regis Sydney This hotel occupies the top 15 floors of a 45-story building and is well placed in the central business district, 2 blocks from Hyde Park and Town Hall. There's nothing spectacular about it, but the rooms are light, modern, and practical. The hotel was refurbished in 2006 and it looks much better for it. Many of the guests are business travelers, which gives the hotel a corporate feel. Nevertheless, it's a relatively good value considering the location. Rooms at the front have views over the city and park. All guests have access to the roof terrace which has a pool and great views.

27 Park St. (at Castlereagh St.), Sydney, NSW 2000. ✆ **1800/060 954** in Australia, or 02/9267 6511. Fax 02/9264 2252. www.leisureinnhotels.com.au. 120 units, all with shower only. A$175 (US$140/UK£70) double; A$198 (US$154/UK£100) suite. Extra person A$22 (US$18/UK£9). Children under 14 stay free in parent's room. Aussie auto club discounts available. AE, DC, MC, V. Parking A$20 (US$16/UK£8). CityRail: Town Hall. Monorail: Park Plaza. **Amenities:** Small heated outdoor pool; concierge; tour desk; 24-hr. room service; babysitting; laundry service; dry cleaning; nonsmoking rooms. *In room:* A/C, TV, fridge, coffeemaker, hair dryer.

MODERATE

Travelodge Hotel Sydney ★ This three-and-a-half-star business-oriented hotel is cheap for Sydney, comfortable, and reasonably well located—making it a good option for travelers who just want to unpack and explore. The rooms are Ikea-like in appearance, with a queen-size bed or twin beds. All come with a kitchenette with a microwave. From here it's a short walk to Oxford Street, Town Hall, Hyde Park, and the monorail to Darling Harbour. The more upmarket **Travelodge Wynyard** (7–9 York St.; ✆ **02 9274 1222**) is more in the heart of the action and is surrounded by cafes and restaurants. It underwent renovation in 2007. Rooms here are nice and plush and cost A$174 (US$139/UK£70) for a standard room, A$195 (US$156/UK£78) for an executive room (with better views), and A$277 (US$221/UK£111) for larger rooms and studio apartments.

27–33 Wentworth Ave., Sydney, NSW 2000. ✆ **1300 886 886** in Australia, or 02/8267 1700. Fax 02/8267 1800. www.travelodge.com.au. 406 units. A$119 (US$95/UK£47) double or twin. Extra person A$16 (US$13/UK£7.50). AE, DC, MC, V. Parking around corner A$17 (US$14/UK£7). CityRail: Museum. **Amenities:** Restaurant; massage; babysitting; nonsmoking rooms. *In room:* A/C, TV, dataport, kitchenette, fridge, coffeemaker, hair dryer, iron/ironing board.

INEXPENSIVE

Sydney Central YHA ★★ *Value* This multiple-award-winning hostel is one of the biggest and busiest in the world. With a 98% year-round occupancy rate, you'll have to book early. It's in a historic nine-story building, and offers far more than standard basic accommodations. In the basement is the Scu Bar, a popular drinking hole with pool tables and occasional entertainment. There's also an entertainment room with more pool tables and e-mail facilities, TV rooms on every floor, and an audiovisual room that shows movies. Rooms are clean and basic. Three dorm rooms hold eight people each; 24 sleep up to six; and 70 accommodate four. The YHA is accessible to travelers with disabilities.

A new hostel, the **Railway Square YHA** (8–10 Lee St., at the corner of Upper Carriage Lane and Lee St., or enter via the Henry Dean Plaza, Sydney, NSW 2000; © **02/9281 9666;** fax 02/9281 9688) opened in 2004. The 64-bed hostel offers four-to-eight-bed dorms and 10 double rooms in a historic 1904 building adjoining "Platform Zero" at Central Railway Station. Some dorm rooms are even located in railway carriages. There's a spa pool, Internet cafe, tour desk, indoor and outdoor communal areas, and a self-catering kitchen. Dorm rooms cost from A$27 to A$33 (US$22–US$26/UK£11–UK£13) a night, doubles with shared bathroom are A$78 (US$62/UK£31), and doubles with bathroom are A$88 (US$70/UK£35).

There are more than 140 YHA hostels in Australia. Check the website for the full list, which includes other hostels in Sydney, such as the **Glebe Point YHA,** the **Sydney Beachhouse YHA** in the beachside suburb of Collaroy, and **Pittwater YHA** in Ku-ring-gai Chase National Park (accessible only by boat, and a fabulous way to experience the "bush" around Sydney).

11 Rawson Place (at Pitt St., outside Central Station), Sydney, NSW 2000. © **02/9281 9111.** Fax 02/9281 9199. www.yha.com.au. 97 dorm units with 448 beds; 54 twin units, 43 with bathroom. A$28–A$33 (US$22–US$26/UK£11–UK£13) dorm bed; A$82 (US$66/UK£33) twin without bathroom; A$94 (US$75/UK£37) twin with bathroom. Non-YHA members are charged an extra A$3.50 (US$2.80/UK£1.40) per night. MC, V. Parking A$12 (US$9.60/UK£4.80). CityRail: Central. **Amenities:** Restaurant; bar; small heated outdoor pool; sauna; 2 kitchens; TV room. *In room:* No phone.

AT DARLING HARBOUR

VERY EXPENSIVE

Star City Hotel ★★ Opened in 1997, this A$900-million (US$720-million/UK£360-million) gambling and entertainment complex includes an AAA-rated five-star hotel, with rooms overlooking Darling Harbour and the architecturally interesting Pyrmont Bridge. Although the four split-level Royal Suites are spectacular—each with three TVs, a giant Jacuzzi, a full kitchen, two bathrooms, its own sauna, and the services of the former butler to the governor of Queensland—the standard rooms are somewhat small. Executive suites are very nice. If you break the casino, use your winnings to pay for a room with views over Darling Harbour. The excellent **Astral** restaurant is on the summit of the hotel tower on Level 17. The views are great, the food is divine, and the menu is varied. A three-course a la carte meal costs A$95 (US76/UK£38) , $A85 for vegetarians).

80 Pyrmont St., Pyrmont, Sydney, NSW 2009. © **1800/700 700** in Australia, or 02/9777 9000. Fax 02/9657 8344. www.starcity.com.au. 491 units. A$350–A$370 (US$280–US$296/UK£140–UK£150) double; from A$510 (US$408/UK£202) and way up suite. Extra person A$40 (US$32/UK£20). Ask about special packages. AE, DC, MC, V. Parking A$20 (US$16/UK£10). Ferry: Pyrmont Bay. Monorail: Harbourside. Light Rail: Star City. **Amenities:** 4 restaurants; large heated outdoor pool; Jacuzzi; sauna; concierge; free shuttle bus from central business district; business center; shopping arcade; salon; 24-hr. room service; massage; laundry service; 2 theaters; currency exchange; casino *In room:* A/C, TV, dataport, minibar, coffeemaker, hair dryer.

EXPENSIVE

Medina Grand, Harbourside ★★ This impressive serviced hotel (which is essentially a furnished apartment with maid service) offers modern, very comfortable rooms at competitive prices. It's a little oddly placed—reached by an offshoot road and a short, unattractive walk from the Sydney Aquarium in Darling Harbour—but it makes up for it by being close to all of the Darling Harbour, Cockle Bay, and Town

Tips Homes Away from Home

Medina, the company behind the Medina Grand, Harbourside, operates several other serviced-apartment complexes in Sydney. They include the **Medina Executive,** Sydney Central (© **02/8396 9800**), in a historic building near Central Station; the pleasant **Medina Classic** in Martin Place (© **02/9224 6400**); coastal **Medina Executive,** near Coogee Beach (© **02/9578 6000**); and the AAA-rated five-star **Medina Grand,** Sydney (© **02/9274 0000**), between Town Hall and Darling Harbour. Check the website (www.medinaapartments.com.au) for prices and details about these highly recommended properties. Rates range from A$165 to A$488 (US$132–US$390/UK£66–UK£195), with many prices and combinations in between.

Hall attractions and shops. You can choose between studio and one-bedroom apartments, which all come with Italian designer furniture, large windows, and balconies (some with good harbor views). Studio units come with a kitchenette, and one-bedroom units come with a fully equipped kitchen and a second TV. All have dataports. Medina offers very good package and weekend rates, which means this place can work out to be a real bargain. Higher prices listed are for water-view units.

Corner of Shelley and King sts., King St. Wharf, Sydney, NSW 2000. © **1300/300 232** in Australia, or 02/9249 7000. Fax 02/9249 6900. www.medinaapartments.com.au. 114 units. A$238–A$254 (US$190–US$203/UK£95–UK£101) studio; A$265–A$330 (US$212–US$264/UK£106–UK£132) 1-bedroom apt. AE, DC, MC, V. CityRail: Town Hall. **Amenities:** Small heated indoor pool; exercise room; concierge; tour desk; business center; laundry service; nonsmoking rooms. *In room:* A/C, TV, dataport, kitchenette, minibar, coffeemaker, hair dryer, iron/ironing board.

MODERATE

Wool Brokers Arms You'll find this friendly 1886 heritage building on the far side of Darling Harbour, next to the prominent AAA-rated four-star Novotel hotel and hidden behind a monstrous aboveground parking garage. It's on a noisy road, so unless you're used to traffic, avoid the rooms at the front. Rooms are simply furnished, with a double bed and a sink. Room no. 3 is one of the nicer ones. Family rooms have a king-size bed, a set of bunks, and two singles through an open doorway. There are 19 shared bathrooms. It's adequate for a few nights.

22 Allen St., Pyrmont, Sydney, NSW 2009. © **02/9552 4773.** Fax 02/9552 4771. www.ozemail.com.au/~woolbrokers. 26 units, none with bathroom. A$89 (US$71/UK£45) double; A$110 (US$88/UK£44) triple; A$130 (US$104/UK£52) family room for 4. Rates include continental breakfast. Extra person A$20 (US$16/UK£8). AE, MC, V. Parking A$11 (US$8.80/UK£4.40) nearby. Bus: 501 from central business district or Central Station. Light Rail: Convention Centre. **Amenities:** Tour desk; coin-op laundry; nonsmoking rooms. *In room:* TV.

IN KINGS CROSS & THE SUBURBS BEYOND

EXPENSIVE

The Kirketon ★ If you want to stay somewhere a bit offbeat and class yourself as a hip, fashionable type, then this boutique hotel in Darlinghurst is a fascinating option. Rooms come with king-size, queen-size, double, or twin beds, and are lightly stocked with modernist furniture and custom-made fittings, including mirrored headboards, sleek bathrooms hidden away behind mirrored doors, and interestingly textured bedspreads and areas of wallpaper. All in all, the decor is fun if you like this sort of thing, although I found it jarred with my more conventional taste. Standard rooms are quite compact, and come with a double bed. Some come with a tub as well as shower. Premium rooms have a queen-size bed. Executive rooms are quite large, have a king-size bed, and some have a small balcony overlooking the main road (the road can be noisy at night). The inside scoop is that the best standard room is no. 330, the best premium room no. 340, and the best executive room no. 323. I would definitely ask for a room away from the main road. The same company operates another stylish boutique hotel, **Medusa,** 267 Darlinghurst Rd. (© **02/9331 1000;** www.medusa.com.au). Rooms start at A$270 (US$216/UK£108) a night here, and the overall size and quality of the rooms reflect the price jumps.

229 Darlinghurst Rd., Darlinghurst, NSW 2010. © **02/9332 2011.** Fax 02/9332 2499. www.kirketon.com.au. 40 rooms. A$145 (US$116/UK£58) junior room; A$175 (US$140/UK£70) premium double; A$175 (US$140/UK£70) executive double. Book these rates over the Internet. Maximum 2 people per room. AE, DC, MC, V. Parking A$25 (US$20/UK£10). **Amenities:** Restaurant; bar. *In room:* A/C, TV, dataport, minibar, hair dryer.

MODERATE

DeVere Hotel The DeVere has been recommended by several readers who commented on the friendly staff and the bargain-basement prices when they booked at the Tourism New South Wales Travel Centre at the Sydney airport. Although the rooms are very modern, they are a little too standard motel-like for the price (unless you get a special deal off the Internet). Superior rooms are a bit larger than standard rooms, and the executive room is larger still and comes with nicer furniture. The suites have views of Elizabeth Bay, a Jacuzzi, and a king-size bed rather than a queen-size. Some suites have a kitchenette with no cooking facilities. Some standard rooms have an extra single bed. Breakfast is available.

44–46 Macleay St., Potts Point, NSW 2011. © **1800/818 790** in Australia, 0800/441 779 in New Zealand, or 02/9358 1211. Fax 02/9358 4685. www.devere.com.au. 100 units. A$180 (US$144/UK£72) double; A$230 (US$184/UK£92) superior room; A$265 (US$212/UK£106) executive room or studio; A$320 (US$256/UK£128) suite. Extra person A$45 (US$36/UK£18). Check website for packages. Children under 12 stay free in parent's room. AE, DC, MC, V. Parking at nearby Landmark Hotel A$15 (US$12/UK£6) per exit. CityRail: Kings Cross. Bus: 311 from Circular Quay. **Amenities:** Tour desk; car-rental desk; business center; laundry service; dry cleaning. *In room:* A/C, TV, fridge, coffeemaker, hair dryer.

Hotel 59 *Kids* This popular and friendly B&B is well worth considering if you want to be near the Kings Cross action, but far enough away to get a decent night's sleep. Deluxe rooms have a queen- or king-size bed and a tub/shower combo, while the smaller standard rooms come with a double bed and a shower. The two large family rooms come with a separate living room, two single beds, and two more that can be locked together to form a king-size. One comes with a small kitchen with a microwave and hot plates. All rooms are well kept and comfortable, with private bathrooms. The cafe below serves breakfast. A flight of stairs and the lack of an elevator might make this a bad choice for travelers with disabilities.

59 Bayswater Rd., Kings Cross, NSW 2011. © **02/9360 5900.** Fax 02/9360 1828. www.hotel59.com.au. 8 units, some with shower only. A$110 (US$88/UK£44) standard double; A$121 (US$97/UK£49) deluxe double; A$132 (US$106/UK£53) family room. Extra person A$15 (US$12/UK£6); extra child 2–12 A$10 (US$8/UK£4). Rates include cooked breakfast. MC, V. No parking. CityRail: Kings Cross. **Amenities:** Cafe; tour desk; car-rental desk; nonsmoking rooms; TV lounge. *In room:* A/C, TV, kitchen, fridge, coffeemaker, hair dryer, iron/ironing board.

Vibe Hotel Rushcutters Bay ★ Vibe Hotels have been making quite an impact over the last couple of years, with new properties opening up in Sydney, Melbourne, and the Gold Coast. This one, on the far side of Kings Cross, is the flagship. Compared to other hotels in this price bracket this really is a bargain, especially when you book online. This large hotel has a good cafe, called Curve, brightly colored rooms with all you need, a heated rooftop swimming pool, and a good gym. Sister hotels **Vibe Hotel Sydney** (111 Goulburn St.; ✆ **02/8372 3300;** rooms A$140–A$170/US$112–US$136/UK£56–UK£68) and **Vibe North Sydney,** are a little less glamorous, but considering their positions and the price of real estate in Sydney these days they too pull off great prices. Vibe North Sydney (88 Alfred St., Milsons Point; ✆ **02/9955 1111;** around A$200/US$160/UK£80 a standard room), is very close to North Sydney Olympic Pool, which almost laps up to the far edge of the Sydney Harbour Bridge. From here, one stop of the CityRail network brings you to Wynyard in the center of the city.

Done100 Bayswater Rd., Rushcutters Bay, NSW 2011. ✆ **02/8353 8988.** Fax 02/8353 8999. www.vibehotels.com.au. 259 units. A$160 (US$128/UK£64) standard room. AE, DC, MC, V. Parking A$30 (US$24/UK£12) CityRail: Kings Cross. **Amenities:** Restaurant; bar; small heated outdoor pool; gym; concierge; tour desk; business center; laundry service; nonsmoking rooms. *In room:* A/C, TV, dataport, minibar, coffeemaker, hair dryer, iron/ironing board.

INEXPENSIVE

Victoria Court Sydney ★ *Value* This cute, well-priced place is made up of two 1881 terrace houses joined together. It's near a string of backpacker hostels and popular cafes on a leafy street running parallel to sleazy Darlinghurst Road. The glass-roofed breakfast room on the ground floor is a work of art, decked out with hanging ferns, giant bamboo, wrought-iron tables and chairs, and a trickling fountain. Just off this space is a peaceful guest lounge stacked with books and newspapers. The very plush rooms come with either king- or queen-size beds, but lack a tub in the bathroom. There's a coin-op laundry just down the road.

122 Victoria St., Potts Point, NSW 2011. ✆ **1800/630 505** in Australia, or 02/9357 3200. Fax 02/9357 7606. www.victoriacourt.com.au. 22 units. A$115 (US$92/UK£46) double; A$165 (US$132/UK£66) deluxe double with sun deck; A$250 (US$200/UK£100) honeymoon suite with balcony. Extra person A$20 (US$16/UK£8). Rates include buffet breakfast. AE, DC, MC, V. Free secure parking. CityRail: Kings Cross. **Amenities:** Guest lounge. *In room:* A/C, TV.

OXFORD STREET/DARLINGHURST

Sullivans Hotel About half of this boutique hotel's guests come from overseas, mainly from the United Kingdom, Europe, and the United States. There's also a small corporate following. Sullivans is right in the heart of the action in one of Sydney's most popular shopping, entertainment, restaurant, and gay pub and club areas. The hotel is particularly popular with Americans during Gay and Lesbian Mardi Gras. All rooms are simple and compact, but are good for a few nights. They come with an attached shower. Standard rooms have two single beds, and the garden rooms have a queen-size bed and pleasant garden views.

21 Oxford St., Paddington, NSW 2021. ✆ **02/9361 0211.** Fax 02/9360 3735. www.sullivans.com.au. 64 units. A$165 (US$132/UK£66) standard double; A$180 (US$144/UK£77) garden room double and triple; A$180 (US$144/UK£77) family room; A$225 (US$128/UK£64) 2 connecting rooms. AE, DC, MC, V. Limited free parking. Bus: 378 from Central Station or 380 from Circular Quay. **Amenities:** Breakfast cafe; small heated outdoor pool; free use of bikes; coin-op laundry; free Internet access. *In room:* A/C, TV w/free movies, fridge, hair dryer, iron/ironing board.

Wattle Private Hotel *Finds* This attractive Edwardian-style house built between 1900 and 1910 offers basic to very pleasant accommodations in the increasingly fashionable inner-city suburb of Darlinghurst, known for its great cafes, nightlife, and restaurants. The hotel was renovated and refurbished in 2004 and a bit more in 2005, and has changed a lot. Double rooms are rather basic and quite small, but large windows open them. Nicer and larger queen rooms have a queen-size bed, king rooms have a king-size bed (some have harbor views), while a deluxe twin room has two king-size beds or a spa. There's also a family room that sleeps up to six people. Expect period features, such as high ceilings and ornate moldings. Rooms are on four stories, but there's no elevator, so if you don't fancy too many stairs, try to get a room on a lower floor. There's a rooftop garden with harbor and city views.

108 Oxford St. (at corner of Palmer St.), Darlinghurst, NSW 2010. ✆ **02/9332 4118.** Fax 02/9331 2074. www.thewattle.com. 11 units. A$100–A$130 (US$80–US$104/UK£40–UK£52) double; A$110–A$140 (US$88–US$112/UK£44–UK£61) queen; A$120–A$160 (US$96–US$128/UK£48–UK£64) king; A$140–A$180 (US$112–US$144/UK£64–UK£72) king with harbor views; A$140–A$180 (US$112–US$191/UK£106–UK£95) deluxe king with spa, or with 2 king-size beds; A$160–A$200 (US$128–US$160/UK£64–UK£80) family unit. More expensive rates are for Fri and Sat nights. Extra person A$30 (US$24/UK£12). Rates include continental breakfast. MC, V. No parking. Bus: Any to Taylor Sq. from Circular Quay. **Amenities:** Coin-op laundry. *In room:* A/C, TV, minibar.

IN NEWTOWN

INEXPENSIVE

Billabong Gardens For that inner-city feel, you can't beat Newtown, with its busy street happenings, cheap restaurants, and grunge look. It's also easy to get to by bus or CityRail. Billabong Gardens is just off the main drag, King Street, and earned a five-star backpackers' rating from the National Roads and Motorists' Association. Rooms are simply furnished in pine and have exposed brickwork. Besides the dormitory accommodations, you might consider the double or twin rooms, which offer pretty good value. The more expensive rooms have their own bathrooms. It's a friendly place with lots of native plants scattered around, and a pool in a pleasant courtyard. On the property are a comfortable TV lounge, a large kitchen, and a barbecue. It's very secure and offers 24-hour access.

5–11 Egan St., Newtown, NSW 2042. ✆ **02/9550 3236.** Fax 02/9550 4352. www.billabonggardens.com.au. 37 units. A$23–A$25 (US$18–US$20/UK£9–UK£10) dorm bed; A$69–A$130 (US$55–US$104/UK£27–UK£52) double or twin. Family rooms available. MC, V. Parking A$5 (US$4/UK£2). CityRail: Newtown. Bus: 422, 423, 426, or 428. **Amenities:** Small heated outdoor pool; Jacuzzi; game room; coin-op laundry; free Internet access. *In room:* No phone.

IN GLEBE

EXPENSIVE

Tricketts Luxury Bed & Breakfast ★★ The *New York Times* published an article in November 2006 in which Tricketts was described as the best bed-and-breakfast accommodations in the Southern Hemisphere. While that's quite a claim, as soon as I walked into this atmospheric old place, I wanted to ditch my modern Sydney apartment and move in. Your first impression as you enter the tessellated, tiled corridor of the 1880s Victorian mansion is the jumble of plants and ornaments, the high ceilings, the Oriental rugs, and the leaded windows. Guests relax over a decanter of port or with a magazine on wicker furniture on the veranda overlooking fairly busy Glebe Point Road. The guest rooms are quiet and homey. My favorites are no. 2, with its wooden floorboards and king-size bed, and The Honey Room Suite—with an 1820s king-size four-poster bed. There's a nice courtyard out back. The owner, Liz Tricketts, is a delight and is a rich source of Sydney's history.

270 Glebe Point Rd., Glebe (the water end), NSW 2037. ✆ **02/9552 1141.** Fax 02/9692 9462. www.tricketts.com.au. 7 units, all with shower only. A$198 (US$158/UK£78) double; A$220 (US$176/UK£88) honeymoon suite. Rates include continental breakfast. MC, V. Free parking. Bus: 431 from George St. **Amenities:** Tour desk; massage; nonsmoking rooms. *In room:* A/C, TV, hair dryer.

MODERATE

Alishan International Guest House The Alishan is a quiet place with a real Aussie feel. It's at the city end of Glebe Point Road, just 10 minutes by bus from the shops around Town Hall. It's a mixture of upmarket youth hostel and typical guesthouse. Standard dorm rooms are spotless, light, and bright, and come with two sets of bunks. Doubles have a double bed, a sofa and armchair, and a shower. Grab room no. 9 if you fancy sleeping on one of two single mattresses on the tatami mat floor, Japanese-style.

100 Glebe Point Rd., Glebe, NSW 2037. ✆ **02/9566 4048.** Fax 02/9525 4686. www.alishan.com.au. 19 units. A$27–A$33 (US$22–US$26/UK£11–UK£13) dorm bed; A$99–A$115 (US$79–US$92/UK£40–UK£46) double; A$154 (US$123/UK£62) family room. Extra person A$16 (US$13/UK£7.50). AE, MC, V. Secured parking for 6 cars; metered street parking. Bus: 431 or 433 from George St., or Kingsford Smith Shuttle from airport. **Amenities:** Coin-op laundry; Internet access. *In room:* TV, fridge.

IN BONDI

Bondi Beach is a good place to stay if you want to be close to the surf and sand, though if you're getting around by public transport you'll need to catch a bus to Bondi Junction, then a train to the city center. (You can stay on the bus all the way, but it takes forever.)

In addition to the properties recommended below, there are two good backpacker hostels. **Surfside Backpackers,** 35a Hall St. (✆ **02/9365 4900;** www.surfsidebackpackers.com.au), offers four- to eight-person dorm rooms for A$18 (US$14/UK£7) in winter and A$22 (US$18/UK£9) in summer, and double rooms in a separate building opposite North Bondi Surf Club for the same price per person. **Noah's,** 2 Campbell Parade (✆ **02/9365 7100**), has a great ambience and offers modern four- to eight-person dorm rooms for A$24 to A$25 (US$19–US$20/UK£9.50–UK£10) as well as doubles for A$55 (US$44/UK£22) and beach doubles for A$65 (US$52/UK£26). Weekly rates range from A$144 to A$330 (US$115–US$264/UK£57–UK£132).

VERY EXPENSIVE

Swiss-Grand Hotel ★★ Right on Bondi Beach, overlooking the Pacific, the Swiss-Grand is the best hotel in Bondi. It occupies a unique position overlooking the waves and sand of one of Australia's most famous cultural icons. The lobby is grand indeed, with high ceilings and stylish furniture. A renovation in 2002 made each room into a suite, with separate bedroom and living room. All suites are spacious, and each comes with a rather luxurious bathroom. All rooms have two TVs; some have Jacuzzis. All oceanfront units have balconies. The general sumptuousness of the accommodations and a terrific day spa help make this a fine place to stay. It's popular with American and European travelers with a bit of money to spend.

Corner of Campbell Parade and Beach Rd. (P.O. Box 219, Bondi Beach, NSW 2026). ✆ **800/344-1212** in the U.S., 1800/655 252 in Australia, 0800/951 000 in the U.K., 0800/056 666 in New Zealand, or 02/9365 5666. Fax 02/9365 9710. www.swissgrand.com.au. 230 units. A$308 (US$246/UK£123) standard double; A$352 (US$281/UK£140) oceanview double; from A$396 (US$317/UK£158) suite. Packages are available on their website. Extra person A$44 (US$35/UK£22). AE, DC, MC, V. Free parking. Bus: 380 or 333 from Circular Quay. **Amenities:** 2 restaurants; rooftop and indoor heated pools; fitness center; Jacuzzi; tour desk. *In room:* A/C, TV, coffeemaker, hair dryer, iron/ironing board.

MODERATE

Ravesi's on Bondi Beach ★★ Right on Australia's most famous golden sands, this boutique property is a AAA-rated three-star hotel, offering modern minimalist rooms with white marble bathrooms—all very chic, with African tribal wall hangings. Standard doubles are spacious; there's a one-bedroom suite, and a split-level one-bedroom option with the bedroom upstairs. Room nos. 5 and 6 and the split-level suite have the best views of the ocean. All rooms have Juliet balconies, and the split-level suite has its own terrace. If you're a light sleeper, request a room on the top floor, because the popular **Ravesi's Restaurant** can be noisy on busy nights. An attractive glass-sided ground-floor bar is the in place on the Bondi scene, with lounge, house, and "chill" music every evening. The bar is a great place to watch the outside street scene.

Corner of Hall St. and Campbell Parade, Bondi Beach, NSW 2026. ✆ **02/9365 4422.** Fax 02/9365 1481. www.ravesis.com.au. 16 units. A$120 (US$96/UK£48) standard double; A$230 (US$184/UK£92) double with side view; A$295 (US$236/UK£118) beachfront room; A$275 (US$220/UK£110) 1-bedroom suite; A$275–A$350 (US$220–US$280/UK£110–UK£140) split-level suite with terrace. Extra person A$30 (US$24/UK£12). 2 children under 12 stay free in parent's room. AE, DC, MC, V. Parking at the Swiss-Grand Hotel nearby A$8 (US$6.40/UK£3.20). CityRail: Bondi Junction; then bus 380. Bus: 380 or 333 from Circular Quay. **Amenities:** Restaurant; bar; tour desk; 24-hr. room service; laundry service; dry cleaning. *In room:* A/C, TV, minibar, hair dryer, iron/ironing board, safe.

IN MANLY

If you decide to stay in my favorite beachside suburb, be aware that ferries from the city stop running at midnight. If you get stranded, you'll be facing an expensive taxi ride (around A$40/US$32/UK£16), or you'll need to make your way to the bus stand behind Wynyard CityRail station to catch a night bus. Consider buying a multiple-ride ticket, which will save you a bit of money if you're staying in Manly for a few days.

Manly has several backpacker places that are worth checking out. The best is **Manly Backpackers Beachside,** 28 Ragland St. (✆ **02/9977 3411;** fax 02/9977 4379; www.manlybackpackers.com.au), which offers dorm beds from A$22 to A$27 (US$18–US$21/UK£9–UK£11), double from A$52 to A$62 (US$42–US$49/UK£21–UK£25). The hostel charges a A$30 (US$24/UK£12) key deposit.

VERY EXPENSIVE

Manly Pacific Hotel ★★ If you could bottle the views from this top-class hotel—across the sand and through the Norfolk Island Pines to the Pacific Ocean—you'd make a fortune. Standing on your private balcony in the evening with the sea breeze in your nostrils and the chirping of hundreds of lorikeets is nothing short of heaven. The Manly Pacific is the only hotel of its class in this wonderful beachside suburb. There's nothing claustrophobic here, from the broad expanse of glittering foyer to the wide corridors and spacious accommodations. Each standard room is light and modern, with two double beds, a balcony, limited cable TV, and all the necessities. Views over the ocean are really worth the extra money. The hotel is a 10-minute stroll, or a A$5 (US$4/UK£2) taxi ride, from the Manly ferry.

55 North Steyne, Manly, NSW 2095. ✆ **02/9977 7666.** Fax 02/9977 7822. www.accorhotels.com.au. 218 units. A$283–A$327 (US$226–US$261/UK£113–UK£130) double; A$512 (US$409/UK£205) suite. Extra person A$32 (US$26/UK£13). AE, DC, MC, V. Parking A$10 (US$8/UK£4). Ferry or JetCat: Manly. **Amenities:** 2 restaurants; 2 bars; heated rooftop pool; exercise room; Jacuzzi; sauna; concierge; tour desk; 24-hr. room service; laundry service. *In room:* A/C, TV, dataport, minibar, coffeemaker, hair dryer, iron/ironing board.

MODERATE

Manly Lodge ★ *Kids* At first sight this ramshackle building halfway between the main beach and the harbor doesn't look like much. But don't let the tattiness—especially the cramped, hostel-like foyer bristling with tourist brochures—put you off. Some of the rooms are lovely, and the whole place has a nice atmosphere and plenty of character. Double rooms are not exceptional. They come with a double bed, stone or carpet floors, a TV and VCR, and either a Jacuzzi or a tub/shower combination. Some of the standard doubles and all of the deluxe doubles have a kitchen. Family rooms have a set of bunk beds and a double in one room, and a shower. Family suites are very classy; each has a Jacuzzi, a small kitchen area, one double and three singles in the bedroom, and two sofa beds in the living area. The lodge also has table tennis and even an Olympic-size trampoline. For purposes of setting room rates, peak season is defined as Christmas, Easter, and school holidays.

22 Victoria Parade, Manly, NSW 2095. ✆ **02/9977 8655.** Fax 02/9976 2090. www.manlylodge.com.au. 24 units. Peak season (Oct 1–Apr 30) A$160 (US$128/UK£114) standard double, A$210 (US$168/UK£84) deluxe double, A$265 (US$212/UK£106) family suite; off season A$120 (US$96/UK£49) standard double, A$160 (US$128/UK£64) deluxe double, A$180 (US$144/UK£72) family suite. Extra person A$35 (US$28/UK£14); extra child under 10 A$20 (US$16/UK£10). Ask about weekly rates and off-season discounts. Rates include continental breakfast. AE, MC, V. Free parking. Ferry or JetCat: Manly. **Amenities:** Exercise room; Jacuzzi; sauna; coin-op laundry. *In room:* A/C, TV.

Manly Paradise Motel and Beach Plaza Apartments ★ I walked into this place after taking a look around the modern Manly Waterfront Apartment Hotel next door and immediately felt more at home here. The motel and apartment complex are separate, but share a reception area. The irregularly shaped rooms are big yet cozy, and come with a shower and a springy double bed. Though there is no restaurant, you can get breakfast in bed; a simple breakfast costs about A$10 (US$8/UK£4). My only concern is that the traffic can make it a little noisy during the day (but you'll probably be on the beach then, anyway). Some rooms have glimpses of the sea. Residents of the apartment complex share the swimming pool (with views) on the roof.

The apartments are magnificent—very roomy, with thick carpets. They're stocked with everything you need, including a washing machine and dryer, a full kitchen with dishwasher, and two bathrooms (one with a tub). The sea views from the main front balcony are heart-stopping.

54 N. Steyne, Manly, NSW 2095. ✆ **1800/815 789** in Australia, or 02/9977 5799. Fax 02/9977 6848. www.manlyparadise.com.au. 40 units, some with shower only. A$110–A$190 (US$88–US$152/UK£44–UK£76) double motel unit; A$220–A$375 (US$176–US$300/UK£88–UK£150) 2-bedroom apt. Higher prices in summer. Extra person A$25 (US$20/UK£10). Ask about long-term discounts. AE, DC, MC, V. Free secured parking. Ferry or JetCat: Manly. **Amenities:** Indoor heated pool; dry cleaning; nonsmoking rooms. *In room:* A/C, TV, dataport, hair dryer, iron/ironing board.

Periwinkle–Manly Cove Guesthouse Nicely positioned across the road from one of Manly's two harbor beaches, the Periwinkle is a short walk from the ferry, the shops along the Corso, and the main ocean beach. Rooms are small and come with a double bed. Some have a shower and toilet (these go for the higher prices noted below), but otherwise you'll have to make do with one of four separate bathrooms (one has a tub). A full kitchen next to a pleasant-enough communal lounge means you could save money by not eating out. Room nos. 5 and 10 are the nicest and have screened balconies overlooking the harbor (but no bathrooms). For atmosphere, I prefer the Manly Lodge (see above). There's no smoking inside.

18–19 E. Esplanade, Manly, NSW 2095. ✆ **02/9977 4668.** Fax 02/9977 6308. www.periwinkle.citysearch.com.au. 18 units, 12 with bathroom. A$135 (US$108/UK£54) double without bathroom; A$165 (US$132/UK£66) double with bathroom. Units with harbor views A$10 (US$8/UK£4) extra. Extra person A$25 (US$20/UK£10). Rates include continental breakfast. MC, V. Free parking. Ferry or JetCat: Manly. **Amenities:** Coin-op laundry; nonsmoking rooms. *In room:* TV, fridge.

AT THE AIRPORT

Stamford Sydney Airport ★★ This is the best airport hotel. It has the largest rooms, each with a king-size bed or two doubles, access to airport information, and a good-size bathroom with tub. Just 7 minutes from the airport, and pickup service is free. Day-use rates are A$85 (US$68/UK£34) for 2 to 4 hours and A$115 (US$92/UK£46) for 4 to 8 hours.

Corner of O'Riordan and Robey sts. (P.O. Box 353), Mascot, Sydney, NSW 2020. ✆ **1300/301 391** in Australia, or 02/9317 2200. Fax 02/9317 3855. www.stamford.com.au. 314 units. A$270 (US$216/UK£108) double; from A$370 (US$296/UK£149) suite. Extra person A$25 (US$20/UK£10). Children under 17 stay free in parent's room. Ask about discount packages and weekend rates. AE, DC, MC, V. A$5 (US$4/UK£2) self-parking for up to 10 days. **Amenities:** 2 restaurants; bar; good-size outdoor pool; fitness center; Jacuzzi; sauna; concierge; business center; 24-hr. room service; babysitting; laundry service; nonsmoking rooms; executive rooms; currency exchange. *In room:* A/C, TV, minibar, dataport, coffeemaker, hair dryer, iron/ironing board.

4 Where to Dine

Sydney is a gourmet paradise, with an abundance of fresh seafood, a vast range of vegetables and fruit always in season, prime meats at inexpensive prices, and top-quality chefs making international names for themselves. Asian and Mediterranean cooking have had a major influence on Australian cuisine, with spices and herbs finding their way into most dishes. Immigration has brought with it almost every type of cuisine, from African to Tibetan, from Russian to Vietnamese. Some areas of the city are dedicated to one type of food, while other areas are melting pots of styles.

Sydney is a great place to try Contemporary, or "Mod Oz," cuisine, which has been applauded by chefs and food critics around the world. Contemporary cuisine emphasizes fresh ingredients and a creative blend of European styles with Asian influences. (Some foodies complain that some restaurants use the label "Contemporary" as an excuse to serve skimpy portions—like one lamb chop atop a tiny mound of mashed potatoes sprinkled with curry sauce.) At its best, Contemporary food is world-class, but you'll probably have to go to the best of Sydney's restaurants to see what the scene is all about.

Australians think American-style coffee tastes like ditch water and favor a range of Italian-style coffee creations. Ask for a latte if you just want coffee with milk. "Bottomless" cups of coffee are rare in Australia. By the way, in Australia, the first course is called the entrée and the second course the main.

I've included the websites of some of the top-class restaurants here as you would be advised to reserve well in advance if you want a table.

NEAR CIRCULAR QUAY

VERY EXPENSIVE

Forty One ★★ FRENCH/CONTEMPORARY Powerful people, international celebrities, and average Sydneysiders out for a special celebration all come here to feel exclusive. It's won plenty of awards. The 41st-floor views over the city and the harbor are terrific, the service is fun, the cutlery is the world's best, and Swiss chef and owner Dietmar Sawyere has given the food a wickedly good Asian slant. In all, it's a glamorous place to experience some of the best of Australian cuisine. The signature dish is roast wild hare, with celeriac and potato purée, Viennese carrots, and chartreuse jus. The menu changes every 2 weeks to keep up with seasonal produce.

Level 42, Chifley Tower, 2 Chifley Sq. ✆ **02/9221 2500.** www.forty-one.com.au. Reservations required. 3-course menu A$125 (US$100/UK£50); 3-course menu with matched wine A$140 (US$112/UK£56); 6 courses with wine A$200 (US$160/UK£80). AE, DC, MC, V. Tues–Fri noon–4pm; Mon–Sat 6–10pm. CityRail: Wynyard.

Guillaume at Bennelong ★★★ FRENCH If you go to Bondi, you have to swim in the Pacific; if you see the Harbour Bridge, you have to walk across it; if you visit

Where to Dine in Sydney

Aria **16**
Ashiana **29**
Bar Coluzzi **33**
Bill's **34**
Bilsons **14**
Botanic Gardens Restaurant **20**
Buena Vista Café **23**
Buon Ricardo **39**
Capitan Torres **30**
Chinta Ria (The Temple of Love) **25**
City Extra **15**
Doyles at the Quay **6**
EST **8**
Fish at The Rocks **2**
Forty One **22**
G'Day Café **5**
Govindas **35**
Guillaume at Bennelong **17**
The Gumnut Café **9**
Hard Rock Cafe **31**
Hernandez **36**

The Italian Village **1**
The Löwenbräu Keller **4**
Marque **32**
Mezzaluna **38**
Nicks Seafood Restaurant **26**
Oh Calcutta **38**
The Old Coffee Shop **24**
Otto Ristorante **21**
Phillip's Foote **10**
Portobello Caffe **18**
Quay **7**
Quay Deli **12**
Rockpool **11**
Rossini **13**
Sailors Thai **11**
Sydney Cove Oyster Bar **19**
Tetsuya's **28**
Waterfront Restaurant **1**
Wolfie's Grill **1**
Yoshii **3**
Zaaffran **27**

See "Dining in The Rocks" map

ELIZABETH BAY
To Watsons Bay
Billyard Ave.
Cowper Wharf Rd.
Challis Ave.
Woolloomooloo Bay
Lincoln Cr.
Mrs. Macquarie's Rd.
Cahill Exp.
Hospital Rd.
Main Pond
Conservatorium of Music
Visitors Centre
Tropical Centre
Shakespeare Pl.
State Library of NSW
Farm Cove
Government House
ROYAL BOTANIC GARDENS
Macquarie St.
Phillip St.
Young St.
Bent St.
Bligh St.
O'Connell St.
Spring St.
Bridge St.
Martin Pl.
Port Jackson
Kirribilli Point
Bennelong Point
Farm Cove Cr.
Sydney Opera House
Circular Quay
Alfred St.
Lotus
Pitt St.
Essex St.
Stock Exchange
Bond
Hunter
Carrington St.
Sydney Harbour Tunnel
To North Shore
Sydney Cove
Manly Jetcat Wharf
Manly Ferry Wharf
CIRCULAR QUAY
Loftus
Sydney Harbour Bridge
Bradfield Highway
Dawes Point
Pier One
Circular Quay West
George St.
Hickson Rd.
LWR Fort St.
THE ROCKS
Cumberland St.
Gloucester St.
Harrington St.
Grosvenor St.
Jamison St.
Lang St.
Margaret
York
Clarence St.
Western Distributor
Wynyard Station
Erskine St.
Church
DAWES POINT
Argyle St.
Sydney Observatory
National Trust
Kent St.
Hickson Rd.
Darling Harbour
MILLERS POINT
Walsh
Sydney Theatre Bay Dance Company
Windmill St.
Argyle Place
North Sydney
Port Jackson
Area of Detail Sydney
Bondi Junction

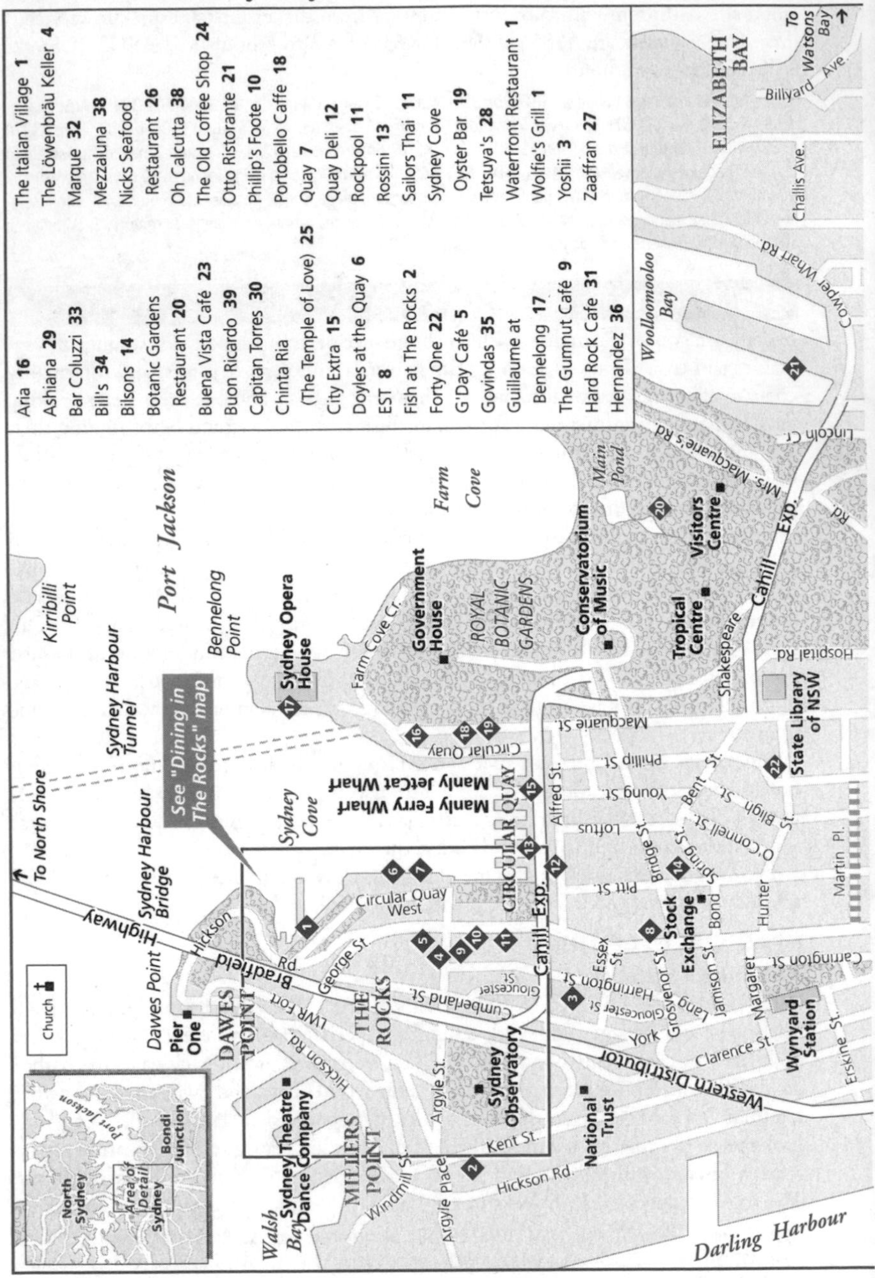

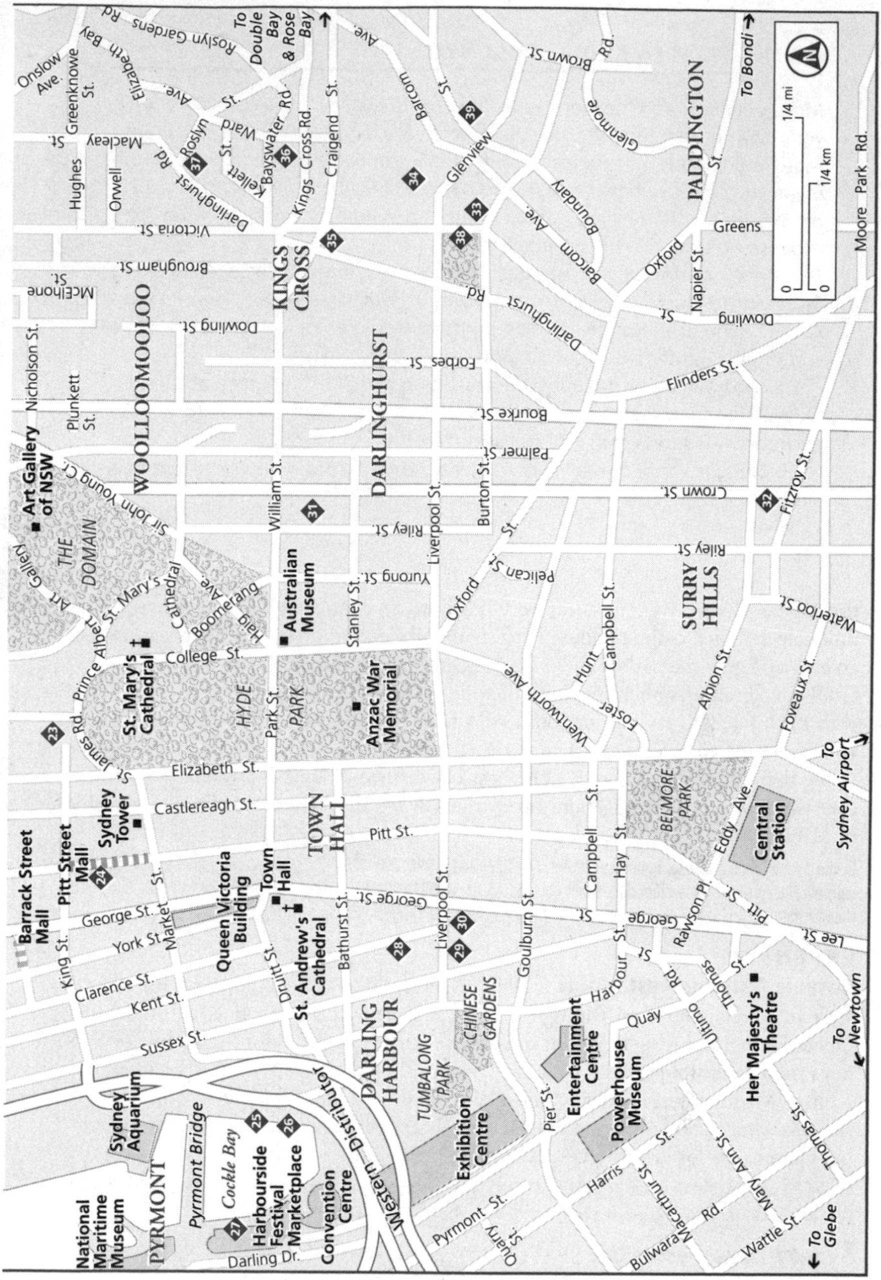
National Maritime Museum
PYRMONT
Sydney Aquarium
Pyrmont Bridge
Cockle Bay
Harbourside Festival Marketplace
Convention Centre
Darling Dr.
Western Distributor
Pyrmont St.
Quarry St.
Exhibition Centre
TUMBALONG PARK
DARLING HARBOUR
CHINESE GARDENS
Pier St.
Entertainment Centre
Powerhouse Museum
Harris St.
Macarthur St.
Bulwara Rd.
Mary Ann St.
Wattle St.
Thomas St.
To Glebe
To Newtown
Her Majesty's Theatre
Ultimo Rd.
Quay St.
Harbour St.
Thomas St.
Sussex St.
Kent St.
Clarence St.
York St.
King St.
George St.
Market St.
Barrack Street Mall
Pitt Street Mall
Sydney Tower
Queen Victoria Building
Town Hall
St. Andrew's Cathedral
Druitt St.
Bathurst St.
Liverpool St.
Goulburn St.
Campbell St.
Hay St.
George St.
Rawson Pl.
Pitt St.
Lee St.
Eddy Ave.
Central Station
To Sydney Airport
BELMORE PARK
TOWN HALL
Pitt St.
Castlereagh St.
Elizabeth St.
St. James Rd.
St. Mary's Cathedral
HYDE PARK
Park St.
Anzac War Memorial
College St.
Prince Albert Rd.
St. Mary's Rd.
Art Gallery Rd.
THE DOMAIN
Art Gallery of NSW
Sir John Young Cr.
Cathedral St.
Boomerang St.
Haig Ave.
Australian Museum
William St.
Stanley St.
Yurong St.
Riley St.
Liverpool St.
Burton St.
Oxford St.
Wentworth Ave.
Foster St.
Hunt St.
Campbell St.
Pelican St.
Albion St.
Foveaux St.
Waterloo St.
SURRY HILLS
Riley St.
Crown St.
Fitzroy St.
Palmer St.
Bourke St.
Flinders St.
Moore Park Rd.
WOOLLOOMOOLOO
DARLINGHURST
Plunkett St.
Nicholson St.
Dowling St.
Forbes St.
McElhone St.
Brougham St.
Victoria St.
KINGS CROSS
Darlinghurst Rd.
Barcom Ave.
Boundary St.
Dowling St.
Napier St.
Greens Rd.
Oxford St.
PADDINGTON
Glenmore Rd.
Brown St.
Glenview St.
Barcom Ave.
Craigend St.
Kings Cross Rd.
Bayswater Rd.
Kellett St.
Roslyn St.
Ward Ave.
Hughes St.
Orwell St.
Macleay St.
Greenknowe St.
Onslow Ave.
Elizabeth Bay Rd.
Roslyn Gardens Rd.
To Double Bay & Rose Bay
To Bondi
0 1/4 mi
0 1/4 km
N
23
24
25
26
27
28
29
30
31
32
33
34
35
36
37
38
39

Value What to Know about BYO

Most moderate and inexpensive restaurants in Sydney are **BYO,** as in "bring your own" bottle, though some places also have extensive wine and beer lists. More moderately priced restaurants are introducing corkage fees, which mean you pay anywhere from A$2 to A$8 (US$1.60–US$6.40/UK80p–UK£3.20) per person for the privilege of the waiter opening your bottle of wine. Very expensive restaurants discourage BYO.

Sydney's **cheap eats** congregate in inner-city areas such as along King Street in Newtown, Crown Street in Darlinghurst, and Glebe Point Road in Glebe. There are also inexpensive joints scattered among the more upscale restaurants in Kings Cross and along trendy Oxford Street.

I would avoid the takeout booths along the ferry wharves at Circular Quay. The fish-and-chip shop opposite the "bottle shop" (liquor store) is an exception—it serves some of the best french fries in Sydney.

Smoking is banned in all Sydney restaurants, except if you're eating at a sidewalk table.

the Opera House, you must eat at Guillaume at Bennelong. The restaurant is as uniquely designed as the building itself, with tall glass windows that furrow around in an arch and grab the harbor and Circular Quay by the throat. Renowned French chef Guillaume Brahimi's offerings could include sealed veal sweetbreads; or chicken breast with duck foie gras raviloli, or confit of Atlantic salmon on braised endive with red-wine sauce. Many would rather miss the first half of the opera they've paid a fortune to see than leave before dessert. The best bar in town is upstairs, where you can see over the water to the bridge and up to the other "sails." Good bar food is available until 11:30pm.

In the Sydney Opera House, Bennelong Point. ✆ **02/9241 1999.** Fax 02/9241 3795. www.guillaumeatbennelong.com.au. Reservations recommended. Main courses A$39 (US$31/UK£15). AE, DC, MC, V. Thurs–Fri noon–3pm; pre-theater menu Mon–Sat 5:30–7:45pm; dinner Mon–Sat 8–10:30pm. CityRail, bus, or ferry: Circular Quay.

EXPENSIVE

Botanic Gardens Restaurant CONTEMPORARY You couldn't ask for a better walk to a restaurant than through the Royal Botanic Gardens, next to the Sydney Opera House. Enjoying lunch on the wisteria-covered balcony in the middle of Sydney's most beautiful park is a treat every visitor should enjoy. Main courses often mix a bit of Mediterranean, French, and Asian. They include the popular white sausage *(boudin blanc)* with lentils and braised fennel. Try perfect crème brûlée with underlying plum purée for dessert (A$12/US$9.20/UK£4.60).

In the Royal Botanic Gardens. ✆ **02/9241 2419.** Reservations recommended. Main courses A$23–A$30 (US$18–US$24/UK£9–UK£12). AE, DC, MC, V. Daily 8am–4:30pm. Bus or ferry: Circular Quay.

Sydney Cove Oyster Bar SEAFOOD Just before you reach the Sydney Opera House, you'll notice a couple of small shedlike buildings with tables and chairs set up to take in the stunning views of the harbor and the Harbour Bridge. The first is a

Sydney institution, serving some of the best oysters in town. Light meals such as Asian-style octopus and seared tuna steak are also on the menu.

No. 1 Eastern Esplanade, Circular Quay East. ✆ **02/9247 2937.** www.sydneycoveoysterbar.com. Main courses A$25–A$35 (US$20–US$28/UK£10–UK£14). 10% surcharge weekends and public holidays. AE, DC, MC, V. Mon–Sat 11am–11pm; Sun 11am–8pm. CityRail, bus, or ferry: Circular Quay.

MODERATE

City Extra ITALIAN/AUSTRALIAN Because this place stays open 24 hours, it's convenient if you get the munchies at a ridiculous hour. It's also nicely placed, right next to the Manly ferry terminal. Over several visits here I've found the food to be pretty variable in quality. The burgers are fine, but some of the pastas are disappointing. Friends of mine complain that it's overpriced for what you get, and the high turnover can tend to lead to a perception of poor service. However, the plastic chairs and outdoor tables make it a pleasant-enough spot for a quick bite at any time of the day or night. A range of salads, pies, steaks, ribs, fish, and Asian-influenced dishes are also available. There's also a fat selection of desserts. In my opinion, the food is much nicer and a better value next door at Rossini (see below).

Shop E4, Circular Quay. ✆ **02/9241 1422.** Reservations not accepted. Main courses A$13–A$26 (US$10–US$21/UK£5–UK£10). 10% surcharge midnight–6am, Sun, public holidays. AE, DC, MC, V. Daily 24 hr. CityRail, bus, or ferry: Circular Quay.

INEXPENSIVE

Portobello Caffé PIZZA/SANDWICHES Sharing the address of the Sydney Cove Oyster Bar (and the same priceless views), the Portobello Caffé offers first-class gourmet sandwiches on Italian wood-fired bread, small but delicious gourmet pizzas, breakfast croissants, snacks, cakes, and hot and cold drinks. Walk off with sensational ice cream in a cone for around A$3.50 (US$2.80/UK£1.40).

No. 1 Eastern Esplanade, Circular Quay East. ✆ **02/9247 8548.** Main courses A$10 (US$8/UK£4). 10% surcharge Sun and public holidays. AE, DC, MC, V. Minimum credit card purchase A$30 (US$24/UK£12). Daily 8am–11:50pm. CityRail, bus, or ferry: Circular Quay.

Rossini ★ *Kids* ITALIAN This cafeteria-style Italian restaurant opposite Ferry Wharf 5 at Circular Quay is wonderfully positioned for people-watching. The outside tables are perfect for breakfast or a quick bite before a show at the Opera House. Breakfast croissants, Italian doughnuts, muffins, and gorgeous Danish pastries cost A$3 (US$2.40/UK£1.20), and bacon and eggs with toast A$12 (US$9.60/UK£4.80). Wait to be seated for lunch or dinner, make your choice, pay at the counter, take a ticket, and then pick up your food. Meals, including veal parmigiana, cannelloni, ravioli, chicken crepes, and octopus salad, are often huge. You could easily get away with

---

What's the Restaurant Surcharge?

Some Australian restaurants charge surcharges on public holidays and Sundays. Typically this can amount to an extra A$2 to up to A$6 (US$1.60–US$4.80/UK80p–UK£2.40) or more per person. Restaurants argue that it's difficult to get staff to work on these days, so they need to provide a cash incentive not to call in with a hangover from the previous night. In Australia waiters rely on their wages rather than tips.

Finds A Great Place for Picnic Grub

If you're looking for something to take with you on a harbor cruise or on a stroll through the Royal Botanic Gardens, you can't go wrong with **Quay Deli,** E5 Alfred St., next to the pharmacy under the Circular Quay CityRail station, facing the road (✆ **02/9241 3571**). You'll find all sorts of goodies, including gourmet sandwiches and takeout foods such as olives, Greek dishes, pasta, salads, meat pies, and the best English-style custard tarts around. Everything is fresh and tasty. Lunch items go for A$1.80 to A$4.50 (US$1.45–US$3.60/UK70p–UK£1.80). It's open Monday through Friday from 5am to 6:45pm, Saturday from 9am to 4pm. No credit cards.

one meal for two people—ask for an extra plate—and while it's not the best Italian you'll ever eat, it is tasty. Coffee fanatics rate the Rossini brew as average.

Shop W5, Circular Quay. ✆ **02/9247 8026.** Main courses A$10–A$22 (US$8–US$18/UK£4–UK£9). No credit cards. Daily 7am–10pm. CityRail, bus, or ferry: Circular Quay.

THE ROCKS

VERY EXPENSIVE

Aria ★★★ MODERN AUSTRALIAN With front-row views of the Harbour Bridge and the Sydney Opera House, Aria stands in one of the most enviable spots in the city. The windows overlooking the water are huge, the atmosphere is elegant and buzzy, and many of the tables have an intimate relationship with the stunning view. The food, created by Matthew Moran, one of Australia's great chefs, is imaginative and mouthwatering. Standout dishes at the time of writing included the pan-fried kingfish filets with a salad of white beans and hazelnut, with a red-wine sauce; and the sweet pork loin with lentil salad and black pudding.

1 Macquarie St., East Circular Quay. ✆ **02/9252 2555.** www.ariarestaurant.com.au. Reservations essential. Main courses A$42–A$49 (US$34–US$39/UK£17–UK£20); pre-theater supper, 1 course A$36 (US$29/UK£18), 2 courses A$58 (US$46/UK£29), 3 courses A$72 (US$57/UK£28). AE, DC, MC, V. Mon–Fri noon–2:30pm; pre-theater daily 5:30–7pm; Mon–Sat 7–11:30pm; Sun 6–11:30pm. CityRail, bus, or ferry: Circular Quay.

Quay ★★★ CONTEMPORARY With its enviable location on top of the cruise-ship terminal, Quay offers another of the loveliest views in the city, and some feel that it's Sydney's best restaurant (though I prefer Tetsuya's). In good weather, the sun sparkles off the water and through the large windows; the Opera House, city skyline, North Shore suburbs, and Harbour Bridge all look magnificent. At night, when the city lights wash over the harbor and bridge and the Opera House's sails are lit up, the view is even better. Chef Peter Gilmore's menu is a revelation of French, Italian, and Australian ideas. Signature dishes include crisped pressed duck with garlic purée and porcini mushrooms, and seared yellowfin tuna with tomato jelly, roasted eggplant, and basil oil. This restaurant has tempted all the big-name visitors to Sydney.

On the upper level of the Overseas Passenger Terminal, Circular Quay West, The Rocks. ✆ **02/9251 5600.** www.quay.com.au. Reservations recommended well in advance. Main courses A$38 (US$30/UK£15). A$6 (US$4.80/UK£2.40) per-person surcharge on public holidays. AE, DC, MC, V. Mon–Fri noon–2:30pm; daily 6–10pm. CityRail, bus, or ferry: Circular Quay.

Where to Dine in The Rocks

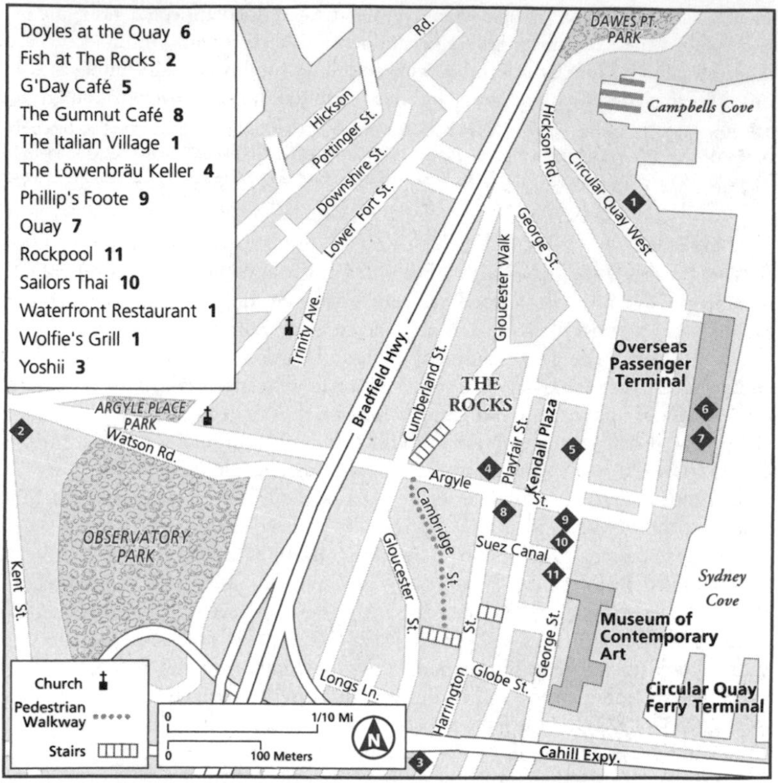

Rockpool ★★★ CONTEMPORARY The Rockpool is an institution in Sydney and is known for its inventive food. It's approached by a steep ramp and opens up into two stories of ocean-green carpet, designer chairs, and stainless steel. Along with the bar, the kitchen—with its busy chefs and copper pots and pans—is very much at the center of things. Rather than serving individual courses, the restaurant favors many smaller offerings. On the chef's menu tasting expect the freshest fish, oysters, quail eggs, abalone, clams, oysters, and all sorts of delicacies, which are expertly parceled-out and served. It's really worth checking out the website and booking well in advance. It's a true Sydney dining experience—if you can afford it!

109 George St., The Rocks. ✆ **02/9252 1888.** www.rockpool.com. Reservations essential. Chef's Tasting Menu A$175 (US$140/UK£70) per person; Five Course Set Price Menu with Selections A$150 (US$120/UK£60) per person. Wine is extra. AE, DC, MC, V. Mon–Sat 6–11pm. CityRail, bus, or ferry: Circular Quay.

Yoshii ★★★ JAPANESE Yoshii is about as far away from the increasingly popular conveyor-belt sushi service as you can imagine. Sit at the sushi counter and watch the chef slice and dice, or in the more intimate, muted tone main restaurant and witness beautiful service. At lunchtime there are seven set menus to choose from, and at dinner two 13-course options: the Yoshii Menu and the Saqura Menu. Tastes from the latter include smoked salmon mousse wrapped in marinated dried apricot, a Tasmania oyster with plum wine jelly, and a grilled persimmon and scallop with saffron *sumiso* sauce. This is a fabulous lunch option too, with several set meal options including a Sashimi Sushi Set that comes with tempura and miso soup too. It's all so overwhelmingly good.

115 Harrington St., The Rocks. © **02/9247 2566.** www.yoshii.com.au. Reservations essential. Lunch menus A$45–A$50 (US$36–US$40/UK£18–UK£20). Dinner: Yoshii Menu A$120 (US$96/UK£48) per person; Saqura Menu A$100 (US$80/UK£40) per person. AE, DC, MC, V. Tues–Fri noon–3pm; Mon–Sat 6–9:30pm. CityRail, bus, or ferry: Circular Quay.

EXPENSIVE

Doyles at the Quay *Overrated* SEAFOOD Just below Quay (see above) is Doyles, a name synonymous with seafood in Sydney. Most customers sit outside to enjoy the fabulous views across the harbor, though green guard railings do somewhat interrupt the view of the Opera House. Businesspeople and tourists come here if they don't want to lay out the cash for Quay or if they fancy a more relaxed style. The most popular dish is basically pricey fish and chips, which costs A$35 (US$28/UK£14). You can also get a dozen oysters for A$30 (US$24/UK£12) or half a lobster for A$65 (US$52/UK£26). One word of advice though, Australian lobsters (crayfish in reality) aren't nearly as tasty as lobsters in other parts of the world in my experience. Still, if you want the views and it's a nice day, then it's a nice place to sit.

A sister restaurant, **Doyles on the Beach** (© **02/9337 2007**), over at Watsons Bay, was slammed by Matthew Evans, the well-respected *Sydney Morning Herald* food critic, who gave it one of the worst reviews that's ever appeared in an Australian newspaper. The fish and chips, at A$35 (US$24/UK£12), is expensive and the service varies. Look up www.eatability.com.au/au/sydney/doyles_on_the_beach.htm for the latest reviews from patrons. In proximity to this eatery is **Doyles Fisherman's Wharf** (© **02/9337 1572**), on the ferry wharf; it used to be a takeout joint and now also has sit-down service. Doyles also runs the food service at the wonderful Watsons Bay Hotel nearby—a fabulous place for a drink on a sunny day. Ferries run to Watsons Bay from Circular Quay from 10:35am and then every half an hour until 3:35pm Monday through Friday, and from 9:20am and then every 45 minutes until 6:15pm on Saturday, Sunday, and public holidays.

Overseas Passenger Terminal, Circular Quay. © **02/9252 3400.** Main courses A$30–A$60 (US$24–US$48/UK£12–UK£24). DC, MC, V. Daily 11:30am–3pm; Mon–Sat 5:30–10:30pm; Sun 5:30–9:30pm. CityRail, bus, or ferry: Circular Quay.

Fish at the Rocks ★★ SEAFOOD This midsize eatery opposite the Lord Nelson Hotel, a 10-minute stroll up the main hill leading from The Rocks, serves delicious food with a focus on fresh seafood. There are a few little tables outside, as well as plenty inside below the photographs of sailing boats. The staff is very friendly and the service very professional. Portions are not huge, so don't expect to fill up on a single main course if you're starving. The dishes are well crafted, though. My favorites here are the Queensland scallops on polenta and braised peas, and the whiting filets (a fish) in a beer-batter. Don't pass on the chocolate mud cake, either—it's stunning.

29 Kent St., The Rocks. © **02/9252 4614.** www.fishattherocks.com.au. Reservations recommended. Main courses A$24–A$29 (US$19–US$23/UK£9.50–UK£12). AE, MC, V. Daily noon–2:30pm and 6–10:30pm. CityRail, bus, or ferry: Circular Quay.

Phillip's Foote ★ BARBECUE Venture behind this historic pub and you'll find a courtyard strung with tables, benches, and large barbecues. Choose your own steak, lemon sole, trout, chicken, or pork, and throw it on the "barbie." It's fun, it's filling, and you might even make some new friends while your meal's sizzling. Some Sydneysiders think A$27 (US$21/UK£11) is a bit pricey, but then again you are eating in prime real estate land. You may even experience an off night, when the salads don't look all that fresh, and the service is barely existent, but there's no excuse if you burn your own steak.

101 George St., The Rocks. ✆ **02/9241 1485.** www.phillipsfoote.com.au. Main courses A$27 (US$21/UK£11). AE, DC, MC, V. Mon–Sat noon–midnight; Sun noon–10pm. CityRail, bus, or ferry: Circular Quay.

Sailors Thai ★ THAI With a reputation as hot as the chiles in its jungle curry, Sailors Thai canteen attracts casual lunchtime crowds who come to eat great-tasting noodles and the likes of pork and prawn wonton soup, red curry with litchis, and Thai salads at its one stainless steel table with some 40 chairs. Four other tables overlook the cruise-ship terminal and the quay. Downstairs, the a la carte restaurant serves inventive food that's a far cry from the fare at your average Thai restaurant, such as stir-fried pineapple curry with chiles and cashew nuts, and wonderfully glutinous coconut ash pudding, made from the ash of burned coconuts cooked with licorice root, coconut water, rice flour, and sugar.

106 George St., The Rocks. ✆ **02/9251 2466.** www.sailorsthai.citysearch.com.au. Reservations required well in advance in restaurant, not accepted in canteen. Main courses A$26–A$35 (US$21–US$28/UK£11–UK£14) in restaurant, A$15–A$23 (US$12–US$18/UK£6–UK£9) in canteen. AE, DC, MC, V. Restaurant Mon–Fri noon–2pm; Mon–Sat 6–10pm. Canteen daily noon–9pm. CityRail, bus, or ferry: Circular Quay.

Waterfront Restaurant ★ CONTEMPORARY You can't help but notice the mast, rigging, and sails that mark this restaurant in a converted stone warehouse. It's one of four in a row (though a Chinese restaurant was closing at the time of writing) next to the water below the main spread of The Rocks. It's popular at lunchtime, when businesspeople snap up the best seats outside in the sunshine. At night, with the colors of the city washing over the harbor, it can be magical. You get a choice of such things as steaks, mud crab, fish filets, or prawns. The seafood platter, at A$132 (US$105/UK£52) for two, includes lobsters, Balmain bugs (small, odd-looking crayfish), prawns, scallops, baby squid, fish pieces, and octopus. The food is simple and fresh, at prices that reflect the glorious position and views. Come here instead of Doyles.

In the same building you'll find sister restaurants **Wolfie's Grill** (✆ **02/9241 5577**), which serves good chargrilled beef and seafood dishes for A$24 to A$34 (US$19–US$27/UK£9.50–UK£13), **The Italian Village** (✆ **02/9247 6111**), which serves regional Italian cuisine for A$24 to A$34 (US$19–US$27/UK£9.50–UK£13), and the Imperial Peking Harbourside which has Pekingese food, such as five spices crispy duckling and salt-and-pepper crab, for between A$23 and A$38 (US$18–US$30/UK£9–UK£15). All four restaurants offer fantastic water views and indoor and outdoor dining.

In Campbell's Storehouse, 27 Circular Quay West, The Rocks. ✆ **02/9247 3666.** www.waterfrontrestaurant.com.au. Reservations recommended. Main courses A$35–A$39 (US$28–US$31/UK£14–UK£16). A$3.50 (US$2.40/UK£1.20) per-person surcharge weekends and public holidays. AE, DC, MC, V. Daily noon–10:30pm. CityRail, bus, or ferry: Circular Quay.

MODERATE

The Gumnut Café Kids CONTEMPORARY A hearty lunch in a courtyard shaded from the sun by giant umbrellas—ah, heaven. With a great location in the heart of The Rocks, this 1890 sandstone cottage restaurant also has an extensive indoor seating area, so it's a perfect place to take a break from all that sightseeing. On weekends live jazz sets the mood. The breakfast specials (A$8.50/US$6.80/UK£3.40) are popular with guests from surrounding hotels, and at lunchtime the cafe bustles with tourists and office workers. Lunchtime blackboard specials cost A$11 (US$8.80/UK£4.40). More regular fare includes the disappointing Ploughman's Lunch (why spoil a traditional English meal of bread, cheese, and pickles by limiting the bread and adding unappealing vegetables and salad?), the better chicken and leek pies, and good pasta and noodle dishes. Filling Turkish sandwiches cost A$7.70 to A$9 (US$6.20–US$7.20). The courtyard is heated in winter, making it cozy. BYO; no corkage fee.

28 Harrington St., The Rocks. ✆ **02/9247 9591.** Main courses A$8.50–A$14 (US$6.80–US$11/UK£3.40–UK£5.50). AE, DC, MC, V. Sun–Wed 8am–5pm; Thurs–Sat 8am–10:30pm. CityRail, bus, or ferry: Circular Quay.

The Löwenbräu Keller ★ BAVARIAN Renowned for celebrating Oktoberfest every day for getting on 30 years, this is the place to watch Aussies let their hair down. Come for lunch and munch a club sandwich or focaccia in the glassed-off atrium while watching the daytime action of The Rocks. For a livelier scene, head here on Friday or Saturday night, when mass beer-sculling (chugging) and yodeling are accompanied by a brass band, and costumed waitresses ferry foaming beer steins about the atmospheric, cellarlike space. Options include hearty southern German and Austrian fare and several varieties of German beers in bottle or on draft (tap). There's a good wine list, and, surprisingly, vegetarians have a few choices, too. A good bargain is the lunchtime special, for just A$12 (US$9.60/UK£4.80). Monday it's salad with grilled chicken, on Tuesday currywurst with french fries, Wednesday goulash with mashed potato, and Thursday pork knuckle with potato salad. Try a good Bavarian beer during the daily happy hour, between 11:30am and 12:30pm, and again from 5pm to 7:30pm.

18 Argyle St. (at Playfair St.), The Rocks. ✆ **02/9247 7785.** www.lowenbrau.com.au. Reservations recommended. Main courses A$17–A$23 (US$9.60–US$18/UK£4.80–UK£9). AE, DC, MC, V. Daily 9:30am–2am (kitchen closes at 11pm). CityRail, bus, or ferry: Circular Quay.

INEXPENSIVE

G'Day Café *Value* CAFE According to the manager, about half the tourists who visit Sydney eat at this little place in the heart of The Rocks. That's not surprising, considering it offers simple, satisfying food at around half the price you'd expect to pay in such a tourist precinct. The interior is uninspiring, but in back there's a leafy courtyard. Among the offerings are focaccia sandwiches, hearty soups, salads, burgers, lasagna, chili con carne, and beef curry.

83 George St., The Rocks. ✆ **02/9241 3644.** Main courses A$3–A$7 (US$2.40–US$5.60/UK£1.20–UK£2.80). AE. Sun–Thurs 5am–midnight; Fri–Sat 5am–3am. CityRail, bus, or ferry: Circular Quay.

Zia Pina PIZZA/PASTA With 10 tables crammed downstairs and another 24 upstairs, there's not much room to breathe in this cramped traditional pizzeria and spaghetti house. But squeeze in between the bare-brick walls and wallow in the clashes and clangs coming from the hardworking chefs in the kitchen. Pizzas come in two sizes; the larger feeds two people. They cost between A$16 and A$20 (US$13–US$16/UK£6.50–8). There are several chicken dishes, seafood dishes, and salads, too.

93 George St., The Rocks. ✆ **02/9247 2255.** www.ziapina.com.au. Reservations recommended. Main courses A$9–A$20 (US$7.20–US$16/UK£3.60–UK£8). AE, DC, MC, V. Daily noon–3pm; Sun–Mon 5–9pm; Tues–Thurs 5–10:30pm; Fri–Sat 5–11:30pm. CityRail, bus, or ferry: Circular Quay.

NEAR TOWN HALL

VERY EXPENSIVE

Bilsons ★★★ FRENCH/CONTEMPORARY Tucked away at the back of the Radisson Plaza Hotel is one of those great restaurants that could easily compete with some of the Michelin-starred classics in Europe. The chef, Tony Bilson, is a well-known Sydney personality and the quality of his French-influenced food is a testament to some 30 years in the business. The restaurant is modern in its look, but comfortable too, and the service is impeccable. Expect something in the same vein as slow-roasted suckling pig with grilled pineapple, or grilled breasts of wild pigeon with foie gras.

The Foyer, Radisson Plaza Hotel, 27 O'Connell St., Sydney. © **02/8214 0496.** www.bilsons.com.au. Reservations essential. Main courses A$40 (US$32/UK£16); 8-course degustation menu A$120 (US$96/UK£48) per person, without wine, and A$200 (US$160/UK£80) per person with wine. AE, DC, MC, V. Mon–Fri noon–2:30pm; Mon–Sat 6–10pm. CityRail or bus: Town Hall or Wynyard.

est. at Establishment Hotel ★★★ MODERN AUSTRALIAN Upstairs in the trendy Establishment Hotel complex you'll find est., a restaurant that culinary luminary Peter Doyle has melded into a Sydney icon. The decor is a sensual masterpiece, with more white columns and rich felt-brown carpets adding to an ambience already sexed up by the coolest lounge music. est. won the ultimate score of three "hats" in the *Sydney Morning Herald's Good Food Guide* in 2004, 2005, 2006, and 2007 (only eight restaurants in Sydney received this score in 2007). It was also honored as Restaurant of the Year in 2006. Dishes that make an appearance on the menu include grilled rock lobster with herbs and lemon butter, and juniper-crusted saddle of venison, with beet-root purée, potato, and semolina gnocchi. It's more laid-back on the top floor, where you'll find the city's best sushi bar—a trendy raw-fish and rice place with one long table bathed in natural light called **Sushi E.** This is partitioned off from Hemisphere—a moody drinking place strung out with leather armchairs and comfy sofas.

Level 1, 252 George St., Sydney. © **02/9240 3010.** www.merivale.com. Reservations essential. Main courses A$43–A$57 (US$34–US$46/UK£17–UK£23). AE, DC, MC, V. Mon–Fri noon–3pm; Mon–Sat 6–10pm. CityRail or bus: Wynyard.

Tetsuya's ★★★ JAPANESE/FRENCH FUSION Tetsuya's was named the fifth-best restaurant in the world in *Restaurant Magazine*'s annual list of the world's 50 best eateries in 2007. Rockpool, the only other Australia or New Zealand restaurant on the top 50 list, slipped three places to 33. Topping the top 50 list was El Bulli in Barcelona, followed by The Fat Duck in Bray, Berkshire, to the west of London. Third was Pierre Gagnaire in Paris, followed by French Laundry in Yountville, California. So what makes Tetsuya's so good? On a recent visit I secured a table right next to the ceiling-to-floor windows, for intimate views across a Japanese-inspired courtyard with maples and waterfall. We chose the wine-matching option to go with our 10 courses, in my opinion the best thing to do here (corkage costs A$20 [US$16/UK£8] if you bring your own wine, and the tasting option means you get to try 10 good wines, several made especially to complement Tetsuya's dishes). The matching wine option costs $85 (US$68/UK£34) per head. The service was impeccable, and the food truly inspired. Small delicate morsels appeared: an incredible shot of pea soup with bitter chocolate sorbet was first, followed by a roulette of chopped smoked ocean trout capped with caviar, then a leek and spanner crab custard. Then came the signature dish: a confit of Tasmanian ocean trout with a crust of konbu seaweed, on a bed of daikon radish and fennel. And so it went on: a real culinary journey from the air and sea to the thick dark forests heady with mushrooms, veal and red wine. It was a once-in-a-lifetime experience. We came out with a bill in excess of A$600 (US$480/UK£240) for two, and then there was the tip! Everybody who is anybody wants to come here—so getting a table is difficult. To have a chance, you need to book when reservations become available, 4 weeks in advance, and reconfirm a few days before.

529 Kent St., Sydney. ✆ **02/9267 2900.** www.tetsuyas.com. Reservations essential; accepted 4 weeks ahead. 10-course degustation menu A$185 (US$148/UK£74) per person. Drinks extra. AE, DC, MC, V. Fri noon–3pm; Tues–Sat 6–10pm. CityRail: Town Hall.

EXPENSIVE

Capitan Torres SPANISH Sydney's Spanish quarter, around Liverpool Street (a 10-min. walk from Town Hall station on your right just past Sydney's main cinema strip), offers some good restaurants, of which Capitan Torres is my favorite. It's not fine dining, and certainly not up there with the best Mexican and Spanish restaurants found in the Spanish-speaking world, but it's a good choice for something casual. Downstairs is a tapas bar with traditional stools, Spanish staff, and lots of authentic dark oak. Upstairs on two floors is a fabulous restaurant with heavy wooden tables and an atmosphere thick with sangria and regional food. The garlic prawns are good, and the whole snapper a memorable experience. The tapas are better at **Asturiana** (✆ **02/9264 1010**), another Spanish restaurant a couple of doors down. Make sure you insist on eating at the bar for that authentic experience. ***Warning:*** Spanish serving staff in Sydney can be a bit gruff, so come armed with your sense of humor.

73 Liverpool St. (just past the cinema strip on George St., near Town Hall). ✆ **02/9264 5574.** Fax 02/9283 2292. Main courses A$23–A$27 (US$18–US$22/UK£9–UK£11); tapas A$12–A$19 (US$9.60–US$15/UK£4.70–UK£7.50). AE, DC, MC, V. Daily noon–3pm; Mon–Sat 6–11pm; Sun 6–10pm. CityRail: Town Hall.

INEXPENSIVE

Buena Vista Cafe ★ *Finds* CAFE If you happen to be in the city center, this fabulous, largely undiscovered restaurant and cafe is a must for the great value and the absolutely fantastic views reaching over Hyde Park and even to the harbor. It's very large inside, has panoramic windows, and serves meals from the counter. Hearty breakfasts include bacon and eggs, omelets, and cereals. All-day dishes run to sandwiches, Caesar salad, homemade pies, pastas, and lasagna. Even if you're not hungry, it's well worth popping in for a coffee.

Level 14, Law Courts Building, 184 Phillip St. (Queens Sq.). ✆ **02/9230 8224.** Main courses A$8–A$13 (US$6–US$10/UK£3–UK£5); coffee and cake A$5 (US$4/UK£2). No credit cards. Mon–Fri 7am–5pm. CityRail or bus: Museum.

NEAR CENTRAL STATION

VERY EXPENSIVE

Marque ★★★ FRENCH Seriously sophisticated, the Marque offers a small menu featuring classic French dishes with pizazz in an eggplant-colored room. Politicians, actors, and food critics all rave about the place. One such scribe, writing for the *New York Times,* wrote lyrically about the beet tart on flaky pastry, and suggested that the "sardine fillet, baked inside a thin, crisp, translucent crust until it looks like a fossil, then served with mackerel jelly" could only have been created by a "culinary wizard." He concluded the story by saying that there may be no better food anywhere in Australia.

4–5/355 Crown St., Surry Hills. ✆ **02/9332 2225.** www.marquerestaurant.com.au. Reservations essential. Main courses A$39–A$43 (US$31–US$34/UK£15–UK£17). AE, DC, MC, V. Mon–Sat 6:30–10:30pm. Taxi, Surry Hills (5 min. drive from Central Station).

DARLING HARBOUR

EXPENSIVE

Nicks Seafood Restaurant ★ *Finds* *Kids* SEAFOOD This nice, indoor, and alfresco eatery overlooking the water on the same side as Darling Harbour (to the left of Sydney Aquarium if you're looking at the boats) offers good cocktails and plenty of seafood. The best seats are outside in the sunshine, where you can watch the world go by over a bottle of wine. My choice of dish is the seafood platter for two, which has enough crab, prawns, fish, oysters, and lobster to satisfy. It costs A$120 (US$96/UK£48). Otherwise there are various fish, prawn, and octopus dishes to choose from. A kids' menu offers either chicken, calamari, or fish, with french fries and a soft drink, followed by ice cream. It costs A$13 (US$10/UK£5). Nicks has another, equally nice eatery, on the other side of the Aquarium called **Nicks Bar & Grill** (✆ **02/9279 0122**) and another, called **Nick's Bar & Grill Bondi Beach** (✆ **02/9365 4122**) in the Bondi Pavillion (across the grass and opposite the beach). The food and prices at all three places are similar. A sister establishment called I'm Angus Steakhouse (✆ **02/9264 5822**) caters to meat-eaters. It's on Cockle Bay Wharf, too.

The Promenade, Cockle Bay Wharf (on the city side of Darling Harbour). ✆ **02/9264 1212.** Reservations recommended. Main courses A$26–A$39 (US$21–US$31/UK£11–UK£15). A$5 (US$4/UK£2) per person surcharge on weekends and public holidays. AE, MC, V. Daily noon–3pm and 6–11pm. Ferry or monorail: Darling Harbour.

Zaaffran ★★ CONTEMPORARY INDIAN Sydney certainly hasn't seen an Indian restaurant quite like this one before. Forget the dark interiors and Indian murals. Here you find white surfaces, a glass-fronted wine cellar, and magnificent views of the water and the Sydney skyline from the far side of Darling Harbour. (An outdoor terrace provides the best views.) The restaurant started when two brothers from Bombay joined forces with chef Vikrant Kapoor, formerly the chef de cuisine at Raffles in Singapore. Together, they've revolutionized classic Indian cuisine. Expect such delights as the famed chicken *biryani,* baked in a pastry case and served with mint yogurt, or the tiger prawns in coconut cream and a tomato broth. Even fans of traditional Indian food are impressed by the creations here.

Level 2, 345 Harbourside Shopping Centre, Darling Harbour. ✆ **02/9211 8900.** Reservations recommended. Main courses A$20–A$26 (US$16–US$21/UK£8–UK£10). AE, DC, MC, V. Daily noon–2:30pm and 6–11pm. Ferry or monorail: Darling Harbour.

MODERATE

Chinta Ria (The Temple of Love) ★ MODERN MALAYSIAN Cockle Bay's star attraction for those who appreciate good food and fun ambience without paying a fortune, Chinta Ria is on the roof of the three-story development. In a round building dominated by a giant golden Buddha in the center, Chinta Ria serves fairly good "hawker-style" (read: cheap and delicious) Malaysian food. While the food is good, the atmosphere is even more memorable. The service is slow, but who cares in such an interesting space, with plenty of nooks, crannies, and society folk to look at. There are seats outside (some within range of the noise of the highway), but the best views unfold inside. Hot-and-sour soup—with tofu, mushrooms, bamboo shoots, and preserved cabbage—makes an interesting starter, and I recommend chile prawns and *hokkeien char* (soft-cooked egg noodles with extras) as main dishes.

Cockle Bay Wharf Complex. ✆ **02/9264 3211.** Main courses A$13–A$26 (US$9.60–US$21/UK£4.70–UK£10). AE, DC, MC, V. Daily noon–2:30pm and 6–11pm. Ferry or monorail: Darling Harbour.

WOOLLOOMOOLOO WHARF

VERY EXPENSIVE

Otto Ristorante ★★ MODERN ITALIAN Recognized as one of Sydney's premier restaurants, Otto boasts lush designer appointments and dim lighting that make it popular with local celebrities and socialites. Outside it's all light and breezy, with nice views of a boardwalk and some harbor water. Menu possibilities include roasted rack of pork with fennel and pork sausage, braised red cabbage, and balsamic peaches; or the veal wrapped in pancetta with fresh fig and polenta. For dessert I recommend the Campari and grenadine poached pear, which is simply out of this world.

8 the Wharf Woolloomooloo, 6 Cowper Wharf Rd. ✆ **02/9368 7488.** www.ottoristorante.com.au. Reservations required. Main courses A$24–A$39 (US$19–US$31/UK£9.50–UK£15). AE, DC, MC, V. Tues–Sun noon–3:30pm; Mon 6–10:30pm; Tues–Sat 6pm–midnight; Sun 6–9pm. Limited street parking. Bus: 311 from Circular Quay. Water taxi: Berth 53.

KINGS CROSS/DARLINGHURST

VERY EXPENSIVE

Mezzaluna ★★ NORTHERN ITALIAN Exquisite food, flawless service, and an almost unbeatable view across the city's western skyline have all helped Mezzaluna position itself firmly among Sydney's top waterside eateries. An open, candlelit place with white walls and polished wooden floorboards, the main dining room opens onto a huge all-weather terrace kept warm in winter by giant overhead fan heaters. The restaurant's owner, Sydney culinary icon Beppi Polesi, provides an exceptional wine list to complement a menu that changes daily. There's always a fabulous risotto on the menu. Other delights may include spatchcock oven roasted with prosciutto, Asiago cheese, and sage, served with a black truffle potato purée and braised leek; oven-roasted lamb rump served with black olive Parmesan gratin, braised tomatoes, and basil oil. Whatever you choose, you can't really go wrong.

123 Victoria St., Potts Point. ✆ **02/9357 1988.** Fax 02/9357 2615. www.mezzaluna.com.au. Reservations recommended. Main courses A$32–A$43 (US$26–US$34/UK£13–UK£17). AE, DC, MC, V. Mon–Fri noon–3pm; Mon–Sat 6–11pm. CityRail: Kings Cross.

EXPENSIVE

Oh Calcutta ★★ *Finds* MODERN INDIAN A tiny terrace, found after an interesting walk (turn right at the exit of Kings Cross CityRail station and ask directions from someone who appears normal) hides two cramped floors of Indian heaven. Apart from the name there's little to suggest it's an Indian eatery, and when it comes to the food any resemblance to what you might find on the subcontinent is hard to grasp, too. Apart from the spices, that is. So, in short, it's Indian and it's not—which makes it all the more intriguing. Some examples include kangaroo with sesame seeds, chile, and lemon; oxtail curry with celeriac and caramelized onion; and the wonderful baby beet root with snow pea leaves, *garam masala,* and mild chile. There are several vegetarian options. The chef and owner, Basil Danielli, makes it all the more fun with his repartee. I highly recommend this place if you don't mind a casual atmosphere, a tight squeeze, and adventurous cuisine. It's a fun and fascinating taste sensation.

251 Victoria St., Darlinghurst. ✆ **02/9360 3650.** www.ohcalcutta.com.au. Reservations essential. Main courses A$19–A$28 (US$15–US$22/UK£7.50–UK£11). AE, MC, V. Mon–Sat 6–11pm. CityRail: Kings Cross.

MODERATE

Hard Rock Cafe AMERICAN The obligatory half-Cadillac through the wall beckons you into this shrine to rock 'n' roll. Among the items on display are costumes worn by Elvis, John Lennon, and Elton John, as well as guitars from Sting and the Bee Gees, drums from Phil Collins and The Beatles, and one of Madonna's bras. The mainstays here are the burgers, with ribs, chicken, fish, salads, and T-bone steaks on the menu, too. Most meals come with french fries or baked potatoes and a salad. It's really busy on Friday and Saturday evenings from around 7:30 to 10:30pm, when you might have to line up to get a seat.

121–129 Crown St., Darlinghurst. ✆ **02/9331 1116.** Reservations not accepted. Main courses A$9.95–A$22 (US$7.80–US$18/UK£3.90–UK£9). 10% surcharge weekends and public holidays. AE, DC, MC, V. Daily noon–midnight. Shop daily 10am–midnight. Closed Dec 25. CityRail: Museum, then walk across Hyde Park, head down the hill past the Australian Museum on William St., and turn right onto Crown St. Sydney Explorer Bus: Stop no. 7.

INEXPENSIVE

Govindas VEGETARIAN When I think of Govindas, I can't help smiling. Perhaps it's because I'm recalling the happy vibe from the Hare Krishna center it's based in, or maybe it's because the food is so cheap! Or maybe it's because they even throw in a decent movie with the meal. (The movie theater is on a different floor.) The food is simple vegetarian, served buffet-style and eaten in a basic room off black-lacquer tables. Typical dishes include pastas and salads, lentil dishes, soups, and casseroles. It's BYO and doctrine-free.

112 Darlinghurst Rd., Darlinghurst. ✆ **02/9380 5155.** www.govindas.com.au. Dinner A$16 (US$13/UK£6.50), including movie. AE, MC, V. Daily 6–11pm. CityRail: Kings Cross.

GLEBE

VERY EXPENSIVE

The Boathouse on Blackwattle Bay ★★ *Finds* SEAFOOD Above Sydney University's rowing club and overlooking a working area of Sydney Harbour, this converted boat shed offers water views across to the city and the Anzac Bridge. It serves terrific French-inspired seafood in an elegant, yet informal, atmosphere of white tablecloths and natural lighting. The service is variable (but hopefully improving after not-so-hot reviews in recent months). Oh, and you can see the chefs at work in the open kitchen. You can't go wrong with the signature dish, the fabulous snapper fish pie with roasted tomatoes and mashed potatoes. There are usually nine varieties of oysters on the menu. A good wine list and delicious desserts cap off a truly memorable experience. I highly recommend The Boathouse, particularly as a lunchtime treat. Catch a taxi—it's a little hard to find.

End of Ferry Rd., Glebe. ✆ **02/9518 9011.** www.boathouse.net.au. Main courses A$37–A$43 (US$30–US$34/UK£15–UK£17). AE, DC, MC, V. Tues–Sun noon–2:30pm and 6:30–10pm. Bus: 431, 433, or 434 from Millers Point, The Rocks (on George St.), or 459 from behind Town Hall.

PADDINGTON

The top end of Oxford Street, which runs from Hyde Park in central Sydney toward Bondi, has a profusion of trendy bars and cafes and a scattering of cheaper eateries among the more glamorous ones.

VERY EXPENSIVE

Buon Ricordo ★★ ITALIAN With yellow walls pinned with antique plates and artwork, and padded-wooden chairs and archways, Buon Ricordo oozes trattoria-style charm. The food is rich and the prices for main courses are high, but the food is just perfection. Dishes might include such seasonal specialties as crispy fried harbor prawns, or a delicious winter salad of raw fennel and artichoke hearts. A favorite is the polenta cake with grilled radicchio flavored with sweet vincotto. The house signature dish is *fettuccine al tartufovo*—fettuccine served in a cream sauce with lightly fried, truffle-infused eggs.

108 Boundary St., Paddington. ✆ **02/9360 6729.** www.buonricordo.com.au. Reservations essential. Pastas A$25–A$30 (US$20–US$24/UK£10–UK£12). Main courses A$38–A$49 (US$30–US$39/UK£15–UK£20). AE, DC, MC, V. Fri–Sat noon–3pm; Tues–Sat 6:30–11pm. Bus: 360 or 361.

CAFE CULTURE

Debate rages over which cafe serves the best coffee in Sydney, which has the best atmosphere, and which has the tastiest snacks. The main cafe scenes center on **Victoria Street** in Darlinghurst, **Stanley Street** in East Sydney, and **King Street** in Newtown. Other places, including Balmoral Beach on the North Shore, Bondi Beach, and Paddington all have their own favored hangouts.

Note: Americans will be sorry to learn that, unlike in the States, free refills of coffee are rare in Australian restaurants and cafes. Sip slowly. Expect a cup of coffee to cost A$2.50 to A$3 (US$2–US$2.40/UK£1–UK£1.40); main courses run A$8 to A$15 (US$6.40–US$12/UK£3.20–UK£6).

This section includes my favorite cafes around town.

Bar Coluzzi Although it may no longer offer the best coffee in Sydney, this cafe's claim to fame is that long ago it served real espresso when the rest of the city was drinking Nescafé. People-watching is a favorite hobby at this fashionably worn-around-the-edges spot in the heart of Sydney's cafe district.

322 Victoria St., Darlinghurst. ✆ **02/9380 5420.** MC, V. Daily 5am–8pm. CityRail: Kings Cross.

Bill's This bright and airy place, strewn with flowers and magazines, serves nouveau cafe-style food. It's so popular you might have trouble finding a seat. The signature breakfast dishes—including ricotta hotcakes with honeycomb butter and banana, and sweet corn fritters with roast tomatoes and bacon—are the stuff of legend.

433 Liverpool St., Darlinghurst. ✆ **02/9360 9631.** Fax 02/9360 7302. AE, MC, V. Mon–Sat 7:30am–3pm. CityRail: Kings Cross.

Café Hernandez ★ *Finds* The walls of this tiny, cluttered cafe are crammed with eccentric fake masterpieces, and the aroma of 20 types of coffee roasted and ground on the premises permeates the air. It's almost a religious experience for discerning inner-city coffee addicts. The Spanish espresso is a treat.

60 Kings Cross Rd., Potts Point. ✆ **02/9331 2343.** www.cafehernandez.com.au. AE, MC, V. Daily 24 hr. CityRail: Kings Cross.

The Old Coffee Shop ★ Sydney's oldest coffee shop opened in the Victorian Strand Arcade in 1891. The shop may or may not serve Sydney's best java, but the old-world feel of the place and the sugary snacks, cakes, and pastries make up for it. It's a good spot to take a break from shopping and sightseeing.

Ground floor, Strand Arcade. ✆ **02/9231 3002.** MC, V. Mon–Fri 7:30am–5pm; Sat 8:30am–5pm; Sun 10:30am–4pm. CityRail: Town Hall.

IN NEWTOWN: GREAT ETHNIC EATS

Inner-city Newtown is three stops from Central Station on CityRail, and 10 minutes by bus from central Sydney. On Newtown's main drag, **King Street,** many inexpensive restaurants offer food from all over the world.

Le Kilimanjaro AFRICAN With so many excellent restaurants in Newtown—they close down or improve quickly enough if they're bad—I picked Kilimanjaro because it's one of the most unusual. It's a tiny place, with limited seating on two floors. Basically, you enter, you choose a dish off the blackboard menu (while standing), and a waiter escorts you to your seat. On a recent visit I had couscous, African bread (similar to Indian chapati), and *saussou-gor di guan* (tuna in a rich sauce). Another favorite dish is *yassa* (chicken in a rich sauce). All meals are served on traditional wooden plates. The servings are rather small though, so order more than you think your stomach can manage.

280 King St., Newtown. ✆ **02/9557 4565.** Reservations not accepted. Main courses A$8.50–A$12 (US$7–US$9.20/UK£3.50–UK£4.60). No credit cards. CityRail: Newtown.

Old Saigon ★ *Finds* VIETNAMESE I highly recommend this place for a cheap night out. Bursting with atmosphere, Old Saigon was owned until 1998 by a former American Vietnam War correspondent who loved Vietnam so much he ended up living there and marrying a local before coming to Australia. Just to make sure you knew his history, he put up his photos on the walls and scattered homemade tin helicopters around the place. His Vietnamese brother-in-law has taken over, but the food is still glorious; the spicy squid dishes are among my favorites. A popular pastime is grilling your own strips of venison, beef, wild boar, kangaroo, or crocodile over a burner at your table, then wrapping the meat in rice paper with lettuce and mint, and dipping it in chile sauce. The salt-and-pepper squid is the best in town. BYO.

107 King St., Newtown. ✆ **02/9519 5931.** Reservations recommended. Main courses A$13–A$43 (US$9.60–US$34/UK£4.80–UK£17); most dishes around A$18 (US$14/UK£7). AE, DC, MC, V. Wed–Fri noon–3pm; Tues–Sun 6–11pm. CityRail: Newtown.

BONDI BEACH

EXPENSIVE

Bondi Icebergs/Icebergs Dining Room & Bar ★★★ SEAFOOD/MEDITERRANEAN This revamped old swimming club complex overlooking Bondi Beach is a truly fabulous place to hang out. From its corner position on the cliffs, the Icebergs Bar looks directly across the beach and water, and its floor-to-roof windows make sure you get to experience what's probably the best view in Sydney. The bar features lots of cushions and even hammocks, and the views stretch on across the balcony and into the restaurant. Inside this highly recommended eating place it's all frosted glass dividers (to match the color of the ocean), and crisp white tablecloths and napkins (to resemble the surf). Not surprisingly, seafood features highly on the menu. You may well find wild scallops; risotto with coral trout and oregano; a fish stew from Livorno; and spaghetti with clams.

Here too is the **Sundeck Café,** which boasts a variety of light snacks and meals ranging from focaccia, salads, and burgers to fresh local seafood and pasta, all served out on a terrace with fantastic views.

1 Notts Ave., Bondi Beach. ✆ **02/9365 9000.** Reservations essential. Main courses A$36–A$44 (US$29–US$35/UK£15–UK£18). AE, DC, MC, V. Tues–Sat noon–3pm and 6:30–10:30pm; Sun noon–3pm and 6:30–9pm. CityRail to Bondi Junction and bus 380 or 333 to Bondi Beach, or bus 380 or 333 from the city.

MODERATE

Thai Terrific THAI Thai Terrific by name, terrific Thai by nature. This simple, but great place on the right night is around the corner from the Bondi Hotel. Sometimes it falls a little short on service and sometimes the food doesn't quite hit the right note, but when it's spot-on it's fabulous. The back room can be noisy, so if you prefer less din with your dinner, sit at one of the sidewalk tables. The servings are enormous—three people could fill up on just two main courses. The *tom yum* (hot-and-sour) soups and spicy prawn or seafood laksa noodle soups (made with coconut milk) are the best I've tasted in Australia and very filling. I also highly recommend the red curries.

Equally nice (and quieter) is the Bangkok-style **Nina's Ploy Thai Restaurant** ★, 132 Wairoa Ave. (✆ **02/9365 1118**), at the corner of Warners Avenue at the end of the main Campbell Parade strip. Main courses here cost A$10 to A$15 (US$8–US$12/UK£4UK£6); cash only.

147 Curlewis St., Bondi Beach. ✆ **02/9365 7794.** Reservations recommended Fri–Sat night. Main courses A$14–A$20 (US$11–US$16/UK£5.50–UK£8). AE, DC, MC, V. Daily noon–11pm. CityRail to Bondi Junction and bus 380 or 333 to Bondi Beach, or bus 380 or 333 from the city.

EXPENSIVE

Ravesi's ★ CONTEMPORARY Set on a corner beside a run of surf shops, Ravesi's is a kind of fish tank, with the water on the outside. Downstairs, it's all glass windows and bar stools—the perfect place to watch the street life go by. On weekend nights the place is packed. Upstairs is a fine casual restaurant with seating both inside and out on the balcony overlooking the beach. On a recent visit I had the smoked chicken salad with avocado, chile, mango, and peanuts and it easily outclassed any salad I've had for a long while. The seafood, meat dishes, and lots of vegetarian options, also make a big impression. Weekend breakfast up here is a wonderful experience, and they do excellent Bloody Marys, comforting after a night on the town.

Corner of Campbell Parade and Hall Street, Bondi Beach. ✆ **02/9365 4422.** Reservations recommended. Main courses A$23–A$29 (US$18–US$23/UK£9–UK£12). Breakfasts A$10–A$22 (US$8–US$18/UK£4–UK£9). AE, MC, V. Mon–Sat noon–3pm and 6–10pm; Sun noon–4pm. Breakfasts Sat–Sun 9am–noon. CityRail to Bondi Junction and bus 380 or 333 to Bondi Beach, or bus 380 or 333 from the city.

INEXPENSIVE

Pompei's ★ *Finds* PIZZA/PASTA/ICE CREAM The recipe is simple: Use good ingredients and you'll get good pizzas—regulars swear they are the best in Sydney. Toppings include figs, prosciutto, fresh goat cheese, and pumpkin. Pompei's also has a selection of pizzas without cheese. And leave some room for the homemade gelati, the best in Sydney by far. The last time I had anything so good was in Pompeii, Italy, itself, and I swore then it was the best I'd ever eaten. Try dense raspberry, thick chocolate, tiramisu, or limoncello. The water views and outside tables are another plus.

126–130 Roscoe St. at Gould St., Bondi Beach. ✆ **02/9365 1233.** Reservations recommended. Pizza A$13–A$17 (US$10–US$14/UK£5–UK£7). AE, DC, MC, V. Tues–Sun 11am–11pm. CityRail to Bondi Junction and bus 380 or 333 to Bondi Beach, or bus 380 or 333 from the city.

MANLY

Manly is 30 minutes from Circular Quay by ferry, or 15 minutes by JetCat. The takeout shops that line **the Corso,** as well as the **pedestrian mall** that runs between the ferry terminal and the main Manly Beach, offer everything from Turkish kabobs to Japanese noodles. There are better restaurants along the seafront (though there's a road between them and the beach). All are pretty good, so just take a lunchtime walk, check out their blackboard menus, and take a seat if something takes your fancy.

INEXPENSIVE

Ashiana ★ INDIAN You'll be hard-pressed to find a better moderately priced Indian restaurant in the Sydney area. Tucked away up a staircase next to the Steyne

Hotel (just off the Corso near the main beach), Ashiana has won prizes for its traditional spicy cooking. I've eaten there for years. Portions are large and filling, though creamy in that kind of pampering-to-Western-tastes style. The service is friendly. The butter chicken is magnificent, while *malai* kofta (cheese and potato dumplings in mild, creamy sauce) is the best this side of Bombay. Beer is the best drink with everything. Work off the excellent meal with a beachside stroll afterward.

Corner of Sydney Rd. and the Corso, Manly. ✆ **02/9977 3466.** Reservations recommended. Main courses A$10–A$19 (US$8–US$16/UK£4–UK£8). AE, MC, V. Daily 5:30–11pm. Ferry or JetCat: Manly.

Green's Eatery VEGETARIAN Of the many eateries in Manly, this nice little vegetarian place, just off the Corso on the turnoff before the Steyne Hotel, does the best lunchtime business. The food is healthy and good quality. The menu includes 11 vegetarian burgers, vegetable curries and noodle dishes, patties and salads, soups, smoothies, and wraps. Green's serves exceptionally nice cakes, too, which despite being wholesome are surprisingly tasty. On a nice day you can sit outside.

1–3 Sydney Rd., Manly. ✆ **02/9977 1904.** Menu items A$1.20–A$7.40 (US95¢–US$5.95/UK45p–UK£3). No credit cards. Daily 8am–7pm. Ferry or JetCat: Manly.

5 What to See & Do in Sydney

The only problem with visiting Sydney is fitting in everything you want to do and see. Of course, you won't want to miss the iconic attractions: the **Opera House** and the **Harbour Bridge.** Everyone seems to be climbing over the arch of the bridge these days on the BridgeClimb Sydney Tour, so look up for the tiny dots of people waving to the ferry passengers below.

You should also check out the native wildlife in **Taronga Zoo** and the **Sydney Aquarium,** stroll around the tourist precinct of **Darling Harbour,** and get a dose of Down Under culture at the not-too-large **Australian Museum.** Also try to take time out to visit one of the nearby national parks for a taste of the Australian bush. If it's hot, take your "cozzie" (swimsuit) and towel to **Bondi Beach** or **Manly.**

I also recommend a quick trip out of town. Go bushwalking in the **Blue Mountains,** wine tasting in the **Hunter Valley,** or dolphin spotting at **Port Stephens** (see chapter 5 for details on all three).

Whatever you decide to do, you won't have enough time. Don't be surprised if you start planning your next visit before your first is even finished.

Attraction Passes are shared by Sydney Tower and OzTrek, Sydney Aquarium, and Wildlife World, and you can buy them online at their websites or at the attractions themselves. The **Aqua + Tower Pass** includes entry to Sydney Aquarium and Sydney Tower + OzTrek. It costs A$47 (US$37/UK£18) for an adult, A$26 (US$20/UK£10)

Value Great Deals on Sightseeing

The **See Sydney & Beyond** card (✆ **02/9247 6611**; www.seesydneycard.com), a cashless smart card packaging more than 40 of the city's main attractions and tours, is valuable for avoiding lines and saving money, although you'll have to plan well to get the most out of it. The card can be purchased for a 1-, 2-, 3-, or 7-day period; the 1-day pass costs A$69 (US$55/UK£27) for adults and A$49 (US$39/UK£20) for children. Buy through their website.

Central Sydney Attractions

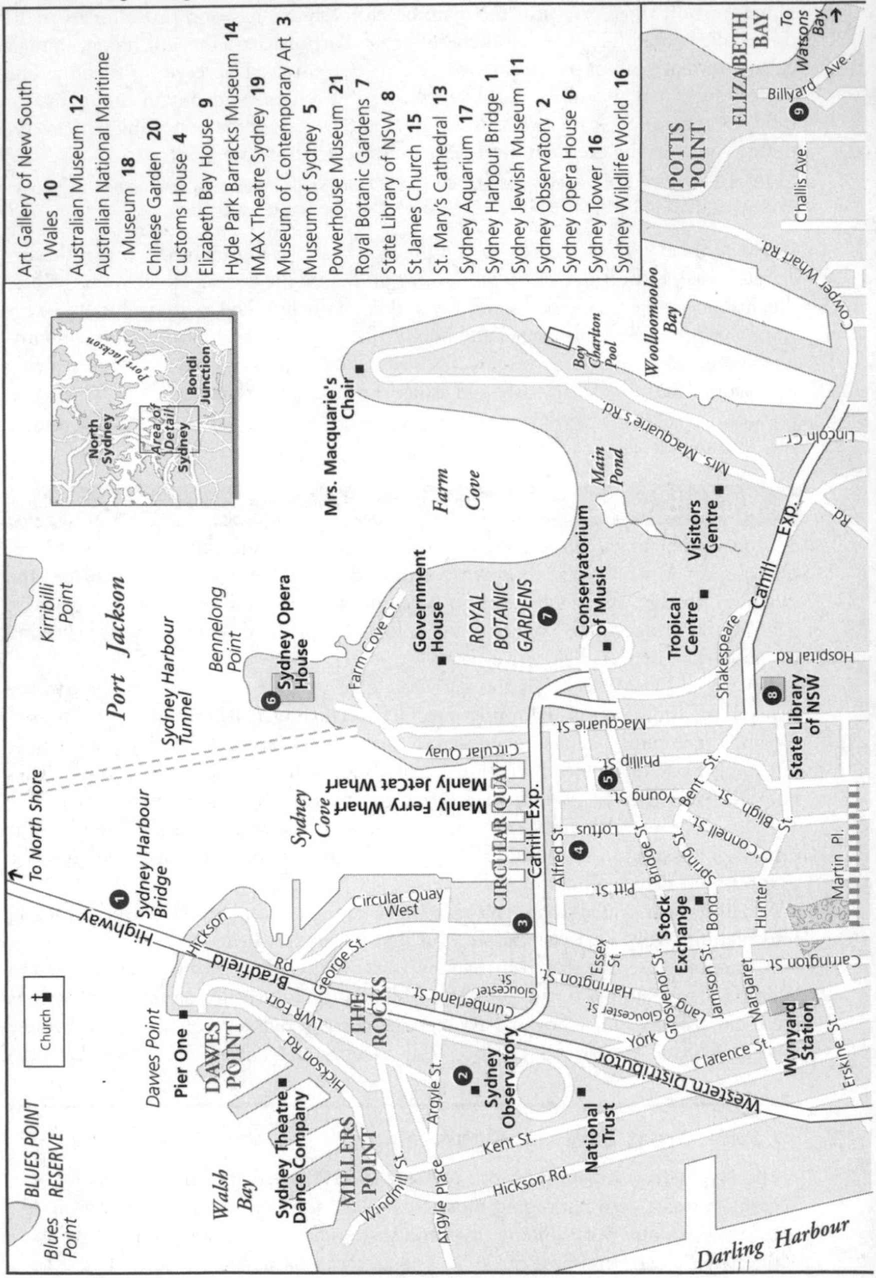

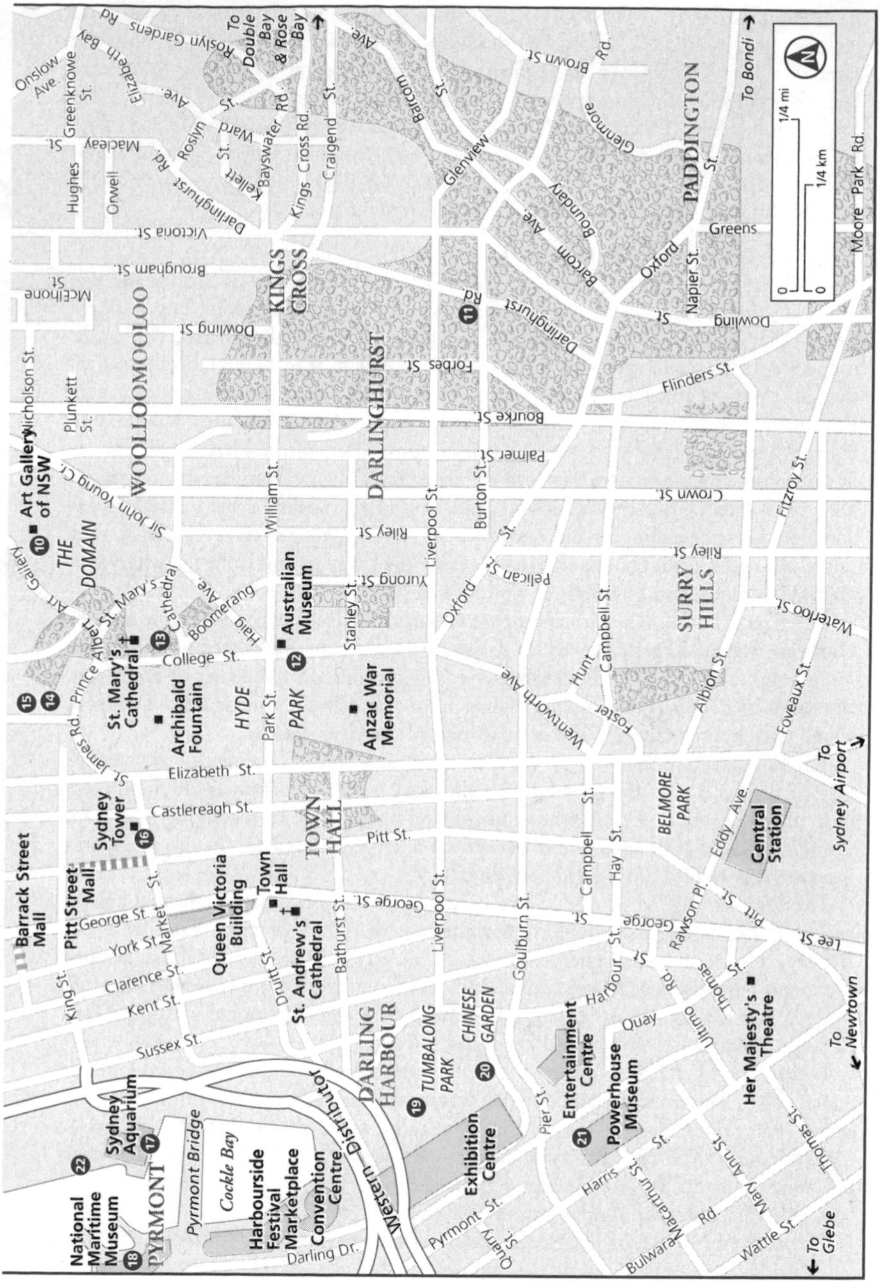

To Double Bay & Rose Bay →
Onslow Ave.
Greenknowe St.
Elizabeth Bay
Roslyn Gardens Rd
Ave.
Roslyn St.
Ward Ave.
Macleay St.
Hughes
Orwell
Darlinghurst Rd.
Kellett St.
Bayswater Rd.
Kings Cross Rd.
Craigend St.
Barcom Ave.
Brown St.
Glenmore Rd.
Glenview St.
Boundary
Barcom Ave.
Victoria St.
Brougham St.
McElhone St.
KINGS CROSS
WOOLLOOMOOLOO
Dowling St.
Nicholson St.
Plunkett St.
Art Gallery of NSW
Sir John Young Cr.
THE DOMAIN
Art Gallery
William St.
DARLINGHURST
Forbes St.
Darlinghurst Rd.
Bourke St.
Palmer St.
Burton St.
Liverpool St.
Riley St.
Yurong St.
Stanley St.
Australian Museum
Boomerang
Haig Ave.
Cathedral
St. Mary's
Prince Albert
St. Mary's Cathedral
Archibald Fountain
College St.
HYDE PARK
Park St.
Anzac War Memorial
Oxford St.
Pelican St.
Wentworth Ave.
Hunt
Campbell St.
Foster
SURRY HILLS
Crown St.
Riley St.
Waterloo St.
Albion St.
Foveaux St.
Fitzroy St.
Flinders St.
Dowling St.
Oxford
Napier St.
Greens
PADDINGTON
Moore Park Rd.
To Bondi →
1/4 mi
1/4 km
0
St. James Rd.
Elizabeth St.
Castlereagh St.
Sydney Tower
Barrack Street Mall
Pitt Street Mall
Market St.
George St.
York St.
Queen Victoria Building
Town Hall
TOWN HALL
Pitt St.
Clarence St.
Kent St.
King St.
Druitt St.
St. Andrew's Cathedral
Bathurst St.
George St.
Liverpool St.
Goulburn St.
Campbell St.
Hay St.
BELMORE PARK
Eddy Ave.
Central Station
To Sydney Airport
Rawson Pl.
Pitt St.
Lee St.
George St.
Harbour St.
Thomas St.
Ultimo Rd.
Her Majesty's Theatre
To Newtown
Sussex St.
DARLING HARBOUR
TUMBALONG PARK
CHINESE GARDEN
Entertainment Centre
Quay St.
Pier St.
Powerhouse Museum
Sydney Aquarium
Pyrmont Bridge
Cockle Bay
National Maritime Museum
PYRMONT
Harbourside Festival Marketplace
Convention Centre
Western Distributor
Exhibition Centre
Darling Dr.
Pyrmont St.
Quarry St.
Harris St.
Macarthur St.
Mary Ann St.
Thomas St.
Bulwara Rd.
Wattle St.
To Glebe

for a child, and A$116 (US$93/UK£46) for a family. The **Wildlife + Tower Pass** includes entry to Sydney Wildlife World and Sydney Tower + OzTrek. This costs the same as above. The **Sydney Attractions Pass** includes entry to Sydney Aquarium, Sydney Wildlife World, and Sydney Tower + OzTrek. It costs A$64 (US$51/UK£25) for an adult, A$35 (US$28/UK£14) for a child, and A$158 (US$126/UK£63) for a family. **Sydney Adventures By Night** includes night entry to Sydney Aquarium, and Sydney Tower + OzTrek. This costs A$47 (US$37/UK£18) for adults, A$26 (US$20/UK£10) for kids, and A$116 (US$93/UK£46) for a family.

SYDNEY HARBOUR & THE ROCKS

Officially called Port Jackson, **Sydney Harbour** is the focal point of Sydney and one of the features—along with the beaches and easy access to surrounding national parks—that makes this city so special. It's entered through **the Heads,** two bush-topped outcrops (you'll see them if you take a ferry or JetCat to Manly), beyond which the harbor laps at some 240km (149 miles) of shoreline before stretching out into the Parramatta River. Visitors are often awestruck by the harbor's beauty, especially at night, when the sails of the Opera House and the girders of the Harbour Bridge are lit up, and the waters are swirling with the reflection of lights from the abutting high-rises—reds, greens, blues, yellows, and oranges. During the day, it buzzes with green-and-yellow ferries pulling in and out of busy Circular Quay, sleek tourist craft, fully rigged tall ships, giant container vessels making their way to and from the wharves of Darling Harbour, and hundreds of white-sailed yachts.

The greenery along the harbor's edges is a surprising feature, thanks to the **Sydney Harbour National Park,** a haven for native trees and plants, and a feeding and breeding ground for lorikeets and other nectar-eating bird life. In the center of the harbor is a series of islands; the most impressive is the tiny isle supporting **Fort Denison,** which once housed convicts and acted as part of the city's defense.

The Rocks neighborhood is on the Harbour Bridge side of Circular Quay. Sydney's historic district is hilly and crosscut with alleyways. Some of Australia's oldest pubs are here, as well as boutique restaurants, stores, and hotels. Pick up a walking map from the visitor center and make sure to get off the main streets and see the original working-class houses that survived the bulldozers.

The Eora Aboriginal people originally inhabited the rocky headland, now known as The Rocks, and the surrounding shoreline for thousands of years. Then in 1788, British convicts and their guards arrived. A jail was built where The Four Seasons Hotel now stands, on George Street, and public hangings were common. Later it evolved into a vibrant port community, though its history is colored with outbreaks of plague, shanghaied sailors, and cut-throat gangs.

By the turn of the 20th century the harbor was polluted and the wharves were not much better. The Sydney Harbour Trust was formed in 1902 to clean things up. That year a report outlined what they retrieved from the water off The Rocks:

"2524 rats, 1068 cats, 283 bags of meat, 305 bags of fish, 1467 fowls, 25 parrots, 23 sheep, 14 pigs, 1 bullock, 9 calves, 9 goats, 5 hares, 3 kangaroos, 162 rabbits, 18 bags of chaff, 8 bales of straw, 3 flying foxes and 2 sharks"

Over the years much of The Rocks was torn down to make way for roads, the Harbour Bridge, and newer housing developments.

In 1973, bulldozers and protesters clashed with police over plans to tear down many of the buildings that remain today. These resulted in the Green Bans, led by unionist Jack Mundey, which halted any further demolition work. In 1975 a compromise was reached and the bans were lifted, in return for heritage protection and community consultation on future projects.

Today, there are 96 heritage buildings in The Rocks. The oldest house is Cadmans Cottage, built in 1815, while the Dawes Point Battery, built in 1791, is the oldest remaining European structure. On Observatory Hill you'll find the three remaining walls of Fort Phillip, built in 1804.

Luna Park *Kids* The huge smiling clown face and the fairground attractions, which are visible from Circular Quay, make up one of Australia's iconic attractions. Opened in 1935 and closed for many years, it reopened in 2004. It's small but fun, with traditional theme-park amusements rather than high-tech rides. It has a carousel, dodge-'em cars, a Ferris wheel, and the like. Several rides are suitable for small children, too. You buy tickets—or "lunas," as they're called—at booths inside the park.

1 Olympic Dr., Milsons Point (across the harbor from the Sydney Opera House). © **02/9922 6646.** www.lunaparksydney.com. Free admission. Rides A$3–A$7 (US$2.40–US$6/UK£1.20–UK£3); day pass with unlimited rides: A$13 (US$10/UK£5) kids under 4, A$26 (US$21/UK£11) kids 4–12, A$36 (US$29/UK£15) kids over 13 and adults, A$109 (US$87/UK£43) family. Mon–Tues 11am–6pm; Fri 11am–10pm; Sat 10am–11pm; Sun 10am–6pm. Open later during school holidays. Ferry or CityRail: Milsons Point.

The Rocks Discovery Museum This small but interesting museum is in a restored 1850s sandstone warehouse. It tells the story of The Rocks from pre-European days to the present. Learn about the area's traditional landowners, the establishment of the English colony, the sailors, whalers, and traders who made the area their home, and the 1970s union-led protests that preserved this unique part of Sydney.

Kendall Lane, The Rocks. © **1800 067 676.** www.rocksdiscoverymuseum.com.au. Free admission. Daily 10am–5pm. Bus: 308, 339, 343, 431, 432, 433, or 434. CityRail: Circular Quay or Wynyard.

Susannah Place Museum ★★ *Finds* This museum, set around a terrace of four houses, built in 1844, is a real highlight of The Rocks area. It provides visitors with the opportunity to explore domestic working-class life from 1844 to 1990. The modest interiors and rear yards illustrate the restrictions of 19th-century inner-city life. The many layers of the paint finishes, wallpapers, and floor coverings that have survived provide a valuable insight into the tastes of the working class. The original brick privies and open laundries are some of the earliest surviving washing and sanitary amenities remaining in the city. There's also a delightful little shop, selling cordials, postcards, old-fashioned candies, and knickknacks. Allow 45 minutes.

58–64 Gloucester St., The Rocks. © **02/9241 1893.** www.hht.net.au. Admission A$8 (US$6.40/UK£3.20) adults, A$4 (US$3.20/UK£1.60) kids, A$17 (US$14/UK£7) family (entry to shop free). Sat–Sun and Tues–Thurs 10am–5pm; also open daily in Jan and NSW school holidays. Bus, Ferry, or CityRail: Circular Quay.

Sydney Harbour Bridge ★★★ One thing few tourists do, although it only takes an hour or so, is to walk across the Harbour Bridge. The bridge, completed in 1932, is 1,150m (3,772 ft.) long and spans 503m (1,650 ft.) from the south shore to the north. It accommodates pedestrian walkways, two railway lines, and an eight-lane road. The 30-minute stroll from one end to the other offers excellent harbor views. From the other side, you can take a CityRail train from Milsons Point back to the city (to Wynyard—change there for Circular Quay, Town Hall, or Central).

As you walk across, stop off at the **Pylon Lookout** (© **02/9247 3408**), at the southeastern pylon. Admission is A$9 (US$7/UK£3.50) for adults, A$3.50 (US$3/UK£1.50) for children over 7. From the top of this bridge support, 89m (292 ft.) above the water, you get panoramic views of Sydney Harbour, the ferry terminals of Circular

Moments Walk on the Wild Side: Climb the Harbour Bridge

At one time, only bridge workers had the opportunity to view Sydney from the top of the main bridge arch. But since October 1998, Sydneysiders and tourists have been able to experience the spectacular view and the exhilarating achievement of climbing to the top of one of Australia's icons on a **BridgeClimb.** In 2006 a second climb opened, called the **Discovery Climb.** This takes climbers into the heart of the bridge. You traverse the suspension arch and then wind your way through a tangle of hatchways and girders suspended above the traffic. You also climb between the arches to the summit. Both experiences take 3 hours from check-in at the **BridgeClimb** ★★ base, 5 Cumberland St., The Rocks (© **02/9240 1100** or 02/8274 7777; fax 02/9240 1122; www.bridgeclimb.com), to completion. The office is open daily from 8am to 6pm, and climbers leave in small groups every 10 minutes or so. Climbers wear "Bridge Suits" and are harnessed to a line. Participants are also breath-tested for alcohol and are banned from carrying anything, including cameras. Climbs cost A$165 (US$132/UK£66) for adults and A$100 (US$80/UK£40) for children 12 to 16 on weekdays during the day and night; and A$185 (US$148/UK£74) for adults and A$125 (US$100/UK£50) for children for climbs on Saturday and Sunday. Daily twilight climbs cost A$245 (US$196/UK£99) for adults and A$185 (US$148/UK£74) for kids. Children under 12 are not allowed to climb. A dawn climb, on the first Saturday of each month, costs A$295 (US$236/UK£118) for adults and A$195 (US$156/UK£78) for kids. Prices keep changing so use these as a general guide.

Quay, and beyond. An interesting museum charts the building of the bridge. The Pylon Lookout is open daily from 10am to 5pm (closed Dec 25). Reach the pylon by walking to the far end of George Street in The Rocks toward the Harbour Bridge. Just past The Mercantile pub, you'll see some stone steps that take you onto Cumberland Street. From there, it's a 2-minute walk to the steps underneath the bridge on your right. Climb four flights to reach the bridge's Western Footway, and then walk along to the first pylon. ***Note:*** Climbing up inside the pylon involves 200 steps.

Sydney Opera House ★★★ Only a handful of buildings around the world are as architecturally and culturally significant as the Sydney Opera House. But what sets it apart from, say, the Taj Mahal and the Great Pyramids of Egypt is that this white-sailed construction caught mid-billow over the waters of Sydney Cove is a working building. Most visitors are surprised to learn it's not just an opera house, but a full-scale performing-arts complex with five major performance spaces. The biggest and grandest is the 2,690-seat **Concert Hall,** which has the best acoustics of any building of its type in the world. Come here to experience opera, chamber music, symphonies, dance, choral performances, and even rock 'n' roll. The **Opera Theatre** is smaller, seating 1,547, and books operas, ballets, and dance. The **Drama Theatre,** seating 544, and the **Playhouse,** seating 398, specialize in plays and smaller-scale performances. The **Boardwalk,** seating 300, is used for dance and experimental music.

The history of the building is as intriguing as the design. The New South Wales Government raised the construction money with a lottery. Danish Architect Jørn

Utzon won an international competition to design it. From the start, the project was controversial, with many Sydneysiders believing it was a monstrosity. Following a disagreement, Utzon returned home without ever seeing his finished project. The interior fell victim to a compromise design, which, among other things, left too little space to perform full-scale operas. And the cost? Initially the project was budgeted at a cool A$7 million (US$5.6 million/UK£2.8 million), but by the time it was finished in 1973 it had cost a staggering A$102 million (US$82 million/UK£41 million), most raised through a series of lotteries. Since then, continual refurbishment and the major task of replacing the asbestos-laden grouting between the hundreds of thousands of white tiles that make up its shell has cost many millions more.

A long-overdue reconstruction is being completed, aimed at putting into practice what Jørn Utzon has long visualized. The tatty old reception hall has already been transformed into an impressive welcome room. Its centerpiece is Utzon's first foray into visual art: a glorious floor-to-ceiling tapestry inspired by Bach's Hamburg Symphonies and Raphael's painting, *Procession to Calvary.*

Also finished is work on the Western Loggia, or colonnade, which opens up the foyers of The Playhouse, Drama Theatre, and The Studio to harbor views and creates spaces for cafes and functions. Investigations are also going ahead into refurbishing the Opera Theatre and improving the acoustics in the Concert Hall.

Tours & Tickets: Guided tours of the Opera House last about an hour and are conducted daily from 9am to 5pm, except Good Friday and December 25. Though guides try to take groups into the main theaters and around the foyers, if you don't get to see everything you want, it's because the Opera House is a working venue. There's almost always some performance, practice, or setting up to be done. Reservations are essential. Tour sizes are limited, so be prepared to wait. Tours include about 200 stairs. (Tours for people with disabilities can be arranged.) Specialized tours, focusing on the building's architecture and engineering, for example, can also be arranged.

The Tourism Services Department at the Sydney Opera House can book **combination packages,** including dinner and a show; a tour, dinner, and a show; or a champagne interval performance. Prices vary depending on shows and dining venues. Visitors from overseas can buy tickets by credit card and pick them up at the box office on arrival, or contact a local tour company specializing in Australia. Advance ticket purchases are a good idea, because performances are very popular. The views from the back rows are hardly worth the effort and expense if you turn up on the day of performance. Tickets for performances vary from as little as A$12 (US$9.60/UK£4.70) for children's shows to A$180 (US$144/UK£72) for good seats at the opera. Plays average A$40 to A$60 (US$32–US$48/UK£16–UK£24).

Free performances take place outside on the Opera House boardwalks on Sunday afternoons and during festival times. The artists range from musicians and performance artists to school groups.

Bennelong Point. ✆ **02/9250 7250** for guided tours and information, or 02/9250 7777 box office. Fax 02/9251 3943. www.sydneyoperahouse.com. Box office Mon–Sat 9am–8:30pm; Sun 2 hr. before performance. Tours A$26 (US$21/UK£11) for adults and A$16 (US$13/UK£6.50) for kids. Tours daily 9am–5pm (every 30 min.), subject to theater availability. Backstage Tour A$150 (US$120/UK£60) starts daily at 7am, for 2 hr., with breakfast. CityRail, bus, or ferry: Circular Quay. Sydney Explorer bus. Parking: Daytime A$9 (US$7/UK£3.50) per hour; evening A$28 (US$22/UK£11) flat rate.

THE HARBOR ON THE CHEAP The best way to see Sydney Harbour is from the water. Several companies operate tourist craft (see "Harbor Cruises & Organized

Seeing Sydney Harbour through Aboriginal Eyes

The *Deerubbun,* a former Australian navy torpedo recovery vessel, makes quite an impression as it pulls up to the dock near the Opera House concourse with speakers blaring out a recording of clapsticks and didgeridoos. The boat, which is owned by the Tribal Warrior Association (an Aboriginal-operated nonprofit organization that aims to provide maritime training programs for Aboriginal youths) revolutionized the multimillion-dollar Sydney cruise industry in late 2006 by offering an Aboriginal perspective of the famous waterway. Tourists learn that Circular Quay was once occupied by the Cadigal people, they learn about Bennelong, the captured Aborigine who once lived on the point where the Opera House now stands, and his wife Barangaroo, who opposed her husband's conciliatory efforts with the Europeans. The boat putters past the Royal Botanic Gardens, and the guide tells stories of the early Europeans and their hopeless farms, and the smallpox epidemic of 1789, which the local Aborigines thought was caused by evil spirits. Mixed in with the observations of the landscape are tales of the first Aboriginal tour guides, who took early settlers inland from the harbor, as well as mentions of soldiers, statesmen, and farmers who came into contact with the Aborigines, and much more. Tourists disembark at Clark Island to see cave shelters with roofs stained black from ancient fireplaces, convict engravings, and a natural fish trap. Two Aboriginal guides, their dark brown bodies plastered in ghostly white ocher, beat a rhythm with hardwood sticks and growl through a didgeridoo, as they beckon the tourists to the Welcoming Ceremony. Then comes a repertoire of haunting songs, music, and dance. Every visitor to Sydney should do this trip. Aboriginal Cultural Cruises depart at 12:45pm, Tuesday to Saturday, from the Eastern Pontoon (near the Sydney Opera House). Cost: A$55 (US$44/UK£22) adults, A$45 (US$36/UK£18) children 5 to 14. Tickets are available from Sydney Visitor Centres. For more information call ✆ **02/9699 3491** or visit www.tribalwarrior.org.

Tours," later in this chapter), but it's easy enough just to hop on a regular passenger ferry (see "Getting Around," earlier in this chapter). The best ferry excursions are over to the beachside suburb of **Manly** (come back after dusk to see the lights ablaze around The Rocks and Circular Quay); to **Watsons Bay,** where you can have lunch and wander along the cliffs; to **Darling Harbour,** for all the area's entertainment and the fact that you travel right under the Harbour Bridge; and to **Mosman Bay,** just for the ride and to see the grand houses that overlook exclusive harbor inlets.

FAST ACTION ON THE HARBOR For a thrill ride, you can board a 420-horsepower jet boat, which zooms about on three high-speed waterway tours at speeds of up to 40 knots (about 80kmph/50 mph), with huge 240-degree turns and instant stops. **Harbour Jet** (✆ **1300/887 373** in Australia, or 02/9212 3555; www.harbourjet.com) offers a 35-minute Jet Blast Adventure costing A$65 (US$52/UK£26) for adults, A$45 (US$36/UK£18) for kids under 15, and A$190 (US$152/UK£76) for a family. It leaves at noon, 2:30pm, and 4:30pm daily. A 50-minute Sydney Harbour Adventure costs A$80 (US$64/UK£37) for adults, A$55 (US$64/UK£32) for kids, and A$243 (US$194/UK£87) for a family. It leaves at 10:30am, 1:30pm, and 3:30pm daily. An 80-minute Middle Harbour Adventure cruise costs A$95 (US$76/UK£38) for adults, A$70 (US$56/UK£28) for kids, and A$297 (US$237/UK£118) for a family. It leaves at 9am on Fridays, Saturdays, and Sundays. Rides are fast and furious and pump with rock music. The boat leaves from the Convention Jetty, between the Convention Centre and the Harbourside Shopping complex on the far side of Darling Harbour. These trips don't operate every day, so check beforehand.

Another option is **Oz Jet Boat** (✆ **02/9808 3700;** www.ozjetboating.com), which departs every hour from the Eastern Pontoon at Circular Quay (on the walkway to the Opera House). These large red boats are a bit more powerful than the blue Harbour Jet ones, but you might not notice the difference. This company offers a 30-minute "thrill ride" for A$55 (US$44/UK£22) for adults, A$40 (US$32/UK£16) for kids, and A$170 (US$136/UK£68) for a family. It leaves every hour from 11am to sunset. There's also a 45-minute "Sydney Spin" ride, departing daily at 1pm, and costing A$80 (US$64/UK£32) for adults, A$55 (US$44/UK£22) for children, and A$240 (US$192/UK£96) for a family.

ATTRACTIONS AT DARLING HARBOUR

Many tourists head to Darling Harbour for the Harbourside Festival Marketplace, a huge structure beside the Pyrmont pedestrian and monorail bridge that's crammed full of cheap eateries and a few interesting shops. However, Sydney's tourist precinct has a lot more to offer.

Australian National Maritime Museum ★ Kids Modern Australia owes almost everything to the sea, so it's not surprising that there's a museum dedicated to ships, from Aboriginal vessels to submarines. You'll find ships' logs and things to pull and tug at. Docked in the harbor are several ships and launches, including an Australian navy destroyer, the *Vampire,* an Oberon Class submarine, and a replica of the *Endeavour,* the ship Captain James Cook commanded when he laid claim to Australia. You can clamber over many of them. Allow 2 hours.

Darling Harbour. ✆ **02/9298 3777.** www.anmm.gov.au. Free admission to main exhibition. Admission to all ships A$30 (US$24/UK£12) adults, A$16 (US$13/UK£6.50) children 5–15, A$65 (US$52/UK£26) families. Navy Package (includes museum and two ships) A$18 (US$14/UK£7) adults, A$9 (US$7/UK£3.50) children, A$40 (US$32/UK£16) families. Admission to single vessels available A$10–A$15 (US$8–A$12/UK£4–UK£6) for adults and A$8–A$16 (US$6.40–US$13/UK£3.20–UK£6.50) for kids. Daily 9:30am–5pm (until 6:30pm in Jan). Ferry: Darling Harbour. Monorail: Harbourside. Sydney Explorer bus.

Chinese Garden The largest Chinese garden of its type outside China offers a pleasant escape from the city concrete. Expert gardeners from China's Guangdong Province designed the garden according to principles of garden design dating to the 5th century. Allow 30 minutes.

Darling Harbour (adjacent to the Entertainment Centre). ✆ **02/9281 6863.** www.chinesegarden.com.au. Admission A$6 (US$4.80/UK£2.40) adults, A$3 (US$2.40/UK£1.20) children, A$15 (US$12/UK£6) families. Daily 9:30am–5pm. Ferry: Darling Harbour. Monorail: Convention. Sydney Explorer bus.

IMAX Theatre Sydney Four different IMAX films are usually showing on the gigantic eight-story-high screen. Each flick lasts about 50 minutes or so. If you've ever been to an IMAX theater before, you know what to expect. As you watch, your mind is tricked into feeling that it's right in the heart of the action. Also shown are 3-D movies, which cost A$1 (US80¢/UK40p) extra.

Southern Promenade, Darling Harbour. ✆ **02/9281 3300.** www.imax.com.au. Admission A$18 (US$15/UK£7.50) adults, A$13 (US$11/UK£5.50) children 3–15, A$50 (US$40/UK£20) families. Sun–Thurs 10am–10pm; Fri–Sat 10am–11:30pm. Ferry: Darling Harbour. Monorail: Convention. Sydney Explorer bus.

Powerhouse Museum *Kids* Sydney's most interactive museum is also one of the largest in the Southern Hemisphere. In the postmodern industrial interior you'll find all sorts of displays and gadgets relating to the sciences, transportation, human achievement, decorative art, and social history. The many hands-on exhibits make this fascinating museum worthy of a couple of hours of your time.

500 Harris St., Ultimo (near Darling Harbour). ✆ **02/9217 0111.** www.powerhousemuseum.com. Admission A$10 (US$8/UK£4) adults, A$5 (US$4/UK£2) students and children 5–15, A$24 (US$19/UK£9.50) families. Free admission 1st Sat of every month. Daily 9:30am–5pm. Ferry: Darling Harbour. Monorail: Harbourside. Sydney Explorer bus.

Sydney Aquarium ★★★ *Kids* This is one of the world's best aquariums and should be near the top of your itinerary. The main attractions are the underwater walkways through two enormous tanks—one full of giant rays and gray nurse sharks and the other where you can see the seals. Other exhibits include a magnificent section on the Great Barrier Reef, where thousands of colorful fish school around coral outcrops. Sit on the steps beside the huge, main Barrier Reef tank, listening to the classical music, and you might never want to leave. Also on display are two saltwater crocodiles and some fairy penguins. A new touch-pool allows you to stroke baby sharks. Try to visit during the week, when it's less crowded. Allow around 2 hours.

Aquarium Pier, Darling Harbour. ✆ **02/8251 7800.** www.sydneyaquarium.com.au. Admission A$27 (US$22/UK£11) adults, A$14 (US$11/UK£5.50) children 3–15, A$66 (US$53/UK£26) families. Daily 9am–10pm. Seal Sanctuary closes at 7pm in summer. CityRail: Town Hall. Ferry: Darling Harbour. Sydney Explorer bus.

OTHER TOP ATTRACTIONS: A SPECTACULAR VIEW, SYDNEY'S CONVICT HISTORY & MORE

Hyde Park Barracks Museum ★ These Georgian-style barracks were designed in 1819 by the convict and architect Francis Greenway. They were built by convicts and inhabited by prisoners. These days they house relics from those early days in modern displays, including log books, early settlement artifacts, and a room full of ships' hammocks in which visitors can lie and listen to fragments of prisoner conversation. If you are interested in Sydney's early beginnings, I highly recommend a visit. The displays are far more straightforward that those at the Museum of Sydney (see listing later in this chapter). The courtyard cafe is excellent. Allow 1 hour or more.

Queens Sq., Macquarie St. ✆ **02/8239 2311.** www.hht.nsw.gov.au. Admission A$10 (US$8/UK£4) adults, A$5 (US$4/UK£2) children, A$20 (US$16/UK£8) families. Daily 9:30am–5pm. CityRail: St. James or Martin Place. Sydney Explorer bus.

Museum of Contemporary Art (MCA) This imposing sandstone museum set back from the water on The Rocks side of Circular Quay offers wacky, entertaining, inspiring, and befuddling displays of what's new (and dated) in modern art. It houses the J. W. Power Collection of more than 4,000 pieces, including works by Andy Warhol, Christo, Marcel Duchamp, and Robert Rauschenberg, as well as temporary exhibits. A fourth floor opened up in 2005 and part of its permanent collection is displayed there. This museum isn't as impressive as major modern art museums in, say, London or New York; still, it's worth at least 1 hour. Free guided tours are conducted midweek at 11am and 1pm and on weekends at noon and 1:30pm. The **MCA cafe** (✆ **02/9241 4253**) is a nice spot, with good views of the harbor and Opera House. It's serves up contemporary food from 10am to 5pm daily.

140 George St., Circular Quay. ✆ **02/9245 2400.** www.mca.com.au. Free admission. Daily 10am–6pm (5pm in winter). CityRail, bus, or ferry: Circular Quay. Sydney Explorer bus.

Sydney Olympic Park ★ The site of the 2000 Olympic games is still very much a tourist attraction as well as a major sporting venue. Most of the Olympic venues are at this dedicated Olympic precinct at Homebush Bay, which also has plenty of bars and restaurants. Start at the **Homebush Bay Information Centre,** which has displays, walking maps, and tour tips. It's open daily from 9am to 5pm.

Nearby is **Telstra Stadium** (✆ **02/8765 2000;** www.telstrastadium.com.au), the site of the opening and closing ceremonies, the track and field events, and some Olympic soccer games. It was called Stadium Australia back then. Today it schedules Australian Rules games and rugby league, rugby union, and soccer matches. A 60-minute tour of the stadium costs a huge A$28 (US$22/UK£11) for adults, A$15 (US$12/UK£6) for children, and A$55 (US$44/UK£22) for a family. Tours leave every half-hour from 10am to 4pm.

Also at the Olympic Park is the **Sydney International Aquatic Centre** (✆ **02/9752 3666;** www.sydneyaquaticcentre.com.au), which comprises the Olympic pool, diving pool, and training facilities. A 60-minute tour of the aquatic center, including a swim and a spa afterward, costs A$19 (US$15/UK£7.50) for adults, A$9.50 (US$7.60/UK£3.80) for kids 4 to 15, and A$59 (US$47/UK£23) for families. They leave at noon, 1pm, and 2pm. Call ✆ **02/9714 7888** to book. Just a swim costs A$5.80 (US$4.60/UK£2.30) adults, A$4.60 (US$3.70/UK£1.80) kids, A$19 (US$15/UK£7.50) families.

A 1-hour "Games Trail" tour is a more general introduction to the Olympic sites. It leaves daily at noon, 1:30pm, and 3pm. The tour costs A$20 for adults (US$16/UK£8), A$15 (US$12/UK£6) for kids, and A$55 (US$44/UK£22) for a family. Call ✆ **02/9714 7888** to book.

All tours leave from the Sydney Olympic Park Visitors Centre, 1 Showground Rd. (corner of Showground Rd. and Murray Rose Ave.).

There are wonderful views of the Sydney Olympic Park and the city from Level 17 of the **Novotel hotel** (✆ **02/8762 1111**), located in the park. Entry to the observation area costs A$4 (US$3.20/UK£1.60) for adults and A$2 (US$1.60/UK80p) for children over 7. One of the best ways to get to the Olympic site is on the Sydney Explorer bus.

Sydney Olympic Site, Olympic Park, Homebush Bay. ✆ **02/9714 7888.** Sydney Olympic Park Visitors Centre. www.sydneyolympicpark.nsw.gov.au. Visitor Centre open daily 9am–5pm. CityRail: Olympic Park. Sydney Explorer bus.

Sydney Tower (aka Centrepoint Tower) ★ *Kids* The tallest building in the Southern Hemisphere is hard to miss—it resembles a giant steel pole skewering a golden marshmallow. Standing more than 300m (984 ft.) tall, the tower offers stupendous 360-degree views across Sydney and as far as the Blue Mountains. Fortunately, an elevator takes you to the indoor viewing platform on the top floor; if you were to walk up, you'd have to climb 1,504 steps. The general ticket price includes admission to **OzTrek,** where visitors are strapped into moving chairs in front of a 180-degree screen. On this simulator ride, you white-water raft in Queensland, climb Uluru (Ayers Rock), and have a close encounter with a saltwater crocodile. It's great fun, and kids love it. Don't be too concerned if you feel the building tremble slightly, especially in a stiff breeze—I'm told it's perfectly natural. Below the tower are three floors of stores and restaurants. Right up at the top, too, is a revolving restaurant and bar if you're keen to stick around. See also Sydney Tower Skywalk (below). Allow 2 hours.

100 Market St. (another entrance on Pitt St. Mall). ✆ **02/9333 9222.** www.sydneytoweroztrek.com.au. Admission A$24 (US$18/UK£9) adults, A$14 (US$11/UK£5.50) children 4–15, A$60 (US$48/UK£24) families. Sun–Fri 9am–10:30pm; Sat 9am–11:30pm. CityRail: St. James or Town Hall. Sydney Explorer bus.

Sydney Tower Skywalk ★★★ The latest addition to the Sydney thrill scene is this heart-stopping experience that is definitely not for people who are scared of heights. The deal is, you don a special suit, walk out onto a glass-floored platform 260m (853 ft.) above the city floor and walk around the building. The views are breathtaking (even between your feet!). You are harnessed to a safety rail with a sliding harness, so there's no chance of falling off, and funny, well-informed guides offer a helping hand to the nervous. Each Skywalk lasts approximately 1 hour and 30 minutes and operates daily from 9am to 10pm, with the last Skywalk departing at 8:15pm. Cameras aren't allowed for safety reasons, but group or individual shots cost from A$20 (US$16/UK£8). Children under 10 aren't allowed on the Skywalk.

Centrepoint Podium Level, 100 Market St. (entrance also through Pitt St. Mall). ✆ **02/9333 9222.** www.skywalk.com.au. Cost: Day Skywalk, daily A$109 (US$87/UK£43) for adults (aged over 16), A$85 (US$68/UK£34) for kids (aged 10–15); Dusk Skywalk, daily A$139 (US$111/UK£55) for adults, A$105 (US$84/UK£42) for kids; Night Skywalk, Mon–Thurs A$109 (US$87/UK£43) for adults, A$85 (US$68/UK£34) for kids, Fri–Sun A$129 (US$103/UK£51) for adults, A$95 (US$76/UK£38) for kids. Daily 9am–10pm (last Skywalk departs 8:15pm). CityRail: St. James or Town Hall. Sydney Explorer bus.

'ROOS, KOALAS & OTHER AUSSIE WILDLIFE

The Sydney Aquarium is discussed on p. 166.

Australian Reptile Park What started as a one-man operation supplying snake antivenin in the early 1950s has become a nature park teeming with the slippery-looking creatures. But it's not all snakes and lizards; you'll also find saltwater crocodiles and American alligators, as well as plenty of somewhat cuddlier creatures, such as koalas, platypuses, wallabies, dingoes, and flying foxes. The park is on beautiful bushland crossed by nature trails. A devastating fire burned down the entire park in mid-2000, killing all of the animals. The staff has worked valiantly to start up a new collection. The park is a short detour off the route heading up to the Hunter Valley, Barrington Tops, and Port Stephens. Somersby is near Gosford, 84km (52 miles) north of Sydney. Several tour operators to the Hunter Valley stop off here.

Pacific Hwy., Somersby. ✆ **02/4340 1022.** www.reptilepark.com.au. Admission A$22 (US$18/UK£9) adults, A$12 (US$9/UK£4.50) children 3–15, A$60 (US$42/UK£21) families. Daily 9am–5pm. Closed Dec 25. CityRail: Gosford (trains leave Central Station every 30 min.), then by taxi. By car: Take the Pacific Hwy. and the Sydney-Newcastle Fwy. (F3); the trip takes about 1 hr.

Featherdale Wildlife Park ★★ *Kids* If you have time to visit only one wildlife park in Sydney, make it this one. The selection of Australian animals is excellent, and, most important, the animals are very well cared for. You could easily spend a couple of hours here despite the park's compact size. You'll have the chance to hand-feed friendly kangaroos and wallabies, and get a photo taken next to a koala. (There are many here, both the New South Wales variety and the larger Victorian type.) The park's newest addition is the **Reptilian Pavilion.** It houses 30 different native species of reptiles in 26 realistic exhibits. If you are heading to the Blue Mountains on a bus tour then you are well advised to choose one that stops off here.

217 Kildare Rd., Doonside. ✆ **02/9622 1644.** www.featherdale.com.au. Admission A$19 (US$15/UK£7.50) adults, A$9.50 (US$7.60/UK£3.80) children 3–15, A$55 (US$44/UK£22) families. Daily 9am–5pm. CityRail: Blacktown station, then bus 725 (ask driver to tell you when to get off). By car: Take the M4 motorway to Reservoir Rd., turn off, travel 4km (2½ miles), then turn left at Kildare Rd.

Koala Park Sanctuary ★ This is probably the only place in the country (unless you travel all the way to Kangaroo Island in South Australia) where you'll be able to spot this many koalas in one place. In all, around 55 koalas roam within the park's leafy boundaries (it's set in 4 hectares/10 acres of rainforest). Free koala cuddling sessions take place at 10:20 and 11:45am, and 2 and 3pm daily. There are wombats, dingoes, kangaroos, wallabies, emus, and native birds here, too. Hitch onto one of the free "hostess" guides who wander around the park like Pied Pipers.

84 Castle Hill Rd., West Pennant Hills. ✆ **02/9484 3141.** www.koalaparksanctuary.com.au. Admission A$19 (US$15/UK£7.50) adults, A$9 (US$7.20/UK£3.60) children. Daily 9am–5pm. Closed Dec 25. CityRail: Pennant Hills station via North Strathfield (45 min.). Cross over railway line and join Glenorie Bus routes 651 to 655. The bus takes about 10 min. to Koala Park.

Oceanworld Manly *Kids* Though not as impressive as the Sydney Aquarium, Oceanworld can be combined with a visit to Manly Beach (see "North of Sydney Harbour," below) for a nice day's outing. There's a decent display of Barrier Reef fish, as well as giant sharks. Also here are the five most venomous snakes in the world. Shark feeding is at 11am on Monday, Wednesday, and Friday. There is also a **"dive with the sharks"** ★★★ program, where you can dive in the tanks with giant gray nurse sharks. It costs A$175 (US$140/UK£70) for qualified divers, A$205 (US$164/UK£82) for qualified divers who have logged less than 15 dives or haven't dived in the last 6 months, or A$235 (US$188/UK£94) for nonqualified divers (includes an introduction to scuba diving course). You must download an application form from the website.

West Esplanade, Manly. ✆ **02/8251 7878.** www.oceanworld.com.au. Admission A$18 (US$14/UK£7) adults, A$9.50 (US$7.60/UK£3.70) children, A$44 (US$35/UK£17) families (15% off admission prices after 3:30pm). Daily 10am–5:30pm. Ferry or JetCat: Manly.

Sydney Wildlife World Opened in late 2006, Sydney Wildlife World shook the tourism world when it announced it would house several thousand animals—a veritable Noah's Ark? Well, no, unless you count all the insects that is, and leave elephants and most of the other large creatures to be stranded over at Taronga Zoo. Still, this place has a few highlights. You get to see a cassowary up close (a flightless bird about the size of an emu, but armed with a dangerous spiked toe) and some endangered yellow-footed rock wallabies. Throw in a few snakes and lizards, some smaller birds, a few nocturnal marsupials and, of course, the inevitable koala, and you have a collection that almost becomes worth the entry money to see them.

Aquarium Pier, Darling Harbour. ✆ **02/9333 9288.** www.sydneywildlifeworld.com.au. Admission A$29 (US$23/UK£12) adults, A$14 (US$11/UK£5.50) kids 3–15, A$68 (US$54/UK£27) family. Discount tickets are available if you book over the Net, and you can buy a special Attractions Pass which allows discounted entry to here, Sydney Aquarium, and Sydney Tower. Daily 9am–10pm. Ferry/Monorail: Darling Harbour.

Taronga Zoo ★ *Kids* Taronga has the best view of any zoo in the world. Set on a hill, it looks out over Sydney Harbour, the Opera House, and the Harbour Bridge. It's easiest on the legs to explore the zoo from the top down. The main attractions are the fabulous chimpanzee exhibit, the gorilla enclosure, and the Nocturnal Houses, where you can see some of Australia's many nighttime marsupials, including the platypus and the cuter-than-cute bilby (the official Australian Easter bunny), out and about. There's an interesting reptile display, a couple of impressive Komodo dragons, a scattering of indigenous beasties—including a few koalas, echidnas, kangaroos, dingoes, and wombats—and lots more. The kangaroo and wallaby exhibit is unimaginative; you'd be better off going to Featherdale Wildlife Park (see above). Animals are fed at various times during the day. The zoo can get crowded on weekends, so I strongly advise visiting during the week or early in the morning on weekends. Interestingly, the three sun bears near the lower ferry entrance and exit were rescued by an Australian businessman, John Stephens, from a restaurant in Cambodia, where they were to have their paws cut off and served in soup. You can pose with a koala for A$4 (US$3.20/UK£1.60), between 11am and 2:45pm daily, and there are eateries and drinks available. Worth watching are the Seal Shows at 1pm and again at 2:15pm, and the Free Flight Bird Show at noon and 3pm. Allow around 3 hours.

Bradley's Head Rd., Mosman. ✆ **02/9969 2777.** Admission A$32 (US$26/UK£13) adults, A$18 (US$14/UK£7) children 4–15, A$84 (US$67/UK£33) family. Admission includes a trip on the Aerial Safari cable car. Daily 9am–5pm (until 9pm Jan). Ferry: Taronga Zoo. Lower zoo entrance is at ferry terminal.

HITTING THE BEACH

One of the big bonuses of visiting Sydney in the summer (Dec–Feb) is that you get to experience the beaches in their full glory.

Most major city beaches, such as Manly and Bondi, have lifeguards on patrol, especially during the summer. They check the water conditions and are on the lookout for **"rips"**—strong currents that can pull a swimmer far out. Safe places to swim are marked by red and yellow flags. You must always swim between these flags. If you are using a foam or plastic body board or "boogie board," it's advisable to use it between the flags. Fiberglass surfboards must be used outside the flags. (Expect a warning from the beach loudspeakers and a A$100/US$80/UK£40 fine if you fail to take notice.)

WHAT ABOUT SHARKS & OTHER NASTIES? One of the first things visitors wonder when they hit the water in Australia is: *Are there sharks?* The answer is yes, but fortunately they are rarely spotted inshore—you are far more likely to spy a migrating whale. In reality, sharks have more reason to be scared of us than we of them; most of them end up as the fish in your average packet of fish and chips. (Shark filets are often sold as "flake.") Though some beaches—such as the small beach next to the Manly ferry wharf and a section of Balmoral Beach in Mosman—have permanent shark nets, most rely on portable nets that are moved from beach to beach.

Another common problem off Sydney's beaches are **"blue bottles"**—small blue jellyfish, often called "stingers" in Australia and "Portuguese-men-o'-war" elsewhere. You'll often find these creatures (which are not the same as the stingers around the Great Barrier Reef) washed up along the beach; they become a hazard for swimmers when there's a strong breeze coming off the ocean and they're blown in to shore (watch out for warning signs erected on the shoreline). Minute individual stinging cells often break off the main body of the creature, and they can cause minor itching or stinging. Or you might be hit by the full force of a blue bottle, which will often stick to your skin and wrap its tentacles around you. Blue bottles deliver a hefty punch from their many stinging cells, causing a severe burning sensation almost immediately. Wearing a T-shirt in the water reduces the risk somewhat (though a pair of waterlogged jeans isn't a good idea). If you are stung, rinse the area liberally with seawater or fresh water to remove any tentacles stuck in the skin. For intense pain, apply heat or cold, whichever feels better. If you experience breathing difficulties or disorientation, seek medical attention immediately.

SOUTH OF SYDNEY HARBOUR

Sydney's most famous beach is **Bondi** ★★. In many ways it's a raffish version of a California beach, with plenty of tanned skin and in-line skaters. Though the beach is nice, it's cut off from the cafe and restaurant strip that caters to beachgoers by a road that pedestrians have to funnel across in order to reach the sand. On summer weekend evenings it's popular with souped-up cars and groups of disaffected youths from the suburbs. To reach Bondi Beach, take the CityRail train to Bondi Junction, then transfer to bus no. 380 or 333 (a 15-min. bus journey). You can also catch bus no. 380 directly from Circular Quay (but it can take an hour or so at peak times), or better still bus no. 333 (a long, bendy bus). This takes about 40 minutes. You will need to buy a ticket for this bus at newsdealers or 7/11 stores.

If you follow the water along to your right at Bondi, you'll come across a scenic cliff-top trail that takes you to **Bronte Beach** (a 20-min. walk), via gorgeous little **Tamarama,** nicknamed "Glamourama" for its trendy sun-worshipers. This boutique beach is known for its dangerous rips. Bronte has better swimming than Bondi. To go straight to Bronte, catch bus no. 378 from Circular Quay, or pick up the bus at the Bondi Junction CityRail station.

Clovelly Beach, farther along the coast, is blessed with a large rock pool carved into a rock platform and sheltered from the force of the Tasman Sea. This beach is accessible for visitors in wheelchairs on a series of ramps. To reach Clovelly, take bus no. 339 from Circular Quay.

The cliff walk from Bondi will eventually bring you to **Coogee,** which has a pleasant strip of sand with a couple of hostels and hotels nearby. To reach Coogee, take bus no. 373 or 374 from Circular Quay (on Pitt, George, and Castlereagh sts., and Taylor Sq. on Oxford St.) or bus no. 314 or 315 from Bondi Junction.

NORTH OF SYDNEY HARBOUR

On the North Shore you'll find **Manly** ★★, a long curve of golden sand edged with Norfolk Island pines. Follow the crowds shuffling through the pedestrian Corso to the main ocean beach. (Don't be fooled by the two small beaches on either side of the ferry

---

Fun Fact Grin & Bare It

If getting an all-over tan is your scene, you have a couple of options in Sydney. The nudist beach at **Lady Jane Bay** is a short walk from Camp Cove Beach. You get there from Cliff Street in Watsons Bay, reached by walking along the strip of sand—to the right as you look at the sea—at the back of the Watsons Bay Hotel. Or you can try **Cobblers Beach,** off the short, but steep, bush track that leads from the far side of the playing field oval next to the main HMAS *Penguin* naval base at the end of Bradley's Head Road in Mosman. (Follow the procession of men in shorts.) Be prepared for a largely male-oriented scene—as well as the odd boatload of beer-swigging peeping toms.

---

terminal, as some people have—including the novelist Arthur Conan Doyle, who traveled to Manly by ferry and, presuming the small beach near the ferry station was the best the suburb had to offer, did not bother to disembark.)

You'll find one of Sydney's nicest walks here, too. Looking at the ocean, head to your right along the beachfront and follow the coastal path to small and sheltered **Shelly Beach** ★, a nice area for snorkeling and swimming. (A small takeout outlet that sells drinks and snacks sits next to the good, but pricey, Le Kiosk beachfront restaurant.) Follow the bitumen path up the hill to the car park. Here, a track cuts up into the bush and leads toward a firewall, which marks the entrance to the Sydney Harbour National Park. Around here you'll have spectacular ocean views across to Manly and the northern beaches (the headland farther in the distance is Palm Beach). The best way to reach Manly is on a ferry or JetCat from Circular Quay.

Farther north along the coast are a string of ocean beaches. They include the surf spots of **Curl Curl, Dee Why, Narrabeen, Mona Vale, Newport, Avalon,** and finally **Palm Beach** ★, a long and beautiful strip of sand separated from the calmer waters of **Pittwater** by sand dunes and a golf course. Here you'll find the Barrenjoey Lighthouse, which offers fine views along the coast. Take bus no. 136 or 139 from Manly to Curl Curl. Bus no. 190 runs from Wynyard to Newport and then via the other northern beaches as far as Palm Beach.

The best harbor beach is at **Balmoral** ★, a wealthy North Shore hangout with some good cafes (the Sandbar is the best for food) and two good, upmarket beach-view restaurants—the **Bathers Pavillion** (✆ **02/9969 5050**) and **The Watermark** (✆ **02/9968 3433**). The beach itself is split into three parts. As you look toward the sea, the middle section is the most popular with sunbathers, and the wide expanse to your left and the sweep of surreally beautiful sand to your right have a mere scattering. There's a caged pool area for swimming. Reach Balmoral on the ferry to Taronga Zoo and then a 5-minute ride on a connecting bus from the ferry wharf, or catch the bus from the stop outside the zoo's top entrance.

MUSEUMS, GALLERIES, HISTORIC HOUSES & MORE

Art Gallery of New South Wales ★ The galleries here present some of the best of Australian art and many fine examples by international artists, including good displays of Aboriginal and Asian art. You enter from The Domain parklands (across the road from the Royal Botanic Gardens) on the third floor of the museum. On the fourth floor you will find an expensive restaurant and a gallery that often mounts free photography displays. On the second floor is a wonderful cafe overlooking the wharves of Woolloomooloo. Every January and February there is a display of the best work created by school students throughout the state. Allow at least 1 hour.

Art Gallery Rd., The Domain. ✆ **02/9225 1744**. www.artgallery.nsw.gov.au. Free admission to most galleries. Special exhibitions vary; usually around A$12 (US$9.60/UK£4.80) adults, A$7 (US$5.60/UK£2.80) children. Thurs–Tues 10am–5pm; Wed 10am–9pm. Tours of general exhibits Sat–Sun 11am, 1pm, and 2pm; Mon 1pm and 2pm; Tues–Fri 11am, noon, 1pm, and 2pm. Tours of Aboriginal galleries Tues–Sun 11am. Free Aboriginal performance Tues–Sat noon. CityRail: St. James. Sydney Explorer bus.

Australian Museum Though nowhere near as impressive as, say, the Natural History Museum in London, Sydney's premier natural history museum is still worth a look. Displays are presented thematically, the best being the Aboriginal section with its traditional clothing, weapons, and everyday implements. There are some sorry examples of stuffed Australian mammals, as well as stuffed birds, an insect display, and a mineral collection. Allow 1 to 2 hours.

6 College St. ✆ **02/9320 6000.** www.austmus.gov.au. Admission A$10 (US$8/UK£4) adults, A$5 (US$4/UK£2) children, A$25 (US$20/UK£13) families. Special exhibits extra. Daily 9:30am–5pm. Closed Dec 25. CityRail: Museum, St. James, or Town Hall. Sydney Explorer bus.

Elizabeth Bay House A good example of colonial architecture, this house was built in 1835 and was described at the time as the "finest house in the colony." Visitors can tour the whole house and get a real feeling of the history of the fledgling settlement. The house is on a headland and has some of the best harbor views in Sydney. Allow 1 hour.

7 Onslow Ave., Elizabeth Bay. ✆ **02/9356 3022.** www.hht.net.au. Admission A$8 (US$6.40/UK£3.20) adults, A$4 (US$3.20/UK£1.60) children, A$17 (US$14/UK£7) families. Tues–Sun 10am–4:30pm. Closed Good Friday and Dec 25. Bus: 311 from Circular Quay or Sydney Explorer.

Museum of Sydney You'll need to have your brain in full working order to make the most of the contents of this three-story postmodern building near Circular Quay, which encompasses the remnants of Sydney's first Government House. The place is far from a conventional showcase of history; instead, it houses a rather minimalist collection of first-settler and Aboriginal objects and multimedia displays that "invite" the museum-goer to discover Sydney's past for him- or herself. Some Frommer's readers have criticized the place—saying it's not just minimalist, it's simply unfathomable—but if you have the time and inclination then give it a go. By the way, that forest of poles filled with hair, oyster shells, and crab claws in the courtyard adjacent to the industrial-design cafe tables is called *Edge of Trees.* It's a metaphor for the first contact between Aborigines and the British. There's a reasonable cafe out front. Allow anywhere from an hour to a lifetime to understand.

37 Phillip St. ✆ **02/9251 5988.** www.hht.net.au. Admission A$10 (US$8/UK£4) adults, A$5 (US$4/UK£2) children under 15, A$20 (US$16/UK£8) families. Daily 9:30am–5pm. CityRail, bus, or ferry: Circular Quay. Sydney Explorer bus.

St. James Church Sydney's oldest surviving colonial church, begun in 1822, was designed by the government architect, and former convict, Francis Greenway. At one time the church's spire served as a landmark for ships coming up the harbor, but today it looks lost amid the skyscrapers. It's worth seeking out, especially for the plaques on the wall, which pay testament to the early days of the colony when people were lost at sea, were "speared by blacks," and died while serving the British Empire overseas.

Queens Sq., Macquarie St. ✆ **02/9232 3022.** www.stjameschurchsydney.org.au. Free admission. Daily 8am–5pm CityRail: St. James.

St. Mary's Cathedral Sydney's most impressive place of worship is a giant sandstone construction between The Domain and Hyde Park. The foundation stone was laid in 1821, but the chapel was destroyed by fire in 1865. Work on the present cathedral began in 1868, but due to lack of funds, it remained unfinished until 2000, when the two spires were completed in extra-quick time for the Olympics. The stained-glass windows are impressive. St. Mary's is Roman Catholic and was built for Sydney's large population of Irish convicts. In perhaps Sydney's worst pre-Olympic planning, the brown sandstone building was marred by a wide stretch of dark gray paving outside—now a battleground contested by skateboarders and city council types.

College and Cathedral sts. ✆ **02/9220 0400.** www.sydney.catholic.org.au/Cathedral/index.shtml. Free admission. Mon–Fri 6:30am–6:30pm; Sat 8am–7:30pm; Sun 6:30am–7:30pm.

State Library of New South Wales The state's main library consists of two side-by-side sections, the Mitchell and Dixon libraries. A newer reference-library complex nearby has two floors of reference materials, local newspapers, and microfiche viewers. Leave your bags in the free lockers downstairs. (You'll need a A$2 coin, which is refundable.) I highly recommend the library's leafy **Glasshouse Café,** in my opinion one of the best walk-in lunch spots in Sydney. The older building contains many older books on the ground floor, and often mounts free art and photography displays in the upstairs galleries.

Macquarie St. ✆ **02/9273 1770.** Free admission. Mon–Thurs 9am–9pm; Fri 9am–6pm; Sat–Sun and selected holidays 11am–5pm. Closed Jan 1, Good Friday, and Dec 25–26. CityRail: Martin Place. Sydney Explorer bus.

Sydney Jewish Museum Harrowing exhibits here include documents and objects relating to the Holocaust and the Jewish culture, mixed with soundscapes, audiovisual displays, and interactive media. There's also a museum shop, a resource center, a small theater, and a traditional kosher cafe. It's considered one of the best museums of its type in the world. Allow 1 to 2 hours.

148 Darlinghurst Rd., Darlinghurst. ✆ **02/9360 7999.** www.sydneyjewishmuseum.com.au. Admission A$10 (US$8/UK£4) adults, A$6 (US$4.80/UK£2.40) children, A$22 (US$18/UK£9) families. Mon–Thurs 10am–4pm; Fri 10am–2pm. Closed weekends, Jewish holidays, Good Friday, and Dec 25. CityRail: Kings Cross.

Sydney Observatory ★ The city's only major museum of astronomy offers visitors a chance to see the southern skies through modern and historic telescopes. The best time to visit is during the night on a guided tour, when you can take a close-up look at some of the planets. Howevera new **Space Theatre 3D ride,** which takes you zooming through the stars is worth doing, too. During the day you can still see the fascinating telescopes. The Space Theatre starts at 2:30pm and 3:30pm Mondays to Fridays, and 11am, noon, 2pm, and 3:30pm on weekends and daily during school holidays. Night tours go from 6:15 to 8pm and 8:15 to 10pm April to September; 8:15 to 10pm October and November; 8:30 to 10:15pm December and January; and 8:15 to 10pm February and March. Schedules are subject to change, so be sure to check the times when you book your tour. The planetarium and hands-on exhibits are also interesting.

Observatory Hill, Watson Rd., Millers Point. ✆ **02/9241 3767.** Daytime A$7 (US$5.60/UK£2.80) adults, A$5 (US$4/UK£2) children, A$20 (US$16/UK£8) family. Guided night tours (reservations required) A$15 (US$12/UK£6) adults, A$10 (US$8/UK£4) children, A$40 (US$32/UK£16) families. Daily 10am–5pm. CityRail, bus, or ferry: Circular Quay.

Vaucluse House Overlooking Sydney Harbour, this house has lavish entertainment rooms and impressive stables and outbuildings. It was constructed in 1803 and was the home of Charles Wentworth, the architect of the Australian Constitution. It's set in 11 hectares (27 acres) of gardens, bushland, and beach frontage—perfect for picnics. Allow 1 hour.

Wentworth Rd., Vaucluse. ✆ **02/9337 1957.** www.hht.nsw.gov.au. Admission A$8 (US$6.40/UK£3.20) adults, A$4 (US$3.20/UK£1.60) children, A$17 (US$14/UK£7) family. House Tues–Sun 10am–4:30pm; grounds daily 7am–5pm. Free guided tours. Closed Good Friday and Dec 25. Bus: 325 from Circular Quay, or Bondi & Bay Explorer.

PARKS & GARDENS

IN SYDNEY

ROYAL BOTANIC GARDENS If you are going to spend time in one of Sydney's green spaces, then make it the **Royal Botanic Gardens** ★ (✆ **02/9231 8111**), next to the Sydney Opera House. The gardens were laid out in 1816 on the site of a farm that supplied food for the colony. They're informal in appearance, with a scattering of duck ponds and open spaces, though several areas are dedicated to particular plant species. These include the rose garden, the cacti and succulent display, and the central palm and rainforest groves (watch out for the thousands of large fruit bats, which chatter and argue among the rainforest trees). **Mrs. Macquarie's Chair,** along the coast path, offers superb views of the Opera House and the Harbour Bridge. The "chair" is a step cut out of sandstone with a huge stone plaque on top. It bears the name of Elizabeth Macquarie (1788–1835), the wife of Gov. Lachlan Macquarie. (It's a favorite stop for tour buses.) The sandstone building dominating the gardens nearest to the Opera House is the **Government House,** once the official residence of the governor of New South Wales. (He moved out in 1996 in the spirit of republicanism.) The gardens are open to the public daily from 10am to 4pm, and the house is open Friday through Sunday from 10am to 3pm. Entrance to both is free. If you plan to park around here, note that parking meters cost upwards of A$5 (US$4/UK£2) per hour, and you need A$1 coins.

A popular walk takes you through the Royal Botanic Gardens to the **Art Gallery of New South Wales.** The gardens are open daily from 7am to dusk. Admission is free.

HYDE PARK In the center of the city is Hyde Park, a favorite with lunching businesspeople. Of note here are the **Anzac Memorial** to Australian and New Zealand troops killed in the wars, and the **Archibald Fountain,** complete with spitting turtles and sculptures of Diana and Apollo. At night, twinkling lights illuminate avenues of trees, giving the place a magical appearance.

MORE CITY PARKS Another Sydney favorite is giant **Centennial Park** (✆ **02/9339 6699**), usually entered from the top of Oxford Street. It opened in 1888 to celebrate the centenary of European settlement, and today encompasses huge areas of lawn, several lakes, picnic areas with outdoor grills, cycling and running paths, and a cafe. It's open from sunrise to sunset. To get there, take bus no. 373, 374, 378, 380, or 3333 from the city, or the Bondi & Bay Explorer.

A hundred years later, **Bicentennial Park,** at Australia Avenue, in Homebush Bay, came along. Forty percent of the park's total 100 hectares (247 acres) is general parkland reclaimed from a city dump; the rest is the largest existing remnant of wetlands on the Parramatta River and is home to many species of local and migratory wading birds, cormorants, and pelicans. Follow park signs. To reach the park, take a CityRail train to Homebush Bay station.

BEYOND SYDNEY

SYDNEY HARBOUR NATIONAL PARK You don't need to go far to experience Sydney's nearest national park. The Sydney Harbour National Park stretches around parts of the inner harbor and includes several small islands. (Many first-time visitors are surprised at the amount of bushland remaining in prime real-estate territory.) The best walk through the Sydney Harbour National Park is the **Manly to Spit Bridge Scenic Walkway** (✆ **02/9977 6522**). This 10km (6-mile) track winds its way from Manly (it starts near the Oceanarium) via Dobroyd Head to Spit Bridge, where you can catch a bus back to the city. The walk takes around 3 hours at a casual pace, and the views across busy Sydney Harbour are fabulous. There are a few Aboriginal stone carvings, which are signposted along the route. Maps are available from the **Manly Visitors Information Centre** in the ferry terminal building.

Other access points to the park include tracks around Taronga Zoo (ask the zoo staff to point you toward the obscured entrances) and above tiny Shelly Beach, opposite the main beach at Manly.

Also part of the national park is the restored **Fort Denison,** that tiny island fort you can see in the middle of the harbor between Circular Quay and Manly. The fort was built during the Crimean War in response to fears of a Russian invasion, and was later used as a penal colony. **Heritage Tours** of the island leave from Cadmans Cottage, 110 George St., in The Rocks (✆ **02/9247 5033**), at 11:30am and 2:30pm Wednesdays to Sundays. They cost A$22 (US$18/UK£9) for adults, A$18 (US$14/UK£7) for students and children, and A$72 (US$58/UK£29) for a family. The return ferry trip, tour, and time spent on the island means you should plan on 3 hours or so. Pick up maps of the Sydney Harbour National Park at Cadmans Cottage.

Another great walk in Sydney can be combined with lunch or a drink at Watsons Bay. A 15-minute bush stroll to **South Head** starts from the small beach outside the Watsons Bay Hotel. Walk to the end of the beach (to your right as you look at the water), up the flight of steps to Short Street, then left along Cliff Street to the end of Camp Cove Beach. Continue along the coast past the nudist Lady Bay Beach to the lighthouse at South Head, where there are some great views (of the coastline, not the nudists). Across the road in front of the Watsons Bay Hotel is another section of the national park, known for its cliff-top views. Here you'll find The Gap, a sheer cliff popular for suicides, sadly. Ferries from Circular Quay and the Bondi & Bay Explorer go to Watsons Bay.

MORE NATIONAL PARKS Forming a semicircle around the city are Sydney's biggest parks of all. To the west is the **Blue Mountains National Park** (see chapter 5); to the northeast is **Ku-ring-gai Chase National Park;** and to the south is the magnificent **Royal National Park.** All three parks are home to marsupials such as echidnas and wallabies, numerous bird and reptile species, and a broad range of native plant life. Walking tracks, which take as little as half an hour to as long as a few days to cover, make each park accessible to the visitor.

Ku-ring-gai Chase National Park (✆ **02/9457 9322** or 02/9457 9310) is a great place to take a bushwalk through gum trees and rainforest on the lookout for wildflowers, sandstone rock formations, and Aboriginal art. There are plenty of tracks through the park; one of my favorites is a relatively easy 2.5km (1½-mile) tramp to **The Basin** (Track 12). The well-graded dirt path takes you down to a popular estuary with a beach and passes some significant Aboriginal engravings. There are also wonderful water views over Pittwater from the picnic areas at **West Head.** Pick up a free walking guide at the park entrance, or gather maps and information in Sydney at the National Parks & Wildlife Service's center at **Cadmans Cottage,** 110 George St., The Rocks (✆ **02/9247 8861**).

The park is open from sunrise to sunset, and admission is A$11 (US$8.80/UK£4.40) per car. You can either drive to the park or catch a ferry from Palm Beach to The Basin (from there, you can walk up Track 12 and back). Ferries run on the hour (except at 1pm) from 9am to 5pm daily and cost A$4.50 (US$3.60/UK£1.80) one-way; call ✆ **02/9918 2747** for details. Shorelink bus no. 577 runs from the Turramurra CityRail station to the nearby park entrance every hour on weekdays and every 2 hours on weekends; call ✆ **02/9457 8888** for details. There is no train service to the park. Camping is allowed only at The Basin (✆ **02/9457 9853**) and costs A$12 (US$9.60/UK£4.80) for two people booked in advance.

If you have a car you can visit the **Ku-ring-gai Wildflower Garden,** 420 Mona Vale Rd., St. Ives (© **02/9440 8609**), which is essentially a huge area of natural bushland and a center for urban bushland education. There are plenty of bushwalking tracks, self-guided walks, and a number of nature-based activities. It's open daily from 8am to 4pm. Admission is A$3 (US$2.40/UK£1.20) for adults, A$2 (US$1.60/UK80p) for children, and A$7 (US$5.60/UK£2.80) for families.

South of Sydney is the remarkable **Royal National Park,** Farrell Avenue, Sutherland (© **02/9542 0648**). It's the world's oldest national park, declared in 1879. (The main competitor to the title is Yellowstone in the United States, which was set aside for conservation in 1872 but not designated a national park until 1883.) There's a visitor center at Audley Weir (past the main park entrance). You'll have to pay a A$11 (US$8.80/UK£4.40) per-car entry fee to enter the park.

There are several ways to reach the park, but my favorites are the little-known access points from Bundeena and Otford. To get to **Bundeena,** take a CityRail train from Central Station to the seaside suburb of Cronulla (around 1 hr.). Just below the train station, through an underpass, you'll find Cronulla Wharf. From there, hop on the delightful little ferry run by **National Park Ferries** (© **02/9523 2990**) to Bundeena, which I highly recommend you visit (I love it so much I live here!). There are three main beaches here, two of them edged by national park. All of them are beautiful. Shops and cafes are also here. Ferries run on the half-hour from Cronulla (except 12:30pm on weekdays). The last one back from Bundeena is at 7pm (6pm in winter). After you get off the ferry, the first turn on your left just up the hill will take you through part of the village to wonderful Jibbon Beach. Walk along the beach to the end, hop up some rocks, and follow the track (about 20 min.) through the park to Jibbon Head, for some stunning ocean views. Look out for the Aboriginal rock carvings off to your right before you reach it (a sign points toward the headland, but the carvings are to your right). It's around a 3-hour round-trip walk to Marley Beach (which has strong surf and dangerous rips) and a 6-hour round-trip to beautiful Wattamolla, where there's safe swimming for children in the salty lagoon. The ferry returns to Cronulla from Bundeena hourly on the hour (except 1pm). The fare is A$5.20 (US$4/UK£2) each way. Look up www.visitbundeena.com for more details.

A good way to see the park from Bundeena is to hire a canoe from **Bundeena Kayaks** (© **02/9544 5294;** www.bundeenakayaks.com.au) at the gorgeous Bonnievale Beach. Single kayaks cost A$15 (US$12/UK£6) per hour, A$40 (US$32/UK£16) for a half-day, and A$55 (US$44/UK£22) for a full day. Kayaks built for two people cost A$25 (US$20/UK£10) per hour, A$70 (US$56/UK£28) for a half-day, and A$90 (US$72/UK£36) for a full day.

If you fancy exploring the water from Cronulla, including the edge of the Royal national park, then make your way to the ferry terminal for an exploration of Port Hacking. **Cronulla Ferries** (© **02/9523 2990;** www.cronullaferries.com.au) runs daily cruises onboard the historic *Tom Thumb III* daily from May to September, and on Sundays, Mondays, Wednesdays, and Fridays from June to August. Three-hour cruises depart at 10:30am and cost A$18 (US$14/UK£7) for adults, A$13 (US$10/UK£5) for kids, and A$50 (US$40/UK£20) for a family. Another operator, **Cronulla Cruises** (© **02/9544 1400;** www.cronullacruises.com.au), runs ecocruises on a flat-bottomed pontoon boat which allows for better views and more maneuverability. Cruises run from 9am every Wednesday, Saturday, and Sunday and cost A$20 (US$16/UK£8) for adults, and A$15 (US$12/UK£6) for kids under 12. The cruise takes 3½ hours, and you can stop off at Audley Weir for 4 hours, which is a bit of a waste of time if you have a packed day ahead of you.

An alternative way to reach the park is to take the train from Central Station to **Otford,** then climb the hill up to the sea cliffs. If you're driving, you might want to follow the scenic cliff-edge road down into Wollongong. The entrance to the national park is a little tricky to find, so you might have to ask directions—but roughly, it's just to the left of a cliff top popular for hang gliding, radio-controlled airplanes, and kites. A 2-hour walk from the sea cliffs through beautiful and varying bushland and a palm forest will take you to Burning Palms Beach. There is no water along the route. The walk back up is steep, so attempt this trek only if you're reasonably fit. Trains to the area are irregular, and the last one departs around 4pm, so give yourself at least 2½ hours for the return trip to the train station to make sure you don't get stranded. It's possible to walk the memorable 26km (16 miles) from Otford to Bundeena, or vice versa, in 2 days. (Take all your food, water, and camping gear.) The track sticks to the coast, crosses several beaches, and is relatively easy to follow.

ESPECIALLY FOR KIDS

Kids can have fun at plenty of places in Sydney, but my choices below are particularly suitable for youngsters. (All are reviewed in full above.)

At **Taronga Zoo** (p. 169), an all-time favorite with kids, the barnyard animals, surprisingly, get as much attention as the koalas. If your kids want hands-on contact with the animals, though, you'd better head to **Featherdale Wildlife Park** (p. 168), where they can get their photo taken next to a koala, and hand-feed and stroke kangaroos and wallabies. You can't stroke koalas in New South Wales. Even more interactive are the exhibits just crying out to be touched and bashed at the **Powerhouse Museum** (p. 166).

The sharks at **Oceanworld** (p. 169) in Manly and at the **Sydney Aquarium** (p. 166) in Darling Harbour are big lures for kids, too, and the thrill of walking through a long Plexiglas tunnel as giant manta rays perch over their heads will lead to more squeals of excitement.

Another outing for both adults and children is to crawl around inside boats and submarines at the **Australian National Maritime Museum** (p. 165).

And what kid wouldn't enjoy a day at the beach? Sydney's got plenty to choose from, like **Bondi** and **Manly.**

6 Harbor Cruises & Organized Tours

For details on the **Sydney Explorer** bus, see "Getting Around," earlier this chapter.

HARBOR CRUISES

The best thing about Sydney is the harbor, and you shouldn't leave without taking a harbor cruise. **Sydney Ferries** (© **13 15 00** in Australia, or 02/9245 5600; www.sydneyferries.info) offers a 1-hour morning harbor cruise with commentary departing Circular Quay, Wharf 4, daily at 10:30am. It costs A$18 (US$14/UK£7) for adults, A$9 (US$7.20/UK£3.60) for children under 16, and A$45 (US$36/UK£18) for families (with any number of children). A 2½-hour afternoon cruise explores more of the harbor; it leaves from Wharf 4 at 1pm on weekdays and 12:30pm on weekends and public holidays. This tour costs A$24 (US$19/UK£9.50) for adults, A$12 (US$9.60/UK£4.80) for children, and A$60 (US$48/UK£24) for families. The highly recommended 1½-hour **Evening Harbour Lights tour,** which takes in the city lights as far east as Double Bay and west to Goat Island, leaves Monday through

Saturday at 8pm from Wharf 4. The evening tour costs A$22 (US$18/UK£9) for adults, A$11 (US$8.80/UK£4.50) for children, and A$55 (US$44/UK£22) for families.

Captain Cook Cruises, departing Jetty 6, Circular Quay (✆ **02/9206 1111;** www.captaincook.com.au), offers several harbor excursions on its sleek vessels, with commentary along the way.

Examples include a 2-hour 20-minute **Coffee Cruise** departing from Jetty 6, Circular Quay, at 10am and 2:15pm daily. It costs A$46 (US$37/UK£18) for adults, A$24 (US$19/UK£9.50) for kids, and A$99 (US$80/UK£40) for a family. Another is a Seafood Buffet Lunch cruise, departing Circular Quay at 12:30pm daily, and costing A$62 (US$50/UK£25) for adults and A$30 (US$24/UK£12) for children.

Its **Sydney Harbour Explorer** cruise is popular and stops off at The Rocks, Watson's Bay, Taronga Zoo, and Darling Harbour. You get on and off when you want. It costs A$29 (US$23/UK£12) for adults, A$15 (US$12/UK£6) for kids, and A$69 (US$55/UK£27) for a family, and leaves Circular Quay at 9:45am, 11:30am, 1:30pm, and 3:30pm daily.

Another favorite is the 1-hour 15-minute **Harbour Highlights Cruise,** which costs A$25 (US$20/UK£10) for adults, A$12 (US$9.60/UK£4.80) for kids, and A$59 (US$47/UK£23) for adults. It leaves Circular Quay at 9:30am, 11am, 12:45pm, 2:30pm, 4pm, 6pm, and 7:30pm. The first and last cruises are only offered if there are sufficient passengers for a trip.

The company also offers a range of dinner cruises.

Captain Cook cruises have ticket booths at Jetty 6, Circular Quay (open 8:30am–7pm daily), and at 1 King Street Wharf, Darling Harbour (near the Sydney Aquarium). It has limited opening hours of 11am to 4pm daily.

Matilda Cruises (✆ **02/9264 7377;** www.matilda.com.au) offers a 1-hour **Rocket Harbour Express** narrated sightseeing tour leaving the pontoon at the far end of Sydney Aquarium at Darling Harbour eight times daily beginning at 9:30am (six times daily in winter, Apr–Sept, beginning at 10:30am). You can stay on for the full hour, or get off and on again at Circular Quay (opposite the Museum of Contemporary Art), the Opera House, Watsons Bay, and Taronga Zoo. The last boat leaves Taronga Zoo at 5:10pm in summer (4:10pm in winter). There's tea and coffee on board. The cruise costs A$25 (US$20/UK£10) for adults, A$17 (US$14/UK£7) for children 5 to 12, and A$59 (US$47/UK£23) for a family.

Boats also zip across from Darling Harbour and Circular Quay to Luna Park on the half-hour from 9:30am to 7pm (and to 10pm on Fri and Sat). The journey costs A$5.70 (US$4.50/UK£2.25) one-way for adults, A$2.80 (US$2.20/UK£1.10) for kids, and A$14 (US$11/UK£5.70) for a family.

The company also offers a **Zoo Express,** including zoo entry, from both Darling Harbour and Circular Quay. It costs A$37 (US$29/UK£15) for adults, A$20 (US$16/UK£8) for kids aged 5 to 14, and A$110 (US$88/UK£44) for a family.

The company also runs morning and afternoon cruises, and lunch and cocktail cruises with good food on a sailing boat. One example is the **Seafood Lunch** cruise, with a seafood buffet. It leaves Darling Harbour at noon and Jetty 6 at Circular Quay at 12:30pm. The 1½-hour cruise costs A$63 (US$50/UK£25) for adults and A$38 (US$30/UK£15) for kids aged 6 to 12.

Matilda Cruises have a ticket booth at Jetty 6 at Circular Quay, and a ticket office next to the Sydney Aquarium at Darling Harbour.

Other cruise operators also have booths and information available at Circular Quay and Darling Harbour.

HARBOR CRUISE TICKETS & INFO

The one-stop shop for tickets and information on all harbor cruises is the **Australian Travel Specialists** (✆ **02/9247 5151;** www.atstravel.com.au). It's a good idea to check websites before you come to Australia, or pop into a ticket office at Darling Harbour or Circular Quay, because cruise options, departure times, and prices change frequently. You can book on the Net, too.

WALKING TOURS

The center of Sydney is compact, and you can see a lot in a day on foot. If you want to learn more about Sydney's early history, then book a guided tour with **The Rocks Walking Tour** ★★ (✆ **02/9247 6678;** www.rockswalkingtours.com.au), based at 23 Playfair St., Rocks Square, The Rocks. Excellent walking tours leave Monday through Friday at 10:30am, 12:30pm, and 2:30pm (in Jan 10:30am and 2:30pm), and Saturday and Sunday at 11:30am and 2pm. The 1½-hour tour costs A$20 (US$16/UK£8) for adults, A$11 (US$8.20/UK£4.10) for children 10 to 16, A$51 (US$40/UK£20) for families, free for accompanied children under 10.

Another interesting experience is **The Rocks Pub Tour** (✆ **02/9240 8788;** www.therockspubtour.com), a journey aimed at illuminating the lives of the sailors and whalers who once lived around here. You get to meet some of the locals, visit three historic pubs, take a wander around the alleyways, try a brew or two, and enjoy special offers for pub meals. The 1½-hour tour departs from Cadmans Cottage at 5pm on Mondays, Wednesdays, Fridays, and Saturdays. It costs A$35 (US$28/UK£14). You must be over 18.

A journey with a difference is **Weird Sydney Ghost and History Tours** (✆ **02/9943 0167;** www.destinytours.com.au). The tour—in a hearse—is fascinating and fun. It explores a section of historic Sydney and more modern additions, including a former VD clinic, the Sydney Opera House, and some buildings along Macquarie Street. It costs A$72 (US$58/UK£29) for adults for the 2½-hour trip and A$36 (US$29/UK£14) for kids. The tour leaves nightly at 8pm (7pm in winter).

MOTORCYCLE TOURS

Blue Thunder Motorcycle Tours (✆ **1800/800 184** in Australia, or 0408/618 982 mobile; www.bluethunder.com.au) runs Harley-Davidson tours of Sydney, the Blue Mountains, and places around New South Wales. A 1-hour ride (you sit on the back of the bike) around the city costs A$95 (US$76/UK£38). A 1½-hour ride through the city and out to Bondi costs A$145 (US$116/UK£58). A 3-hour trip to the northern beaches or down the south coast through the Royal National Park costs A$225 (US$180/UK£112), including lunch. Full-day trips including lunch and snacks, go to the Hunter Valley, the south coast, Bathurst, or the Blue Mountains.

If you love motorbikes and want to take one out on your own for a self-guided or guided tour, contact **Bikescape** (✆ **02/9356 2453;** www.bikescape.com.au). It will rent you a bike to go around Sydney, or as far afield as Byron Bay or the Great Ocean Road in Victoria.

Sydney by Helicopter

If you have the cash, then a scenic tour of Sydney Harbour and beyond will be a nice investment in time. **Sydney Helicopters,** 25 Wentworth St., Granville (✆ **02/9637 4455;** www.sydneyhelicopters.com.au), offers short flights from A$425 (US$340/UK£170) per person, and longer ones—including a country pub crawl.

7 Staying Active

BIKING The best place to cycle in Sydney is Centennial Park. Rent bikes from **Centennial Park Cycles,** 50 Clovelly Rd., Randwick (✆ **02/9398 5027**), which is 200m (656 ft.) from the Musgrave Avenue entrance. (The park has five main entrances.) Mountain bikes cost A$12 (US$9.60/UK£4.80) for the first hour, A$17 (US$14/UK£7) for 2 hours, A$22 (US$18/UK£9) for 4 hours, and A$40 (US$32/UK£16) for a full day. Longer rental works out cheaper.

Bonza Bike Tours (✆ **02/9331 1127;** www.bonzabiketours.com) runs regular bike tours of the city, and also hires out bikes. A half-day city tour costs A$60 (US$48/UK£24) for adults and A$45 (US$36/UK£18) for kids, and includes a bike and helmet. They also offer tours of Manly, and another which takes you across Sydney Harbour Bridge. Bike hire alone costs A$55 (US$44/UK£22) a day and A$49 (US$39/UK£20) a half-day, plus a A$20 (US$16/UK£8) delivery fee.

FITNESS CLUBS The **City Gym,** 107 Crown St., East Sydney (✆ **02/9360 6247**), is a busy 24-hour gym near Kings Cross. Drop-in visits are A$10 (US$8/UK£4).

GOLF Sydney has over 90 golf courses and plenty of fine weather. The 18-hole championship course at **Moore Park Golf Club,** Cleveland Street and Anzac Parade, Waterloo (✆ **02/9663 1064**), is the nearest to the city. Greens fees are A$40 (US$32/UK£16) Monday through Friday, and A$45 (US$22/UK£27) Saturday and Sunday.

For general information on courses, call the **New South Wales Golf Association** (✆ **02/9264 8433**).

IN-LINE SKATING The best places to skate are along the beachside promenades at Bondi and Manly beaches and in Centennial Park. **Manly Blades,** 49 N. Steyne (✆ **02/9976 3833**), rents skates for A$15 (US$12/UK£6) for 1 hour, A$20 (US$16/UK£8) for 2 hours, A$25 (US$20/UK£10) overnight, and A$30 (US$24/UK£15) for 24 hours. It also hires bicycles and skateboards. Lessons are A$30 (US$24/UK£15), including 1-hour skate rental and a half-hour lesson. **Total Skate,** 36 Oxford St., Paddington, near Centennial Park (✆ **02/9380 6356**), rents skates for A$10 (US$8/UK£4) for the first hour, A$5 (US$4/UK£2) for subsequent hours, and A$30 (US$24/UK£12) for 24 hours. Ask about a free lesson.

JOGGING The **Royal Botanic Gardens, Centennial Park,** and any **beach** are the best places to kick-start your body. You can also run across the Harbour Bridge, though you'll have to put up with the car fumes. Another popular spot is along the sea cliffs from Bondi Beach to Bronte Beach.

SCUBA DIVING Plenty of people learn to dive in Sydney before taking off for the Barrier Reef. Don't expect coral reefs, though. **Pro Dive,** 27 Alfreda St., Coogee (✆ **1800 820 820** in Australia, or 02/9255 0300; www.prodive.com), offers a 4-day learn-to-dive program (Mon–Thurs, or over two weekends) costing A$295 (US$236/UK£118), which includes four ocean dives.

SEAPLANE Sydney by Seaplane, Rose Bay Seaplane Base, Lyne Park, Rose Bay (✆ **02/9974 1455;** www.sydneybyseaplane.com), offers scenic flights over Sydney Harbour, Bondi Beach, the Northern Beaches and beyond, plus several flight and dining packages. A 15-minute scenic flight costs A$135 (US$108/UK£54) for adults and A$101 (US$81/UK£50) for kids under 13. A 30-minute flight costs A$220 (US$176/UK£110) for adults and A$165 (US$132/UK£66) for kids. Sydney Harbour

Finds A Surf Adventure

If you've always fancied learning to surf, then head for **Waves Surf School** (© **1800/851 101** in Australia, or 02/9369 3010; www.wavessurfschool.com.au). It takes budding surfers on 1-day trips from Sydney to the Royal National Park. Trips cost A$75 (US$60/UK£30), including equipment and lunch. If you're young enough to spend the night in a "double-decker party bus," then you might consider a 2-day surfing trip to Seal Rocks, north of Sydney, for A$199 (US$160/UK£80). The company also takes adventurous travelers on a 4-day surfing trip from Sydney to Byron Bay for A$439 (US$351/UK£175).

Seaplanes, same address as above (© **02/9388 1978;** www.seaplanes.com.au), offers similar packages, but doesn't have a discount rate for children.

SURFING **Bondi Beach** and **Tamarama** are the best surf beaches on the south side of Sydney Harbour. **Manly, Narrabeen, Bilgola, Collaroy, Long Reef,** and **Palm** beaches are the most popular on the north side. Most beach suburbs have surf shops where you can rent a board. At Bondi Beach, **Lets Go Surfing,** 128 Ramsgate Ave. (© **02/9365 1800;** www.letsgosurfing.com.au), rents surfboards for A$25 (US$20/UK£10) for 2 hours or A$40 (US$32/UK£16) all day. There are discounts for all-week hire and you can also hire wet suits. The company also offers a range of surfing lessons, both in a group and individually. A 2-hour session in a small group costs between A$69 and A$75 (US$55–US$60/UK£27–UK£30), and three 2-hour sessions cost between A$165 and A$175 (US$132–US$140/UK£66–UK£70). In Manly, **Aloha Surf,** 44 Pittwater Rd. (© **02/9976 3732**), rents surfboards. **Manly Surf School** (© **02/9977 6977;** www.manlysurfschool.com) offers 2-hour small-group surf classes for A$50 (US$40/UK£20). The more lessons you take the cheaper each one turns out. Private lessons cost A$80 (US$64/UK£32) per hour.

SWIMMING If you don't mind the trek to get there, the best place to swim indoors in Sydney is the **Sydney Aquatic Centre,** at Olympic Park, Homebush Bay (© **02/9752 3666**). It's open Monday through Friday from 5am to 9:45pm, and Saturday, Sunday, and public holidays from 6am to 7:45pm (6:45pm May–Oct), and charges A$5.80 (US$4.60/UK£2.30) adults, A$4.60 (US$3.70/UK£1.80) children 4 to 15, A$19 (US$15/UK£7.50) families.

The most central of Sydney's pools is **Cook and Phillip Park,** 4 College St., at William Street (© **02/9326 0444**). The center has three pools: one for serious swimmers, another with a wave machine, and a hydrotherapy pool with easy ramp access and bubble jets. Entry is A$5.80 (US$4.60/UK£2.30) for adults and A$4.20 (US$3.40/UK£1.70) for kids. To find it, walk to the cathedral across Hyde Park, and continue for a couple of minutes along the dark paved area outside the cathedral's front entrance (keeping Hyde Park on your right). Look for signs directing you down some stairs to the entrance. It's open daily from 6am to 10pm.

Another good pool is the **Andrew (Boy) Charlton Swimming Pool,** The Domain, Mrs. Macquaries Road, near the Royal Botanical Gardens (© **02/9358 6686**). From this heated outdoor pool there are fabulous views across Sydney Harbour. There's also a learner's pool and a toddler's pool. Entry is A$5.20 (US$4/UK£2.60) for adults and A$3.60 (US$2.90/UK£1.80) for kids. It's open from 6am to 7pm daily.

Across the Harbour Bridge, near Luna Park, is the **North Sydney Olympic Pool,** Alfred South Street, Milsons Point (✆ **02/9955 2309**). You can refresh yourself in this outdoor pool after a walk over the bridge. Entry costs A$3.50 (US$2.80/UK£1.40) for adults and A$1.65 (US$1.30/UK65p) for children. There's a separate indoor pool, too. It's open from 5:30am to 9pm Monday to Friday, and 7am to 7pm on weekends.

The **Bondi Icebergs Club,** 1 Notts Ave. (✆ **02/9130 4804**), at Bondi Beach, on the rocks to the right of the beach as you look at the sea, has an Olympic-size pool and a children's pool. Entrance costs A$4 (US$3.20/UK£1.60) for adults and A$2.50 (US$2/UK£1.25) for kids, and includes a sauna. It's open from 6am to 7pm Monday to Friday and 6:30am to 6:30pm on weekends.

TENNIS There are hundreds of places around the city to play one of Australia's most popular sports. A nice spot is the **Miller's Point Tennis Court,** Kent Street, The Rocks (✆ **02/9256 2222**). It's run by the Observatory Hotel and is open daily from 7:30am to 10pm. The court costs A$20 (US$16/UK£8) per hour. Racket hire is A$5 (US$4/UK£2.50) per hour. The **North Sydney Tennis Centre,** 1A Little Alfred St., North Sydney (✆ **02/9371 9952**), has three courts available daily from 6am to 10pm. They cost A$18 (US$14/UK£7) until 5pm on weekdays and A$22 (US$18/UK£9) at other times.

YACHTING **Sydney by Sail** (✆ **02/9280 1110;** www.sydneybysail.com.au) offers sailing courses on Sydney Harbour. A skippered, 3-hour sail costs A$130 (US$104/UK£52) for adults and A$65 (US$52/UK£26) for kids.

8 Spectator Sports

CRICKET The **Sydney Cricket Ground,** at the corner of Moore Park and Driver Avenue, is famous for its 1-day and test matches, played October through March. Tickets cost from A$44 (US$35/UK£17). Over the winter months Aussie Rules games, featuring the Sydney Swans, are also played here. Look up www.sydneycricketground.com.au for match details. Tours of the stadium start at 10am and 1pm Monday to Friday and at 10am on Saturday. They cost A$25 (US$20/UK£10) for adults, A$17 (US$14/UK£7) for kids, and A$65 (US$52/UK£26) for a family. Call ✆ **1300 724 737** to book.

FOOTBALL In this city, "football" means rugby league. If you want to see burly chaps pound into each other while chasing an oval ball, then be here between May and September. The biggest venue is the **Sydney Football Stadium,** Moore Park Road, Paddington (✆ **02/9360 6601,** or 1900/963 133 for match information). Buy tickets through **Ticketek** (✆ **02/9266 4800**).

HORSE RACING Sydney has four horse-racing tracks: Randwick, Canterbury, Rosehill, and Warwick Farm. The most central and best known is **Randwick Racecourse,** Alison Street, Randwick (✆ **02/9663 8400**). The biggest race day of the week is Saturday. Entry costs from A$10 (US$8/UK£4). Call the **Sydney Turf Club** (✆ **02/9930 4000**) with questions about Rosehill and Canterbury, and the Randwick number for Warwick Farm.

SURFING CARNIVALS Every summer these uniquely Australian competitions bring crowds to Sydney's beaches to watch surf clubs compete in various watersports. Contact the **Surf Lifesaving Association** (✆ **02/9597 5588**) for times and locations.

Other beach events include Iron Man and Iron Woman competitions, during which Australia's fittest struggle it out in combined swimming, running, and surfing events.

YACHT RACING Sailing competitions take place on the harbor most summer weekends, but the start of the **Sydney to Hobart Yacht Race** on Boxing Day (Dec 26) is a must-see. The race starts from the harbor near the Royal Botanic Gardens.

9 Shopping

You'll find plenty of places to keep your credit cards in action in Sydney. Most shops of interest to the visitor are in **The Rocks** and along **George and Pitt streets** (including the shops below the Sydney Tower and along Pitt Street Mall). Other precincts worth checking out are **Mosman** on the North Shore and **Double Bay** in the eastern suburbs for boutique shopping, **Chatswood** for its shopping centers, the **Sydney Fishmarket** for the sake of it, and various **weekend markets** (listed below).

Don't miss the **Queen Victoria Building (QVB),** on the corner of Market and George streets. This Victorian shopping arcade is one of the prettiest in the world and has some 200 boutiques—mostly men's and women's fashion—on four levels. The arcade is open 24 hours, but the shops do business Monday through Saturday from 9am to 6pm (Thurs to 9pm) and Sunday from 11am to 5pm.

Several other arcades in the city center also have potential, including the **Sydney Central Plaza,** beside the Myer department store on Pitt Street Mall; and the **Skygarden Arcade,** which runs from Pitt Street Mall to Castlereagh Street. The **Strand Arcade** (between Pitt St. Mall and George St.) was built in 1892 and is interesting for its architecture and small boutiques, food stores, and cafes, and the Down Town Duty Free store on the basement level.

On **Pitt Street Mall** you'll find record shops, including HMV, a branch of The Body Shop, and boutiques such as Just Jeans, Jeans West, Katies, and Esprit.

Oxford Street runs from the city to Bondi Junction through Paddington and Darlinghurst and is home to countless clothing stores for the style conscious. You could easily spend anywhere from 2 hours to a whole day making your way from one end to the other. Detour down William Street once you get to Paddington to visit the headquarters of celebrated international Australian designer Collette Dinnigan. On the same street are the trendy boutiques Belinda and Corner Store (cutting-edge designs), and Pelle and Di Nuovo (luxury recycled goods).

Tip: American Express cards seem to be unpopular with many shop owners.

SHOPPING HOURS Regular shopping hours are generally Monday through Wednesday and Friday from 8:30 or 9am to 6pm, Thursday from 8:30 or 9am to 9pm, Saturday from 9am to 5 or 5:30pm, and Sunday from 10 or 10:30am to 5pm. Exceptions are noted in the store listings below.

SYDNEY SHOPPING FROM A TO Z

ABORIGINAL ARTIFACTS & CRAFTS

Gavala Aboriginal Art & Cultural Education Centre I'd head here first if I were in the market for a decent boomerang or didgeridoo. Gavala is owned and operated by Aborigines, and it stocks plenty of authentic Aboriginal crafts, including carved emu eggs, grass baskets, cards, and books. A first-rate painted didgeridoo will cost anywhere from A$100 to A$450 (US$80–US$360/UK£40–UK£180). Gavala also sponsors cultural talks, didgeridoo-making lessons, and storytelling sessions. Open daily from 10am to 9pm. Shop 131, Harbourside, Darling Harbour. © **02/9212 7232.**

Finds A World-Class Gallery of Aboriginal Art

Quality Aboriginal art from some of Australia's best-known painters is on sale at **Original & Authentic Aboriginal Art** at 79 George St., The Rocks (✆ **02/9251 4222**). Artists whose work is represented include Paddy Fordham Wainburranga, whose paintings hang in the White House in Washington, D.C., and Janet Forrester Nangala, whose work has been exhibited in the Australian National Gallery in Canberra. Expect to pay in the range of A$1,000 to A$4,000 (US$800–US$3,200/UK£400–UK£1,600) for the larger paintings. There are some nice painted pots here, too, costing A$30 to A$80 (US$24–US$64/UK£15–UK£32). Open daily from 10am to 6pm.

ANTIQUES

Bottom of the Harbour Antiques This Rocks institution has recently moved to a new home farther toward the Harbour Bridge. It sells a wide range of maritime-related antiques, including clocks, shells, books, brass items, statues, compasses, and other things. A real treasure chest. Open daily 10am to 6pm. 31 George St., The Rocks. ✆ **02/9247 8107.**

ART PRINTS & ORIGINALS

Billich Charles Billich has a fine-arts gallery worth of paintings here, all done by himself. Sydney scenes intermingle with Asian-influenced works of grand scale. Open daily from 9am to 8pm. 104 George St., The Rocks. ✆ **02/9252 1481.**

Done Art and Design Ken Done is well known for having designed his own Australian flag, which he hopes to raise over Australia should it abandon its present one following the formation of a republic. The art here is his. The clothing designs—which feature printed sea- and beachscapes, the odd colorful bird, and lots of pastels—are by his wife, Judy. Open daily from 10am to 5:30pm. 1 Hickson Rd., off George St., The Rocks. ✆ **02/9247 2740.**

Ken Duncan Gallery This photographer-turned-salesman is making a killing from his exquisitely produced large-scale photographs of Australian scenery. Open daily from 9am to 8pm (to 9pm Thurs) in summer, 9am to 7pm in winter. 1 Hickson Rd., The Rocks. ✆ **02/9247 2740.**

BOOKS

You'll find a good selection of books on Sydney and Australia for sale at the **Art Gallery of New South Wales,** the Garden Shop in the **Royal Botanic Gardens,** the **Museum of Contemporary Art,** the **Museum of Sydney,** the **Australian Museum,** and the **State Library of New South Wales.** See listings earlier in this chapter.

Abbey's Bookshop This interesting, centrally located shop specializes in literature, history, and mystery, and has a whole floor on language and education. 131 York St., behind the QVB. ✆ **02/9264 3111.**

Angus & Robertson Bookworld One of Australia's largest bookshops, with two stories of books—including a good guidebook and Australiana section—and games. 168 Pitt St., Pitt Street Mall. ✆ **02/9235 1188.**

Borders Now ranked as one of the best general bookstores in Sydney, Borders has a wonderful magazine section as well as thousands of titles. Skygarden, 77 Castlereagh St. (entrance also on Pitt Street Mall). ✆ **02/9235 2433.**

Gleebooks Bookshop Specializing in art, general literature, psychology, sociology, and women's studies, Gleebooks also has a secondhand store (with a large children's department) down the road at 191 Glebe Point Rd. Open daily 8am to 9pm. 49 and 191 Glebe Point Rd., Glebe. © **02/9660 2333.**

Goulds Book Arcade Come here to search for unusual dusty volumes. About a 10-minute walk from the Newtown CityRail station, the place is bursting with thousands of secondhand and new books, all in rough order. You can browse for hours here. Open daily from 8am to midnight. 32 King St., Newtown. © **02/9519 8947.**

Travel Bookshop Hundreds of travel guides, maps, Australiana titles, coffee-table books, and accessories line the shelves of this excellent bookshop. There's also an Amex counter. Open Monday through Friday from 9am to 6pm and Saturday from 10am to 5pm. Shop 3, 175 Liverpool St. (across from the southern end of Hyde Park, near the Museum CityRail station). © **02/9261 8200.**

CRAFTS

Collect Some of Australia's most respected craft artists and designers are represented here. There are some wonderful glass, textile, ceramic, jewelry, metal, and wood-turned items for sale. Open daily from 9:30am to 5:30pm.–88 George St., The Rocks. © **02/9247 7984.**

DEPARTMENT STORES

The two big names in Sydney shopping are David Jones and Myer. Both stores are open Monday through Wednesday and Friday through Saturday from 9am to 6pm, Thursday from 9am to 9pm, and Sunday from 11am to 5pm.

David Jones (© **02/9266 5544**) is the city's largest department store, selling everything from fashion to designer furniture. You'll find the women's section on the corner of Elizabeth and Market streets, and the men's section on the corner of Castlereagh and Market streets. The food section here is the best in Australia by far.

Myer (© **02/9238 9111**), formally Grace Brothers, is similar to David Jones, but the building is newer and flashier. It's on the corner of George and Market streets.

DUTY-FREE SHOPS

Sydney has several duty-free shops selling goods at a discount. To take advantage of the bargains, you need a passport and a flight ticket, and you must export what you buy. The duty-free shop with the best buys is **Downtown Duty Free,** which has two city outlets, one on the basement level of the Strand Arcade, off Pitt Street Mall © **02/9233 3166**), and one at 105 Pitt St. (© **02/9221 4444**). Five more stores are at Sydney International Airport and are open from the first to the last flight of the day.

FASHION

The best places to shop for fashion are the **QVB** and the **Sydney Central Plaza** (on the ground floor of the mall next to the Myer department store on Pitt St. Mall). Fashion-statement stores featuring the best of Australian design at the QVB include Oroton, Country Road, and the fabulous woman's clothing designer Lisa Ho. In the **Strand Arcade,** off Pitt Street Mall, find Third Millennium, Allanah Hill, and Wayne Cooper. The major Pitt Street Mall outlets will also keep you up-to-date.

Other fashion shopping meccas in or close to Pitt Street Mall include the Glasshouse and the MLC Centre which are linked to one another via a covered overpass. Farther down toward Circular Quay is Chifley Plaza, home to a selection of the world's most famous and stylish international brands. For really trendy clothing, walk up Oxford Street to **Paddington,** and for alternative clothes, go to **Newtown.**

Australian Outback Clothing

R.M. Williams Moleskin trousers may not be the height of fashion at the moment, but you never know. R.M. Williams boots are famous for being both tough and fashionable. You'll find Akubra hats, Driza-bone coats, and kangaroo-skin belts here, too. 389 George St. (between Town Hall and Central CityRail stations). ✆ **02/9262 2228.**

Thomas Cook Boot & Clothing Company Located between Town Hall and Central CityRail stations, this place specializes in Australian boots, Driza-bone coats, and Akubra hats. There's another shop at 129 Pitt St., near Martin Place (✆ **02/9232 3334**). 790 George St., Haymarket. ✆ **02/9212 6616.** www.thomascookclothing.com.au.

Men's Fashion

Esprit Mens Not so cheap but certainly colorful clothes come out of this designer store where bold hues and fruity patterns are the in thing. Quality shirts cost around A$60 (US$48/UK£24). Shop 10G, Sydney Central Plaza, 450 George St. ✆ **02/9233 7349.**

Outdoor Heritage Quality clothing with a yachting influence is what you'll find at this good-looking store specializing in casual, colorful gear. Shop 13G, Sydney Central Plaza, 450 George St. ✆ **02/9235 1560.**

Unisex Fashion

Country Road This chain has outlets all across Australia as well as in the United States. The clothes, for both men and women, are good quality but tend to be quite expensive (though you might find something smart). Other branches are in the QVB, the Skygarden Arcade, Bondi Junction, Darling Harbour, Double Bay, Mosman, and Chatswood. 142–146 Pitt St. ✆ **02/9394 1818.**

Mostrada If you're looking for good-quality leather items at very reasonable prices, then this is your place. Leather jackets for men and women go for A$199 to A$899 (US$159–US$719/UK£80–UK£360), with an average price of around A$400 (US$320/UK£160). There are also bags, belts, and other leather accessories. Store 15G, Sydney Central Plaza, 450 George St. ✆ **02/9221 0133.**

Robby Ingham The collection here is made up of men's and women's brand names like Hugo Boss and Chloe. The MLC building, 19 Martin Place, ✆ **02/9232 6466** and 424–428 Oxford St., Paddington. ✆ **02/9332 2124.**

Women's Fashion

In addition to the places listed below, head to **Oxford Street** (particularly Paddington) for more avant-garde designers.

Akira Isagawa Internationally lauded and locally adored, few have left such an indelible watermark on the Australian fashion pages. 12a Queen St., Woollahra. ✆ **02/9361 5221.**

Belinda For those who love shoes you can't go past this cute little shop just off Oxford Street. 39 William St., Paddington. ✆ **02/9380 8728.**

Collette Dinnigan Cinema sirens, pop royalty, and the world's most glamorous women all appreciate her seriously sexy designs; Collette's exquisite choice of fabrics has helped bring her prominence as a renowned ready-to-wear and couture designer. 33 William St., Paddington. ✆ **02/9360 6691.**

Zimmerman Zimmerman is a real Saturday-afternoon fix for lots of Sydney girls. Looking for an outfit for a big night out, or some funky swimwear? Then Zimmerman is the place to go. 24 Oxford St., Woollahra. ✆ **02/9360 5769.**

FOOD

The goodies you'll find downstairs in the food section of **David Jones** department store on Castlereagh Street (the men's section) are enough to tempt anyone. The store sells the best local and imported products to the rich and famous (and the rest of us).

Coles One of the few supermarkets in the city center, this place is a good bet if you want to cook for yourself or are after ready-made food (including tasty sandwiches) and cheap soft drinks. There's another Coles beneath the giant Coca-Cola sign on Darlinghurst Road, Kings Cross. Open daily from 6am to midnight. Wynyard station, Castlereagh St., Wynyard (opposite the Menzies Hotel and the public bus stands). ✆ **02/9299 4769.**

Darrell Lea Chocolates This is the oldest location of Australia's most famous chocolate shop. Pick up some wonderful handmade chocolates as well as other unusual candies, including the best licorice this side of the Casbah. At the corner of King and George sts. ✆ **02/9232 2899.**

Sydney Fishmarket Finding out what people eat can be a good introduction to a new country and, in my opinion, nowhere is this more fascinating than at the local fish market. Here you'll find seven major fish retailers selling everything from shark to Balmain bugs (small crayfish), with hundreds of species in between. Watch out for the local pelicans being fed the fishy leftovers. There's also a Doyles restaurant and a sushi bar, a couple of cheap seafood eateries, a fruit market, and a good deli. The retail sections are open daily from 7am to 4pm. At the corner of Bank St. and Pyrmont Bridge Rd., Pyrmont. ✆ **02/9004 1100.**

GIFTS & SOUVENIRS

The shops at **Taronga Zoo,** the **Oceanarium** in Manly, the **Sydney Aquarium,** and the **Australian Museum** are all good sources for gifts and souvenirs. Many shops around **The Rocks** are worth browsing, too.

Australian Geographic A spinoff of the Australian version of *National Geographic* magazine, this store sells good-quality crafts and Australiana. On hand are camping gadgets, telescopes, binoculars, garden utensils, scientific oddities, books, calendars, videos, music, toys, and lots more. Harbourside Festival Marketplace, Darling Harbour. ✆ **02/9212 6539.** Sydney Tower, Pitt St. ✆ **02/9231 5055.**

Ikonstore This interesting little store on the pedestrian pathway to the Sydney Opera House from Circular Quay has a fascinating collection of watches and gadgets for the gourmet collector. 16 Opera Quays, East Circular Quay. ✆ **02/9252 6352.**

National Trust Gift and Bookshop You can pick up some nice souvenirs, including books, Australiana crafts, and indigenous foodstuffs here. An art gallery on the premises presents changing exhibits of paintings and sculpture by Australians. There's also a cafe. Closed Monday. Observatory Hill, The Rocks. ✆ **02/9258 0154.**

The Wilderness Society Shop Australiana is crawling out of the woodwork at this cute little crafts emporium dedicated to spending all its profits on saving the few remaining untouched forests and wilderness areas of Australia. You'll find some quality crafts items, cute children's clothes, books, cards, and knickknacks. Sydney Tower, Castlereagh St. ✆ **02/9233 4674.**

MARKETS

Balmain Market Active from 8:30am to 4pm every Saturday, this market has some 140 vendors selling crafts, jewelry, and knickknacks. Take the ferry to Balmain (Darling St.); the market is a 10-minute walk up Darling Street. On the grounds of St. Andrew's Church, Darling St., Balmain ✆ **02/9555 1791.**

Bondi Markets A nice place to stroll around on Sunday after your brunch on Campbell Parade and discover the upcoming young Australian designers. This market specializes in clothing and jewelry, new, secondhand, and retro. It's open Sunday from 9am to 5pm. Bondi Beach School, Campbell Parade. ✆ **02/9398 5486.**

Paddington Bazaar At this Saturday-only market you'll find everything from essential oils and designer clothes to New Age jewelry and Mexican hammocks. Expect things to be busy from 10am to 4pm. Take bus no. 380 or 389 from Circular Quay and follow the crowds. On the grounds of St. John's Church, Oxford St., on the corner of Newcome St. ✆ **02/9331 2646.**

Paddy's Markets A Sydney institution, Paddy's Markets has hundreds of stalls selling everything from cheap clothes and plants to chickens. It's open Thursday through Sunday from 9am to 5pm. Above Paddy's Markets is **Market City** (✆ **02/9212 1388**), which has three floors of fashion stalls, food courts, and specialty shops. Of particular interest is the largest Asian-European supermarket in Australia, on level 1. At the corner of Thomas and Hay sts., Haymarket, near Chinatown. ✆ **1300/361 589** in Australia, or 02/9325 6924.

The Rocks Market Held every Saturday and Sunday, this touristy market has more than 100 vendors selling everything from crafts, housewares, and posters to jewelry and curios. The main street is closed to traffic from 10am to 4pm to make it easier to stroll around. George St., The Rocks. ✆ **02/9255 1717.**

MUSIC

Birdland This is the best store in Sydney for jazz and blues, and it stocks a sizable collection of rare items. The staff is very knowledgeable. 3 Barrack St. ✆ **02/9299 8527.** www.birdland.com.au.

HMV This is one of the best music stores in Sydney. The jazz section is impressive. CDs in Australia are not cheap, with most new releases costing around A$30 to A$35 (US$24–US$28/UK£12–UK£14). Pitt St. Mall. ✆ **02/9221 2311.**

Red Eye Records These two shops, tucked away downstairs in a small arcade not far from Pitt Street Mall and the Strand Arcade, are directly across from one another. The larger store sells a wide range of modern CDs, and the smaller store stocks a great collection of quality secondhand and end-of-the-line CDs for around A$20 (US$16/UK£8) each. Tank Stream Arcade (downstairs), at the corner of King and Pitt sts. (near Town Hall). ✆ **02/9233 8177** (new recordings), or 02/9233 8125 (secondhand CDs). www.redeye.com.au.

Sounds Australian You can find anything you've ever heard that sounds Australian here. From rock and pop to didgeridoo and country, it's all here. And if you haven't a clue what's good and what's bad, you can spend some time listening before you buy. The management is quite knowledgeable. In the Argyle Stores department store, The Rocks. ✆ **02/9247 7290.**

OPALS

There are plenty of opal shops around in Sydney, but don't expect to walk away with any bargains. Better just to choose one you like than haggle.

Altman & Cherny A good selection of opals—black, white, and boulder varieties—as well as jewelry is on sale here. Ask to see "The Aurora Australis," the world-famous black opal valued at A$1 million (US$800,000/UK£400,000). 19–31 Pitt St. (near Circular Quay). ✆ **02/9251 4717.**

Australian Opal Cutters Learn more about opals before you buy at this shop. The staff will give you lessons about opals to help you compare pieces. Suite 10, Level 4, National Building, 250 Pitt St. ✆ **02/9261 2442.**

WINE

Australian Wine Centre This is one of the best places in the country to pick up Australian wines by the bottle or the case. The shop stocks a wide range of wines from all over Australia, including bottles from small boutique wineries you're unlikely to find anywhere else. Individual tastings are possible at any time, and there are formal tastings every Thursday and Friday from 4 to 6pm. Wine is exported all over the world from here, so if you want to send home a crate of your favorite, you can be assured it will arrive in one piece. The center owns the wine bar and bistro next door, which is open Monday through Saturday from 6am until 10pm. You can drink here without dining. 1 Alfred St., Shop 3 in Goldfields House, Circular Quay. ✆ **02/9247 2755.**

10 Sydney After Dark

Australians are party animals when they're in the mood; whether it's a few beers around the barbecue with friends or an all-night rave at a trendy dance club, they're always on the lookout for the next event. You'll find that alcohol plays a big part in the Aussie culture.

WHERE TO FIND OUT WHAT'S ON

The best way to find out what's on is to get hold of the "Metro" section of the Friday *Sydney Morning Herald* or the "Seven Days" pullout from the Thursday *Daily Telegraph.*

THE PERFORMING ARTS

If you have an opportunity to see a performance in the **Sydney Opera House,** jump at it. The "House" is actually not that impressive inside, but the walk back after the show toward the ferry terminals at Circular Quay, with the Sydney Harbour Bridge lit up and the crowd all around you debating the best part of this play or who dropped a beat in that performance—well, it's like hearing Gershwin on the streets of New York. You'll want the moment to stay with you forever. For details on Sydney's most famous performing-arts venue, see "What to See & Do in Sydney," earlier in this chapter.

THE OPERA, SYMPHONY & BALLET

Australian Ballet Based in Melbourne, the Australian Ballet tours the country with its performances. The Sydney season, at the Opera House, is from mid-March until the end of April. A second Sydney season runs November through December. Level 15, 115 Pitt St. ✆ **02/9223 9522.** www.australianballet.com.au.

Australian Chamber Orchestra Based in Sydney, this well-known company performs at various venues around the city, from nightclubs to specialized music venues,

Tips **It's a Festival!**

If you happen to be in Australia in January, plan to attend one of the many events that are part of the annual **Sydney Festival.** The festival kicks off just after New Year's and continues through the month, with recitals, plays, films, and performances at venues throughout the city, including Town Hall, the Royal Botanic Gardens, the Sydney Opera House, and Darling Harbour. Some events are free. "Jazz in The Domain" and "Symphony in The Domain" are two free outdoor performances held in the Royal Botanic Gardens, generally on the third and fourth weekends in January; each event attracts thousands of Sydneysiders. For more information, contact **Festival Ticketek** (© **02/9266 4111;** fax 02/9267 4460). Buy tickets and find out about performances on the Web at **www.sydneyfestival.org.au.**

including the Concert Hall in the Sydney Opera House. Opera Quays, 2 East Circular Quay. © **02/9357 4111,** or 02/8274 3888 box office. www.aco.com.au.

Opera Australia Opera Australia performs at the Sydney Opera House's Opera Theatre. The opera runs January through March and June through November. 480 Elizabeth St., Surry Hills. © **02/9699 1099,** or 02/9319 1088 bookings. www.opera-australia.org.au.

Sydney Symphony Orchestra The renowned Edo de Waart conducts Sydney's finest symphony orchestra. It performs throughout the year in the Opera House's Concert Hall. The main symphony season runs March through November, and there's a summer season in February. Level 5, 52 William St., East Sydney. © **02/9334 4644,** or 02/9334 4600 box office.

THEATER

Sydney's blessed with plenty of theaters, many more than I have space for here—check the *Sydney Morning Herald,* especially the Friday edition, for information on what's currently in production.

Belvoir Street Theatre The hallowed boards of the Belvoir are home to Company B, which pumps out powerful local and international plays upstairs in a wonderfully moody main theater, formerly part of a tomato-sauce factory. Downstairs, a smaller venue generally shows more experimental productions, such as Aboriginal performances and dance. 25 Belvoir St., Surry Hills. © **02/9699 3444.** Tickets around A$34 (US$27/UK£13).

Capital Theatre Sydney's grandest theater plays host to major international and local productions like (cough) Australian singing superstar Kylie Minogue. It's also been the Sydney home of musicals such as *Miss Saigon* and *My Fair Lady.* 13–17 Campbell St., Haymarket, near Town Hall. © **02/9320 5000.** Ticket prices vary.

Her Majesty's Theatre A quarter of a century old, this large theater is still trawling in the big musicals. Huge productions that have run here include *Evita* and *The Phantom of the Opera.* 107 Quay St., Haymarket, near Central Station. © **02/9212 3411.** Ticket prices average A$55–A$75 (US$44–US$60/UK£22–UK£30).

Wharf Theatre This wonderful theater is on a refurbished wharf on the edge of Sydney Harbour, just beyond the Harbour Bridge. The long walk from the entrance of the pier to the theater along old creaky wooden floorboards builds up excitement for the show. Based here is the Sydney Theatre Company, a group well worth seeing, whatever the production. Dinner before the show at the Wharf's restaurant offers special views of the harbor. Pier 4, Hickson Rd., The Rocks. ✆ **02/9250 1777.** www.sydneytheatre.com.au. Ticket prices vary.

THE CLUB & MUSIC SCENE

JAZZ, FOLK & BLUES

The Basement ★ Australia's hottest jazz club also manages to squeeze in plenty of blues, folk, and funk. Acts appear every night, and it's best to book ahead. Call for the schedule, pick up one at the club, or visit the website. 29 Reiby Place, Circular Quay. ✆ **02/9251 2797.** Cover A$15–A$20 (US$12–US$16/UK£6–UK£8) for local acts, A$20–A$40 (US$16–US$32/UK£8/UK£16) for international performers.

side-on café Known by locals as one of the few live venues in Sydney to showcase diverse jazz nearly every night, this surprisingly decent restaurant is part of an arts complex and serves a two-course meal for A$27 (US$22/UK£11). Patrons are a blend of artists, musicians, and jazz lovers. The side-on endeavors to promote upcoming local talent as well as established acts, and is also home to an art gallery upstairs. Located just over 5km (3 miles) from the center of town, it's not all that central but is easily reached by public transport and well worth the detour. Daily 7pm until late. 83 Parramatta Rd., Anandale, near Anandale Hotel. Cover A$13 (US$10/UK£5).

ROCK

Metro A medium-size rock venue with space for 1,000, the Metro is the best place in Sydney to see local and international acts. Tickets sell out quickly. 624 George St. ✆ **02/9264 2666.**

DANCE CLUBS

Clubs come and go, and change names and music, so check the latest with a phone call. You can also check the "Metro" section in the Friday *Sydney Morning Herald;* free giveaway newspapers available in some bars along Oxford Street have info about the latest clubs.

Nightclub entrance charges change regularly, but generally are A$15 to A$20 (US$12–US$16/UK£6–UK£8).

Dragonfly An alleyway club tucked away in less salubrious surrounds, Dragonfly features a cocktail bar, dance floor, and booths flush with leather chairs. Dress trendy in your designer jeans or best dancing outfit. There's R&B on weekdays and house music on weekends. Weekends attract a hip crowd in their 30s. Open Wednesdays, and Friday to Saturday from 9pm to 5am. 1 Earl St., Potts Point. ✆ **02/9356 2666.**

Home Cavelike in shape and feel, with a balcony to look down upon the throng. There's a padded "silver room" for serious ravers. Friday nights are big for trance and hip-hop, and Saturdays for house music. For the serious clubber. Open Friday and Saturday 11pm until dawn. Cockle Bay Wharf, Darling Harbour. ✆ **02/9267 0654.**

Lady Lux Sophisticated and intimate, Lady Lux throbs to the latest party sounds. Getting in might be tricky unless you dress and act the part. It's open Thursday to Sunday from 10pm until late. 2 Roslyn St., Potts Point (near Kings Cross). ✆ **02/9361 5000.**

Q Bar If you are in town any night of the week then the Q Bar will be open for you. It attracts a varied crowd from youngsters to wrinklies, and has everything from a serious dance spot to pool tables. Expect house music every night, with some funk on Sunday and classic hits and disco on Thursdays. Open 9pm until 7am. 44 Oxford St. ✆ **02/9360 1375.**

Tank House music, of course, is the name-of-the-game at this below-ground offshoot of the Establishment Hotel, the city's trendiest historic hot spot. The surrounds, which include three bars on two levels, attract models and film stars when they are in town. Dress casual but designer. Open Friday and Saturday from 10pm until 6am. 3 Bridge Lane, Sydney. ✆ **02/9240 3094.**

GAY & LESBIAN CLUBS

Sydney has a huge gay community, so there's a very happening scene. The center of it all is Oxford Street, though Newtown has established itself as a gay hangout, too. For information on events, pick up a copy of the *Sydney Star Observer* or *Lesbians on the Loose,* available at art-house cinemas, cafes, and stores around Oxford Street. Nightclub covers generally range from A$10 to A$15 (US$8–US$12/UK£4–UK£6).

Arq This 24-hour club has an amazing light show and some of the best DJs in town. A very big place specializing in the latest dance tunes. Dress in drag or get buffed up. Open Thursday to Sunday 9pm to 9am. 16 Flinders St., Taylors Square, Darlinghurst. ✆ **02/9380 8700.**

Civic This original Art Deco hotel has been tastefully spruced up to accommodate three levels of entertainment. There's a theater on the lower first floor (basement), a saloon bar on the ground floor, and an Australian restaurant with live jazz upstairs, as well as an outdoor cocktail terrace. Great bands. Corner of Pitt and Goulburn sts., Sydney. ✆ **02/8267 3181.**

Columbian Hotel An enormous heritage building plays host to a thriving gay scene with heterosexual undercurrents. There's a bar with music videos downstairs, and a nightclub on top with a sparkling ruby chandelier. It's tasteful in its attention to detail, and both throbbing and intimate when it counts. It's open to at least 4am daily. 117–123 Oxford St., Darlinghurst. ✆ **02/9360 2152.**

Gilligan's & Ginger's A cocktail bar on the first floor of the Oxford Hotel, Gilligan's & Ginger's is home to a thriving social scene and great views of Oxford Street and the city skyline. DJs spin the latest handbag hits for the drag queens. 134 Oxford St., Darlinghurst, corner of Taylor Sq. ✆ **02/9331 3467.**

The Stonewall Hotel An institution with three levels of entertainment and many special nights. Don't miss Sydney's Diva, Ricca Paris, at the pickup night Malebox on Wednesdays. Daily noon to 5am. 175 Oxford St., Darlinghurst. ✆ **02/9360 1963.** Free entry most nights.

Tips Sydney Gay & Lesbian Mardi Gras

Each March, some 450,000 people pack into the city center, concentrated on Oxford Street, to watch as members of Sydney's GLBT communities pack a punch with colorful floats and frocks. The crowd is diverse, from kids to grannies, and those in the know bring a stepladder or milk crate to get a better view. Sydney's hotels are at their busiest during Mardi Gras, particularly anything with a view of the route. The post-parade party is an affair not for the fainthearted! Sequins, tight pants, and anything outrageously glamorous goes. Some 19,000 revelers attend. For more information check out the official Mardi Gras website: **www.mardigras.org.au**.

Taxi Club "Tacky Club," as it's affectionately known, is a Sydney institution good for "handbag music"—or old pop and new pop. 40 Flinders St., Darlinghurst (near Taylor Sq., Oxford St.). ✆ **02/9331 4256.**

THE BAR SCENE

Most of Australia's drinking holes are known as "hotels," after the tradition of providing room and board alongside a good drink in the old days. Occasionally you might hear them referred to as pubs. The term *bar* tends to apply in upscale hotels and trendy establishments. Bars close at various times, generally from midnight to around 3am. Unless the listing says otherwise, these bars do not charge a cover.

Bondi Hotel This huge conglomerate across the road from Bondi Beach offers pool upstairs, a casual beer garden outside, and a resident DJ Thursday through Sunday from 8pm to 4am. There's also a free nightclub on Friday nights. Watch yourself; too much drink and sun turns some people nasty here. 178 Campbell Parade, Bondi Beach. ✆ **02/9130 3271.**

Cargo Bar & Lounge This split-level waterfront bar on the city side of Darling Harbour (past the Sydney Aquarium) has a large ground-floor bar with access to an outdoor beer garden. The lounge upstairs features trendy leather and red footstools (apparently you sit on them). Cocktails and cigars are upstairs and more casual beers downstairs. Some nice pizzas here, too—if you like them topped with emu, crocodile, or kangaroo. 52–60 The Promenade, King St. Wharf. ✆ **02/9262 1777.**

The Establishment If you want to see Sydney at its sexiest and most sophisticated then head to this four-level venue where style is everything. Swing through the ground floor entrance on George Street near Wynyard CityRail station and you enter a world of phallic columns and a huge cream-washed space with a long white marble bar. It's a seriously sexy place—and it doesn't end here. Upstairs there are the famous eateries, est. and Sushi E, as well as Hemisphere—a moody drinking place strung out with leather armchairs and ottomans. 252 George St., City. ✆ **02/9240 3040.**

The Friend in Hand In the same location as the fantastically cheap Caesar's No Names spaghetti house, The Friend in Hand offers cheap drinks, poetry readings on Tuesday at 8:30pm, a trivia night on Thursday at 8:30pm, and the distinctly unusual Crab Racing Party every Wednesday at around 8pm. Crab fanciers buy a crustacean for around A$5 (US$4/UK£2), give it a name, and send it off to do battle in a race against about 30 others. There are heats and finals, and victorious crustaceans win their owners prizes. 58 Cowper St., Glebe. ✆ **02/9660 2326.**

Hero of Waterloo Hotel ★ This sandstone landmark, built in 1845, was once reputedly the stalking ground of press gangs, who'd whack unsuspecting landlubbers on the head, push them down a trapdoor, and cart them out to sea. Today, the strangely shaped drinking hole is popular with the locals. It schedules old-time jazz bands (the musicians are often in their 70s and 80s) on Saturday and Sunday from 1:30 to 6:30pm, and Irish and cover bands Friday to Sunday at 8:30pm. 81 Lower Fort St., The Rocks. ✆ **02/9252 4553.**

Jacksons on George A popular drinking spot, this place has four floors of drinking, eating, dancing, and pool playing, and is a popular haunt of tourists and after-work office staff. The nightclub plays dance music, and there's a smart-casual dress code. During happy hour (Mon–Fri 5–7pm), drinks cost around one-third less than normal. If your hotel breakfast seems expensive then come here from 7:30am Monday to Friday. There's a good choice of items on the menu, including Jacksons Big Breakfast (two eggs, sausages, bacon, tomato, hash browns, and toast) for A$13 (US$10/UK£5). 178 George St., The Rocks. ✆ **02/9247 2727.** Cover A$10 (US$8/UK£4) for nightclub Fri–Sat after 10pm.

Lord Dudley Hotel This great English-style pub has the best atmosphere of just about any drinking hole in Sydney, with log fires in winter, couches to relax on, three bars, and a restaurant. The best way to get here is from the Edgecliff CityRail station (between Kings Cross and Bondi Junction, which makes it a bit out-of-the-way if you're staying in the city). From there, bear right along the edge of the bus station, walk up the hill for 5 minutes, then take a right onto Jersey Road—ask the railway staff for the correct exit if you can find anyone working. 236 Jersey Rd., Woollahra. ✆ **02/9327 5399.**

Lord Nelson Hotel ★ *Value* A sandstone landmark, the Lord Nelson rivals the Hero of Waterloo (above) for the title of Sydney's oldest pub. The drinks are sold English-style, in pints and half pints, and the landlord makes his own prizewinning beers. Of those, Three Sheets is the most popular—but if you can't handle falling over on your way home, you might want to try a drop of Quail (a pale beer), Victory (based on an English bitter), and a dark beer called Admiral. You can get some reasonable pub grub here in the style of hot meat pie and mashed potatoes. Upstairs there's a more formal brasserie. Kent and Argyle sts., The Rocks. ✆ **02/9251 4044.**

Marble Bar Inside the Hilton Hotel complex, the Marble Bar is unique: the only grand cafe–style drinking hole in Australia. With oil paintings, marble columns, and brass everywhere, the Marble Bar is the picture of 15th-century Italian Renaissance architecture—despite being crafted in 1893. It's a tourist attraction in itself. Live music, generally jazz or soul, plays here Tuesday through Saturday beginning at 8:30pm. Dress smart on Friday and Saturday evenings. In the Sydney Hilton, 259 Pitt St. ✆ **02/9266 2000.**

The Mercantile Sydney's original Irish bar is scruffy and loud when the Irish music's playing in the evening, but it's an essential stop on any pub-crawl in The Rocks. The Guinness is some of the best you'll taste in Sydney. Irish bands kick off every night around 8pm. 25 George St., The Rocks. ✆ **02/9247 3570.**

Slip Inn This multifunction bar and nightclub setup is a popular place to drink and meet. There's a garden bar downstairs in a courtyard, and a Thai bistro, too. Dug out below is a serious nightclub, the Chinese Laundry, which features house, hip-hop, and electro on Fridays and Saturdays. On Sundays, from noon until dusk, the garden bar attracts university students and 30-somethings who like to boogie. 111 Sussex St., Darling Harbour. ✆ **02/8295 9911.** A 2-min. walk toward the city from the Town Hall/Cockle Bay side of the pedestrian bridge across to Darling Harbour.

Watson's Bay Hotel ★★ *Finds* If it's a sunny afternoon, get over to Watsons Bay for the best food you'll find in the sun anywhere. Formally called the Watson's Bay Hotel (everyone knows it by that name), it has a glorious beer garden serving good seafood and barbecue meat dishes. The views of the harbor make this one of Sydney's best sunny-day options. 1 Military Rd., Watsons Bay. ✆ **02/9337 4299.**

MOVIES

The city's major movie houses, **Hoyts** (© **13 27 00** in Australia), **Greater Union** (© **02/9267 8666**), and **Village** (© **02/9264 6701**), are right next to each other on George Street just past Town Hall. They tend to show big-budget movie releases. Other options are the **Dendy Cinemas,** 19 Martin Place (© **02/9233 8166**); 261–263 King St., Newtown (© **02/9550 5699**); and 2 East Circular Quay, just before you reach the Opera House (© **02/9247 3800**). All show art-house movies; the Dendy Quay allows wine and beer bought on the premises to be consumed in the cinema. In Paddington, the **Palace Verona,** 17 Oxford St. (© **02/9360 6099**), and the **Academy Twin,** 2 Oxford St. (© **02/9361 4455**), conveniently located next to each other, always screen the best local and foreign films in Sydney.

Another exceptional art house and recent-blockbuster cinema is the **Hayden Orpheum Picture Palace,** 380 Military Rd., Cremorne (© **02/9908 4344**). This eight-screen Art Deco gem is an experience in itself, especially on Saturday and Sunday evenings when a Wurlitzer pops up from the center of the Cinema 2 stage, and a musician in a tux gives a stirring rendition of times gone by. Eat "Jaffas," round candy-coated chocolates, if you want to fit in.

Movie prices hover around A$15 (US$12/UK£6), with half-price night generally on Tuesday.

THE CASINO

Star City This huge entertainment complex has 15 main bars, 12 restaurants, two theaters—the Showroom, which presents Las Vegas–style revues, and the Lyric, Sydney's largest theater—as well as a huge complex of retail shops. All the usual gambling tables are here, in four main gambling areas. In all, there are 2,500 slot machines to gobble your change. You must be over 18 to gamble. Open 24 hours. 80 Pyrmont St., Pyrmont (adjacent to Darling Harbour). © **02/9777 9000.** Ferry: Pyrmont (Darling Harbour). Monorail: Casino.

5

New South Wales

by Marc Llewellyn

With so much to experience in a state as big as New South Wales, you're not going to see all the major attractions in one hit, so you must prioritize. If you have just a few days to spare, you should certainly head out to the Blue Mountains, part of the Great Dividing Range that separates the lush eastern coastal strip from the more arid interior. Although these mountains are more like hills, they are spectacular, with tall eucalyptus trees, deep river valleys, waterfalls, and craggy cliffs. Or spend a day in the vineyards of the lower Hunter (also known as the Hunter Valley). If you have a few more days, I recommend heading to Barrington Tops National Park, north of the Hunter, for the rainforest and native animals, or down to the pristine beaches of Jervis Bay for gorgeous scenery and great bushwalks.

For longer trips, you can head north toward the Queensland border on the 964km (598-mile) route to Brisbane. You'll pass pretty seaside towns, deserted beaches, and tropical hinterland. Another option is to travel along the south coast 1,032km (640 miles) to Melbourne. Along the way are some of the country's most spectacular beaches, quaint hamlets, opportunities to spot dolphins and whales, and extensive national parks. If you want to experience the Outback, then head west across the Blue Mountains. You are sure to see plenty of kangaroos, emus, reptiles, and giant wedge-tailed eagles. The main Outback destination is the extraordinary opal-mining town of Lightning Ridge, where you can meet some of the most eccentric fair-dinkum (that means "authentic" or "genuine") Aussies you'll come across anywhere.

EXPLORING THE STATE

VISITOR INFORMATION The **Sydney Visitor Centre at The Rocks,** First Floor, The Rocks Centre, Corner of Argyle and Playfair streets, The Rocks (✆ **02/9240 8788;** www.sydneyvisitorcentre.com), will give you general information on what to do and where to stay throughout the state. **Tourism New South Wales** (✆ **02/9931 1111**) will direct you to the regional tourist office in the town or area you are interested in.

GETTING AROUND **By Car** From Sydney, the **Pacific Highway** heads along the north coast into Queensland, and the **Princes Highway** hugs the south coast and runs into Victoria. The **Sydney-Newcastle Freeway** connects Sydney with its industrial neighbor and the vineyards of the Hunter. The **Great Western Highway** and the **M4 motorway** head west to the Blue Mountains. The **M5 motorway, Hume Highway,** is the quickest way to get to Melbourne (via Canberra).

The state's automobile association, the **National Roads and Motorists' Association (NRMA),** 151 Clarence St., Sydney (✆ **13 11 22** in Australia), offers free maps and touring guides to members of overseas motoring associations, including AAA in the United States, CAA in Canada, AA and RAC in the United Kingdom, and NZAA in New Zealand.

By Train **Countrylink** (✆ **13 22 32** in Australia) trains travel to most places of interest in the state and as far south as Melbourne in Victoria and across the border into southern Queensland. Countrylink also has special rates for car rental through Thrifty.

By Plane **Qantas** (✆ **13 13 13** in Australia) and **Eastern Australia Airlines** (book through Qantas) fly to most major cities and towns in the state.

1 The Blue Mountains ★★

The **Blue Mountains** offer breathtaking views, rugged tablelands, sheer cliffs, deep, inaccessible valleys, enormous chasms, colorful parrots, cascading waterfalls, historic villages, and stupendous walking trails. In 2000, UNESCO classified it as a World Heritage Area. Although the Blue Mountains are where Sydneysiders go now to escape the humidity and crowds of the city, in the early days of the colony, the mountains kept at bay those who would explore the interior. In 1813, three explorers—Gregory Blaxland, William Charles Wentworth, and William Lawson—managed to conquer the cliffs, valleys, and dense forest, and cross the mountains (which are hardly mountains, but rather a series of hills covered in eucalyptus and ancient fern trees) to the plains beyond. There they found land the colony urgently needed for grazing and farming. The **Great Western Highway** and **Bells Line of Road** are the access roads through the region today—winding and steep in places, they are surrounded by the Blue Mountains and Wollemi national parks.

The whole area is known for its spectacular scenery, particularly the cliff-top views into the valleys of gum trees and across to craggy outcrops that tower from the valley floor. It's colder up here than down on the plains, and clouds can sweep in and fill the canyons with mist in minutes, while waterfalls cascade down sheer drops, spraying the dripping fern trees that cling to the gullies. You'll need at least a couple of days up here to get the best out of it—a single-day tour, with all the traveling involved, can only just scratch the surface.

The Blue Mountains are also one of Australia's best-known adventure playgrounds. Rock climbing, caving, abseiling (rappelling), bushwalking, mountain biking, horseback riding, and canoeing are practiced here year-round.

BLUE MOUNTAIN ESSENTIALS

VISITOR INFORMATION You can pick up maps, walking guides, and other information and book accommodations at **Blue Mountains Tourism,** Echo Point Road, Katoomba, NSW 2780 (✆ **1300/653 408** in Australia, or 02/4739 6266). The information center is an attraction itself, with glass windows overlooking a gum forest, and cockatoos and lorikeets feeding on seed dispensers. It's open from 9am to 5pm daily (the office at Glenbrook closes at 4:30pm Sat–Sun).

Fun Fact **Color Me Blue**

The Blue Mountains derive their name from the ever-present blue haze that is caused by light striking the droplets of eucalyptus oil that evaporate from the leaves of the dense surrounding forest.

New South Wales

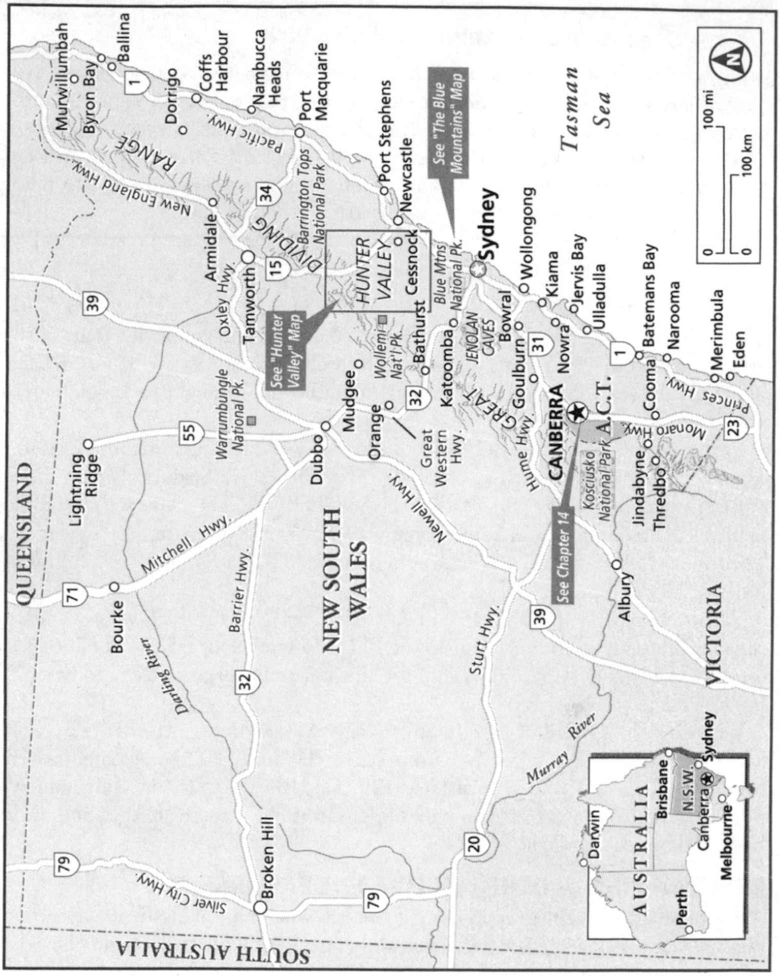

The **National Park Shop,** Heritage Centre, end of Govetts Leap Road, Blackheath (✆ **02/4787 8877;** www.npws.nsw.gov.au), is run by the National Parks and Wildlife Service and offers detailed information about the Blue Mountains National Park. The staff can also arrange personalized guided tours of the mountains. It's open daily from 9am to 4:30pm (closed Dec 25).

Check the great website, www.bluemts.com.au, for more information on the area, including bushwalks.

GUIDED TOURS FROM SYDNEY Many private bus operators offer day trips from Sydney, but it's important to shop around. Some offer a guided coach tour during which you just stretch your legs occasionally, while others let you get your circulation going with a couple of longish bushwalks. One highly recommended operator

Tips **Timing Is Everything: When to Visit**

If you can, try to visit the Blue Mountains on **weekdays,** when most Sydneysiders are at work and prices are lower. Note that the colder winter months (June–Aug) are the busiest season. This period is known as **Yuletide**—the locals' version of the Christmas period, when most places offer traditional Christmas dinners and roaring log fires. It's kind of, almost, just nearly, authentic. Not. But it's fun if a year between Christmases is just a little too long.

is **Oz Trek Adventure Tours** (© **1300 661 234** in Australia, or 02/9666 4262; www.oztrek.com.au). Its trips include a tour of the Sydney Olympic site, tours of all the major Blue Mountain sites, and a 1½-hour bushwalk. It costs A$55 (US$44/UK£22) for adults and A$44 (US$35/UK£18) for kids. You can add overnight packages, horseback riding, and abseiling.

Sydney Tours-R-Us (© **02/9498 4084;** www.sydneytoursrus.com) runs minicoaches to the Blue Mountains, stopping off at the Telstra Stadium (where the Sydney Olympics were held) and Featherdale Wildlife Park. Then you see all the major sights in the mountains and come home via ferry from Parramatta to Circular Quay. The trip costs A$93 (US$74/UK£37) for adults and A$65 (US$52/UK£26) for kids. It's a big 10-hour day.

Wonderbus (© **1300/556 357** in Australia, or 02/9630 0529; www.wonderbus.com.au) offers an exceptional tour to the Blue Mountains for A$87 (US$70/UK£35) for adults and A$65 (US$52/UK£26) for kids including all entry fees and lunch. You can also come back by ferry.

Grayline (© **1300/858 687** in Australia; www.grayline.com) offers several Blue Mountains trips in large coaches from A$78 (US$62/UK£31). A combined Blue Mountains/Jenolan Caves trip costs A$129 (US$103/UK£52) for adults and A$65 (US$52/UK£26) for kids. If you hate big-group travel, choose another option. It's a huge 11-hour day, though.

BUSHWALKING & OTHER ACTIVE ENDEAVORS

Almost every other activity costs money, but bushwalking (hiking) is the exception to the rule that nothing in life is free. There are some 50 walking trails in the Blue Mountains, ranging from routes you can cover in 15 minutes to the 3-day **Six Foot Track** ★ that starts outside Katoomba and finishes at Jenolan Caves. The staff at the tourist offices and national park office will be happy to point you in the right direction, whether it be for an hour's stroll or a full day's hike.

One of the best adventure operators in the area, **High 'n' Wild,** 3–5 Katoomba St., Katoomba, NSW 2780 (© **02/4782 6224;** www.high-n-wild.com.au), offers a series of canyoning expeditions, taking in scenic rainforest gullies and caverns made up of dramatic rock formations and fern-lined walls. There's a bit of swimming and plenty of walking, wading, and squeezing through tight spaces involved—and sometimes rappelling (called "abseiling" in Australia)—but fortunately, being double-jointed is not a prerequisite.

If you really want to test your head for heights, try High 'n' Wild's 150m (492-ft.) "Mega Jump"—the highest continuous rappel in the Southern Hemisphere. This heart-pumping descent down a sheer cliff is suitable for the fearless beginner, but the

staff assures me you soon settle in by learning the ropes on the 10-story-high junior slopes beforehand.

If that's too much to handle, you could always try a day on an inflatable raft between huge towering rock walls on the Wollangambe River. There are a few minor rapids to navigate, and the bushwalk down to the river and back up again can be a little testing, but it's certainly suitable for a family outing. Prices start at A$95 (US$76/UK£38) for abseiling and A$155 (US$124/UK£62) for canyoning. Guided mountain biking costs A$145 (US$116/UK£58) for a full day.

Other excellent adventure operators are the **Blue Mountains Adventure Company,** 84a Bathurst Rd. (P.O. Box 242), Katoomba, NSW 2780 (© **02/4782 1271;** www.bmac.com.au), located above the Summit Gear Shop; and the **Australian School of Mountaineering,** 166 Katoomba St., Katoomba, NSW 2780 (© **02/4782 2014**). Both offer rock climbing, rappelling, and canyoning trips. The Adventure Company also offers caving and mountain biking, and the School of Mountaineering offers bushcraft and survival training.

If you feel like some adventure on your own, you can rent a mountain bike from **Velo Nova,** 182 Katoomba St., Katoomba (© **02/4782 2800**). Standard mountain bikes cost A$25 (US$20/UK£10) for a half-day and A$40 (US$32/UK£16) for a full day.

KATOOMBA: GATEWAY TO THE BLUE MOUNTAINS

114km (71 miles) W of Sydney

Katoomba (pop. 11,200) is the largest town in the Blue Mountains and the focal point of the Blue Mountains National Park. It's an easy 1½- to 2-hour trip from Sydney by train, bus, or car. The town is a low-socioeconomic pocket in a very affluent region, with one of the highest unemployment rates in the state.

GETTING THERE By car from central Sydney, travel along Parramatta Road and turn off onto the M4 motorway (around 2 hr. to Katoomba). Another route is via the Harbour Bridge to North Sydney, along the Warringah Freeway (following signs to the M2). Then take the M2 to the end and follow signs to the M4 and the Blue Mountains. This takes around 1½ hours.

Frequent rail service connects Sydney to Katoomba from Central Station; contact **CityRail** (**© 13 15 00**) or **Countrylink** (**© 13 22 32;** www.countrylink.info) for details. The train trip takes 2 hours. Trains leave almost hourly from platform nos. 12 and 13, stopping at Katoomba, and then at Mount Victoria and Lithgow. An adult same-day round-trip ticket costs around A$15 (US$12/UK£6) off-peak, and A$22 (US$18/UK£9) during commuter hours. A child's ticket costs A$3 (US$2.40/UK£1.20).

GETTING AROUND The best way to get around the Blue Mountains without your own transport is the **Blue Mountains Explorer Bus** (**© 02/4782 4807;** www.explorerbus.com.au). The double-decker bus leaves from outside Katoomba train station every hour from 9:30am until 4:30pm and stops at 27 attractions, resorts, galleries, and tearooms in and around Katoomba and Leura. You can get on and off as often as you want. Tickets cost A$32 (US$26/UK£13) for adults, A$16 (US$13/UK£6.50) for children, and A$75 (US$60/UK£30) for a family; prices include discounts on the Scenic Railway and the Skyway (see "Exploring the Area," below), and at some other attractions and restaurants. Interestingly, you can also link this tour bus with the CityRail train from Sydney, and some prices are cheaper! The **Blue Mountains Explorer Link Ticket,** available from CityRail stations, includes same-day, round-trip train fare and Explorer Bus tickets and costs A$42 (US$34/UK£17) for adults, A$17 (US$13/UK£6.50) for children, and A$65 (US$52/UK£26) for a family. A 3-day ticket, allowing you to travel by CityRail train on 2 days and stay a whole day in the mountains, costs A$58 (US$46/UK£23) for adults and A$24 (US$19/UK£9.50) for kids. There's no family ticket. If you are spending a few days in the mountains then you might want to consider the Explorer Bus Pass allowing up to 7-day's travel in the mountains. It costs an extra A$32 (US$26/UK£13) for adults, A$16 (US$13/UK£6.50) for kids, and A$80 (US$64/UK£32) for adults.

Another option is **Trolley Tours** (**© 1800/801 577** in Australia; www.trolleytours.com.au), which is a kind of tram on wheels with commentary. An all-day pass costs A$15 (US$12/UK£6) and includes stops at 29 various attractions around Katoomba and Leura, too. The trolley leaves Katoomba Station each hour, connecting with the trains from Sydney.

EXPLORING THE AREA

The most visited and photographed attractions in the Blue Mountains are the rock formations known as the **Three Sisters** ★★. For the best vantage point, head to **Echo Point Road,** across from the Blue Mountains Tourism office. Or try Evans Lookout, Govetts Leap, and Hargreaves Lookout, all at Blackheath (see "Blackheath," later in

The Legend of Three Sisters

The Aboriginal Dreamtime legend has it that three sisters, Meehni, Wimlah, and Gunnedoo, lived in the Jamison Valley as members of the Katoomba tribe. These beautiful young ladies had fallen in love with three brothers from the Nepean tribe, yet tribal law forbade them to marry. The brothers were not happy to accept this law and so decided to use force to capture the three sisters, which caused a major tribal battle. As the lives of the three sisters were seriously in danger, a witch doctor from the Katoomba tribe took it upon himself to turn the three sisters into stone to protect them from any harm. While he had intended to reverse the spell when the battle was over, the witch doctor himself was killed. As only he could reverse the spell to return the ladies to their former beauty, the sisters remain in their magnificent rock formation as a reminder of this battle for generations to come.

this chapter)—none of which is on the Blue Mountains Explorer Bus or Trolley Tours route.

One thing you have to do in the Blue Mountains is ride the **Scenic Railway,** the world's steepest—follow the road signs to Scenic World. It consists of a carriage on rails that is lowered 415m (1,361 ft.) into the Jamison Valley at a maximum incline of 52 degrees. It's *very* steep and quite a thrill. Originally the rail line was used to transport coal and shale from the mines below in the 1880s. The trip takes only a few minutes; at the bottom are some excellent walks through forests of ancient tree ferns. Another popular attraction is the **Skyway,** a cable car that travels 300m (984 ft.) above the Jamison Valley. The round-trip takes 6 minutes. The Scenic Railway and the Skyway (© **02/4782 2699**) each cost A$16 (US$13/UK£6.50) round-trip for adults, A$8 (US$6.40/UK£3.20) for children, and A$40 (US$32/UK£16) for a family. They operate from 9am to 5pm daily (last trip at 4:50pm). They depart from the ticket office at 1 Violet St., Katoomba (follow the signs). I'd advise taking the Scenic Railway down, going for a walk, and taking the cable car back up.

Canyons, waterfalls, underground rivers—the Blue Mountains have them all, and before you experience them in person you can catch them on the (giant) screen at the **MAXVISION Cinema,** 225–237 Great Western Hwy., Katoomba (© **02/4782 8900**). The special effects shown on the screen, 18m (59 ft.) high and 24m (79 ft.) wide, make you feel like you're part of the action. At the time of writing, the 38-minute film *The Edge* was being shown every day at 10:20am, 11:05am, 12:10pm, 1:30pm, 2:13pm, and 5:30pm. It would be worth ringing ahead as these times seem to change from time to time. Tickets cost A$13 (US$10/UK£5) for adults, A$11 (US$8.80/UK£4.40) for students, and A$7.50 (US$6/UK£3) for children. The cinema is a 5- to 10-minute walk from the train station. Recently released movies play on part of the giant screen in the evening. A restaurant and a snack bar are on the premises.

To get back to Sydney, I highly recommend taking the Bells Line of Road through Bilpin. This route takes up to 3 hours, but you can stop off at the wonderful **Mount Tomah Botanic Gardens** ★. (You can't miss the large sign on your right about 10 min. before you get to Bilpin.) An adjunct of the Royal Botanic Gardens in Sydney, Mount Tomah is dedicated to cold-climate plants. It's compact and has a very good cafe serving lunch daily. Allow around 2 hours for a stop here.

Tips **Seeing the Blue Mountains from the Back of a Harley**

A thrilling way to see the Blue Mountains is on the back of a chauffeur-driven Harley-Davidson. **Blue Thunder Bike Tours (© 1800/800 184** in NSW, or 02/9438 3122; www.bluethunder.com.au) leaves from Manly Wharf in Sydney (but will pick you up anywhere in the city). Rides cost A$400 (US$320/UK£160) for a full day with lunch to the Blue Mountains. The company offers lots of cheaper Sydney rides.

WHERE TO STAY

Very Expensive

Echoes Hotel & Restaurant, Blue Mountains ★ *Finds* Lilianfels (see below) might be more expensive, but Echoes, just across the road on a cliff overlooking the Jamison Valley, has superior views. Large windows, balconies, and a sizable deck allow guests to soak up the fantastic scenery. Rooms are simply furnished and smaller than those at Lilianfels; all have underfloor heating and are recommended if you're cashed up. As an idea of a package price, expect to pay at least A$295 (US$236/UK£118) for 1 night midweek including breakfast.

3 Lilianfels Ave., Katoomba, NSW 2780. © **02/4782 1966.** Fax 02/4782 3707. www.echoeshotel.com.au. 12 units. Weekend A$833 (US$666/UK£333) 2-night double including breakfast, A$950 (US$760/UK£380) 2-night suite; weekday A$335 (US$268/UK£134) double, A$385 (US$308/UK£154) suite. Packages are available. AE, DC, MC, V. Free parking. **Amenities:** Restaurant; bar; Jacuzzi; sauna; nonsmoking rooms. *In room:* A/C, TV, minibar, coffeemaker, hair dryer, iron/ironing board.

Lilianfels Blue Mountains ★★ Set just over a road from Echo Point, this Victorian country-house hotel—a member of the Small Luxury Hotels of the World—is a full-service yet cozy establishment. Rooms are spacious, expensive, and furnished with antiques. Most have king-size beds. Those with views are more expensive. The living areas are just as grand, with roaring log fires and more antiques. Views are impressive, especially from the lounge, which overlooks the Jamison Valley. On the grounds is an 1889 cottage. Meant for two, it has a sitting room, a bedroom with a four-poster bed, a Jacuzzi, an intimate fireplace, and its own gardens. Among the other offerings at Lilianfels are a billiards room, a library and reading room, and a lawn for French boules. The restaurant here, **Darley's,** serves great Contemporary food and a two-course meal will cost around A$68 (US$54/UK£28) per person. It's open for lunch on Sunday noon to 2:30pm, and for dinner Tuesday to Saturday from 6:15 to 9:30pm.

Lilianfels Ave., Katoomba, NSW 2780. © **1800/024 452** in Australia, or 02/4780 1200. Fax 02/4780 1300. www.slh.com. 85 units, 1 cottage. A$530–A$630 (US$448–US$504/UK£224–UK£252) double; A$635–A$870 (US$508–US$696/UK£252–UK£350) suite. Extra person A$55 (US$44/UK£22). Ask about off-season packages. AE, DC, MC, V. Free parking. **Amenities:** 2 restaurants; small indoor pool; health club w/flotation tank; exercise room; Jacuzzi; sauna; bike rental; tour desk; secretarial services; 24-hr. room service; massage; laundry service; dry cleaning; nonsmoking rooms. *In room:* A/C, TV, minibar, coffeemaker, hair dryer, iron/ironing board.

Moderate

The Carrington Hotel ★★ *Finds* Construction started on this grand Victorian hotel in 1880, and it reopened in 2000 after a major renovation. A ramshackle structure, The Carrington is a must-stay if you're into buildings of the British Raj style. Downstairs are a restaurant and breakfast room (once a ballroom), a couple of lounges with antiques, and a gorgeous wood-paneled billiard room. Chandeliers and

1930s-style lamps reflecting off silver trophies won by the local Rifle Club give everything a warm glow. Unfortunately, heavy Plexiglas doors greet you as you enter each of the many corridors—a necessary fire precaution. All the rooms are delightful, with royal gold and blue carpets and drapes that would probably be gaudy if they didn't fit in with the overall style. Traditional rooms share bathrooms; colonial rooms come with a deep tub in the bathroom (with a noisy fan) and no view to speak of; deluxe colonial rooms have a balcony and mountain views; premier rooms have Jacuzzis and great views; and the suites are fit for a duke and duchess. Dinner here costs A$100 (US$80/UK£40) per person, and the breakfast is one of the best I've encountered.

15–47 Katoomba St. (P.O. Box 28), Katoomba, NSW 2780. ✆ **02/4782 1111.** Fax 02/4782 7033. www.thecarrington.com.au. 63 units. Traditional double A$119 (US$95/UK£48) Sun–Thurs, A$139 (US$111/UK£55) Fri–Sat; colonial double A$170 (US$136/UK£68) Sun–Thurs, A$190 (US$152/UK£76) Fri–Sat; deluxe colonial double A$205 (US$164/UK£82) Sun–Thurs, A$225 (US$180/UK£90) Fri–Sat; premier double (no view) A$205 (US$164/UK£82) Sun–Thurs, A$225 (US$180/UK£90) Fri–Sat; premier double (with view) A$245 (US$196/UK£99) Sun–Thurs, A$265 (US$212/UK£106) Fri–Sat; suite A$315–A$445 (US$252–US$356/UK£126–UK£178) Sun–Thurs, A$335–A$465 (US$268–US$372/UK£134–UK£186) Fri–Sat. Ask about weekend packages. Rates include full breakfast. AE, DC, MC, V. **Amenities:** Restaurant; bar. *In room:* TV, coffeemaker, iron/ironing board.

Echo Point Holiday Villas ★ These are the closest self-contained accommodations to the Three Sisters Lookout. The two front-facing villas are the best because of their beautiful mountain views. Some villas have one double and two single beds, plus a fold-out double bed in the lounge room. There are barbecue facilities in the backyard. The two cottages are also fully self-contained, sleeping up to eight, and have a tub, central heating, and access to nice gardens.

36 Echo Point Rd., Katoomba, NSW 2780. ✆ **02/4782 3275.** Fax 02/4782 7030. www.echopointvillas.com.au. 5 villas, all with shower only, 2 cottages. Villa A$140 (US$112/UK£56) Fri–Sat and public holidays, A$110 (US$88/UK£44) Sun–Thurs; A$160 (US$128/UK£64) cottage for 2. Cottage 2-night minimum. Extra person A$12 (US$10/UK£5). AE, DC, MC, V. *In room:* TV, kitchen, fridge, hair dryer, iron/ironing board.

Inexpensive

Katoomba YHA Hostel ★ This wonderful YHA hostel has won several major tourism awards. It's set in a former 1930s cabaret club and still retains some of the fun atmosphere. It's very roomy, and friendly, and also well located in the heart of Katoomba. There's a log fire in the living room, a communal kitchen, dining room, game room with billiards table, and a television. Also here is a nice balcony and barbecue area. Some double rooms include a set of bunks for kids. Dorm rooms accommodate four to eight people. People from all walks of life, and of all ages, stay here and rave about the place.

207 Katoomba St., Katoomba. ✆ **02/4782 1416.** Fax 02/4782 6203. www.yha.com.au. 57 rooms, 29 doubles/twin/family rooms. A$64 (US$51/UK£26) double with shared bathroom; A$72 (US$58/UK£28) double with private bathroom; A$22–A$24 (US$18–US$19/UK£9–UK£10) dorm. MC, V. **Amenities:** Bike rental; tour desk; coin-op laundry. *In room:* No phone.

WHERE TO DINE

Katoomba Street has many ethnic dining choices, whether you're hungry for Greek, Chinese, or Thai. Restaurants in the Blue Mountains are generally more expensive than equivalent places in Sydney. As well as the ones below, try **The Elephant Bean,** at 159 Katoomba Rd. (✆ **02/4782 4620**), for hearty soups, burgers, muffins, and good coffee. You may want to eat breakfast, or brekkies as they often call it in Australia, at a cafe rather than in your hotel. It can work out cheaper, and you often get more of a choice. The **Stockmarket Café** (179 The Mall, Leura; ✆ **02/4784 3121**) is small and casual with good coffee ordered at the counter. They have good eggs (and great soups, pies and stews at lunchtime, by the way). For an unusual breakfast treat try the poached eggs on spinach risotto with Parmesan shavings. That will set you back around A$16 (US$12/UK£6). The **Fresh Espresso and Food Bar** (181 Katoomba St., Katoomba; ✆ **02/4782 3602**) has a large range of coffees to choose from and does good scrambled eggs. The signature breakfast dishes here are the basins of porridge, either with fresh ricotta, strawberries, honey, and cinnamon, or yogurt and rhubarb compote, for A$9.50 (US$7.60/UK£3.80).

Expensive

Lindsay's ★★ INTERNATIONAL Swiss chef Beat Ettlin has been making waves in Katoomba ever since he left some of the best European restaurants behind to try his hand at dishes such as pan-fried crocodile nibbles on pumpkin scones with ginger dipping sauce. The food in this upscale, New York–style speak-easy is as glorious as its decor—Tiffany lamps, sketches by Australian artist Norman Lindsay, and booths lining the walls. The three-level restaurant is warmed by a cozy fire surrounded by an antique lounge stage and resounds every night to piano, classical music, or a jazz band. The menu changes every few weeks, but a recent popular dish was grilled veal medallions topped with Balmain bugs (small, saltwater crayfish), with potato and béarnaise sauce.

122 Katoomba St., Katoomba. ✆ **02/4782 2753.** Reservations recommended. Main courses A$14–A$24 (US$11–US$19/UK£5.50–UK£9.50). AE, MC, V. Wed–Sun 6pm–midnight.

TrisElies GREEK Perhaps it's the belly dancers, the plate smashing, or the smell of moussaka, but as soon as you walk through the door of this lively eatery you feel as if you've been transported to an authentic Athenian *taverna.* The restaurant folds out onto three tiers of tables, all with a good view of the stage where Greek or international performances take place every night. The food is solid Greek fare—souvlakia, traditional dips, fried halloumi cheese, Greek salads, casseroles like Mother could have made, whitebait (tiny fried fish), and sausages in red wine—with a few Italian and Spanish extras. In winter, warm up beside one of two log fires.

287 Bathurst Rd., Katoomba. ✆ **02/4782 4026.** Fax 02/4782 1128. www.triselies.com.au. Reservations recommended. Main courses A$17–A$26 (US$14–US$21/UK£7–UK£11). AE, DC, MC, V. Sun–Thurs 5pm–midnight; Fri–Sat 5pm–3am.

Inexpensive

Chork Dee Thai Restaurant THAI Loved by the locals, Chork Dee offers good Thai food in a pleasant but modest setting. It serves the usual Thai fare, including satay, spring rolls, and fish cakes to start, followed by lots of curries, noodles, and sweet-and-sour dishes. While vegetarians won't find any starters without meat or fish, plenty of veggie and tofu dishes are available as main courses. BYO.

216 Katoomba St., Katoomba. ✆ **02/4782 1913.** Main courses A$7.70–A$17 (US$6.15–US$14/UK£3/UK£7). AE, MC, V. Sun–Thurs 5:30–9pm; Fri–Sat 5:30–10pm.

Paragon Café *Value* CAFE The Paragon has been a Blue Mountains institution since it opened for business in 1916. Inside, it's decked out with dark-wood paneling, bas-relief figures guarding the booths, and chandeliers. The homemade soups are delicious. The cafe also serves pies, pastas, grills, seafood, waffles, cakes, and a Devonshire tea of scones and cream.

65 Katoomba St., Katoomba. ✆ **02/4782 2928.** Menu items A$3–A$10 (US$2.40–US$8/UK£1.20–UK£4). AE, MC, V. Tues–Fri 10am–3:30pm; Sat–Sun 10am–4pm.

LEURA

107km (66 miles) W of Sydney; 3km (2 miles) E of Katoomba

The fashionable capital of the Blue Mountains, Leura is known for its gardens, its attractive old buildings (many holiday homes for Sydneysiders), and its cafes and restaurants. The National Trust has classified Leura's main street as an urban conservation area. Just outside Leura is the **Sublime Point Lookout,** which has spectacular views of the Three Sisters in Katoomba. From the southern end of **Leura Mall,** a cliff drive takes you all the way back to Echo Point in Katoomba; along the way you'll enjoy spectacular views across the Jamison Valley.

There are a couple of high-class dining options here, the best being **Solitary,** at 90 Cliff Dr., Leura Falls (✆ **02/4782 1164**). It's open for lunch on weekends and dinner from Wednesday to Sunday and serves excellent Contemporary food such as roast lamb rump, and fish tartare with prawns and wasabi. The **Stockmarket Café,** at 179 Leura Mall (✆ **02/4784 3121**), is a good option for a fried breakfast, as well as gourmet sandwiches and hot soups.

WENTWORTH FALLS ★★

103km (64 miles) W of Sydney; 7km (4½ miles) E of Katoomba

This pretty town has numerous crafts and antiques shops, but the area is principally known for its 281m (922-ft.) waterfall, situated in **Falls Reserve.** On the far side of the falls is the **National Pass Walk**—one of the best in the Blue Mountains. It's cut into a cliff face with overhanging rock faces on one side and sheer drops on the other. The views over the Jamison Valley are spectacular. The track takes you down to the base of the falls to the **Valley of the Waters.** Climbing up out of the valley is quite a bit more difficult, but just as rewarding.

A NICE SPOT FOR LUNCH

Conservation Hut Café ★ CAFE This pleasant cafe is in the national park on top of a cliff overlooking the Jamison Valley. It's a good place for a bit of lunch on the balcony after the Valley of the Waters walk, which leaves from outside. It serves the usual cafe fare—burgers, salads, sandwiches, and pastas—but they are far from average. There are vegetarian options, too. Breakfasts are served, too. There's a nice log fire inside in winter.

At the end of Fletcher St., Wentworth Falls. ✆ **02/4757 3827.** Menu items A$17–A$25 (US$14–US$20/UK£7–UK£10). AE, MC, V. Daily 9am–5pm.

MEDLOW BATH

150km (93 miles) W of Sydney; 6km (3¾ miles) NW of Katoomba

Between Katoomba and Blackheath, Medlow Bath is a cozy place, with its own railway station, a secondhand bookstore, and a few properties hidden between the trees. Its one claim to fame is the **Hydro Majestic Hotel** (✆ **02/4788 1002**), a must-do stop for any visitor to the Blue Mountains. The historic Hydro Majestic has fabulous views over the Megalong Valley; the best time to appreciate the views is at sunset with a drink on the terrace. Otherwise, it sells Devonshire tea all day, and plenty of cakes, snacks, coffee, and tea.

WHERE TO STAY

Mercure Grand Hydro Majestic Hotel ★★ The most famous hotel in the Blue Mountains was built in 1904 by Mark Foy, a retail baron, world traveler, sportsman, and hypochondriac. Once called "A Palace in the Wilderness," this former health resort underwent a huge renovation and reopened in 2001 in the style Mr. Foy might have liked. The long, whitewashed building, with great bushland views from the restaurant and many of its more expensive rooms, is reminiscent of the grand hotels of Queen Victoria's time. The property even has a croquet lawn and English lawn bowls. The standard Heritage rooms are furnished in Art Deco style and have views of the garden. The similar Gallery rooms have slightly better views, some with valley glimpses. Cloister rooms, mostly in another wing, are decorated in both Art Deco and Edwardian (think country-style), and have valley views. Some of these have Jacuzzis. Rooms in the Delmonte Wing, decorated in French Provincial style, also have views. The suites are sumptuous. Higher rates in the ranges below apply on Friday and Saturday.

Medlow Bath, NSW 2780. ✆ **02/4788 1002.** Fax 02/4788 1063. www.hydromajestic.com.au. 84 units. A$250–A$290 (US$200–US$232/UK£100–UK£116) Heritage double; A$290–A$330 (US$232–US$264/UK£116–UK£132) Gallery double; A$330–A$370 (US$264–US$296/UK£132–UK£150) Cloister double; A$370–A$410 (US$296–US$328/UK£150–UK£164) Cloister double with Jacuzzi; A$830–A$1,070 (US$664–US$856/UK£332–UK£428) suite. Rates include breakfast. Extra person A$30 (US$24/UK£12). Check the website for great deals, such as a A$150 (US$120/UK£60) per-night double room. AE, MC, V. **Amenities:** Restaurant; bar; 2 outdoor lit tennis courts; health club; tour desk; limited room service. *In room:* TV, minibar, coffeemaker, hair dryer.

BLACKHEATH

114km (71 miles) W of Sydney; 14km (8¾ miles) NW of Katoomba

Blackheath is the highest town in the Blue Mountains at 1,049m (3,441 ft.). The **Three Brothers** at Blackheath are not as big or as famous as the Three Sisters in Katoomba, but you can climb two of them for fabulous views. Or you could try the **Cliff Walk** from **Evans Lookout** to **Govetts Leap** (named after a surveyor who mapped the region in the 1830s), where there are magnificent views over the **Grose Valley** and **Bridal Veil Falls.** The 1½-hour tramp passes through banksia, gum, and wattle forests, with spectacular views of peaks and valleys. If you want a guide in the area, contact **Blue Mountains Magic** (✆ **02/4787 6354;** www.bluemts.com.au), based in Blackheath. The guide, Phil Foster, is a trained botanist.

Blackheath has some interesting tearooms and antiques shops.

The best restaurant here is **Vulcans,** at 33 Govetts Leap Rd., Blackheath (✆ **02/4787 6899**). It's a seriously good eatery with mains costing around A$32 (US$26/UK£13). The chef makes good use of the wood-fired oven. The signature dish is the glazed duck sausage with pickled beet root. It's open for lunch and dinner Friday to Sunday. Book ahead.

GETTING THERE The Great Western Highway takes motorists from Katoomba to Blackheath. CityRail trains also stop at Blackheath.

VISITOR INFORMATION The **Heritage Centre** (✆ **02/4787 8877;** www.npws.nsw.gov.au), operated by the National Parks and Wildlife Service, is close to Govetts Leap Lookout on Govetts Leap Road. It has information on guided walks, camping, and hiking, as well as information on local European and Aboriginal historic sites. It's open daily from 9am to 4:30pm.

EXPLORING THE AREA ON HORSEBACK

One of the nicest ways to get around is on horseback. **Werriberri Trail Rides** (✆ **02/4787 9171;** fax 02/4787 6680), at the base of the Blue Mountains, 10km (6 miles) from Blackheath on Megalong Road in the Megalong Valley, offers guided multiday rides through the Megalong Valley and beyond. Suitable for beginners to advanced riders.

WHERE TO STAY

Jemby-Rinjah Lodge ★ The Blue Mountains National Park is just a short walk away from this interesting alternative accommodations option. There are nine standard cabins (seven two-bedroom cabins, and two one-bedroom loft cabins), one deluxe cabin called Treetops Retreat, and three pole-frame lodges good for groups. The well-spaced cabins are right in the bush and can sleep up to six people. Each has a slow-combustion heater, carpets, a bathroom, a fully equipped kitchen, and a lounge and dining area. There are laundry and barbecue areas nearby. The lodges have five bedrooms, two bathrooms, and a common lounge area with a circular fireplace. You can rent linens, but bring your own food. Free pickup can be arranged from Blackheath train station. Treetops Retreat has a Japanese hot tub, TV, VCR, stereo, and three private balconies with bush views. It sleeps two, making it a perfect romantic getaway. The nearby walking trails take you to the spectacular Grand Canyon; the Grose Valley Blue Gum forests; and Walls Cave, a resting place for local Aborigines 10,000 years ago.

336 Evans Lookout Rd., Blackheath, NSW 2785. ✆ **02/4787 7622.** Fax 02/4787 6230. www.jembyrinjahlodge.com.au. 10 cabins, 3 lodges. Standard 1- and 2-bedroom cabins A$150 (US$120/UK£60) Mon–Thurs, A$199 (US$159/UK£80) Fri–Sun; deluxe cabins A$199 (US$159/UK£80) Mon–Thurs, A$250 (US$200/UK£100) Fri–Sun; Ecolodges (8 adults/group booking) A$79 (US$63/UK£32) per person Mon–Thurs, A$95 (US$76/UK£38) per person Fri–Sun. Extra adult A$30 (US$24/UK£12), extra child A$22 (US$18/UK£9). Linen A$14 (US$11/UK£5.50) per bed. AE, DC, MC, V. **Amenities:** Restaurant w/lounge area; coin-op laundry; nonsmoking rooms. *In room:* TV, kitchenette, fridge, coffeemaker.

JENOLAN CAVES ★

182km (113 miles) W of Sydney; 70km (43 miles) SW of Katoomba

The winding road from Katoomba eventually takes you to a spur of the Great Dividing Range and a series of underground limestone caves considered some of the world's best. Known to the local Aborigines as Binoomea, meaning "dark place," the caves are an impressive amalgamation of stalactites, stalagmites, and underground rivers and pools. They have been open to the public since 1866.

GETTING THERE From Sydney, take the M4 Motorway traveling west through the Blue Mountains, Katoomba, and Mt. Victoria. Find the Jenolan Caves turnoff just past the village of Hartley. There is no fuel available at Jenolan. When traveling from Sydney the last service station is at Mount Victoria or Lithgow. It's a 1½-hour drive from Katoomba to the caves. CityRail trains run to Katoomba and link up with daily Jenolan Caves excursions run by **Fantastic Aussie Tours** (✆ **02/4782 1866,** or 1300/300 915 in Sydney; www.fantastic-aussie-tours.com.au). The day tour departs Katoomba at 10:30am and returns at 5:15pm. It costs A$75 (US$60/UK£30) for adults, A$38 (US$30/UK£15) for children, and A$200 (US$160/UK£80) for a family. The company also runs transfers to Jenolan from Katoomba, departing at 10:30am and leaving Jenolan at 3:45pm daily. They cost A$85 (US$68/UK£34) for adults and A$43 (US$34/UK£17) for kids. The company can transfer you to Jenolan Caves for A$50 (US$40/UK£20) for adults and A$25 (US$20/UK£10) for kids. Ask about family fares.

Another option is to go from Katoomba to Jenolan with **Jenolan 4WD Adventures** (✆ **02/6335 6239**). Four-wheel-drive tours cost from A$80 (US$64/UK£32) for a half-day to A$180 (US$144/UK£72) for a full day.

EXPLORING THE CAVES

Nine caves are open for exploration, with guided tours operated by **Jenolan Caves Reserves Trust** (© **02/6359 3311;** www.jenolancaves.org.au). The first cave tour starts at 10am weekdays and 9:30am weekends and holidays. The final tour departs at 4:30pm (5pm in warmer months). Tours last 1 to 2 hours, and each costs A$16 to A$23 (US$13–US$18/UK£7.50–UK£9) for adults, A$10 to A$15 (US$8–US$12/UK£4–UK£6) for children under 15. Family rates and multiple cave packages are available. The best all-around cave is **Lucas Cave; Imperial Cave** is best for seniors. Adventure Cave Tours, which include canyoning, last 3 hours to a full day and cost A$55 to A$188 (US$44–US$150/UK£22–UK£75) per person.

WHERE TO STAY

A relatively inexpensive option is to stay at **Jenolan Cabins** (© **02/6335 6239**). These cozy wood cabins, set up high on a ridge, accommodate six people, with one queen-size bed and two sets of bunks. There's a kitchenette, so bring your own food. Bed linens cost an extra A$15 (US$12/UK£6) for the queen-size bed and A$10 (US$8/UK£4) for each single bed. There's a TV. Cabins cost A$98 (US$79/UK£40) per night midweek, and A$115 (US$92/UK£46) on Friday and Saturday nights.

Jenolan Caves House ★ This heritage-listed hotel built between 1888 and 1906 is one of the most outstanding structures in New South Wales. The main part of the enormous three-story building is made of sandstone and fashioned in Tudor-style black and white. Around it are several cottages and former servants' quarters. Accommodations within the main house vary, from simple "traditional" rooms with shared bathrooms to "classic" rooms with private bathrooms. The traditional and classic rooms are old-world and cozy, with heavy furniture and views over red-tile rooftops or steep slopes. Classic rooms have views of Jenolan Caves Valley and gardens; "grand classic" rooms have spectacular views across the hills and countryside. "Mountain lodge" rooms, in a building behind the main house, are more motel-like. The 2-night weekend rates show why you should avoid this place on weekends.

Jenolan Caves Village, NSW 2790. © **02/6359 3322**. Fax 02/6359 3227. www.jenolancaves.com. 101 units, 87 with bathroom. A$190–A$250 (US$152–US$200/UK£76–UK£100) traditional double; A$280–A$380 (US$224–US$304/UK£112–UK£152) classic double; A$330–A$450 (US$264–US$360/UK£132–UK£180) grand classic double; A$370–A$450 (US$296–US$360/UK£150–UK£180) classic suite; A$400–A$560 (US$320–US$448/UK£160–UK£224) grand classic suite; A$210–A$280 (US$168–US$224/UK£85–UK£112) mountain lodge double. Rates include dinner. Higher rates are for Fri–Sun and public holidays. 2-night minimum on weekends. Extra person A$60 (US$48/UK£24). AE, DC, MC, V. **Amenities:** 2 restaurants; bar; tour desk; nonsmoking rooms. *In room:* TV, coffeemaker, hair dryer.

2 The Hunter Valley: Wine Tasting & More ★

Cessnock: 190km (118 miles) N of Sydney

The Hunter Valley (or "the Hunter," as it's also called) is the oldest commercial wine-producing area in Australia, as well as a major site for coal mining. Internationally acclaimed wines have poured out of the Hunter since the early 1800s. Though the region falls behind the major wine-producing areas of Victoria in terms of volume, it has the advantage of being just 2 hours from Sydney.

People come here to visit the vineyards' "cellar doors" for free wine tasting, to enjoy the scenery, to sample the area's highly regarded cuisine, or to escape from the city for a romantic weekend. The whole area is dedicated to the grape and the plate, and you'll find many superb restaurants amid the vineyards and farmland.

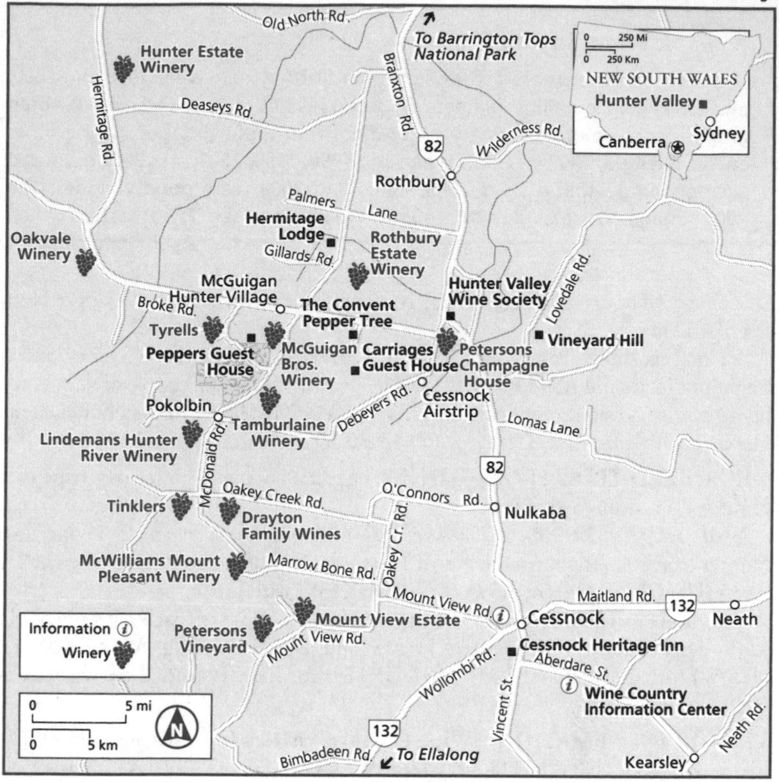

In the **Lower Hunter,** centered on the towns of Cessnock and Pokolbin, are around 110 wineries and cellar doors, including well-known producers such as Tyrell, Rothbury, Lindemans, Draytons, McGuigans, and McWilliams. Many varieties of wine are produced here, including semillon, Shiraz, chardonnay, cabernet sauvignon, and pinot noir.

Farther north, the **Upper Hunter** represents the very essence of Australian rural life, with its sheep and cattle farms, historic homesteads, more wineries, and rugged bushland. The vineyards here tend to be larger than those in the south, and they produce more aromatic varieties, such as traminers and Rieslings. February through March is harvest time.

The Upper Hunter gives way to the forested heights of the World Heritage–listed Barrington Tops National Park. The ruggedly beautiful park is home to some of the highest Antarctic beech trees in the country. It abounds with animals, including several marsupial species and a profusion of birds.

HUNTER VALLEY ESSENTIALS

GETTING THERE To get to the wine-producing regions of the Hunter, leave Sydney by the Harbour Bridge or Harbour Tunnel and follow the signs for Newcastle. Just before Hornsby, turn off the highway and head up the National 1/F3 freeway. After around an hour, take the Cessnock exit and follow signs to the vineyards. The trip will

Tips A Wine-Buying Tip

The best years ever for red wines in this part of Australia were 1998 and 2000, and 2004 when long, hot summers produced fewer but more intensely flavored grapes. Stock up on anything you can find from those vintages. At the other end of the scale, 1997 was a bad year, and 1996, 1999, 2001, and 2002 produced average vintages. The years 2003, 2005, and 2006 were good vintages. The 2007 vintage was small due to drought. We've yet to see how it tastes.

take about 2½ hours. Barrington Tops National Park is reached via the Upper Hunter town of Dungog.

A rental car should cost at least A$45 (US$36/UK£18) a day from Sydney, and you might put in around A$40 (US$32/UK£16) worth of gas for a couple of days of touring (the price hovers around A$1.40/US$1.10/UK55p a liter). In the Hunter, contact **Hertz,** 1A Aberdare Rd., Cessnock (✆ **13 30 39** in Australia, or 02/4991 2500).

ORGANIZED TRIPS FROM SYDNEY Several companies offer **day trips** to the Hunter Valley from Sydney.

Visitours (✆ **02/9909 0822;** www.visitours.com.au) takes small groups to the Hunter to visit up to six wineries as well as cheese and fudge producers. The trip costs A$85 (US$68/UK£34), or A$95 (US$76/UK£38) with lunch.

Grayline (✆ **1300/858 687;** www.grayline.com.au) offers coach trips to the vineyards every Tuesday, Wednesday, Friday, and Sunday costing A$143 (US$114/UK£57) for adults and A$72 (US$57/UK£29) for kids. It visits three wineries and includes lunch.

VISITOR INFORMATION **Wine Country Visitors Information Centre,** Main Road, Pokolbin, NSW 2325 (✆ **02/4990 4477;** fax 02/4991 4518; www.winecountry.com.au), is open Monday through Friday from 9am to 5pm, Saturday from 9:30am to 5pm, and Sunday from 9:30am to 3:30pm. The staff can make accommodations bookings and answer any questions. The **Dungog Visitors Information Centre,** Dowling Street, Dungog (✆ **02/4992 2212**), has plenty of information on the Barrington Tops area. A good general website is www.winecountry.com.au. Pick up a copy of the free Hunter Valley Wine Country Visitors Guide in any visitor center in Sydney or the Hunter Valley.

VISITING THE WINERIES

Many people start their journey through the Hunter by popping into the **Hunter Valley Wine Society,** 455 Wine Country Dr., Pokolbin (✆ **1300/303 307** in Australia, or 02/4941 3000). The club basically acts as a Hunter Valley wine clearinghouse, sending bottles and cases to members all over Australia, and some overseas. It's also a good place to talk to experts about the area's wines, and to taste a few of them. It's open daily from 9am to 5pm.

You might also like to visit the **Small Winemakers Centre,** 426 McDonalds Rd., Pokolbin (✆ **02/4998 7668**). At any one time it represents around six of the region's smaller producers.

Most of the wineries in the region are open for cellar-door tastings, and it's perfectly acceptable just to turn up, taste a couple of wines or more, and then say your goodbyes without buying anything. Though you will come across some unusual vintages, especially at the boutique wineries, don't expect to find any bargains—city bottle shops buy in bulk and at trade price, which means you can probably get the same bottle of wine for less in Sydney than at the cellar door in the Hunter.

If you're not traveling by car, see the following section for information about day tours of the wineries.

Drayton Family Wines Drayton's produces some spectacular Shiraz. Open Monday to Friday 9am to 5pm; Saturday and Sunday 10am to 5pm. Tours Monday to Friday 11am. 555 Oakey Creek Rd., Pokolbin. ✆ **02/4998 7513.**

Lindemans Hunter River Winery This famous winery offers an interesting sparkling red Shiraz. Open Monday to Friday 9am to 4:30pm; Saturday and Sunday 10am to 4:30pm. McDonald Rd., Pokolbin. ✆ **02/4998 7684.**

McGuigan Brothers Cellers A winery worth visiting, McGuigan also has a cheese factory and bakery on the site. Open daily 9:30am to 5pm with tours at noon. Corner of Broke and McDonalds roads, Pokolbin. ✆ **02/4998 7402.**

McWilliams Mount Pleasant Winery Famous for its Elizabeth Semillon, which has won 39 trophies and 214 gold medals since 1981, and its Lovedale Semillon, which has won 39 trophies and 74 gold medals since 1984. Open daily 10am to 4:30pm with tours at 11am. Marrowbone Rd., Pokolbin. ✆ **02/4998 7505.**

Peterson's Champagne House This is the only specialist champagne winery in the Hunter. Open daily 9am to 5pm. At the corner of Broke and Branxton roads, Pokolbin. ✆ **02/4998 7881.**

Peterson's Vineyard Peterson's produces fine chardonnay, semillon, and Shiraz. Open Monday to Saturday 9am to 5pm, Sunday 10am to 5pm. Mount View Rd., Mount View. ✆ **02/4990 1704.**

Rothbury Estate ★ This very friendly winery produces the magnificent Brokenback Shiraz and the nice Mudgee Shiraz. Open daily 9:30am to 4:30pm. Broke Rd., Pokolbin. ✆ **02/4998 7555.**

Tamburlaine Winery Don't miss this boutique winery, the winner of many wine and tourism awards. Open daily 9:30am to 5pm. 358 McDonald Rd., Pokolbin. ✆ **02/4998 7570.**

Tinklers If you want to taste grapes in season, head to Tinklers. It sells some 30 different varieties of eating grapes between December and March, and nectarines, plums, peaches, and vegetables at other times of the year. It also offers wine tasting and free vineyard walks at 11am Saturday and Sunday. Open daily 10am to 4pm. Pokolbin Mountains Rd., Pokolbin. ✆ **02/4998 7435.**

Tyrell's Tyrell's has produced some famous wines and exports all over the world. Tours Monday to Saturday 1:30pm. Broke Rd., Pokolbin. ✆ **02/4993 7000.**

Tips **Remember a Designated Driver!**

Australia's drunk-driving laws are strict and rigidly enforced. Both easily identifiable and unmarked police cars patrol the vineyard regions. If you are interested in tasting some grapes in the Hunter Valley, choose a designated driver or take a guided tour (see above).

Tips **A Wine-Tasting Tip**

Some wineries routinely offer some of their inferior wines for tastings. We've made a habit of asking for a list of their premium wines available for tasting. Most wineries usually have a bottle or two of their better wines uncorked for those with a serious interest.

DAY TOURS, HOT-AIR BALLOON RIDES & OTHER FUN STUFF

If you don't have a car, you'll have to get around as part of a tour, because no public transport runs between the wineries.

Trekabout Tours (**© 02/4990 8277;** www.hunterweb.com.au/trekabout) offers half-day and full-day winery tours for a maximum of six people. Half-day tours cost A$35 (US$28/UK£14), with visits to five or six wineries; full-day tours cost A$45 (US$36/UK£18) and take in up to nine wineries, mostly boutique ones. The company can pick you up from your hotel in Cessnock or Pokolbin.

Also offering local pickup is **Hunter Vineyard Tours** (**© 02/4991 1659;** www.huntervineyardtours.com.au), which has a full-day tour on a 12- or 21-seat bus, taking in five wineries. It costs A$50 (US$40/UK£20), or A$74 (US$59/UK£30) with a two-course meal.

A tranquil way to see the wineries is from above. **Balloon Aloft,** in Cessnock (**© 1800/028 568** in Australia, or 02/4938 1955; www.balloonaloft.com.au), offers year-round dawn balloon flights that include postflight champagne and optional breakfast costing A$16 (US$13/UK£6.50). Flights last about an hour and cost A$280 (US$224/UK£112) for adults and A$170 (US$136/UK£68) for kids ages 8 to 12.

If you like adventure, try **Grapemobile Bicycle and Walking Tours** (**© 0500/804 039** in Australia, or ©/fax 02/4991 2339. This company supplies you with a mountain bike, helmet, guide, and support bus, and takes you on a peaceful meander through the wineries. Tours cost A$98 (US$78/UK£39), including lunch in a restaurant. The firm also rents bicycles—A$22 (US$18/UK£9) for a half-day and A$30 (US$24/UK£12) for a full day.

WHERE TO STAY

The Hunter Valley is far more expensive on weekends and during public holidays than on weekdays. Room prices jump significantly, and some properties insist on a 2-night stay. It's worth checking out the information board in the Wine Country Visitors Information Centre (see "Visitor Information," above) for special deals, including self-contained accommodations, cottages, resorts, and guesthouses.

IN CESSNOCK

Staying in Cessnock is a good idea if you don't have a car and are relying on local tour companies to pick you up and show you around the area.

Cessnock Heritage Inn This 1920s building, built as a pub, is right in the center of Cessnock, so there's easy access to pubs and restaurants. All the rooms are simple and done in country style, with dried grasses, floral bedspreads, and the like. All are quite large, with high ceilings, but differ greatly—the smallest room has a double bed, others have queen-size beds and singles, and there are two family rooms (sleeping five). There's a guest lounge with a hideous carpet where you can chat with the owners.

Tips **Bunking Down in a Caravan, Man**

Two trailer (caravan) parks offer reasonably comfortable accommodations in trailers and cabins. **Cessnock Cabins and Caravan Park** (✆ **02/4990 5819**; fax 02/4991 2944), Allandale/Branxton Road, Nulkaba (2km/1¼ miles north of Cessnock), has four on-site vans for A$30 to A$40 (US$24–US$32/UK£16–UK£30), and a double and 12 cabins with shower for A$48 to A$69 (US$38–US$55/UK£19–UK£28)—the more expensive prices for weekends. There are also camping sites for A$14 (US$11/UK£5.50) and powered sites for A$16 (US$13/UK£6.50).

The **Valley Vineyard Tourist Park** (✆/fax **02/4990 2573**) on Mount View Road (on the way to the vineyards) has five trailers for A$35 (US$28/UK£14) and 12 cabins with shower for A$55 (US$44/UK£22). Two two-bedroom units cost A$75 (US$60/UK£30). Powered sites cost A$16 to A$20 (US$13–US$16/UK£6.50–UK£8) and a camping site A$12 (US$10/UK£5). There are a BYO restaurant, a campers' kitchen, and a swimming pool on-site.

Vincent St. (P.O. Box 714), Cessnock, NSW 2325. ✆ **02/4991 2744.** Fax 02/4991 2720. www.hunterweb.com.au/heritageinn.html. 13 units. Weekend A$120 (US$96/UK£48) double, A$200 (US$160/UK£80) 2-night package; weekday A$90 (US$72/UK£36) double. Rates include breakfast. AE, MC, V. **Amenities:** Tour desk; nonsmoking rooms. *In room:* A/C, TV w/free videos, minibar, coffeemaker, ceiling fan.

IN POKOLBIN

Very Expensive

Casuarina Restaurant and Country Inn ★★ *Finds* Now, this place is really an oddity. Each of its very different suites has an unusual theme. Just naming them will give you an idea: the Moulin Rouge, the Oriental, the Bordello, Casanova's Loft, the Mariners Suite, British Empire, Out of Africa, Edwardian, Palais Royale, and Romeo's Retreat. The most popular is the Bordello, with a pedestaled king-size bed, voluptuous pink curtains, and strategically placed mirrors. To get the full picture, it's well worth roaming around the website before you book. The award-winning **Casuarina Restaurant** serves Mediterranean-style food.

Hermitage Rd., Pokolbin, NSW 2321. ✆ **02/4998 7888.** Fax 02/4998 7692. www.casuarinainn.com.au. 10 units. A$285–A$310 (US$212–US$248/UK£106–UK£124) weekday; A$310–A$350 (US$248–US$280/UK£124–UK£140) weekend. 2-night minimum on weekends. AE, DC, MC, V. **Amenities:** Restaurant; large heated outdoor pool; laundry service; nonsmoking rooms. *In room:* A/C, TV, coffeemaker, hair dryer.

Peppers Convent Hunter Valley ★★ Originally a convent for Brigidine nuns in the early part of the 20th century, this building was transported some 600km (372 miles) from Coonamble in central New South Wales to its present location in 1990. A year later, it opened as a hotel. Rooms are elegant and spacious, with baroque decor, including plaster frieze ceilings and thick, rich drapes. French doors open onto private verandas overlooking patches of bushland. King rooms are larger and have wicker lounge areas. There is an elegant sitting area where drinks are served, and a light and airy breakfast room serving the best breakfasts in the Hunter (A$28/US$22/UK£11).

The Pepper Tree Complex includes Pepper Tree Wines and the excellent **Robert's Restaurant.** Check the website for ever-changing packages.

In the Pepper Tree Complex, Halls Rd., Pokolbin, NSW 2320. ✆ **02/4998 7764.** Fax 02/4998 7323. www.peppers.com.au. 17 units. Weekend A$323–A$387 (US$258–US$309/UK£128–UK£155) double; weekday A$291–A$332 (US$233–US$265/UK£117–UK£133) double. Extra adult A$44 (US$35/UK£18). Extra child 5–15 A$22 (US$18/UK£9). Children under 5 stay free in parent's room. 2-night minimum on weekends. Ask about packages and check website the week before for specials. AE, DC, MC, V. **Amenities:** Restaurant (see "Where to Dine," below); medium-size heated outdoor pool; outdoor lit tennis court; Jacuzzi; free use of bikes; concierge; tour desk; car-rental desk; business center; massage; babysitting; laundry service; dry cleaning; nonsmoking rooms. *In room:* A/C, TV, minibar, coffeemaker, hair dryer, iron/ironing board.

Peppers Guest House This tranquil escape is set in beautiful bush gardens. The spot is so peaceful that kangaroos hop up to the veranda in the evenings looking for treats. The "classic" rooms downstairs have French doors that you can fling open; upstairs rooms have just a tad more old-fashioned charm and come with air-conditioning. All rooms have king-size beds and are furnished with colonial antiques. Guests don't come here for action; they come to relax. The Pampering Place offers massages and facials, and a gentle 30-minute trail winds through the bush. There's a pleasant guest lounge with an open fireplace and a bar. The restaurant, **Chez Pok,** is an upscale establishment with mismatched china and pretty good country food.

Ekerts Rd., Pokolbin, NSW 2321. ✆ **02/4998 7596.** Fax 02/4998 7739. www.peppers.com.au. 47 units, 1 cottage. Weekend A$277 (US$221/UK£110) colonial double, A$303 (US$242/UK£121) classic double, A$315 (US$252/UK£126) vintage double, A$347 (US$277/UK£139) heritage suite; weekday A$273 (US$218/UK£109) colonial double, A$283 (US$226/UK£113) classic double, A$292 (US$233/UK£117) vintage double, A$327 (US$261/UK£131) heritage suite. 2-night minimum on weekends. Weekday rates include buffet breakfast. AE, DC, MC, V. **Amenities:** Restaurant; small heated indoor pool; outdoor lit tennis court; bike rental; laundry service; nonsmoking rooms. *In room:* A/C, TV, minibar, coffeemaker, hair dryer, iron/ironing board.

Expensive

Carriages Guest House ★★ Tucked away on 15 hectares (37 acres), a kilometer off the main road, Carriages is a secluded retreat in the heart of Pokolbin. A two-suite cottage, the Gatehouse, is on a separate part of the grounds. In the main two-story house, a veranda circles downstairs rooms, which are furnished in antique country pine. Upstairs, the two lofty gable suites center on huge fireplaces. The Gatehouse suites offer incredible luxury; although relatively new, the stained-glass windows and rescued timber give them a rustic feel (these two Jacuzzi rooms share a lounge with a full kitchen and an open fire). There are open fires in six of the rooms. (The two standard doubles don't have them.) Breakfast is served in your room, and Robert's Restaurant is next door. The friendly owner, Ben Dawson, assures me he'll take Frommer's readers up to the top of a nearby hill where they can see plenty of wild kangaroos.

Halls Rd., Pokolbin, NSW 2321. ✆ **02/4998 7591.** Fax 02/4998 7839. www.thecarriages.com.au. 10 units. A$150–A$195 (US$148–US$156/UK£75–UK£78) double; A$195–A$275 (US$156–US$220/UK£78–UK£110) suite; A$235–A$295 (US$188–US$236/UK£94–UK£118) Jacuzzi suite. Rates include breakfast. 2-night minimum on weekends. AE, MC, V. **Amenities:** Large heated outdoor pool; outdoor lit tennis court; Jacuzzi; massage; babysitting, laundry service; nonsmoking rooms. *In room:* A/C, TV, kitchenette, fridge, coffeemaker, hair dryer, iron/ironing board.

Hermitage Lodge ★ If you want to be in the heart of vineyard country, stay at this property, which is surrounded by vineyards. Standard rooms are large, sunny, and nicely decorated; they come with a queen-size bed and a double sofa bed. The spa suites are larger, with queen-size beds (two also come with double sofa beds), cathedral ceilings, Jacuzzis, and separate showers. Continental breakfast is served in all rooms, and a cooked one is available on request. **Il Cacciatore** restaurant is one of the best in the region and was awarded "Best Italian Restaurant" for the Hunter Region from 2001 to 2005. The owners built 11 new rooms in 2006, and will follow with a refurbishment of the older ones. Two of the new rooms are two-story suites, each with a nice living area, king-size bed, and a big deck with a spa tub overlooking the vineyard. Five of them have fireplaces.

At Gillards and McDonalds roads, Pokolbin, NSW 2320. ✆ **02/4998 7639.** Fax 02/4998 7818. www.hermitagelodge.com.au. 20 units. Weekend A$230 (US$184/UK£92) standard double, A$250 (US$200/UK£100) spa suite; weekday A$155 (US$124/UK£62) standard double, A$175 (US$140/UK£70) spa suite. Extra person A$20 (US$16/UK£8). Kids under 5 stay free in parent's room. 2-night minimum on weekends. Rates include continental breakfast. Ask about packages. AE, DC, MC, V. **Amenities:** Restaurant; bar; medium-size outdoor pool; golf course nearby; limited room service; babysitting; free self-service laundry; nonsmoking rooms. *In room:* A/C, TV, fridge, coffeemaker, hair dryer, iron/ironing board.

Moderate

Vineyard Hill ★ Fully self-contained chalets here are modern and spacious, with a separate bedroom, a lounge and dining area, a full kitchen, and a balcony with views across a valley of vineyards to the Brokenback Ranges in the distance. It's all terrifically rural, with cows wandering about the 13-hectare (32-acre) property and kangaroos and possums creeping around at dusk. There's no restaurant, but there is a gourmet deli on the premises, and you can choose your own meats for a barbecue. In the garden are a large pool and a nice Jacuzzi.

Lovedale Rd., Pokolbin, NSW 2321. ✆ **02/4990 4166.** Fax 02/4991 4431. www.vineyardhill.com.au. 8 units. Weekend A$155 (US$124/UK£62) 1-bedroom unit; weekday A$107 (US$86/UK£43) 1-bedroom unit. Extra person A$20 (US$16/UK£8). Ask about weekday and long-weekend packages. AE, MC, V. **Amenities:** Large heated outdoor pool; Jacuzzi; limited room service; massage; babysitting; free laundry service; nonsmoking rooms. *In room:* A/C, TV, kitchen, minibar, fridge, coffeemaker, hair dryer, iron/ironing board.

IN THE UPPER HUNTER

Barrington Guest House ★★ Barrington Guest House is in a valley just outside the Barrington Tops National Park, 1½ hours from the main Hunter wine region. It retains an old-world charm and serves bacon and eggs for breakfast, scones and cream, and vegetables boiled soft enough for your dentures. The place has lace tablecloths in the dining room, a log fire beneath a higgledy-piggledy brick chimney, mahogany walls, high ceilings, and personalized service—despite the communal mealtimes and the lack of a menu. Rooms come with or without private bathroom; they're basic (no TV) but comfortable enough, and can be noisy if a party's in full swing in the dining room. This place is very popular with seniors during the week but appeals to a range of ages on weekends. The guesthouse grounds attract plenty of animals and act as a wildlife reserve for several rescued kangaroos. Activities include horseback riding, guided walks through the rainforest, "billy tea" tours, night spotting for quolls (native cats) and possums, bush dancing, tennis, film evenings, and skeet shooting. It can be a very social scene, too. Several luxury rainforest cottages are also available. They sleep up to five people and come with a master bedroom, a loft bedroom, a full bathroom with spa, a lounge, a dining room and full kitchen, a gas log fire, and a separate barbecue area and tennis court; and they have views over the National Park, State Forest, and the Guest House.

Salisbury (3½ hr. from Sydney), NSW 2420. ✆ **02/4995 3212.** Fax 02/4995 3248. www.barringtonguesthouse.com.au. 21 guesthouse units, 13 with bathroom. Weekend A$230 (US$184/UK£92) double for 2 nights without bathroom, A$260 (US$208/UK£104) double with bathroom; weekday A$95 (US$76/UK£38) double without bathroom, A$130 (US$104/UK£52) double with bathroom. Rates include all meals and activities. 2-night minimum on weekends. Ask about packages and child rates. AE, DC, MC, V. Free pickup from Dungog railway station. **Amenities:** Restaurant; bar; 2 lit tennis courts; tour desk; massage; laundry service; nonsmoking rooms. *In room:* Cottages only: TV, kitchen, fridge, coffeemaker, hair dryer, iron/ironing board.

Moments **Staying at a Hunter Cattle Station**

Just off the Golden Highway, 2½ hours west of Cessnock and 4 hours northwest of Sydney, **Runnymede,** Golden Highway, Runnymede, Cassilis, NSW 2329 (✆ **02/6376 1183;** fax 02/6376 1187), is an 800-hectare (2,000-acre) sheep-and-cattle ranch where you can get a taste of Aussie ranch life. The ranch—called a "station" in Australia—offers farm-style lodgings in a 1930s California-style bungalow. Two rooms have private bathrooms with shower, and the third shares the hosts' bathroom down the hall. The homestead has an open fire in the living room (and a rarely used TV). There are plenty of native birds in the gardens, and kangaroos are common. May is the best time to see sheep shearing, and August is the best time to witness lambing and calving. Guests rave about hosts Libby and David Morrow, and according to the guest-book it was a real highlight for many of them. David offers 1-hour tours of the property and other tours throughout the district. Bed-and-breakfast costs A$130 (US$104/UK£52) per couple, and dinner, bed, and breakfast and a fabulous farm tour costs A$238 (US$190/UK£80) for two. No credit cards. Bring your own wine or beer.

WHERE TO DINE

IN CESSNOCK

Amicos MEXICAN/ITALIAN/PIZZA You can't mistake the Mexican influence in the decor—bunches of chile peppers, cow skulls, ponchos, masks, and frescoes—but the Mediterranean/Italian connection is more evident in the menu. Mexican dishes include the usual nachos, enchiladas, burritos, barbecued chicken, and the like, and there are a few pastas and Mediterranean dishes, such as crumbed lamb brains. The pizzas are pretty good, and one could just about serve four people. The restaurant will deliver, too.

138 Wollombi Rd., Cessnock. ✆ **02/4991 1995.** Fax 02/4990 9302. Reservations recommended. Main courses A$12–A$20 (US$9.60–US$16/UK£4.80–UK£8); pizzas A$14–A$18 (US$11–US$14/UK£5.50–UK£7). MC, V. Daily 6–10pm.

IN POKOLBIN

The three restaurants in the Hunter with the biggest reputations are **Robert's Restaurant,** in the Peppers Convent Hunter Valley guesthouse; **Chez Pok,** in Peppers Guest House; and **Casuarina Restaurant.** See "Where to Stay," above. Another good offering is **Beltree@Margan,** 266 Hermitage Rd., Pokolbin (✆ **02/6574 7216**), which serves Mediterranean-influenced food either out on a courtyard or in front of a fireplace. It's open for a lingering lunch daily from 10am to 5pm.

For good coffee don't go past **Bliss Coffee Roasters,** shop 2, Hunter Valley Gardens Shopping Centre, Broke Road, Pokolbin (✆ **02/4998 6700**).

Café Enzo MODERN AUSTRALIAN This charming little cafe offers a nice ambience and good cuisine. Pastas, pizzettas, antipasti, and steaks dominate the menu. The pizzetta with chargrilled baby octopus, squid, king prawns, Kalamata olives, fresh chile, onion, and freshly shaved Parmesan is particularly nice. Cakes and cheese plates are a specialty.

At the corner of Broke and Ekerts roads (adjacent to Peppers Creek Antiques, near Peppers Guest House), Pokolbin. ✆ **02/4998 7233.** Main courses A$10–A$18 (US$8–US$14/UK£4–UK£7); Devonshire tea A$7.50 (US$6/UK£3). AE, DC, MC, V. Wed–Fri and Sun 10am–5pm; Sat 10am–10pm.

Robert's at Peppertree ★★ EUROPEAN Chef and owner Robert Molines has become a legend in Hunter Valley gourmet circles for coming up with great dishes that perfectly complement the region's wines. His restaurant is known for its eclectic mix of antiques and his country-style dishes, such as rabbit with olives and vegetables, and the signature dish, twice-roasted duckling with braised savoy cabbage and pear glaze. Other nice dishes could include the lamb rack Provençal, and venison steaks on a beet root and baby onion confit, with muscat sauce.

In the Pepper Tree complex, Halls Rd., Pokolbin. ✆ **02/4998 7330.** www.robertsrestaurant.com. Main courses A$38–A$42 (US$30–US$34/UK£15–UK£17). A$5 (US$4/UK£2) per-person surcharge weekends and public holidays. AE, DC, MC, V. Daily noon–5pm and 7pm–midnight.

3 Port Stephens: Dolphin- & Whale-Watching ★★

209km (130 miles) N of Sydney

Port Stephens, just 2½ hours north of Sydney, should be at the top of any New South Wales itinerary. It's a perfect add-on to a trip to the Hunter Valley (p. 210). Though you can come up from Sydney for the day, I recommend staying in the general area for at least 1 night. The sheltered Port Stephens bay is more than twice the size of Sydney Harbour, and is as clean as a newly poured bath. The sea literally jumps with fish, and the creamy islands and surrounding Tomaree National Park boast more species of birds than even Kakadu National Park in the Northern Territory. Two pods of bottle-nosed dolphins, around 70 individuals in all, call the bay home, and you are almost certain to see some on a dolphin-watching cruise. Port Stephens is also a fabulous place to watch whales during their migration to the breeding grounds farther north (roughly from June to mid-Nov—though they are less frequently seen in Aug). There is also a large breeding colony of koalas in Lemon Tree Passage on the south side of the Tomaree Peninsula, which makes up the southern shoreline of the bay.

The main town, **Nelson Bay** (pop. 7,000), is on the northern side of the peninsula. The township of Shoal Bay, farther along the peninsula, has a spectacular beach edged with wildflowers. Another small resort town, **Anna Bay,** is the largest development on the southern side of the peninsula, and has excellent surf beaches. The Stockton Bight stretches some 32km (20 miles) from Anna Bay south to the large industrial town of Newcastle. The beach here is popular with ocean fishermen who have the awful habit of driving their four-wheel-drives along it. The first 500m (1,640 ft.) of the beach is for swimming and surfing only. The Stockton Sand Dunes, which run behind the beach, are the longest in the Southern Hemisphere.

Opposite the Tomaree Peninsula, across the bay, are the small tourist townships of Tea Gardens and Hawks Nest, both at the mouth of the Myall River.

ESSENTIALS

GETTING THERE To get to Port Stephens, take the Sydney-Newcastle Freeway (F3) to its end, then follow the Pacific Highway signs to Hexham and Port Stephens. **Port Stephens Coaches** (✆ **1800/045 949** in Sydney, or 02/4982 2940; www.pscoaches.com.au) travels between Port Stephens and Newcastle, and to Nelson Bay from Sydney daily at 2pm. Buses from Sydney leave from Eddy Avenue, near

Finds Through the Dunes on Horseback

You can ride a horse through the dunes with **Sahara Horse Trails** (**© 02/4981 9077;** www.saharatrails.com). The barn is on Port Stephens Road, before you reach Nelson Bay. Sahara Trails also has accommodations options. A 2-hour trip costs A$60 (US$48/UK£24), and a half-day excursion is A$120 (US$96/UK£48). Bookings required 1 day in advance.

Central Station; the journey takes 3½ hours. Round-trip tickets cost around A$48 (US$38/UK£19) for adults and A$32 (US$26/UK£13) for children. There's no train service to Port Stephens. You must book ahead.

VISITOR INFORMATION The **Port Stephens Visitor Information Centre,** Victoria Parade, Nelson Bay (**© 02/4980 6900;** www.portstephens.org.au), is open Monday through Friday from 9am to 5pm and Saturday and Sunday from 9am to 4pm.

SEEING THE AREA

Several operators offer **dolphin- and whale-watching cruises.** Some of the best are aboard ***Imagine*** (**© 02/4984 9000;** www.imaginecruises.com.au), a 15m (49-ft.) catamaran operated by Frank Future and Yves Papin, two real characters. They offer a daily Island Discovery trip that includes dolphin-watching and a trip around the offshore islands. The 4-hour cruise departs from D'Albora Marina in Nelson Bay from Thursday to Sunday at 12:30pm from mid-December to March only. It costs A$45 (US$36/UK£18) for adults, A$20 (US$16/UK£8) for children 1 to 14, and A$145 (US$116/UK£58) for families, including lunch.

Four-hour whale-watching tours cost the same and leave at 11am from June 1 to November 15. You are most likely to spot humpback whales, but there's also a chance to see minke and southern right whales.

A dolphin-watching cruise runs from 10:30am to 12:30pm, and 2:30pm daily during summer, and Thursday to Sunday at 10am from November to May. It costs A$22 (US$18/UK£9) for adults, A$14 (US$11/UK£5.50) for children aged 1 to 14, and A$58 (US$46/UK£23) for families. If you happen to be around on the weekend nearest a full moon, ask about overnight Full Moon Tours.

The **Port Stephens Ferry Service** (**© 02/4984 1262**) operates a 2½-hour Early Bird Dolphin Watch, with a stop at Tea Gardens township, daily at 8:30am. A similar 3½-hour cruise departs at noon (you can eat lunch in Tea Gardens), and a 2-hour dolphin-watching cruise departs at 3:30pm. All cruises cost A$17 (US$14/UK£7) for adults, A$9 (US$7.20/UK£3.60) for children 4 to 17, and A$40 (US$32/UK£16) for families.

WHERE TO STAY

Port Stephens is very popular with Sydneysiders, especially during the Christmas holidays, January, and Easter, so you'll need to book well in advance then.

Peppers Anchorage Port Stephens ★★ This low-rise resort, split into a main guesthouse and four separate lodges, is built onto a headland and runs almost directly into the bay—it's stopped from sliding in by a boardwalk and a picturesque marina. Rooms are light and luxurious; the suites each have a good-size Jacuzzi, perfect for two. Rooms on the top floor have a large balcony, from which uninterrupted views take in the bay and the islands; those below have private verandas. Two rooms are designed for wheelchairs. A nearby beach is the perfect spot for a sunset stroll.

Corlette Point Rd., Corlette, NSW 2315. ✆ **1800/809 142** in Australia, or 02/4984 2555. Fax 02/4984 0300. www.peppers.com.au. 80 units. Weekend, 2-night stay, A$377 (US$301/UK£150) double, A$449–A$764 (US$359–US$611/UK£180–UK£306) suite; weekday, single-night stay, A$148 (US$119/UK£59) double, A$181–A$306 (US$145–US$245/UK£73–UK£123) suite. Ask about packages. AE, DC, MC, V. **Amenities:** Restaurant; bar; good-size heated outdoor pool; exercise room; Jacuzzi; sauna; children's program (public holidays only); tour desk; 24-hr. room service; massage; babysitting; laundry service; nonsmoking rooms. *In room:* A/C, TV, fax, dataport, minibar, coffeemaker, hair dryer, iron/ironing board.

Port Stephens Motor Lodge Surrounded by tall trees and gardens, this motor lodge a short stroll from the main township is a peaceful place to stay. The standard rooms are quite plain, with raw-brick walls, a comfy double bed (and an extra single bed in most rooms), a private balcony, and an attached shower with half-tub. Adjacent to the lodge is a self-contained family unit for four; it has two bedrooms, a laundry, and water views. There's a barbecue area on the grounds. Rates peak during the Christmas holiday period.

44 Mangus St., Nelson Bay, NSW 2315. ✆ **02/4981 3366.** Fax 02/4984 1655. psmlodge@aol.com. 17 units. A$60–A$120 (US$48–US$96/UK£24–UK£48) standard double; A$88 (US$70/UK£35) family unit weekday, A$120 (US$96/UK£48) family unit weekend. Extra adult A$10 (US$8/UK£4); extra child under 15 A$5 (US$4/UK£2). AE, DC, MC, V. **Amenities:** Heated outdoor pool; coin-op laundry; nonsmoking rooms. *In room:* A/C, TV, coffeemaker, hair dryer, iron/ironing board.

Salamander Shores ★ Salamander Shores looks like a beached, ramshackle paddle steamer—it's all white-painted bricks and rails and stairs, fixed to the bay by a jetty. Set in a well-tended, sloping garden, this five-story hotel retains a certain 1960s charm, despite undergoing selective modernization. Standard rooms are similar to most motel rooms, but you really should throw caution to the wind and get a sea-view room—you won't regret it. These rooms have Jacuzzis and large balconies with extensive views of the bay. When the sun rises over the water and the garden is full of lorikeets and corellas, it couldn't be more picture-perfect. Down below is a pub and shop selling alcohol.

147 Soldiers Point Rd., Soldiers Point, NSW 2317. ✆ **1800/655 029** in Australia, or 02/4982 7210. Fax 02/4982 7890. www.salamander-shores.com. 90 units. A$145 (US$116/UK£58) standard double; A$160 (US$128/UK£64) garden-view double; A$175 (US$140/UK£70) sea-view double. Extra person A$20 (US$16/UK£8). Ask about packages. AE, DC, MC, V. **Amenities:** 2 restaurants; bar; small heated outdoor pool; sauna; tour desk; babysitting; laundry service; nonsmoking rooms. *In room:* A/C, TV, minibar, coffeemaker, hair dryer, iron/ironing board.

WHERE TO DINE

Most people head to **Nelson Bay** for their meals because of the great views. You'll find a host of cheap takeout joints and a few pleasant sit-down eateries.

Sinclair's ★ SEAFOOD/PASTA It's a bit noisy inside, but the lunchtime food makes up for it. The fish and chips are nice, as is the linguine. Outside is a small section where you can buy an excellent range of local oysters for A$2.50 (US$2/UK£1) each.

D'Albora Marinas. ✆ **02/4984 4444.** Reservations recommended. Main courses A$12–A$22 (US$9.60–US$18/UK£4.80–UK£9). MC. V. Daily noon–3pm and 6–10pm.

4 North of Sydney along the Pacific Highway: Australia's Holiday Coast

The Pacific Highway leads over the Sydney Harbour Bridge and merges into the Sydney-Newcastle Freeway. It continues to the industrial coast town of Newcastle, bypassing Tuggerah Lake and Lake Macquarie (neither of real interest compared to what follows). From here, the Pacific Highway stays close to the coast until it reaches Brisbane, some 1,000km (620 miles) from Sydney.

Though the road is gradually being upgraded, conditions vary, and distances are long. Travelers should be aware that the route is renowned for its accidents. Though you could make it to Brisbane in a couple of days, you could also easily spend more than a week stopping off at the attractions along the way. The farther north you travel, the more tropical the landscape gets. By the time visitors reach the coastal resort town of Coffs Harbour, temperatures have noticeably increased, and banana palms and sugar-cane plantations start to appear.

Along the coast, you'll find excellent fishing and some superb beaches, most of them virtually deserted. Inland, the Great Dividing Range, which separates the wetter eastern plains from the dry interior, throws up rainforests, extinct volcanoes, and hobby farms growing tropical fruit as you head farther north toward Queensland. Along the way are a series of national parks, most of them requiring detours of several kilometers. Those you shouldn't miss include the **Dorrigo** and **Mount Warning** national parks, both of which encompass some of the country's best and most accessible rainforests.

PORT MACQUARIE

423km (262 miles) N of Sydney

Port Macquarie (pop. 28,000), about halfway between Sydney and the Queensland border, boasts some fabulous beaches; Flynn's Beach in particular is a haven for surfers. Boating and fishing are other popular pastimes. It used to be a penal colony for convicts who found life in Sydney Cove a touch too easy.

ESSENTIALS

GETTING THERE From Sydney, motorists follow the Pacific Highway and then the Sydney-Newcastle Freeway (F3). **Eastern Australia Airways** (✆ **02/9691 2333**) flies between Sydney and Port Macquarie. The coach trip from Sydney takes about 7 hours.

VISITOR INFORMATION The **Port Macquarie Visitor Information Centre,** at the corner of Clarence and Hay streets, under the Civic Centre (✆ **1800/025 935** in Australia, or 02/6581 8000; www.portmacquarieinfo.com.au), is open Monday through Friday from 8:30am to 5pm and Saturday and Sunday from 9am to 4pm.

EXPLORING THE AREA

The Billabong Koala and Wildlife Park, 61 Billabong Dr., Port Macquarie (✆ **02/6585 1060**), is a family-owned nature park where you can get up close to hand-raised koalas, kangaroos, emus, wombats, many types of birds, and fish. You can pat (but not hold) the koalas at 10:30am, 1:30pm, and 3:30pm. There are also barbecue facilities, picnic grounds, and a restaurant. Allow 2 hours to fully experience this recommended wildlife park. It's open daily from 9am to 5pm; admission is A$15 (US$12/UK£6) for adults and A$6 (US$4.80/UK£2.40) for children.

The 257-passenger vessel ***Port Venture*** (✆ **02/6583 3058**) offers a 2-hour scenic cruise on the Hastings River. It leaves from the wharf at the end of Clarence Street Tuesday and Thursday through Sunday at 10am and 2pm. Cruises cost A$25 (US$20/UK£10) for adults, A$12 (US$9.60/UK£4.80) for children 6 to 14, and A$65 (US$39/UK£20) for families. Reservations are essential. The boat also travels up the river on a 5-hour Barbecue Cruise most Wednesdays at 10am. It docks at a private bush park along the way, and passengers can tuck into a traditional Aussie barbecue of steaks, fish, and salad. You can then fish, take a bushwalk, swim, or take a 20-minute four-wheel-drive trip. The cruise costs A$60 (US$48/UK£24) for adults, A$20 (US$16/UK£8) for children, and A$120 (US$96/UK£48) for families. A 4-hour cruise leaves on Wednesdays, when the 5-hour cruise isn't running, also at 10am. It costs A$40 (US$32/UK£16) for adults, A$20 (US$16/UK£8) for children, and A$100 (US$80/UK£40) for families.

WHERE TO STAY

El Paso Motor Inn Right on the waterfront, the El Paso offers a bit-better-than-standard motel-type rooms; the more expensive deluxe doubles are a little larger and have newer furniture. Two rooms have Jacuzzis, and some come with kitchenettes. The third-floor three-room suite has good ocean views and a kitchenette.

29 Clarence St., Port Macquarie, NSW 2444. ✆ **1800/027 965** in Australia, or 02/6583 1944. Fax 02/6584 1021. 53 units. A$115 (US$92/UK£46) standard double; A$129 (US$103/UK£52) deluxe double; A$195 (US$156/UK£78) Jacuzzi room; A$129 (US$103/UK£52) suite. Extra person A$10 (US$8/UK£4). A$30 (US$24/UK£12) surcharge per room per night Easter, Christmas, and some long weekends. DC, MC, V. **Amenities:** Restaurant; bar; good-size heated outdoor pool; Jacuzzi; sauna; game room; tour desk; babysitting; nonsmoking rooms. *In room:* A/C, TV, minibar, coffeemaker, hair dryer, iron/ironing board.

COFFS HARBOUR: BANANA CAPITAL OF AUSTRALIA

554km (344 miles) N of Sydney; 427km (265 miles) S of Brisbane

Rainforests, beaches, and sand surround the relaxed capital of Australia's Holiday Coast, the state's "banana republic" headquarters—the area used to produce more bananas than any area in Australia (but you have to go farther north for the huge plantations these days). It's still bordered by hillsides furrowed with rows of banana palms, though. Farther inland, the rolling hills plateau into Dorrigo National Park, one of the best examples of accessible rainforests anywhere. Also inland is the Nymboida River, known for its excellent white-water rafting.

Coffs Harbour is a rather disjointed place, with an old town-center retail area; the Jetty Strip (with restaurants and fishing boats) near the best swimming spot, Park Beach; and a new retail area called the Plaza. Wide sweeps of suburbia separate the three areas; it's a difficult town to negotiate if you don't have a car.

ESSENTIALS

GETTING THERE It takes around 7 hours to drive from Sydney to Coffs Harbour without stops; from Brisbane it takes around 5 hours. The Pacific Highway in this region is notoriously dangerous; many serious accidents have involved drivers enduring long hours behind the wheel. Ongoing road-widening projects should improve things. **Qantas** (✆ **13 13 13** in Australia) flies nonstop to Coffs Harbour from Sydney. Several coach companies, including **Greyhound Australia** (✆ **13 14 99** in Australia, or 07/4690 9950; www.greyhound.com.au), make the trip from Sydney in about 9 hours. A **Countrylink** (✆ **13 22 32** in Australia) train from Sydney costs A$79 (US$63/UK£32).

VISITOR INFORMATION The **Coffs Harbour Visitors Information Centre** (© **1300/369 070** in Australia, or 02/6652 1522; www.coffscoast.com.au) is just off the Pacific Highway, at the corner of Grafton and McLean streets. It's open daily from 9am to 5pm. A good general website is www.holidaycoast.com.au.

GETTING AROUND If you don't have a car, you can get around on **Coffs Harbour Coaches** (© **02/6652 2877**), which runs day trips around the local area on weekdays.

VISITING THE BIG BANANA & OTHER THINGS TO DO

You can't miss the 10m (33-ft.) reinforced-concrete banana alongside the highway at the **Big Banana Theme Park** (© **02/6652 4355;** www.bigbanana.com), 3km (2 miles) north of town. The adjoining park offers ice-skating and other attractions. It's open daily from 9am to 4:30pm (3pm in winter). Admission to the Big Banana is free. I had my doubts about this place before I visited, but I ended up charmed—even if it was simply by the wackiness of the place.

The **Coffs Harbour Zoo** (© **02/6656 1330**), 10 minutes north of town on the Pacific Highway, has plenty of koalas, as well as wombats, kangaroos, dingoes, Tasmanian devils, water birds, and aviaries. The award-winning native gardens are full of wild birds expecting a feed. The zoo is open daily from 8:30am to 4pm. Admission is A$15 (US$12/UK£6) for adults, A$7.50 (US$6/UK£3) for children, and A$35 (US$28/UK£14) for families.

A free natural attraction is **Mutton Bird Island,** which you can get to from the Coffs Harbour jetty. A steep path leads up the side of the island, but views from the top are worth it. Between September and April the island is home to thousands of shearwaters (mutton birds), which make their nests in burrows in the ground.

If you prefer fish, try diving with gray nurse sharks, manta rays, and moray eels with **Island Snorkel and Dive** (© **02/6654 2860**) or **Dive Quest** (© **02/6654 1930**). The ***Pamela Star*** (© **02/6658 4379**) offers good-value deep-sea-fishing trips.

For a taste of gold fever, head to **George's Gold Mine,** 40km (25 miles) west of Coffs Harbour on Bushman's Range Road (© **02/6654 5355** or 02/6654 5273). You get to go into an old-time gold mine, see the "stamper battery" crushing the ore, and pan for gold yourself. The mine is open Wednesday through Sunday (daily during school and public holidays) from 10:30am to 4pm. Admission is A$10 (US$8/UK£4) for adults, A$5 (US$4/UK£2) for children, and A$28 (US$22/UK£11) for families.

Kiwi Down Under Farm (© **02/6653 4449**) is a fascinating organic farm growing kiwi fruit and macadamia nuts, among other things. No nasty sprays are used here. Free 30- to 45-minute guided tours of the property leave at 2, 3, and 4pm on weekends and school holidays. The tea shop on the premises serves amazing scones and jam and excellent vegetarian lunches. The farm is 14km (8½ miles) south of Coffs Harbour; turn off at Gleniffer Road, just south of Bonville, and follow signs for 4km (2½ miles).

EXPLORING THE RAINFORESTS & OTHER OUTDOOR ADVENTURES

Coffs Harbour's main advantage is its position as a good base for exploring the surrounding countryside. You must see the World Heritage–listed **Dorrigo National Park** ★★, 68km (42 miles) west of Coffs Harbour, via Bellingen. Perched on the Great Dividing Range that separates the lush eastern seaboard from the arid interior, the rainforest here is one of the best I've seen in Australia. (It's a pity that so much fell to the axes of early settlers.) Entry is free.

The **Dorrigo Rainforest Centre** (✆ **02/6657 2309**) is the gateway to the park and has extensive information on the rainforest. Just outside is the 21m-high (69-ft.) **Skywalk,** which offers a bird's-eye view of the forest canopy. Several walks leave from the Rainforest Centre, the Glade Picnic Area (about 1km/½ mile away), and the Never-Never Picnic Area (a 10km/6¼-mile drive along Dome Rd.). Most tracks are suitable for wheelchairs. Bring a raincoat or an umbrella; it is a rainforest, after all! The **Dorrigo Tourist Information** office (✆ **02/6657 2486**) is in the center of Dorrigo township.

One of the best tour operators in the area is the award-winning **Mountain Trails 4WD Tours** (✆ **02/6658 3333;** fax 02/6658 3299). Full-day tours that include visits to two rainforest areas and a good lunch cost A$80 (US$64/UK£32) for adults and A$60 (US$48/UK£24) for children under 16. Half-day tours of one rainforest cost A$56 (US$45/UK£23) for adults and A$40 (US$32/UK£16) for children.

For a bit more personal action, try horseback riding through the rainforest 23km (14 miles) southwest of Coffs Harbour with **Valery Trails** (✆ **02/6653 4301;** www.valerytrails.com.au). Two-hour rides leave at 10am and 2pm daily and cost A$45 (US$36/UK£18) per person. Reservations are essential.

Looking for an adrenaline rush? Then head to the **Raleigh International Raceway** (✆ **02/6655 4017**), where you can zip around the track behind the wheel of your very own go-kart. It's 23km (14 miles) south of Coffs Harbour and 3km (2 miles) along Valery Road off the Pacific Highway north of Nambucca Heads. Eleven high-speed laps cost A$27 (US$22/UK£11), and 16 cost A$38 (US$30/UK£15). It's open daily from 9am to 5pm (to 6pm in summer).

WHERE TO STAY

Coffs Harbour is a popular beachside holiday spot, with plenty of motels along the Pacific Highway offering standard roadside rooms for A$35 to A$49 (US$28–US$39/UK£14–UK£20). Vacancy signs are common outside Australian school holiday periods and the Christmas and Easter periods (when Coffs really fills up). A few to try are the **Caribbean Motel,** 353 High St., Coffs Harbour, NSW 2450 (✆ **02/6652 1500;** fax 02/6651 4158), with doubles ranging from A$55 to A$120 (US$44–US$96/UK£22–UK£48), depending on the season and the view; and the **Coffs Harbour Motor Inn,** 22 Elizabeth St., Coffs Harbour, NSW 2450 (✆ **02/6652 6388;** fax 02/6652 6493), with doubles for A$72 to A$108 (US$57–US$86/UK£29–UK£43), depending on the season.

Pelican Beach Resort Australis ★ *Value* This Bali-style resort complex is 7km (4½ miles) north of Coffs Harbour beside a long stretch of creamy sand. (The beach is dangerous for swimming.) Terraced over six levels, the resort's rooms all have balconies, and many have ocean views. Standard rooms are light and modern, with either twin or queen-size beds. Family rooms have a kitchenette, a dining area, and one queen-size and two single beds divided by a half wall. Suites have a separate bedroom, kitchenette, lounge area, and Jacuzzi. Two rooms are equipped for travelers with disabilities. The highest rates apply from December 26 through January 18. Outside in the landscaped gardens are a minigolf course and a volleyball court.

Pacific Hwy., Coffs Harbour, NSW 2450. ✆ **1300/650 464** in Australia, or 02/6653 7000. Fax 02/6653 7066. 112 units. www.australishotels.com. A$120–A$215 (US$96–US$172/UK£48–UK£86) double; A$184–A$330 (US$147–US$264/UK£74–UK£132) family room for up to 4; A$236–A$463 (US$153–US$300/UK£77–UK£150) suite. Extra person A$33 (US$26/UK£13). Ask about packages and discounts. AE, DC, MC, V. **Amenities:** Restaurant; bar; large lagoon-style pool; 3 tennis courts; exercise room; 2 Jacuzzis; sauna; children's center (weekends); game room;

concierge; tour desk; car-rental desk; 24-hr. room service; babysitting; massage; free self-service laundry; dry cleaning; nonsmoking rooms. *In room:* A/C, TV, dataport, minibar, hair dryer, iron/ironing board.

Sanctuary Motor Inn Resort If you like animals, you'll love this animal sanctuary and guesthouse complex 2km (1¼ miles) south of town. Wandering around the grounds are wallabies, kangaroos, peacocks, and several species of native birds. The rooms are comfortable; the more expensive units are larger and more recently renovated. The executive room comes with a Jacuzzi. Four units have kitchens.

Pacific Hwy., Coffs Harbour, NSW 2450. © **02/6652 2111.** Fax 02/6652 4725. www.plazahotels.com.au. 38 units. A$88 (US$70/UK£35) standard double; A$94 (US$75/UK£38) superior double; A$150 (US$120/UK£60) executive double. Extra person A$15 (US$12/UK£6). Holiday surcharge A$25 (US$20/UK£10) per room per night. Ask about Aussie auto club discounts. AE, DC, MC, V. **Amenities:** Restaurant; bar; large heated outdoor pool; minigolf; lit tennis and squash courts; Jacuzzi; sauna; room service (7–9am and 6–8pm); coin-op laundry. *In room:* A/C, TV w/free satellite channels, fridge, coffeemaker, hair dryer.

WHERE TO DINE

The Jetty on Harbour Drive is where you'll find most of the main eateries. Some good ones include the **Foreshore's Café,** 394 Harbour Dr. (© **02/6652 3127**), which serves huge breakfasts and lunches on an oceanview terrace; and **Crying Tiger,** 386 Harbour Dr. (© **02/6650 0195**), which has good Thai food at dinnertime.

Tide & Pilot Oyster Bar & Sea Grill This bi-level restaurant offers superb views out to sea and serves up great seafood. The downstairs cafe is cheaper and has tables inside and outside. A great place for bacon and eggs.

Marina Dr. © **02/6652 2811.** Reservations recommended. Main courses A$20–A$30 (US$16–US$24/UK£8–UK£12). AE, MC, V. Winter daily 9am–6pm; summer daily 9am–8pm.

BYRON BAY: A BEACH BOHEMIA ★

790km (490 miles) N of Sydney; 200km (124 miles) S of Brisbane; 78km (48 miles) SE of Murwillumbah

At the easternmost point on the Australian mainland, the sun's rays hit Byron before anywhere else. This geographical position is good for two things: It's attractive to the town's "alternative" community, and you can spot migrating whales. The humpback migration begins in May/June when they head north to warmer waters to breed, and they return south around September/October when they often come into the Bay and breach and frolic with their calves. Painters, craftspeople, glass blowers, and poets are so plentiful they almost fall from the macadamia trees. The place is loaded with float tanks, "pure body products," beauty therapists, and massage centers. Though it attracts squadrons of backpackers to its party scene and discos each summer, many of the locals simply stay at home, sipping their herbal tea and preparing for the healing light of the coming dawn. Families love Byron Bay for the beautiful beaches, and surfers flock here for some of the best waves in the world.

ESSENTIALS

GETTING THERE If you're driving up the north coast, leave the Pacific Highway at Ballina and take the scenic coast road via Lennox Head. It's around 10 hours by car from Sydney, and 2 hours from Brisbane.

Regional Express (© **13 17 13** in Australia; www.regionalexpress.com.au) flies from Sydney to Ballina, south of Byron Bay. The round-trip fare is around A$280 (US$224/UK£112). **Virgin Blue** (www.virginblue.com.au) also flies to Ballina. **Byron Bus Transfers** (© **02/6681 3354**) meets all flights and transfers to Byron Bay for A$20 (US$16/UK£8) single and A$35 (US$28/UK£14) round-trip. **Coolangatta**

Airport is 1 hour north of Byron Bay (112km/69 miles). **Countrylink** (© **13 22 32** in Australia) runs daily trains from Sydney to Byron Bay; the one-way fare is around A$98 (US$78/UK£39) for adults and A$47 (US$37/UK£19) for children, and the trip takes 13 hours. **Greyhound Australia** (© **13 14 99** in Australia, or 07/4690 9950; www.greyhound.com.au) buses from Sydney take 14 hours; the one-way coach fare is A$69 (US$55/UK£28).

ORGANIZED TOURS FROM SYDNEY An unusual way to get to Byron is on a 5-day surf safari from Sydney with **Surfaris** (© **1800/634 941** in Australia; www.surfaris.com). You can learn to surf along the way as you stop off at several beaches, camping overnight. Trips leave Sydney on Monday morning and Byron Bay on Sunday morning. The safari costs A$549 (US$439/UK£220), all-inclusive—though you need to bring a sleeping bag.

Another great trip is with **Ando's Outback Tours** (© **1800/228 828** in Australia; www.outbacktours.com.au), which operates from Sydney every Sunday. It heads inland deep into the Outback on a 5-day trip and returns to Byron Bay. Among the highlights are visits to Lightning Ridge and the wild Glengarry opal fields (see "Outback New South Wales," later in this chapter). The trip costs A$435 (US$348/UK£174). A return trip to Sydney from Byron Bay costs A$35 (US$28/UK£14).

VISITOR INFORMATION The **Byron Visitors Centre,** 80 Jonson St., Byron Bay, NSW 2481 (© **02/6680 9271;** www.visitbyronbay.com), is open daily from 9am to 5pm.

A half-hour farther south is the **Ballina Tourist Information Centre,** on the corner of Las Balsas Plaza and River Street, Ballina (© **02/6686 3484**), open daily from 9am to 5pm.

SPECIAL EVENTS Byron really goes to town during 4 days over the Easter weekend with the **East Coast Blues & Roots Festival** (www.bluesfest.com.au). Up to 30,000 people camp out to listen to up to 80 acts, including the likes of Ben Harper, Midnight Oil, and Joan Armatrading. Book tickets on the Web. On the first Sunday of every month, the extraordinary local **crafts market** brings hippies and funky performers out from the hinterland. Byron Bay is very popular over the Christmas period, so book well in advance.

HITTING THE SURF & SAND

Many accommodations in Byron Bay offer free surfboards for guests. If yours doesn't, head to the **Byron Surf Shop,** Lawson Street at the corner of Fletcher Street (© **02/6685 7536**), which rents boards. The shop can also arrange surf lessons for around A$25 (US$20/UK£10) per hour. The **Byron Bay Surf School,** 127 Jonson St. (© **1800 707 274**), offers surfing classes from A$60 (US$48/UK£24).

Wategos Beach and an area off the tip of Cape Byron called **"The Pass"** are two particularly good surf spots—and since each of the beaches faces a different direction, you are bound to find the surf is up on at least one. **Main Beach,** which stretches along the front of the town (it's actually some 50km/31 miles long), is good for swimming. West of Main Beach is **Belongil Beach,** the unofficial nudist beach (when authorities aren't cracking down on covering up). **Clarke's Beach** curves away to the east of Main Beach toward Cape Byron.

The **Cape Byron Lighthouse** on Cape Byron is one of Australia's most powerful. It's eerie to come up here at night to watch the stars and see the light reach some 40km

(25 miles) out to sea. A nice walk just south of town goes through the rainforest of the **Broken Heads Nature Reserve.**

The best place to dive around Byron Bay is at **Julian Rocks,** about 3km (2 miles) offshore. Cold currents from the south meet warmer ones from the north here, which makes it a good spot to find a large variety of marine sea life. **Byron Bay Dive Centre,** 111 Jonson St. (© **02/6685 7149;** www.byronbaydivecentre.com.au), offers a range of diving and snorkeling tours and runs dive courses, too.

EXPLORING THE HILLS & RAINFORESTS

Behind Byron you'll find hills that could make the Irish weep, as well as rainforests, waterfalls, and small farms burgeoning with tropical fruits. A good operator taking trips inland is **Forgotten Country Ecotours** (© **02/6687 7843**).

Byron Bay to Bush Tours (© **02/6685 6889** or 0418/662 684; bush@mullum.com.au) operates day trips to the hippie hangout of **Nimbin** ★—where during my last visit I was approached four times in 10 minutes by people selling marijuana—and up into the rainforest, where you visit a macadamia-nut farm and have a barbecue on the company's organic farm. The trip leaves at 11am Monday through Saturday and costs A$35 (US$28/UK£14). This company also operates trips to the Sunday market at Channon the second Sunday of each month and to the market at Bangalow on the fourth Sunday.

The **Nimbin Shuttle** (© **02/6680 9189**) operates a shuttle bus service to Nimbin from Byron Bay Monday to Saturday for A$12 (US$9.60/UK£4.80) one-way. The Nimbin Market is on every third Sunday in the month. If you like that sort of thing you could also visit the Hemp Embassy (© **02/6689 1842;** www.hempembassy.net) for all things marijuana-related. There are a couple of interesting art galleries in Nimbin, too.

WHERE TO STAY

Real-estate agents **Elders R Gordon & Sons** (© **02/6685 6222;** eldersbb@omcs.com.au) can book rooms and cottages in Byron Bay and in the hinterland. The **Byron Bay Accommodation Booking Office** (© **02/6680 8666;** www.byronbayaccom.net) is very helpful for booking places to stay before you arrive.

Arts Factory Lodge *Finds* This is a wacky kind of place. Once famous as a music club popular with American draft-dodgers during the Vietnam War, it's now big with young travelers seeking an alternative place to stay and older folk who cut their hair short years ago. Accommodations include tepees, tents, rooms made from bark strips, and funky indoor "cubes." The so-called Love Shack is more standard, and quite tropical in appearance. Workshops include didgeridoo making, massage, yoga, and even boxing! The entertainment lineup includes live music, fire shows, Aboriginal culture, and sports. A cafe serves vegetarian meals, and the property has a great outdoor pool and lush gardens.

Skinners Shoot Rd., Byron Bay, NSW 2481. © **02/6685 7709.** Fax 02/6685 8534. www.artsfactory.com.au. A$25 (US$20/UK£10) dorm; A$63 (US$52/UK£26) cube; A$70 (US$56/UK£28) Love Shack. 3-night minimum. Discounts for 5 nights. AE, DC, MC, V. **Amenities:** Cafe; outdoor pool; free use of bikes; free minibus to town.

The Byron at Byron Resort & Spa ★★★ The number-one place to stay at Byron Bay, the relatively new Byron at Byron is set within a stunning 18-hectare (45-acre) lush rainforest, just a short distance out of town. Each one-bedroom suite has a king-size bed, kitchen, separate lounge and dining area, and a plasma TV, as well as two enclosed balconies. Luxurious bathrooms have deep free-standing bathtubs and separate shower. The main building opens onto large verandas that overlook the rainforest canopy.

There are six luxurious treatment rooms, offering hot stone massages, body wraps, facials, hydrotherapy treatments, and specialized spa therapies. The large infinity pool is very inviting. You can hire bikes here, too. It's a harmonious, gorgeous place, and well worth the money.

77–79 Broken Head Rd., Suffolk Park, Byron Bay, NSW 2481. ✆ **1300 554 362.** www.byronatbyron.com.au. 92 units. A$300 (US$240/UK£120) per night. 2-night minimum. AE, DC, MC, V. **Amenities:** Restaurant; bar; 25m (82-ft.) outdoor heated pool; tennis court; gym; spa; Jacuzzi; bike hire; laundry service. *In room:* A/C, TV, minibar, coffeemaker, hair dryer, iron/ironing board.

The Byron Bay Waves Motel (The Waves) ★ This exceptional motel is only 60m (197 ft.) from Main Beach and just around the corner from the town center. Each of the standard suites comes with a queen-size bed, a marble bathroom with shower, and a king-size tub. They also have a pullout sofa bed. Toasters, in-house massage, and beauty treatments are also available. There are two State Suites: The Bay Suite has stunning beach and ocean views, and a large private terrace, while the Lawson Suite has views of the hinterland and its own private terrace, too. Each of these has a king-size bed. The penthouse is a very plush, fully self-contained one-bedroom apartment. A new beachfront terrace studio sleeps four, has great ocean views, a large plasma TV with a DVD/CD player, a king-size bed, and an enclosed courtyard with barbecue. The first room rate below is based on low season (essentially winter), and the second rate on high season (Christmas and New Year). Mid-season rates are somewhere in between.

Corner of Lawson and Middleton sts. (P.O. Box 647), Byron Bay, NSW 2481. ✆ **02/6685 5966.** Fax 02/6685 5977. www.wavesbyronbay.com.au. 20 units. A$185–A$370 (US$148–US$296/UK£75–UK£148) standard suite; A$250–A$475 (US$200–US$380/UK£100–UK£190) state suite; A$275–A$475 (US$220–US$380/UK£110–UK£190) beachfront terrace; A$400–A$650 (US$320–US$520/UK£160–UK£260) penthouse. Extra person A$50 (US$40/UK£20). AE, DC, MC, V. **Amenities:** Massage; babysitting; laundry service; nonsmoking rooms. *In room:* A/C, TV, fax, minibar, coffeemaker, hair dryer, iron/ironing board, safe.

Byron Central Apartments If you don't want to eat out all the time, then this is the place for you. The self-contained apartments come with a queen-size bed and free in-house movies. First-floor units have balconies. There are also a few loft-style apartments with separate dining, lounge, and sleeping areas. Units for people with disabilities are available. The landscaped garden has a barbecue. The apartments are a 2-minute walk from the beach and town. Rates are at their highest in the Christmas and New Year period; low season is April through September.

Byron St., Byron Bay, NSW 2481. ✆ **02/6685 8800.** Fax 02/6685 8802. www.byroncentral.com. 26 units. A$150–A$160 (US$120–US$128/UK£60–UK£65) standard apt. Ask about long-term discounts. AE, DC, MC, V. **Amenities:** Medium-size saltwater pool; coin-op laundry; nonsmoking rooms. *In room:* TV, kitchen, fridge, coffeemaker, hair dryer.

WHERE TO DINE

Byron Bay's **Jonson Street** is crammed with eateries, so you certainly won't starve.

Dish ★ MEDITERRANEAN This down-to-earth restaurant with its classical white-cloth tables and long opening onto the street scene is a Byron institution, which keeps getting better. The menu is small but enticing, and though it changes regularly, you can get an idea from a couple of regulars: the Atlantic salmon filet with roasted garlic purée, sweet corn oil, red-wine sauce, crushed new potatoes, and a confit of onion; and the filet of aged beef served with shiitake mushrooms, glazed carrots, blue cheese gratin, and tarragon.

Corner Jonson and Marvel sts. ✆ **02/6685 7320.** Reservations recommended. Main courses A$26–A$35 (US$21–US$28/UK£11–UK£14). AE, MC, V. Daily 6pm–midnight.

Fins ★★ SEAFOOD The best seafood place in Byron Bay is located in the popular Beach Hotel. The food is inspired by the chef's travels, and she uses locally caught seafood and fresh ingredients, including herbs from her own garden. The signature dish is the **Cataplana of Seafood** (for two people). It's a Southern Portuguese bouillabaisse-style dish of local seafood and potatoes poached in a saffron and star anise–flavored broth. It costs A$75 (US$60/UK£30).

In the Beach Hotel, at Bay and Jonson sts. ✆ **02/6685 5029.** Main courses A$28–A$37 (US$22–US$30/UK£11–UK£15). AE, MC, V. Daily noon–3pm and 6–10pm.

Olivo ★ CONTEMPORARY Warm service, a laid-back atmosphere, a wafer-thin room, bare-brick walls, an open kitchen, chic mirrors, and beige leather seating all add up to make Olivo one of Byron's in places to eat. Expect the likes of pork belly layered with roasted figs, and Spanish mackerel sashimi.

34 Jonson St. ✆ **02/6685 7950.** Reservations recommended. Main courses A$24–A$28 (US$19–US$22/UK£10–UK£11). AE, MC, V. Daily 6:30–9pm.

Rae's on Watego's ★ MODERN AUSTRALIAN/SEAFOOD You can't beat Rae's for its location or its food. It's right on the beach, about a 2-minute drive from the town center, and has a secluded, privileged air about it—in the nicest of ways. Inside it's all Mediterranean blue and white, perfectly complementing the waves hitting the sand. The menu changes daily, but you may find the likes of grilled Atlantic salmon, red curry of roast beef filet, braised lamb shanks, and yellowfin tuna. If you have any special dietary requirements, tell the chef, and he will go out of his way to please you. Next door to the restaurant, but part of the same establishment, is **Rae's on Watego's,** an exclusive AAA-rated five-star guesthouse offering luxury accommodations. There are seven units; prices run from A$350 (US$280/UK£140) for a double suite to A$990 (US$792/UK£396) for the penthouse suite.

Watago's Beach, Byron Bay. ✆ **02/6685 5366.** Fax 02/6685 5695. www.raes.com.au. Reservations recommended. Main courses A$30–A$35 (US$24–US$28/UK£12–UK£14) lunch, A$35–A$50 (US$28–US$42/UK£14–UK£21) dinner. AE, DC, MC, V. Daily 7–10pm; Sat–Sun noon–3pm.

MURWILLUMBAH

321km (199 miles) N of Coffs Harbour; 893km (554 miles) N of Sydney; 30km (19 miles) S of Queensland border

The main town of the Tweed Valley, Murwillumbah is a good base for touring the surrounding area, which includes **Mount Warning,** picturesque towns, and countryside dominated by sugar cane and banana.

ESSENTIALS

GETTING THERE Murwillumbah is inland from the Pacific Highway. The nearest airport is at **Coolangatta,** 34km (21 miles) away, over the Queensland border. **Countrylink** trains (✆ **13 22 42** in Australia) link Murwillumbah with Sydney, taking around 13 hours. The one-way fare is A$110 (US$88/UK£44) in standard class, A$149 (US$119/UK£60) in first class. **Greyhound Australia** (✆ **13 14 99** in Australia, or 07/4690 9950; www.greyhound.com.au) runs from Sydney to Murwillumbah; the trip takes 15 hours.

VISITOR INFORMATION The **Murwillumbah Visitors Centre,** at the corner of the Pacific Highway and Alma Street, Murwillumbah, NSW 2484 (✆ **02/6672 1340;** www.tweed-coolangatta.com), is worth visiting before heading out to see more of the Tweed Valley or the beaches to the east. Another option is the **Tweed Heads**

604-925-0618

INSON@SHAW.CA

LEN + FREDA

Visitors Centre, at the corner of Bay and Wharf streets, Tweed Heads, NSW 2485 (© **07/5536 4244**). Both are open Monday through Friday from 9am to 5pm, and Saturday from 9am to 1pm.

SEEING THE AREA

If you're looking for a Big Avocado to go with your Coffs Harbour Big Banana, head for **Tropical Fruit World,** on the Pacific Highway (© **02/6677 7222;** www.tropicalfruitworld.com.au), 15km (9½ miles) north of Murwillumbah and 15km (9½ miles) south of Coolangatta. The Tweed Valley's top attraction grows some 400 varieties of tropical fruit, which you can discover on an interesting 1½-hour tractor-train tour of the 81-hectare (200-acre) plantation, as well as on four-wheel-drive rainforest drives and riverboat rides. It's open daily from 10am to 4pm. Also on the property are a kiosk, fruit market, and gift shop. Admission to food and shopping areas is free. Guided tours cost A$30 (US$24/UK£12) for adults, A$15 (US$12/UK£6) for children 4 to 12.

The 1,154m (3,785-ft.) **Mount Warning** is part of the rim of an extinct volcano formed some 20 to 23 million years ago. You can hike around the mountain and to the top on trails in the Mount Warning World Heritage Park.

WHERE TO STAY & DINE

Crystal Creek Rainforest Retreat ★★ Crystal Creek is tucked away in a little valley of rainforest just 25 minutes by car from the Pacific Highway. Self-contained cabins skirt the edge of the rainforest that borders the Border Ranges National Park, a World Heritage Site. There are plenty of native birds, possums, echidnas, wallabies, and bandicoots around and about. Guests can swim in the cold natural pools and laze around on hammocks strung up in the bush. Cabins have two comfortable rooms, a balcony, a kitchen, a barbecue, and plenty of privacy. Two glass-terrace cabins overlook the rainforest and mountain. All rooms have a king-size bed and a double Jacuzzi—with no curtains in the bathroom, because the rainforest gives enough privacy. Several tours are offered, including four-wheel-drive rainforest tours and visits to local country markets and arts-and-crafts galleries, as well as walking tours around the property. Guests cook their own food (bring it with you) or eat at the casual restaurant.

Brookers Rd., Upper Crystal Creek, Murwillumbah, NSW 2484. © **02/6679 1591.** Fax 02/6679 1596. www.crystalcreekrainforestretreat.com.au. 7 cabins. A$285–A$345 (US$228–US$276/UK£114–UK£138) double. Ask about weekday specials. AE, DC, MC, V. Pickup service from the airport, bus, and train stations available. Children not accepted. **Amenities:** Restaurant; Jacuzzi; 24-hr. room service; massage; nonsmoking rooms. *In room:* TV, kitchen, fridge, coffeemaker, hair dryer, iron/ironing board, CD player.

THE TWEED VALLEY AFTER DARK

The clubs up here on the border of Queensland are huge and offer cheap bistro meals as well as pricier ones in more upscale restaurants, inexpensive drinks at the bar, entertainment, and hundreds of poker machines. The biggest in New South Wales is the **Twin Towns Services Club,** Wharf Street, Tweed Heads (© **07/5536 2277**). Another worth checking out is **Seagulls Rugby League Club,** Gollan Drive, Tweed Heads (© **07/5536 3433**). Major entertainers such as Tom Jones and Joe Cocker have played here over the last few years. It's open 24 hours. To gain admittance to these "private" clubs, you must sign the registration book just inside the door. Tweed Heads is 40km (25 miles), or about a 30-minute drive, from Murwillumbah.

5 South of Sydney along the Princes Highway

Two main roads lead south out of Sydney: the M5, which turns into the Hume Highway, and the Princes Highway. Both routes connect Sydney to Melbourne, but the M5/Hume Highway route is quicker. A favorite with truckers and anyone in a hurry, the M5/Hume Highway will get you to Melbourne in about 12 hours. The Princes Highway is a scenic coastal route that can get you to Melbourne in 2 days, though the many attractions along the route make it well worth taking longer.

KIAMA

119km (74 miles) S of Sydney

Kiama (pop. 10,300) is famous for its **blowhole.** In fact, there are two, a large one and a smaller one; both spurt seawater several meters into the air. The larger of the two can jet water up to 60m (197 ft.), but you need a large swell and strong southeasterly winds to force the sea through the rock fissure with enough force to achieve that height. The smaller of the two is more consistent but fares better with a good northeasterly wind.

Pick up a map from the **Kiama Visitors Centre** (see below) to guide you on a Heritage Walk through the historic district of this quaint village, where you can tour a row of National Trust workers' cottages built in 1896. There's little reason to stay the night—plenty of more scenic places await farther south.

ESSENTIALS

GETTING THERE From Sydney, travel south on the Princes Highway via the steelworks city of Wollongong. There's also regular train service from Sydney, and **Greyhound Australia** (© **13 14 99** in Australia, or 07/4690 9950; www.greyhound.com.au) coach service. The trip by coach takes about 2 hours, the train trip a little less.

VISITOR INFORMATION The **Kiama Visitors Centre,** Blowhole Point, Kiama (© **02/4232 3322;** fax 02/4226 3260; www.kiama.net/default.htm), is open daily from 9am to 5pm.

JERVIS BAY: AN OFF-THE-BEATEN-TRACK GEM ★★

182km (113 miles) S of Sydney

Booderee National Park, at Jervis Bay, is nothing short of spectacular. How does this grab you—miles of deserted beaches, the whitest sand imaginable, kangaroos you can stroke, lorikeets that mob you for food during the day and possums that do the same at night, pods of dolphins, great walks through gorgeous bushland, and a real Aboriginal spirituality-of-place? I could go on, but see for yourself. A word of warning though, just don't turn up and expect to see wildlife everywhere, and don't come if you don't like walking. Most marsupials come out in the evening, and you'll only get the best from the place if you bring your walking shoes and spend a couple of days. A car will get you from beach to beach and to various walking tracks.

ESSENTIALS

GETTING THERE It's best to reach Jervis Bay via Huskisson, 24km (15 miles) southeast of Nowra on the Princes Highway. Approximately 16km (10 miles) south of Nowra, turn left onto the Jervis Bay Road to Huskisson. The entrance to Booderee National Park—formally named Jervis Bay National Park—is just after Huskisson. It's about a 3-hour drive from Sydney. You'll probably need at least 2 days to get to know the area. Watch out for the black cockatoos.

Australian Pacific Tours (✆ **02/9247 7222;** fax 02/9247 2052; www.aptours.com.au) runs a dolphin-watching cruise to Jervis Bay from Sydney every day between early October and mid-April, and Monday and Thursday in winter. The 12-hour trip—7 hours of which are on the coach—includes a visit to the Kiama blowhole, a 3-hour luncheon cruise looking for bottlenose dolphins, and a stop on the way back at Fitzroy Falls in the Southern Highlands. The trip costs A$117 (US$94/UK£47) for adults and A$109 (US$87/UK£44) for children.

VISITOR INFORMATION For information on the area, contact the **Shoalhaven Visitors Centre,** at the corner of Princes Highway and Pleasant Way, Nowra (✆ **1800/024 261** in Australia, or 02/4421 0778; www.shoalhaven.nsw.gov.au). Pick up maps and book camping sites at the **Booderee National Park** office (✆ **02/4443 0977**), located just beyond Huskisson; it's open daily from 9am to 4pm. **Hyams Beach Store** (✆ **02/4443 0242**) has an accommodations guide listing 34 rental properties for A$100 (US$80/UK£40) and up for a weekend.

SEEING THE AREA

If you want to see the best spots, you'll need to pay the park-entrance fee of A$11 (US$8.80/UK£4.40) per day; a standard NSW National Parks Pass doesn't work here. Places to visit include **Hyams Beach** ★, reputed to have the whitest sand in the world. Notice how it squeaks when you walk on it. Wear sunscreen! The reflection off the beach can burn your skin in minutes even on a cloudy day. **Hole in the Wall Beach** has interesting rock formations and a lingering smell of natural sulfur. Secluded **Summer Cloud Bay** offers excellent fishing.

Dolphin Watch Cruises, 74 Owen St., Huskisson (✆ **1800/246 010** in Australia, or 02/4441 6311; www.dolphinwatch.com.au), runs a hardy vessel out of Huskisson on the lookout for the resident pod of bottlenose dolphins—you have "more than a 95% chance of seeing them," the company claims. A 2-hour coffee cruise runs at 10am on Saturday and Sunday, public holidays, and school holidays, and costs A$20 (US$16/UK£8) for adults and A$10 (US$8/UK£4) for children. A 2½-hour dolphin watch and bay cruise leaves at 1pm and costs A$25 (US$20/UK£10) for adults and A$12 (US$9.60/UK£4.80) for children. It's possible to see humpback and southern right whales in June and July and from mid-September to mid-November. A 3-hour whale-watch cruise costs A$40 (US$32/UK£16) for adults and A$30 (US$24/UK£12) for children.

WHERE TO STAY & DINE

If you have a tent and camping gear, all the better. **Caves Beach** is a quiet spot (except when the birds chorus at dawn) just a stroll away from a good beach; it's home to eastern gray kangaroos. A campsite here costs A$8.65 (US$6.90/UK£3.50) per tent in winter and A$11 (US$8.60/UK£4.30) in summer and on public holidays. It's about a 250m (about ⅒-mile) walk from the car park to the campground. **Greenpatch** is more dirt than grass, but you get your own area, and it's suitable for motor homes. It's infested with overfriendly possums around dusk. A camp spot here costs A$13 (US$10/UK£5) in winter and A$16 (US$13/UK£6.50) in summer.

For supplies, head to the area's main towns, **Huskisson** (pop. 930) and **Vincentia** (pop. 2,350). The **Huskisson RSL Club,** overlooking the wharf area on Owen Street (✆ **02/4441 5282**), has a good bistro and a bar. You'll have to sign in inside the main entrance. The Huskisson Hotel (also called the "Husskie Pub") is down the road and has a nice beer garden and cheapish meals at lunchtime.

Tips A Safety Warning

Jervis Bay is notorious for its car break-ins, a situation the local police force has been unable to control. If you park your car anywhere in the national park, remove all valuables, including things in the trunk.

Huskisson Beach Tourist Resort This resort is the very pinnacle of cabin accommodations on this part of the east coast. Cabins vary in price depending on size, but even the smallest has room enough for a double bed, triple bunks, and a small kitchen with microwave. Larger cabins have two separate bedrooms. There's a game room and barbecue facilities. Weekend prices are huge, so best to stay weekdays. Rates also rise significantly over Christmas and Easter.

Beach St., Huskisson, Jervis Bay, NSW 2540. ✆/fax **02/4441 5142.** www.huskissonbeachtouristresort.com.au. 38 cabins. Weekdays A$75–A$140 (US$60–US$112/UK£30–UK£56); weekends A$140–A$320 (US$112–US$256/UK£56–UK£128). DC, MC, V. **Amenities:** Small heated outdoor pool; lit tennis court; coin-op laundry; nonsmoking rooms. *In room:* TV, kitchen, fridge, coffeemaker, hair dryer, iron/ironing board.

Jervis Bay Guest House ★ This relatively new guesthouse has four distinctly different rooms (different color schemes, beds, and so on), each with a private bathroom. One room has a Jacuzzi, and two rooms face the water and have coffeemakers. Breakfast is a hearty affair that could include emu sausages and thick slabs of bacon followed by a tropical fruit platter.

1 Beach St., Huskisson, NSW 2540. ✆ **02/4441 7658.** Fax 02/4441 7659. www.jervisbayguesthouse.com.au. 4 units. A$145–A$220 (US$116–US$176/UK£58–UK£88) double. Rates include breakfast. AE, DC, MC, V. After the Jervis Bay Hotel, take the 2nd road to the left (Nowra St.) and follow it to the end. Children under 16 not accepted. **Amenities:** Lounge and game room; tour desk; massage; nonsmoking rooms. *In room:* A/C, hair dryer, iron/ironing board.

ULLADULLA

220km (136 miles) S of Sydney

Very much a supply town as well as a fishing center, especially for tuna, Ulladulla is a pleasant stopover on your journey south. This is also a good place to stock up on supplies from local supermarkets. On the outskirts of town (just to the south) are a series of saltwater lakes with good fishing, though you'll have competition from the pelicans. Inland is the giant Morton National Park, marked by the peak of Pigeonhouse Mountain. The 3- to 4-hour walk to the top and back starts at a parking lot a 30-minute drive from Ulladulla. The going is steep at first, but the trail levels out as it crosses a sandstone plateau. Another upward climb and you're rewarded with a magnificent view of peaks and ocean.

Several side roads worth exploring spur off between Ulladulla and Batemans Bay (see below). These lead to the tiny villages of Bawley Point and Kioloa, where holiday cottages nestle between isolated beaches, gum forests, and green patches studded with gray kangaroos.

There are more kangaroos at pristine **Pebbly Beach** ★ in Murramarang National Park, a short hop—20 minutes south—of Ulladulla. The furry creatures actually wander around the beach and adjacent campsite, or gather on the grassy dunes to graze. It's a good area for birding, too.

ESSENTIALS

GETTING THERE Ulladulla is about a 3-hour drive from Sydney Central Business District down the Pacific Highway.

VISITOR INFORMATION **Ulladulla Visitors Centre,** Civic Center, Princes Highway (✆ **02/4455 1269;** www.shoalhaven.nsw.gov.au), is open Monday through Friday from 10am to 5pm, Saturday and Sunday from 9am to 5pm.

WHERE TO STAY & DINE

Ulladulla is well known for its food (particularly seafood and beef) and wine (there are a few boutique wineries in the area). For some of the best fish in Australia, head to one of the fish-and-chips shops on Wason Street, close to the harbor. The best is **Tiger Fish and Chips** (no phone). On the same street is **Torys Takeaway** (✆ **02/4454 0888**), where you can buy good fish and chips on the ground floor for about a third of the price at the very nice restaurant above (**Torys Seafood Restaurant;** open in the evenings; same number) and stroll down to the harbor to eat among the seagulls.

Ulladulla Guest House ★★★ This fabulous, award-winning property is one of the best places to stay in Australia. Run by the friendly Andrew and Elizabeth Nowosad—try and guess his accent—the Ulladulla Guest House is an impressive AAA-rated five-star establishment. It's surrounded by small but lovely tropical gardens—Andrew insists his coconut palms are the only ones this far south—and overlooks the harbor. Unusually, the house is also a registered art gallery, and the walls are festooned with paintings for sale. Past the cozy lounge are three types of rooms. Two self-contained units with private entrances to the garden are the lowest in price. The one-bedroom unit has a queen-size bed and a fold-out sofa bed, and the two-bedroom unit has a double bed in one room, two singles in another, and a double foldout sofa bed in the lounge. Luxury rooms have a queen-size bed, custom-made furniture, and original artwork. Executive rooms come with a marble bathroom and a Jacuzzi. There are three masseurs on standby. In the rates listed below, peak periods are weekends, public holidays, Easter, and Christmas school holidays. The hotel prides itself on its food, too.

39 Burrill St., Ulladulla, NSW 2539. ✆ **02/4455 1796.** Fax 02/4454 4660. www.guesthouse.com.au. 10 units. Garden room A$208 (US$166/UK£83); luxury room A$228 (US$182/UK£91); family room or executive room A$278 (US$222/UK£111). 2-night minimum on weekends. 3-course dinner A$50 (US$40/UK£20). AE, DC, MC, V. **Amenities:** Restaurant; lagoon-style heated outdoor pool; golf course nearby; exercise room; Jacuzzi; watersports equipment rental; bike rental; room service (7am–10pm); in-room massage; babysitting; laundry service; dry cleaning; nonsmoking rooms. *In room:* A/C, TV, fax, dataport, fridge, coffeemaker, hair dryer, iron/ironing board.

BATEMANS BAY

275km (171 miles) S of Sydney

This laid-back holiday town offers good surfing beaches, arts-and-crafts galleries, boat trips up the Clyde River, good game fishing, and bushwalks in the Morton and Deua national parks.

ESSENTIALS

GETTING THERE Batemans Bay is a 3- to 4-hour drive from Sydney, depending on the traffic. (Avoid leaving Sydney at rush hour, and prepare for long delays on holidays.) **Premier Motor Service** (✆ **1300/368 100** in Australia, or 02/4423 5233) runs coaches to Batemans Bay from Sydney's Central Station.

VISITOR INFORMATION **Batemans Bay Visitor Information Centre,** at the corner of Princes Highway and Beach Road (✆ **1800/802 528** in Australia, or 02/4472 6800), is open daily from 9am to 5pm.

GAME FISHING & A RIVER CRUISE

If you fancy some serious fishing, contact **OB1 Charters,** Marina, Beach Road, Batemans Bay (✆ **1800/641 065** in Australia, 02/4471 2738, or 0416/241 586 mobile; www.southcoast.com.au/ob1). The company runs full-day game-fishing trips and morning snapper-fishing trips (afternoon snapper trips in summer, too). Expect to encounter black marlin, blue marlin, giant kingfish, mako sharks, albacore tuna, yellowfin tuna, and blue tuna from November through June. The trip includes all tackle, bait, and afternoon and morning tea, but you must provide your own lunch. It costs A$900 (US$720/UK£360) to hire the six-person boat for the day; if there are just a couple of you, the charter company may be able to fill the rest of the boat if you make reservations far enough in advance. Trips to catch snapper (a nice-tasting fish, which is not the same as red snapper) include all gear, bait, and morning or afternoon tea for A$80 (US$64/UK£32) per person; these last about 6 hours.

A river cruise on **MV *Merinda,*** Innes Boatshed, Orient Street, Batemans Bay (✆ **02/4472 4052;** fax 02/4472 4754), is a pleasant experience. The 3-hour cruise leaves at 11:30am daily and travels inland past townships, forests, and farmland. It costs A$22 (US$18/UK£9) for adults, A$11 (US$8.80/UK£4.40) for children, and A$50 (US$40/UK£20) for families; a fish-and-chips lunch is A$6 (US$4.80/UK£2.40) extra, and a seafood basket for two is A$12 (US$9.60/UK£4.80).

A NICE PLACE TO STAY

The Bay Soldiers Esplanade Motor Inn ★ *Kids* This AAA-rated four-star motel right on the Batemans Bay river estuary has fabulous views and is close to the town center. Rooms are light and well furnished, and all have balconies (some with water views). Some doubles and suites have Jacuzzis; they cost the same as non-Jacuzzi rooms, so specify if you want one when booking. Eat at the hotel's restaurant or at the Batemans Bay Soldiers' Club, just opposite, which has a restaurant, a bistro, cheap drinks, and a free evening kids' club.

23 Beach Rd. (P.O. Box 202), Batemans Bay, NSW 2536. ✆ **1800/659 884** in Australia, or 02/4472 0200. Fax 02/4472 0277. www.esplanade.com.au. 23 units. A$115–A$139 (US$92–US$111/UK£46–UK£55) double (the 2nd rate is for a room with water views); A$167–A$241 (US$133–US$193/UK£67–UK£97) suite. Extra person A$12 (US$9.60/UK£4.80). Children under 18 stay free in parent's room. AE, DC, MC, V. **Amenities:** Restaurant; coin-op laundry; nonsmoking rooms. *In room:* A/C, TV, kitchenette, fridge, coffeemaker, hair dryer, iron/ironing board.

NAROOMA ★

345km (214 miles) SW of Sydney

Narooma is a seaside town with beautiful deserted beaches, a golf course right on a headland, a natural rock formation in the shape of Australia (popular with camera-wielding tourists), and excellent fishing. However, its major attraction is **Montague Island** ★★, the breeding colony for thousands of shearwaters (or mutton birds, as they're also called) and a hangout for juvenile seals.

Just 18km (11 miles) farther south is **Central Tilba** ★, one of the prettiest towns in Australia and the headquarters of the boutique ABC Cheese Factory. You'll kick yourself if you miss this charming historic township (pop. 35; 1 million visitors annually).

Waltzing the Tilbas

The south coast of New South Wales hides two little gems between hills the color of emeralds. It's hard to believe we're in Australia; the countryside is just so remarkably green. The rolling hills in front of us are studded with contented cows. Frogs are croaking from the verges in the valley, and a couple of long-neck turtles are stumbling across the laneway toward the creek. We are sitting on a wide veranda belonging to a charming bed-and-breakfast stopover called **Green Gables** (269 Corkhill Dr., Tilba Tilba; ✆ **02/4473 7435**; www.greengables.com.au; A$140 (US$112/UK£56) per night, extra person A$20–A$40 (US$16–US$32/UK£8–UK£16). This former Temperance Hall was built in 1879 to serve the gold rush town of tiny Tilba Tilba.

From across the road at the historic Pam's Store you can start off on the Tilba Tilba Track, which leads to the top of Gulaga (or Mount Dromedary). This ancient extinct volcano is heavily wooded and topped with rainforest. It's a moderate walk, with some relatively steep sections toward the top. Allow 5 hours return. The mountain is the spiritual heart of the local Yuin Aboriginal people. The highlight of Tilba Tilba itself is **Foxglove Spires** (open to the public daily; admission A$7.50/US$6/UK£3), a complex of businesses including antiques and gift shops, a fabulous cafe, a gorgeous nursery specializing in rare herbs and perennials, and one of the best open gardens in Australia. The gardens are set around a 100-year-old cottage, and run to nearly 1.6 hectares (4 acres) of flower beds, oak trees, rambling roses, and half-wild fruit trees. Areas of note include a secluded woodland that tumbles downhill to a large swampy frog pond, and a long shady arbor of trained Manchurian pears. The colors are amazing in autumn. Plan your whole day around lunch at the associated **Love at First Bite Café** (✆ **02/4473 7055**). This is a seriously good eatery, with a wood-dominated interior, groovy jazz, and a huge range of meals including gourmet sandwiches and fresh vegetable and fruit juices. Standout dishes include the Thai chicken laksa and a legendary lentil burger.

A short drive away is **Central Tilba**—like its smaller twin it's classified as a heritage village under the National Trust. The quaint wooden buildings here make it perhaps the most attractive of all the historic settlements in Australia. We soon had a soft spot for the village's **Old Time Lolly Shop,** and just loved the warm feeling of the **Tilba Teapot Café.** We tried on clothes shipped in from Nepal and smelled incense sticks, new leather, and the best homemade pies around. There were antiques stores and art galleries, and shops selling crystals and jewelry. Our favorite was the **Tilba Woodturning Gallery,** which specializes in carved bowls, wind chimes, rocking horses, and so much more. We left with fine-spun jumpers from the **Tilba Alpaca Shop,** Tilba Famous Fudge from the general store, and some Applebox Smoke and Summer Herb cheeses from the famous **ABC Cheese Factory.** With a bottle or two from Tilba Valley Wines, and a loaf of granary bread from the local bakery, we were well set up for tomorrow's lunch. We'd follow it with a snooze to the tune of mooing cows perhaps. After all, that's what a real getaway is all about.

For more information, visit **www.tilba.com.au**.

ESSENTIALS

GETTING THERE Narooma is a 7-hour drive from Sydney down the Princes Highway. **Premier Motor Service** (✆ **1300/368 100** in Australia, or 02/4423 5233) runs coaches to Narooma from Sydney's Central Station.

VISITOR INFORMATION The **Narooma Visitors Centre,** Princes Highway, Narooma (✆ **1800 240 003** in Australia, or 02/4476 2881; fax 02/4476 1690; www.naturecoast-tourism.com.au), is open daily from 9am to 5pm.

WHAT TO SEE & DO: WHALES, GOLF & MORE

A must if you're visiting the area is a boat tour with **Narooma Charters** (✆ **02/4476 2240;** www.naroomacharters.com.au). It offers spectacular tours of the coast on the lookout for dolphins, seal colonies, and little penguins, and also includes a tour of Montague Island. Morning and afternoon tours take 3½ hours and cost A$99 (US$40/UK£20) for adults, A$88 (US$70/UK£35) for children. A 4½-hour tour includes some of the world's best whale-watching (between mid-Sept and early Dec) and costs the same. The last time I went on this trip, we saw no fewer than eight humpback whales, some of them mothers with calves. The company also offers game fishing from February to the end of June and standard fishing trips of 4 hours for A$89 (US$71/UK£36) for adults and A$79 (US$63/UK£32) for kids. A full-day's fishing costs A$195 (US$156/UK£78) for adults and A$175 (US$140/UK£70) for kids. You may also see giant fish-eating gray nurse sharks, dolphins, and even orcas. Dives cost A$77 (US$61/UK£31) for a double dive. Ask about family prices.

Narooma Golf Club, Narooma (✆ **02/4476 2522**), has one of the most interesting and challenging coastal courses in Australia. A round of golf will cost you A$25 (US$20/UK£10).

While you're in the area, I recommend stopping off at the **Umbarra Aboriginal Cultural Centre** ★, Wallaga Lake, off the Princes Highway on Bermagui Road (✆ **02/4473 7232;** umbarra@acr.net.au). It's 20km (12 miles) south of Narooma. The center offers activities such as boomerang throwing, spear throwing, and painting with natural ochers for A$6.25 (US$5/UK£2.50) per person, or A$20 (US$16/UK£8) per family. There are also discussions, Aboriginal archival displays, and a retail store. It's open Monday through Friday from 9am to 5pm, Saturday and Sunday from 9am to 4pm (closed Sun in winter). The center's guides also offer 2- to 4-hour four-wheel-drive/walking trips of nearby **Mount Dromedary** ★ and **Mumbulla Mountain,** taking in sacred sites. The tours cost A$45 (US$36/UK£18) per person. Reservations are essential.

If you want to attempt Mount Dromedary without a guide, ask for directions in Narooma. The hike to the top takes around 3 hours.

WHERE TO STAY

Whale Motor Inn ★ This nice, quiet motor inn has the best panoramic ocean views on the south coast and the largest rooms in town. Standard rooms have a queen-size bed and a single-person sofa bed. Standard suites have a separate bedroom, two sofa beds, and a kitchenette. Spacious executive and Jacuzzi suites are better furnished, and have a kitchenette and a balcony or patio.

Princes Hwy., Narooma, NSW 2546. ✆ **02/4476 2411.** Fax 02/4476 1995. www.whalemotorinn.com.au. 17 units. A$90–A$145 (US$72–US$116/UK£36–UK£58). Extra person A$10 (US$8/UK£4). AE, DC, MC, V. **Amenities:** Restaurant; small unheated outdoor pool; nonsmoking rooms. *In room:* A/C, TV, fridge, coffeemaker, hair dryer, iron/ironing board.

MERIMBULA

480km (298 miles) S of Sydney; 580km (360 miles) NE of Melbourne

This seaside resort (pop. approximately 7,000) is the last place of interest before the Princes Highway crosses the border into Victoria. Merimbula is a good center from which to discover the surrounding **Ben Boyd National Park** and **Mimosa Rocks National Park;** both offer bushwalking. Another park, **Bournda National Park,** surrounds a lake and has good walking trails and a surf beach.

Golf is the game of choice in Merimbula, and the area's most popular venue is the **Pambula-Merimbula Golf Club** (© **02/6495 6154**). You can spot kangaroos grazing on the fairways of the 27-hole course. It costs A$14 (US$11/UK£5) for 9 holes, or A$25 (US$20/UK£10) for the day. Another favorite is **Tura Beach Country Club** (© **02/6495 9002**), which is known for its excellent coastal views. A round of 18 holes costs A$20 (US$16/UK£8).

Eden, 20km (13 miles) south of Merimbula, was once a major whaling port. The rather gruesome **Eden Killer Whale Museum,** on Imlay Street in Eden (© **02/6496 2094;** www.killerwhalemuseum.com.au), is the only reason to stop here. It has a dubious array of relics, including boats, axes, and remnants of the last of the area's killer whales, called Old Tom. The museum is open Monday through Saturday from 9:15am to 3:45pm, Sunday from 11:15am to 3:45pm. In January it's open daily from 9:15am to 4:45pm. Admission is A$6 (US$4.80/UK£2.40) for adults and A$2 (US$1.60/UK80p) for children. You can still see a scattering of whales off the coast in October and November.

ESSENTIALS

GETTING THERE The drive from either Sydney or Melbourne takes about 7 hours. The **Greyhound Australia** (© **13 14 99** in Australia, or 07/4690 9950; www.greyhound.com.au) bus trip from Sydney takes more than 8 hours.

VISITOR INFORMATION The **Merimbula Tourist Information Centre,** Beach Street, Merimbula (© **1800/150 457** in Australia, or 02/6495 1129; fax 02/6495 1250), is open daily from 9am to 5pm (10am–4pm in winter).

SPECIAL EVENTS Jazz fans should head for the **Merimbula Jazz Festival** held over the long Queens Birthday weekend, the second weekend in June. A country-music festival takes place the last weekend in October.

WHERE TO STAY

Ocean View Motor Inn This pleasant motel has good water views from 12 of its rooms (the best are nos. 9, 10, and 11). The rooms are spacious and modern, with plain brick walls, patterned carpets, and one long balcony serving the top six rooms. Fourteen units have kitchenettes. All have showers. It's a friendly place. Breakfast is delivered to your room for A$7.70 (US$6.15/UK£3.10) extra.

Merimbula Dr. and View St., Merimbula, NSW 2548. © **02/6495 2300.** Fax 02/6495 3443. www.oceanviewmotorinn.com.au. 20 units. A$70–A$125 (US$56–US$100/UK£28–UK£50) double. Higher rate at Christmas and Easter. Extra person A$11 (US$8.80/UK£4.40). MC, V. **Amenities:** Medium-size solar-heated outdoor pool; limited room service; babysitting; coin-op laundry; nonsmoking rooms. *In room:* A/C, TV, kitchenette, fridge, coffeemaker.

6 The Snowy Mountains: Australia's Ski Country (★

Thredbo: 519km (322 miles) SW of Sydney; 208km (129 miles) SW of Canberra; 543km (337 miles) NE of Melbourne

Made famous by Banjo Paterson's 1890 poem "The Man from Snowy River," the Snowy Mountains are most commonly used for what you'd least expect in Australia—skiing. It starts to snow around June and carries on until September. During this time hundreds of thousands of people flock here to ski at the major ski resorts—Thredbo and Perisher Blue, and, to a lesser extent, Charlotte Pass and Mount Selwyn. It's certainly different skiing here, with ghostly white gum trees as the obstacles instead of pine trees.

The whole region is part of the **Kosciuszko** (pronounced Ko-zi-*os*-co) **National Park,** the largest alpine area in Australia. During the summer months the park is a beautiful place for walking, and in spring the profusion of wildflowers is exquisite. A series of lakes in the area, including the one in the resort town of Jindabyne, are favorites with trout fishermen.

Visitors stay in **Jindabyne,** 62km (38 miles) south of Cooma, or **Thredbo Village,** 36km (22 miles) southwest of Jindabyne. Jindabyne is a bleak-looking resort town on the banks of the man-made Lake Jindabyne, which came into existence when the Snowy River was dammed to provide hydroelectric power.

Thredbo Village is set in a valley of Mount Crackenback and resembles European-style resorts. From here, the Crackenback Chairlift provides access to an easy-grade pathway that leads to the top of Mount Kosciuszko, which at 2,228m (7,308 ft.) is Australia's highest peak. The mountain has stunning views of the alpine region and some good walks.

SNOWY MOUNTAIN ESSENTIALS

GETTING THERE From Sydney, take the Eastern Distributor road toward Sydney Airport and turn right just before the planes, following the signs to Wollongong, and then Canberra, on the M5 motorway and the Hume Highway. Follow the Hume Highway south to Goulburn, where you turn onto the Federal Highway toward Canberra. From there take the Monaro Highway to Cooma, then follow the Alpine Way through Jindabyne and on to Thredbo. Tire chains may be necessary on the slopes in winter and can be rented from local service stations. The trip takes around 6 hours from Sydney with short breaks.

Qantas (© **13 13 13** in Australia) has daily flights from Sydney to Cooma. A connecting bus to the ski fields takes about 1 hour and operates from June through October. It's run by **Snowy Mountain Hire Cars** (© **02/6456 2957**) and costs A$48 (US$38/UK£19) one-way.

In winter only (around June 19–Oct 5), **Greyhound Australia** (© **13 14 99** in Australia, or 07/4690 9950; www.greyhound.com.au) operates daily buses between Sydney and Cooma, via Canberra. The journey takes around 7 hours from Sydney and 3 hours from Canberra. A one-way ticket costs around A$50 (US$40/UK£20).

VISITOR INFORMATION Pick up information about the ski fields and accommodations options at the **Cooma Visitors Centre,** 119 Sharp St., Cooma, NSW 2630 (© **02/6450 1740;** fax 02/6450 1798); or at the **Snowy Region Visitor Centre,** Kosciuszko Road, Jindabyne, NSW 2627 (© **02/6450 5600;** fax 02/6456 1249; srvc@npws.nsw.gov.au). A good website is **www.perisherblue.com.au.**

HITTING THE SLOPES & OTHER ADVENTURES

Obviously, skiing is the most popular activity here. More than 50 ski lifts serve the fields of Perisher Valley, Mount Blue Cow, Smiggins Holes, and Guthega. Perisher Valley offers the best overall slopes; Mount Blue Cow is generally very crowded; Smiggins Holes offers good slopes for beginners; and Guthega has nice light, powdery snow and is less crowded. Thredbo has some very challenging runs and the longest downhill runs, but I prefer Perisher for atmosphere. A day's ski pass costs around A$87 (US$69/UK£35) for adults, A$48 (US$38/UK£19) for children 6 to 14.

> *Tips* **Ski Condition Updates**
>
> For up-to-date ski field information, call the **Snowy Region Visitor Centre** (**✆ 02/6450 5600**).

A ski-tube train midway between Jindabyne and Thredbo on the Alpine Way travels through the mountains to Perisher Valley and then to Blue Cow. (A "ski-tube train" is a train that goes through a mountain tunnel.) It costs A$34 (US$27/UK£19) return for adult skiers and A$19 (US$15/UK£7.50) for kids. Ski gear can be rented at numerous places in Jindabyne and Thredbo.

In summer, the region is popular for hiking, canoeing, fishing, and golf. Thredbo Village has tennis courts, a 9-hole golf course, and mountain-bike trails.

WHERE TO STAY

You'll have to book months ahead to find a place during the ski season (especially on weekends). And don't expect to find a lot of bargains. The **Kosciuszko Accommodation Centre,** Nuggets Crossing, Jindabyne, NSW 2627 (**✆ 1800/026 354** in Australia, or 02/6456 2022; fax 02/6456 2945), can help you find and book accommodations in the area. Other private agents who can help find you a spot for the night include the **Snowy Mountains Reservation Centre** (**✆ 02/6456 2633**) and the **Thredbo Resort Centre** (**✆ 1800/020 622** in Australia).

IN THREDBO

Riverside Cabins These self-contained studio and one-bedroom cabins sit above the Thredbo River and overlook the Crackenback Range. They're also a short walk from the Thredbo Alpine Hotel and local shops. Most rooms have balconies. Rates vary wildly from weekday to weekend and season to season.

Thredbo, NSW 2625. **✆ 02/6459 4196** in Australia, or 02/6459 4299. Fax 02/6459 4195. www.thredbo.com. 36 units. Winter A$160–A$516 (US$128–US$412/UK£65–UK£206) double; summer A$117–A$164 (US$94–US$131/UK£47–UK£66) double. Ask about weekly rates. AE, DC, MC, V. *In room:* TV, kitchen, fridge, coffeemaker, hair dryer, iron/ironing board, coin-op laundry.

Thredbo Alpine Apartments These apartments are very similar to the Riverside Cabins (see above) and are managed by the same people. All have balconies with mountain views. Some have queen-size beds. There's limited daily maid service, and free in-room movies. Winter rates apply from July 30 through September 2.

Thredbo, NSW 2628. **✆ 1800/026 333** in Australia, or 02/6459 4299. Fax 02/6459 4195. 35 units. Winter weekends A$210–A$441 (US$168–US$353/UK£84–UK£178) 1-bedroom apt, A$289–A$628 (US$231–US$502/UK£116–UK£251) 2-bedroom apt, A$394–A$770 (US$315–US$616/UK£157–UK£308) 3-bedroom apt, weekday rates about 20% cheaper; summer A$127–A$164 (US$101–US$131/UK£51–UK£66) 1-bedroom apt, A$159–A$190 (US$127–US$152/UK£65–UK£76) 2-bedroom apt, A$180–A$210 (US$144–US$16/UK£72–UK£8) 3-bedroom apt. Ask about weekly rates. AE, DC, MC, V. Covered parking. **Amenities:** Coin-op laundry. *In room:* TV, kitchen, fridge, coffeemaker, hair dryer, iron/ironing board.

Moments In the Footsteps of the Man from Snowy River

Horseback riding is a popular activity for those wanting to ride like the "Man from Snowy River." **Reynella Kosciusko Rides,** in Adamanaby, 44km (27 miles) northwest of Cooma (✆ **1800/029 909** in Australia, or 02/6454 2386; fax 02/6454 2530; www.reynellarides.com.au), offers multinight rides through the Kosciuszko National Park from October to the end of April. Three-day, 4-night rides cost around A$799 (US$639/UK£320), and the 5-day, 6-night ride A$1,207 (US$965/UK£483). Transfers from Cooma cost around A$35 (US$28/UK£14) each way. The trips are all-inclusive and include camping and homestead accommodations. Shorter rides are offered by **Jindabyne Trail Rides** (✆ **02/6456 2421**; fax 02/6456 1254). Gentle, 1½-hour rides on the slopes above Jindabyne cost A$25 (US$20/UK£10) per person.

Thredbo Alpine Hotel After the skiing is finished for the day, the center of activity in Thredbo is this large resort-style lodge. Rooms vary; those on the top floor of the three-story hotel have a king-size bed instead of a standard queen-size. The rooms are all wood-paneled and have free in-house movies. Thredbo's only nightclub is here.
P.O. Box 80, Thredbo, NSW 2625. ✆ **02/6459 4200.** Fax 02/6459 4201. www.thredbo.com.au. 65 units. Winter A$198–A$498 (US$158–US$396/UK£79–UK£200) double; summer A$129–A$189 (US$103–US$151/UK£52–UK£76) double. Rates include breakfast. Ask about weekly rates and packages. AE, DC, MC, V. **Amenities:** 2 restaurants; bistro; 4 bars; heated outdoor pool; golf course nearby; 3 lit tennis courts; Jacuzzi; sauna; tour desk; massage; room service (winter only); coin-op laundry; nonsmoking rooms. *In room:* TV/VCR, minibar, coffeemaker, hair dryer.

7 Outback New South Wales

The Outback is a powerful Australian image. Hot, dusty, and prone to flies, it can also be a romantic place where wedge-tailed eagles float in the shimmering heat as you spin in a circle, tracing the unbroken horizon. If you drive out here, you have to be constantly on the lookout for emus, large flightless birds that dart across roads open-beaked and wide-eyed. When you turn off the car engine, it's so quiet you can hear the scales of a sleepy lizard, as long as your forearm, scraping the rumpled track as it turns to taste the air with its long, blue tongue.

The scenery is a huge canvas with a restricted palette: blood red for the dirt, straw yellow for the blotches of Mitchell grass, searing blue for the surreally large sky. There is room to be yourself in the Outback, and you'll soon find that personalities often tilt toward the eccentric. It's a hardworking place, too, where miners and sheep and cattle farmers try to eke out a living in Australia's hard center.

BROKEN HILL ★★

1,157km (717 miles) W of Sydney; 508km (315 miles) NE of Adelaide

At heart, Broken Hill—or "Silver City," as it's been nicknamed—is still very much a hardworking, hard-drinking mining town. Its beginnings date to 1883, when the trained eye of a boundary rider named Charles Rasp noticed something odd about the craggy rock outcrops at a place called the Broken Hill. He thought he saw deposits of tin, but they turned out to be silver and lead. Today, the city's main drag, Argent Street, bristles with finely crafted colonial mansions, heritage homes, hotels, and public buildings. Look deeper and you see the town's quirkiness. Around one corner you'll find the radio station, built to resemble a giant wireless set with round knobs for windows, and around another the headquarters of the Housewives Association, which ruled the town with an iron apron for generations. Then there's the Palace Hotel—made famous in the movie *The Adventures of Priscilla, Queen of the Desert*—with its high painted walls and a mural of Botticelli's *Birth of Venus* on the ceiling two flights up.

Traditionally a hard-drinking but religious town, Broken Hill has 23 pubs (down from 73 in its heyday) and plenty of churches, as well as a Catholic cathedral, a synagogue, and a mosque to serve its 21,000 inhabitants.

ESSENTIALS

GETTING THERE By car, take the Great Western Highway from Sydney to Dubbo, then the Mitchell Highway to the Barrier Highway, which will take you to Broken Hill. **Southern Australian Airlines** (book through Qantas, ✆ **13 13 13** in Australia) also connects Broken Hill to Adelaide, Melbourne, and Mildura.

The ***Indian Pacific*** train stops here on its way from Sydney to Perth twice a week. It takes nearly 16 hours, leaving Sydney at 2:55pm on Saturday and Wednesday and arriving in Broken Hill at 6:40am the next day. The fare from Sydney is A$564 (US$451/UK£226) for adults and A$473 (US$378/UK£180) for children in a first-class sleeper, A$375 (US$300/UK£150) for adults and A$283 (US$226/UK£113) for children in an economy sleeper, and A$225 (US$180/UK£90) for adults and A$120 (US$96/UK£48) for children in an economy seat. Contact **Great Southern Railways** (✆ **08/8213 4530;** www.gsr.com.au) for timetables, fares, bookings, and more information.

Greyhound Australia (✆ **13 14 99** in Australia, or 07/4690 9950; www.greyhound.com.au) runs buses from Adelaide for around A$60 (US$48/UK£24); the trip takes 7 hours. The 16-hour trip from Sydney costs from A$96 (US$77/UK£38).

VISITOR INFORMATION The **Broken Hill Visitors Information Centre,** Blende and Bromide streets, Broken Hill, NSW 2880 (✆ **08/8087 6077;** fax 08/8088 5209; www.visitbrokenhill.com.au), is open daily from 8:30am to 5pm. The **National Parks & Wildlife Service (NPWS)** office is at 183 Argent St. (✆ **08/8088 5933**); and the **Royal Automobile Association of South Australia,** which offers reciprocal services to other national and international auto-club members, is at 261 Argent St. (✆ **08/8088 4999**).

Note: The area code in Broken Hill is **08,** the same as the South Australia code, not 02, the New South Wales code.

GETTING AROUND Free, volunteer-led tours lead off from the Visitor's Centre at 10am on Mondays, Wednesdays, and Fridays from March to October. **Silver City Tours,** 380 Argent St. (✆ **08/8087 3144**), conducts tours of the city and surrounding Outback. City tours take around 4 hours and cost A$45 (US$36/UK£18) for adults and A$20 (US$16/UK£8) for children. The company also offers a range of other tours of the area.

Fun Fact **What Time Is It, Anyway?**

Broken Hill runs its clocks on Central Standard Time, to correspond with South Australia. The surrounding country, however, runs half an hour faster at Eastern Standard Time.

Other good operators are **Tri State Safaris** (**© 08/8088 2389;** www.tristate.com.au) which runs many multiday tours into the Outback, and **Broken Hill's Outback Tours** (**© 08/8087 7800;** www.outbacktours.net).

Hertz (**© 08/8087 2719;** fax 08/8087 4838) rents four-wheel-drive vehicles suitable for exploring the area.

EXPLORING THE TOWN: GALLERIES, A MINE TOUR & THE WORLD'S LARGEST SCHOOLROOM

With the largest regional public gallery in New South Wales and 27 private **galleries,** Broken Hill has more places per capita to see art than anywhere else in Australia. The **Broken Hill Regional Art Gallery,** Chloride Street, between Blende and Beryl streets (**© 08/8088 5491**), houses an extensive collection of Australian colonial and Impressionist works. Look for the *Silver Tree,* a sculpture created out of the pure silver mined beneath Broken Hill. This is also a good place to see works by the "Brushmen of the Bush," a well-known group of artists, including Pro Hart, Jack Absalom, Eric Minchin, and Hugh Schultz, who spend many days sitting around campfires in the bush trying to capture its essence in paint. The gallery is open Monday through Friday from 10am to 5pm, and Saturday and Sunday from 1 to 5pm. Admission is A$3 (US$2.40/UK£1.20) for adults, A$2 (US$1.60/UK80p) for children, and A$6 (US$4.80/UK£2.40) for families.

Other galleries worth visiting around town include **Absalom's Gallery,** 638 Chapple St. (**© 08/8087 5881**), and the **Pro Hart Gallery,** 108 Wyman St. (**© 08/8087 2441**). Both are open daily. Pro Hart's gallery is really worth a look. Apart from his own works—including pieces based on incidents and scenes relating to Broken Hill—his gallery is crammed with everything from a bas-relief of Salvador Dalí to a landscape by Claude Monet.

Be sure not to miss the School of the Air and the Royal Flying Doctor Service base, both of which help show the enormity of the Australian interior. The **School of the Air**—the largest schoolroom in the world, with students scattered over 800,000 sq. km (312,000 sq. miles)—conducts lessons via two-way radios. Visitors can listen in on part of the day's first teaching session Monday through Friday at 8:30am (except public holidays). Bookings are essential and must be made through the **Broken Hill Visitors Information Centre** (see "Visitor Information," above). Tours costs A$3.50 (US$2.80/UK£1.40) for adults and A$2.50 (US$2/UK£1) for kids. The **Royal Flying Doctor Service base** is at the Broken Hill Airport (**© 08/8080 1777**). The service maintains communication with more than 400 Outback stations, ready to fly at once in case of an emergency. The base at Broken Hill covers 25% of New South Wales, as well as parts of Queensland and South Australia. Explanations of the role of the flying doctor service run continuously at the base Monday through Friday from 9am to 5pm. Admission is A$6 (US$4.80/UK£2.40) for adults, and A$3 (US$2.40/UK£1.20) for children.

Join the **Bush Mail Run** (**© 02/8087 2164,** or mobile 0411 102 339), an Outback mail delivery service that operates every Wednesday and Saturday. The day starts at 7am and you cover roughly 500km (310 miles). You stop at various homesteads. The run costs A$120 (US$96/UK£48).

OTHER THINGS TO SEE & DO NEARBY

VISITING A GHOST TOWN At least 44 movies have been filmed in the Wild West town of **Silverton** ★ (pop. 50), 23km (14 miles) northwest of Broken Hill. It's the Wild West Australian-style, though, with camels instead of horses sometimes placed in front of the **Silverton Pub,** which is well worth a visit for its kitschy Australian appeal. Silverton once had a population of 3,000, following the discovery of silver here in 1882, but within 7 years almost everyone had left. There are some good art galleries here, as well as a restored jail and hotel.

DISCOVERING ABORIGINAL HANDPRINTS **Mutawintji National Park** ★ (also known and pronounced by its old name, Mootwingee), 130km (81 miles) northeast of Broken Hill, was one of the most important spiritual meeting places for Aborigines on the continent. Groups came from all over to peck out abstract engravings on the rocks with sharpened quartz tools and to sign their handprints to show they belonged to the place. The ancient, weathered fireplaces are still here, laid out like a giant map to show where each visiting group came from. Hundreds of ocher outlines of hands and animal paws, some up to 30,000 years old, are stenciled on rock overhangs. The fabulous 2-hour Outback trip from Broken Hill to Mootwingee is along red-dirt tracks not really suitable for two-wheel-drives. It should not be attempted after a heavy rain.

Mootwingee Heritage Tours (✆ **08/8088 7000**) organizes inspections of the historic sites every Wednesday and Saturday at 10:30am Broken Hill time (11am Mootwingee, or Eastern Standard, time). The tours may be canceled in very hot weather. The **NPWS office** in Broken Hill (✆ **08/8088 5933**) also has details. You can camp at the **Homestead Creek** campground for A$11 (US$8.80/UK£4.40) a night. It has its own water supply.

EXPLORING WHITE CLIFFS ★★ White Cliffs, 290km (180 miles) east of Broken Hill, is an opal-mining town that's bigger than it looks. To escape the summer heat, most houses are built underground in mine shafts, where the temperature is a constant 72°F (22°C). Unlike Lightning Ridge (below), which produces mainly black opals, White Cliffs is known for its less valuable white opals—as is Coober Pedy in South Australia (see chapter 11). Prospecting started in 1889, when kangaroo shooters found the colorful stones on the ground. A year later the rush was on, and by the turn of the 20th century about 4,000 people were digging and sifting in a lawless, waterless hell of a place. White Cliffs is smaller than Coober Pedy and less touristy—which is its great charm. You also have more freedom to wander around the old opal tailings here, which is discouraged in Coober Pedy. Given the choice between White Cliffs and Lightning Ridge, I'd opt for the latter—though if you have time, you should see both.

The countryside here looks like an inverted moonscape, pimpled with bone-white heaps of gritty clay dug from the 50,000 mine shafts that surround the town. These days, White Cliffs is renowned for its eccentricity. Take **Jock's Place,** for instance, an

---

Finds A Fabulous Place to Enjoy the Sunset

Just outside Broken Hill in the **Living Desert Nature Park** is the best collection of sculptures this side of Stonehenge. Twelve sandstone obelisks, up to 3m (10 ft.) high and carved totemlike by artists from as far away as Georgia, Syria, Mexico, and the Tiwi Islands, make up the Sculpture Symposium. Surrounding them on all sides is brooding mulga scrub. It's fantastic at sunset.

---

underground museum full to the beams with junk pulled from old mine shafts. Then there's a house made of beer flagons, and a 9-hole **dirt golf course** where locals play at night with fluorescent green balls.

WHERE TO STAY: ABOVEGROUND & BELOW

One option is to rent a local cottage from **Broken Hill Historic Cottages** (© **08/8087 9966**) for A$80 (US$64/UK£32) a night.

Best Western Broken Hill Oasis Motor Inn This is my favorite place to stay in Broken Hill, although admittedly that's not really saying much in this Outback town. It's set way back from the road, has nice green areas and barbecue facilities, and is very quiet. The more expensive AAA-rated four-star rooms are much nicer than the cheaper options and considerably larger. Two family rooms sleep up to six in a combination of single and queen-size beds. You can order off several menus supplied by local restaurants; the hotel supplies plates and cutlery.

142 Iodide St., Broken Hill, NSW 2880. © **08/8088 2566,** or reserve through Best Western (© **800/780-7234** in the U.S. and Canada, 0800/39 3130 in the U.K., 0800/237 893 in New Zealand, 13 17 79 in Australia). Fax 08/8088 4377. http://book.bestwestern.com/bestwestern/productInfo.do?propertyCode=90401. 15 units. A$85–A$135 (US$68–US$108/UK£34–UK£54) double; A$135 (US$108/UK£54) 2-bed unit. Extra person A$10 (US$8/UK£4). AE, DC, MC, V. **Amenities:** Small heated outdoor pool; sauna; tour desk; laundry service; dry cleaning; nonsmoking rooms. *In room:* A/C, TV, dataport, fridge, coffeemaker, hair dryer, iron/ironing board.

Mario the Palace Hotel *Value* With its high painted walls, a mural of Botticelli's *Birth of Venus* on the ceiling two flights up, and an office crammed with stuffed animal heads and crabs, the Palace Hotel is an intriguing sanctuary. The owners have put a lot of work into restoring the place. The more expensive doubles are larger and come with a small lounge area, but all are comfortable and cool. Ten double rooms come with an attached shower. The Priscilla Suite is famous because that's where the transvestites stayed in *The Adventures of Priscilla, Queen of the Desert.* Mario owned the place for "donkey's years," as he says; he's now retired, and his family runs the hotel.

227 Argent St., Broken Hill, NSW 2880. © **08/8088 1699.** Fax 08/8087 6240. mariospalace@bigpond.com. 51 units, 10 with bathroom. A$44 (US$35/UK£18) double without bathroom; A$53–A$70 (US$42–US$56/UK£21–UK£28) double with bathroom; A$90 (US$72/UK£36) Priscilla suite for 2. AE, MC, V. **Amenities:** Bar; dining room. *In room:* A/C, TV, fridge, coffeemaker, iron/ironing board.

Underground Motel ★★ I love this place; it's worth making the scenic trip out to White Cliffs just to stay here for the night. All but two of the rooms are underground; they're reached by a maze of spacious tunnels dug out of the rock and sealed with epoxy resin to keep out the damp and the dust. The temperature below ground is a constant 72°F (22°C), which is decidedly cooler than a summer day outside. Rooms are comfortable though basic, with shared toilets and showers. Turn the light off, and it's dark as a cave. Every night guests sit around large tables and dig into the roast of the day. (Vegetarians have options, too.) The three-course meal costs A$25 (US$20/UK£10).

Smiths Hill, White Cliffs (P.O. Box 427), NSW 2836. © **1800/021 154** in Australia, or 08/8091 6677. Fax 08/8091 6654. 30 units, none with bathroom. A$83 (US$66/UK£33) double. Extra person A$24 (US$19/UK£10). MC, V. **Amenities:** Restaurant; bar; small heated outdoor pool; coin-op laundry; nonsmoking rooms.

WHERE TO DINE

The best place for a meal Aussie-style is a local club. You'll find one of the best bistros at the **Barrier Social & Democratic Club,** 218 Argent St. (© **08/8088 4477**). It serves breakfast, lunch, and dinner. Another good one is at the Southern Cross Hotel, at 357 Cobalt St. (✆ **02/8088 4122**). Interestingly, the fresh fish is a standout. Locals go for steaks at the Sturt Club, at 321 Blende St. (✆ **02/8087 4541**).

LIGHTNING RIDGE: OPALS GALORE ★★

793km (492 miles) NW of Sydney; 737km (457 miles) SW of Brisbane

Lightning Ridge, or "The Ridge" as the locals call it, is perhaps the most fascinating place to visit in New South Wales. Essentially, it's a hardworking opal-mining town in the arid northern reaches of New South Wales—where summer temperatures hover around the 113°F (45°C) mark. Lightning Ridge thrives off the largest deposit of black opals in the world. Good-quality opals can fetch a miner around A$8,000 (US$6,400/UK£3,200) per carat, and stones worth more than A$500,000 (US$400,000/UK£200,000) each are not unheard of. Tourists come to get a taste of life in Australia's "Wild West." A popular activity in the opal fields is to pick over the old heaps of mine tailings. Stories (perhaps tall tales) abound of tourists finding overlooked opals worth thousands.

I strongly recommend you visit the **Grawin** and **Glengarry opal fields** ★★, both about an hour or so from Lightning Ridge on a dirt track suitable for two-wheel-drive cars in dry weather only. (Check with the Tourist Information Centre before you go.) Bristling with drills and hoists pulling out bucket-loads of dirt, these frontier townships buzz with news of the latest opal rush. If you can convince a local to take you there, all the better—the tracks can be misleading. **Ando's Outback Tours** (see "Byron Bay: A Beach Bohemia," earlier in this chapter) takes in Glengarry and Lightning Ridge on its 5-day trip.

ESSENTIALS

GETTING THERE From Sydney, it takes about 9 hours to drive to Lightning Ridge, via Bathurst, Dubbo, and the fascinating town of Walgett. **Airlink** (✆ **02/6884 2435**) flies to Lightning Ridge from Sydney via Dubbo. Countrylink (✆ **13 22 32**) runs trains from Sydney to Dubbo and then it's a bus from there. The trip from Dubbo takes around 4½ hours and costs A$60 (US$48/UK£24).

VISITOR INFORMATION The **Lightning Ridge Tourist Information Centre,** Morilla Street (P.O. Box 1779), Lightning Ridge, NSW 2834 (✆ **02/6829 0565;** fax 02/6829 0565), is open Monday through Friday from 8:30am to 4pm. On weekends, call ✆ **02/6829 0429** or e-mail lridge@walgettshire.com.

SPECIAL EVENTS If you're in Australia around Easter, make sure you come to Lightning Ridge for the **Great Goat Race** and the rodeo. A decent website for information is www.lightningridge.net.au.

SEEING THE TOWN

Any visit to Lightning Ridge should start with an orientation trip with **Black Opal Tours** (✆ **02/6829 0368;** fax 02/6829 1206; www.blackopaltours.com). The company offers both a 3-hour morning tour and an afternoon tour for A$25 (US$20/UK£10) for adults and A$22 (US$18/UK£9) for kids.

Among the points of interest is the 15m-tall (49-ft.) **Amigo's Castle,** which dominates the worked-out opal fields surrounding the modern township of Lightning Ridge. Complete with turrets, battlements, dungeons, and a wishing well, the castle has been rising out of these arid lands for the past 18 years, with every rock scavenged from the surrounding area and lugged in a wheelbarrow or in a rucksack on Amigo's back. The wonderful Amigo hasn't taken out insurance on the property, so there are no official tours, though if he feels like a bit of company he'll show you around.

The **Artesian Bore Baths,** 2km (1¼ miles) from the post office on Pandora Street, are free, open 24 hours a day, and said to have therapeutic value. The water temperature hovers between 104°F and 122°F (40°C–50°C). A visit at night when the stars are out is amazing.

The **Bevan's Black Opal & Cactus Nursery** (✆ **02/6829 0429**) contains more than 2,000 species of cactus and succulent plants, including rare specimens. Betty Bevan cuts opals from the family's mine, and many are on display. Admission is A$5 (US$4/UK£2) to the cactus nursery, free to see the opals.

Lightning Ridge has plenty of opal shops, galleries, walk-in opal mines, and other unique things to see. You might want to take a look at **Gemopal Pottery** (✆ **02/6829 0375**), on the road to the Bore Baths. The resident potter makes some nice pots out of clay mine tailings and lives in one of his five old Sydney railway carriages.

WHERE TO STAY & DINE

An interesting addition to the Lightning Ridge lodging scene is the **Lightning Ridge Hotel/Motel** (✆ **02/6829 0304**), set on 4 hectares (10 acres) of bush, complete with a birdbath to attract the native parrots. There are 40 log cabins here, as well as a trailer park (for your own trailer or motor home) and camping sites. Cabins cost A$56 (US$45/UK£23) without bathroom, A$58 (US$46/UK£23) with a bathroom; motel rooms go for A$77 (US$62/UK£32) double, A$87 (US$69/UK£35) triple, A$145 (US$118/UK£59) quad. If you want to stay at the Glengarry opal fields, your only option is the **Glengarry Hilton,** a rustic Outback pub (not associated with the major hotel chain). Here you stay in mobile units sleeping 24. A night costs A$15 (US$12/UK£6).

The Wallangulla Motel My choice of the four motels in town, The Wallangulla offers two standards of rooms, the cheaper ones being in an older section of the property. Newer rooms are better furnished and generally nicer; they're worth the extra money. Two large family rooms each have two bedrooms and a living room; one has a Jacuzzi. Guests can use the barbecue facilities. The Lightning Ridge Bowling Club across the road has a restaurant with pretty good food and a very cheap bistro; motel guests can charge meals to their room bills.

Morilla St. (at Agate St.), Lightning Ridge, NSW 2834. ✆ **02/6829 0542.** Fax 02/6829 0070. www.wj.com.au/wallangulla. 43 units. A$60–A$100 (US$48–US$80/UK£24–UK£40) double; A$80–A$115 (US$64–US$92/UK£32–UK£46) triple; A$90–A$125 (US$72–US$100/UK£36–UK£50) family room with Jacuzzi. AE, DC, MC, V. **Amenities:** Coin-op laundry; nonsmoking rooms. *In room:* A/C, TV, coffeemaker.

6

Brisbane

by Lee Mylne

Queensland's capital is relaxed, laid-back, and subtropical. Set along the banks of the wide, brown Brisbane River, this is a city that has grown up in recent years, confident in its appeal. It's one of those places that people don't always appreciate until they spend time there, but where the welcome is as warm as the weather. The city is green and leafy: Moreton Bay fig trees give shade, and in summer, the purple haze of jacarandas competes with the scarlet blaze of poinciana trees. A mango tree in the backyard is practically de rigueur.

The theme parks are south of the city, on the Brisbane–Gold Coast corridor. Brisbane folk don't consider that a drawback. They'll urge you to discover the city, rich in history and character, and get to know the locals. That's easy—friendly locals will start chatting with just about anyone.

Brisbane (pronounced *Briz*-bun) is known for its timber "Queenslanders," cottages and houses set high on stumps to catch the breeze, with wide verandas to keep out the midday sun. In some suburbs, Queenslanders have been converted to trendy cafes, restaurants, and shops selling antiques, clothes, and housewares.

In the city center, gracious colonial sandstone buildings stand next to modern glass towers. Wander in the city botanic gardens, in-line skate or bike along the riverfront pathways, have a drink in a pub beer garden, or get out on the river on a CityCat ferry. Several bridges cross the river, the most famous and attractive being the Story Bridge, on the Town Reach of the river (see "Brisbane's Bridge Climb," later in this chapter). Getting around is cheap and easy, good food—including fantastic seafood—is abundant, and accommodations are affordable, especially in some of the city's comfortable, elegant B&Bs.

Brisbane is in the southeast corner of the state, flanked by the Sunshine Coast, about 2 hours to the north, and the Gold Coast, 1 hour to the south. The Brisbane River flows into Moreton Bay, dotted with beautiful islands you can explore.

1 Orientation

ARRIVING

BY PLANE About 20 international airlines serve Brisbane from Europe, Asia, and New Zealand, including Qantas, Air New Zealand, Pacific Blue, Singapore Airlines, Thai International, Malaysia Airlines, and Cathay Pacific. From North America, you can fly direct from Los Angeles to Brisbane on Qantas, but from other places you will likely fly to Sydney and connect on Qantas, or fly direct from Auckland, New Zealand.

Qantas (✆ **13 13 13** in Australia; www.qantas.com.au) and its subsidiary **QantasLink** (book through Qantas) operate daily flights from state capitals, Cairns,

Townsville, and several other towns. No-frills **Jetstar** (✆ **13 15 38** in Australia; www.jetstar.com.au) has daily service from Proserpine, Hamilton Island, Melbourne's Avalon airport, and Hobart and Launceston in Tasmania. **Virgin Blue** (✆ **13 67 89** in Australia; www.virginblue.com.au) offers direct services from all capital cities as well as Cairns, Townsville, Hamilton Island and Proserpine in the Whitsundays, Mackay and Rockhampton in Queensland, and Newcastle in New South Wales.

Brisbane International Airport is 16km (10 miles) from the city, and the domestic terminal is 2km (1¼ miles) farther away. The arrivals floor, on Level 2, has an information desk to meet all flights, help with flight inquiries, dispense tourist information, and make hotel bookings, and a check-in counter for passengers transferring to domestic flights. The international terminal is undergoing a major expansion and upgrade, expected to be completed by the end of 2008.

Travelex currency-exchange bureaus are on the departures and arrivals floors. **Avis** (✆ **07/3860 4200**), **Budget** (✆ **07/3860 4466**), **Europcar** (✆ **07/3874 8150**), **Hertz** (✆ **07/3860 4522**), and **Thrifty** (✆ **1300/367 227**) have desks on Level 2; in the airport there is also a free call-board connecting you to smaller local car-rental companies that sometimes offer better rates. On levels 2, 3, and 4 you will find ATMs, free showers, and baby-changing rooms.

The domestic terminal has a Travelex currency-exchange bureau, ATMs, showers, and the big four car-rental desks. (Call the telephone numbers above.)

For security reasons, luggage lockers are not available at either terminal.

Coachtrans (✆ **07/3238 4700;** www.coachtrans.com.au) runs a shuttle between the airport and Roma Street Transit Centre every 30 minutes from 5am to 11pm. The one-way cost is A$9 (US$7.20/UK£3.60) or A$11 (US$8.80/UK£4.40) for hotel drop-off. The round-trip fare is A$15 (US$12/UK£6) or A$18 (US$14/UK£7). Family tickets are A$24 (US$19/UK£9.60) or A$29 (US$23/UK£12) one-way. The trip takes about 40 minutes, and reservations are not needed. No public buses serve the airport. A **taxi** to the city costs around A$25 (US$20/UK£10) from the international terminal and A$30 (US$24/UK£12) from the domestic terminal, plus A$2 (US$1.60/UK80p) for departing taxis.

Airtrain (✆ **07/3216 3308;** www.airtrain.com.au), a rail link between the city and Brisbane's domestic and international airport terminals, runs every 15 minutes from around 6am to 7:30pm daily. Fares from the airport to city stations are A$12 (US$9.60/UK£4.80) per adult, A$6 (US$4.80/UK£2.40) per child. The trip takes about 20 minutes. Airtrain also links the airport with the Gold Coast.

The Airtrain fare between the international and domestic terminals is A$4 (US$3.20/UK£1.60). A taxi between terminals costs about A$10 (US$8/UK£4).

BY TRAIN **Queensland Rail** (✆ **13 22 32** in Queensland; www.qr.com.au) operates several long-distance trains to Brisbane from Cairns. The high-speed Tilt Train takes about 25 hours and costs A$303 (US$242/UK£121) for business class. The slower *Sunlander* takes 32 hours and costs A$207 (US$166/UK£83) for a sitting berth, A$265 (US$212/UK£106) for an economy-class sleeper, A$409 (US$327/UK£164) for a first-class sleeper, or A$743 (US$594/UK£297) for the all-inclusive Queenslander class. **Countrylink** (✆ **13 22 32** in Australia; www.countrylink.info) runs two daily train services to Brisbane from Sydney. The 7:15am departure arrives in the town of Casino, south of the border, at 6:34pm, where passengers transfer to a bus for the rest of the trip to Brisbane, arriving at 10:20pm. The trip costs A$124

(US$99/UK£50) for an adult seat. The overnight train, which leaves Sydney at 4:20pm and arrives in Brisbane at 6:30am the next day, costs A$175 (US$140/UK£70) for a seat or an extra A$88 (US$70/UK£35) for a sleeper. Ask about off-peak discounts, depending on the time of year.

All intercity and interstate trains pull into the city center's **Brisbane Transit Centre at Roma Street,** often called the Roma Street Transit Centre. From here, most city and Spring Hill hotels are a few blocks' walk or a quick cab ride away. The station has food outlets, showers, tourist information, and lockers.

Queensland Rail CityTrain (© **13 12 30** in Queensland) provides daily train service from the Sunshine Coast and plentiful service from the Gold Coast.

BY BUS All intercity and interstate coaches pull into the Brisbane Transit Centre (see "By Train," above). **Greyhound Australia** (© **13 14 99** in Australia, or 07/4690 9950; www.greyhound.com.au) serves the city several times daily. A one-way Cairns-Brisbane ticket costs A$234 (US$187/UK£94); the trip takes 30 hours. The Sydney-Brisbane trip takes 17 hours and costs A$116 (US$93/UK£46) one-way. Coachtrans provides daily service from the Gold Coast. Call **Transinfo** (© **13 12 30**) for details.

BY CAR The Bruce Highway from Cairns enters the city from the north. The Pacific Highway enters Brisbane from the south.

VISITOR INFORMATION

The Brisbane Visitor Information Centre (© **07/3006 6290**) is in the Queen Street Mall, between Edward and Albert streets. It's open Monday through Thursday from 9am to 5:30pm, Friday 9am to 7pm or later, Saturday 9am to 5pm, Sunday 9:30am to 4:30pm, and public holidays 9am to 4:30pm. The official website, www.our brisbane.com, and the Brisbane Transit Centre (© **07/3236 2020;** see "By Train," above) are other good sources of information.

CITY LAYOUT

The city center's office towers shimmer in the sun on the north bank of a curve of the Brisbane River. At the tip of the curve are the lush Brisbane City Gardens (sometimes called the City Botanic Gardens). The 30m (98-ft.) sandstone cliffs of Kangaroo Point rise on the eastern side of the south bank; to the west are the South Bank Parklands and the Queensland Cultural Centre, known as South Bank. The **Goodwill Bridge,** for pedestrians and bikes only, links South Bank with the City Gardens. To the west 5km (3 miles), Mount Coot-tha (pronounced *Coo*-tha) looms out of the flat plain.

MAIN ARTERIES & STREETS It's easy to find your way around central Brisbane once you know that the east-west streets are named after female British royalty, and the north-south streets are named after their male counterparts. The northernmost is Ann, followed by Adelaide, Queen, Elizabeth, Charlotte, Mary, Margaret, and Alice. From east to west, the streets are Edward, Albert, George, and William, which becomes North Quay, flanking the river's northeast bank.

Queen Street, the main thoroughfare, becomes a pedestrian mall between Edward and George streets. Roma Street exits the city diagonally to the northwest. Ann Street leads all the way east into Fortitude Valley. The main street in Fortitude Valley is Brunswick Street, which runs into New Farm.

STREET MAPS The **Brisbane Map,** free from the Brisbane Visitor Information Centre (see "Visitor Information," above) or your concierge, is a lightweight map that shows the river and suburbs, as well as the city. It's great for drivers because it shows parking lots and one-way streets on the city-center grid. It can also be downloaded from **www.ourbrisbane.com**. Rental cars usually come with street directories. Newsdealers and some bookstores sell this map; the state auto club, the **RACQ,** in the General Post Office, 261 Queen St. (© **13 19 05**), is also a good source.

NEIGHBORHOODS IN BRIEF

City Center The vibrant city center is where residents eat, shop, and socialize. Queen Street Mall, in the heart of town, is popular with shoppers and moviegoers, especially on weekends and Friday night (when stores stay open until 9pm). The Eagle Street financial and legal precinct has great restaurants with river views and, on Sunday, markets by the Riverside Centre tower and the Pier. Much of Brisbane's colonial architecture is in the city center, too. Strollers, bike riders, and in-line skaters shake the summer heat in the green haven of the Brisbane City Gardens at the business district's southern end.

Fortitude Valley "The Valley," as locals call it, was once one of the sleazier parts of town. Today, it is a stamping ground for street-smart young folk who meet in restored pubs and eat in cool cafes. The lanterns, food stores, and shopping mall of Chinatown are here, too. Take Turbot Street to the Valley's Brunswick Street, or venture a little farther to trendy James Street.

New Farm Always an appealing suburb, New Farm is an in-spot for café-hopping. Merthyr Street is where the action is, especially on Friday and Saturday night. From the intersection of Wickham and Brunswick streets, follow Brunswick southeast for 13 blocks to Merthyr.

Paddington This hilltop suburb, a couple of miles northwest of the city, is one of Brisbane's most attractive. Brightly painted Queenslander cottages line the main street, Latrobe Terrace, as it winds west along a ridge top. Many of the houses have been turned into shops and cafes, where you can browse, enjoy coffee and cake, or just admire the charming architecture.

Milton & Rosalie Park Road in Milton might not quite be a little bit of Europe, but it tries hard—right down to a replica Eiffel Tower above the cafes and shops. Italian restaurants line the street, buzzing with office workers who down cappuccinos at alfresco restaurants, scout interior design stores for a new objet d'art to grace the living room, and stock up on European designer rags. A few minutes' drive away, Baroona Road and Nash Street, in Rosalie, are catching up.

West End This small inner-city enclave is alive with ethnic restaurants, cafes, and the odd, interesting housewares or fashion store. Most action centers on the intersection of Vulture and Boundary streets, where Asian grocers and delis abound.

Bulimba One of the emerging fashionable suburbs, Bulimba has a long connection with the river through the boat-building industry. One of the nicest ways to get there is by CityCat. Oxford Street is the main drag, lined with trendy cafes and shops.

2 Getting Around

BY PUBLIC TRANSPORTATION

TransLink operates a single network of buses, trains, and ferries. For timetables and route inquiries, call **TransInfo** (✆ **13 12 30;** www.translink.com.au; Mon–Thurs 6am–9pm, and continuously 6am Fri–9pm Sun, although hours may vary on public holidays). An integrated ticket system operates, and the easiest place to buy your tickets is on the buses or at the train stations. You can also buy tickets and pick up maps and timetables at the Queen Street bus station information center (in the Myer Centre, off Queen St. Mall) and the Brisbane Visitor Information Centre in the Queen Street Mall. Tickets are also sold at some inner city newsdealers.

A trip in a single sector or zone on the bus, train, or ferry costs A$2.20 (US$1.75/UK90p). A single ticket is good for up to 2 hours on a one-way journey on any combination of bus, train, or ferry. When traveling with a parent, kids under 5 travel free and kids 5 to 14 and students pay half fare. If you plan on using public transport a lot, a 10-trip ticket may be a good investment.

You will probably not need to travel farther than four zones on the transport system. This will cost you the princely sum of A$3.40 (US$2.70/UK£1.35) each way. A 1-day ticket for four zones will cost A$6.80 (US$5.45/UK£2.70).

On weekends and public holidays, it's cheaper to buy an **Off-Peak ticket,** which lets you travel all day for A$3.30 (US$2.65/UK£1.30) for adults. The Off-Peak ticket is also available on weekdays, but you must plan your sightseeing around the fact that it cannot be used before 9am or between 3:30 and 7pm.

The **Brisbane Mobility Map,** produced by the Brisbane City Council, outlines wheelchair access to buildings in the city center and includes a detailed guide to the Queen Street Mall and a map of the Brisbane Botanic Gardens Mount Coot-tha. The council's disability-services unit also has a range of publications, including a Braille Trail and an access guide to parks, available from council customer service centers (✆ **07/3403 8888**).

BY BUS Buses operate from around 5am to 11pm weekdays, with less service on weekends. On Sunday, many routes stop around 5pm. Most buses depart from City Hall at King George Square, from Adelaide or Ann Street. The Downtown Loop is a free bus service that circles the city center. The Loop's distinctive red buses run on two routes, stopping at convenient places including Central Station, Queen Street Mall, City Botanic Gardens, Riverside Centre, and King George Square. Look for the red bus stops. They run every 10 minutes from 7am to 5:50pm Monday through Friday.

BY FERRY The fast **CityCat** ferries run to many places of interest, including South Bank and the Queensland Cultural Centre; the restaurants and Sunday markets at the Riverside Centre; and New Farm Park, not far from the cafes of Merthyr Street. They run every half-hour between Queensland University, about 9km (5½ miles) to the south, and Brett's Wharf, about 9km (5½ miles) to the north. Slower but more frequent CityFerry service (**Inner City** and **Cross River** ferries) stops at a few more points, including the south end of South Bank Parklands, Kangaroo Point, and Edward Street right outside the Brisbane City Gardens. Ferries run from around 6am to 10:30pm daily. Two hours on the CityCat takes you the entire length of the run.

BY TRAIN Brisbane's suburban rail network is fast, quiet, safe, and clean. Trains run from around 5am to midnight (until about 11pm on Sun). All trains leave Central Station, between Turbot and Ann streets at Edward Street.

Brisbane Accommodations, Dining & Attractions

ACCOMMODATIONS ■
Eton **9**
Hotel George Williams (YMCA) **10**
Hotel Ibis Brisbane **11**
Novotel Brisbane **7**
Quay West Suites **20**
Stamford Plaza Brisbane **18**
Thornbury House Bed & Breakfast **4**

DINING ◆
e'cco bistro **3**
Govinda's **21**
Jo Jo's **14**
Pier Nine **15**
Plough Inn **25**
Story Bridge Hotel **17**
Tognini's BistroCafeDeli **5**
Walt Moden Dining **2**

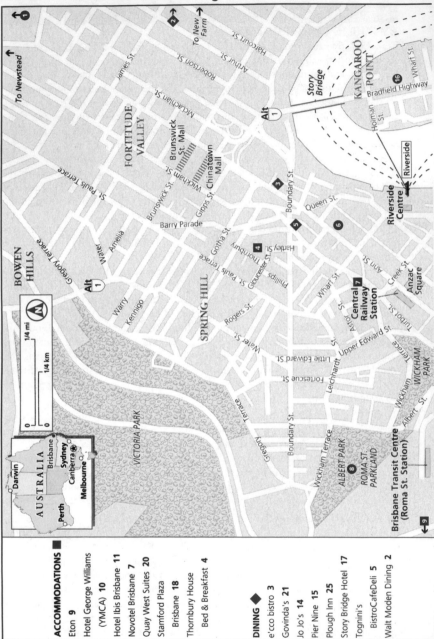

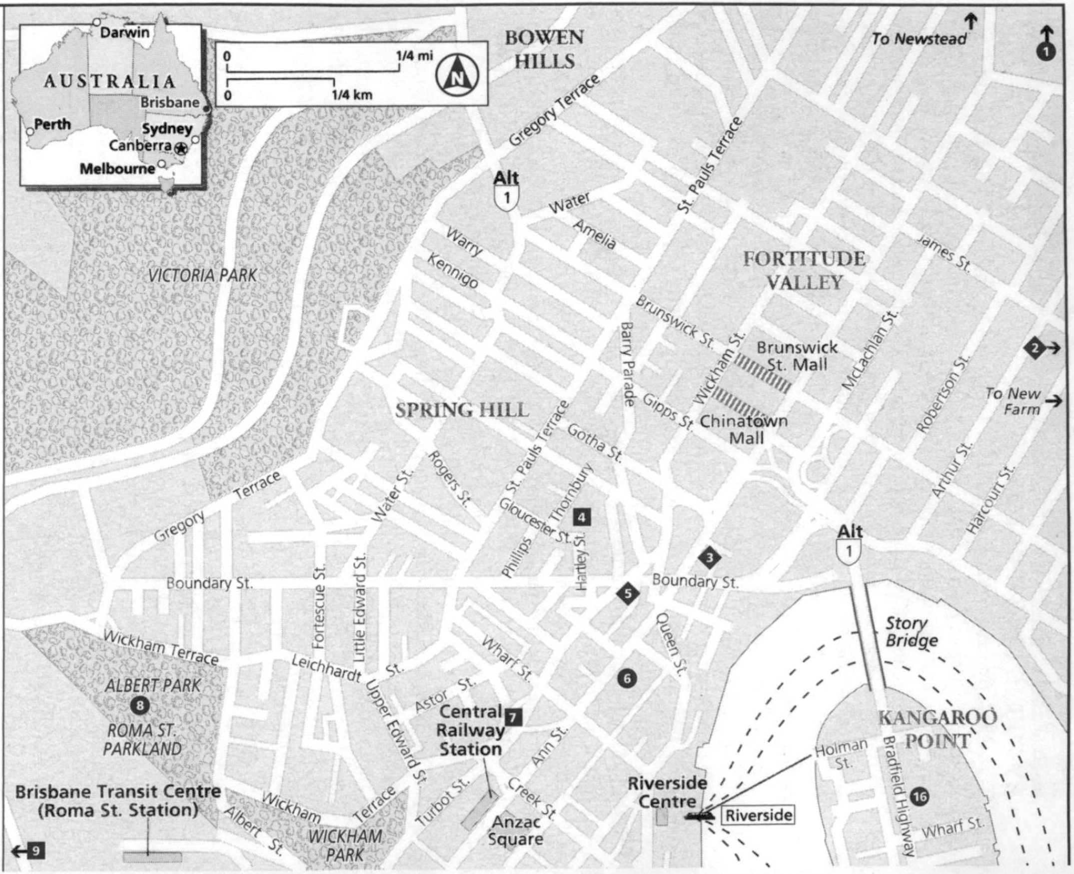

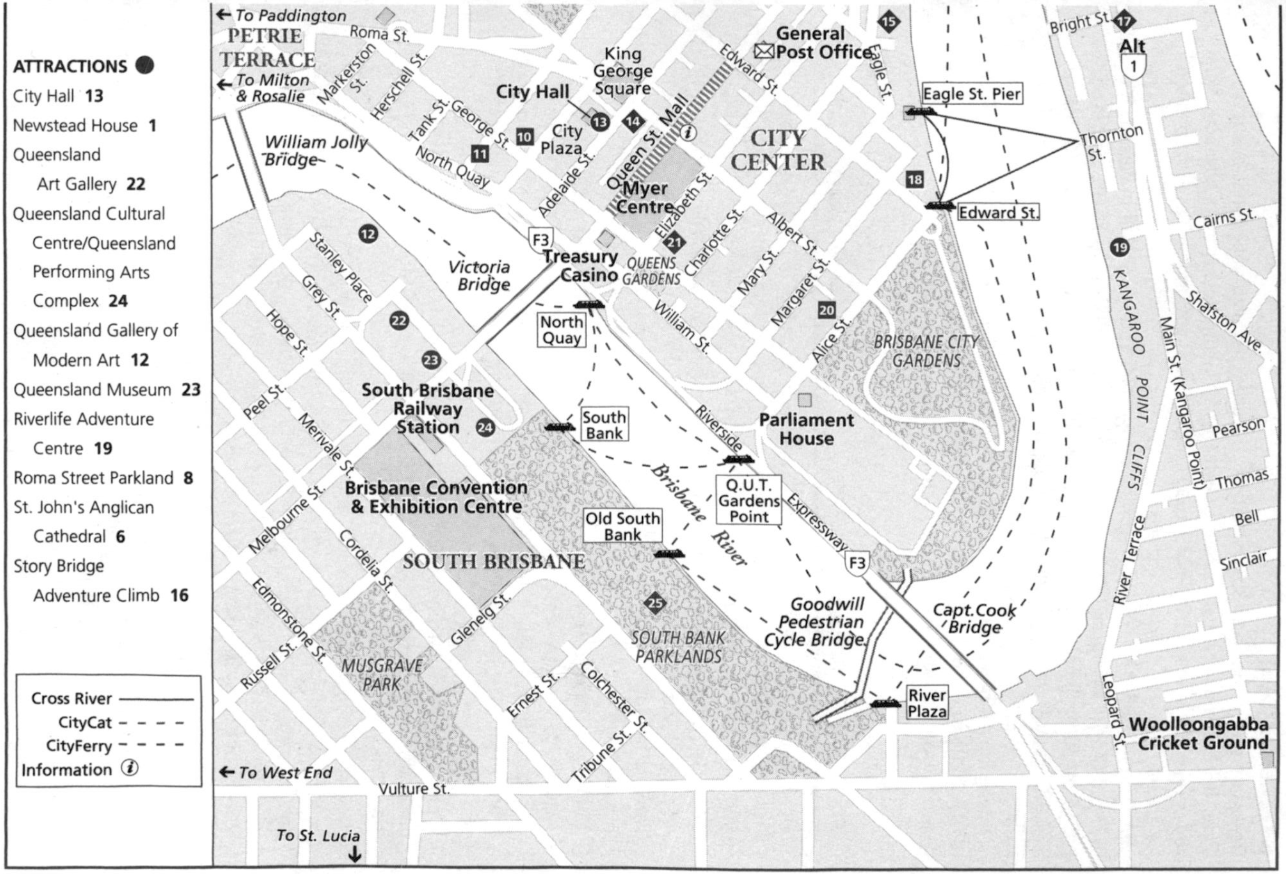
ATTRACTIONS
City Hall 13
Newstead House 1
Queensland Art Gallery 22
Queensland Cultural Centre/Queensland Performing Arts Complex 24
Queensland Gallery of Modern Art 12
Queensland Museum 23
Riverlife Adventure Centre 19
Roma Street Parkland 8
St. John's Anglican Cathedral 6
Story Bridge Adventure Climb 16
Cross River
CityCat
CityFerry
Information
To Paddington
PETRIE TERRACE
To Milton & Rosalie
Roma St.
Markerston St.
Herschell St.
Tank St.
George St.
North Quay
City Hall
King George Square
City Plaza
Queen St. Mall
Edward St.
General Post Office
Eagle St.
Eagle St. Pier
Edward St.
Thornton St.
Bright St.
Alt 1
CITY CENTER
Myer Centre
Adelaide St.
Elizabeth St.
Charlotte St.
Albert St.
Mary St.
Margaret St.
Alice St.
William St.
QUEENS GARDENS
Treasury Casino
William Jolly Bridge
Victoria Bridge
North Quay
Stanley Place
Grey St.
Hope St.
Peel St.
Merivale St.
Melbourne St.
South Brisbane Railway Station
South Bank
Riverside
Parliament House
BRISBANE CITY GARDENS
Brisbane River
Q.U.T. Gardens Point
Expressway
Old South Bank
Brisbane Convention & Exhibition Centre
SOUTH BRISBANE
Cordelia St.
Glenelg St.
Edmonstone St.
Russell St.
MUSGRAVE PARK
Ernest St.
Colchester St.
Tribune St.
SOUTH BANK PARKLANDS
Goodwill Pedestrian Cycle Bridge
Capt. Cook Bridge
River Plaza
To West End
Vulture St.
To St. Lucia
Cairns St.
KANGAROO POINT CLIFFS
Main St. (Kangaroo Point)
Shafston Ave.
Pearson
Thomas
Bell
Sinclair
River Terrace
Leopard St.
Woolloongabba Cricket Ground

BY CAR OR TAXI

Brisbane's grid of one-way streets can be confusing, so plan your route before you leave. Brisbane's biggest parking lot is at the Myer Centre (enter from Elizabeth St.) and is open 24 hours (© **07/3229 1699**). Most hotels and motels have free parking for guests.

Avis (© **13 63 33** or 07/3221 2900), **Budget** (© **1300/362 848** in Australia, or 07/3220 0699), **Europcar** (© **13 13 90** in Australia, or 07/3006 7440), and **Hertz** (© **13 30 39** or 07/3221 6166) all have outlets in the city center. **Thrifty** (© **1300/ 367 227** in Australia) is on the edge of the city center at 49 Barry Parade, Fortitude Valley.

For a taxi, call **Yellow Cabs** (© **13 19 24** in Australia) or **Black and White Taxis** (© **13 10 08** in Australia). There are taxi stands at each end of Queen Street Mall, on Edward Street and on George Street (outside the Treasury Casino).

FAST FACTS: Brisbane

American Express The office at 131 Elizabeth St. (© **1300/139 060**) cashes traveler's checks, exchanges foreign currency, and replaces lost traveler's checks. It's open 9am to 5pm Monday to Friday and 9am to noon Saturday.

Business Hours Banks are open Monday through Thursday from 9:30am to 4pm, until 5pm on Friday. See "The Shopping Scene," later in this chapter, for store hours. Some restaurants close Monday night, Tuesday night, or both; bars are generally open from 10 or 11am until midnight.

Currency Exchange **Travelex,** in the Myer Centre, Queen Street Mall (© **07/ 3210 6325;** www.travelex.com.au), is open Monday through Thursday from 9am to 5:30pm, Friday 9am to 8pm, Saturday from 9am to 5pm, and Sunday from 10am to 4pm. Locations at the airport are open whenever flights are arriving.

Dentist The **Adelaide and Albert Dental Centre,** Level 1, 245 Albert St. at Adelaide Street, opposite City Hall (© **07/3229 4121**), is open Monday through Friday from 8am to 6pm.

Doctor The **Travellers' Medical and Vaccination Centre** (© **07/3221 9066;** www.thetraveldoctor.com.au) is on Level 5 of the Qantas building, 247 Adelaide St., between Creek and Edward streets. It is open Monday and Friday from 8am to 5pm, Tuesday 8am to 7pm, Wednesday 8am to 9pm, Thursday 8am to 4:30pm, and Saturday 8:30am to 2pm. For after-hours emergencies, call © **0408/199 166.**

Embassies & Consulates The United States, Canada, and New Zealand have no representation in Brisbane; see chapter 4, "Sydney," for those countries' nearest offices. The British Consulate-General is at Level 26, Waterfront Place, 1 Eagle St. (© **07/3223 3200**).

Emergencies Dial © **000** for fire, ambulance, or police help in an emergency. This is a free call from a private or public telephone.

Hospitals The nearest one is **Royal Brisbane Hospital,** about a 15-minute drive from the city at Herston Road, Herston (© **07/3636 8111**).

Hot Lines **Lifeline** (**© 13 11 14**) is a 24-hour emotional crisis counseling service.

Internet Access The **South Bank Visitor Information Centre,** Stanley Street Plaza, South Bank Parklands, offers Internet access daily from 9am to 4:30pm and charges A$1 (US80¢/UK40p) per 10 minutes. There are several Internet cafes on Adelaide Street, including the **Cyber Room,** 25 Adelaide St. (**© 07/3012 9331**), and **Netparadise,** 198 Adelaide St. (**© 07/3211 8218**).

Luggage Storage & Lockers **The Brisbane Transit Centre** on Roma Street (**© 1800/632 640**) has baggage lockers. Medium-size lockers are also available to hire at **South Bank Parklands,** in the Stanley Street Plaza near Streets Beach. The cost is A$3 (US$2.40/UK£1.20) for 3 hours or A$6 (US$4.80/UK£2.40) for 6 hours storage.

Newspapers & Magazines The *Courier-Mail* (Mon–Sat) and the *Sunday Mail* are Brisbane's daily newspapers. Another good news source is the online newspaper *Brisbane Times,* www.brisbanetimes.com.au. The free weekly *Brisbane News* magazine is a good guide to dining, entertainment, and shopping.

Pharmacies (Chemist Shops) **T & G Corner Day & Night Pharmacy,** 141 Queen St. Mall (**© 07/3221 4585**), is open Monday through Thursday from 7am to 9pm, Friday from 7am to 9:30pm, Saturday from 8am to 9pm, Sunday from 8:30am to 5:30pm, and public holidays from 9am to 7:30pm.

Police Dial **© 000** in an emergency, or **© 07/3364 6464** for police headquarters. Police are stationed 24 hours a day at 65–69 Adelaide St. (**© 07/3224 4444**) in the city.

Safety Brisbane is relatively crime free, but as in any large city, be aware of your personal safety, especially when you're out at night. Stick to well-lit streets and busy precincts.

Time Zone The time in Brisbane is Greenwich Mean Time plus 10 hours. Brisbane does not observe daylight saving time, which means it's on the same time as Sydney and Melbourne in winter, and 1 hour behind those cities October through March. For the exact local time, call **© 1194.**

Weather Call **© 1196** for the southeast Queensland weather forecast.

3 Where to Stay

IN THE CITY CENTER

VERY EXPENSIVE

Stamford Plaza Brisbane ★★★ The Stamford is one of Brisbane's most beautiful hotels; brocade chairs and sofas, enormous still-life oils, gilt mirrors, and palms dot the marble lobby. It's also one of the few city hotels with river views from every room—especially stunning from the southern rooms at night, when the Story Bridge lights up. The plush rooms are not enormous, but all fit a king-size bed or two twins. What must be the biggest bathrooms in Brisbane sport small TVs. A riverside boardwalk leads from the hotel to the Eagle Street Pier restaurants, and the Brisbane City Gardens abut the hotel. In a historic 19th-century sandstone building adjacent to the hotel is one of Brisbane's grandest fine-dining restaurants, **Siggi's,** which also boasts a wine and tapas bar.

Edward and Margaret sts. (adjacent to the Brisbane City Gardens), Brisbane, QLD 4000. ✆ **1800/773 700** in Australia, or 07/3221 1999. Fax 07/3221 6895. www.stamford.com.au. 252 units. A$300–A$650 (US$240–US$520/UK£120–UK£260) double; A$690–A$3,500 (US$552–US$2,800/UK£276–UK£1,400) suite. Extra person A$40 (US$32/UK£16). Children under 12 stay free in parent's room with existing bedding. Ask about packages. AE, DC, MC, V. Covered parking. Train: Central, then taxi or walk 6 blocks. Bus: Downtown Loop. Ferry: Riverside Centre, Eagle St. **Amenities:** 3 restaurants; 3 bars; small outdoor heated lap pool; health club; Jacuzzi; sauna; bike rental; concierge; tour desk; car-rental desk; business center; salon; 24-hr. room service; in-room massage; babysitting; dry cleaning; 24-hr. butler service (for a fee); nonsmoking rooms. *In room:* A/C, TV/VCR w/pay movies, dataport, minibar, coffeemaker, hair dryer, iron.

EXPENSIVE

Novotel Brisbane ★ This well-appointed contemporary hotel, a short walk from Brisbane's main shopping areas, is popular with both families and business travelers. The modern, stylish rooms and suites are spacious and have superb views over the city. The lap pool is very inviting and has terrific city views. There's live music in the Spring Bar each night, and kids' meals are offered in both the upmarket **Cilantro** restaurant or the more casual **Loose Goose** cafe.

200 Creek St., Brisbane, QLD 4000. ✆ **1300/656 565** in Australia, 800/221-4542 in the U.S. and Canada, 0870/609 0961 in the U.K., 0800/44 4422 in New Zealand, or 07/3309 3309. Fax 07/3309 3308. www.accorhotels.com.au. 296 units. A$226–A$246 (US$181–US$197/UK£90–UK£98) double. Children under 16 stay free in parent's room with existing bedding. Ask about packages. AE, DC, MC, V. Free undercover parking. Train: Central. **Amenities:** 2 restaurants; bar; outdoor heated pool; gymnasium; sauna; concierge; car-rental desk; tour desk; business center; 24-hr. room service; babysitting; coin-op laundry; laundry service; dry cleaning; nonsmoking rooms. *In room:* A/C, TV w/pay movies, dataport, minibar, coffeemaker, hair dryer, iron.

Quay West Suites ★★ When the business folk go home on Fridays, they leave available this glamorous all-suite hotel, just 4 blocks from Queen Street Mall; you'll find excellent package deals here. A one-bedroom suite will sleep four with the sofa bed. The suites have all the amenities of a five-star hotel—daily servicing, concierge, a bar and restaurant with a lovely outdoor terrace—and their own laundry, dining area, separate bedroom, and fully equipped kitchen. Pamper yourself in the plunge pool or Jacuzzi; then back in your room get into your bathrobe, gaze over the Botanic Gardens, read the free newspaper, turn up your CD player, or watch one of the two TVs.

132 Alice St. (between Albert and George sts.), Brisbane, QLD 4000. ✆ **1800/672 726** in Australia, or 07/3853 6000. Fax 07/3853 6060. www.mirvachotels.com.au. 70 apts. A$295 (US$236/UK£118) 1-bedroom apt; A$405 (US$324/UK£162) 2-bedroom apt. Extra person A$35 (US$28/UK£14). Ask about special packages. AE, DC, MC, V. Undercover secure valet parking A$18 (US$14/UK£7). Bus: Downtown Loop. Ferry: Edward St. (Inner City and Cross River Ferry); or Riverside (CityCat), then a 10-min. stroll. **Amenities:** Restaurant; bar; outdoor pool; Jacuzzi; concierge; business center; 24-hr. room service; valet dry cleaning or laundry service. *In room:* A/C, TV w/in-house movies, dataport, kitchen, minibar, hair dryer, iron, safe, laundry.

MODERATE

Hotel Ibis Brisbane You get what you pay for at this AAA-rated three-star sister property to the Novotel Brisbane (see above). In this case, it is basically a room, with few amenities you might expect in a large hotel. But if you don't mind doing without river views, porters, a pool, or other small luxuries, this could be the place for you. The hotel has rooms—refurbished in early 2006 and much larger than those in most three-star hotels—furnished in contemporary style, with sizable work desks and small but smart bathrooms.

27–35 Turbot St. (between North Quay and George St.), Brisbane, QLD 4000. ✆ **1300/656 565** in Australia, 800/221-4542 in the U.S. and Canada, 020/8283 4500 in the U.K., 0800/44 4422 in New Zealand, or 07/3237 2333.

Fax 07/3237 2444. www.accorhotels.com.au. 218 units. A$149 (US$119/UK£60) double. Extra person A$30 (US$24/UK£12). Children under 16 stay free in parent's room with existing bedding. Ask about packages. AE, DC, MC, V. Parking A$10 (US$8/UK£4). Train: Roma St. Bus: Downtown Loop. Ferry: North Quay (CityCat or CityFerry). **Amenities:** 2 restaurants; 2 bars; car-rental desk; airport shuttle; coin-op laundry; laundry service; dry cleaning; nonsmoking rooms. *In room:* A/C, TV w/pay movies, fridge, coffeemaker, hair dryer, iron.

INEXPENSIVE

Eton ★ *Finds* This heritage-listed cottage, not far from the Brisbane Transit Centre, has five rooms and an attic suite that sleeps three, all with en-suite bathrooms. The attic suite is a self-contained apartment with its own entrance and kitchen. Room no. 1, at the front of the house, is my pick—it has a claw-foot bathtub and king-size bed. Out the back is a garden courtyard, where you can have breakfast among the palms, ferns, and frangipani trees. No children under 4. There's no smoking indoors.

436 Upper Roma St., Brisbane, QLD 4000. ✆ **07/3236 0115.** www.babs.com.au/eton. 6 units, 5 with shower only. A$110–A$130 (US$88–US$104/UK£44–UK£52) double; A$490 (US$392/UK£196) apt weekly. Rates include breakfast (except apt). AE, MC, V. Limited free parking. Train: Roma St. **Amenities:** Access to guest laundry and kitchen; wireless Internet access and Internet-enabled PC available. *In room:* A/C, TV, coffeemaker, hair dryer, iron.

Hotel George Williams ★ *Value* This 7-year-old hotel is so smart it's hard to believe it's a YMCA. Accommodations have vivid bedcovers, chrome chairs, and artsy bedside lamps on chrome stands. Rooms are small but some can sleep up to four adults. Among the useful facilities are a 24-hour front desk, safe-deposit boxes, and a hip cybercafe (and there's also wireless broadband access from your room). Hair dryers are available on request. Guests have free access to the City Y health club, the largest hotel gym in Australia, which offers aerobics classes, personal trainers, and massage (for an extra fee). Four rooms are designed for guests with disabilities, and there is also easy access to the gym.

317–325 George St. (between Turbot and Ann sts.), Brisbane, QLD 4000. ✆ **1800/064 858** in Australia, or 07/3308 0700. Fax 07/3308 0733. www.hgw.com.au. 81 units, most with shower only. A$95–A$175 (US$76–US$140/UK£38–UK£70) double. Extra person A$25 (US$20/UK£10). Children under 4 stay free in parent's room. Ask about packages. AE, DC, MC, V. Limited free parking. Train: Roma St. Bus: Downtown Loop. Ferry: North Quay (CityCat or CityFerry). **Amenities:** Cafe; bar; health club; tour desk; coin-op laundry w/iron and ironing board; laundry service; dry cleaning; nonsmoking rooms. *In room:* A/C, TV, fridge, coffeemaker.

Thornbury House Bed & Breakfast ★ *Finds* A 15-minute walk to Spring Hill from the city center brings you to this 1886 Queenslander cottage on a quiet street. Hosts Christine and Gerry Scanlan have decked out every room individually with Oriental rugs, comfortable beds, bathrobes, and lovely old furniture and knickknacks. Those without attached bathrooms have their own private bathrooms down the hall. The attic suite sleeps three and has two bedrooms, a sitting room, and a bathroom. Two of the rooms have direct access to the front veranda. Breakfast is served in the ferny courtyard (a cool and restful place on a humid day), where you can help yourself to tea, coffee, cookies, and the newspaper any time of day. Guests have access to the house's washer, dryer, iron, fridge, and microwave. The airport bus stops at the front door.

1 Thornbury St., Spring Hill, Brisbane, QLD 4000. ✆ **07/3839 5334.** www.babs.com.au/thornbury. 6 units, 5 with shower only. A$100–A$110 (US$80–US$88/UK£40–UK£44) double; A$140 (US$112/UK£56) apt. Rates include breakfast. AE, MC, V. Limited free parking; metered street parking A$5 (US$4/UK£2). Train: Central. **Amenities:** Access to nearby pools, golf club, and health club; play area and toys; dry cleaning; nonsmoking rooms; fax, computer, and dataport available; pay phone. *In room:* A/C, TV, hair dryer.

IN PADDINGTON

Aynsley B&B ★ *Finds* In a quiet street just off the main shopping and restaurant strip in Paddington, this restored 1905 Queenslander house retains most of its original features, such as leadlight windows, tongue-and-groove walls, high ceilings, and polished timber floors. The two air-conditioned guest bedrooms are nicely furnished and have good quality, comfy mattresses. Each has its own en-suite bathroom. Your hosts, Gena and Garth Evans, have been in the B&B business for 7 years, both in Sydney and Brisbane, and know how to look after their guests. A rear deck on both levels overlooks mango trees, busy with birdlife, and its hard to believe you are only 3km (2 miles) from the city center. There's also a large swimming pool. There's no smoking indoors.

14 Glanmire St., Paddington, Brisbane, QLD 4064. ✆ **07/3368 2250,** or 0417 482 021 mobile. Fax 07/3368 2250. www.aysnley.com.au. 2 units, both with shower only. A$155–A$165 (US$124–US$132/UK£62–UK£66) double. Weekly rates available. Rates include full breakfast. MC, V. Free off-street parking. Bus: 375 or 377; stop 200m (656 ft.) away. **Amenities:** Outdoor pool; coin-op laundry; nonsmoking rooms; safe. *In room:* A/C, TV, Internet access, fridge, coffeemaker, hair dryer, iron.

4 Where to Dine

Visitors are often surprised to find that Brisbane has a sophisticated dining scene. Stylish bistros and cafes line Merthyr Street in New Farm; cute cafes are plentiful in Paddington; Asian eateries are a good choice around the intersection of Vulture Street and Boundary Street in West End; and in Fortitude Valley ("the Valley" for short), you'll find Chinatown. A street full of upscale but laid-back restaurants, many with a Mediterranean flavor, sits under the kitsch replica Eiffel Tower on Park Road in Milton, and in the city center you can find slick riverfront restaurants at Eagle Street Pier and Riverside. The intersection of Albert and Charlotte streets buzzes with inexpensive, good-quality cafes.

IN THE CITY CENTER

EXPENSIVE

e'cco bistro ★★★ CONTEMPORARY "Here it is" is one translation of the Italian *e'cco,* and that's the philosophy behind the food at this award-winning bistro. It serves simple food, done exceptionally well and with passion. In a former tea warehouse on the city fringe, it's one of Australia's best. Dishes include such delights as duck breast with Peking duck consommé, wombok, broccolini, chile, and ginger; or grilled white fish with a cassoulet of white beans, clams, mussels, parsley, and peppers. The bistro is enormously popular, and bookings are essential. Large windows, bold colors, and modern furniture make it a pleasant setting in a small but popular restaurant enclave. The price structure is simple (each course's offerings are all the same price), and there's an extensive wine list—many by the glass.

100 Boundary St. (at Adelaide St.). ✆ **07/3831 8344.** Fax 07/3831 8460. www.eccobistro.com. Reservations required. Starters A$22 (US$18/UK£9); main courses A$37 (US$30/UK£15); desserts A$15 (US$12/UK£6). AE, DC, MC, V. Tues–Fri noon–2:30pm; Tues–Sat 6–10pm. Metered street parking or nearby parking buildings.

Pier Nine ★★★ CONTEMPORARY/SEAFOOD Ask the locals for the best seafood in town, and they'll send you to this light-filled contemporary restaurant overlooking the river and Story Bridge. The menu changes daily; specialties include oysters shucked to order and served several ways or *au naturel* for the purist, fresh local Moreton Bay bugs (a kind of crustacean), mud crab, and wild barramundi. There are plenty of options for meat-lovers and vegetarians, but the emphasis is on fresh seafood—try the shredded omelet with sand crab, shrimp, and fine egg noodles or the blackened fish with chickpea, celery, and raisin salad, and burnt orange yogurt. It's always busy, so if you don't have a reservation, prepare to hang out at the oyster bar.

Eagle St. Pier, 1 Eagle St. ✆ **07/3226 2100.** Reservations recommended. Main courses A$21–A$48 (US$17–US$38/UK£8.40–UK£19). AE, DC, MC, V. Mon–Fri 11:30am–10pm; Sat 5–10pm; closed Sun and public holidays. Underground parking. Ferry: Riverside (CityCat); Edward St. or Riverside (CityFerry); Eagle St. Pier (Cross River Ferry).

Watt Modern Dining ★★ MODERN AUSTRALIAN Whether it's for a leisurely weekend breakfast, lunch, or dinner before a show at the Brisbane Powerhouse, this is a bright spot to be. With a menu of modern fare with Asian, Middle Eastern, and European influences, and a terrific wine list, Watt is one of my favorite places to eat out in Brisbane—partly because of the riverside setting in New Farm Park, and partly because of the great food. Dishes include interesting things like blackened duck breast with sea scallops, pickled cucumber and star anise broth, or a Thai green vegetable curry with fried shallots and jasmine rice. The whole place was given a revamp in mid-2006. The Park Lounge is great for drinks and light meals before the theater.

Brisbane Powerhouse, 119 Lamington St., New Farm (near the river). ✆ **07/3358 5464.** www.watt.net.au. Reservations recommended. Main courses A$25–A$37 (US$20–US$30/UK£10–UK£15). AE, DC, MC, V. Tues–Fri 10am–late; Sat–Sun 8am–late. Ample nearby parking.

MODERATE

Jo Jo's INTERNATIONAL/CAFE FARE A spectacular timber, limestone, and glass bar dominates the center of this casual cafe-style eating spot, housing more than 1,000 bottles of wine. Four menus—chargrill, Thai, pizza, and Mediterranean—are available, and the locals have dropped in here for years for a shopping pit stop or a post-cinema meal. The food is well priced and good. You order at the bar and meals are delivered to the table (try to get one on the balcony overlooking the Queen St. Mall). Among your options are steaks and seafood from the grill; curries and stir-fries from the Thai menu; Mediterranean pastas, antipasto, and designer sandwiches; and gourmet toppings on wood-fired-oven pizzas.

1st floor, Queen St. Mall at Albert St. ✆ **07/3221 2113.** www.jojos.com.au. Main courses A$10–A$30 (US$8–US$24/UK£4–UK£12). AE, DC, MC, V. Daily 9:30am–midnight; happy hour daily 4:30–6pm. Train or bus: Central.

INEXPENSIVE

Govinda's *Value* VEGETARIAN If you're on a budget, or a committed vegetarian, seek out the Hare Krishnas' chain of Govinda restaurants. This one serves vegetable casserole, dal soup, samosas, and other tasty stuff with a north Indian influence. The atmosphere is pretty spartan, but the food is very satisfying. This is a stimulant-free zone, so don't come expecting alcohol, tea, or coffee—you're likely to get something like homemade ginger and mint lemonade instead.

99 Elizabeth St. (opposite Myer Centre), 2nd floor. ✆ **07/3210 0255.** A$9 (US$7.20/UK£3.60) all-you-can-eat; A$8 (US$6.40/UK£3.20) student/senior rates, A$6 (US$4.80/UK£2.40) students (2–3pm only). No credit cards. Mon–Thurs 11am–3pm (takeout 4:30–6:30pm); Fri 11am–8:30pm; Saturday 11am–2:30pm. Sun Feast from 5pm, with lectures and dancing, costs A$5 (US$4/UK£2). Bus: Downtown Loop.

IN SPRING HILL

MODERATE

Tognini's BistroCafeDeli MODERN AUSTRALIAN Owners Mark and Narelle Tognini run this relaxed modern bistro, incorporating an extensive deli and walk-in cheese room. Popular with inner-city dwellers and business folk, it serves gourmet delights to eat in or take out. Sit at one of the communal tables and try salmon and sweet potato fish cakes with Asian noodle salad, or maybe crab and asparagus risotto with lemon and chile. Don't pass up the vanilla panna cotta for dessert—it's divine. There's another Tognini's at Baroona Road, Milton, and the brand-new Tognini's Café WineBar at the new State Library at South Bank.

Turbot and Boundary sts., Spring Hill. ✆ **07/3831 5300.** Fax 07/3831 5311. www.togninis.com. Reservations not accepted. Main courses A$15–A$23 (US$12–US$18/UK£6–UK£9). AE, DC, MC, V. Mon–Fri 7am–6pm; Sat–Sun 8am–4pm. Closed Easter and Dec 25.

IN MOUNT COOT-THA

EXPENSIVE

The Summit ★★ MODERN AUSTRALIAN It would be hard to find a better view of Brisbane than from this spot. A teahouse of some kind has been on this mountaintop for more than a century. Part 19th-century Queenslander house and part modern extension, the restaurant has wraparound covered decks with a view of the city and Moreton Bay. A changing menu features local produce teamed with Australian wines. Try saltwater barramundi (fish) filet, or pan-seared kangaroo loin medallions. The early-bird offer—A$30 (US$24/UK£12) for three courses if you finish by 7pm—is available starting at 5pm. There's also a kids' menu of two courses for less than A$15 (US$12/UK£6). And when you've finished dining, spend some time on the observation deck—at night the city lights provide a glittering panorama.

At the Mt. Coot-tha Lookout, Sir Samuel Griffith Dr., Mt. Coot-tha. ✆ **07/3369 9922.** Fax 07/3369 8937. www.brisbanelookout.com. Reservations recommended Fri–Sat night. Main courses A$29–A$38 (US$23–US$30/UK£12–UK£15). AE, DC, MC, V. Daily 11:30am–midnight; Sun brunch 8–10:30am. Closed for lunch Jan 1, Good Friday, Dec 26; closed for dinner Dec 25. Free parking. Bus: 471. From Roma St. Transit Centre, take Upper Roma St. and Milton Rd. 3.5km (2¼ miles) west to the Western Fwy. roundabout at Toowong Cemetery, veer right into Sir Samuel Griffith Dr., and go approximately 3km (2 miles).

IN EAST BRISBANE

MODERATE

Green Papaya ★ *Value* NORTH VIETNAMESE After 12 years of delighting Brisbane diners—and visitors to the city—with her clean, fresh, and simple dishes, owner-chef Lien Yeoman sold her famous restaurant in 2007. I haven't been back since the hand-over, but the new owner has kept on chef Thang, who has worked with Lien since 1998, as well as the same staff and menu. So I trust that when you visit, the same quality for which this restaurant has been known has been maintained. There are two chic, cheerful rooms, usually crowded with a faithful clientele. If you don't know your *bo xao cay ngot* (spicy beef) from your *nom du du* (green papaya salad), the staff willingly gives advice. The restaurant is licensed, but you can bring your own wine (no beer or spirits) for a corkage charge of A$3 (US$2.40/UK£1.20) per person. The restaurant also does takeout.

898 Stanley St. E. (at Potts St.), 1 block from Woolloongabba Cricket Ground, East Brisbane. ✆ **07/3217 3599.** www.greenpapaya.com.au. Reservations recommended. Main courses A$25–A$36 (US$20–US$29/UK£10–UK£14); banquet menus (for minimum of 4 people) A$50–A$60 (US$40–US$48/UK£20–UK£24). Minimum charge A$30 (US$24/UK£12) per person. AE, DC, MC, V. Tues–Sun 5:30–10pm; Thurs–Fri lunch by reservation only. Closed Good Friday and Dec 25 to early Jan. Parking at rear of restaurant and on-street. Train: Woolloongabba.

IN ALBION

MODERATE

Breakfast Creek Hotel ★ STEAK A A$4.5-million (US$3.6-million/UK£1.8-million) renovation and restoration in 2002 gave fresh life to this Brisbane treasure. Built in 1889 and listed by the National Trust, the French Renaissance–style pub is fondly known as the Brekky Creek—or simply "the Creek." The quintessentially

Queensland establishment is famed for its gigantic steaks (choose your own), served with baked potato, bacon sauce, coleslaw, and salad, and for serving beer "off the wood" (from the keg). Also on the premises, the Spanish Garden restaurant and the beer garden are always popular, and an outdoor dining area overlooks Breakfast Creek. The Substation No. 41 bar, created in the shell of a derelict electricity substation next to the hotel, makes the most of its exposed brick walls and soaring ceilings. The 4.5m-long (15-ft.) wooden bar is just the place to sip the latest cocktail.

2 Kingsford Smith Dr. (at Breakfast Creek Rd.), Albion. ✆ **07/3262 5988.** www.breakfastcreekhotel.com. Main courses A$17–A$25 (US$14–US$20/UK£7–UK£10). AE, DC, MC, V. Daily 11:30am–2:30pm; Mon–Fri 5:30–9:30pm; Sat 5–9:30pm; Sun 5–8:30pm. Pub Sun–Thurs 10am–10pm; Fri–Sat 10am–11pm. Substation No. 41 daily noon–late; Sunday 8–10:30am for breakfast. Bus: 300 or 322. Wickham St. becomes Breakfast Creek Rd.; the hotel is just off the route to the airport.

5 Exploring Brisbane

CUDDLING A KOALA & OTHER TOP ATTRACTIONS

Brisbane Botanic Gardens Mount Coot-tha These 52-hectare (128-acre) gardens at the base of Mount Coot-tha feature Aussie natives and exotics you probably won't see at home, including an arid zone, a Tropical Dome conservatory housing rainforest plants, a cactus house, a bonsai house, fragrant plants, a Japanese garden, African and American plants, wetlands, and a bamboo grove. There are lakes and trails, usually a horticultural show or arts-and-crafts display in the auditorium on weekends, and a cafe. Free 1-hour guided tours leave the kiosk at 11am and 1pm Monday through Saturday (except public holidays and between mid-Dec and mid-Jan). The Sir Thomas Brisbane Planetarium & Cosmic Skydome (see below) is also in the botanic gardens.

Mt. Coot-tha Rd., Toowong, 7km (4 miles) from the city. ✆ **07/3403 2535.** www.brisbane.qld.gov.au. Free admission to Botanic Gardens. Sept–Mar daily 8am–5:30pm; Apr–Aug daily 8am–5pm. Free parking. Bus: 471.

City Hall Once the tallest building in Brisbane, City Hall is now dwarfed by the office blocks that surround it. Nevertheless, a ride in the old elevator to the top of the sandstone clock tower (at 92m/302 ft.) gives you a different perspective on the city center. A cheery elevator operator will give you a history of the building on your short ride to the third floor before letting you out into the glassed-in observation floor in the bell tower. Or you can take a 90-minute guided tour on weekdays between 8:30am and 4:30pm. If you're there on the quarter-hour, you'll get a close-up experience of the chimes. Try not to be there at midday, when the clock chimes 12—it's deafening.

King George Sq. (Ann and Adelaide sts.). ✆ **07/3403 8888.** Free admission to City Hall; free admission to clock tower; tours cost A$5 (US$4/UK£2) adults, A$2 (US$1.60/UK80p) children over 5 and students (bookings essential). City Hall weekdays 8am–5pm, weekends 10am–5pm; clock tower Mon–Fri 10am–3pm, Sat 10am–2:30pm (closed Sun and public holidays). Train: Roma Street. Bus: City Circle.

Lone Pine Koala Sanctuary ★★ *Kids* This is the best place in Australia to cuddle a koala—and one of the few places where koala cuddling is still allowed. Banned in New South Wales and Victoria, koala cuddling is allowed in Queensland under strict conditions that ensure that each animal is handled for less than 30 minutes a day—and gets every third day off! When it opened in 1927, Lone Pine had only two koalas, Jack and Jill; it is now home to more than 130. You can cuddle them anytime and have a photo taken holding one for A$15 (US$12/UK£6); once you've purchased a photograph, your companions can take as many photos of you as they like with their own cameras. Lone Pine isn't just koalas—you can also hand-feed kangaroos and wallabies and get up close with emus, snakes, baby crocs, parrots, wombats, Tasmanian devils, skinks, lace monitors, frogs, bats, turtles, possums, and other native wildlife. There is a currency exchange, a gift shop, and a restaurant and cafe. You can also take advantage of the picnic and barbecue facilities.

The nicest way to get to Lone Pine is a cruise down the Brisbane River aboard MV *Mirimar* (© **1300/729 742** in Australia or 0412 749 426 mobile phone), which leaves the Cultural Centre pontoon at South Bank Parklands at 10am. The 19km (12-mile) trip to Lone Pine takes 90 minutes and includes commentary. You have 2 hours to explore Lone Pine before returning, arriving in the city at 2:45pm. The fare is A$48 (US$38/UK£19) for adults and A$27 (US$22/UK£11) for children aged 3 to 13 or A$135 (US$108/UK£54) for a family of five, including entry to Lone Pine. Cruises run daily except April 25 (Anzac Day) and December 25.

Jesmond Rd., Fig Tree Pocket. © **07/3378 1366.** Fax 07/3878 1770. www.koala.net. Admission A$20 (US$16/UK£8) adults, A$15 (US$12/UK£6) children 3–13, A$52 (US$42/UK£21) families of 5. AE, DC, MC, V. Daily 8:30am–5pm; 1:30–5pm Apr 25 (Anzac Day); 8:30am–4:30pm Dec 25. By car (20 min. from the city center), take Milton Rd. to the roundabout at Toowong cemetery, then Western Fwy. toward Ipswich. Signs point to Fig Tree Pocket and Lone Pine. Ample free parking. Bus: 430 from the city center hourly 8:45am–3:40pm weekdays, 8:30am–3:30pm weekends and public holidays; 445 at 8:45am and 3:45pm, and hourly from 9:10am–2:10pm weekdays, 7:55am–2:55pm Sat. Bus fare A$2.90 (US$2.30/UK£1.15) adults, A$1.50 (US$1.20/UK60p) children. Taxi from the city center about A$24 (US$19/UK£9.60).

Museum of Brisbane This smallish museum in the historic City Hall is designed to capture the history and essence of Brisbane. There's a theater that shows a short film about the city and a shop that stocks "made in Brisbane" items. Changing exhibitions relate the stories, events, and ideas that have shaped the city, as well as giving practical information for visitors. It is a good starting point for your visit.

City Hall, King George Sq. © **07/3403 8888.** Free admission. Daily 10am–5pm. Closed Jan 1, Good Friday, Dec 25 and 26, and until 1pm Apr 25 (Anzac Day). Train: Roma Street. Bus: City Circle.

Newstead House ★ Brisbane's oldest surviving home has been restored to its late Victorian splendor in a peaceful park overlooking the Brisbane River. Wander the rooms, admire the gracious exterior dating from 1846, and on Sunday between March and November, take Devonshire tea. The U.S. Army occupied the house during World War II, and the first American war memorial built in Australia stands on Newstead Point, on the grounds.

Newstead Park, Breakfast Creek Rd., Newstead. © **1800/061 846** or 07/3216 1846. www.newsteadhouse.com.au. A$4.50 (US$3.60/UK£1.80) adults, A$3.50 (US$2.80/UK£1.40) seniors and students, A$2.50 (US$2/UK£1) children 6–16, A$12 (US$9.60/UK£4.80) families. Free admission on the first Fri of each month. Mon–Fri 10am–4pm; Sun 2–5pm. Last admittance 30 min. before closing. Closed Sat, Good Friday, Apr 25 (Anzac Day), Dec 24–Jan 1, and other public holidays. Limited parking. Bus: 300 or 302.

Queensland Cultural Centre *Kids* This modern complex stretching along the south bank of the Brisbane River houses many of the city's performing arts venues as well as the state art gallery, museum, and library. With plenty of open plazas and fountains, it is a pleasing place to wander or just sit and watch the river and the city skyline. It's a 7-minute walk from town.

The **Queensland Performing Arts Centre** (© **07/3840 7444** administration Mon–Fri 9am–5pm, or 13 62 46 for all bookings; www.qpac.com.au) houses the 2,000-seat Lyric Theatre for musicals, ballet, and opera; the 1,800-seat Concert Hall for orchestral performances; the 850-seat Playhouse theater for plays; and the 315-seat Cremorne Theatre for theater-in-the-round, cabaret, and experimental works. The complex has a restaurant and a cafe. Guided tours of the theaters and public and backstage areas leave from the box office at 11:30am on Fridays (except holidays) and take about 90 minutes. Reservations are advisable during school holidays (© **07/3840 7444**). The cost is A$7.50 (US$6/UK£3) adults and A$5 (US$4/UK£2) children.

The **Queensland Art Gallery** ★ (© **07/3840 7303;** www.qag.qld.gov.au) is one of Australia's most attractive galleries, with vast light-filled spaces and interesting water features inside and out. It is a major player in the Australian art world, attracting blockbuster exhibitions of works by the likes of Renoir, Picasso, and van Gogh, and showcasing diverse modern Australian painters, sculptors, and other artists. It also has an impressive collection of Aboriginal art. Admission is free. There is a gift shop and bistro. The new **Queensland Gallery of Modern Art,** next door, opened in late 2006, providing more space for the collections of modern and contemporary Australian, indigenous Australian, Asian, and Pacific art. The **Australian Cinémathèque,** located at the Gallery of Modern Art, has two cinemas in which it presents retrospective and thematic film programs, as well as a gallery dedicated to screen-related exhibitions. Both galleries are open Monday through Friday 10am to 5pm, weekends 9am to 5pm; closed Good Friday, December 25, and until noon on April 25 (Anzac Day).

The **Queensland Museum** (© **07/3840 7555;** www.qmuseum.qld.gov.au), on the corner of Grey and Melbourne streets, underwent a major revamp in 2003 and looks the better for it. The museum houses an eclectic collection ranging from natural history specimens and fossils to a World War I German tank. Children will like the blue whale model; the dinosaurs, which include Queensland's own Muttaburrasaurus; and the interactive Sciencentre on Level 1. The museum has a cafe and gift shop. Admission is free, except to the Sciencentre and traveling exhibitions. It's open daily 9:30am to 5pm; closed Good Friday, December 25, and until 1:30pm on April 25 (Anzac Day).

Adjacent to South Bank Parklands, across Victoria Bridge at western end of Queen St. © **07/3840 7100.** Admission to Sciencentre A$9.50 (US$7.60/UK£3.80) adults, A$7.50 (US$6/UK£3) children 5–16, A$29 (US$23/UK£12) family of 6. Plentiful underground parking. Ferry: South Bank (CityCat) or Old South Bank (Inner City Ferry). Bus: Numerous routes from Adelaide St. (near Albert St.), including 100, 111, 115, and 120, stop outside.

Roma Street Parkland Thousands of plants, including natives and some of the world's most endangered, have been used to create lush subtropical gardens in an unused railway yard. The effect is stunning. Free 1-hour guided walks leave from the Hub, near the Spectacle Garden entrance at 10am and 2pm daily (excluding Good Friday and Christmas Day), and there are also self-guided walks for each themed area of the gardens. The "art walk" helps visitors discover the interesting public art on display. The park also has barbecues, picnic areas, a playground, and cafe. From King George Square, it is about a 500m (1,640-ft.) walk along Albert Street.

Roma St.; information booths in Spectacle Garden and at Activity Centre. © **07/3006 4545.** www.romastreetparkland.com. Free admission. Daily 24 hr.; Spectacle Garden daily dawn–dusk. Train: Roma St. Station. By car, enter from Roma St. or the Wickham Terrace/College Rd./Gregory Terrace intersection.

Sir Thomas Brisbane Planetarium & Cosmic Skydome *Kids* After a major upgrade in early 2004, the planetarium has new seating and new digital multimedia systems that present real-time digital star shows and computer-generated images in the Cosmic Skydome theater. The popular and fascinating 40-minute astronomical show includes a re-creation of the Brisbane night sky using a Ziess star projector. There are special shows designed for kids between 5 and 8 at 11:30am on weekends; the planetarium is not recommended for younger children. Kids shows cost A$5.90 (US$4.70/UK£2.35) adults and children.

In Brisbane Botanic Gardens Mt. Coot-tha, Mt. Coot-tha Rd., Toowong. ✆ **07/3403 2578.** www.brisbane.qld.gov.au/planetarium. A$12 (US$9.60/UK£4.80) adults, A$9.70 (US$7.75/UK£3.90) seniors and students, A$6.90 (US$5.50/UK£2.75) children under 15, A$32 (US$26/UK£13) family of 4. Tues–Fri 2:30–4:30pm; Sat 11am–7:30pm; Sun 11am–4:15pm. Shows Tues–Fri 3:15pm; Sat 12:30, 2, 3:15, 6, and 7:30pm; Sun 12:30, 2, and 3:15pm. Closed public holidays. Reservations recommended. Bus: 471, 598, or 599.

South Bank Parklands *Kids* Follow the locals' lead and spend some time at this delightful 16-hectare (40-acre) complex of parks, restaurants, shops, playgrounds, street theater, and weekend markets. There's a man-made beach, lined with palm trees, with real waves and sand, where you can swim, stroll, and cycle the meandering pathways. Or sit over a cafe latte in one of the cafes and enjoy the city views. From the parklands it's an easy stroll to the museum, art gallery, and other parts of the adjacent **Queensland Cultural Centre** (see above). The South Bank Parklands are a 7-minute walk from town.

South Bank. ✆ **07/3867 2051** for Visitor Information Centre. www.south-bank.net.au. Free admission. Park daily 24 hr.; Visitor Information Centre daily 9am–5pm. From the Queen St. Mall, cross the Victoria Bridge to South Bank or walk across Goodwill Bridge from Gardens Point Rd. entrance to Brisbane City Gardens. Plentiful underground parking in Queensland Cultural Centre. Train: South Brisbane. Ferry: South Bank (CityCat or Cross River Ferry). Bus: Numerous routes from Adelaide St. (near Albert St.), including 100, 111, 115, and 120, stop at the Queensland Cultural Centre; walk through the Centre to South Bank Parklands.

St. John's Anglican Cathedral ★★ Brisbane's stunning neo-Gothic Anglican cathedral is in the final stages of completion—a mere 100 years after it was begun. This is the last Gothic-style cathedral to be completed anywhere in the world. There may still be some scaffolding or cranes around when you visit, as stonemasons use traditional medieval building techniques to complete this wonderful building. The interior was completed in 2007 and the western towers and spires will complete the final picture by 2009. Friendly, knowledgeable volunteer guides run tours and will point out some of the details that make this cathedral uniquely Queensland—like the carved possums on the organ screen and the hand-stitched cushions.

373 Ann St. (between Wharf and Queen sts.). ✆ **07/3835 2248.** www.stjohnscathedral.com.au. Daily 9:30am–4:30pm; free tours Mon–Sat 10am, daily 2pm. Closed to visitors, except for services, Apr 25 (Anzac Day), Dec 25, and some other public holidays. Train: Central Station.

TAKING A CITY STROLL

Because Brisbane is leafy, warm, and full of colonial-era Queenslander architecture, it is a great city for strolling. Pick up one of the free Heritage Trail Maps from the Brisbane Visitor Information Centre (see "Visitor Information," earlier in this chapter) and explore on your own. The map books include a history of the area and excellent detailed information of historic buildings and other sights along the way.

A "floating" **River Walk** connects more than 20km (13 miles) of pathways, roads, bridges, and parks along the Brisbane River. You can stroll along River Walk on the north bank of the river between the University of Queensland at St. Lucia and Teneriffe, and on the south bank from the West End ferry terminal at Orleigh Park to Dockside at Kangaroo Point.

For information on organized walking tours, see below.

6 Organized Tours

RIVER CRUISES The best way to cruise the river, in my view, is aboard the fast **CityCat ferries** ★★. Board at Riverside and head downstream under the Story Bridge to New Farm Park, past Newstead House to the restaurant row at Brett's Wharf; or cruise upriver past the city and South Bank to the University of Queensland's lovely campus. (Take a look at its impressive Great Court while you're there.) This trip in either direction will set you back a whole A$2.60 (US$2.10/UK£1.05). Or you can stay on for the full trip, which takes about 2 hours. For more information, see "Getting Around," earlier in this chapter.

For those who'd like commentary and a meal as they cruise, the **Kookaburra River Queen** paddle-wheelers (✆ **07/3221 1300;** www.kookaburrariverqueens.com) are a good option. You can choose from a lunch or dinner cruise, and from a three-course menu or a seafood platter. Lunch cruises cost A$48 (US$38/UK£19) and A$70 (US$56/UK£28) for seafood; dinner cruises are A$65 (US$52/UK£26) and A$85 (US$68/UK£34). Prices are A$10 (US$8/UK£4) higher on Friday and Saturday nights and public holidays. The boat departs from the Eagle Street Pier (parking is available under the City Rowers tavern on Eagle St.). Devonshire tea and wine-and-cheese options are also available for A$30 (US$24/UK£12) per person.

BUS TOURS For a good introduction to Brisbane, look no further than a City Sights bus tour run by **Brisbane City Council** (✆ **13 12 30** in Australia). **City Sights** buses stop at 19 points of interest in a continuous loop around the city center, Spring Hill, Milton, South Bank, and Fortitude Valley, including Chinatown. They take in various historic buildings and places of interest. The driver of the blue-and-yellow bus narrates, and you can hop on and off at any stop you like. The tour is a good value—your ticket also gives unlimited access to buses, ferries, and CityCats for the day, as well as discounts to some attractions. The bus departs every 45 minutes from 9am to 3:45pm daily except Good Friday, April 25 (Anzac Day), and December 25. The whole trip, without stopping, takes 90 minutes. Tickets cost A$22 (US$18/UK£8.80) for adults, A$16 (US$13/UK£6.40) for children 5 to 14. Buy your ticket on board. You can join anywhere along the route, but the most central stop is City Hall, stop 2, on Adelaide Street at Albert Street.

WALKING TOURS The Brisbane City Council has a wonderful program called **Gonewalking** (✆ **07/3403 8888**). About 80 free guided walks are run each week from somewhere in the city or suburbs, exploring all kinds of territory, from bushland to heritage buildings to riverscapes to cemeteries. The walks are aimed at locals, not tourists, so you get to explore Brisbane side by side with the townsfolk. Every walk has a flexible distance option and usually lasts about an hour. Most are easy, but some are more demanding. Most start and finish near public transport and end near a food outlet.

Prepare for shivers up your spine if you take one of Jack Sim's **Ghost Tours** ★ (✆ **07/3344 7265;** www.ghost-tours.com.au), which relive Brisbane's gruesome past. You can take a Saturday night Haunted Brisbane tour or Bloody Brisbane crime and murder tour for A$45 (US$36/UK£18) adults or A$23 (US$18/UK£9.20) children aged 12 to 17 or combine them for A$75 (US$60/UK£30). Other regular tours take in the historic Toowong and South Brisbane cemeteries. The cost is A$35 (US$28/UK£14) adults or A$18 (US$14/UK£7) children. Reservations are essential; no children under 12.

Free guided walks of the **City Botanic Gardens** at Alice Street leave from the rotunda at the Albert Street entrance Monday through Saturday at 11am and 1pm (except public holidays). They take about 1 hour. Bookings are not necessary.

7 Enjoying the Great Outdoors

OUTDOOR ACTIVITIES

ABSEILING The Kangaroo Point cliffs just south of the Story Bridge are a breeze for first-time abseilers (rappellers)—or so they say. The **Riverlife Adventure Centre** (© **07/3891 5766;** www.riverlife.com.au), in the old naval stores building at the base of the cliffs, runs daily abseiling and rock-climbing classes. Both activities cost A$29 (US$23/UK£12) per person, with nighttime rock climbing on Fridays from 6:30pm costing A$39 (US$31/UK£16).

BIKING Bike tracks, often shared with pedestrians and in-line skaters, stretch for 400km (248 miles) around Brisbane. One great scenic route, about 9km (5½ miles) long, starts just west of the Story Bridge, sweeps through the Brisbane City Gardens, and follows the river all the way to the University of Queensland campus at St. Lucia. **Brisbane Bicycle Sales and Hire,** 87 Albert St. (© **07/3229 2433**), will rent you a bike and furnish you with the Brisbane City Council's free detailed bike maps. Rentals start at A$12 (US$9.60/UK£4.80) for 1 hour and go up to A$25 (US$20/UK£10) for the day; overnight rentals (A$45/US$36/UK£18) are available. **Valet Cycle Hire** (© **0408 003 198** mobile; www.cyclebrisbane.com) operates from the bicycle station in the City Botanic Gardens, near the Alice Street gate, from 9:30am until dark. The cost is A$15 (US$12/UK£6) for 1 hour and A$5 (US$4/UK£2) each extra hour up to A$35 (US$28/UK£14). You can also have your bike "valet" delivered to all city area accommodations at extra cost and can rent for a week for A$100 (US$80/UK£40). All rentals include helmets, which are compulsory in Australia. The Brisbane City Council at City Hall (© **07/3403 8888**) and Brisbane Visitor Information Centre (see "Visitor Information," earlier in this chapter) also give out bike maps.

BUSHWALKING **Brisbane Forest Park** ★★, a 28,500-hectare (70,395-acre) expanse of bushland, waterfalls, and rainforest a 20-minute drive north of the city, has hiking trails ranging from just a few hundred meters up to 8km (5 miles). Some tracks have themes—one highlights the native mammals that live in the park, for example, and another, the 1.8km (just over 1-mile) **Mount Coot-tha Aboriginal Art Trail,** showcases contemporary Aboriginal art, with tree carvings, rock paintings, etchings, and a dance pit. Because the park is so big, most walks depart from one of the seven regional centers, which are up to a 20-minute drive from headquarters—you will need a car. Make a day of it and pack a picnic. At Park Headquarters, 60 Mount Nebo Rd., The Gap (© **1300/723 684;** www.epa.qld.gov.au/projects/park/index.cgi?parkid=2), you will find a wildlife display, a restaurant, a crafts shop, and an information center.

IN-LINE SKATING In-line skaters can use the network of bike and pedestrian paths. See "Biking," above, for locations that distribute maps, or head down to the Brisbane City Gardens at Alice Street and find your way along the river. **SkateBiz,** 101 Albert St. (© **07/3220 0157**), rents blades for around A$15 (US$12/UK£6) for 2 hours, or A$25 (US$20/UK£10) for up to 24 hours. Protective gear is included. Take a photo ID. The store is open from 9am to 5:30pm Monday through Thursday, 9am to 9pm Friday, 9am to 4pm Saturday, and 10am to 4pm Sunday.

KAYAKING To get out on the Brisbane River, you can rent a kayak from **Riverlife Adventure Centre** (© **07/3891 5766;** www.riverlife.com.au), at the base of the Kangaroo Point cliffs, for A$25 (US$20/UK£10) per person for an hour. Classes, in which you will learn how to launch, paddle, turn the kayak, stay out of the path of the CityCats, and much more, are run daily and cost A$29 (US$23/UK£12) per

Moments **Brisbane's Bridge Climb**

Brisbane boasts nine bridges across its wide river. The most interesting is the Story Bridge, built in 1940. If you are over 12 years old and at least 130 centimeters (just over 4 ft. 3 in.) tall, you can "climb" this overgrown Meccano set. The **Story Bridge Adventure Climb** (✆ **1300/254 627** in Australia, or 07/3514 6900; www.storybridgeadventureclimb.com.au) peaks at a viewing platform on top of the bridge, 44m (143 ft.) above the roadway and 80m (262 ft.) above the Brisbane River. Launched in late 2005, this is only the third "bridge climb" in the world (after Sydney's and Auckland's), so make the most of the chance. You'll be rewarded with magnificent 360-degree views of the city, river, and Moreton Bay and its islands. Climbs operate Wednesday to Sunday, and start from the base headquarters at 170 Main St. (at Wharf St.), Kangaroo Point. Day climbs cost A$110 (US$88/UK£44) adults and A$83 (US$66/UK£33) children aged 12 to 16 on weekdays and A$130/A$98 (US$104/US$78 or UK£52/UK£39) weekends. Twilight climbs cost A$130 (US$104/UK£52) adults and A$98 (US$78/UK£39) children. Night climbs are A$120 (US$96/UK£48) adults and A$90 (US$72/UK£36) children weekdays and A$130/A$98 (US$104/US$78 or UK£52/UK£39) weekends. Dawn climbs, only on Saturday and Sunday, cost A$130 (US$104/UK£52) adults and A$98 (US$78/UK£39) children. Children must be accompanied by an adult.

person. Night kayaking lessons are run on Tuesday and Thursday from 6:30pm and cost A$39 (US$31/UK£16) per person. The center is open 9am to 6:30pm daily.

8 The Shopping Scene

Brisbane's best shopping centers on **Queen Street Mall,** which has around 500 stores. Fronting the mall at 171–209 Queen St., under the Hilton, is the three-level **Wintergarden** shopping complex (✆ **07/3229 9755;** www.wgarden.com.au), housing upscale jewelers and Aussie fashion designers. Farther up the mall at 91 Queen St. (at Albert St.) is the **Myer Centre** (✆ **07/3223 6900**), which has Brisbane's biggest department store and five levels of moderately priced stores, mostly fashion. The **Brisbane Arcade,** 160 Queen St. Mall (✆ **07/3221 5977**), abounds with the boutiques of local Queensland designers. Just down the mall from it is the **Broadway on the Mall** arcade (✆ **07/3229 5233;** www.broadwayonthemall.com.au), which stocks affordable fashion, gifts, and accessories on two levels. Across from the Edward Street end of the mall is a smart new fashion and lifestyle shopping precinct, **MacArthur Central** (✆ **07/3007 2300;** www.macarthurcentral.com), right next door to the GPO on the block between Queen and Elizabeth streets. This is where you'll find top-name designer labels, Swiss watches, galleries, and accessory shops.

The trendy suburb of **Paddington,** just a couple of miles from the city by cab (or take the no. 144 bus to Bardon), is the place for antiques, books, art, crafts, one-of-a-kind clothing designs, and unusual gifts. The shops—colorfully painted Queenslander cottages—line the main street, Given Terrace, which becomes Latrobe Terrace. Don't miss the second wave of shops around the bend.

Finds Fireworks for Your Wall

If the Aboriginal art you see in the usual tourist outlets doesn't do it for you, what you'll see at Brisbane's **Fire-Works Gallery** will. Upstairs in an old printery at 11 Stratton St., Newstead (© **07/3216 1250**; www.fireworksgallery.com.au), this renowned gallery shows art by established and emerging artists from all over Australia. You may pale at some of the prices, but the stockroom at the back of the gallery may have something in your range. The staff will get your new acquisition shipped home for you. Open Tuesday to Friday 11am to 5pm, Saturday 11am to 4pm, or by appointment.

SHOPPING HOURS Brisbane shops are open Monday through Thursday from 9am to 6pm, Friday 9am to 9pm, Saturday 9am to 5:30pm, and Sunday 10am to 6pm. On Friday evening in the city, the Queen Street Mall is abuzz with cinema-goers and revelers; the late (until 9pm) shopping night in Paddington is Thursday.

MARKETS Authentic retro '50s and '60s fashion, offbeat stuff like old LPs, secondhand crafts, fashion by up-and-coming young designers, and all kinds of junk and treasure are for sale at Brisbane's only alternative market, **Valley Markets,** Brunswick Street and Chinatown malls, Fortitude Valley (© **07/3854 0860**). Hang around in one of the many coffee shops and listen to live music. It's open Saturday and Sunday from 8am to 4pm.

Friday night is a fun time to visit the **South Bank Lifestyle Markets,** Stanley Street Plaza, South Bank Parklands, when fairy lights illuminate the buzzing outdoor market. The market is open Friday from 5 to 10pm, Saturday and Sunday from 10am to 5pm.

Brisbane folk like trawling the **Riverside Markets** ★ at the Riverside Centre, 123 Eagle St., and the adjacent **Eagle Street Pier Art & Craft Markets** for housewares, colorful pottery, wooden blanket chests, handmade toys, painted flowerpots, and other stylish wares. They both open on Sunday from around 8am to 3pm.

For an authentic taste of Queensland's best produce, the **Farmers Markets** ★★ (© **0439/999 009;** www.janpower.com) operate on the second and fourth Saturday of each month, from 7am to noon, in the grounds of the Brisbane Powerhouse, Lamington Street, New Farm. Here you'll find much to tempt your palate, brought into the city by farmers from around the southeast part of the state. There are about 100 stalls, selling everything from fresh fruit and vegetables to homemade chutneys, quail, fresh seafood, free-range eggs, and pâtés. Foodies will be in heaven.

9 Brisbane After Dark

You can find out about festivals, concerts, and events, and book tickets through **Ticketek** (© **13 28 49** in Queensland; www.ticketek.com). You can book in person at Ticketek agencies, the most convenient of which are on Level E at the Myer Centre, 91 Queen St. Mall, and in the Visitor Information Centre at South Bank Parklands. Or try **Ticketmaster** (© **13 61 00;** www.ticketmaster.com.au).

QTIX (© **13 62 46** in Australia; www.qtix.com.au) is a major booking agent for performing arts and classical music, including all events at the Queensland Performing Arts Complex (QPAC). There is a A$2.75 (US$2.20/UK£1.10) booking fee per ticket.

You can also book in person at the box office at QPAC between 8:30am and 9pm Monday to Saturday, and at the South Bank Parklands Visitor Information Centre.

The free weekly magazine *Brisbane News* lists performing arts, jazz and classical music performances, art exhibitions, rock concerts, and public events. The free weekly *TimeOff,* published on Wednesday and available in bars and cafes, is a good guide to live music, as is Thursday's *Courier-Mail* newspaper.

THE PERFORMING ARTS

Many of Brisbane's performing arts events are at the **Queensland Performing Arts Centre (QPAC)** in the Queensland Cultural Centre (see "Exploring Brisbane," earlier in this chapter). The city also has a lively independent theater scene, with smaller companies making an increasing impact. To find out what's playing and to book tickets, contact QTIX (see above).

Queensland Theatre Company (✆ **07/3010 7600** for information; www.qldtheatreco.com.au), the state theater company, offers eight or nine productions a year, from the classics to new Australian works. It attracts some of the country's best actors and directors. Most performances are at the Playhouse or Cremorne Theatre at the Queensland Performing Arts Centre (QPAC), South Bank. Tickets cost from A$26 (US$21/UK£10)—if you are under 25—to A$68 (US$54/UK£27).

La Boite Theatre ★ (✆ **07/3007 8600** administration; www.laboite.com.au) is a well-established innovative company that performs contemporary Australian plays in the round. La Boite performs in the 400-seat Roundhouse Theater, 6 Musk Ave., Kelvin Grove. Take bus no. 390 from the city to Kelvin Grove Road and get off at stop 7. Tickets cost A$35 to A$55 (US$28–US$44/UK£14–UK£22), previews A$35 (US$28/UK£14). If you are 25 or under, they cost A$22 (US$18/UK£8.80).

Brisbane Powerhouse–Centre for the Live Arts, 119 Lamington St., New Farm (✆ **07/3358 8600;** www.brisbanepowerhouse.org), is a venue for innovative (some might say fringe) contemporary works. A former electricity powerhouse, the massive brick factory—which underwent another refurbishment in 2007—is now a dynamic art space for exhibitions, contemporary performance, and live art. The building retains its unique character, an industrial mix of metal, glass, and stark surfaces etched with 20 years of graffiti. It's a short walk from the New Farm ferry terminal along the riverfront through New Farm Park.

The state opera company, **Opera Queensland** (✆ **07/3735 3030** administration; www.operaqueensland.com.au), performs a lively repertoire of traditional as well as modern works, musicals, and choral concerts. Free talks on the opera you are about to see start in the foyer 45 minutes before every performance. Free close-up tours of the set are held after every performance (except the final night); book ahead through QTIX (✆ **13 62 46;** www.qtix.com.au). Most performances take place at the Queensland Performing Arts Centre (QPAC). Tickets range from A$39 to A$138 (US$31–US$110/UK£16–UK£55), or A$44 (US$35/UK£18) at some performances if you're age 30 or under.

The **Queensland Orchestra** (✆ **07/3377 5000** for administration; www.thequeenslandorchestra.com.au) provides classical music lovers with a diverse mix of orchestral and chamber music, with the odd foray into fun material, such as movie themes, Cole Porter hits, and gospel music. It schedules about 30 concerts a year. Free talks in the foyer begin 1 hour before major performances. The orchestra plays at the Concert Hall in the Queensland Performing Arts Centre (QPAC) or City Hall; more

Finds Brisbane's Historic Pubs

Brisbane's attractive historic pubs, many of them recently revitalized, have wide, shady verandas and beer gardens just perfect for whiling away a sunny afternoon or catching a quick meal at night.

The best known is the **Breakfast Creek Hotel,** 2 Kingsford Smith Dr., Breakfast Creek (✆ **07/3262 5988;** see "Where to Dine," earlier in this chapter). Built in 1889, the hotel is a Brisbane institution. For many people, a visit to the city isn't complete without a steak and beer "off the wood" at the Brekky Creek.

Another landmark is the **Regatta Hotel,** 543 Coronation Dr., Toowong (✆ **07/3871 9595;** www.regattahotel.com.au). This heritage hotel with three stories of iron lace balconies is the perfect spot for a cool drink overlooking the Brisbane River. After a multimillion-dollar renovation in 2002, the place now bursts at the seams on weekends. Its **Boatshed restaurant** (✆ **07/3871 9533**) is popular but not inexpensive—tables around the hotel verandas are a better choice.

Not far from the Regatta is the **Royal Exchange Hotel,** 10 High St., Toowong (✆ **07/3371 2555**). Known simply as "the RE," it's popular with students, probably because of its proximity to the University of Queensland. It has a great garden bar at the back.

The **Story Bridge Hotel,** 200 Main St., Kangaroo Point (✆ **07/3391 2266;** www.storybridgehotel.com.au), is well known as the venue for some of Brisbane's most unusual events, such as the annual Australia Day (Jan 26) cockroach races. Built in 1886, the pub is also a great place to find live music. In 2003 it was refurbished to the tune of A$3.2 million (US$2.5 million/UK£1.2 million), creating a new restaurant and bar literally built into the base of the bridge, and a new beer garden under the bridge.

In Red Hill, on the city fringe, is the **Normanby Hotel,** 1 Musgrave Rd. (✆ **07/3831 3353;** www.thenormanby.com.au), built in 1872 and recently stylishly revamped. Features are the giant Moreton Bay fig tree in the beer garden and the biggest outdoor TV screen in town.

Another of the city's oldest pubs is the **Plough Inn** (✆ **07/3844 7777;** www.ploughinn.com.au) at South Bank Parklands, which has stood its ground through major changes in the neighborhood since 1885. There's even a ghost, they say . . .

intimate works sometimes play at the Conservatorium Theatre, South Bank. Occasional "Tea and Symphony" concerts at City Hall include tea and coffee. Tickets for the Maestro concert series cost A$50 to A$66 (US$40–US$53/UK£20–UK£26), A$35 (US$28/UK£14) if you are a student or under 26.

NIGHTCLUBS & BARS

Friday's This indoor/outdoor bar, restaurant, and nightclub complex overlooking the Brisbane River is a haunt for "the Zoolander generation" of 18- to 40-year-olds. Gather on the large outdoor terrace with its huge island bar, or head for the restaurant, supper club, or dance floor. Music spans acid jazz, urban groove, and dance anthems from resident DJs, with the latest R&B, soul, and funk by live bands. Wednesday through Saturday nights see some kind of happy-hour deal, cocktail club, or drinks special; the dance action starts pumping around 9pm on Friday and Saturday. Upstairs in Riverside Centre, 123 Eagle St. ✆ **07/3832 2122.** Cover A$7–A$10 (US$5.60–US$8/UK£2.80–UK£4). Ferry: CityCat to Riverside.

Treasury Casino This lovely heritage building—built in 1886 as, ironically enough, the state's Treasury offices—houses a modern casino. Three levels of 100 gaming tables offer roulette, blackjack, baccarat, craps, sic-bo, and traditional Aussie two-up. There are more than 1,000 slot machines, five restaurants, and seven bars. It's open 24 hours. Live bands appear nightly in the Livewire Bar, and there's stand-up comedy on Wednesday night in the Premier's Bar. Queen St. between George and William sts. ✆ **07/3306 8888.** Must be 18 years old to enter; neat casual attire required (no beachwear or thongs). Closed Good Friday, Dec 25, and until 1pm Apr 25 (Anzac Day). Train: Central or South Brisbane, then walk across the Victoria Bridge.

Zenbar Minimalist Manhattan-style interiors with an 8m-high (26-ft.) glass wall overlooking a bamboo garden make this one of the hippest joints in town. It's a restaurant as well, but the bar is packed on Friday and Saturday night with office workers and beautiful people. There are about 40 wines by the glass, but in this kind of place you should be drinking a margarita or martini. The music ranges from '70s underground jazz and lounge to ultramodern funk house on Friday; on Saturday, the mood changes to easy background music. Park level, Post Office Sq., 215 Adelaide St. ✆ **07/3211 2333.** Train: Central.

COOL SPOTS FOR JAZZ & BLUES

The Bowery Exposed brick walls, wooden booths and a comfortable courtyard set the scene for one of Brisbane's most intimate and sophisticated jazz venues. This atmospheric cocktail bar, modeled on Prohibition-era speakeasies, has live jazz during the week and on Sundays—usually from around 8pm or 8:30pm—and DJs on Friday and Saturday from 9pm. Open Tuesday to Sunday 5pm to 3am. 676 Ann St., Fortitude Valley. ✆ **07/3252 0202.** Train: Brunswick St.

Brisbane Jazz Club ★ *Finds* On the riverfront under the Story Bridge, this is the only Australian jazz club still featuring big band dance music (every Sun night). Watch out for the slightly sloping dance floor—it was once a boat ramp! Traditional and mainstream jazz is featured on Saturday nights. It's open Fridays 6:30 to 11:30pm, Saturday 7 to 11:30pm, Sunday 5:30 to 8:30pm, and on Thursdays from 6:30 to 9pm there's a casual jazz appreciation session; phone and check what's on before heading over. Bookings are necessary for some events. 1 Annie St., Kangaroo Point. ✆ **07/3391 2006.** www.brisbanejazzclub.com.au. Cover usually A$15 (US$12/UK£6), higher for some guest acts. Free parking lot. Ferry: CityCat to Holman St.

10 Brisbane's Moreton Bay & Islands

The Brisbane River runs into Moreton Bay, which is studded with hundreds of small islands—and a few large ones. Some of them can be reached only by private vessel. Others are national parks and are accessible by tour boat or public ferry.

NORTH STRADBROKE ISLAND ★★

Affectionately called "Straddie" by the locals, the island was once home to a large Aboriginal population and still retains much of their history. The town of Dunwich was used as a convict outstation, Catholic mission, quarantine station, and benevolent institution. The **historical museum** at Dunwich (✆ **07/3409 9699**) has a display of historical photographs, items salvaged from shipwrecks, and information about the early settlement of the island; it's open from 10am to 2pm Wednesday, Friday, and Saturday. Entry costs A$3.30 (US$2.65/UK£1.30) adults and A$1.10 (US90¢/UK45p) children. Pick up a booklet which will guide you along a heritage trail which features 30 points of interest at Dunwich, Amity, and Lookout Point, as well as detailing the history of the Dunwich Cemetery. The booklet is available at visitor centers on the mainland and at Dunwich, at the museum and at tourist attractions on the island. Another "must" for visitors is the North Gorge Headlands Walk, for breathtaking views and for spotting turtles, dolphins, and whales.

GETTING THERE & GETTING AROUND **Stradbroke Ferries** (✆ **07/3286 2666**) operates water-taxi service from Toondah Harbour, Middle Street, Cleveland, to Dunwich (about 30 min.); the round-trip adult fare is A$17 (US$14/UK£6.80), A$10 (US$8/UK£4) for children 5 to 14. The vehicle barge takes walk-on passengers for A$11 (US$8.80/UK£4.40) round-trip; the trip takes about 45 minutes. A bus meets almost every water taxi or ferry at Dunwich and connects it with the other two main settlements, Amity and Point Lookout. The trip to either place takes about 30 minutes and costs A$9.50 (US$7.60/UK£3.80) round-trip for adults, A$5 (US$4/UK£2) for children 5 to 14.

To get to Cleveland by public transport from Brisbane, take the train from Central Station to Cleveland Station (A$4.20/US$3.35/UK£1.70), then walk about 300m (½ mile) to Middle Street or take a bus from the station to the ferry terminal, which costs A$2 (US$1.60/UK80p).

VISITOR INFORMATION The **Stradbroke Island Tourism** information center (✆ **07/3409 9555**) is on Junner Street, Dunwich, about 200m (656 ft.) from the ferry terminal. It is open weekdays from 8:30am to 5pm and weekends 9am to 4pm.

SOUTH STRADBROKE ISLAND ★★

A turn-of-the-20th-century shipwreck (with a cargo of whiskey and explosives) weakened the link between this lovely island and North Stradbroke, and nature did the rest. South Stradbroke is less well known than its sister island, but that's changing. The island has four camping grounds and three resorts. South Stradbroke Island is accessible from Hope Harbour, about a 45-minute drive south of Brisbane.

GETTING THERE & GETTING AROUND From Brisbane, take the Pacific Highway exit after Dreamworld (exit 57), and follow signs to Hope Harbour and to the departure terminal for the island. The resorts run boats for guests only; the only other way to get there is by water taxi. **Gold Coast Water Taxi** (✆ **0418 759 789**) takes groups to the island for A$150 (US$120/UK£60) per transfer (10 people with no luggage, or six people plus camping gear). **Couran Cove Island Resort** (✆ **1800/268 726** or 07/5597 9995; www.couran.com) runs day tours. Prices start at A$65 (US$52/UK£26) adults, A$35 (US$28/UK£14) children or A$175 (US$140/UK£70) for a family of four, which includes return transfers from Hope Harbour, lunch, and use of resort facilities. The Fastcat ferry leaves Hope Harbour at 10:30am, and you can return on the 3, 5, or 7pm boat.

Moreton Bay & Islands

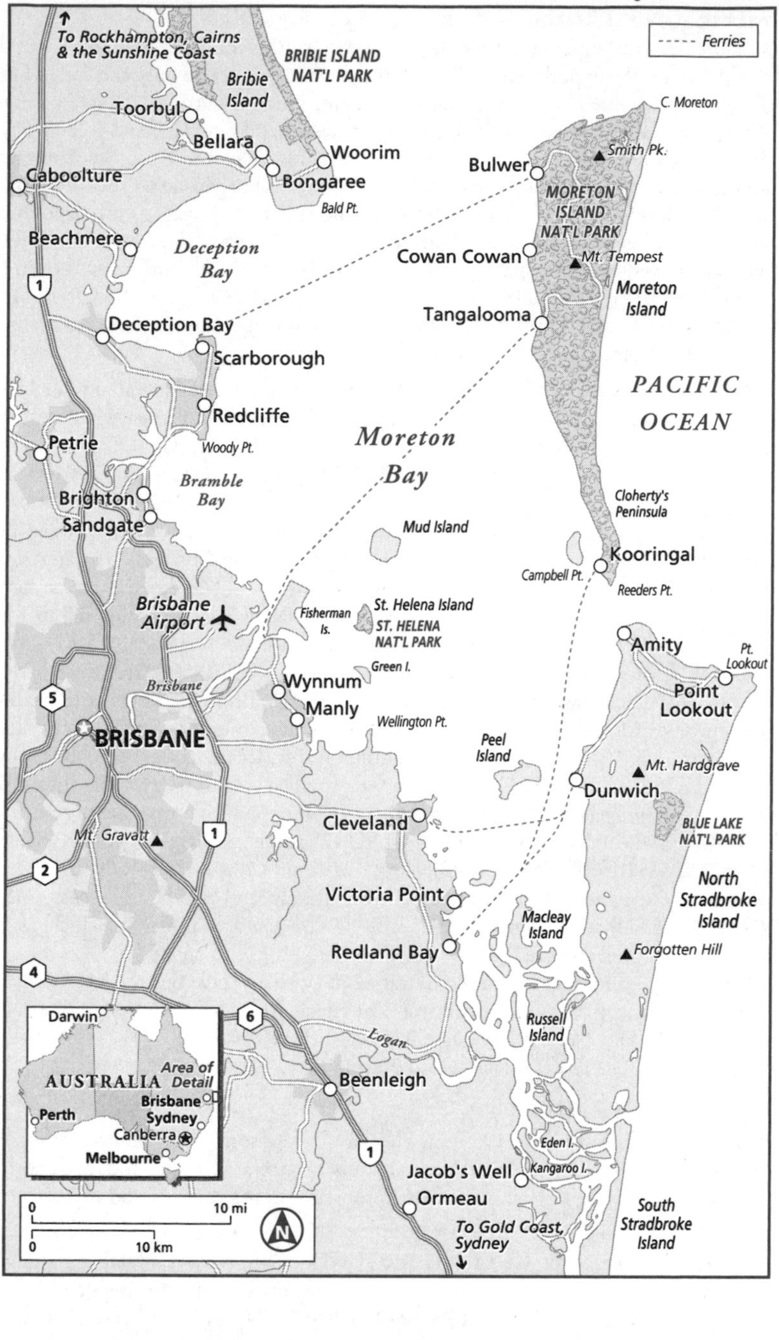

Ferries
To Rockhampton, Cairns & the Sunshine Coast
BRIBIE ISLAND NAT'L PARK
Bribie Island
Toorbul
Bellara
Woorim
Bongaree
Bald Pt.
Caboolture
Beachmere
Deception Bay
Deception Bay
Scarborough
Redcliffe
Woody Pt.
Petrie
Bramble Bay
Brighton
Sandgate
Brisbane Airport
Brisbane
BRISBANE
Wynnum
Manly
Mt. Gravatt
C. Moreton
Smith Pk.
Bulwer
MORETON ISLAND NAT'L PARK
Cowan Cowan
Mt. Tempest
Moreton Island
Tangalooma
PACIFIC OCEAN
Moreton Bay
Cloherty's Peninsula
Mud Island
Kooringal
Campbell Pt.
Reeders Pt.
Fisherman Is.
St. Helena Island
ST. HELENA NAT'L PARK
Green I.
Amity
Pt. Lookout
Point Lookout
Wellington Pt.
Peel Island
Mt. Hardgrave
Dunwich
Cleveland
BLUE LAKE NAT'L PARK
North Stradbroke Island
Victoria Point
Macleay Island
Redland Bay
Forgotten Hill
Russell Island
Logan
Beenleigh
Darwin
AUSTRALIA
Area of Detail
Brisbane
Perth
Sydney
Canberra
Melbourne
Eden I.
Kangaroo I.
Jacob's Well
Ormeau
To Gold Coast, Sydney
South Stradbroke Island
0
10 mi
0
10 km
N

MORETON ISLAND ★★

At more than 200 sq. km (78 sq. miles), Moreton is the second-largest sand mass in the world (after Queensland's Fraser Island) and has the world's largest sand hill, Mount Tempest. It's home to three settlements and the Tangalooma Wild Dolphin Resort, where guests and visitors on an extended day cruise can take part in hand-feeding a pod of wild dolphins that comes to the jetty each evening. Moreton has other attractions: You can visit the 42-hectare (104-acre) "desert" and toboggan down the sand dunes, snorkel around the 12 wrecks just north of the resort, and visit historical points of interest, including the sandstone lighthouse at Cape Moreton, built in 1857. A four-wheel-drive vehicle is essential for getting around, but the resort runs tours. Permits for access (A$34/US$27/UK£14 per vehicle) and camping (A$4.50/US$3.60/UK£1.80 per person or A$18/US$14/UK£7 for a family) are available from national park rangers and ferry operators.

GETTING THERE & GETTING AROUND High-speed catamarans (✆ **1300/652 250** in Australia, or 07/3268 6333) leave Brisbane's Pinkenba wharf at Eagle Farm for Tangalooma on Moreton Island three times daily, at 8am, 10am, and 5pm (1pm on Mon, Sat, and Sun). The trip takes 75 minutes. For a A$5 (US$4/UK£2) charge, coaches pick up passengers at the Roma Street Transit Centre to connect with the launch, and will pick up from city hotels on request. Return transfers leave Tangalooma at 9am and 4pm and after the evening dolphin feeding session at 7pm every day. On weekends and Mondays, they also leave at 2pm. The day trip return fare is A$40 (US$32/UK£16) for adults and A$25 (US$20/UK£10) for children 3 to 14 or A$100 (US$80/UK£40) for a family of four (extra child A$10/US$8/UK£4). The ***Combie Trader*** vehicular and passenger ferry (✆ **07/3203 6399;** www.moreton-island.com) departs from Scarborough on the Redcliffe Peninsula for Bulwer Wednesday through Monday. The trip takes about 2 hours; round-trip fares for walk-on passengers are A$40 (US$32/UK£16) adults, A$35 (US$28/UK£14) students over 15, and A$25 (US$20/UK£10) children 5 to 15. The cost to take a four-wheel-drive and two passengers is A$185 (US$148/UK£74). Day trips operate on Saturday (8am–3:30pm) and cost A$30 (US$24/UK£12) adults, A$20 (US$16/UK£8) children, and A$105 (US$84/UK£42) family of four. *Combie Trader* also runs four-wheel-drive trips to the island on Monday, Saturday, and Sunday. The cost—A$85 (US$68/UK£34) adults and A$60 (US$48/UK£24) children under 14—includes the ferry crossing, full day tour, and lunch. Times are subject to change.

To reach Scarborough by public transit from Brisbane, take bus no. 315 (Redcliffe Express) from stop 59, on Queen Street near Creek Street, to Scarborough North and walk about 500m (½ mile). The fare is A$4.40 (US$3.50/UK£1.75) for adults, half price for children. The trip takes 60 to 90 minutes.

ST. HELENA ISLAND ★★

For 65 years, from 1867 to 1932, St. Helena was a prison island, known as "the hell hole of the Pacific" to the nearly 4,000 souls incarcerated there. Today, the prison ruins are a tourist attraction, with a small museum in the restored and reconstructed Deputy Superintendent's Cottage.

GETTING THERE & GETTING AROUND Entry to the island is by guided tour only. Excellent tours, most involving a reenactment of life on the island jail, are run by **AB Sea Cruises** (✆ **07/3893 1240;** 8:30am–4:30pm Mon–Sat) on the launch

Cat-o-Nine-Tails, leaving from Manly Boat Harbour. The cost is A$69 (US$55/UK£28) adults, A$59 (US$47/UK£24) seniors and students, A$39 (US$31/UK£16) children aged 17 and under. Tours operate on Wednesdays, leaving at 9:15am and returning at 2:15pm, and on Sundays leaving at 10am and returning at 3pm. The price includes a box lunch. **St. Helena By Night Ghost Tours** run from Manly Boat Harbour on Saturday nights. They include dinner, a dramatized version of life in the prison, and a few spooky surprises. Night tours leave at 7pm and return at 11:15pm; they cost A$85 (US$68/UK£34) adults, A$80 (US$64/UK£32) seniors and students, and A$44 (US$35/UK£18) children. Reservations are essential.

To reach Manly Boat Harbour from Brisbane, take the train from Central Station to Manly (A$3.40/US$2.70/UK£1.35) and walk about 100m (328 ft.). The trip takes about 50 minutes.

WHERE TO STAY ON THE ISLANDS

Moreton and South Stradbroke islands have resorts, and North Stradbroke has plenty of low-key accommodations. The smaller islands offer a variety of motels, cabins, motor-home parks, and camping grounds.

Couran Cove Island Resort ★★★ *Finds* You'll be lucky to find a more peaceful resort than this one, which is an island idyll in a class of its own. South Stradbroke Island has no cars—everyone gets around on foot, bicycle, or silent electric shuttle. You can hang around the pools or lagoon, head to the spectacular surf beach about 2km (1¼ miles) from the main resort, or stroll through remnants of primeval rainforest. The resort is committed to environmentally friendly practices, and is unique for its range of more than 100 recreational and sporting activities, including a 9m (30-ft.) rock-climbing wall, three-lane sprint track, baseball and softball pitching cage, and High Ropes Challenge course. There's also beach volleyball, bocce and lawn bowls, shuffleboard, surfing, fishing, a stargazing observatory, an extensive day spa, and a resident artist who gives lessons. There are lots of accommodations choices. I like the colorful waterfront units, which have water views and are close to the restaurants and spa. All have kitchens, and there's a general store and "pantry service" that delivers supplies to your room. Waterfront units are air-conditioned, and other accommodations have ceiling fans; marine resort rooms have minibars. Smoking is allowed only in designated outdoor areas and on balconies, and no tobacco products are sold at the resort.

South Stradbroke Island, Moreton Bay (P.O. Box 224, Runaway Bay), QLD 4216. ✆ **1800/268 726** or 07/5509 3000. Fax 07/5509 3001. www.couran.com. 223 units. A$333 (US$266/UK£133) double. Children under 12 stay free in parent's room using existing bedding. Extra person A$40 (US$32/UK£16) per night. AE, DC, MC, V. **Amenities:** 4 restaurants; poolside cafe; 10-lane heated pool and children's pool; driving range; putting green; free transfers to mainland golf courses; 2 tennis courts; 2 fully equipped exercise rooms; spa; extensive watersports equipment rentals; bike rental; children's programs; .25-hectare (½-acre) adventure playground; game room; tour desk; massage; babysitting; laundry service; dry cleaning. *In room:* TV w/pay movies, VCR, fax, dataport, kitchen, hair dryer, safe.

Tangalooma Wild Dolphin Resort ★ *Kids* Once the Southern Hemisphere's largest whaling station, Tangalooma is the only resort on Moreton Island. Its big attraction is the pod of wild dolphins that visits the jetty each evening. Guests are guaranteed one chance during their visit to hand-feed the dolphins, but you can't swim with or touch them. The feeding is regulated, and your turn is over in a few seconds. Day-trippers can also take part in dolphin feeding for a cost of A$90 (US$72/UK£36) adults and A$50 (US$40/UK£20) children 3 to 14, as part of a day cruise.

Tangalooma is a good base for exploring the island, and a variety of tours are available, among them seasonal (late June to Oct) whale-watching cruises for a rate of A$98 (US$78/UK£39) adults, A$60 (US$48/UK£24) children. A dolphin research center is also based here. In 2002, the resort gained 96 new hotel rooms; 56 modern two-story family villas are only a year or so older. Villas are pricier than regular rooms, and a little farther from the resort facilities. Each has a full kitchen. The new hotel rooms sleep up to four and have such amenities as air-conditioning, minibars, and hair dryers, which the other rooms do not. However, older rooms have kitchenettes. Units in the main resort area sleep four to five people, and each has a private balcony. A general store is on-site.

Moreton Island, off Brisbane (P.O. Box 1102, Eagle Farm), QLD 4009. © **1300/652 250** or 07/3268 6333. Fax 07/3268 6299. www.tangalooma.com. 286 units, all with shower only. A$280–A$370 (US$224–US$296/UK£112–UK£148) double; A$330–A$390 (US$264–US$312/UK£132–UK£156) double for 1-bedroom apt (sleeps 5); A$370–A$470 (US$296–US$376/UK£148–UK£376) double villa (sleeps 8). Extra adult A$30 (US$24/UK£12). Children 3–14 sharing with adults A$30 (US$24/UK£12). Rates include dolphin feeding. AE, DC, MC, V. **Amenities:** 2 restaurants; cafe; 2 outdoor pools; driving range; putting green; tennis and squash courts; Jacuzzi; watersports equipment rental; children's programs; playground; tour desk; 4WD rental; babysitting; coin-op laundry; archery. *In room:* TV, minibar, fridge, coffeemaker.

7

Queensland & the Great Barrier Reef

by Lee Mylne

Three times the size of Texas, with a population that clings to the coast but embraces the Outback for its icons, Queensland is a sprawling amalgam of stunning scenery, fantastic yarns, and eccentric personalities. Its most famous attraction is the Great Barrier Reef—by no means the only thing worth seeing.

White sandy beaches grace almost the entire coastline, and a string of islands and coral atolls dangles just offshore. At the southern end, Gold Coast beaches and theme parks keep tourists happy. In the north, from Townsville to Cape York, the rainforest teems with flora and fauna.

Brisbane is the state capital, a former penal colony that today brims with style. While Brisbane boasts world-class theater, shopping, markets, art galleries, and restaurants, it retains the relaxed warmth of a country town. For more on this city, see chapter 6.

Less than an hour's drive south of Brisbane is the **Gold Coast** "glitter strip," with its 35km (22 miles) of surf and sandy beaches. North of Brisbane lies the aptly named **Sunshine Coast**—more sandy beaches, crystal-clear waters, and rolling mountains dotted with villages.

Don't miss the wild beauty of the largest sand island in the world, **Fraser Island.** Each year from August to October, humpback whales frolic in the waters between Fraser Island and Hervey Bay—if you're in the area at this time, you won't want to miss the opportunity to experience the whales firsthand.

As you travel north, you'll be tempted by one tropical island after another until you hit the cluster of 74 that makes up the **Whitsunday** and **Cumberland** groups.

Then you enter a land where islands, rainforest, mountains, and rivers unite. Green sugar-cane fields are everywhere—**Mackay** is the largest sugar-producing region in Australia. This attractive city has its own beach, and the harbor is a departure point for cruises to the Great Barrier Reef and the Whitsunday Islands. The Whitsundays are on the same latitude as Tahiti, and for my money are equally lovely. The idyllic island group is laced with coral reefs rising out of calm, blue waters teeming with colorful fish—warm enough for swimming year-round.

North of the Whitsundays are **Dunk Island** and the rainforest settlement of **Mission Beach**—a perfect illustration of the contrasts in Tropical North Queensland. **Townsville** boasts 320 days of sunshine a year and marks the start of the Great Green Way—an area of lush natural beauty on the way to Cairns.

Then you come to **Cairns,** with rainforest hills and villages to explore and a harbor full of boats waiting to take you to the Reef. Cairns is a good base, but savvy travelers head an hour north to the village of **Port Douglas.**

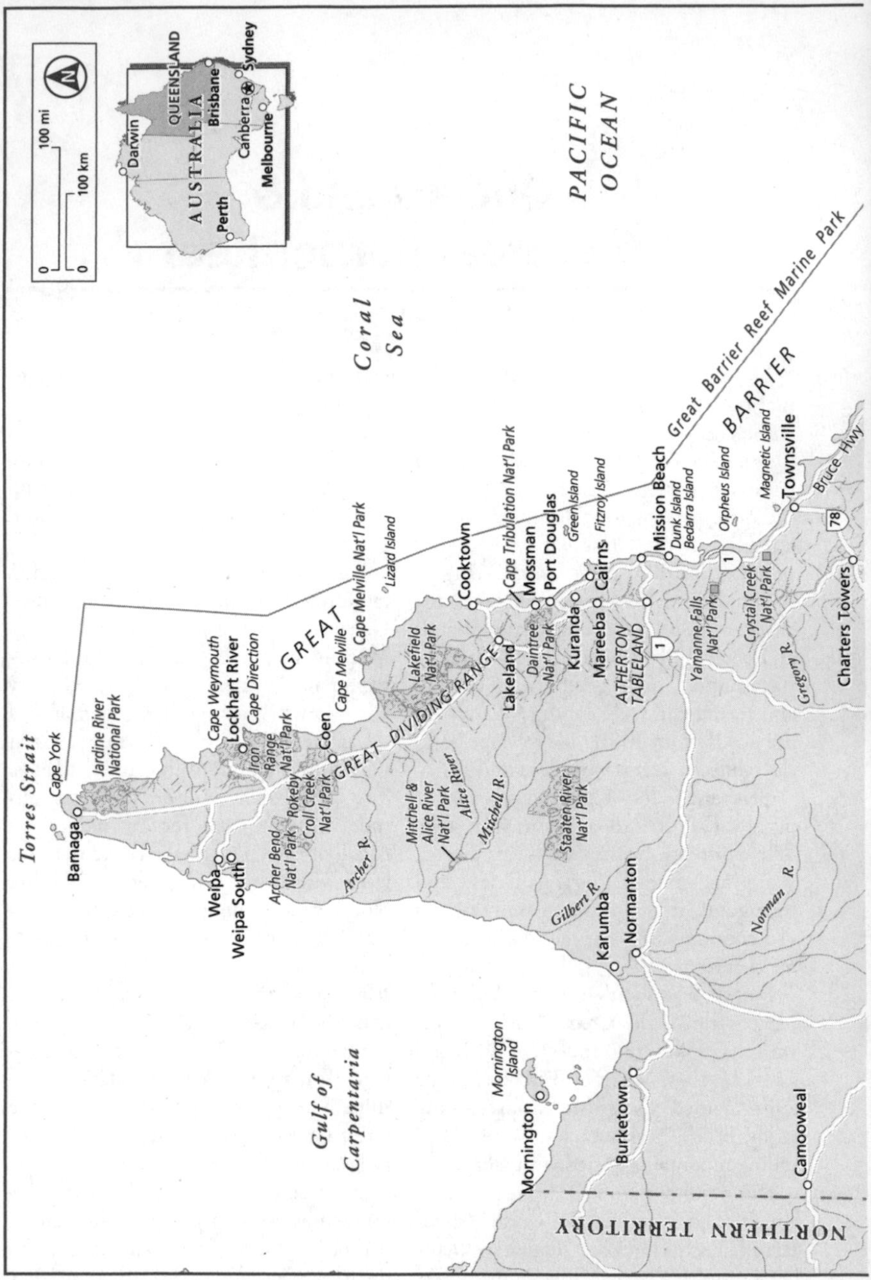
0
100 mi
0
100 km
AUSTRALIA
QUEENSLAND
Darwin
Perth
Brisbane
Canberra
Sydney
Melbourne
PACIFIC OCEAN
Coral Sea
Great Barrier Reef Marine Park
GREAT BARRIER
Torres Strait
Cape York
Bamaga
Jardine River National Park
Weipa
Weipa South
Archer Bend Nat'l Park
Archer R.
Rokeby Croll Creek Nat'l Park
Iron Range Nat'l Park
Cape Weymouth
Lockhart River
Cape Direction
Coen
Cape Melville
Cape Melville Nat'l Park
Lizard Island
Lakefield Nat'l Park
GREAT DIVIDING RANGE
Mitchell & Alice River Nat'l Park
Alice River
Mitchell R.
Cooktown
Lakeland
Cape Tribulation Nat'l Park
Mossman
Port Douglas
Daintree Nat'l Park
Green Island
Fitzroy Island
Kuranda
Cairns
Mareeba
ATHERTON TABLELAND
Mission Beach
Dunk Island
Bedarra Island
Yamanne Falls Nat'l Park
Orpheus Island
Magnetic Island
Townsville
Bruce Hwy
Crystal Creek Nat'l Park
Gregory R.
Charters Towers
Staaten River Nat'l Park
Gilbert R.
Karumba
Normanton
Norman R.
Gulf of Carpentaria
Mornington Island
Mornington
Burketown
Camooweal
NORTHERN TERRITORY
1
78

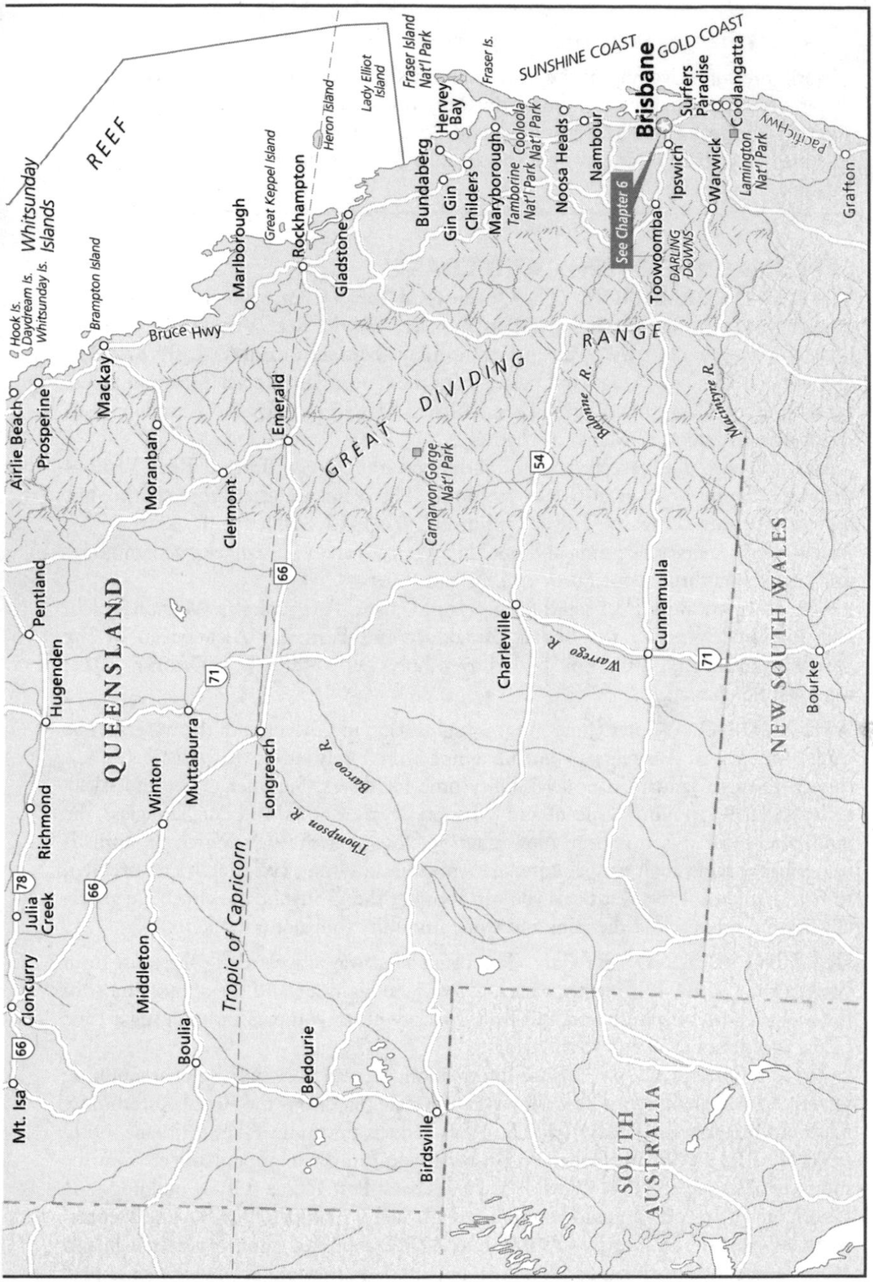

REEF
Whitsunday Islands
Hook Is.
Daydream Is.
Whitsunday Is.
Brampton Island
Airlie Beach
Proserpine
Mackay
Bruce Hwy
Marlborough
Great Keppel Island
Rockhampton
Heron Island
Lady Elliot Island
Gladstone
Bundaberg
Gin Gin
Childers
Maryborough
Hervey Bay
Fraser Island Nat'l Park
Fraser Is.
Tamborine Nat'l Park
Cooloola Nat'l Park
Noosa Heads
Nambour
SUNSHINE COAST
Brisbane
GOLD COAST
Surfers Paradise
Coolangatta
See Chapter 6
Toowoomba
DARLING DOWNS
Ipswich
Warwick
Lamington Nat'l Park
Pacific Hwy
Grafton
Moranbah
Clermont
Emerald
GREAT DIVIDING RANGE
Carnarvon Gorge Nat'l Park
Balonne R.
Macintyre R.
54
Pentland
QUEENSLAND
66
Charleville
Cunnamulla
Warrego R.
71
NEW SOUTH WALES
Bourke
Hugenden
Muttaburra
Longreach
Barcoo R.
Thompson R.
Winton
Richmond
Julia Creek
78
Middleton
Tropic of Capricorn
Cloncurry
Mt. Isa
Boulia
Bedourie
Birdsville
SOUTH AUSTRALIA

Tips When to Visit the Reef

April through November is the best time to visit the Great Barrier Reef. December through March can be uncomfortably hot and humid, particularly as far north as the Whitsundays, Cairns, and Port Douglas. In the winter months (June–Aug), the water can be a touch chilly (Aussies think so, anyway), but it rarely drops below 72°F (22°C).

EXPLORING THE QUEENSLAND COAST

VISITOR INFORMATION The **Queensland Travel Centre** is a great resource on traveling and touring the state, including the Great Barrier Reef. Visit the Destination Queensland website at **www.queenslandholidays.com.au** or call © **1300/872 835** in Australia. Tourism Queensland, which runs the Queensland Travel Centre and Destination Queensland, has offices in the United States and the United Kingdom—see "Visitor Information & Maps" in chapter 2.

You will also find excellent information on the **Great Barrier Reef Visitors Bureau**'s website (www.great-barrier-reef.com). This is not an official tourist office but part of a private company, **Travel Online** (© **07/3512 8100;** fax 07/3876 4645), which offers itinerary planning and booking services for a wide range of accommodations and tours throughout north Queensland.

For information on B&Bs and farmstays in Cairns, Port Douglas, Mission Beach, and Townsville, contact the **Bed & Breakfast and Farmstay Association of Far North Queensland,** P.O. Box 595, Ravenshoe, QLD 4888 (© **07/4097 7022;** www.bnbnq.com.au).

WHEN TO GO Winter (June–Aug) is high season in Queensland; the water can be chilly—at least to Australians—but its temperature rarely drops below 72°F (22°C). August through January is peak visibility time for divers. Summer is hot and sticky across the state. In North Queensland (Mission Beach, Cairns, and Port Douglas), the monsoonal Wet season is from November or December through March or April. It brings heavy rains, high temperatures, extreme humidity, and cyclones. It's no problem to visit then, but if the Wet turns you off, consider the Whitsundays, which are generally beyond the reach of the rains and worst humidity (but not of cyclones).

GETTING AROUND **By Car** The Bruce Highway travels along the coast from Brisbane to Cairns. It is mostly a narrow two-lane highway, and the scenery most of the way is eucalyptus bushland, but from Mackay north you pass through sugar-cane fields, adding some variety to the trip.

Tourism Queensland (see "Visitor Information," above) publishes regional motoring guides. All you are likely to need, however, is a state map from the **Royal Automobile Club of Queensland (RACQ),** 300 St. Pauls Terrace, Fortitude Valley, Brisbane, QLD 4006 (© **13 19 05** in Australia). In Brisbane, you can get maps and advice from the more centrally located RACQ office in the General Post Office (GPO) building, 261 Queen St. For recorded road condition reports, call © **1800/629 501.** The **Department of Natural Resources** (© **07/3896 3216**) publishes Sunmaps that highlight tourist attractions, national parks, and so on, although they are of limited use as road maps. You can get them at newsdealers and gas stations throughout the state.

By Train Queensland Rail's **Traveltrain** (**✆ 1300/131 722** in Australia; www.traveltrain.com.au) operates two long-distance trains along the Brisbane-Cairns route, a 32-hour trip aboard the ***Sunlander*** or about 8 hours less on the high-speed **Tilt Train.** Traveltrain also operates trains to Outback towns. See the "Getting Around Australia" section in chapter 2 for more details.

By Plane This is the fastest way to see a lot in such a big state. **Qantas** (**✆ 13 13 13** in Australia; www.qantas.com.au) and its subsidiaries **QantasLink** and the no-frills Jetstar (**✆ 13 15 38** in Australia; www.jetstar.com.au) serve most coastal towns from Brisbane, and a few from Cairns. **Virgin Blue** (**✆ 13 67 89** in Australia; www.virginblue.com.au) services Brisbane, Cairns, Townsville, Mackay, Proserpine and Hamilton Island in the Whitsundays, Rockhampton, Hervey Bay, the Gold Coast, and Maroochydore on the Sunshine Coast.

1 Exploring the Great Barrier Reef

It's the only living structure on earth visible from the moon; at 348,700 sq. km (135,993 sq. miles), it's bigger than the United Kingdom; it's over 2,000km (1,240 miles) long, stretching from Lady Elliot Island off Bundaberg to just south of Papua New Guinea; it's home to 1,500 kinds of fish, 400 species of corals, 4,000 kinds of clams and snails, and who knows how many sponges, starfish, and sea urchins. The Great Barrier Reef is a World Heritage Site and is the biggest marine park in the world.

There are three kinds of reef on the Great Barrier Reef—fringing, ribbon, and platform. **Fringe reef** is the stuff you see just off the shore of islands and along the mainland. **Ribbon reefs** create "streamers" of long, thin reef along the outer edge of the Reef, and are only found north of Cairns. **Platform** or **patch reefs** are splotches of coral emerging off the continental shelf all the way along the Queensland coast. Platform reefs, the most common kind, are what most people think of when they refer to the Great Barrier Reef. Island resorts in the Great Barrier Reef Marine Park are either "continental," meaning part of the Australian landmass, or "cays," crushed dead coral and sand amassed over time by water action. Dazzling coral and marine life surround cays. On continental islands, the coral can be of varying quality.

Apart from the impressive fish life around the corals, the Reef is home to large numbers of green and loggerhead turtles, one of the biggest dugong (manatee) populations in the world, sharks, giant manta rays, and sea snakes. In winter (June–Aug), humpback whales gather in the warm waters around Hervey Bay and the Whitsunday Islands to give birth to calves.

To see the Reef, you can snorkel, dive, fish, or fly over it. For most people, the Great Barrier Reef means the Outer Reef, the network of platform and ribbon reefs that lie

---

Tips The Reef Tax

Every passenger over 4 years old must pay a A$5 (US$4/UK£2) daily Environmental Management Charge (EMC), commonly called "reef tax," every time they visit the Great Barrier Reef. This money goes toward the management and conservation of the Reef. Your tour operator will collect it from you when you pay for your trip.

---

an average of 65km (40 miles) off the coast (about 60–90 min. by boat from the mainland). You should get out and see that, but there is plenty of fringing reef to explore around islands closer to the mainland.

Learning about the Reef before you get there will enhance your visit. **Reef Teach** ★★ (© **07/4031 7794**) is an evening multimedia presentation by a team of experienced marine biologists, conservationists, and researchers. You will learn everything you need to know about the Reef, from how it was formed and how coral grows, to what dangerous creatures to avoid and how to take successful underwater photos. The presentation takes place throughout the year at 14 Spence St., Cairns, Monday through Saturday from 6:30 to 8:30pm, and costs A$13 (US$10/UK£5.20) adults and A$7 (US$5.60/UK£2.80) children under 14.

Townsville is the headquarters of the Great Barrier Reef Marine Park Authority, and a visit to its showcase, **Reef HQ** (p. 332), is a superb introduction. The star attraction at the aquarium is a re-created living-reef ecosystem in a massive viewing tank. Find out more about the Reef from the **Great Barrier Reef Marine Park Authority** (© **07/4750 0700;** fax 07/4772 6093; www.gbrmpa.gov.au or www.reefhq.com.au).

DISCOVERING THE REEF

Snorkeling the Reef can be a wondrous experience. Green and purple clams, pink sponges, red starfish, purple sea urchins, and fish from electric blue to neon yellow to lime are truly magical sights. The rich colors of the coral only survive with lots of light, so the nearer the surface, the brighter and richer the marine life. That means snorkelers are in a prime position to see it at its best.

If your Reef cruise offers a guided snorkel tour or "snorkel safari," take it. Some include it as part of the price, but even if you pay an extra A$30 (US$24/UK£12) or so, it is worth it. Most safaris are suitable for both beginners and advanced snorkelers, and are led by marine biologists who tell you about the sea creatures you are seeing. Snorkeling is easy to master, and crews on cruise boats are always happy to tutor you.

A day trip to the Reef also offers a great opportunity to go scuba diving—even if you have never dived before. Every major cruise boat listed in "Day Trips to the Reef" (below) and many dedicated dive boats listed in "Diving the Reef" (later in this chapter) offers introductory dives that allow you to dive without certification to a depth of 6m (20 ft.) in the company of an instructor. You will need to complete a medical questionnaire and undergo a 30-minute briefing on the boat. (Intro dives are also called resort dives because many resorts offer something similar, giving you 1 or 2 hr. instruction before taking you to a nearby reef to dive.)

CHOOSING A GATEWAY TO THE REEF

Cairns and **Port Douglas** are good places from which to visit the Reef—but the quality of the coral is just as good off any town along the coast between **Gladstone** and Cairns. The Reef is pretty much equidistant from any point on the coast—about 90 minutes away by high-speed catamaran. An exception is **Townsville,** where the Reef is about 2½ hours away. Think carefully about where to base yourself.

The main gateways, north to south, are **Port Douglas, Cairns, Mission Beach, Townsville, the Whitsunday Islands, Gladstone** (for Heron Island), and **Bundaberg.** The Whitsundays have the added attractions of dazzling islands to sail among; beautiful island resorts offering a wealth of watersports and other activities; and a large array of diving, fishing, and day cruises. Most important, you can snorkel every day

The Great Barrier Reef

off your island or join a sailing or cruise day trip to a number of magnificent inner reefs much nearer than the main Outer Reef. Many people stay in Cairns simply because of its easy international airport access.

If you are a nonswimmer, choose a Reef cruise that visits a coral cay, because a cay slopes gradually into shallow water and the surrounding coral. The **Low Isles** at Port Douglas; **Green Island, Michaelmas Cay,** or **Upolu Cay** off Cairns; **Beaver Cay** off Mission Beach; and **Heron Island** are all good locations.

DAY TRIPS TO THE REEF

The most common way to get to the Reef is on one of the motorized catamarans that carry up to 300 passengers each from Cairns, Port Douglas, Townsville, Mission Beach, and the Whitsunday mainland and islands. The boats are air-conditioned and have a bar, videos, and educational material, as well as a marine biologist who gives a talk on the Reef's ecology en route. The boats tie up at their own private permanent pontoons anchored to a platform reef. The pontoons have glass-bottom boats for passengers who don't want to get wet, dry underwater viewing platforms, usually a bar, sun decks, shaded seats, and often showers.

An alternative to traveling on a big tour boat is to go on one of the many smaller boats. These typically visit two or three Reef sites rather than just one. There are usually no more than 20 passengers, so you get more personal attention, and you get to know the other passengers. Another advantage is that you will have the coral pretty much all to yourself. The drawbacks of a small boat are that you have only the cramped deck to sit on when you get out of the water, and your traveling time to the Reef may be longer. If you're a nervous snorkeler, you may feel safer on a boat where you will be swimming with 300 other people.

Most day-trip fares include snorkel gear—fins, mask, and snorkel (plus wet suits in winter, although you rarely need them)—free use of the underwater viewing chambers and glass-bottom-boat rides, a plentiful buffet or barbecue lunch, and morning and afternoon refreshments. Diving is an optional activity for which you pay extra. The big boats post snorkeling scouts to keep a lookout for anyone in trouble and to count heads periodically. If you wear glasses, ask whether your boat offers prescription masks—this could make a big difference to the quality of your experience! Don't forget, you can travel as a snorkel-only passenger on most dive boats, too.

The major launching points for day trips to the Reef are Port Douglas, Cairns, Mission Beach, Townsville, and the Whitsundays (see individual sections on these regions later in this chapter).

Tips Reef Health & Safety Warnings

Coral is very sharp, and coral cuts get infected quickly and badly. If you cut yourself, ask the staff on your cruise boat for antiseptic cream, and apply it to grazes as soon as you come out of the water.

The sun and reflected sunlight off the water can burn you fast. Remember to put sunscreen on your back and the back of your legs, especially around your knees and the back of your neck, and even behind your ears—all places that rarely get exposed to the sun but will be exposed as you swim facedown. Apply more when you leave the water.

MAJOR REEF SITES

FROM CAIRNS Approximately 20 reefs lie within a 1½- to 2-hour boat ride from Cairns. These are the reefs most commonly visited by snorkelers and divers on day trips, because they are so close and so pretty. Some reefs are small coral "bommies," or outcrops, that you can swim completely around in a matter of minutes, whereas others are miles wide. Some reefs have more than one good dive site; Norman Reef, for example, has at least four. Three of the most popular reefs with both snorkelers and divers are **Hastings, Saxon,** and **Norman** ★, which are all within a short boat ride of one another. Each has a wonderful array of coral, big colorful reef fish, schools of pretty rainbow-hued small reef fish, and the odd giant clam. Green sea turtles and white-tip reef sharks are common, especially at Saxon, though you will not necessarily spot one every day. Divers may see a moray eel and a grouper or two, barracuda, reef sharks, eagle and blue-spotted rays, and octopus. Norman is an especially lovely reef with several nice sites. South Norman has lovely sloping coral shelves. If you are an experienced diver and like swim-throughs, the Caves at Norman is a good spot; it has boulder and plate corals.

Some of the best diving anywhere on the Great Barrier Reef is on the **Ribbon Reefs** ★ on the outer Reef edge, which fringes the continental shelf off Cairns and Port Douglas. Glorious coral walls, abundant fish, and pinnacles make these a rich, colorful dive area with lots of variety. The currents can be stronger here, because the reefs are the last stop between the open sea, so drift dives are a possibility. The Ribbon Reefs are beyond the reach of day boats, but are commonly visited by live-aboard boats (see below). For divers, experts recommend **Steve's Bommie** and **Dynamite Pass.** Steve's Bommie is a coral outcrop in 30m (98 ft.) of water, topped with barracudas, and covered in colorful coral and small marine life. You can swim through a tunnel here amid crowds of fish. Dynamite Pass is a channel where barracuda, trevally, grouper, mackerel, and tuna gather to feed in the current. Black coral trees and sea whips grow on the walls, patrolled by eagle rays and reef sharks.

Cairns's most famous dive site is **Cod Hole** ★, where you can hand-feed giant potato cod as big as you are, or bigger. The site also has Maori wrasse, moray eels, and coral trout. Cod Hole is about 20km (13 miles) off Lizard Island, 240km (149 miles) north of Cairns, so it is not a day trip unless you are staying at exclusive Lizard Island (see "Where to Stay," later in this chapter). However, it is a popular stop with just about every live-aboard vessel, often combined in a trip to the Ribbon Reefs lasting about 4 days, or in a trip to the Coral Sea (see below) lasting between 4 and 7 days. Either itinerary makes an excellent dive vacation.

Keen divers looking for adventure in far-flung latitudes can visit the **Far Northern** region of the Great Barrier Reef, much farther north than most dive boats venture. Up in this region you will find a wide choice of good sites, little explored by the average diver. Visibility is always clear. **Silvertip City** on Mantis Reef has sharks, pelagics, potato cod, and lionfish that patrol a wall up to 46m (150 ft.) deep. Another goodie is the **Magic Cave** swim-through adorned with lots of colorful fans, soft corals, and small reef fish. Sleeping turtles are often spotted in caves on the reefs off **Raine Island,** the world's biggest green turtle rookery. Visibility averages 24m (80 ft.) at Rainbow Wall, a colorful wall that makes a nice gentle drift dive with the incoming tide.

Some 100 to 200km (63–126 miles) east of Cairns, out in the **Coral Sea,** isolated mountains covered in reefs rise more than a kilometer (½ mile) from the ocean floor

Moments Overnighting on the Reef

Down Under Dive (✆ **1800/079 099** in Australia, or 07/4052 8300; fax 07/4031 1373; www.downunderdive.com.au) in Cairns offers a chance to "sleep on the Reef" aboard the 36m (120-ft.) *Spirit of Freedom,* a sleek, modern motor yacht with electronic stabilizers, wide-screen TV/DVD, comfortable lounge areas, sun decks, and 11 luxury double or quad share cabins, each with an en-suite bathroom. There are 3-, 4-, and 7-day cruises to choose from. You will visit the popular Cod Hole and Ribbon Reef and on the 4- and 7-day trips, venture into the Coral Sea. A 3-day, 3-night trip will cost A$1,100 to A$1,750 (US$880–US$1,400/UK£440–UK£700) depending on your choice of cabin, and ends with a 193km (120-mile) one-way low-level flight from Lizard Island back to Cairns. The 4-day, 4-night cruise begins with the flight and then cruises from Lizard Island back to Cairns. It costs between A$1,375 (US$1,100/UK£550) and A$2,100 (US$1,680/UK£840) and includes up to 16 dives. A 7-day cruise, priced from A$2,325 to A$3,700 (US$1,860–US$2,960/UK£930–UK£1,480), is a combination of both shorter trips. On a 3-day trip you will fit in up to 11 dives, and up to 27 on the 7-day trip. Prices include meals and pickup from your Cairns accommodations. Allow around A$100 (US$80/UK£40) extra for equipment rental.

to make excellent diving. Although not within the Great Barrier Reef Marine Park, the Coral Sea is often combined into an extended live-aboard trip that also takes in Cod Hole and the Ribbon Reefs. The whole trip usually takes 4 to 7 days. In addition to showing you huge schools of pelagic and reef fish big and small, a wide range of corals, and gorgonian fans, the area is a prime place to spot sharks. The most popular site is **Osprey Reef,** a 100-sq.-km (39-sq.-mile) reef with 1,000m (3,300-ft.) drop-offs, renowned for its year-round visibility of up to 70m (230 ft.). The highlight of most Osprey Reef itineraries is a **shark feeding** session. White-tip reef sharks are common, but the area is also home to gray reef sharks, silvertips, and hammerheads. Green turtles, tuna, barracuda, potato cod, mantas, and grouper are also common.

Closer to shore, Cairns has several coral cays and reef-fringed islands within the **Great Barrier Reef Marine Park.** Less than an hour from the city wharf, **Green Island** is a 15-hectare (37-acre) coral cay with snorkeling equal to that on the Great Barrier Reef. It is also a popular diving spot. You can visit it in half a day if time is short.

The **Frankland Islands** are a pristine group of uninhabited rainforested isles edged with sandy beaches, reefs, and fish 45km (28 miles) south of Cairns. The islands are a rookery for **green sea turtles,** which snorkelers and divers often spot in the water. In February and March, you may even be lucky enough to see dozens of baby turtles hatching in the sand. **Michaelmas Cay** and **Upolu Cay** are two pretty coral sand blips in the ocean, 30km (19 miles) and 25km (16 miles) off Cairns, surrounded by reefs. Michaelmas is vegetated and is home to 27,000 seabirds; you may spot dugongs (manatees) off Upolu. Michaelmas and Upolu are great for snorkelers and introductory divers, but experienced divers are probably better off visiting the excellent sites at such reefs as Norman, Hastings, or Saxon.

FROM PORT DOUGLAS The waters off Port Douglas boast just as many wonderful reefs and marine life forms as the waters around Cairns; the reefs are equally close to shore and equally colorful and varied. Some of the most visited reefs are

Tongue, Opal, and **St. Crispin Reefs.** The **Agincourt** complex of reefs also has many excellent dive sites; experts recommend the double-figure-eight swim-through at the **Three Sisters,** where baby gray whaler sharks gather, and the wonderful coral walls of **Castle Rock,** where stingrays often hide in the sand. **Nursery Bommie** is a 24m (79-ft.) pinnacle that is a popular haunt with big fish like barracuda, rays, sharks, and moray eels; under the big plate corals of **Light Reef,** giant grouper hide out. Other popular sites are the staghorn coral garden (so named because the coral looks like a stag's antlers) at the **Playground;** one of the region's biggest swim-throughs at **The Maze,** where parrot fish and an enormous Maori wrasse hang out; the **Stepping Stones,** home of the exquisitely pretty clownfish (like Nemo!); **Turtle Bommie,** where hawksbill turtles are frequently sighted; and **Harry's Bommie,** where divers see the occasional manta ray. Among the 15-plus dive sites visited by *Poseidon* (see below) are **Turtle Bay,** where you may meet "Killer," a friendly Maori wrasse; the **Cathedrals,** a collection of coral pinnacles and swim-throughs; and **Barracuda Pass,** home to coral gardens, giant clams, and schooling barracudas.

The closest Reef site off Port Douglas, the **Low Isles,** lies only 15km (9 miles) northeast. Coral sand and 22 hectares (55 acres) of coral surround these two tiny coral cays, which are covered in lush vegetation and are home to many seabirds. The coral is not quite as dazzling as the outer Reef's—head to the outer Reef if you have only 1 day to spend on the Great Barrier Reef—but the fish life here is rich, and you may spot sea turtles. Because you can wade out to the coral right from the beach, the Low Isles are a good choice for nervous snorkelers. A half-day or day trip to the Low Isles makes for a more relaxing day than a visit to outer Reef sites, because in addition to exploring the coral, you can walk or sunbathe on the sand or laze under palm-thatched beach umbrellas. ***Note:*** If you visit the Low Isles, wear old shoes, because the coral sand can be rough underfoot.

FROM MISSION BEACH Mission Beach is the closest point on the mainland to the Reef, 1 hour by boat. The main site visited is **Beaver Cay,** a sandy coral cay surrounded by marine life. The waters are shallow, making the cay ideal for both snorkelers eager to see the coral's vibrant colors and novice divers still getting a feel for the sport. It's a perfect spot for an introduction dive.

FROM TOWNSVILLE Townsville's waters boast hundreds of large patch reefs, some miles long, and many almost never visited by humans. Here you can find excellent coral and fish life, including mantas, rays, turtles, and sharks, and sometimes canyons and swim-throughs in generally good visibility. One of the best reef complexes is **Flinders Reef.** Actually located in the Coral Sea, beyond the Great Barrier Reef Marine Park boundaries, we mention it here because many dive trips incorporate it in Great Barrier Reef itineraries. At 240km (149 miles) offshore, it has 30m (100-ft.) visibility, plenty of coral, and big walls and pinnacles with big fish to match, like whaler shark and barracuda.

Fun Fact **The Floating P.O.**

Australia's only floating post office is on **Agincourt Reef,** about 72km (45 miles) off Port Douglas. The facility floats on the Quicksilver Connections pontoon, and your letter or postcard will be stamped with a postmark from the Great Barrier Reef.

What draws most divers to Townsville, though, is one of Australia's best wreck dives, **SS *Yongala*** ★. Still largely intact, the sunken remains of this steamer lie 90km (56 miles) from Townsville, 16km (10 miles) off the coast, in 15 to 30m (50–98 ft.) of water with visibility of 9 to 18m (approximately 30–60 ft.). A cyclone sent the *Yongala* and its 49 passengers and 72-member crew to the bottom of the sea in 1911. Today it's surrounded by a mass of coral and marine life, including barracuda, enormous grouper, rays, sea snakes, turtles, moray eels, shark, cod, and reef fish. You can even enter the ship and swim its length, with care.

The *Yongala* is not for beginners—the boat is deep, and there is a strong current. Most dive companies require their customers to have advanced certification or to have logged a minimum of 15 dives with open-water certification. The boat is usually visited on a live-aboard trip of at least 2 days, but some companies run day trips. There are also open-water certification dive courses that finish with a dive on the *Yongala,* but freshly certified scuba hounds might be wise to skip this advanced dive.

FROM THE WHITSUNDAYS Visitors to the Whitsundays get to have their cake and eat it too; they can visit the outer Reef and enjoy some good dive and snorkel sites in and around the islands. Many islands have rarely visited fringing reefs, which you can explore in a rented dinghy. The reef here is just as good as off Cairns, with many drop-offs and drift dives, a dazzling range of corals, and a rich array of marine life, including whales, mantas, shark, reef fish, morays, turtles, and pelagics. Visibility is usually around 15 to 23m (49–75 ft.).

The Stepping Stones on 800-hectare (1,976-acre) **Bait Reef** is one of the most popular sites on the outer Reef. It is made up of a series of pinnacles that abound with fish life and offer caverns, swim-throughs, and channels. A family of grouper often greets divers at Groupers Grotto on **Net Reef,** and a pod of dolphins hang around Net Reef's southeast wall. **Oublier Reef** has plate corals over 2m (7 ft.) wide in its coral gardens.

Among the island sites, most folks' favorite is **Blue Pearl Bay** ★ off Hayman Island, whether they're snorkeling or diving. It has loads of corals and some gorgonian fans in its gullies, and heaps of reef fish, including Maori wrasse and sometimes even manta rays. It's a good place to make an introductory dive, walking right in off the beach. **Mantaray Bay** on Hook Island is renowned for its range of marine life, from small reef fish and nudibranchs to bigger pelagics farther out. Mantas hang around here in November. Another good snorkel and dive spot is **Black Reef** ★, called **Bali Hai Island,** between Hayman and Hook islands. You'll see soft shelf and wall coral, tame Maori wrasse, octopus, turtles, reef shark, various kinds of rays including mantas, eagles and cow-tails, plus loads of fish. Divers may even see hammerhead shark.

FROM BUNDABERG The southern reefs of the Great Barrier Reef are just as prolific, varied, and colorful as the reefs farther north off Cairns. However, because this part of the coast is less settled, fewer snorkel and dive boats visit them. Many are the virgin reefs in these parts that have never seen a diver.

The only reef visited by snorkelers and divers on a daily basis from Bundaberg is pretty **Lady Musgrave Island,** a vegetated 14-hectare (35-acre) national-park coral cay, 52 nautical miles off the coast. It is surrounded by a lagoon 8km (5 miles) in circumference, filled with hundreds of corals and some 1,200 of the 1,500 species of fish and other marine creatures found on the Great Barrier Reef.

Lady Musgrave Island is one of the **Bunker Group** of islands and reefs, which lie approximately 80km (50 miles) due north of Bundaberg. They are due east of Gladstone and closer to that town, but no boats visit them from there. Little explored by divers, these vividly colored reefs are some of the most pristine on the Great Barrier Reef. Farther south of Bunker Group is **Lady Elliot Island.** Although it lies outside the borders of the Great Barrier Reef Marine Park, Bundaberg's **Woongarra Marine Park** is a popular destination for divers visiting the Reef. This small park hugs the town's coastline in an area known as Bargara, and has loads of soft and hard corals, nudibranchs, wobbegongs, epaulette sharks, sea snakes, some 60 fish species, and frequent sightings of green and loggerhead turtles. Most of this is in water less than 9m (30 ft.) deep, and you can walk right into it off the beach.

Beyond Woongarra, 2.5 nautical miles (4.6km) offshore, is **Cochrane artificial reef,** where a few Mohawk and Beechcraft aircraft have been dumped to make a home for fish. Other sites off Bunbaberg in about 23m (75 ft.) of water include the **manta "cleaning station"** at Evan's Patch, a **World War II Beaufort bomber** with lots of marine life.

DIVING THE REEF ★

Divers have a big choice of dive boats that make 1-day runs to the Outer Reef and live-aboard dive boats for excursions that last up to a week. As a general rule, on a typical 5-hour day trip to the Reef, you will fit in about two dives. The companies listed below give you an idea of the kinds of trips available and how much they cost. This is by no means an exhaustive list—there are far too many to include here. "The Active Traveler" in chapter 2 has more tips for finding a dive operator. Prices quoted include full gear rental; knock off about A$20 (US$16/UK£8) if you have your own gear.

FROM CAIRNS **Tusa Dive Charters** (✆ **07/4040 6464;** www.tusadive.com) runs two 24m (72-ft.) dive boats daily to two dive sites from a choice of 21 locations on the Outer Reef. The day costs A$190 (US$152/UK£76) for divers and A$130 (US$104/UK£52) adult or A$80 (US$64/UK£32) child ages 4 to 14 for snorkelers, with wet suits, guided snorkel tours, lunch, and transfers from your Cairns or northern beaches hotel. If you want to be shown the best spots, you can take a guided dive for an extra A$20 (US$16/UK£8). Day trips for introductory divers cost A$195 (US$156/UK£78) for one dive or A$240 (US$192/UK£96) for two. The groups have a maximum of 28 people, so you get personal attention. The company is the Nitrox and Rebreather facility for north Queensland, and certified divers can take two introductory dives on Nitrox/Safe Air in 1 day for A$220 (US$176/UK£88).

FROM PORT DOUGLAS The waters off Port Douglas are home to dramatic coral spires and swim-throughs at the Cathedrals; giant clams at Barracuda Pass; a village of parrot fish, anemone fish, unicorn fish, and two moray eels at the pinnacle of Nursery Bommie; fan corals at Split-Bommie; and many other wonderful sites.

Poseidon (✆ **1800/085 674** in Australia, or 07/4099 4772; www.poseidon-cruises.com.au) is a fast 24m (79-ft.) vessel that visits three Outer Reef sites. The day-trip price of A$155 (US$124/UK£62) for adults, A$120 (US$96/UK£48) for kids 3 to 12 includes snorkel gear, a marine biology talk, snorkel safaris, lunch, and pickups from Port Douglas hotels. Certified divers pay A$40 (US$32/UK£16) extra for two dives or A$55 (US$44/UK£22) extra for three, plus A$20 (US$16/UK£8) gear rental. Guides will accompany you, free of charge, to show you great locations. Introductory divers pay A$50 (US$40/UK£20) extra for one dive, and A$40 (US$32/UK£16) each for the second and third. The vessel carries no more than 48 passengers, less than half its capacity, and gets you to the Reef in just over an hour, giving you 5 hours on the coral. The boat departs Marina Mirage daily at 8:30am. Transfers from Cairns and the Northern Beaches cost an extra A$15 (US$12/UK£6) per adult and A$10 (US$8/UK£4) per child.

FROM TOWNSVILLE Off Townsville, you can dive not only the Reef but also a wreck, the ***Yongala*** ★, which lies off the coast in 30m (98 ft.) of water with good visibility. **Adrenalin Dive (✆ 07/4724 0600;** www.adrenalindive.com.au) runs day trips in which you will do two dives on the *Yongala.* The cost is A$199 (US$159/UK£80), plus A$35 (US$28/UK£14) for gear hire and A$30 (US$24/UK£12) per dive for a guide if you have logged fewer than 15 dives.

FROM THE WHITSUNDAYS In and around the Whitsunday Islands, you can visit the Outer Reef and explore the many excellent dive sites close to shore. **H20 Sportz (✆ 07/4946 9888;** www.h20sportz.com.au), based at Hamilton Island marina, runs day tours to **Bait Reef,** one of the best known locations on the Great Barrier Reef. Tours are limited to 30 passengers and leave at 9:30am, returning 5pm. That gives you 3½ hours at the Reef, allowing plenty of time for lots of snorkeling or two dives. The cost is A$161 (US$129/UK£64) adults, A$81 (US$65/UK£32) kids aged 4 to 13. One child 13 years or under travels free when accompanied by two adults. The cost includes lunch, snacks, all snorkel equipment, and wet suit.

DIVE COURSES

Many dive companies in Queensland offer instruction, from initial open-water certification all the way to dive master, rescue diver, and instructor level. To take a course, you will need to have a medical exam done by a Queensland doctor. (Your dive school will arrange it; it costs about A$55/US$40/UK£20.) You will also need two passport photos for your certificate, and you must be able to swim! Courses usually begin every day or every week. Some courses take as little as 3 days, but 5 days is regarded as the best. Open-water certification usually requires 2 days of theory in a pool, followed by 2 or 3 days on the Reef, where you make four to nine dives. Prices vary, but are generally around A$600 (US$480/UK£240) for a 5-day open-water certification course, or A$500 (US$400/UK£200) for the same course over 4 nights.

Deep Sea Divers Den (✆ 07/4046 7333; fax 07/4031 1210; www.divers-den.com) has been in operation since 1974 and claims to have certified about 55,000 divers. The 5-day open-water course involves 2 days of theory in the pool in Cairns, and 3 days and 2 nights on a live-aboard boat. The course costs A$690 (US$552/UK£276) per person, including all meals on the boat, nine dives (one a guided night dive), all your gear, a wet suit, and transfers from your city hotel. The same course over 4 nights, with 1 night on the boat and five dives, costs A$555 (US$444/UK£222). New courses begin every day of the week.

Virtually every Great Barrier Reef dive operator offers dive courses. Most island resorts offer them, too. You will find dive schools in Cairns, Port Douglas, Mission Beach, Townsville, and the Whitsunday Islands.

Companies offering dive courses appear under the relevant regional sections throughout this chapter.

Tips **Diving Reminders**

Don't forget your "C" certification card. Bringing along your dive log is also a good idea. Remember not to fly for 24 hours after diving.

---

2 Cairns

346km (215 miles) N of Townsville; 1,807km (1,120 miles) N of Brisbane

This part of Queensland is the only place in the world where two World Heritage–listed sites—the Great Barrier Reef and the Wet Tropics Rainforest—lie side by side. In parts of the far north, the rainforest touches the Reef, reaching right down to sandy beaches from which you can snorkel the Reef. Cairns is the gateway to these natural attractions, as well as man-made tourist destinations such as the Skyrail Rainforest Cableway. It's also a steppingstone to islands of the Great Barrier Reef and the grasslands of the Gulf Savannah.

When international tourism to the Great Barrier Reef boomed a decade or two ago, the small sugar-farming town of Cairns boomed along with it. The town now boasts outstanding hotels, offshore island resorts, big Reef-cruise catamarans in the harbor, and too many souvenir shops. The only beach right in town is a man-made 4,000-sq.-m (43,000-sq.-ft.) saltwater lagoon and artificial beach on the Esplanade, which opened in early 2003 as part of a multimillion-dollar redevelopment of the city and port.

The 110-million-year-old rainforest, the Daintree, where plants that are fossils elsewhere in the world exist in living color, is just a couple of hours north of Cairns. The Daintree is part of the Wet Tropics, a World Heritage–listed area that stretches from north of Townsville to south of Cooktown, beyond Cairns, and houses half of Australia's animal and plant species.

If you are spending more than a day or two in the area, consider basing yourself on the city's pretty northern beaches, in Kuranda, or in Port Douglas (see "Port Douglas, Daintree & the Cape Tribulation Area," later in this chapter). Although prices will be higher in the peak season (Australian winter and early spring, July–Oct), affordable accommodations are available year-round.

ESSENTIALS

GETTING THERE **By Plane** **Qantas** (© **13 13 13** in Australia) has direct flights throughout the day to Cairns from Sydney and Brisbane, and at least one flight a day from Darwin, Uluru (Ayers Rock), and Perth. From Melbourne you can sometimes fly direct, but most flights connect through Sydney or Brisbane. **QantasLink** also flies from Townsville, Hamilton Island in the Whitsundays, and Alice Springs. **Virgin Blue** (© **13 67 89** in Australia) flies to Cairns direct from Brisbane, Sydney, and Melbourne. **Jetstar** (© **13 15 38** in Australia) flies from Brisbane, Sydney, Adelaide, and Melbourne. Qantas international subsidiary **Australian Airlines** (© **1300/799 798** in Australia) links Cairns with Sydney, and several international carriers serve Cairns from various Asian cities and New Zealand.

Cairns Airport is 8km (5 miles) north of downtown. The domestic and international terminals are linked by a covered walkway—it takes about 5 minutes to walk between the two. **Airport Connections** (© **07/4099 5950;** www.tnqshuttle.com) will meet all flights at both terminals. Transfers to the city cost A$11 (US$8.80/UK£4.40) adults and A$5.50 (US$4.40/UK£2.20) children 4 to 14, and they also run transfers to as far as Cape Tribulation, Mission Beach, and Dunk Island. **Sun Palm Express Coaches** (© **07/4084 2626;** www.sunpalmtransport.com) provides transfers from the airport to the city and northern beaches. The one-way fare is A$10 (US$8/UK£4) adults and A$5 (US$4/UK£2) children 2 to 12 to the city, and A$16 (US$13/UK£6.40) adults and A$8 (US$6.40/UK£3.20) children to Palm Cove.

A taxi from the airport costs around A$15 (US$12/UK£6) to the city, A$30 (US$24/UK£12) to Trinity Beach, and A$40 (US$32/UK£16) to Palm Cove. Call **Black & White Taxis** (© **13 10 08** in Australia).

Avis, Budget, Hertz, and **Thrifty** all have car-rental offices at the domestic and international terminals (see "Getting Around," below).

By Train Long-distance trains operated by Queensland Rail's **Traveltrain** (© **1300/131 722** in Queensland; www.traveltrain.com.au) run from Brisbane several times a week. The 160kmph (100-mph) **Tilt Train** takes about 25 hours and costs A$295 (US$236/UK£118) for business class. Northbound trains leave Brisbane at 6:25pm on Monday and Friday; southbound runs depart Cairns at 8:15am on Wednesday and Sunday. The train features luxury business-class seating, with an entertainment system for each seat, including multiple movie and audio channels.

The ***Sunlander,*** which runs four times a week between Brisbane and Cairns, takes 32 hours and costs A$207 (US$166/UK£83) for a sitting berth, A$265 (US$212/UK£106) for an economy-class sleeper, A$409 (US$327/UK£166) for a first-class sleeper, or A$725 (US$580/UK£290) for all-inclusive Queenslander class (only available twice a week). Trains pull into the Cairns Central terminal (© **1300 131 722** in Australia for reservations, or 07/4036 9250 for the terminal) on Bunda Street in the center of town. The station has no showers, lockers, or currency exchange booths, but you will find 24-hour ATMs outside the Cairns Central shopping mall, right above the terminal.

By Bus **Greyhound Australia** (© **13 14 99** in Australia, or 07/4690 9950) buses pull into Trinity Wharf Centre on Wharf Street in the center of town. Buses travel from the south via all towns and cities on the Bruce Highway, and from the west from Alice Springs and Darwin via Tennant Creek on the Stuart Highway and the Outback mining town of Mount Isa to Townsville, where they join the Bruce Highway and head north. The 46-hour Sydney-Cairns trip costs A$350 (US$280/UK£140); the 30-hour trip from Brisbane is A$234 (US$187/UK£94); and from Darwin, the journey takes about 38 hours and costs A$517 (US$414/UK£207).

By Car From Brisbane and all major towns in the south, you'll enter Cairns on the Bruce Highway. To reach the northern beaches or Port Douglas from Cairns, take Sheridan Street in the city center, which becomes the Captain Cook Highway.

VISITOR INFORMATION Tourism Tropical North Queensland's **Gateway Discovery Centre,** 51 The Esplanade, Cairns, QLD 4870 (© **07/4051 3588;** fax 07/4051 2509; www.tropicalaustralia.com), has information on Cairns and its environs,

---

Finds Staying Connected

You can surf the Web, check your e-mail, eat, drink, read, listen to live music, and much more at the **Inbox Café,** 119 Abbot St. (© **07/4041 4677;** fax 07/4041 4322). It's open daily from 7am to midnight (and 2am on Fri and Sat nights). All computers have high-speed broadband, CD burners, and a live webcam. This is Cairns's only licensed Internet cafe, and the food is fresh, tasty, and affordable. There is a bar with lots of newspapers and magazines, and resident DJs play groovy tunes to set a relaxed mood.

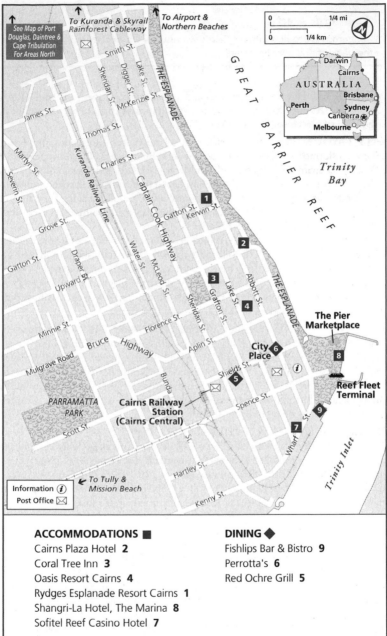

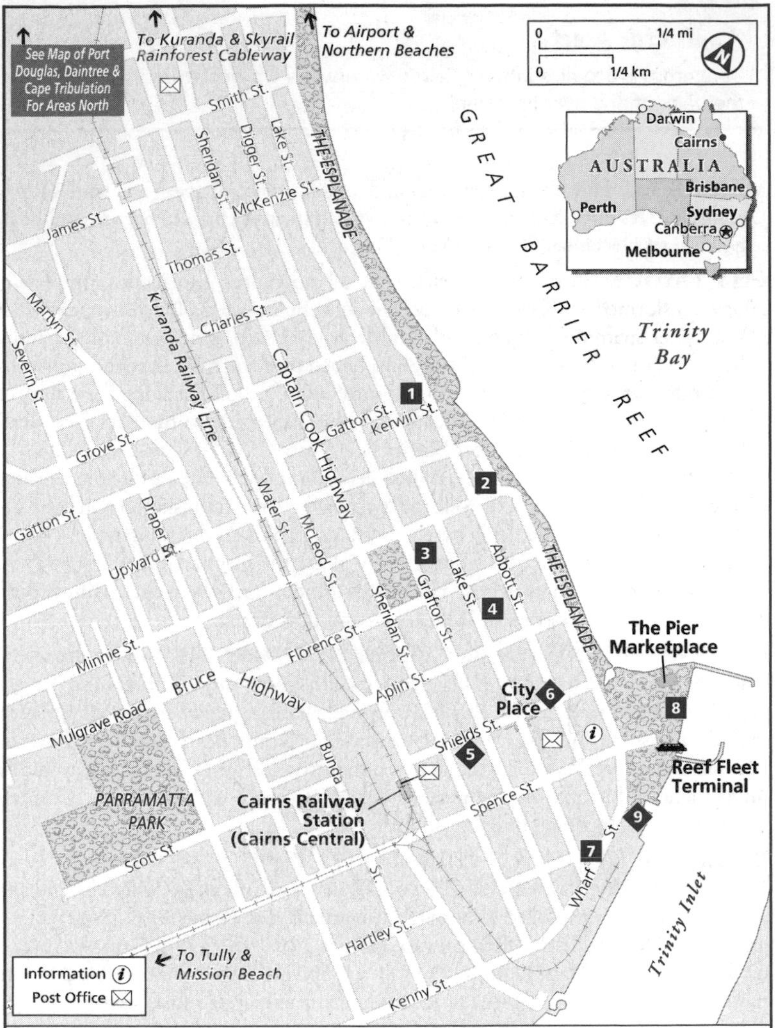

ACCOMMODATIONS ■

Cairns Plaza Hotel **2**
Coral Tree Inn **3**
Oasis Resort Cairns **4**
Rydges Esplanade Resort Cairns **1**
Shangri-La Hotel, The Marina **8**
Sofitel Reef Casino Hotel **7**

DINING ◆

Fishlips Bar & Bistro **9**
Perrotta's **6**
Red Ochre Grill **5**

Tips **Croc Alert!**

Dangerous crocodiles inhabit Cairns waterways. Do not swim in, or stand on the bank of any river or stream.

Mission Beach, Port Douglas, the Daintree Rainforest, Cape York, and Outback Queensland. It's open daily from 8:30am to 6:30pm, and 10am to 6pm on public holidays. Closed December 25, New Year's Day, and Good Friday.

CITY LAYOUT A major redevelopment of the Cairns Esplanade, completed in 2003, transformed the face of the city. The focal point is a 4,000-sq.-m (43,000-sq.-ft.) saltwater swimming lagoon with a wide sandy beach and surrounding parkland with public artworks and picnic areas. Suspended over the mud flats and providing a platform for birding, a timber boardwalk runs 600m (1,968 ft.) along the waterfront, and is lit for nighttime use. A walkway links the Esplanade to the Reef Fleet Terminal, the departure point for Great Barrier Reef boats.

Downtown Cairns is on a grid 5 blocks deep, bounded in the east by the Esplanade on the water and in the west by McLeod Street, where the train station and the Cairns Central shopping mall are. In between are shops, offices, and restaurants.

Heading 15 minutes north from the city along the Captain Cook Highway, you come to the **northern beaches:** Holloway's Beach, Yorkey's Knob, Trinity Beach, Kewarra Beach, Clifton Beach, Palm Cove, and Ellis Beach.

GETTING AROUND **By Bus** **Sunbus** (© **07/4057 7411**) buses depart City Place Mall at the intersection of Lake and Shields streets. Buy all tickets and passes on board, and try to have correct change. You can hail buses anywhere it's convenient for the driver to stop. Bus nos. 1X, 2, and 2A travel to Trinity Beach and Palm Cove. The N route is an express bus that runs between the city and Palm Cove on Friday and Saturday nights only. Routes and timetables change, so check with the driver. Most buses run from early morning until almost midnight.

By Car **Avis** (© 07/4051 5911), **Budget** (© 07/4051 9222), **Hertz** (© 07/4051 6399), and **Thrifty** (© 1300/367 227 in Australia) have offices in Cairns city and at the airport. One long-established local outfit, **Sugarland Car Rentals** (© 07/4052 1300), has reasonable rates. **Britz Campervan Rentals** (© 1800/331 454 in Australia, or 07/4032 2611) and **Maui Rentals** (© 1300/363 800 in Australia, or 07/4032 2065) rent motor homes. Britz and most major rental-car companies rent four-wheel-drive vehicles.

By Taxi Call **Black & White Taxis** (© **13 10 08**).

DAY TRIPS TO THE REEF

Large-scale operator **Great Adventures** (© **1800/079 080** in Australia, or 07/4044 9944; www.greatadventures.com.au) does daily cruises from Cairns in fast, air-conditioned catamarans to a three-level pontoon on the Outer Reef. The pontoon has a children's swimming area, a semisubmersible, and an underwater observatory. You get at least 3 hours on the Reef. The cost for the day is A$174 (US$139/UK£70) for adults, A$87 (US$70/UK£35) for children 4 to 14, and A$429 (US$343/UK£172) for families. Hotel transfers are available from Cairns, the northern beaches, and Port Douglas for an extra cost. The boat departs the Great Adventures terminal at the new Reef Fleet Terminal at 10:30am.

You can also depart Cairns with Great Adventures at 8:30am and spend 2 hours on Green Island en route. This gives you time to walk nature trails, rent snorkel gear and watersports equipment, or laze on the beach before continuing to the Outer Reef. This cruise costs an extra A$20 (US$16/UK£8) per adult and A$10 (US$8/UK£4) per child or A$50 (US$40/UK£20) per family.

Sunlover Cruises (✆ **1800/810 512** in Australia, or 07/4050 1333; www.sunlover.com.au) heads its large, fast catamarans to Moore Reef on the Outer Reef. The day costs A$186 (US$149/UK£74) for adults, A$103 (US$82/UK£41) for children 4 to 14, and A$494 (US$395/UK£198) for a family of four, including transfers from city and northern beaches hotels. This trip includes a glass-bottom boat ride and semisubmersible viewing. You spend about 4 hours on the Reef. Introductory dives cost A$109 (US$87/UK£44). Certified divers pay A$69 (US$55/UK£28) for one dive or A$124 (US$99/UK£50) for two, including all gear. The cruise includes lunch and transfers from Cairns and northern beaches hotels, and leaves from the Reef Fleet Terminal in Cairns at 10am daily.

You can also take a coach transfer from Cairns or Palm Cove to join the **Quicksilver Wavepiercer** (✆ **07/4087 2100**) based in Port Douglas, for a day trip to the Outer Reef (p. 286). Transfers cost A$16 (US$13/UK£6.40) per adult or A$8 (US$6.40/UK£3.20) per child.

Great Adventures, Quicksilver, and Sunlover all offer helicopter flights over the Reef from their pontoons—a spectacular experience! There are also fly-cruise trips.

An alternative to motoring to the Reef is to sail to it. **Ocean Spirit Cruises** (✆ **1800/644 227** in Australia, or 07/4031 2920; www.oceanspirit.com.au) operates two sailing cats that take no more than 150 passengers to Michaelmas Cay or Upolu Cay, lovely white-sand cays on the Outer Reef surrounded by rich reefs. This trip is a good value; it includes a pleasant 2-hour sail to either cay, a guided snorkeling safari, a guided beach walk, and a glass of bubbly and live music on the way home—in addition to the usual reef ecology talks, semisubmersible rides, lunch, and transfers from your Cairns or northern beaches hotel. Another plus is that you spend your out-of-water time on a beautiful beach, not on a pontoon or boat deck. You get about 4 hours on the Reef.

The day trip to Michaelmas Cay is A$179 (US$143/UK£72) for adults, A$88 (US$70/UK£35) for children 4 to 14, including transfers from Cairns (from Port Douglas they are A$39/US$31/UK£16 per person extra). The day trip to Upolu Cay costs A$110 (US$88/UK£44) for adults, A$76 (US$61/UK£30) for kids. Transfers

---

Tips Diving Made Easy

Can't swim? Don't want to get your hair wet? Don't worry—you can still get underwater and see the wonders of the Reef. Several companies offer travelers the chance to don a dive helmet and "walk" underwater. Similar to old-style diving helmets, which allow you to breathe underwater, the helmet has air pumped into it by a hose. You walk into the water to a depth of about 4m (13 ft.), accompanied by instructors, and the Reef is right before you. **Quicksilver Cruises** calls it "Ocean Walker"; with **Sunlover Cruises** and at **Green Island Resort** it's "Sea Walker." You must be at least 10 or 12 years old. The cost is about A$135 (US$108/UK£54) for 20 minutes.

---

from Cairns and the northern beaches are A$15 (US$12/UK£6) per person, and from Port Douglas they cost an extra A$39 (US$31/UK£16) per person. Introductory dives cost A$95 (US$76/UK£38) for one or A$150 (US$120/UK£60) for two, certified divers pay A$65 (US$52/UK£26) for one or A$110 (US$88/UK£44) for two, all gear included, at Michaelmas Cay, less at Upolu. The boats depart Reef Fleet Terminal at 8:30am daily.

WHAT TO SEE & DO IN & AROUND CAIRNS

If you're staying in Cairns, also check out activities in and around Port Douglas (see section 3 of this chapter) and Mission Beach (see section 4 of this chapter). Many tour operators in Port Douglas, and a few in Mission Beach, offer transfers from Cairns.

LEARNING ABOUT ABORIGINAL CULTURE

Tjapukai Aboriginal Cultural Park ★ Whether you choose the day or night experience, the Tjapukai (pronounced Jab-*oo*-guy) Aboriginal Cultural Park is one of the best chances you'll have to discover the history and culture of the Aborigines without going to Central Australia. However, it is a much different experience from that which you would have in the Red Centre. Perhaps because it was founded by American theater director Don Freeman and his French-Canadian dancer wife, Judy—working with the local Aborigines who now own 51% of the business—this seems more about show business than about an authentic cultural experience. Despite this, the park has won multiple international awards since it began in 1987, and is worth a look.

Housed in a striking modern building that incorporates Aboriginal themes and colors, the Tjapukai experience needs at least 2 to 3 hours. Start in the Creation Theatre, where performers use the latest in illusion, theatrics, and technology to tell the story of the creation of the world according to the spiritual beliefs of Tjapukai people. Actors work with special effects and holographic images to illustrate the legends. The production is performed in the Tjapukai language, translated through headsets.

Move on through the Magic Space museum and gallery section of the complex to the History Theatre, where a 20-minute film relates the history of the Tjapukai people since the coming of white settlers 120 years ago.

Outside, there's a cultural village where you can attempt boomerang and spear throwing, fire-making and didgeridoo playing, and learn about bush foods and medicines. Shows and demonstrations are planned so visitors can move from one to another easily, without missing anything. The complex also includes a restaurant and coffee shop. An arts-and-crafts gallery and shop stocks the work of Aboriginal artists and crafts workers.

Tjapukai by Night tours run daily from 7:30 to 10pm. They include interactive time in the Magic Space museum, a Creation Show performance, and an outdoor Serpent Circle—an interactive show featuring tap sticks for each guest to use, a join-in corroboree (an Aboriginal nighttime dance), and a ceremony involving fire and water. Following are a buffet dinner and dance show, and the chance to meet the dancers. The cost is A$103 (US$82/UK£41) adults, A$52 (US$42/UK£21) children, or A$258 (US$206/UK£53) for a family of four, including transfers to and from Cairns.

Captain Cook Hwy. (beside the Skyrail terminal), Smithfield. ✆ **07/4042 9900.** Fax 07/4042 9990. www.tjapukai.com.au. Admission A$30 (US$24/UK£12) adults, A$16 (US$13/UK£6.40) children 4–14, A$78 (US$62/UK£31) families. Ask about packages that include transfers, lunch, and a guided Magic Space tour, or Skyrail and/or Scenic Rail travel to and from Kuranda. Daily 9am–5pm. Closed Jan 1 and Dec 25. Free parking. Bus: 1C or 1E. Book shuttle transfers from Cairns hotels (A$11/US$8.80/UK£4.40 adults and A$5.40/US$4.30/UK£2.15 children, one-way) through the park. Park is 15 min. north of Cairns and 15 min. south of Palm Cove.

MORE ATTRACTIONS

In Cairns

Cairns Tropical Zoo *Kids* Get a dose of your favorite Aussie wildlife here—some kind of talk or show takes place about every 15 or 30 minutes throughout the day, including koala cuddling (have your photo taken for an extra A$15/US$12/UK£6), saltwater crocodile and lorikeet feedings, and cane toad racing. Lots of other animals are on show, too, like kangaroos (which you can hand-feed for A$1/US80¢/UK40p a bag), emus, cassowaries, dingoes, and native birds in a walk-through aviary. The park also runs a nocturnal tour, during which you can see many of the more elusive creatures on show. To take the park's 3-hour Cairns Night Zoo tour (www.cairnsnightzoo.com), book by 4pm on the same day (Mon–Thurs and Sat), earlier if you want transfers. The evening starts at 7pm and includes a wildlife spotlighting walk, during which you can pat a koala and a possum and feed kangaroos; a stargazing interlude; a barbecue dinner with beer and wine, billy tea, and damper; and dancing to an Aussie bush band.

Captain Cook Hwy. (22km/14 miles north of the city center), Palm Cove. ✆ **07/4055 3669.** Fax 07/4059 1160. www.cairnstropicalzoo.com. Admission A$28 (US$22/UK£11) adults, A$14 (US$11/UK£5.60) children 4–15. Cairns Night Zoo experience A$87 (US$70/UK£35) adults, A$44 (US$35/UK£18) children 4–15 (more if you want transfers from Cairns or Port Douglas). Daily 8:30am–5pm. Closed Dec 25. Free parking. Bus: 1B. Transfers from Cairns through Down Under Tours (✆ **07/4035 5566**) or from Port Douglas with Wildlife Discovery Tours (✆ **07/4099 6612**).

Cairns Wildlife Dome For some visitors to Cairns, exploring the rainforest and its wildlife doesn't even involve leaving the hotel, thanks to the city's newest attraction. Here, 200 animals—including a huge saltwater crocodile called Goliath—are housed in a 20m-high (66-ft.) glass dome on the rooftop of the Hotel Sofitel Reef Casino (see "Where to Stay," later in this chapter). You can get up close with koalas, lizards, kookaburras, frogs, pademelons, turtles, and snakes. There are wildlife presentations and free guided tours throughout the day.

In the Hotel Sofitel Reef Casino, 35–41 Wharf St., Cairns. ✆ **07/4031 7250.** Fax 07/4031 5265. www.cairnsdome.com.au. Admission A$22 (US$18/UK£8.80) adults, A$11 (US$8.80/UK£4.40) children 4–14, A$55 (US$44/UK£22) for a family of 4. Daily 8am–6pm. Closed Dec 25.

Hartley's Crocodile Adventures ★★ *Kids* Hartley's is the original Australian croc show, and quite possibly the best. What makes it different from others is the fantastic natural setting—a 2-hectare (5-acre) lagoon surrounded by melaluca (Paperbark) and bloodwood trees and home to 23 estuarine crocs. The best time to visit is for the 3pm "croc attack" show, when you can witness the saltwater crocodile "death roll" during the 45-minute performance. At 11am you can see these monsters get hand-fed or hear an eye-opening talk on the less aggressive freshwater crocodiles. There are tours of the croc farm at 10am and 1:30pm; at 2pm there is a snake show; and 4:30pm is koala-feeding time. Cassowaries are fed at 9:30am and 4:15pm. This attraction makes a good stop en route to Port Douglas.

Capt. Cook Hwy. (40km/24 miles north of Cairns; 25km/16 miles south of Port Douglas). ✆ **07/4055 3576.** Fax 07/4059 1017. www.crocodileadventures.com. Admission (good for 3 days) A$29 (US$23/UK£12) adults, A$15 (US$12/UK£6) children 4–15, A$73 (US$58/UK£29) families. Daily 8:30am–5pm. Closed Dec 25. Free parking. Transfers from Cairns available through Down Under Tours (✆ **07/4035 5566**) or from Cairns and Port Douglas through Wildlife Discovery Tours (✆ **07/4099 6612**).

Royal Flying Doctor Visitors Centre The Royal Flying Doctor Service (RFDS), the free aeromedical service that provides a "mantle of safety" for all Outback Australians, has a base in Cairns. Tours of the center start every 30 minutes from 9am to 4:30pm. You can also watch a film, attend a talk on how the service began, browse through memorabilia, and board a former RFDS plane. Allow about 45 minutes.

1 Junction St., Edge Hill. ✆ **07/4053 5687.** Admission A$5.50 (US$4.40/UK£2.20) adults, A$2.75 (US$2.20/UK£1.10) children, A$17 (US$14/UK£6.80) families. Mon–Sat 8:30am–5pm. Closed Sun and public holidays. Bus: 6 or 6A.

EXPLORING THE ISLANDS

You don't have to go all the way to the Outer Reef to see coral. Less than an hour from the city wharf, Green Island has snorkeling equal to that on the Great Barrier Reef. Fitzroy Island has rainforest walks, coral accessible by dive and snorkel boat trips from the island, and watersports. See "Where to Stay," later in this section, for details about the resorts on both islands.

GREEN ISLAND This 15-hectare (37-acre) coral cay, surrounded by dazzling coral and marine life, is just 27km (17 miles) east of Cairns. You can rent snorkel gear, windsurfers, and paddle-skis; take glass-bottom-boat trips; go parasailing; take an introductory or certified dive; walk vine-forest trails; or laze on the beach. The beach is coral sand, so it's a little rough underfoot. Day visitors have access to one of Green Island Resort's pools, its main bar, casual or upscale restaurants, and lockers and showers. Ask the beach staff to recommend the best snorkeling spots. If you don't snorkel, it's worth the admission charge to see the display of clown fish, potato cod, and anemones at the little underwater observatory, despite its cloudy old viewing windows. The island has a small attraction called **Marineland Melanesia** (✆ **07/4051 4032**), where you can see old nautical artifacts, primitive art, a turtle and reef aquarium, and live crocodiles. Admission is A$11 (US$8.80/UK£4.40) adults, A$5 (US$4/UK£2) kids; croc shows are at 10:30am and 1:45pm.

Great Adventures (✆ **07/4044 9944;** www.greatadventures.com.au) and **Big Cat Green Island Reef Cruises** (✆ **07/4051 0444;** www.bigcat-cruises.com.au) run to Green Island from Cairns. A half-day trip with snorkel gear or a glass-bottom-boat cruise with Great Adventures costs A$60 (US$48/UK£24), with full-day trips starting at A$102 (US$82/UK£41) from Cairns. Big Cat makes a day trip for A$62 (US$50/UK£25). Big Cat's boat is slightly slower, but you still get more than 5 hours on the island. Great Adventures also has transfer-only rates of A$60 (US$48/UK£24), which also gives access to the island's day facilities. Both companies pick up from hotels in Cairns, the northern beaches, and Port Douglas for an extra cost; Big Cat also runs to the island direct from Palm Cove.

FITZROY ISLAND Scenic Fitzroy Island (**www.fitzroyisland.com.au**), a rainforested national park 45 minutes from Cairns, offers good diving. The island's only resort closed for redevelopment in 2006 and was still closed at press time for this book, but by the time you get here it may be operating again (reopening was scheduled for late 2007). However, you can still take a day trip there for diving, watersports, or just to take a hike to the lighthouse at the top of the hill. A day trip can cost as little as the round-trip ferry fare, A$47 (US$38/UK£19) adults and A$26 (US$21/UK£10) for kids 4 to 14. Departures from Cairns are daily at 8:30 and 10:30am, returning at 9:30am and 3pm. Make reservations through **Raging Thunder Adventures** (✆ **07/4030 7990;** www.ragingthunder.com.au). Raging Thunder also runs full-day guided sea kayak expeditions to Fitzroy Island. Sea kayak trips include 3 hours of kayaking, snorkeling gear, a picnic lunch on a deserted beach, and a rainforest walk to the lighthouse. Trips cost A$170 (US$136/UK£68) per person from Cairns, and participants must be over 12.

EXPLORING THE WET TROPICS RAINFOREST

The 110-million-year-old World Heritage–listed Daintree Rainforest, 2 hours north of Cairns, gets most of the attention (see "Port Douglas, Daintree & the Cape Tribulation Area," later in this chapter), but tracts of rainforest closer to Cairns are just as pristine. These rainforests and the Daintree are part of the Wet Tropics, a World Heritage area that stretches from Cape Tribulation to Townsville. This dense, lush environment has remained unchanged by ice ages and other geological events, and the plants and animals retain primitive characteristics. In the tract's mangroves, eucalyptus woodlands, and tropical rainforest are 65% of Australia's bird species, 60% of its butterfly species, and many of its frogs, reptiles, bats, marsupials, and orchids.

Because so much rainforest wildlife is nocturnal and often difficult to spot, consider joining **Wait-a-While Rainforest Tours** (© **07/4098 2422;** www.waitawhile.com.au) on a day-into-night tour into Daintree and Cape Tribulation national parks. The tours cost A$176 to A$259 (US$141–US$207/UK£70–UK£104), depending on your pickup point, and are designed to maximize your encounters with the wild things. They begin from Cairns at 2pm and finish at about 11:30pm.

A SIDE TRIP TO KURANDA, A RAINFOREST VILLAGE ★

Few travelers visit Cairns without making at least a day trip to the mountain village of **Kuranda,** 34km (21 miles) northwest of Cairns near the Barron Gorge National Park. Although it's undeniably touristy, the cool mountain air and mist-wrapped rainforest refuse to be spoiled, no matter how many tourists clutter the streets. The shopping in Kuranda—for leather goods, Australian-wool sweaters, opals, crafts, and more—is more unusual than in Cairns, and the handful of cafes and restaurants are much more atmospheric. The town is easy to negotiate on foot; pick up a visitors' guide and map at the Skyrail gondola station or train station (see below) when you arrive.

GETTING THERE

Getting to Kuranda is part of the fun. Some people drive up the winding 25km (16-mile) mountain road, but the most popular approaches are to chuff up the mountainside in a scenic train, or to glide silently over the rainforest canopy in the world's longest gondola cableway, the Skyrail Rainforest Cableway.

The most popular round-trip is one-way on the Skyrail (mornings are best for photography) and the other way on the train.

BY SKYRAIL The **Skyrail Rainforest Cableway** ★★★ (© **07/4038 1555;** www.skyrail.com.au) is a magnificent feat of engineering and one of Australia's top tourism attractions. There are about 114 six-person gondolas, which leave every few seconds from the terminal in the northern Cairns suburb of Smithfield for the 7.5km (4½-mile) journey. The view of the coast as you ascend is so breathtaking that even those afraid of heights will find it worthwhile. As you rise over the foothills of the coastal range, watch the lush green of the rainforest take over beneath you. Looking back, you have spectacular views over Cairns and north toward Trinity Bay. On a clear day, you can see Green Island. There are two stops during the 90-minute trip, at Red Peak and Barron Falls. After about 10 minutes, you reach Red Peak. You are now 545m (1,788 ft.) above sea level, and massive kauri pines dominate the view. You must change gondolas at each station, so take the time to stroll around the boardwalks for the ground view of the rainforest. Guided walks start every 20 minutes.

You'll continue on to Barron Falls station, built on the cleared site of an old construction camp for workers on the first hydroelectric power station on the Barron River in the 1930s. A rainforest information center has been established here, and there are boardwalks to the lookouts for wonderful views of the Barron Gorge and Falls. From Barron Falls station, the gondola travels over the thick rainforest of the range. It's easy to spot ferns and orchids and the brilliant blue butterflies of the region. As you reach the end of the trip, the gondola passes over the Barron River and across the Kuranda railway line into the station.

A one-way ticket is A$37 (US$30/UK£15) for adults and A$19 (US$15/UK£7.60) for children 4 to 14 or A$93 (US$74/UK£37) for families of four; a round-trip ticket, including transfers from your Cairns or northern beaches hotel, is A$73 (US$58/UK£29) for adults, A$37 (US$30/UK£15) for children, A$183 (US$146/UK£73) for families; from Port Douglas, it's A$88 (US$70/UK£35) for adults, A$44 (US$35/UK£18) for children, A$220 (US$176/UK£88) for families. You must make a reservation to travel within a 15-minute time frame. Don't worry if it rains on the day you go—one of the best trips I've made on Skyrail was in a misty rain, which added a new dimension to the rainforest. The cableway operates daily except December 25 from 8:30am to 5:30pm, with the last boarding at the Cairns end at 4:15pm. The Skyrail terminal is on the Captain Cook Highway at Kamerunga Road, Caravonica Lakes, 15km (9½ miles) north of Cairns's city center.

BY SCENIC RAILWAY The 34km (21-mile) **Kuranda Scenic Railway** (**© 07/4036 9333;** www.kurandascenicrailway.com.au) is one of the most scenic rail journeys in the world. The train snakes through the magnificent vistas of the Barron Gorge National Park, past gorges and waterfalls on the 90-minute trip from Cairns to Kuranda. It rises 328m (1,076 ft.) and goes through 15 tunnels before emerging at the pretty Kuranda station, which is smothered in ferns. Built by hand over 5 years in the late 1880s, the railway track is today a monument to the 1,500 men who toiled to link the two towns, and the ride on the steam train adds to the atmosphere. The train departs Cairns Central at 8:30am and 9:30am daily (except Dec 25), and leaves Kuranda at 2pm and 3:30pm. The one-way fare is A$37 (US$30/UK£15) for adults, A$19 (US$15/UK£7.60) for children 4 to 14, and A$93 (US$74/UK£37) for a family of four.

SKYRAIL/TRAIN COMBINATION TICKETS In most cases, these packages represent convenience rather than savings. A package combining one-way travel on the Skyrail and a trip back on the Scenic Railway is A$74 (US$59/UK£30) for adults and A$37 (US$30/UK£15) for children; A$93 (US$74/UK£37) for adults and A$47 (US$38/UK£19) for kids with round-trip transfers from Cairns or the northern beaches. Skyrail runs a shuttle bus from most Cairns hotels. A package including the Skyrail, the Scenic Railway, and entry to the Tjapukai Aboriginal Cultural Park (see earlier in this chapter) is A$115 (US$92/UK£46) for adults, A$58 (US$46/UK£23) for kids, and A$369 (US$295/UK£148) for a family of four, including transfers from Cairns, the northern beaches, or Palm Cove. An option including the Skyrail, Scenic Railway, and Rainforestation (see below) is A$148 (US$118/UK£59) for adults, A$74 (US$59/UK£30) for kids, and A$369 (US$295/UK£148) for a family of four including transfers from Cairns. All packages can upgrade to Gold Class service on the train for an extra A$43 (US$34/UK£17) per person. Book packages through Skyrail, Queensland Rail, or Tjapukai.

BY BUS **Whitecar Coaches** (**© 07/4091 1855**) operates a bus to Kuranda from Cairns. The fare is A$4 (US$3.20/UK£1.60) per person. Catch it at stop D in the city mall, Cairns.

EXPLORING KURANDA

Kuranda is known for its markets that sell locally made arts and crafts, fresh produce, boomerangs, T-shirts, and jewelry. There are two true markets—the small "original" markets at 7 Therwine St., behind Kuranda Market Arcade (open Wed–Fri and Sun 8am–3pm), which mainly sell cheap imports; and the 90-stall Heritage Market (open daily 9am–3pm), which offers a wider variety of goods. Try to visit Kuranda when both markets are open. The New Kuranda Markets, in an undercover complex in Coondoo Street, houses a range of stalls and shops including an Aboriginal art gallery.

Because even the Heritage Market has been invaded by imported products, a group of about 50 local artisans sell their work in the **Kuranda Arts Co-Operative** ★, Shop 6, 43 Rob Veivers Dr., next to the Butterfly Sanctuary (**© 07/4093 9026**). It's open from 10am to 4pm daily. You will find quality furniture crafted from recycled Australian hardwoods, jewelry, and handicrafts, among other items.

You can explore the rainforest, the river esplanade, or Barron Falls along a number of easy walking trails. If you want to learn about the rainforest, explore it with Brian Clarke of **Kuranda Riverboat Tours** (**© 07/4093 7476** or 0412/159212), who runs informative 45-minute river cruises. The cruises depart hourly from 10:30am to 2:30pm from the riverside landing across the footbridge near the train station. Brian is a former crocodile hunter and has lived in the rainforest for more than 30 years. The cruise costs A$14 (US$11/UK£5.60) for adults, A$7 (US$5.60/UK£2.80) for children 5 to 15, and A$35 (US$28/UK£14) for a family of four. Buy your tickets on board.

KURANDA'S NATURE PARKS

Birdworld (**© 07/4093 9188**), behind the Heritage markets off Rob Veivers Drive, has eye-catching macaws, a pair of cassowaries, and Australia's largest collection of free-flying birds. Birdworld is open daily from 9am to 4pm (closed Dec 25); admission is A$12 (US$9.60/UK£4.80]) for adults, A$5 (US$4/UK£2) for children 4 to 14, A$29 (US$23/UK£12) for families.

Kuranda Koala Gardens (**© 07/4093 9953;** www.koalagardens.com) is a small wildlife park at the Heritage Markets. Here you can cuddle a koala and have your photo taken, and check out other animals including freshwater crocodiles, wombats, lizards, and wallabies. Not for the fainthearted, take a stroll through the walk-through snake enclosure, while they slither at your feet. A small display about Kuranda's pioneers is made up of photos from the owners' family albums. Kuranda Koala Gardens is open daily from 9am to 4pm, and costs A$15 (US$12/UK£6) adults and A$7.50 (US$6/UK£3) children 4 to 15. It is packaged with Birdworld and the Australian Butterfly Sanctuary (see below) as the Kuranda Wildlife Experience, and a pass to all three can be bought on arrival at any of the three attractions for A$36 (US$29/UK£14) adults and A$18 (US$14/UK£7.20) children.

Australian Butterfly Sanctuary ★ *Kids* A rainbow-hued array of 1,500 tropical butterflies—including the electric-blue Ulysses and Australia's largest species, the

Cairns bird wing—occupies a lush walk-through enclosure here. Take the free guided tour and learn about the butterfly's fascinating life cycle. The butterflies will land on you if you wear pink, red, and other bright colors, and don't be put off if it's raining—this attraction is good in any weather.

8 Rob Veivers Dr. © **07/4093 7575.** Fax 07/4093 8923. www.australianbutterflies.com. Admission A$15 (US$12/UK£6) adults, A$7.50 (US$6/UK£3) children 4–15, A$38 (US$30/UK£15) families of 4. Daily 9:45am–4pm. Free guided tours every 15 min. 10am–3:15pm. Closed Dec 25. Street parking. Bus stop 7 min. from sanctuary.

Rainforestation Nature Park At this 40-hectare (99-acre) nature and cultural complex, you can take a 45-minute ride into the rainforest in a World War II amphibious Army Duck. You'll hear commentary on orchids and other rainforest wildlife along the way. You can also see a performance by Aboriginal dancers; learn about Aboriginal legends and throw a boomerang on the Dreamtime Walk; or have your photo taken cuddling a koala in the wildlife park. You can do any of these activities separately, or do them all (except cuddle a koala) for one price. Koala photos are A$12 (US$9.60/UK£4.80). The Army Duck runs on the hour beginning at 10am; the Aboriginal dancers perform at 10:30am, noon, and 2pm; and the 30-minute Dreamtime Walk leaves at 10, 11, and 11:30am, 12:30, 1:30, and 2:30pm.

Kennedy Hwy., a 5-min. drive from the center of Kuranda. © **07/4085 5008.** Fax 07/4085 5016. www.rainforest.com.au. A$36 (US$29/UK£14) for adults, A$18 (US$14/UK£7.20) for kids 4–14, A$90 (US$72/UK£36) for a family of 4. Daily 8:30am–4pm. Closed Dec 25. Free parking. Shuttle from the Butterfly Sanctuary, Rob Veivers Dr., every 30 min. 10:45am–2:45pm for A$7 (US$5.60/UK£2.80) adults, A$3.50 (US$2.80/UK£1.40) children, A$18 (US$14/UK£7.20) families, round-trip.

WHITE-WATER RAFTING & OTHER THRILLS

RnR Rafting ★ (© **07/4041 9444;** www.raft.com.au) and **Raging Thunder Adventures** (© **07/4030 7990;** www.ragingthunder.com.au) serve as one-stop booking shops for action pursuits in and around Cairns, including hot-air ballooning, sky diving, jet-boating, horseback riding, ATV (all-terrain vehicle) safaris, parasailing, and rafting. Ask about multipursuit packages.

BUNGEE JUMPING Contact **A. J. Hackett Bungy** (© **1800/622 888** in Australia, or 07/4057 7188). The cost is A$102 (US$82/UK£41) per person including transport to the site, which is 20 minutes north of town on McGregor Road.

FISHING Cairns is the world's giant black marlin capital. Catches of more than 1,000 pounds hardly raise an eyebrow in this neck of the woods. The game-fishing season is September through December, with November the busiest. Book early—game boats are reserved months in advance. Game fishers can also battle Pacific sailfish, dogtooth and yellowfin tuna, Spanish mackerel, wahoo, dolphin fish, barracuda, and tiger shark. Reef anglers can expect to land coral trout, red emperor (sea perch), and sweetlip. Mangrove jack, barramundi, and tarpon lurk in the estuaries. Contact **Fishing Cairns** (© **07/4041 1169;** www.fishingcairns.com.au) to book a charter. Expect to pay around A$400 (US$320/UK£160) per person or about A$1,900 (US$1,520/UK£760) per day for a sole charter for heavy-tackle game fishing, A$375 (US$300/UK£150) per person for light-tackle fishing, at least A$185 (US$148/UK£74) for reef fishing, and A$155 (US$124/UK£62) for a day or A$85 (US$68/UK£34) for a half-day in Cairns' Trinity Inlet estuary.

WHITE-WATER RAFTING Several companies offer exciting white-water-rafting trips from Cairns on the Class III to IV **Tully River** ★★, 90 minutes south of Cairns near Mission Beach; the Class III Barron River in the hills behind the city; and the

Class IV to V rapids of the inland Johnstone River. One of the best is **RnR Rafting** (**© 07/4041 9444**).

One-day trips on the Tully are the most popular (see "Mission Beach: The Cassowary Coast," later in this chapter). The trip costs A$155 (US$124/UK£62) from Cairns or the northern beaches, including transfers.

Closer to Cairns, the gentler **Barron River** is a good choice for the timid. A half-day trip with RnR Rafting costs A$98 (US$78/UK£39) from Cairns or A$116 (US$93/UK£46) from Port Douglas, including pickup and 2 hours of rafting. Prices do not include a A$25 (US$20/UK£10) levy for national park and other fees.

WHERE TO STAY

High season in Cairns includes 2 weeks at Easter, the period from early July to early October, and the Christmas holiday through January. Book ahead in those periods. In low season (Nov–June), many hotels offer discounts or are willing to negotiate.

Cairns has a good supply of affordable accommodations, both in the heart of the city and along the northern beaches. You can also stay in the peaceful village of Kuranda, or get away from it all at an island resort.

Don't think you have to stay in Cairns city if you don't have a car. Most tour and cruise operators will pick you up and drop you off in Cairns, on the northern beaches, or even in Port Douglas (see section 3, later in this chapter).

IN CAIRNS

Unless noted otherwise, all accommodations below are within walking distance of shops, restaurants, cinemas, the casino, the tourist office, bus terminals, the train station, and the departure terminals for Great Barrier Reef cruises.

Very Expensive

Shangri-La Hotel, The Marina ★ After a A$35-million-plus (US$28-million/UK£14-million) renovation, this hotel became part of the swish Shangri-La group in mid-2004 and has a modern, sophisticated new look. Overlooking the marina, 36 new rooms are part of the exclusive Horizon Club and all have broadband and wireless Internet connectivity (as does the business center). These rooms are contemporary in style and exceptionally spacious—more than 56 sq. m (603 sq. ft.), with 3.3m (11-ft.) ceilings. Bathrooms have ocean views, and the rooms have large terraces looking to the moored yachts and the mountains. The AAA-rated five-star hotel adjoins the Pier Shopping Centre and the new Esplanade lagoon, and is not far from the Reef Fleet Terminal.

Pierpoint Rd., Cairns, QLD 4870. **© 1800/222 448** in Australia, 0800/442 179 in New Zealand, 800/942 5050 in the U.S. and Canada, 020/8747 8485 in the U.K., or 07/4031 1411. Fax 07/4031 3226. www.shangri-la.com. 256 units. A$397–A$444 (US$318–US$355/UK£159–UK£178) double; A$601–A$1,133 (US$481–US$906/UK£240–UK£453) suite. Children under 18 stay free in parent's room with existing bedding. AE, DC, MC, V. Free outdoor and covered self-parking. **Amenities:** 1 restaurant; 2 bars; large outdoor pool and children's pool; nearby golf course; health club; Jacuzzi; sauna; video arcade; concierge; tour desk; car-rental desk; airport shuttle (on request); business center; shopping arcade; 24-hr. room service; in-room massage; babysitting; laundry services; dry cleaning; executive-level rooms. *In room:* A/C, TV/VCR w/pay movies, fax, dataport, minibar, coffeemaker, hair dryer, iron, safe.

Sofitel Reef Casino Cairns ★ Arguably the most stylish property in Cairns, this six-story hotel is 1 block from the water, with partial water views from some rooms, and city/hinterland outlooks from others. All the rooms have lots of light, high-quality amenities, Jacuzzis, bathrobes, and small balconies with smart timber furniture. The **Reef Casino** is attached to the hotel (see "Cairns After Dark," later in this chapter).

35–41 Wharf St., Cairns, QLD 4870. ✆ **1800/808 883** in Australia, 800/221-4542 in the U.S. and Canada, 020/8283 4500 in the U.K., 0800/44 4422 in New Zealand, or 07/4030 8888. Fax 07/4030 8777. www.accorhotels.com. 128 units. A$370–A$395 (US$296–US$316/UK£148–UK£158) double; A$480–A$585 (US$384–US$468/UK£192–UK£234) suite; A$1,865 (US$1,492/UK£746) presidential suite. AE, DC, MC, V. Free valet and self-parking. **Amenities:** 4 restaurants; 3 bars; small rooftop pool; health club; Jacuzzi; sauna; concierge; tour desk; airport shuttle; business center; 24-hr. room service; babysitting; laundry service; dry cleaning. *In room:* A/C, TV/VCR, dataport and Wi-Fi, minibar, hair dryer, iron, safe.

Expensive

Oasis Resort Cairns *Value* The large pool, complete with swim-up bar and a little sandy beach, is the focus of this attractive six-story resort built in 1997. All the colorful, contemporary rooms have balconies with views over the tropical gardens, the mountains, or the pool. The suites, with a TV in the bedroom and a large Jacuzzi bathtub, could well be the best-value suites in town.

122 Lake St., Cairns, QLD 4870. ✆ **07/4080 1888.** Fax 07/4080 1889. www.oasis-cairns.com.au. 314 units. A$285–A$315 (US$228–US$252/UK£114–UK£126) double; A$455 (US$364/UK£182) suite. Extra person A$45 (US$36/UK£18). Children under 16 stay free in parent's room with existing bedding. Free crib. Ask about packages. AE, DC, MC, V. Free valet and self-parking. **Amenities:** Restaurant; 2 bars; outdoor pool; health club; concierge; tour desk; airport shuttle; limited room service; babysitting; coin-op laundry; laundry service; dry cleaning. *In room:* A/C, TV w/pay movies, dataport, minibar, coffeemaker, hair dryer, iron, safe.

Rydges Esplanade Resort Cairns Despite its lack of glitz, this 14-story hotel has been the choice of a number of movie stars—most famously Marlon Brando—while on location in Cairns. A 20-minute waterfront walk from downtown, the hotel offers a range of accommodations, from hotel rooms to penthouse apartments. The one- and two-bedroom apartments look out to the sea; hotel rooms have sea or mountain views. Some units have dataports; kitchenettes are in studios and apartments; and hotel rooms and apartments have minibars. The rooms are spacious, but the bathrooms are not, perhaps reflecting the hotel's Japanese market. Out back are cheaper studios and apartments, with upgraded furnishings; out front are a pool and sun deck.

The Esplanade (at Kerwin St.), Cairns, QLD 4870. ✆ **1800/079 105** in Australia, or 07/4031 2211. Fax 07/4031 2704. 342 units. A$320–A$350 (US$256–US$280/UK£102–UK£140) double; A$290 (US$232/UK£116) double 1-bedroom studio, or A$350 (US$280/UK£140) for up to 4 people; A$330 (US$264/UK£132) double 2-bedroom studio, or A$475 (US$380/UK£190) for up to 4; A$295–A$375 (US$236–US$300/UK£118–UK£150) tower apt for up to 4; A$395 (US$316/UK£158) double 2-bedroom apt, A$475 (US$380/UK£190) for up to 4. Ask about packages. AE, DC, MC, V. Free covered parking. Bus stop about 100m (328 ft.) from the hotel. **Amenities:** 2 restaurants; 3 bars; 3 outdoor pools; golf course about 20 min. away; 2 lit tennis courts; health club w/aerobics classes; Jacuzzi; sauna; bike rental; concierge; tour desk; car-rental desk; airport transfers; shuttle service around city; salon; 24-hr. room service; in-room massage; babysitting; coin-op laundry; laundry service; dry cleaning; nonsmoking rooms. *In room:* A/C, TV w/pay movies, hair dryer, iron, safe.

Moderate

Cairns Plaza Hotel The harbor views at this seven-story complex are better than those at most of the more luxurious hotels in Cairns. Two blocks from town, the accommodations are a good size, with fresh, appealing furnishings and modern bathrooms. Suites and studios have kitchenettes. If your balcony does not have a water vista, you overlook a nice aspect of the city or mountains instead. Families can book a connecting suite and standard room to create more space and privacy.

145 The Esplanade (at Minnie St.), Cairns, QLD 4870. ✆ **1800/117 787** in Australia, or 07/4051 4688. Fax 07/4051 8129. www.cairnsplaza.com.au. 60 units. A$130 (US$104/UK£52) double; A$160 (US$128/UK£64) suite. Rates include continental breakfast. AE, DC, MC, V. Limited free parking. **Amenities:** Restaurant; bar; small outdoor pool; golf course nearby; 4 lit tennis courts nearby; access to nearby health club; Jacuzzi; tour desk; car-rental desk; limited

room service; massage; babysitting; coin-op laundry; dry cleaning. *In room:* A/C, TV w/free movies, dataport, minib..., coffeemaker, hair dryer, iron.

Inexpensive

Coral Tree Inn *Value* The focal point of this airy, modern resort-style motel a 5-minute walk from the city center is the friendly communal kitchen that overlooks the palm-lined saltwater pool and paved sun deck. It's a great spot to cook a steak or reef fish filet on the free barbecue and join other guests at the big shared tables. Local restaurants deliver, you can order a continental breakfast for A$9 (US$7.20/UK£3.60) per person, free fresh-roasted coffee is on the boil all day, and a vending machine sells wine and beer, so you don't even have to go down to the pub for supplies! The small-ish, basic but neat motel rooms have painted brick walls, terra-cotta tile or carpeted floors, and new bathrooms with marble-look laminate countertops. In contrast, the eight suites, which have kitchenettes, are huge and stylish enough for any corporate traveler. They are some of the best-value accommodations in town. All rooms have a balcony or patio; some look out onto the commercial buildings next door, but most face the pool. Ask about packages that include cruises and other tours.

166–172 Grafton St., Cairns, QLD 4870. ✆ **07/4031 3744.** Fax 07/4031 3064. www.coraltreeinn.com.au. 58 units. A$120 (US$96/UK£48) double; A$148 (US$118/UK£59) suite. Extra person A$10 (US$8/UK£4). AE, DC, MC, V. Limited free parking; ample street parking. **Amenities:** Bar; outdoor saltwater pool; access to nearby health club; bike rental; tour desk; car-rental desk; airport shuttle; babysitting; coin-op laundry; laundry service; dry cleaning; nonsmoking rooms; safe (at reception). *In room:* A/C, TV, dataport, fridge, coffeemaker, hair dryer, iron.

Lilybank Bed & Breakfast ★ This 1870s Queenslander homestead, originally a mayor's residence, is in a leafy suburb 6km (3¾ miles) from the airport and a 10-minute drive from the city. The large, attractive guest rooms, individually decorated with such features as wrought-iron beds and patchwork quilts, have good-size bathrooms. The largest room has French doors opening onto a "sleep-out" (an enclosed veranda with two extra beds). You can also stay in the gardener's cottage, with slate floors, stained-glass windows, a king-size bed, and a bar. The house is set in gardens with an attractive rock-lined saltwater pool. Breakfast is served in the garden room by the fishpond. Gregarious hosts Mike and Pat Woolford share their house with two poodles, a galah (an Australian parrot) called Chook, and a giant green tree frog. There's a guest TV lounge and kitchen, and phone, fax, and e-mail access. Many tours pick up at the door, and several good restaurants are a stroll away, so you don't need a car to stay here. A taxi from the airport costs approximately A$15 (US$12/UK£6). No smoking indoors.

75 Kamerunga Rd., Stratford, Cairns, QLD 4870. ✆ **07/4055 1123.** Fax 07/4058 1990. www.lilybank.com.au. 6 units, 4 with shower only. A$99–A$121 (US$79–US$97/UK£40–UK£49) double. Extra person A$33 (US$26/UK£13). Rates include full breakfast. AE, MC, V. Free parking. Bus: 1E or 1G. Bus stop 120m (394 ft.) away. Children not accepted. **Amenities:** Outdoor pool; tour desk; massage (on request); coin-op laundry; nonsmoking rooms. *In room:* A/C, hair dryer, no phone.

ON THE NORTHERN BEACHES

A string of white sandy beaches starts 15 minutes north of the city center. Trinity Beach, 15 minutes from the airport, is secluded, elegant, and scenic. The most upscale is Palm Cove, 20 minutes from the airport. Here rainbow-hued shops and tasteful apartment blocks nestle among giant Paperbarks and palms fronting a postcard-perfect beach. It has several advantages over other beach suburbs: A 9-hole resort golf course and a gym are within walking distance, the Quicksilver Wavepiercer Great Barrier Reef cruise boat picks up passengers here daily, and it has the greatest choice of places to eat. Add 5 to 10 minutes to the traveling times above to reach the city.

nsive

l Reef House & Spa Palm Cove ★★★ Picture yourself in a Somerset m novel—substituting the Queensland tropics for Singapore—and you've got it. This is one of the most romantic hotels in Queensland, or all of Australia. The Reef House's guest list reads like an excerpt from Who's Who—the most recent addition being Bob Dylan and his band. But no matter who you are, you will not want to leave. The white walls are swathed in bougainvillea, and the beds with mosquito netting. Airy interiors feature handmade artifacts and white wicker furniture. The Verandah Spa rooms, which have a Jacuzzi on the balcony, overlook the pool, waterfalls, and lush gardens. They have extra touches such as bathrobes and a CD player, as well as balconies within earshot of the ocean. The beachfront **restaurant,** on a covered wooden deck beneath towering Paperbarks, is a favorite with locals and tourists alike for its unsurpassed ocean views, gentle breezes, and unpretentious food.

99 Williams Esplanade, Palm Cove, Cairns, QLD 4879. ✆ **1800/079 052** in Australia, or 07/4055 3633. Fax 07/4055 3305. www.reefhouse.com.au. 69 units, 14 with shower only. A$405–A$573 (US$324–US$458/UK£162–UK£229) double; A$520–A$730 (US$416–US$584/UK£208–UK£292) suite. AE, DC, MC, V. Free limited covered parking; ample street parking. Bus: 1, 1B, 1X, 2X, or N. **Amenities:** Restaurant; bar; cafe; honor bar; 3 small heated outdoor pools; nearby golf course; spa; access to nearby health club; concierge; tour desk; airport shuttle; limited room service; massage; babysitting; coin-op laundry; laundry service; dry cleaning. *In room:* A/C, TV/VCR, kitchenette, minibar, coffeemaker, hair dryer, iron, safe.

Expensive

Outrigger Beach Club & Spa ★ Set behind a grove of melaluca trees across the street from the beach, the main hotel in this resort, which opened in late 2002, has rooms and apartments with touches of Queensland colonial style. Hotel rooms are small but have Jacuzzis and timber outdoor furniture on the decks. Eight penthouses (three floors up) have private rooftop terraces and pools, but there's no elevator. A further 25 penthouses have Jacuzzis. The large lagoon-style pool has a sandy beach and swim-up bar. Coconut palms with white-painted trunks surround the lagoon, which is lit by flaming torches at night. A "resort within the resort," the Serenity Wing, has 42 suites and a private rainforest pool. The suites are secluded, with kitchens, gas barbecues, washers and dryers, and state-of-the-art entertainment units, including DVDs and flatscreen televisions. Pampering awaits you at the Sanctum Spa, which has seven wet and dry treatment rooms and offers yoga classes as well as beauty and massage treatments for both men and women. If you are staying 5 nights or more at full rates and want to arrive in style, order the free limousine or Rolls-Royce transfers from Cairns Airport to Palm Cove. For guests staying 3 nights or more, the room rate includes coach transfers to the airport.

123 Williams Esplanade, Palm Cove, Cairns, QLD 4879. ✆ **800/688-7444** in the U.S., 1800/134 444 in Australia, or 07/4059 9200. Fax 07/4059 9222. www.outrigger.com. 220 units. A$295–A$360 (US$236–US$288/UK£118–UK£144) double with Jacuzzi; A$371–A$460 (US$297–US$368/UK£149–UK£184) double 1-bedroom suite; A$469–A$502 (US$375–US$402/UK£188–UK£201) double 1-bedroom suite with Jacuzzi; A$533–A$656 (US$426–US$525/UK£213–UK£262) 2-bedroom suite with Jacuzzi for up to 4; A$1,056 (US$845/UK£422) 2-bedroom penthouse suite for up to 4 with plunge pool. Extra person A$35 (US$28/UK£14). 3-night minimum at Easter and Christmas to mid-Jan. AE, DC, MC, V. Secure parking. **Amenities:** 4 restaurants; 3 outdoor pools; golf course nearby; tennis court; gym; spa; concierge; tour desk; nonsmoking rooms. *In room:* A/C, TV w/pay movies, DVD player, dataport, fridge, coffeemaker, hair dryer, iron, safe, CD player, Jacuzzi.

Moderate

Ellis Beach Oceanfront Bungalows ★ *Finds* On arguably the loveliest of the northern beaches, about 30 minutes from Cairns, these bungalows and cabins sit under palm trees between the Coral Sea and a backdrop of mountainous rainforest.

Tips **Safe Swimming**

All of the northern beaches have small, netted enclosures for safe swimming from October through May, when deadly stingers (box jellyfish) render all mainland beaches in north Queensland off-limits.

Lifeguards patrol the beach, and there are stinger nets in season as well as a shady pool and toddlers' wading pool. There's plenty of privacy, and the accommodations are basic but pleasant. You can sit on the veranda and gaze at the ocean. Keep an eye out for dolphins. Each bungalow and cabin sleeps four and has full kitchen facilities (with microwave, fridge, and freezer), but cabins have no en-suite bathroom (they use the communal facilities at the campground in the same complex). The property has coin-operated barbecues and phone and fax facilities.

Captain Cook Hwy., Ellis Beach, QLD 4879. ✆ **1800/637 036** in Australia, or 07/4055 3538. Fax 07/4055 3077. www.ellisbeach.com. 15 units, all with shower only. A$68–A$80 (US$54–US$64/UK£27–UK£32) double cabin; A$100–A$180 (US$80–US$144/UK£40–UK£72) double bungalow. Extra person A$15 (US$12/UK£6) cabin, A$25 (US$20/UK£10) bungalow. 3-night minimum June–Sept; 2-night minimum Oct–May. AE, MC, V. **Amenities:** Restaurant; 2 outdoor pools; golf course nearby; tour desk; car-rental desk; coin-op laundry. *In room:* A/C, TV, kitchen, iron, ceiling fans, no phone.

The Reef Retreat ★★ Tucked back one row of buildings from the beach is this little gem—a low-rise collection of contemporary studios and suites built around a swimming pool in a grove of palms and silver Paperbarks. All the rooms have cool tile floors and smart teak and cane furniture and were all renovated and refurbished in 2006. The studios are a terrific value and much larger than the average hotel room. Some suites have two rooms; others have a Jacuzzi and a kitchenette outside on the balcony. There are also two-bedroom villas, and across the road from the complex is a two-bedroom town house, all of which sleep up to six people. There's a barbecue and a Jacuzzi on the grounds. There's no elevator. Units are serviced once for every 5-day stay. Extra cleanings A$20 to A$30 (US$16–US$24/UK£8–UK£12).

10–14 Harpa St., Palm Cove, Cairns, QLD 4879. ✆ **07/4059 1744.** Fax 07/4059 1745. www.reefretreat.com.au. 36 units, all with shower only. A$170 (US$136/UK£68) studio double; A$185 (US$148/UK£74) suite; A$195 (US$156/UK£78) suite with Jacuzzi; A$295 (US$236/UK£118) 2-bedroom villa for up to 4; A$230 (US$184/UK£92) town house for up to 4. Extra person A$25 (US$20/UK£10). Children under 3 stay free in parent's room with existing bedding. Crib A$25 (US$20/UK£10). AE, MC, V. Free parking. Bus: 1, 1B 1X, 2X, or N. **Amenities:** Outdoor saltwater pool; nearby golf course; nearby tennis courts; Jacuzzi; tour desk; car-rental desk; coin-op laundry; laundry service; dry cleaning. *In room:* A/C, TV, dataport, kitchenette, fridge, coffeemaker, hair dryer, iron.

ISLAND RESORTS

Several island resorts are within the Great Barrier Reef Marine Park off Cairns. They afford safe swimming year-round, because the infestations of deadly marine stingers that plague this area from October through May don't make it to the islands. They also offer snorkeling and diving opportunities every day.

The only true budget choice in the islands, the no-frills **Fitzroy Island Resort** (www.fitzroyisland.com.au), closed in early 2006 for overnight visitors for a A$10-million-plus (US$8-million/UK£4-million) redevelopment which will see an upgrade of the existing cabin/bunkhouse accommodations and the addition of 48 new two-bedroom apartments. You can still make a day trip to the island. The resort is set to welcome overnight guests again by the end of 2007. The project will also include a new spa, bar and restaurant, dive shop, general store, coffee shop, bakery, and conference rooms. It had not reopened at press time.

VERY EXPENSIVE

Green Island Resort ★ Step off the beach at this Great Barrier Reef national park island, and you are surrounded by acres of coral. The resort is a high-class cluster of rooms tucked away in a dense vine forest. Each room is private, roomy, and elegantly outfitted, with polished wooden floors and a balcony looking into the forest. Windsurfing, surf-skiing, canoeing, diving and snorkeling (both on the island and on day trips to the outer Reef), glass-bottom-boat trips, self-guided rainforest walks, parasailing, and beach volleyball are among the activities available, or you can simply laze on the white-coral sand or by the guests-only pool. Helicopter and seaplane flights and cruises are available. Room rates include many activities and equipment, such as non-motorized sports, snorkel gear, and glass-bottom-boat trips; there's a charge for scuba diving and other activities using fuel. Both the resort and the island are small (you can walk around it in 45 min.), and it is a popular day-tripper destination. But after they leave at 4:30pm, the place is blissfully peaceful.

Green Island, 27km (17 miles) east of Cairns (P.O. Box 898), Cairns, QLD 4870. ✆ **1800/673 366** in Australia, or 07/4031 3300. Fax 07/4052 1511. www.greenislandresort.com.au. 46 units. A$495–A$595 (US$396–US$476/UK£198–UK£238) double. Extra person A$93 (US$74/UK£37). Rates include launch transfers. Ask about packages. AE, DC, MC, V. Helicopter and seaplane transfers available. **Amenities:** 2 restaurants; 2 bars; 2 outdoor saltwater pools; spa; wide array of watersports equipment available; concierge; tour desk; laundry service; coin-op laundry. *In room:* A/C, TV, minibar, hair dryer, safe.

Lizard Island ★★★ Luxury lodges, huge potato cod so tame divers can pet them, snorkeling off the beach, and isolation—that's what lures the well-heeled to this small, exclusive resort. Lizard is a rugged 1,000-hectare (2,470-acre) national park island on the Great Barrier Reef, sparsely vegetated but stunningly beautiful, ringed by 24 white sandy beaches, with fringing reefs that support a multitude of marine life including giant clams. No day-trippers are allowed. Room rates include many activities: snorkeling and glass-bottom-boat trips, catamarans, paddle-skis, fishing tackle, tennis, and hiking trails, such as the muscle-straining 545m (½-mile) climb to Cook's Look, where Captain Cook spied his way out of the treacherous reefs in 1770. You pay for fishing and diving trips to nearby Reef sites, including Cod Hole. Introductory dive lessons and night dives are available.

The 40 villas, elegant free-standing lodges tucked under palms along the beach or perched on cliff tops overlooking the bay, were renovated in 2000. They are built of timber and stone, in a casual tropical style, with earth and sea tone finishes. A guest lounge has Internet facilities, TV and video, bar facilities, and a book and games library. The recently expanded Azure Spa offers a Vichy shower, double-massage room and steam room, and a new range of therapies.

The most exclusive accommodations option, **The Pavilion,** is a villa offering complete privacy, sheer luxury, and spectacular panoramic views. It has private decks leading down to its own plunge pool, and comes with extras such as a laptop, binoculars, and Bollinger on arrival.

Lizard Island, 240km (149 miles) north of Cairns; 27km (17 miles) offshore (Voyages, G.P.O. Box 3589, Sydney, NSW 2001). ✆ **1300/134 044** in Australia, or 02/8296 8010 (Sydney reservations office). Fax 02/9299 2103 (Sydney reservations office). www.voyages.com.au. 40 units, all with shower only. A$1,584 (US$1,267/UK£634) double; A$1,974 (US$1,579/UK£790) villa double; A$2,058 (US$1,646/UK£823) suite double; A$3,500 (US$2,800/UK£1,400) Pavilion double. Extra person A$465 (US$372/UK£186). Rates include all meals and many activities. AE, DC, MC, V. Air transfers daily from Cairns take 1 hr. and cost around A$398 (US$318/UK£159) per person round-trip. Aircraft luggage limit

15 kilograms (33 lb.) per person. Air-charter transfers available. Children under 10 not accepted. **Amenities:** Restaurant; freshwater pool; lit tennis court; gym; spa; laundry service. *In room:* A/C, dataport, minibar, coffeemaker, hair dryer, iron, fans.

WHERE TO DINE

IN CAIRNS

For cheap eats, head to the Esplanade along the seafront; it's lined with cafes, pizzerias, fish-and-chips places, food courts, and ice-cream parlors.

Expensive

Fishlips Bar & Bistro ★★ CONTEMPORARY/SEAFOOD This popular Cairns institution has moved, and is now located inside the Cairns Yacht Club, with views over the Cairns Inlet. But the essentials haven't changed, with chef Ian Candy still serving up the innovative seafood dishes that have kept the locals patronizing his restaurant for years. The huge menu features "everything from burgers to lobster," and there are up to 15 specials daily. The local barramundi, or "barra," shows up in several incarnations, maybe in spring rolls with chilli plum sauce, beer-battered, or pan-fried with meuniere on potato mash. There's also pasta, steaks, and Thai-inspired curries. For dessert, have the homemade ice cream with flavors that change each week. There's live jazz on Thursday nights and a singer/guitarist on Friday nights. You'll find the drink prices more than reasonable.

4 Wharf St. ✆ **07/4031 2750.** www.fishlips.com.au. Reservations recommended. Main courses A$12–A$27 (US$9.60–US$22/UK£4.80–UK£11). AE, DC, MC, V. Daily for lunch from 11:30am–2:30pm, for dinner from 5:30pm–late. Club is open until midnight.

Red Ochre Grill ★ Kids GOURMET BUSH TUCKER You could accuse this restaurant/bar of using weird and wonderful Aussie ingredients as a gimmick to pull in crowds, but the diners who have flocked here for the past decade or so know good food when they taste it. Daily specials are big on fresh local seafood, and the regular menu—which changes often—lets you devour the Aussie coat of arms in several different ways. Try salt-and-native-pepper crocodile and prawns with Vietnamese pickles and lemon aspen sambal, chargrilled kangaroo sirloin with a quandong chile glaze, sweet potato fritter, and bok choy, or maybe a Queensland ostrich filet with refried kipfler potatoes, crisp pancetta, and green beans. It's slick enough for a big night out but still informal enough for a casual meal. It's independent, not part of the chain that has a branch in Alice Springs. There's also a kids' menu.

43 Shields St. ✆ **07/4051 0100.** www.redochregrill.com.au. Reservations recommended. Main courses A$16–A$33 (US$13–US$26–UK£6.40–UK£13) at lunch, A$21–A$33 (US$17–US$26/UK£8.40–UK£13) at dinner. Australian game platter A$45 (US$36/UK£18) per person; seafood platter A$66 (US$53/UK£26) per person. Tastes of Australia 4-course set menu A$60 (US$48/UK£24) per person (minimum 2 people). AE, DC, MC, V. Daily noon–midnight; public holidays 6pm–midnight. Closed Dec 25.

Moderate

Perrotta's MODERN AUSTRALIAN The locals flock here for brunch and lunch, particularly on weekends, and you can team it with a visit to the Cairns Regional Art Gallery (the cafe is just outside). Breakfast differs from the usual bacon and eggs or pancakes, offering delights such as smoked salmon and sweet-potato hash browns with sour cream, and avocado. Sweet tooths may go for French toast with cinnamon, caramelized apples, and honey mascarpone. For lunch there's a choice of bruschettas, focaccia, or panini, pasta dishes, or more individual dishes such as barbecued Cajun Spanish mackerel with tomato and basil salad. At dinner, try wild barramundi, braised duck leg, or lamb shanks. Remember to check out the specials board.

Abbott and Shields sts. ✆ **074031 5899.** Reservations recommended. Breakfast A$2.50–A$8 (US$2–US$6.40/UK£1–UK£3.20); lunch A$6.50–A$12 (US$5.20–US$9.60/UK£2.60–UK£4.80); main courses at dinner A$13–A$24 (US$10–US$19/UK£5.20–UK£9.60). MC, V. Daily 8:30am–late.

ON THE NORTHERN BEACHES

Colonies MODERN AUSTRALIAN It may not have the ocean frontage of the grander restaurants along Williams Esplanade, but the veranda of this cheery little aerie upstairs behind a seafront building is still within earshot of the waves. The atmosphere is simple, and the menu includes loads of inexpensive choices, such as pastas, soups, green chicken curry, and seafood. Licensed and BYO.

Upstairs in Paradise Village shopping center, Williams Esplanade, Palm Cove. ✆ **07/4055 3058.** Fax 07/4059 1559. www.palmcoveonline.com/colonies. Reservations recommended. Main courses A$16–A$29 (US$13–US$23/UK£6.40–UK£12). AE, DC, MC, V. Daily 10am–10:30pm. Closed mid-Jan to mid-Mar. Bus: 1, 1B, 1X, 2X, or N.

Far Horizons MODERN AUSTRALIAN You can't quite sink your toes into the sand, but you are just yards from the beach at this pleasant restaurant in the Angsana Resort. The laid-back fine-dining fare includes plenty of fresh seafood—try offerings such as red emperor with roasted fennel and tomato salad, kipfler potato and truffle cream dressing, or Hinchinbrook bluewater barramundi with brandade mash and saffron beurre blanc. The restaurant sometimes sets up tables on the lawn among the palm trees beside the beach. The service is relaxed and friendly, and the crowd is a mix of guests from this and other nearby resorts.

In the Angsana Resort, 1 Veivers Rd. (southern end of Williams Esplanade), Palm Cove. ✆ **07/4055 3000.** Reservations recommended. Main courses A$25–A$30 (US$20–US$24/UK£10–UK£12). AE, DC, MC, V. Daily 6:30pm–midnight (last orders at 9:30pm). Bus: 1, 1B, 1X, 2X, or N.

CAIRNS AFTER DARK

Pick up a copy of the free entertainment newspaper *Barfly*, published on Thursday, for a guide to the week's after-hours action in Cairns. Top spots recommended by the locals include **Met Bar,** upstairs at 15 Spence St. (✆ **07/4041 0258**), which is popular with the 25-to-45 market and features a sophisticated chocolate decor and a cigar lounge. Younger people and backpackers flock to **Gilligan's Bar,** 57–89 Grafton St. (✆ **07/4041 6566**), where the 1000-person beer hall doubles as a nightclub with dance floor, DJs, live bands, and sport and music on the giant video screens. The **Hotel Sofitel Reef Casino,** 35–41 Wharf St. (✆ **07/4030 8888**), has two levels of blackjack, baccarat, reef routine, roulette, sic-bo, money wheel, paradise pontoon, keno, and slot machines. It's open Sunday through Thursday 10am to 3am, and from 10am Friday and Saturday until 5am the next day. It's closed Good Friday, April 25 (Anzac Day), and December 25. No entry for children under 18.

3 Port Douglas ★★, Daintree & the Cape Tribulation Area

Port Douglas: 67km (42 miles) N of Cairns; Mossman: 19km (12 miles) N of Port Douglas; Daintree: 49km (30 miles) N of Port Douglas; Cape Tribulation: 34km (21 miles) N of Daintree

The tiny fishing village of Port Douglas is where the rainforest meets the Reef. Just over an hour's drive from Cairns, through rainforest and along the sea, Port Douglas may be a one-horse town, but stylish shops and seriously trendy restaurants line the main street, and beautiful Four Mile Beach is not to be missed. This is a favorite spot with celebrities big and small—you may find yourself dining next to anyone from Bill Clinton to Kylie Minogue, Sean Penn to rock bands or minor soap stars.

Port Douglas, Daintree & Cape Tribulation

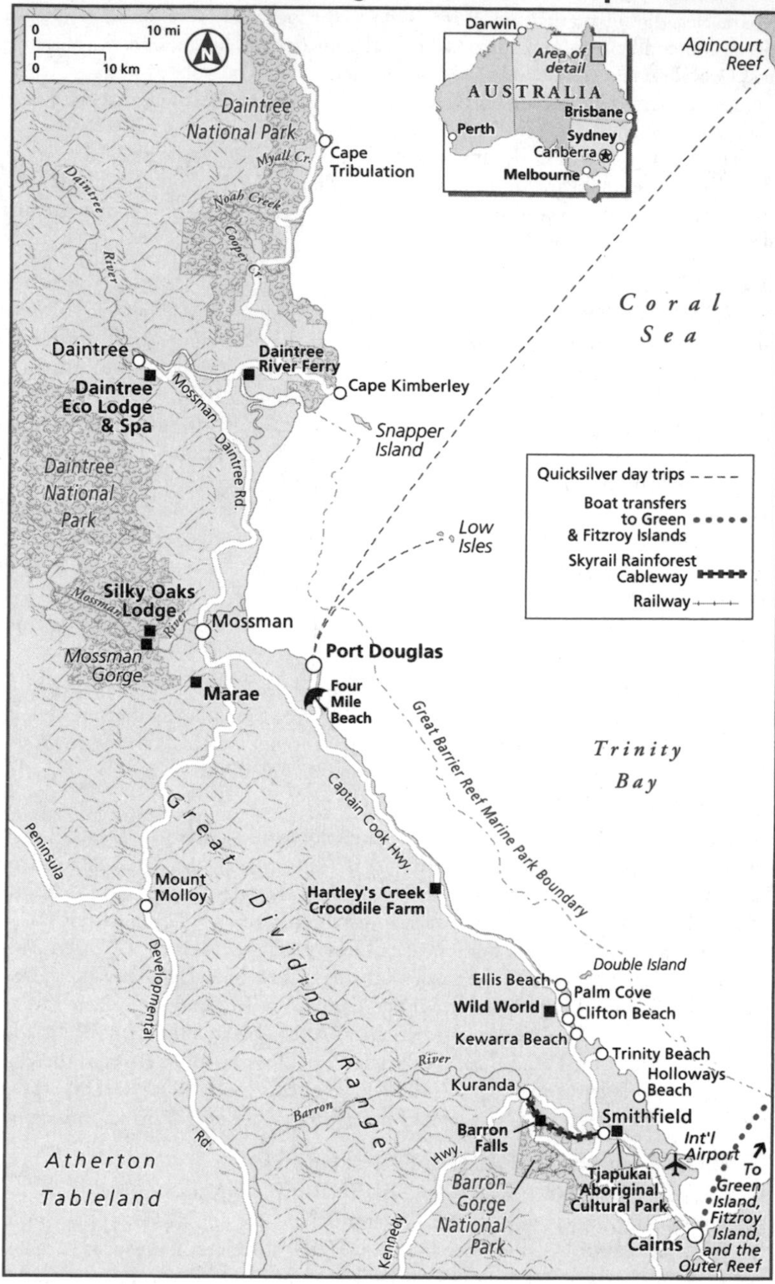

Travelers often base themselves in "Port," as the locals call it, rather than in Cairns, because they like the rural surroundings, the uncrowded beach, and the absence of tacky development (so far, anyway). Don't think you will be isolated—many Reef and rainforest tours originate in Port Douglas, and many of the tours discussed in the Cairns section above pick up from Port Douglas.

Daintree National Park lies just north of Port Douglas; just north of that is Cape Tribulation National Park, another wild tract of rainforest and hilly headlands sweeping down to the sea. Exploring these two national parks is easy on a four-wheel-drive day safari from Port Douglas.

ESSENTIALS

GETTING THERE Port Douglas is a scenic 65-minute drive from Cairns, in part along a narrow winding road that skirts the coast. Take Sheridan Street north out of the city as it becomes the Captain Cook Highway; follow the signs to Mossman and Mareeba until you reach the Port Douglas turnoff on your right.

A one-way ticket aboard **Sun Palm Express Coaches** (✆ **07/4084 2626**) to Port Douglas hotels is A$30 (US$24/UK£12) from the Cairns airport. Fares for children 2 to 12 are half price. If you are staying in Cairns but taking a **Quicksilver** ★ (✆ **07/4087 2100**) cruise to the Great Barrier Reef for the day, you can take a bus transfer to Port Douglas for A$16 (US$13/UK£6.40) adults, half price for kids.

A **taxi** from Cairns runs around A$100 (US$80/UK£40); call **Black & White Taxis** (✆ **13 10 08** in Cairns).

There is no train to Port Douglas, and no scheduled air service. A small airport handles light aircraft and helicopter charters.

VISITOR INFORMATION There is no official visitor information office in Port Douglas. Instead, visitors should stop into a private tour information and booking center in town. One of the biggest and most centrally located is the **Port Douglas Tourist Information Centre,** 23 Macrossan St. (✆ **07/4099 5599**), open from 7:30am to 6pm daily.

GETTING AROUND Of the major rental companies, **Avis** (✆ **07/4099 4331**), **Budget** (✆ **07/4099 5702**), and **Thrifty** (✆ **07/4069 9977**) have offices in Port Douglas. Check out the local companies, including **Port Douglas Car Rental** (✆ **07/4099 4988**). All rent regular vehicles as well as four-wheel-drives, which you need if you plan to drive to Cape Tribulation. For a taxi, call **Port Douglas Taxis** (✆ **07/4084 2650**).

A good way to get around the town's flat streets is by bike. **Holiday Bike Hire,** 40 Macrossan St. (✆ **07/4099 6144**), is open daily from 8am to 6pm or later and rents a large range of mountain bikes; prices start at A$11 (US$8.80/UK£4.40) for a half-day, A$17 (US$14/UK£6.80) for a full day. **Port Douglas Bike Hire,** at the corner of Warner and Wharf streets (✆ **07/4099 5799**), rents bikes for A$10 (US$8/UK£4) for a half-day, A$14 (US$11/UK£5.60) for a full day. It's open 9am to 5pm daily.

EXPLORING THE REEF & THE RAINFOREST

DISCOVERING THE GREAT BARRIER REEF Without a doubt, the most glamorous large vessels visiting the Outer Reef are the **Quicksilver Wavepiercers** (✆ **07/4087 2100**) based in Port Douglas. These ultrasleek, high-speed, air-conditioned 37m (121-ft.) and 46m (151-ft.) catamarans carry 300 or 440 passengers to Agincourt Reef, a ribbon reef 39 nautical miles (72km/45 miles) from shore on the outer edge of the Reef. After the 90-minute trip to the Reef, you tie up at a two-story pontoon, where you spend 3½ hours.

Quicksilver departs Marina Mirage at 10am daily except December 25. The cost for the day is A$186 (US$149/UK£74) for adults and A$93 (US$74/UK£37) for kids 4 to 14. Guided snorkel safaris cost A$58 (US$46/UK£23) per person, and introductory dives cost A$134 (US$107/UK£54) per person. Qualified divers take a dive-tender boat to make one dive for A$92 (US$74/UK£37) or two dives for A$134 (US$107/UK£54) per person, all gear included. Because Quicksilver carries so many passengers, booking snorkel safaris and dives in advance is a good idea.

The dive boat ***Poseidon*** (see "Diving the Reef," earlier in this chapter) welcomes snorkelers. It presents a Reef ecology talk and takes you on a guided snorkel safari. The price of A$155 (US$124/UK£62) for adults and A$120 (US$96/UK£48) for children 3 to 12 includes lunch and transfers from Port Douglas hotels.

Snorkeling specialist boat ***Wavelength*** (**© 07/4099 5031;** www.wavelength.com.au) does a full-day trip to the Outer Reef for A$160 (US$128/UK£64) for adults, A$110 (US$88/UK£44) for children 2 to 12, A$485 (US$388/UK£194) for a family of four. The trip visits three different snorkel sites each day and incorporates a guided snorkel tour and a reef presentation by a marine biologist. It carries up to 30 passengers and includes snorkel gear, sunsuits, lunch, and transfers from your hotel. Both beginners and experienced snorkelers will like this trip. It departs daily at 8:15am from the Wavelength jetty, Wharf Street.

Another way to spend a pleasant day on the Great Barrier Reef, closer to shore, is to visit the **Low Isles,** 15km (9½ miles) northeast of Port Douglas. The isles are 1.5-hectare (3¾-acre) coral-cay specks of lush vegetation surrounded by white sand and 22 hectares (54 acres) of coral—which is what makes them so appealing. The coral is not quite as good as the outer Reef's, but the fish life is rich, and the proximity makes for a relaxing day.

The trip aboard the 30m (98-ft.) luxury sailing catamaran ***Wavedancer*** (**© 07/4087 2100**), operated by Quicksilver, is A$132 (US$106/UK£53) for adults, A$66 (US$53/UK£26) for kids 4 to 14, and A$330 (US$264/UK£132) for families. You have the option of making an introductory scuba dive for an extra A$112 (US$90/UK£45) per person. Coach transfers are available through Quicksilver from Cairns and Palm Cove for A$16 (US$13/UK£6.40) adults, half price for children.

EXPLORING DAINTREE NATIONAL PARK & CAPE TRIBULATION The World Heritage–listed Daintree Rainforest has remained largely unchanged over the past 110 million years. It is now home to rare plants that provide key links in the evolution story. In the 56,000-hectare (138,320-acre) **Daintree National Park,** you will find cycads, dinosaur trees, fan palms, giant strangler figs, and epiphytes like the basket fern, staghorn, and elkhorn. Nighttime croc-spotting tours on the Daintree River vie for popularity with early-morning cruises to see the rich bird life. Pythons, lizards, frogs, and electric-blue Ulysses butterflies attract photographers, and sport fishermen come here to do battle with big barramundi.

Just about everyone who visits Port Douglas takes a guided four-wheel-drive day trip into the beautiful Daintree and Cape Tribulation rainforests. Although they are two separate national parks, the forests merge into one.

You can rent a four-wheel-drive and explore on your own, but you won't understand much about what you are seeing unless you have a guide. Most companies basically cover the same territory and sights, including a 1-hour Daintree River cruise to spot crocs, a visit to the Marrdja Botanical Walk, a stroll along an isolated beach, lunch at a pretty spot somewhere in the forest, and a visit to Mossman Gorge. Some tours also go to the picturesque Bloomfield Falls in Cape Tribulation National Park. Expect to pay about A$140 (US$112/UK£56) per adult and about A$95 (US$76/UK£38) per child. Trips that include Bloomfield Falls cost more. A company that provides an excellent, gently adventurous alternative is Pete Baxendell's **Heritage & Interpretive Tours** ★ (✆ **07/4098 7897;** www.nqhit.com.au). On a daylong bushwalk into a tract of privately owned rainforest with Pete, a naturalist and professional tour guide, you taste green ants (be brave—it's quite an experience) and other native "bush tucker," discover how to rustle up a toothbrush from a shrub if you forgot to pack yours, learn about bush medicine and the wildlife around you, and clamber up a stream to a waterfall. He takes a maximum of six people at a time. Lunch and Port Douglas pickups are included in the price of A$130 (US$104/UK£52) per person. Pickups from Cairns and the northern beaches can be organized through BTS Tours (see below) for an extra cost. Walks run Tuesday and Saturday, leaving Port at 8:30am.

You can **charter** Pete and his 4WD on other days for day bushwalks for A$185 (US$148/UK£74) per person (minimum of two). A longer "go anywhere" adventure costs A$650 (US$520/UK£260) per day, including Cairns and northern beaches pickups. The charter prices compare favorably to a regular Daintree four-wheel-drive tour if there are three or more of you—and you get a tailored itinerary, Pete's knowledge, and the vehicle all to yourself. He often takes charter customers inland to Outback gold mining ghost towns, or north to tiny Cooktown, which boasts an excellent museum devoted to Australia's "discoverer," Capt. James Cook. If you have 2 days, he can take you farther west to see Aboriginal rock art and stay at a permanent safari camp, or to the amazing Undara Lava Tubes.

Other established operators are **Trek North Safaris** (✆ **07/4033 2600**) and **BTS Tours** (✆ **07/4099 5665**). As is the case in most tourist hot spots, some tour operators battle fiercely to pay tour desks the highest commission to recommend their tours, even though those tours may not necessarily be the best for your needs. Take tour desks' recommendations with a grain of salt, and ask other travelers for their recommendations. You may not see too much wildlife—rainforest animals are shy, camouflaged, nocturnal, or all three! Most four-wheel-drive tours will pick you up in Port Douglas at no charge; there is usually a fee from Cairns and the northern beaches. Floods and swollen creeks can quash your plans to explore the Daintree in the Wet season (Dec–Mar or Apr), so keep your plans flexible.

If your chosen safari does not visit **Mossman Gorge,** 21km (13 miles) northwest of Port Douglas near the sugar town of Mossman, try to get there under your own steam. The gushing river tumbling over boulders, and the short forest walks are magical. (Don't climb on the rocks or enter the river, because strong currents are extremely dangerous and have claimed at least one life in recent years.)

Most four-wheel-drive Daintree tours include a 1-hour cruise on the **Daintree River** ★, but if yours does not, or you want to spend more time on the river, cruises are available on a variety of boats, ranging from open-sided "river trains" to small fishing boats. One of the best is with **Dan Irby's Mangrove Adventures** ★ (✆ **07/4090 7017;** www.mangroveadventures.com.au), whose small open boat can get up side creeks the bigger boats can't. Originally from Tonkawa, Oklahoma, Dan has been in Australia for 34 years and is extremely knowledgeable about the wildlife and habitat. He takes no more than 10 people at a time on 2- to 4-hour cruises. It is very important to make advance reservations with Dan (at least 24 hr. ahead, if possible) to determine which days he is operating, departure times, and seat availability. Chances are you will spot lots of fascinating wildlife on his 2-hour night cruise, but even if you don't, it's worth it just to see the stars! A 2-hour trip costs A$45 (US$36/UK£18). The early-morning sunrise tours and night tours leave from Daintree Eco Lodge, 20 Mossman Daintree Rd., 4km (2½ miles) south of Daintree village; day tours leave from the public jetty next to the Daintree River ferry crossing. You can combine both, taking an afternoon tour, followed by a 45-minute break for a snack at Daintree Eco Lodge, then the night tour. Take the Captain Cook Highway north to Mossman, where it becomes the Mossman Daintree Road, and follow it for 24km (15 miles) to the signposted turnoff for the ferry on your right. The ferry is 5km (3 miles) from the turnoff. You'll need a car to get there, as Dan does not do transfers from hotels.

Birders love the Wet Tropics rainforests of which the Daintree and Cape Tribulation national parks are part. More than half of Australia's bird species have been recorded within 200km (120 miles) of this area. **Fine Feather Tours** (© **07/4094 1199;** www.finefeathertours.com.au) has a full-day bird-watching safari through the Wet Tropics to the edge of the Outback for A$225 (US$180/UK£90), an afternoon cruise on the Daintree River for A$165 (US$132/UK£66), and other tours.

Rainforest Habitat wildlife sanctuary (© **07/4099 3235;** www.rainforesthabitat.com.au) is a great place to see the animals that are too shy to be spotted in the wild. Here, 180 animal species from the Wet Tropics are in one place for you to see up close. You can see saltwater and freshwater crocodiles, hand-feed kangaroos, and have your photo taken beside (but not holding) a koala (10–11am and 3–4pm for the cost of a donation). The highlight is the walk-through aviary, which houses more than 100 Wet Tropics bird species, including cassowaries. You'll get the most out of your visit if you take one of the excellent free guided tours that leave every half-hour from 9am to 3pm. Rainforest Habitat is on Port Douglas Road at the turnoff from the Captain Cook Highway. Open daily (except Dec 25) from 8am to 5:30pm (last entry at 4:30pm). Admission is A$28 (US$22/UK£11) for adults, A$14 (US$11/UK£5.60) for kids 4 to 14, or A$70 (US$56/UK£28) for a family of four. Between 8am and 11am, the park serves a champagne buffet breakfast for A$39 (US$31/UK£16) for adults, A$20 (US$16/UK£8) for kids, or A$98 (US$78/UK£39) families, including admission. Allow at least 2 hours here.

DISCOVERING ABORIGINAL CULTURE Members of the native KuKu-Yalanji tribe will teach you about bush medicines and food, Dreamtime legends, and the sacred sites their families have called home for thousands of years. **KuKu-Yalanji Dreamtime Walks** ★ (© **07/4098 2595;** www.yalanji.com.au) offers a guided walk through the rainforest to see cave paintings and visit "special sites." The tour is followed by a Dreamtime story and didgeridoo performance over billy tea and damper in a bark *warun* (shelter). You can buy artifacts from the information center, gift shop, and art gallery (open 8:30am–5pm Mon–Sat). Walks last 90 minutes and leave Monday through Friday at 9am, 11am, 1pm, and 3pm from the Kuku-Yalanji community, on the road to Mossman Gorge (1km/½ mile before you reach the Gorge parking lot). Tours cost A$25 (US$20/UK£10) for adults, A$15 (US$12/UK£6) children under 12, A$65 (US$52/UK£26) for a family of four.

MORE TO SEE & DO

Some companies in Cairns that offer outdoor activities will pick up from Port Douglas hotels. See "White-Water Rafting & Other Thrills," in the Cairns section earlier in this chapter for details.

Tips **The Secret of the Seasons**

High season in Port Douglas is roughly June 1 through October 31.

The best outdoor activity in Port Douglas, however, is to do absolutely nothing on spectacular **Four Mile Beach** ★★. From May through September, the water is stinger-free. From October through April, swim in the stinger safety net. **Extra Action Water Sports** (✆ **07/4099 3175**) offers parasailing, jet-skiing, and tube rides on Four Mile Beach. A half-hour on a jet ski or parafly is A$70 (US$56/UK£28) solo or A$90 (US$72/UK£36) tandem. The booking office is at the end of the jetty on the Port Douglas slipway.

Visitor greens fees at the championship **Sheraton Mirage** golf course on Port Douglas Road are A$145 (US$116/UK£58) for 18 holes or A$85 (US$68/UK£34) for 9 holes, including a cart. Club rental costs A$38 to A$60 (US$30–US$48/UK£15–UK£24). Whacking a ball on the hotel's aquatic driving range costs A$6.50 (US$5.20/UK£2.60) for a bucket of 25, A$13 (US$10/UK£5.20) for 50 balls, plus A$2.15 (US$1.70/UK85p) for club rental. Contact the **Pro Shop** (✆ **07/4099 5537**).

Wonga Beach Equestrian Centre (✆ **07/4098 7583**) does 3-hour horseback rides through the rainforest and along Wonga Beach, 35 minutes north of Port Douglas, for A$109 (US$87/UK£44) per person, plus A$10 (US$8/UK£4) per person for insurance. Transfers from Port Douglas are included. Rides start at 8:30am and 3pm. Riders must be aged 7 or over.

Every Sunday from 7:30am to 1pm, a colorful handicrafts and fresh food market sets up on the lawns under the mango trees beside Dickson Inlet at the end of Macrossan Street. Stalls offer everything from foot massages to fresh coconut milk. While you're here, take a peek, or attend a non-denominational service inside the pretty timber St. Mary's by the Sea church.

WHERE TO STAY

Port Douglas Accommodation Holiday Rentals (✆ **1800/645 566** in Australia, or 07/4099 4488; www.portdouglasaccom.com.au) has a wide range of apartments and homes for rent.

VERY EXPENSIVE

Sheraton Mirage Port Douglas ★★★ One of Australia's most luxurious properties, this low-rise Sheraton has 2 hectares (5 acres) of saltwater pools and a championship Peter Thomson–designed 18-hole golf course. It is a bit too far from Port's main street by foot, but a free shuttle runs from 9am to 6pm to the golf course's country club and health center, to Marina Mirage shopping center, and into town. All the rooms are large and light-filled, and the resort has undergone extensive refurbishment in the past year, with new color schemes, furniture, and artwork, and extras like ministereo systems. All rooms have minibars, PlayStations, and Internet access. You might upgrade to a Mirage room with a Jacuzzi and king-size beds, but I thought the standard rooms just fine. The Sheraton handles rental of the 101 privately owned two-, three-, and four-bedroom luxury villas with golf course, garden, or sea views; the decor varies, but each has a kitchenette, a Jacuzzi, and two bathrooms.

Davidson St. (off Port Douglas Rd.), Port Douglas, QLD 4877. ✆ **1800/073 535** in Australia; 800/325-3535 in the U.S. and Canada; 00800/325 353535 in the U.K., Ireland, and New Zealand; or 07/4099 5888. Fax 07/4099 4424, or

Starwood Hotels reservation fax 07/4099 5398. www.sheraton-mirage.com.au. 394 units, including 101 villas. A$619–A$830 (US$495–US$664/UK£248–UK£332) double; A$2,500 (US$2,000/UK£1,000) suite; A$950–A$1,150 (US$760–US$920/UK£280–UK£460) 2-, 3-, or 4-bedroom villa. Extra person A$92 (US$74/UK£37). Children under 17 stay free in parent's room with existing bedding. Discounts available. AE, DC, MC, V. Free valet and self-parking. Helicopter transfers available. **Amenities:** 3 restaurants; 2 bars; 25m (82-ft.) outdoor lap pool; 18-hole championship golf course w/country club and pro shop, aquatic driving range (w/targets in a lake), putting green, and golf clinics; 9 lit tennis courts; health club; spa; Jacuzzi; bike rental; daily day care for kids under 5 and kids' club for children 5–15 during school vacations (fee); concierge; tour desk; car-rental desk; business center (fee for Internet access); salon; 24-hr. room service; massage; babysitting; dry cleaning; nonsmoking rooms. *In room:* A/C, TV, dataport, coffeemaker, hair dryer, iron, safe.

EXPENSIVE

Port Douglas Peninsula Boutique Hotel ★★ This intimate studio apartment hotel fronting Four Mile Beach is one of the nicest places to stay in town. Every apartment features an open-plan living room/bedroom, a contemporary kitchenette (with microwave and dishwasher), and a groovy bathroom boasting a giant double tub (or Jacuzzi, in some units). Corner apartments are a little bigger. The decor is a stylish mélange of terra cotta, mosaic tiles, granite, and wicker, with classy extra touches like a CD player and boxed Twining's teas. Most units have great beach views from the roomy balcony or patio; a few look onto the green and mauve complex of petite Art Deco–ish pools, waterfalls, hot and cold Jacuzzis, and sun deck rising and falling on several levels. A 2-minute walk brings you to the main street.

9–13 The Esplanade, Port Douglas, QLD 4877. ✆ **1800/676 674** in Australia, or 07/4099 9100. Fax 07/4099 5440. www.peninsulahotel.com.au. 34 units. A$340–A$460 (US$272–US$368/UK£136–UK£184) double. Rates include full breakfast and round-trip transfers from Cairns airport. Ask about packages and seasonal specials. AE, DC, MC, V. Free covered parking. Children under 15 not accepted. **Amenities:** Restaurant; small bar; large outdoor pool; hot and cold Jacuzzis; bike rental; tour desk; free guest laundry; laundry service; dry cleaning. *In room:* A/C, TV/VCR, dataport, kitchenette, coffeemaker, hair dryer, iron, safe.

MODERATE

Archipelago Studio Apartments ★ You won't find a friendlier or more convenient place to stay in Port Douglas than these apartments, 10 seconds from the beach and less than 10 minutes' walk from town. Hosts Wolfgang Klein and Christel Bader are eager to help with tour bookings and to give advice—and they also speak fluent German, conversational French, and some Spanish. The apartments are on the small side (most suit only three people), but all are well cared for. You can opt for a tiny Garden apartment with a patio; Balcony and Seaview apartments are a bit larger and have private balconies. Seaview apartments are quite roomy, and have side views of Four Mile Beach. Towels are changed daily and linen weekly, but general housekeeping service will cost A$20 (US$16/UK£8) extra. There's no elevator and no porter, so be prepared to carry your luggage upstairs.

72 Macrossan St., Port Douglas, QLD 4877. ✆ **07/4099 5387.** Fax 07/4099 4847. www.archipelago.com.au. 21 units, all with shower only. High season (June–Oct) A$133–A$235 (US$106–A$188/UK£53–UK£94) double; low season A$113–A$190 (US$90–US$152/UK£45–UK£76) double. Additional person A$20 (US$16/UK£8). 3-night minimum. MC, V. Free covered parking. Children under 6 not accepted. **Amenities:** Outdoor saltwater pool; nearby golf course; 6 nearby lit tennis courts; access to nearby health club; Jacuzzi; tour desk; coin-op laundry; laundry service; nonsmoking rooms. *In room:* A/C, TV, kitchenette, fridge, coffeemaker, hair dryer.

Port Douglas Retreat This well-kept two-story studio apartment complex on a quiet street, featuring the white-battened balconies of the Queenslander architectural style, is a good value. Even some of the ritzier places in town can't boast its lagoonlike saltwater pool, surrounded by dense jungle and wrapped by an ample shady sun deck that cries out to be lounged on with a good book and a cool drink. The apartments are not enormous, but they're fashionably furnished with terra-cotta tile floors, wrought-iron beds, cane seating, and colorful bedcovers. All have large furnished balconies or patios looking into tropical gardens; some on the ground floor open onto the common-area boardwalk, so you might want to ask for a first-floor (second-story) unit. The town and beach are 5 minutes walk away. There's no smoking indoors.

31–33 Mowbray St. (at Mudlo St.), Port Douglas, QLD 4877. ✆ **07/4099 5053.** Fax 07/4099 5033. www.portdouglasretreat.com.au. 36 units, all with shower only. High season (June–Oct) A$145–A$169 (US$116–A$135/UK£58–UK£68) double; low season (Nov–May) A$79–A$110 (US$63–US$88/UK£32–UK£44) double. Crib A$5.50 (US$4.40/UK£2.20) per night. Minimum 3-night stay. AE, MC, V. Secure covered parking. **Amenities:** Outdoor saltwater pool; tour desk; car-rental desk; coin-op laundry; nonsmoking rooms. *In room:* A/C, TV w/free movies, kitchenette, iron.

INEXPENSIVE

Port O'Call Lodge There's a nice communal feeling to this modest motel on a suburban street a 10-minute walk from town. Backpackers, families, and travelers on a budget seem to treat it like a second home, swapping stories as they cook a meal in the communal kitchen and dining room. The rooms are light, cool, and fresh with tile floors, loads of luggage and bench space, and small patios. New double and quad rooms were added in 2004, and half the double rooms have king-size beds. The hostel rooms have private bathrooms and no more than five beds or bunks in each. A 24-bed bunkhouse has facilities for travelers with disabilities. At night the lively poolside Port O'Call Bistro is the place to be. Other features include free board games, a pay phone, Internet access, and a kiosk selling refreshments.

Port St. at Craven Close, Port Douglas, QLD 4877. ✆ **1800/892 800** in Australia, or 07/4099 5422. Fax 07/4099 5495. www.portocall.com.au. 28 units, all with shower only. A$69–A$119 (US$55–US$95/UK£28–UK£48) double. Extra person A$15 (US$12/UK£6). Hostel quad rooms A$29 (US$23/UK£12) YHA/Hostelling International members, or A$30 (US$24/UK£12) nonmembers; bunkhouse A$24 (US$19/UK£9.60) YHA/Hostelling International members, A$25 (US$20/UK£10) nonmembers. Children under 3 stay free in parent's room. MC, V. Free parking. Free once-daily shuttle to and from Cairns and the airport Mon–Sat. Bus: 1X (stop at front door). **Amenities:** Restaurant (see "Where to Dine in Port Douglas," below); outdoor pool; 3 golf courses nearby; access to nearby health club; bike rental; tour desk; coin-op laundry; nonsmoking rooms. *In room:* A/C, TV, fridge, coffeemaker, hair dryer, iron (motel rooms only), safe.

A LUXURY B&B IN THE COUNTRY

Marae ★★ John and Pam Burden's architecturally stunning timber home, on a hillside 15km (9½ miles) north of Port Douglas, is a glamorous and restful retreat. The rustic-meets-sleek contemporary bedrooms have white mosquito nets and smart linens on king-size beds, and elegant bathrooms. The garden room opens onto a plunge pool overlooking the valley, and there is also a lap pool. Wallabies and bandicoots (small marsupials) feed in the garden, kingfishers and honeyeaters use the pools, and butterflies are everywhere. A delicious tropical breakfast is served on the west deck in the company of a flock of red-browed finches and peaceful doves. Afterward you can wander the rainforest trails of Mossman Gorge, just a few miles away.

Lot 1, Chook's Ridge, Shannonvale (P.O. Box 133), Port Douglas, QLD 4877. ✆ **07/4098 4900.** Fax 07/4098 4099. www.marae.com.au. 3 units, 2 with shower only. A$180 (US$144/UK£72) double. 2-night minimum. Rates include full breakfast. MC, V. Covered parking. From Port Douglas, take Captain Cook Hwy. toward Mossman for 10km (6¼ miles), go left onto Mt. Molloy turnoff for 1km (½ mile), then right onto Ponzo Rd. for 2km (1¼ miles); Chook's Ridge is on your left. Children under 13 not accepted. **Amenities:** Outdoor plunge pool; nearby golf courses; tour desk; laundry service; nonsmoking rooms. *In room:* A/C, TV, hair dryer.

RAINFOREST HIDEAWAYS

Silky Oaks Lodge & Healing Waters Spa ★★ Relax in the hammock on your veranda and listen to the waters of the Mossman River gushing through the rainforest.

Stroll down for a swim—no crocs here. Despite its popularity, this luxury resort tucked away at the edge of cane fields exudes a restful feeling. Treehouses are scattered through the rainforest and gardens, each in its own private part of the gardens and rainforest; the five Riverhouses overlook the river frontage, and all have Jacuzzis. Each unit has timber floors, attractive furnishings, a king-size bed, bathrobes, a CD player—but no TV—and a double hammock. The resort's most recent renovation included the addition of the Healing Waters Day Spa, where I had the best facial of my life. The spa has since tripled in size (no doubt word of how good it is has got out), and the central lodge and **Treehouse Restaurant** have a fresh, contemporary new look. Rates include guided nature walks, tennis, mountain bikes, and kayaking or snorkeling in the Mossman River, and there is a daily activities program. To reach Mossman Gorge's lovely walking trails, across the river, you'll need a car.

Finlayvale Rd., Mossman, 7km (4½ miles) west of Mossman township; 27km (17 miles) from Port Douglas (c/o Voyages, G.P.O. Box 3589, Sydney, NSW 2001). ✆ **1300/134 044** in Australia, 02/8296 8010 (Sydney reservations office) or 07/4098 1666 (lodge). Fax 02/9299 2103 (Sydney reservations office) or 07/4098 1983 (lodge). www.voyages.com. 50 units. A$590–A$780 (US$472–US$624/UK£236–UK£312) double. Extra person A$58 (US$46/UK£23). Rates include full breakfast, some activities, and a morning and afternoon shuttle from Port Douglas. Ask about packages. AE, DC, MC, V. Town-car transfers A$145 (US$116/UK£58) per car one-way from Cairns city or airport; stretch limousine transfers A$250 (US$200/UK£100). Take Captain Cook Hwy. to Mossman, where it becomes the Mossman-Daintree Rd.; follow approximately 3.5km (2¼ miles) past Mossman and turn left onto Finlayvale Rd. at the small white-on-blue SILKY OAKS sign. Children under 15 not accepted. **Amenities:** Restaurant; bar; outdoor pool; lit tennis court; spa; tour desk; coin-op laundry; laundry service. *In room:* A/C, ceiling fans, minibar, coffeemaker, hair dryer, iron.

Thala Beach Lodge ★★ "Where are the walls?" may be your first question on arriving at this Balinese-style luxury hideaway in the rainforest outside Port Douglas. The reception area and lobby are open, to stunning effect. From the elevated restaurant, the impact is even greater, with sweeping views from the Daintree to Cape Grafton, south of Cairns. Thala (pronounced *Ta*-la) Beach is on a 59-hectare (146-acre) private peninsula, bordered on three sides by private beaches and coves. Owners Rob and Oonagh Prettejohn also own the well-established Kewarra Beach Resort on Cairns's northern beaches. Thala Beach opened in 1998, taking its inspiration from the flora and fauna of the World Heritage area that surrounds it. The secluded bungalows are spacious and comfortable, with timber-paneled walls and your choice of king-size or twin beds. All are built on high poles in the trees, where dazzling lorikeets and small red-faced flying foxes feed on blossoms and hang contentedly from the branches. The 16 Coral Sea bungalows overlook the ocean; the rest have forest and mountain views. Some of the bungalows are a bit of a hike from the public areas, but I thought it was a small price to pay for the privacy and the rainforest setting.

16km (10 miles) south of Port Douglas (P.O. Box 199), Smithfield, Cairns, QLD 4878. ✆ **1800/251 958** in Australia (Small Luxury Hotels of the World), or 07/4098 5700 (lodge). Fax 07/4098 5837. www.slh.com/thala. 85 units. A$440–A$680 (US$352–US$544/UK£176–UK£272) double. AE, DC, MC, V. Free valet parking. Transfers from Cairns A$26 (US$21/UK£10) per person. **Amenities:** Restaurant; bar; 2 outdoor pools; nearby golf course; tour desk. *In room:* A/C, ceiling fans, TV, minibar, coffeemaker, hair dryer, iron, safe.

A SPA IN THE RAINFOREST

Daintree Eco Lodge & Spa ★ Check in and head straight for the Daintree Spa. Here you can relax and soak up all kinds of pampering treatments, including the 2-hour, A$280 (US$224/UK£112) Walbul-Walbul body treatment, in which you are wrapped in mud as you recline on a magnificent carved timber "wet bed," and the Yiri Jalaymba rain therapy treatment. It's bliss.

A multiple award winner for "green tourism," this lodge in the primeval forest books only a small number of guests. Don't think "eco" means sacrificing creature comforts: The large rooms boast marble floors, timber and bamboo furniture, and tiled bathrooms with robes. Five have Jacuzzis on their screened balconies.

You can join a yoga or Ki (based on Japanese aikido) session, laze by the small solar-heated pool, walk rainforest trails, join members of the local Aboriginal Kuku tribe on a bush tucker and native medicine stroll, or take a four-wheel-drive day trip to modern-day Aboriginal communities. The **Julaymba Restaurant** overlooks a lily pond and serves food with a gourmet bush-tucker slant. The lodge is 98km (61 miles) north of Cairns and 40km (25 miles) north of Port Douglas.

20 Daintree Rd. (4km/2½ miles south of Daintree village), Daintree, QLD 4873. ✆ **1800/808 010** in Australia, or 07/4098 6100. Fax 07/4098 6200. www.daintree-ecolodge.com.au. 15 units, 10 with shower only. A$530–A$580 (US$424–US$464/UK£212–UK£232) double. Extra person A$55 (US$44/UK£22). Rates include full breakfast. Ask about packages. AE, DC, MC, V. Once-a-day scheduled minibus service to or from Mossman A$25 (US$20/UK£10), to or from Port Douglas hotels A$60 (US$48/UK£24), to or from Cairns hotels or Cairns airport A$80 (US$64/UK£32) per person, one-way. On-call transfers A$160 (US$128/UK£64) per car from Port Douglas, A$210 (US$168/UK£84) per car (maximum 2 passengers) from Cairns, one-way. Take Captain Cook Hwy. north to Mossman, where it becomes the Mossman-Daintree Rd.; follow to lodge. The road is paved all the way. No children under 7. **Amenities:** Restaurant; pool; spa; tour desk; laundry service. *In room:* A/C, TV, minibar, coffeemaker, hair dryer.

WHERE TO DINE IN PORT DOUGLAS

Nautilus ★★ TROPICAL/SEAFOOD Bill and Hillary Clinton dined here during a visit Down Under, and by all accounts loved it. So did I. The restaurant, which has been keeping the locals happy since 1953, is set under the palm trees and stars, with a clever seating plan and unusual high-backed chairs that create a wonderfully intimate atmosphere. Local produce and seafood are the mainstays of the menu, which features such delights as wok-tossed whole North Queensland mud crab dressed with spiced vanilla champagne butter, watercress or chile jam, kaffir lime, and tamarind. For true indulgence, order the seven-course degustation menu for your table, at A$110 (US$88/UK£44) per person, with six matched wines for an extra A$50 (US$40/UK£20). There is also a vegetarian menu.

17 Murphy St. (entry also from Macrossan St.), Port Douglas. ✆ **07/4099 5330.** www.nautilus-restaurant.com.au. Reservations recommended. Main courses A$34–A$40 (US$27–US$32/UK£14–UK£16). AE, DC, MC, V. Daily 5:30–10:30pm or until the last diners leave. Closed Feb. Children under 8 not accepted.

Port O'Call Bistro *Kids* CAFE/BISTRO Locals patronize this poolside bistro and bar at the Port O'Call Lodge (p. 320) almost as often as guests do, because it offers good, honest food like lamb shanks and steaks in hearty portions at painless prices. The atmosphere is fun and friendly. There are pasta and curry dishes, and every night you can try one of the chef's blackboard surprises, including local seafood. There are kids' meals for A$9 (US$7.20/UK£3.60) as well as burgers, chicken, and Asian stir-fries to appeal to everyone.

In the Port O'Call Lodge, Port St. at Craven Close. ✆ **07/4099 5422.** Main courses A$14–A$20 (US$11–US$16/UK£5.60–UK£8). MC, V. Daily 6pm–midnight.

Salsa Bar & Grill ★★ *Kids* MODERN/TROPICAL This trendy restaurant, in a timber Queenslander with wraparound verandas, has terrific food, great prices, and lively, fun service. Here you can choose simple fare such as gnocchi, Caesar salad, or Thai chicken spring rolls with banana mayo and Asian greens, or such mouthwatering delights as a sumac-crusted lamb loin with canellini bean and potato galette; or pan-fried barramundi with crocodile won ton and water chestnut sauce. This is not a place to resist dessert. The buttermilk-and-almond-nougat panna cotta I tried was to-die-for.

26 Wharf St. (at Warner St.). ✆ **07/4099 4922.** www.salsa-port-douglas.com.au. Reservations required. Main courses A$15–A$35 (US$12–US$28/UK£6–UK£14). AE, DC, MC, V. Mon–Sat 10am–midnight; Sun 8am–midnight.

4 The North Coast: Mission Beach ★★, Townsville & the Islands

For years the lovely town of **Mission Beach** was a well-kept secret. Farmers retired here; then those who liked to drop out and chill out discovered it; today, it's a small, prosperous, stunningly pretty rainforest town. The beach here is one of the most beautiful in Australia, a long white strip fringed with dense tangled vine forests, the only surviving lowlands rainforest in the Australian tropics. It is also one of the least crowded and least spoiled, so clever has Mission Beach been at staying out of sight, out of mind, and off the tourist trail.

The nearby **Tully River** is white-water-rafting heaven for thrill-seekers. You can also bungee jump and tandem sky dive when you're not rushing down the rapids, flanked by lush rainforest.

From Mission Beach it's a short ferry ride to **Dunk Island,** a large resort island that welcomes day-trippers. You can even sea kayak here from the mainland. Mission Beach is closer to the Great Barrier Reef than any other point along the coast—just an hour—and cruise boats depart daily from the jetty, stopping en route at Dunk Island.

A few hours' drive south brings you to the city of **Townsville,** also a gateway to the Great Barrier Reef, but more important to visitors as a gateway to Magnetic Island, a picturesque, laid-back haven for hikers and watersports enthusiasts.

MISSION BEACH: THE CASSOWARY COAST

140km (87 miles) S of Cairns; 240km (149 miles) N of Townsville

Tucked away off the Bruce Highway, the township of Mission Beach has managed to duck the tourist hordes. It's actually a conglomeration of four beachfront towns: South Mission Beach, Wongaling Beach, Mission Beach proper, and Bingil Bay. Most commercial activity centers on the small nucleus of shops and businesses at Mission Beach proper. It's so isolated that signs on the way into town warn you to watch out for cassowaries emerging from the jungle to cross the road. Rainforest hides the town from view until you round the corner to Mission Beach proper and discover appealing hotels, neat shops, and smart little restaurants. Just through the trees is the fabulous beach. A mile or so north of the main settlement is Clump Point Jetty.

ESSENTIALS

GETTING THERE From Cairns, follow the Bruce Highway south. The Mission Beach turnoff is at the tiny town of El Arish, about 15km (9½ miles) north of Tully. Mission Beach is 25km (16 miles) off the highway. It's a 90-minute trip from Cairns. If you're coming from Townsville, a turnoff just north of Tully leads 18km (11 miles) to South Mission Beach.

Mission Beach Connections (✆ **07/4059 2709**) operates door-to-door shuttles three times a day from Cairns and Cairns Airport for A$38 (US$30/UK£15) adults and A$19 (US$15/UK£7.60) children, and from the northern beaches for A$49 (US$39/UK£20) adults and A$25 (US$20/UK£10) children.

Tips **Mission Beach Money Matters**

There's no bank in Mission Beach; the only ATM in the township is at Mission Beach Resort, Wongaling Beach, so come with enough cash, traveler's checks, and credit cards to cover your expenses.

Greyhound Australia (✆ **13 14 99** in Australia) coaches stop in Mission Beach proper (not South Mission Beach) several times daily on the Cairns-Brisbane-Cairns runs. The fare is A$29 (US$23/UK£12) from Cairns, A$227 (US$182/UK£908) for the 26-hour-plus trip from Brisbane.

Five **trains** a week on the Cairns-Brisbane-Cairns route serve the nearest station, Tully, about 20km (13 miles) away. One-way travel from Cairns on the Tilt Train costs A$46 (US$37/UK£18) for the 2-hour, 50-minute journey. From Brisbane, fares range from A$179 (US$143/UK£72) in an economy seat to A$367 (US$294/UK£147) for a first-class sleeper on the *Sunlander* or A$661 (US$529/UK£264) for Queenslander Class. For more information, call Queensland Rail's long-distance division, **Traveltrain** (✆ **1300/131 722** in Australia, or 07/3235 1133; www.traveltrain.com.au). A taxi from Tully to Mission Beach with **Supreme Taxis** (✆ **07/4068 3937**) is about A$40 (US$32/UK£16).

VISITOR INFORMATION The **Mission Beach Visitor Information Centre,** Porters Promenade, Mission Beach, QLD 4852 (✆ **07/4068 7099;** fax 07/4068 7066; www.missionbeachtourism.com), is at the northern end of town. It's open daily from 9am to 5pm (except Dec 25).

GETTING AROUND **Trans North Bus & Coach** (✆ **07/4068 7400**) provides bus service linking the beach communities from Bingal Bay to South Mission Beach. Just flag the bus down outside your accommodations or wherever you see it. **Sugarland Car Rentals** (✆ **07/4068 8272**) is the only rental-car company in town. For Mission Beach taxi service, call ✆ **0429/689366.**

WHAT TO SEE & DO

EXPLORING THE REEF Mission Beach is the closest point on the mainland to the Reef, just 1 hour by the high-speed **Quick Cat Cruises** catamaran (✆ **07/4068 7289**). The trip starts with an hour at Dunk Island, 20 minutes offshore, where you can walk rainforest trails, play on the beach, or parasail or jet-ski for an extra fee. Then it's a 1-hour trip to Beaver Cay on the Outer Reef, where you have 3 hours to snorkel or to check out the coral from a glass-bottom boat. There's no shade on the cay, so bring a hat and sunscreen. The trip departs daily from Clump Point Jetty at 9:30am. It costs A$144 (US$115/UK£58) for adults, A$72 (US$58/UK£29) for children 4 to 14. An introductory scuba dive costs A$80 (US$64/UK£32) for the first dive and A$35 (US$28/UK£14) for the second. You should pre-book your introductory scuba dive to ensure a place. Qualified divers pay A$60 (US$48/UK£24) for the first dive, A$35 (US$28/UK£14) for the second, all gear included. Free pickups from Mission Beach are included. You can also join this trip from Cairns; coach connections from your Cairns or northern beaches hotel will cost extra.

WHITE-WATER RAFTING ON THE TULLY A day's rafting through the rainforest on the Class III to IV Tully River is an adventure you won't soon forget. In raft-speak,

The North Coast

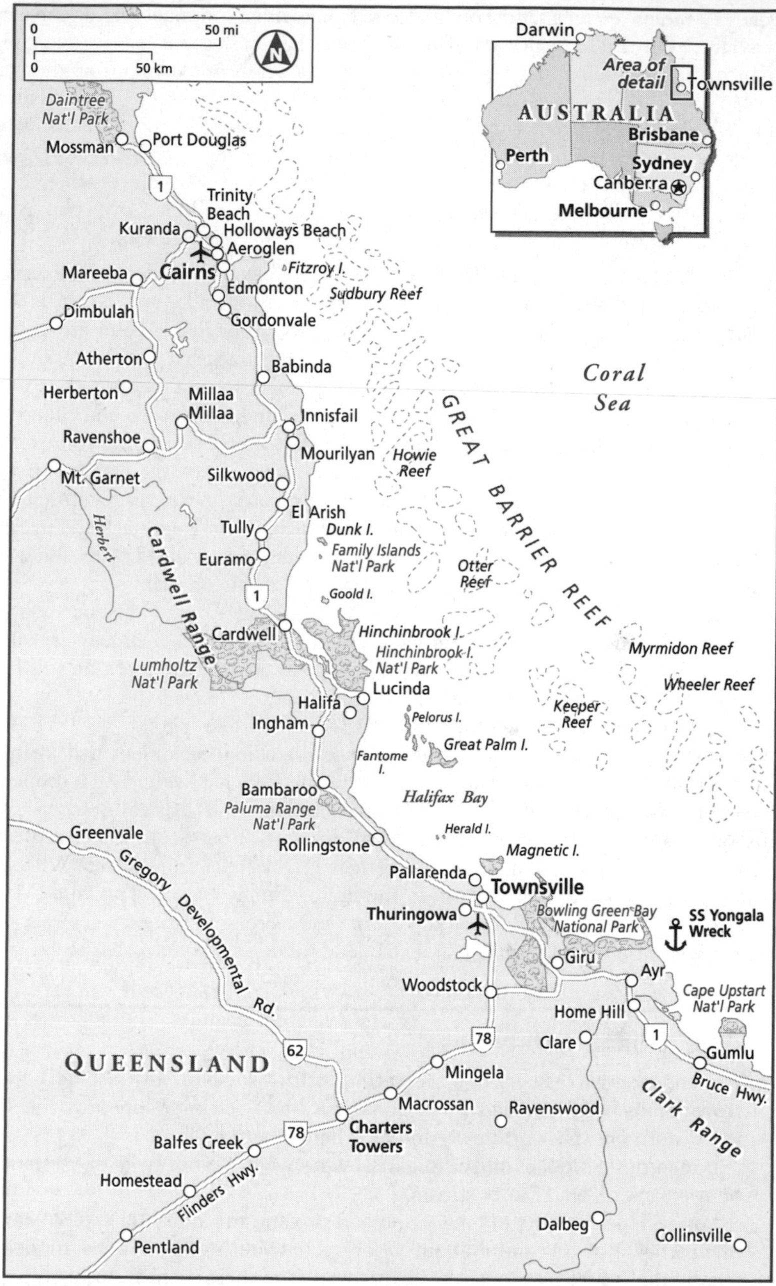

Class IV means "exciting rafting on moderate rapids with a continuous need to maneuver rafts." On the Tully, that translates to regular hair-raising but manageable rapids punctuated by calming stretches that let you float downstream. You don't need experience, just a decent level of agility and an enthusiastic attitude. **RnR Rafting** (**© 07/4041 9444**) runs a daily trip that includes 5 hours on the river with fun, expert guides, a barbecue lunch in the rainforest, and a video screening of your adventure. With transfers, the day costs A$145 (US$116/UK£58) from Mission Beach; A$155 (US$124/UK£62) from Cairns, the northern beaches, or Palm Cove, plus A$25 (US$20/UK£10) for national park and other fees. You must be age 13 or over.

EXPLORING THE RAINFOREST & COAST Walking, wildlife spotting, canoeing in the forest, and kayaking along the pristine coast are all worth doing. Hiking trails abound through national parks, in rainforests, through fan palm groves, and along the beach. The 8km (5-mile) **Licuala Fan Palm** track starts at the parking lot on the Mission Beach–Tully Road about 1.5km (1 mile) west of the turnoff to South Mission Beach. The track leads through dense forest and over creeks, and comes out on the El Arish–Mission Beach Road about 7km (4½ miles) north of the post office. When you come out, you can cross the road and keep going on the 1km (less than a mile) Lacey Creek loop in the Tam O'Shanter State Forest. A shorter Rainforest Circuit leads from the parking lot at the start of the Licuala Fan Palm track and makes a 1km (less than a mile) loop incorporating a fan palm boardwalk. There's also a 10-minute "follow the cassowary footprints to the nest" children's walk.

If you would rather see the sea, take the 7km (4½-mile) Edmund Kennedy track, which starts below The Horizon resort at the southern end of the Kennedy Esplanade in South Mission Beach. You get views of the ocean and the rainforest on this trail. The Mission Beach Visitor Centre has free trail maps.

Coral Sea Kayaking (**© 07/4068 9154,** or mobile phone 0419 782453; www.coralseakayaking.com) offers a range of sea-kayaking expeditions that interpret the rich environment around you. Groups are usually between five and eight people, so you get personal attention and time to ask questions. The half-day sea-kayak trip (A$60/US$48/UK£24 per person) follows the coast near South Mission Beach. Between mid-May and mid-November, owners David Tofler and Atalanta Willy also run a 3-day sea kayak camping trip to the nearby Family Islands. This costs A$570 (US$456/UK£228), including pickup from your accommodations, all meals, and equipment including snorkeling gear. Extended 5- and 7-day paddles are also available.

Tips Wildlife Safety Tips

The endangered cassowary (a spectacular ostrichlike bird with a blue bony crown on its head) can kill with its enormous claws, so never approach one. If you disturb one, back off slowly and hide behind a tree.

Dangerous crocodiles inhabit the local waterways. Do not swim in, or stand on the bank of, any river or stream.

You will spend plenty of time lazing and strolling the area's 14km (8¾ miles) of beaches, but be careful about where you swim. Deadly marine stingers inhabit the sea from October through May; during these months, swim only in the stinger nets erected at Mission Beach and South Mission Beach.

HITTING THE BEACH Relaxing on the uncrowded beach is why everyone comes to Mission Beach. From June through September, you can swim anywhere, and the water is warm; October through May, stick to areas with stinger nets at Mission Beach proper (behind Castaways resort) and South Mission Beach.

A DAY TRIP TO DUNK ISLAND If you're a beachcomber at heart, Dunk will fulfill your dreams. Just 5km (3 miles) offshore from Mission Beach, Dunk was the inspiration for writer E. J. Banfield's book *Confessions of a Beachcomber.* Banfield moved to Dunk at the turn of the 20th century to live out what he thought would be a short life. He lived another 23 years, which must say something about the restorative powers of a piece of paradise. Ed and Bertha Banfield's graves are alongside the track to Mount Kootaloo.

Thick bushland and rainforest cover much of the island's 12 sq. km (4¾ sq. miles), most of which is a national park. The island is renowned for its myriad birds and electric-blue Ulysses butterflies.

You can stay at the upscale Dunk Island resort (see below) or pop over for the day to snorkel, hike in the forest, or do all sorts of watersports. **Quick Cat Cruises** (**© 07/4068 7289**) runs transfers for A$48 (US$38/UK£19) adults round-trip, half price for kids 4 to 14, free for kids under 4. Daily departures are from Clump Point Jetty at 8:30 and 10am and 2pm, returning at 1:30, 3:30, and 4:30pm. You can also get to Dunk by **water taxi** (**© 07/4068 8310**), which runs five times a day from Wongaling Beach and takes 10 minutes. Ask at your hotel about transfers between Clump Point and South Mission Beach.

Once on Dunk, you pay as you go for activities and equipment rental. Everything from water-skiing to catamaran sailing is available, and Dunk has lovely beaches and half a dozen rainforest walking trails, ranging in duration from 15 minutes to 4 hours. On Monday and Thursday mornings, you can visit an artist's gallery reached on a 40-minute trail through the rainforest; admission is A$4 (US$3.20/UK£1.60).

Coral Sea Kayaking (**© 07/4068 9154,** or mobile phone 0419 782453; www.coralseakayaking.com) runs full-day guided paddles to Dunk Island. It takes about 90 minutes to reach the small islands near Dunk and you may see dolphins and turtles. There's a stop at a nearby island for a midmorning snack, and while on Dunk Island you can walk in the rainforest, and swim or snorkel in a secluded bay. The trip costs A$101 (US$81/UK£40) per person, including park fees, lunch, and snacks.

WHERE TO STAY IN MISSION BEACH

The Horizon ★ With its beguiling views across the pool to Dunk Island, its rainforest setting, and its impressive rooms, this resort perched on a steep hillside is one of the most comfortable and beautiful you will find. Even the least expensive rooms are spacious and have luxurious bathrooms. All but a handful of rooms have some kind of sea view; a half-dozen retain the older-style bathrooms from a previous resort development, but the sea views from these rooms are the best. It's just a minute or two down the rainforest track to the beach.

Explorer Dr., South Mission Beach, QLD 4852. © **1800/079 090** in Australia, or 07/4068 8154. Fax 07/4068 8596. www.thehorizon.com.au. 55 units. A$220–A$420 (US$176–US$336/UK£88–UK£168) double; A$260 (US$208/UK£104) suite; A$290–A$350 (US$232–US$280/UK£116–UK£140) family room (sleeps 5). Extra child 4–14 A$15 (US$12/UK£6). Ask about packages and specials. Rates higher Dec 22–Jan 2. AE, DC, MC, V. **Amenities:** 3 restaurants; bar; large saltwater pool; lit tennis courts; tour desk. *In room:* A/C, TV, minibar, coffeemaker, hair dryer, iron.

Mackays *Value* This delightfully well-kept motel is one of the best deals in town. It's just 80m (262 ft.) from the beach and 400m (¼ mile) from the heart of Mission Beach. The friendly Mackay family repaints the rooms annually, so the place always looks brand-new. All the rooms are pleasant and spacious, with white-tiled floors, cane sofas, colorful bedcovers, and very clean bathrooms. Some have views of the attractive granite-lined pool and gardens. Rooms in the older painted-brick wing have garden views from a communal patio. Apartments have kitchenettes but only have air-conditioning in the main bedrooms. Ask about special packages; they can be extremely good deals and may include extras like rafting on the Tully River and day trips to the Reef and Dunk Island.

7 Porter Promenade, Mission Beach, QLD 4852. ✆ **07/4068 7212.** Fax 07/4068 7095. www.mackaysmissionbeach.com. 22 units, 12 with bathroom, 10 with shower only. A$95–A$110 (US$76–US$88/UK£38–UK£44) double; A$110–A$155 (US$88–US$124/UK£44–UK£62) 1- and 2-bedroom apt. Extra adult A$20 (US$16/UK£8); extra child under 14 A$10 (US$8/UK£4). Crib A$10 (US$8/UK£4). Ask about packages. AE, DC, MC, V. Free covered parking. **Amenities:** Outdoor pool; access to nearby tennis courts; access to bike rental; tour desk; car-rental desk; room service at breakfast; in-room massage; babysitting; coin-op laundry; nonsmoking rooms. *In room:* A/C, TV, fax, fridge, safe.

WHERE TO STAY ON DUNK ISLAND

Dunk Island ★ *Kids* Families love Dunk Island because there's so much to do, but it's just as appealing for honeymooners or retired couples. For those who are more inclined to relaxation, Dunk has beautiful beaches and pastimes like champagne sunset cruises. Just 5km (3 miles) offshore from Mission Beach, Dunk is a rainforested 12-sq.-km (7½-sq.-mile) island that attracts everyone. The island is renowned for bird life and neon-blue Ulysses butterflies, which you will see everywhere.

Among the free activities are windsurfing, catamaran sailing, paddle skiing, tennis and squash courts, fitness classes and aqua-aerobics, beach and pool volleyball, badminton, bocce, and archery. You pay for a range of other activities, including guided jet-ski tours, parasailing, water-skiing, tube rides, tandem sky diving, game-fishing trips, motorboats, sunset wine-and-cheese cruises, and horse riding. The 18-hole golf course is Australia's only island resort course. A yacht calls to make trips around nearby islands, and a game-fishing boat picks up here. The kids will love the playground and a visit to Coonanglebah (the island farm), as well as the kids' club. An artists' colony in the rainforest sells works Monday and Thursday, from 10am to 1pm.

All four kinds of low-rise (two-story) accommodations were refurbished and restyled in 2003. The top-of-the-range units are the bright, spacious Bayview suites, which have virtually uninterrupted views over Brammo Bay and direct access to the beach. Set in small groups of four units (two units upstairs, two downstairs), suites have king-size beds, luxurious bathrooms, large L-shaped balconies, and extras such as CD players, bathrobes, and stocked minibars. Beachfront rooms are just that, with views over Brammo Bay from most units. Upstairs rooms have balconies, downstairs rooms have patios and open onto the gardens and the beach, and some have family configurations with one king-size and two single beds. Connecting rooms are available. A short stroll from the central complex, resort facilities, and beach are the Garden Cabanas as well as the Banfield rooms, which are great for families. To truly relax, visit the **Spa of Peace and Plenty,** two tropical-style buildings connected by a floating boardwalk on a man-made lake, for a facial, massage, body wrap, or other pampering.

Off Mission Beach (c/o Voyages, G.P.O. Box 3589, Sydney, NSW 2001). ✆ **1300/134 044** in Australia, or 02/8296 8010 (Sydney reservations office); resort 07/4068 8199. Fax 02/9299 2477 (Sydney reservations office). www.voyages.com.au. 146 units, 72 with shower only. A$316–A$556 (US$253–US$445/UK£127–UK£223) double. Rates include full breakfast. Extra adult A$58 (US$46/UK£23). Children under 12 stay free in parent's room using existing bedding. Ask about packages. AE, DC, MC, V. Daily 45-min. flights operate from Cairns (book through Qantas or the resort).

Aircraft luggage limit 16 kilograms (35 lb.) per person. Quick Cat Cruises (© **07/4068 7209**) makes round-trip ferry transfers from Mission Beach for A$48 (US$38/UK£19) adults, half price kids. Including the ferry fare, the company does daily door-to-door coach connections from Port Douglas for A$84 (US$67/UK£34), Cairns for A$59 (US$47/UK£24), and Cairns northern beaches for A$70 (US$56/UK£28) adult, one-way. Fares for children 4–14 are half price. Disembarkation from the ferry is sometimes into shallow water—be prepared to get your feet wet! Airport pickups must be booked. Transfers also available by air charter. **Amenities:** 3 restaurants; bar; 2 large outdoor pools; 18-hole golf course; 3 lit tennis courts (1 indoor); exercise room; spa; extensive watersports equipment rental; bike rental; daily kids' club for ages 3–12 (fee); babysitting; coin-op laundry. *In room:* A/C, ceiling fans, TV, minibar (beachfront units and suites only), fridge, coffeemaker, hair dryer, iron.

BEDARRA ISLAND: THE ULTIMATE LUXURY GETAWAY

Only a mile long, Bedarra is home to an exclusive 15-room resort favored by the rich, famous, and anyone who desires privacy. The staff is discreet, and day-trippers are banned. Rainforested and fringed by beaches, Bedarra is a few miles south of Dunk Island.

Bedarra Island ★★★ Bedarra is one of those rare and fabulous places that throws not just meals but vintage French champagne, fine cognac and wine, and other potable treats into the price, shocking though that price may be. If you feel like Louis Roederer Champagne at 3am, help yourself. The private villas have large verandas, and there's a sense of light and space in the public areas. The lobby, restaurant, and 24-hour bar are open, with ironbark and recycled timber beams, and feature panels of volcanic stone. Each villa, tucked into the rainforest, has a balcony and sea views. All come with generous living areas, king-size beds, CD players, bathrobes, and the important things in life, like double hammocks on the veranda, big double bathtubs, and aromatherapy oil-burners. Bathrooms offer divine pampering treats including signature Bedarra aromatherapy oils.

Four exclusive villas sit away from the main resort, perched on cliff tops overlooking Wedgerock Bay. The Pavilions at Bedarra and The Point offer superior facilities, including separate living and sleeping areas, large decks, and an outdoor area with a private plunge pool.

The emphasis here is on relaxation. Walk along rainforest trails, fish off the beach, snorkel. Take a catamaran, paddle-ski, or windsurf out on the water. These activities are free; chartering a yacht or game-fishing boat costs extra. To visit the Great Barrier Reef, you will need to transfer to Dunk Island to join the Quick Cat catamaran (see "Exploring the Reef," above). The Beachclub offers watersports facilities and a gym and massage therapy room as well as a lounge area with Internet access. Many guests do nothing more strenuous than have the chef pack a gourmet picnic with a bottle of bubbly and set off in search of a deserted beach. Dress at night is smart casual.

Off Mission Beach (c/o Voyages, G.P.O. Box 3589, Sydney, NSW 2001). © **1300/134 044** in Australia, or 02/8296 8010 (Sydney reservations office). Fax 02/9299 2477 (Sydney reservations office). www.voyages.com.au. 16 villas. A$1,584–A$1,912 (US$1,267–US$1,530/UK£634–UK£765) double villas; A$2,990 (US$2,392/UK£1,196) double at The Point and Pavilions. Rates include all meals, 24-hr. open bar, transfers from Dunk Island. Ask about packages. AE, DC, MC, V. Air or coach/ferry transfer to Dunk Island from Cairns (see above), then 15-min. boat transfer. Water transfers from Mission Beach available. Children under 16 not accepted. **Amenities:** Restaurant; bar; secluded outdoor pool w/private Jacuzzi area; lit tennis court; gym; watersports; massage; laundry service. *In room:* A/C, ceiling fan, TV/VCR, minibar, hair dryer, iron.

WHERE TO DINE IN MISSION BEACH

Friends Restaurant MEDITERRANEAN/SEAFOOD The cozy interior and a hearty menu favoring local seafood make this place a long-standing favorite with locals. Appetizers include mussels Normandy, oysters done three ways, and garlic prawns. Main courses feature lamb shanks; steak with mushrooms or green peppercorn sauce; and chicken hot pot. Settle in with a homemade dessert and liqueur coffee after dinner. Licensed.

Porters Promenade (opposite Campbell St.), Mission Beach. ✆ **07/4068 7107.** Reservations recommended. Main courses A$15–A$25 (US$12–US$20/UK£6–UK£10). AE, MC, V. Tues–Sat (also Sun on long weekends) 6:30–10:30pm or until the last diners leave. Closed 1 month during Feb–Mar.

TOWNSVILLE & MAGNETIC ISLAND

346km (215 miles) S of Cairns; 1,371km (850 miles) N of Brisbane

With a population of 140,000, Townsville claims to be Australia's largest tropical city. Because of its size, and an economy based on mining, manufacturing, education, and tourism, it is sometimes overlooked as a holiday destination. Unjustly so, I think. The people are friendly, the city is pleasant, and there's plenty to do. The town nestles by the sea below the pink face of Castle Rock, which looms 300m (about 1,000 ft.) directly above. The beachfront had a A$29-million (US$23-million/UK£11.6-million) revamp a couple of years ago.

Townsville's major attraction is the world-class **Museum of Tropical Queensland,** where a full-size replica of HMS *Pandora* is the stunning centerpiece. The museum is next door to one of the city's most enduring attractions, the Reef HQ aquarium.

Remnants of bygone times are apparent in some of the surrounding towns, particularly **Charters Towers** and **Ravenswood,** which retain splendid examples of colonial architecture, historic hotels, museums, and displays of old gold mining machinery and cottages.

Cruises depart from the harbor for the Great Barrier Reef, about 2½ hours away. Just 8km (5 miles) offshore is Magnetic Island—"Maggie" to the locals—a popular place for watersports, hiking, and spotting koalas in the wild.

Although Townsville can be hot and humid in the summer—and sometimes in the path of cyclones—it is generally spared the worst of the Wet-season rains.

ESSENTIALS

GETTING THERE Townsville is on the Bruce Highway, a 3-hour drive north of Airlie Beach and 4½ hours south of Cairns. The Bruce Highway breaks temporarily in the city. From the south, take Bruce Highway Alt. 1 route into the city. From the north, the highway leads into the city. The drive from Cairns to Townsville through sugar-cane fields, cloud-topped hills, and lush bushland is a pretty one—one of the most picturesque stretches in Queensland.

Qantas (✆ **13 13 13** in Australia; www.qantas.com.au) flies direct from Brisbane. **QantasLink** flies from Cairns, Brisbane, Hamilton Island in the Whitsundays, and Mackay. **Jetstar** (✆ **13 15 38** in Australia) flies from Brisbane, Sydney, and Melbourne's Tullamarine airport, and **Virgin Blue** (✆ **13 67 89** in Australia) flies direct to Townsville from Brisbane and Sydney daily.

Abacus Charters & Tours (✆ **07/4775 5544**) runs a door-to-door airport shuttle. It meets all flights from Brisbane, and from Cairns or elsewhere if you book in advance. A trip into town is A$8 (US$6.40/UK£3.20) one-way. A **taxi** from the airport to most central hotels costs about A$15 (US$12/UK£6).

Seven **Queensland Rail** (✆ **1300 131 722** in Queensland, or 07/3235 1122; www.traveltrain.com.au) long-distance trains stop at Townsville each week. The 19-hour Tilt Train journey from Brisbane costs A$263 (US$210/UK£105). The 24-hour *Sunlander* journey costs A$179 (US$143/UK£72) for an economy seat, A$237 to

A$367 (US$190–US$294/UK£95–UK£147) for a sleeper, and A$661 (US$529/UK£264) in the luxury Queenslander Class.

Greyhound Australia (✆ **13 14 99** in Australia) coaches stop at Townsville many times a day on their Cairns-Brisbane-Cairns routes. The fare from Cairns is A$62 (US$50/UK£25); trip time is 6 hours. The fare from Brisbane is A$200 (US$160/UK£80); trip time is 23 hours.

VISITOR INFORMATION For an information packet, contact **Townsville Enterprise Limited,** P.O. Box 1043, Townsville, QLD 4810 (✆ **07/4726 2728;** www.townsvilleonline.com.au). It has two Information Centres. One is in the heart of town on Flinders Mall (✆ **1800/801 902** in Australia, or 07/4721 3660); it's open Monday through Friday from 9am to 5pm, and weekends from 9am to 1pm. The other is on the Bruce Highway 10km (6¼ miles) south of the city (✆ **07/4778 3555**); it's open daily from 9am to 5pm. For information on Magnetic Island, also check www.magnetic-island.com.au or www.magneticisland.info.

GETTING AROUND Local **Sunbus** (✆ **07/4725 8482**) buses depart Flinders Mall. Car-rental chains include **Avis** (✆ **07/4721 2688**), **Budget** (✆ **07/4725 2344**), **Hertz** (✆ **07/4775 4821**), and **Thrifty** (✆ **07/4725 4600**).

Detours Coaches (✆ **07/4771 3986**) runs tours to most attractions in and around Townsville. For a taxi, call ✆ **13 10 08.**

DAY TRIPS TO THE REEF

Most boats visiting the Reef from Townsville are live-aboard vessels that make trips of 2 or more days, designed for serious divers. **Barrier Reef Dive, Cruise & Travel** (✆ **1800/636 778** in Australia, or 07/4772 5800; www.divecruisetravel.com) runs day trips to Wheeler Reef and John Brewer Reef. It takes only 1½ hours to reach John Brewer Reef, where you can make introductory dives for A$229 (US$183/UK£92) for the first and A$274 (US$219/UK£110) for two, and certified divers can make two dives for A$244 (US$195/UK£98); all gear is included. The cruise costs A$139 (US$111/UK£56) for adults, A$125 (US$100/UK£50) for seniors, A$84 (US$67/UK£34) for children 5 to 15, and A$357 (US$287/UK£143) for a family of four. The price includes lunch and morning and afternoon tea. There are freshwater showers on board. Cruises depart Townsville at 8:30am, with a pickup at Magnetic Island en route, and return by 5pm. Several other operators, including **Adrenalin Dive** (✆ **07/4724 0600;** www.adrenalindive.com.au), have trips to the *Yongala*, the Coral Sea, and the Reef.

THE TOP ATTRACTIONS

Museum of Tropical Queensland ★★ A stunning addition to Townsville's skyline is this A$22-million (US$17.6-million/UK£8.8-million) museum, with its curved roof reminiscent of a ship in full sail. In pride of place is the amazing exhibition of relics salvaged from the wreck of HMS *Pandora,* which lies 33m (108 ft.) underwater on the edge of the Great Barrier Reef, 120km (74 miles) east of Cape York. The *Pandora* exhibit includes a full-scale replica of a section of the ship's bow and its 17m-high (56-ft.) foremast. Standing three stories high, the replica and its copper-clad keel were crafted by local shipwrights for the museum. *Pandora* sank in 1791, and the wreck was discovered in 1977. The exhibition traces the ship's voyage and the retrieval of the sunken treasure. The museum has six galleries, including a hands-on science center, and a natural history display that looks at life in tropical Queensland—above and below the water. Another is dedicated to north Queensland's indigenous heritage, with items from Torres Strait and the South Sea Islands as well as stories from people of different cultures about the settlement and labor of north Queensland. Touring exhibitions change every 3 months. Allow 2 to 3 hours.

70–102 Flinders St. (next to Reef HQ). ✆ **07/4726 0600**, or 07/4726 0606 info line. www.mtq.qld.gov.au. Admission A$12 (US$9.60/UK£4.80) adults, A$8 (US$6.40/UK£3.20) seniors and students, A$7 (US$5.60/UK£2.80) children 4–16, A$30 (US$24/UK£12) family of 5. Daily 9:30am–5pm. Closed Good Friday, Dec 25, and until 1pm Apr 25 (Anzac Day).

Reef HQ ★ *Kids* Reef HQ is the education center for the Great Barrier Reef Marine Park Authority's headquarters and is the largest living coral reef aquarium in the world. The highlight is walking through a 20m-long (66-ft.) transparent acrylic tunnel, gazing into a giant predator tank where sharks cruise silently. The wreck of SS *Yongala* provides an eerie backdrop for blacktip and whitetip reef sharks, leopard sharks, and nurse sharks, sharing their 750,000-liter (195,000-gal.) home with stingrays, giant trevally, and a green turtle. Watching them feed is quite a spectacle. The tunnel also reveals the 2.5-million-liter (650,000-gal.) coral reef exhibit, with its hard and soft corals providing a home for thousands of fish, giant clams, sea cucumbers, sea stars, and other creatures. During the scuba show, the divers speak to you over an intercom while they swim with the sharks and feed the fish. Other highlights include a touch tank and a wild sea-turtle rehabilitation center, plus interactive activities for children. Reef HQ is an easy walk from the city center.

2–68 Flinders St. ✆ **07/4750 0800**. www.reefhq.com.au. Admission A$22 (US$18/UK£8.80) adults, A$17 (US$14UK£7) seniors and students, A$11 (US$8.80/UK£4.40) children 4–16, A$54 (US$43/UK£22) family of 5. Daily 9:30am–5pm. Closed Dec 25. Public parking lot opposite Reef HQ. Bus: 1, 1A, or 1B (stop 3-min. walk away).

MORE THINGS TO SEE & DO

The Strand is a 2.5km (1½-mile) strip with safe swimming beaches, a fitness circuit, a great water park for the kids, and plenty of covered picnic areas and free gas barbecues. Stroll along the promenade or relax at one of the many cafes, restaurants, and bars while you gaze across the Coral Sea to Magnetic Island. For the more active, there are areas to in-line skate, cycle, walk, or fish, and a basketball half-court. Four rocky headlands and a picturesque jetty adjacent to Strand Park provide good fishing spots, and there are two surf lifesaving clubs to service the three swimming areas along The Strand. With 300 days of sunshine each year, Townsville is a place where you'll enjoy cooling off—in the Olympic-size Tobruk Pool, the seawater Rockpool, or at the beach itself. During summer (Nov–Mar), three swimming enclosures operate to keep swimmers safe from marine stingers. If watersports are on your agenda, try a jet ski, hire a canoe, or take to the latest in pedal skis. A state-of-the-art water park has waterfalls, hydrants, water slides, and water cannons, plus a huge bucket of water that continually fills until it overturns and drenches laughing children.

Don't miss the views of Cleveland Bay and Magnetic Island from **Castle Hill;** it's a 2.5km (1½-mile) drive or a shorter, steep walk up from town. To drive to the top, follow Stanley Street west from Flinders Mall to Castle Hill Drive; the walking trails up are posted en route.

At the **Billabong Sanctuary** (✆ **07/4778 8344;** www.billabongsanctuary.com.au) on the Bruce Highway 17km (11 miles) south of town, you can see Aussie wildlife in a natural setting and hand-feed kangaroos. You can also be photographed (starting at A$10/US$8/UK£4) holding a koala, a (baby) crocodile, a python, a wombat, and other creatures. Talks and shows run continuously starting at 8:30am; one of the most popular is the saltwater-crocodile feeding at noon and 2:45pm. There are also gas barbecues, a food kiosk, and a pool. Admission is A$26 (US$21/UK£10) for adults,

A$24 (US$19/UK£9.60) for students, A$15 (US$12/UK£6) for kids 4 to 16, and A$80 (US$64/UK£32) for a family of five. The sanctuary is open every day except December 25 from 8am to 5pm.

WHERE TO STAY

Holiday Inn Townsville The "Sugar Shaker" (you'll know why when you see it) has been Townsville's favorite hotel for years. Right on Flinders Mall, it's a stroll from Reef HQ, Museum of Tropical Queensland, and Magnetic Island ferries. The rooms are fitted out in sleek blond wood, and because the 20-story building is circular, every one faces the city, the bay, or Castle Hill. Suites have kitchenettes. The star attractions are the rooftop pool and sun deck with barbecues.

334 Flinders Mall, Townsville, QLD 4810. ✆ **1800/079 903** in Australia, 800/835-7742 in the U.S. and Canada, 0345/581 666 in the U.K. or 020/8335 1304 in London, 0800/801 111 in New Zealand, or 07/4729 2000. Fax 07/4721 1263. www.ichotelsgroup.com. 230 units. A$140–A$165 (US$112–US$132/UK£56–UK£66) double; A$170–A$180 (US$136–US$144/UK£68–UK£72) suite. Extra person A$40 (US$32/UK£16). Children stay free in parent's room with existing bedding. Free crib. Ask about weekend rates, advance-purchase rates, and packages. AE, DC, MC, V. Parking A$7 (US$5.60/UK£2.80) per day, free valet parking. **Amenities:** Restaurant; 2 bars; rooftop pool; free access to nearby gym; bike rental; secretarial services; 24-hr. room service; massage; babysitting; coin-op laundry; laundry service; dry cleaning. *In room:* A/C, TV w/pay movies, dataport, minibar, coffeemaker, hair dryer, iron, safe.

Seagulls Resort This popular low-key resort, a 5-minute drive from the city, is built around an inviting free-form saltwater pool in 1.2 hectares (3 acres) of dense tropical gardens. Despite the Esplanade location, the motel-style rooms do not boast waterfront views, but they are comfortable and a good size. The larger deluxe rooms have painted brick walls, a sofa, dining furniture, and a kitchen sink. Studios and family rooms have kitchenettes; executive suites have Jacuzzis. Apartments have a main bedroom and a bunk bedroom (sleeps three), a kitchenette, dining furniture, and a roomy balcony. The whole resort is wheelchair friendly, with bathroom facilities for people with disabilities. The accommodations wings surround the pool and its pretty open-sided restaurant, which is popular with locals. It's a 10-minute walk to The Strand, the local bus to the city costs only A$3 (US$2.40/UK£1.20) and most tour companies pick up at the door.

74 The Esplanade, Belgian Gardens, QLD 4810. ✆ **1800/079 929** in Australia, or 07/4721 3111. Fax 07/4721 3133. www.seagulls.com.au. 70 units, all with shower only. A$110–A$140 (US$88–US$112/UK£44–UK£56) double; A$150 (US$120/UK£60) 2-bedroom apt; A$170 (US$136/UK£68) executive suite. Extra adult A$20 (US$16/UK£8); extra child under 14 A$10 (US$8/UK£4). Crib A$10 (US$8/UK£4). AE, DC, MC, V. Free parking. Bus: 7. **Amenities:** Restaurant; bar; 2 large outdoor saltwater pools; children's wading pool; access to nearby golf course; small tennis court; access to nearby health club; playground; tour desk; airport shuttle (A$3/US$2.40/UK£1.20 one-way or A$5/US$4/UK£2 round-trip); business center; room service (dinner); coin-op laundry; laundry service (Mon–Fri); dry cleaning. *In room:* A/C, TV w/free movies, dataport, fridge, coffeemaker, hair dryer, iron.

WHERE TO DINE

Along with the suggestions below, there are restaurants and cafes on **Palmer Street,** an easy stroll across the river from Flinders Mall, Flinders Street East, and The Strand.

Michel's Cafe and Bar MODERN AUSTRALIAN This big contemporary space is popular with Townsville's in crowd. Choose a table on the sidewalk, or opt for air-conditioning inside. Owner-chef Michel Flores works in the open kitchen where he can keep an eye on the excellent servers. You might choose vanilla-scented slow-cooked duck legs with caramelized sweet potato, steamed broccolini, and orange marmalade, or roasted sweet pork cutlet with braised red cabbage, hazelnuts, and spiced apple chutney, or something more casual, like the stylish pastas, seafood, or warm salads.

7 Palmer St. ✆ **07/4724 1460.** Reservations recommended. Main courses A$15–A$25 (US$12–US$20/UK£6–UK£10). AE, DC, MC, V. Tues–Fri 11:30am–2:30pm; Tues–Sat 5:30pm–late.

Zouí Alto ★★ MODERN AUSTRALIAN This is not just one of the best restaurants in Townsville, it's one of the best in the country. Chef Mark Edwards, who has cooked for the king of Norway, turns out terrific food. His effusive wife, Eleni, runs the front of the house, which is idiosyncratically decked out in primary splashes and Greek urns. Main courses include ravioli with choice of filling—pumpkin and blue-vein cheese, sweet potato and ginger, or sun-dried tomato and goat's cheese. Arrive before sunset, to make the most of the spectacular 14th-floor views of Castle Hill on one side and the bay on the other.

At Aquarius on the Beach, 75 The Strand. ✆ **07/4721 4700.** Reservations recommended. Main courses A$18–A$22 (US$14–US$18/UK£7–UK£9). AE, MC, V. Tues–Sat 6:30–9:30pm. Bus: 1B.

A SIDE TRIP TO MAGNETIC ISLAND

8km (5 miles) E of Townsville

"Maggie" is a delightful 51-sq.-km (20-sq.-mile) national park island 20 minutes from Townsville by ferry. About 2,500 people live here, and it's popular with Aussies, who love its holiday atmosphere. It is a busy little place where visitors and locals zip about between the small settlements that dot the coast; in fact, the island has a good range of restaurants, laid-back cafes, and takeout joints. But peace-seeking visitors will find plenty of unspoiled nature to restore their souls. Most people come for the 20 or so pristine (and amazingly uncrowded) bays and white beaches, but hikers, botanists, and birders may want to explore the eucalyptus woods, patches of gully rainforest, and granite tors. (The island got its name when Captain Cook thought the "magnetic" rocks were interfering with his compass readings.) The place is famous for wild koalas that are easily spotted up in the gum trees by the side of the road; ask a local to point you to the nearest colony. Rock wallabies are often spotted in the early morning. Maggie, by and large off the tourist trail, is definitely a flip-flops kind of place.

VISITOR INFORMATION There is no information center on Magnetic Island. Stop off at the **Flinders Mall Visitor Information Centre** (✆ **1800/801 902** in Australia, or

---

Tips Magnetic Island Travel Tips

If you're going to Magnetic Island for the day, pick up a copy of the free *Magnetic Island Guide* from any tourist information center or hotel lobby or at the ferry terminal in Townsville before you go. Because there are so many activities and tours, it will help if you plan your day before you arrive. Also, there is no bank on the island, so carry cash (not every business will cash traveler's checks) and a credit card.

Be warned: Deadly marine stingers make swimming and snorkeling a bad idea October through May, except at the safe swimming enclosures at Picnic Bay and Horseshoe Bay. Lifeguards sweep and patrol Alma Bay, so it is usually safe. You can still do watersports on top of the water if your rental outlet provides a protective Lycra stinger suit, but you won't want to wear one of those in the sticky summer heat from November through March.

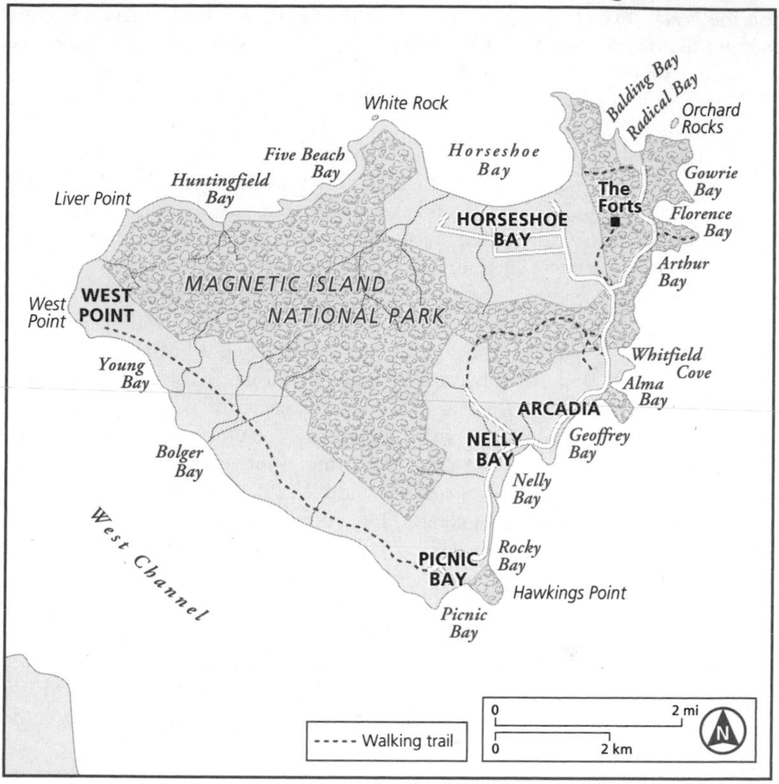

07/4721 3660) in Townsville before you cross to the island. It's open Monday through Friday from 9am to 5pm, and weekends from 9am to 1pm.

GETTING THERE & GETTING AROUND **Sunferries** (© **1800/447 333** in Australia, or 07/4771 3855) runs 15 round-trips a day from the Breakwater terminal on Sir Leslie Thiess Drive. Round-trip tickets are A$26 (US$21/UK£10) for adults, A$13 (US$10/UK£5) for children 5 to 15, and A$56 (US$45/UK£22) for a family of five. The trip takes about 25 minutes.

You can take your car on the ferry, but most people get around by renting an open-sided minimoke (similar to a golf cart) from the many rental outfits on the island. Minimokes are unlikely to go much over 60kmph (36 mph). **Moke Magnetic** (© **07/4778 5377**) rents them for around A$68 (US$54/UK£27) a day. The **Magnetic Island Bus Service** (© **07/4778 5130**) runs a 3-hour guided tour of the island for A$35 (US$28/UK£14) for adults, A$18 (US$14/UK£7.20) for kids 5 to 15, or A$88 (US$70/UK£35) for a family of four. Tours leave at 9am and 1pm daily from Nelly Bay Harbour, and the price includes travel on the buses for the rest of the day.

Out & About on the Island

There is no end to the things you can do on Maggie—snorkeling, swimming in one of a dozen or more bays, catamaran sailing, water-skiing, paraflying, horseback riding on the beach, biking, tennis or golf, scuba diving, sea kayaking, sailing or cruising around the island, taking a Harley-Davidson tour, fishing, and more. Equipment for all these activities is for rent on the island.

Most activities spread out around Nelly Bay (where the ferry pulls in); the island's other two settlements, Arcadia and Horseshoe Bay; and Picnic Bay.

The island is not on the Great Barrier Reef, but surrounding waters are part of the Great Barrier Reef Marine Park. There is good reef snorkeling at Florence Bay on the southern edge, Arthur Bay on the northern edge, and Geoffrey Bay, where you can even reef-walk at low tide. (Wear sturdy shoes and do not walk directly on coral to avoid damaging it.) First-time snorkelers will have an easy time of it in Maggie's weak currents and softly sloping beaches. Outside stinger season, there is good swimming at any number of bays all around the island. Reef-free Alma Bay, with its shady lawns and playground, is a good choice for families; Rocky Bay is a small, secluded cove.

One of the best, and therefore most popular, of the island's 20km (13 miles) of hiking trails is the Nelly Bay–Arcadia trail, a one-way journey of 5km (3 miles) that takes 2½ hours. The first 45 minutes, starting in rainforest and climbing to a saddle between Nelly Bay and Horseshoe, are the most interesting. Another excellent walk is the 2km (1¼-mile) trail to the Forts, remnants of World War II defenses, which, not surprisingly, have great 360-degree sea views. The best koala spotting is on the track up to the Forts off Horseshoe Bay Road. Carry water when walking—some bays and hiking trails are not near shops.

If you feel like splurging, consider a jet-ski circumnavigation of the island with **Adrenalin Jet Ski Tours & Hire** (✆ **07/4778 5533**). The half-day tour on two-seat jet skis costs A$175 (US$140/UK£70) per person, which includes your wet suit, life jacket, and stinger suits in season. Tours depart from Horseshoe Bay morning and afternoon. Keep your eyes peeled for dolphins, dugongs (manatees), and sea turtles.

ORPHEUS ISLAND

80km (50 miles) N of Townsville; 190km (118 miles) S of Cairns

From the moment the small white seaplane bringing you to Orpheus lands—either within stepping distance of the beach, or at the floating pontoon offshore—you'll know you're somewhere special. The waters surrounding Orpehus Island are home to 340 of the 350 or so coral species found on the Great Barrier Reef, 1,100 species of fish, green and loggerhead turtles, dolphins, manta rays, and, from June through September, humpback whales. With a maximum of 42 guests and no day-trippers, the only other people you will see are the attentive but unobtrusive resort staff and the occasional scientist from the James Cook University marine research station in the next bay. It's no wonder that since the 1930s, those seeking seclusion have headed to this beautiful island—among them actress Vivien Leigh, novelist Zane Grey, and more recently, rock star Elton John. One of the Great Barrier Reef's most exclusive retreats, Orpheus Island Resort is also a popular getaway for executives, politicians, honeymooners, and any savvy traveler eager for peace and beauty.

Transfers are by eight-seat Cessna seaplane from Townsville and Cairns daily. Fares are A$450 (US$360/UK£180) from Townsville, A$780 (US$624/UK£312) from Cairns, or A$640 (US$512/UK£256) originating in one place and returning to the other, per person round-trip. Book through the resort. Luggage limit is 15 kilograms (55 lb.) per person.

Orpheus Island Resort ★ If seclusion and tranquillity are what you are looking for, this is the place to find them. The resort is a cluster of rooms lining one of the prettiest turquoise bays you'll find anywhere. Most guests spend their time snorkeling over coral reefs, chilling with a good book or magazine in the Quiet Lounge, or lazing in a hammock. Free activities include tennis, snorkeling, catamaran sailing, canoeing, paddle-skiing, fishing, and taking a motorized dinghy around the shore to explore some of the island's 1,300 national park hectares (3,211 acres). You can pay to go game fishing, charter a boat or seaplane to the outer Reef, or do a dive course. A seven-course degustation-style menu is served nightly in the restaurant.

All the rooms and suites on Orpheus are beachfront. Most of the 17 Orpheus Retreats are in blocks of three, and each has a personal patio and a Jacuzzi. Four Nautilus Suites are more spacious, with separate lounge and bedroom areas, large private patios, and large Jacuzzis. Two have enclosed garden courtyards.

Orpheus Island, Great Barrier Reef (P.M.B. 15), Townsville, QLD 4810. ✆ **07/4777 7377.** Fax 07/4777 7533. www.orpheus.com.au. 21 units. A$1,450 (US$1,160/UK£580) Orpheus Retreat double; A$1,700 (US$1,360/UK£680) Nautilus Suite double. Rates include all meals but not drinks. Ask about packages. AE, DC, MC, V. Children under 15 not accepted. **Amenities:** Restaurant; bar; 2 small outdoor pools, 1 w/swim-up bar; lit tennis court; exercise room; Jacuzzi; watersports rentals; concierge; business center with 24-hr. Internet access. *In room:* A/C, minibar, coffeemaker, hair dryer, iron, CD player, no phone.

5 The Whitsunday Coast & Islands

A day's drive or a 1-hour flight south of Cairns brings you to the dazzling collection of 74 islands known as the Whitsundays. No more than 3 nautical miles (3.4km/2 miles) separate most of the islands, and altogether they represent countless bays, beaches, dazzling coral reefs, and fishing spots that make up one fabulous Great Barrier Reef playground. Sharing the same latitude as Rio de Janeiro and Hawaii, the water is at least 72°F (22°C) year-round, the sun shines most of the year, and in winter you'll require only a light jacket at night.

All the islands consist of densely rainforested national park land, mostly uninhabited. The surrounding waters belong to the Great Barrier Reef Marine Park. Don't expect palm trees and coconuts—these islands are covered with dry-looking pine and eucalyptus forests full of dense undergrowth, and rocky coral coves far outnumber the few sandy beaches. More than half a dozen islands have resorts that offer just about all the activities you could ever want—snorkeling, scuba diving, sailing, reef fishing, water-skiing, jet-skiing, parasailing, sea kayaking, hiking, rides over the coral in semisubmersibles, fish feeding, putt-putting around in dinghies to secluded beaches, playing tennis or squash, and aqua-aerobics classes. Accommodations range from small, low-key wilderness retreats to midrange family havens to Australia's most luxurious resort, Hayman.

The village of Airlie Beach is the center of the action on the mainland. The Whitsundays are just as good a steppingstone to the outer Great Barrier Reef as Cairns, and some people consider them better, because you don't have to make the 90-minute trip to the Reef before you hit coral. Just about any Whitsunday island has fringing reef around its shores, and there are good snorkeling reefs between the islands, a quick boat ride away from your island or mainland accommodations.

ESSENTIALS

GETTING THERE **By Car** The Bruce Highway leads south from Cairns or north from Brisbane to Proserpine, 26km (16 miles) inland from Airlie Beach. Take the Whitsunday turnoff to reach Airlie Beach and Shute Harbour. Allow a good 8

Tips Safety Tips

Although they have not been sighted at Airlie Beach for several years, deadly marine stingers may frequent the shorelines from October through April. The best place to swim is in the beachfront Airlie Beach lagoon.

The rivers in these parts are home to dangerous saltwater crocodiles (which mostly live in fresh water, contrary to their name), so don't swim in streams, rivers, and water holes.

hours to drive from Cairns. There are several car-storage facilities at Shute Harbour. **Whitsunday Car Security** (✆ **07/4946 9955**) will collect your car anywhere in the Whitsunday area and store it in locked covered parking for A$10 (US$8/UK£4) per day or A$15 (US$12/UK£6) overnight.

By Plane There are two air routes into the Whitsundays: Hamilton Island Airport and Whitsunday Coast Airport at Proserpine on the mainland. **QantasLink** (✆ **13 13 13** in Australia) flies direct to Hamilton Island from Cairns and Townsville. **Virgin Blue** (✆ **13 67 89** in Australia) flies to Proserpine direct from Brisbane and Sydney, and with connections from Canberra, Melbourne, Adelaide, Perth, Hobart, and Launceston, and direct from Brisbane to Hamilton Island. **Jetstar** (✆ **13 15 38** in Australia) flies from Brisbane and Sydney to Proserpine and from Adelaide, Brisbane, Melbourne, and Sydney to Hamilton Island. If you stay on an island, the resort may book your launch transfers automatically. These may appear on your airline ticket, in which case your luggage will be checked through to the island.

By Train Several **Queensland Rail** (✆ **1300 131 722** in Australia; www.traveltrain.com.au) long-distance trains stop at Proserpine every week. The one-way fare from Cairns on the Tilt Train is A$144 (US$115/UK£58). There is a bus link to Airlie Beach. Brisbane fares range from A$233 (US$186/UK£93) on the Tilt Train to A$336 (US$269/UK£134) for a first-class sleeper on the *Sunlander* or A$606 (US$485/UK£242) for the all-inclusive Queenslander Class service.

By Bus **Greyhound Australia** (✆ **13 14 99** in Australia) operates plentiful daily services to Airlie Beach from Brisbane (trip time: around 19 hr.) and Cairns (trip time: 10 hr.). The fare is A$173 (US$138/UK£69) from Brisbane and A$108 (US$86/UK£43) from Cairns.

Whitsunday Transit (✆ **07/4946 1800**) meets all flights and trains at Proserpine and provides door-to-door transfers to Airlie Beach hotels or to Shute Harbour. The fare from the airport is A$17 (US$14/UK£7) adults and A$9 (US$7.20/UK£3.60) children to Airlie Beach or Shute Harbour. From the train station, it is A$8.20 (US$6.55/UK£3.30) adults and A$4.20 (US$3.35/UK£1.70) children to Airlie Beach or A$11 (US$8.80/UK£4.40) adults and A$5.50 (US$4.40/UK£2.20) children to Shute Harbour.

Fantasea Cruises' Blue Ferries (✆ **1800/650 851** in Australia, or 07/4946 5111) makes ferry transfers from Hamilton Island Airport to Shute Harbour, Daydream Island, Long Island and for guests only to Lindeman Island. The one-way fare is A$37 (US$30/UK£15) adults and A$20 (US$16/UK£8) children, or A$2 (US$1.60/UK80p) extra to Lindeman Island. Make sure you book an airport transfer, not the service that will drop you at Hamilton Island marina.

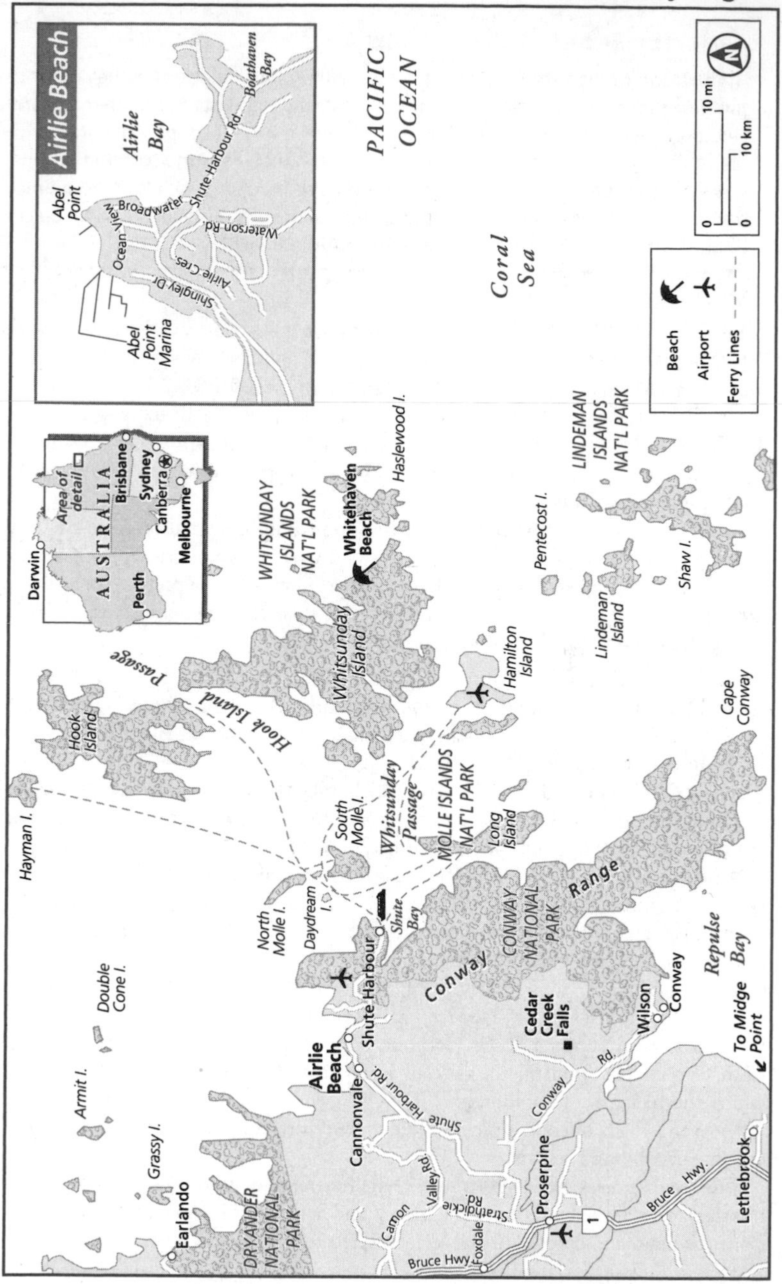
Airlie Beach
Abel Point
Airlie Bay
Boathaven Bay
Broadwater
Ocean View
Shute Harbour Rd.
Waterson Rd.
Airlie Cres.
Shingley Dr.
Abel Point Marina
PACIFIC OCEAN
Coral Sea
0
10 mi
0
10 km
Beach
Airport
Ferry Lines
Darwin
AUSTRALIA
Area of detail
Brisbane
Sydney
Canberra
Melbourne
Perth
Haslewood I.
WHITSUNDAY ISLANDS NAT'L PARK
Whitehaven Beach
LINDEMAN ISLANDS NAT'L PARK
Pentecost I.
Shaw I.
Lindeman Island
Hamilton Island
Whitsunday Island
Hook Island Passage
Hook Island
Cape Conway
Hayman I.
South Molle I.
Whitsunday Passage
MOLLE ISLANDS NAT'L PARK
Long Island
North Molle I.
Daydream I.
Shute Bay
Shute Harbour
Conway Range
CONWAY NATIONAL PARK
Repulse Bay
Double Cone I.
Airlie Beach
Cedar Creek Falls
Wilson
Conway
To Midge Point
Armit I.
Cannonvale
Shute Harbour Rd.
Conway Rd.
Grassy I.
Earlando
Valley Rd.
Proserpine
Lethebrook
DRYANDER NATIONAL PARK
Strathdickie Rd.
Canon
Bruce Hwy.
Foxdale
1

Tips The Secret of the Seasons

High season in the Whitsundays coincides with school vacations, which occur in January, in mid-April, from late June to early July, from late September to early October, and in late December. The Aussie winter, June through August, is popular, too. You have to book months ahead to get high-season accommodations, but any other time you can get some good deals indeed. Specials on accommodations, sailing trips, day cruises, and diving excursions fairly leap off the blackboards outside the tour-booking agents in Airlie Beach.

VISITOR INFORMATION For information before you travel, contact **Tourism Whitsundays,** P.O. Box 83, Whitsunday, QLD 4802 (www.whitsundaytourism.com). The **Whitsundays Information Center** (✆ **1800/801 252** in Australia, or 07/4945 3711; fax 07/4945 3182) is in Proserpine, on the Bruce Highway in the town's south. It's open Monday to Friday from 8:30am to 5pm and weekends and public holidays (except Good Friday and Dec 25) from 9am to 3pm. Another useful website is www.whitsunday.net.au.

If you're staying in Airlie Beach, it's easier to pick up information from the private booking agents lining the main street. All stock a vast range of cruise, tour, and hotel information, and make bookings free of charge. They all have pretty much the same stuff, but because some represent certain boats exclusively, and because prices can vary a little from one to the next, shop around.

GETTING AROUND Island ferries and Great Barrier Reef cruises leave from Shute Harbour, a 10-minute drive south of Airlie Beach on Shute Harbour Road. Most other tour-boat operators and bareboat charters anchor at Abel Point Marina, a 15-minute walk west from Airlie Beach.

Avis (✆ **07/4946 6318**), **Hertz** (✆ **07/4946 4687**), and **Thrifty** (✆ **07/4946 7727**) have outlets in Airlie Beach and Proserpine Airport (telephone numbers serve both locations). Budget has no Whitsundays office.

Whitsunday Transit (✆ **07/4946 1800**) runs half-hourly buses between Airlie Beach and Shute Harbour to meet all ferries. The fare is A$4.65 (US$3.70/UK£1.85). A **Ten Trip Ticket,** valid for 1 month and able to be used by more than one person, can be used to travel between Shute Harbour, Airlie Beach, Cannonvale, and Proserpine. It costs A$23 (US$18/UK£9.20) adults and A$12 (US$9.60/UK£4.80) children, which means A$2.25 (US$1.80/UK90p) per trip. An **Explorer Pass,** good for unlimited travel between Shute Harbour, Airlie Beach, Cannonvale, and Proserpine from 6am to 10:30pm on the date of issue, costs A$8.50 (US$6.80/UK£3.40) for adults and half price for children.

Most tour-boat operators pick up guests free from Airlie Beach hotels and pick up at some or all island resorts.

Fantasea Cruises (✆ **1800/650 851** in Australia, or 07/4946 5111) makes ferry transfers from Shute Harbour to the islands and between the islands. One-way transfers from the mainland cost A$26 (US$21/UK£10) to Long and Daydream islands; A$39 (US$31/UK£16) to Hamilton Island. Children 4 to 14 pay A$17 (US$14/UK£6.80) and A$21 (US$17/UK£8.40). Reservations are not necessary, but do book your arrival and departure ferry so that you don't miss your connections. Most islands receive a boat only every 2 to 4 hours, so it's a long wait if you miss your boat.

CHOOSING A WHITSUNDAY BASE

The advantages of staying on the mainland are cheaper accommodations, a choice of restaurants, and the freedom to visit a different island each day. The mainland has jet-skiing, kayaking, parasailing, catamaran rental, and windsurfing.

The main advantage of staying on an island is that swimming, snorkeling, bush-walking, and a huge range of watersports, many of them free, are right outside your door. The deadly stingers that can infest Airlie's shores do not make it to the islands, so swimming in the islands is safe year-round. You won't be isolated if you stay on an island, because most Great Barrier Reef cruise boats, "sail and snorkel" yacht excursions, Whitehaven Beach cruises, dive boats, fishing tour vessels, and so on stop at the island resorts every day or on a frequent basis. Be warned, however, that once you're "captive" on an island, you may be slugged with high food and drink prices. Bear in mind, too, that although most island resorts offer nonmotorized watersports, such as Windsurfers and catamarans, free of charge, you will pay for activities that use fuel, such as parasailing, water-skiing, and dinghy rental.

In some places in the Whitsundays, extreme low tides may reveal rocky mud flats below the sand line. Watersports can be limited then because of the low water level.

EXPLORING THE ISLANDS & THE REEF

REEF CRUISES **Fantasea Cruises** (**© 07/4946 5111;** www.fantasea.com.au) makes a daily trip to Hardy Reef from Shute Harbour, near Airlie Beach, in a high-speed, air-conditioned catamaran. The boat has a bar, and a biologist gives a marine ecology talk en route. You anchor at the massive Fantasea Reefworld pontoon, which holds up to 600 people, and spend up to 3½ hours on the Reef. The day trip costs A$176 (US$141/UK£70) for adults, A$150 (US$120/UK£60) for seniors and students, A$30 (US$24/UK£12) for children 4 to 14. Up to five children may travel with each full paying adult. Guided snorkel safaris cost A$25 (US$20/UK£10) extra or A$75 (US$60/UK£30) for a family of four. Cruise-dive packages are available for A$89 (US$71/UK£36) extra for both introductory and certified dives, or you can book one on board for A$95 (US$76/UK£38) for first-time divers and A$80 (US$64/UK£32) for certified dives. Cruises depart at 8am and pick up passengers at Daydream and Hamilton island resorts. Passengers from Long Island can connect by water taxi.

A fun alternative is Fantasea's 2-day, 1-night **ReefSleep,** during which you spend the night on the pontoon. This gives you a fabulous chance to snorkel at night when the coral is luminescent in the moonlight and nocturnal sea creatures get busy. The trip includes a marine biologist's slide presentation, two scuba dives, plenty of night snorkeling, two buffet lunches, dinner under the stars with wine, and breakfast and

---

Moments Whale-Watching in the Whitsundays

Humpback whales migrate to the Whitsundays July through September to give birth. These fearless giants of the deep come right up to the boat. **Fantasea Adventure Cruising** (**© 07/4946 5111;** www.fantasea.com.au) runs whale-watching cruises in season; trips feature an onboard talk and videos. The cost is about A$100 (US$80/UK£40) per adult. If you don't see whales, you can go free another day, or choose another of Fantasea's cruises as an alternative.

Moments Come Sail with Me

If "bareboating" is a mystery to you, take heart. You're not alone—it simply means you are sailing the boat yourself. And if that seems daunting, rest assured that thousands of people do it safely every year. Most of the many yacht-charter companies in the islands will want one person on the boat to have a little experience at the helm of a vessel, but don't worry if you're a total novice. You do not need a license, and sailing is surprisingly easy in these uncrowded waters, where the channels are deep and hazard-free and the seas are protected from big swells by the Great Barrier Reef. The 74 islands are so close to each other that one is always in sight, and safe anchorages are everywhere.

If you have no boating experience, the company may require you to take a skipper along for the first day at an extra cost of around A$200 (US$160/UK£80) a day or A$275 (US$220/UK£110) overnight. And if you think you know what you're doing but just want extra reassurance, you can take a skipper along for the first couple of hours for A$60 (US$48/UK£24) to help you get the hang of things. Most companies mail you a preparation kit before you leave home. Before departure they give you a thorough 2- to 3-hour briefing and easy-to-read maps marking channels, anchorage points, and the very few dangerous reefs. Your charter company will radio in once or twice a day to check that you're still afloat, and you can contact the staff anytime for advice.

Most yachts are fitted for two to eight passengers. Try to get a boat with two berths more than you need if your budget will bear it, because space is always tight. The boats usually have a galley kitchen, a barbecue mounted to the stern, hot showers, a toilet, linens, a radio or stereo (or both), a motorized dinghy, and snorkeling equipment. Sleeping quarters are usually not all that luxurious and include a mix of single galley berths and one or two very compact private cabins. You can buy your own provisions or have the charter company stock the boat at an extra cost of about A$40 (US$32/UK£16) per person per day. Most operators will load a Windsurfer, fishing tackle, and scuba-diving equipment on request for an extra fee, if they are not standard.

more snorkeling on the second day. You can stay in a clean, comfortable bunkroom for four for A$395 (US$316/UK£158) per person, or in the double cabin, which has a king-size bed, for A$495 (US$396/UK£198) per person. With so few guests per night, you have the Reef all to yourself.

SAILING & SNORKELING TRIPS ★ A cheaper alternative to skippering your own yacht—also called "bareboating"—around the Whitsundays (see the box "Come Sail with Me," above) is a journey on one of the many yachts offering 3-day, 2-night sailing adventures around the islands. You can get involved with sailing the boat as much or as little as you want, snorkel to your heart's content over one dazzling reef after another, beach comb, explore national park trails, learn to sail, stop at secluded bays, swim, sunbathe, and generally have a laid-back good time. A few companies offer introductory and qualified scuba diving for an extra cost per dive. Most boats

In peak season you may have to charter the boat for a week. At other times, most companies impose a minimum of 5 days, but many will rent for 3 nights if you ask, rather than let a vessel sit idle. Five nights is a good length; it allows you to get familiar enough with the boat to relax and enjoy yourself.

In peak season, expect to pay A$615 to A$790 (US$492–US$632/UK£246–UK£316) per night for a four- to six-berth yacht. Rates in the off season, and even in the Whitsundays' busiest time, June through August, will be anywhere from A$100 to A$200 (US$80–US$160/UK£40–UK£80) less. If you are prepared to book within 14 days of when you want to sail, the deals can be even better; you should be able to find a boat that late in the off season. You will be asked to post a credit card bond of around A$2,000 (US$1,600/UK£800). Mooring fees apply if you want to stop at one of the island resorts overnight. A number of bareboat-charter companies offer "sail 'n' stay" packages that combine a few days of sailing with a few days at an island resort.

Most bareboat-charter companies will make complete holiday arrangements for you in the islands, including accommodations, transfers, tours, and sporting activities. Most companies operate out of Airlie Beach, Hamilton Island, or both. Well-known operators include **Whitsunday Rent-A-Yacht** (✆ **1800/075 000** in Australia, or 07/4946 9232; www.rentayacht.com.au); **Queensland Yacht Charters** (✆ **1800/075 013** in Australia, or 07/4946 7400; fax 07/4946 7698; www.yachtcharters.com.au); **Sail Whitsunday** (✆ **07/4946 7070**; fax 07/4946 7044; www.sailwhitsunday.com.au); and **The Moorings** (✆ **888/952-8420** in the U.S., or 07/4948 9509 in Australia; www.moorings.com). Tourism Whitsundays (see "Visitor Information," above) can furnish you with a complete list of operators.

If you don't want to sail yourself, countless skippered sailing trips go through the islands (see "Sailing & Snorkeling Trips," below).

carry a maximum of 12 passengers, so the atmosphere is always friendly and fun. The food is generally good, the showers are usually hot, and you sleep in comfortable but small berths off the galley. Some have small private twin or double cabins.

Prices usually include all meals, Marine Park entrance fees, snorkel gear, and transfers to the departure point (Abel Point Marina or Shute Harbour). In the off season, the boats compete fiercely for passengers; you'll see signboards on the main street in Airlie Beach advertising standby deals.

Among the better-known operators are ***Ragamuffin*** (✆ **07/4946 7777**), a 17m (56-ft.) oceangoing yacht; and **Prosail** (✆ **1800/810 116** in Australia, or 07/4946 5433; www.prosail.com.au), which runs trips on a fleet of 28 yachts. Prosail's 2-day, 2-night guided sailing trips through the Marine and Great Barrier Reef Marine parks cost A$340 (US$272/UK£136) plus A$30 (US$24/UK£12) in marine park fees. All

Finds Hitting the Sand at Whitehaven Beach

The 6km (3¾-mile) stretch of pure-white silica sand on **Whitehaven Beach** ★★ will leave you in rapture. The beach, on uninhabited Whitsunday Island, does not boast a lot of coral, but the swimming is good, and the forested shore is beautiful. Take a book and chill out. Some sailboat day trips visit it, as do some motorized vessels, including **Fantasea Adventure Cruising (© 07/4946 5111)**. Expect to pay around A$95 (US$76/UK£38) per adult and A$55 (US$44/UK£22) per child for the day, with lunch.

trips include sailing, snorkeling, scuba diving, and bushwalking, and you can sail on maxi-yachts such as *Matador, Condor, Apollo, Broomstick,* and *Hammer.* The company also offers 3- and 6-day packages. Contact **Tourism Whitsundays** (see "Visitor Information," above) for details on other charters.

ISLAND HOPPING Day-trippers to Hamilton, Daydream, South Molle, Club Crocodile Long Island, and Hook Island resorts can rent the hotels' watersports equipment, laze by the beaches and pools, scuba dive, join the resorts' activities programs, hike their trails, and eat at some or all of their restaurants. See "The Whitsunday Island Resorts," below, for details on where to stay. Club Crocodile's Long Island Resort is rather noisy but unpretentious, with plentiful watersports, picturesque hiking trails, wild wallabies, and a large beach–cum–tidal flat where you can relax on sun lounges.

You can get to the islands on your own by ferry (see "Getting Around," above), or take an organized day trip that visits one, two, or even three islands in a day. **Fantasea Cruises** (**© 1800/650 851** in Australia, or 07/4946 5111; www.fantasea.com.au) and **Whitsunday Island Adventure Cruises** (**© 07/4946 5255** for the booking agent) all offer them, as do several yachts.

SCENIC FLIGHTS Expect to pay around A$300 (US$240/UK£120) for a 30-minute flight over the Whitsundays (a spectacular sight from the air), a seaplane flight to a Reef pontoon to snorkel for a couple of hours, or for a helicopter to drop you on an island with a champagne picnic and snorkel gear. **Hamilton Island Aviation** (**© 07/4946 8249**) and **Air Whitsunday** (**© 07/4946 9111**) offer a range of tours.

FISHING Reef fishing is superb throughout the islands; red emperor, coral trout, sweetlip, and snapper are common catches. One of the most popular charter vessels is the 16m (52-ft.) timber cruiser ***Moruya*** (**© 07/4946 7127,** or 0415/185 653 mobile; www.fishingwhitsunday.com.au). Day trips depart Shute Harbour daily at 9:30am and return at 5:30pm. They include lunch, bait, and fishing rods. The crew will even clean your catch for you. Adults pay A$120 (US$96/UK£48), seniors A$110 (US$88/UK£44), children 4 to 14 A$75 (US$60/UK£30), and a family of four A$315 (US$252/UK£126).

If you want to undertake your own fishing expedition, **Harbourside Boat Hire,** in Shute Harbour (**© 07/4946 9330**), rents motorized dinghies for A$60 (US$48/UK£24) for a half-day or A$90 (US$72/UK£36) for a full day. Half-cabin cruisers cost A$90 (US$72/UK£36) for a half-day, A$150 (US$120/UK£60) for a full day. They also rent fishing rods and sell tackle, bait, ice, and all your fishing needs.

ECOTOURS Visitors to the Whitsundays can get up close and personal with crocodiles in their natural habitat with **Proserpine River Eco Tours** (book through Fantasea

Cruises, ✆ **07/4946 5111**), which combines an open-air wagon ride through the pristine Goorganga wetlands and a boat trip on the river to learn more about one of Queensland's major crocodile-breeding grounds. This is the only place to see crocs in safety in the wild south of the Daintree. Bus pickups operate from Airlie Beach, Cannonvale, and Proserpine for the tours, which run about 4 hours, depending on tides, and cost A$89 (US$71/UK£36) for adults, A$57 (US$46/UK£23) for kids 4 to 14, and A$235 (US$188/UK£94) for a family of four. Back on land, you'll enjoy billy tea, the best damper I've ever tasted (and they'll even give you the recipe), and a talk on native wildlife over a barbecue lunch.

GOLF Serious golfers should not miss a round on arguably Australia's best resort course, the championship **Turtle Point golf course** ★ at Laguna Whitsundays Resort, Kunapipi Springs Road, Midge Point (✆ **07/4947 7777**), a 45-minute drive south of Airlie Beach. An 18-hole round dodging wallabies, goannas, and kookaburras on the difficult fairways will set you back around A$95 (US$76/UK£38), plus A$25 (US$20/UK£10) for club hire.

SEA KAYAKING ★ If you have strong arms, sea kayaking is a wonderful way to enjoy the islands. Daydream Island and the beaches and bays of the North, Mid, and South Molle group of islands are all within paddling distance of the mainland. It's common to see dolphins, turtles, and sharks along the way. One long-established operator is **Salty Dog Sea Kayaking** (✆ **07/4946 1388;** www.saltydog.com.au), which takes escorted trips through the islands. Half-day trips run on Tuesday, Wednesday, and Saturday, and full-day trips on Monday, Thursday, and Friday, departing Airlie Beach at 8:30am. A half-day trip is A$70 (US$56/UK£28) per person and a day trip is A$125 (US$100/UK£50) per person. Two- and 6-day trips, during which you camp out, are

---

Tips Great Whitsunday Walking

The Whitsundays Great Walk—one of six **Great Walks of Queensland**—covers 36km (22 miles) in Conway State Forest and Conway National Park, behind Airlie Beach. The trail starts in the parking lot at the end of Brandy Creek Road, a short drive from Cannonvale, and winds in three stages from Brandy Creek to Airlie Beach, with two campsites at 12km (7½-mile) intervals. The hills here are rich in giant strangler figs, ferns, and palms, and if you're lucky, you'll spot a giant blue Ulysses butterfly. Walkers should carry drinking water, because the water in natural systems is not good for drinking.

A permit is required for overnight walks, and must be booked in advance (✆ **13 13 04** in Australia 24-hr.; or online at www.qld.gov.au/camping). The cost is A$4.50 (US$3.60/UK£1.80) per person or A$18 (US$14/UK£7.20) for a family of two adults and children aged 5 to 17. More information on the Great Walk and shorter walks can be obtained from the Queensland Parks and Wildlife Service information center, Shute Harbour Road at Mandalay Road (✆ **07/4946 7022**) 2.5km (1½ miles) northeast of Airlie Beach. It's open Monday through Friday from 8:30am to 5pm and most, but not all, Saturdays from 9am to 1pm.

Other Great Walks are on Fraser Island (p. 362), the Wet Tropics near Cairns, the Sunshine Coast hinterland, near Mackay, and in the Gold Coast hinterland. For more details on all walks, log onto **www.epa.qld.gov.au**.

A$365 (US$292/UK£146) and A$1,490 (US$1,192/UK£596). All rates include snorkel gear, meals, pickup, and, on overnight trips, camping gear. The company also delivers sea kayaks anywhere in the Whitsundays. Rental prices start at A$50 (US$40/UK£20) for a single kayak, A$80 (US$64/UK£32) for a double for a half-day, including delivery and pickup and safety equipment. A deposit of A$200 (US$160/UK£80) is required for rentals.

AIRLIE BEACH

640km (397 miles) S of Cairns; 1,146km (711 miles) N of Brisbane

The little town of Airlie Beach is the focal point of activity on the Whitsunday mainland. The town is only a few blocks long, but you will find an adequate choice of decent accommodations, a small selection of good restaurants and bars, a nice boutique or two, and facilities such as banks and a supermarket. Cruises and yachts depart from Shute Harbour, a 10-minute drive south on Shute Harbour Road, and Abel Point Marina, a 10-minute walk west along the foreshore or a quick drive over the hill on Shute Harbour Road.

Airlie Beach has a massive beachfront artificial lagoon, with sandy beaches and landscaped parkland, which solves the problem of where to swim in stinger season. The lagoon is the size of about six full-size Olympic swimming pools, set in 4 hectares (10 acres) of botanic gardens, with a children's pool, plenty of shade, barbecues, picnic shelters, toilets, showers, and parking.

Perched on the edge of the Coral Sea, with views across Pioneer Bay and the Whitsunday Passage, Airlie Beach has a village atmosphere; life revolves around the beach and marina by day, and the bars and restaurants by night.

The spit of land between Airlie Bay and Boathaven Bay is home to the Airlie Beach Sailing Club. Shute Harbour, 11km (7¾ miles) from Airlie Beach, is one of Queensland's busiest ports, filled with yachts, cruisers, water taxis, ferries, and fishermen. For a bird's-eye view, head to the Lions Lookout.

WHERE TO STAY

Airlie Beach Hotel In the heart of Airlie Beach, this large hotel complex offers fairly standard accommodations but is ideal if you like to be in the thick of things. The hotel straddles a whole block, giving it frontage on both the Esplanade and the main street. Rooms are spacious and well-appointed, with views over the inlet. There are standard motel rooms, or newer hotel rooms as well as executive-style suites with kitchens. My pick is the rooms at the front, overlooking the Esplanade and the inlet, which have a small balcony.

16 The Esplanade (at Coconut Grove), Airlie Beach, QLD 4802. © **1800/466 233** in Australia, or 07/4964 1999. Fax 07/4964 1988. www.airliebeachhotel.com.au. 80 units. A$119–A$158 (US$95–US$126/UK£48–UK£63) double standard motel room; A$169–A$208 (US$135–US$166/UK£68–UK£83) double standard hotel room; A$189–A$228 (US$151–US$182/UK£76–UK£91) double executive room; A$278 (US$222/UK£111) double suite. Crib A$21 (US$17/UK£8.40). AE, DC, MC, V. Free covered parking. **Amenities:** 3 restaurants; 3 bars; heated outdoor saltwater pool; tour desk; coin-op laundry; dry cleaning; nonsmoking rooms. *In room:* A/C, ceiling fans, TV, dataport, minibar, coffeemaker, hair dryer, iron.

Coral Sea Resort ★ In Airlie Beach's best location, on the edge of Paradise Point, with 280-degree views of the ocean, this 6-year-old resort is one of the best places to stay on the Whitsunday mainland. The wide range of great accommodations styles suits everyone from honeymooners to families, and although it's relatively sprawling, the design is such that you can easily feel you're alone. All the rooms have a nautical feel. The Coral Sea suites are divine, complete with a Jacuzzi and double hammock on the balcony. There are four styles of suites, apartments, and family units. Bayview suites have a Jacuzzi inside. It's a 3-minute walk along the waterfront to Airlie Beach village.

25 Oceanview Ave., Airlie Beach, QLD 4802. ✆ **1800/075 061** in Australia, or 07/4946 6458. Fax 07/4946 6516. www.coralsearesort.com.au. 78 units. A$220–A$260 (US$176–US$208/UK£88–UK£104) double; A$300–A$360 (US$240–US$288/UK£120–UK£144) double suite; A$320 (US$256/UK£128) double 1-bedroom apt; A$335–A$365 (US$268–US$292/UK£134–UK£146) 2-bedroom beach house apt; A$500 (US$400/UK£200) 3-bedroom beach house apt; A$320 (US$256/UK£128) family unit for up to 5; A$375 (US$300/UK£150) 1-bedroom penthouse; A$510 (US$408/UK£204) double 2-bedroom penthouse; A$715 (US$572/UK£286) double 3-bedroom penthouse. Extra person A$40 (US$32/UK£16). Crib A$15 (US$12/UK£6). 3-night minimum at Easter and Dec 26–Jan 5. Ask about packages. AE, DC, MC, V. Free parking. **Amenities:** Restaurant; bar; 25m (82-ft.) outdoor pool; exercise room; game room; tour desk; car-rental desk; 24-hr. room service; massage; babysitting; coin-op laundry; dry cleaning. *In room:* A/C, ceiling fans, TV w/satellite and free movies, kitchenette, minibar, coffeemaker, hair dryer, iron.

Martinique Whitsunday Resort ★ Apartments in this French Caribbean–style complex high on the hill above Airlie Beach have views that make the short but very steep walk from the town well worthwhile. The one-, two-, and three-bedroom apartments are roomy and light, and each has a big balcony. The wet-edge lap pool also overlooks the Coral Sea, and is surrounded by tropical gardens and waterfalls. There's a barbecue area, and you can also order kitchen supplies to be ready when you arrive. Apartments are serviced weekly, and each has a washing machine and dryer.

18 Golden Orchid Dr. (off Shute Harbour Rd.), Airlie Beach, QLD 4802. ✆ **07/4948 0401.** Fax 07/4948 0402. www.martiniquewhitsunday.com.au. A$200 (US$160/UK£80) double 1-bedroom apt; A$260 (US$208/UK£104) 2-bedroom apt for 4 people; A$360 (US$288/UK£144) 3-bedroom apt for up to 6. Extra person A$25 (US$20/UK£10). AE, DC, MC, V. Free covered parking. **Amenities:** Outdoor lap pool; exercise room; 2 Jacuzzis; tour desk. *In room:* A/C, ceiling fans, TV, kitchen, minibar, hair dryer, iron.

Whitsunday Organic B&B ★ This is a B&B with a difference. Owners John Sergeant and Sharini Kumarage are committed to organic practices and sustainable tourism, which means that almost everything you eat here will have been organically grown. Ask John for a tour of his garden, in which you will find native trees and exotic fruits. Sharini's Sri Lankan heritage influences her menu (dinners on request), which is served up at a fantastic handcrafted table, hewn from one piece of camphor-laurel—or, if you prefer, at a private table on the balcony. The stylish house has been designed with sustainable features such as solar panels, an ecofriendly cooling insulation system, rainwater tank, and recycled building materials. They even use biodegradable, chemical-free cleaning products, and 20% of profits are invested in sustainable agriculture and environmental projects. Artworks by local Aboriginal people are exhibited and for sale.

8 Lamond St., Airlie Beach, QLD 4802. ✆ **07/4946 7151.** Fax 07/4946 7152. www.whitsundaybb.com.au. A$165–A$195 (US$132–US$156/UK£66–UK£78) double. Ask about packages and specials. AE, DC, MC, V. Limited off-street parking. **Amenities:** Tour desk; massage. *In room:* A/C, ceiling fans, hair dryer.

WHERE TO DINE

Mangrove Jack's Café Bar PIZZA/CAFE FARE Bareboat sailors, local sugar farmers, Sydney yuppies, and European backpackers all flock to this big, open-fronted sports bar and restaurant. The mood is upbeat and pleasantly casual, the surroundings are spick-and-span, and the food passes muster. Wood-fired pizza with trendy toppings is the specialty. There is no table service; place your order at the bar and collect your food when your number is called. There are kids' meals for A$8.50 (US$6.80/UK£3.40). More than 50 wines come by the glass.

In the Airlie Beach Hotel, 16 The Esplanade (enter from Shute Harbour Rd.). ✆ **07/4946 6233.** Reservations recommended. Pizzas A$19–A$24 (US$15–US$19/UK£7.60–UK£9.60); main courses A$12–A$26 (US$9.60–US$21/UK£4.80–UK£10). AE, DC, MC, V. Mon–Fri 11:30am–2:30pm and 5:30pm–9:30pm (10pm on Fri); Sat 11am–10pm; Sun 11am–9:30pm.

On AquA Restaurant & Bar CONTEMPORARY With ocean views and fantastic food, you could not find a better place than this for a long lunch or an intimate dinner. A 200m (660 ft.) walk from the main street will bring you to one of Airlie Beach's newest restaurants, opened in 2006 by one of the region's best chefs, Damien Orth. Focusing on seasonal produce, Damian is serving up such delights as Tasmanian salmon filet on local mud crab–infused mash with wilted baby spinach, green beans, and a champagne brie cream, or charred Burdekin pork cutlet on Mediterranean roasted vegetables with a fig compote and salsa verde. Save room for a "summer berry orgy"—that's a wild berry fonde suisse with caramel shards and a basil-infused orange reduction—or perhaps the Aussie-inspired gum-leaf-infused crème brûlée.

Shute Harbour Rd., Airlie Beach. ✆ **07/4948 AQUA (2782).** Reservations recommended. Main courses A$29–A$35 (US$23–US$28/UK£12–UK£14). AE, DC, MC, V. Open for dinner Wed–Sun.

THE WHITSUNDAY ISLAND RESORTS

There are about 10 resorts of varying degrees of splendor; accommodations range from positively plush to comfortably midrange to downright old-fashioned.

VERY EXPENSIVE

Hayman ★★★ This is the most luxurious, glitzy, and glamorous resort in Australia. And a A$30-million (US$24-million/UK£12-million) redevelopment in 2003 made it even more so. Check-in is done over a glass of bubbly aboard the resort's sleek launch, which meets you at Hamilton Island Airport. On arrival, you won't take long to find your way through the open-air sandstone lanais, cascading ponds, and tropical foliage to the fabulous hexagonal complex of swimming pools by the sea. Despite the luxury, Hayman is relaxed. Dress is beachwear by day, smart casual at night (pack something elegant for dinner, if you wish). An impressive lineup of activities is available, and it's probably fair to say the staff at Hayman can organize almost anything you desire.

While Hayman is renowned for the antiques, artworks, and fine objets d'art gracing its public areas, the accommodations are welcoming. Every room, suite, villa, and penthouse has a balcony or terrace, bathrobes, and valet service (and butler service in the penthouses). Pool Wing rooms with marble floors and bathrooms and tropically elegant furnishings have views over the pool, and to the sea from the third and fourth floors. Lagoon Wing rooms overlook a lagoon and have sea views from the third floor. The resort has new Lagoon rooms, suites and penthouses, 16 Retreat Rooms (each with private veranda, open patios, and outdoor rinse showers), a Jacuzzi, and a contemporary beachfront restaurant. For even greater privacy, the **Beach Villa** has a private Balinese-style courtyard, walled gardens, a private infinity plunge pool, and personalized concierge service. The latest addition to the facilities in 2006 is **Spa Chakra Hayman,** which has 13 treatment rooms, two relaxation lounges including a meditation suite, a hydrotherapy area, saunas, and steam rooms.

Hayman Island (33km/20 miles from Shute Harbour), Great Barrier Reef, QLD 4801. ✆ **1800/075 175** in Australia, 800/745-8883 in the U.S. and Canada, 0800/1010-1111 in the U.K. and Ireland, 0800/44 1016 in New Zealand (Leading Hotels of the World), 02/8272 7070 (Sydney sales office), or 07/4940 1234 (the island). Fax 02/8272 7010 (Sydney sales office) or 07/4940 1567 (the island). www.hayman.com.au. 228 units. A$665–A$1,150 (US$532–US$920/UK£266–UK£460) double; A$2,200 (US$1,760/UK£880) suite; A$2,800–A$4,500 (US$2,240–US$3,600/UK£1,120–UK£1,800) penthouse; A$3,600 (US$2,880/UK£1,440) Beach Villa. 2-night minimum and 10% surcharge Dec 24–Jan 7. Children under 13 stay free in parent's room; A$140 (US$112/UK£56) child over 12 sharing parent's room; 50% of room rate for child under 13 in adjoining room. Dining for children 5–12 half price. Ask about packages. AE, DC, MC, V. Resort launch meets all flights at Hamilton Island Airport for the 55-min. transfer. Helicopter and seaplane transfers available. **Amenities:** 4 restaurants; 2 bars; 3 pools (1 saltwater, 2 heated freshwater); beachside 9-hole golf putting green; 5 lit tennis courts (w/ball machine and coaching); extensive health club; spa; outdoor Jacuzzi; watersports (including parasailing; water-skiing; windsurfing; catamarans; dive center offering dive day trips, courses, and gear rental); daily kids' club (ages 5–14), day care for younger kids; game room; concierge; tour desk; business center; shopping arcade; salon; 24-hr. room service; babysitting; laundry service; dry cleaning. *In room:* A/C, TV w/free and pay movies, fax, minibar, fridge, coffeemaker, hair dryer, iron, safe.

Peppers Palm Bay ★ A A$7-million (US$5.6-million/UK£2.8-million) upgrade in 2001 transformed this Long Island hideaway, giving its beachfront *bures* (a kind of hut common in Polynesia) a glamorous Balinese style, with new decks and furnishings. The dining and bar area overlooks the gorgeous pool area, which is surrounded by timber decking, and a day spa is one of the attractions. This is a private and romantic spot, with no phone, radio, television, or air-conditioning in the rooms, but each veranda has a hammock. A recent addition is Platinum House, a luxury two-bedroom house on the hill behind the bures. Each bedroom has its own private entry and bathroom, and features a separate lounge with large plasma TVs and stereo. A wide wraparound deck has views of the Whitsunday Passage. For those who want to be active, there are non-motorized watersports such as kayaks available.

Palm Bay, Long Island (16km/10 miles southeast of Shute Harbour), Whitsunday Islands (P.M.B. 28), Mackay, QLD 4741. ✆ **1800/095 025** in Australia, or 07/4946 9233. Fax 07/4946 9309. www.peppers.com.au. 21 units. A$460 (US$368/UK£184) double cabin; A$658 (US$526/UK£263) double bure; A$777 (US$622/UK£311) 2-bedroom bungalow; A$1,199 (US$959/UK£480) house. Extra person (aged 13 and over) A$100 (US$80/UK£40) per night. Rates include breakfast. Ask about packages. AE, DC, MC, V. Fantasea Cruises (✆ **1800/650 851** in Australia, or 07/4946 5111) launches transfers from Hamilton Island Airport; water taxi transfers available from Shute Harbour. **Amenities:** Restaurant and bar; outdoor pool; lit tennis court; Jacuzzi; watersports; tour desk; spa; coin-op laundry; laundry service; dry cleaning. *In room:* Ceiling fan, minibar, coffeemaker, hair dryer, iron, no phone.

South Long Island Nature Lodge ★★★ No glass in your windows, no locks on your doors, no telephone in your room. And you don't need any of them. This environmentally sensitive lodge was designed to show off the Whitsundays' natural beauty with minimal impact on it. Tucked in a cove under towering hoop pines and palms, it appeals to people who want to explore the wilderness in comfort, without the crowds, noisy watersports, or artificial atmosphere of a resort. Wildlife abounds, including wallabies and abundant birdlife. No ferries or cruise boats stop here and the lodge is inaccessible to day-trippers. A maximum of 14 guests stay in 10 smart cabins—refurbished in mid-2006—facing the sea, each with a modern bathroom, and private deck facing the sea. Solar power rules, so there is no air-conditioning or TVs, hair dryers, irons, or mobile phone reception (there is one public phone). Social life centers on an open-sided gazebo by the beach, equipped with a natural-history library and CDs, where everyone dines together on fabulous meals whipped up by your private chef and swaps stories of their travels. Access is only by a short but stunning helicopter flight from Hamilton Island. Sounds like heaven? It's close.

Daily excursions include sailing on the lodge's gleaming 10m (33-ft.) catamaran, sea kayaking the mangroves to spot giant green sea turtles (which are common around the lodge), snorkeling the fringing reef on uninhabited islands, or bushwalking to a magical milkwood grove no one else knows about. Or you may prefer to just laze in a hammock or head off with a free sea kayak and snorkel gear. A half-day helicopter tour to the Outer Reef is available for an extra A$600 (US$480/UK£240) per person. This tour is exclusively for lodge guests; you will be flown to Fantasea's Reefworld pontoon in the early morning before the boat loads of tourists arrive. This is an exclusive experience not available to the general public. Guests can spend an hour and a half snorkeling the spectacular coral and fish surrounding the pontoon.

Paradise Bay, Long Island (16km/10 miles southeast of Shute Harbour), Whitsunday Islands (P.O. Box 842), Airlie Beach, QLD 4802. ✆ **07/4946 9777.** Fax 07/4946 9777. www.southlongisland.com. 10 units, all with shower only. A$2,950 (US$2,360/UK£1,180) per person for a minimum 5–night stay. A$400 (US$320/UK£160) per person extra nights. No single supplement. Rates include all meals, helicopter transfers from Hamilton Island Airport, daily excursions, and equipment. MC, V. Children under 14 not accepted. *In room:* Fridge, coffeemaker, no phone.

EXPENSIVE

Daydream Island Resort ★★ Kids One of the Whitsundays' oldest resorts is now one of Australia's most extensive and modern spa resorts. Daydream Island has a mixed clientele consisting of families and those seeking pampering and luxury. Features such as the outdoor cinema and kids' club have always made it popular with families, but the 16 therapy rooms at the **Rejuvenation Spa** appeal to those who are seeking one of the most sophisticated and well-equipped health spas in Australia. The state-of-the-art spa has an in-house naturopath and a range of computerized health analyses using equipment and tests usually found only in clinics in Europe and the United States, such as iridology and measurement of vitamin and mineral imbalances and antioxidant levels. Rooms are large, smart, and comfortable, with uninterrupted ocean views. The "village" at the southern end of the island, a short stroll along the boardwalk from the resort, has shops, cafes, a pool and bar, a water-activities center, and a tavern serving bistro-style meals. A rainforest walk stretches almost the entire length of the kilometer-long (just over half a mile) island; other activities include snorkeling, sailboarding, jet-skiing, parasailing, coral viewing, reef fishing, diving and dive school, tennis, volleyball, and minigolf.

Daydream Island (40km/25 miles northeast of Shute Harbour), Whitsunday Islands (P.M.B. 22), Mackay, QLD 4741. ✆ **07/4948 8488.** Fax 07/4948 8499. www.daydreamisland.com. 296 units. A$330–A$450 (US$264–US$360/UK£132–UK£180) double; A$495–A$801 (US$396–US$641/UK£198–UK£321) suite; A$594–A$695 (US$475–US$556/UK£238–278) family suite. Children under 15 stay free in parent's room with existing bedding. Ask about packages. AE, MC, V. Fantasea Cruises (✆ **1800/650 851** in Australia, or 07/4946 5111) provides launch transfers from Shute Harbour (15 min.) and from Long Island, South Molle, and Hamilton Island. Cruise Whitsundays (✆ 07/4946 4662) also offers launch transfers from Shute Harbour and Hamilton Island to Daydream. **Amenities:** 3 restaurants; 3 bars; 3 freshwater outdoor pools (1 heated); 2 lit tennis courts; 3 Jacuzzis; watersports equipment; tour desk; coin-op laundry. *In room:* A/C, TV w/pay movies and PlayStation, dataport, minibar, coffeemaker, hair dryer, iron.

Hamilton Island ★★ Kids More a vacation village than a single resort, Hamilton has the widest range of activities, accommodations styles, and restaurants of any Great Barrier Reef island resort. Thanks to a A$80-million (US$64-million/UK£32-million) refurbishment over the past 5 years, the place is looking fresh. Accommodations choices are extralarge rooms and suites in the high-rise hotel; high-rise one-bedroom apartments; Polynesian-style bungalows in tropical gardens (ask for one away from the road for real privacy); and glamorous rooms in the two-story, adults-only Beach Club (with minimalist decor, a personal "host" to cater to every whim, and private restaurant, lounge, and pool for exclusive use of Beach Club guests); as well as one-, two-, three-, and four-bedroom apartments and villas. The best sea views are from the second-floor Beach Club rooms, from floors 5 to 18 of the Reef View Hotel, and from most apartments and villas. The hotel and Beach Club have concierge service. In-room amenities vary depending on your accommodations choice (for example, apartments have kitchens), so check when booking.

On one side of the island is a marina village with cafes, restaurants, shops, and a yacht club. On the other are the accommodations, a large free-form pool and swim-up bar, and the curve of Catseye Beach. Hamilton offers a huge range of watersports, fishing trips, cruises, speedboat rides, go-karts, a "wire flyer" flying-fox hang glider, a pistol/clay target/rifle range, minigolf, an aquatic driving range, beach barbecue safaris, hiking trails, a wildlife sanctuary where you can cuddle a koala or hold a baby crocodile, and an extensive daily activities program. Because a steep hill splits the resort, the best way to get around is on the free bus service which operates on three loops around the island from 7am to 11pm, or by golf buggy (A$40/US$32/UK£16 per hour or A$80/US$64/UK£32 for 24 hr.). To get away from the main resort area, hit the beach or the hiking trails—most of the 750-hectare (1,853-acre) island is virgin bushland. The biggest drawback is that just about every activity costs extra (and it's usually not cheap), so you are constantly adding to your bill.

Hamilton Island (16km/10 miles southeast of Shute Harbour), Whitsunday Islands, QLD 4803. © **13 73 33** in Australia, 02/9433 3333 (Sydney reservations office), or 07/4946 9999 (the island). Fax 02/9433 0488 (Sydney reservations office), or 07/4946 8888 (the island). www.hamiltonisland.com.au. 820 units, some with shower only. A$299–A$365 (US$239–US$292/UK£120–UK£146) Palm Bungalow or Palm Terrace; A$277–A$458 (US$222–US$366/UK£111–UK£183) hotel double; A$378–A$458 (US$302–US$366/UK£151–183) suite. A$655–A$740 (US$524–US$592/UK£328–296) Beach Club double. A$570–A$645 (US$456–US$516/UK£228–UK£258) Whitsunday Holiday Apartments. Standard self-catering accommodations (4-night minimum): A$493 (US$394/UK£197) 1-bedroom; A$573 (US$458/UK£229) 2-bedroom; A$625 (US$500/UK£250) 3-bedroom. Superior self-catering accommodations: A$578 (US$462/UK£231) 1-bedroom; A$658 (US$526/UK£263) 2-bedroom; A$737 (US$590/UK£295) 3-bedroom; A$669–A$817 (US$535–US$654/UK£268–UK£327) 4-bedroom. Deluxe self-catering accommodations: A$597–A$743 (US$478–US$594/UK£239–UK£297) 2-bedroom; A$675–A$822 (US$540–US$658/UK£270–UK£329) 3-bedroom; A$762–A$923 (US$610–US$738/UK£305–UK£369) 4-bedroom. Luxury self-catering accommodations: A$1,221–A$1,576 (US$977–US$1,261/UK£489–UK£631) 3-bedroom. Minimum 4-night stay for all self-catering accommodations. Children 14 years and under stay free in parent's room using existing bedding and eat free from kids' menu at some restaurants before 7pm (not applicable to Hamilton Island Holiday Properties guests). Rates include airport transfers. Ask about packages for stays of 4 nights or more. AE, DC, MC, V. Airlines fly into Hamilton Island Airport. Fantasea Cruises (© **1800/650 851** in Australia, or 07/4946 5111) provides launch transfers from Shute Harbour and most other islands. No children in Beach Club. **Amenities:** 10 restaurants; 7 bars; 7 outdoor pools; minigolf and driving range; lit tennis courts; health club; extensive range of watersports and activities; child-care center for kids from 6 weeks to 14 years (in 3 groups); tour desk; business center; shopping arcade; salon; limited room service; massage; babysitting; coin-op laundry; laundry service (hotel only). *In room:* A/C, TV, fax, minibar, coffeemaker, hair dryer, iron, safe.

MODERATE

Hook Island Wilderness Resort This humble collection of cabins and campsites on a white sandy beach is one of the few really affordable island resorts on the Great Barrier Reef. That makes it popular with backpackers and anybody who just wants to dive, rent canoes, play beach volleyball, visit the underwater observatory, hike, fish in the four-person flat-bottom boat, laze in the pool and Jacuzzi, or chill out. Good snorkeling is footsteps from shore, and the resort's dive center conducts first-time and regular dives off the beach. Hook is a national park and the second-largest Whitsunday island. The cabins are very basic, with beds or bunks sleeping six or eight. All come with fresh bed linens; bring your own bath towels. A store sells essentials for campers, but the camp kitchen is not available to guests staying in cabins or bunkhouses.

Hook Island (40km/25 miles northeast of Shute Harbour), Whitsunday Islands (P.M.B. 23), Mackay, QLD 4741. © **07/4946 9380.** Fax 07/4946 9470. www.hookislandresort.com. 20 tent sites, 6 10-bed dormitories, 8 cabins (4 with bathroom, shower only). A$100 (US$80/UK£40) cabin without bathroom double; extra adult A$45 (US$36/UK£18), extra child 2–18 A$25 (US$20/UK£10). A$140 (US$112/UK£56) cabin with bathroom double; extra person A$65 (US$52/UK£26), extra child A$25 (US$20/UK£10). Dorm bed A$35 (US$28/UK£14) adult, A$25 (US$20/UK£10) child 2–18. Tent site A$25 (US$20/UK£10) per adult, A$15 (US$12/UK£6) per child. Ask about packages. MC, V. Transfers from mainland A$50 (US$40/UK£20) per person, round-trip. Boat leaves Shute Harbour 9am, Hook Island 2pm. Book through resort. **Amenities:** Restaurant; bar; outdoor pool; Jacuzzi; watersports equipment (snorkel gear, canoes, sea kayaks); tour desk. *In room:* A/C, minifridge, coffeemaker.

6 The Capricorn Coast & the Southern Reef Islands

South of the Whitsundays, the Bruce Highway travels through rural country until it hits the beaches of the Sunshine Coast north of Brisbane. It may not be the tourism heartland of the state, but there's plenty to discover. The most spectacular of the Great Barrier Reef islands, Heron Island, is off the coast from Gladstone. Heron's reefs are a source of enchantment for divers and snorkelers; its waters boast 21 dive sites. In summer giant turtles nest on its beaches, and in winter humpback whales cruise by.

North of Gladstone are Rockhampton and the Capricorn Coast, named after the tropic of Capricorn that runs through it. Rockhampton is also a steppingstone to the resort island of Great Keppel. The reefs and islands off Rockhampton are not a commonly visited part of the Great Barrier Reef, yet they offer some good dive sites, most of them not far out to sea. To the south, off the small town of Bundaberg, lies another tiny coral cay, Lady Elliot Island, which is a nesting site for tens of thousands of seabirds and has a first-rate fringing reef. Two little-known attractions in Bundaberg are its good shore scuba diving and a loggerhead turtle rookery that operates in summer on the beach. Farther south lies the world's largest sand island, the World Heritage–listed Fraser Island, which can be negotiated only on foot or by four-wheel-drive (see section 7 in this chapter).

ROCKHAMPTON: THE BEEF CAPITAL

1,055km (654 miles) S of Cairns; 638km (396 miles) N of Brisbane

You may hear Queenslanders talk dryly about "Rockvegas." Don't be fooled. "Rocky" is the unofficial capital of the sprawling beef-cattle country inland, and the gateway to Great Keppel Island, which boasts some of the few inexpensive island retreats in Queensland, but it bears no resemblance to Las Vegas. Heritage buildings line the Fitzroy River, where barramundi await keen fishermen. At least once a month, on a Saturday night, at the Great Western Hotel, Stanley and Denison streets (✆ **07/4922 3888**), you can see bull-riding cowboys take to the rodeo ring to test their skills against local Brahma bulls.

ESSENTIALS

GETTING THERE Rockhampton is on the Bruce Highway, a 3½-hour drive south of Mackay, and about 90 minutes north of Gladstone.

QantasLink (✆ **13 13 13** in Australia) has flights from Brisbane, Mackay, and Gladstone. **Virgin Blue** (✆ **13 67 89** in Australia) flies direct from Brisbane and Sydney. **Jetstar** (✆ **13 15 38** in Australia) flies from Brisbane.

Queensland Rail (✆ **1300 131 722** in Queensland; www.traveltrain.com.au) trains stop at Rockhampton daily. The trip from Brisbane takes just 7 hours on the high-speed Tilt Train; the fare is A$102 (US$82/UK£41) in economy class and A$151 (US$121/UK£60) in business class.

Greyhound Australia (✆ **13 14 99** in Australia) serves Rockhampton on its many daily runs between Brisbane and Cairns. The fare is A$106 (US$85/UK£42) from Brisbane (trip time: 12 hr.) and A$164 (US$131/UK£66) from Cairns (trip time: 18 hr.).

The Central Queensland Coast

VISITOR INFORMATION Drop by the **Capricorn Tourism** information center, at the city's southern entrance on Gladstone Road at the Capricorn Spire (✆ **1800/ 676 701** in Australia, or 07/4927 2055; www.capricorntourism.com.au). It's open daily from 9am to 5pm.

GETTING AROUND **Avis** (✆ **07/4927 3344**), **Budget** (✆ **07/4922 8064**), **Hertz** (✆ **07/4927 8700**), and **Thrifty** (✆ **07/4927 8755**) have offices in Rockhampton. The local bus is **Sunbus** (✆ **07/4936 2133**).

EXPLORING: CAVERNS, ABORIGINAL CULTURE & MORE

The **Capricorn Caves** ★ (✆ **07/4934 2883;** wwwcapricorncaves.com.au), 23km (14 miles) north of Rockhampton at Olsen's Caves Road, off the Bruce Highway, have been a popular attraction in this part of the world ever since Norwegian pioneer John Olsen stumbled upon them in 1882. The limestone caves originated in an ancient coral reef (380 million years old) and today are a maze of small tunnels and larger chambers. The 1-hour tour, which winds through large caverns with stalactite and stalagmite formations before entering the 20m-high (66-ft.) Cathedral Cave, is A$20 (US$16/UK£8) for adults, A$10 (US$8/UK£4) for children 5 to 15. It departs daily (except Dec 25) on the hour from 9am to 4pm (closing time is 5pm). Spelunkers over age 16 can squeeze through tunnels and chimneys and rock climb on a 3-hour adventure tour that costs A$65 (US$52/UK£26); minimum of two required. Book 24 hours ahead for this. From December 1 to January 10, you can catch the Summer Solstice light cave on a tour departing every morning at 11am. On the longest day of the year, the sun moves slowly over the tropic of Capricorn, and a ray of pure light pours through a hole in the limestone caves. It's known as the Summer Solstice phenomenon and takes place at the only time of year when the sun is directly over the tropic of Capricorn. The caves are also home to thousands of small insectivorous bats, which leave the cave at sunset to feed. Plan enough time here to walk the 30-minute dry rainforest trail, watch the video on bats in the interpretive center, and feed the wild kangaroos. If you want to stay, a motor-home park and campground are attached. Bus tours operate from Rockhampton; contact the Caves for details.

The **Dreamtime Cultural Centre** (✆ **07/4936 1655;** www.dreamtimecentre.com.au), on the Bruce Highway opposite the Yeppoon turnoff, 6km (3¾ miles) north of town, showcases Aboriginal culture. There's a sandstone cave replica, a display on the dugong (manatee) culture of the Torres Strait Islanders, and an Aboriginal crafts shop. The center is open Monday to Friday from 10am to 3:30pm. Admission, including a tour, is A$13 (US$10/UK£5.20) for adults, A$9 (US$7.20/UK£3.60) for seniors, A$6 (US$4.80/UK£2.40) for children, and A$11 (US$8.80/UK£4.40) for students and backpackers. Tours of burial sites and rock art, with didgeridoo demonstrations and boomerang-throwing, start at 10:30am.

Rockhampton has two free public botanic gardens, both nice for a stroll and a picnic. The **Kershaw Gardens,** which display Aussie rainforest, wetland, and fragrant plants from north of the 30th parallel, also have a monorail and a pioneer-style slab hut where Devonshire teas are served. Enter off Charles Street. The **Rockhampton Botanic Gardens** (✆ **07/4922 1654**), established in 1869, are quite lovely. Admission is free to the small zoo inside the grounds, which features 'roos, koalas, lorikeets, cassowaries, and a range of other creatures, including—rather bizarrely—two rather sad looking chimpanzees in a concrete enclosure. The gardens are open 6am to 6pm daily, the zoo daily from 8am to 5pm. Enter off Ann Street or Spencer Street.

WHERE TO STAY

Rydges Capricorn Resort ★ The 20km (13 miles) of unbroken beach that fronts this resort—and the fact that it is the only resort of any size or style in this region—are reasons enough to visit. The resort is about 9km (5½ miles) from the pretty seaside town of Yeppoon, about 45km (28 miles) north of Rockhampton Airport. Open since 1986, the resort was built and is owned by Japanese businessman Yohachiro Iwasaki, and you will still hear the locals refer to it as "the Iwasaki Resort" despite its several changes of name over the years. Now showing its age a little, the resort is nevertheless cheerful and pleasant, and the rooms are spacious.

The best of the three accommodations blocks is The Palms, with views over the beach and out to Great Keppel Island. The main resort block is dominated by one of the largest freshwater swimming pools in the Southern Hemisphere, popular with visiting local families, especially on weekends. Accommodations vary: Some suites and all apartments have kitchenettes, hotel rooms have minibars, and two-bedroom apartments and Capricorn suites with kitchens have a washing machine and dryer. Set in 8,910 hectares (22,000 acres) of bushland, the resort also has extensive wetlands teeming with bird life. Wetlands tours are available for a fee, as are horseback riding, land yachting, fishing, canoeing, clay-pigeon shooting, WaveRunners, and rifle shooting. This is not the place for a quiet getaway—it is popular with large and sometimes noisy conference groups—but there are lots of activities, and it may be just the place to break up your coastal trek.

Farnborough Rd. (P.O. Box 350), Yeppoon, QLD 4703. ✆ **1300/857 922** in Australia, or 07/4925 2525. www.rydges.com. 281 units. A$320 (US$256/UK£128) double; A$370 (US$296/UK£148) junior suite; A$395 (US$316/UK£158) junior suite with kitchenette; A$445 (US$356/UK£178) Capricorn suite; A$470 (US$376/UK£188) Capricorn suite with kitchenette; A$440 (US$352/UK£176) 1-bedroom apt; A$490 (US$392/UK£196) 2-bedroom apt. Free crib. Packages, including golf packages, available year-round. Transfers from airport or train station A$20 (US$16/UK£8) adults, A$10 (US$8/UK£4) child 2–12. Rates include watersports and some other activities. AE, DC, MC, V. Free covered parking. **Amenities:** 4 restaurants; 2 bars; outdoor freshwater pool w/adjoining heated beach-style pool; 2 18-hole golf courses; 4 lit tennis courts; exercise room; outdoor Jacuzzi; sauna; extensive watersports and other activities; bike rental; free daytime kids' club (fee for evening sessions); playground; game room for children over 14; concierge; tour desk; car-rental desk; business center; salon; limited room service; in-room and poolside massage; babysitting; laundry service; coin-op laundry; dry cleaning. *In room:* A/C, TV w/pay movies, dataport, fridge, coffeemaker, hair dryer, iron.

GREAT KEPPEL ISLAND

15km (9½ miles) E of Rockhampton

This 1,454-hectare (3,591-acre) island is home to one major resort, for the 18-to-35s, and a couple of smaller, family-oriented resorts. You can stay at one of the resorts or take a day trip from the mainland and pay to use many of the facilities, including watersports equipment, pools, and food outlets. Seventeen beaches on the island are accessible by walking trails or dinghy (which you can rent). The shallow waters and fringing reef make the island a good choice for beginner divers; experienced divers will see corals, sea snakes, turtles, and rays. If you stay overnight, you will most likely be rewarded with one of the spectacular sunsets for which the island is famous.

GETTING THERE **Freedom Fast Cats** (✆ **1800/336 244** in Australia, or 07/4933 6244) operates launches that make the 30-minute crossing from Rosslyn Bay Harbour, about 55km (34 miles) east of Rockhampton, three times daily. The round-trip costs A$37 (US$30/UK£15) for adults, A$19 (US$15/UK£7.60) for children 4 to 14, and A$93 (US$74/UK£37) for a family of four. A water taxi will cost around A$60 (US$48/UK£24).

From Rockhampton, take the Capricorn Coast scenic drive Route 10 to Emu Park and follow the signs to Rosslyn Bay Harbour. If you're coming to Rockhampton from the north, the scenic drive turnoff is just north of the city, and from there it's 46km (29 miles) to the harbor. You can leave your car in covered storage at **Great Keppel Island Security Car Park,** 422 Scenic Hwy., near the harbor (✆ **07/4933 6670**), for A$7 to A$9 (US$5.60–US$7.20/UK£2.80–UK£3.60) per day.

Rothery's Coaches (✆ **07/4922 4320**) runs from Kern Arcade on Bolsover Street in Rockhampton to Rosslyn Bay Harbour, and back, twice a day. You can request pickup from the airport, train station, or your hotel. One-way fares from town are A$9.75 (US$7.80/UK£3.90) for adults, A$4.90 (US$3.90/UK£1.95) for children aged 4 to 15, A$24 (US$19/UK£9.60) for a family of four. The one-way airport fare is A$19 (US$15/UK£7.60) for adults, A$9.65 (US$7.70/UK£3.85) for children, and A$48 (US$38/UK£19) for families of four. Round-trip fares cost double.

Guests at Great Keppel Island Resort can take a charter flight from Rockhampton airport on a light plane, which meets most scheduled flights (three times a day) and takes about 20 minutes. The cost is A$55 (US$44/UK£22) per person one-way, but a minimum of two passengers is required, so if you are alone you may have to buy two tickets. Special charter flights can be organized at a time suitable to the individual

Great Keppel Island

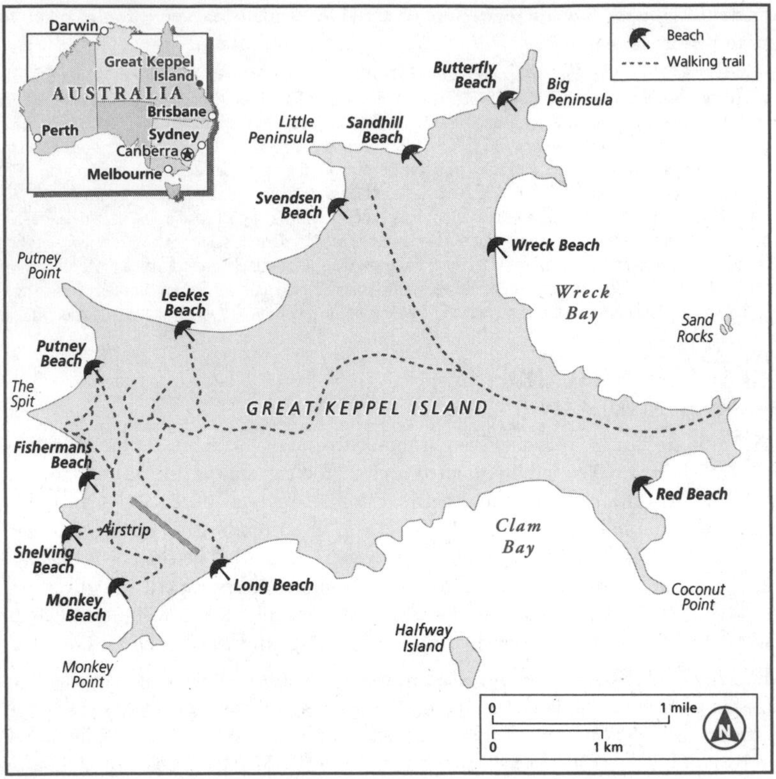

guests, at a cost of A$120 (US$96/UK£48) per person one-way (minimum of two). Luggage restrictions apply and vary depending on aircraft size and number of guests traveling. Bookings can be made through the resort (see below) or ✆ **1800/245 658.**

VISITOR INFORMATION Pick up information about accommodations and activities on Great Keppel at the **Capricorn Tourism** information center (at the Capricorn Spire), on Gladstone Road, Rockhampton (✆ **1800/676 701** in Australia, or 07/4927 2055; www.capricorntourism.com.au). It's open daily from 9am to 5pm. You will also find some information at the ferry terminal at Rosslyn Bay Harbour.

WHERE TO STAY& DINE

Great Keppel Island Holiday Village *Value* Great Keppel Island Holiday Village is located in a garden setting less than a minute's walk to two great swimming beaches. Accommodations include six-bed dormitory rooms; twin or double rooms; twin or double canvas tents erected on timber decks and en-suite cabins, sleeping four. Also available are two self-contained houses suitable for families of up to six people. The private two-bedroom Dolphin House has a queen-size bed in one room and a double bed and bunks in the other. The two-story, solar powered Keppel House is set among large shade trees on the southern end of Fisherman's Beach, and sleeps up to six. Verandas off the spacious lounge room offer plenty of shade, and there is a barbecue outside. All linen is provided (except towels for Keppel House) as well as snorkeling gear to use during your stay. There is a fully equipped communal kitchen for those in the tents and cabins, with gas stoves, refrigerators, and microwave available, as well as a barbecue. Basic grocery items such as milk, bread, and soft drinks, and some food items are available to buy. Kayaking and snorkeling tours are offered.

Great Keppel Island, off Rockhampton, QLD 4700. © **1800 180 235** in Australia, or 07/4939 8655. www.gkiholidayvillage.com.au. 19 units. A$33 (US$26/UK£13) dorm bed per person. A$76 (US$61/UK£30) tent per person twin/double, A$54 (US$43/UK£22) single. A$120 (US$96/UK£48) cabin (all with bathroom, shower only) twin or double; additional person A$20 (US$16/UK£8) extra. A$210 (US$168/UK£84) houses for up to 4 people, A$20 (US$16/UK£8) extra person. MC, V. **Amenities:** Watersports rentals. *In room:* TV (houses only), fridge, coffeemaker (in cabins), ceiling fan.

Great Keppel Island Resort There are plenty of reasons why Great Keppel Island Resort has been a popular holiday destination for Aussies for generations—but the main one is probably its versatility. It's the kind of place that appeals to—and tries to cater for—everyone. Great Keppel made its name in Australia in the '70s, and has undergone many incarnations since then. In 2005, it was completely refurbished and some new family-friendly features introduced, such as a kids' club for 3- to 12-year-olds. It offers about 40 water- and land-based activities, and about 25 of them, including catamarans, paddle-skis, and windsurfers, are free. Activities that cost extra include scuba diving, water-skiing, wakeboarding, coral cruises, jet-skiing, sunset champagne sails, and camel treks, to name only a few. There are three types of accommodations: Hillside Villas with sea or bush views, garden rooms, and beachfront units—my pick because of their location.

Great Keppel Island, QLD 4700. © **1800/245 658** in Australia, or 07/4939 5044. Fax 07/4939 1775. www.greatkeppelresort.com.au. 181 units. A$147 (US$118/UK£59) double Garden View room; A$177 (US$142/UK£71) Beachfront rooms; A$197 (US$158/UK£79) double hillside villas. Ask about packages. AE, DC, MC, V. **Amenities:** 3 restaurants; 3 bars; 5 outdoor pools; 9-hole golf course; 3 lit tennis courts; gym; 2 Jacuzzis; kids' club (A$20/US$16/UK£8 per 4-hr. session); extensive watersports equipment and rental; tour desk; massage; coin-op laundry; nonsmoking rooms. *In room:* A/C (villas only), TV, fridge, coffeemaker, hair dryer, iron, ceiling fan.

GLADSTONE: GATEWAY TO HERON ISLAND

550km (341 miles) N of Brisbane; 1,162km (720 miles) S of Cairns

The industrial port town of Gladstone is the departure point for beautiful Heron Island. It is also home to the delectable mud crab, best savored over a glass of wine at the award-winning **Flinders Restaurant** (© **07/4972 8322**). About 25km (16 miles) south of the town (but off the Bruce Hwy.) are the twin beach towns of Boyne Island and Tannum Sands, which are worth the detour.

ESSENTIALS

GETTING THERE & GETTING AROUND Gladstone is on the coast 21km (13 miles) off the Bruce Highway. **QantasLink** (book through Qantas) has daily flights from Brisbane (trip time: 75 min.), Rockhampton, and Mackay.

Queensland Rail (© **1300/131 722** in Queensland; www.traveltrain.com.au) operates trains to Gladstone from Brisbane and Cairns most days. The economy fare on the high-speed Tilt Train from Brisbane (trip time: 6 hr.) is A$92 (US$74/UK£37); from Cairns (trip time: 17½ hr.) it is A$243 (US$194/UK£97). Fares from Cairns on the *Sunlander* (trip time: 20 hr.) range from A$167 (US$134/UK£67) for a seat to A$663 (US$530/UK£265) for a sleeper in the luxury Queenslander Class.

Greyhound Australia (✆ **13 14 99** in Australia) operates daily coaches to Gladstone on the Brisbane-Cairns run. The fare is A$97 (US$78/UK£39) from Brisbane (trip time: 10 hr.), A$180 (US$144/UK£72) from Cairns (trip time: 20 hr.).

Avis (✆ 07/4978 2633), **Budget** (✆ 07/4972 8488), **Hertz** (✆ 07/4978 6899), and **Thrifty** (✆ 07/4972 5999) have offices in Gladstone.

VISITOR INFORMATION The **Gladstone Visitor Information Centre** is in the ferry terminal at Gladstone Marina, Bryan Jordan Drive, Gladstone, QLD 4680 (✆ **07/4972 9000;** www.gladstonholidays.info). It's open from 8:30am to 5pm Monday through Friday, and from 9am to 5pm Saturday and Sunday.

WHERE TO STAY

Country Plaza International This four-level hotel in the center of town runs a free shuttle to the wharf for guests bound for Heron Island. Gladstone's largest and best hotel, it caters primarily to business travelers, so it has ample facilities—spacious rooms with balconies, modern bathrooms, an upscale seafood restaurant, and a pool and sun deck. Most rooms have views over the port or the city. There are six three-bedroom apartments and one two-bedroom apartment.

100 Goondoon St., Gladstone, QLD 4680. ✆ **07/4972 4499.** Fax 07/4972 4921. www.plazahotels.com.au/gladstone.htm. 107 units. A$140 (US$112/UK£70) double; A$150–A$160 (US$120–US$128/UK£60–UK£64) apt. Rates include transfers from airport, coach terminal, marina, and train station. AE, DC, MC, V. Free covered parking. **Amenities:** Restaurant; bar; outdoor pool; business center; 24-hr. room service; laundry service; dry cleaning. *In room:* A/C, TV w/free movies, fax, dataport, minibar, coffeemaker, hair dryer, iron.

HERON ISLAND: JEWEL OF THE REEF ★★★

72km (45 miles) NE of Gladstone

The difference between Heron and other islands is that once there, you have no need to travel farther to the Reef. Step off the beach and you enter magnificent fields of coral that seem to stretch for miles. And the myriad life forms that abound here are accessible to everyone through diving, snorkeling, or reef walks at low tide, or aboard a semisubmersible vessel that allows you to view the ocean floor without getting wet. When geologist Joseph Bette Jukes named this piece of paradise in 1843, he overlooked the turtles for which it is now famous in favor of the reef herons that abounded. There has been a resort on Heron since 1932, and in 1943 the island became a national park. It is a haven for wildlife and people, and an experience of a lifetime is almost guaranteed at any time of year. Heron is a rookery for giant green and loggerhead turtles. Resort guests gather on the beach from late November to February to watch the female turtles lay eggs, and from February to mid-April to see the hatched babies scuttle down the sand to the water. Humpback whales pass through from June through September.

Three days on Heron gives you plenty of time to see everything. The island is so small that you can walk around it at a leisurely pace in about half an hour. One of the first things to do is to take advantage of the organized activities that operate several times a day and are designed so guests can plan their own days. Snorkeling and reef walking are major occupations for visitors—if they're not diving, that is. The island is home to 21 of the world's most stunning dive sites.

Guided walks provide another way to explore the island. Walks include a visit to the island's research station. As for the reef walk, just borrow a pair of sand shoes, a balance pole, and a viewing bucket, and head off with a guide at low tide. The walk

Moments Up Close & Personal with a Turtle

The egg in my hand is warm, soft, and about the size of a Ping-Pong ball. At our feet, a giant green turtle sighs deeply as she lays a clutch of about 120 eggs in a pear-shaped chamber dug from the sand. A large tear rolls from her eye. In the distance, the wedge-tailed shearwaters call eerily to each other, backed by the sound of the ocean.

The egg-laying ritual of the turtles is central to a trip to **Heron Island** in the summer months. At night and in the early morning, small groups of people gather on the beaches to witness as the turtles lumber up the beach, dig holes in the sand, and lay their eggs. (The turtles are not easily disturbed, and you can get very close.) Every night during the season, volunteer guides from the University of Queensland research station on the island are on hand; you can watch and ask questions as the researchers tag and measure the turtles before they return to the water. The laying season runs December through February, and only one in 5,000 hatchlings will live to return in about 50 years to lay their own eggs.

Another good place to watch the turtles nesting is Mon Repos Beach, outside Bundaberg. **Mon Repos Conservation Park** is one of the two largest loggerhead-turtle rookeries in the South Pacific. The visitor center by the beach has a great display on the turtle life cycle and shows films at approximately 7:30pm daily in summer. There is a strict booking system for turtle-watching tours, to help cope with the crowds. Access to the beach is by ticket only, and you must book your visit to Mon Repos during the turtle season. Tickets are sold through the Bundaberg City Visitor Information Centre (✆ **07/4153 8888**) at 189 Bourbong St., Bundaberg. Tours start at 7pm and you will be given a time for your tour, which saves waiting around in a long queue of people. Nesting happens around high tide; hatching usually occurs between 8pm and midnight. Take a flashlight if you can, and a sweater, as it can get quite cool.

The **Mon Repos Turtle Rookery** ★ (✆ **07/4159 1652** for the visitor center) is 14km (8¾ miles) east of Bundaberg's town center. Follow Bourbong Street out of town toward Burnett Heads as it becomes Bundaberg-Bargara Road. Take the Port Road to the left and look for the Mon Repos signs to the right. During turtle nesting season (Nov to late Mar) the park and information center is open 24 hours a day. Public access to the beach is closed from 6pm to 6am. Turtle viewing tours run from 7pm until 1am daily (except for Dec 24, 25, and 31). From April to early November (when there are no turtles around) the information center is open Monday to Thursday from 7:30am to 4pm and Friday 7:30am to noon. The park is open 24 hours. Admission to the visitor center is free from April through November but when the turtles start nesting, you pay A$8.70 (US$6.95/UK£3.50) for adults, A$4.60 (US$3.70/UK£1.85) for children ages 5 to 17, or A$21 (US$17/UK£8.40) for a family.

can take up to 90 minutes, but there's no compulsion to stay; if it gets too hot, you can head to the sanctuary of your room or the shady bar area.

A fishing trip should also be on the agenda, even for the most inexperienced. The reef fish seem to just jump onto the hook, and the resort chef is happy to cook them for you for dinner!

GETTING THERE A courtesy coach meets flights from Brisbane (with connections from other cities) at Gladstone airport at 10:30am to take guests to Gladstone Marina for the launch transfer to the island; it departs 11am daily (except Dec 25). Round-trip transfers aboard the sleek 130-seater catamaran *Heron Spirit* cost A$200 (US$160/UK£80) for adults, half price for kids 3 to 14. Trip time is around 2 hours or 2 hours 30 minutes. Helicopter transfers can be arranged for A$291 (US$233/UK£116) per adult or A$145 (US$116/UK£58) per child one-way.

WHERE TO STAY ON HERON ISLAND

Heron Island Resort ★★★ Kids This lovely, low-key resort has been transformed over the past few years, and changes to the accommodations mix and cosmetics continue. The latest additions are the chic Wistari Suites, each with a private garden and veranda. But new accommodations, a revamped central complex, and a stylish, contemporary new look have not changed the focus on the outdoors. The brilliant colors of the island's surrounding water and Reef are reflected in the interiors, and everything is light-filled and breezy. Heron's central complex is equal parts grand Queenslander home and sophisticated beach house, with smart bar and lounge areas open to ocean views and sunsets. Duplex-style Turtle rooms are designed for couples or families, with a casual living area and a veranda, or you can go for greater luxury in the suites or the private beach house.

The property has a lounge with a TV, public phones (only the four Point suites and the Beach House have private phones), and Internet access. The **Aqua Soul Spa** offers double treatment rooms, therapies designed for two, and the usual spa treatments and pampering. The spa complex is in a secluded spot on the edge of the island's pisonia forests, removed from the main resort.

Heron Island, off Gladstone, QLD 4680 (Voyages, G.P.O. Box 3589, Sydney, NSW 2001). ✆ **1300/134 044** in Australia, or 02/8296 8010 (Sydney reservations office). Fax 02/9299 2103 (Sydney reservations office). www.voyages.com.au. 109 units, some with shower only. A$370 (US$296/UK£148) Turtle room double; A$440 (US$352/UK£176) Reef suite double; A$590 (US$472/UK£236) Heron Beachside suite double; A$830 (US$664/UK£332) Point suite, Wistari suite, or Beach House double. Extra adult A$58 (US$46/UK£23). Children 3–12 stay free in parent's room. Free crib. Rates include all meals and many activities. Ask about special packages. AE, DC, MC, V. No children allowed in Point and Wistari suites or Beach House. **Amenities:** Restaurant; bar; outdoor pool; 2 lit tennis courts; spa; Jacuzzi; limited watersports equipment rental; Heron Kids Junior Rangers program (ages 7–12) during Australian school vacations; game room; activities desk; babysitting; coin-op laundry. *In room:* Fridge, coffeemaker, hair dryer, iron, ceiling fan.

BUNDABERG: GATEWAY TO LADY ELLIOT ISLAND

384km (238 miles) N of Brisbane; 1,439km (892 miles) S of Cairns

The small sugar town of Bundaberg is the closest to the southernmost point of the Great Barrier Reef. If you visit the area between November and March, allow an evening to visit the Mon Repos Turtle Rookery. Divers may want to take in some of Australia's best shore diving right off Bundaberg's beaches.

GETTING THERE & GETTING AROUND Bundaberg is on the Isis Highway, about 50km (31 miles) off the Bruce Highway from Gin Gin in the north and 53km (33 miles) off the Bruce Highway from just north of Childers in the south.

QantasLink (✆ **13 13 13** in Australia) flies from Brisbane daily and from Gladstone three times a week.

Queensland Rail (✆ **1300 131 722** in Queensland; www.traveltrain.com.au) trains stop in Bundaberg every day en route between Brisbane and Cairns. The fare is A$65 (US$52/UK£26) from Brisbane in economy class or A$96 (US$77/UK£38) business class on the Tilt Train; fares range from A$179 (US$143/UK£72) for a seat to A$678 (US$542/UK£271) for a sleeping berth in luxury Queenslander Class on the *Sunlander* from Cairns. The trip takes 4½ hours from Brisbane and 8¼ hours from Cairns on the Tilt Train; the *Sunlander* takes 6¾ hours from Brisbane and 25 hours from Cairns.

Greyhound Australia (✆ **13 14 99** in Australia) stops here many times a day on runs between Brisbane and Cairns. The 6½-hour trip from Brisbane costs A$74 (US$59/UK£30). From Cairns it is a 22-hour trip, and the fare is A$200 (US$160/UK£80).

Avis (✆ 07/4152 1877), **Budget** (✆ 07/4151 1355), **Hertz** (✆ 07/4151 2099), and **Thrifty** (✆ 07/4151 6222) all have offices in Bundaberg.

VISITOR INFORMATION The **Bundaberg City Visitor Information Centre,** at 186 Bourbong St., Bundaberg, QLD 4670 (✆ **1800/308 888** in Australia, or 07/4153 8888; www.bundabergregion.org) is open Monday to Friday from 9am to 5pm and Saturday and Sunday from 9am to noon. Closed public holidays. There is another information center at 271 Bourbong St. (at Mulgrave St.), Bundaberg West.

WHAT TO SEE & DO

The best shore diving in Queensland is in Bundaberg's **Woongarra Marine Park.** It has soft and hard corals, urchins, rays, sea snakes, and 60 fish species, plus a World War II Beaufort bomber wreck. There are several scuba operators. **Dive Musgrave** (✆ **1800/552 614** in Australia; www.divemusgrave.com.au) runs 3-day, 3-night dive cruises to Lady Musgrave Island twice a week. The cruise costs A$595 (US$476/UK£238), plus reef tax of A$6 (US$4.80/UK£2.40) per day, including all meals and 8 to 10 dives. Equipment rental, including a dive computer, is A$85 (US$68/UK£34) per person.

WHERE TO STAY

Sun City Motel *Value* This basic but neat and tidy motel is a short stroll across the river from the town center. The rooms are clean and well kept, and have a ceiling fan, toaster, and tea- and coffeemaking facilities. Two family rooms have a double bed and twin bunks. Home-cooked meals can be delivered to your room or you can use the guest barbecue and outdoor dining area. Hosts Sue and Steve will pick you up from the bus, train, or airport.

11a Hinkler Ave., North Bundaberg, QLD 4670. ✆ **1800/308 888** in Australia, or 07/4152 1099. Fax 07/4153 1510. www.suncitymotel.com.au. 12 units, all with shower only. A$70 (US$56/UK£28) double; A$85 (US$68/UK£34) family room (sleeps 4). Extra adult A$12 (US$9.60/UK£4.80), extra child under 12 A$10 (US$8/UK£4). AE, DC, MC, V. Free covered parking. **Amenities:** Outdoor saltwater pool; nearby golf course; access to nearby health club; tour desk; limited room service; coin-op laundry; dry cleaning; nonsmoking rooms. *In room:* A/C, TV, fridge, coffeemaker, hair dryer, iron.

LADY ELLIOT ISLAND ★

80km (50 miles) NE of Bundaberg

The southernmost Great Barrier Reef island, Lady Elliot is a 42-hectare (104-acre) coral cay ringed by a wide, shallow lagoon filled with dazzling coral life. Reef walking, snorkeling, and diving are the main reasons people come to this coral cay, which is so small you can walk across it in 15 minutes. You may snorkel and reef walk during only the 2 to 3 hours before and after high tide, so plan your schedule accordingly. You will see dazzling corals and brilliantly colored fish, clams, sponges, urchins, and anemones. Divers will see a good range of marine life, including green and loggerhead turtles (which nest on the beach Nov–Mar). Whales pass by from June through September.

Lady Elliot is a sparse, grassy island rookery, not a lush tropical paradise, so don't expect white sand and palm trees. Some people will find it too spartan; others will relish chilling out in a beautiful, peaceful location with reef all around. Just be prepared for the smell and constant noise of those birds.

GETTING THERE You reach the island by a 30-minute flight from Bundaberg or Hervey Bay, which run three times a day. Book your air travel with your accommodations. Round-trip fares from both departure points are A$219 (US$175/UK£88) for adults and A$119 (US$95/UK£48) for children 3 to 12. There is a 10-kilogram (22-lb.) luggage limit. **Seair** (© **07/5599 4509;** www.seairpacific.com.au) operates day tours from Brisbane, the Gold Coast, and Sunshine Coast for A$599 (US$479/UK£240) adults and A$330 (US$264/UK£132) children. Prices for all day trips include flights, snorkel gear, glass-bottom-boat ride, lunch, and guided activities.

WHERE TO STAY

Lady Elliot Island Eco Resort ★ Accommodations here are fairly basic, but visitors come for the Reef, not the room. Because of the relatively low number of guests, you pretty much get the Reef to yourself. Top of the range are Island suites, which have one or two separate bedrooms, and great sea views from the deck. Most Reef rooms have a double bed and two bunks, and a deck with views through the trees to the sea. Shearwater bunk rooms sleep up to six. All room types have modern private bathrooms. The cool, spacious safari-tent ecocabins have four bunks, electric lighting, and timber floors, but share the public toilets and showers used by day guests. The limited facilities include a boutique, an education center, and a dive shop which runs both shore and boat dives, introductory dives, and rents equipment. The resort has no air-conditioning, no keys (secure storage is at the front desk), no TVs, no radio, and one public telephone. The food is basic. A low-key program of mostly free activities includes glass-bottom boat rides, badminton, guided walks, and beach volleyball.

Great Barrier Reef, off Bundaberg (P.O. Box 348), Runaway Bay, QLD 4216. © **1800/072 200** in Australia, or 07/4156 4444. Fax 07/4156 4400. www.ladyelliot.com.au. 40 units, 20 with bathroom with shower only. A$290–A$340 (US$232–US$272/UK£116–UK£136) tent cabin double; A$350–A$378 (US$280–US$302/UK£140–UK£151) Shearwater bunk room double; A$424–A$456 (US$339–US$365/UK£170–UK£183) Reef double; A$494–A$620 (US$395–US$496/UK£196–UK£248) 1-bedroom Island suite double; A$528–A$562 (US$422–US$450/UK£211–UK£225) 2-bedroom Island suite double; A$904–A$960 (US$723–US$768/UK£362–UK£384) 2-bedroom Island suite for 4. 3-night minimum Dec 24–Jan 5; 2-night minimum for suites. Ask about packages. Rates include breakfast and dinner. AE, DC, MC, V. **Amenities:** Cafe/bistro; dining room; saltwater pool; children's program (ages 3–12) during Queensland school holidays. *In room:* Ceiling or wall fans, no phone.

7 Fraser Island: Ecoadventures & Four-Wheel-Drive Fun

1,547km (959 miles) S of Cairns; 260km (161 miles) N of Brisbane; 15km (9½ miles) E of Hervey Bay

The biggest sand island in the world, this 162,000-hectare (400,140-acre) World Heritage–listed island off the central Queensland coast attracts a mix of ecotourists and Aussie fishermen. Fraser is a pristine vista of eucalyptus woodlands, dunes, clear creeks, ancient rainforest, blue lakes, ocher-colored sand cliffs, and a stunning 121km-long (75-mile) beach. For four-wheel-drive fans, Fraser's beauty lies in its absence of paved roads. On weekends when the fish are running, it's nothing to see 100 four-wheel-drives lining 75-mile Beach, which is an authorized road. Pedestrians, beware!

You'll need more than a day here to see everything and to truly appreciate how stunning this place is. Allow at least 3 days to soak it all up, and to allow for the slow pace dictated by the sandy trails that pass for roads.

ESSENTIALS

GETTING THERE Hervey (pronounced *Har*-vey) Bay is the main gateway to the island. Take the Bruce Highway to Maryborough, then the 34km (21-mile) road to Hervey Bay. From the north, turn off the highway at Torbanlea, north of Maryborough, and cut across to Hervey Bay. Allow 3 hours from the Sunshine Coast, a good 5 hours from Brisbane.

Virgin Blue (© **13 67 89** in Australia) flies direct from Sydney to Hervey Bay four times a week, with connections from Adelaide, Perth, and Melbourne. **Jetstar** (© **13 15 38** in Australia) flies direct from Sydney.

Greyhound Australia (© **13 14 99** in Australia) coaches stop in Hervey Bay on the Brisbane-Cairns-Brisbane routes. The 5-hour trip from Brisbane costs A$57 (US$46/UK£23). From Cairns, the fare is A$213 (US$170/UK£85) and the trip is almost 24 hours.

The nearest **train** station is in **Maryborough West,** 34km (20 miles) from Hervey Bay. Passengers on the high-speed **Tilt Train** (Sun–Fri) can book connecting bus service to Pialba (a suburb of Hervey Bay) through **Queensland Rail** (© **1300/131 722** in Queensland; www.traveltrain.com.au). The fare from Brisbane for the 3½-hour Tilt Train trip is A$67 (US$54/UK£27) in economy class and A$96 (US$77/UK£38) in business class, including the bus fare. Fares are A$193 (US$154/UK£77) in a seat and A$389 (US$311/UK£156) in a first-class sleeper from Cairns (trip time: just under 27 hr.). Train passengers from the north must take a courtesy shuttle from Maryborough West to Maryborough Central, then take the next available local bus to Pialba.

Guests at Kingfisher Bay Resort (p. 366) can get to the resort aboard the **Kingfisher Bay Fastcat,** which departs Urangan Boat Harbour at Hervey Bay at 8:45am, noon, 4pm, 6:30pm (7pm Fri–Sat), and 10pm. Round-trip fare for the 40-minute crossing is A$50 (US$40/UK£20) adults and A$25 (US$20/UK£10) kids 4 to 14. The resort runs a shuttle from Hervey Bay's airport and coach terminal to the harbor; the cost is A$7 (US$5.60/UK£2.80) adults, half price for kids. You can park free at the Fastcat terminal. Drive to the terminal first to unload your luggage at the Kingfisher Bay reception desk, then return to the parking lot and walk back (only 100m/328 ft.).

MI Helicopters (© **1800/600 345** in Australia, or 07/4125 1599; www.mihelicopters.com.au) provides transfers from Hervey Bay to Kingfisher Bay Resort for A$176 (US$141/UK£70) per person round-trip (minimum 2 people) as well as other parts of Fraser Island.

GETTING THERE & GETTING AROUND BY FOUR-WHEEL-DRIVE Four-wheel-drives are the only vehicle transportation on the island. Many four-wheel-drive-rental outfits are based in Hervey Bay. You must be 21 or over to rent a 4WD. You'll pay around A$200 (US$160/UK£80) a day, plus around A$20 to A$35 (US$16–US$28/UK£8–UK£14) per day to reduce the deductible (usually A$4,000/US$3,200/UK£1,600), plus a bond (typically A$500/US$400/UK£200). You must also buy a government Vehicle Access Permit, which costs A$33 (US$26/UK£13) from your rental-car company, Urangan Boat Harbour, or the River Heads boat ramp; or A$40 (US$32/UK£16) from a Queensland Parks and Wildlife Service office on the island.

Bay 4WD Centre (✆ **1800/687 178** in Australia, or 07/4128 2981; www.bay4wd.com.au) rents four-wheel-drives and camping gear, offers four-wheel-drive packages that include camping or accommodations, organizes Vehicle Access Permits, barge bookings, camping permits, and secure storage for your car and will pick you up from the airport, the coach terminal, or your hotel. **Aussie Trax 4x4 Rentals** (✆ **1800/062 275** in Australia, or 07/4124 4433; www.fraserisland4wd.com.au), has offices in Hervey Bay and at Kingfisher Bay Resort on Fraser Island (see below). A four-wheel-drive will cost you between about A$175 (US$140/UK£70) and A$240 (US$192/UK£96) a day, plus a A$33 (US$26/UK£13) Fraser Island driving permit and a A$500 (US$400/UK£200) security deposit (by credit card) held until return of the vehicle in the original condition. The company allows 1-day rentals. Rates are cheaper if you book for a week. Book well in advance.

Four-wheel-drives reach the island on the **Fraser Venture** barge (✆ **07/4125 4444**), which runs three times a day (four times on Sat) from River Heads, 17km (11 miles) south of Urangan Boat Harbour. Kingfisher Bay Resort (see below) also runs a barge from River Heads. The round-trip fare for a vehicle with up to four occupants is A$130 (US$104/UK£52), plus A$8 (US$6.40/UK£3.20) per extra passenger. It is a good idea to book a place for the 45-minute crossing.

The **Rainbow Venture** and **Fraser Explorer** barges (✆ **07/5486 3154**) provide access to Rainbow Beach and operate continuously between Inskip Point and Hook Point between 6am and 5:30pm daily. The cost is A$75 (US$60/UK£30) return for a vehicle and four passengers.

Fraser Island Taxi Service (✆ **07/4127 9188,** or 0429 379 188 mobile phone) is another option for getting around. There is only one taxi on the island (a 4WD, of course), so it's important to book ahead. They will pick you up anywhere on the island, and will give you a quote on price before you set off. The taxi seats five, and there's also room for your luggage and fishing rods.

VISITOR INFORMATION The **Hervey Bay Visitor Information Centre** is at 262 Urraween Rd. at Maryborough–Hervey Bay Road, Pialba (✆ **1800/811 728** in Australia, or 07/4215 9855; www.frasercoastholidays.info). It is open daily 9am to 5pm, except Good Friday and Christmas Day. Another online source of information is www.hervey.com.au. The **Marina Kiosk** (✆ **07/4128 9800**) at Urangan Boat Harbour is a one-stop booking and information agency for all Fraser-related travel. Several Queensland Parks and Wildlife Service information offices are on the island.

Tips Please Don't Feed the Dingoes

The dingoes that roam the island are emboldened by visitors who have—sometimes deliberately, sometimes unwittingly—fed them over the years. These dangerous wild animals have been responsible for one death and several serious attacks in recent years. Do not feed them, and keep your distance. If you don't, rangers can impose on-the-spot fines of A$225 (US$180/UK£90). And be warned: The laws are strictly enforced by the rangers and the maximum penalty is A$3,000 (US$2,400/UK£1,200).

Fraser Island

There are no towns and very few facilities, food stores, or services on the island, so if you're camping, take all supplies with you.

ECOEXPLORING THE ISLAND

Fraser's turquoise lakes and tea-colored "perched" lakes in the dunes are among the island's biggest attractions. Brilliant blue **Lake McKenzie** is absolutely beautiful; a swim here may be the highlight of your visit. Lake Birrabeen is another popular swimming spot. Don't miss a refreshing swim in the fast-flowing clear shallows of **Eli Creek.** Wade up the creek for a mile or two and let the current carry you back down. You should also take the boardwalk through a verdant forest of palms and ferns along the banks of Wanggoolba Creek.

Don't swim at **75-mile Beach,** which hugs the eastern edge of the island—it has dangerously strong currents and a healthy shark population. Instead, swim in the **Champagne Pools** (also called the Aquarium)—pockets of soft sand protected from the worst of the waves by rocks. The bubbling seawater turns the pools into miniature spas. The pools are just north of **Indian Head,** a 60m (197-ft.) rocky outcrop at the northern end of the beach.

View the island's famous colored sand in its natural setting—the 70m (230-ft.) cliffs called **the Cathedrals,** which stretch for miles north of the settlement of Happy Valley on the eastern side of the island.

Some of Queensland's best fishing is on Fraser Island. Anglers can throw a line in the surf gutters off the beach. (Freshwater fishing is not allowed.) Bream, whiting, flathead, and swallowtail are the beach catches. Indian Head is good for rock species and tailor; the waters east off **Waddy Point** yield northern and southern reef fish. **Kingfisher Bay Resort** (see below) offers free fish clinics, rents tackle, and organizes half-day fishing jaunts.

From August through October, tour boats crowd the straits to see humpback whales returning to Antarctica with calves in tow. Kingfisher Bay Resort runs a whale-watching cruise from Urangan Harbour.

WHERE TO STAY

Fraser Island Wilderness Retreat ★ *Finds* This is the wild side of Fraser Island, just minutes from 75-mile Beach. Don't come expecting a luxury resort—this one has comfortable timber cottages and all the amenities you need. There's a small pool, surrounded by a deck and deck chairs, and each cottage has a small veranda. The rooms all have fans, limited cooking facilities, and a VCR. (You can rent videos.) The bar-bistro is open for all meals, but be warned that day-tour buses stop here for lunch, so it can be crowded at that time. If you want to cook for yourself, there's a general store selling food and liquor. The store also has fuel, ice, and gas for campers. You can also hire a four-wheel-drive from the resort. There's a public phone. The only access is by plane (**Air Fraser Island, ✆ 1800/247 992** in Australia, or 07/4125 3600) or bus. **The Fraser Island Company** (**✆ 07/4125 3933**) will transfer guests to the resort from Hervey Bay; it also runs day tours of the island for A$169 (US$135/UK£68) adults and A$119 (US$95/UK£48) children 4 to 14.

Happy Valley, Fraser Island, QLD 4650. **✆ 07/4127 9144.** Fax 07/4127 9131. www.fraserislandco.com.au. 9 units, all with shower only. A$140–A$180 (US$112–US$144/UK£56–UK£72) 1-bedroom lodge for up to 3; A$180–A$220 (US$144–US$176/UK£72–UK£88) family lodge for up to 5. Ask about packages. AE, MC, V. **Amenities:** Restaurant; bar; outdoor pool; tour desk; car-rental desk; babysitting; coin-op laundry. *In room:* TV/VCR, kitchenette, small fridge, no phone.

Kingfisher Bay Resort ★★ *Kids* This sleek, environment-friendly ecoresort lies low along Fraser's west coast. Hotel rooms are smart and contemporary, with air-conditioning and a Japanese-style screen opening onto a balcony looking into the bush, but my pick is the two- and three-bedroom villas just a short walk from the main resort area and pools. The hillside villas, which have Jacuzzis on their balconies, are fairly luxurious, but guests must contend with that long haul up the hill. Each villa has a kitchen, washing machine, and dryer, but if you want daily service it will cost A$95 to A$120 (US$76–US$96/UK£38–UK£48) per night extra. Two new houses—one with three bedrooms, one with four—are now available for those who want extra privacy away from the resort area. The only draw-back is that you must have your own

Moments Another Great Walk

The stunning Fraser Island World Heritage Area is the location for Queensland's six Great Walks (p. 345). The **Fraser Island Great Walk** (© 1 **04** in Australia; www.epa.qld.gov.au) follows a winding track from Dilli Villag to Lake Garawongera. The main trail is 85km (53 miles) long and takes 6 to 8 days to complete, but offshoots provide short, full-day, overnight, and 2- to 3-day walks. Overnight walkers must book huts and need a permit, which costs A$4.50 (US$3.60/UK£1.80) per person or A$18 (US$14/UK£7.20) for a family of four or more with children aged 17 or under. The walk takes you to many of the island's popular landmarks, such as Lake McKenzie, Central Station, Wangoolba Creek, Valley of the Giants, and Lake Wabby.

vehicle, as transport is not provided to get to them. An impressive lineup of eco-educational activities includes daily four-wheel-drive tours with a ranger to points of interest around the island, free guided walks daily, and an excellent free Junior Eco-Ranger program on weekends and during school vacations. You can also join bird-watching tours, guided canoe trips, sunset champagne sails, and dolphin and dugong (manatee) spotting cruises. Wildlife videos play continuously in the lobby, and the on-site ranger office lists the animals and plants you are most likely to spot.

Fraser Island (P.M.B. 1), Urangan, QLD 4655. © **1800/072 555** in Australia, or 07/4120 3333. Fax 07/4120 3326. www.kingfisherbay.com. 262 units. A$285–A$315 (US$228–US$252/UK£114–UK£126) hotel double; A$304–A$420 (US$243–US$336/UK£122–UK£168) 2-bedroom villa for up to 5; A$352–A$520 (US$282–US$416/UK£141–UK£208) 3-bedroom villa for up to 6; A$550–A$650 (US$440–US$520/UK£220–UK£260) for houses. 3-night minimum (5-night for houses) in peak season; 2-night minimum in low season. Free crib. Ask about packages. AE, DC, MC, V. **Amenities:** 3 restaurants; 4 bars; 4 outdoor saltwater pools (1 w/water slide); lit tennis courts; Jacuzzi; watersports equipment rental and fishing tackle rental; kids' club; game room; tour desk; babysitting. *In room:* TV, fridge, coffeemaker, hair dryer, iron.

8 The Sunshine Coast

Warm weather, miles of pleasant beaches, trendy restaurants, and a relaxed lifestyle attract Aussies to the Sunshine Coast in droves. Despite some rather unsightly commercial development in recent years, the Sunshine Coast is still a great spot if you like lazing on sandy beaches and enjoying a good meal.

The Sunshine Coast starts at **Caloundra,** 83km (51 miles) north of Brisbane, and runs all the way to **Rainbow Beach,** 40km (25 miles) north of **Noosa Heads** ★, where the fashionable crowd goes. There's a wide range of accommodations, from inexpensive motels and holiday apartments to AAA-rated five-star hotels and resorts.

Most of Noosa's sunbathing, dining, shopping, and socializing takes place on trendy Hastings Street, in Noosa Heads, and on adjacent Main Beach. The commercial strip of Noosa Junction is a 1-minute drive away; a 3-minute drive west along the river takes you to the low-key town of Noosaville, where Australian families rent holiday apartments. Giving Noosa a run for its money in recent years is newly spruced-up Mooloolaba, about 30km (19 miles) south, which has a better beach and about 90 great restaurants.

A short drive away, in the hinterland, mountain towns like **Maleny, Montville,** and **Mapleton** lead to the stunning beauty of the **Glass House Mountains,** a dramatic series of 16 volcanic plugs.

SENTIALS

you're **driving** from Brisbane, take the Bruce Highway theme park at Palmview, exit onto the Sunshine Motorway dore, or Noosa Heads. The trip takes about 2 hours. **89** in Australia) flies direct from Melbourne and Sydney. ustralia) flies direct from Sydney, Adelaide, and Melbourne **Henry's Airport Bus Service** (✆ **07/5474 0199;** www. flights; door-to-door transfers to Noosa Heads are A$20 (US$16/UK£8) ... s, A$10 (US$8/UK£4) for kids 4 to 14, or A$50 (US$40/UK£20) for a family of four, one-way. Bookings are essential, and should be made 24 hours ahead if possible. A taxi from the airport will cost around A$15 (US$12/UK£6) to Maroochydore or A$45 (US$36/UK£18) to Noosa.

The nearest **train** station to Noosa Heads is in **Cooroy,** 25km (16 miles) away. **Queensland Rail** (✆ **13 16 17** in Queensland; www.qr.com.au) serves Cooroy once daily from Brisbane on its **CityTrain** (✆ **07/3606 5555;** www.citytrain.com.au) network. The trip takes about 2½ hours, and the fare is A$17 (US$14/UK£6.80). Other trains will take you there via Nambour or Caboolture, but you will have to then get a bus connection to get to Noosa Heads. Queensland Rail's long-distance trains from Brisbane pick up but do not drop off passengers in Cooroy, with the exception of the high-speed **Tilt Train** (which runs Sun–Fri). The fare is A$28 (US$22/UK£11). The *Sunlander* makes several trips from Cairns each week; the fare is A$183 (US$146/UK£73) for a seat, A$345 (US$276/UK£138) for a first-class sleeper. **Sunbus** (✆ **13 12 30** in Australia, or 07/5450 7888) meets most trains at Cooroy station and travels to Noosa Heads; take bus no. 631.

Several **coach** companies have service to Noosa Heads from Brisbane, including **Suncoast Pacific** (✆ **07/5443 1011**). **Greyhound Australia** (✆ **13 14 99** in Australia) has many daily services from all major towns along the Bruce Highway between Brisbane and Cairns. Trip time to Noosa Heads is 2 hours and 35 minutes from Brisbane, and just over 27 hours from Cairns. The fare is A$25 (US$20/UK£10) from Brisbane and A$228 (US$182/UK£91) from Cairns.

VISITOR INFORMATION Contact **Tourism Sunshine Coast,** Level 1, The Wharf Complex, Mooloolaba, QLD 4557 (✆ **07/5452 2501;** www.sunshinecoast.org). In Noosa, drop into the **Noosa Visitor Information Centre,** at the eastern roundabout on Hastings Street where it intersects Noosa Drive (✆ **07/5447 4988;** fax 07/5474 9494; www.tourismnoosa.com.au). It's open daily from 9am to 5pm. Other tourist information centers are: **Maroochy Tourism,** Sunshine Coast Airport (✆ **07/5479 1566**), and Sixth Avenue and Melrose Parade, Maroochydore (✆ **07/5479 1566**); and **Caloundra Visitor Information Centre,** 7 Caloundra Rd., Caloundra (✆ **07/5420 6240**).

GETTING AROUND Major car-rental companies on the Sunshine Coast are **Avis** (✆ **07/5443 5055** Sunshine Coast Airport, or 07/5447 4933 Noosa Heads), **Budget** (✆ **07/5448 7455** airport, or 07/5474 2820 Noosa Heads), **Hertz** (✆ **07/5448 9731** airport, or 07/5447 2253 Noosa Heads), and **Thrifty** (✆ **1300/367 227**). Many local companies rent cars and four-wheel-drives, including **Trusty** (✆ **07/5491 2444**).

The local bus company is **Sunbus** (✆ **07/5450 7888,** or 13 12 30 in Australia).

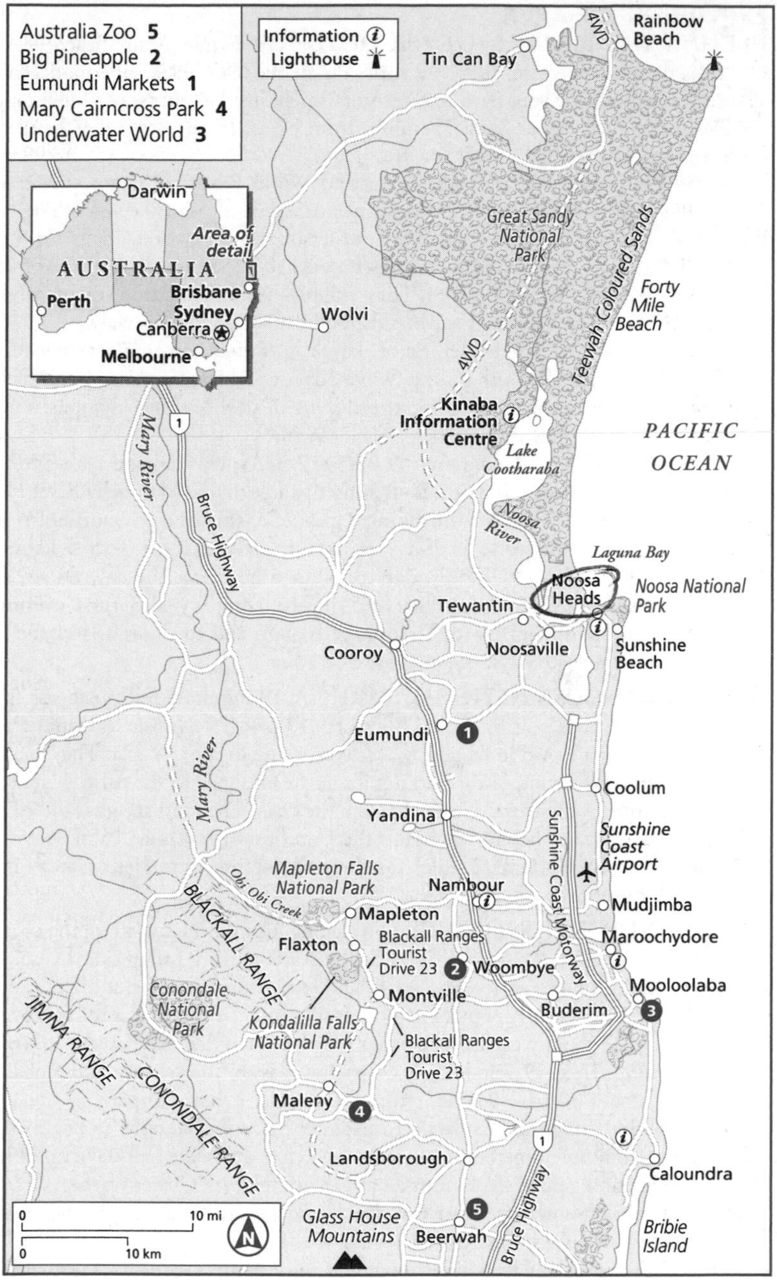
Australia Zoo 5
Big Pineapple 2
Eumundi Markets 1
Mary Cairncross Park 4
Underwater World 3
Information
Lighthouse
Darwin
Area of detail
AUSTRALIA
Perth
Brisbane
Sydney
Canberra
Melbourne
Tin Can Bay
Rainbow Beach
4WD
Great Sandy National Park
Teewah Coloured Sands
Forty Mile Beach
Wolvi
Kinaba Information Centre
Lake Cootharaba
PACIFIC OCEAN
Mary River
Bruce Highway
Noosa River
Laguna Bay
Noosa Heads
Noosa National Park
Tewantin
Noosaville
Sunshine Beach
Cooroy
Eumundi
Coolum
Yandina
Sunshine Coast Airport
Sunshine Coast Motorway
Mapleton Falls National Park
Obi Obi Creek
Nambour
Mudjimba
Mapleton
Maroochydore
Flaxton
Blackall Ranges Tourist Drive 23
Woombye
Mooloolaba
BLACKALL RANGE
Montville
Buderim
Conondale National Park
Kondalilla Falls National Park
JIMNA RANGE
CONONDALE RANGE
Maleny
Landsborough
Caloundra
0
10 mi
10 km
N
Glass House Mountains
Beerwah
Bribie Island

EXPLORING THE AREA

HITTING THE BEACH & OTHER OUTDOOR FUN Main Beach, Noosa Heads, is the place to swim, surf, and sunbathe. If the bikini-clad supermodel look-alikes are too much for you, head to Sunshine Beach, just behind Noosa Junction off the David Low Way, about 2km (1¼ miles) from Noosa Heads. It's just as beautiful. Both beaches are patrolled 365 days a year.

Learn to surf with two-time Australian and World Pro-Am champion **Merrick Davis** (✆ **0418/787 577** mobile; www.learntosurf.com.au), who's been teaching here since 1992. Merrick and his team run 2-hour lessons on Main Beach daily for A$55 (US$44/UK£22), 3-day certificate courses for A$150 (US$120/UK£60), and 5-day courses for A$220 (US$176/UK£88). They will pick you up and drop you off at your accommodations. They also rent surfboards, body boards, and sea kayaks.

If you want to rent a Windsurfer, canoe, kayak, surf ski, catamaran, jet ski, or fishing boat that you can play with on the Noosa River or take upriver into Great Sandy National Park (see below), check out the dozens of outfits along Gympie Terrace between James Street and Robert Street in Noosaville.

The **Aussie Sea Kayak Company** (✆ **07/5477 5335;** www.ausseakayak.com.au), at The Wharf, Mooloolaba, runs a 2-hour sunset paddle on the Maroochy River every day for A$45 (US$36/UK£18)—including a glass of champagne on your return as a reward for all the hard work! Half-day tours run every day for 3 to 4 hours at Mooloolaba (A$65/US$52/UK£26), day tours for 6 hours on Tuesday, Friday, and Saturday at Noosa (A$135/US$108/UK£54). The company also runs overnight adventures to Moreton and North Stradbroke Islands, and to Fraser Island and the Whitsundays for up to 6 days.

EXPLORING NOOSA NATIONAL PARK A 10-minute stroll northeast from Hastings Street brings you to the 432-hectare (1,067-acre) **Noosa National Park.** Anywhere you see a crowd looking upward, you're sure to spot a koala. They're often seen in the unlikely setting of the parking lot at the entrance to the park. A network of well-signposted walking trails leads through the bush. The most scenic is the 2.7km (1½-mile) coastal trail. The shortest trail is the 1km (just over ½-mile) Palm Grove circuit; the longest is the 4.8km (3-mile) Tanglewood trail inland to Hell's Gates—definitely worth the effort.

GREAT SANDY NATIONAL PARK Stretching north of Noosa along the coast is the 56,000-hectare (138,320-acre) Great Sandy National Park (often called Cooloola National Park). It's home to forests, beach, and freshwater lakes, including the state's largest, Lake Cootharaba. A popular activity is to cruise the Everglades formed by the Noosa River and tributary creeks. The park's information office, the **Kinaba Information Centre** (✆ **07/5449 7364;** daily 9am–3pm), is on the western shore of Lake Cootharaba, about 30km (19 miles) from Noosaville. It has a display on the area's geography and a mangrove boardwalk to explore; it's accessible only by boat, which you can rent from the numerous outfits in Noosaville. There are half-day cruises into the Everglades, and guided kayak tours that explore the park's lower reaches.

The other option is to take a four-wheel-drive along Forty-mile Beach, a designated highway with traffic laws, for a close-up view of the Teewah colored sand cliffs. This is a great place to get away from the crowds and enjoy nature's wonders. Lifeguards do not patrol the beach, so do not swim alone, and take care. Tours are available, or you can rent a four-wheel-drive and explore on your own. To reach the beach, cross the

Noosa River on the ferry at Tewantin, then take Maximilian Drive for 4km (2½ miles) to the beach. Stock up on water, food, and gas in Tewantin. The ferry (© **07/5447 1321**) costs A$10 (US$8/UK£4) per vehicle round-trip; it operates from 5:30am to 10:15pm Sunday through Thursday, and 5:30am to midnight Friday and Saturday.

WILDLIFE PARKS & THEME PARKS Small theme parks seem to thrive on the Sunshine Coast. Don't expect thrill rides, but you might find some of them a pleasant way to spend a few hours.

A transparent tunnel with an 80m (262-ft.) moving walkway that takes you through a tank filled with sharks, stingrays, groupers, eels, and coral is the highlight at **Underwater World** (© **07/5458 6222;** www.underwaterworld.com.au) at The Wharf, Parkyn Parade, Mooloolaba. Kids can pick up starfish and sea cucumbers in the touch pool, and there are displays on whales and sharks, shark breeding, freshwater crocodile talks, an otter enclosure, and a 30-minute seal show. You can swim with the seals (A$76/US$61/UK£30) or dive with the sharks (A$99/US$79/UK£40 for certified divers, including gear, or A$165/US$132/UK£66 for nondivers). Age restrictions apply. It's open daily (except Dec 25) from 9am to 6pm (last entry at 5pm). Admission is A$26 (US$21/UK£10) for adults, A$18 (US$14/UK£7.20) for seniors and students,

---

Remembering the Croc Hunter

Fans of crocodile hunter, TV star, and conservationist Steve Irwin will find a poignancy in a visit to the amazing **Australia Zoo** ★ (© **07/5436 2000;** www.australiazoo.com.au), on Glass House Mountains Tourist Drive, at Beerwah, off the Bruce Highway. Little has changed in the day-to-day running of the zoo since Irwin died in a diving accident in north Queensland in 2006, his legacy being the continuation of his work by his family and staff. With his widow Terri at the helm, the zoo continues with the expansion which has made it a world-class attraction covering 100 hectares (251 acres). The highlight is the "crocoseum," a 5,000-seat stadium in which the daily croc feedings are held at noon. Other demonstrations and feedings are held throughout the day, and you can also hand-feed 'roos, pat a koala, check out foxes and camels, and watch (even hold!) venomous snakes and pythons. You can tour the Koala and Wildlife Hospital next door to see how sick and injured animals are cared for. There are also lots of exotic animals: check out the new Tiger Temple, home to five tigers and four cheetahs. The Irwin family has named November 15 "Steve Irwin Day" at the zoo, so for fans this might be the time to visit. Admission is A$49 (US$39/UK£20) for adults, A$38 (US$30/UK£15) for seniors and students, A$29 (US$23/UK£12) for kids 3 to 14, and A$147 (US$118/UK£59) for a family of four. The park is open daily from 9am to 4:30pm. Closed December 25. Courtesy buses operate daily from 8:30am with pickups at Noosa and other spots around the Sunshine Coast, arriving at the zoo at 10:20am. The return bus leaves at 4pm. The courtesy bus will also pick up train passengers at Beerwah railway station. Bookings are essential, so call ahead to the zoo. **Sunbus** (© **07/5450 7888,** or 13 12 30 in Australia) services run to Australia Zoo from Maroochydore's Sunshine Plaza shopping center, Mooloolaba, and Landsborough railway station. Take bus no. 615.

A$15 (US$12/UK£6) for children 3 to 15, and A$69 (US$55/UK£28) for a family of five. Allow 2 hours to see everything, more if you want to attend all the talks.

At the **Big Pineapple** (✆ **07/5442 1333**), 6km (3¾ miles) south of Nambour on the Nambour Connection Road in Woombye—don't worry, you can't miss the 16m-tall (52-ft.) monument—you can take a train ride through a pineapple plantation, ride through a rainforest and a macadamia farm in a macadamia nut–shaped carriage, and visit a baby animal farm. It's open daily from 9am to 5pm (rides start at 10am); it opens later on April 25 (Anzac Day) and December 25 (call for exact time). Entry is free, but you pay for tours. The train ride costs A$12 (US$9.60/UK£4.80) adults and A$9.50 (US$7.60/UK£3.80) children 4 to 14; the macadamia tour costs A$7.50 (US$6/UK£3) adults and A$5.50 (US$4.40/UK£2.20) children. The best option is a family pass, A$55 (US$44/UK£22) for two adults and up to four children.

A MOUNTAINTOP DRIVE THROUGH THE SUNSHINE COAST HINTERLAND

A leisurely drive along the lush green ridge top of the **Blackall Ranges** ★ behind Noosa is a popular half- or full-day excursion. Mountain villages, full of crafts shops and cafes, and terrific views of the coast, are the main attractions. Macadamia nuts, peaches, and other local produce are often for sale by the road at dirt-cheap prices.

On Saturday from 6:30am to 2pm or Wednesday from 8am to 1:30pm, head to the colorful outdoor **Eumundi Markets** ★★ in the historic village of Eumundi, 13km (8 miles) west of Noosa along the Eumundi Road. Locals and visitors wander under the huge shady trees among dozens of stalls selling locally grown organic lemonade, fruit, groovy hats, teddy bears, antique linen, homemade soaps, handcrafted hardwood furniture—even live emu chicks! Get your face painted, your palm read, or your feet massaged. Listen to some didgeridoo music or bush poetry. When shopping's done, everyone pops into the cafes on Eumundi's main street.

From Eumundi, take the Bruce Highway to Nambour and turn right onto the **Nambour-Mapleton Road.** (The turnoff is just before you enter Nambour; if you hit the town, you've gone too far.) A winding 12km (7½-mile) climb up the range between rolling farmland and forest brings you to Mapleton. Stop at the pub for some spectacular views from the veranda. From here, detour almost 4km (2½ miles) to see the 120m (394-ft.) Mapleton Falls. A 200m (656-ft.) bushwalk departs from the picnic grounds and ends with great views over the Obi Obi Valley. There is also a 1.3km (¾-mile) circuit.

Back on the main **Mapleton-Maleny Road,** head south 3.5km (2 miles) through lush forest and farms to Flaxton Gardens. Perched on the cliff with breathtaking coast views is a wine cellar offering tastings and sales, plus a pottery, cafe, and gift shop. A bit farther south, you can detour right and walk the 4.6km (2¾-mile) round-trip trail to the base of 80m (262-ft.) Kondalilla Falls. You can swim here, too. It's a slippery downhill walk, and the climb back up can be tough.

Take the main road south for 5.5km (3½ miles) to **Montville.** This English-style village has become such a popular stop that it has lost some of its character, and lots of people decry its touristy facade. But everyone still ends up strolling the tree-lined streets and browsing the gift shops and galleries.

About 13km (8 miles) down the road is **Maleny,** more modern and less commercialized than Montville. Be sure to follow the signs to **Mary Cairncross Park** for spectacular views of the **Glass House Mountains** ★★, 16 volcanic plugs protruding out of the plains. The park has a food kiosk, a playground, free wood barbecues, and a rainforest information center; a 1.7km (1-mile) walking trail loops through the rainforest past some giant strangler figs.

You can either return to Noosa the way you came or, if you're in a hurry, drive down to Landsborough and rejoin the Bruce Highway.

WHERE TO STAY

EXPENSIVE

Hyatt Regency Coolum ★★ A couple of hours under the expert care of the therapists at the Sun Spa, and you'll feel years younger! This is one of the reasons the well-heeled flock to this sprawling bushland resort. The other is its 18-hole Robert Trent Jones, Jr.–designed golf course. The Sun Spa does everything from aromatherapy baths to triglyceride checks—130 treatments in all—and has massage rooms, aqua-aerobics, yoga, a 25m (82-ft.) lap pool, and much more. The golf course has been rated as one of the top five resort courses in Australia. Golf widows and widowers can play tennis, do decoupage in the Creative Arts Center, take the twice-daily free shuttle into Noosa to shop, and surf at the resort's private beach.

So spread out are the low-rise accommodations that guests rent a bike to get around, wait 15 minutes for the two free resort shuttles (frustrating sometimes!), or get into the healthy swing of things and walk. Accommodations all have contemporary decor and come as "suites" (one room divided into living and sleeping quarters); two-bedroom President's Villas with a kitchenette; villas in the Ambassador Club, which has its own concierge, pool, tennis court, and lounge; and two-story, three-bedroom Ambassador Club residences boasting rooftop terraces with a Jacuzzi. All the rooms were refurbished in 2004–05.

The Village Square is just that: an attractive cluster of shops, restaurants, bars, and takeout joints that makes up the heart of the resort.

Warran Rd., off David Low Way (approximately 2km/1¼ miles south of town), Coolum Beach, QLD 4573. ✆ **13 12 34** in Australia, 800/633-7313 in the U.S. and Canada, 0845/758 1666 in the U.K. or 020/8335 1220 in London, 0800/44 1234 in New Zealand, or 07/5446 1234. Fax 07/5446 2957. www.coolum.regency.hyatt.com. 324 units. A$240–A$285 (US$192–US$228/UK£96–UK£114) double; A$385–A$1,480 (US$308–US$1,184/UK£154–UK£592) villa; A$1,025–A$1,305 (US$820–US$1,044/UK£410–UK£522) Ambassador Residence. Rates include continental breakfast. Extra person A$45 (US$36/UK£18). Children under 13 stay free in parent's room with existing bedding. Ask about golf, spa, and other packages. AE, MC, V. Valet parking A$18 (US$14/UK£7.20). Free self-parking. Resort shuttle (A$18/US$14/UK£7.20 per person, one-way) meets all flights at Sunshine Coast Airport. Town-car transfers from Brisbane Airport A$79 (US$63/UK£32) per person, one-way. Limousine transfers available. **Amenities:** 3 restaurants; 3 bars; 9 outdoor pools (2 heated); golf course; 9 night/day tennis courts; health club and spa; watersports equipment rental; bike rental; children's programs daily for kids ages 6 weeks to 12 years (fee); concierge; tour desk; car-rental desk; business center; shopping arcade; limited room service; massage; babysitting; dry cleaning; nonsmoking rooms; executive rooms. *In room:* A/C, TV w/pay movies, fax, dataport, kitchenette, minibar, coffeemaker, hair dryer, iron, safe.

Sheraton Noosa Resort & Spa ★★★ A great place to enjoy a day spa by the sea is Noosa's first AAA-rated five-star resort. Right in the heart of Hastings Street, the Sheraton has a prime spot. There are several styles of rooms, but the best in my book are those with views away from the beach looking down the Noosa River to the mountains. Sit on the balcony at sunset and drink it in. All the rooms are extralarge, and all have Jacuzzis. You'll pay more for two-level poolside villas, which have private access to the pool area but no view. Some rooms have ocean (but not beach) views. The Aqua Day Spa has a Roman-bathhouse feel and offers a wide range of treatments. The restaurant, **Cato's**—named for the late Australian novelist Nancy Cato, who lived in Noosa—fronts Hastings Street and is a great place to people-watch.

Hastings St., Noosa Heads, QLD 4567. ✆ **1800/073 535** in Australia, 888/625-5144 in the U.S., or 07/5449 4888. Fax 07/5449 2230. www.sheraton.com. 175 units. A$295–A$490 (US$236–US$392/UK£118–UK£196) double. Extra adult A$50 (US$40/UK£20). AE, DC, MC, V. Free covered parking, valet parking. **Amenities:** Restaurant; 2 bars; outdoor heated pool; health club and sauna; spa; Jacuzzi; concierge; tour desk; 24-hr. room service; poolside and in-room massage; babysitting; use of free guest laundry; laundry service; dry cleaning. *In room:* A/C, TV w/free and pay movies, kitchenette w/microwave, minibar, fridge, coffeemaker, hair dryer, iron, safe.

MODERATE

Noosa Village Motel *Value* All the letters from satisfied guests pinned up on the wall here are a testament to owners John and Mary Skelton's hard work in continually sprucing up this bright little motel in the heart of Hastings Street. The pleasant rooms are spacious and freshly painted, with a cheerful atmosphere, and all have ceiling fans. And at these rates, it's one of Hastings Street's best values.

10 Hastings St., Noosa Heads, QLD 4567. ✆ **07/5447 5800.** Fax 07/5474 9282. www.noosavillage.com.au. 11 units, all with shower only. A$115–A$125 (US$92–US$100/UK£46–UK£50) double; A$155–A$165 (US$124–US$132/UK£62–UK£66) suite (sleeps 4); A$230–A$240 (US$184–US$192/UK£92–UK£96) 2-bedroom unit (sleeps 6). Extra person A$10–A$15 (US$8–US$12/UK£4–UK£6). Rates may be higher in peak season. Ask about specials. MC, V. Free parking. **Amenities:** Bike rental; tour desk; car-rental desk; room service (breakfast); babysitting; coin-op laundry; nonsmoking rooms. *In room:* TV, kitchenette, fridge, hair dryer.

IN THE HINTERLAND

Avocado Grove Bed & Breakfast Joy Barron and Brian Baxter's modern, red-cedar Queenslander home is in a peaceful rural setting in the middle of an avocado grove just off the ridge-top road. The cozy, comfortable rooms have country-style furniture, full-length windows opening onto private verandas, and oil heaters for cool mountain nights. The big suite downstairs has a TV and kitchen facilities. Parrots and other birds are a common sight. Guests are welcome to picnic on the sloping lawns, which have wonderful views west to Obi Obi Gorge in the Connondale Ranges.

10 Carramar Court, Flaxton via Montville, QLD 4560. ✆/fax **07/5445 7585.** www.avocadogrove.com.au. 4 units, 3 with bathroom with shower only, 1 with private adjacent bathroom. A$110–A$130 (US$88–US$104/UK£44–UK£52) double; A$130–A$150 (US$104–US$120/UK£52–UK£60) suite. Rates include full breakfast. Ask about weekend and midweek packages. MC, V. Turn right off ridge-top road onto Ensbey Rd.; Carramar Court is the 1st left. **Amenities:** Tour desk; in-room massage; nonsmoking rooms. *In room:* Coffeemaker, hair dryer, ceiling fan.

WHERE TO DINE

Noosa's **Hastings Street** comes alive at night with vacationers wining and dining at restaurants as sophisticated as those in Sydney and Melbourne. Just stroll along and see what appeals to you—but make a reservation in high season. The best breakfast in town is at **Bistro C,** one of the few restaurants offering beachfront dining, but **Café Le Monde** at the southern end of Hastings Street (opposite the back of the Surf Club) is a Noosa institution and you'll still find a crowd there. Noosa Junction is a less attractive place to eat, but the prices are cheaper. There are about 90 restaurants at Mooloolaba.

Tips The Seasons of the Sunshine Coast

Room rates on the Sunshine Coast are mostly moderate, but they jump sharply in the Christmas period from December 26 to January 26, during school holidays, and in the week following Easter. Book well ahead at these times. Weekends are often busy, too.

Madame Fu's ★★ MODERN ASIAN In the heart of Hastings Street, Madame Fu's is a welcome addition to the Noosa restaurant scene, as the only Asian restaurant in this strip. The food is interesting, the staff friendly and helpful, and the decor stylish. House specialties include chilli-salted squid with dry fired onion, slated duck egg and mustard green sauce, and caramelized beef cheek with lemon, cucumber, radish, and watercress. Delicious! There are plenty of noodle dishes, and when we visited plans were underway to create an oyster bar. They also do takeout.

8 Hastings St., Noosa Heads. ✆ **07/5447 2433.** Reservations recommended. Main courses A$17–A$35 (US$14–US$28/UK£7–UK£14). AE, DC, MC, V. Daily 11:30am–3pm and 5:30pm–late.

Season ★ MODERN AUSTRALIAN With one of the few beachfront restaurant locations, this is one of Noosa's most popular restaurants. Former Sydney chef Gary Skelton has maintained his following, with vacationers from southern states rediscovering Season, and even if the locals balk at the A$10 (US$8/UK£4) corkage fee for BYO wine, the food remains superb. Breakfast dishes can be as simple as muffins, or you can indulge yourself with buttermilk-and-banana pancakes (with palm sugar butter and maple syrup). For dinner? How about the pan-fried snapper with honey-roasted pumpkin, green beans, chèvre, and a cabernet dressing, or even simpler, crisp fried fish and chips with tartar sauce and fresh lemon? Smoking is not permitted.

25 Hastings St., Noosa Heads. ✆ **07/5447 3747.** Reservations essential for dinner; accepted same day only. Main courses A$22–A$33 (US$18–US$26/UK£9–UK£13); breakfast items A$5–A$15 (US$4–US$12/UK£2–UK£6). AE, DC, MC, V. Daily 8am–10pm.

Spirit House ★ ASIAN It's worth making the effort to get to this amazing restaurant—you will be thinking and talking about it long after you've left. Walk along the jungle paths to the hidden building and you'll start to get an idea of what's in store. Tables are set around a lagoon and among the trees, with massive statues and other artworks scattered throughout. At night the effect is enhanced by torches and lighting. But it won't prepare you for the flavors which come out of this kitchen, mainly Thai but with other Asian influences. Dishes like whole crispy fish with tamarind and chile sauce, palm sugar, and lime poached schnappers, or Penang chicken curry with snake beans and caramelized pumpkin with coconut, Thai basil, and peanuts. I defy you to leave without buying the cookbook or signing up for the cooking classes.

20 Ninderry Rd., Yandina. ✆ **07/5446 8994.** www.spirithouse.com.au. Reservations essential. Main courses A$27–A$34 (US$22–US$27/UK£11–UK£14). AE, DC, MC, V. Daily for lunch from noon; Wed–Sat from 6pm.

9 The Gold Coast

Love it or hate it, the Gold Coast is one of Australia's icons. Bronzed lifeguards, bikini-clad meter maids, tanned tourists draped with gold jewelry, high-rise apartment towers that cast long shadows over parts of the beach . . . but the glitz, the glitter, and the overdevelopment pale as soon as you hit the beach. The white sands stretch uninterrupted for 70km (43 miles), making up for the long strips of neon-lit motels and souvenir shops. Since the '50s, Australians have flocked to this strip of coastline, and that hasn't changed. Today, they're lining up with tourists from around the world to get into the theme parks, but everyone can still find a quiet spot on the beach.

The Gold Coast's theme parks are not as large or as sophisticated as Disney World, but they're exciting. Apart from the three major parks—Dreamworld, Warner Bros. Movie World, and Sea World—there are of plenty of smaller ones. There are also 40 golf courses, dinner cruises, and loads of adrenaline-fueled outdoor activities, from bungee jumping to jet-skiing. The best activity on the Gold Coast, though, is the natural kind, and it doesn't cost a cent—hitting the surf and lazing on the beach.

GOLD COAST ESSENTIALS

GETTING THERE **By Car** Access to the Gold Coast Highway, which runs the length of the Coast, is off the Pacific Highway from Sydney or Brisbane. The drive takes about 80 minutes from Brisbane. From Sydney it's an 11-hour trip, sometimes longer, on the crowded, run-down Pacific Highway.

By Plane Domestic flights land at Gold Coast Airport, Coolangatta, 25km (16 miles) south of Surfers Paradise. **Qantas** (✆ **13 13 13**) offers direct flights from Sydney. **Virgin Blue** (✆ **13 67 89**) flies from Sydney, Melbourne, and Adelaide. **Jetstar** (✆ **13 15 38** in Australia) flies from Melbourne, Newcastle, and Adelaide. The **Gold Coast Tourist Shuttle** (✆ **13 12 30**) meets every flight and will take you to your accommodations; the fare is A$18 (US$14/UK£7.20) one-way and A$33 (US$26/UK£13) round-trip for adults, A$9 (US$7.20/UK£3.60) one-way or A$17 (US$14/UK£6.80) round-trip for kids ages 4 to 13, A$45 (US$36/UK£18) one-way or A$83 (US$66/UK£33) round-trip for families of four. A better deal if you are going to use buses a lot is to buy a Freedom Pass (see "Getting Around" below) which includes your airport transfers. A **taxi** from the airport to Surfers Paradise is about A$30 (US$24/UK£12) but may be higher if traffic is heavy.

The nearest international gateway is **Brisbane International Airport** (see chapter 6). The **Coachtrans Airporter** bus meets most flights and makes about 20 trips a day from the domestic and international terminals at Brisbane Airport to Gold Coast accommodations for A$35 (US$28/UK£14) adults, A$18 (US$14/UK£7.20) children 4 to 13, or A$89 (US$71/UK£36) for a family of four. The trip takes about 90 minutes to Surfers Paradise. You do not need to book in advance unless you are on an evening flight; if you are, call ✆ **1300/664 700** in Queensland, or 07/3358 9700.

AirtrainConnect links Brisbane Airport and the Gold Coast by train and bus for A$37 (US$30/UK£15) adults, A$19 (US$15/UK£7.60) children 5 to 14, or A$93 (US$74/UK£37) for a group of four. Take Airtrain to the Gold Coast, then an air-conditioned coach shuttle to any accommodations between Southport Spit at the northern end of the Gold Coast and Burleigh Heads to the south. Airtrain's SmartPass, for A$112 (US$90/UK£45) per adult, A$56 (US$45/UK£22) per child, or A$280 (US$224/UK£112) for a family of four for 3 days, covers AirtrainConnect transfers, as well as unlimited door-to-door theme park transfers on the Gold Coast Tourist Shuttle and use of the local Surfside bus network, 24 hours a day. Passes are also available for 5, 7,10, and 14 days.

By Bus **Coachtrans** (✆ **13 12 30** in Queensland, or 07/3238 4700) runs between Brisbane and Gold Coast hotels. The fare is A$26 (US$21/UK£10) adults one-way, A$15 (US$12/UK£6) for kids 4–13; A$67 (US$54/UK£27) for a family of four.

Greyhound Australia (✆ **13 14 99**) makes daily stops at Surfers Paradise from Sydney and Brisbane. The trip from Sydney takes 14 to 15 hours, and the fare is A$112 (US$90/UK£45). Trip time from Brisbane is 90 minutes, and the fare is A$24 (US$19/UK£9.60).

By Train Suburban trains (call **Queensland Rail CityTrain;** ✆ **07/3235 5555**) depart Brisbane Central and Roma Street stations every 30 minutes for the 70-minute

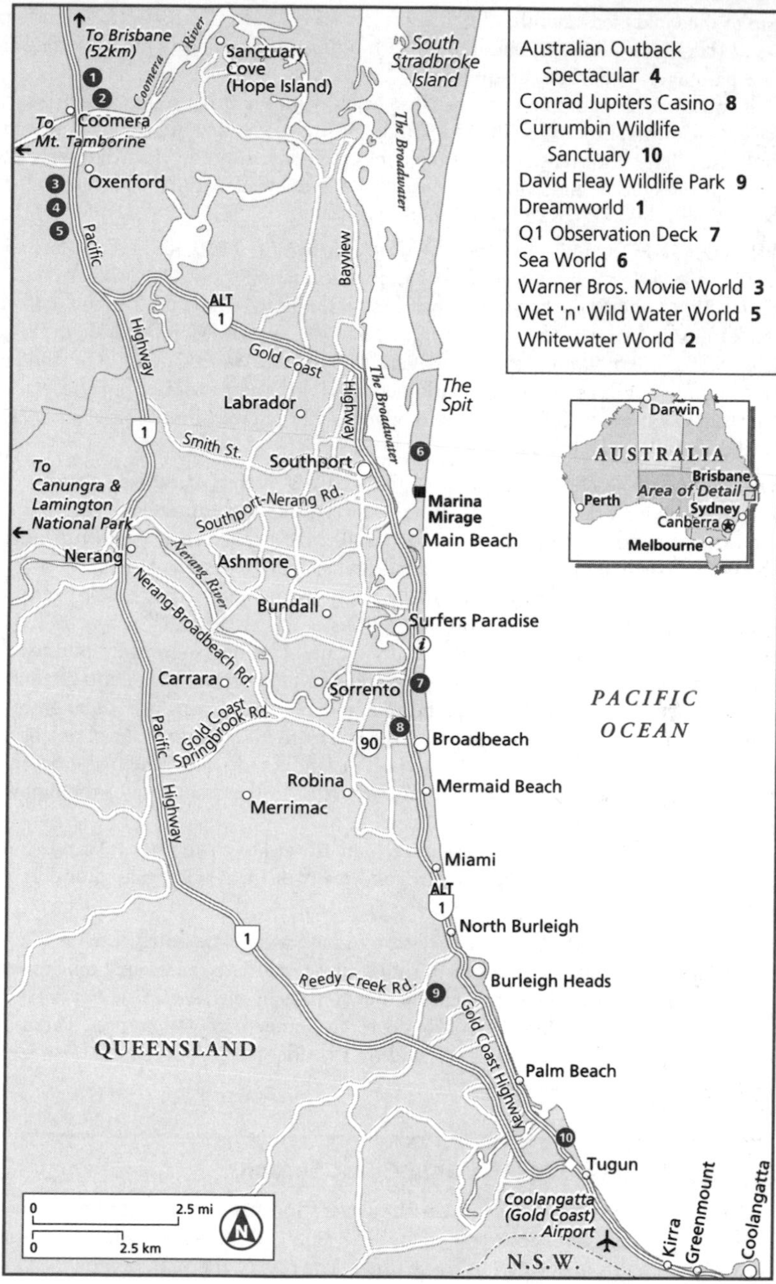

To Brisbane (52km)
Sanctuary Cove (Hope Island)
South Stradbroke Island
Coomera River
Coomera
To Mt. Tamborine
Oxenford
The Broadwater
Pacific Highway
Bayview
ALT 1
Gold Coast Highway
Labrador
The Spit
Smith St.
Southport
To Canungra & Lamington National Park
Southport-Nerang Rd.
Marina Mirage
Main Beach
Nerang
Nerang River
Ashmore
Nerang-Broadbeach Rd.
Bundall
Surfers Paradise
Carrara
Sorrento
Gold Coast Springbrook Rd.
Broadbeach
90
Robina
Merrimac
Mermaid Beach
PACIFIC OCEAN
Miami
North Burleigh
Burleigh Heads
Reedy Creek Rd.
QUEENSLAND
Palm Beach
Tugun
Coolangatta (Gold Coast) Airport
N.S.W.
Kirra
Greenmount
Coolangatta
0 2.5 mi
0 2.5 km
N
Australian Outback Spectacular 4
Conrad Jupiters Casino 8
Currumbin Wildlife Sanctuary 10
David Fleay Wildlife Park 9
Dreamworld 1
Q1 Observation Deck 7
Sea World 6
Warner Bros. Movie World 3
Wet 'n' Wild Water World 5
Whitewater World 2
AUSTRALIA
Darwin
Brisbane
Area of Detail
Perth
Sydney
Canberra
Melbourne

trip to the Gold Coast suburb of Nerang. The fare is A$23 (US$18/UK£9.20) adults, A$12 (US$9.60/UK£4.80) children 5 to 14. Numerous local buses meet the trains to take passengers to Surfers Paradise.

If you come by train to Surfers Paradise from Sydney or other southern cities, service is on **Countrylink** (✆ **1300 131 722** in Australia; www.countrylink.nsw.gov.au), and you will need to transfer to a connecting coach in Casino or Murwillumbah, just south of the Queensland border. The trip from Sydney takes 14 to 15 hours and the fare is A$96 (US$77/UK£38) for a first-class seat.

VISITOR INFORMATION **Gold Coast Tourism** (✆ **1300 309 440** in Australia, or 07/5538 4419; www.verygc.com) has an information kiosk on Cavill Avenue in Surfers Paradise. It is stacked with brochures on things to see and do, and the staff will book tours and arrange accommodations. The kiosk is open Monday through Friday from 8:30am to 5:30pm, Saturday 8:30am to 5pm, and Sunday and public holidays from 9am to 4pm. A second information booth is at the corner of Griffith and Warner streets in Coolangatta. It is open from 8:30am to 5:30pm weekdays, from 8am to 2pm weekends and public holidays.

ORIENTATION The heart of the Gold Coast is **Surfers Paradise**—"Surfers" to the locals—a high-rise forest of apartment towers, shops, cheap eateries, taverns, and amusement parlors. The pedestrian-only Cavill Mall in the center of town connects the Gold Coast Highway to The Esplanade, which runs along the beach.

The Gold Coast Highway is the main artery that connects the endless beachside suburbs lining the coast. Just north of Surfers is **Main Beach** ★★, where Tedder Avenue abounds with shops, restaurants, and cafes. Heading south from Surfers, the main beach centers are **Broadbeach,** where retail complexes and restaurants are mushrooming; family-oriented **Burleigh Heads;** and the twin towns of **Coolangatta** in Queensland and **Tweed Heads** just over the border in New South Wales. Coolangatta still has a sleepy small-town feel that's ideal for families, despite some major development in the past few years. Gold Coast Airport is on the other side of the highway from Coolangatta township.

West of Surfers Paradise and Broadbeach are the affluent suburbs of **Ashmore** and **Nerang,** where luxury residential estates and many of the region's championship golf courses have sprung up.

GETTING AROUND It's not necessary to have a car. The hotels listed below are within walking distance of the beach, shops, and restaurants, and many tour companies pick up at hotels. You can reach the theme parks by bus. A car is handy for a day trip to the hinterland, and to get around to restaurants and golf courses. Parking is cheap and plentiful in numerous lots and on the side streets between the Gold Coast Highway and The Esplanade.

Tips The Secret of the Gold Coast Seasons

School holidays, especially the Christmas vacation from mid-December to the end of January, are peak season on the Gold Coast. Accommodations are booked months in advance at these times. The rest of the year, occupancy levels plummet—and so do rates! Packages and deals abound in the off season, so make sure you ask.

Avis (© 07/5539 9388), **Budget** (© 07/5538 5470), **Hertz** (© 07/5538 5366), and **Thrifty** (© 07/5570 9999) have outlets in Surfers Paradise and at Gold Coast Airport. Endless local outfits rent cars at cheap rates.

Surfside Buslines (© **13 12 30** in Australia, or 07/5571 6555) is the local bus company. Its best deal is the **Freedom Pass,** which allows you to hop on and off the buses anytime you like. The 3-day pass costs A$58 (US$46/UK£23) adults and A$29 (US$23/UK£12) children or A$145 (US$116/UK£58) for a family of four; 5-, 7-, 10-, and 14-day passes are also available. The pass gives you door to door return Gold Coast Airport transfers, unlimited door-to-door transfers to Dreamworld, Warner Bros. MovieWorld, Sea World, Wet 'n' Wild Water World, and Currumbin Wildlife Sanctuary, as well as unlimited use of the Surfside bus network, 24 hours a day.

WHAT TO SEE & DO ON THE COAST

HITTING THE BEACHES

The white sandy beaches are the number-one attraction on the Gold Coast. No fewer than 35 patrolled beaches stretch almost uninterrupted from the Spit north of Surfers Paradise to Rainbow Bay, south of Coolangatta. In fact, the Gold Coast is just one long fabulous beach—all you need do is step onto it at any point, and you will spot the nearest set of red and yellow flags that signal safe swimming. The most popular beaches are **Main Beach** ★★, **Surfers North, Elkhorn Avenue, Surfers Paradise, Mermaid Beach, Burleigh Heads, Coolangatta,** and **Greenmount.** All are patrolled 365 days a year.

DOING THE THEME PARKS

The big three—Dreamworld, Sea World, and Warner Bros. Movie World—have been joined in 2006 by the new **Australian Outback Spectacular,** also owned by Warner Bros. located between Movie World and Wet 'n' Wild Water World.

Sea World is the only major theme park in the center of town. The others are in northern bushland on the Pacific Highway, about 15 to 20 minutes away from Surfers Paradise. You can ride to the theme parks on the Gold Coast Tourist Shuttle (see above) or on **Surfside Buslines** (© **13 12 30** in Queensland) buses. Take bus no. TX1 or TX2 to the Dreamworld, Movie World, and Wet 'n' Wild; and bus no. 750 from Surfers Paradise or 9 from Southport to get to Sea World.

If you are driving, take the M1 Pacific Motorway for about 15 to 20 minutes north of the Gold Coast or 40 minutes south of Brisbane for Wet 'n' Wild, Warner Bros. Movie World, and Dreamworld. Exits are all well signposted. All the theme parks have huge free parking lots.

Trains (© **13 12 30**) run to Coomera and Helensvale on the Brisbane–Gold Coast line. Queensland Rail CityTrain sells tickets to the theme parks at attended stations, including Brisbane Central.

Australian Outback Spectacular This A$23-million (US$18-million/UK£9.2-million) extravaganza is part theme park, part dinner show. Aimed at introducing a largely international audience to the spirit of the Outback, the show features "wild horses, stampeding cattle, an array of bush vehicles and an unforgettable display of horsemanship." There's even a helicopter that dives into the arena to round up the cattle! With seating for 1,000, the evening begins with pre-show entertainment and a three-course Aussie barbecue-style meal. The 90-minute show is staged during dinner. Part of the show is built around the competitive spirit of Australians. The audience is

Value Money-Saving Theme Park Passes

Sea World, Warner Bros. Movie World, and Wet 'n' Wild sell a **Fun Pass** that gives you 1 day's entry to each park over a 5-day period. It costs A$135 (US$108/UK£54) for adults and A$86 (US$69/UK£34) for kids 4 to 13. A Super Pass gives unlimited entry to all three for 14 days, and costs A$170 (US$136/UK£68) adults and A$112 (US$90/UK£45) for kids. You can buy passes at the parks, online, from a travel agency, or at most Gold Coast hotels, apartments, and tour desks. Sea World and Warner Bros. Movie World sell a return pass for A$32 (US$26/UK£13) extra adult or A$21 (US$17/UK£8.40) children, but you must use the second day within 14 days of your first visit. Wet 'n' Wild's second-day pass is A$21 (US$17/UK£8.40) adults and A$14 (US$11/UK£5.60) children. **Dreamworld** and **WhiteWater World** have a 2-day pass to both for A$99 (US$79/UK£40) adults, A$66 (US$53/UK£26) kids aged 4 to 13, or A$297 (US$238/UK£119) for a family of four.

split into two groups after receiving free stockmen's hats whose headbands depict the respective station for which they are encouraged to cheer. The "station muster" is billed as the most breathtaking part of the show, highlighting the skills of horse and rider.

Pacific Hwy. (21km/13 miles north of Surfers Paradise), Oxenford. © **13 33 86** in Australia, or 07/5519 6200. www.outbackspectacular.com.au. Admission A$95 (US$76/UK£38) adults, A$65 (US$52/UK£26) children 4–13. Bookings essential. Tues–Sun doors open 6:15pm, entertainment starts 6:45pm. Closed Dec 25. Ample free parking. Coach transfers (© 13 33 86) from Gold Coast accommodations cost A$15 (US$12/UK£6) per person round-trip.

Dreamworld ★ *Kids* Adrenaline-crazed thrill-seekers will love the action rides, such as the aptly named Giant Drop, in which you free-fall 39 stories in 5 seconds, and the Tower of Terror, which propels you forward and upward at 4.5Gs before you fall backward 38 stories in 7 seconds. They'll also get a kick out of the hair-raising Cyclone roller coaster, with its 360-degree loop, and the Wipeout, which spins, twists, and tumbles you upside down in a random sequence (but only exerts a sissy 2.5Gs units of pressure). These high-octane offerings make the park's other attractions look tame. Dreamworld is a family-fun park, Disney-style—except that here giant koalas called Kenny and Belinda roam the streets instead of Mickey Mouse. Kids will love Nick Central, the only Nickelodeon cartoon attraction outside the U.S.

Other activities include an IMAX theater, a wildlife park where you can cuddle a koala and hand-feed kangaroos, river cruises livened up by a bushranger shootout, and a carousel and other rides for young kids. A big highlight is to watch trainers swim, wrestle, and play with Bengal tigers on Tiger Island. Souvenir stores, restaurants, cafes, and ice-cream shops abound, and there's a water-slide park, so bring your swimsuit.

Pacific Hwy. (25km/16 miles north of Surfers Paradise), Coomera. © **1800/073 300** in Australia, 07/5588 1111, or 07/5588 1122 (24-hr. info line). www.dreamworld.com.au. Admission (all-inclusive except skill games, souvenir photos, and helicopter rides) A$64 (US$51/UK£26) adults, A$42 (US$34/UK£17) children 4–13. Daily 10am–5pm; Main St., Plaza Restaurant, and Koala Country open at 9am. Closed Dec 25 and until 1:30pm Apr 25 (Anzac Day). Extended hours during Easter and Dec–Jan. Free parking for 1,600 cars.

Sea World ★★ *Kids* Four polar bears—Lia and Lutik, and Canadian orphan cubs Hudson and Nelson—are the star attractions at this marine park, and crowds flock to see them frolic, dive, and hunt for fish in a large pool. The cubs are usually out in the morning, and the bigger bears on show in the afternoon, but you'll probably make a day of it, so you'll get to see them all. Sea World may not be as sophisticated as similar parks in the United States, but it has its own charm, plus all the things you'd expect to see—performing dolphins and sea lions, ski shows, an aquarium, shark feeding, and an array of rides. The newest attraction is Shark Bay, a A$13-million (US$10-million/UK£5-million) exhibit where you can see some of the larger and more dangerous species, such as tiger sharks. You can also snorkel with the sharks for A$60 (US$48/UK£24) per person (if you are 10 or over) or dive with them if you are a certified diver for A$90 (US$72/UK£36).

A monorail gets you around the park, and there's a free water-slide playground. Watersports are available for an extra fee. Adults (14 and over) can snorkel with seals or dolphins for A$135 or A$165 (US$108–US$132/UK£54–UK£66), including a souvenir photo. An hour-long Dolphin Dive Encounter uses "ocean-walker" technology to allow guests without dive qualifications to have a divelike encounter with dolphins. It costs A$250 (US$200/UK£100) per person (you must be 14 or over). Younger kids can attend a 30-minute dolphin talk, pat one, and have their photo taken with one for A$90 (US$72/UK£36).

Sea World Dr. (3km/1¾ miles north of Surfers Paradise), The Spit, Main Beach. ✆ **07/5588 2222,** or 07/5588 2205 (24-hr. info line). Fax 07/5591 1056. www.seaworld.com.au. Admission (all-inclusive except animal experiences, helicopter rides, and powered watersports) A$64 (US$51/UK£26) adults, A$42 (US$34/UK£17) children 4–13. Daily 10am–5pm; 1:30–6:30pm Apr 25 (Anzac Day). Closed Dec 25. Free parking.

Warner Bros. Movie World ★ *Kids* Australia's answer to Universal Studios just about matches its U.S. counterpart for thrills and spills. The park is based around working studios where *Scooby-Doo,* starring Sarah Michelle Gellar and Freddie Prinze, Jr.; *The Phantom,* starring Billy Zane; *20,000 Leagues Under the Sea,* with Michael Caine; and *Street Fighter,* with Jean-Claude Van Damme, were filmed. If you already know how Superman flies over skyscrapers and you've heard a Foley sound studio in action, the train ride around the sets might not interest you, but it's a great introduction to cinema tricks for first-timers. The newest attractions are the Shrek 4D movie, and the Superman Escape roller coaster, which joins other hair-raising, tummy-turning rides like the indoor Scooby-Doo Spooky Coaster roller coaster, the Lethal Weapon roller coaster, and the simulated high-speed chase of Batman—The Ride. Don't miss the hilarious Police Academy Stunt Show. Young kids can take rides and see stage shows by Yosemite Sam and Porky Pig in the Looney Tunes Village, and there's a Looney Tunes Parade through the streets each day. Most parades and shows take place between 11am and 4pm.

Pacific Hwy. (21km/13 miles north of Surfers Paradise), Oxenford. ✆ **07/5573 3999,** or 07/5573 8485 (recorded info). www.movieworld.com.au. Admission (all-inclusive) A$62 (US$50/UK£25) adults, A$40 (US$32/UK£16) children 4–13. Daily 9:30am–5:30pm; rides and attractions operate 10am–5pm. Closed Dec 25 and until 1:30pm Apr 25 (Anzac Day). Free parking.

EXPLORING THE WILDLIFE PARKS

Currumbin Wildlife Sanctuary ★ *Kids* Currumbin began life as a bird sanctuary, and it is almost synonymous with the wild rainbow lorikeets that flock here by the hundreds twice a day for feeding. It's quite an experience—flocks of chattering birds descend onto visitors holding trays of food for them. Photographers go crazy, and tourists love it. The amazingly beautiful birds have a vivid green back, blue head, and red-and-yellow chest. Lorikeet feeding is at 8am and 4pm, and lasts for about 90 minutes. Don't miss it.

You can also have your photo taken cuddling a koala, hand-feed kangaroos, take a free miniature steam-train ride through the park, and attend animal talks and feeding

Getting Wet ('n Wild!)

Long-established water park **Wet 'n' Wild Water World** (✆ **07/5556 1610** or 07/5573 2255 for 24-hr. recorded info; www.wetnwild.com.au) has got competition from a newcomer, **WhiteWater World by Dreamworld** (✆ **1800/073 300** in Australia, or 07/5588 1111; www.whitewaterworld.com.au). The A$60-million (US$48-million/UK£24-million) new kid on the block opened in late 2006, and is a colorful addition with some of the most modern water slides and thrill rides in the world. It has some terrifying turns and waves, and is themed around Australian surf culture. The Super Tubes HydroCoaster is a "roller coaster on water" and is one of only two in the world; the Blue Ringed Octopus (BRO) is the world's only eight-lane Octopus Racer—you get the idea? For families, there's Nickelodeon's Pipeline Plunge, a playground for kids aged 5 to 12. Across the highway at Wet 'n' Wild, hurtling down a seven-story piece of fiberglass at 70kmph (43 mph) is just one of many water-slide options, all with names like Double Screamer, Mammoth Falls, the Twister, Terror Canyon, and White Water Mountain. Scaredy-cats can stick to the four regular white-water flumes, float gently past palm-studded "islands" at Calypso Beach, swim in the artificial breakers in the Wave Pool or in the regular pool, or soak in a spa at Whirlpool Springs. There's also a water playground for young kids. Wet 'n' Wild's point of difference—but one that won't matter to most teenagers—is that every night in January, and Saturday night September through April, is Dive-In Movie night, during which film fans can recline on a rubber tube in the pool while watching the flick on a giant screen. These are hugely popular nights, which get very crowded, and to get a tube or a seat you have to get there early. The water at both parks is heated April to September, there are lifeguards on duty, you can rent towels and lockers, and you can use showers. Both parks are open every day, except Christmas Day (Dec 25) and Anzac morning (Apr 25). WhiteWater World's hours are 10:30am to 4:30pm every day of the year (but may be extended during summer). Wet 'n' Wild opens at 10am daily but closes at 4pm May to August, 5pm September 1 to December 26 and January 26 to April 30, and stays open until 9pm December 27 to January 25 and on Dive-In movie nights. Entry to the parks costs the same: A$42 (US$34/UK£17) adults, A$28 (US$22/UK£11) kids aged 4 to 13. Wet 'n' Wild offers an "afternoon rate" of A$21 (US$17/UK£8.40) adults and A$14 (US$11/UK£5.60) children after 2pm or 3pm for the final 2 hours of operation each day, or after 5pm on Dive-In Movie nights.

demonstrations. An Aboriginal song-and-dance show takes place daily. The park's 27 hectares (67 acres) are home to 1,400 native birds and animals, including two saltwater crocodiles, and the wetlands on the grounds attract lots of native birds. Allow several hours to see everything. A highlight is the free-flight birds show at 11am and 2pm. Wildnight tours are run daily at 7:15pm, and last for around 2½ hours. They cost A$49 (US$39/UK£20) adults and A$27 (US$22/UK£11) children 4 to 13.

28 Tomewin St., Currumbin (18km/11 miles south of Surfers Paradise). ✆ **07/5534 1266.** www.currumbin-sanctuary.org.au. Admission A$30 (US$24/UK£12) adults, A$20 (US$16/UK£8) children 4–13. Daily 8am–5pm. Closed Dec 25 and until 1pm Apr 25 (Anzac Day). Ample free parking. Bus: 700, 760, or 765 (stop 15m/49 ft. from entrance).

David Fleay Wildlife Park ★ *Value* Established in 1952 by Australian naturalist David Fleay, this is one of Australia's premier wildlife parks. You'll see a platypus, saltwater and freshwater crocodiles, wallabies, kangaroos, glider possums, dingoes, wombats, the rare Lumholtz's tree kangaroo, and a big range of Australian birds, including emus, cassowaries, wedge-tailed eagles, black swans, and lorikeets. You walk on a series of raised boardwalks through picturesque mangrove, rainforest, and eucalyptus habitats, where most of the animals roam free. The nocturnal house, open from 11am to 5pm daily, is where you'll see many of the most elusive animals, including Australia's answer to the Easter bunny, the bilby.

Talks and feeding demonstrations throughout the day include a reptile show and saltwater-croc feeding—usually only October through April, when the crocs are hungry. Aboriginal rangers give talks about weaponry, bush medicine, and their links with this region. Volunteers also give free guided tours throughout the day. The Queensland National Parks and Wildlife Service (QNPWS) has run the park since 1983; David Fleay continued to live here until his death in 1993. Because the QNPWS frowns on handling animals, you can't cuddle a koala or hand-feed kangaroos here. There's a cafe, gift shop, and picnic tables.

Kabool Rd. (17km/11 miles south of Surfers Paradise), West Burleigh. © **07/5576 2411.** Admission A$15 (US$12/UK£6) adults, A$10 (US$8/UK£4) seniors and students, A$7.20 (US$5.75/UK£2.90) children 4–17, A$39 (US$31/UK£16) family of 6. Daily 9am–5pm. Closed Dec 25. Ample free parking.

WHERE TO STAY

VERY EXPENSIVE

Palazzo Versace You almost have to see this to believe it. In the unlikely location of the Australian Gold Coast, fashion designer Donatella Versace has created a tribute to her late brother, Gianni, in the form of an extravagantly opulent resort, furnished exclusively with Versace gear. You'll either love it or hate it—there's no in-between. Everything was imported from Italy, from the river stones that pave the *porte-cochere* to the massive antique chandelier that dominates the vast, marbled lobby. Vaulted ceilings are hand-detailed in gold, and huge marble columns dominate. The rooms are decorated in four colors (red, blue, gold, and orange), and are less confronting than the public areas. Everything in them—furniture, cutlery, crockery, toiletries, the lot—is Versace (either from the home wares collection or specially created for the hotel). Many of the rooms overlook the huge pool, the Broadwater (a stretch of ocean), and the marina. As you'd expect, everything is beautifully appointed, and you'll enjoy strolling the corridors lined with Gianni's artwork and designs. There's an extensive spa and health club in the basement. You can choose from eight room types (Donatella stays in the A$3,500/US$2,800/UK£1,400 Imperial Suite) or from a pool of two- and three-bedroom condominiums. All rooms and suites have Jacuzzis; condos have kitchens. And of course, should you get the urge to shop, there's a Versace boutique.

94 Sea World Dr., Main Beach, QLD 4217. © **1800/098 000** in Australia, or 07/5509 8000. Fax 07/5509 8888. www.palazzoversace.com. 205 units, 72 condos. A$410–A$725 (US$328–US$580/UK£164–UK£290) double superior room; A$475–A$790 (US$380–US$632/UK£190–UK£316) double superior suite; A$495–A$810 (US$396–US$648/UK£198–UK£324) double lagoon room; A$615–A$930 (US$492–US$744/UK£246–UK£372) deluxe suite; A$775–A$1,090 (US$620–US$872/UK£310–UK£436) Broadwater suite; A$2,500–A$3,500 (US$2,000–US$2,800/UK£1,000–UK£1,400) Imperial suite. AE, DC, MC, V. **Amenities:** 3 restaurants; 2 bars; saltwater heated lagoon pool and 27 other pools (some exclusive to condos); health club and spa; wet and dry sauna; concierge; tour desk; business center; salon; 24-hr. room service; massage; laundry service; dry cleaning; nonsmoking rooms. *In room:* A/C, TV w/pay movies, dataport, minibar, fridge, coffeemaker, hair dryer, iron, safe, Jacuzzi, PlayStation.

Tips Good Value Vacation Apartments

Apartments make good sense for families and for any traveler who wants to self-cater to save money. Because the Gold Coast has a dramatic oversupply of apartments that stand empty except during school vacations, you can get a spacious modern unit with ocean views for the cost of a midrange hotel. Apartment-block developers got in quick to snag the best beachfront spots when the Gold Coast boomed in the 1970s, so apartment buildings, not hotels, have the best ocean views. The **Gold Coast Booking Centre** (© **1300/737 111;** www.gcbc.com.au) is a centralized booking service that offers great deals at more than 1,200 apartments in Surfers Paradise and Broadbeach.

MODERATE

Paradise Resort Gold Coast ★ *Value* *Kids* Parents, if your idea of a holiday is to not even see your kids for most of the day, this place is for you. The resort has a licensed child-care center for little ones as young as 6 weeks and up to 5 years old. For 5- to 12-year-olds, there's the Zone 4 Kids, complete with pedal minicars, the Leonardo painting room, and an underwater themed pirate adventure world. You can laze around the leafy pool area and watch the kids play on the water slide. The child-care center charges moderate fees, and the Zone 4 Kids is free; both operate daily year-round. The low-rise building is comfortable, and rooms have views of the pool or the gardens. Family quarters sleep up to five in two separate rooms, and some (the family studios) have kitchenettes. Junior Bunkhouse rooms have a queen-size bed in the main room and brightly painted bunks in a separate kids' area, complete with their own TVs with Nickelodeon kids' channel, PlayStation, chalkboard, and play desk.

The resort rents a wide range of kiddy stuff such as prams (strollers), bottle warmers, car seats, and PlayStations, and it has a mini-supermarket and takeout meal service. The big range of activities makes this a great value for families, and the center of Surfers Paradise and the patrolled beach are a few blocks across the highway. Some rooms are near the highway, so ask for a quiet spot.

122 Ferny Ave., Surfers Paradise, QLD 4217. © **1800/074 111** in Australia, or 07/5579 4444. Fax 07/5579 4492. www.paradiseresort.com.au. 405 units. A$138–A$178 (US$110–US$142/UK£55–UK£71) resort room for up to 4; A$218 (US$174/UK£87) Junior Bunkhouse rooms (sleeps 4); A$238 (US$190/UK£95) resort family room for up to 5; A$268 (US$214/UK£107) interconnecting room (sleeps 6). Ask about special packages. AE, DC, MC, V. Free covered secure parking. Bus: 1 or 1A (stop outside the resort). **Amenities:** 2 restaurants; cafe/sandwich bar; bar; 4 outdoor pools; 2 tennis courts; exercise room; Jacuzzi; sauna; child-care center and kids' club; game room/video arcade; concierge; tour desk; shuttle bus; business center; babysitting; coin-op laundry; dry cleaning. *In room:* A/C, TV/VCR w/free and pay-per-view movies, kitchenette, fridge, coffeemaker, hair dryer, iron, safe.

Q1 ★ This is the best view in town, and that's really saying something. Q1 opened in late 2005, as the world's tallest residential tower—it reaches 323m (1,058 ft.). From your aerie, you can truly look down on everyone else on the Gold Coast, especially if you are staying at level 46 or higher, which dwarfs all other Gold Coast buildings. From inside, or on your glass-enclosed balcony, you can see much of the wide expanse of the coast or hinterland—and for the complete 360-degree experience, head to the 77th floor for the **Observation Deck** (p. 385). Each apartment has a luxury kitchen, dining and lounge area, and is given a daily miniservice. It's all glass, granite, and stainless steel, but there are nice personal touches (I liked the idea of the old-fashioned hair curlers in the bathroom drawer). Each apartment has laundry facilities, and two- and three-bedroom apartments have two bathrooms.

Hamilton Ave. (at Northcliffe Terrace), Surfers Paradise, QLD 4217. ✆ **1300/792 008** in Australia, or 07/5630 4500. Fax 07/5630 4555. www.Q1.com.au. 527 units. A$240–A$380 (US$192–US$304/UK£96–UK£152) 1-bedroom apt; A$325–A$490 (US$260–US$392/UK£130–UK£196) 2-bedroom apt; A$425–A$550 (US$340–US$440/UK£170–UK£220) 3-bedroom apt. Extra person A$35 (US$28/UK£14). Crib A$40 (US$32/UK£16) per week. 3-night minimum stay (5 nights in high season, mid-Dec to mid-Jan). AE, DC, MC, V. **Amenities:** Restaurant; bar; 2 lagoon pools and an indoor heated lap pool; health club and spa; sauna; 24-hour concierge; business center; nonsmoking rooms; cinema. *In room:* A/C, TV w/pay movies, dataport, minibar, fridge, coffeemaker, hair dryer, iron, safe.

WHERE TO DINE

The Gold Coast is full to the rafters with good restaurants. Many stylish new restaurants and cafes, most reasonably priced, are springing up around **Surf Parade** and **Victoria Avenue** in Broadbeach, as well as in the nearby **Oasis shopping mall.** Other trendy spots are the stylish **Marina Mirage** shopping center, opposite the Sheraton on Sea World Drive in Main Beach, and the hip **Tedder Avenue** cafes in Main Beach.

Elephant Rock Cafe ★ *Finds* MODERN AUSTRALIAN Take your seat under the pavilion overlooking Currumbin Beach and be mesmerized by the waves. The food's good too, but the view is something else. Elephant Rock Cafe is a chic, modern restaurant that's one of the best on the Gold Coast. Whether you go for breakfast, lunch, or dinner you'll not be disappointed with food that includes gourmet vegetarian choices as well as something for those who like more traditional fare. Lunch and dinner menus change seasonally, and the wines are usually from small boutique wineries. The cakes and biscuits are made at the cafe, and there are burgers and bagels and more. There's also a kids' menu for A$7 to A$8 (US$5.60–US$6.40/UK£2.80–UK£3.20). You can BYO; corkage is A$3 (US$2.40/UK£1.20) per person.

776 Pacific Parade, Currumbin. ✆ **07/5598 2133.** Breakfast A$4.20–A$14 (US$3.35–US$11/UK£1.70–UK£5.60). Main courses A$14–A$23 (US$11–US$18/UK£5.60–UK£9.20) at lunch, A$20–A$26 (US$16–US$21/UK£8–UK£10) at dinner. AE, DC, MC, V. Daily 7am–10pm.

Moments On Top of the World

The Gold Coast's newest, tallest building is Q1, a gleaming steel-and-glass tower, inspired by the Sydney 2000 Olympic torch. It's a stunner. Entry is on Surfers Paradise Boulevard, where you take the super-fast elevator for just 43 seconds to reach the **Q1 Observation Deck** (✆ **07/5630 4700;** www.Q1observationdeck.com.au), 230m (754 ft.) above the ground on levels 77 and 78 of the building. From there, you can gaze down on all the Gold Coast has to offer, with 360-degree views. A small theater in the Skyline Room shows a short film on the history of the Gold Coast, or you can stop in at the cafe for a piece of Q1-shaped cake and a coffee. Better still, head up there before sunset for a cocktail in the Skybar. The Observation Deck is open 9am to 9pm Sunday to Thursday, and until midnight Friday and Saturday. Entry costs A$18 (US$14/UK£7) adults, A$13 (US$10/UK£5) seniors and students, A$10 (US$8/UK£4) children aged 5 to 14, and A$45 (US$36/UK£18) family of four (extra children A$8.50/US$6.80/UK£3.40 each). All admissions are A$10 (US$8/UK£4) after 8pm Friday and Saturday. Last tickets are sold 45 minutes prior to closing time.

Tips Book Ahead for Indy & Easter Madness!

Most accommodations require a 1-week minimum stay during school holiday periods and a 4-day minimum stay at Easter. When the Gold Coast Indy car race takes over the town for 4 days in October, hotel rates skyrocket and most hostelries demand a minimum stay of 3 or 4 nights. Don't leave accommodations to the last minute! Contact the **Gold Coast Tourism Bureau (© 07/5538 4419**; www.verygc.com.au) to find out the exact dates.

Ristorante Fellini ★ ITALIAN Locals and visitors flock here for the flavors of Italy—mainly from Naples and Tuscany—as well as the fantastic views of the marina and Broadwater. When the temperature is right, the huge windows are opened to let in the sea breeze, and the split-level design means every table gets the same view. For so stylish a place, you'd expect the prices to be sky high, but they're not. Family owned, the restaurant is friendly and welcoming but the service is snappy. The menu includes pasta dishes such as ravioli filled with roasted duck and vegetables cooked in a light sauce of butter, fresh sage, and grated Parmesan topped with poppy seeds, and a range of chicken, beef, and seafood dishes including fresh snapper filets pan-fried in olive oil with zucchini, shallots, slow-roasted tomato, fresh thyme, and white wine and served baked in a paper envelope.

Level 1, Marina Mirage, Sea World Dr., Main Beach. © **07/5531 0300.** Main courses A$31–A$36 (US$25–US$29/UK£12–UK£14). AE, DC, MC, V. Daily noon–10:30pm.

THE GOLD COAST AFTER DARK

There's a genuine Rolls-Royce parked in the corner at **Rolls** nightclub, at the Sheraton Mirage, Sea World Drive, Main Beach (© **07/5591 1488**). You can reserve it as your booth for the night. A mixed-age crowd of sophisticated locals rubs shoulders with hotel guests. There is a A$5 (US$4/UK£2) cover; the club opens Friday and Saturday night. At 10:30pm they push back the tables at **Saks,** Marina Mirage, Sea World Drive, Main Beach (© **07/5591 2755**), and the elegant cafe and wine bar turns into a dance floor for fashionable 20- and 30-somethings. Friday, Saturday, and Sunday are the coolest nights to turn up, and there's a live band Sundays; no cover.

It's not as big as some Vegas casinos, but **Conrad Jupiters Casino,** Gold Coast Highway, Broadbeach (© **07/5592 8282**), has plenty to keep the gambler amused—70 gaming tables and 1,300-plus slot machines with roulette, blackjack, Caribbean stud poker, baccarat and minibaccarat, craps, Pai Gow, and sic-bo. The 1,100-seat Jupiter's Theatre stages floor shows and concerts; and there are three bars, including an English-style pub. Of the five restaurants, the good-value **Food Fantasy** buffet is outrageously popular, so be prepared to wait. The casino is open 24 hours. You must be 18 to enter, and smart, casual dress is required.

10 The Gold Coast Hinterland: Back to Nature

The cool, green Gold Coast hinterland is only a half-hour drive from the coast, but it is a world away from the neon lights, theme parks, and crowds. Up here, at an altitude of 500 to 1,000m (1,640–3,280 ft.), the tree ferns drip moisture, the air is crisp, and the pace is slow.

Mount Tamborine shelters several villages known for their crafts shops, galleries, cafes, and B&Bs. Easy walking trails wander from the streets through rainforest and eucalyptus woodland, and as you drive you will discover magnificent views.

The impressive 20,200-hectare (49,895-acre) **Lamington National Park** lies south of Mount Tamborine. The park, at around 1,000m (3,328 ft.) above sea level, is a eucalyptus and rainforest wilderness crisscrossed with walking trails. It's famous for its colorful bird life, wallabies, possums, and other wildlife. The road to the park is full of twists and turns, and as you wind higher and higher, tangled vines and dense eucalyptus and ferns make a canopy across the road—it's so dark you need headlights. The park is about 90 minutes from the coast, but once you're ensconced in your mountain retreat, the world will seem remote.

The hinterland is close enough to the Gold Coast and Brisbane to make a pleasant day trip, but you will almost certainly want to stay overnight, or longer, once you breathe that restorative mountain air.

MOUNT TAMBORINE

40km (25 miles) NW of Surfers Paradise; 70km (43 miles) S of Brisbane

Crafts shops, teahouses, and idyllic vistas are Mount Tamborine's attractions. The mountaintop is more a plateau than a peak, and it's home to a string of villages, all a mile or two apart—Eagle Heights, North Tamborine, and Mount Tamborine proper. Many shops and cafes are open only Thursday through Sunday.

ESSENTIALS

GETTING THERE & GETTING AROUND From the Gold Coast, head to Nerang and follow signs to Beaudesert. The Mount Tamborine turnoff is off this road. Alternatively, take the Pacific Highway north to Oxenford and take the Mount Tamborine turnoff, the first exit after Warner Bros. Movie World. Many tour operators run minibus and four-wheel-drive day trips from the Gold Coast, and some run tours from Brisbane. A fun thing to do is take a tour with the **Tamborine Trolley Co.** buses (✆ **07/5545 4321**), modeled on early-20th-century trams, which have a variety of tours to wineries and other attractions. A 3-hour winery tour costs A$45 (US$36/UK£18) per person, while a full-day food and wine tour costs A$95 (US$76/UK£38) with pickup from your accommodations.

VISITOR INFORMATION Head to **Gold Coast Tourism's** Visitor Information centers (see under "The Gold Coast," earlier in this chapter) to stock up on information and tourist maps before you set off. Brisbane Visitor Information Centre (see "Visitor Information" in chapter 6) also has information. The **Tamborine Mountain Information Centre** is in Doughty Park, where Geissmann Drive joins Main Western Road in North Tamborine (✆ **07/5545 3200;** www.tamborinemtncc.org.au). It's open daily from 10:30am to 3:30pm.

EXPLORING THE MOUNTAIN

With a map at hand, you are well equipped to drive around Mount Tamborine's roads, admire the views over the valleys, and poke around the shops. New Age candles, homemade soaps, maple-pecan fudge, tropical watercolors, German cuckoo clocks, and Aussie antiques are some of the things you can buy in the many stores. The best place to shop is the quaint strip of galleries, cafes, and shops known as **Gallery Walk** on Long Road, between North Tamborine and Eagle Heights. Eagle Heights has few shops but great views back toward the coast. North Tamborine is mainly a commercial center with the odd nice gallery or two. Mount Tamborine itself is mainly residential.

Allow time to walk some of the trails that wind through forest throughout the villages. Most are reasonably short and easy. The Mount Tamborine Information Centre has maps marking them.

WHERE TO STAY

Tamborine Mountain Bed & Breakfast ★ Ideally situated close to rainforest walks, arts and craft shops, wineries, and restaurants, Tony and Pam Lambert's restful timber home has stunning 180-degree views to the ocean from the breakfast balcony. Laze by the open fire in the timber-lined living room, or on the lovely veranda where rainbow lorikeets, kookaburras, and crimson rosellas flit about over the bird feeders. The ferny gardens have four purpose-built rustic timber rooms, each individually decorated in cottage style and linked to the house by covered walkways. Rooms are heated in winter. Hair dryers are available on request. There's no smoking indoors.

19–23 Witherby Crescent, Eagle Heights, QLD 4721. ✆ **07/5545 3595.** Fax 07/5545 3322. www.tmbb.com.au. 4 units, all with shower only. A$145 (US$116/UK£58) double midweek; A$175 (US$140/UK£70) double weekend. Rates include continental breakfast Mon–Fri, full breakfast weekends. MC, V. Free parking. Children under 12 not accepted. **Amenities:** Nonsmoking rooms. *In room:* A/C, TV/VCR, small fridge, coffeemaker, iron.

LAMINGTON NATIONAL PARK ★★

70km (43 miles) W of Gold Coast; 115km (71 miles) S of Brisbane

Subtropical rainforest, 2,000-year-old moss-covered Antarctic beech trees, giant strangler figs, and misty mountain air characterize Lamington's high, narrow ridges and plunging valleys. Its stretches of dense rainforest make it one of the most important subtropical parks in southeast Queensland, and one of the loveliest. The park has 160km (99 miles) of walking trails that track through thick forest, past ferny waterfalls, and along mountain ridges with soaring views across green valleys. The trails vary in difficulty and length, from 1km (½-mile) strolls to 23km (14-mile) treks.

The park is a haven for bird lovers, who come to see and photograph the rosellas, bowerbirds, rare lyrebirds, and other species that live here, but that's not the only wildlife you will see. Groups of small wallabies, called pademelons, graze outside your room. In summer you may see giant carpet pythons curled up in a tree or large goannas sunning themselves on rock ledges. Near streams you may be stopped by a hissing Lamington spiny crayfish, an aggressive little monster 6 inches long, patterned in royal blue and white. The park comes alive with owls, possums, and sugar-gliders at night.

Most visitors are fascinated by the park's Antarctic beech trees, which begin to appear above the 1,000m (3,280-ft.) line. Like something from a medieval fairy tale, these mossy monarchs of the forest stand 20m (66 ft.) tall and measure up to 8m (26 ft.) in girth. They are survivors of a time when Australia and Antarctica belonged to the supercontinent Gondwana, when it was covered by wet, tropical rainforest. The species survived the last Ice Age, and the trees at Lamington are about 2,000 years old, suckered off root systems about 8,000 years old. The trees are a 2½-hour walk from O'Reilly's Rainforest Guesthouse (see below).

EXPLORING LAMINGTON NATIONAL PARK

The easiest way to explore the park is to base yourself at **O'Reilly's Rainforest Guesthouse** in the Green Mountains section of the park, or at **Binna Burra Mountain Lodge** in the Binna Burra section (see "Where to Stay & Dine," below). Most of the trails lead from one or the other of these resorts, and a 23km (14-mile) **Border Trail** connects them; it follows the New South Wales–Queensland border for much of the way, and most reasonably fit folk can walk it in a day. Guided walks and activities at both resorts are for guests only; however, both properties welcome day visitors who want to walk the trails (which is free). Both have inexpensive cafes for day-trippers.

It is a good idea to bring a torch (flashlight) and maybe binoculars for wildlife spotting. The temperature is often 10° to 20°F cooler than on the Gold Coast, so bring a sweater in summer and bundle up in winter when nights get close to freezing. September through October is orchid season, and the frogs come out in noisy abundance in February and March.

GETTING THERE By Car O'Reilly's is 37km (23 miles) from the town of Canungra. The road is twisty and winding, so take it slow. Allow an hour from Canungra to reach O'Reilly's, and plan to arrive before dark. Binna Burra is 35km (22 miles) from Nerang via Beechmont, or 26km (16 miles) from Canungra, on a winding mountain road. From the Gold Coast go west to Nerang, where you can turn off to Binna Burra via Beechmont, or go on to Canungra, where you will see the O'Reilly's and Binna Burra turnoffs. From Brisbane, follow the Pacific Highway south and take the Beenleigh/Mount Tamborine exit to Mount Tamborine. From there, follow signs to Canungra. Allow a good 2½ hours to get to either resort from Brisbane, and 90 minutes from the Gold Coast. Binna Burra sells unleaded fuel; O'Reilly's has emergency supplies only.

By Coach The **Mountain Coach Company** (✆ **07/5524 4249**) does daily transfers to O'Reilly's and Binna Burra from the Gold Coast, leaving the airport at 8am, picking up at hotels along the way, and arriving at O'Reilly's at around noon. The return trip leaves O'Reilly's at 2:30pm, arriving at the airport by 6pm. **Allstate Scenic Tours** (✆ **07/3003 0700;** www.daytours.com.au) makes a daily coach run from outside the Roma Street Transit Centre in Brisbane at 8:30am, arriving at O'Reilly's at 12:30pm. The return trip leaves O'Reilly's at 2pm and gets to Brisbane at 6pm. The cost is A$73 (US$58/UK£29) adults and A$39 (US$31/UK£16) children.

The Binna Burra resort runs a shuttle from Gold Coast Airport at 1:30pm daily and from Nerang railway station at 2pm (to meet the noon Airtrain from Brisbane Airport), arriving at Binna Burra at 3pm. If you are on the Gold Coast, buses run every 15 minutes from Pacific Fair shopping center at Broadbeach to Nerang Station. Bookings are essential and made at least 24 hours in advance. It's A$40 (US$32/UK£16) adults and A$20 (US$16/UK£8) children 5 to 16 from the airport and A$30 (US$24/UK£12) adults and A$15 (US$12/UK£6) children from Nerang station.

VISITOR INFORMATION The best sources of information on hiking are O'Reilly's Rainforest Guesthouse and Binna Burra Mountain Lodge (see "Where to Stay & Dine," below); ask them to send you copies of their walking maps. There is a national parks information office at both properties. For detailed information on hiking and camping in the park, contact the ranger at Lamington National Park, Green Mountains section (at O'Reilly's), Canungra, QLD 4211 (✆ **07/5544 0634**). The office is open 9 to 11am and 1 to 3:30pm weekdays.

WHERE TO STAY & DINE

Both of these mountaintop retreats have long and interesting histories. Both offer walking trails of a similar type and distance; guided walks, including nighttime wildlife-spotting trips; hearty food; and a restful, enjoyable experience. They offer similar experiences; the differences are perhaps in style, with O'Reilly's having become a more sophisticated and modern operation in recent years. Look into the special-interest workshops both properties run throughout the year, which can be anything from gourmet weekends to mountain-jogging programs.

Binna Burra Mountain Lodge ★★ *Kids* Binna Burra is a postcard-perfect mountain lodge. The original cabins, built in 1935, are still in use; they've been outfitted with modern comforts but not with contemporary "inconveniences," such as telephones, televisions, radios, and clocks. All the accommodations have pine-paneled walls, floral bedcovers, heaters, and electric blankets. The most attractive and spacious are the mud-brick and weatherboard Acacia cabins, which have private bathrooms and the best views over the Numinbah Valley. The two kinds of Casuarina cabins are less expensive—the nicest are the small and cozy huts with a pitched ceiling, a washbasin, and a nice aspect into the forest and over the valley. Less atmospheric are the bunkroom-style units that sleep four to six people—good for families and groups of friends. Guests in Casuarina cabins share bathroom facilities, which include a Jacuzzi.

Meals are served in the stone-and-timber dining room. Seating is communal, so you get to meet other travelers. Free tea and coffee are on the boil all day. Also here are a crafts shop, a natural history library, and conference rooms.

Beechmont via Canungra, QLD 4211. ✆ **1800/074 260** in Australia, or 07/5533 3622. Fax 07/5533 3658. www.binnaburralodge.com.au. 41 cabins, 22 with bathroom with shower only. A$110–A$210 (US$88–US$168/UK£44–UK£84) double; A$150–A$225 (US$120–US$180/UK£60–UK£90) B&B-only double; A$240–A$340 (US$192–US$272/UK£96–UK£136) double with all meals. Extra person A$30–A$100 (US$24–US$80/UK£12–UK£40). Extra child 5–12 A$20–A$50 (US$16–US$40/UK£8–UK£20). Crib A$10 (US$8/UK£4) per night. Ask about packages. MC, V. **Amenities:** Restaurant; bar; free kids' club (ages 5–12) during school vacations; babysitting; coin-op laundry. *In room:* Minibar, fridge, coffeemaker, no phone.

O'Reilly's Rainforest Guesthouse ★★ *Kids* Highlights of your stay will be the chance to hand-feed brilliantly colored rainforest birds every morning and the fact that the staff will remember you by name. Nestled high on a cleared plateau, the buildings are closed in on three sides by dense tangled rainforest and open to picturesque mountain views to the west. The timber resort complex is inviting, with upmarket new suites and a major refurbishment of older rooms adding a touch of luxury. The comfortable guest lounge has an open fire, old-fashioned sofas and chairs, and an upright piano. The six rooms in the Toolona block, built in the 1930s, have communal bathrooms and basic furniture. The six refurbished motel-style Garden View rooms have handcrafted maple furniture. The seven Bithongabel rooms are singles. Mountain View rooms look out to the McPherson Ranges and have balconies; the six family rooms in this block have bunks for kids, and two rooms have wheelchair access. Three large Canopy Suites have a king-size four-poster bed, fireplace, Jacuzzi, library, stereo/CD player, minibar, and bar. One of the former O'Reilly family homes has been transformed into two new guest units, called "Vince" and "Lona" after the second-generation couple who raised their 10 children in the house. Each unit has two bedrooms (one with a king-size four-poster), two bathrooms, a separate living room, and a two-way fireplace. The large decks have a Jacuzzi, from which you can look out to magical sunsets. Polished timber floors, cedar shutters, handcrafted maple furniture, a minibar, and a stereo add the final touches.

At mealtime, the maitre d' assigns you to a table, so you get to meet other guests. If you do not buy a meal package, buffet breakfasts and lunches cost A$26 (US$21/UK£10) each, and a three-course dinner is A$48 (US$38/UK£19). Before dinner, head to the hexagonal timber bar, perched up high for great sunset views, for half-price cocktails (5–6:30pm). Among other facilities are a cafe and gift shop, a basketball court, and free tea, coffee, and cookies all day.

Via Canungra, Lamington National Park Rd., Lamington National Park, QLD 4275. ✆ **1800/688 722** in Australia, or 07/5502 4911. www.oreillys.com.au. 72 units. A$250–A$290 (US$200–US$232/UK£100–UK£116) double; A$450 (US$360/UK£180) canopy suite; A$650 (US$520/UK£260) 2-bedroom suite. Free crib. Rates include all meals and activities. Children under 18 stay free in parent's room with existing bedding. 4-night minimum New Year's, Easter, Christmas. Ask about 2-night and longer packages. Meal plan A$84 (US$67/UK£34) adults, A$42 (US$34/UK£17) children 11–15, A$26 (US$21/UK£10) children 4–10 for 3 meals per day; 2-meal packages available. AE, DC, MC, V. **Amenities:** Restaurant; bar; heated outdoor plunge pool; lit tennis court; Jacuzzi; sauna; kids' club (age 6 and up) on weekends and school vacations; game room; massage; babysitting; coin-op laundry. *In room:* Fridge, coffeemaker.

8

The Red Centre

by Marc Llewellyn

The Red Centre is the landscape many of us conjure up when we think of the Outback—vast horizons, red sand as far as the eye can see, mysterious monoliths, cloudless blue sky, harsh sunlight, and the rhythmic twang of the didgeridoo. It's home to sprawling cattle ranches, ancient mountain ranges, "living fossil" palm trees that survived the Ice Age, cockatoos and kangaroos, red gorges, pretty water holes, and Ayers Rock, now officially called by its Aboriginal name, Uluru.

Aboriginal people have lived here for thousands of years, since long before the Pyramids were a twinkle in a pharaoh's eye, but the Centre is still largely unexplored by non-Aboriginal Australians. One highway cuts from Adelaide in the south to Darwin in the north, and a few roads and four-wheel-drive tracks make a lonely spider web across it; in many areas, non-Aborigines have never set foot.

Alice Springs is the only big town in central Australia. So let's get one thing straight—Alice Springs and Uluru are *not* side by side. Uluru is 462km (286 miles) away. You can see it in a day from Alice Springs, but it's an effort.

The Red Centre is more than just the Rock. Give yourself a few days to experience all there is—visiting the impressive Olgas (or Kata Tjuta, its Aboriginal name) near Uluru (Ayers Rock), walking the rim of Kings Canyon, riding a camel down a dry riverbed, poking around Aboriginal rock carvings, swimming in water holes, or staying at an Outback homestead. Alice Springs gives you a better flavor for the Outback than Uluru. If you base yourself there, it's easy to radiate out to less crowded but still beautiful attractions like Palm Valley, Ormiston Gorge, and Trephina Gorge Nature Park, each an easy day trip. Too many visitors jet in, snap a photo of the Rock, and head home, only to miss the essence of the desert.

1 Exploring the Red Centre

VISITOR INFORMATION The **Central Australian Tourism Industry Association** (see "Visitor Information" under "Alice Springs," below) can send you a brochure pack. It is your best one-stop source of information.

Most of the Red Centre lies within the Northern Territory. The **Northern Territory Tourist Commission,** Tourism House, 43 Mitchell St., Darwin, NT 0800 (© **13 61 10** in Australia, or 08/8999 3900), maintains a site for travelers at www.ntholidays.com. The commission publishes a helpful annual guide to central Australia that details hotels, tour operators, car-rental companies, and attractions, and operates a division that offers package deals on complete trips, as well as lots of information on local Aboriginal culture and Aboriginal tours.

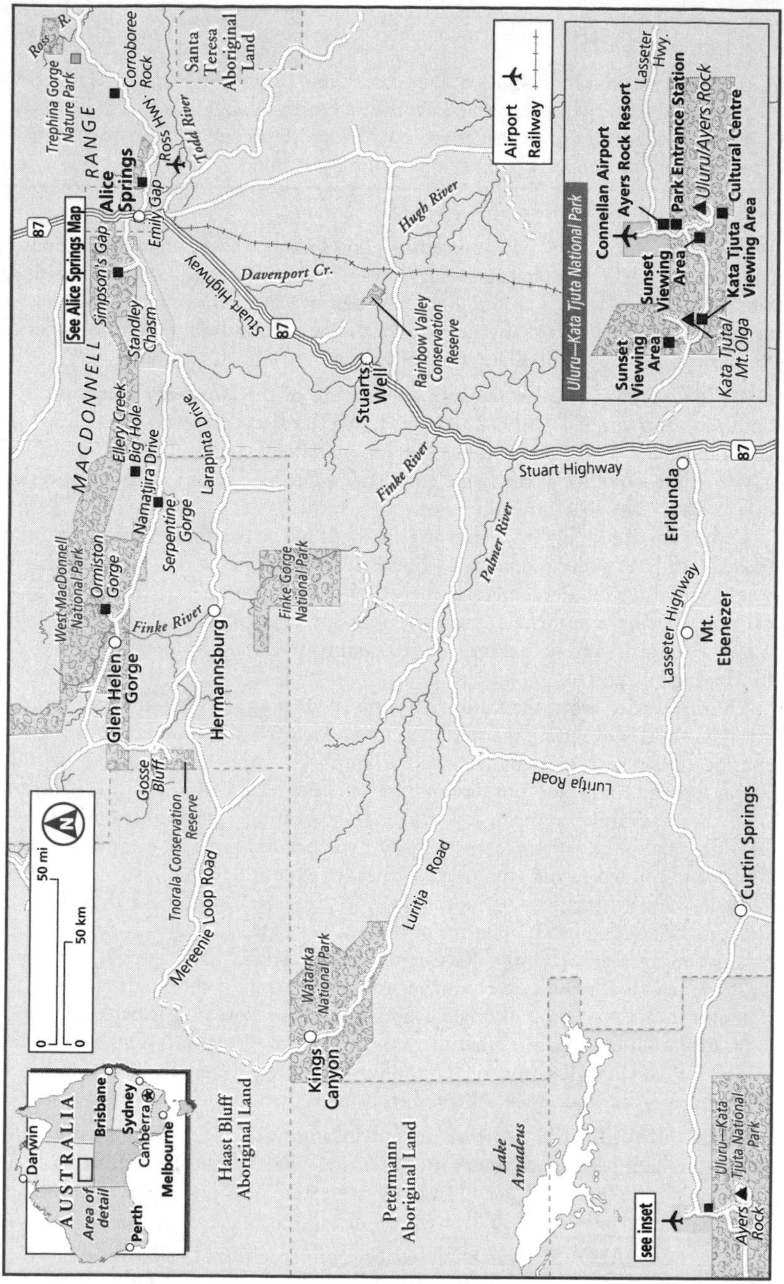
Alice Springs
See Alice Springs Map
MACDONNELL RANGE
Trephina Gorge Nature Park
Ross R.
Corroboree Rock
Ross Hwy.
Todd River
Santa Teresa Aboriginal Land
Emily Gap
Simpson's Gap
Standley Chasm
Stuart Highway
Davenport Cr.
Hugh River
Rainbow Valley Conservation Reserve
Stuarts Well
Ellery Creek Big Hole
Namatjira Drive
Serpentine Gorge
Larapinta Drive
West MacDonnell National Park
Ormiston Gorge
Finke River
Glen Helen Gorge
Hermannsburg
Finke Gorge National Park
Palmer River
Erldunda
Lasseter Highway
Mt. Ebenezer
Gosse Bluff
Tnorala Conservation Reserve
Mereenie Loop Road
Luritja Road
Curtin Springs
Watarrka National Park
Kings Canyon
Haast Bluff Aboriginal Land
Petermann Aboriginal Land
Lake Amadeus
Uluru—Kata Tjuta National Park
Ayers Rock
see inset
Airport
Railway
Uluru—Kata Tjuta National Park
Connellan Airport
Ayers Rock Resort
Lasseter Hwy.
Park Entrance Station
Uluru/Ayers Rock
Cultural Centre
Kata Tjuta Viewing Area
Sunset Viewing Area
Sunset Viewing Area
Kata Tjuta/ Mt. Olga
0
50 mi
0
50 km
N
AUSTRALIA
Darwin
Area of detail
Perth
Brisbane
Sydney
Canberra
Melbourne
87

Tips Buzz Off!

Uluru is notorious for plagues of flies in summer. Don't be embarrassed to cover your head with the fly nets sold in souvenir stores—you'll look like the Dreamtime Beekeeper from Outer Space, but there will be "no flies on you, mate," an Aussie way of saying you are doing the right thing.

WHEN TO GO April, May, September, and October have sunny days (coolish in May, hot in Oct). Winter (June–Aug) means mild temperatures with cold nights. Summer (Nov–Mar) is ferociously hot and best avoided. In summer, limit exertions to early morning and late afternoon, and choose air-conditioned accommodations. Rain is rare but can come at any time of year.

DRIVING TIPS The **Automobile Association of the Northern Territory,** 79–81 Smith St., Darwin, NT 0800 (✆ **08/8981 3837**), offers emergency breakdown service to members of affiliated overseas automobile associations and dispenses maps and advice. It has no office in the Red Centre. For a recorded report of **road conditions,** call ✆ **1800/246 199** in Australia.

Only a handful of highways and arterial roads in the Northern Territory are sealed (paved) roads. A conventional two-wheel-drive car will get you to 95% of what you want to see, but consider renting a four-wheel-drive for complete freedom. All the big car-rental chains have them. Some attractions are on unpaved roads good enough for a two-wheel-drive car, but your car-rental company will not insure a two-wheel-drive for driving on them.

Outside settled areas, the territory has no speed limit, but before you hit the gas, consider the risk of hitting the wildlife: camels, kangaroos, and other protected native species. Locals stick to a comfortable 120kmph (75 mph) or less. Avoid driving at night, early morning, and late afternoon, when 'roos feed; beware of cattle lying down on the warm bitumen at night. A white road sign bearing a black circle outline crossed by a diagonal black line indicates the point when speed restrictions no longer apply. Make sure you have a full tank of gas before setting out.

Road trains (trucks hauling more than one container) and fatigue caused by driving long distances are two other major threats. For details on safe driving, review the tips in the "By Car" section of "Getting Around Australia" in chapter 2.

If you plan to "go bush" in remote regions not covered by this guide, you may need a permit from the relevant Aboriginal lands council to cross Aboriginal land. This can be a drawn-out bureaucratic affair that takes weeks, so plan ahead. The Northern Territory Tourist Commission (see "Visitor Information," above) can put you in touch with the appropriate council. All good road maps mark Aboriginal lands clearly.

OTHER TRAVEL TIPS **Always carry drinking water.** When hiking, carry 4 liters (about a gallon) per person per day in winter, and a liter (¼ gal.) per person per hour in summer. Wear a broad-brimmed hat, high-factor sunscreen, and insect repellent.

Bring warm clothing for chilly evenings in winter.

TOUR OPERATORS Numerous coach, minicoach, and four-wheel-drive tour operators run tours that take in Alice Springs, Kings Canyon, and Uluru. They depart from Alice Springs or Uluru, offering accommodations ranging from spiffy resorts, comfortable motels, and basic cabins to shared bunkhouses, tents, or swags (sleeping bags) under the stars. Most pack the highlights into a 2- or 3-day trip, though leisurely trips of 6 days or more are available. Many offer one-way itineraries between Alice and the Rock (via Kings Canyon if you like), or vice versa, which will allow you to avoid backtracking.

Among the reputable companies are **AAT Kings** (**© 1800/334 009** in Australia, or 03/9274 7422 for the Melbourne central reservations office; www.aatkings.com), which specializes in coach tours but also has four-wheel-drive camping itineraries; **Alice Springs Holidays** (**© 08/8953 1411;** www.alicespringsholidays.com.au), which does upscale soft-adventure tours for groups; **Sahara Adventures** (**© 08/8252 5333;** www.saharaadventures.com.au), which conducts camping safaris in small groups for all ages; and **Discovery Ecotours** (**© 08/8956 2563;** www.ecotours.com.au), which specializes in ecotours for groups. **Tailormade Tours** (**© 08/8952 1731;** www.tailormadetours.com.au) and **VIP Travel Australia** (**© 1800/806 412** in Australia, or 08/8956 2388; www.vipaustralia.com.au) customize luxury tours in limos, minicoaches, and four-wheel-drives, and offer treats like desert barbecues and champagne tailgate dinners overlooking the Rock or the Olgas.

Aboriginal Desert Discovery Tours (**© 08/8952 3408;** www.aboriginalart.com.au), owned by Alice Springs Aboriginal people, teams up its Aboriginal guides with Alice-based tour companies to offer tours with an Aboriginal slant.

2 Alice Springs

462km (286 miles) NE of Uluru (Ayers Rock); 1,491km (924 miles) S of Darwin; 1,544km (957 miles) N of Adelaide; 2,954km (1,831 miles) NW of Sydney

"The Alice," as Australians fondly dub it, is the unofficial capital of Outback Australia. In the early 1870s, a handful of telegraph-station workers struggled nearly 1,600km (992 miles) north from Adelaide through the desert to settle by a small spring in what must have seemed like the ends of the earth. Alice Springs, as the place was called, was just a few huts around a repeater station on the ambitious telegraph line that was to link Adelaide with Darwin and the rest of the world.

Today Alice, as it's also known, is a city of 27,000 people, with supermarkets, banks, and the odd nightclub. It's a friendly, rambling, unsophisticated place. No matter what direction you come from, you will soar for hours over a vast, flat landscape to get here. That's why folks are so surprised when they reach Alice Springs and see low but dramatic mountain ranges, rippling red in the sunshine. Many people excitedly mistake them for Uluru, but that baby is about 462km (286 miles) down the road. The craggy hills close by are the **MacDonnell Ranges.**

Many tourists visit Alice only to get to Uluru, but Alice has charms all its own, albeit mostly of a small-town kind. The red folds of the MacDonnell Ranges hide lovely gorges with shady picnic grounds. A planned 250km (155-mile) hiking trail is partly ready for your boots now. The area has an old gold-rush town to poke around in, quirky little museums, wildlife parks, a couple of cattle stations (ranches) that welcome visitors, a couple of nice day trips, and one of the world's top 10 desert golf courses. You could easily fill 2 or 3 days.

This is the heart of the Aboriginal Arrernte people's country, and Alice is a rich source of tours, shops, and galleries for those interested in Aboriginal culture, art, or souvenirs. There is a sad side to this story. Not every Aborigine succeeds in splicing his or her ancient civilization with the 21st century, and the result is dislocated communities living in the riverbed with only alcohol for company.

ESSENTIALS

GETTING THERE **By Plane** **Qantas** (✆ **13 13 13** in Australia) flies direct from Sydney, Adelaide, Darwin, Cairns, Broome, and Uluru (Ayers Rock). Flights from most other cities connect via Sydney or Adelaide. **Virgin Blue** (✆ **13 67 80** in Australia; www.virginblue.com.au) flies to Alice Springs direct from Sydney, with connections from Adelaide, Brisbane, the Gold Coast, and Melbourne. The company offers heavily discounted prices if you book online well in advance. Prices start at around A$570 (US$456/UK£228) for a two-way trip.

The **Alice Springs Airport Shuttle** (✆ **08/8953 0310;** office: Gregory Terrace) meets all major flights, but not always those from small towns like Tennant Creek. It transfers you to your Alice hotel door for A$12 (US$9.60/UK£4.80) one-way or A$20 (US$16/UK£8) round-trip. A taxi from the airport to town, a distance of 15km (9⅓ miles), is around A$25 (US$20/UK£10).

By Train The ***Ghan*** train, named after Afghan camel-train drivers who carried supplies in the Red Centre during the 19th century, makes the trip from Adelaide to Alice every week, continuing to Darwin. The twice-weekly Adelaide-Alice service (leaving Adelaide on Sun and Wed at 12:20pm and Alice Springs on Thurs and Sat) takes roughly 24 hours. The *Ghan* departs Alice Springs for Darwin on Monday and Thursday at 6pm, arriving in Katherine on Tuesday and Friday mornings, and Darwin in the afternoon. The service from Darwin departs on Wednesday and Saturday. Stopovers in Katherine last at least 4 hours. The route is often treeless and empty, if fascinatingly so; don't be concerned that you'll miss it by overnighting on the train. The train has sleeper berths. For information, contact **Great Southern Railway** (✆ **13 21 47** in Australia, or 08/8213 4592; www.gsr.com.au) or see "Getting Around Australia," in chapter 2, for its booking agencies abroad.

The Airport Shuttle (✆ **08/8953 0310**) runs between the station and the town center for A$5 (US$4/UK£2) one-way and A$8 (US$6.40/UK£3.20) round-trip. A taxi costs about A$7 (US$5.60/UK£2.70) for the trip.

By Bus **Greyhound** (✆ **13 14 99** in Australia, or 07/4690 9950; www.greyhound.com.au) runs from Adelaide and Darwin. It's a 21-hour trip from Adelaide, and the fare is around A$220 (US$176/UK£88). The 21-hour trip from Darwin costs about A$240 (US$192/UK£96). The 36-hour trip from Cairns costs A$410 (US$328/UK£164). A daily 5¾-hour run connects with Uluru (Ayers Rock); the fare is around A$75 (US$60/UK£30).

By Car Alice Springs is on the Stuart Highway linking Adelaide and Darwin. Allow a very long 2 days or a more comfortable 3 days to drive from Adelaide, the same from Darwin. From Sydney, connect to the Stuart Highway via Broken Hill and Port Augusta north of Adelaide; from Cairns, head south to Townsville, then west via the town of Mount Isa to join the Stuart Highway at Tennant Creek. Both routes are long and dull. From Perth it is an even longer, duller drive across the Nullarbor Plain to connect with the Stuart Highway at Port Augusta. If you fancy a driving holiday of

---

Tips **Safety in the Centre**

Alice is a safe place, but steer clear of dark streets and the riverbed at night, when some teenagers can make a nuisance of themselves.

Alice Springs

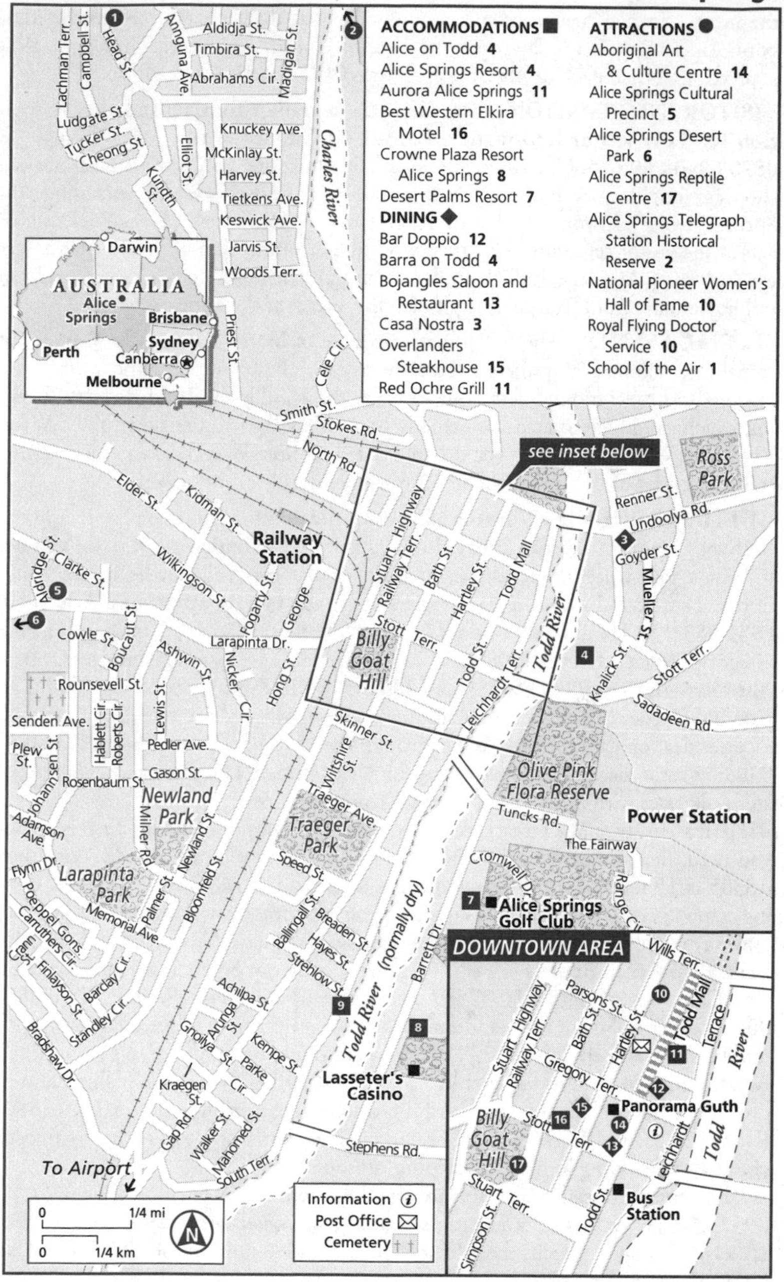

ACCOMMODATIONS ■
Alice on Todd **4**
Alice Springs Resort **4**
Aurora Alice Springs **11**
Best Western Elkira
 Motel **16**
Crowne Plaza Resort
 Alice Springs **8**
Desert Palms Resort **7**

DINING ◆
Bar Doppio **12**
Barra on Todd **4**
Bojangles Saloon and
 Restaurant **13**
Casa Nostra **3**
Overlanders
 Steakhouse **15**
Red Ochre Grill **11**

ATTRACTIONS ●
Aboriginal Art
 & Culture Centre **14**
Alice Springs Cultural
 Precinct **5**
Alice Springs Desert
 Park **6**
Alice Springs Reptile
 Centre **17**
Alice Springs Telegraph
 Station Historical
 Reserve **2**
National Pioneer Women's
 Hall of Fame **10**
Royal Flying Doctor
 Service **10**
School of the Air **1**

AUSTRALIA
Darwin
Alice Springs
Perth
Brisbane
Sydney
Canberra
Melbourne

see inset below

Ross Park

Railway Station

Billy Goat Hill

Olive Pink Flora Reserve

Power Station

Newland Park

Traeger Park

Larapinta Park

The Fairway

Alice Springs Golf Club

DOWNTOWN AREA

Lasseter's Casino

Panorama Guth

Bus Station

Billy Goat Hill

To Airport

0 1/4 mi
0 1/4 km

Information ⓘ
Post Office ✉
Cemetery

the area, with rental car and accommodations included, then check out **www.ntholidays.com**. An example is a 6-day trip from Alice to Uluru/Ayers Rock, The Olgas, Kings Canyon, and then back to Alice Springs for A$952 (US$761/UK£380).

VISITOR INFORMATION The **Central Australian Tourism Industry Association (CATIA) Visitor Information Centre,** 60 Gregory Terrace, Alice Springs, NT 0870 (© **08/8952 5800;** www.centralaustraliantourism.com), is the official one-stop shop for bookings and touring information for the Red Centre, including Alice Springs, Kings Canyon, and Uluru–Kata Tjuta National Park (Ayers Rock). It also acts as the visitor center for the Parks & Wildlife Commission of the Northern Territory. It's open Monday through Friday from 8:30am to 5:30pm and weekends and public holidays from 9am to 4pm. It also has a desk at the airport.

SPECIAL EVENTS The town hosts a couple of bizarre events. The **Camel Cup** camel race takes place on the second Saturday in July. In late September, folks from hundreds of miles around come out to cheer the **Henley-on-Todd Regatta** ★, during which gaudily decorated, homemade bottomless "boats" race down the dry Todd River bed. Well, what else do you do on a river that flows only 3 days a year? See "Australia Calendar of Events" in chapter 2 for more details on this event.

GETTING AROUND Virtually all tours pick you up at your hotel.

If your itinerary traverses unpaved roads, as it may in outlying areas, you will need to rent a four-wheel-drive vehicle, because regular cars will not be insured on an unpaved surface. However, a regular car will get you to most attractions. **Avis** (© 08/8953 5533; 52 Hartley St.), **Budget** (© 08/8952 8899; Shop 6, Capricornia Centre, Gregory Terrace), **Hertz** (© 08/8952 2644; 76 Hartley St.), local company **Outback Auto Rentals** (© 08/8953 5333), and **Thrifty** (© 08/8952 9999; corner of Stott Terrace and Hartley St.) all rent conventional and four-wheel-drive vehicles. You may get a better deal on car rental by going through the **Outback Travel Shop** (© 08/8955 5288; www.outbacktravelshop.com.au) in Alice Springs, a booking agent that negotiates bulk rates with most Alice car-rental companies.

Hertz, Thrifty, and Outback Auto Rentals rent **camping kits** holding everything you need, including a tent, sleeping bags, and a gas stove. A kit usually costs around A$385 (US$308/UK£154) for two people for 5 days. Book them in advance. Carrying camping gear, as well as your luggage, probably means you have to hire a larger car!

Many rental outfits for motor homes (camper vans) have Alice offices. They include **Britz Campervan Rentals** (© 08/8952 8814; corner of Stuart Hwy. and Power St.), **Kea Campers** (© 08/8955 5525; 7 Kidman St.), and **Maui Rentals** (© 08/8952 8049; corner of Stuart Hwy. and Power St.). As an example of price, another outfitter, **Apollo Campers** (© 1800/777 779 in Australia; www.apollocamper.com), rents two- to three-berth vans for around A$100 (US$80/UK£40) a day, with pickup and drop-off at several major centers. A four-wheel-drive version costs A$165 to A$220 (US$132–US$175/UK£66–UK£87) a day. This can work out to be significantly cheaper than staying in hotels and going on tours.

The **Stuart Tourist and Caravan Park,** Lerapinta Drive, Alice Springs (© **08/8952 2547;** www.stuartcaravanpark.com.au), has powered sites costing A$26 (US$21/UK£10) a night. Cabins here cost between A$58 and A$80 (US$46–US$64/UK£23–UK£37) per night.

The best way to get around town without your own transport is aboard the **Alice Wanderer** bus (see "Organized Tours," below). Taxi fares are exorbitant, presumably because there's only one main outfit in town, **Alice Springs Taxis** (✆ **13 10 08** or 08/8952 1877). They congregate on the corner of Todd Street and Gregory Terrace.

CITY LAYOUT **Todd Mall** is the heart of town. Most shops, businesses, and restaurants are here or within a few blocks' walk. Most hotels, the casino, the golf course, and many of the town's attractions are a few kilometers outside of town. The dry Todd River "flows" through the city east of Todd Mall.

SEEING THE SIGHTS IN ALICE

Aboriginal Art & Culture Centre Set up by the Southern Arrernte Aboriginal people, this center houses a small, intriguing museum with exhibits on Aboriginal life. It displays a timeline of the Aboriginal view of history since "contact" (the arrival of Europeans). It's worth a visit if you're interested in indigenous cultures. It sells artifacts and art. Allow 15 to 60 minutes.

86 Todd St. ✆ **08/8952 3408.** Free admission. Daily 8am–5pm.

Alice Springs Cultural Precinct At least one or two of the attractions here will probably pique your interest. All of them are within walking distance of each another. The **Museum of Central Australia** mostly shows local fossils, natural history displays, and meteorites. Some impressive Aboriginal and contemporary Aussie art is on display at the **Araluen Centre** (✆ **08/8951 1122**), the town's performing arts hub; check out the "Honey Ant Dreaming" stained-glass window in its foyer. Aviation nuts may want to browse the old radios, aircraft, and wreckage in the **Aviation Museum,** which preserves the territory's aerial history. You can buy stylish crafts, and sometimes catch artists at work, in the **Territory Craft** gallery. You may want to amble among the outdoor sculptures, including the 15m (49-ft.) *Yeperenye Dreamtime Caterpillar,* or among the gravestones in the cemetery, where "Afghani" camel herders (from what is now Pakistan) are buried facing Mecca. To reach the precinct, take a cab, Alice Wanderer bus, or Desert Park Transfers. There is a picnic area, but save your meal for the Alice Springs Telegraph Station Historical Reserve (below).

Larapinta Dr. at Memorial Ave., 2km (1¼ miles) south of town. ✆ **08/8951 1120.** Admission (includes Museum of Central Australia, Araluen Centre, Central Australian Aviation Museum, Territory Craft, and Memorial Cemetery) A$9 (US$7.30/UK£3.70) adults; A$6 (US$4.80/UK£2.40) seniors, students, and children 5–16; A$23 (US$18/UK£9) families. Mon–Fri 10am–4pm; Sat–Sun 11am–4pm. Closed Good Friday and Dec 25.

Alice Springs Desert Park ★ By means of an easy 1.6km (1-mile) trail through three reconstructed natural habitats, this impressive wildlife and flora park shows you 120 or so of the animal species that live in the desert around Alice but that you won't spot too easily in the wild (including kangaroos you can walk among). Most of the creatures are small mammals (like the big-eared bilby), reptiles (cute thorny devil lizards), and birds. Don't miss the excellent **Birds of Prey** ★★ show. There's a cafe here, too. The **Alice Wanderer** bus (✆ **1800/722 111** in Australia, or 08/8952 2111; www.alicewanderer.com.au) has an add-on visit to the park with its town tour (see Alice Wanderer, below). Allow 2 to 3 hours.

Larapinta Dr., 6km (3¾ miles) west of town. ✆ **08/8951 8788.** www.alicespringsdesertpark.com.au. Admission A$18 (US$14/UK£7) adults, A$9 (US$5.85/UK£3) students and children 5–16, A$40 (US$32/UK£16) families. Daily 7:30am–6pm (last suggested entry 4pm; 'roo and emu exhibit closes 4:30pm). Closed Dec 25.

Alice Springs Reptile Centre *Kids* Kids can walk around with pythons or bearded dragons (lizards) on their shoulders, all day if they want, at this Aussie reptile park. The easygoing proprietor lifts up the cages' glass fronts for better photos and lets kids hand-feed bugs to the animals at feeding time. Some 30 species are on display, including the world's deadliest land snake—the taipan—and big goannas. Also here are brown snakes, death adders, and mulga, otherwise known as king brown snakes. Don't miss the saltwater croc exhibit featuring underwater viewing. Allow an hour.

9 Stuart Terrace (opposite the Royal Flying Doctor Service). ✆ **08/8952 8900.** www.reptilecentre.com.au. Admission A$8 (US$6.40/UK£3.20) adults, A$4 (US$3.20/UK£1.60) children under 17, A$20 (US$16/UK£8) families. Daily 9am–5pm. Closed Jan 1 and Dec 25.

Alice Springs Telegraph Station Historical Reserve ★ *Finds* Alice Springs began life in 1872 as this charming telegraph repeater station, set by a pretty water hole amid red bouldery hills, sprawling gums full of parrots, and mercifully green lawns. An oasis in the harsh Alice landscape, it's a place tourists often overlook. Arm yourself with the free map or join a free 45-minute tour. You can wander around the old stationmaster's residence; the telegraph office, with its Morse code machine tap-tapping away; the shoeing yard packed with blacksmith's equipment; and the stables, housing vintage buggies and saddlery. From the on-site computer, you can "telegraph" e-mails to your friends. May through October, "kitchen maids" in period dress serve scones (biscuits) and damper (campfire bread) from the original wood-fired ovens. The park has pet camels, and sometimes orphaned kangaroo joeys. Allow a good hour, more to walk one of the several hiking trails leading from the extensive grounds. This is a lovely picnic spot. There is a gift shop, and coffee and snacks are for sale, too. To get there, take a cab or Alice Wanderer bus (see "Organized Tours," below) or the 4km (2½-mile) riverside pedestrian/bike track that starts near the corner of Wills Terrace and Undoolya Road. Section One of the Larapinta Trail to Simpsons Gap starts here. Walkers are advised to register with the Walker Registration Scheme through the Parks and Wildlife Office or by phoning ✆ **1300 650 730.**

Stuart Hwy., 4km (2½ miles) north of town (beyond the School of the Air turnoff). ✆ **08/8952 3993.** Free admission to picnic grounds and trails; station A$7 (US$5.60/UK£3.30) adults, A$3.75 (US$3/UK£1.50) children 5–15. Daily 8am–5pm (picnic grounds and trails 'til 9pm). Station closed Dec 25.

Royal Flying Doctor Service Alice is a major base for this airborne medical service that treats people living and traveling in the vast Outback. An interesting 20-minute tour runs every half-hour, featuring a video and a talk in the communications room; allow another 30 minutes or so to browse the small museum. Some of the recorded conversations between doctors and patients are intriguing. There is a nice garden cafe and a gift shop.

8–10 Stuart Terrace (at end of Hartley St.). ✆ **08/8952 1129.** www.flyingdoctor.net. Admission A$6.50 (US$5.20/UK£2.60) adults, A$3 (US$2.40/UK£1.20) children 6–15. Mon–Sat 9am–5pm (last tour 4pm); Sun and public holidays 1–5pm. Closed Jan 1 and Dec 25.

School of the Air Sitting in on school lessons may not be your idea of a vacation, but this school is different—it broadcasts by radio to a 1.3-million-sq.-km (507,000-sq.-mile) "schoolroom" of 140 children on Outback stations. That's as big as Germany, Great Britain, Ireland, New Zealand, and Japan combined—or twice the size of Texas. Visitors watch and listen in when classes are in session; outside class hours, you may hear taped classes. You can browse the kids' artwork, photos, video, and other displays in the well-organized visitor gallery. Free 30-minute tours run throughout the day.

80 Head St. (2.5km/1½ miles from town). ✆ **08/8951 6834.** Admission A$6.50 (US$5.20/UK£2,80) adults, A$4 (US$3.20/UK£1.60) children 5–16, A$16 (US$13/UK£6.50) families. Mon–Sat and public holidays 8:30am–4:30pm; Sun 1:30–4:30pm. Closed Jan 1 and Dec 25–26. Bus: 3 or Alice Wanderer (see "Organized Tours," below).

ORGANIZED TOURS

AROUND TOWN & OUT IN THE DESERT The **Alice Wanderer** bus (✆ **1800/722 111** in Australia, or 08/8952 2111; www.alicewanderer.com.au) does a running loop of 12 town attractions every 70 minutes starting at 9am, with the last departure at 4pm. Hop on and off as you please, and enjoy the commentary from the driver. The bus departs daily from the south end of Todd Mall. Tickets are sold on board and cost A$40 (US$32/UK£16) for adults, and A$30 (US$24/UK£12) for kids 4 to 14. Call for free pickup from your hotel. The ticket lasts for 2 days and you can use it on non-consecutive days. The company also runs full-day tours to outlying areas, including to the West MacDonnell Ranges, costing A$105 (US$84/UK£42) for adults and A$75 (US$60/UK£30) for kids; to Bond Springs Cattle Station, costing A$95 (US$76/UK£38) for adults and A$65 (US$52/UK£26) for kids; and to Santa Teresa Aboriginal Community. Here you can meet local Aborigines, and view and purchase their artwork. This half-day tour costs a whopping A$130 (US$104/UK£52) for adults and A$100 (US$40/UK£20) for kids. There are also half- and full-day tours of the West Macdonnell Ranges (see later).

The bus calls at most of the attractions above, plus the **Old Ghan Museum & Road Transport Hall of Fame,** housing the original *Ghan* train that plied the Adelaide–Alice Springs line from 1929 to 1980; and **Panorama Guth,** an art gallery housing a 360-degree painting of central Australian landscapes by artist Henk Guth.

It's well worth checking out the Alice Wanderer website to help you plan your time before you visit.

Many Alice-based companies offer minicoach or four-wheel-drive day trips and extended tours of Alice and of outlying areas including the East and West Macs, Hermannsburg, and Finke Gorge National Park. Among the well-regarded ones are: **Discovery Ecotours** (✆ **08/8956 2563;** www.ecotours.com.au); **Alice Springs Holidays** (✆ **1800/801 401** in Australia, or 08/8953 1411; www.alicespringsholidays.com.au); and **Alice Springs Tour Professionals** (✆ **1800/673 391** in Australia, or 08/8953 0666).

Several companies run tours by motorcycle or four-wheel-drive ATV (all-terrain vehicle). One option is **Central Oz Tours** (✆ **08/8953 4755;** www.centraloz.biz).

ABORIGINAL TOURS I recommend a visit to the **Aboriginal Art & Culture Centre** (6 Todd St., Alice Springs; www.aboriginalart.com.au). Tours, with Aboriginal leaders, are very pricey, but then Aboriginal tours often come with a premium attached. The **half-day tour** ★ features an explanation of the Dreamtime creation era; a gentle bush tucker walk; a chance to throw a boomerang and spear; talks about tools and weapons over billy tea and damper; and a dance performance at which you can have a go yourself, and have your photo taken with the dancers. You may have seen the dancers performing in the opening ceremony of the Sydney 2000 Olympic games. Threaded through all this is an ongoing discussion of Aboriginal culture, beliefs, family relationships, and a view of history both ancient and modern through Aboriginal eyes. You have a chance to buy art. The experience wraps up with a didgeridoo lesson. The tour departs daily at 8am and costs A$94 (US$75/UK£37) for adults and A$56 (US$45/UK£22) for children under 12, including hotel pickup. A full-day tour, including the West MacDonnell Ranges, costs A$165 (US$132/UK£66) for adults and A$66 (US$53/UK£27) for kids. The center also advertises an "Alice Springs/Red Centre Dreaming dinner," with lots of dancing, atmosphere, and twinkling stars. Dinner includes kangaroo and barramundi fish. The performance, with dinner and wine,

Moments Billy Tea & Damper

Any tour in the Outback isn't complete without the traditional bushman's meal of billy tea and damper. Billy tea is made from tea leaves, and sometimes eucalyptus leaves, put into water (traditionally from a water hole or river) and boiled in an open-topped canister on an open fire. You don't have to stir it; the trick is to pick up the canister by the wire handle and swing the whole thing around, sometimes over your head—centrifugal force keeps the liquid in (don't try this at home, though). Damper is simply flour, water, and salt mixed into dough and thrown in the ashes of the fire to cook into bread. Yummy.

costs A$98 (US$78/UK£39) for adults and A$55 (US$44/UK£22) for kids. Call ✆ **08/8950 4444** to book.

CAMEL SAFARIS You might not associate camels with Australia, but the camel's ability to get by without water was key to opening the arid inland parts of the country to European settlement in the 1800s. With the advent of cars, they were released into the wild, and today more than 200,000 roam central Australia. Australia even exports them to the Middle East! **Frontier Camel Tours** (✆ **08/8950 3030;** http://cameltours.ananguwaai.com.au) runs camel rides daily, with pickup from your hotel. A 1-hour Camel Ramble with associated activities costs A$45 (US$36/UK£18) for adults and A$25 (US$20/UK£10) for kids aged 5 to 12. A 1-hour sunset tour with dinner at the company's camel farm, where you can browse its camel museum and shop, costs A$110 (US$88/UK£44) for adults and A$80 (US$64/UK£32) for kids 5 to 12. It departs daily at 4pm April through October, and at 5pm November through March, and gets back around 5½ hours later. Kids under 6 can join the ride if the Cameleer on duty agrees. A 1-hour sunset ride without dinner costs A$45 (US$36/UK£18) for adults and A$25 (US$20/UK£10) for kids. A breakfast ride, leaving at 6:30am and returning at 9:30am, costs A$85 (US$68/UK£34) for adults and A$50 (US$40/UK£20) for children. The company also runs camel tours near Uluru (Ayers Rock).

HOT-AIR BALLOON FLIGHTS Dawn balloon flights above the desert are popular in central Australia. You have to get up 90 minutes before dawn, though. Several companies offer flights. **Outback Ballooning** (✆ **1800/809 790** in Australia, or 08/8952 8723; www.outbackballooning.com.au) is one of the most upscale. A 1-hour flight followed by champagne breakfast in the bush costs A$360 (US$288/UK£144), with a 20% discount for kids under 17. A 30-minute breakfast flight costs A$230 (US$184/UK£92). Kids under 6 are discouraged from participating because they cannot see over the basket. Don't make any other morning plans—you probably won't get back to your hotel until close to noon.

ACTIVE PURSUITS

BIKING A gently undulating 17km (11-mile) **bike trail** weaves from John Flynn's Grave on Larapinta Drive, 7km (4⅓ miles) west of town, through the bushland and desert foothills of the MacDonnell Ranges to Simpson's Gap (p. 409). **Centre Cycles,** Lindsay Avenue at Undoolya Road (✆ **08/8953 2966**), rents bikes for around A$10 (US$8/UK£4) for 4 hours (plus a A$50/US$40/UK£20 refundable deposit). ***Note:*** Carry water, because the two taps en route are a long way apart. Bike in cooler months only.

BUSHWALKING The 223km (138-mile) **Larapinta Trail** winds west from Alice through the sparse red ranges, picturesque semidesert scenery, and rich bird life of the West MacDonnell National Park (p. 408). This long-distance walking track is divided into 12 sections, each a 1- to 2-day walk. Sections range from easy to hard. The shortest is 8km (5 miles), ranging up to several 23-to-29km (14–18-mile) stretches. The Larapinta Trail begins at the old Alice Springs Telegraph Station and meanders through many gaps and sheltered gorges and climbs steeply over rugged ranges. Each section is accessible to vehicles (some by high clearance 4WD only), so you can join or leave the trail at any of the trail heads. Camping out under a sea of stars in the Outback is a highlight of the experience. Although they vary, most campsites offer picnic tables and hardened tent sites—all trail heads have a water supply and some have free gas barbecues. The **Parks & Wildlife Commission of the Northern Territory** office in Alice Springs (✆ **08/8951 8211**) and the **CATIA Visitor Information Centre** (see "Visitor Information," earlier in this chapter) dispense trail maps and information. Check www.nt.gov.au/nreta/parks/walks/larapinta for detailed information on the trail and downloadable maps. ***Warning:*** *Always* carry drinking water. The trail may close in extremely hot summer periods.

The Alice Wanderer (✆ **1800/72 2111** in Australia, or 08/8952 2111) runs to road access points along the trail, where you can mostly pick up a choice of 1-, 2-, or 3-day hikes. Several outfitters run guided, supported hikes along trail sections.

GOLF The **Alice Springs Golf Club** ★, 1km (just over ½ mile) from town on Cromwell Drive (✆ **08/8952 5440**), boasts a Thomson-Wolveridge course rated among the world's top desert courses by touring pros. The course is open from sunup to sundown. Nine holes cost A$20 (US$16/UK£8); 18 holes, A$30 (US$24/UK£12). Club rental costs A$25 (US$20/UK£10), and a cart, which many locals don't bother with, goes for A$30 (US$24/UK£12). It's best to book a tee time.

SHOPPING AT THE SOURCE FOR ABORIGINAL ART

Alice Springs is the best place in Australia to buy **Aboriginal art and crafts** ★. You will find no shortage of stuff: linen and canvas paintings, didgeridoos, spears, clapping sticks, *coolamons* (a dish used by women to carry anything from water to babies), animal carvings, baskets, and jewelry, as well as books, CDs, and all kinds of non-Aboriginal merchandise printed with Aboriginal designs. Prices can soar into the thousands for large canvases by world-renowned painters, but you will find plenty of small works for under A$250 (US$200/UK£100). Major artworks sell unmounted for ease of shipment, which most galleries arrange. Store hours can vary with the seasons and the crowds, so it pays to check ahead.

Papunya Tula Artists, 78 Todd St. (✆ **08/8952 4731**), sells paintings on canvas and linen from Papunya and other artists living in the desert as far as 700km (434 miles) west of Alice Springs.

If you're interested in investing in serious artwork, speak to Roslyn Premont, proprietor of **Gallery Gondwana,** 43 Todd Mall (✆ **08/8953 1577**). She has written a book on desert art, and her gallery sells only top-notch works.

The outdoor **Todd Mall Markets** (✆ **08/8952 9299**) are held every second Sunday morning from late February to December. Expect local arts, crafts, food, and buskers.

A MUSEUM & GALLERY

Mbantua Gallery ★★★ *Finds* Raucously colorful paintings line the walls like dot candy at this museum-gallery, which is one of the most reliable sources of authentic

Aboriginal art. The selection is dizzying, but prices can be affordable, and chances are good that an artist or two will be tooling around when you visit. The art comes from a harsh desert region ironically called Utopia, two hours by car from Alice Springs, where indigenous Australians live in encampments akin to Native American reservations in the U.S. Mbantua owner Tim Jennings began supplying locals with paints and canvas during food deliveries to Utopia, first as sheriff then as concerned general store owner. Every two weeks, he drops off new materials and pays the artists for finished works. More than 75 Utopia residents paint; the website features artists' portraits and bios, in conjunction with their work. Some have garnered international recognition; in 2007, *The New York Times* praised the work of Barbara Weir, Gloria Petyarre, and the late painters Emily Kangwarre and Minnie Pwerle. Predictably, as Aboriginal artwork grows in value, forgeries are on the rise. Jennings authenticates every piece of art; he and his gallery employees photograph the artist with the work and elicit the Aboriginal dreaming, or traditional meaning, behind it. Works by established artists can range in price from $850 to tens of thousands; in early 2007, a painting by Kangwarre broke a record for Aboriginal art by fetching more than A$1 million. A couple hundred bucks, however, will fetch you work by lesser known but talented painters. The artists earn a fraction of what the art is worth, but they still fare better at galleries such as Mbantua, which pays them in cash or essential goods, rather than alcohol or other dubious collateral.

1 Gregory Terrace, (PO Box 8118), Alice Springs 0871. ✆ **08/8952-5571**. Fax: 08/8952-5191. www.mbantua.com/au. Open Mon–Fri 9am–6pm; Sat 9:30am–5pm; Sun 1pm–5pm. AE, DC, MC, V.

WHERE TO STAY

Alice's hotel stock is not grand. Many properties have dated rooms and modest facilities; they're no match for the gleaming **Ayers Rock Resort** (described later in this chapter). You may pay lower rates than those listed in the summer off season (Dec–Mar), and even as late as June. Peak season typically runs from July through October or November. Besides the more upmarket properties below, there are several backpacker resorts offering dorm rooms and doubles. One of the best is **Annie's Place,** 4 Traegar Ave., Alice Springs, NT 0870 (✆ **1800/359 089** in Australia, or 08/8952 1545; www.anniesplace.com.au). Doubles cost between A$50 (US$28/UK£14) for a room with shared bathroom and A$60 (US$48/UK£24) for one with your own. Annie's Place runs **Mulgas Adventures,** which operates a 3-day backpackers tour of the area for A$250 (US$200/UK£100), with most things included.

EXPENSIVE

Alice Springs Resort ★ This friendly, well-run, low-rise property is a 3-minute walk from town over the Todd River. Standard rooms are quite pleasant, while deluxe rooms are a touch plusher and have outlooks across the Todd River or the gardens, In summer, it's nice to repair to the pool under a couple of desert palms after a hot day's sightseeing. A fire glows in the **Gumtree Lounge** bar on winter evenings.

34 Stott Terrace, Alice Springs, NT 0870. ✆ **800/225-9849** in the U.S., 1300/134 044 in Australia, or 08/8951 4545. Fax 08/8953 0995. www.alicespringsresort.com.au. 144 units, 108 with shower only. A$150–A$240 (US$120–US$192/UK£60–UK£96) double. Extra person A$25 (US$20/UK£10). Children under 12 stay free in parent's room with existing bedding. Ask about packages with Ayers Rock Resort and Kings Canyon Resort. AE, DC, MC, V. Free parking. **Amenities:** Restaurant; 2 bars; solar-heated outdoor pool; bike rental; concierge; tour desk; airport shuttle; secretarial services; limited room service; in-room massage; babysitting; laundry service; dry cleaning. *In room:* A/C, TV w/pay movies, minibar, hair dryer, iron.

Bond Springs Outback Retreat ★ *Finds* This working 1,515-sq.-km (591-sq.-mile) cattle ranch is a great place to get a taste of Outback life with a real Aussie family. A reader said it reminded her of the kind of place you'd see in *The Thorn Birds*. Janice Heaslip welcomes guests to her homestead, inviting them to join country dinners with the family and accommodating them in two appealing cottages. The first is Corkwood Cottage, which was originally built for the station's head stockman and his family. The main bedroom features a queen-size bed, and two other bedrooms each have twin beds and a single bed. There's a comfortable lounge and dining room, a fully equipped kitchen, and an outdoor barbecue. The second cottage, called "The Wurlie," has a main bedroom with a queen-size bed and a second bedroom with twin beds. There's a lounge and dining room, which includes a kitchenette. Gourmet breakfasts are delivered to both cottages. The owners run a range of day trips, overnight bush camps, and tours throughout the Red Centre, making this a good base for exploring. Ask about 3- and 5-day packages, some of which include tours and accommodations at Kings Canyon Resort and Ayers Rock Resort. There's no smoking indoors.

Note: All but the last 6km (3¾ miles) of the road to the ranch is paved. Car-rental companies do not allow driving on unpaved roads, but they may permit it here; check with your company.

25km (16 miles) north of Alice Springs (P.O. Box 4), Alice Springs, NT 0870. ✆ **08/8952 9888.** Fax 08/8953 0963. www.outbackretreat.com.au. 2 cottages. A$277 (US$221/UK£111) Corkwood Cottage; A$231 (US$185/UK£93) The Wurlie Cottage. Rates include full breakfast. Extra adult A$58 (US$46/UK£23); extra child 6–15 A$47 (US$38/UK£19). Dinner A$55 (US$44/UK£22) per person. MC, V. Closed Dec 25–Jan. Transfers from Alice Springs A$40 (US$32/UK£16) from town, A$80 (US$64/UK£32) from airport, one-way, per vehicle. **Amenities:** Unheated outdoor pool; outdoor tennis court; laundry service. *In room:* A/C, fridge, hair dryer, no phone.

MODERATE

Alice on Todd ★ *Kids* A new addition to the Alice accommodations scene, Alice on Todd has nice one- and two-bedroom apartments. It's a very good option, particularly if you have kids (if they're under 4 they stay free). The hotel overlooks the Todd River and is just a short stroll from town. The two luxury two-bedroom apartments each have an extra sofa bed.

Strehlow St. and South Terrace (P.O. Box 8454), Alice Springs, NT 0870. ✆ **08/8953 8033.** www.aliceontodd.com. 34 units. A$105 (US$84/UK£42) studio apt; A$130 (US$104/UK£52) 1-bedroom apt; A$160 (US$128/UK£64) 2-bedroom apt; A$180 (US$144/UK£72) luxury 2-bedroom apt. Additional person A$20 (US$16/UK£8). AE, MC, V. **Amenities:** Outdoor pool; game room. *In room:* A/C, TV, kitchenette, fridge, coffeemaker, iron, washing machine.

Aurora Alice Springs This pleasant hotel is smack in the center of town. Rooms in the newer wing are standard motel-style lodgings, all large and decorated nicely. Those in the original wing are small and a little dark; they have a pretty heritage theme, with floral bedcovers and lace curtains. New Executive rooms have a king-size bed and private balconies facing the Todd River. Deluxe and Standard rooms have one double bed and one single bed. Family rooms have a double bed and a set of bunks. The courtyard has a barbecue, and the front desk loans hair dryers. The tiny pool and Jacuzzi are tucked away in a corner, so this is not the place for chilling out poolside; stay here to be within walking distance of shops and restaurants.

Leichhardt Terrace (backing onto Todd Mall), Alice Springs, NT 0870. ✆ **08/8950 6666.** Fax 08/8952 7829. www.aurora resorts.com.au. 108 units, all with shower only. A$99–A$199 (US$80–US$160/UK£40–UK£80) double. Extra person A$20 (US$16/UK£8). Children under 14 stay free in parent's room with existing bedding. AE, DC, MC, V. Free parking. Hotel provides transfers from airport (A$11/US$8.80/UK£4.40 per person one-way); also picks up from train. **Amenities:** Restaurant (Red Ochre Grill; see "Where to Dine," below); small heated outdoor pool; Jacuzzi; tour desk; airport shuttle; limited room service; babysitting; laundry service; dry cleaning. *In room:* A/C, TV w/pay movies, minibar, fridge, iron.

Crowne Plaza Resort Alice Springs ★ *Value* Next to the golf club and near Lasseter's Casino, this is one of Alice's fanciest resorts. Three stories of rooms wrap around the pool and an ample sun deck. All rooms are spacious. Each has a balcony—some look onto the pool, some toward town, some over the red ranges. Barbecues take place around the pool at lunch and dinner from September through March.

Barrett Dr. (1.5km/1 mile from town center), Alice Springs, NT 0870. © **1800/000 867** in Australia, or 08/8950 8000. Fax 08/8953 0475. www.rydges.com. 236 units. A$160–A$215 (US$128–US$172/UK£64–UK£86) double; A$350–A$500 (US$280–US$400/UK£140–UK£200) suite. Extra person A$25 (US$20/UK£10). Children under 13 stay free in parent's room with existing bedding. Free cribs. Ask about packages. AE, DC, MC, V. Free parking. **Amenities:** Restaurant; bar; heated outdoor pool; 2 lit tennis courts; exercise room w/plunge pool; Jacuzzi; sauna; bike rental; tour desk; airport shuttle; secretarial services; 24-hr. room service; babysitting; laundry service; dry cleaning. *In room:* A/C, TV w/pay movies, dataport, minibar, hair dryer, iron.

INEXPENSIVE

Best Western Elkira Motel The cheapest rooms in the heart of town—decent ones, that is—are at this unpretentious motel. Standard rooms are dated, with lots of wood and tile floors, and a fridge and shower. Two standard family rooms come with a double bed and three singles. Deluxe rooms have a little more space; some have microwaves, and some have queen-size beds, yet more have a spa tub. Family rooms are nicer still, and come with a kitchenette. They cost the same as normal deluxe rooms and are well worth asking for even if you're traveling as a couple. All deluxe family rooms and a few deluxe doubles have bathrooms. The seven budget rooms are a little dated, and though small, they are comfortable and quiet. They come with a double bed, TV, shower, fridge, and hair dryer. Two units have Jacuzzis. Ask for a room away from the road, because the traffic is noisy during the day.

65 Bath St. (opposite Kmart), Alice Springs, NT 0870. © **08/8952 1222.** Fax 08/8953 1370. www.elkira.com.au. 58 units, some with shower only. A$110–A$180 (US$88–US$144/UK£44–UK£72) double or family room. Extra adult A$15 (US$12/UK£6); extra child under 3 A$5 (US$4/UK£2). AE, DC, MC, V. Free parking. **Amenities:** 2 restaurants; unheated outdoor pool; nearby golf course; Jacuzzi; tour desk; car-rental desk; airport shuttle; limited room service; laundry service; dry cleaning; nonsmoking rooms. *In room:* A/C, TV, fax, dataport, fridge, coffeemaker, hair dryer, iron, safe.

Desert Palms Resort ★ *Value* Next to Lasseter's Casino (where the food can be awful) and the Alice Springs Golf Club (where guests have honorary membership), these cheery cabins behind manicured palms and pink bougainvillea are one of the nicest places to stay in Alice. Don't be deterred by their prefab appearance; inside they are surprisingly large, well kept, and inviting, with a pine-pitched ceiling, a minikitchen, a sliver of bathroom sporting white tiles and fittings, and a furnished front deck. Four rooms are suitable for travelers with disabilities. A sun deck and pool with its own little island is out front. The pleasant staff at the front desk loans hair dryers, processes film, does laundry, sells basic grocery and liquor supplies, and books tours.

74 Barrett Dr. (1km/½ mile from town), Alice Springs, NT 0870. © **1800/678 037** in Australia, or 08/8952 5977. Fax 08/8953 4176. www.desertpalms.com.au. 80 units, all with shower only. A$120 (US$96/UK£48) double; A$135 (US$108/UK£54) triple; A$145 (US$116/UK£58) quad. Extra person A$10 (US$8/UK£4). AE, DC, MC, V. Amenities: Large unheated outdoor pool; golf course nearby; half-size tennis court; access to nearby health club; tour desk; car-rental desk; free coach station/train station/airport shuttle twice daily; free resort-to-town shuttle 4 times daily; massage; laundry service; dry cleaning; nonsmoking rooms. In room: A/C, TV, dataport, kitchenette, fridge, coffeemaker.

A LUXURY STAY ON TRIBAL LAND

Gunya Titjikala ★★★ For a steep fee, these all-inclusive luxury safari tents afford visitors the precious chance to interact with indigenous Australians as guests on their land. The project is a joint venture between Gunya Tourism and the Titjikala Aboriginal community in the Simpson desert, 120km (74 miles) outside Alice Springs. Proceeds go toward sustaining the community's traditional way of life. The tents are posh as tents go, with plumbing though no electricity; three daily meals are included in the price, as are nonalcoholic beverages (Titjikala is dry). A visionary amateur anthropologist named Steve Watkins helps the community manage the site and the money. Guests can custom-design their itineraries, but a typical day might involve the female guests foraging for witchetty grubs with the women, while the menfolk hunt kangaroo, butcher their catches, and roast them for that night's dinner. One constant's guaranteed: As members of the world's oldest culture fighting for its life, the residents of Titjikala will blow your mind and break your heart.

Information/ reservations, see website or contact Level 57, MLC Centre, 19 Martin Place, Sydney, NSW 2000. ✆ **02/9211-2322.** Fax 02/9211-3569. www.gunya.com/au. Double tents A$1,300 (US$1,040/UK£520) per night (minimum 2 night stay; each extra adult A$200 (US$160/UK£80) per night; children under 15 free with existing bedding). Price includes 3 meals/day and non-alcoholic beverages. AE, MC, V.

WHERE TO DINE

EXPENSIVE

Barra On Todd ★★ MODERN AUSTRALIAN Ask the locals for the best chow in town, and this is where they'll send you. This, the former Palms Restaurant, is part of the Alice Springs Resort. There are usually two or three barramundi dishes on the menu, as well as lamb shanks, steak, flambéed prawns (in malibu, with garlic and sweet chile cream sauce, rice, and asparagus), and roasted chicken roulade (with bacon, leek and sweet-potato filling, parsnip and cream cheese mash, and oven-roasted tomato salsa). It does a good breakfast menu and all-day-dining by the pool (with dishes costing just A$15/US$12/UK£6). Live piano music plays nightly.

At the Alice Springs Resort, 34 Stott Terrace. ✆ **08/8951 4545.** Reservations recommended at dinner. Main courses A$18–A$28 (US$14–US$22/UK£7–UK£11). AE, DC, MC, V. Daily 6am–9:30pm.

Overlanders Steakhouse ★ STEAK/AUSSIE TUCKER This landmark on the Alice dining scene is famous for its "Drover's Blowout" menu, which assaults the megahungry with soup and damper, then a platter of crocodile *vol-au-vents,* camel and kangaroo filet, and emu medallions—these are just the *appetizers*—followed by Scotch filet, or barramundi (freshwater fish), and dessert. There's a regular menu with a 700-gram (1-lb., 10-oz.) steak, plus lots of lighter fare like oysters and spinach crepes. The barnlike interior is Outback all through, from the rustic bar to the saddlebags hanging from the roof beams. An "Overlanders' Table" seats solo diners together.

72 Hartley St. ✆ **08/8952 2159.** Reservations required in peak season. Main courses A$23–A$35 (US$18–US$28/UK£9–UK£14); Drover's Blowout A$45 (US$36/UK£18). AE, DC, MC, V. Daily 6–10pm.

MODERATE

Casa Nostra ★★ *Value* ITALIAN The only difference between this cheery homespun family eatery and every other Italian restaurant in the world is that this one has autographed photos of Tom Selleck pinned to the wall. Judging by his scrawled praise, Tom loved eating here (when on location in Alice filming *Quigley Down Under*) as much as the locals do. You've seen the red-checked tablecloths and the basket-clad chianti bottles before, but the food is surprisingly good. A long list of pastas (including masterful carbonara), pizzas, and chicken and veal dishes are the main offerings. All meals are available to take out. BYO.

Corner of Undoolya Rd. and Sturt Terrace. ✆ **08/8952 6749.** Reservations recommended. Main courses A$13–A$22 (US$10–US$18/UK£5–UK£9). MC, V. Mon–Sat 5–10pm. Closed Dec 25–Jan.

Red Ochre Grill ★ GOURMET BUSH TUCKER If you've never tried wallaby mignons on a bed of native pasta and polenta cake with native berry and red-wine cream sauce, or barramundi (fish) baked in Paperbark with wild lime and coriander butter, here's your chance. The chef at this upscale chain fuses native Aussie ingredients with dishes from around the world. Although it might seem a touristy formula, the food is mouthwatering. Dine in the contemporary interior fronting Todd Mall, or outside in the attractive courtyard.

Todd Mall. ✆ **08/8952 9614.** www.redochregrill.com.au. Reservations recommended at dinner. Main courses A$9–A$21 (US$7.20–US$17/UK£3.60–UK£8.50) lunch, A$15–A$23 (US$12–US$19/UK£6–UK£16) dinner; A$13–A$16 (US$11–US$13/UK£5.50–UK£6.50) buffet breakfast. AE, DC, MC, V. Daily 6:30am–9:30pm.

INEXPENSIVE

Bar Doppio ★ EAST/WEST CAFE FARE If you're in need of a dose of cool—style, as well as air-conditioning—this arcade cafe is the place to chill over good coffee and feast on cheap, wholesome food. Sacks of coffee beans are stacked all over, Gypsy music plays, no tables and chairs match, and the staff doesn't care if you sit here all day. It's largely vegetarian, but fish and meat figure on the blackboard menu. Try lamb chermoula cutlets on Gabriella potatoes with rocket, red onion, and tomato salad; chickpea curry; warm Turkish flatbread with dips; or spuds with hot toppings. Hot and cold breakfast choices stay on the menu until 11am. Takeout is available. It's BYO.

2 and 3 Fan Arcade (off the southern end of Todd Mall). ✆ **08/8952 6525.** Main courses A$7–A$16 (US$5.60–US$13/UK£2.80–UK£6.50); sandwiches average A$6 (US$4.80/UK£2.40). No credit cards. Mon–Fri 7:30am–5:30pm; Sat 7:30am–4:30pm; Sun 10am–4:30pm; Fri–Sat 6–9pm. Closed holidays and Dec 25–Jan 1.

Bojangles Saloon and Restaurant ★ BURGERS/STEAKS/MODERN AUSTRALIAN Swing open the saloon doors and enter a world of cowhide seats, thick wooden tables, Western-style knickknacks, original American Civil War guns, and so on. The front bar is friendly and serves good beers by the bottle or schooner, and food such as burgers, nachos, salads, and fish and chips. The restaurant out back has more gourmet offerings, but either way it's a great atmosphere. Aussie-style country and folk singers strum away in the evenings, and the bar staff is terrific.

80 Todd St. ✆ **08/8952 2873.** Main courses A$7–A$18 (US$5.60–US$15/UK£2.70–UK£7.50) front bar, A$12–A$25 (US$9.60–US$20/UK£4.80–UK£10) restaurant. AE, DC, MC, V. Daily noon–3pm and 6–10pm.

3 Road Trips from Alice Springs

The key attraction of a day trip to the MacDonnell Ranges is unspoiled natural scenery and few crowds. Many companies run coach or four-wheel-drive tours—half- or full-day, sometimes overnight—to the West and East Macs. Some options appear in "Organized Tours" in the "Alice Springs" section, earlier in this chapter. Expect to pay about A$100 (US$80/UK£40) for a full-day trip. Families and backpackers alike love getting around with **Wayward Bus** ★ (✆ **08/8410 8833;** www.waywardbus.com.au). The company runs buses across the desert from Alice Springs on a 3-night camping trip stopping off at Kings Canyon and Uluru. You can sleep in a tent or a "swag"—a heavy waterproof sleeping bag (you can see the stars as you drop off). Tours cost A$395 (US$316/UK£158) with discounts for kids.

THE WEST MACDONNELL RANGES ★

WEST MACDONNELL NATIONAL PARK The 300km (186-mile) round-trip drive west from Alice Springs into West MacDonnell National Park is a stark but picturesque trip to a series of red gorges, semidesert country, and the occasional peaceful swimming hole. The 12-stage, 242km (150-mile) **Larapinta Walking Trail** takes you along the backbone of the West MacDonnell Ranges through some of the most unique and isolated country in the world. The hills, colors, birds, water holes, gorges, and the never-ending diversity of this trail will leave you spellbound by the beauty of Central Australia. The track stretches from the Telegraph Station in Alice Springs to Mount Sonder, past Glen Helen Gorge. Detailed track notes are on the website of the Parks & Wildlife Commission (**www.nt.gov.au/ipe/pwcnt**), and at the visitor information center in Alice Springs. Don't attempt the walk in the height of summer unless you are very well prepared. For great tips, and other information, look up the Alice Wanderer website (**www.alicewanderer.com.au**).

From Alice, take Larapinta Drive west for 18km (11 miles) to the 8km (5-mile) turnoff to Simpson's Gap, a water hole lined with ghost gums. Black-footed rock wallabies hop out on the cliffs in the late afternoon (so you may want to time a visit here on your way back to Alice). There are a couple of short trails, including a .5km (⅓-mile) Ghost Gum circuit, and a 17km (11-mile) round-trip trail to Bond Gap. Swimming is not permitted. The place has an information center/ranger station and free use of barbecues.

Twenty-three kilometers (14 miles) farther down Larapinta Road, 9km (5½ miles) down a turnoff, is **Standley Chasm** (**© 08/8956 7440**). This rock cleft is only a few meters wide but 80m (262 ft.) high, reached by a 10-minute creek-side trail. Aim to be here at midday, when the walls glow orange in the overhead sun. A kiosk sells snacks and drinks. Admission is A$6.50 (US$5.20/UK£2.60) for adults and A$5.50 (US$4.40/UK£2.20) for seniors and children 5 to 14. The chasm is open daily from 8am to 6pm (last entry at 5pm; closed Dec 25).

Six kilometers (3¾ miles) past Standley Chasm, you can branch right onto Namatjira Drive or continue to Hermannsburg Historical Precinct (see below). If you take Namatjira Drive, you'll go 42km (26 miles) to picturesque **Ellery Creek Big Hole.** The spring-fed water is so chilly that the tourism authority warns swimmers to take a flotation device in case of cramping. A 3km (2-mile) walking trail explains the area's geological history.

Eleven kilometers (7 miles) farther along Namatjira Drive is **Serpentine Gorge,** where a trail leads up to a lookout for a lovely view of the ranges through the gorge walls. Another 12km (7½ miles) on are **ocher pits,** which Aboriginal people quarried for body paint and for decorating objects used in ceremonial performances. Twenty-six kilometers (16 miles) farther west, 8km (5 miles) from the main road, is **Ormiston Gorge and Pound** (**© 08/8956 7799** for the ranger station/visitor center). This is a good spot to picnic, swim in the wide deep pool below red cliffs, and walk a choice of trails, such as the 30-minute Ghost Gum Lookout trail or the easy 7km (4⅓-mile) scenic loop (allow 3–4 hr.). The water is warm enough for swimming in the summer. You can camp here for A$6.60 (US$5.30/UK£2.70) per adult, and A$3.30 (US$2.60/UK£1.30) per child 5 to 15. The campground has no powered sites but does have hot showers, toilets, and free barbecues.

Farther on is **Glen Helen Gorge,** where the Finke River cuts through the ranges, with more gorge swimming, a walking trail, guided hikes, and helicopter flights. Modest **Glen Helen Resort** (**© 1800/896 110** in Australia, or 08/8956 7489; www.glenhelen.com.au) has 25 motel rooms (A$143/US$114/UK£57 double); bunkhouses for four (A$19/US$15/UK£7.50 per person); and campgrounds (A$9/US$7.20/

Tips Road Trips to the East & West Macs

Facilities are scarce outside Alice, so bring food (perhaps a picnic, or meat to barbecue), drinking water, and a full gas tank. Leaded, unleaded, and diesel fuel are for sale at Glen Helen Resort and Hermannsburg. Wear walking shoes.

Many of the water holes dry up too much to be good for swimming—those at Ellery Creek, Ormiston Gorge, and Glen Helen are the most permanent. Being spring-fed, they can be intensely cold, so take only short dips to avoid cramping and hypothermia, don't swim alone, and be careful of underwater snags. Don't wear sunscreen, because it pollutes drinking water for native animals.

Two-wheel-drive rental cars will not be insured on unsealed (unpaved) roads—that means the last few miles into Trephina Gorge Nature Park, and the 11km (7-mile) road into N'Dhala Gorge Nature Park, both in the East Macs. If you are prepared to risk it, you will probably get into Trephina in a two-wheel-drive car, but you will need a four-wheel-drive for N'Dhala and Arltunga. The West MacDonnell road is paved to Glen Helen Gorge; a few points of interest may require driving for short lengths on unpaved road. Before setting off, drop into the **CATIA Visitor Information Centre** (see "Visitor Information," earlier in this chapter) for tips on road conditions and for details on the free ranger talks, walks, and slide shows that take place in the West and East Macs from April through October. Entry to all sights, parks, and reserves (except Standley Chasm) is free.

UK£3.60 per person for a tent site, A$22/US$18/UK£9 double for a powered campsite). There's a restaurant serving three meals a day; a bar; and barbecues for which the resort sells meat packs. They offer 2-day trips of the area.

GETTING THERE You can arrange to be dropped off by the **Alice Wanderer** (✆ **08/8952 2111;** www.alicewanderer.com.au) at several stops in the Ranges. It costs around A$80 (US$64/UK£32) for two people for the return trip to Simpson's Gap; A$100 (US$80/UK£40) to Standley Chasm; A$180 (US$144/UK£72) to Serpentine Gorge; and A$210 (US$168/UK£84) to Ormiston Gorge. If you plan to camp out, call ✆ **1300 650 730** to register your intentions (it's voluntary but worth it if you get lost—a rescue team will try to find you). You must pay a A$50 (US$40/UK£20) refundable deposit by credit card. Take plenty of water. The Alice Wanderer also does group tours to the area.

HERMANNSBURG HISTORICAL PRECINCT An alternative to visiting the West Mac gorges is to stay on Larapinta Drive all 128km (79 miles) from Alice Springs to the old **Lutheran Mission** at the **Hermannsburg Historical Precinct** (✆ **08/8956 7402**). Some maps show this route as an unpaved road, but it is paved. Settled by German missionaries in the 1870s, this is a cluster of restored farmhouse-style mission buildings. There are a museum, a gallery housing landscapes by Aussie artist Albert Namatjira, and tearooms serving apple strudel from an old German recipe. The mission is open daily from 9am to 4pm (10am–4pm Nov–Mar). Admission to the precinct with tea or coffee is A$4.50 (US$3.60/UK£1.80) for adults, A$3 (US$2.40/UK£1.20) for school-age kids, or A$12 (US$9.60/UK£4.80) for a family, plus A$3.50 (US$2.80/UK£1.40) per adult or A$2.50 (US$2/UK£1) per child for a guided gallery tour, which departs every hour. The precinct is closed from December 24 to January 2 or 3, and on Good Friday.

FINKE GORGE NATIONAL PARK Just west of Hermannsburg is the turnoff to the 46,000-hectare (113,620-acre) **Finke Gorge National Park,** 16km (10 miles) to the south on an unpaved road (or about a 2-hr. drive west of Alice Springs). Turn south off Larapinta Dr. just west of Hermannsburg. Access along the last 16km (10 miles) of road, which follows the sandy bed of the Finke River, is limited to 4WD vehicles only. Heavy rains may cause this section of the road to be impassable. The park is most famous for **Palm Valley,** where groves of rare *Livistona mariae* cabbage palms have survived since central Australia was a jungle millions of years ago. You will need a four-wheel-drive to explore this park. Four walking trails between 1.5km (1 mile) and 5km (3 miles) take you among the palms or up to a lookout over cliffs; one is a signposted trail exploring Aboriginal culture. There is a campsite about 4km (2½ miles) from the palms; it has showers, toilets, and free barbecues. Collect your firewood outside the park. Camping is A$6.60 (US$5.30/UK£2.70) for adults, A$3.30 (US$2.60/UK£1.30) for kids 5 to 15. For information, call the CATIA Visitor Information Centre in Alice Springs before you leave, because there is no visitor center in the park. The ranger station (© **08/8956 7401**) is for emergencies only.

THE EAST MACDONNELL RANGES

Not as many tourists tread the path on the Ross Highway into the East Macs, but if you do, you'll be rewarded with lush walking trails, fewer crowds, and traces of Aboriginal history. I even spotted wild camels on my visit.

The first points of interest are **Emily Gap,** 10km (6 miles) from Alice, and **Jessie Gap,** an additional 7km (4⅓ miles), a pretty picnic spot. You can cool off in the Emily Gap swimming hole if there is any water. Don't miss the "Caterpillar Dreaming" Aboriginal art on the wall, on your right as you walk through.

At **Corroboree Rock,** 37km (23 miles) farther, you can make a short climb up the outcrop, which was important to local Aborigines. The polished rock "seat" high up in the hole means Aboriginal people must have used this rock for eons.

Twenty-two kilometers (14 miles) farther is the turnoff to **Trephina Gorge Nature Park,** an 18-sq.-km (7-sq.-mile) beauty spot with peaceful walking trails ranging from 45 minutes to 4½ hours. The last 5km (3 miles) of the 9km (5½-mile) road into the park are unpaved, but you can make it in a two-wheel-drive car.

N'Dhala Gorge Nature Park, 10km (6 miles) past Trephina Gorge Nature Park, houses an "open-air art gallery" of rock carvings, or petroglyphs, left by the Eastern Arrernte Aboriginal people. An interesting 1.5km (1-mile) signposted trail explains the Dreamtime meanings of a few of the 6,000 rock carvings, hundreds or thousands of years old, that are thought to be in this eerily quiet gorge. A four-wheel-drive vehicle is a must to traverse the 11km (7-mile) access road.

The Ross Highway is paved all the way to Ross River Resort, 86km (53 miles) from Alice Springs.

4 Kings Canyon ★

Anyone who saw the movie *The Adventures of Priscilla, Queen of the Desert* will remember the stony plateau the transvestites climb to gaze over the plain below. You can stand on that same spot (wearing sequined underpants is optional) at **Kings Canyon** ★ in **Watarrka National Park** (✆ **08/8956 7460** for park headquarters). As the crow flies, it is 320km (198 miles) southwest of Alice Springs. The sandstone walls of the canyon drop about 100m (330 ft.) to rock pools and centuries-old gum trees. There is little to do except walk the dramatic canyon rim for a sense of the peaceful emptiness of the Australian Outback.

GETTING THERE The best way is to drive. There's no regular air service to Kings Canyon.

Numerous **four-wheel-drive** tour outfits head to Kings Canyon from Alice Springs or Uluru (Ayers Rock), with time allowed for the rim walk. See "Exploring the Red Centre," earlier in this chapter, for recommended companies.

With a four-wheel-drive, you can get to Kings Canyon from Alice Springs on the unpaved Mereenie Loop Road. The regular route is the 480km (298-mile) trip from Alice Springs south on the Stuart Highway, then west onto the Lasseter Highway, then north and west on the Luritja Road. All three roads are paved. Uluru (Ayers Rock) is 306km (190 miles) to the south on a paved road; from Yulara, take the Lasseter Highway east for 125km (78 miles), turn left onto Luritja Road and go 168km (104 miles) to Kings Canyon Resort. The resort sells leaded and unleaded petrol and diesel.

GETTING AROUND **AAT Kings** (✆ **1800/334 009** in Australia, or 08/8956 2171; www.aatkings.com) provides a 1-day tour to Kings Canyon from the Ayers Rock Resort for A$103 (US$82/UK£41) per person. You can book through AAT Kings or the resort.

EXPLORING THE PARK

The way to explore the canyon is on the 6km (3¾-mile) **walk** up the side (short but steep!) and around the rim. Even if you're in good shape, it's a strenuous 3- to 4-hour hike. It leads through a maze of rounded sandstone formations called the Lost City, across a bridge to a fern-fringed pocket of water holes called the Garden of Eden, and back along the other side through more sandstone rocks. There are lookout points en route. If you visit after the odd rainfall, the walls teem with waterfalls. In winter, don't set off too early, because sunlight doesn't light up the canyon walls to good effect until midmorning.

If you're not up to making the rim walk, take the shady 2.6km (1½-mile) round-trip trail along the mostly dry **Kings Creek bed** on the canyon floor. It takes about an hour. Wear sturdy boots, because the ground can be rocky. This walk is all right for young kids and travelers in wheelchairs for the first kilometer (½ mile).

Both walks are signposted. Avoid the rim walk in the middle of the day between September and May, when it's too hot.

An exhilarating option is a guided tour of Kings Creek Station on your own four-wheel **quad bike.** You journey through the rugged Outback taking in spectacular scenery, including red sand dunes, on the search for wildlife. Your adventure takes you through the cattle country where you will often see santa/shorthorn cattle and occasionally surprise camels, kangaroos, and dingoes. Kings Creek Station is approximately 20 minutes drive south of Kings Canyon Resort (below) and the tours are booked though the resort. It costs A$65 (US$52/UK£26) for 30 minutes, A$75 (US$60/UK£30) for an hour, and A$160 (US$128/UK£64) for 2 hours. The minimum age is 16.

Professional Helicopter Services (✆ **08/8956 7873;** www.phs.com.au) makes 15-minute flights over the canyon for A$115 (US$92/UK£46) per person.

WHERE TO STAY & DINE

Apart from campgrounds, the only place to stay in Watarrka National Park is at Kings Canyon Resort.

Kings Canyon Resort ★ This attractive, low-slung complex 7km (4⅓ miles) from Kings Canyon blends into its surroundings. All but four of the larger deluxe rooms were built in 1999 and have desert views from glass-enclosed Jacuzzis. The remaining rooms are typical hotel accommodations, comfortable enough, with range views from the balcony. Thirty-two units have Jacuzzis. The double/twin, shared quad, and family lodge rooms are adequate low-budget choices, with a communal kitchen and bathroom facilities. Children are not permitted in lodge (dorm-style) rooms unless you book the entire room. The resort has a well-stocked minimart where you can buy meat for the barbecues. Live entertainment plays some nights, and a ranger gives a slide show several nights a week. Internet access is available. The resort runs and books several tours

Luritja Rd., Watarrka National Park, NT 0872. ✆ **1800/817 622** in Australia, or 08/8956 7442. Fax 08/8956 7426. www.voyages.com.au, or www.kingscanyonresort.com.au. 164 units, 128 with bathroom; 72 powered campsites and tent sites. July–Nov A$330–A$397 (US$264–US$317/UK£132–UK£158) hotel double; Dec–June A$277–A$343 (US$221–US$275/UK£110–UK£138) hotel double. Extra adult A$27 (US$22/UK£11). Children under 16 stay free in parent's room with existing bedding. July–Nov A$100 (US$80/UK£40) lodge double, A$168 (US$135/UK£68) quad, A$185 (US$148/UK£74) family unit for up to 5; Dec–June A$98 (US$78/UK£39) lodge double, A$163 (US$130/UK£65) quad, A$178 (US$142/UK£71) family. Tent site A$28 (US$22/UK£11) double; powered site A$32 (US$26/UK£13) double. Extra adult A$11 (US$8.80/UK£4.40); extra child 6–15 A$5 (US$4/UK£2) in powered campsite. Children under 16 dine free at restaurant breakfast and dinner buffets with an adult. Ask about packages with Ayers Rock Resort and Alice Springs Resort. AE, DC, MC, V. **Amenities:** Restaurant; cafe; 2 bars; 2 outdoor unheated pools; outdoor lit tennis court; bike rental (from nearby gas station); tour desk; limited room service; coin-op laundry; volleyball court. *In room:* A/C, TV, fridge. Hotel only: TV w/pay movies, minibar, hair dryer, iron.

5 Uluru–Kata Tjuta National Park (Ayers Rock/The Olgas) ★

462km (286 miles) SW of Alice Springs; 1,934km (1,199 miles) S of Darwin; 1,571km (974 miles) N of Adelaide; 2,841km (1,761 miles) NW of Sydney

Uluru (Ayers Rock) is the Australian tourism industry's pinup icon, a glamorous red stone that has probably been splashed on more posters than Cindy Crawford has been on magazine covers. Just why people trek from all over the world to gawk at it is a bit of a mystery. For its size? Hardly—nearby Mount Conner is three times as big. For its shape? Probably not—most folks agree the neighboring Kata Tjuta (the Olgas) is more picturesque. You can put its popularity down to the faint shiver up the spine and the indescribable sense of place it evokes in anyone who looks at it. Even Aussie bushmen reckon it's "got somethin' spiritual about it."

In 1985 the **Uluru–Kata Tjuta National Park** ★ was returned to its Aboriginal owners, the Pitjantjatjara and Yankunytjatjara people, known as the Anangu, who manage the property jointly with the Australian government. People used to speculate that the Rock was a meteorite, but we now know it was formed by sediments laid down 600 million to 700 million years ago in an inland sea and thrust up aboveground 348m

Tips The Rock in a Day?

It's a loooong day to visit Uluru in a day from Alice by road. Many organized coach tours pack a lot—perhaps a Rock base walk or climb, Kata Tjuta (the Olgas), the Uluru–Kata Tjuta Cultural Centre, and a champagne sunset at the Rock—into a busy trip that leaves Alice around 5:30 or 6am and gets you back late at night. **Murray Cosson's Australian Outback Flights (✆ 08/8953 1444;** www.australianoutbackflights.com.au) offers an aerial day trip from Alice Springs that includes flights over Kings Canyon, Gosse Bluff meteorite crater, and Lake Amadeus; a rental car at Uluru (Ayers Rock); national park entry fee; and lunch. It costs A$900 (US$720/UK£360) per person (minimum two passengers). There are more tour options, too, including an 8-hour excursion taking in Kings Canyon for A$560 (US$448/UK£224)

You should consider a day trip only between May and September. At other times, it's too hot to do much from early morning to late afternoon.

(1,141 ft.) by geological forces. With a circumference of 9.4km (6 miles), the Rock is no pebble, especially because two-thirds of it is thought to be underground. On photos it looks like a big smooth blob. In the flesh, it's more interesting—dappled with holes and overhangs, with curtains of stone draping its sides, creating little coves hiding water holes and Aboriginal rock art. It also changes color from pink to a deep wine red depending on the slant of the sun.

Don't think a visit to Uluru is just about snapping a few photos and going home. You can walk around the Rock, climb it (although the local Aborigines prefer you don't), fly over it, ride a camel to it, circle it on a Harley-Davidson, trek through the Olgas, eat in an outdoor restaurant, tour the night sky, and join Aboriginal people on guided walks.

Give yourself at least a day in the Uluru area; you could easily stay 2 or 3.

Isolation (and a lack of competition) makes things like accommodations, meals, and transfers expensive. A coach tour or four-wheel-drive camping safari is often the cheapest way to see the place. See "Exploring the Red Centre," at the beginning of this chapter, for recommended tour companies.

ESSENTIALS

GETTING THERE By Plane Qantas (✆ **13 13 13** in Australia) flies to Ayers Rock (Connellan) Airport direct from Sydney, Alice Springs, Perth, and Cairns. Flights from other airports go via Alice Springs. The airport is 6km (3¾ miles) from Ayers Rock Resort. Expect to pay around A$320 (US$256/UK£128) one-way. A free shuttle ferries all resort guests, including campers, to their door.

By Car Take the Stuart Highway south from Alice Springs 199km (123 miles), turn right onto the Lasseter Highway, and go 244km (151 miles) to Ayers Rock Resort. The Rock is 18km (11 miles) farther on. (Everyone mistakes the flat-topped mesa they see en route for Uluru; it's Mount Conner.)

Only Avis, Hertz, and Thrifty have Uluru depots: Thrifty charges around A$110 (US$88/UK£44) a day for bookings under 3 days; Hertz charges A$137 (US$109/UK£55) a day for bookings under 7 days; and Avis charges A$137 (US$109/UK£55) a day for bookings of 2 days or fewer. If you want to rent a car in Alice Springs and drop it at Uluru, brace yourself for a one-way penalty.

VISITOR INFORMATION For information before you leave, contact the **Central Australian Tourism Industry Association (CATIA),** 60 Gregory Terrace, Alice Springs (© **08/8952 5800;** www.centralaustraliantourism.com), or drop into its **Visitor Information Centre** in Alice Springs. One of the best online sources is Ayers Rock Resort's site (www.voyages.com.au).

The **Ayers Rock Resort Visitor Centre,** next to the Desert Gardens Hotel (© **08/8957 7377**), has displays on the area's geology, wildlife, and Aboriginal heritage, plus a souvenir store. It's open daily from 8:30am to 7:30pm. You can book tours at the **tour desk** in every hotel at Ayers Rock Resort, or visit the **Ayers Rock Resort Tour & Information Centre** (© **08/8957 7324**) at the shopping center in the resort complex. It dispenses information on and books tours as far afield as Kings Canyon and Alice Springs. It's open daily from 7:30am to 8:30pm.

One kilometer (½ mile) from the base of the Rock is the **Uluru–Kata Tjuta Cultural Centre** ★ (© **08/8956 3138**), owned and run by the Anangu, the Aboriginal owners of Uluru. It uses eye-catching wall displays, frescoes, interactive recordings, and videos to tell about Aboriginal Dreamtime myths and laws. It's worth spending some time here to understand a little about Aboriginal culture. A National Park desk has information on ranger-guided activities and animal, plant, and bird-watching checklists. The center also has a cafe, a souvenir shop, and two Aboriginal arts and crafts galleries. It's open daily from early in the morning to after sundown; exact hours vary from month to month.

PARK ENTRANCE FEES Entry to the Uluru–Kata Tjuta National Park is A$25 (US$20/UK£10) per adult, free for children under 16, valid for 3 days. The cost of many organized tours includes the entry fee.

ETIQUETTE The Anangu ask you not to photograph sacred sites or Aboriginal people without permission, and to approach quietly and respectfully.

GETTING AROUND

Getting around the park is expensive. Ayers Rock Resort runs a **free shuttle** every 15 minutes or so around the resort complex from 10:30am to after midnight, but to get to the Rock or Kata Tjuta (the Olgas), you will need to take transfers, join a tour, or have your own wheels. The shuttle also meets all flights.

BY SHUTTLE **Uluru Express** (© **08/8956 2152;** www.uluruexpress.com.au) provides a minibus shuttle from Ayers Rock Resort to and from the Rock about every 50 minutes from before sunrise to sundown, and several times a day to the Olgas. The basic shuttle costs A$35 (US$28/UK£14) for adults and A$20 (US$16/UK£8) for kids (including to see the sunset); a sunrise trip costs A$60 (US$48/UK£24) for adults and A$30 (US$24/UK£12) for kids. To the Olgas, it costs A$55 (US$44/UK£22) for adults and A$25 (US$20/UK£10) for children. A 3-day pass covering as many trips as you like to both sites costs A$150 (US$120/UK£60) for adults and A$60 (US$48/UK£24) for kids. A combined Uluru and Olgas trip costs A$60 (US$48/UK£24) for adults and A$30 (US$24/UK£12) for kids. All fares are round-trip.

Tips **Water, Water . . .**

Water taps are scarce and kiosks nonexistent in Uluru–Kata Tjuta National Park. Always carry your own drinking water when sightseeing.

BY CAR If there are two of you, the easiest and cheapest way to get around is likely to be a rental car. All roads in the area are paved, so a four-wheel-drive is unnecessary. Expect to pay around A$70 to A$95 (US$56–US$76/UK£28–UK£38) per day for a medium-size car. Rates drop a little in low season. Most car-rental companies give you the first 100km (63 miles) free and charge A30¢ (US25¢/UK15p) per kilometer after that. Take this into account, because the round-trip from the resort to the Olgas is just over 100km (63 miles), and that's without driving about 20km (13 miles) to the Rock and back. **Avis** (✆ **08/8956 2266**), **Hertz** (✆ **08/8956 2244**), and **Thrifty** (✆ **08/8956 2030**) book four-wheel-drives through their Darwin offices. All rent regular cars and four-wheel-drives.

The **Outback Travel Shop** ★ (✆ **08/8955 5288;** www.outbacktravelshop.com.au), a booking agent in Alice Springs, often has better deals on car-rental rates than you'll get by booking direct.

BY ORGANIZED TOUR Several tour companies run a big range of daily sunrise and sunset viewings, circumnavigations of the Rock by coach or on foot, guided walks at the Rock or the Olgas, camel rides, observatory evenings, visits to the Uluru–Kata Tjuta Cultural Centre, and innumerable permutations and combinations of all of these. Some offer "passes" containing the most popular activities. Virtually every company picks you up at your hotel. Among the most reputable are **Discovery Ecotours** (formerly Uluru Experience and Alice Experience), **AAT Kings, Tailormade Tours,** and **VIP Travel Australia** (see "Exploring the Red Centre" at the start of this chapter for details).

ABORIGINAL TOURS Because **Anangu Tours** ★★ (✆ **08/8950 3030;** www.anangutours.com.au) is owned and run by the Rock's Aboriginal owners, its tours give you firsthand insight into Aboriginal culture. Tours are in the Anangu language and translated by an interpreter. They are not cheap, but if you are going to spend money on just one tour, this group is a good choice.

The company does a **Kuniya** walk during which you visit the Uluru–Kata Tjuta Cultural Centre and the Mutitjulu water hole at the base of the Rock, learn about bush foods, and see rock paintings, before watching the sunset. It departs daily at 2:30pm March through October, 3:30pm November through February. With hotel pickup, the tour costs A$99 (US$80/UK£40) for adults and A$55 (US$44/UK£22) for children. There's also a 4½-hour breakfast tour costing A$119 (US$95/UK£48) for adults and A$79 (US$63/UK£32) for children. It includes a base tour and demonstrations of bush skills and spear-throwing. A standard tour during the day costs A$75 (US$60/UK£30) for adults and A$49 (US$39/UK£20) for kids. Dot-painting workshops at the Uluru Cultural Centre cost A$79 (US$63/UK£32) for adults and A$56 (US$45/UK£23) for kids.

DISCOVERING ULURU (AYERS ROCK)

AT SUNRISE & SUNSET The peak time to catch the Rock's beauty is sunset, when oranges, peaches, pinks, reds, and then indigo and deep violet creep across its face as if it were a giant opal. Some days it's fiery, other days the colors are muted. A sunset-viewing car park is on the Rock's western side. Plenty of sunset and sunrise tours operate from the resort. A typical sunset tour is that offered by **AAT Kings** (✆ **08/8956 2171;** www.aatkings.com): It departs 90 minutes before sunset, includes a free glass of wine with which to watch the "show," and returns 20 minutes after sundown; the cost is A$40 (US$32/UK£16) for adults, A$28 (US$22/UK£11) for

Moments **Dinner in the Desert**

Why sit in a restaurant when you can eat outside in the dust? Because you came to the Outback to be outside, that's why. Ayers Rock Resort's **Sounds of Silence dinner** ★ makes outside eating a fascinating event. In an outdoor clearing, you sip champagne and nibble canapés as the sun sets over the Rock to the strains of a didgeridoo played by a white man (the excuse is that didgeridoos don't come from this part of the world but from Arnhemland—though there seem to be plenty of local Aboriginals who play). We hope you've zeroed in on people you want to sit with by now, because you head to communal white-clothed, candlelit tables and a serve-yourself meal of kangaroo and barramundi (a large freshwater fish). Last time I was here, they served pretty poor pumpkin soup to begin, the main courses varied from bland to nice, and the Aussie wines were bad examples. However, after dinner, the lanterns fade, and you are left with stillness (apart from an occasional dingo looking for scraps). It is the first time some city folk have ever heard silence. Next, an astronomer points out the constellations of the Southern Hemisphere, and you have a chance to see the stars through telescopes. Sounds of Silence is held nightly, weather permitting, and costs A$149 (US$119/UK£60) for adults and A$75 (US$60/UK£30) for children under 15, including transfers from Ayers Rock Resort. It's mighty popular, so book 3 months ahead in peak season. Book through the Ayers Rock Resort office in Sydney (© **1300/139 889** in Australia, or 02/9339 1040).

children 4 to 14. AAT Kings offers several other tours around the area, so if large-group touring is your thing then I really suggest you check out their website before leaving home.

At sunrise the colors are less dramatic, but many folks enjoy the spectacle of the Rock unveiled by the dawn to birdsong. You'll need an early start—most tours leave about 75 minutes before sunup.

CLIMBING IT Aborigines refer to tourists as *minga*—little ants—because that's what we look like crawling up Uluru. Climbing this thing is no picnic—there's sometimes a strong wind that can blow you right off, the walls are almost vertical in places (you have to hold onto a chain), and it can be freezing cold or insanely hot. Quite a few people climbing the rock have died from heart attacks, heat stress, or falling off. If you're not in good shape; have breathing difficulties, heart trouble, or high or low blood pressure; or are just plain scared of heights, don't do it. The Rock is closed to climbers during bad weather; when temperatures exceed 97°F (36°C), which they often do from November to March; and when wind speed exceeds 25 knots, so climb in the stillness of early morning. ***Warning:*** Wherever you go at Uluru and Kata Tjuta (the Olgas), bring lots of drinking water with you from the resort.

If that doesn't put you off, you'll be rewarded with views of the plain, Kata Tjuta (the Olgas), and Mount Conner. The surface is rutted with ravines about 2.5m (8¼ ft.) deep, which demand scrambling. The climb takes at least 1 hour up for the fit, and 1 hour down. The less sure-footed should allow 3 to 4 hours all told.

Note: The Anangu do not like people climbing Uluru, because the climb follows the trail their ancestral Dreamtime Mala men took when they first came to Uluru. They allow people to climb but strongly prefer that they don't.

WALKING, DRIVING, OR BUSING AROUND IT A paved road runs around the Rock. The easy 9.4km (6-mile) **Base Walk** circumnavigating Uluru takes about 2 hours, but allow time to linger around the water holes, caves, folds, and overhangs that make up its walls. A shorter walk is the easy 1km (½-mile) round-trip trail from the **Mutitjulu** parking lot to the pretty water hole near the Rock's base, where there is some rock art. The **Liru Track** is another easy trail; it runs 2km (1¼ miles) from the Cultural Centre to Uluru, where it links with the Base Walk.

Make time for the free daily 2km (1¼-mile) **Mala Walk** ★, where the ranger, who is often an Aborigine, explains the Dreamtime myths behind Uluru, talks about Aboriginal lifestyles and hunting techniques in days past, and explains the significance of the rock art and other sites you see along the way. The 90-minute trip leaves the Mala Walk sign at the base of the Uluru climb at 10am May through September, and at a cooler 8am October through April.

Before setting off on any walk, it's a good idea to arm yourself with the self-guided walking notes available from the Cultural Centre (see "Visitor Information," above).

Most companies offer base tours. As an example, **Discovery Ecotours** (**© 1800/803 174;** www.discoveryecotours.com.au) conducts a 5-hour guided base tour that gives you insight into natural history, rock art, and Dreamtime beliefs. It's scheduled to coincide with sunrise. The tour costs A$115 (US$92/UK£46) for adults and A$87 (US$70/UK£35) for children 6 to 15, but it's not suitable for kids under 10. The company also runs a 4-hour sunset trip to the Olgas for A$84 (US$67/UK£34) for adults and A$62 (US$50/UK£25) for kids.

FLYING OVER IT Several companies do scenic flights by light aircraft or helicopter over Uluru, Kata Tjuta (the Olgas), nearby Mount Conner, the vast white saltpan of Lake Amadeus, and as far as Kings Canyon. Helicopters don't land on top of the Rock, however. As a guide to the flights available, **Professional Helicopter Services** (**© 08/8956 2003;** www.phs.com.au) does a 12- to 15-minute flight over Uluru for A$115 (US$92/UK£46) per adult, and a 25- to 30-minute flight, which includes the Olgas, for A$220 (US$176/UK£88). Kids under 13 usually pay half price (depending more on their weight than on their age). You can drive to the helicopter site on a Harley-Davidson for A$60 (US$48/UK£24) one-way and A$100 (US$80/UK£40) round-trip.

MOTORCYCLING AROUND IT Harley-Davidson tours are available as sunrise or sunset rides, laps of the Rock, and various other Rock and Kata Tjuta (Olgas) tours with time for the Olgas walks. A blast out to the Rock at sunset with **Uluru Motorcycle Tours** (**© 08/8956 2019**) will set you back A$145 (US$116/UK£58), which includes a glass of champagne. The guide drives the bike; you sit behind and hang on.

Tips **Travel Tip**

Most tourists visit Uluru in the mornings and Kata Tjuta (the Olgas) in the afternoon. Reverse the order (do the Valley of the Winds walk in the morning and Uluru in the afternoon) and you'll find both spots a little more silent and spiritual.

Self-ride tours are available, too, at a hefty price. You can rent a Harley for a half-day for around A$365 (US$292/UK£146).

VIEWING IT ON CAMELBACK Legend has it that a soul travels at the same pace as a camel; it's certainly a peaceful way to see the Rock. **Anangu Tours** (**✆ 08/8950 3030;** www.anangutours.com.au) makes daily forays aboard "ships of the desert" to view Uluru. Amble through red-sand dunes with great views of the Rock, dismount to watch the sun rise or sink over it, and ride back to the depot for billy tea and beer bread in the morning, or champagne in the evening. The 1-hour rides depart Ayers Rock Resort 1 hour before sunrise or 1½ hours before sunset, and cost A$95 (US$76/UK£38) per person, including transfers from your hotel. All tours leave from the Camel Depot at the Ayers Rock Resort.

EXPLORING THE OLGAS

Although not everyone has heard of massive **Mount Olga** ★ (or "the Olgas"), a sister monolith an easy 50km (31-mile) drive west of Uluru, many folks who have say it's lovelier and more mysterious, and I agree. Known to the Aborigines as Kata Tjuta, or "many heads," the Olgas' 36 momentous red domes bulge out of the earth like turned clay on a potter's wheel. The tallest dome is 200m (656 ft.) higher than Uluru. The Olgas are more important in Aboriginal Dreamtime legend than Uluru.

Two walking trails take you in among the domes: the 7.4km (4½-mile) **Valley of the Winds** ★ walk, which is fairly challenging and takes 3 to 5 hours, and the easy 2.6km (1½-mile) **Gorge** walk, which takes about an hour. The Valley of the Winds trail is the more rewarding in terms of scenery. Both have lookout points and shady stretches. The Valley of the Winds trail closes when temperatures rise above 97°F (36°C).

WHERE TO STAY & DINE

Ayers Rock Resort not only is in the township of Yulara—it is the township. Located about 30km (19 miles) from the Rock, outside the national park boundary, it is the only place to stay. It is an impressive, contemporary complex, built to a high standard, efficiently run, and attractive—all things you can end up paying an arm and a leg for. Because everyone either is a tourist or lives and works here, it has a village atmosphere—with a supermarket; a bank; a post office; a newsdealer; babysitting services; a medical center; a beauty salon; several gift, clothing, and souvenir shops; a place to buy beer; and a gas station.

You have a choice of seven places to stay within the complex, from hotel rooms and apartments to luxury and basic campsites. In keeping with this village feel, no matter where you stay, even in the campground, you are free to use all the pools, restaurants, and other facilities of every hostelry, except the rather glamorous Sails in the Desert pool, which is reserved for Sails guests.

Voyages Hotels & Resorts manages Ayers Rock Resort, Alice Springs Resort, and Kings Canyon Resort. You can book accommodations for all three properties through the central reservations office in Sydney (**✆ 1300/139 889** in Australia, or 02/9339 1040; fax 02/9332 4555; www.voyages.com.au). Ask about packages that include one, two, or all three resorts. Prices tend to work out cheaper per night if you stay more than 1 night, too. ***Warning:*** Shop around for prices on the Internet and with travel agencies. My experience is that people staying here have paid a whole range of prices.

High season is July through November. Book well ahead.

A tour desk, same-day dry-cleaning and laundry service, and babysitting are all available at each hostelry and campground.

In addition to the dining options below, the resort's small shopping center has the pleasant **Gecko's Café,** which offers wood-fired pizzas, pastas, and sandwiches; a bakery; an ice creamery; and takeout. Sails in the Desert, Desert Gardens, and the Outback Pioneer Hotel & Lodge can provide picnic hampers and breakfast backpacks. Kids under 15 dine free at any of the hotels' buffets in the company of an adult. It's a good idea to bring some wine with you, because the place really has things sewn up, including prices.

VERY EXPENSIVE

Longitude 131 ★★★ You can find this African-style luxury safari camp, with perfect views of Uluru, in the sand dunes a mile or two from the main complex. The camp was finished in June 2002, mostly burned down in 2003, and reopened in July 2004. It offers 15 top-class air-conditioned tents, each with a private bathroom and a balcony overlooking the rock. The resort is promoting them as "six star." (How long until we have a seven star?) Whatever—A$9 million (US$7.2 million/UK£3.6 million) on 15 tents makes them pretty expensive. A central facility, **Dune House,** holds a restaurant (with superb food), bar, library, and shop.

Yulara Dr., Yulara, NT 0872. ✆ **08/8957 7888.** Fax 08/8957 7474. 15 units. A$1,980 (US$1,584/UK£792) tent for 2. Rates include walking and bus tours around the area, meals, selected drinks. 2-night minimum. AE, DC, MC, V. **Amenities:** Restaurant; bar; unheated outdoor pool; free airport shuttle. *In room:* No phone.

Sails in the Desert ★★ This top-of-the-range hotel offers expensive, contemporary-style rooms, many overlooking the pool and six with Jacuzzis (though watch your head on the glass doors leading to the private balcony, if you have one—I had a bruise for days). You can't see the Rock from your room, but most guests are too busy sipping cocktails by the pool to care. The pool area is shaded by white "sails" and surrounded by sun lounges. The lobby art gallery has artists in residence. The **Kuniya** restaurant serves elegant a la carte fine-dining fare with bush tucker ingredients; **Winkiku** is a smart a la carte and buffet venue; and the lively **Rockpool** (open seasonally) serves Thai fare poolside.

Yulara Dr., Yulara, NT 0872. ✆ **08/8957 7888.** Fax 08/8957 7474. 232 units. High season A$548–A$640 (US$438–US$512/UK£219–UK£256) double, A$894 (US$715/UK£358) suite; low season A$442–A$514 (US$354–US$411/UK£178–UK£206) double, A$880 (US$704/UK£352) suite. Extra person A$36 (US$30/UK£15). AE, DC, MC, V. **Amenities:** 3 restaurants; bar; large unheated outdoor pool; 2 outdoor lit tennis courts; free airport shuttle; limited room service. *In room:* A/C, TV w/pay movies, dataport, minibar, hair dryer, iron.

EXPENSIVE

Desert Gardens Hotel ★ This is the only hotel with views of the Rock (albeit rather distant ones), from some of the 84 deluxe rooms. The accommodations are not as lavish as Sails in the Desert, but they're equally comfortable and have elegant furnishings. In 2002, 34 new rooms were built, and in 2001 the existing 100 standard rooms were refurbished with new bathrooms, bedding, and carpets. The **White Gums** restaurant serves a la carte flame grill and buffet meals.

Yulara Dr., Yulara, NT 0872. ✆ **08/8957 7888.** Fax 08/8957 7716. 218 units, 100 with shower only. High season A$448–A$520 (US$358–US$416/UK£179–UK£208) double; low season A$354–A$412 (US$283–US$330/UK£142–UK£165) double. Extra person A$36 (US$29/UK£15). AE, DC, MC, V. **Amenities:** 2 restaurants; bar; unheated outdoor pool; free airport shuttle; limited room service. *In room:* A/C, TV w/pay movies, minibar, hair dryer, iron.

Emu Walk Apartments ★ These bright, contemporary apartments have full kitchens, separate bedrooms, and roomy living areas. They have daily maid service. There's no restaurant or pool, but Gecko's Café and the market are close, and you can cool off in the Desert Gardens Hotel pool next door.

Moments When You See the Southern Cross for the First Time

Light pollution is extremely low in the Red Centre, so the night sky is a dazzler. At the Ayers Rock Observatory, you can check out your zodiac constellation and take a 1-hour tour of the Southern Hemisphere heavens (they're different from the Northern Hemisphere stars).

To visit the observatory, you must join a tour with **Discovery Ecotours** (✆ **1800/803 174** in Australia, or 08/8956 2563; www.discoveryecotours.com.au), which provides hotel pickup and a tour. Tours depart twice a night; times vary. They cost A$33 (US$26/UK£13) for adults, A$25 (US$20/UK£10) for children 6 to 15. Family rates are available on request.

Yulara Dr., Yulara, NT 0872. ✆ **08/8957 7888.** Fax 08/8957 7742. 59 apts, all with shower only. High season A$436 (US$349/UK£175) 1-bedroom apt, A$540 (US$432/UK£216) 2-bedroom apt for 4; low season A$354 (US$283/UK£142) 1-bedroom apt, A$448 (US$358/UK£179) 2-bedroom apt for 4. Extra person A$36 (US$29/UK£15). AE, DC, MC, V. **Amenities:** Free airport shuttle; limited room service. *In room:* A/C, TV w/pay movies, kitchen, minibar, hair dryer, iron.

The Lost Camel ★ This AAA-rated three-and-a-half-star hotel opened its doors in late 2002 on the site of the resort's demolished Spinifex Lodge, which once offered the best budget deals outside the campgrounds. It's aimed at young urbanites and is as bright, crisp, and modern as something you might find in Sydney's Darlinghurst. (Don't you just love that urban feel in the red dirt? You could forget you are in the Outback altogether.) The Red Camel offers lush courtyards and a generous swimming pool. Bang goes that budget, though.

Yulara Dr., Yulara, NT 0872. ✆ **08/8957 7888.** Fax 08/8957 7474. 99 units. High season A$404 (US$323/UK£162) double; low season A$296 (US$237/UK£119) double. AE, DC, MC, V. **Amenities:** Bar; unheated outdoor pool; free airport shuttle. *In room:* A/C, minibar, hair dryer, iron, safe.

Outback Pioneer Hotel and Lodge A happy all-ages crowd congregates at this midrange collection of hotel rooms, budget rooms, shared bunkrooms, and dorms. Thirty new rooms were added in 2002, offering clean, simple accommodations with private bathrooms; these are cheaper than the standard hotel rooms but more expensive than the existing budget rooms. Standard rooms come with a queen-size bed and a single; these have TVs with pay movies, a fridge, a minibar, and a phone. Some budget rooms have a TV and a fridge; 24 of the budget rooms come with two bunk beds and have private bathrooms. A dozen budget rooms have a double bed and a bunk; these share bathrooms. Each quad bunkroom holds two sets of bunk beds; these are coed and share bathrooms. Children under 16 aren't allowed in bunkrooms unless you book the entire room. Plenty of lounge chairs sit by the pool, and there's also an Internet lounge. The Bough House Restaurant offers buffets, and a dirt-cheap kiosk sells burger-style fare. What seems like the entire resort gathers nightly at the great-value **Outback Pioneer Barbeque** ★★. This barn with big tables, lots of beer, and live music is the place to join the throngs throwing a kangaroo steak or emu sausage on the communal cook-it-yourself barbie.

Yulara Dr., Yulara, NT 0872. ✆ **08/8957 7888.** Fax 08/8957 7615. 125 units, all with private bathroom; 12 budget rooms without bathroom; 30 budget rooms with bathroom; 32 quad bunkrooms; 20-bed male-only dorm without bathroom, 20-bed female-only dorm without bathroom. High season A$404 (US$323/UK£162) double, A$206 (US$165/UK£83) budget room with bathroom, A$180 (US$144/UK£72) budget room without bathroom; low season

A$296 (US$237/UK£118) double, A$192 (US$154/UK£77) budget room with bathroom, A$170 (US$136/UK£68) budget room without bathroom. Bunkroom bed A$40 (US$32/UK£16), dorm bed A$32 (US$26/UK£13) year-round. AE, DC, MC, V. **Amenities:** 2 restaurants; bar; unheated outdoor pool; free airport shuttle. *In room:* A/C.

INEXPENSIVE

Moderately priced cabins and inexpensive bunkhouse and dorm beds are available at the Outback Pioneer Hotel and Lodge, above.

Ayers Rock Campground Instead of red dust you get green lawns at this campground, which has barbecues, a playground, Internet access, a small general store, and clean communal bathrooms and kitchen. If you don't want to camp but want to travel cheap, consider the modern cabins. They're a great value; each has air-conditioning, a TV, a kitchenette with a fridge, dining furniture, a double bed, and four bunks. They book up quickly in winter.

Yulara Dr., Yulara, NT 0872. ✆ **08/8956 2055.** Fax 08/8956 2260. 220 tent sites, 198 powered sites, 14 cabins, none with bathroom. A$150 (US$120/UK£60) cabin for up to 6; A$29 (US$23/UK£12) double tent site; A$34 (US$27/UK£14) powered motor-home site. AE, DC, MC, V. **Amenities:** Unheated outdoor pool; playground; free airport shuttle; coin-op laundry. *In room:* No phone.

Thrifty (✆ **08/8956 2030**) at Uluru rents its customers a complete camping kit with sleeping bags, tents, cooking equipment, and so on for A$401 (US$320/UK£160) for 5 days out of Ayers Rock. You must hire as part of a car deal (a medium-size car with camping gear for 5 days, plus good insurance will cost around A$1,070/US$856/UK£428). You need to book hire cars in Uluru at least 2 weeks ahead. Contact **Hertz** (✆ **08/8956 2244**) for a similar deal.

9

The Top End

by Lee Mylne

The "Top End" is a last frontier, a vast sweep of barely inhabited country from Broome on the west coast to Arnhemland in the Northern Territory and eastern Queensland. Most of it is in the Northern Territory, and the term also differentiates the northern part of the Territory from the Red Centre. It is a place of wild, rugged beauty and, sometimes, hardship.

The Northern Territory's capital, Darwin, is a small city, rich, modern, and tropical. Katherine is famous for its river gorge. Visit an Aboriginal community, canoe along lonely rivers, and soak in thermal pools. To the east of Darwin is Kakadu National Park, home to wetlands teeming with crocs and birds; one-third of the country's bird species are here. Farther east is Arnhemland, a stretch of rocky escarpments and rivers owned by Aborigines and seen by few others.

Life in the Top End is different from life elsewhere in Australia. Its slightly lawless image is one the locals enjoy. Isolation, the summer Wet season, monsoons, predatory crocodiles, and other dangers make 'em tough up here.

1 Exploring the Top End

Read "Exploring the Red Centre," in chapter 8; it contains information on traveling the entire Northern Territory.

VISITOR INFORMATION The **Northern Territory Tourist Commission,** Tourism House, 43 Mitchell St., Darwin, NT 0800 (✆ **13 67 68** in Australia, or 08/8951 8471; www.travelnt.com), can supply information on Darwin, Litchfield National Park, Kakadu National Park, Katherine, and other destinations in the territory. The website has special sections tailored for international travelers (choose your country) and for the self-drive market. It can help you find a travel agent who specializes in the Northern Territory, details many hotels, tour operators, rental-car companies, and attractions, and features a special fishing guide. The Commission's Territory Discoveries division (**www.holidaysnt.com**) offers package deals.

The **Tourism Top End** information center in Darwin and **Katherine Visitor Information Centre** (listed in the "Katherine" section, later in this chapter) can supply information about the Top End in addition to their local regions.

WHEN TO GO Most folks visit the Top End in the winter **Dry season** ("the Dry"). It's more than likely that not a cloud will grace the sky, and temperatures will be comfortable, even hot in the middle of the day. The Dry runs from **late April to late October/early November.** It is high season, so book every hotel or tour in advance.

Tips Croc Alert!

Saltwater crocodiles are a threat in the sea, estuaries, lakes, wetlands, pools, and rivers of the Top End—even well inland. They live in fresh water, too. *Never* jump in the water or stand on the bank unless you are willing to risk becoming a croc's lunch!

The **Wet season** ("the Wet") runs from **November through March or April,** sometimes starting as early as October and sometimes lasting a few weeks longer in the Kimberley. While rain does not fall 24 hours a day, it comes down in buckets for an hour or two each day, mainly in the late afternoon or at night. The land floods as far as the eye can see, the humidity is murderous, and the temperatures hit nearly 104°F (40°C). The floods cut off many attractions, and some tour companies close for the season. Cyclones may hit the coast during the Wet, with the same savagery and frequency as hurricanes hit Florida. Many people find the "buildup" to the Wet, in October and November, when clouds gather but do not break, to be the toughest time.

Despite that, many people love traveling in the Wet. Waterfalls become massive torrents, lightning storms crackle across the afternoon sky, the land turns green, cloud cover keeps the worst of the sun off you, crowds vanish, and there is an eerie beauty to it all. Keep your plans flexible to account for floods, take it slowly in the heat, and carry lots of drinking water. Even if you normally camp, sleep in air-conditioned accommodations now. Book tours ahead, because most operate on a reduced schedule. See the tips about traveling in the Wet, below.

GETTING AROUND The **Automobile Association of the Northern Territory (AANT),** 79–81 Smith St., Darwin, NT 0800 (✆ **08/8981 3837;** www.aant.com.au), is a good source of maps and road advice. See also the Northern Territory Tourist Commission's site (**www.travelnt.com**), which has sections designed specifically for those setting out on a driving holiday.

Until 2006, the Northern Territory had no open-road speed limits. Normal restricted speed limits apply in all urban areas, and the new speed limits on highways are still considerably higher than in other states. The speed limit is set at 130kmph (81 mph) on the Stuart, Arnhem, Barkly, and Victoria highways, while rural roads are designated 110kmph (68 mph) speed limits unless otherwise signposted. Drivers should be careful to keep to a reasonable speed and leave enough distance to stop safely. The road fatality toll in the Northern Territory is high: 27 fatalities per 100,000 people each year, compared with the Australian average of 8 per 100,000.

Most Aboriginal land is open to visitors, but in some cases you must obtain a permit first. If you are taking a tour, this will be taken care of, but independent travelers should apply to the relevant Aboriginal Land Council for permission.

Always carry 4 liters (1 gal.) of **drinking water** per person a day when walking (increase to 1 liter/¼ gal. per person per hour in summer). Wear a broad-brimmed hat, high-factor sunscreen, and insect repellent containing DEET (such as Aerogard and RID brands) to protect against the dangerous Ross River Fever virus carried by mosquitoes in these parts.

The Northern Territory

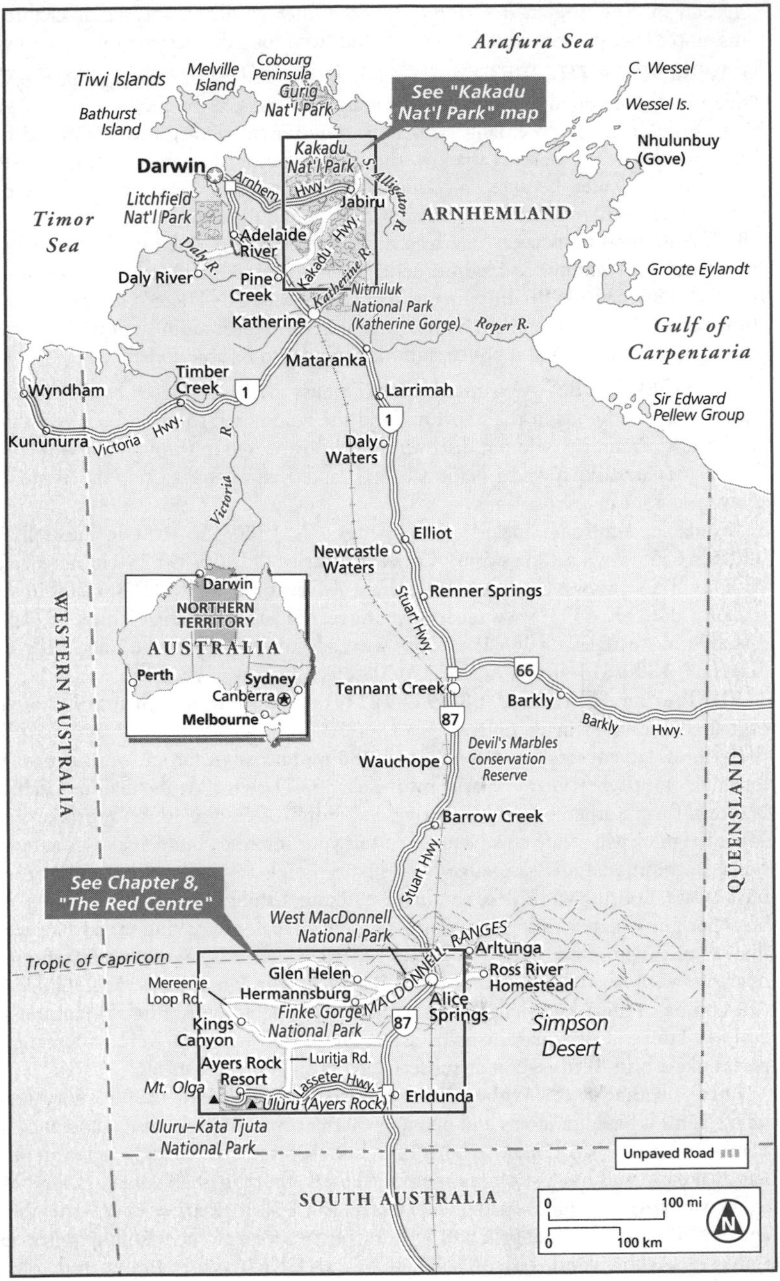

Deadly **marine stingers** (see "Bugs, Bites & Other Wildlife Concerns" in chapter 2) put a stop to ocean swimming in the Top End from roughly October to April or May.

TRAVELING IN THE WET Some roads will be underwater throughout the Wet, while others can flood unexpectedly, leaving you cut off for hours, days, or even months. Flash floods pose dangers to unwary motorists. Don't cross a flooded road unless you know the water is shallow, the current gentle, and the road intact. Never wade into the water, because crocodiles may be present. If you're cut off, the only thing to do is wait, so it's smart to travel with food and drinking water in remote parts. Check road conditions every day by calling the Northern Territory Department of Infrastructure, Planning & Environment's 24-hour recorded **report on road conditions** (✆ **1800/246 199**); dropping into or calling the AANT (see "Getting Around," above) in Darwin during office hours; or tuning in to local radio stations. Tour companies, tourist bureaus, and police stations should also be able to help.

TOUR OPERATORS Organized tours can bust the hassles posed by distance, isolation, and Wet floods in the Top End, and the guides will show and tell you things you almost certainly would not discover on your own. A loop through Darwin, Litchfield National Park, Kakadu National Park, and Katherine is a popular route that shows you a lot in a short time.

Reputable companies include **AAT Kings** (✆ **1300/556 100** in Australia, or 08/8923 6555; www.aatkings.com); **Odyssey Safaris** (✆ **1800/891 190** in Australia, or 08/8984 3504; www.odysaf.com.au); **Sahara Adventures** (✆ **1800/806 240** in Australia, or 08/8252 5333; www.saharaadventures.com.au); **Adventure Tours** (✆ **1300/654 604** in Australia, or 08/8132 8230; www.adventuretours.com.au); and **Billy Can Tours** (✆ **1800/813 484** in Australia, or 08/8947 1877; www.billycan.com.au).

VIP Touring Australia (✆ **08/8947 1211**; www.viptouring.com.au) offers luxury organized and tailor-made tours.

Far Out Adventures ★ (✆ **0427/152 288** mobile; www.farout.com.au) does tailor-made four-wheel-drive safaris into Kakadu, Darwin, Arnhemland, Litchfield National Park, Katherine, the Kimberley, and more Top End regions. Proprietor-guide Mike Keighley will create an adventure to suit your interests, budget, and time restrictions. Accommodations can range from luxury hotels to "under the stars" in Aussie bush swags. Touring with Mike can involve hiking, fishing, meeting or camping with his Aboriginal mates, canoeing, seeing Aboriginal rock art, taking extras like scenic flights, and swimming under (croc-free) waterfalls. Mike is one of a select group of operators with Australia's Advanced Eco Tour Accreditation and Savannah Guide status, and has a great knowledge of the Top End's geography, Aboriginal culture, and ecology. Fun and personal, his trips are accompanied by good wine (sometimes in places like a bird-filled lagoon at sunset) and "bush gourmet" meals.

Lord's Kakadu & Arnhemland Safaris (✆ **08/8948 2200**; www.lords-safaris.com) is based in Jabiru and operates charter tours throughout Kakadu and Arnhemland. Owner Sab Lord was born on a buffalo station in Kakadu before it was a national park, and has a strong rapport with local Aborigines. His small-group 4WD tours, which can be tailor-made, visit the Injalak Hill rock-art sites in Arnhemland and the arts center at Oenpelli and have exclusive access to the Minkinj Valley. Day tours to Arnhemland cost A$189 (US$151/UK£76) for adults and A$149 (US$119/UK£60) for children under 14. They operate May to November. The company also runs tours to Jim Jim and Twin Falls.

2 Darwin

1,489km (923 miles) N of Alice Springs

Australia's proximity to Asia is never more apparent than when you are in Darwin. The northernmost capital, named after Charles Darwin, is an exotic blend of frontier town, Asian village, and modern life. With a population of about 90,000, Darwin has had a turbulent history—and it shows. This city has battled just about everything that man and nature could throw at it. Most of its buildings date from the mid-1970s; Cyclone Tracy wiped out the city on Christmas Eve 1974. Don't bother bringing a jacket and tie here. Shorts and sandals will get you most places—even the swankiest official state invitations stipulate "Territory Rig" dress, meaning long pants and a short-sleeved open-neck shirt for men.

Darwin is most commonly used as a gateway to Kakadu National Park, Katherine Gorge, and the Kimberley, and many Australians have never bothered to visit—or at least not for long. And that's a shame, because it is an attractive and interesting place. Give yourself a day or two to wander the pleasant streets and parklands, visit the wildlife attractions, and discover some of the city's rich history. Then take time for some wetlands fishing, or shop for Aboriginal art and the Top End's South Sea pearls. An easy day trip is **Litchfield National Park** ★★, one of the Territory's best-kept secrets, boasting waterfalls to swim under that you only see on holiday brochures.

ESSENTIALS

GETTING THERE **Qantas** (✆ **13 13 13** in Australia; www.qantas.com) serves Darwin daily from most state capitals; flights either are direct or connect in Alice Springs. Qantas also flies direct from Cairns. **Virgin Blue** (✆ **13 67 89** in Australia; www.virginblue.com) flies direct to Darwin from Brisbane, Newcastle, and Melbourne, with connections from Sydney, Cairns, Canberra, the Gold Coast, Adelaide, Perth, and Tasmania, as well as other regional centers. **Airnorth** (✆ **1800/627 474** in Australia, or 08/8920 4001; www.airnorth.com.au) flies from Broome and Kununurra in Western Australia. There are also direct flights to Darwin from Asia.

Darwin Airport Shuttle Services (✆ **1800/358 945** in the Northern Territory, or 08/8981 5066) meets every flight and delivers to any hotel between the airport and city for A$8.50 (US$6.80/UK£3.40) one-way or A$15 (US$12/UK£6) round-trip. Children 6 to 13 pay A$4.50 (US$3.60/UK£1.80), or A$8 (US$6.40/UK£3.20) round-trip. Bookings aren't essential. A cab to the city is around A$25 (US$20/UK£10). **Avis, Budget, Europcar, Hertz,** and **Thrifty** have airport desks (see "Getting Around," below, for phone numbers).

Greyhound Australia (✆ **13 14 99** in Australia; www.greyhound.com.au) makes a daily coach run from Alice Springs. The trip takes around 20 hours, and the fare is A$278 (US$222/UK£111). Greyhound also has a daily service from Broome via Kununurra and Katherine; this trip takes around 24 hours and costs A$353 (US$282/UK£141). They also run from Cairns via Townsville and Tennant Creek, a 40-hour trip costing A$517 (US$414/UK£166).

The opening of the Alice Springs–Darwin railway line in 2004 gave the Top End its only rail link. Great Southern Railway's ***Ghan*** (✆ **13 21 47** in Australia; www.trainways.com.au) runs a twice-weekly round-trip between the two cities, leaving Alice on Mondays and Saturdays, arriving in Darwin about 24 hours later. The return trip leaves Darwin on Wednesdays and Mondays. The adult one-way fare is A$355

(US$284/UK£142) for a "day-nighter" seat, A$705 (US$564/UK£226) for a sleeper, or A$1,095 (US$876/UK£438) for a first-class sleeper.

Darwin is at the end of the Stuart Highway. Allow at least 2 long days, 3 to be comfortable, to drive from Alice. The nearest road from the east is the long and dull Barkly Highway, which connects with the Stuart Highway at Tennant Creek, 922km (572 miles) south. The nearest road from the west is Victoria Highway, which joins the Stuart Highway at Katherine, 314km (195 miles) to the south.

VISITOR INFORMATION **Tourism Top End** runs the official visitor center, Knuckey Street at Mitchell Street, Darwin, NT 0800 (✆ **08/8936 2499;** www.tourismtopend.com.au). It is the place to go for maps, bookings, national park notes, and information on Darwin and other regions throughout the Northern Territory, including Arnhemland, Katherine, and Kakadu and Litchfield national parks. It's open Monday to Friday from 8:30am to 5:45pm, Saturday from 9am to 2:45pm, and Sunday and public holidays from 10am to 1:45pm.

CITY LAYOUT The city heart is the **Smith Street pedestrian mall.** One street over is the **Mitchell Street Tourist Precinct,** with backpacker lodges, cheap eateries, and souvenir stores. Two streets away is the harborfront **Esplanade.** In the old **Wharf Precinct,** a walk from town, are a couple of tourist attractions, a jetty popular with fishermen, and a working dock. **Cullen Bay Marina** is a hub for restaurants, cafes, and expensive boats; it's about a 25-minute walk northwest of town. Northwest of town is **Fannie Bay,** where you'll find the Botanic Gardens, sailing club, golf course, museum and art gallery, and casino.

GETTING AROUND For car and four-wheel-drive rentals, call **Avis** (✆ 08/8981 9922), **Budget** (✆ 08/8981 9800), **EuropCar** (✆ 08/8941 0300), **Hertz** (✆ 08/8941 0944), or **Thrifty** (✆ 08/8924 0000).

By Bus **Darwinbus** (✆ **08/8924 7666**) is the local bus company. A A$2 (US$1.60/UK80p) adult or A50¢ (US40¢/UK20p) child bus fare gives unlimited travel for 3 hours. A Show&Go ticket gives unlimited bus travel for 1 day for A$5 (US$4/UK£2) or for a week (valid Mon–Sun) for A$15 (US$12/UK£6). The city terminus is on Harry Chan Place (off Smith St., near State Sq.). Get timetables there, or from the Tourism Top End visitor center (see "Visitor Information," above).

Darwin Day Tours (✆ **1300/721 365** in Australia, or 08/8923 6523) has a range of sightseeing tours.

By Taxi **Darwin Radio Taxis** (✆ **13 10 08**) is the main cab company. Taxi stands are at the Knuckey Street and Bennett Street ends of Smith Street Mall.

EXPLORING DARWIN

Darwin's parks, harbor, and tropical clime make it lovely for strolling during the Dry. The tourist office distributes a free map showing a Historical Stroll of 17 points of

---

Tours of Darwin

The **Tour Tub bus** (✆ **08/8985 6322**) does a loop of most city attractions and major hotels between 9am and 4pm daily. Hop on and off all day for A$25 (US$20/UK£10) for adults, A$15 (US$12/UK£6) for children 4 to 12. It departs the Knuckey Street end of Smith Street Mall, opposite Woolworths, every hour.

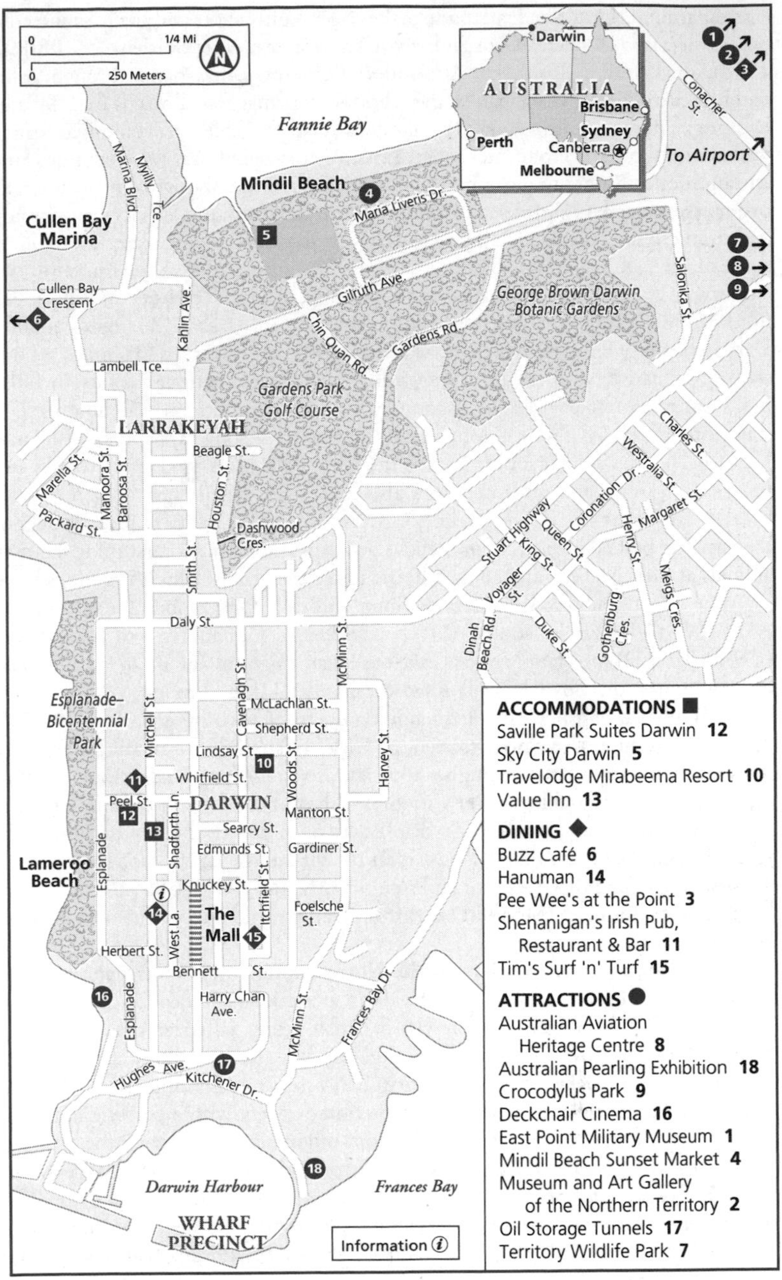

Darwin

0 — 1/4 Mi
0 — 250 Meters

Fannie Bay

Cullen Bay Marina

Mindil Beach **4**

5

Maria Liveris Dr.

Cullen Bay Crescent

6

Gilruth Ave.

Kahlin Ave.

Chin Quan Rd.

Gardens Rd.

George Brown Darwin Botanic Gardens

Salonika St.

7
8
9

Lambell Tce.

Gardens Park Golf Course

LARRAKEYAH

Beagle St.

Houston St.

Marella St.
Manoora St.
Baroosa St.
Packard St.

Dashwood Cres.

Smith St.

Daly St.

Charles St.

Westralia St.

Coronation Dr.

Henry St.

Margaret St.

Meigs Cres.

Gothenburg Cres.

Stuart Highway

Queen St.

King St.

Voyager St.

Dinah Beach Rd.

Duke St.

Esplanade–Bicentennial Park

Mitchell St.

Cavenagh St.

McLachlan St.
Shepherd St.

Woods St.

McMinn St.

Harvey St.

Lindsay St.

Whitfield St.

10

DARWIN

Manton St.

11
12
13

Peel St.
Shadforth Ln.

Searcy St.
Edmunds St.
Gardiner St.

Esplanade

Lameroo Beach

Knuckey St.

Litchfield St.

Foelsche St.

14

i

The Mall **15**

Herbert St.
West La.

Bennett St.

16

Harry Chan Ave.

Esplanade

Frances Bay Dr.

17

Hughes Ave.

Kitchener Dr.

Darwin Harbour

Frances Bay

18

WHARF PRECINCT

Information *i*

AUSTRALIA

• Darwin

Brisbane
Sydney
Canberra ★
Melbourne

Perth

Conacher St.

To Airport

1
2
3

ACCOMMODATIONS ■
Saville Park Suites Darwin **12**
Sky City Darwin **5**
Travelodge Mirabeema Resort **10**
Value Inn **13**

DINING ◆
Buzz Café **6**
Hanuman **14**
Pee Wee's at the Point **3**
Shenanigan's Irish Pub,
 Restaurant & Bar **11**
Tim's Surf 'n' Turf **15**

ATTRACTIONS ●
Australian Aviation
 Heritage Centre **8**
Australian Pearling Exhibition **18**
Crocodylus Park **9**
Deckchair Cinema **16**
East Point Military Museum **1**
Mindil Beach Sunset Market **4**
Museum and Art Gallery
 of the Northern Territory **2**
Oil Storage Tunnels **17**
Territory Wildlife Park **7**

interest around town. The **Esplanade** makes a pleasantly short and shady saunter, and the 42-hectare (104-acre) **George Brown Darwin Botanic Gardens** (**© 08/8981 1958**), on Gardens Road 2km (1¼ miles) from town, has paths through palms, orchids, every species of baobab in the world, and mangroves. Entry is free. Take bus no. 4 or 6; the buses drop you at the Gardens Road entrance, but you might want to walk straight to the visitor center (open 8:30am–4pm daily) near the Geranium Street entrance (open 24 hr.) to pick up self-guiding maps to the Aboriginal plant-use trails.

The pleasant 5km (3-mile) trail along **Fannie Bay** from the Skycity Darwin hotel and casino to the East Point Military Museum is also worth doing. Keep a lookout for some of the 2,000 wild wallabies on the east side of the road near the museum.

Darwin has two wildlife parks worth visiting. At the **Territory Wildlife Park** (**© 08/8988 7200;** www.territorywildlifepark.com.au), 61km (38 miles) south of Darwin at Berry Springs, you can take a free shuttle or walk 6km (3¾ miles) of bush trails to see native Northern Territory wildlife in re-created natural habitats, including monsoon rainforest boardwalks, lagoons with hides (shelters for watching birds), a walk-through aviary, a walk-through aquarium housing sting rays and sawfish, and a nocturnal house with marsupials such as the bilby. Bats, birds, spiders, crocs, frill-neck lizards, kangaroos, and other creatures also make their homes here (but not koalas, because they don't live in the Territory). A program of animal talks runs throughout the day. The best is the birds of prey show, at 10am and 3pm. Go first thing to see the animals at their liveliest, and allow 4 hours to see everything, plus 45 minutes traveling time. Open daily from 8:30am to 6pm, and closed December 25. Admission is A$20 (US$16/UK£8) for adults, A$10 (US$8/UK£4) for children 5 to 16, and A$55 (US$44/UK£22) for a family of six. Take the Stuart Highway for 50km (31 miles) and turn right onto the Cox Peninsula Road for another 11km (7 miles).

In addition to housing a small crocodile museum, **Crocodylus Park** (**© 08/8922 4500**), a 15-minute drive from town at 815 McMillan's Rd., Berrimah (opposite the police station), holds croc-feeding sessions and free hour-long guided tours at 10am, noon, and 2pm. It doubles as Darwin's zoo, with exotic species including lions, Bengal tigers, leopards, and monkeys on display. It's open daily from 9am to 5pm (closed Dec 25). Admission is A$25 (US$20/UK£10) for adults, A$20 (US$16/UK£8) for seniors, A$13 (US$10/UK£5) for children 3 to 15, and A$65 (US$52/UK£26) for a family group. Bus no. 5 (Mon–Fri only) from Darwin will drop you about a 5-minute walk from the park entrance.

The **Museum and Art Gallery of the Northern Territory,** Conacher Street, Bullocky Point (**© 08/8999 8264**), also holds an attraction for crocodile fans—the preserved body of **Sweetheart,** a 5m (16-ft.) man-eating saltwater croc captured in Kakadu National Park. The museum and gallery is a great place to learn about Darwin's place in Australia's modern history. It has sections on Aboriginal, Southeast Asian, and Pacific art and culture, and a maritime gallery with a pearling lugger and other boats that have sailed into Darwin from Indonesia and other northern parts. A highlight is the Cyclone Tracy gallery, where you can stand in a small, dark room as the sound of the cyclone rages around you. The gallery and museum are open from 9am to 5pm Monday through Friday, and 10am to 5pm weekends and public holidays; closed January 1, Good Friday, and December 25 and 26. The cafe has lovely bay views. Admission is free to the permanent exhibits. Take bus no. 4 or 6.

Darwin was bombed 64 times during World War II, and 12 ships were sunk in the harbor. It was an Allied supply base, and many American airmen were based here. The

East Point Military Museum, East Point Road, East Point (© **08/8981 9702**), housed in a World War II gun command post, plays a video of the 1942 and 1943 Japanese bombings. It has small but fine displays of photos, memorabilia, artillery, armored vehicles, weaponry old and new, and gun emplacements outside. Open daily from 9:30am to 5pm (closed Good Friday and Dec 25). Admission is A$10 (US$8/UK£4) adults, A$9 (US$7.20/UK£3.60) seniors, A$5 (US$4/UK£2) children, and A$28 (US$22/UK£11) families.

Even if you are not a military or aircraft buff, you may enjoy the excellent **Australian Aviation Heritage Centre** ★, 557 Stuart Hwy., Winnellie (© **08/8947 2145**). A B-52 bomber on loan from the United States is the prized exhibit, but the center also boasts a B-25 Mitchell bomber, Mirage and Sabre jet fighters, rare Japanese Zero fighter wreckage, and funny, sad, and heartwarming (and heart-wrenching) displays on World War II and Vietnam. Hours are daily from 9am to 5pm (closed Good Friday, Dec 25). Admission is A$11 (US$8.80/UK£4.40) for adults, A$8 (US$6.40/UK£3.20) for seniors and students, A$6 (US$4.80/UK£2.40) for children 6 to 12, and A$28 (US$22/UK£11) for families. Guided tours are at 10am, 2pm, and 4pm. The Heritage Centre is 10 minutes from town; take the no. 5 or 8 bus.

Empty **World War II oil storage tunnels** (© **08/8985 6333**), on Kitchener Drive in the Wharf Precinct, house a collection of black-and-white photographs of the war in Darwin, each lit up in the dark. The simple but haunting attraction is worth a visit. Admission is A$5 (US$4/UK£2) adults and A$3 (US$2.40/UK£1.20) children. The tunnels are closed in December and February. They open from 9am to 4pm daily May through September; October through April, hours are Tuesday through Sunday (and public holidays) from 9am to 1pm.

On the Esplanade stands a monument to the destroyer **USS *Robert E. Peary,*** which went down in Darwin Harbour, with a loss of 88 lives.

Despite all this destruction, some of Darwin's historic buildings—or at least parts of them—have survived, and you can see them around the city center.

For an insight into Darwin's pearling industry, visit the **Australian Pearling Exhibition** (© **08/8999 6573**), on Kitchener Drive near the Wharf Precinct. It has displays following the industry from the days of the lugger and hard-hat diving to modern farming and culture techniques. It's open from 10am to 5pm daily, except January 1, Good Friday, and December 25 and 26. Tickets cost A$6.60 (US$5.30/UK£2.65) for adults, A$3.30 (US$2.65/UK£1.30) for children, and A$17 (US$14/UK£7) for a family of five.

If you have an evening free, get out on the harbor. **Australian Harbour Cruises** (© **08/8941 4000;** www.australianharbourcruises.com.au) offers 3-hour sunset cruises aboard the restored lugger *Anniki.* They leave Cullen Bay Marina daily at 4:45pm and cost A$50 (US$40/UK£20) for adults and A$30 (US$24/UK£12) for kids 3 to 15. The price includes a glass of bubbly and some nibbles, and you can buy more drinks. **Darwin Harbour Cruises** (© **08/8942 3131;** www.darwinharbour cruises.com.au) operates a sunset champagne cruise aboard the sailing schooner *Tumlaren,* which costs A$60 (US$48/UK£24) per adult and A$39 (US$31/UK£16) for children 4 to 14. A sit-down three-course dinner cruise aboard the *Alfred Nobel* costs A$90 (US$72/UK£36) adults and A$59 (US$47/UK£24) children 2 to 12. Both cruises leave Cullen Bay Marina at 5pm.

The Top End's wetlands and warm oceans are **fishing** ★ heaven. The big prey is barramundi, or "barra." Loads of charter boats conduct jaunts of up to 10 days in the river and wetland systems around Darwin, Kakadu National Park, and into remote Arnhemland.

The same company that runs Darwin's Tour Tub bus runs the **Northern Territory Fishing Office** (✆ **1800/632 225** in Australia, or 08/8985 6333; www.ntfishingoffice.com.au), a booking agent for a number of fishing charter boats offering barramundi day trips and extended wetland safaris, reef fishing, light tackle sportfishing, fly-fishing, and estuary fishing. A day's barra fishing on wetlands near Darwin will cost around A$300 (US$240/UK£120) per person; for an extended barra safari, budget about A$1,440 (US$1,152/UK£576) per person for a 3-day trip. If you simply want to cast a line in Darwin Harbour for trevally, queenfish, and barra, the company will take you out for A$90 (US$72/UK£36) per person (or A$70/US$56/UK£28 for kids under 12) for a half-day, or A$165 (US$132/UK£66) per adult and A$145 (US$116/UK£58) kids under 12 for a full day. It also rents skipper-yourself fishing boats and tackle. Also check out the fishing section on **www.travelnt.com** for detailed information on fishing tours, guides, and everything you need to know to make your arms ache from reeling 'em in!

THE DARWIN SHOPPING SCENE

Darwin's best buys are Aboriginal art and crafts, pearls, opals, and diamonds.

For a good range of authentic Aboriginal artworks and artifacts at reasonable prices, check out **Raintree Aboriginal Fine Arts Gallery,** Shop 5, 20 Knuckey St. (✆ **08/8941 2732**). To make a heavyweight investment in works by internationally sought-after artists, visit the Aboriginal-owned **Aboriginal Fine Arts Gallery,** on the second floor at the corner of Knuckey and Mitchell streets (✆ **08/8981 1315;** www.aaia.com.au). Its website is a useful guide to art and artists.

The world's best South Sea pearls are farmed in the Top End seas. Buy, or just drool in the window, at **Paspaley Pearls,** off Smith Street Mall on Bennett Street (✆ **08/8982 5515**). **The World of Opal,** 52 Mitchell St. (✆ **08/8981 8981**), has a re-creation of an opal mine in the showroom. If you fancy a pink diamond (the world's rarest) from the Argyle Diamond Mine in Kununurra (see "Kununurra" in chapter 10), you can get them at **Creative Jewellers,** 27 Smith St. Mall (✆ **08/8941 1233**), an Argyle-appointed supplier that buys direct from the mine. It also stocks the champagne diamonds for which Argyle is renowned and other Argyle diamond colors, as well as South Sea pearls and opals. The jewelers try to fashion pieces for overseas visitors in a short time to match your traveling schedule.

Jokes about "snapping handbags" abound in croc country. For your own croc-skin fashion statement, head to **di Croco,** in the Paspaley Pearls building in Smith Street Mall (✆ **08/8941 4470**). You'll find bags, purses, wallets, card holders, belts, pens, and other accessories, all made from saltwater croc skins farmed locally.

WHERE TO STAY

April through October is the peak Dry season; hotels usually drop their rates from November through March (the Wet).

EXPENSIVE

Saville Park Suites Darwin ★★ This eight-floor apartment hotel, a block from Smith Street Mall and overlooking the Esplanade, is one of Darwin's most comfortable, elegant lodgings. Rich, dark cane lobby armchairs and sofas are welcoming and rooms feature sleek contemporary-style spacious studios and one- and two-bedroom apartments that boast their own private balcony with great views. Premium Harbour View apartments have an eclectic blend of Asian-style teak, mahogany, and wicker furniture.

The kitchens feature new modern granite bench tops and stainless steel appliances and the two penthouses include 104-centimeter (40-in.) plasma screens with digital surround sound. An extensive upgrade to the whole hotel, completed in early 2005, includes a smart new color scheme throughout the guest rooms and a warm inviting new lobby, befitting the hotel's tropical surroundings. All rooms and apartments have city or harbor views. A pantry-stocking service does grocery shopping. Premium apartments have CD players and all apartments have separate dataports. Some rooms don't have balconies but are a generous size.

88 The Esplanade (at Peel St.), Darwin, NT 0800. ✆ **1300/881 686** in Australia, or 08/8943 4333. Fax 08/8943 4388. www.savillesuites.com.au. 204 units. A$255–A$280 (US$204–US$224/UK£102–UK£112) double; A$270 (US$216/UK£108) studio apt; A$280–A$315 (US$224–US$252/UK£112–UK£126) 1-bedroom apt; A$485–A$520 (US$388–US$416/UK£194–UK£208) 2-bedroom apt; A$650–A$660 (US$520–US$528/UK£260–UK£264) 3-bedroom apt. Children under 15 stay free in parent's room with existing bedding. AE, DC, MC, V. Parking A$5.50 (US$4.40/UK£2.20). Bus: 4. **Amenities:** Restaurant; bar; outdoor pool; access to nearby golf course and health club; Jacuzzi; bike rental; concierge; tour desk; car-rental desk; business center; salon; limited room service (5:30am–10pm); massage; babysitting; laundry service; dry cleaning (Mon–Sat); nonsmoking rooms; executive-level rooms. *In room:* A/C, TV w/pay movies, minibar, coffeemaker, hair dryer, iron.

Skycity Darwin ★ *Value* A A$10-million (US$8-million/UK£4-million) refurbishment of the whole complex including the addition of 10 AAA-rated five-star Superior Rooms and an infinity-edged lagoon style swimming pool in 2005, has given this upscale hotel a whole new look. Over 2008, the complex will gain a new outdoor restaurant and bar as well as expanded dining facilities to further increase the entertainment options on offer. Attached to Darwin's casino on Fannie Bay, the hotel is now owned by the Skycity Entertainment Group. The complex resembles a tropical palace, with white blocky architecture and 7 hectares (18 acres) of gardens on Mindil Beach, next to the Botanic Gardens. The rooms are a cocktail of European-style, contemporary Spanish furniture, and tropical elegance. All have balconies. It's worth paying a little extra for an ocean-facing room so you can watch Darwin's great Dry season sunsets and spectacular monsoon season lightening storms. Superior Rooms feature luxurious spa tubs and cool marble in the bathrooms. Full-length glass windows provide views over a private balcony terrace to lush tropical gardens and Mindil beach. All rooms have free broadband Internet access, and there is wireless access in all guest areas. A short beachside stroll brings you to the Museum and Art Gallery, and the Mindil Beach Sunset Markets take place right outside on Thursday and Sunday nights in the Dry season. A free shuttle runs four times a day to and from the city. There are also 10 rooms for families and travelers with disabilities.

Gilruth Ave., Mindil Beach, Darwin, NT 0800. ✆ **1800/891 118** in Australia, or 08/8943 8888. Fax 08/8943 8999. www.skycitydarwin.com.au. 117 units. A$220 (US$176/UK£88) double; A$330 (US$264/UK£132) suite. Extra person A$50 (US$40/UK£20). Children under 14 stay free in parent's room with existing bedding. AE, DC, MC, V. Free valet and self-parking. Bus: 4 or 6. **Amenities:** 3 restaurants; 5 bars; heated outdoor pool; free access to nearby 9-hole

---

Tips **Where Can I Swim?**

Crocodiles and stingers render Darwin's beaches a no-swim zone year-round. Locals sunbathe on Casuarina Beach and swim within view of the sea in **Lake Alexander** in East Point Reserve. About an hour's drive from the city, on the way to the Territory Wildlife Park, **Berry Springs Nature Park** has swimming holes along Berry Creek, with steps for easy access, and small waterfalls that create natural whirlpool action. They may be closed in the Wet season.

---

golf course and 20 tennis courts; exercise room; Jacuzzi; sauna; concierge; tour desk; car-rental desk; business center; 24-hr. room service; massage; babysitting; free guest laundry; laundry service; dry cleaning; VIP suites. *In room:* A/C, TV/DVD w/pay movies, dataport, minibar, fridge, coffeemaker, hair dryer, iron.

MODERATE

Travelodge Mirambeena Resort You're just a stone's throw from the city center at this modern hotel complex, where the tempting swimming pools and the Tree Tops restaurant, all shaded by the leaves of a sprawling strangler fig, have a castaway-island feel. Each room is a decent size and has a garden or pool view. Loft apartments with kitchenettes are good for families, if you can handle sharing the compact bathroom with your kids, and sleep up to five. All rooms have broadband Internet access.

64 Cavenagh St., Darwin, NT 0800. ✆ **1800/891 100** in Australia, or 08/8946 0111. Fax 08/8981 5116. www.travelodge.com.au. 225 units, all with shower only. A$185–A$245 (US$148–US$196/UK£74–UK£98) double; A$275 (US$220/UK£110) loft apt for up to 3. Extra person A$30 (US$24/UK£12). Children under 12 stay free in parent's room. AE, DC, MC, V. Free off-street parking. Bus: 4, 5, 6, 8, or 10. **Amenities:** Restaurant; poolside cafe; 2 bars; 2 outdoor pools; children's pool; exercise room; 2 Jacuzzis; bike rental; game room; tour desk; secretarial services; limited room service; babysitting; coin-op laundry; laundry service; dry cleaning. *In room:* A/C, TV w/pay movies, minibar, hair dryer, iron, safe.

INEXPENSIVE

Value Inn *Value* The cheerful rooms at this neat little hotel in the Mitchell Street Tourist Precinct are compact but tidy, with colorful modern fittings. Each room is just big enough to hold both a queen-size and a single bed, and a small writing table. The views aren't much, but you'll probably spend your time in the nearby cafes. Smith Street Mall and the Esplanade walking path are 2 blocks away. There are a pay phone, cold drink and coffee vending machines, an iron on each floor, microwave ovens on the first and second floors, and a very small garden swimming pool off the parking lot.

50 Mitchell St., Darwin, NT 0800. ✆ **08/8981 4733.** Fax 08/8981 4730. www.valueinn.com.au. 93 units, all with shower only. A$69–A$115 (US$55–US$92/UK£28–UK£46) double. AE, MC, V. Limited free parking. Bus: 4. **Amenities:** Outdoor pool; tennis courts; access to nearby golf course and gym; bike rental; tour desk; car-rental desk; coin-op laundry; dry cleaning. *In room:* A/C, TV, fridge, no phone.

WHERE TO DINE

Cullen Bay Marina, a 25-minute walk or a short cab ride from town, is packed with trendy restaurants and cafes. If it's Thursday, don't even think about eating anywhere other than the **Mindil Beach Sunset Market** ★★. And on Saturday, head to the suburban Parap markets for Asian goodies (see the box, "Cheap Eats & More!" below). The cool crowd hangs at **Roma Bar Cafe,** 9 Cavenagh St. (✆ **08/8981 6729**), for good coffee and a cheap nosh; it's open from 7am to 5pm Monday through Friday, from 8am to 2pm Saturday and Sunday.

EXPENSIVE

Buzz Café ★★ CONTEMPORARY This smart, busy waterfront cafe is as well known for its "loo with a view" as it is for its terrific food and relaxed atmosphere. The men's bathroom just nudges out the women's for interest value. Ladies, get a man to take you in there to see what I mean—everybody does! The food is flavorsome East-meets-West fare like jungle curry of chicken with snake beans and green peppercorns, and pan-fried barramundi on potato mash in lemon-butter sauce; the lamb shanks are so huge almost no one can finish them. Wash it down with a cocktail.

Marina Blvd., Cullen Bay. ✆ **08/8941 1141.** Reservations recommended in the Dry (May–Oct). Main courses A$17–A$30 (US$14–US$24/UK£7–UK£12). AE, DC, MC, V. Mon–Fri noon–2am; Sat–Sun 10:30am–2am (brunch until 11:30am). Bus: 4 or 6.

Value Cheap Eats & More!

If it's Thursday, join the entire city at the **Mindil Beach Sunset Market** ★★ to feast at the 60 terrific (and cheap—most dishes are A$5–A$8/US$4–US$6.40/UK£2–UK£3.20 a serving!) Asian, Greek, Italian, and Aussie food stalls; listen to live music; wander among almost 200 arts-and-crafts stalls; and mix and mingle with masseurs, tarot card readers, and street performers as the sun sets into the sea. The action runs from 5 to 10pm in the Dry (approximately May–Oct). A smaller market of about 50 stalls runs Sunday from 4 to 9pm. The markets' season changes from year to year, so if you're visiting on the seasonal cusp, in April or September, check whether they are on by calling the organizers (✆ **08/8981 3454;** or visit www.mindil.com.au). The beach is about a A$10 (US$8/UK£4) cab ride from town, or take bus no. 4. The Tour Tub's last run of the day, at 4pm (see "Getting Around," earlier this chapter), goes by the markets.

On Saturdays (7:30am–1:30pm), head to suburban **Parap Markets** ★, which transform a small street into a corner of Asia. The focus is on food, with a sprinkling of arts and crafts, and it's a favorite place for locals to have breakfast or brunch, choosing from the Southeast Asian soups, noodle dishes, and satays, washed down with fresh-squeezed tropical fruit drinks. The market stalls cover only about a block, on Parap Road in Parap (✆ **0438/882 373** mobile).

Hanuman ★ CONTEMPORARY THAI/NONYA/TANDOORI Elegant black walls and a moody Eastern atmosphere make this city restaurant popular as a business venue by day and as a rendezvous for couples, families, and more business folk by night. "Nonya"-style cuisine is a fusion of Chinese and Malaysian style cooking. You can rely on it for dishes such as roasted duck in a red curry of coconut, litchis, kaffir lime, and sweet basil, or barramundi grilled and served with a ginger, tamarind, and passionfruit sauce. There is also a tandoori menu. Service is prompt and friendly.

28 Mitchell St. ✆ **08/8941 3500.** Reservations recommended. Main courses A$20–A$30 (US$16–US$24/UK£8–UK£12). AE, DC, MC, V. Mon–Fri noon–2:30pm; daily 6:30–11pm.

Pee Wee's at The Point ★★ CONTEMPORARY Surrounded on three sides by forest, this steel-and-glass venue affords views of Fannie Bay from just about every table, inside, out on the deck, or down on the lawn. The owners—two chefs and a sommelier—offer an extensive wine list that includes some older and hard-to-find Australian wines. The food emphasizes fresh local produce and employs some dishes that have an Asian twist. An example: miso baked locally caught crisp skin saltwater barramundi filet on wok charred choy sum, with kaffir lime and ginger fish cakes and a Thai-style coleslaw with mango chutney. Get there in time to watch the sun set.

Alec Fong Lim Dr., East Point Reserve (4km/2½ miles from town). ✆ **08/8981 6868.** Reservations recommended, especially in the Dry (May–Oct). Main courses A$25–A$46 (US$20–US$37/UK£10–UK£19). AE, DC, MC, V. Daily 6pm–late. Closed Dec 26. Free parking. Cab fare from the city about A$15 (US$12/UK£6).

MODERATE

Shenanigan's ★ IRISH PUB FARE Hearty Irish stews and braised beef-and-Guinness pies (plus the odd pint of Guinness itself) get everyone in the mood for eating, talking, and dancing at this convivial bar and restaurant. A friendly mix of solo travelers, families, seniors, and backpackers eat and drink in atmospheric wooden booths, standing up at bar tables, or by the fire. Besides hearty meat dishes, there is lighter stuff including vegetarian dishes and a good smattering of local produce. Try the "Taste of the Territory"—crocodile, kangaroo, and barramundi served on spinach mash with pepper-leaf and mustard glaze. There are also daily chef's specials. There's also entertainment every night, either live bands, a quiz, or karaoke.

69 Mitchell St. (at Peel St.). ✆ **08/8981 2100.** Reservations recommended. Main courses A$15–A$28 (US$12–US$22/UK£6–UK£11). AE, DC, MC, V. Daily 10:30am–2am.

INEXPENSIVE

Tim's Surf 'n' Turf ★ *Value* *Kids* STEAK/SEAFOOD This Darwin favorite has a new look and a new location after a move in 2005 to a classic elevated Darwin home that has been transformed into a modern restaurant. Diners can choose between the air-conditioned open plan dining and bar area, its walls hung with Top End Aboriginal artworks, or head outside to sit under the shady trees and palms. The lunch menu offers a range of A$10 (US$8/UK£4) specials including salads, baguettes and rolls, or hot dishes such as crocodile schnitzels, Malay curries, crumbed barramundi, and salmon fettuccine. At dinner the menu offers includes steaks, seafood platters, oysters, and vegetarian dishes, along with a range of salads, chicken, and pasta dishes. The wine list features mostly Australian wines, with around half offered by the glass.

10 Litchfield St. ✆ **08/8981 1024.** Main courses A$14–A$21 (US$11–US$17/UK£5.60–UK£8.40). AE, DC, MC, V. Mon–Fri noon–2pm; daily for dinner.

Moments Movie Stars under the Stars

Lie back in a canvas deck chair under the stars at the **Deckchair Cinema** (✆ **08/8981 0700;** www.deckchaircinema.com) to watch Aussie hits, foreign films, and cult classics. A move in 2004 to a new setting on the edge of Darwin Harbour (opposite Parliament House on the Esplanade) gave a new lease on life to this Darwin institution, run by the Darwin Film Society. Take a picnic dinner and get there early to soak up the scene: the twinkling lights from boats anchored in the Arafura Sea, and the fabulous sunsets. A smart new kiosk sells wine, beer, soft drinks, and snacks. There are 250 deck chairs as well as about 100 straight-backed seats, and staffers can supply cushions and even insect repellent if you need it. Entry is by a walkway from the Esplanade, or by car off Kitchener Drive (there's a parking lot). The box office and kiosk open at 6:30pm and movies start at 7:30pm daily in the Dry (Apr–Nov), with double features on Friday and Saturday. Tickets are A$13 (US$10/UK£5.20) adults, A$6 (US$4.80/UK£2.40) children, and A$30 (US$24/UK£12) for a family of four, or A$20 (US$16/UK£8) adults, A$9 (US$7.20/UK£3.60) children, and A$45 (US$36/UK£18) family for double features. (In the Wet, the movies screen indoors so call for details of the current venue.)

DARWIN AFTER DARK

The gaming tables at the **Skycity Darwin Casino,** Gilruth Avenue, Mindil Beach (✆ **08/8943 8888**), are in play from noon until 4am Sunday to Thursday, until 6am Friday and Saturday. Slot machines operate 24 hours. The dress code allows neat jeans, shorts, and sneakers, but men's shirts must have a collar.

A good spot to catch Darwin's Technicolor sunsets is the supercasual **Darwin Sailing Club,** Atkins Drive on Fannie Bay (✆ **08/8981 1700**). Ask the manager to sign you in. Dine on affordable meals outdoors while a family of goannas (monitor lizards) swirls around your feet looking for meaty scraps. The bar is open from 10am until midnight Sunday through Thursday, and until 2am Friday and Saturday.

The cafes and restaurants of **Cullen Bay Marina** are a good place to be day or night, but especially for Dry season sunsets.

If it's Thursday, you are mad to be anywhere except the **Mindil Beach Sunset Market** ★★ (see "Cheap Eats & More!" above).

A SIDE TRIP TO LITCHFIELD PARK

120km (74 miles) S of Darwin

An easy 90-minute drive south of Darwin is a miniature Garden of Eden full of forests, waterfalls, rocky sandstone escarpments, glorious swimming holes, and prehistoric cycads that look as if they belong on the set of *Jurassic Park.* Litchfield National Park is much smaller (a mere 146,000 hectares/360,620 acres) and much less famous than its big sister, Kakadu, but it is no less stunning.

The park's main attractions are the spring-fed swimming holes, like the magical plunge pool at **Florence Falls** ★★★, 29km (18 miles) from the forest. It's a 15-minute hike down stairs to the water, so the easily accessible pool at **Wangi Falls** ★, 49km (30 miles) from the eastern entrance, gets more crowds. (It's a beautiful spot, surrounded by cliffs and forests with a lookout from the top.) More idyllic grottoes are 4km (2½ miles) from Florence Falls at **Buley Rockhole,** a series of tiered rock pools and waterfalls. You can't swim at **Tolmer Falls,** but during the Wet when they're flowing, take the boardwalk about 400m (1,312 ft.) to the lookout and see the cascade against a backdrop of red cliffs.

There are a number of short **walking trails** through the park, such as the half-hour Shady Creek Circuit from Florence Falls up to the parking lot.

Parts of the park are also home to thousands of 2m-high (6½-ft.) **"magnetic" termite mounds,** so called because they run north-south to escape the fierce midday heat. (See a picture of the mounds in the color insert at the front of this book!) A display hut and a viewing point are 17km (11 miles) from the park's eastern entrance.

Most of the park's swimming holes are regarded as crocodile-free; the same is *not* true of the Finniss and Reynolds rivers in the park, so no leaping into those!

To get there from Darwin, head south for 86km (53 miles) on the Stuart Highway and follow the park turnoff on the right through the town of Batchelor for 34km (21 miles). A number of minicoach and four-wheel-drive day trips run from Darwin. Katherine-based tour operator **Travel North** (✆ **1800/089 103** in Australia, or 08/8971 9999) runs a day tour to Litchfield that starts in Darwin and ends in Katherine, a convenient way to combine sightseeing and transport if you plan to visit both. It costs A$149 (US$119/UK£60) adults and A$125 (US$100/UK£50) children 5 to 15. Crowds of locals can shatter the peace in Litchfield on weekends, especially in the Dry season, but the park is worth visiting, crowds or no crowds. Entry to the park is free.

Roads to most swimming holes are paved, although a few are accessible only by four-wheel-drive. In the Wet season (approximately Nov–Apr), some roads—usually the four-wheel-drive ones—may be closed, and the Wangi water hole may be off-limits due to turbulence and strong currents. Check with the **Parks & Wildlife Commission** (✆ **08/8999 4555**) before you leave Darwin during this time.

A number of locations in the park have basic campsites. The camping fee per night is A$6.60 (US$5.30/UK£2.65) for adults, A$3.30 (US$2.65/UK£1.30) for kids under 16, or A$15 (US$12/UK£6) for a family of two adults and four kids. A kiosk at Wangi Falls sells some supplies, but stock up on fuel and alcohol in Batchelor.

3 Kakadu National Park ★

257km (159 miles) E of Darwin

Kakadu National Park, a World Heritage area, is Australia's largest national park, covering a massive 1.7 million hectares (4.2 million acres).

Cruising the lily-clad wetlands to spot crocodiles, plunging into exquisite natural swimming holes, hiking through spear grass and cycads, fishing for prized barramundi, soaring in a light aircraft over torrential waterfalls during the Wet season, photographing thousands of birds flying over the eerie red sandstone escarpment that juts 200m (650 ft.) above the flood plain, and admiring some of Australia's most superb Aboriginal rock-art sites—these are the activities that draw people to Kakadu. Some 275 species of birds and 75 species of reptiles inhabit the park, making it one of the richest wildlife habitats in the country.

Kakadu is an ecological jewel. But be aware that the vast distances between points of interest in the park, and the sameness that infects so much Australian landscape, can detract from Kakadu's appeal for some people. Wildlife here is not the breathtaking equivalent of an African game park, where herds roam the plains—which is why even Australians get so excited when they spot a kangaroo in the wild. It is best in the late Dry, around September and October, when crocs and birds gather around shrinking water holes. Wildlife viewing is not particularly good in the Wet season, when birds disperse widely and you may not see a single croc.

The name "Kakadu" comes from "Gagudju," the group of languages spoken by Aborigines in the northern part of the park, where they and their ancestors are believed to have lived for 50,000 years. Today, Aborigines manage the park as its owners with the Australian government. This is one of the few places in Australia where some Aborigines stick to a traditional lifestyle of hunting and living off the land. You won't see them, because they keep away from prying eyes, but their culture is on display at a cultural center and at rock-art sites. Kakadu and the wilds of Arnhemland to the east are the birthplace of the "X-ray" style of art for which Aboriginal artists are famous.

JUST THE FACTS

VISITOR INFORMATION Both the park entrances—the northern station on the Arnhem Highway used by visitors from Darwin and the southern station on the Kakadu Highway for visitors from Katherine—hand out free visitor guides with maps. In the Dry they also issue a timetable of free ranger-guided bushwalks, art-site talks, and slide shows taking place that week. Entry to the park is free.

You can get a lot of information at the **Bowali Visitor Centre** (✆ **08/8938 1120**), on the Kakadu Highway, 5km (3 miles) from Jabiru, 100km (62 miles) from the northern entry station, and 131km (81 miles) from the southern entry station. The

Kakadu National Park

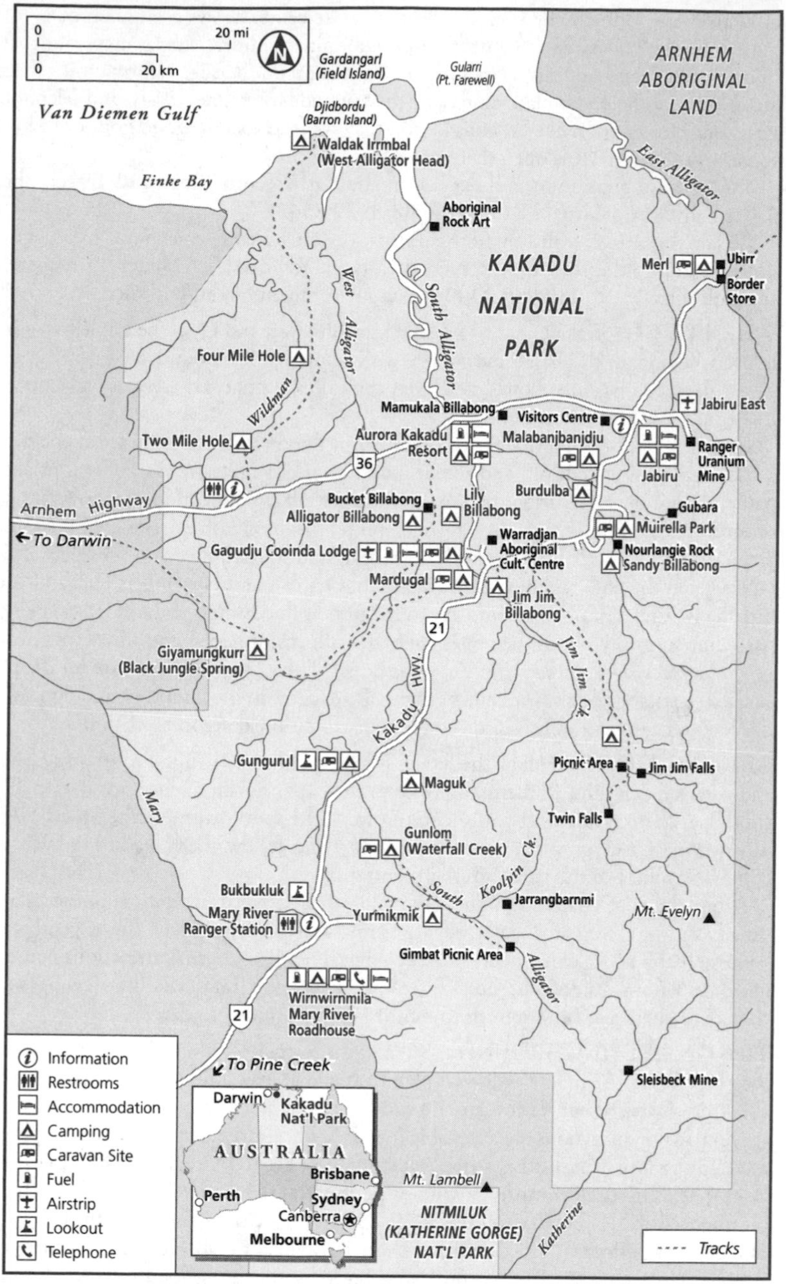

0
20 mi
0
20 km
N
Gardangarl
(Field Island)
Gularri
(Pt. Farewell)
ARNHEM
ABORIGINAL
LAND
Van Diemen Gulf
Djidbordu
(Barron Island)
Waldak Irrmbal
(West Alligator Head)
Finke Bay
East Alligator
Aboriginal
Rock Art
KAKADU
NATIONAL
PARK
Merl
Ubirr
Border
Store
West Alligator
South Alligator
Four Mile Hole
Wildman
Jabiru East
Mamukala Billabong
Visitors Centre
Aurora Kakadu
Resort
Malabanjbanjdju
Ranger
Uranium
Mine
Jabiru
Two Mile Hole
36
Burdulba
Bucket Billabong
Lily
Billabong
Alligator Billabong
Gubara
Arnhem Highway
To Darwin
Muirella Park
Warradjan
Aboriginal
Cult. Centre
Nourlangie Rock
Sandy Billabong
Gagudju Cooinda Lodge
Mardugal
Jim Jim
Billabong
21
Giyamungkurr
(Black Jungle Spring)
Jim Jim Ck.
Kakadu Hwy.
Gungurul
Picnic Area
Jim Jim Falls
Maguk
Mary
Twin Falls
Gunlom
(Waterfall Creek)
Koolpin Ck.
South
Bukbukluk
Jarrangbarnmi
Mary River
Ranger Station
Yurmikmik
Mt. Evelyn
Gimbat Picnic Area
Alligator
Wirnwirnmila
Mary River
Roadhouse
21
To Pine Creek
Sleisbeck Mine
Information
Restrooms
Accommodation
Camping
Caravan Site
Fuel
Airstrip
Lookout
Telephone
Darwin
Kakadu
Nat'l Park
AUSTRALIA
Brisbane
Perth
Sydney
Canberra
Melbourne
Mt. Lambell
NITMILUK
(KATHERINE GORGE)
NAT'L PARK
Katherine
Tracks

attractive, environmentally friendly Outback-style center shows a program of 1-hour videos on the park's natural history and Aboriginal culture, stocks maps and park notes, has a library and displays, and has a gift shop and a cafe. Information officers are on hand to help you plan your visit (they provide tour times, costs, and telephone numbers, but do not make bookings). You may want to spend a good hour or so here, more to see a video. It is open daily from 8am to 5pm.

You can also book tours and get information at **Kakadu Tours and Travel,** Shop 6, Tasman Plaza, Jabiru, NT 0886 (✆ **08/8979 2548**).

Before you arrive, you can find information on Kakadu, and book tours at the Tourism Top End information center in Darwin. You can also contact the rangers at the park directly (✆ **08/8938 1100;** www.environment.gov.au/parks/kakadu).

WHEN TO GO Kakadu has two distinct seasons: Wet and Dry. The Dry (May–Oct) is overwhelmingly the best time to go, with temperatures around 86°F (30°C) and sunny days. Many tours, hotels, and even campsites are booked a year in advance, so make sure you have reservations.

In the Wet season, November through April, floodwaters cover much of the park, some attractions are cut off, and the heat and humidity are extreme. Some tour companies do not operate during the Wet, and ranger talks, walks, and slide shows are not offered. The upside is that the crowds vanish, the brownish vegetation bursts into green, waterfalls swell from a trickle to a roar, and lightning storms are spectacular, especially in the hot "buildup" to the season in October and November. The landscape can change dramatically from one day to the next as floodwaters rise and fall, so be prepared for surprises—both nice ones (like giant flocks of geese) and unwelcome ones (like blocked roads). Although it can pour down all day, it's more common for the rain to fall in late-afternoon storms and at night. Take it easy in the humidity, and don't even think about camping in this heat—stay in air-conditioned accommodations.

GETTING THERE Follow the Stuart Highway 34km (21 miles) south of Darwin, and turn left onto the Arnhem Highway to the park's northern entrance station. The trip takes 2½ to 3 hours. If you're coming from the south, turn off the Stuart Highway at Pine Creek onto the Kakadu Highway, and follow the Kakadu Highway for 79km (49 miles) to the park's southern entrance.

A big range of coach, minibus, and four-wheel-drive tours and camping safaris, usually lasting 1, 2, or 3 days, depart from Darwin daily. These are a good idea, because many of Kakadu's geological, ecological, and Aboriginal attractions come to life only with a guide. The best water holes, lookouts, and wildlife-viewing spots change dramatically from month to month, even from day to day.

TIPS ON GETTING AROUND Kakadu is a big place—about 200km (124 miles) long by 100km (62 miles) wide—so plan to spend at least a night. Day trips are available from Darwin, but it's too far and too big to see much in a day.

Most major attractions are accessible in a two-wheel-drive vehicle on sealed (paved) roads, but a four-wheel-drive vehicle allows you to get to more falls, water holes, and campsites. Car-rental companies will not permit you to take two-wheel-drive vehicles on unpaved roads. **Thrifty** (✆ **08/8979 2552**) rents cars at the Gagudju Crocodile Holiday Inn, Flinders Street, Jabiru; otherwise, rent a car in Darwin. If you rent a four-wheel-drive in the Wet season (Nov–Apr), always check floodwater levels on all roads at the **Bowali Visitor Centre** (✆ **08/8938 1120**). The Bowali Visitor Centre, many attractions such as Nourlangie and Yellow Water Billabong, and the towns of Jabiru and Cooinda usually stay above the floodwaters year-round.

Tips **Never Smile at a You-Know-What!**

The Aboriginal Gagudju people of the Top End have long worshiped a giant crocodile called Ginga, but the way white Australians go on about these reptilian relics of a primeval age, you'd think they worshiped them, too. There is scarcely a soul in the Northern Territory who will not regale you with his or her personal croc story, and each one will be more outrageous than the last.

Aussies may be good at pulling your leg with tall tales, but when they warn you not to swim in crocodile country, they're deadly serious. After all, crocodiles are good at pulling your leg, too—literally. Here are some tips:

1. There are two kinds of crocodile in Australia: the highly dangerous and enormously powerful saltwater or "estuarine" croc; and the "harmless" freshwater croc, which will attack only if threatened or accidentally stood on. Saltwater crocs can and do swim in the ocean, but they live in fresh water.
2. Don't swim in *any* waterway, swimming hole, or waterfall unless you have been specifically told it is safe. Take advice only from someone like a recognized tour operator or a park ranger. You can never be sure where crocodiles lurk from year to year, because during every Wet season crocs head upriver to breed, and they spread out over a wide flooded area. As the floodwaters subside, they are trapped in whatever water they happen to be in at the time—so what was a safe swimming hole last Dry season might not be croc-free this year.
3. Never stand on or walk along a riverbank, and stand well back when fishing. A 6m (20-ft.) croc can be 1 inch beneath the surface of that muddy water yet remain invisible. It moves fast, so you won't see it until you're in its jaws.
4. Plant your campsite and clean your fish at least 25m (82 ft.) from the bank.

And if you do come face to face with a crocodile? There is little you can do. Just don't get into this situation in the first place!

Facilities are limited. The only town of any size is **Jabiru** (pop. 1,455), a mining community where you can find banking facilities and a few shops. The only other real settlements are the park's four accommodations houses.

SEEING THE HIGHLIGHTS

EN ROUTE TO KAKADU

En route to the park, stop in at the **Fogg Dam Conservation Reserve** (© **08/8988 8009** is the ranger station), 25km (16 miles) down the Arnhem Highway and 7km (4⅓ miles) off the highway. You'll get a close-up look at geese, finches, ibis, brolgas, and other wetland birds from lookouts over ponds of giant lilies, or by walking through monsoon forests to viewing blinds. There are two lookouts on the road and three walks, two of 2.2km (1½ miles) round-trip and one of 3.6km (2¼ miles) round-trip. Entry is free. Crocs live here, so don't swim, and keep away from the water's edge. To take a ranger-guided walk, reserve by calling © **08/8999 4555.**

Four kilometers (2½ miles) down the Arnhem Highway at Beatrice Hill, you can stop at the **Window on the Wetlands Visitor Centre** (✆ **08/8988 8188**), which offers views across the Adelaide River flood plain and displays and touch-screen information on the wetlands' ecology. It's free and open daily from 8am to 7pm.

Just past Beatrice Hill on the highway at the Adelaide River Bridge (look out for the statue of a grinning croc), **Adelaide River Queen Cruises** (✆ **1800/888 542** in Australia, or 08/8988 8144) runs the **jumping crocodiles cruise.** From the relative safety of a restored paddle steamer or a smaller boat, you can watch wild crocodiles leap out of the water for hunks of meat dangled over the edge by the boat crew—but don't lean out too far! It's an unabashed tourist trap, with a souvenir shop that sells all things croc, including crocodile toilet seat covers. It may not be to my, or your, taste, but because crocs typically move fast only when they attack, it may be your only chance to witness their immense power and speed. The cruises depart at 9 and 11am and 1:30 and 3pm April through October, and 9am, 11am, and 3pm November through March (closed Dec 24–25). The cost is from A$30 (US$24/UK£12) for adults and A$20 (US$16/UK£8) for children 5 to 15, depending on which cruise and which vessel you choose. Children aged 4 or under cannot travel for safety reasons. If you need transport, **Darwin Day Tours** (✆ **08/8924 1111**) and **Goanna Eco Tours** (✆ **1800/003 880** in Australia) both run tours from Darwin that include the cruise.

TOP PARK ATTRACTIONS

WETLANDS CRUISES One of Kakadu's biggest attractions is **Yellow Water Billabong,** a lake 50km (31 miles) south of the Bowali Visitor Centre at Cooinda (pop. about 20). It's rich with freshwater mangroves, Paperbarks, pandanus palms, water lilies, and masses of birds gathering to drink—sea eagles, honking magpie geese, kites, china-blue kingfishers, and jaçanas, called "Jesus birds" because they seem to walk on water as they step across the lily pads. This is one of the best places in the park to spot saltwater crocs. Cruises in canopied boats with running commentary depart near Gagudju Lodge six times a day starting at 6:45am in the Dry (Apr–Nov) and four times a day starting at 8:30am in the Wet (Dec–Mar). A 90-minute cruise is A$43 (US$34/UK£17) for adults and A$22 (US$18/UK£9) for children 2 to 14. A 2-hour cruise (available in the Dry only) is A$50 (US$40/UK£20) for adults, A$25 (US$20/UK£10) for children. Book through **Gagudju Lodge Cooinda** (p. 447).

Fair warning: In the Wet, when the Billabong floods and joins up with Jim Jim Creek and the South Alligator River, the bird life spreads far and wide over the park and the crocs head upriver to breed, so don't expect wildlife viewing to be spectacular.

Another good cruise is the **Guluyambi East Alligator River Cruise** (✆ **1800/089 113** in Australia, or 08/8979 2411). The East Alligator River forms the border between Kakadu and isolated Arnhemland. Unlike the Yellow Water cruise, which focuses on crocs, birds, and plants, this excursion teaches you about Aboriginal myths, bush tucker, and hunting techniques. The cruise lasts about 1 hour and 45 minutes, starting at 9 and 11am, and 1 and 3pm daily May through October. A free shuttle will take you from the Border Store, at Manbiyarra just before the river, to the boat ramp. It costs A$40 (US$32/UK£16) for adults and A$20 (US$16/UK£8) for children 4 to 14.

ABORIGINAL ART & CULTURE There are as many as 5,000 art sites throughout the park, though for cultural reasons the Aboriginal owners make only a few accessible to visitors. Dating the rock art is controversial, but some paintings may be 50,000 years old. The best are **Nourlangie Rock** and **Ubirr Rock.** Nourlangie, 31km (19 miles) southeast of the Bowali Visitor Centre, features "X-ray"-style paintings of

Moments A Side Trip to a Tiwi Island

Separated from the northern mainland by a narrow strait are the Tiwi Islands, Bathurst and Melville. The Tiwi culture is distinct from that of the Aborigines, and one of the main reasons for visiting is to see firsthand their distinctive art style. **Tiwi Tours** (© **1300/721 365** in Australia, or 08/8923 6523) takes small groups on 1- and 2-day tours to Bathurst Island (Melville Island is closed to the public). They include visits to two art centers where you can watch artists at work and buy their paintings, carvings, silk-screen printing, and basketwork at "island prices"—usually up to a third cheaper than buying the same item in Darwin. You will learn the history of the islands, have tea with some Tiwi women and see them making baskets, and visit a mock burial site. The 2-day tour includes overnight camping. There are no commercial accommodations on the island, and the 1-day tour probably satisfies most people's curiosity. The 1-day tour costs A$369 (US$295/UK£148) adults and A$269 (US$215/UK£108) children; the 2-day tour is A$645 (US$516/UK£258) adults and A$490 (US$392/UK£196) children. Both include the round-trip light-plane airfare from Darwin (it's about a 20-min. flight) and meals. Tours operate Monday to Friday, except public holidays.

animals; a vivid, energetic striped Dreamtime figure of **Namarrgon** ★, the "Lightning Man"; and modern depictions of a white man in boots, a rifle, and a sailing ship. You'll also find rock paintings at **Nanguluwur,** on the other side of Nourlangie Rock, and a variety of excellent sites at Ubirr Rock, which is worth the 250m (820-ft.) climb for the additional sites higher up, and for views of the flood plain.

Ubirr Rock can be cut off in the Wet, but the views of afternoon lightning storms from the top at that time are breathtaking.

Unlike most sites in Kakadu, Ubirr is not open 24 hours—it opens at 8:30am April through November and at 2pm December through March, and closes at sunset year-round. There are a 1.5km (1-mile) signposted trail past Nourlangie's paintings (short trails to the art sites shoot off it), an easy 1.7km (1-mile) trail from the parking lot into Nanguluwur, and a 1km (½-mile) circuit at Ubirr. Access to the sites is free.

Displays and videos about bush tucker, Dreamtime creation myths, and lifestyles of the Bininj Aborigines are at the **Warradjan Aboriginal Cultural Centre** ★ (© **08/8979 0145**) at Cooinda. This building was built in the shape of a pig-nose turtle at the direction of the Aboriginal owners. It has a quality gift shop selling items like didgeridoos, bark paintings by local artists, and baskets woven from pandanus fronds. The center is open daily from 9am to 5pm, and admission is free. A 1km-long (½-mile) trail connects it to Gagudju Lodge Cooinda and the Yellow Water Billabong.

SCENIC FLIGHTS Scenic flights over the flood plains and the rainforest-filled ravines of the escarpment are worth taking if the strain is not too great on your wallet. They're much more interesting in the Wet than in the Dry, because the flood plains spread and Jim Jim Falls and Twin Falls swell from their Dry season trickle to a flood. Viewing it from the air is also the best way to appreciate the clever crocodile shape of the Gagudju Crocodile Holiday Inn. **North Australian Helicopters**

(✆ **1800/898 977** in Australia, or 08/8972 2444) operates flights from Jabiru from A$170 (US$136/UK£68) per person, but to see Jim Jim and Twin Falls, you must take the flight costing A$420 (US$336/UK£168) per person. **Kakadu Air Services** (✆ **1800/089 113** in Australia, or 08/8979 2411) runs 30-minute fixed-wing flights from Jabiru and Cooinda for A$110 (US$88/UK£44) per person, as well as heli flights.

SWIMMING, FISHING & BUSHWALKING IN THE PARK

In the eastern section of the park rises a massive red-sandstone escarpment that sets the stage for two waterfalls, **Jim Jim Falls** and **Twin Falls.** In the Dry, the volume of water may not be all that impressive, but the settings are magical. Both are accessible by four-wheel-drive only, and neither is open in the Wet. At Twin Falls, you must swim or float the last 500m (1,640 ft.) to the base of the falls—and be warned that saltwater crocodiles have been found in this area.

A campground near Jim Jim Falls and Twin Falls has sites for 200 people. **Garnamarr Campground** (named for the red-tailed black cockatoo commonly found in Kakadu) doesn't accept reservations, so check at the Bowali Visitor Centre (✆ **08/8938 1121**) before driving there, to see whether it is full. The campground manager collects the fee of A$5.40 (US$4.30/UK£2.15) per adult per night (cash only). A gate at the campground controls access to Jim Jim and Twin Falls and is locked between 8:30pm and 6:30am.

WHERE CAN I SWIM?

Some people swim at spots that are generally regarded as croc-free, such as Jim Jim Falls and water holes such as Gubara (it's a long walk, but it can be lovely in the Wet), Maguk, and Koolpin Gorge. However, you do so at your own risk. Although rangers survey the swimming holes at the start of the season, and crocodiles are territorial creatures that stick to one spot, no one can guarantee that a saltwater crocodile has not moved into a swimming hole.

A good indication that a hole is croc-free is the presence of other people swimming. Crocs tend to eat whatever's moving, so if people are swimming happily, the pool is almost certainly croc-free! Macabre it may be, but it's a tool many people use to gauge a pool's safety. Ask at the Bowali Visitor Centre which pools are croc-free that year (it can change from year to year) before setting off into the park. If you are unsure about a water hole's safety, the only place rangers recommend you swim is your hotel pool. Water hole depths change dramatically with the season. Check with the Bowali Visitor Centre for the swimming spots that are best at the time you visit.

A 1km (½-mile) walk over rocks and through rainforest leads to a **deep green plunge pool** ★ at Jim Jim Falls, 103km (64 miles) from the Bowali Visitor Centre. An almost

---

Tips Glowing Attraction?

Not all of Kakadu's attractions are natural. Tours of the **Ranger Uranium Mine,** 13km (8 miles) east of the Bowali Visitor Centre, reveal how this extremely controversial material is extracted from a large open-cut mine and turned into yellowcake to fire nuclear power plants around the world. Ninety-minute tours depart daily May through October at 10:30am and 1:30pm and cost A$25 (US$20/UK£10) adults, A$10 (US$8/UK£4) kids ages 4 to 14. The tours depart by bus from Jabiru Airport, which is near the mine. Book through **Kakadu Tours** (✆ **1800/089 113** in Australia, or 08/8979 2411).

Moments **A Swim in the Falls**

Remember the idyllic pool that Paul Hogan and Linda Koslowski plunged into in *Crocodile Dundee?* That was **Gunlom Falls,** 170km (105 miles) south of the Bowali Visitor Centre. A climb to the top rewards you with great views of southern Kakadu. It is generally regarded as croc-free and safe for swimming. Access is by four-wheel-drive; it is cut off in the Wet.

perfectly circular 150m (492-ft.) cliff surrounds the water. Allow 2 hours to drive the final 60 unpaved kilometers (37 miles) off the highway. Due to floodwaters, Jim Jim Falls may not open until as late as June. At Twin Falls, the waterfalls descend into a natural pool edged by a sandy beach, surrounded by bush and high cliffs.

Kakadu Gorge and Waterfall Tours ★ (book through Gagudju Lodge Cooinda; ✆ **08/8979 0145**) runs an excellent small-group day trip for active people. You bushwalk into Jim Jim Falls for a swim and morning tea, four-wheel-drive through the bush, and then paddle in a canoe past a "friendly" freshwater crocodile (the kind that does not typically attack humans) to Twin Falls for swimming and lunch. Tours depart daily from Jabiru and Cooinda from May through November and cost A$140 (US$112/UK£56) for adults, A$120 (US$96/UK£48) for kids 4 to 14 (no kids under 4 allowed). Book in advance for July, the busiest month.

Kakadu's wetlands are brimful of barramundi, and Territorians like nothing more than to hop in a tin dinghy barely big enough to resist a croc attack and go looking for them. **Kakadu Fishing Tours** (✆ **08/8987 2025** or book through Gagudju Lodge Cooinda) takes you fishing in a 5m (17-ft.) sportfishing boat. Tours depart from Jabiru, 5km (3 miles) east of the Bowali Visitor Centre, and cost A$144 (US$115/UK£58) per person for 5 hours and A$260 (US$208/UK£104) per person for a full day.

Wide-ranging **bush and wetlands walking trails,** including many short strolls and six half- to full-day treks, lead throughout the park. Typical trails include a .75km (less than ½-mile) amble through the Manngarre Monsoon Forest near Ubirr Rock; an easy 3.8km (2½-mile) circular walk at the Iligadjar Wetlands near the Bowali Visitor Centre; and a tough 12km (7½-mile) round-trip trek through rugged sandstone country at Nourlangie Rock.

One of the best wetlands walks is at **Mamukala wetlands,** 29km (18 miles) from Jabiru. Thousands of magpie geese feed here, especially in the late Dry season around October. An observation platform gives you a good view, and a sign explains the dramatic seasonal changes the wetlands undergo. Choose from a 1km (½-mile) or 3km (1¾-mile) round-trip meander. The Bowali Visitor Centre sells hiking-trail maps. There are also some challenging unmarked trails along creeks and gorges, for which you will need good navigational skills.

WHERE TO STAY & DINE

High season is usually from April 1 to late October or early November.

Aurora Kakadu This property is near the northern entrance to the park. The downside is that it is the farthest accommodations from major attractions like Yellow Waters and Nourlangie, although many tour operators pick up here. The upside is that the resort's green lawns and tropical gardens adorned with wandering peacocks and goannas and chattering native birds are a wonderfully restful haven from the harsh surroundings of Kakadu outside. Don't yield to the temptation to dive into the lily-filled lagoon down the back—like every other waterway in Kakadu, it is home to saltwater crocs! A 3.6km (2-mile) nature trail winds from the hotel through monsoon forest and past a billabong. All but the end rooms of the neatly decorated motel-style accommodations have pitched timber ceilings, and all have restful views from a balcony or patio. Budget rooms have two sets of bunks. All rooms are nonsmoking. Hair dryers are free at reception, and there are barbecues on the grounds. Keep an eye out for regular special deals on offer. There are also 60 unpowered campsites.

Arnhem Hwy., South Alligator (41km/25 miles west of Bowali Visitor Centre), Kakadu National Park, NT 0886. ✆ **1800/818 845** in Australia, or 08/8979 0166. Fax 08/8979 0147. www.auroraresorts.com.au. 138 units. A$157 (US$126/UK£63) double; extra person A$42 (US$34/UK£17). Children under 14 free when sharing with 2 adults. Free crib. Budget rooms A$104 (US$83/UK£42) for private use or A$26 (US$21/UK£10) per person for 4-share by gender. Family rooms double rate plus A$84 (US$67/UK£34). AE, DC, MC, V. Free parking. **Amenities:** Restaurant; cafe; bar; shaded outdoor pool; day/night tennis court; Jacuzzi; tour desk; coin-op laundry. *In room:* A/C, TV, fridge, coffeemaker.

Bamurru Plains ★★ The best way to get to this stylish safari camp is by light plane, a 20-minute flight from Darwin. If you drive to this working buffalo station, you will have to leave your car at the gate, and a staff member will pick you up for the 20-minute drive to your accommodations. Bamurru Plains, set on the edge of the Mary River flood plains, between the coast and the western boundary of Kakadu National Park, is about 3 hours drive from Darwin and 2½ hours from Jabiru. Your luxury tent has a timber floor, fine linens on the bed, and a high-pressure shower in the bathroom but no phone, TV, or other distractions. You can lie in bed and look out through the screen walls to the flood plains. Meals are served at the main lodge building and feature crocodile, emu, and other local delicacies. Activities include guided walks, river cruises, fishing, 4WD safaris to view wildlife (Bamurru is the Aboriginal name for the magpie geese you will see in the thousands), and day trips to Kakadu and Arnhem Land by light plane to see Aboriginal rock art.

Swim Creek Station, Harold Knowles Rd. (P.O. Box 1020), Humpty Doo, NT 0836. ✆ **1300/790 561** in Australia, or 02/9231 2923. www.bamurruplains.com. 9 units. A$850 (US$340/UK£170) double; A$425 (US$340/UK£170) children under 16 sharing with adults; A$765 (US$612/UK£306) children under 16 sharing a separate room. Minimum 2-night stay. Rates include all meals, drinks, and activities. AE, DC, MC, V. Closed Nov 1–Jan 31. No children under 12. **Amenities:** Restaurant; bar; swimming pool.

Gagudju Crocodile Holiday Inn ★ Some people think this hotel is kitsch; others declare it an architectural masterpiece. I liked it. It was built to the specifications of its owners, the Gagudju Aborigines, in the form of their spirit ancestor, a giant crocodile called Ginga. The building's entrance is the "jaws," the two floors of rooms are in the "belly," the circular parking lot clusters are "eggs," and so on. From the ground, it's hard to see, but from the air, the shape is quite distinct. Love it or hate it, it is the most luxurious place to stay in Kakadu, a stylish modern hotel with basic but comfortable rooms. Guests can use the town's 9-hole golf course, tennis courts, and Olympic-size swimming pool a few blocks away. The lobby doubles as an art gallery selling the works of local Aborigines, and a trail leads to the Bowali Visitor Centre.

1 Flinders St. (5km/3 miles east of Bowali Visitor Centre), Jabiru, NT 0886. ✆ **1800/007 697** in Australia, 800/465-4329 in the U.S. and Canada, 0800/405060 in the U.K., 1800/553 155 in Ireland, 0800/322 222 in New Zealand, or 08/8979 9000. Fax 08/8979 2707. 110 units. A$155–A$250 (US$124–US$200/UK£62–UK£100) double. Discounts often available in the Wet. Children under 20 stay free in parent's room with existing bedding. Free crib. AE, DC, MC, V. **Amenities:** Restaurant; 2 bars; small outdoor pool; concierge; tour desk; car-rental desk; secretarial services; limited room service; babysitting; coin-op laundry; laundry service. *In room:* A/C, TV w/free movies, minibar, coffeemaker, hair dryer, iron.

Gagudju Lodge Cooinda These modest but pleasant accommodations are set among tropical gardens at the departure point for Yellow Water Billabong cruises. The simply furnished tile-floor bungalows are big and comfortable, and there are four family rooms that sleep up to four. Budget rooms are twin or triple share (four have double beds) in an air-conditioned corrugated iron demountable, or portable cabin, with shared bathrooms. The lodge is something of a town center, with a general store, gift shop, currency exchange, post office, fuel, and other facilities. Cook up a steak at the do-it-yourself barbecue in the rustic and ultracasual **Barra Bistro and Bar,** or go for the bush tucker a la carte meals at lunch or dinner in **Mimi's** ★, which has a nice "bush sophisticated" ambience. The Barra Bistro serves a full buffet breakfast and an all-day snack menu, with live entertainment in the Dry season. Dining options can be limited between December and March, in the Wet. Scenic flights take off from the lodge's airstrip, and the Warradjan Aboriginal Cultural Centre is a 15-minute walk.

Kakadu Hwy. (50km/31 miles south of Bowali Visitor Centre), Jim Jim, NT 0886. ✆ **1800/500 401** in Australia, 800/835-7742 in the U.S. and Canada, 0800/897 121 in the U.K., 1800/553 155 in Ireland, 0800/801 111 in New Zealand, or 08/8979 0145. Fax 08/8979 0148. www.gagudjulodgecooinda.com.au. 48 bungalows, all with shower only, 24 budget rooms, none with bathroom, 80 powered and 300 unpowered campsites. Lodge: A$155–A$250 (US$124–US$200/UK£62–UK£100) double. Budget rooms: A$70 (US$56/UK£28) double; A$31 (US$25/UK£12) per person for twin or triple share. Campsites: A$30–A$35 (US$24–US$28/UK£12–UK£14) for powered sites; A$15 (US$12/UK£6) unpowered. Children under 14 stay free in campsites. Bungalow and budget room discounts often available in Wet season. AE, DC, MC, V. **Amenities:** 2 restaurants; small outdoor pool; tour desk; babysitting; coin-op laundry. *In room (lodge only):* A/C, TV, coffeemaker, hair dryer (on request), iron.

4 Katherine

314km (195 miles) S of Darwin; 512km (317 miles) E of Kununurra; 1,177km (730 miles) N of Alice Springs

The key draw to the farming town of Katherine (pop. 11,000) is Katherine (Nitmiluk) Gorge. It's small by the standards of, say, the Grand Canyon, but its dramatic sheer orange walls dropping to a blue-green river make it an unexpected delight in the middle of the dry Arnhemland plateau that stretches to the horizon.

The gorge and its surrounding river ecosystem are in the 292,008-hectare (721,260-acre) **Nitmiluk National Park.** In the Dry, the gorge is a haven not just for cruisers but for canoeists, who must dodge the odd "friendly" freshwater crocodile as they paddle between the walls. In the Wet, the gorge can become a torrent, and jet boating is sometimes the only way to tackle it. Hikers will find trails any time of year throughout the park. Farther afield are hot springs, water holes, uncrowded rivers to canoe, and Aboriginal communities where visitors can make dot paintings and find bush tucker.

ESSENTIALS

GETTING THERE **Greyhound Australia** (✆ **13 14 99** in Australia) buses stop in Katherine on their Darwin–Alice Springs routes. From Darwin, it's about a 4½-hour trip costing A$76 (US$61/UK£30). From Alice, with departures once a day, it's about a 15-hour journey, for which the fare is A$225 (US$180/UK£90). Greyhound also runs to Katherine daily from Broome via Kununurra, a journey of about 23 hours costing A$290 (US$232/UK£116).

Visitors to Katherine can hop aboard the ***Ghan*** (see "Getting Around Australia" in chapter 2) in Adelaide or Alice Springs and hop off in Katherine. The train leaves Adelaide on Sundays and Wednesdays at 12:20pm and Alice Springs on Sundays and Thursdays at 6pm. The trip from Alice takes about 15 hours. One-way fares are A$355

(US$284/UK£142) for a "day-nighter" seat or A$740 to A$1,095 (US$592–US$876/UK£296–UK£428) for a sleeper from Alice. Contact **Great Southern Railways** (✆ **13 21 47** in Australia; www.trainways.com.au) for details on connections from Sydney and Melbourne.

At press time, there were currently no airlines operating flights into Katherine.

Katherine is on the Stuart Highway, which links Darwin and Alice Springs. From Alice Springs, allow a good 2 days to make the drive. The Victoria Highway links Katherine with Kununurra to the west. There is no direct route from the east; from, say, Cairns, you need to go via Townsville, Mount Isa, and Tennant Creek, a long, dull journey.

VISITOR INFORMATION The **Katherine Visitor Information Centre,** Lindsay Street at Katherine Terrace, Katherine, NT 0850 (✆ **1800/653 142** or 08/8972 2650; www.krta.com.au), has information on things to see—not only all around Katherine, but as far afield as Kakadu National Park and the Kimberley. It's open Monday through Friday from 8:30am to 6pm and weekends from 10am to 3pm in the Dry season; in the Wet it's open Monday through Friday from 9am to 5pm.

The **Nitmiluk Visitor Centre,** on the Gorge Road, 32km (20 miles) from town (✆ **08/8972 1886**), dispenses information on the Nitmiluk National Park and sells tickets for gorge cruises, which depart outside. The center has maps; displays on the park's plant life, birds, geology, and Aboriginal history; a gift shop; and a cafe. It's open daily from 7am to 7pm, sometimes closing a little earlier in the Wet. Entry to the park is free.

GETTING AROUND **Hertz** (✆ **08/8971 1111**), **Europcar** (✆ **08/8971 2777**), and **Thrifty** (✆ **08/8972 3183**) have outlets in Katherine.

Travel North (✆ **1800/089 103** in Australia, or 08/8971 9999) makes transfers from Katherine hotels to the cruise, canoe, and helicopter departure points at the Nitmiluk Visitor Centre three times a day. Round-trip fares are A$24 (US$19/UK£10) for adults and A$12 (US$10/UK£4.80) for children. Most Katherine activities and attractions can be booked through Travel North. The company runs many tours and activities, such as horseback cattle musters, visits to an old homestead, half-day trips to Mataranka Thermal Pools (see below), and tours of up to 5 days taking in Katherine, Darwin, Litchfield and Kakadu national parks, and outlying Aboriginal communities.

For personalized tours both off the beaten path and around town, contact **Far Out Adventures** ★ (✆ **0427/152 288** mobile), described below.

EXPLORING KATHERINE GORGE (NITMILUK NATIONAL PARK)

Cruising the gorge in an **open-sided boat** is the most popular way to appreciate its beauty. Katherine Gorge is actually a series of 13 gorges, but most cruises ply only the first two, because the second gorge is the most photogenic.

Nitmiluk Tours (✆ **08/8972 1253;** www.nitmiluktours.com.au) operates all cruises. Most people take a 2-hour cruise, available four times a day. The morning cruises, at 9am and 11am, are cultural cruises and cost A$50 (US$40/UK£20) for adults and A$29 (US$23/UK£12) for children 5 to 15. The afternoon cruises, at 1pm and 3pm, cost A$45 (US$36/UK£18) adults and A$19 (US$15/UK£7.60) children. There is also a 4-hour cruise at least once daily, although you will probably be satisfied with 2 hours. An 8-hour cruise-hike safari to the fifth gorge is available from about May to mid-October only. Wear sturdy shoes; because each gorge is cut off from the next by rapids, all the cruises involve some walking along the bank.

In the height of the Wet season, the cruises may not operate when the floodwaters really start to swirl. Instead, a **jet boat** runs as far as the third gorge. This 45-minute adventure costs A$53 (US$42/UK£21) for adults and A$38 (US$30/UK£15) for kids 5 to 15. Departure times vary with the floodwater conditions.

Cruising is nice, but in a **canoe** ★ you can discover sandy banks and waterfalls, and get up close to the gorge walls, the birds, and those crocs. (Don't worry—they're the freshwater kind and not typically regarded as dangerous to humans.) Rocks separate the gorges, so be prepared to carry your canoe quite often. You may even want to camp out on the banks overnight. A half-day canoe rental from Travel North is A$35 (US$28/UK£14) for a single canoe and A$53 (US$42/UK£21) for a double, with a A$20 (US$16/UK£8) cash deposit. Canoeing the gorge is popular, so book canoes ahead, especially in the Dry season.

Guided paddles are a good idea, because you will learn and see more. The most knowledgeable company is **Gecko Canoeing** ★ (✆ **1800/634 319** in Australia, or 08/8972 2224; www.geckocanoeing.com.au), whose tours are known for their eco-tourism content. Gecko's guides have Australia's elite Savannah Guide status. They offer 3- to 7-day canoeing-camping safaris on the Katherine River, as well as a 1-day canoe safari at a cost of A$188 (US$150/UK£75) per person. The company also runs canoeing and camping safaris (with any other activities you like, such as mountain biking, rock climbing, wildlife photography, hiking, or fishing) of up to 10 days in little-explored wildernesses and river systems across the Top End. Tours run between April and November, with departures on request, and can be tailored to your needs.

Some 100km (62 miles) of **hiking trails** crisscross Nitmiluk National Park, ranging in duration from 1 hour to the lookout to 5 days to Edith Falls (see below). Trails—through rocky terrain and forests, past water holes, and along the gorge—depart the Nitmiluk National Park ranger station, in the Nitmiluk Visitor Centre, where you can pick up trail maps. Overnight walks require a deposit of A$20 to A$50 (US$16–US$40/UK£8–UK£20) per person, and a A$3.30 (US$2.65/UK£1.30) per-person camping permit, payable at the Nitmiluk Visitor Centre.

One of the nicest spots in the park is 42km (26 miles) north of Katherine, 20km (13 miles) off the Stuart Highway. **Edith Falls** ★ is an Eden of natural (croc-free) swimming holes bordered by red cliffs, monsoonal forest, and pandanus palms. Among the bushwalks leading from Edith Falls is a 2.6km (1½-mile) round-trip trail, which takes about 2 hours and incorporates a dip at the upper pool en route.

More than the gorge itself, the aerial views of the ravine-ridden Arnhem Plateau, which stretches uninhabited to the horizon, are arresting. **North Australian Helicopters** (✆ **1800/621 717** in Australia, or 08/8972 1666) offers daily flights over the gorges, starting at A$189 (US$151/UK£76) per person. To see all 13 gorges will cost you A$278 (US$222/UK£111) per person.

ABORIGINAL CULTURE TOURS, HOT SPRINGS & MORE

On a 1-day visit to the **Manyallaluk Aboriginal community** ★, a 90-minute drive southeast from Katherine, you chat with Aborigines about how they balance traditional ways with modern living; take a short bushwalk to look for native medicines and bush tucker like green ants (they're refreshing!); try lighting a fire with two sticks, weaving baskets, throwing spears, painting on bark, and playing a didgeridoo; and take a dip in a water hole. You can buy locally made Aboriginal art and artifacts at better prices than you may find elsewhere. Lunch is a barbecue featuring stuff like high-grade kangaroo filet, kangaroo tail, Scotch filet steak, or barramundi cooked on hot coals. Some visitors rush into these tours and expect the community to be a kind of Aboriginal theme park with a new attraction every 10 minutes, but that's not how it is. It's an unstructured experience (this is the community's home), so it's up to you to take part.

A 1-day tour from Katherine costs A$177 (US$142/UK£71) for adults and A$88 (US$70/UK£35) for children 5 to 15, or A$135 (US$108/UK£54) adults and A$78 (US$62/UK£31) for kids if you drive yourself. There are basic camping facilities, including tent sites and powered and unpowered sites. The last 35km (22 miles) of road is unsealed (unpaved), and rental cars will be insured only if they are four-wheel-drive. The tour runs Monday through Friday from April to October, but hours may be reduced, or the place may close, in the Wet. Call ahead before setting off no matter what the time of year, because sometimes it may be closed for cultural reasons. Call Manyallaluk—The Dreaming Place (✆ **08/8975 4727**), or book through Travel North (see "Getting Around," above).

About 110km (68 miles) south of Katherine, you can soak your aches away at the **Mataranka Thermal Pools.** The man-made pools are fed by 93°F (34°C) spring water, which bubbles up from the earth at a rate of 16,495 liters (4,124 gal.) per minute! It's a little paradise, surrounded by palms, pandanus, and a colony of flying foxes. The pools are open 24 hours and admission is free. They are 7km (4⅓ miles) along Homestead Road, off the Stuart Highway 1.5km (1 mile) south of Mataranka township. They make a welcome stop on the long drive from Alice Springs.

If you can't be bothered to drive to Mataranka, you can soak in the pleasantly warm **Katherine Hot Springs,** under shady trees 3km (2 miles) from town on Riverbank Drive. Entry is free.

At the **School of the Air,** Giles Street (✆ **08/8972 1833**), you can sit in on an 800,000-sq.-km (312,000-sq.-mile) "classroom" as children from the Outback do their lessons by radio. Forty-five-minute tours begin on the hour at 9, 10, and 11am from mid-March to mid-November. Tours also run during school holidays and public holidays, minus the on-air classes. Admission is A$5 (US$4/UK£2) for adults and A$2 (US$1.60/UK80p) for school-age kids.

Mike Keighley of **Far Out Adventures** ★ (✆ **0427/152 288**) runs upmarket tailor-made tours that include areas around Katherine such as the 5,000-sq.-km. (1,930-sq.-mile or 1.2-million-acre) Elsey Cattle Station, 140km (87 miles) southeast of Katherine, made famous as the setting of the Aussie book and film *We of the Never Never.* Meet children of the Mangarrayi Aborigines, sample bush tucker, learn a little bush medicine, and swim in a vine-clad natural "spa-pool" in the Roper River. Mike has been accepted as an honorary family member of the Mangarrayi people and is a mine of information about Aboriginal culture and the bush.

WHERE TO STAY

The Nitmiluk National Park ranger station in the Nitmiluk Visitor Centre has maps of available "bush campsites" throughout the park. These are very basic sites—no showers, no soaps or shampoos allowed (they pollute the river system), and simple pit toilets or none at all. Most are beside natural swimming holes. You must stop for a camping permit at the ranger station beforehand; the camping fee is A$3.30 (US$2.65/UK£1.30) per person per night.

There are caravan and camping sites at **Springvale Homestead** (✆ **08/8972 1355** or book through Travel North), 7km (4⅓ miles) from Katherine township on the banks of the Katherine River. Sites are in a shady park, and there's a licensed bistro and kiosk, swimming pool, and children's water slide. Wallabies roam freely. Fees are

A$9 (US$7.20/UK£3.60) per adult, A$5 (US$4.40/UK£2.20) per child for a tent site, and A$23 (US$18/UK£9) double for a powered site (A$9/US$7.20/UK£3.60 for each extra person).

Knotts Crossing Resort At this low-key resort, you have a choice of huge, well-furnished motel rooms, some with kitchenettes, minibars, and in-room dataports and fax machines; cabins with a kitchenette inside and a private bathroom just outside the door (but no phone); or campgrounds, all located amid the tropical landscaping. The "village" rooms are a good budget choice, built in 1998 and smartly furnished with a double bed and bunks, a kitchenette, and a joint veranda facing a small private pool with a barbecue. Locals meet at the casual bar beside the pool, and **Katie's Bistro** is one of the smartest places to eat in town.

Corner of Giles and Cameron sts., Katherine, NT 0850. ✆ **1800/222 511** in Australia, or 08/8972 2511. Fax 08/8972 2628. www.knottscrossing.com.au. 123 units, some with shower only, 75 powered and unpowered campsites. A$80 (US$64/UK£32) double cabin; A$95 (US$76/UK£38) double "village" room; A$127–A$152 (US$102–US$122/UK£51–UK£61) double motel room; A$172 (US$138/UK£69) motel family room for 4. Extra adult A$10 (US$8/UK£4); extra child under 13 A$5 (US$4/UK£2). Unpowered site A$10 (US$8/UK£4) per person per night. Powered site A$22 (US$18/UK£9) per night single or double; extra adult A$10 (US$8/UK£4); extra child A$5 (US$4/UK£2). Rates include transfers from airport or bus stop. AE, DC, MC, V. **Amenities:** Restaurant; bar; 2 outdoor pools (1 large and attractive, 1 small); Jacuzzi; tour desk; car-rental desk; limited room service; coin-op laundry; laundry service; dry cleaning. *In room:* A/C, TV w/pay movies, fridge.

10

Perth & Western Australia

by Ron Crittall

Western Australia (WA) is the "Boom State," with incredible growth thanks to international demand for its natural resources, especially iron ore, nickel, aluminum, and natural gas. There's low unemployment and a buzz in the air. The downside for visitors is that some businesses (including restaurants and hotels) are continually short-staffed.

The other thing about WA is how big and empty it is. WA covers one-third of Australia at over 2.5 million sq. km (1 million sq. miles) but has only 2.1 million inhabitants of whom almost 75% (1.5 million) live in Perth. And Perth is the most remote large city on earth—Adelaide is 2,700km (1,700 miles) to the east. You don't get here by accident.

The state may be enormous but there are several jewels to entice and entertain. Domestic flights are not expensive and international travelers can use air passes (see chapter 2). It's worth the trip for great wine regions, some of Australia's best snorkeling and diving, historic towns, splendid natural scenery, and a chance to really go "Outback." Every spring (Aug–Oct), wildflowers carpet much of the state. The capital, **Perth** ★, has a fabulous outdoor life with parks, rivers and beaches, great walking and biking trails, excellent food, and a beautiful historic port, Fremantle.

The **Southwest** ★★★ corner of the state, below Perth, is the prettiest part of Western Australia. Vineyards and pastures sit between massive stands of karri and jarrah trees, the surf is world-class, there are sparkling limestone caverns, and the coastline is rugged. The Margaret River region has some of Australia's most acclaimed wines, and many top-notch eateries. En route to the Southwest you can swim with **wild dolphins** by the town of Bunbury—if they are in the mood for socializing.

Head east 596km (372 miles) inland from Perth and you strike what, in the 1890s, was the richest square mile of gold-bearing earth the world has seen. The mining town of **Kalgoorlie** ★ is a repository of ornate 19th-century architecture, and still Australia's biggest gold producer (nearly 2,000 oz. a day). It's a heady mix and, if Australia has an answer to the Wild West, Kalgoorlie is it.

Head north of Perth and you reach the Outback. Red sand, scrubby trees, and spinifex grass are all you see for hundreds of miles. About 855km (534 miles) north of Perth, **wild dolphins** ★ make daily visits to the shores of Monkey Mia. Another 713km (445 miles) on is Exmouth, entry point to one of Australia's best-kept secrets, a 300km (187-mile) coral reef called **Ningaloo** ★★, along the Outback shore.

The rugged northern portion of Western Australia is known as **the Kimberley** ★★. It's been called Australia's last frontier, a vast empty region of cattle ranching, a few Aboriginal settlements, and the exotic coastal town of Broome. This is a rocky region of red cliffs, strange bulbous boab trees, waterfalls, and billabongs. You can visit a 405,000-hectare (million-acre) cattle station (ranch), see Aboriginal rock art, ride a camel on the beach, and shop for the world's biggest South Sea pearls.

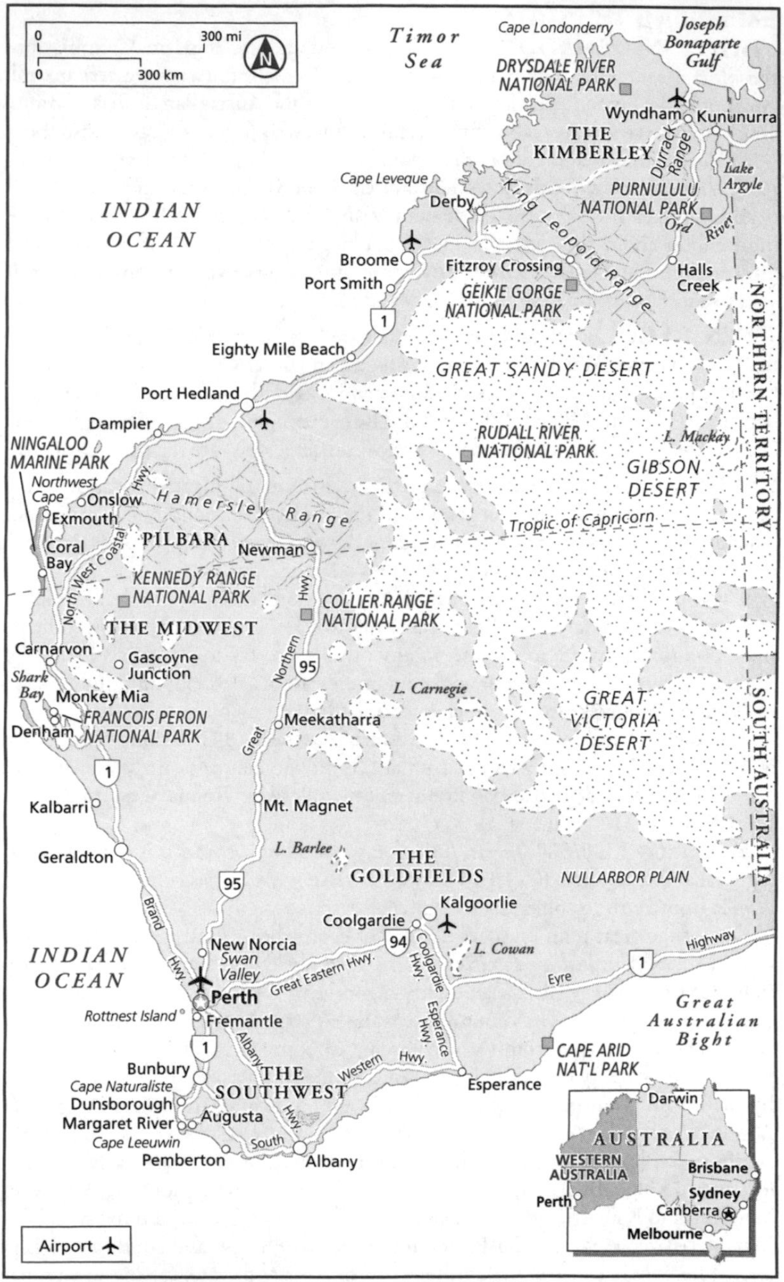
0 300 mi
0 300 km
N
Timor Sea
Cape Londonderry
Joseph Bonaparte Gulf
DRYSDALE RIVER NATIONAL PARK
Wyndham
Kununurra
THE KIMBERLEY
Durrack Range
Lake Argyle
Cape Leveque
PURNULULU NATIONAL PARK
Derby
King Leopold Range
Ord River
INDIAN OCEAN
Broome
Fitzroy Crossing
Halls Creek
Port Smith
GEIKIE GORGE NATIONAL PARK
NORTHERN TERRITORY
1
Eighty Mile Beach
GREAT SANDY DESERT
Port Hedland
Dampier
RUDALL RIVER NATIONAL PARK
L. Mackay
NINGALOO MARINE PARK
GIBSON DESERT
Northwest Cape
Onslow
Hwy.
Hamersley Range
Exmouth
Tropic of Capricorn
PILBARA
Coral Bay
Newman
North West Coastal
KENNEDY RANGE NATIONAL PARK
Hwy.
COLLIER RANGE NATIONAL PARK
THE MIDWEST
Carnarvon
Gascoyne Junction
Northern
95
Shark Bay
L. Carnegie
Monkey Mia
GREAT VICTORIA DESERT
SOUTH AUSTRALIA
FRANCOIS PERON NATIONAL PARK
Meekatharra
Denham
Great
1
Kalbarri
Mt. Magnet
L. Barlee
Geraldton
THE GOLDFIELDS
NULLARBOR PLAIN
95
Brand
Kalgoorlie
Coolgardie
94
Coolgardie Hwy.
L. Cowan
INDIAN OCEAN
New Norcia
Swan Valley
Hwy.
Great Eastern Hwy.
Highway
1
Eyre
Perth
Rottnest Island
Fremantle
Esperance Hwy.
Great Australian Bight
1
Albany
Bunbury
THE SOUTHWEST
Western Hwy.
CAPE ARID NAT'L PARK
Cape Naturaliste
Esperance
Dunsborough
Hwy.
Augusta
Margaret River
Cape Leeuwin
South
Pemberton
Albany
Darwin
AUSTRALIA
WESTERN AUSTRALIA
Brisbane
Perth
Sydney
Canberra
Melbourne
Airport

EXPLORING THE STATE

VISITOR INFORMATION The **Western Australian Tourism Commission** is the official source of information on the state. Its website (**www.westernaustralia.com**) provides a good overview, and you may find the **Australian Tourist Commission**'s website (**www.australia.com**) useful, or the Web pages of local tourism boards (see "Visitor Information" in each regional section of this chapter). A private company, **Visit WA** (**www.visitwa.com.au**), offers an online tour-planning service.

Also contact the **Western Australian Visitor Centre** in Perth, which dispenses information about the state and makes bookings. See section 1 of this chapter for information. The **Department of Environment & Conservation** website (**www.dec.wa.gov.au**) has information on national and marine parks.

WHEN TO GO Perth and the southwest are blessed with long, dry summers and mild, wet winters. You'll want some warm gear in winter, but temperatures rarely hit freezing point. Far north of Perth, summer is seriously hot; temperatures soar to between 104°F and 120°F (40°C–49°C). The cooler months of May through September (for the Kimberley) or October (for the Outback Coast) are the times to go north.

GETTING AROUND Before you plan a driving tour of this state, consider the distances (it's three times as big as Texas) and the mostly flat, monotonous countryside. The forests, coastal scenery, and vineyards of the Southwest make for pleasant driving; otherwise you should fly, especially if time is a factor.

If you do hit the road, remember that gas stations (keep the gas tank full!) and emergency help are far apart. Road trains (up to 53m/174 ft. long) and wildlife pose more of a threat on the roads than in any other state. Try to avoid driving at night, dusk, and dawn—all prime animal-feeding times. Read "Road Conditions & Safety," in "Getting Around Australia" in chapter 2, before setting off.

The **Royal Automobile Club of Western Australia,** 832 Wellington St., Perth, WA 6000 (✆ **13 17 03;** www.rac.com.au), is a good source of maps and motoring advice. For a recorded road-condition report, call **Main Roads Western Australia** (✆ **1800/013 314** in Australia).

Skywest (✆ **1300/660 088** in Australia; www.skywest.com.au) is the state's major regional airline. **Qantas** (✆ **13 13 13** in Australia; www.qantas.com.au) also provides service from Perth to some smaller centers.

One of the great train journeys of the world provides a passenger service from the eastern states. The ***Indian Pacific*** ★ runs twice weekly on a continent-covering 66-hour trip from Sydney via Adelaide and Kalgoorlie to Perth (see "Getting Around Australia," in chapter 2). **Greyhound Australia** (✆ **13 14 99** in Australia) has one interstate coach service, from Darwin through Broome to Perth.

Inside the state, passenger trains run only in the southern third. They are operated by the **Public Transport Authority (PTA),** also known as **TransWA** (✆ **1300/662 205** in Western Australia, or 08/9326 2600; www.transwa.wa.gov.au), from Perth to Bunbury, 2¼ hours south of Perth; to Northam, an hour or so east in the Avon Valley; and to Kalgoorlie. TransWA also runs coach services throughout the southwest of WA, north to Kalbarri, Geraldton, and Meekatharra; to the wine and forest regions of Margaret River, Augusta, and Pemberton; south to Albany; and southeast to Esperance. The only railways in the northern part of WA are private, carting vast tonnages of iron ore; no passengers.

All major car- and motor-home-rental companies have offices in Perth.

Moments Tiptoeing through the Wildflowers

Every year from August to mid-November, the southern half of Western Australia is blessed with a magnificent range of **wildflowers** ★★. The drier, more northerly areas produce great carpets of white, yellow, pink, and red daisylike everlastings, while the southern reaches have an incredible variety of individual flowering plants.

Wildflower shows and festivals in country towns throughout the state accompany the annual blossoming, and coach- and rail-tour companies carry enthusiasts from all around the globe on wildflower tours. You can check out the wildflowers on day trips from Perth or on longer jaunts of up to 5 days or so. Late August through October is the peak time.

If time is short, you can go to Perth's **Kings Park & Botanic Garden** (p. 474), which has a 5-day Wildflower Festival every September.

The display of everlastings is not constant, but varies from year to year depending on winter rains. The Western Australian Visitor Centre (see "Visitor Information," below) can keep you up to speed on whatever spot is blooming brightest that week, and the staff can book you on one of the wildflower tours. The Tourism Commission produces a 40-page **Wildflower Holiday Planner** brochure that describes self-drive wildflower routes, accommodations and events en route, and wildflower tour operators. Download it from the commission's website (**www.westernaustralia.com**).

Interstate buses and trains, and local hotels fill up fast in wildflower season, so book ahead.

TOUR OPERATORS Western Australia's two biggest coach tour companies, **Australian Pinnacle Tours** (✆ **1800/999 069** in Australia, or 08/9417 5555; www.pinnacletours.com.au) and **Feature Tours** (✆ **1800/999 819** in Australia, or 08/9475 2900; www.ft.com.au) serve Perth, the Southwest, Monkey Mia, the Northwest Cape, and attractions about a day's drive away, such as Wave Rock, and the Pinnacles (see the box "Dragon's Teeth in the Dunes" below). Australian Pinnacle Tours also does four-wheel-drive tours. **Global Gypsies** (✆ **08/9341 6727**; www.globalgypsies.com.au) runs four-wheel-drive tag-along safaris into the Outback, including Ningaloo and the Kimberley. The tours are fully escorted and catered, and there is limited passenger seating (three seats per tour). Global Gypsies can help with the hire of 4WD vehicles and all equipment.

Aerial tours make sense in Western Australia. Look into the personalized or set tours offered by **Complete Aviation Services** (✆ **1800/632 221** in Australia, or 08/9478 2749; www.casair.com.au) or **Kookaburra Air** (✆ **08/9354 1158**; www.kookaburra.iinet.net.au). Tours from Perth can take you throughout Western Australia, including the Kimberley, the Top End, and the Red Centre.

Landscope Expeditions ★★ is an excellent tour program run by the state Department of Environment and Conservation. The University of Western Australia handles bookings (✆ **08/6488 2433**; fax 08/6488 1066 for a free schedule; www.dec.wa.gov.au). You'll be helping scientists on research projects, such as monitoring endangered

Moments Dragon's Teeth in the Dunes

The **Pinnacles** ★★, a 3-hour drive north of Perth, attracts thousands of visitors each year. Masses of limestone pillars, from a few inches to over 3m (10 ft.) high, simply rise up out of golden sand dunes. Some small ones are just a fragile tracery, some are tall, solid mushroom-headed giants, while the sharp jagged versions could well be taken for fossilized dragon's teeth. From a distance they can look like the remnants of a deserted city, and are best seen around dawn or dusk. See "Tour Operators" above for details on two companies that stop here.

loggerhead turtles on Dirk Hartog Island, studying Australia's sea lion colonies in the Abrolhos Islands near the edge of the continental shelf, or recording animal and plant species in Cape Arid National Park on the south coast, among others.

1 Perth ★

4,405km (2,731 miles) W of Sydney; 2,389km (1,481 miles) S of Broome

Perth is probably the most outdoorsy of all Aussie cities. The climate, Perth's brilliant setting along both the Swan River and the Indian Ocean, and the abundance of parkland mean that it's almost obligatory to get outside and enjoy the sun and fresh air. One of Perth's great advantages is that virtually the entire river and seafront is public land; everyone can stroll, cycle, or picnic along the waterfront—and they do.

Perth is a sunshine capital with a wonderful Mediterranean climate that gives it more hours of sun than any other major city in Australia from October right through to April. It's also home to a thousand mining and exploration companies, which bring a touch of the Outback to the city. All these facts give Perth a youthful, energetic vibrancy. It has a superb position alongside a broad stretch of the Swan River, and its tall silver buildings glint in a brilliantly blue sky, while a sparkling ocean and glorious white beaches are just a bus ride from downtown. It's a friendly city; partly because of the outdoor openness, partly it's the Outback influence, and then there's a high proportion of migrants attracted by the climate and the lifestyle. There's much to do here, though the city center tends to be rather dead once the shops close. Wander through the restored historic warehouses, museums, and working docks of bustling **Fremantle;** stock up at the Aboriginal art and souvenir stores; visit art galleries and museums; eat at some of the country's best restaurants; enjoy the riverside parks and gardens; catch a few waves at one of the beaches; bushwalk through a 400-hectare (1,000-acre) park in the middle of the city; and pedal your bike to a great snorkeling spot on **Rottnest Island** ★★, a miniature reef resort 19km (12 miles) offshore.

More than most other Aussie capitals, Perth gives you good choices of side trips: Drop in on the Benedictine monks in the Spanish Renaissance monastery town of **New Norcia** ★, nip out to the **Swan Valley** ★ vineyards, or spend a few days in **Margaret River** ★★★ country, one of Australia's top wine regions.

Perth's climate is pleasant throughout the year. Most visitors focus on the brilliant summer months of December through March, with lots of sun, sea, and sand, though the sea breeze can get (annoyingly) strong. The winter months of June to August can

ACCOMMODATIONS ■
Medina Executive Barrack Plaza **17**
The Melbourne Hotel **6**
Miss Maud Swedish Hotel **18**
The Outram **7**
Parmelia Hilton Hotel **12**
River View on Mount Street **10**
The Sebel Residence West Perth **21**
Sullivans Hotel **11**

DINING ◆
44 King Street **14**
Chinatown **4**
Fast Eddy's Café **5**
Fraser's **8**
Jackson's **24**
Lamont's East Perth **22**
Miss Maud Swedish Restaurant **18**
Must Wine Bar **25**
Romany Restaurant **1**

ATTRACTIONS ●
Art Gallery of Western Australia **3**
His Majesty's Theatre **13**
Holmes à Court Gallery **23**
Kings Park & Botanic Garden **9**
Perth Concert Hall **19**
Perth Mint **20**
Perth Zoo **16**
Swan Bells **15**
Western Australian Museum **2**

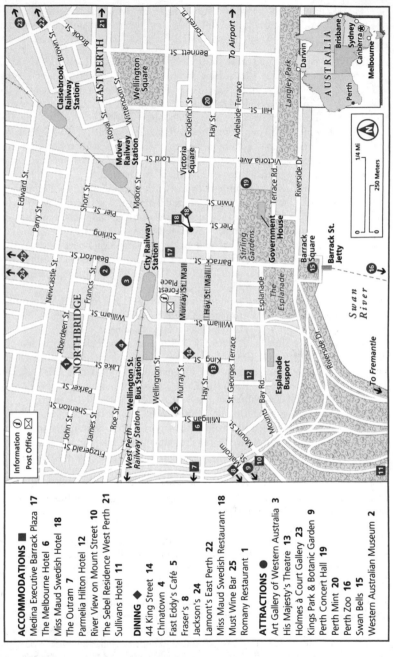

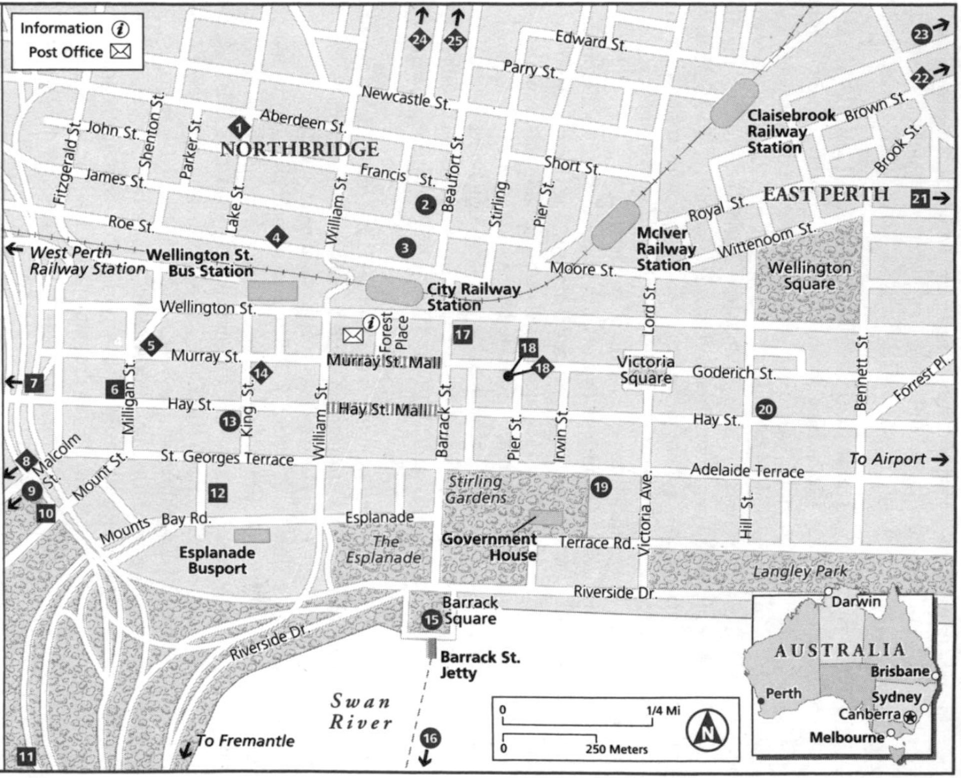

be cold and rainy but still average 6 hours of sun a day, while the in-between times of April to May and September to November are often superb with mild, fine, still days.

ORIENTATION

ARRIVING By Plane Qantas, or its subsidiary **Qantaslink** (✆ **13 13 13** in Australia; www.qantas.com.au), flies at least once a day from all mainland capitals as well as Broome, Alice Springs, and Uluru (Ayers Rock). It also services several mining towns in Western Australia. **Virgin Blue** (✆ **13 67 89** in Australia; www.virginblue.com.au) flies direct from Sydney, Melbourne, Adelaide, Brisbane, the Gold Coast, and Broome, with connections from other cities. **Jetstar** (✆ **13 15 38** in Australia; www.jetstar.com) has a daily flight from Melbourne, with connections from other eastern states cities. **Skywest** (✆ **1300/660 088** in WA; www.skywest.com.au) connects Perth to all significant towns in WA and to Darwin.

Perth Airport is 12km (7½ miles) northeast of the city. Allow 15 to 20 minutes to transfer between the international and domestic terminals. Both have ATMs, showers, baby-changing rooms, a mailbox (newsdealers sell stamps), and limited tourist information. Internet kiosks and currency-exchange bureaus are in the international and Qantas domestic terminals. The international terminal has cellphones for rent. At the international terminal, look out for volunteer Customer Service Officers called "Gold Coats," mostly in departures, and "WOWs" (West Oz Welcomers) wearing ocher jackets and Akubra hats in arrivals.

Avis (✆ 08/9277 1177 domestic terminal, 08/9477 1302 international terminal), **Budget** (✆ 08/9277 9277), **Europcar** (✆ 08/9237 4320), **Hertz** (✆ 08/9479 4788), and **Thrifty** (✆ 08/9464 7333) have desks at both terminals.

The **Airport City Shuttle** (✆ **08/9277 7958**) aims to meet all flights within 30 to 45 minutes of Customs clearance, or luggage collection for domestic flights. There is no need to book. City transfers from the international terminal cost A$15 (US$12/UK£6.15) adults one-way and A$25 (US$20/UK£10) return; from the domestic terminal, A$12 (US$9.60/UK£4.90) adults one-way, A$22 (US$18/UK£9) return.

The **Fremantle Airport Shuttle** (✆ **1300/668 687** in Australia, or 08/9335 1614) operates regular services each day from both airport terminals to hotels or anywhere else in Fremantle. You must reserve for the return trip. The fare is A$30 (US$24/UK£12) per person and gets cheaper the bigger your group is—down to A$10 (US$8/UK£4.10) per person for five or more people traveling together.

Transfers between terminals operate regularly from 5am to 5pm daily, with limited service until 9:30pm. Qantas/One World inter-flight transfers are free, otherwise it will cost you A$8 (US$6.40/UK£3.30); taxis between the terminals are about A$24 (US$19/UK£7.75).

Public **bus** no. 37 runs to the city from the domestic terminal. No buses run from the international terminal. A **taxi** to the city is about A$40 (US$32/UK£16) from the international terminal and A$32 (US$26/UK£13) from the domestic terminal, including a A$2 (US$1.60/UK£0.80) fee for picking up a taxi at the airport.

By Train The 3-day journey to Perth from Sydney via Broken Hill, Adelaide, and Kalgoorlie aboard the ***Indian Pacific*** ★, operated by Great Southern Railway (✆ **13 21 47** in Australia; www.trainways.com.au), is a great experience. It has the world's longest straight stretch of rail (over 483km/300 miles) along the Nullarbor Desert. The train runs twice a week in each direction, and can carry your vehicle. The one-way fare ranges from A$1,790 (US$1,432/UK£731) in first class with meals and en-suite bathroom, to

A$1,320 (US$1,056/UK£539) in comfy, but cramped if you're large or tall, second class (meals cost extra, and bathrooms are shared), down to A$680 (US$544/UK£278) for sit-up-all-the-way coach class (not a good idea). Connections are available from Melbourne on the ***Overland*** train. See "Getting Around Australia" in chapter 2 for contact details in Australia and abroad. The **Prospector** train makes the 6¾-hour trip from Kalgoorlie daily; call the **Public Transport Authority (PTA; ✆ 1300/662 205** in Western Australia; www.transwa.wa.gov.au).

All long-distance trains pull into the East Perth Terminal, Summers Street off Lord Street, East Perth. A taxi to the city center costs about A$17 (US$14/UK£6.95).

By Bus **Greyhound Australia** (**✆ 13 14 99** in Australia) no longer has a service from the eastern states; there's only a daily service from Darwin via Kununurra and Broome (about 59 hr.) and the fare is A$715 (US$572/UK£292).

By Car There are only two interstate routes—the 2,389km (1,481-mile) route from Broome in the north, and the 2,708km (1,679-mile) odyssey from Adelaide, which has some of the world's straightest and most featureless roads on the trek across the Nullarbor Plain. Arm yourself with up-to-date details on sightseeing (yes, there is some, including whale-watching), and the limited accommodations before setting off. The South Australian or Western Australian state auto clubs (listed under "Getting Around Australia," in chapter 2) can provide advice and information. Both routes are pretty boring with very few towns en route, but they really bring home how big and empty is much of Australia.

VISITOR INFORMATION The **Western Australian Visitor Centre,** Albert Facey House, 469 Wellington St. at Forrest Place, Perth (**✆ 1300/361 351** in Australia; www.westernaustralia.com), is the official visitor information source for Perth and the state. It's open Monday through Thursday from 8:30am to 6pm (to 5:30pm in winter, May–Aug), Friday from 8:30am to 7pm (to 6pm in winter), Saturday from 9:30am to 4:30pm, and Sunday 12:00 to 4:30pm year-round. The City of Perth's **i-City Information Kiosk,** in the Murray Street Mall near Forrest Place, is open Monday to Thursday and Saturday 9:30am to 4:30pm, Friday 9:30am to 8pm, and Sunday noon to 4:30pm (closed public holidays).

Volunteers lead free 90-minute guided tours around the city, Monday to Friday at 11am and 2pm, Saturday at 11am, and Sunday at 2pm. The morning and Sunday sessions are general city orientation tours, while the other afternoon tours are more heritage-oriented. There's no need to book. Another source of information and maps (plus a free booking service) is **Perth Tourist Lounge,** Level 2, Carillon Arcade off 207 Murray St. Mall (**✆ 08/9481 4400;** www.perthtourist.com.au), open Monday through Saturday 9:30am to 4:30pm (closed Sun, public holidays).

For an untouristy lowdown on the city's restaurants, cultural life, shops, bars, nightlife, concerts, and the like, buy the excellent glossy quarterly magazine ***Scoop*** (A$9.95/US$7.95/UK£4; **www.scoop.com.au**), available in bigger newsstands.

CITY LAYOUT The city center is 19km (12 miles) upriver from the Indian Ocean, on the north bank of a broad reach of the Swan River. Four long avenues run east-west between riverside parkland and the railway reserve. **St. Georges Terrace** (it becomes Adelaide Terrace at Victoria Ave.) is the main thoroughfare and commercial and banking address, while **Hay Street** and **Murray Street** are the major retail avenues with pedestrian malls in the central blocks. Arcades link all three, plus Wellington Street, which has Perth's suburban railway station on its northern side.

MAPS Of the many free pocket guides to Perth available at tour desks and in hotel lobbies, *Your Guide to Perth & Fremantle* (Countrywide Publications) has the **best street map.** It shows one-way streets, public toilets and telephones, taxi stands, post offices, police stations, and street numbers, as well as most attractions and hotels. The **Royal Automobile Club of Western Australia** (see "Exploring the State," earlier in this chapter) is a good source of maps to the state, as is **The Perth Map Centre,** 900 Hay St. (✆ **08/9322 5733**). You will find tourist maps at the Western Australian Visitor Centre and the Perth Tourist Lounge (see "Visitor Information," above).

NEIGHBORHOODS IN BRIEF

City Center The central business district (the CBD) is home to offices, shops, and department stores. It has a modest collection of 19th-century heritage buildings, especially convict-built Government House and Town Hall. A good introduction to Perth's charms is to take in the views from the pathway that skirts the river along Riverside Drive. Within walking distance is **Kings Park & Botanic Garden** ★★.

Northbridge Most of Perth's nightclubs, and a good many of its cool restaurants, bars, and cafes, are in this 5-block precinct north of the railway line. It's within easy walking distance of the city center, or take the free Blue CAT buses. The rough boundaries are William, James, Aberdeen, and Parker streets. The Cultural Centre is here too, with a tightly knit collection of Western Australian Museum, Art Gallery of Western Australia, State Library, and Perth Institute of Contemporary Arts.

Subiaco This well-heeled inner suburb is on the other side of Kings Park. Take a stroll through "Subi's" villagelike concoction of restaurants, cafes, markets, boutiques, antiques shops, pubs, and galleries. Most of the action is near the intersection of Hay Street and Rokeby (pronounced *Rock*-er-bee) Road, with the Subiaco Hotel and Art Deco Regal Theatre on opposing corners. Take the train to Subiaco station.

Fremantle Not only is "Freo" a working port, it's also Perth's second city heart, and a favorite weekend spot to eat, drink, shop, and sail. A 1980s restoration of Victorian warehouses and hotels turned Freo into a marvelous example of a 19th-century seaport, although a takeover of many buildings by Notre Dame University has taken away some of the old vibrancy. Fremantle is 19km (12 miles) downriver, at the mouth of the Swan.

Scarborough Beach This is one of Perth's prize beaches, 12km (7½ miles) north of the city center. The district is a little tatty, with an oversupply of cheap takeout food outlets, but if you like sun, sand, and surf, this is the place to be. You will find bars, restaurants, and surf-gear rental stores here. Allow 20 to 30 minutes to get here by car, 50 minutes by public transport.

Cottesloe Beach This is another great beach, quieter, safer, and less frenetic than Scarborough, with a protective rocky groyne (jetty) to one side. The surrounding area is very pleasant with grassy slopes, good hotels, and cafes, and the whole suburb is defined by towering Norfolk pines. Allow 20 minutes to get here by car, 30 minutes by bus or train.

Burswood/East Perth These two areas are on opposite sides of the Swan River just upstream of Perth city. Both are on land reclaimed from earlier industrial use, and show enlightened development with parkland, pathways, and artworks. Burswood has major entertainment complexes, a public golf course, and superb gardens. East Perth is mostly modern housing, parks, galleries, and restaurants, based around a river inlet with walkways.

GETTING AROUND

BY PUBLIC TRANSPORTATION **Transperth** (www.transperth.wa.gov.au) runs Perth's buses, trains, and ferries. For route, bus stop, and timetable information, call ✆ **13 62 13** in Western Australia, or drop into the Transperth InfoCentres at the Plaza Arcade off Hay Street Mall, the Perth Train Station, the Wellington Street Bus Station, or the Perth Esplanade Busport on Mounts Bay Road. You can transfer between bus, ferry, and train services for up to 2 hours (Zones 1–4) or 3 hours (Zones 5–8). Travel costs A$2.10 (US$1.70/UK£0.85) in one zone (to Subiaco, for instance), and A$3.20 (US$2.55/UK£1.05) in two, which gets you most places, including Fremantle, with discounts for kids ages 5 to 14.

By Bus The Wellington Street Bus Station (close to Perth Train Station) and the Perth Esplanade Busport on Mounts Bay Road are the two main arrival and departure points. The vast majority of buses travel along St. Georges Terrace. You must hail the

Tips Take a Free Ride

A welcome freebie in Perth is the availability of free public transport within the city center and some nearby areas. It's a great facility. There are the **CAT** (Central Area Transit) buses (see below), and there is the **Free Transit Zone (FTZ).** You can travel free on all buses within this zone any hour, day or night. For free train travel in the FTZ, a **SmartRider** (see below) must be used, and is less practical for most visitors. The FTZ is bounded by Kings Park Road, Fraser Avenue, Thomas Street, and Loftus Street in the west; Newcastle Street in the north; and the river in the south and east. Basically, this means you can travel to Kings Park, Northbridge, east to major sporting grounds, and anywhere in the city center free. Signs mark the FTZ boundaries; just ask the driver if you're unsure. FTZ boundaries for trains are City West station on the Fremantle line and Claisebrook on the Midland and Armadale lines.

SmartRider can save up to 25% off the cash fare depending on how you add value to the card, but involves a basic A$10 (US$8/UK£4.10) cost plus minimum A$10 (US$8/UK£4.10) travel component, so of doubtful value to most tourists. Check the website or an InfoCentre for more information. To use the passes, you need to validate them in the machines on the bus, train platform, or ferry wharf. A **DayRider** ticket can be purchased to allow 1 day of unlimited travel after 9am on weekdays and all day on weekends and public holidays for A$7.70 (US$6.15/UK£3.15). A **FamilyRider** pass is valid for unlimited all-day travel to any destination and back, for a group of up to seven people with a maximum of two adults, but only on weekends and public holidays, also for A$7.70 (US$6.15/UK£3.15).

bus to ensure that it stops. Buy tickets from the driver. Buses run from about 5:30am until about 10:30 or 11:30pm, depending on the route.

The best way to get around town is on the free **CAT** buses that run a continual loop of the city and Northbridge. The Red CAT runs east-west every 5 minutes, Monday through Friday from 6:50am to 6:20pm, and every 25 minutes from 10am to 6:15pm weekends. The Blue CAT runs north-south, between Northbridge and Barrack Street Jetty every 7 minutes from 6:50am. The last Blue CAT service is at 6:20pm Monday through Thursday, but on Friday it runs every 15 minutes from 6:20pm until 1am Saturday. Saturday it runs from 8:30am to 1am the next day every 15 minutes, and Sunday every 15 minutes from 10am to 6:15pm. The Yellow CAT runs between East Perth and West Perth every 10 minutes from 6:50am to 6:20pm weekdays, and every 30 minutes 10am to 6:10pm weekends. There are no CAT services on public holidays. Look for the silver CAT bus stops with the black cat on them. Transperth InfoCentres (see above) dispense free route maps. For beach services, check **www.transperth.wa.gov.au**.

Perth Tram Co. tours (see "Whale-Watching Cruises, Tram Trips & Other Tours," later in this chapter) are a good way to get around, too.

By Train Trains are fast, clean, and safe. They start at about 5:30am and run every 15 minutes or more often during the day, and every half-hour at night until midnight. All trains depart from Perth Train Station opposite Forrest Place on Wellington Street. Buy your ticket before you board, at the vending machines on the platform. There are five lines: north to Joondalup; northeast to Midland; southeast to Armadale; southwest to Fremantle; and (opening late 2007) south to the resort town of Mandurah.

By Ferry You will use ferries to visit South Perth and Perth Zoo. They run every half-hour or so, more often in peak hours, every day from 6:50am weekdays and 7:50am weekends and public holidays, until 7:24pm (or until 9:15pm Fri–Sat in summer, Sept–Apr) from the Barrack Street Jetty to Mends Street in South Perth. Buy tickets before you board from the vending machine on the wharf. The trip takes approximately 7 minutes.

By Taxi Perth's two biggest taxi companies are **Swan Taxis** (✆ **13 13 30**) and **Black & White Taxis** (✆ **13 10 08**). Ranks (stands) are at Perth Railway Station and at the Barrack Street end of Hay Street Mall.

By Car Perth's signposting is reasonably good for helping drivers find their way around. The major car-rental companies are **Avis** (✆ 08/9325 7677), **Budget** (✆ 08/9480 3111), **Europcar** (✆ 08/9277 9144), **Hertz** (✆ 08/9321 7777), and **Thrifty** (✆ 08/9464 7444). All except Hertz also have outlets in Fremantle.

Tips **Bring Your Bike, Too!**

You are allowed, even encouraged, to take your bicycle on Perth's suburban trains and ferries. The only limitations are to avoid the Monday to Friday peak services—toward the city between 7 and 9am, and away from the city between 4:30 and 6:30pm—and not have your bike at Perth Train Station during either of these times.

FAST FACTS: Perth

American Express The office at 645 Hay St. Mall (✆ **1300/139 060**) is open Monday through Friday from 9am to 5pm and Saturday from 9am to noon.

Business Hours Banks are open Monday through Thursday from 9:30am to 4pm and until 5pm Friday. Shopping hours are usually from 9am to 5:30pm Monday through Friday (until 9pm on Thurs in the suburbs and Fremantle, and until 9pm Fri in the city), and from 9am to 5pm on Saturday. On Sunday most (but not all) major stores open from noon to 4pm or later in the city, and from noon to 6pm in Fremantle.

Currency Exchange Go to the American Express office (see above) or **Interforex,** Shop 24, London Court, off Hay Street Mall (✆ **08/9325 7418;** Mon–Sat 8am–6pm, until 8pm Fri, Sun 10am–5pm). Interforex has a Fremantle bureau at the corner of William and Adelaide streets (✆ **08/9431 7022;** Mon–Sat 8am–5:30pm, until 6pm Fri, Sun 10am–5:30pm).

Dentist **LifeCare Dental** (✆ **08/9221 2777,** or 08/9383 1620 after-hours) is on the Upper Walkway Level, Forrest Chase shopping complex, 425 Wellington St., opposite Perth Railway Station. Open daily from 8am to 8pm.

Doctor **Central City Medical Centre** is on the Perth Railway Station concourse, 420 Wellington St. (✆ **08/9221 4747**). Open daily 8am to 6pm.

Embassies & Consulates The **United States Consulate-General** is at 16 St. Georges Terrace (✆ **08/9202 1224**). The **Canadian Consulate** is at 267 St. Georges Terrace (✆ **08/9322 7930**). The **British Consular Agency** is at 77 St. Georges Terrace (✆ **08/9224 4700**).

Emergencies Dial ✆ **000** for fire, ambulance, or police in an emergency. This is a free call; no coins are needed from a public phone.

Hospitals **Royal Perth Hospital** in the city center has a public emergency/casualty ward (✆ **08/9224 2244**). Enter from Victoria Square, which is off Murray Street.

Luggage Storage & Lockers The **Perth Tourist Lounge** (see "Visitor Information," above) stores luggage, and there are baggage lockers at the international and domestic terminals at the airport.

Pharmacies **Forrest Chase Pharmacy** (✆ **08/9221 1691**), on the upper level of the Forrest Chase shopping center, 425 Wellington St. (near the dentist's office listed above), is open Monday through Thursday from 8am to 7pm (and until 9pm Fri), Saturday from 8:30am to 6pm, and Sunday from 10am to 6pm. Most pharmacies will make local deliveries—try either Friendlies or Amcal Chemist branches as defined in the telephone directory.

Police Dial ✆ **000** in a life-threatening emergency, otherwise ✆ **13 14 44** to be connected to the nearest station. **Perth Police Station,** 60 Beaufort St. (✆ **08/9223 3715**), and **Fremantle Police Station,** 45 Henderson St. (✆ **08/9430 1222**), are open 24 hours.

Safety Perth is safe, but steer clear of the back streets of Northbridge and the city center malls late at night—where groups of teenagers tend to congregate—even if you are not alone.

Time Zone Western Australian time (WST) is Greenwich Mean Time plus 8 hours and is on a 3-year trial of daylight saving, so GMT plus 9 hours October through March. It is 2 hours behind Sydney and Melbourne. Call ✆ **1194** for the exact local time.

Weather Call ✆ **1196** for a recorded local weather forecast.

WHERE TO STAY

The city center has loads of hotels. That means competition for your business can be high, especially Friday through Sunday when the business travelers go home, so ask about lower rates on weekends. You may strike a deal on a weeknight if business is slow. Many hotels throw breakfast or some other feature into weekend packages. Most hotels have rooms for travelers with disabilities.

IN OR NEAR THE CITY CENTER

Expensive

The Melbourne Hotel This 1897 hotel in Perth's downtown West End was restored to its gold rush–era looks in 1997 and updated again in 2003, though the interior is looking a bit tired now. The exterior retains its original appearance with ornate first-floor balcony, but the interior has been lifted to 21st-century standards while still retaining the restaurant's superb plaster ceiling and tall mirrors, the elegant timber staircase, and original paneled elevator. Suites are a large single room with sitting area. Go for the outside rooms which open onto the wide veranda, and have a drink in the atmospheric street-front **Melbourne Bar.**

Corner of Hay and Milligan sts., Perth, WA 6000. ✆ **1800/685 671** in Australia, or 08/9320 3333. Fax 08/9320 3344. www.melbournehotel.com.au. 36 units, all with shower only. A$240 (US$192/UK£98) double; A$280 (US$224/UK£114) suite. Ask about packages. AE, DC, MC, V. Valet parking A$17 (US$14/UK£6.95). Bus: Red CAT Stop 19 (QVI) 1 block away in St. Georges Terrace. **Amenities:** Restaurant; cafe; bar; access to nearby health club and tennis courts; car-rental next door; airport shuttle; room service; babysitting; dry cleaning. *In room:* A/C, brass ceiling fans, TV w/free movies, minibar, coffeemaker, hair dryer, iron.

The Outram ★★ *Finds* Discreet and intimate are the key words for this small but elegant hotel, plus friendly service. Opened in 2005 it is Perth's only member of the Small Luxury Hotels of the World group, and was built partly to provide a suitable city link to some of the upmarket Margaret River establishments. Tucked away in West Perth, it's 2 short blocks from Kings Park and within easy reach of the city center. Privacy is paramount, with full key-card access control. The rooms are large but not opulent, with king-size beds, open-plan bathrooms, "his and her" basins, a walk-through shower, and tiny balcony. Most rooms have double spas. The foyer-level Club Room (with terrace extension) serves complimentary breakfasts, coffee and cake, and evening hors d'oeuvres with drinks. It's a smoke-free property.

32 Outram St., West Perth, WA 6005. ✆ **1800/251 958** SLH in Australia, or 08/9322 4888. Fax 08/9322 1138. 18 units, 15 with double spas. A$395 (US$316/UK£161) double; A$365 (US$292/UK£149) single, including breakfast. AE, DC, MC, V. Basement parking A$15 (US$12/UK£6.15). Bus: Red CAT Stop 24 right outside. No children under 12 years. **Amenities:** Club Room cafe/terrace (guests only); limited room service; daily laundry and dry cleaning service. *In room:* A/C, TV/DVD w/free movies, free broadband, minibar, coffeemaker, hair dryer, iron, safe.

Parmelia Hilton Hotel ★★ Perth's first Hilton five-star hotel and still one of the best. If you want a city center hotel with style, this is it. It's steps from the Perth Convention Centre, with the Swan River not far away. The elegant marble foyer has a brass plaque commemorating the SS *Parmelia,* which brought 150 of the first settlers to these shores. The river views have mostly been built out, so ask for rooms from the seventh floor upward (no extra charge). The hotel has subtly striped wallpaper throughout, the spacious standard rooms and deluxe rooms are decorated in cool relaxing shades, while the suites boast separate living, working, and dining areas. Soft furnishings have been replaced since the last refurbishment in 1999. There is key-card elevator access. The **Globe Restaurant** has one of Perth's most innovative menus, and hosts regular fashion and winemaker events.

14 Mill St. (just off St. Georges Terrace), Perth, WA 6000. ✆ **1300/445 866** Hilton in Australia, or 08/9215 2000. Fax 08/9215 2001. www1.hilton.com/en_US/hi/hotel/PERHITW-Parmelia-Hilton-Perth-hotel/index.do. 284 units. A$225–A$295 (US$180–US$236/UK£92–UK£120) double; A$345–A$520 (US$276–US$416/UK£141–UK£212) suite. Ask about packages and specials, especially on weekends. AE, DC, MC, V. Valet parking A$30 (US$24/UK£9.80) per 24 hr. Bus: Blue CAT Stop 1 (St. Georges Terrace). **Amenities:** 2 restaurants; 2 bars; outdoor heated pool; gym and sauna; concierge; airport shuttle; business center; meeting rooms; secretarial service; salon; room service; babysitting service; laundry/valet service; dry cleaning; barbershop; luggage hold. *In room:* A/C, TV w/pay movies, high-speed Internet, minibar, coffeemaker, hair dryer, iron, safe.

Moderate

Medina Executive Barrack Plaza ★ *Kids* This is a modern apartment hotel with contemporary styling in central Perth, within easy walking distance of the pedestrian malls, railway station, Cultural Centre, and Northbridge eateries. It opened in July 2006 and appeals to the corporate market but is also geared toward families. Most units are one-bedroom apartments of a good size, especially the living area. There are studio rooms and two-bedroom apartments, with an option to link these for secure family use. All units have small balconies, with the north-facing units best in the cooler months, getting the most sun. Apartments have full kitchen facilities, while studios have kitchenettes with microwave but no stove or washing machine. You'll get much better rates if you book online, so head for the website if this is your choice. You'll also find very good deals in December and January (though not New Year's).

138 Barrack St. (between Murray and Wellington sts.), Perth, WA 6000. ✆ **1300/633 462** Medina in Australia, or 08/9267 0000. Fax 08/9267 0199. www.medina.com.au. 99 units. A$190 (US$152/UK£78) studio; A$215–A$230 (US$172–US$184/UK£88–UK£94) 1-bedroom apt; A$280–A$320 (US$224–US$256/UK£114–UK£131) 2-bedroom apt. Extra person/rollaway A$40 (US$32/UK£16), crib A$5 (US$4/UK£2.05). AE, DC, MC, V. Parking A$17 (US$13/UK£6.50). Train: Perth. Bus: All Cats nearby. **Amenities:** Cafe next door with room service and charge-back available; 12m (39-ft.) lap pool; small gym and sauna; in-room massage; dry cleaning. *In room:* A/C, TV w/pay movies, broadband, kitchenette, coffeemaker, hair dryer, iron, safe, stereo with CD.

The Sebel Residence East Perth ★★★ This 4-year-old hotel is in a great location in East Perth, this contemporary development just minutes from the city. It's quiet, and has good views across Claisebrook (a broad pool, lined with artworks and upmarket housing) and down to the Swan River. Galleries, restaurants, parks, and riverside walkways are a few steps away. A barbecue area and 25m (82-ft.) lap pool are outside overlooking Claisebrook. There is no restaurant but the corner cafe will deliver breakfast, and it and other local restaurants, including **Lamont's** (p. 469), and a wine shop, offer charge-back facilities to the hotel. Each one-bedroom apartment has a full kitchen with microwave, washer and dryer, and balcony. The best overlook Claisebrook. Studios have kitchenette and shower only. You can combine a studio and a one-bedroom apartment to make a private two-bedroom apartment. Internet access is also available in the lobby, and the staff is friendly and helpful.

60 Royal St. (at Plain St.), East Perth, WA 6004. ✆ **1800/010 559** Mirvac in Australia, or 08/9223 2500. Fax 08/9223 2590. www.mirvachotels.com.au. 57 units. A$195–A$215 (US$156–US$172/UK£80–UK£88) studio; A$245–A$265

(US$196–US$212/UK£100–UK£108) 1-bedroom apt double; A$310 (US$248/UK£127) 2-bedroom apt. AE, DC, MC, V. Free covered parking. Train: Claisebrook. Bus: Yellow CAT stops 5 and 32. **Amenities:** Heated outdoor lap pool; small well-equipped gym; guest laundry; dry cleaning. *In room:* A/C, TV w/free movies, DVD, kitchenette, fridge, coffeemaker, hair dryer, iron, safe, stereo.

Inexpensive

Miss Maud Swedish Hotel ★ *Value* This hotel offers a fresh European *pension*-style presence in the heart of the city, 1 block from the Murray Street Mall. It's a 1911 building so a bit of a rabbit warren. The whole place has been refurbished over the last 5 years, but still retains its Swedish ambience. It has a comfortable "feel," with wallpaper used throughout. Miss Maud is real—Maud Edmiston who started the hotel and restaurant 35 years ago. Many staff have been with her for years and there's a loyal customer base. Single women find it a safe and comfortable place to stay. Sixty percent of visitors are corporate, and there's a strong European market. There are six single rooms. Two principal aims are to provide sleeping comfort and a good breakfast, so large beds are provided—and the fabulous buffet next door in **Miss Maud Swedish Restaurant** (p. 470). All windows are double glazed to eliminate traffic noise.

97 Murray St. (at Pier St.), Perth, WA 6000. ✆ **1800/998 022** in Australia, or 08/9325 3900. Fax 08/9221 3225. www.missmaud.com.au. 52 units, 35 with shower only. A$159 (US$127/UK£65) standard room double; A$139 (US$111/UK£57) standard room single; A$219 (US$175/UK£89) standard room triple; A$179 (US$143/UK£73) superior double; A$159 (US$127/UK£65) superior single. Rates include smorgasbord breakfast. Great Night Out package includes smorgasbord dinner A$183 (US$146/UK£75) Sun–Thurs, A$199 (US$159/UK£81) Fri–Sat. AE, DC, MC, V. Parking A$12 (US$9.60/UK£4.90) 1 block away. Bus: Red CAT Stop 1 (Pier St.); Blue CAT Stop 5 (Murray St. Mall E.). **Amenities:** Restaurant; takeout pastry shop; discounted access to nearby health club; tour desk; car-rental desk; airport shuttle; room service; babysitting; coin-op laundry; laundry service; dry cleaning. *In room:* A/C, flatscreen TV/VCR w/free cable, minibar, coffeemaker, hair dryer.

River View on Mount Street On a quiet, leafy street a short walk from both the city and Kings Park, these roomy studio apartments in a 1960s block were refurbished in 1999. The exterior and passages are a dull brick, but the interiors have pleasant modern surroundings, and are equipped with smart-looking fittings. The result is reasonable style at a good price. Some rooms sleep three. Try for the front Riverview rooms with balconies. Maid service is weekly. The helpful on-site managers loan hair dryers and irons. You can have breakfast at Cimbalino's, the downstairs cafe. No smoking.

42 Mount St., Perth, WA 6000. ✆ **08/9321 8963.** Fax 08/9322 5956. www.riverviewperth.com.au. 50 units, all with shower only. A$110–A$120 (US$88–US$96/UK£45–UK£49) standard apartments; A$125–A$135 (US$100–US$108/UK£51–UK£55) Riverview. Weekly rates available. AE, MC, V. Limited free parking. Bus: Red CAT Stop 19 in Hay St. (QVI), over freeway footbridge. **Amenities:** Cafe; coin-op laundry; laundry service; dry cleaning; nonsmoking rooms. *In room:* A/C, TV, dataport, kitchenette, fridge, coffeemaker, hair dryer, iron.

Sullivans Hotel ★ *Value* *Kids* This small intimate family-owned hotel about 1.5km (1 mile) from town is immediately below Kings Park, close to the Swan River. It's popular with British and other Europeans for its small-scale ambience and friendly service. The rooms are simply furnished, not glamorous but roomy. Larger deluxe rooms come with balconies and views over parkland and the freeway to the river. There is one two-bedroom apartment with kitchenette. Out back is a pleasant little pool with a sun deck and barbecue. Use of bikes is free, the restaurant is affordable, and the front desk has free Internet access for guests. The city, Swan River, and Kings Park are just a stroll away.

166 Mounts Bay Rd., Perth, WA 6000. ✆ **08/9321 8022.** Fax 08/9481 6762. www.sullivans.com.au. 71 units, 69 with shower only, 5 family rooms. A$130–A$150 (US$104–US$120/UK£53–UK£61) standard/deluxe double; A$160 (US$128/UK£65) 1-bedroom apt; A$200 (US$160/UK£82) 2-bedroom apt. Winter package—pay for 3 days, stay 4. Weekly rates available. AE, DC, MC, V. Free parking. Bus: Blue Cat by front door, otherwise hotel is within Free Transit

Zone. **Amenities:** Restaurant/bar; small outdoor pool; free bikes; tour desk; airport shuttle; coin-op laundry; dry cleaning; free Internet access. *In room:* A/C, TV w/free movies, coffeemaker, hair dryer.

IN BURSWOOD

InterContinental Burswood Hotel ★★★ It's the setting that first grabs your attention, the distinctively tiered building set within parkland right next to the Swan River, overlooking the city. Then you walk into the full-height, glass-ceilinged atrium, all set about with high-flying triangular sails. Glass-sided elevators ascend one wall. The foyer and public facilities have all been upgraded since 2003, and the suites will follow in 2008. The hotel is part of an entertainment complex that includes Perth's only casino, a large theater, another hotel (Holiday Inn), and a public 18-hole golf course. The surrounding parks and gardens include lakes and fountains, free barbecue facilities, a heritage walk, an outdoor summer cinema, a tourist helipad, and children's playground. Being outside the city center, the main focus is on tourists not corporate travelers. The real stars are the spacious suites with large balconies, facing straight downriver; otherwise ask for river-view rooms. The fitness center is staffed 6am to 9pm.

1 Bolton Ave. (off Great Eastern Hwy. by the Causeway), Burswood, WA 6100. ✆ **13 83 88** (reservations) in Australia, or 08/9362 8888. www.burswood.com.au/hotels. 408 units. A$184–A$335 (US$147–US$268/UK£75–UK£137) standard rooms, room only; add A$100 (US$80/UK£41) for Club service (includes breakfast, valet parking, and club access); A$724–A$905 (US$579–US$724/UK£296–UK£369) suites. Max usage 3 adults in twin, or with 2 children using existing bedding. AE, DC, MC, V. Valet parking A$20 (US$16/UK£8.15) per day to max A$50 (US$40/UK£20) per stay; some free parking available. Bus: numerous along Great Eastern Hwy. Starting point for Perth Tram. Train: Burswood station. **Amenities:** 2 restaurants; 2 bars (more in casino); enormous free-form pool; heated indoor pool; tennis courts; well-equipped fitness center and sauna (available 24 hr.); yoga/Pilates classes; day/beauty spa with 13 treatment rooms; bikes for hire; concierge; airline/car rental/tour desk; business center 8:30am–5pm Mon–Fri; secretarial services; hairdresser; 24-hr. room service; dry cleaning/laundry service; lobby shop; florist. *In room:* A/C, TV w/pay movies, broadband, minibar with freezer, hair dryer, iron, choice of 4 pillow types.

ON THE BEACH

Hotel Rendezvous Observation City Perth ★ Kids If you're looking for absolute beach frontage this is it. The only high-rise along Perth's Indian Ocean coast, it has superb views up and down Scarborough's long sandy beach. A surf lifesaving club, beach amphitheater, children's playground, and part of the coastal bike/walking track are right there. Surfing lessons and bike hire are available, and the Australian Life Saving Championships will be here late March 2008 and 2009. The hotel's no-fuss ambience makes it popular with vacationers from around the world and families. Most of the rooms, refurbished in 2004, have private balconies with ocean views; some are interconnected. Bed configurations are king-size, queen-size plus single, or two doubles. The suites have prime position on the top floors with spacious balconies. It has the largest hotel gym in Perth (re-fitted mid-2006), and a large pool area with palm trees and waterfall—sheltered from the sea breeze.

The Esplanade, Scarborough Beach, WA 6019. ✆ **1800/067 680** in Australia, or 08/9245 1000. Fax 08/9245 1345. www.rendezvoushotels.com. 327 rooms, 6 suites. A$130–A$210 (US$104–US$168/UK£53–UK£86) standard rooms (limited views/balconies); A$166–A$246 (US$133–US$197/UK£68–UK£100) deluxe; from A$566 (US$453/UK£231) suites. Prices for rooms as configured. Ask about packages. AE, DC, MC, V. Valet parking A$20 (US$16/UK£6.55); self-parking A$7 (US$5.60/UK£2.85). Bus: 400. **Amenities:** 2 restaurants; cafe; 3 bars (1 British pub–style); heated outdoor pool; children's wading pool; 2 outdoor day/night tennis courts; fitness center and steam rooms; spa; Jacuzzi; limited watersports equipment rentals; bike rental; concierge; tour desk; daily courtesy shuttle between hotel, Perth city, Fremantle, local mall; business center; salon; room service; babysitting; coin-op laundry; laundry service; dry cleaning; executive-level rooms top 3 floors. *In room:* A/C, TV w/pay movies, high-speed Internet most rooms A$25 (US$20/UK£10) per day, minibar, coffeemaker, hair dryer, iron.

IN FREMANTLE

There's something of a perpetual holiday atmosphere in this picturesque port city. Public transport, for the 19km (12-mile) journey to Perth's city center, is good, especially the train. So you can happily explore all of Perth from here—and many top attractions are here in Freo. There are good restaurants and a happening nightlife, too.

Esplanade Hotel Fremantle ★★ Freo's best hotel is this low-rise 1897 colonial building wrapped by two verandas, now modernized and extended, and centered on the original glass and iron four-story atrium. It's opposite a leafy park close to the Fishing Harbour, and within walking distance of all Freo's cafes, shops, and attractions. A major expansion in 2003 added 41 rooms and a 1,000-seat convention center. Several room types were refurbished in 2006. The rooms are all of reasonable size, with the suites especially spacious and having large balconies. Some studio units have Jacuzzis. Eleven rooms are designed for wheelchair access. The larger pool in the courtyard is a good place to chill out without getting buffeted by the pesky local sea breeze, the "Fremantle Doctor."

Marine Terrace at Essex St., Fremantle, WA 6160. ✆ **1800/998 201** in Australia, or 08/9432 4000. Fax 08/9430 4539. www.esplanadehotelfremantle.com.au. 300 units, some with shower only. A$330–A$370 (US$234–US$260/UK£135–UK£151) double; A$400–A$419 (US$270–US$335/UK£163–UK£171) studio; A$445–A$619 (US$356–US$495/UK£182–UK£253) suite. Extra person A$38 (US$30/UK£16). Children under 13 stay free in parent's room with existing bedding. Crib free. There are several 1- and 2-night packages, and attractive Internet rates. AE, DC, MC, V. Valet parking A$25 (US$15/UK£10); paid street parking nearby. Train: Fremantle. Fremantle Airport Shuttle (see "Arriving: By Plane," earlier in this chapter). **Amenities:** 2 restaurants; cafe; 2 bars (1 poolside); 2 heated outdoor pools; small gym; 3 outdoor spas; sauna; bike rental; concierge; tour desk; business center; room service; in-room massage; babysitting; coin-op laundry; laundry service; dry cleaning (Mon–Sat). *In room:* A/C, TV w/pay movies, broadband in most rooms, minibar, coffeemaker, hair dryer, iron.

Fothergills of Fremantle ★★ *Finds* One of Perth's best bed-and-breakfast establishments, it's located in two lovely old restored 1890s limestone mansions. Fremantle with all its charms is a 10-minute walk, and Fremantle Prison (see "Seeing the Sights in Fremantle," later in this chapter) is a block away. The houses have been extensively and tastefully modernized, and owner David Cooke has spread his extensive art collection throughout, bringing color, light, and life. The upstairs balconies have views over the roofs of Fremantle to the Indian Ocean, ideal for evening sundowners. Most rooms have queen-size beds while the O'Connor suite has a king-size and double fold-out bed. There's no lounge but the courtyards are quiet restful havens. Interiors are nonsmoking.

18–20 Ord St., Fremantle, WA 6160. ✆ **08/9335 6784**. Fax 08/9430 7789. www.babs.com.au/fothergills. 10 units, most with shower only. A$140–A$200 (US$112–US$160/UK£57–UK£82) double. Extra adult A$50 (US$40/UK£20); extra child 3–12 A$10 (US$8/UK£4.10). Minimum stay 2 nights; extra A$10 (US$8/UK£3.30) if 1 night. Week-stay package. Full breakfast included. MC, V. Street parking. Bus: Fremantle Cat, stop 4 (High St.), 2 blocks away. **Amenities:** 2 breakfast rooms; seating in courtyards and balconies. *In room:* A/C, TV/DVD, broadband, fridge, coffeemaker, hair dryer, iron.

WHERE TO DINE

An array of upscale choices plus terrific cheap ethnic spots make Perth's restaurant scene as sophisticated as Sydney's and Melbourne's—which is to say, excellent. You'll find a great range in "restaurant city," Northbridge. Friday and Saturday nights tend to be very busy, so service can suffer. Midweek is less busy, quieter, and generally more pleasant.

Many outlets emphasize the use of fresh local produce. Western Australia is blessed with several climate zones plus pristine ocean waters so look out for seasonal berry, stone, citrus, and tropical fruit; lamb, beef, veal, and goat; seafood such as rock lobster, abalone, and prawns; freshwater crustaceans such as marron and yabbies; and superb fish including dhufish, snapper, red emperor, and cobbler.

For inexpensive pasta, a Turkish bread sandwich, or excellent coffee and cake, you can't beat Perth's homegrown **DOME** chain of cafes. Look for the dark green logo at Trinity Arcade between Hay Street Mall and St. Georges Terrace (✆ **08/9226 0210**); 149 James St., Northbridge (✆ **08/9328 8094**); 13 S. Terrace, Fremantle (✆ **08/9336 3040**); 26 Rokeby Rd., Subiaco (✆ **08/9381 5664**); in Rendezvous Observation City (✆ **08/9205 1665**); and Henderson Street on Rottnest Island (✆ **08/9292 5026**)—to name just a few.

Western Australian law bans smoking in enclosed public spaces, including restaurants.

IN OR NEAR THE CITY CENTER

Expensive

Fraser's ★★★ *Moments* MODERN AUSTRALIAN What a sensational view! You look past spiky grass trees and towering lemon-scented gums to Perth's panoply of skyscrapers and the Swan River. Even better, the victuals match the vista. Executive chef Chris Taylor changes the menu daily to focus on the very latest fresh produce, with seafood and fish especially prominent. This place was awarded a national title for "Best informal dining in Australia" in 2006. "Fraser's three taste" brings together beef, lobster, and salmon in a great starter, while crisp fried soft shell crabs married with turmeric and pumpkin curry comes as a starter or entree, and whitebait fritters are served with a tamarind sauce. To maximize the view, ask for a seat on the terrace.

Fraser Ave. (near the Information Kiosk), Kings Park. ✆ **08/9481 7100.** Reservations required. Main courses A$30–A$55 (US$24–US$44/UK£12–UK£22). 10% Sun surcharge. AE, DC, MC, V. Breakfast weekends and public holidays from 8am. Daily noon–late. Closed Good Friday. Bus: 37 and 39 stop behind the Information Kiosk. Red CAT Stop 26 (Havelock St.) is 2 blocks from the gates.

Jackson's ★★★ *Moments* MODERN AUSTRALIAN/INTERNATIONAL Understated contemporary design and ambience only help to emphasize the quality of the food here. Chef Neil Jackson has a loyal clientele, and a host of awards for his ability to bring out the best in local produce, with some quirky touches based partly on his English background. This place is a short distance out of town but worth the trip. The menu changes seasonally but with a reputation for duck dishes and soufflés, both sweet and savory. His degustation menu, called "the dego," offers nine courses, with suggested matching wines. Friday and Saturday are booked out weeks ahead, and diners are warned "this food may contain traces of nuts, love, quality produce, and passion!"

483 Beaufort St., Highgate. ✆ **08/9328 1177.** Reservations essential. Main courses A$38 (US$30/UK£16); "the dego" A$95 (US$76/UK£39) or A$150 (US$120/UK£61) with wines. AE, DC, MC, V. Mon–Sat 7pm–late. Closed Good Friday. Bus: 21 or 67 (limited night services) by Queen's Tavern.

Lamont's East Perth ★★★ MODERN AUSTRALIAN Kate Lamont has a well-deserved reputation for the flavor-driven food she produces at her three restaurants, in Margaret River, Swan Valley, and here. The menu changes regularly depending on the availability of seasonal produce. Marron (a local crustacean) is a specialty, presented in various manners, especially a poached version with pea risotto. Desserts are tapas-style, encouraging shared tastings. Weekend breakfast features a triple layer pyramid of various ingredients; more of a brunch offering. The modern glass-fronted restaurant faces directly on to Claisebrook Inlet, with the Swan River 50m (164 ft.) away, and the Holmes à Court Gallery is right next door. There's an extensive wine list, with the option to take away the Lamont family wines, at cellar door prices.

11 Brown St., East Perth. ✆ **08/9202 1566.** Reservations essential. Main courses A$36–A$42 (US$29–US$34/UK£15–UK£17). AE, DC, MC, V. Tues 10am–5pm; Wed–Fri 10am–late; Sat 9am–late; Sun 9am–5pm. Closed public holidays. Bus: Yellow Cat Stop 5 (Trafalgar Rd.) then cross Claisebrook bridge.

Must Wine Bar ★ BISTRO This place has one of Australia's finest wine lists, and there's some pretty good food, too. Check out the cool contemporary design, with suspended wine rack separating bar from restaurant. It's a trendy hangout especially on Friday and Saturday nights. There are 600 wines in stock, with some 50 available by the glass. Food is contemporary French, with a charcuterie plate (shared appetizer) and beef cheek ravioli specialties.

519 Beaufort St., Highgate (close to Jackson's). ✆ **08/9328 8255.** Reservations recommended on weekends. Main courses A$24–A$38 (US$19–US$30/UK£9.80–UK£16). AE, DC, MC, V. Daily noon–late. Closed public holidays. Bus: 21 or 67 (limited night services) by Queen's Tavern.

Moderate

44 King Street ★★ BISTRO Socialites, hip corporate types, and plain casuals adorn this bustling sophisticated hangout—for a meal, a snack, or just good coffee, roasted on-site. The interior is a mix of industrial design and European cafe, with dark timber tables, exposed air ducts, and windows onto the street. The open kitchen produces all its own bread and pastries, and has a weekly changing menu with some weird and wonderful choices—such as fennel-roasted duck with paella of Valencia, or Cajun pink snapper with sweet-potato frites and avocado sour cream. The menu helpfully lists wine suggestions for each dish, and offers over 70 wines by the glass from around A$8 (US$6.40/UK£3.30), and taster glasses too. There's also a good beer selection.

44 King St. ✆ **08/9321 4476.** Reservations not accepted. Breakfast A$10–A$17 (US$8–13/UK£4–6.80), lunch and dinner A$18–A$38 (US$14–US$30/UK£7.35–UK£16). 10% surcharge weekends and public holidays. AE, DC, MC, V. Daily 7am–late. Closed Dec 25 and Good Friday. Bus: Red CAT Stop 29 (King St.); Blue CAT Stop 1 (Cloisters).

Miss Maud Swedish Restaurant ★ *Value* INTERNATIONAL "Good food and plenty of it" is the motto at Miss Maud's homey establishment, and the crowds packing the place prove it works. Most diners skip the a la carte menu and go straight for the smorgasbord. At breakfast, that means 50 dishes, including pancakes cooked before your eyes. At lunch and dinner you can tuck into soup, 10 salads, a big range of seafood (including oysters at dinner), cold meats, roasts, hot vegetables, pasta, cheeses, European-style breads, half a dozen tortes, fruit, and ice cream—65 dishes in all. Service is fast and polite.

97 Murray St. (at Pier St.), below the Miss Maud Swedish Hotel. ✆ **08/9325 3900.** Reservations recommended. Smorgasbord breakfast A$22 (US$18/UK£9) Mon–Sat, A$24 (US$19/UK£9.80) Sun and holidays; lunch A$30 (US$24/UK£12) Mon–Sat, A$34 (US$27/UK£14) Sun and holidays; dinner A$39 (US$31/UK£16) Sun–Fri, A$43 (US$34/UK£18) Sat and holidays. Significant discounts for children 4–13. A la carte main courses, sandwiches, and light meals A$8–A$30 (US$6.40–US$24/UK£3.30–UK£12). AE, DC, MC, V. Daily smorgasbord times 6:45–10am (11am on Sun and holidays), noon–2:30pm (3pm on Sun and holidays), and 5pm–late. A la carte, coffee, and cake served all day. Bus: Red CAT Stop 1 (Pier St.); Blue CAT Stop 5 (Murray St. Mall E.).

Inexpensive

Fast Eddy's Café FAST FOOD This place is open 24/7. A hefty menu of steaks, burgers, sandwiches, soups, pancakes, sundaes, shakes, and full fry-up brekkies (breakfasts) are served all hours at this popular chain. The interior sports 1930s soap-powder posters and Coca-Cola advertisements. One side is table service; the same food minus the side orders will cost you about half the already-low prices at the Victorian-era-meets-1950s counter-service diner and takeout section on the other side.

454 Murray St. (at Milligan St.). ✆ **08/9321 2552.** Main courses A$10–A$30 (US$8–US$24/UK£4.10–UK£9.80). MC, V. Daily 24 hr. Bus: Red CAT Stop 28 (Milligan St.).

IN NORTHBRIDGE

The area is jampacked with cafes and restaurants, many reflecting the waves of migration that have made this part of Perth a staging point in their assimilation. Italian, Greek, Chinese, and Vietnamese have all lived here and now cook here.

Romany Restaurant ITALIAN In new premises since October 2006 this long-lasting traditional Italian restaurant has a new life. It has a classy but comfortable appearance with maroon (a subtle version) chairs and walls, in and out, which show up the brilliant white tablecloths. The effect is to make you feel that you could happily spend several hours here, and the staff wouldn't mind. The mains are mainstream Italian, featuring dishes such as veal parmigiana with spaghetti, *osso buco,* and *capretto* (baby goat). A lot of regulars appear at lunch and weekends.

105 Aberdeen St., Northbridge. ✆ **08/9328 8042.** Reservations recommended for dinner Fri–Sat. Main courses A$19–A$27 (US$15–US$22/UK£7.75–UK£11). 10% surcharge public holidays. AE, DC, MC, V. Mon–Fri noon–2:30pm (last orders) and 5:30pm–9:30pm (last orders); Sat 5:30pm–late. Closed Good Friday, Apr 25, and for 3 weeks from Dec 24. Bus: Blue CAT Stop 11.

IN SUBIACO

Star Anise ★★ *Finds* ASIAN-INFLUENCED AUSTRALIAN In 9 years chef/owner David Coomer has taken this small restaurant in a quiet suburban street to be rated perhaps best in Perth. The converted house features several dining areas including a small open courtyard, and the decor is clean and subtle with Asian influences and contemporary artworks. The innovative menu is done daily and features a Signature Menu of six fixed courses (with suggested wines). The a la carte section is kept simple with five courses listed in each of the appetizer, main, and dessert sections. Among David's noted creations are crispy aromatic duck, seared scallops, and licorice ice cream. Tuesday is an optional BYO (bring your own alcohol) night.

225 Onslow Rd., Shenton Park (next to Subiaco). ✆ **08/9381 9811.** Reservations recommended. Main courses A$39–A$58 (US$31–US$46/UK£16–UK£24); Signature Menu A$110 (US$88/UK£45) food only, A$160 (US$128/UK£65) with wine. AE, DC, MC, V. Tues–Sat 6:30–10:30pm. Closed Good Friday, Apr 25, Christmas, and Dec 31. Train: Shenton Park, but taxi preferable.

Witch's Cauldron ★★ MODERN AUSTRALIAN Australia's best garlic prawns arrive preceded by a wafting cloud of sizzling garlic. The Cauldron has twice been voted as Perth's favorite restaurant. Started in a single room in 1971, its owners Geoff and Tanis Gosling have expanded it into a large double-story establishment but without

---

Tips **Late-Nite Bites**

Eating after midnight in Perth can be a problem. Fast Eddy's (see above) and Vulture's (✆ **08/9227 9087**; corner William and Francis streets; open 'til midnight Sun-Thurs, until 3am Fri-Sat) are options; otherwise try Chung Wah Lane in Northbridge. It's more China-alley than Chinatown, with several Chinese restaurants, including **Uncle Bill,** tucked behind a red gilt Chinese gateway at 60 Roe St. (between William and Lake sts., behind the Bus Station). They all open daily between 5pm and 6pm, and close at 4am.

---

compromising style or standards. They have even bought some street-side parking bays, effectively extending the restaurant right across the sidewalk. Numerous witches, including political cartoons, adorn the walls and ceilings without being kitsch. One feature is a series of circular banquettes for cozy dining for groups of four to six. Service is brisk, friendly, and efficient. Besides the garlic prawns there's an emphasis on simple cooking of quality fish and steak. Try tournedos chasseur or cobbler (or dhufish) meuniere. Also open for breakfast (but without garlic prawns).

89 Rokeby Rd. (near Hay St.), Subiaco ✆ **08/9381 2508.** Reservations recommended, especially when major events at nearby Subiaco Oval. Main courses A$27–A$48 (US$22–US$38/UK£11–UK£20); lunch includes set menus, A$30 (US$24/UK£12) 2 courses, A$42 (US$34/UK£17) 3 courses. AE, DC, MC, V. Daily 7:30–11am, noon–5pm, and 6pm–late. Closed Good Friday, Apr 25, Christmas, and Dec 31. Train: Subiaco.

AT THE BEACH

The Blue Duck *Kids* INTERNATIONAL/PIZZA For ocean views and a lively atmosphere, it's hard to beat this casual restaurant perched right over the sand. The balcony has pride of place and is always booked out, but the interior doesn't miss out with full-length picture windows. It's popular throughout the day, with sunset time especially appealing, but recent reports suggest that standards can slip when the place is busy. North Cottesloe Beach is a favorite spot for early-morning bathers, so breakfast is served from 6:30am, with the full menu available from noon. The menu has light choices with a variety of salads, while the seafood tasting plate is always popular.

151 Marine Parade, North Cottesloe. ✆ **08/9385 2499.** Reservations recommended. Breakfast A$10–A$20 (US$8.90–US$16/UK£4–UK£8); main courses A$24–A$34 (US$19–US$27/UK£9.80–UK£14), pizzas A$15–A$21 (US$12–US$17/UK£6.15–UK£8.60). Kids' menu A$7–A$10 (US$5.60–US$8/UK£2.85–UK£4.10). AE, MC, V. Daily 6:30am–10:30pm. Bus: 102 or 381.

IN FREMANTLE

The Capri *Value* ITALIAN A Fremantle institution, this place has been owned by the Pizzale family for 50 years, and the decor probably hasn't changed in that time. This is dining as it once was—no fussy furnishings, just good honest Italian grub. Free bread and water are served immediately, and complimentary soup with main courses. It's unlicensed so BYO. Here you'll find standard Italian fare, such as spaghetti marinara and scallopine, available in small or large servings. It's right in the middle of the Cappuccino Strip.

21 South Terrace, Fremantle. ✆ **08/9335 1399.** Main courses A$20–A$25 (US$16–US$20/UK£8.15–UK£10). AE, DC, MC, V. Daily noon–2pm and 5–10pm. Train: Fremantle.

Cicirello's *Value* *Kids* SEAFOOD Right on Fremantle's Fishing Boat Harbour, this is one of several places offering freshly cooked, tasty fish and chips—and other seafood. It's a functional, volume restaurant but still has character. Large fish tanks (for show) are the decorative feature, and floor-to-ceiling glass doors lead out to the broad timber balcony, also with seating, directly above the water. Fishing boats are moored next door. The food comes battered and fried, or grilled, but the essential meal is fish and chips. There's a kid's menu.

44 Mews Rd. (Fishermans Wharf), Fremantle. ✆ **08/9335 1911.** Main courses A$10–A$25 (US$8–US$20/UK£4.10–UK£10). AE, DC, MC, V. Daily 9am–9pm. Closed Dec 25. Train: Fremantle.

The Essex ★★ *Moments* MODERN AUSTRALIAN For a quiet, elegant, romantic night out The Essex is hard to beat. Located just off Fremantle's Cappuccino Strip, and up the road from the Esplanade Hotel, it's in a restored 120-year-old limestone cottage, with the dining areas spread among several rooms. The service is discreet but

Tips **Cappuccino Strip**

Don't leave Freo without a "short black" (that's an espresso) or a "flat white" (coffee with milk) at one of the many alfresco cafes along South Terrace. On weekends the street bursts at the seams with locals flocking to Italian-style eateries that serve good coffee and excellent focaccia, pasta, and pizza. **DOME, Old Papa's,** and **Gino's** are three to look for.

can leave you unattended at times. Try the Balmain bugs (a curiously flattened, but tasty, crustacean) and ravioli, or the beef Gabrielle filled with scallops.

20 Essex St., Fremantle. ✆ **08/9335 5725.** Reservations recommended. Main courses A$30–A$52 (US$24–US$42/UK£12–UK£21); lunch A$32 (US$26/UK£13) 2 courses, A$39 (US$31/UK£13) 3 courses. AE, DC, MC, V. Daily 6pm–late; lunches Wed–Fri and Sun from noon. Train: Fremantle. Bus: Fremantle Cat (South or Marine Terrace)—does not run at night.

Little Creatures PUB/PIZZA This place is hard to categorize but is essentially a noshery serving good cheap food to showcase the beers made on-site. Half the huge tin shed (which once housed boats) is the award-winning microbrewery, also called Little Creatures, with the stainless-steel tanks in full view of bar and eating area, and with an open kitchen. It's all rather barnlike with ultra-simple furnishings but there's a lively atmosphere. The wood-fired pizzas, tapas-type dishes, and freshly cut frites are best known. The staff, known as "creatures," are young but friendly.

40 Mews Rd., Fremantle. ✆ **08/9430 5155.** Mains A$12–A$20 (US$9.60–US$16/UK£4–UK£8.15). MC, V. Mon–Fri 10am–midnight; Sat–Sun brunch from 9am. Closed Dec 25. Train: Fremantle.

WHAT TO SEE & DO IN PERTH

AQWA (Aquarium of Western Australia) ★ *Kids* There are no performing dolphins, but there's plenty to see, including Australia's largest walk-through aquarium, where you are surrounded by 4m (13-ft.) sharks, rays, turtles, and hundreds of colorful fish. AQWA specializes in the various ocean ecosystems around WA, and has a touch pool, a great attraction for small (and bigger) kids; a lagoon full of stingrays; and the Seal Island underwater viewing area to watch endangered sea lions at play. You can come face to fin with pretty leafy sea dragons, and observe some of the ocean's deadliest such as blue-ringed octopus and stonelike stonefish. Keepers feed the sharks and the touch-pool creatures daily, and a program of talks and movies on marine creatures runs throughout the day. For A$125 (US$100/UK£51) plus A$20 (US$16/UK£8.15) for snorkel gear or A$40 (US$32/UK£16) for dive gear (diving qualifications required), you can **swim with the sharks** (daily 1pm and 3pm). Advance bookings essential. Allow half a day here.

Sorrento Quay at Hillarys Boat Harbour, 91 Southside Dr., Hillarys. ✆ **08/9447 7500.** www.aqwa.com.au. Admission A$25 (US$20/UK£10) adults, A$18 (US$14/UK£7.35) seniors and students, A$14 (US$11/UK£5.70) children 4–15, free for children under 4, A$65 (US$52/UK£27) family of 4. Daily 10am–5pm; sometimes later in Jan. Closed Dec 25. Train: Joondalup line to Warwick, transfer to bus 423. By car, take Mitchell Fwy. 23km (14 miles) north, turn left onto Hepburn Ave. and proceed to roundabout at entrance to Hillarys Boat Harbour; AQWA is at the western end of the harbor.

Art Gallery of Western Australia This is a well-laid-out and attractive gallery. Most outstanding among the international and Australian sections is the Aboriginal art collection, regarded as the finest in Australia. There are regular visiting exhibitions. Free 1-hour tours of a particular collection run Tuesday through Thursday and Sunday at 11am and 1pm; Friday tours are at 12:30pm and 2pm; Saturday at 1pm.

Roe St. and Beaufort St. (enter near the walkway opposite Perth Railway Station), Northbridge. ✆ **08/9492 6600** administration, or 08/9492 6622 recorded info line. www.artgallery.wa.gov.au. Free admission. Entry fee may apply to special exhibitions. Daily 10am–5pm. Closed Good Friday, Dec 25, and until 1pm Apr 25 (Anzac Day). Train: Perth. Bus: Blue CAT Stop 7 (Museum).

Cohunu Koala Park *Kids* WA allows koala cuddling, and this large park set in bushland is the only place to do so. You can also feed kangaroos, wallabies, and emus wandering in natural enclosures, see wombats and dingoes, walk through an aviary housing Aussie native birds, and see wild water birds on the ponds. The Caversham Wildlife Park in the Swan Valley (see "Side Trips from Perth," later in the chapter) has a bigger, more intriguing range of native species, but does not allow koala cuddling. It's hard to get here without a car; if you don't have one, a taxi will cost about A$50 (US$40/UK£20).

Off Mills Rd. E., Martin (Gosnells). ✆ **08/9390 6090**; www.cohunu.com.au. Admission A$25 (US$20/UK£10) adults, A$12 (US$9.60/UK£4.90) children 5–14. Koala-cuddling A$25 (US$20/UK£10) and you take your own photo/video. Daily 9:30am–5pm (winter 10am); koala photo sessions 10am–4pm. Closed Dec 25. Train: Armadale line to Gosnells, then cab (about A$15/US$12/UK£6.15). Train: Armadale Line to Gosnells, then taxi. Bus: 219. By car, take Riverside Dr. across Swan River onto Albany Hwy., follow for approximately 25km (16 miles) to Gosnells, turn left onto Tonkin Hwy. and right onto Mills Rd. E. (about 35-min. drive from city) to the top of the hills.

His Majesty's Theatre and King Street ★★ A lovely old wedding cake of an Edwardian theater, the venue was rescued and revamped in 1979. It's Perth's major venue for the WA Ballet and Opera companies and visiting theater productions, including those for the Perth International Arts Festival. Friends (volunteers) of His Majesty's are on hand Monday to Friday 10am to 4pm, to provide information and tours of the theater (unless it's in use) and public areas for a donation. Downstairs houses the Museum of Performing Arts with an engrossing collection of costumes and other memorabilia. A modern cafe, **Barre,** occupies part of the ground floor. King Street, just north of the theater, is a charming little thoroughfare with numerous restored buildings housing upmarket bistros, galleries, and fashion stores.

Theater on corner of Hay St. and King St., Perth. ✆ **08/9265 0900** administration. www.hismajestystheatre.com.au. Or check daily newspapers for current productions. Performing Arts Museum Mon–Fri 10am–4pm with gold coin donation. King St. outlets include 44 King Street (see "Where to Dine," earlier in this chapter) and Creative Native (see "The Shopping Scene," later in this chapter).

Holmes à Court Gallery This small riverside gallery (next to Lamont's Restaurant) offers rotating exhibitions from one of the country's most outstanding private art collections, that of Janet Holmes à Court, Australia's richest woman. Many of the works are Aboriginal or by well-known Australian artists such as Sidney Nolan.

11 Brown St., East Perth. ✆ **08/9218 4540.** Free admission. Wed–Sun noon–5pm. Closed public holidays. Train: Claisebrook.

Kings Park & Botanic Garden ★★★ In prime position, overlooking both the city and Swan River, is this 406-hectare (1000-acre) hilltop jewel of parkland, botanical gardens, and native bush. The main entry, along Fraser Avenue, is lined with magnificent

---

Moments **Picture-Perfect**

For the only photo of Perth you'll need, snap the view over the city and river from the lookout in Kings Park—it's superb day or night.

Moments Anzac Day Dawn Service

Anzac Day (Apr 25), which commemorates the Australian landings at Gallipoli in 1915 which helped to define the nation, is the most poignant public holiday in Australia. The Perth Dawn Service is held by the War Memorial in Kings Park. You arrive in the dark and ease your way into the throng. The muffled tapping of a drum marks the official procession to the memorial, then the service starts as the pre-dawn light reveals a hushed crowd of over 30,000, young and old. The sun rises behind the memorial, silhouetted against the Swan River, and the Last Post sounds.

lemon-scented gums. You can inspect Western Australian flora; experience the solitude of the bush; and bike, stroll, or drive an extensive network of roads and trails. A walk through the Botanic Garden showcases many of the state's plant species, including banksias and boabs, and leads to the Federation Walkway, a glass arched bridge that soars through the treetops. Visiting the spring **wildflower displays** (which peak Aug–Oct) is a highlight for many, with an excellent Wildflower Festival in late September. There are barbecue and picnic facilities, several extensive playgrounds, tearooms, an Information Centre manned by volunteer guides, the stylish **Aspects of Kings Park** craft shop (p. 484), and the incomparable **Fraser's** restaurant (p. 469).

Pick up self-guiding maps from the Visitor Information Centre, or join one of the free guided walks leaving from opposite the Centre. Walks depart daily at 10am and 2pm and take 1½ hours, or 2 or 3 hours for bushwalks (May–Oct only). The **Perth Tram Co.** (✆ **08/9322 2006**) runs half-hour (hop on and off) tours of the park in replica wooden trams. Tours depart from the main car park off Fraser Avenue daily at 11am, 12:15pm, 1:05pm, and 2:25pm. Tickets cost A$6 (US$4.80/UK£2.45) for adults, A$3 (US$2.40/UK£1.25) for children. Buy tickets on board.

Fraser Ave. off Kings Park Rd. ✆ **08/9480 3634** Information Centre, or 08/9480 3600 administration. www.bgpa.wa.gov.au. Free admission. Park daily 24 hr. Information Centre daily 9:30am–4pm (closed Dec 25). Bus: 33 stops outside the Information Centre and extends into the park on Sat afternoon, and much of the day Sun and public holidays. Red CAT Stop 25 (Havelock St.) is 1 block north of the entrance.

Perth Mint ★ This lovely historic building—built in the 1890s to refine gold and mint currency from the Kalgoorlie gold rush—is one of the world's oldest mints operating from its original premises. It now produces legal-tender precious metal coins and commemorative medallions for investors and collectors around the world, and bullion is still traded here. The "Gold Exhibition" allows visitors to see Australia's biggest collection of nuggets, watch gold coins being minted, handle a 400-ounce gold bar, and engrave their own medallion. Tours start with a guided heritage walk on the half-hour, and lead on to the molten gold pouring demonstration (on the hour 10am–4pm weekdays, and 10am–noon on weekends and public holidays). The shop sells gold coins and nugget jewelry, and the Tea Garden provides a quiet spot to relax.

310 Hay St. (at Hill St.), East Perth. ✆ **08/9421 7223.** www.perthmint.com.au. Admission to the Gold Exhibition A$15 (US$12/UK£6.15) adults, A$13 (US$10/UK£5.30) seniors and students, A$5 (US$4/UK£1.65) school-age children. Shop admission free. Mon–Fri 9am–5pm; Sat–Sun and holidays 9am–1pm. Closed Jan 1, Good Friday, Apr 25 (Anzac Day), and Dec 25. Bus: Red CAT Stop 10 (Perth Mint).

Perth Zoo *Kids* This is an excellent modern zoo—with re-created natural habitats and no cages in sight. It has several successful breeding programs, including being a

Moments Catch the Fireworks

Australia Day (Jan 26) commemorates the arrival of the First Fleet in Australia. The main celebrations in Perth are around Perth Water, climaxing with a massive fireworks display set off from moored barges. It's free and draws over 300,000 people so you need to stake out a vantage point early or, if you're staying in a hotel with river views, make sure you're at the window!

world leader with orangutans. Others cover white rhinos, African painted dogs, and a number of West Australian fauna, including the numbat, which is WA's animal emblem. This is a good place to see a wide range of Australian wildlife such as kangaroos, koalas, wombats, quokkas, emus, echidnas (the Aussie answer to the porcupine), and penguins, and there's a walk-through aviary. Exotic animals include other apes, Rothschild's giraffes, lions, tigers, meerkats, and elephants. Feeding demonstrations and talks run throughout the day. Volunteer guides, called docents, are always around to provide information, and conduct free daily walking tours at 1:30pm and 11am (Sept–Apr). You can do a behind-the-scenes Close Encounters Tour (with 3 weeks notice), and buy paintings by the zoo's elephants.

20 Labouchere Rd., South Perth. © **08/9474 3551** for recorded information, or 08/9474 0444 administration. www.perthzoo.wa.gov.au. Admission A$17 (US$14/UK£6.95) adults, A$8.50 (US$6.80/UK£3.50) children 4–15, A$45 (US$36/UK£16) family of 4. Zebra car tour A$3.50 (US$2.80/UK£1.45) adults, A$2.50 (US$2/UK£1) student/senior rate. Daily 9am–5pm. Ferry: Barrack St. Jetty to Mends St. Jetty, South Perth. Bus: 30 or 31.

Swan Bells A needlelike tower, wrapped in copper sails, was specially built to house a complete "ring" of 18 bells, 12 with centuries of history from London's St. Martin-in-the-Fields (given to Perth for Australia's Bi-Centenary), and the others specially cast. The tower stands out above Barrack Street Jetty on the Swan River, immediately below the city. It has had to be soundproofed to minimize disturbing people working nearby but, as a result, can hardly be heard away from the jetty.

Barrack Square, Perth. © **08/9218 8183.** www.swanbells.com.au. Admission A$10 (US$8/UK£4.10) adults, A$7 (US$5.60/UK£2.85) student/senior rate, children under 5 free. Daily from 10am. Closed Good Friday and Dec 25. Full bell ringing Mon, Tues, Thurs, and weekends noon–1pm. Bus: Blue CAT to Barrack Square.

Swan River ★★ The river is a great natural and free asset to the city. Perth Water, immediately below the CBD, is a superb foreground and mirror to the city—best seen from South Perth, and stunning at and just after sunset. The South Perth ferry (see "Getting Around" earlier in this section) is the easiest way of getting there. Perth Water is shallow, so ideal for "messing about in boats," and small catamarans can be hired on the South Perth foreshore. Once past the Narrow Bridge, the river widens out and becomes home to several yacht clubs. Biking along riverside pathways is a great way to enjoy the city, the river, and the weather. You can rent both boats and bikes (information below).

Surfcat hire: South Perth foreshore. © **0408 926 003** in Australia. www.funcats.com.au. Bike rental: corner Riverside Drive and Plain St. © **08/9221 2665.** www.aboutbikehire.com.au.

Western Australian Museum *Kids* Kids will like the dinosaur gallery, the drawers full of insects, the blue whale skeleton on the well-stocked aquatic zoology floor, the "megamouth" shark preserved in a tank in the ground in the courtyard, and assorted other examples of Australia's weird natural creatures. The main attraction for grown-ups is one of Australia's best displays of Aboriginal culture and heritage ("Listen to our stories"), and rare photographs, many housed in the Old Gaol (1856). Allow 90 minutes to see most highlights.

Off James St. Mall, Cultural Centre, Northbridge. ✆ **08/9212 3700.** Enter by gold coin donation. Fee may apply for temporary exhibitions. Daily 9:30am–5pm. Closed Good Friday, Dec 25–26, and until 1pm Apr 25 (Anzac Day). Train: Perth. Bus: Blue CAT Stop 8 (Museum).

Yanchep National Park *Kids* This is the best place in Perth to see some traditional Aboriginal culture, with presentations three times a day on Saturdays and Sundays. The park is 51km (32 miles) north of the city, set in glorious natural woodland, around a reed-fringed lake. You can follow a boardwalk through the koala enclosure, hire a rowboat, take a limestone cavern tour, have a coffee and snack (or beer) at the historic Tudor-style Yanchep Inn, or admire the wildlife. Kangaroos abound, there are resident (and noisy) black cockatoos, and other birds include swans, pelicans, wrens, parrots, and kookaburras.

Off Wanneroo Rd., Yanchep. ✆ **08/9561 1004.** Entry fee A$10 (US$8/UK£4.10) per vehicle. Tours, including the Aboriginal presentation, A$6.50 (US$5.20/UK£2.65) adults, A$3.50 (US$2.80/UK£1.45) children, A$16 (US$12/UK£6.55) families (2 adults, 2 children). Daily 9:15am–4:30pm. Aboriginal tours Sat–Sun at 1pm, 2pm, and 3pm. By car, take Wellington St. west and turn into Thomas St., which feeds into Wanneroo Rd. Follow this for about 45km (28 miles) to the park turnoff.

HITTING THE BEACHES

Perth shares Sydney's good luck in having beaches in the metropolitan area—in an almost continuous line from Cottesloe in the south to Quinns Rocks in the north, including a section called the Sunset Coast. Mornings are usually best, because the sea breeze can make the afternoons unpleasant in summer. Evenings and sunsets are lovely on quiet days. Always swim between the red and yellow flags, which denote a safe swimming zone.

Bus nos. 400 and 408 run to Scarborough Beach every 15 minutes each day, while 102 goes to Cottesloe every 30 minutes. Bus no. 458 operates a summer timetable along the northern beaches from Scarborough to Hillarys, half-hourly on weekends and public holidays and hourly on weekdays, in both directions. Surfboards under 1.2m (4 ft.) can be carried on 400, 408, and 458. Bus no. 381 operates a weekday service between Fremantle and Warwick, with stops at both Cottesloe and Scarborough.

The three most popular beaches are Cottesloe, Scarborough, and Trigg.

COTTESLOE This pretty crescent, graced by the Edwardian-style Indiana Tea House, is Perth's most fashionable beach. It has grassed slopes overlooking the beach, safe swimming, and a small surf break. Some good cafes and hotels are nearby. Train: Cottesloe, then walk several hundred meters (between a quarter- and a half-mile). Bus: 102.

SCARBOROUGH Scarborough's white sands stretch for miles from the base of the **Hotel Rendezvous Observation City** (p. 467). Swimming is generally safe, and

Tips **Going with the Gold**

Australia has $1 and $2 coins which are a dull bronze but generally known as "gold." It's common for attractions or charities to request "gold coin" contributions as an entry fee.

A Pesky Sea Breeze

In the summer, Perth gets an easterly offshore breeze in the morning then, as the land heats up, it switches to be a southwesterly on-shore wind. This is called the "Fremantle Doctor" because it blows up the river from Fremantle and provides relief on hot summer days. The timing and strength of the breeze varies and it can be almost gale force, whipping up the sand on exposed beaches. Check the daily weather forecast for likely wind strength.

surfers are always guaranteed a wave, although inexperienced swimmers should take a rain check when the surf is rough. The Australian Surf Life Saving Championships will be held here in late March 2008 and 2009. The busy shopping precinct across the road means there's always somewhere to buy lunch and drinks. Bus: 400.

TRIGG Surfers like Trigg best for its consistent swells, but it can have dangerous rips. Stay within the flags. Bus: 400 to Scarborough, then walk, or bus 458 (summer).

A DAY OUT IN FREMANTLE ★★

The heritage port precinct of **Fremantle,** 19km (12 miles) from downtown Perth on the mouth of the Swan River, is probably best known outside Australia as the site of the 1987 America's Cup challenge. In the lead-up to that event, the city embarked on a major restoration of its gracious warehouses and Victorian buildings. Today "Freo" is a bustling district of 150 National Trust buildings, alfresco cafes, museums, galleries, pubs, markets, and shops in a masterfully preserved historical atmosphere. European influences are strong, thanks to the migrant fishermen, especially Italians, who made Fremantle their new home. It's still a working port, so you can see fishing boats unloading in the Fishing Harbour on one side, and yachts and container ships gliding in and out of the main commercial river-mouth harbor on the other. Much of the buzz has gone from the historic heart with many buildings taken over by the local Notre Dame University. Weekends are best, with a wonderful hubbub of buzzing shoppers, merchants, coffee drinkers, locals, tourists, and fishermen. Allow a full day to take in even half the sights—and don't forget to knock back a beer or two on the veranda of one of the gorgeous old pubs.

ESSENTIALS

GETTING THERE Parking is plentiful, but driving is frustrating in the maze of one-way streets. Most attractions are within walking distance (or accessible on the free CAT bus), so take the train to Fremantle and explore on foot.

A nice way to get to Freo and see Perth's river suburbs is on the cruises that run once or twice a day from Barrack Street Jetty. See "Whale-Watching Cruises, Tram Trips & Other Tours," below, for cruise operators.

GETTING AROUND The orange Fremantle CAT bus makes a comprehensive running loop of local attractions every 10 minutes Monday through Friday from 7:30am to 6:30pm, and on weekends and holidays from 10am to 6:30pm, except Good Friday and December 25 and 26. It is free and departs from the train station.

VISITOR INFORMATION The **Fremantle Visitors Centre** is in Town Hall, Kings Square (at High St.), Fremantle, WA 6160 (© **08/9431 7878;** www.fremantlewa.com.au). It's open Monday through Friday from 9am to 5pm, Saturday 10am to 3pm, Sunday 11:30am to 2:30pm, closed public holidays. The best website is that of the Fremantle Council, **www.fremantle.wa.gov.au**.

Fremantle

ACCOMMODATIONS ■
Esplanade Hotel **12**
Fothergill's **17**

DINING ◆
The Capri **14**
Cicirello's **10**
The Essex **13**
Little Creatures **11**

ATTRACTIONS ●
E-Shed Markets **5**
Fremantle Arts Centre/ History Museum **1**
Fremantle Fishing Boat Harbour **9**
Fremantle Markets **15**
Fremantle Prison **16**
Fremantle Railway Station **4**
High Street Shopping Mall **3**
The Roundhouse **7**
Shipwreck Galleries **8**
Town Hall (Visitor Centre) **2**
Western Australia Maritime Museum **6**

Pedestrian Only
Tourist Information

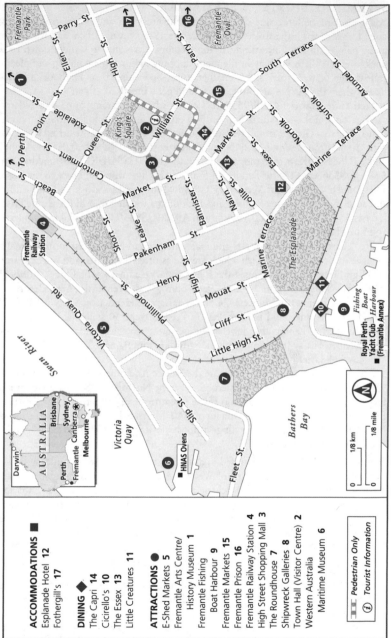

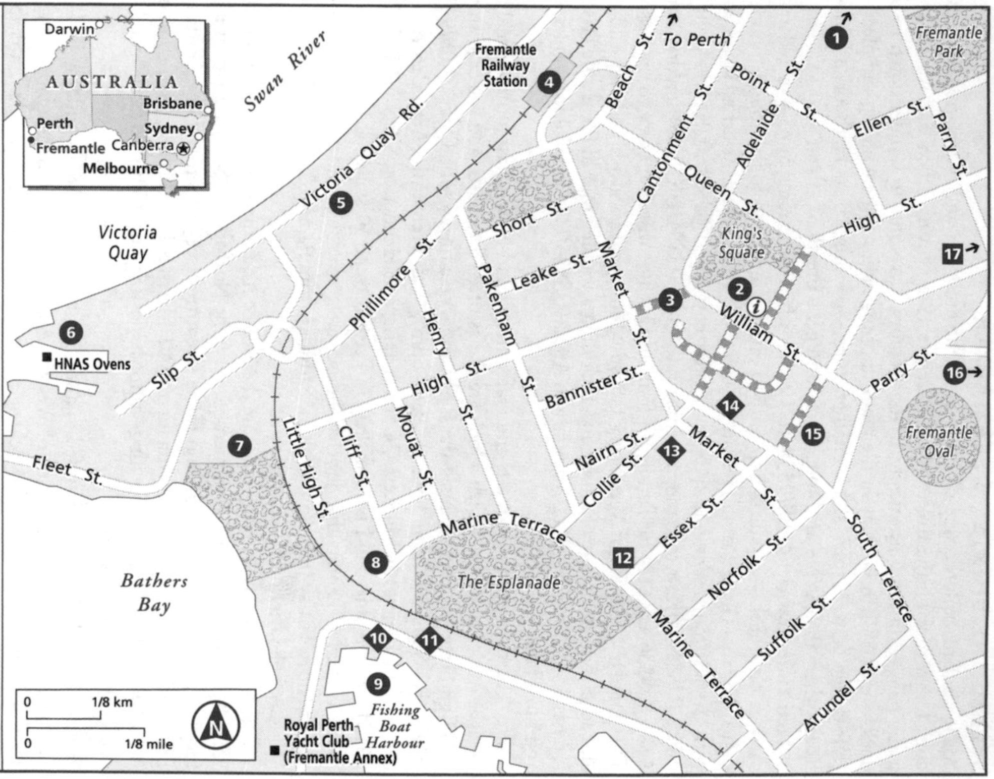

SEEING THE SIGHTS IN FREMANTLE

You'll want to explore some of Freo's excellent museums and other attractions, but don't forget to stroll the streets and admire the 19th-century offices and warehouses, many painted in rich, historically accurate colors. Take time to wander down to the docks—either Victoria Quay in the main shipping harbor, where sailing and pleasure craft dodge between tugs and container ships, or Fishing Boat Harbour, off Mews Road, where the catches are brought in—and get a breath of salt air.

Fremantle Trams (© **08/9339 8719;** www.fremantletrams.com)—an old tram carriage on wheels—conducts hop on/hop off commentated tours around the main sights. The tours depart from Fremantle Town Hall 10 times a day starting at 9:45am, with the last tour leaving at 2:45pm. Tickets cost A$20 (US$16/UK£8.15) adults, A$15 (US$12/UK£6.15) student/senior rate, A$5 (US$4/UK£2.05) children, and A$45 (US$36/UK£18) for families of four, and include discount entry to the Prison. The popular Friday-night Very Scary Ghostly Tour includes a fish-and-chips dinner and admission to a range of attractions, including a walking tour of Fremantle Prison. It costs A$48 (US$38/UK£20) adults and A$32 (US$26/UK£13) children under 15. You must book for this.

Freo's best **shopping** is for arts and crafts, from hand-blown glass to Aboriginal art to alpaca-wool clothing. Worth a look are the assorted art, crafts, and souvenir stores on **High Street** west of the mall; the **E Shed markets** on Victoria Quay © **08/9430 6393** (Fri–Sun and Mon holidays 9am–6pm); and **Fremantle Arts Centre** (see below). The **Fremantle Markets,** 74 South Terrace at Henderson Street (© **08/9335 2515**), are the oldest and best markets in Perth. Over 150 stalls sell local as well as cheap imported handicrafts, jewelry, housewares, clothing, and inexpensive food. They're open Friday from 9am to 9pm, Saturday from 9am to 5pm, and Sunday and Monday holidays from 10am to 5pm.

The most popular watering holes are the **Sail & Anchor,** 64 South Terrace (© **08/9335 8433**), which has its own microbrewery; the **Norfolk,** 47 South Terrace at Norfolk Street (© **08/9335 5405**); and **Little Creatures** (see "Where to Dine," earlier in this chapter) brewery bar and restaurant, 40 Mews Rd. in Fishing Boat Harbour (© **1300/722 850**). The happening "cappuccino strip" on South Terrace is good for people-watching—and coffee.

Fremantle Arts Centre Housed in a striking neo-Gothic 1860s building built by convicts, this center contains one of Western Australia's best contemporary arts-and-crafts galleries, with a constantly changing array of works. A shop sells crafts from Western Australia, a bookstore stocks Australian art books and literature, and the leafy courtyard cafe is the perfect place to hang out. Free concerts play on the lawn every Sunday and public holiday from October to April, from 2 to 4pm. Also here is the Fremantle History Museum (see below).

1 Finnerty St. at Ord St. © **08/9432 9555.** Free admission. Daily 10am–5pm. Closed Jan 1, Good Friday, and Dec 25–26.

Fremantle History Museum ★ Housed in a convict-built former lunatic asylum next to the Fremantle Arts Centre, this small but densely packed museum uses lots of old photographs and personal possessions to paint a realistic picture of what life was like for Fremantle's first settlers, the Aborigines they displaced, and later generations up to the present day, especially the post–World War II immigration boom.

In the Fremantle Arts Centre (see above), 1 Finnerty St. at Ord St. © **08/9430 7966.** Admission by gold coin donation. Mon–Fri 10am–4:30pm; Sat and public holidays 1–5pm; Sun 10:30am–4:30pm. Closed Jan 1, Good Friday, and Dec 25–26.

Fremantle Prison ★ Even jails boasted attractive architecture in the 1850s. This limestone jail, built to house 1,000 inmates by convicts who no doubt ended up inside it, was Perth's maximum-security prison until 1991. Take the 75-minute main tour "Doing Time" to see cells re-created in the style of past periods of the jail's history, bushranger (highwayman) Joe Moondyne's "escape-proof" cell, the gallows, workshops, chapel, jailers' houses, and cell walls featuring artwork by the former inmates. The ticket price includes an additional 45-minute tour (the precinct tour) that visits other areas, including the women's prison and commissariat, hourly after the main tour. You must book ahead for the 90-minute **torchlight tours** ★ on Wednesday and Friday only, and the 2½ hour **tunnel tour,** which takes you by foot and boat through limestone tunnels 20m (66 ft.) down.

1 The Terrace. ✆ **08/9336 9200.** www.fremantleprison.com. Free admission to prison gatehouse and visitor center. Day Tours A$16 (US$13/UK£6.55) adults, A$13 (US$10/UK£5) seniors and students, A$8 (US$6.40/UK£3.25) children 4–15 and people with disabilities A$42 (US$34/UK£17) families (maximum 3 children). Torchlight tour A$20 (US$16/UK£8.15) adults, A$16 (US$13/UK£6.55) seniors and students, A$11 (US$8.40/UK£4.50) children and people with disabilities A$50 (US$40/UK£20) families. Tunnel tour A$55 (US$44/UK£22) adults, A$38 (US$30/UK£16) children 12–15. Daily 10am–5pm. Main tours every 30 min. Precinct tours every hour 11:30am–4:30pm. Torchlight tours Wed and Fri every 20 min. from sunset. Tunnel tours hourly 9am–3:20pm. Closed Good Friday and Dec 25.

The Roundhouse This 12-sided jail is the oldest public building in the state (built in 1831). It's worth a visit for history's sake, and for the one o'clock gun. The time cannon (a replica of a gun salvaged from an 1878 wreck) is fired and a **time ball** dropped at 1pm daily, just as it was in the early 1900s, from a deck overlooking the ocean. You might be that day's honorary gunner chosen from the crowd! Volunteer guides are on hand to explain it all.

10 Arthur Head (enter over the railway line from High St.). ✆ **08/9336 6897.** Admission by gold coin donation, A$1 or A$2 (US80¢ or US$1.60/UK£.040–UK£0.80). Daily 10:30am–3:30pm. Closed Good Friday and Dec 25.

Shipwreck Galleries The massive remnant hulk of the Dutch ship ***Batavia,*** wrecked north of Perth in 1629, will stop you in your tracks as you enter one of the first displays in this fascinating museum, located in a lovely old 1850s limestone building. The *Batavia*'s story is of survival and betrayal; most of the survivors of the wreck were massacred by a handful of mutineers. The mutiny and massacre have been the subject of films and an opera. You will love the tales of old wrecks and displays of pieces of eight, glassware, cannon, and other deep-sea treasure recovered off the Western Australian coast. Displays date from the 1600s, when Dutch explorers became the first Europeans to encounter Australia. The museum is world-renowned for its work in maritime archaeology and preservation.

Cliff St. at Marine Terrace. ✆ **08/9431 8444.** Admission by gold coin donation. Daily 9:30am–5pm. Closed Good Friday, Dec 25, and until 1pm Apr 25 (Anzac Day) and Dec 26. Free tours daily 10am, 11am, 2pm, and 3pm (check at reception).

Western Australian Maritime Museum ★★ This fascinating museum at the western end of Fremantle's main harbor faces straight out through tall glass panels to the Indian Ocean. The museum looks at Fremantle's history and operations as a port, shipping in both Indian Ocean and Swan River, signaling and piloting, current sailing technology, naval defense, and Aboriginal maritime heritage. It also features historic boats, including *Australia II* (the Aussie yacht that won the America's Cup back in 1983). You can tour HMAS *Ovens,* an Oberon-class submarine, every half-hour from 10am to 4:30pm. You can buy a ticket just for the sub, or a joint one for the museum and sub, at a discount.

Victoria Quay. ✆ **08/9431 8444.** Admission A$10 (US$8/UK£4.10) adults, A$5 (US$4/UK£2.05) seniors and students, A$3 (US$2.40/UK£1.20) children 5–15, A$22 (US$18/UK£9) family (up to 6). Free admission 2nd Tues of each month. Admission to submarine only A$8 (US$6.40/UK£3.30) adults, A$5 (US$4/UK£1.65) seniors and students, A$3 (US$2.40/UK£1.20) children 5–15, A$22 (US$18/UK£9) family. Daily 9:30am–5pm. Closed Good Friday, Dec 25, and until 1pm Apr 25 (Anzac Day) and Dec 26.

WHALE-WATCHING CRUISES, TRAM TRIPS & OTHER TOURS

Oceanic Cruises (✆ **08/9325 1191**) and **Captain Cook Cruises** (✆ **08/9325 3341**) run a wide assortment of cruises on the Swan River. Some go downriver to Fremantle and return, with options to spend time in the harbor city and/or to take lunch. Full-day cruises go upstream to historic homes and vineyards in the Swan Valley. Captain Cook has a dinner cruise on the Swan River viewing the city lights, at A$89 (US$71/UK£36) adults, A$84 (US$67/UK£34) seniors, A$60 (US$48/UK£25) children 4 to 14. Oceanic Cruises offers a lunch cruise to see wild sea lions at Carnac Island, off Fremantle; the cruise from Perth costs A$99 (US$79/UK£40) adults, A$89 (US$71/UK£36) children 13 to 17, A$59 (US$47/UK£24) kids 4 to 12 (less from Fremantle).

From September through November, Perth's ocean waters are alive with humpback **whales** returning from the north with their calves. To join a 2- or 3-hour jaunt to watch them, contact **Rottnest Express** (✆ **08/9421 5888**) or Oceanic Cruises. Departure days and times vary from year to year with each operator, so check ahead. Prices are about A$35 (US$28/UK£14) adults and A$19 (US$15/UK£7.75) from Fremantle and A$56 (US$45/UK£23) or A$30 (US$24/UK£12) from Perth.

The **Perth Tram Co.** (✆ **08/9322 2006;** www.perthtram.com.au) makes a daily loop of the city, the casino, and Kings Park in replica 1899 wooden trams; hop on and off as often as you wish. Tickets, which you buy on board, cost A$24 (US$19/UK£9.80) for adults, A$10(US$8/UK£4.10) for children 4 to 14, and A$48 (US$38/UK£20) for families (up to six). City-to-casino or Kings Park single legs are also available. Join anywhere; the tram starts at 565 Hay St. at 8:30am and makes nine 90-minute narrated loops a day, every day.

Feature Tours (✆ **1800/999 819** in Australia, or 08/9475 2900; www.ft.com.au) runs a comprehensive series of half- and full-day coach tours to attractions in and around Perth, including to the Pinnacles and Margaret River.

Heli West (✆ **08/9414 1000;** www.heliwest.com.au) offers three helicopter trips: around the city for A$60 (US$48/UK£25); down the Swan River to Fremantle and return for A$150 (US$120/UK£61); and along the northern beaches and back up the Swan for A$240 (US$192/UK£98). Takeoff and landing are at Burswood Park by the river, 7 days a week.

ACTIVE PURSUITS

BIKING Perth's superb bike-track network stretches for miles along the Swan River, through Kings Park, around Fremantle, and all the way along the beaches. A great 9.5km (6-mile) track enables a complete loop around Perth Water, the broad expanse of river in front of the central business district. The state Department of Transport's cycling division, Bikewest, publishes a range of useful bike-route maps to the city. They are available in bike shops, from most newsdealers, and at the **Perth Map Centre,** 900 Hay St. (✆ **08/9322 5733**).

Rental from **About Bike Hire** by the Swan River at the corner of Riverside Drive and Plain Street (✆ **08/9221 2665;** www.aboutbikehire.com.au), about 2km (1¼ miles) from the city center, is A$9 (US$7.20/UK£3.70) for an hour, or A$30

(US$24/UK£12) for a 24-hour day for adults, and A$6 (US$4.80/UK£2.45) or A$18 (US$14/UK£7.35) for children under 12. The day rate, which reduces the longer you have the bike, requires a credit card imprint as deposit, and includes a complimentary helmet (required by law in Australia), lock, and pump. Kayaks and in-line skates can also be hired. It's open 10am to 5pm Monday to Saturday, 9am to 5pm Sunday.

GOLF Most convenient to the city is **Burswood Park Public Golf Course,** adjacent to (but not part of) the Burswood International Resort Casino, across the river on the Great Eastern Highway, Burswood (✆ **08/9362 7576** pro shop; www.burswoodpark golfcourse.com). A 9-hole round is just A$17 (US$14/UK£6.95) weekdays and A$22 (US$18/UK£9) weekends and public holidays; 18 holes are A$25 (US$20/UK£10) or A$32 (US$26/UK£13). A cart is A$22 (US$18/UK£9) and club rental A$17 (US$14/UK£5.70) for 9 holes.

Even more scenic are the 27 championship fairways designed by Robert Trent Jones, Jr., at **Joondalup Resort,** Country Club Boulevard, Connolly, a 25km (16-mile) drive north of Perth (✆ **08/9400 8811** pro shop; www.joondalup resort.com.au); and **The Vines** in the Swan Valley (✆ **08/9297 3000** resort, or 08/9297 0777 pro shop; www.vines.com.au), which has two 18-hole championship bushland courses. Joondalup has twice been ranked the number-one Resort Golf Course in Australia by *Golf Australia* magazine. Kangaroos are seen regularly on both courses. You'll pay around A$65 (US$52/UK£20) for 9 holes or A$115 (US$92/UK£47) for 18 holes weekdays at Joondalup; and A$90 (US$72/UK£37) or A$140 (US$112/UK£57) on Saturdays and Sundays; all including use of a cart. At The Vines, fees are around A$50 (US$40/UK£20) for 9 holes Monday to Friday, A$64 (US$51/UK£26) weekends, and A$85 (US$68/UK£35) Monday to Friday or A$99 (US$79/UK£40) weekends for 18 holes. Add A$25 (US$20/UK£10) per person for a buggy. Dress standards apply at all courses (that is, in general shirts with collars, closed footwear, socks, no jeans or running suits; dress shorts are acceptable.)

SAILING The tallest Tall Ship in Australia, the barquentine (three-masted) **STS *Leeuwin II*** (✆ **08/9430 4105;** www.leeuwin.com), sails from B Shed at Victoria Quay, Fremantle, when it is not on voyages around Western Australia. You get the chance to try your hand at sailing the way it used to be, even clambering up the rigging. The ship takes 2½-hour twilight or brunch trips at A$75 (US$60/UK£31) adults or A$40 (US$32/UK£16) children 3 to 12, or 4-hour half-day sails at A$99 (US$79/UK£40) adults or A$69 (US$55/UK£28) children.

Experienced sailors can sometimes find a spot in Thursdays' summer twilight events with members of the **Royal Perth Yacht Club,** Australia II Drive, Crawley (✆ **08/9389 1555,** ask for the sailing administrator), if there is a place available. It's not spinnaker sailing, so the action is at an easy pace. All-white dress standards apply.

SCUBA DIVING & SNORKELING Just 19km (12 miles) off Perth, Rottnest Island's corals, reef fish, wrecks, and limestone caverns, in 18-to-35m (59–115-ft.) visibility, are a gift from heaven to Perth divers and snorkelers. Contact **Rottnest Malibu Diving** (✆ **08/9292 5111**) on Rottnest Island (see "Side Trips from Perth," below) to rent gear or join a dive trip.

SURFING You will find good surfing at many city beaches, Scarborough and Trigg in particular. See the "Hitting the Beaches" section, earlier in this chapter. Rottnest Island (see "Side Trips from Perth," below) also has a few breaks. **Murray Smith Surf Centre,** Shop 14, Luna Maxi Mart, Scarborough (✆ **08/9245 2988**), rents long boards for A$20 (US$16/UK£8.15) for half a day or A$30 (US$24/UK£12) for the day, plus a A$100 (US$80/UK£41) refundable deposit. It also rents body boards. **Surfing WA** (© **08/9448 0004;** www.surfingaustralia.com) runs surfing classes for A$50 (US$40/UK£20) per person per hour for groups of up to eight people. It gets cheaper the bigger your group is. Boards, wet suits, and sunscreen are provided.

THE SHOPPING SCENE

Most major shops are downtown on the parallel **Hay Street** and **Murray Street malls,** and in the network of arcades running off them, such as the Plaza, City, Carillon, and Tudor-style **London Court** arcades. Off Murray Street Mall on Forrest Place is the **Forrest Chase shopping complex,** housing the Myer department store and boutiques on two levels. The other major department store, David Jones, opens on to both malls. Add to your collection of international designer brands on posh **King Street,** in the west end. **Harbourtown,** at the western edge of the city, is a large complex housing "factory outlets" of numerous retail chains.

If you want to avoid the chains, spend half a day in **Subiaco** ★ or "Subi," where Hay Street and Rokeby Road are lined with smart boutiques, galleries, cafes, antiques shops, and markets. The Colonnade shopping center at 388 Hay St. showcases some groovy young Aussie fashion designers.

Fremantle's shopping is mostly limited to a good selection of crafts, markets, and Aboriginal souvenirs, with several galleries in High Street.

Shops are open until 9pm on Friday in the city, and until 9pm on Thursday in Subiaco and Fremantle.

LOCAL ART & CRAFTS Two shops showcase contemporary ceramic, textile, glass, and jewelry products: **form** at 357 Murray St. just round the corner from King St.; and **Aspects of Kings Park** behind the Visitor Centre.

ABORIGINAL ARTS & CRAFTS **Creative Native,** 32 King St. (© **08/9321 5470**), stocks Perth's widest range of Aboriginal arts and crafts. Upstairs is a gallery selling original works by some renowned Aboriginal artists. There's another branch at 65 High St., Fremantle (© **08/9335 7438**).

Indigenart, 115 Hay St., Subiaco (© **08/9388 2899**), and 82 High St., Fremantle (© **08/9335 2911**), stocks works on canvas, paper, and bark, as well as artifacts, textiles, pottery, didgeridoos, boomerangs, and sculpture, by Aboriginal artists from all over Australia.

JEWELRY Western Australia is renowned for farming the world's best **South Sea pearls** off Broome, for Argyle **diamonds** mined in the Kimberley, and for being one of the world's biggest **gold** producers.

Finds Aboriginal Fine Art

Japingka Gallery, 47 High St., Fremantle (© **08/9335 8265**), is dedicated to encouraging and exhibiting Aboriginal art from around Australia. It has a large stock of certificated art covering a broad cross section of areas and styles. There's an ongoing exhibition program, which usually involves having the artist present for discussion and explanation. The gallery is based over two floors in a historic building in central High Street.

Moments Movies & Stars

Catch an art house movie in the superb tree-lined Somerville Auditorium in the grounds of the University of WA. Picnic on the grass beforehand (you can buy food and drinks) while the sun sets, then watch the film from rows of deck chairs, with the stars visible overhead. The season runs nightly at 8:30pm from December through March, as part of the Perth International Arts Festival.

Artisans of the Sea, corner of Marine Terrace and Collie Street, Fremantle (✆ **08/9336 3633**), sells elegant South Sea pearls and gold jewelry.

Some of Perth's other leading jewelers, where you can buy opals, Argyle diamonds, and Broome pearls, are **Costello's,** Shop 5–6, London Court (✆ **08/9325 8588**), and **Linneys,** 37 Rokeby Rd., Subiaco (✆ **08/9382 4077**).

For opals to suit all budgets, head to the Perth outlet of **Quilpie Opals,** Shop 6, Piccadilly Arcade off Hay Street Mall (✆ **08/9321 8687**).

PERTH AFTER DARK

Scoop (see "Visitor Information," earlier in this chapter) is a good source of information on festivals and concerts, theater, classical music, exhibitions, and the like. Your best guide to dance clubs, rock concerts, gig listings, and art-house cinemas is the free weekly ***X-press*** magazine, available at pubs, cafes, and music venues every Thursday. The ***West Australian*** (especially the Sat edition) and ***Sunday Times*** newspapers publish entertainment information, including cinema guides.

Two ticket agencies handle most of the city's major performing arts, entertainment, and sporting events: the performing arts–oriented **BOCS** (✆ **1800/193 300** in Australia, or 08/9484 1133; www.bocsticketing.com.au) and the sports-and-family-entertainment-oriented **Ticketmaster** (✆ **13 61 00;** www.ticketmaster.com.au). Book opera, ballet, the orchestra, and the Black Swan Theatre Company (see below) through BOCS.

THE PERFORMING ARTS The **West Australian Opera** (✆ **08/9278 8999** administration) and **West Australian Ballet** (✆ **08/9481 0707** administration) usually perform at **His Majesty's Theatre,** 825 Hay St. (see earlier in "What to See & Do in Perth"). Perth's leading theater company, the **Black Swan Theatre Company** (✆ **08/6389 0311** administration), plays at theaters around town. The **West Australian Symphony Orchestra** (✆ **08/9326 0000**) usually performs at the **Perth Concert Hall,** 5 St. Georges Terrace, but with other performances in **Kings Park** (open-air summer concerts) and the **Art Gallery.** Perth Concert Hall has the best acoustics of any such venue in Australia, and features a wide range of other artists.

Perth is an outdoors kinda place. In summer, look for outdoor concerts or jazz at **Perth Zoo** (✆ **08/9474 3551** for recorded information, or 08/9474 0444 administration); movies at Perth's several outdoor cinemas; and open-air concerts, plays, and movies in **Kings Park** (✆ **08/9480 3600** administration; **08/9480 3666** 24-hr. events information).

The **Perth International Arts Festival** ★ (✆ **08/6488 2000** administration; www.perthfestival.com.au; bookings through BOCS) is the oldest arts festival in the Southern Hemisphere, producing 3½ weeks of local and international theater, dance, music, and a wide variety of free performances every February. It makes great use of Perth's weather and outdoor venues, especially with its 4-month film festival (see below).

PUBS, BARS & NIGHTCLUBS Northbridge houses most of the city's lively pubs and dance clubs. Don't forget that Freo has good pubs, too (see "A Day Out in Fremantle," earlier in this chapter).

For a take on the traditional pub, head to the **Brass Monkey,** 209 William St. at James Street, Northbridge (© **08/9227 9596**). Downstairs are several bars, including a wine bar serving gourmet pizzas, and a beer garden. Wednesday to Saturday, head upstairs to the Glasshouse for live entertainment, including the Laugh Resort comedy club at 8pm Wednesday for a A$10 (US$8/UK£4.10) cover.

The "Subi," also known as the **Subiaco Hotel,** 465 Hay St. at Rokeby Road, Subiaco (© **08/9381 3069**), is a popular historic pub with a stylish cafe, great cocktails, and live jazz on Wednesday and Saturday nights.

The biggest and swingiest place on the nightclub scene is **Metro City**, 146 Roe Street Northbridge (© **08/9228 0500**) with 10 bars over three levels. It opens every Saturday night from 10pm with its "Super Club," featuring R&B music. The cover of A$10 (US$8/UK£5) increases to A$15 (US$12/UK£7.50) after 11pm. It opens frequently on other weekend nights, with varying cover charge, for special events with visiting bands and artists. Visit **www.metrocity.com.au** for details.

In Fremantle, the **Metropolis,** 58 S. Terrace (© **08/9336 1880**), is a complex of four dance floors and eight bars on several levels. It's open Friday 9pm to 5am, Saturday 9pm to 6am, and Sunday 9pm to 1am. The cover varies depending on the entertainment, but is usually in the A$15 (US$12/UK£6) range.

CASINO **Burswood International Resort Casino** complex, on the Great Eastern Highway just over the river from the city (© **08/9362 7777** for information) is WA's only legal casino, with 137 tables and 1,500 gaming machines, and the premium gaming Pearl Room. Some of the casino's most popular games include roulette, keno, blackjack, and two-up. The casino operates 24 hours every day except Good Friday and December 25 (closed 3am–10pm), and April 25 (Anzac Day) (closed 3am–noon), and is open to everyone over the age of 18. Dress code is "neat and tidy," with smarter standards after 7pm. There are seven restaurants and bars, a 900-seat nightclub, and a 2,300-seat theater which features numerous major international acts. Live bands, disco, cabaret performers, or karaoke play nightly. It's about a A$22 (US$18/UK£9) cab ride from the city, or take a train to Burswood station.

2 Side Trips from Perth

ROTTNEST ISLAND: GETTING FACE TO FACE WITH THE FISHES ★★

19km (12 miles) W of Perth

The delightful wildlife reserve of Rottnest Island, off the Perth coast, has been WA's favorite holiday island for a hundred years. It's surrounded by sheltering reefs, which ensure safe swimming and snorkeling in glorious, protected bays. Its jewel-bright waters, warmed by a south-flowing current, harbor **coral outcrops** and 360 kinds of fish. The island is also home to 10,000 **quokkas,** cute otterlike marsupials that reach up to your knees when they sit up asking for a piece of lettuce (though you're not supposed to feed them). The island has that wonderful Mediterranean visual impact of light and water. Rottnest is publicly owned and accessible to all. It's the sort of place where you feel your cares fall away as soon as you arrive, and it's almost decadent in the way that everything is laid-back and casual.

The island is only 11km (7 miles) long and 4.5km (3 miles) across at its widest point with two main areas of settlement, where self-catering cottages and villas can be rented from the **Rottnest Island Authority.** Getting about is restricted to walking and cycling, with a few buses taking visitors around the island or linking the settlements. There are strong historical links. Following mainland clashes between settlers and Aborigines, Rottnest was a "Native Prison" from 1839 until 1902. The main settlement now has WA's oldest and most intact precinct of heritage buildings and an Aboriginal cemetery. The island was also a major military base during World War II.

ESSENTIALS

GETTING THERE **Rottnest Express** (✆ **08/9421 5888** Perth, or **08/9335 6406** Fremantle) and **Oceanic Cruises** (✆ **08/9325 1191**) operate trips from Perth (trip time: about 1 hr., 45 min.) and, more frequently, from Fremantle (trip time: about 30 min.). Round-trip fares average about A$69 (US$55/UK£28) from Perth, or about A$53 (US$42/UK£21) from Fremantle. Rottnest Express and Oceanic pick you up free from most Perth and Fremantle hotels. You pay about A$5 (US$4/UK£2.05) more if you return on a later day, for Fremantle trips only. Most boat operators offer day-trip and accommodations packages. You may find references elsewhere to Boat Torque Cruises; they've been taken over by Rottnest Express.

Rottnest Air Taxi (✆ **1800/500 006** in Western Australia, or 08/9292 5027; www.rottnest.de) provides aerial transfers in four- or six-seater (including the pilot) aircraft. A same-day round-trip in a four-seater costs A$240 (US$192/UK£98) for the whole plane. **Kookaburra Air** (✆ **08/9354 1158;** www.kookaburra.iinet.net.au) also operates a range of tours to Rottnest. Both operate from Jandakot Airport, 18km (11 miles) south of Perth.

VISITOR INFORMATION The **Rottnest Island Visitor & Information Centre** (✆ **08/9372 9752**) is right at the end of the jetty on the island. The center is run by the **Rottnest Island Authority** (✆ **08/9432 9111;** www.rottnest.wa.gov.au), as is the entire island. The Western Australian Visitor Centre (see "Visitor Information" in the Perth section, earlier in this chapter) also has information.

GETTING AROUND Ferries pull into the jetty in Thomson Bay, which has most of the facilities and accommodations (it's often just called The Settlement) lining its shores. **Rottnest Bike Hire** (✆ **08/9292 5105**), next to the Rottnest Hotel near the jetty, rents 1,300 bikes of every size, speed, and type, as well as trailers or carriers for everything from surfboards to babies. An 18-speed bike is A$23 (US$18/UK£9.40) for a 24-hour day (plus a A$25/US$20/UK£10 refundable deposit) including a helmet (compulsory in Australia) and lock. The price reduces for subsequent days.

The yellow **Bayseeker** ★★ bus does half-hourly circumnavigations, calling at 18 stops, including all the best bays. You can get on and off as often as you like, with an all-day ticket costing A$7.50 (US$6/UK£3.05) for adults, A$3.80 (US$3/UK£1.55) for children 4 to 12, and A$18 (US$14/UK£7.35) for families of four. Buy tickets on board.

A free bus runs regularly between the airport and Thomson Bay, and the secondary settlement at Geordie, Fay's, and Longreach Bays on the northern shore. It does not run to the Basin, which is a 15-minute walk from the Settlement.

ISLAND ORIENTATION TOURS

Many first-time visitors take the 2-hour **Island Coach Tour,** a good introduction to the bays and the island's cultural and natural history—and it includes a stop to see the quokkas. It costs A$24 (US$19/UK£9.80) for adults, A$12 (US$9.75/UK£4.90) for kids 4 to 12, and A$55 (US$44/UK£22) for families of four. Departure times vary, but you can expect tours to run twice a day, usually around 10:30am and 1:30pm. The **Wadjemup Lighthouse Tour** takes people to the main lighthouse in the middle of the island and you can climb 155 steps to the best view on the island. Tour frequency varies according to the season, and it costs A$15 (US$12/UK£6.15) adults, A$6 (US$4.80/UK£2.45) kids 4 to 12, and A$36 (US$29/UK£15) families.

Tickets for these tours and the **Train Ride** (see "For History Buffs" below) can be bought at the Ticket Booth by the main bus stop from December through April and during school holidays; at other times from the Visitor Centre.

SNORKELING, DIVING, SURFING & FISHING

Most people come to Rottnest to snorkel, swim, surf, dive, or fish. As soon as you arrive, rent a bike and your preferred aquatic gear, and pedal around the coast until you come to a beach that suits you. (Don't forget to carry drinking water and food, because the only shops are at The Settlement and Geordie Bay.) The Basin, Little Parakeet Bay, Little Armstrong Bay, Little Salmon Bay, and Parker Point are good **snorkel** spots. There are two snorkel trails, with underwater information points, at Little Salmon and Parker Point. **Surfers** should try Cathedral Rocks or Strickland Bay. **Fishermen** will catch squid, herring, and tailor, as well as all kinds of reef fish, but several areas are now off-limits to fishing. The island's dive shop, **Rottnest Malibu Diving** (© **08/9292 5111;** www.rottnestdiving.com.au), near the jetty, rents snorkel gear, dive gear, wet suits, surfboards, body boards, aqua-bikes, and fishing tackle. The company conducts two daily boat trips to some of the 100-plus dive sites around Rottnest. Some feature limestone caverns and a few of the island's 14 shipwrecks. A boat dive with all gear included is A$80 (US$64/UK£33), or A$165 (US$132/UK£37) round-trip from Perth. If you have never dived before, a 1- to 2-hour theory lesson followed by a boat dive is A$200 (US$160/UK£82), including round-trip transport from Perth. There are also snorkel tours at A$28 (US$22/UK£11), all gear included, running three times a day in summer.

FOR HISTORY BUFFS

Rottnest has a lot to offer for history buffs. There are numerous heritage buildings especially along the Thomson Bay foreshore, dating from when the island was a prison and convict labor was employed. It became a major base during World War II, protecting the sea lane to Fremantle, and the Oliver Hill 9¼-inch guns are still there. Guided 1-hour tours (gold coin fee) take visitors around them as well as the battery tunnels housing an engine room, a plotting room, and observation posts. You can make your own way there, or take a train (see below). The tours start at 9:30am or on the hour from 11am to 2pm. The train, the *Captain Hussey,* departs from the station near the Visitor Centre hourly from 10:30am to 2:30pm. The fare is A$17 (US$13/UK£6.95) for adults, A$8.30 (US$6.65/UK£3.40) for children 4 to 12, and A$41 (US$33/UK£17) for families of four, including the tour (except the last trip, which starts after the last tour).

Volunteer guides run several free 1-hour walking tours. One is a historical tour around Thomson Bay, including the governor's residence, chapel, octagonal prison, small **museum** (© **08/9372 9752;** open daily 10:45am–3:30pm), and the former Boys' Reformatory. Another heritage trail takes you to the memorial commemorating

Kids A Great & Safe Place

Rottnest is an ideal place to spend a few days with young kids. Drivers of the (few) service vehicles give way to cyclists and walkers, especially younger ones; the beaches shelve gradually and are sheltered from the waves by the offshore reefs. Two areas of accommodations are particularly popular with families: South Thomson Bay (sometimes known as "Nappy Row") and Geordie Bay. The children can safely roam the streets, play in the sand, and paddle in the shallows.

de Vlamingh, the Dutch explorer who named the island *Rottenest* (Rat's Nest) in 1696 when he mistook quokkas for (very large) rats. There are also quokka walks, and the "Reefs, Wrecks and Daring Sailors" tour which includes a walk to Bathurst lighthouse.

WHERE TO STAY & DINE

Call the **Rottnest Island Authority's accommodations booking service** (© **08/9432 9111**) to book one of the island's 250-plus holiday homes, villas, or historic cottages, or the campground. Don't expect anything grand, and there is no air-conditioning. Book well in advance all through summer; accommodations during the WA school vacation times are allocated through a ballot system, for which you must submit an application. Reduced pricing applies during winter, June through August.

The Authority's units are all self-catering, with gas stoves and barbecues. Both hotels (listed below) have good restaurants; otherwise, dining is available at the licensed Rottnest Tearooms (meals 11am–8pm, or 9pm Fri–Sat), the Geordie Bay Café (Thurs–Sat evenings, summer only), the DOME Café (being re-built in 2007), and a couple of lackluster takeout joints.

Quokka Arms Formerly the Rottnest Hotel, this 1864 building near the jetty began life as the state governor's summer residence, and underwent a major renovation in 2004. Now, day-trippers gather in the sports bar or the large open-air beer garden to admire the setting over an ale or two. The hotel contains pleasant, motel-style rooms, some with a small patio and sea views. There's a large upstairs apartment with lounge, kitchen/dining, four doubles, and great views; sadly no access to the veranda for safety reasons. Guests have the use of a barbecue. No smoking indoors.

Bedford Ave., Rottnest Island, WA 6161. © **08/9292 5011.** Fax 08/9292 5188. www.axismgt.com.au/rottnesthotel. 18 units, all with shower only. Peak season (Dec–Jan) A$230–A$250 (US$184–US$200/UK£94–UK£102) double; shoulder season A$200–A$220 (US$160–US$176/UK£82–UK£90) double; low season A$140–A$160 (US$112–US$128/UK£57–UK£65) double. Extra person A$40 (US$32/UK£16). Crib A$15 (US$12/UK£6.15). Apt A$250–A$600 (US$200–US$480/UK£102–UK£245). Rates include continental breakfast. Ask about midweek packages. AE, DC, MC, V. **Amenities:** 2 restaurants; 2 bars; beer garden; nonsmoking rooms. *In room:* TV, fridge, coffeemaker, no phone.

Rottnest Lodge This former colonial barracks and prison has been heavily modified to provide attractive, comfortable visitor accommodations, with newer units added at the rear, facing across salt lakes to the main Rottnest Lighthouse. The Premium Lakeside rooms, updated in 2005, are the island's most luxurious accommodations. They have king-size beds, flagstone floors, private balconies, and a spacious living area with a wood fire. The standard Lakeside rooms are set up with both queen-size and single beds and also have balconies, but with limited views. The remaining rooms are in the historic quarters. The Deluxe rooms are bright and cheery, with courtyard entry and French windows opening on to a colonial veranda. The two-bedroom family rooms have the advantage of a kitchen and laundry. The area known as the Quod has budget accommodations. The lodge is just a short stroll from the jetty and Visitor Centre.

Kitson St., Rottnest Island, WA 6161. ✆ **08/9292 5161.** Fax 08/9292 5158. www.rottnestlodge.com.au. 80 units, all with shower only. A$215–A$290 (US$172–US$232/UK£88–UK£118) Deluxe double; A$180–A$240 (US$144–US$192/UK£73–UK£98) Standard double; A$225–A$300 (US$180–US$240/UK£92–UK£122) Lakeside double; A$260–A$345 (US$208–US$276/UK£106–UK£141) Premium Lakeside double; A$445–A$535 (US$356–US$428/UK£182–UK£218) Family apt. Extra person A$65 (US$52/UK£27). Rates include continental breakfast and are seasonal. Ask about packages. AE, DC, MC, V. **Amenities:** Restaurant; 2 bars; small lagoon-style pool. *In room:* Ceiling fan, TV w/pay movies, fridge, coffeemaker, hair dryer, iron.

IN PURSUIT OF THE GRAPE IN THE SWAN VALLEY ★

20km (13 miles) NE of Perth

You don't have to go all the way to Margaret River to find rolling vineyards, local produce, and good wine and food. The Swan Valley is only 20 minutes from the Perth city center, but has 30 or so wineries, a wildlife park, antiques shops, galleries, several restaurants, and Australia's best golf resort. Some outlets are closed Monday to Wednesday. Good times to visit are during two annual festivals, "Spring in the Valley" (second weekend in Oct), and "Taste the Valley" (during Apr).

Lord Street from the Perth city center becomes Guildford Road and takes you to the historic town of Guildford at the start of the Swan Valley. The **Swan Valley and Eastern Region Visitors Centre** is at the corner of Meadow and Swan streets, Guildford (✆ **08/9379 9400;** www.swanvalley.com.au). It's open daily except Christmas from 9am to 4pm. It provides helpful information, advice, and maps, and separate sheets listing the venues that are open on Mondays, Tuesdays, or Wednesdays. Several companies (see "Whale-Watching Cruises, Tram Trips & Other Tours," earlier in this chapter) run day tours or day cruises from Perth, and local companies run tours by black cab or Rolls-Royce.

TOURING THE WINERIES & OTHER THINGS TO DO

Most Swan wineries are small, family-run affairs, many with links to early Italian or Yugoslav origins. An exception is **Houghton Wines,** Dale Road, Middle Swan (✆ **08/9274 9540;** www.houghton-wines.com.au), Western Australia's oldest, biggest, and most venerable winery. The new (2006) tasting room is light, airy, and appealing. and there are lovely picnic grounds, where mauve jacaranda trees blossom gloriously in November. There's the Jacaranda Cafe, and an art gallery, housed in old beamed timber cellars lined with barrels (still in use), open 10am to 5pm daily except Good Friday, December 25 and 26, and some public holidays.

In general, the tastings at the Swan wineries are free, with some wineries charging a small fee for their premium offerings.

The other big-name winery is **Sandalford Wines,** 3210 W. Swan Rd., Caversham (✆ **08/9374 9374;** www.sandalford.com). It has twice-daily 90-minute winery tours (minimum five people), which take you along walkways over the high-tech production areas. The A$22 (US$18/UK£9) fee includes a tasting of premium wine and a wine-education kit. A very popular tour is "Become a Winemaker for a Day." Besides the winery tour you get a chance to blend your own wine which you can then drink over a three-course lunch. The winery also has a good gift shop and a pleasant restaurant (lunch noon–3pm) with a pretty vine-covered alfresco area. Open 10am to 5pm daily except Good Friday, December 25 and 26, and some public holidays.

The popular **Margaret River Chocolate Company** has an outlet at 5123 W. Swan Rd. (near the Reid Hwy.), West Swan (✆ **08/9250 1588**). It offers tastings, and you can watch chocolate making through the viewing window. Open daily from 10am to 5pm. A recent addition to the sweet scene is **Mondo Nougat,** with a migrant family following their southern Italian traditions. There's a viewing window and cafe.

Caversham Wildlife Park (✆ **08/9248 1984;** www.cavershamwildlife.com.au) is a large reserve of 4,300 hectares (10,621 acres) with smart new homes (since its move in 2003) for the collection of 200 species of mostly Western Australian wildlife, kept in mostly natural surroundings. You can stroke koalas (but not hold them), feed kangaroos, pet farm animals, take a camel ride, and, sometimes, cuddle joeys and wombats. There are barbecue and picnic sites, train and tram rides, and a cafe. It's at Whiteman Park, West Swan, and open daily from 8:30am to 4:30pm, closed December 25. Admission is A$17 (US$13/UK£6.95) for adults, A$6.50 (US$5.20/UK£2.65) for children 2 to 14.

Antiques lovers should browse the strip of shops on James Street, Guildford (most shops are open daily), or visit **Woodbridge House,** a beautifully restored 1883 manor house on Ford Street, West Midland (✆ **08/9274 2432**). The house is open daily from 1 to 4pm; closed all of July, and December 12 to January 31. Admission is A$5 (US$4/UK£1.65) for adults, A$3 (US$2.40/UK£1.20) for seniors and children under 16, and A$12 (US$9.60/UK£4.90) for a family of six. Its river-view tearooms serve lunch.

Drop into **Guildford Village Potters** (✆ **08/9279 9859**), 22 Meadow St. (next to the Visitors Centre), to check out work by about 20 local women. You may find it hard to resist the raku (open-fired) glazes. Open 10am to 4:30pm weekdays, 9:30am to 4:30pm weekends and holidays. One of Perth's finest galleries is half-hidden within woodland just off the Roe Highway. The **Gomboc Gallery and Sculpture Park** (✆ **08/9274 3996;** www.gomboc-gallery.com.au) at 50 James Rd., Middle Swan, has been in operation for 25 years. The grounds feature an eclectic array of sculptures, while the gallery houses regular exhibitions of major WA artists. Gomboc is the main outlet for one of Australia's greatest contemporary artists, Robert Juniper.

WHERE TO STAY

Grandis Cottages ★★ Two excellently furnished two-bedroom cottages sit in a rural setting, looking over rolling lawns, a small dam, and a large bed of roses. Birds include kookaburras, cockatoos, and blue wrens, while kangaroos roam the back lawn. A breakfast hamper is supplied, otherwise they're self-catering with full kitchen and comfortable lounge featuring gas log fire stove and two recliners. The large veranda has a seating area with gas barbecue. The water supply is 100% rainwater, and all waste water is recycled.

45 Casuarina Place (off West Swan Rd.), Henley Brook, WA 6055. ✆ **08/9296 3400.** Fax 08/9296 3500. www.grandiscottages.com.au. 2 self-contained cottages, 1 with facilities for people with disabilities. Sun–Thurs A$180 (US$144/UK£72) double; Fri–Sat A$205 (US$164/UK£84) double. Extra adult A$30 (US$24/UK£12), extra child (to 12 years) A$15 (US$12/UK£6.15). Ask about packages. AE, DC, MC, V. Take West Swan Rd. to Henley Brook, turn left onto Woolcott St. and right into Casuarina Place. *In room:* A/C, TV/DVD, hair dryer, iron, laundry facilities, CD, spa and shower.

Hansons Swan Valley ★★ Sleek and sophisticated sums up this boutique B&B surrounded by vineyards and paddocks. The river's only a short stroll away, with river gums and arum lilies lining the brown waterway. There's constant birdsong. The 10 rooms of what was a family mansion offer simple but contemporary decor, full of light and artworks. Comfort and style go hand in hand, and a swimming pool sits invitingly close by.

Six rooms have spas and king-size beds, four have queen-sized beds and showers, and there's a two-bedroom cottage. Start the day with hearty fare in the sunny breakfast room, and then take in a few wineries. This is a nonsmoking indoors property.

60 Forest Rd., Henley Brook, WA 6055. ✆ **08/9296 3366.** Fax 08/9296 3332. www.hansons.com.au. 10 units and 1 cottage. Sat and long weekends A$260–A$360 (US$208–US$288/UK£106–UK£147) double; Sun–Fri A$180–A$250 (US$144–US$200/UK£74–UK£102) double; A$350–A$490 (US$280–US$294/UK£143–UK£200) cottage. Rates include full breakfast. Ask about packages. Not recommended for children. AE, DC, MC, V. Take West Swan Rd. to Henley Brook and turn right at Little River Winery onto Forest Rd.; Hansons is on the left at the end of the road. **Amenities:** Small outdoor pool; in-room spa treatments (with 2-hr. notice); laundry service; dry cleaning; nonsmoking rooms. *In room:* A/C, TV/DVD w/in-house movies, minibar, hair dryer, iron.

Novotel Vines Resort ★ This rural retreat has one of the best resort golf courses in Australia, and is the most upmarket place in the Swan Valley. Most rooms or apartments in the low-rise accommodations have balconies looking onto the 36-hole championship golf course or over the pool or vineyard. Kangaroos are a regular sight along the bush-fringed fairways. The rooms are of a high standard, if a bit stiff and citified. A suite consists of a room with a living area and some feature a spa. There's no smoking allowed.

Verdelho Dr., Belhus (near Upper Swan), WA 6069. ✆ **1300/656 565** Accor in Australia, 800/221 4542 in the U.S. and Canada, or 08/9297 3000. Fax 08/9297 3333. www.vines.com.au. 103 hotel rooms and 54 apartments. A$240 (US$192/UK£98) double; A$305 (US$244/UK£124) suite; A$290 (US$232/UK£118) 2-bedroom apt; A$345 (US$276/UK£141) 3-bedroom apt. Children under 16 stay free in parent's room with existing bedding. Ask about packages. AE, DC, MC, V. Take West Swan Rd. to Upper Swan and turn left on to Millhouse Rd. The resort entrance is about 1.5km (1 mile) on the right. **Amenities:** 2 restaurants; 2 cafes; 2 bars; large outdoor pool; golf course (guest discounts available); 4 tennis courts (2 floodlit); exercise room; outdoor heated Jacuzzi; salon; room service; laundry service; dry cleaning; 2 squash courts. *In room:* A/C, TV w/pay movies, dataport, minibar, coffeemaker, hair dryer, iron.

WHERE TO DINE

Chesters ★ MODERN AUSTRALIAN The simple casual setting, with semi-open kitchen, provides a good venue for easy dining. Originally a fruit shed, it has views past gum trees to open paddocks. The food is excellent once one gets past the strange menu titles, such as "Chairmains (sic) of the Board," with various combinations a specialty. The lamb composition is one such, and there's a yabbie cheesecake. It was a Gold Plate winner in 2006.

8691 West Swan Rd., Henley Brook. ✆ **08/9296 3444.** www.heafodglenwine.com.au. Reservations recommended at weekends. Main courses A$30–A$35 (US$24–US$28/UK£12–UK£14). AE, DC, MC, V. Wed–Fri 11am–3:30pm; Sat–Sun and public holidays noon–3:30pm; Fri–Sat 6pm–late. Closed Good Friday.

Lamont Winery Cellar Door ★ TAPAS STYLE The cellar door kitchen serves food all day Saturday, Sunday, and public holidays from a "grazing menu" which features fresh seasonal produce for eating outside at the farm tables. A gallery on the grounds shows Western Australian art and crafts. The cellar door is open daily for wine sales and tasting.

85 Bisdee Rd. (off Moore Rd.), Millendon, near Upper Swan. ✆ **08/9296 4485.** Reservations recommended. A$8–A$15 (US$6.40–US$12/UK£3.30–UK£6.15) the various platters. AE, DC, MC, V. Sat–Sun and holidays 10am–5pm. Closed Dec 25–26, Jan 1, and Good Friday. Take the Great Northern Hwy. to Baskerville, near Upper Swan, take a right onto Haddrill Rd. for 1.6km (1 mile), turn right onto Moore Rd. for 1km (just over ½ mile), and make a right onto Bisdee Rd.

NEW NORCIA: A TOUCH OF SPAIN IN AUSTRALIA ★

132km (82 miles) N of Perth

It's the last thing you expect to see in the Australian bush—a Benedictine monastery town with elegant European architecture, a fine museum, and a collection of Renaissance art—but New Norcia is no mirage. Australia's only monastic town (and still a

Finds **A Fun, Quirky Cafe**

Taylor's art and coffee house is a quirky, even eccentric, cafe that is simple yet appealing. Siblings Michael and Caroline Taylor have converted their old family home, with corrugated iron walls and polished floorboards, into an intriguing venue—part cafe, part gallery. The outside has a broad paved shady courtyard with a varied mix of tables, chairs, and sculptures, many made by Michael. Running down one side is "The Shed," an old workshop which is the venue for quarterly professional theater productions (seating for 150). Open for "brekky" and lunch Wednesday to Sunday, and dinner Saturday. The food is tasty and cheap (510 Great Northern Hwy., Middle Swan; ✆ **08/9250 8838;** www.taylorstudio.com.au).

working community) retains an aura of peace and quiet and calming spirituality. The pretty town and the surrounding 8,000-hectare (19,760-acre) farm were established in 1846 by Spanish Benedictine missionaries. Visitors can tour beautifully frescoed chapels, marvel at one of the finest religious art collections in Australia, attend prayers with the 15 monks who live here, and stock up on famous New Norcia nut cake from the monastery's 120-year-old wood-fired ovens, or olive oil from WA's oldest grove.

Ten kilometers (6¼ miles) south of the town is the **New Norcia Deep Space Ground Station,** run by the European Space Agency. It's not open to the public, but visitors can learn about it at the town's Education Centre.

New Norcia is an easy 2-hour drive from Perth. From downtown, take Lord Street, which becomes Guildford Road, to Midland, and follow the Great Northern Highway to New Norcia. The **Public Transport Authority (PTA; ✆ 1300/662 205** in Western Australia, or 08/9326 2000; www.transwa.wa.gov.au) runs a coach from Perth on Tuesday and Thursday at 9:30am, returning at 2:50pm from the roadhouse, at A$18 (US$14/UK£7.35) one-way. Day tours from Perth are available.

You can get information and book tours at the **New Norcia Tourist Information Centre,** New Norcia, WA 6509 (✆ **08/9654 8056;** www.newnorcia.wa.edu.au), in the Museum and Art Gallery, off the highway behind St. Joseph's. It keeps the same hours as the museum (see below). Reserve accommodations and tours in advance, especially in wildflower season from August through October.

EXPLORING THE TOWN & MONASTERY

The intriguing 2-hour **walking tours** are a must. Tickets cost A$23 (US$18/UK£9.40) for adults and A$12 (US$9.60/UK£4.90) for children 12 to 17, free for younger children, and include entrance to the museum and art gallery, and tastes of local produce. Tours depart daily except December 25 at 11am and 1:30pm, and they allow time for you to attend prayers with the monks if you wish. The guide leads you around some of the town's 27 National Trust–classified buildings and gives insight into the monks' lifestyle. You will also see the frescoes in the old monastery chapel and in St. Ildephonsus's and St. Gertrude's colleges. Free heritage walking-trail maps are available at the Tourist Information Centre.

The **Museum and Art Gallery** ★ is full of relics from the monks' past—old mechanical and musical instruments, artifacts from the days when New Norcia was an

Moments A Monk's Point of View

One of the more enthralling options at New Norcia is to "Meet a Monk." You get to sit down and have a half-hour conversation with one of the monks about life in the monastery, and life in general, from the Benedictine point of view. Available Monday to Friday 10:30am (just before the 11am tour), Saturday 4:30pm, Sunday 10am.

Aboriginal mission, gifts to the monks from the queen of Spain, and an astounding collection of paintings by Spanish and Italian artists, dating from the 1400s. Give yourself at least an hour here. The museum and gallery are open daily August through October from 9:30am to 5pm, and November through July from 10am to 4:30pm (closed Dec 25). Admission is A$10 (US$8/UK£4.10) for adults, and A$6 (US$4.80/UK£2.45) for children 12 to 17, free for younger children. Don't leave the gift shop without some of the famous New Norcia nut cake, made at the monastery bakery.

Apart from joining the monks for 15-minute prayers in the monastery chapel five times a day (noon and 2:30pm are the most convenient for day visitors), you can join them for Mass in the Holy Trinity Abbey Church Monday through Saturday at 7:30am and on Sunday at 9am, or at 5:30pm for vespers.

WHERE TO STAY & DINE

St. Benedict's rules of hospitality are paramount, which means that part of the monastery is open to guests, but really for those who are looking for a quiet, reflective place to stay and don't mind abiding by a few rules. The accommodations are spartan, and the cost is a donation, with A$70 (US$56/UK£29) as the suggested amount. Call the guesthouse (© **08/9654 8002**) to book. For others, the hotel (below) is the best bet.

New Norcia Hotel When they thought a Spanish royal visit to New Norcia was imminent in 1926, the monks built this grandiose hotel fit for, well, a king. Sadly, the royals never materialized, and the building was used for parents visiting children boarding at the town's colleges. In 1955, it became a hotel. The grand central staircase, soaring pressed-metal ceilings, and imposing Iberian facade hint at its former splendor. The rooms are simple but comfortable. About 5 years ago, they gained new carpets, curtains, and beds, but there are only shared facilities. It's nice to eat a meal at the bar or the charmingly faded dining room, and to wander out of your room to sit on the massive veranda upstairs. The bar gets jumping (everything is relative) on Friday and Saturday nights when local farmers come to town. No smoking.

Great Northern Hwy., New Norcia, WA 6509. © **08/9654 8034.** Fax 08/9654 8011. hotel@newnorcia.wa.edu.au. 17 units, 1 with bathroom. A$85 (US$68/UK£35) double without bathroom. Extra person A$19 (US$15/UK£7.75). AE, MC, V. **Amenities:** Restaurant; bar; nonsmoking rooms. *In room:* Fridge, coffeemaker, iron, no phone.

3 Margaret River & the Southwest: Wine Tasting among the Forests ★★★

Margaret River: 277km (173 miles) S of Perth

For most Australians, the words "Margaret River" are synonymous with great wine. It is also a region "where every prospect pleases," and U.S.-based "Wine Market Report" in 2006 gave it the award for "Wine Tourism Region of the World." It commented that "many consider (it) to be the most remote wine region on the planet," but it's a mere 3 hours' drive from Perth.

Forty years ago this was a quiet backwater, a simple countryside of dairy farms and forest, with a few insiders aware of some great surfing spots. A survey then found that the climate was remarkably similar to that of Bordeaux, and the first vineyards were planted. The area now has over 80 wineries and, while they produce only about 1% of Australia's wine output, they turn out around 10% of the country's top "premium" wines. There's a growing selection of quality lodges and B&Bs, galleries, gourmet food outlets, and super restaurants. Many crafts people have set up here, together with producers of venison, cheese, chocolate, and olive oil. Statuesque forests of gracious karri trees (the world's third-tallest species) create beautiful dappled drives; the west coast has spectacular surf breaks and cliffs perfect for abseiling (rappelling) and rock climbing; the northern coast has wonderfully peaceful safe beaches; and there's a honeycomb of limestone caves filled with stalagmites and stalactites. Whales pass by June through December, wildflowers line the roads August through October, and wild birds, kangaroos, and shingle-backed lizards are everywhere.

Moments **Taking a Dip with Flipper**

The wild dolphins that come to Monkey Mia's shore (see "The Coral Coast: Where the Outback Meets the Sea," later in this chapter) are justly famous. But just 2 hours' drive south of Perth, en route to Margaret River, is a place where you can ***swim*** ★★ with these creatures.

At the **Dolphin Discovery Centre,** Koombana Drive, Bunbury (✆ **08/9791 3088;** http://dolphins.mysouthwest.com.au), bottlenose dolphins come into shore in Koombana Bay. You can "float" with them free in the waist-deep "interaction zone" on the beach, under the watchful eye of volunteer guides. The dolphins don't show up about a third of the time (the best chance of seeing them is 8am–noon), and the water does not usually have the same clear visibility as at Monkey Mia. Reservations are not necessary.

From November to April (weather dependent), the center runs 2-hour **"Swim on the Wild Side"** tours where, accompanied by a marine biologist, you can snorkel with some of the bay's 100-plus dolphins in deeper water for A$125 (US$100/UK£51) including equipment; you must be over 8. **Naturaliste Charters** (✆ **08/9755 2276;** www.whales-australia.com) runs excellent 90-minute **dolphin watch cruises** twice daily (except Dec 25 or in bad weather) from the center at 11am and 2pm; they cost A$37 (US$30/UK£15) adults, A$24 (US$19/UK£9.80) kids 4 to 12, A$28 (US$22/UK£11) for kids 13 to 17, or A$109 (US$87/UK£44) family of 2 adults, 2 children. The center has showers, a cafe, and a good little ecodisplay on the dolphin life cycle; admission to that is A$6 (US$4.80/UK£2.45) adults; A$3 (US$2.40/UK£1.20) seniors, students, and children; A$15 (US$12/UK£6.15) families. The center is open daily from 8am to 4pm (Sept–May) and from 9am to 3pm (June–Aug); closed December 25.

Note: You can hand-feed wild dolphins at **Tangalooma Wild Dolphin Resort** near Brisbane (see chapter 6).

Moments Under the Stars with the Stars

Every February or March, **Leeuwin Estate Winery** (**© 08/9759 0000;** www.leeuwin estate.com.au) stages its **Leeuwin Concert Series** ★★ starring leading showbiz lights (past performers have included Sting, kd lang, Dame Kiri Te Kanawa, Julio Iglesias, and Diana Ross) and usually a major orchestra, attended by 6,000 picnicking guests. Tickets are about A$120 (US$96/UK£49). This is a major event, which sells out months ahead. It's held in the open air, below the winery and accompanied by kookaburras calling in the surrounding karri trees.

The Margaret River region isn't very large, so is easy to get around. It reaches 120km (75 miles) from Cape Naturaliste in the north to Cape Leeuwin on the southwest tip of Australia, both with attendant lighthouses. If you like hiking, pack your boots, because there are plenty of trails, from a 15-minute stroll around Margaret River township, or an hour's stroll along the Dunsborough beaches, to a 6-day Cape-to-Cape trek along the sea cliffs.

The main settlements are Dunsborough in the north, Margaret River township in the center, and Augusta in the south. Busselton is the gateway to the region, though not really part of it.

ESSENTIALS

GETTING THERE It's a 3-hour drive to Margaret River from Perth; take the inland South Western Highway or the more scenic Old Coast Road to Bunbury, and pick up the Bussell Highway to Busselton, the gateway to the region.

Air Australia (**© 08/9332 5011;** www.airaustralia.net) operates charter flights from Perth's Jandakot airport, for A$550 (US$440/UK£224) same day return for up to three passengers. **Leeuwin Estate** winery (**© 08/9430 4099;** www.leeuwinestate.com.au) arranges charter flights from Perth for A$405 (US$324/UK£165) per person (based on two passengers), including flight, tea tour and tastings, and a la carte lunch in the restaurant.

Southwest Coachlines (**© 08/9324 2333**) runs a daily service to Margaret River from Perth for about A$31 (US$25/UK£13). The **Public Transport Authority (PTA; © 1300/602 205** in Western Australia, or 08/9326 2600; www.transwa.wa.gov.au) also runs a coach service from Perth. The services take between 4½ and 5½ hours, so are not recommended. There is no train service to Margaret River, though the twice-daily *Australind* train does run from Perth to Bunbury, with coach connections onward.

Self-drive is the best way to get here and have the necessary freedom to get around.

VISITOR INFORMATION The **Margaret River Visitor Centre** is one of the best and most useful in the country. It's at 100 Bussell Hwy. (at Tunbridge St.), Margaret River, WA 6285 (**© 08/9757 2911;** www.margaretriverwa.com). Pick up a winery guide, a guide to the artisans of the region, and maps, here or at the **Dunsborough Visitor Centre,** Shop 14, Dunsborough Park Shopping Centre, Dunsborough, WA 6281 (**© 08/9755 3299;** www.geographebay.com). Both are open daily from 9am to 5pm; closed December 25.

GETTING AROUND Two north-south roads service the area, Bussell Highway and the slower, winding Caves Road. Numerous smaller roads connect the two, or loop down to bayside settlements renowned for their surfing opportunities. The Bussell

Tips A Pretty Jetty

Busselton has the longest wooden jetty in the Southern Hemisphere, stretching 1,841m (over 1 mile) out into shallow Geographe Bay. An underwater observatory has been built at the end, allowing visitors to go 8m (26 ft.) down and look out at the marine life that congregates around the massive 140-year-old timber supports. The observatory is open daily except December 25, weather permitting, from 8am to 5pm in summer, and 10am to 4pm winter. Observatory tours are A$20 (US$16/UK£8.15) adults, A$12 (US$9.20/UK£4.90) children 3 to 14.

Highway turns due south 9km (5½ miles) past Busselton, and runs down the middle of the region, through Margaret River town to Augusta and windswept Cape Leeuwin. Caves Road runs past Dunsborough then swirls southward, closer to the coast, past limestone caves and karri forests toward Augusta.

A car is close to essential. **Hertz** (✆ **13 30 39** in Australia, or 08/9758 8331) has an office in Margaret River, or call **Avis** (✆ **1800/679 880** in Australia for reservations in the Southwest). For a taxi, call **Margaret River Taxi Service** (✆ **13 10 08** or 08/9757 3444).

Several companies run sightseeing and winery tours from Margaret River or Perth.

TOURING THE WINERIES

Fans of premium wines will have a field day. Cabernet sauvignon and merlot are the star red varieties, with most wineries making a straight cabernet and/or cabernet/merlot blend. Shiraz is also popular and Cape Mentelle makes a powerful zinfandel. Chardonnay is the standard single variety white wine, while fresh vibrant semillon/sauvignon blanc blends have become synonymous with the region. A few wineries make (Australian-style) Rieslings. Most wineries offer free tastings from 10am to 4:30pm daily. There are two main clusters of vineyards; the biggest grouping is in the northern half in the Willyabrup area, with a smaller number, including several big names, around Margaret River township.

The region's best known winery, and one of the very best, is **Leeuwin Estate** ★, Stevens Road, Margaret River (✆ **08/9430 4099**). It has a towering reputation, with its Art Series chardonnay often rated Australia's finest. Winery tours run three times a day. A relative newcomer, **Voyager Estate** ★★, Stevens Road, Margaret River (✆ **08/9757 6354**), has exquisite rose gardens and a South African Cape Dutch–style cellar and restaurant. The three pioneer vineyards from the late 1960s, Moss Wood, Vasse Felix, and Cullen's, are all still rated very highly. Other labels to look for are Cape Mentelle, Devil's Lair, Madfish (Howard Park Wines), Lenton Brae, Pierro, Woodlands, and Cape Grace Wines. Ashbrook takes a very serious approach to style and quality, and makes one of the best WA Rieslings. Some wineries make excellent "quaffers"—Aussie slang for easy-drinking, inexpensive wines. Vasse Felix makes Theatre Red and Theatre White, while Cape Mentelle sells 1.5-liter bottles of both its red and white CMV wines.

BEYOND THE WINERIES: CAVES, BUSH TUCKER & MORE

Six of the Southwest's 350 or so limestone caves are open to the public. Some contain elaborate formations and have lighting, stairs, and boardwalks to help you along the way. Stop at **CaveWorks** eco-interpretive center, Lake Cave, Caves Road (✆ **08/9757 7411**),

Tips A Wine-Buying Tip

Most wineries don't deliver internationally, and the wine you like might not be exported to your country of residence, so use the services of the **Margaret River Regional Wine Centre,** 9 Bussell Hwy., Cowaramup (**© 08/9755 5501;** www.mrwines.com). It stocks about every local wine; does daily tastings of select vintages; and sells maps, visitor guides, and winery guides. The expert staff will help you make your choices, and even tailor your day's foray. It is open Monday through Saturday from 10am to 8pm, and Sunday from noon to 6pm (closed Good Friday, Dec 25, and sometimes Jan 1). You can also order through the website.

before or after you visit the caves. It's open daily except December 25 from 9am to 5pm. Entry is free if you tour Lake, Jewel, or Mammoth cave, otherwise A$2 (US$1.60/UK£0.80) per person.

Lake Cave, outside CaveWorks and 300 steps down an ancient sinkhole, contains a tranquil pond that reflects the exquisite formations. Four kilometers (2½ miles) north along Caves Road is **Mammoth Cave,** where you can see the fossilized jaw of an extinct giant wombat. **Jewel Cave** ★, 8km (5 miles) north of Augusta on Caves Road, is the prettiest. Tours of Lake and Jewel and self-guided tours (using a CD audio system) of Mammoth each cost A$17 (US$14/UK£6.95) for adults, A$8.50 (US$6.80/UK£3.50) for children 4 to 16, A$46 (US$37/UK£19) for a family of four. A Grand Tour Pass to all three plus CaveWorks saves you a little money. Mammoth is open from 9am to 5pm (last tour at 4pm); tours of Lake and Jewel run hourly from 9:30am to 3:30pm. Sometimes extra tours are scheduled during school vacations. The caves are open every day except December 25. Booking is not required.

Calgardup and Giants caves, run by the Department of Environment and Conservation, are more challenging. The caves are not electrically lit, and there are no guides. Visitors receive helmets, lamps, and information, and may spend as long as they like exploring. **Calgardup Cave** goes to a depth of 27m (89 ft.) and has boardwalks to help negotiate it. Calgardup is on Caves Road, about 12 minutes' drive south of Margaret River and 3 minutes north of the Conto's Road turnoff. It is open from 9am to 4:15pm (last entry) daily. **Giants Cave,** 20 minutes south of Margaret River on Caves Road, is one of the largest and deepest caves on the Leeuwin-Naturaliste Ridge, and requires the ability to deal with vertical ladders and some rock-clambering. It is a "through" cave 800m (2,624 ft.) long, with a different entrance and exit. It's open 9:30am to 3:30pm (last entry) during school holidays, and some other times when groups have been booked (check beforehand). Entry to Calgardup or Giants costs A$12 (US$9.60/UK£4.90) adult, A$6 (US$4.80/UK£2.45) child 6 to 15, including helmets and lamps. Buy tickets at the **National Park Information Centre** (**© 08/9757 7422**) at Calgardup Cave. The center also has walking maps and information on camping sites and activities in the Leeuwin-Naturaliste National Park.

Another "adventure cave" where you get down-and-dirty crawling on your hands and knees, and even sliding on your stomach—in the protective clothing supplied—is **Ngilgi Cave,** Caves Road, Yallingup (**© 08/9755 2152**), for A$110 (US$88/UK£45) for anyone over 15. A guided tour departs daily at 9:30am depending on demand, and takes at least 3 hours. "Short" adventure tours are less demanding and take 1½ hours, at A$30 (US$24/UK£12) adults, A$18 (US$14/UK£7.35) children 10 to 16. Torchlight tours are spooky but you don't see the caves at their best, and cost A$19 (US$15/UK£7.75) adults and A$13 (US$10/UK£5.30) children. Both this and the short adventure tour are dependent on numbers. Book all tours at least 24 hours ahead. Beautiful translucent stalactite "shawls" are found in Ngilgi's main chamber which anyone can explore on semi-guided tours (guides are available to answer questions but do not conduct tours). These cost A$17 (US$14/UK£6.95) for adults, A$8 (US$6.40/UK£3.27) for children 5 to 17, or A$44 (US$35/UK£18) for a family of four, and run half-hourly from 9:30am to 3:30pm (4pm during school vacations). The cave is open every day except December 25.

Food-based attractions are opening up in the area all the time. You can pick your own kiwi, raspberries, and other fruit at the **Berry Farm,** 222 Bessell Rd., outside Margaret River (© **08/9757 5054**), or buy them ready-made as attractively packaged (fruit-based) wines, jams, and vinegars. At the **Margaret River Chocolate Company** ★, Harman's Mill Road (at Harman's Rd. S.), Metricup (© **08/9755 6555**), you can participate in free tastings, watch the candy-making through a window, and, of course, buy up the sweet stuff and coffees. Open daily 9am to 5pm. **Olio Bello** ★★, on the corner of Armstrong Road and Cowaramup Bay Road, Cowaramup (© **08/9755 9771**), was the 2006 Australian Olive Grower of the Year. You can buy a range of olive oils, soaps, and body creams, dips, and tapenades. Olio Bello also has macadamias, fruit trees, and native shrubs so the place is full of birds. Open daily 10am to 4:30pm; closed Good Friday and December 25.

Margaret River Venison, Caves Road, Margaret River (just south of Olio Bello), is a family-run enterprise, selling products derived from deer raised on the property. Open daily 9am to 6pm. The **Margaret River Dairy Company,** Bussell Highway, Cowaramup (just north of the village) (© **08/9755 7588**), uses local milk to make a range of cheeses and yogurts. Open 9:30am to 5pm; closed Good Friday, December 25 and 26, and January 1. Some of WA's finest ice cream is made at **Simmo's Ice Creamery** ★, Commonage Road, Dunsborough (southeast of town) (© **08/9755 3745**), open 10am to 5:30pm. Closed December 25.

Try to make time for a **Margaret River with Neil McLeod** ★ tour. Neil was raised in the area on his parents' dairy farm, and now runs illuminating 5-hour morning tours of the area. The tour covers aspects of the region's early history, the links between Prevelly Beach and Prevelli in Crete, visits to Surfer's Point and Redgate Beach, the karri forest, a major vineyard, wildflowers, and his own bush-lined property abounding with kangaroos. Billy tea and "Mum's fruit cake" are served on the banks of a stream. Tours depart daily at 8am, from the Margaret River Visitor Centre, and cost A$75 (US$60/UK£31) adult, A$45 (US$36/UK£18) children 14 and under.

Moments Scenic Drives

Boranup Drive ★ is a magical detour off Caves Road through towering karris (keep in mind that your rental car is not insured on unpaved surfaces). It leaves Caves Road 6km (3¾ miles) south of Mammoth Cave and rejoins it after a glorious 14km (8¾-mile) meander. Boranup Forest, despite its impressive height, is regrowth, the entire area having been logged in the early 20th century.

Moments **Kings of the Surfing World**

Margaret River Pro ★ is the West Australian leg of the international surfing circuit, attracting the world's top surfers. It's held at Surfer's Point, Prevelly, just 10km (6¼ miles) west of Margaret River town, in late March or early April. Check with Margaret River Visitor Centre for actual dates.

Surfing lessons ★ from four-time Western Australian professional surfing champion **Josh Palmateer** (© **08/9757 3850,** or 0418/958 264 mobile; www.mrsurf.com.au) are a must! Two-hour lessons in the gentle surf at Margaret River mouth (they will pick you up and take you to the beach) cost A$110 (US$88/UK£45) for an individual lesson, A$60 (US$48/UK£25) per person in a private group up to eight people, and A$4 (US$36/UK£1.65) per person if you join a group (daily 11am–1pm), including use of wet suits and boards. Lessons run November through June. They also rent boards and wet suits and offer surf-guiding tours if you are already a Master of the Surf Universe and want to try any of the legendary breaks along the coast. Canoes and kayaks are available for hire, for paddling up the river.

From June through December, **whales** play just offshore all along the coast. There is a whale lookout near the Cape Naturaliste lighthouse. Daily 3-hour whale-watching cruises with **Naturaliste Charters** ★ (© **08/9755 2276**) depart June through August from Augusta, around Flinders Bay where you'll probably see both humpback and southern right whales, and often dolphins. September through December, the cruise departures switch to Dunsborough, where the migrating humpbacks rest their calves in sheltered Geographe Bay. The boat is fitted with an underwater camera connected to a TV and a hydrophone, so you can see and hear the creatures. Cruises cost A$60 (US$48/UK£25) for adults, A$44 (US$35/UK£18) for students 13 to 17, A$33 (US$26/UK£13) for children 4 to 12, and A$170 (US$136/UK£69) for a family of four.

WHERE TO STAY

There's an amazing selection of places to stay in **Margaret River** town and **Dunsborough,** and around the vineyards. A couple of medium-size hotels can be found near Dunsborough on the edge of Geographe Bay, otherwise there are B&B establishments, self-catering villas and cottages, camping ground chalets, and a range of excellent lodges. Some places may require a minimum 2-night stay on weekends. The **Margaret River Visitor Centre** is a good place to get advice and suggestions. Nowhere here is far away, so the best idea is to find a place that really suits your style and wallet and book that.

Cape Lodge ★★★ A lovely secluded lodge in Cape Dutch style, it has been voted in the world's top 100 hotels, and was rated Australia's best regional hotel in 2006. A member of the Small Luxury Hotels of the World group, it's set within 16 hectares (40 acres) of vineyards and natural forest, with lakes, rolling lawns, and rose beds. The immediate impression is of space and tranquillity, accompanied by birdsong. A number of small blocks, or wings, are strategically located so there are uninterrupted views and you're never really aware of other people. The rooms are large and elegantly furnished with king-size beds, and balcony or small courtyard. The Lodge Suite, in the original homestead, has an extremely comfortable lounge and two en-suite bathrooms. The restaurant, incorporating a guest lounge, has a glass wall and decking on the edge of the main lake. It has won several awards and opens for breakfast and dinner, with limited evening space for nonguests. About 50% of guests are international, mostly from the U.K. There's no smoking in any of the rooms.

Caves Rd. (between Abbey Farm and Johnson roads), Yallingup, WA 6282. ✆ **08/9755 6311.** Fax 08/9755 6322. www.capelodge.com.au. 22 units, with tub or spa and shower; unit for those with disabilities has shower only. A$365–A$425 (US$292–US$340/UK£149–UK£173) garden suites; A$495–A$595 (US$396–US$476/UK£202–UK£243) superior and forest suites; A$650 (US$520/UK£265) lodge suite. 2-night stay required on weekends. Inclusive packages at Christmas, Easter, and for special events. Rates include gourmet breakfast. AE, DC, MC, V. Free parking. Children not recommended. **Amenities:** Licensed restaurant (14,000-bottle cellar); golf nearby; tennis court; laundry and dry cleaning service; Internet access. *In room:* A/C, TV/DVD, minibar, coffeemaker, hair dryer, iron, safe, CD.

Heritage Trail Lodge ★ Although it's on the highway right "in" Margaret River (within walking distance of restaurants), this row of salmon-pink cabin-style rooms, built in 1997 and renovated in 2007, sits in a serene karri forest, out of sight of town. Each spacious unit (including one for travelers with disabilities) has a veranda and king-size double or king-size twin beds, and a double Jacuzzi, from which you can see the forest. The rooms back onto a number of bushwalk trails. No smoking indoors.

31 Bussell Hwy. (almost .5km/¼ mile north of town), Margaret River, WA 6285. ✆ **08/9757 9595.** Fax 08/9757 9596. www.heritage-trail-lodge.com.au. 10 units, all with shower and spa tub A$229–A$329 (US$183–US$263/UK£93–UK£134) double. Extra person A$75 (US$60/UK£31). Rates include gourmet continental breakfast. Ask about midweek and romantic packages. AE, DC, MC, V. Children under 16 not accepted. **Amenities:** Nonsmoking rooms. *In room:* A/C, TV/DVD, Internet access, minibar, coffeemaker, hair dryer, iron, CD.

Tips Galleries Galore

The natural beauty of the Margaret River region and the associated lifestyle have inspired many artists to make their homes here. You can watch them work and perhaps buy a unique souvenir from around 35 studios and galleries, mostly found close to Dunsborough or Margaret River town. Follow the **Artisans Map,** available from tourist information centers, hotels, and galleries.

Near Dunsborough, **Jewel of the Capes** ★, 136 Marrinup Dr. (off Caves Rd.), Yallingup (✆ **08/9756 6336**), showcases the creative handcrafted jewelry of John Miller. Others in the "don't miss" category here are **Gunyulgup Galleries,** Gunyulgup Valley Drive (off Caves Rd.) near Yallingup (✆ **08/9755 2177**), and **Yallingup Galleries** on Caves Road (✆ **08/9755 2372**), where you can see the work of many fine Australian artists, jewelers, and craftspeople. Not far away is **Happs Vineyard and Pottery,** Commonage Road, Dunsborough (✆ **08/9755 3479**). Miles Happ runs the pottery side while his father is in charge of the winery.

Just outside Margaret River, stop off to see potters Rod Dilkes and Tova Hoffman creating their lustrous "phoenix" bowls with iridescent glazes. The **Dilkes-Hoffman Ceramics** is on Caves Road, 4km (2½ miles) north of Walcliffe Road (✆ **08/9757 2998**). Serious lovers of glass art should head to **Fox Galleries,** Karridale, south of Margaret River (✆ **08/9758 6712**), which master glassmaker Alan Fox only opens by appointment. His superb creations are in numerous private and public collections, including Buckingham Palace. Beautiful furniture is made at several places, using the magnificent local jarrah timber. The best is at **Boranup Gallery** ★★, Caves Road (close to the Boranup Rd. turnoff) (✆ **08/9757 7585**), featuring stunning jarrah burl inlays.

Redgate Beach Escape ★★ Four comfortable contemporary cottages sit on a hill, looking out across native bush to an expanse of ocean. There is no noise, just the breeze, birdsong, and the distant sound of the sea, with an occasional eagle floating past. The nearest traffic lights are 30 minutes away! The fully furnished cottages have a Balinese theme, have full-height doors and windows facing the ocean, and are self-catering. Hosts Roger and Mim Budd built with a philosophy of clean uncluttered lines and sustainability. All services are underground including a 250-kiloliter rainwater tank which supplies the cottages. Several gourmet-produce outlets, and the Margaret River supermarket, are nearby. There's no smoking indoors.

Lot 14 Redgate Rd., off Caves Rd., (12km/7½ miles southwest of) Margaret River, WA 6285. ✆ **08/9757 6677**, or mobile 0437 770 107. www.redgatebeachescape.com.au. 4 2-bedroom cottages, with indoor and outdoor showers. A$200–A$300 (US$160–US$240/UK£82–UK£122) double. A$20 (US$16/UK£8.15) per extra person. Reduced rates for over 2 nights. AE, DC, MC, V. *In room:* A/C, TV/DVD, full kitchen and barbecue, fridge, coffeemaker, hair dryer, iron, washing machine, stereo, linen provided, no phone.

WHERE TO DINE

Some of WA's finest dining is to be found here, with quality chefs attracted by the opportunities, the produce, and the lifestyle. Many of the better wineries have restaurants, with several superb examples, but most are not open in the evening, and there are other good options elsewhere. Besides the wineries listed below you should consider: Driftwood Estate, Brookland Valley Vineyard (Flutes Restaurant), Amberley Estate, Wise Vineyard, Lamont's Margaret River (see also "Where to Dine" in "Perth," earlier), and Rivendell Wines. **Leeuwin Estate's restaurant** ★★, Stevens Road, Margaret River (✆ **08/9430 4099**), has terrific food. It's cozy in winter, and in summer its deck overlooking lawns is just the spot for lunch; it is open Saturday night.

Cullen Wines ★★ MODERN AUSTRALIAN/ORGANIC Owner and winemaker Vanya Cullen operates in a simple and holistic manner, aiming for simplicity, integrity, and sustainability, using organic principles. Both vineyard and kitchen garden are certified biodynamic. The granite-and-timber restaurant is unpretentious but comfortable, with a shady outdoor option, and offers casual, relaxed dining, using totally fresh biodynamic and organic local produce. All dishes are labeled as organic, biodynamic, gluten-free, vegetarian, or free range. Try the Organic Platter. Cullen's produces an excellent semillon/sauvignon blanc blend, and its Diane Madeleine cabernet/merlot is perhaps the best in Margaret River.

Caves Rd. just north of Harmans South Rd., Cowaramup. ✆ **08/9755 565.** Reservations recommended, especially on weekends. Main courses A$28–A$40 (US$22–US$32/UK£11–UK£16) lunch only. AE, DC, MC, V. Daily 10am–4pm.

Newtown House ★★ MODERN FRENCH/AUSTRALIAN Folks come from far and wide to savor owner/chef Stephen Reagan's dishes, such as rare local venison with roast pears, beets, and red-wine glaze. Desserts are no letdown—caramel soufflé with lavender ice cream and hot caramel sauce is typical. The menu changes seasonally. Located in a historic 1851 veranda-ed homestead, the restaurant consists of two simple, intimate rooms with contemporary, boldly colored walls. Log fires burn in winter and in summer there's the choice to eat outside, and it's BYO. You can also drop by for morning or afternoon tea. Voted Best Country Restaurant in WA five times.

737 Bussell Hwy. (9km/5½ miles past Busselton), Vasse. ✆ **08/9755 4485.** Reservations recommended, especially for dinner. Main courses about A$34 (US$27/UK£14). AE, DC, MC, V. Tues–Sat lunch from 10am and dinner from 6:30pm.

Vasse Felix ★★ MODERN AUSTRALIAN One of Margaret River's original wineries, the restaurant and cellar door are set within forest and vineyards 2km (1¼ miles) from Caves Road. They occupy an attractive modern two-story building, with the upstairs dining area presenting fresh regional cuisine. Some of the extensive Holmes à Court family art collection is displayed downstairs. For a simple fresh dish it's hard to improve upon the grilled sand whiting with panzanella salad and roast almond aioli.

Corner Caves Rd. and Harmans South Rd., Cowaramup. ✆ **08/9756 5000.** Reservations recommended, especially at weekends. Main courses A$30–A$44 (US$24–US$35/UK£12–UK£18) lunch only. AE, DC, MC, V. Daily 10am–5pm.

Vat 107 ★ MODERN AUSTRALIAN Touted by many locals as "one of the best restaurants in Australia," Vat 107 serves undeniably very good food. It's a slick, smart, city-bistro type place which puts it slightly at odds with the usual Margaret River laid-back style, but it's attractive and appealing. Dishes include seared duck breast with herb spaetzle and warm cherry purée, and slow-cooked salmon with truffled orzo and roasted forest mushroom and, for dessert, a delectable chocolate trio.

107 Bussell Hwy., Margaret River. ✆ **08/9758 8877.** Reservations recommended. Main courses A$28–A$37 (US$22–US$30/UK£11–£15). 15% public holiday surcharge. AE, MC, V. Daily 11am–late.

Voyager Estate ★★★ *Finds* MODERN AUSTRALIAN Nothing has been spared in attention to style and detail in aiming to create WA's finest winery and restaurant. Palatial white gates lead into spotless grounds, lined with rose gardens, and with what surely is the tallest flagpole in WA. In one corner, tucked behind a formal Cape-style garden, is the elegant white Cape Dutch cellar and restaurant (based on the mansions and wineries in South Africa's Cape region). The restaurant is in a long timber-vaulted room strung with chandeliers, and won WA's award for Top Restaurant in 2006, and Best Winery Restaurant for the third successive year. The menu is imaginative and varies seasonally, and comes with recommended wines (available by the glass). Try the Taste Plate or Seafood Assiette, and leave room for the specially selected range of cheeses.

Stevens Rd., (just south of) Margaret River. ✆ **08/9757 6354.** Reservations recommended, especially at weekends. Main courses A$27–A$42 (US$22–US$34/UK£11–UK£17) lunch only. AE, DC, MC, V. Daily 10am–4pm.

Watershed Wines ★ *Kids* MODERN AUSTRALIAN Most restaurants here have beautiful settings, but Watershed tops the lot. You sit on the balcony, looking out over serried vineyards with a stunningly blue lake sitting in the middle distance. It's enough to make you forget your lunch—almost. Once again, quality food is married with wine by the glass, with the restaurant winning an award for best family dining 2 years

---

Tips If Wine Is Not Your Tipple

If your tastes run more to beer than champagne, or you need a "cleansing ale," head for **Bootleg Brewery,** Pusey Road, Wilyabrup (✆ **08/9755 6300**). You'll find a range of amber fluids, all brewed on the premises. There's a tasty golden pils, and a real snorter—a prizewinning porter called Raging Bull at 7.1% alcohol. Complementing the great beers is a menu of tasty dishes such as Raging Bull Beef Pie and a Brewers Platter, as well as the usual pub-style food. Main courses cost around A$20 to A$29 (US$16–US$23/UK£8–UK£12), and the lakefront setting—complete with a playground—is a relaxing spot for lunch after a tough morning on the tourist trail. Open daily 10am to 4:30pm; lunch served noon to 3pm. Make a reservation on weekends and holidays.

---

in a row. There's also a cafe which caters to kids and more casual dining, with an adjacent playground. Try the crispy duck breast with seared scallops.

Corner Bussell Hwy. and Darch Rd., Margaret River. ✆ **08/9758 8633.** Reservations recommended, especially at weekends. Main courses A$25–A$33 (US$20–US$26/UK£10–UK£13) lunch only. AE, DC, MC, V. Daily noon–3pm; cafe 10am–5pm.

4 The Goldfields ★

595km (369 miles) E of Perth

The twin city of Kalgoorlie-Boulder is a wonderful repository of gloriously extravagant 100-year-old buildings, cheek-by-jowl with the scale and innovation of 21st-century mining. After Paddy Hannan struck gold in 1893 in WA's vast Outback, a "Gold Rush" of almost biblical proportions ensued, leading to the development of dozens of mines, and creation of the cities of Kalgoorlie and Boulder. The area between the two became known as the "Golden Mile," the richest square mile of gold-bearing earth in the world. Today **Kalgoorlie** ★ (pop. 32,000) is once again a boomtown, with nickel as well as gold dominating exploration and conversation. The city has retained most of its original, gold-fuelled architectural extravagances with wrought-iron lace verandas, which now contrast with 21st-century hustle and bustle, for which the broad streets (designed to turn a camel train) are entirely suitable. It's like stumbling onto a Western movie set, and countless bars still enjoy the roaring trade they did in the 1890s, serving young miners with often more money than they know what to do with.

Kalgoorlie is semi-desert (260 millimeters/10 in. annual rainfall) though you wouldn't know it, given the vast and unique woodland (salmon gums up to 25m/82 ft. high) that surrounds the town. But the lack of water was a serious problem, both for the population and the mining processes, until one of the world's great engineering projects pumped water from the hills outside Perth some 600km (372 miles) to Kalgoorlie. The Goldfields Pipeline still supplies water to the city and to a vast area of the state.

Where dozens of head frames and chimneys were once starkly silhouetted against the skyline there is now an enormous, terraced hole. Roads, mines, processing sheds, and slag heaps have all been moved to make way for the mining of the 21st century; from Golden Mile to Super Pit in 100 years. The Super Pit, the world's biggest open-cut gold mine, is unbelievably big: 3.5km (2¼ miles) long, 1.5km (1 mile) wide, and 360m (1,181 ft.) deep. That's large enough to totally hide the Perth CBD.

Not all the old mining centers are still vibrant. Just 39km (24 miles) down the road is **Coolgardie** (pop. 1,100), another 1890s boomtown whose gold ran out in 1963. The town's semi-abandoned air is a sad foil to Kalgoorlie's energy. Much of the lovely architecture remains, and you can wander the gracious streets and a few museums for a pleasant nostalgia buzz.

ESSENTIALS

GETTING THERE **Qantas** (✆ **13 13 13** in Australia; www.qantas.com.au) has several flights a day between Kalgoorlie and Perth. **Skywest** (✆ **1300/660 088** in Australia; www.skywest.com.au) also flies from Perth daily.

Goldrush Tours (✆ **1800/620 440** in Australia, or 08/9021 2954) runs a 7-hour express coach service from Perth Sunday through Friday for A$70 (US$56/UK£29) adults, A$43 (US$34/UK£18) children under 15.

Kalgoorlie is a stop on the 3-day ***Indian Pacific*** ★ train service, which runs between Sydney and Perth twice a week in both directions. See section 13, "Getting

Fun Fact Streets Paved with . . . Gold?

In Kalgoorlie's early days, its streets were paved with a blackish spoil from the mining process called "tellurides." When someone realized tellurides contain up to 40% gold and 10% silver, those streets were ripped up in one big hurry. The city fathers had paved the streets with gold and didn't even know it!

Around Australia," in chapter 2, for contact details. The new ***Prospector*** train makes nine trips a week from Perth to Kalgoorlie in just under 7 hours, for A$72 (US$58/UK£29) adults, A$36 (US$29/UK£15) kids under 16. Contact the **Public Transport Authority** (© **1300/602 205** in Western Australia, or 08/9326 2600; www.transwa.wa.gov.au).

Driving from Perth, take the Great Eastern Highway, through the Perth Hills and the Wheatbelt on to Coolgardie and Kalgoorlie. The otherwise boring trip can be livened up by following the **Golden Pipeline Heritage Trail** ★ (map and booklet available from the National Trust; © **08/9321 6088;** www.ntwa.com.au), which celebrates the Goldfields' Pipeline, with its old pumping stations, reservoirs, and isolation. Both pipeline and highway follow much the same track and, at times, both they and the railway line loop together across the countryside. If you want to make the long and monotonous 2,182km (1,353-mile) journey on the Eyre Highway from Adelaide, contact the South Australian or Western Australian state auto clubs listed under "Getting Around Australia," in chapter 2, for advice.

VISITOR INFORMATION The **Kalgoorlie Goldfields Visitor Centre,** 250 Hannan St., Kalgoorlie, WA 6430 (© **1800/004 653** in Australia, or 08/9021 1966; www.kalgoorlie.info, dispenses information on Kalgoorlie, Coolgardie, and outlying regions. The center's inexpensive walking trail map (A$3.50 (US$2.80/UK£1.40).to the town's heritage is worth buying. The center is open Monday through Friday from 8:30am to 5pm, and Saturday, Sunday, and public holidays from 9am to 5pm. The **Coolgardie Visitor Centre,** 62 Bayley St., Coolgardie, WA 6429 (© **08/9026 6090**), is open daily from 9am to 5pm.

GETTING AROUND **Avis** (© 08/9021 1722), **Budget** (© 08/9093 2300), **Europcar** (© 08/9022 4922), and **Thrifty** (© 08/9021 4722) have offices in Kalgoorlie. Bear in mind that many outlying attractions will involve driving on unsealed roads, which is not permitted with the hire of ordinary 2WD vehicles.

Local tour operators offer coach and four-wheel-drive bush tours, including gold prospecting, around the Goldfields. Tours range from half a day to several days.

WHAT TO SEE & DO

As you might guess, gold is a common thread running through many of the town's attractions. One of the best is the **Mining Hall of Fame** ★ (© **08/9026 2700;** www.mininghall.com), Broad Arrow Road, 6km (3¾ miles) north of the Tourist Centre on the Goldfields Highway. Opened in late 2001, it has five interactive galleries focusing on modern high-tech mining, plus a number of historic mining and processing facilities, including several derricklike head frames. Find out how prospecting is done, learn how the business of mining is conducted, and then re-visit the old days. You can go 36m (118 ft.) underground in a mining cage and explore the tunnels where "real" miners once worked. You can pan for gold, watch a gold pour, see a video in a

Tips Time for the Gee-Gees

The Kalgoorlie Race Round is the high point in the local social calendar, with 3 weeks of horse races, the World Two Up Championship, and a variety of events in and around Kalgoorlie, including a bush picnic. The Round starts with the Coolgardie Cup, and finishes with over half of the town partying at the Kalgoorlie Cup. Usually held in early September.

re-created miner's tent, and pore over an extensive collection of mining memorabilia, machinery, and huts in a miners' village. The site is open daily from 9am to 4:30pm, except January 1 and December 25 and 26. Admission for aboveground activities only is A$17 (US$14/UK£6.95) for adults, A$14 (US$11/UK£5.70) for seniors and students, A$9 (US$7.20/UK£3.70) for children, and A$45 (US$36/UK£18) for families. If you want to add the underground tour, the prices are A$24 (US$19/UK£9.80) adults, A$18 (US$14/UK£7.35) seniors and students, A$14 (US$11/UK£5.70) children, and A$60 (US$48/UK£25) families. Underground tours and gold panning start four times a day, more often during school holidays. Allow half a day to see everything.

The **WA Museum Kalgoorlie-Boulder,** 17 Hannan St. (**© 08/9021 8533;** www.museum.wa.gov.au), is worth a look. You'll find it easily, with its enormous red head frame dominating Hannan Street and making a grand entrance statement. A glass elevator within it takes you to a great view over the city. You'll see the first 400-ounce gold bar minted in town, nuggets and jewelry, and historical displays. It is open daily from 10am to 4:30pm, closed Good Friday and December 25. Admission is free (donation requested). Tours are at 11am and 2:30pm. Allow an hour.

Don't leave town without goggling at the **Super Pit** ★★ open-cut mine—it makes giant dump trucks (which carry 225 tons of ore) look like ants. The lookout is at Outram Street in Boulder, off the Goldfields Highway. It's open daily from about 7am to about 9pm, but may be temporarily closed during the daily blast; check the time with the visitor center. Entry is free.

The **Royal Flying Doctor Service** (**© 08/9093 7595**) base at Kalgoorlie-Boulder Airport is open for visitors to browse memorabilia, see a video, and look over an aircraft (if one is in). It is open Monday through Friday from 10am to 3pm. Admission is by A$2 (US$1.60/UK£0.85) donation. Tours run on the hour, the last one at 2pm, and take 45 minutes.

Kalgoorlie's—and maybe Australia's—most unusual attraction must be **Langtrees 181,** 181 Hay St. (**© 08/9026 2181**), a working brothel styled into a sex-industry museum in the heart of Kalgoorlie's (in)famous red-light district. Despite laws to the contrary, Kalgoorlie's brothels flourished in red and pink corrugated-iron sheds festooned with colored lights, known as "starting stalls," and became a popular drive-by spot for gawping tourists. Langtrees is a swish modern establishment offering 90-minute tours, which are fun rather than sleazy, showing some of the 12 themed (and unoccupied) rooms, at a cost of A$35 (US$28/UK£14), A$25 (US$20/UK£10) for seniors! Tours depart at 1pm, 3pm, and 6pm daily.

The two town halls are both worth a visit. **Kalgoorlie Town Hall** has a statue of Paddy Hannan (the prospector who started the region's Gold Rush) inside, with a replica (complete with drinking fountain) outside, while the **Boulder Town Hall** has the magnificent 100-year-old Goatcher Theatre Curtain depicting the Bay of Naples.

It's lowered for viewing Wednesdays from 10am to noon and 1 to 3pm, and on Boulder Market Days (third Sun every month) from 9:30am to 1pm.

Wandering **Coolgardie's** quiet streets, which are graced with historic facades, is a stroll back in time. More than 100 signboards throughout the town, many with photos, detail what each site was like at the turn of the 20th century. The **Goldfields Exhibition,** 62 Bayley St. (✆ **08/9021 1966**), tells the town's story in a lovely 1898 building once used as the mining warden's courthouse. (The Tourist Bureau is also here.) Admission is free, and it's open daily except December 25, from 9am to 5pm.

"Inside Australia" ★★ is a series of sculptures scattered across a salt lake 187km (116 miles) north of Kalgoorlie. Fifty-one metal figures, derived from computer scans of the residents of nearby Menzies, were created by the renowned British sculptor Antony Gormley in 2003. They are spread in lonely splendor across the brilliant white salt surface of Lake Ballard, creating an eerily beautiful effect. Sunset can be particularly evocative. You can drive here, getting supplies and meals at Menzies, or Goldrush Tours offers trips with a minimum of 10 passengers.

The **Golden Quest Discovery Trail** is a 965km (598-mile) self-drive tour through old and new mining areas to the north of Kalgoorlie, including ghost towns and the Inside Australia statues. A comprehensive guidebook, with associated CDs, adds immeasurably to the drive and can be bought at all local visitor centers.

If you fancy trying your hand at a bit of prospecting, grab a half- or full-day tour with **Finders Keepers Prospecting Adventures** (✆ **0439 032 180** mobile). The tours provide an introduction to the local bush, and a chance to use a metal detector (with tuition). You keep any gold that you find. A half-day tour costs A$85 (US$68/UK£35) adults, A$50 (US$40/UK£20) children, while the full-day Gold Prospectors Discovery Trail is A$130 (US$104/UK£53) adults, and A$85 (US$68/UK£35) children.

WHERE TO STAY

The **Kalgoorlie Goldfields Visitor Centre** offers a free accommodations booking service (✆ **08/9021 1966;** fax 08/9021 2180; kbtc@emerge.net.au).

Broadwater Resort Hotel ★★ Kalgoorlie's only AAA-rated five-star hotel, opened in 2003, brings much-needed luxury accommodations for this major mining center and has already won awards for both its accommodations and dining. The studios are comfortable and spacious, and there are 10 one- and two two-bedroom apartments—all with spa tubs It's set in landscaped gardens about 2km (1¼ miles) from town center, and has a free shuttle service to Hannan Street. The low-profile blocks of units are set around the outdoor pool, and the rooms are elegantly furnished with quality modern amenities.

21 Davidson St., Kalgoorlie, WA 6430. ✆ **1800/198 001** in Australia, or 08/9080 0800. Fax 08/9080 0900. www.broadwaters.com.au. 92 units. A$265 (US$212/UK£108) deluxe studio; A$339 (US$271/UK£138) 1-bedroom apt; A$477 (US$382/UK£195) 2-bedroom apt (sleeps 4). Ask about packages. AE, DC, MC, V. Free parking. **Amenities:** Restaurant; bar; outdoor and indoor pool; adjacent golf course and night driving range; outdoor spa; bike hire; tour and car rental bookings; secretarial services available; coin-op laundry; dry-cleaning service. *In room:* A/C, TV/VCR w/in-house movies, fridge, coffeemaker, hair dryer, iron.

Palace Hotel The Grand Old Lady of Kalgoorlie was built 110 years ago at the height of the Gold Rush, on the town's principal intersection. It was the most luxurious hotel outside Perth and has been restored to its original grandeur. An elegant two-story building, it's graced with a splendid balcony, part of which is now the Balcony Restaurant (see below), and the rest provides private settings for the superior rooms. It retains a more genteel atmosphere than some of the other, rowdier, pubs, and has a magnificent sideboard/dresser donated by mining engineer Herbert Hoover (later U.S. president) to the barmaid with whom he fell in love when he was working on the Goldfields. It has a number of single rooms and some family rooms. No smoking indoors.

137 Hannan St. corner Boulder Rd., Kalgoorlie, WA 6430. © **08/9021 2788.** Fax 08/9021 1813. www.palacehotel.com.au. 50 units, some with shared facilities. A$120 (US$96/UK£49) Balcony double; A$90 (US$72/UK£37) Balcony single; A$75–A$85 (US$60–US$68/UK£31–UK£35) standard double; A$110 (US$88/UK£45) standard family; A$35–A$65 (US$28–US$52/UK£14–UK£26) budget rooms (men only). AE, DC, MC, V. Free parking. **Amenities:** Restaurant; cafe; 3 bars; coin-op laundry; dry cleaning service. *In room:* (Not budget rooms) A/C, TV w/in-house movies, fridge, coffeemaker.

WHERE TO DINE

Balcony Restaurant ★ MODERN AUSTRALIAN/TAPAS The restaurant is on the first floor balcony of the Palace Hotel, overlooking Hannan Street and some of the Goldfields' finest buildings, with a tree-lined horizon beyond. The food is almost as good as the setting, ideal for a sunset drink followed by dinner or a tapas plate as the evening closes in. Transparent plastic blinds can be rolled down when the weather doesn't suit (it's not always hot and dry in Kalgoorlie), but it's best when the evening air and the sounds of the passing crowds and traffic come wafting in.

137 Hannan St. (inside Palace Hotel), Kalgoorlie. © **08/9021 2788.** Reservations recommended. Main courses A$20–A$36 (US$16–US$29/UK£8–UK£15); tapas plates come in 3 sizes for sharing A$19–A$32 (US$15–US$26/UK£7.75–UK£13). AE, DC, MC, V. Mon–Sat 6pm–late.

Saltimbocca Restaurant ★ ITALIAN It must surely be Kal's favorite eatery with good crowds even on Monday nights. Its central location helps, but so does the modern decor, friendly service, and good candlelit atmosphere. Opened in 2003, it seems to have captured the hearts and stomachs of the locals. It serves up modern takes on the standard Italian fare, with the veal saltimbocca a standout.

90 Egan St. (1 block from Hannan St.), Kalgoorlie. © **08/9022 8028.** Reservations recommended. Main courses A$23–A$30 (US$18–US$24/UK£9.40–UK£12). AE, DC, MC, V. Mon–Sat 6pm–late.

5 The Coral Coast: Where the Outback Meets the Sea ★★

There is magic in the waters of the Indian Ocean where it brushes the shores of the northern portions of Western Australia's west coast. Brilliant coral reefs just meters offshore, whale sharks and dolphins, turtles and manta rays make this one of the world's most marvelous (and accessible) marine environments. Much of this is paradoxically due to the fact that inland is largely treeless semi-desert, occupied by vast sheep stations and a mere handful of people. This is real Outback with soaring summer temperatures and little rain, but this means that there are no rivers to carry sediments and pollutants to the sea. The ocean is untainted and has been able to develop some glorious natural attractions.

Since the 1960s, a pod of **bottlenose dolphins** has been coming into shallow water at **Monkey Mia** ★, in the World Heritage–listed Shark Bay Marine Park, to greet shore-bound humans. The dolphins' magical presence has drawn people from every corner of the globe.

Another 730km (453 miles) by road north on the Northwest Cape, adventure seekers from around the world come to **swim with the whale sharks** ★★★—measuring up to 18m (59 ft.) long—from March to early June. The Cape's parched shore and green waters hide another dazzling secret, though—a fringing coral reef 300km (186 miles) long called **Ningaloo** ★★, protected by a Marine Park. It contains 250 species of coral and 450 kinds of fish, dolphins, mantas, whales, turtles, and dugongs (manatees). Even the Great Barrier Reef can't beat Ningaloo Reef's proximity to shore—just a step or two off the beach delivers you into a wondrous underwater garden. What is amazing is that so few people seem to know about it. That and the remoteness means beaches you'll have pretty much to yourself, seas teeming with life because humans haven't scared (or fished) it away, unspoiled scenery, and a genuine sense of the frontier. There are also carpets of everlastings (daisylike wildflowers) stretching across vast areas in August and September in good years.

This coast, called both Coral and Outback, is lonely, remote, and too hot, and often windy, to visit between November and March. The best time to visit is April through October when it is warm enough to swim and the weather is balmy, though snorkelers might want a wet suit June and July. Humidity is always low. Facilities, gas, and fresh water are scarce, and distances are immense, so be prepared.

SHARK BAY (MONKEY MIA) ★

857km (535 miles) N of Perth; 1,867km (1,157 miles) SW of Broome

Monkey Mia's celebrity dolphins may not show on time—but they rarely pass up a visit. Apart from these delightful sea mammals, Shark Bay's waters heave with fish, turtles, the world's biggest population of dugongs (11,000 at last count), manta rays, sea snakes, and, June through October, humpback whales.

Shark Bay is an enormous body of clean clear shallow water, sheltered by a line of islands, and protected by its status as a Marine Park and World Heritage Site. The Peron Peninsula, a strangely shaped prong of land, juts far out into the bay and features white beaches composed entirely of shells, and "living fossils"—rocklike structures by the shore (called **stromatolites**) that are earth's first life. On the northern tip of the peninsula, **Francois Peron National Park** is home to many endangered species, thanks to a fence built across the narrowest point to keep out feral cats and foxes. The bay's only municipality is the one-time pearling town of **Denham** (pop. 500), 129km (80 miles) from the main coastal highway. It has a couple of hotels, a bakery, a newsdealer, some fishing-charter and tour operators, and the World Heritage Discovery Centre. Monkey Mia, 25km (16 miles) away on the opposite side of the peninsula, exists purely because of the dolphins. It has a dolphin information center and the pleasant but basic Monkey Mia Dolphin Resort (p. 512).

ESSENTIALS

GETTING THERE **Skywest Airlines** (✆ **1300/660 088** in Australia; www.skywest.com.au) has 1 hour, 45-minute flights from Perth, on Fridays through Sundays and Tuesdays. Skywest also links Monkey Mia to other Coral Coast destinations such as Carnarvon and Exmouth. Airfares start at approximately A$220 (US$176/UK£90) one-way. The **Shark Bay Airport Bus** (✆ **08/9948 1358**) meets every flight and transfers you to Monkey Mia Dolphin Resort for A$10 (US$8/UK£4.10) per person one-way.

Greyhound Australia (✆ **13 14 99** in Australia) travels daily between Perth and Broome. A separate service runs three times a week between Monkey Mia and the Overlander Roadhouse at the Shark Bay turnoff on the North West Coastal Highway. Its timing connects with the service from Broome (and Exmouth). Coming from Perth requires an overnight stay at Overlander. From Broome it costs A$308 (US$246/UK£126) and takes about 25 hours through featureless landscape—not recommended.

If driving yourself, beware of wildlife on the lonely 10-hour trip from Perth, and keep the gas tank full. From Perth, take the Brand Highway 424km (263 miles) north to Geraldton, then the North West Coastal Highway for 278km (172 miles) to the Overlander Roadhouse. Turn left onto the Denham-Hamelin Road and follow it for 154km (96 miles) to Monkey Mia. If you want to break the journey, the **All Seasons Inn Geraldton,** Brand Highway, Geraldton, WA 6530 (✆ **08/9921 2455**), has smart, clean motel rooms. Rates are A$147 (US$118/UK£60) double; specials are available most nights. It also has a relaxing restaurant and bar, swimming pool, free in-house movies, and a children's playground.

Numerous tour companies, including **Australian Pinnacle Tours** (✆ **1800/999 069** in Australia, or 08/9417 5555; www.pinnacletours.com.au) and **Feature Tours** (✆ **1800/999 819** in Australia, or 08/9475 2900; www.ft.com.au) offer package trips to Monkey Mia.

VISITOR INFORMATION Wide-ranging ecological information on Shark Bay Marine Park, Francois Peron National Park, and Hamelin Pool Marine Nature Reserve, as well as details on local tours, is available at the **Monkey Mia Dolphin Interpretive Centre** (✆ **08/9948 1366**) in Monkey Mia Dolphin Resort (see "Where to Stay & Dine," below). Videos run throughout the day, and researchers give free talks and slide shows most nights. The state Department of Environment and Conservation (✆ **08/9948 1208;** www.dec.wa.gov.au) runs the center. The official information outlet is the **Shark Bay World Heritage Discovery Centre,** 71 Knight Terrace, Denham, WA 6537 (✆ **08/9948 1590;** www.sharkbayinterpretivecentre.com.au), which is open daily from 8am to 5pm (until 6pm in winter).

GETTING AROUND **Shark Bay Car Hire** (✆ **08/9948 1247**) delivers cars and four-wheel-drives to the airport and the resort from its Denham office. Several local companies run tours to the various attractions.

FAST FACTS Admission to the **Monkey Mia Reserve,** in which Monkey Mia Dolphin Resort is located, is A$6 (US$4.80/UK£2.45) per adult, A$2 (US$1.60/UK£0.80) per child under 16, and A$12 (US$9.60/UK£4.90) per family. Resort guests as well as day-trippers pay this daily fee.

There are ATMs at the **Heritage Resort,** 73 Knight Terrace (at Durlacher St.), Denham (✆ **08/9948 1133**), and the local supermarket, but no banks. A banking agency is in the post office in Denham.

MEETING THE DOLPHINS ★

At 7am, guests at Monkey Mia Dolphin Resort are already gathering on the beach (as are the resident pelicans) in quiet anticipation of the dolphins' arrival. By 8am three or more dolphins usually show, and they come and go until the early afternoon. Because of the crowds the dolphins attract (about 40 people a session in low season, busloads in high season), park rangers instruct everyone to line up knee-deep in the water as the playful swimmers cruise by your legs. You may not approach them or reach out to pat them, but they sometimes come up to touch people of their own accord. Feeding times are different each day, and the quantities are strictly limited, so the dolphins won't become dependent on the food. Apart from the Monkey Mia Reserve entry fee, there is no charge to see the creatures.

A GREAT SEA-LIFE CRUISE, "LIVING FOSSILS" & MORE

Don't do what so many visitors do—see the dolphins, then shoot off to your next fast-sight. Stay to see Shark Bay's incredible marine life on the sailing maxi-catamaran

Tips Where Can I See the Dolphins?

The main advantages to making the trek to **Monkey Mia** ★★ is that dolphin sightings are virtually guaranteed every day, they swim and lie in the ultra-clear shallow water, and you can watch them being fed and interacting with the rangers. But it's crowded, and rangers strictly monitor behavior with the dolphins—not the interactive frolic you might have imagined. The first sightings, generally around 8am, are the most popular and crowded, after which the tour groups all disappear. If you stay around, the dolphins will often return and you can have a much more satisfying encounter. At **Bunbury** ★, a 2-hour drive south of Perth, you can *swim* with wild dolphins (see "Taking a Dip with Flipper," earlier in this chapter), but here the critters show up only about two-thirds of the time.

Shotover ★ (© **1800/241 481** in Australia, or 08/9948 1481; www.monkeymiawildsights.com.au). During a 2½-hour dugong (manatee) cruise, you will see a huge range of creatures, possibly hammerhead sharks, sea snakes, turtles, dolphins, and, of course, dugongs. Every passenger is given polarized sunglasses, which help you spot underwater animals. Sometimes you see dozens of dugongs (though they leave the area from mid-May to Aug). The cruise departs from Monkey Mia Dolphin Resort at 1pm daily and costs A$64 (US$51/UK£26) adults, half price children 7 to 16. The *Shotover* also runs a fascinating 2-hour dolphin cruise at 10:30am—worth doing even if you've already seen the dolphins on the shore. It costs A$59 (US$47/UK£24) adults, free for children under 17. Sunset cruises are a fast-sailing summer option, September through January, at A$49 (US$39/UK£20) adults, half price children 7 to 16.

On your way in or out of Monkey Mia, stop by **the Hamelin Pool Historic Telegraph Station** (© **08/9942 5905**), 29km (18 miles) from the highway turnoff. A small museum houses old equipment, farming tools, and historical odds and ends from the 19th-century days when this was a telegraph repeater station. The A$4 (US$3.20/UK£1.65) admission fee to the museum includes an explanation of the **stromatolites,** rocky formations about a foot high that were created by the planet's first oxygen-breathing cells—in other words, earth's first life. You might want to skip the museum, but do wander down to the shoreline and stroll out along a boardwalk to see them close-up (warning: they look, and act, just like rocks!).

Nearby **Shell Beach,** ★ 43km (27 miles) from the highway, is amazing. The beach is said to be 110km (68 miles) long and over 10m (33 ft.) deep, made up of billions of tiny snow-white shells; the numbers are incalculable. They crunch beneath your feet as you walk along and stretch beneath the rich, clear blue water. Solidified blocks of the shells were quarried nearby to build many local buildings. There is a cafe and gift store.

An electronic fence has been built across the peninsula at its narrowest point here, to keep out cats and foxes; there's even an electronic barking "dog" to deter the predators. This is an essential element of Project Eden which is re-introducing and protecting various endangered marsupials. The northern part of the peninsula, beyond Denham and Monkey Mia, is the 52,500-hectare (129,675-acre) **Francois Peron National Park.** You can explore its salt pans, dunes, coastal cliffs, beaches, and old homestead, either alone (you will need a four-wheel-drive, but stay on the marked

Value Save on Park Passes

Entry to many national parks in Western Australia, including Cape Range and Francois Peron, costs A$10 (US$8/UK£4.10) per car per day. If you are planning to visit a few, a **Holiday Park Pass** is worth the money. It costs A$35 (US$28/UK£14) for a vehicle carrying up to eight people and is valid for 4 weeks. Obtain passes from the Department of Environment and Conservation (**www.dec.wa.gov.au**). The passes are not valid for Monkey Mia Dolphin Reserve.

road—the claypans known as *birridas* are seriously boggy) or on a half- or full-day tour with **Monkey Mia Wildsights** (✆ **1800/241 481;** www.monkeymiawildsights.com.au). The scenery is harsh but with great coastal beauty where red cliffs meet beaches fringed with vivid turquoise water. You should spot wallabies, birds, and emus, and you may see turtles, dolphins, rays, dugongs, and sharks from the cliffs. Other activities include game and deep-sea-fishing trips from Denham, scuba diving, excursions to the deserted beaches and 180m (590-ft.) cliffs of nearby Dirk Hartog Island, and a couple of pearl-farm tours.

WHERE TO STAY & DINE

Monkey Mia Dolphin Resort Set right on the beach the dolphins visit, this oasis of green lawns and palms doubles as a town settlement, and is the only place to stay at Monkey Mia (all other accommodations are 25km/16 miles away, in Denham). The beachside Dolphin Lodge (and backpacker lodge) opened in 2004, offering 24 motel-style units. Each has a king-size bed, private bathroom, and hair dryer. Ground-floor units open right onto the dolphin beach, and first-floor units have balconies with views across the bay. The backpacker lodge, with its own Monkey Bar and large communal kitchen, is behind the lodge. It holds four- and seven-bed dormitories as well as shared and family rooms with bathrooms. The new accommodations complement the existing villas (which sleep three to five people); air-conditioned demountable (portable cabin) "park homes" with cooking facilities; and trailer and camping sites. The pleasant open-sided all-day restaurant overlooks the sea; the resort has a minimarket, an Internet cafe, and a dive shop; and you can hire a kayak or boat. Most tours in the area depart from here. A 1.5km (1-mile) nature trail leads from the resort.

Monkey Mia Rd., Shark Bay (P.O. Box 119), Denham, WA 6537. ✆ **1800/653 611** in Australia, or 08/9948 1320. Fax 08/9948 1034. www.monkeymia.com.au. 57 powered trailer sites, 20 tent sites; 13 park homes, 6 with bathroom; 60 villas; 24 motel units, all with shower only. A$12 (US$9.60/UK£4.90) per person tent site; A$24 (US$19/UK£9.80) per person in backpacker dorm; A$109 (US$87/UK£44) park home for up to 4; A$205 (US$164/UK£84) double or triple Garden Villa; A$275 (US$220/UK£112) double or triple Beachfront Villa; A$205 (US$164/UK£84) Beachside Dolphin Unit. Extra person A$20 (US$16/UK£8.15). Weekly rates available. AE, DC, MC, V. Free parking. **Amenities:** 2 restaurants; 2 bars; takeout cafe; outdoor pool; outdoor tennis court; Jacuzzi (fed by naturally warm underground water); use of snorkel gear; tour desk; car-rental desk; massage; babysitting; coin-op laundry. *In room:* A/C, TV, small fridge, coffeemaker, hair dryer, iron.

THE NORTH WEST CAPE & NINGALOO

Exmouth: 1,260km (781 miles) N of Perth; 1,567km (972 miles) SW of Broome

Driving along the only road on the Exmouth Peninsula toward North West Cape is surreal. Hundreds of anthills march through the scrub and away to the horizon, clumps of spinifex dot the red earth, occasional sheep and 'roos threaten to get under the wheels, and the sun shines down from a cloudless blue sky. On the western shore is the tiny reef resort settlement of **Coral Bay** (pop. 120), a cluster of dive shops, backpacker lodges, a low-key resort, and charter boats nestled on sand so white, water so blue, and ocher dust so orange you'd think the townsfolk had computer-enhanced the colors. Away from the settlement are sandy beaches edged by coral. Another 141km (88 miles) farther north is **Exmouth** (pop. 3,500), born in 1967 as a support town to the Harold E. Holt Naval Communications Station, a joint Australian–United States center. It has become the principal center for trips and tours to Ningaloo and has a new marina.

Apart from swimming with the whale shark, the reason you come here is to scuba dive and snorkel in the **Ningaloo Marine Park** ★★, which hugs the peninsula's western shores. You can also take four-wheel-drive trips into and over the **Cape Range National Park,** which covers much of the northern portion, and the surrounding sheep stations.

Exmouth is on the eastern shore, facing Exmouth Gulf, and tends to be several degrees warmer than the west (Ningaloo-facing) coast, including Coral Bay. Coral Bay is one of Australia's most casual resorts, but it has divine diving, swimming, and snorkeling. It has no ATMs. Exmouth can be hot and charmless, but it has more facilities, including a supermarket, ATMs, an outdoor cinema, rental cars, and smarter accommodations and dining options. Most tours pick up or leave from Exmouth. Both places have plenty of dive, snorkel, fishing, and whale-watch companies. Wherever you stay, it's best to book ahead in whale shark season (from late Mar to June), and school holidays. Carry drinking water everywhere you go.

ESSENTIALS

GETTING THERE **Skywest** (✆ **1300/660 088** in Australia; www.skywest.com.au) flies from Perth daily. A shuttle bus meets every flight and takes you to your Exmouth hotel for A$20 (US$16/UK£8.15) one-way. Reservations can be made with **Exmouth Bus Charter** (✆ **08/9949 4623;** exmouthbuscharter@bigpond.com). (Have the cash on you; there's no ATM at the airport.) **Coral Bay Adventures** (✆ **08/9942 5955**) makes transfers, on demand, from the airport to Coral Bay, approximately 120km (74 miles) away, for A$75 (US$60/UK£31) adults, A$35 (US$28/UK£14) children under 13, one-way.

Greyhound Australia (✆ **13 14 99** in Australia) has a service to Coral Bay and Exmouth from Minilya on the Great Northern Highway. It connects with both the Perth-Broome and Broome-Perth services, in the wee hours of the morning, Monday to Saturday. The trip time from Perth is 19 hours, and the fare is A$229 (US$183/UK£93).

The 14-hour drive from Perth (plus rest stops) is through lonely country on a two-lane highway. Check that your contract allows you to drive your rental car this far north, and includes unlimited mileage. Wildlife can be thick on the ground, and gas stations thin. From Perth, take the Brand Highway north to Geraldton, 424km (263 miles)

Tips 'Roos and Wedgies

Driving between Shark Bay and Exmouth you need to be aware not just of kangaroos on the road (mostly at dusk, dawn, and at night), but also of the ones that didn't make it, and who have attracted scavengers, mostly crows and wedge-tailed eagles. The crows are not a problem but the wedgies are large and ponderous when trying to get out of your way. You don't want one of these in your windshield, so slow down when you see a large bird ahead.

---

away, then the North West Coastal Highway for 618km (386 miles) to Minilya gas station; the Exmouth turnoff is 7km (4⅓ miles) north of Minilya. The Coral Bay turnoff is 79km (49 miles) farther north, and Exmouth another 145km (90 miles). Overnight at the **Wintersun Hotel/Motel Geraldton,** 44 Chapman Rd., Geraldton, WA 6530 (**© 08/9923 1211;** A$95/US$76/UK£39 or A$120/US$96/UK£49 family room), or in Carnarvon, the only town between Geraldton and Exmouth. Everything else that looks like a town on your map is just a roadhouse (a gas station with shop, cafe, and perhaps some limited accommodations). But keep in mind that even the roadhouses can be 200km (124 miles) apart. The longer drive from Broome is even less recommended.

VISITOR INFORMATION The **Exmouth Visitor Centre,** Murat Road, Exmouth, WA 6707 (**© 1800/287 328** in Western Australia, or 08/9949 1176), is open weekdays, and weekends April through September, from 9am to 5pm, but weekends October through March from 9am to 1pm. The **Milyering Visitors Centre,** on the west coast, 52km (32 miles) from Exmouth, is the Cape Range and Ningaloo National Parks' information center, run by the Department of Environment and Conservation (DEC). It is open daily from 10am to 12:30pm and 1:15 to 4pm. You can also pick up information, including a hiking-trail map of the Cape Range park from DEC's office on Nimitz Street, Exmouth. **Coastal Adventure Tours** runs an information and booking center, and Internet cafe, in Coral Bay Shopping Arcade, Coral Bay, WA 6701 (**© 08/9948 5190;** www.coralbaytours.com.au).

GETTING AROUND Tour and dive operators pick up from either Exmouth or Coral Bay accommodations. The roads to Exmouth and Coral Bay are paved, as is most of the only road that runs from Exmouth along the west (Ningaloo) coast. **Avis** (**© 08/9949 2492**), **Europcar** (**© 08/9949 2940**), and local operator **Allens Car Hire** (**© 08/9949 2403**) have offices in Exmouth; there is no car rental in Coral Bay.

Ningaloo Reef Bus (**© 1800/999 941**) runs from Exmouth hotels to various beaches along the Ningaloo coast, stopping at the Milyering Visitors Centre en route. It runs Monday, Tuesday, Friday, and Saturday April through October, and daily November through March. The round-trip fare to the snorkel beauty spot of Turquoise Bay is A$20 (US$16/UK£8.15) adults, A$15 (US$12/UK£6.15) children, and A$60 (US$48/UK£25) families of 2 adults, 2 children. You can hire a snorkel and fins on the bus for A$10 (US$8/UK£4.10). Hotel pickup is about 9am, and leaves Turquoise Bay again at about 2:30pm, so you need to bring food, water, and sun protection.

SWIMMING WITH WHALE SHARKS ★★★

Whale sharks are sharks, not whales, and are the world's biggest fish, reaching a railway engine size of 12 to 18m (39–58 ft.) in length. Terrified? Don't be. Their gigantic size belies their gentle nature and swimming speed; despite having mouths big enough to swallow a boatload of snorkelers, they eat plankton. Several boat operators take people out to swim alongside the whale sharks when they appear from late March to mid-June. You simply float in the water wearing mask and snorkel and watch this magnificent spotted fish moving effortlessly past you; it's mind-blowing that you can be so close to such a huge, beautiful and harmless creature. A day trip with one of the longest established whale-shark companies, **Exmouth Diving Centre** (**© 08/9949 1201;** www.exmouthdiving.com.au), or its Coral Bay sister company, **Ningaloo Reef Diving Centre** (**© 08/9942 5824;** www.ningalooreefdive.com), costs A$350 (US$280/UK£143) for snorkeling or A$375 (US$300/UK£153) including a subsequent scuba dive, including all gear.

DIVING, SNORKELING, FISHING & 4WD TOURS

Dive and snorkel ★ Ningaloo's unspoiled waters, and you will see marvelous reef formations, groper, manta rays, octopus, moray eels, potato cod (which you can hand-feed), and other marvels at a dozen or more sites. Divers often spot humpback and false killer whales and large sharks, while snorkelers may see dolphins, dugongs, manta rays, and turtles. Loads of dive companies in Exmouth and Coral Bay (including the two listed in "Swimming with Whale Sharks," above) rent gear and run daily dive trips and learn-to-dive courses. A two-dive day trip costs A$185 (US$148/UK£76) with all gear supplied.

Three great snorkeling spots are: right off the shore at Coral Bay, where you can stroll up the beach, put on your mask and snorkel, and drift with the current past corals and limitless fish, then climb out and do it all over again; Pilgramunna Ledges, 72km (45 miles) from Exmouth, where you're rarely more than 10m (33 ft.) from the beach; and sheltered **Turquoise Bay** ★★, a 60km (37-mile) drive from Exmouth, which also has a drift option, but you do need to be a reasonable swimmer. In deeper waters off Coral Bay, you can snorkel with **manta rays** ★ with a "wingspan" of up to 7m (23 ft.). If you're lucky the rays may encounter a good feeding patch, when they will perform a series of backward somersaults to keep themselves within the same area. Companies in both towns run manta and reef-snorkel trips, and rent snorkel gear. The Ningaloo shores have loads of swimming beaches; for safety's sake, never swim alone.

Reef fish, tuna, and Spanish mackerel are common catches in these waters, and black, blue, and striped marlin run outside the reef September through January. Up to a dozen boats operate reef and **game-fishing day trips** ★ out of Exmouth and Coral Bay, and tackle and tin fishing dinghies are easy to rent in either town.

Green and loggerhead **turtles** ★ lay eggs at night from November through February or March on the Cape's beaches. Take a flashlight and go looking for them, or join one of several turtle-watch tours from either town. August through October, boats run cruises from either town to spot **humpback whales.**

Because the Cape has few roads, take an off-road 240km (149-mile) four-wheel-drive escapade with **Ningaloo Safari Tours** (✆ **08/9949 1550;** www.ningaloosafari.com). You will explore the arid limestone ridges of 50,581-hectare (124,935-acre) Cape Range National Park, snorkel Turquoise Bay, climb a lighthouse, and cruise orange-walled Yardie Creek Gorge to spot rock wallabies. This full-day trip departs your Exmouth hotel at 7:30am and returns at 6pm. It costs A$175 (US$140/UK£71) for adults and A$125 (US$100/UK£51) for children under 13. A 5-hour afternoon tour and full day snorkeling tour are also available depending on numbers.

Coral Bay's **Coastal Adventure Tours** (✆ **08/9948 5190**) has quad bike tours which head off to quiet deserted beaches via bush tracks and over sand dunes. Three-hour snorkel treks are A$90 (US$72/UK£37) and a 2-hour sunset trek is A$75 (US$60/UK£31), or less when people share the same bike.

WHERE TO STAY & DINE

IN OR NEAR EXMOUTH

Ningaloo Reef Retreat ★★ If you want a quiet and remote, but environmentally sensitive, place to stay, this is it. Set in Cape Range National Park, within sight and smell of the Indian Ocean, it's a small ecocamp where you stay in spacious tents with queen-size bed, hammock, composting toilet, and solar shower. You can also sleep in a swag (bedroll) under the magnificent southern sky. The swags are an essential option when families bring a child with them. Boardwalks connect to the "Retreat" which contains lounge, dining area, kitchen, sun deck, and small reference library. All meals, guided snorkeling and kayaking tours, park fees, and transfers from Exmouth are included. Fresh food is delivered daily from Exmouth, with some guests assisting in preparation of meals such as kangaroo curry with banana and yogurt sauce. Bring your own drinks. Evenings are special, with the sun setting over a quiet sea and, almost invariably, kangaroos in the foreground.

Yardie Creek Rd., Cape Range National Park, 66km (41 miles) from Exmouth, WA 6707. ✆ **1800/999 941** within Australia, or 08/9949 1776. www.ningalooreefretreat.com. 5 tents, with solar shower. A$720 (US$576/UK£294) double. Inquire about packages. DC, MC, V. Ningaloo Reef Bus provides courtesy transfers from Exmouth. **Amenities:** Dining tent; lounge with library; guided snorkeling and kayaking; fruit, tea, coffee, juices, water available 24 hr.; cots available. *In room:* Hammock. No smoking in covered areas.

Potshot Hotel Resort The grounds can be hot and dusty, but the hotel is in a modern complex, within easy walking distance of town center. The brick motel rooms are cool and spacious; the homestead rooms are smaller, older, and more basic (they don't have phones). There are two-bedroom apartments, and across the road are newer three-bedroom apartments, some with Jacuzzis. The cocktail bar around the pool is the only shady place in town to enjoy a drink, which explains its popularity with locals. The restaurant is scant on atmosphere but has a long menu, good food, and a nice wine list. Prices are between A$15 and A$30 (US$12–US$24/UK£6.15–UK£12). There's a seafood buffet on Friday and Saturday nights.

Murat Rd., Exmouth, WA 6707. ✆ **08/9949 1200.** Fax 08/9949 1486. www.potshotresort.com. 97 units, all with shower only. A$89 (US$71/UK£36) double homestead room; A$139 (US$111/UK£57) resort studio room for 2 or 3; A$159 (US$127/UK£65) 1-bed king spa room; A$149–A$175 (US$119–US$140/UK£61–UK£71) 2-bedroom apt; A$190 (US$152/UK£78) 3-bedroom apt. Extra person A$12–A$15 (US$9.60–US$12/UK£4.90–UK£6.15). Maid service in apt A$22–A$33 (US$18–US$26/UK£9–UK£13) per day. AE, DC, MC, V. Easy free parking. **Amenities:** 2 restaurants; 4 bars; 3 small outdoor pools; coin-op laundry. *In room:* A/C, TV, full kitchen in apt, fridge, coffeemaker, hair dryer, iron.

IN CORAL BAY

Ningaloo Reef Resort *Kids* This low-rise complex of motel rooms, studios, and apartments stands out as the best place to stay among Coral Bay's profusion of backpacker hostels. Located on a blissfully green lawn with a swimming pool overlooking the bay, the rooms are nothing fancy or new, but they're clean, with views toward the bay and the pool. Some have kitchens. The place has a nice communal air, thanks to the bar doubling as the local pub.

1 Robinson St., Coral Bay, WA 6701. ✆ **08/9942 5934.** Fax 08/9942 5953. www.ningalooreefresort.com.au. 34 units, all with shower only. A$175–A$195 (US$140–US$156/UK£71–UK£80) double; A$200–A$260 (US$160–US$208/UK£82–UK£106) apt. Extra person A$18 (US$14/UK£7.35). Weekly rates available. MC, V. **Amenities:** Restaurant; bar; outdoor pool; coin-op laundry; guest barbecue. *In room:* A/C, cooking facilities in apt, coffeemaker, hair dryer, iron, no phone.

6 The Kimberley: A Far-Flung Wilderness ★★

Most Aussies would be hard put to name a single settlement, river, or mountain in the Kimberley, so rarely visited and sparsely inhabited is this wilderness. It has been called Australia's "Last Frontier." This vast empty rugged chunk in the far north of Western Australia pushes out into the Timor Sea like a giant fist. Dry in winter and impassable in summer after one of the regular cyclones passes through, it is an area of endless bush punctuated with enormous boab trees whose trunks are shaped like giant bottles, a lonely island-strewn coastline, long rocky ridges, and a surprising number of running rivers. The dry spreading scenery calls to mind parts of Africa or India.

The Kimberley Region

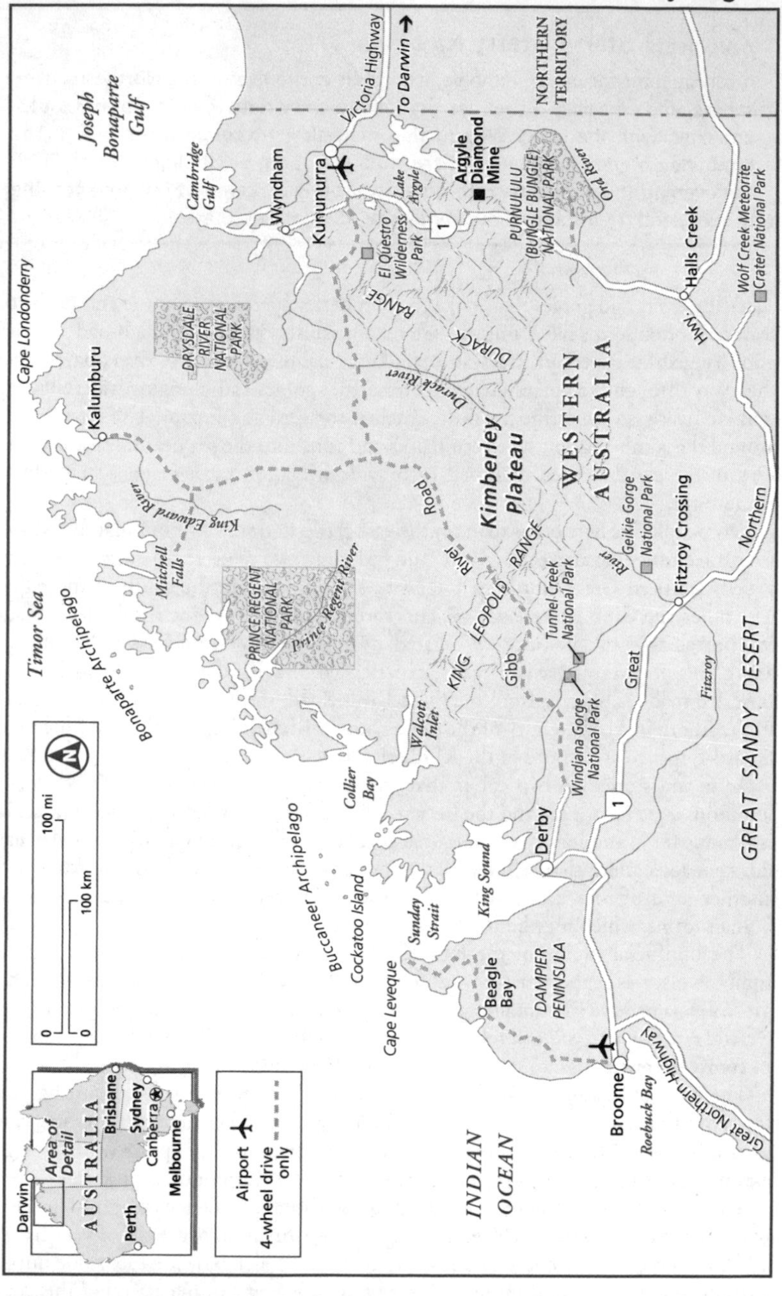

Moments Starry, Starry Nights

It can be hard for people who've lived their entire lives in the Northern Hemisphere, and especially if they are city folk, to appreciate the glory of the southern skies, with the Milky Way curving majestically through the heavens. The Kimberley is one place where there is no pollution, or city lights, to diminish the evening show. Find time to go away from your camp or lodge, lie on the ground, and try to take in the immensity of what's up there.

It's the rivers and gorges that make the Kimberley special even at the end of the dry season. It often seems like a miracle, after a long dusty drive, to find a broad sparkling pool fringed by Paperbark trees and pandanus palms. Where the rivers have carved their way through the ranges there are spectacular gorges and plunging waterfalls. Two massive river systems define the outer reaches: the Ord and Fitzroy. The Fitzroy loops around the south and southwestern flanks and runs into the sea near Derby, while the Ord in the east has been dammed to provide irrigation for a major scheme below Kununurra.

Few people live here other than on the vast cattle stations or Aboriginal reserves. It's over three times the area of England, but with only two roads traversing it. One is the sealed, sanitized Great Northern Highway, skirting around the south of the region. The other, the **Gibb River Road** ★, cuts through the heart of the Kimberley. Most of it is unsealed—a rough, dusty, corrugated, death-to-all-RVs, route. If you haven't been along this road, you haven't really experienced the Kimberley. One other rough unsealed road leads north from the Gibb River Road, the Kalumburu Road that leads to the Aboriginal community of the same name. **Mitchell Falls** ★★, one of the major if hard-to-get-to attractions of the Kimberley, is accessible from the Kalumburu Road.

Aqua and scarlet are two colors that will hit you in the eye in the Kimberley—a luminous aqua for the sea and the fiery red of the fine soil called "pindan." The region is famous for Wandjina-style Aboriginal rock art depicting people with circular hairdos that look more than a little like beings from outer space. It is also known for another kind of rock art known as "Bradshaw figures," sticklike representations of human forms, which may be the oldest art on earth.

The unofficial capital of the East Kimberley is **Kununurra.** The small agricultural town serves as the base for wildlife cruises on the Ord; tours to the **Bungle Bungle** ★★★, a massive labyrinth of beehive-shaped rock formations; and **El Questro** ★★, a cattle ranch where you can hike, fish, and cruise palm-filled gorges by day and sleep in comfy permanent safari tents or glamorous homestead rooms by night.

The town of **Broome** ★★ is the gateway to the West Kimberley and starting point for most tours. It's not really of the Kimberley, but rather an exotic resort which started life as a 19th-century pearling port. Its waters now give up the world's biggest and best South Sea pearls, and it has become a major winter holiday resort.

The coast between Broome and Kununurra is littered with islands, gulfs, and long inlets, almost all uninhabited and with no trace of human activity. Everything is affected by the region's massive tides of up to 10m (33 ft.), which create some impressive effects when funneled through narrow passages. Some of the appeal of this coastline lies in the knowledge that so few people have visited it since the first explorers of the 17th century.

ESSENTIALS

VISITOR INFORMATION **Australia's North West Tourism,** P.O. Box 554, Broome, WA 6725 (© **08/9193 6660;** www.australiasnorthwest.com), supplies information on the entire region. The **Kununurra Visitor Centre** (p. 521) and the **Broome Visitor Centre** (p. 525) also handle inquiries about things to see and do across the entire Kimberley, and you can drop into their offices once you arrive.

Best of the Kimberley (© **1800/450 850** in Australia, or 08/9192 6070; www.kimberleytravel.net) is a Broome-based one-stop agency marketing a large range of tours and experiences, and it specializes in personalized vacations. Visits to the remote Dampier Peninsula to fish and go mud-crabbing with an Aboriginal family, and self-fly packages around this vast region for private pilots (aircraft rental included) are among the agency's more unusual offerings.

GETTING AROUND Enormous distances, high gasoline costs (A$1.50 per liter, or US$5.45 per gallon or more), Wet season floods, and very limited roads and facilities can make traveling the Kimberley expensive and time-consuming. Some attractions are so remote they can only be reached by aerial tours or charter boats. Many more are accessible only on unsealed roads, for which a two-wheel-drive rental car is totally unsuitable. If you don't want to rely on tours, rent a four-wheel-drive (available in Broome and Kununurra). Allow for an average speed of 80kmph (50 mph) on the area's rough unsealed roads, but be prepared for unexpected dips and patches where the road surface has collapsed. Most outfits will allow one-way rentals between Broome and Kununurra, or vice versa, at a surcharge of approximately A$350 to A$550 (US$280–US$440/UK£143–UK£224). Review "Road Conditions & Safety," "What If Your Vehicle Breaks Down?" and "Tips for Four-Wheel Drivers," in the "Getting Around Australia" section of chapter 2 before starting.

Kimberley Camping & Outback Supplies, 65 Frederick St., Broome (© **08/9193 5909;** fax 08/9193 6878; www.kimberleycamping.com.au), sells and rents every piece of camping equipment you need, from tents and "mozzie" (mosquito) nets to cooking utensils and outdoor clothing.

Taking a guided four-wheel-drive camping or accommodated safari is usually the best way to travel the Kimberley. Safaris depart Broome, Kununurra, or Darwin, and last between 2 days and 2 weeks. Popular tours are the cross-Kimberley journey between Broome and Kununurra, especially along the **Gibb River Road,** and into the **Bungle Bungle.**

Most safaris run only in the Dry season, April or May through October or November. Respected operators include **APT Kimberley Wilderness Adventures** (© **1800/675 222** in Australia; www.kimberleywilderness.com.au); **East Kimberley Tours** (© **08/9168 2213;** www.eastkimberleytours.com.au); **Australian Adventure Travel** (© **1800/621 625** in Australia, or 08/9284 2355; www.safaris.net.au); and **Kimberley Wild** (© **1300/738 870** in Australia, or 08/9193 7778; www.kimberleywild.com).

Both APT Kimberley Wilderness and East Kimberley operate semi-permanent, catered, and environmentally sensitive camps in remote scenic spots. They are primarily for people on their tours, but the APT facilities may be available to independent travelers, from A$150 (US$120/UK£61) per person, dinner, bed, and breakfast. Book well ahead at © **1800/889 389.**

Broome Aviation (© **1300/136 629** in Australia, or 08/9192 1369; www.broomeaviation.com) and **King Leopold Air** (© **08/9193 7155;**

Tips **Aboriginal Culture**

The Kimberley is one area where Aboriginal culture has, to a larger extent than elsewhere, remained intact. Try to get involved with some aspects. Find a gallery that encourages and stocks the work of local artists, such as the Warmun (Turkey Creek) school which owes much to the superb interpretations of Rover Thomas. An Aboriginal commentary on the Kimberley landscape and/or the Wandjina rock art can add immeasurably to one's understanding. You have a good chance of getting this when staying at Kooljaman Resort or traveling on an APT Kimberley Wilderness Adventure—both are at least part-owned by local Aboriginal communities.

www.kingleopoldair.com.au), based in Broome, and **Alligator Airways** (© **1800 632 533** in Australia, or 08/9168 1333; www.alligatorairways.com.au) and **Slingair Heliwork** (© **1800/095 500** in Australia, or 08/9169 1300; www.slingair.com.au), based in Kununurra, run a range of flight-seeing tours all over the Kimberley, lasting from a couple of hours to several days. Some involve sightseeing on the ground, hiking, four-wheel-drive trips, overnights at fishing camps, or stops at cattle stations.

KUNUNURRA

827km (513 miles) SW of Darwin; 1,032km (640 miles) E of Broome

Given the generally arid conditions in the Kimberley, it's quite a surprise to swoop over a field of sugar cane as you come in to land at Kununurra. This relatively new town (pop. 6,000) was developed as an agricultural center based on major irrigation works created by the damming of the mighty Ord River. There are two dams: **Lake Argyle,** Australia's largest, and the smaller Lake Kununurra that actually feeds the irrigation areas.

Kununurra (the name is Aboriginal for "meeting of big waters") has become the base for visiting several outstanding attractions, and is now a significant tourist center. A cruise or canoe trip down the **Ord River** ★★ to see real wilderness, birds, dramatic cliffs, and crocs is a must. So is a flight over, or a trip into, the **Bungle Bungle** ★★★, monumental striped domes of rock that look like giant beehives. The world's biggest diamond mine is not in South Africa but out in the rugged Kimberley wilds near Kununurra, and it can be visited by air. The town is a gateway to the Kimberley proper via the **Gibb River Road** ★. **El Questro Wilderness Park** ★★ is a million-acre cattle station (ranch) where you can hike magnificent gorges, fish, cruise rivers, ride horses, and see some of Australia's most breathtaking Aboriginal art. The port of Wyndham, terminus for many Kimberley cruises, and with a superb lookout over Cambridge Gulf, is 101km (63 miles) away on a sealed road.

ESSENTIALS

GETTING THERE **Air North** (© **1800 627 474** in Australia, or 08/8920 4001; www.airnorth.com.au) flies from Broome and Darwin daily. **Skywest** (© **1300/660 088** in Australia; www.skywest.com.au) flies from and to Broome on Tuesday and Thursday, with connections to Perth. **Greyhound Australia** (© **13 14 99** in Australia) serves the town daily from Perth via Broome and daily from Darwin via Katherine. From Perth the trip takes about 48 hours, from Broome about 14 hours. The one-way fare from Perth is A$601 (US$481/UK£245). From Darwin, the trip time is around 10 hours, and the fare is A$194 (US$155/UK£79).

Kununurra is 512km (317 miles) west of Katherine on the Victoria Highway. The Great Northern Highway from Broome connects with the Victoria Highway 45km (28 miles) west of Kununurra. The Gibb River Road connects with the Great Northern Highway 53km (33 miles) west of Kununurra.

VISITOR INFORMATION The **Kununurra Visitor Centre** is at Coolibah Drive, Kununurra, WA 6743 (© **08/9168 1177;** www.kununurratourism.com). Hours change with the season, but it's usually open daily from 8am to 5pm weekdays and 9am to 4pm weekends and holidays April to October, and from 9am to 4pm weekdays November to March (closed Sat, Sun, and public holidays during this time).

GETTING AROUND **Avis** (© 08/9169 1258), **Budget** (© 08/9168 2033), **Europcar** (© 08/9168 3385), **Hertz** (© 08/9169 1424), and **Thrifty** (© 08/9169 1911) all rent four-wheel-drive vehicles. Hertz also rents camping gear.

WHAT TO SEE & DO

ON THE ORD RIVER Several cruise outfits offer trips on the Ord River and/or Lake Argyle, a man-made inland sea ringed by red hills and bigger than 19 Sydney Harbours. Go for the Ord. The Ord River is one of the most picturesque waterways in Australia, lined with raw scenery, and teeming with all kinds of wetland birds and freshwater crocodiles. **Triple J Tours** ★★ (© **1800/242 682** in Australia, or 08/9168 2682; www.triplejtours.net.au) runs excellent cruises, with several itineraries which vary from Dry season to Wet. The most popular starts with a 70km (43-mile) narrated coach ride to Lake Argyle, including a visit to the historic Durack homestead, and ends with a 55km (34-mile) cruise down the Ord back to Kununurra. The boat travels fast, through rock-lined gorges and along still satiny reaches, and pulls in at numerous tranquil spots. This costs A$135 (US$108/UK£55) for adults and A$95 (US$76/UK£39) for children 4 to 15, including pickup from your hotel, and afternoon tea. You usually catch the sunset and flocks of birds going home over the river as the cruise is finishing.

Big Waters Kimberley Canoe Safaris (© **1800/641 998** in Australia, or 08/9169 1998; www.adventure.kimberley.net.au) offers a popular 3-day self-guided canoeing and camping safari down the Class I (that means "gentle") Ord River, from Lake Argyle to Kununurra, in two-person Canadian canoes (equipment supplied). It costs A$165 (US$132/UK£67) per person.

A day on the river to fish for barramundi with Greg Harman's **Ultimate Adventures** (© **08/9168 2310;** www.ultimateadventures.citysearch.com.au) costs around A$290 (US$232/UK£118) per person, more if there is only one of you. Greg also offers trips of up to 7 days at his Hairy Dog's Fishing Camp.

Triangle Tours (© **08/9168 1272**) has half-day tours to the Ord River irrigation area at A$70 (US$56/UK£29) adults, A$40 (US$32/UK£16) children; and full-day tours to the historic port of Wyndham at A$165 (US$132/UK£67) adults, and A$90 (US$72/UK£37) children.

DIAMONDS IN THE ROUGH Turning out an impressive 38 million carats a year is the world's biggest diamond mine, the **Argyle Diamond Mine,** 176km (109 miles) from Kununurra. It is the only mine in the world that produces pink diamonds in commercial quantities; champagne, cognac, yellow, green, and white ones are also found. **Slingair Heliwork** (© **1800/095 500** in Australia, or 08/9169 1300; www.slingair.com.au) can take visitors to the mine. The visits include the process plant and diamond display room (closed shoes must be worn for security reasons!), and are part of two all-day tours. The flights also go over nearby Purnululu (Bungle Bungle) National Park and Lake Argyle, while one includes a helicopter trip around the Bungles. Costs are A$480 (US$384/UK£195), or A$745 (US$596/UK£304) with the helicopter flight. Kids under 12 are not permitted on mine tours.

SPENDING A DAY OR MORE AT VOYAGES EL QUESTRO WILDERNESS PARK ★★ You do not have to stay at El Questro (see "Where to Stay," below), in the eastern Kimberley, to enjoy the wonderful facilities. The million-acre cattle ranch has been turned it into a kind of Outback resort which provides a good introduction to the nature and attractions of the Kimberley without the distances and discomfort. It's still a working cattle station with 5,000 head of Brahman cattle, but visitors can't be involved in this side of the operation.

You can go barramundi fishing and heli-fishing in pristine wetlands and rivers; soak under palm trees in the thermal waters of Zebedee Springs; hike gorges, with pockets of rainforest; take four-wheel-drive fishing safaris; cruise tranquil Chamberlain Gorge; horseback ride across stony plains; join rangers on bird-watching or "bush tucker" tours; or gaze upon Aboriginal rock paintings. It's an unspoiled, primeval place.

If you're short on time, the station's 12-hour ranger-guided **day trips** from Kununurra are a good idea, for A$165 (US$132/UK£67) per person.

El Questro is open from April 1 to October 31 (closed during the Wet), and offers a variety of accommodations options (see below). All visitors must purchase a **Wilderness Park Permit,** valid for 7 days, for A$15 (US$12/UK£6.15); children under 12 free.

Four-wheel-drive transfers for guests operate from Kununurra; a ranger drives and gives a commentary en route. The cost is A$150 (US$120/UK£61) per adult round-trip to Emma Gorge, or A$180 (US$144/UK£74) to Station Township; children under 12 are half price. If you are driving yourself, take the Great Northern Highway 58km (36 miles) from Kununurra toward Wyndham, then the (unsealed) Gibb River Road 25km (16 miles) to Emma Gorge Resort at the foot of the Cockburn Range. A separate turnoff 11km (7 miles) farther on leads to Station Township (16km/10 miles), and the Homestead (another 9km/5½ miles). You can take a flight from Kununurra to El Questro for A$470 (US$376/UK£192).

Station Township has the main facilities (bungalows, restaurant, airstrip, camping areas, stables, and so forth), and most tours and activities depart from here. Hiring a four-wheel-drive in Kununurra is recommended, to allow you to explore at your leisure, and avoid the cost of transfers to and within the resort.

WHERE TO STAY

At Voyages El Questro

All of the accommodations accept American Express, MasterCard, and Visa. All have public pay phones, but no in-room phones or TVs.

El Questro Homestead ★★★ Perched over the Chamberlain River on the edge of a gorge, this homestead is one of the world's most luxurious yet simple getaways. Visitors (make that *wealthy* visitors) come for the sense of seclusion and the wilderness experience. You stay in airy rooms furnished in a blend of Aussie country style and Indonesian antiques, with a view of the gardens and the river from your veranda.

Voyages. Mailing address: GPO Box 3589, Sydney NSW 2001 ✆ **1300/134 044** in Australia, or 08/9169 1777. Fax 08/9169 1383. www.elquestro.com.au. 6 units, all with shower only (Chamberlain Suite has a tub on the veranda). A$890 (US$712/UK£291) per person per night double or twin. Rates include all meals, open bar, laundry service, and all activities except helicopter flights. 2-night minimum. Children under 12 not accepted. **Amenities:** Small outdoor pool; tennis court; Jacuzzi; tour bookings; laundry service. *In room:* A/C, hair dryer.

Emma Gorge Resort ★★ The neatly kept oasis of permanent tents mounted on lush lawns under pandanus palms sits at the foot of the soaring red Cockburn Range. The "tents" are very comfortable, and those without bathrooms share clean and modern facilities. The rustic restaurant serves gourmet bush-tucker meals and has a retractable roof for stargazing.

See contact details for El Questro Homestead, above. 55 tented cabins, 37 with bathroom with shower only. A$248 (US$198/UK£101) deluxe tented cabins for up to 4. **Amenities:** Restaurant; bar; outdoor pool; tour desk; coin-op laundry. *In room:* No phone.

Station Township Bungalows These basic but comfortable bungalow-style rooms are good for anyone without their own transportation—tours depart from right outside. The nicest units are the eight new-ish ones with balconies overhanging the Pentecost River. Two of the four original stone bungalows sleep six but rent for the same price. The **Steakhouse** restaurant and bar serves three meals a day of the steak and barramundi kind, and there is often live entertainment at the Swinging Arm Bar.

See contact details for El Questro Homestead, above. 12 bungalows, with shower only. A$298 (US$238/UK£122) bungalow for up to 4. Transfers A$70 (US$56/UK£29) per person. AE, MC, V. **Amenities:** Restaurant; bar; tour desk; four-wheel-drive rental desk; coin-op laundry. *In room:* A/C, fridge, coffeemaker, no phone.

Station Township Riverside Camping There are two camping areas with a total of 73 campsites. All campsites are A$15 (US$12/UK£6.15) per person per night; free for children under 12. Campers share shower facilities and a laundry, and use the **Steakhouse** restaurant.

In Kununurra

Country Club Plaza Resort Just down the road from the tourist bureau, this low-rise hotel is your best bet among Kununurra's modest choice of accommodations. Set in tropical gardens, it has a lovely shaded pool with sun lounges and a bar, and a couple of simple dining and bar venues. The rooms are nothing flashy, but they're neat and clean, with plenty of space. The front desk lends hair dryers.

47 Coolibah Dr., Kununurra, WA 6743. ✆ **1800/808 999** in Australia, or 08/9168 1024. Fax 08/9168 1189. www.countryclubhotel.com.au. 88 units, 80 with shower only. Dry season (Apr–Oct) A$192 (US$154/UK£78) double, A$222 (US$178/UK£91) triple, A$252 (US$202/UK£103) 2-bedroom apt; Wet season (Nov–Mar) A$172 (US$138/UK£70) double, A$202 (US$162/UK£82) triple, A$232 (US$186/UK£95) 2-bedroom apt. Extra person A$30 (US$24/UK£12). AE, DC, MC, V. **Amenities:** 2 restaurants; 3 bars; outdoor pool; tour desk; airport transfers; scooter hire; coin-op laundry. *In room:* A/C, TV/in-house movies, fridge, coffeemaker, hair dryer.

PURNULULU (BUNGLE BUNGLE) NATIONAL PARK ★★★

250km (155 miles) S of Kununurra

Rising precipitously out of the landscape 250km (155 miles) south of Kununurra are thousands of enormous sandstone domes 200 to 300m (656–984 ft.) high called the Bungle Bungle, and often simply the Bungles. They are thought to have been named after either "bundle bundle" grass or the bungle beetle. The Bungle Bungle get their distinctive orange-and-gray stripes from algae found in the permeable layers and mineral graining in non-permeable layers. The domes look spectacular from the air, which is the only way to see them in the Wet, when the roads are closed. They are even better from close up with sheer cliffs, and extremely narrow gorges slicing deep into the massif. Several of the gorges end in enormous precipitous amphitheaters, where giant boulders squat like king-size dollops of nutty cake mix. High up, straight up, watercourses come to an abrupt end where the runoff just drops into the gorge.

Moments Midday & Sunset

Try to be in **Echidna Chasm** at midday. This incredibly narrow gorge runs straight back into the rock. The walls rise to impossible heights, curving and slipping out of sight somewhere high above. At midday the dark impenetrable shadows give way to roseate glows, and sudden, blinding, glaring flashes of direct sunlight. A great sunset spot is on a small ridge to the west of the massif, which turns orange and fiery red in the fading light. If you're lucky you may then get a great big fat full moon rising over the Bungles.

Highlights are the beehive-shaped walls of Cathedral Gorge, the rock pool at Frog Hole Gorge, and palm-filled Echidna Chasm. Keep an eye peeled for rainbow bee-eaters, flocks of budgerigars, and rare nail-tailed wallabies. The Bungles aren't intimidating but this is one place where you feel incredibly small and insignificant. It's quiet, contemplative, and dramatic.

VISITOR INFORMATION For information, call the **Department of Environment and Conservation** (**© 08/9168 4200**) in Kununurra. There's also a **visitor center/ranger station** (**© 08/9168 7300**) in the park.

GETTING THERE & GETTING AROUND One road leads into the Bungles, a 52km (32-mile) bone-shaker 4WD drive; no caravans allowed. The access road is closed to ground traffic January 1 to March 31. Scenic flights over the park from Kununurra are available with **Slingair Heliwork** (**© 1800/095 500** in Australia, or 08/9169 1300) or **Alligator Airways** (**© 1800/632 533** in Australia, or 08/9168 1333). The flight takes about 2 hours, incorporates a flight over Lake Argyle and Argyle Diamond Mine, and costs A$250 (US$200/UK£10) for adults and A$200 (US$160/UK£160) for children 3 to 12. Both companies also do day trips that combine the flight with ground tours, though they're pricey, starting at A$520 (US$416/UK£212) for adults and A$470 (US$376/UK£192) for kids. Slingair has a helicopter option from Turkey Creek (Warnum) on the Great Northern Highway 196km (122 miles) from Kununurra, with a 45-minute trip from A$265 (US$212/UK£108) for adults and A$215 (US$172/UK£88) kids. **APT Kimberley Wilderness Adventures** and **East Kimberley Tours** (see "Getting Around," in the Kimberley section, earlier in this chapter) run an array of four-wheel-drive and fly-drive camping (using semi-permanent camps), including some 1-day "express" versions.

BROOME ★★

2,389km (1,481 miles) N of Perth; 1,859km (1,152 miles) SW of Darwin

Part rough Outback town, part glam seaside resort, the pearling port of **Broome** (pop. 11,000) is a hybrid of Australia and Asia you won't see anywhere else. Chinese and Japanese pearl divers worked the pearling luggers (for the pearl shell to make buttons) in the old days, and brought some of their distinctive architecture. The result is **Chinatown,** with neat rows of corrugated iron buildings wrapped by verandas and trimmed with Chinese peaked roofs. One experience not matched anywhere is an evening sitting in the deck chairs watching a film at **Sun Pictures** ★.

Broome is a marine oasis, mere kilometers from the Great Sandy Desert, with dramatic colors, swaying palm trees, and masses of blooming bougainvillea and frangipani. The culture is different too, part Asian part Aussie, with a wonderfully casual, free-and-easy atmosphere. Many Japanese divers died here—cyclones and the "bends" took their toll, and the legacy is the **Japanese Cemetery,** with ornate inscriptions on 900 rough-hewn headstones.

Broome is situated on a small peninsula that partially defines the broad **Roebuck Bay** to the east of the town. The mangrove-fringed bay is shallow and changes dramatically between high and low tide. At low tide, masses of mudflats are exposed, while at high tide the water has a vivid milky turquoise color. It's stunning. The old pearling luggers used to tie up here, and so this was where **Chinatown** developed. On the western side, **Cable Beach** ★★ faces straight out on to the Indian Ocean, and is where many of the modern developments have taken place.

For such a small and remote place, Broome is surprisingly sophisticated. Walk the streets of Chinatown and you'll rub shoulders with Aussie tourists, itinerant workers, Asian food-store proprietors, tough-as-nails cattle hands, and well-heeled visitors from Europe and America who down good coffee at a couple of trendy cafes. Broome's South Sea pearls are its bread and butter (together with tourism), but the old timber pearling luggers have been replaced with gleaming high-tech vessels.

To be honest, it's kind of hard to explain Broome's appeal. There is not much to do, but it's like nowhere else in Australia and it's such a pleasant relaxing place to be. Most people simply come to laze by the jade-green Indian Ocean on Cable Beach, ride camels along the sand as the sun plops into the sea, fish the pristine seas, mosey around the art galleries and jewelry stores, and soak up the atmosphere.

Broome is the main departure point for tours into the Kimberley, whether by boat or by 4WD along the **Gibb River Road** ★.

ESSENTIALS

GETTING THERE **Qantas/Qantaslink** (✆ **13 13 13** in Australia) flies direct from Perth, and Sydney and Melbourne in peak season. **Virgin Blue** (✆ **13 67 89** in Australia) flies direct to Broome from Perth and Adelaide, with connections from other cities. **Skywest** (✆ **1300/660 088** in Australia; www.skywest.com.au) flies from Perth daily. Landing at Broome is surreal, either sweeping across a broad golden beach or roaring in at rooftop height over the town. Never mind inner-city suburbs, this is inner-city airport—literally within walking distance.

Greyhound Australia (✆ **13 14 99** in Australia) has a daily service from Perth, taking around 34 hours. The fare is A$381 (US$305/UK£156). Greyhound's daily service from Darwin via Katherine and Kununurra takes around 24 hours; the one-way fare is A$367 (US$294/UK£150).

Broome is 34km (21 miles) off the Great Northern Highway, which leads from Perth in the south and Kununurra to the east.

VISITOR INFORMATION The **Broome Visitor Centre** on the Broome Highway at Bagot Street, Broome, WA 6725 (✆ **1800/883 777** in Australia, or 08/9192 2222; www.broomevisitorcentre.com.au), provides information and a booking service. It's open Monday through Friday from 8am to 5pm; Saturday, Sunday, and public holidays from 8:30am to 4pm.

Book hotels and tours well in advance of the peak June-through-August season.

GETTING AROUND **Avis** (✆ 08/9193 5980), **Budget** (✆ 08/9193 5355), **Europcar** (✆ 08/9193 7788), **Hertz** (✆ 08/9192 1428), and **Thrifty** (✆ 08/9193 7712) all rent conventional cars and four-wheel-drives. Hertz also rents camping-gear kits and car-top tents that affix to the larger four-wheel-drives. Among the motor-home companies are **Britz** (✆ **1800/331 454** in Australia, or 08/9192 2647), and **Australian Pinnacle Tours** (✆ mobile **0417 946 505**).

The **Town Bus Service** (✆ **08/9193 6585**) does an hourly loop of most attractions, including Chinatown and Cable Beach, from 7:10am to 6:30pm daily. From May to October, it also runs every half-hour from 8:30am to 4:30pm. A single adult fare is A$3 (US$2.40/UK£1.20), a day-pass is A$9 (US$7.20/UK£3.70), and a five-trip multi-rider is A$14 (US$11/UK£5.70). Children to 16 travel free if with a parent, otherwise A$1.30 (US$1/UK£0.55).

There are several taxi companies, including **Broome Taxis** (✆ **08/9192 1133**) and **Roebuck Taxis** (✆ **1800/880 330**).

Many companies (including those listed under "Essentials" in the "Kimberley" section, earlier in this chapter) run a variety of day tours of the town, plus trips to natural attractions farther afield, like Windjana and Geikie Gorges, Tunnel Creek, and the Dampier Peninsula (described in "Beyond Broome & the Gibb River Road" below), or four-wheel-drive camping safaris along the Gibb River Road.

WHAT TO SEE & DO

When you arrive, head to **Chinatown,** in the town center on Carnarvon Street and Dampier Terrace, to get a feel for the town. The wide streets, the tropical-style buildings with their broad verandas and Chinese influences, the corrugated iron frontages, and the **Sun Pictures** ★ outdoor cinema (see below) are typical Broome. All the main shops and cafes are here, with every corner featuring a pearl shop, which reflects the growth of both the pearling and the tourist industries.

Probably the most popular pastime is lazing on the 22km (14 miles) of glorious, white sandy **Cable Beach** ★★. The beach is 6km (3¾ miles) out of town; the bus runs there regularly. In the Wet, about November through April, the water is off-limits due to marine stingers. Crocodiles, on the other hand, seem not to like surf, so you should be safe swimming here. Go to the beach for at least one of the magnificent sunsets, when the sun sinks into the sea behind the romantic outlines of a pearling lugger, while strings of camels sway along the edge of the water. The sand is very firm so don't be surprised to find you're sharing beach and sunset with dozens of 4WDs parked facing put to sea—with tables, chairs, and drinks (this is Broome after all).

A novel way to experience the beach is on a **camel ride.** Several outfits offer rides, with sunset the most popular time. A 1-hour sunset ride with **Red Sun Camels** (✆ **08/9193 7423**) costs A$55 (US$44/UK£22) adults, A$35 (US$28/UK£14) kids 6 to 16. Kids under 6 pay A$10 (US$8/UK£4.10), but they must sit in an adult's lap.

Four-time state surf champ **Josh Palmateer** ★ (✆ **0418/958 264** mobile) gives 2-hour surf lessons on the beach in August and September for A$100 (US$80/UK£41) per person, or A$55 (US$44/UK£22) per person for two (cheaper if you join a group). He supplies the boards and the wet suits, and the lessons are great fun.

Don't miss the **Pearl Luggers** ★★, 31 Dampier Terrace (✆ **08/9192 2059**). A 1-hour tour includes a look over two restored Broome pearling luggers, a browse through a small pearling museum, and a riveting and hilarious talk about pearl diving by former pearl divers. Admission is A$19 (US$15/UK£7.75) adults, A$17 (US$14/UK£6.95) seniors and students, A$9 (US$7.20/UK£3.65) kids over 9, A$50 (US$40/UK£20) family of 2 adults and 2 children. Tours depart at 9am, 11am, and 2pm, with extra sessions May to September. Closed December 25. The Pigram Brothers, a local country folk band, play here on Thursday evenings at 6:30pm, for $A25 (US$20/UK£10)per head (food and bar available).

Moments Staircase to the Moon

On the happy coincidence of a full moon and low tide (which happens on about 3 consecutive nights a month Mar–Oct), nature treats the town to a show. The light of the rising moon falls on the remnant channels between the exposed mudflats in Roebuck Bay, with the reflections creating a "staircase to the moon." The best places to see it are from the cliff-top restaurant at the **Mangrove Resort Hotel,** or adjacent **Moonlight Bay Suites** (see "Where to Stay & Dine," below), and from the food and crafts markets at Town Beach. Live music plays at the Mangrove most staircase nights, including a didgeridoo player to accompany the rising moon.

A **dinosaur footprint** 120 million years old is on show at very low tide on the cliff at Gantheaume Point, 6km (3¾ miles) from town. The town authorities have set a plaster cast of it higher up on the rocks, so you can see it anytime. Bring your camera to snap the point's breathtaking palette of glowing scarlet cliffs, white beach, and jade-turquoise water.

You should also take a walk through the haunting **Japanese pearl divers' cemetery** on Port Drive. Entry is free.

During a tour of the **Willie Creek Pearl Farm** ★★ (✆ **08/9192 6000**), 38km (24 miles) north of town, you will see the delicate process of an oyster getting "seeded" with a nucleus to form a pearl, learn about pearl farming, and discover what to look for when buying a pearl. You can also buy them in the showroom. The tour costs A$33 (US$26/UK£13) adults, A$15 (US$12/UK£6.15) children, and A$85 (US$68/UK£35) for a family of four. You must book the tour whether you drive yourself or not. Tides can cut off the four-wheel-drive-only road to the farm, so it could be wise to take a coach tour, which costs A$65 (US$52/UK£27) adults, A$33 (US$26/UK£13) children 6 to 16, and A$175 (US$140/UK£71) families, including pickup and drop-off at your hotel. Willie Creek won WA's top tourism award in 2006.

If you have not seen any crocs in the wild during your travels, you can take a 1-hour tour at the **Broome Crocodile Park,** next to Cable Beach Club Resort Broome, Cable Beach Road (✆ **08/9193 7824**). Admission is A$23 (US$18/UK£9.40) for adults, A$20 (US$16/UK£8.15) for seniors, backpackers, and students, A$15 (US$12/UK£6.15) for kids 5 to 15, and A$55 (US$44/UK£22) for families with up to three children. The **Malcolm Douglas Wildlife Wilderness Park** (about 16km/10 miles out of town), scheduled to open late 2007, will be devoted to Australia's rare and endangered animals. For information, contact the crocodile park.

Several art galleries sell vivid oil and watercolor Kimberley landscapes and a range of Aboriginal art. A historic pearling master's house, **Monsoon Gallery,** 60 Hamersley St. (✆ **08/9193 5811**), stocks a large range of European and Aboriginal paintings, sculpture, pottery, carvings, and books, and has regular exhibitions by noted artists. **Matso's,** next door, has a lovely veranda cafe and a boutique brewery that turns out unusual recipes like alcoholic ginger beer, and displays many of the Monsoon pictures. The gallery is open daily from 10am to 5pm, and the cafe from 8am until late.

On Saturday from 8am to 1pm, browse the **markets** in the gardens of the colonial Courthouse at the corner of Frederick and Hamersley streets. It used to be the official station for the telegraph cable from Broome to Java.

A number of boats, including a restored pearling lugger, run **sunset cruises** off Cable Beach. **Fishing** ★ for trevally, barracuda, barramundi, queenfish, tuna, shark, sailfish, marlin, salmon (in the May–Aug run), and reef fish is excellent around Broome; fly- and sportfishing are also worth a go. Rent tackle and try your luck from the deepwater jetty beyond Town Beach 2km (1¼ miles) south of town, or join one of several charter boats, such as **FAD Game Fishing Charters** (✆ **0410/649 135;** www.fadcharters.com.au), for a day, or longer, trip. **Pearl Sea Coastal Cruises** (see "Boating the Kimberley Coast," below) runs live-aboard fishing safaris up the coast. Cyclones, rain, and strong tides restrict fishing December through April.

More than one-third of Australia's bird species live in the Kimberley, and Roebuck Bay has the greatest diversity of shorebird species anywhere, with over 800,000 birds visiting every year. **The Broome Bird Observatory** research station ★★ (✆ **08/9193 5600;** www.broomebirdobservatory.com), 25km (16 miles) out of town on Roebuck Bay, monitors the thousands of migratory wetlands birds that gather here from Siberia. Entry is A$5 (US$4/UK£2.05) per person, while a 2½-hour tour from Broome costs A$90 (US$72/UK£37) or A$60 (US$48/UK£25) self-drive. Tour timings depend on the tides; check the excellent website. There are basic accommodations and camping facilities at the observatory.

Australia's first family of pearling, the Paspaleys, sell their wonderfully elegant jewelry at **Paspaley Pearls,** Carnarvon Street at Short Street (✆ **08/9192 2203**). **Linneys** (✆ **08/9192 2430**) is another reputable jeweler nearby.

Don't leave without taking in a movie at **Sun Pictures** ★, Carnarvon Street (✆ **08/9192 1077**). Built in 1916, these are the oldest "picture gardens" in the world. The occasionally vocal audience sits in canvas deck chairs, and the show may be interrupted by the evening flight roaring just meters overhead. Tickets are A$15 (US$12/UK£6.15) adults, A$10 (US$8/UK£4.10) children, A$42 (US$34/UK£17) families. Open nightly except December 25—even through the Wet.

WHERE TO STAY & DINE

Broome has developed enormously over the last 5 years, leading to a large increase in the number of places offering accommodations. The **Broome Visitor Centre** (✆ **1800/883** 777 in Australia) can provide expert advice and bookings. As far as dining is concerned, both hotels listed below have good restaurants, and there are numerous cafes/restaurants including **Matso's** (see above under "What to See & Do") and the **Old Zoo Restaurant** mentioned below.

Cable Beach Club Resort Broome ★★★ For some Aussies, a visit to Broome is just an excuse to stay at this chic Asia-meets-Outback resort—corrugated-iron walls inside as well as out, verandas, Aboriginal art—blended with red-and-green latticework, pagoda roofs, and Asian cotton bedcovers. A A$15-million (US$12-million/UK£6-million) refurbishment was completed in 2007. The huge standard rooms are gorgeous and have a decent-size living area and balcony. Bungalows (which sleep up to seven) have central bedrooms wrapped on three sides by a veranda, and kitchens. The luxury private villas have private courtyards and plunge pools, and Pool Terrace studios have direct access to the adults-only pool. For glamour, the colonial-pearling-master suites are lavishly decked out with eye-popping Asiatic antiques and valuable Australian art. These are truly to die for, so ask about suite packages. A dune blocks full sea views, except for the suites and Ocean View Studios. The resort also has a guest-activities program and an art gallery and pearl boutique.

Cable Beach Rd., Broome, WA 6725. © **1800/199 099** in Australia, or 08/9192 0400. Fax 08/9192 2249. www.cablebeachclub.com. 263 units, some with shower only. Apr–May 2008 A$307 (US$246/UK£125) Garden View Studio, A$509 (US$407/UK£208) Deluxe Bungalow, A$869 (US$695/UK£355) Villa; June–Oct 2008 A$376 (US$301/UK£153) Garden View Studio, A$587 (US$470/UK£240) Deluxe Bungalow, A$1,049 (US$839/UK£428) Villa. Extra person A$40 (US$32/UK£16). Prices based on minimum 4-night stay. Children under 12 stay free in parent's room with existing bedding. Ask about packages. AE, DC, MC, V. Free on-site parking. Town bus. **Amenities:** 3 restaurants (2 seasonal); cafe; bar; 2 outdoor pools (family pool and adults-only saltwater pool, both chilled in Wet season and heated in winter); golf course nearby; 2 floodlit tennis courts; gymnasium; spa; kids' club (ages 2–12); concierge; tour desk; airport shuttle; room service; babysitting; laundry service; dry cleaning. *In room:* A/C, TV w/free movies, minibar, coffeemaker, hair dryer, iron.

Mangrove Resort Hotel ★ The best public views in Broome across Roebuck Bay are from this recently refurbished, modest but appealing cliff-top hotel, a 5-minute walk from town. There's no faulting the well-kept, roomy deluxe rooms with sea views. Sixteen extra-large executive rooms were added in 2002, and there are four suites with kitchenettes. **The Tides** ★ is a lovely outdoor restaurant serving fresh, affordable food, with its tables and chairs set out on the lawns under the palms and along the cliff edge. Inside, **Charters** restaurant is one of Broome's best.

47 Carnarvon St., Broome, WA 6725. © **1800/094 818** in Australia, or 08/9192 1303. Fax 08/9193 5169. www.mangrovehotel.com.au. 70 units, 66 with shower only. Apr–Sept A$170–A$205 (US$136–US$164/UK£69–UK£84) double, A$265–A$295 (US$212–US$236/UK£108–UK£120) suite; Oct–Mar A$145–A$178 (US$116–US$142/UK£59–UK£73) double, A$235–A$275 (US$188–US$220/UK£95–UK£112) suite. Extra person A$35 (US$28/UK£14). Children under 3 stay free in parent's room. Ask about Wet season packages. AE, DC, MC, V. **Amenities:** 2 restaurants; 2 bars; 2 outdoor pools; spa; 2 Jacuzzis; tour desk; courtesy car from airport; limited room service; coin-op laundry; laundry service; dry cleaning. *In room:* A/C, TV w/free movies, fridge, coffeemaker, hair dryer, iron.

Moonlight Bay Suites ★ This apartment complex is set around a large sparkling pool, well above Roebuck Bay and its fringing belt of mangroves. A broad stretch of lawn is ideal for watching Staircase to the Moon. While hundreds of people cram into the nearby Mangrove Hotel (see above) to witness this phenomenon, here at Moonlight Bay everyone has a front-row seat. The one- and two-bedroom apartments are fully furnished, comfortable, and self-catering with all facilities. It's within easy walking distance of Chinatown. Some rooms are available for smokers.

51 Carnarvon St., Broome, WA 6725. © **08/9193 7888.** Fax 08/9193 7999. www.kimberleyaccommodation.com.au. 51 units, some with spa. A$207–A$243 (US$166–US$194/UK£84–UK£99) 1-bedroom suites; A$228–A$269 (US$182–US$215/UK£93–UK£110) 1-bedroom bay-view; A$259–A$316 (US$207–US$253/UK£106–UK£129) 2-bedroom suite; A$305–A$404 (US$244–US$323/UK£124–UK£165) 2-bedroom deluxe. Children under 14 stay free in parent's room with existing bedding. AE, DC, MC, V. Free on-site parking. Town bus stops outside. **Amenities:** Outdoor pool and spa; small gymnasium; beauty and relaxation center; airport shuttle; coin-op laundry. *In room:* A/C, TV w/free movies, full kitchen, fridge, coffeemaker, hair dryer, iron.

Old Zoo Restaurant ★ Originally part of a zoo that no longer exists, this very pleasant, quiet, and casual restaurant is half enclosed and half alfresco in a tropical garden setting. It has a good ambience and is close to Cable Beach.

2 Challenor Dr., Cable Beach, Broome, WA 6725. © **08/9193 6200.** Reservations recommended for weekend evenings. Mains A$17–A$29 (US$13–US$23/UK£6.95–UK£12); tapas plates A$9 (US$7.20/UK£3.70). MC, V. Daily 7am–late.

BEYOND BROOME & THE GIBB RIVER ROAD ★

North and East of Broome, the Kimberley is wilderness at its best, suited to those who love nature at its most raw and isolated. Swimming in the ocean and river mouths is off-limits due to crocodiles, although many of the inland rivers and pools provide welcome relief from heat and dust.

Fun Fact One Big River

The Fitzroy River is Australia's largest wild river. It has no dams, it's totally unfettered, and its flow (after one of the summer cyclones) has been rated among the highest in the world. This makes its waters highly desirable to Australia's drying cities well to the south so there are regular (and perhaps not totally far-fetched) plans to harness it and carry the precious water thousands of kilometers south. The Greens do not agree! Most visitors only see the Fitzroy in the Dry, either at Geikie Gorge or the long Willare Bridge east of Broome, when it is but a quiet and unremarkable river.

Stretching 220km (136 miles) north of Broome, the **Dampier Peninsula** is home to several Aboriginal communities and a small resort at the northern tip of Cape Leveque. The 4WD Cape Leveque Road runs through the fine red dust called "pindan," past **Beagle Bay's** wonderful pearl-shell church built by missionaries, and up to the remote red-cliffed cape. The Aboriginal-run Kooljaman Resort here has cabins and deluxe safari tents gazing out over an empty azure sea.

Traveling the **Gibb River Road** is not for everyone, being rough, remote, and dusty, and lacking the world's little luxuries. It's for those who love wilderness and adventure in a primal land. Facilities really are few and far between. Both this road and the Kalumburu Road are classified as 4WD; certainly off-limits for your rented 2WD. The roads are often closed during the Wet from December to April; check with Main Roads at ✆ **13 81 38** for up-to-date road conditions.

The western part of the Kimberley is the most accessible and can be explored on a long day trip from Broome. The 350-million-year-old **Windjana Gorge,** 240km (149 miles) east of Broome, has tall gray limestone cliffs enclosing long silent pools separated by enormous sand banks, basking placees for freshwater crocodiles. Another unsealed road leads south, past **Tunnel Creek,** a limestone cavern through which you can walk, to the Great Northern Highway. Some 100km (62 miles) farther east is **Geikie Gorge** (pronounced *Geek*-ee), or 418km (259 miles) east of Broome. Its 30m-high (98-ft.) walls are part of the same ancient coral-reef system as Windjana; you explore Geikie Gorge on walking trails or on a short cruise run by rangers.

Traveling farther along the Gibb River Road you wind through rough rocky ranges, with detours to take in the delights of stunning pools and waterfalls such as those at Bell and Manning Gorges. One hundred thirty kilometers (81 miles) up the Kalumburu Road is the turnoff to **Mitchell Plateau.** The plateau is heavily dissected and marked by tall mop-headed livistonia palms. Some rock outcrops contain superb painted images, particularly the Wandjina; vivid haloed figures, sometimes with a body, or simply a head, but never a mouth. The Bradshaw Figures, or Gwion, are also found here; stylized human figures, many having sticklike images, which could be the oldest human art in the world.

There's a scenic 3.5km (2¼-mile) walk to the **Mitchell Falls** ★★, although you can take a helicopter transfer. The longest and best chopper trip goes from the falls way out to Admiralty Gulf, a milky turquoise sea with sharks and crocs visible in the shallows, and back along the lower Mitchell River gorge. The flight shows up the immensity and emptiness of the Kimberley, bringing a superb vista of rocky terraces, islands, mangroves, bays, and creeks extending in all directions—with absolutely nothing else to be seen.

The main operators offering tours along the Gibb River Road are listed in "Getting Around" at the beginning of the Kimberley section, earlier in this chapter.

BOATING THE KIMBERLEY COAST

Boating this vast, unspoiled Kimberley coastline is a true adventure. There are no towns, marinas, or service facilities. You take everything with you. But it allows some unforgettable experiences: magnificent if stark scenery, the utter isolation, showering under pristine waterfalls, experiencing the size and power of the tides including the so-called "Horizontal Falls," and the magnificent starry skies.

Several boat operators run fishing and adventure trips from Broome, Derby (221km/137 miles northeast of Broome), or Kununurra. Others operate cruises that can only be described as luxurious. North Star Cruises (below) even travels with its own helicopter for flight-seeing and heli-fishing. Some boats take scuba divers and snorkelers to Rowley Shoals, a marvelous outcrop of coral reef and giant clams 260km (161 miles) west of Broome. Find a trip and vessel that suits you—some provide comfortable en-suite private cabins, while others are camp-on-the-beach jobs.

Some of the most established operators are **North Star Cruises** (**© 08/9192 1829;** www.northstarcruises.com.au), **Pearl Sea Coastal Cruises** (**© 08/9193 6131;** www.kimberleyquest.com.au), **Coral Princess Cruises** (**© 07/4040 9999;** www.coralprincesscruises.com), all operating from Broome; and **Buccaneer Sea Safaris** (**© 08/9191 1991;** www.buccaneerseasafaris.com) operating out of Derby. The cruises run only in the Dry, generally between April and October, and tend to book up well in advance, with many 2008 trips already sold out.

The 34m (112-ft.) ***North Star*** can carry 36 passengers on 13-day cruises between Broome and Wyndham at A$13,995 to A$20,995 (US$11,200–US$16,800/UK£5,712–UK£8,569) per person, and with some shorter options and October trips to Rowley Shoals. Pearl Sea carries 18 passengers onboard the 25m (82-ft.) ***Kimberley Quest II,*** with its 13-day Broome-Wyndham prices ranging from A$10,995 to A$17,595 (US$8,800–US$14,080/UK£4,488–UK£7,182). Coral Princess has the largest vessels, the 35m (115-ft.) ***Coral Princess*** and the 63m (207-ft.) ***Oceanic Discoverer,*** with 10 night cruises between Broome and Darwin for A$6,200 to A$8,100 (US$4,960–US$6,480/UK£2.531–UK£3,306). Buccaneer has beach camping and mostly shorter trips but its 14-day Derby-Wyndham prices are A$6,490 (US$5,192/UK£2,649). You need to check what is supplied with the cruises in the way of excursions or transfers, such as seaplane and/or helicopter flights.

11

Adelaide & South Australia

by Marc Llewellyn

Adelaide (pop. 1 million) has a major advantage over the other state capitals in that it has Outback, vineyards, wetlands, animal sanctuaries, a major river, and mountain ranges virtually on its doorstep. Meals and lodgings are cheaper in Adelaide than in Sydney or Melbourne. If you plan to travel outside the city, a trip to one of the winegrowing areas has to be on your itinerary. Of all the wine areas, the **Barossa Valley** is the most interesting. Centered on Tanunda, the Barossa is known for its German architecture as well as its dozens of pretty hamlets, fine restaurants, and vineyards offering cellar-door tastings.

If you want to see animals instead of, or in addition to, grapes, you're in luck. You're likely to come across the odd kangaroo or wallaby near the main settlements, especially at dusk, or you could visit one of the area's wildlife reserves. Otherwise, head into the Outback or over to **Kangaroo Island,** without a doubt the best place in Australia to see concentrated numbers of native animals in the wild.

Another place well worth visiting is the craggy **Flinders Ranges,** some 460km (285 miles) north of Adelaide. Though the scenery along the way is mostly unattractive grazing properties devoid of trees, the Flinders Ranges offer an incredible landscape of multicolored rocks, rough-and-ready characters, and even camel treks in the semidesert. On the other side of the mountains, the real Outback starts.

The **South Australian Outback** is serenely beautiful, with giant skies, red earth, little water, and wildflowers after the rains. Out here you'll find bizarre opal-mining towns, such as **Coober Pedy,** where summer temperatures can reach 122°F (50°C) and where most people live underground to escape the heat.

If you prefer your landscape with more moisture, head to the **Coorong,** a water-bird sanctuary rivaled only by Kakadu National Park in the Northern Territory (see chapter 9).

EXPLORING THE STATE

VISITOR INFORMATION **The South Australia Visitor & Travel Centre,** 18 King William St. (© **1300/655 276** in Australia, or 08/8303 2033; fax 08/8303 2249; www.southaustralia.com), is the best place to find information on Adelaide and South Australia. It's open weekdays from 8:30am to 5pm and weekends from 9am to 2pm. There's also an information booth at the King William Street end of Rundle Mall.

For general information about South Australia's national parks, contact the **Department of Environment and Natural Resources Information Centre,** Australis House, 77 Grenfell St., Adelaide, SA 5000 (© **08/8204 1910**). It's open Monday through Friday from 9am to 5pm.

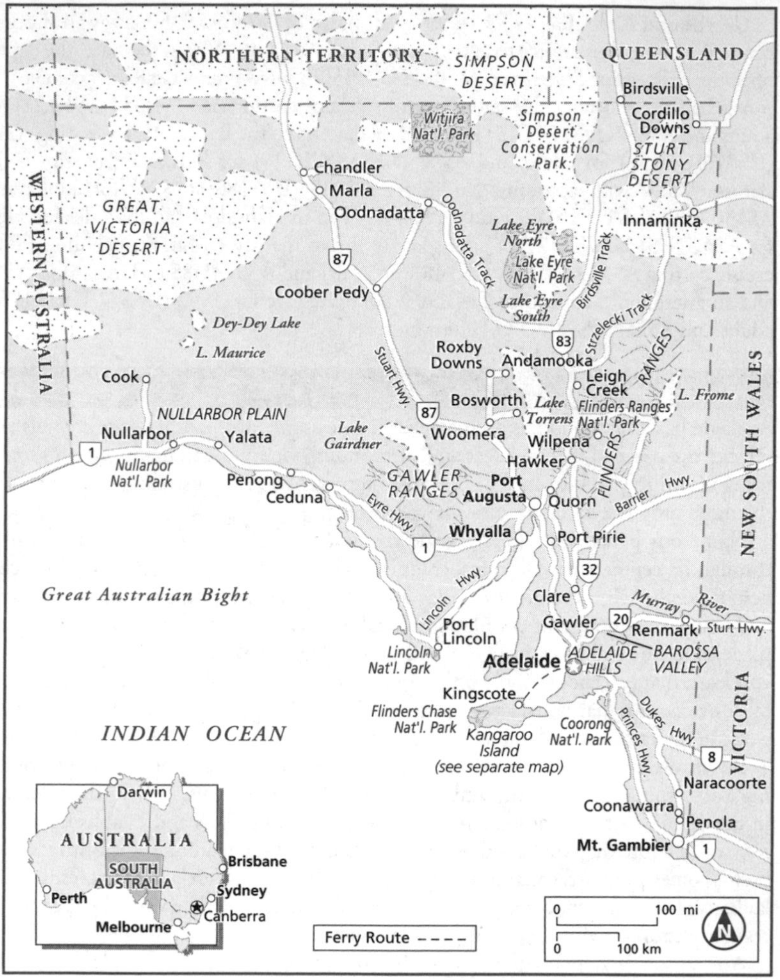

GETTING AROUND South Australia, at four times the size of the United Kingdom, has a lot of empty space between places of interest. The best way to see it is by car. Limited rail service connects Adelaide with some areas. The Stuart Highway bisects the state from south to north; it runs from Adelaide through the industrial center of Port Augusta (gateway to the Flinders Ranges), and through Coober Pedy to Alice Springs in the Red Centre. The Eyre Highway travels westward along the coastline and into Western Australia, and the Barrier Highway enters New South Wales just before the mining city of Broken Hill (see chapter 5). The Princes Highway takes you east to Melbourne. If you plan to drive into the Outback regions, contact the **Royal Automobile Association of South Australia (RAA),** 41 Hindmarsh Sq., Adelaide, SA 5000 (✆ **13 11 11** in South Australia, or 08/8202 4600; www.raa.net). The RAA provides route maps and emergency breakdown service.

Greyhound Australia (© **13 14 99** in Australia, or 07/4690 9950; www.greyhound.com.au) operates bus service to and around South Australia. Within the state, the largest operator is **Premier Stateliner** (© **08/8415 5500;** www.premierstateliner.com.au). It runs a half-day morning city-sights tour of Adelaide costing A$52 (US$42/UK£21) for adults and A$26 (US$21/UK£11) for kids; a day trip to the Barossa Valley costing A$95 (US$76/UK£38) for adults and A$48 (US$38/UK£19) for kids; a 2-day trip to the Barossa Valley with accommodations for A$235 (US$188/UK£94) for adults and A$130 (US$104/UK£52) for kids; a half-day trip to Hahndorf and the Adelaide Hills for A$42 (US$33/UK£17) for adults; a day trip to the River Murray, including a boat cruise, costing A$119 (US$95/UK£48) for adults and A$57 (US$46/UK£23) for kids; and an afternoon excursion to Cleland Wildlife Reserve for A$52 (US$42/UK£21) for adults and A$26 (US$21/UK£11) for kids.

1 Adelaide

Adelaide has a reputation as a quieter place than some of the other state capitals and relishes the peace of its parklands and surrounding vineyards. In many ways it's something of a throwback to the comfortable lifestyle of 1950s Australia—a lifestyle that the more progressive state capitals have left behind.

Numerous parks and gardens, wide tree-lined streets, the River Torrens running through its center, sidewalk cafes, colonial architecture, and, of course, the churches help make the "city of churches" a pleasant, open city, perfect for strolling or bicycling.

Though the immigrant population has added a cosmopolitan flair to the restaurant scene, Adelaide still has a feeling of old England about it. That's not surprising when you learn that Adelaide was the only capital settled by English free settlers rather than by convicts, and that it attracted more after World War II, when Brits flocked here to work in the city's car and appliance factories.

But it was earlier immigrants, from Germany, who gave Adelaide and the surrounding area a romantic twist. Arriving as refugees fleeing religious strife in their country in the 1830s, German immigrants brought winemaking skills and established wineries. Today, more than one-third of all Australian wine—including some of the world's best—comes from areas within about an hour's drive from Adelaide. As a result, Adelaidians of all socioeconomic groups are more versed in wine than even the French and regularly compare vintages, winegrowing regions, and winemaking trends.

Any season is a good time to visit Adelaide, though May through August can be chilly and January and February hot.

ESSENTIALS

GETTING THERE **By Plane** **Qantas** (© **13 13 13** in Australia) flies to Adelaide from the other major state capitals. The discount carrier **Virgin Blue** (© **13 67 89** in Australia; www.virginblue.com.au) flies direct from Melbourne, with connections from other state capitals and some major towns. Check the website for cheap deals. Adelaide International Airport is 5km (3 miles) west of the city center. Major car-rental companies (Avis, Budget, Hertz, and Thrifty) have desks in both the international and domestic terminals.

The **Skylink** (© **08/8332 0528;** www.skylinkadelaide.com) connects the airport with major hotels and the rail and bus stations. On weekdays, buses leave the terminals at 30-minute intervals from 5:30am to 9:30pm, and on weekends and public holidays

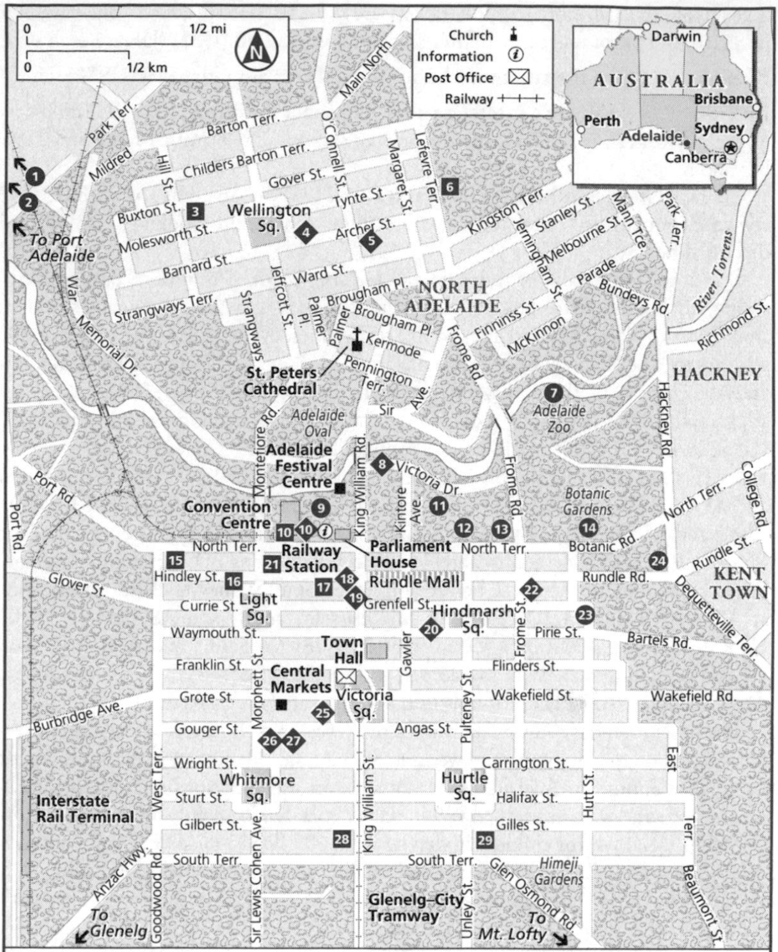

ACCOMMODATIONS ■

Adelaide City Park Motel **29**
Hilton Adelaide **25**
Hyatt Regency Adelaide **10**
Mercure Grosvenor Hotel **21**
Moore's Brecknock Hotel **28**
North Adelaide Heritage Group **3**
Novotel Adelaide on Hindley **17**
Princes Lodge Motel **6**
Rockford Adelaide **16**
Saville Park Suites Adelaide **15**

DINING ◆

Amalfi **22**
Gaucho's Argentinian Restaurant **26**
The Grange **25**
Jasmin Indian Restaurant **20**
Jolleys Boathouse Restaurant **8**
The Manse **4**
Matsuri **27**
Mekong Thai **18**
Ned Kelly's Restaurant **5**
Rigoni's Bistro **19**
Shiki **10**

ATTRACTIONS ●

Adelaide Casino **9**
Adelaide Zoo **7**
Art Gallery of South Australia **13**
Botanic Gardens **14**
National Railway Museum **2**
National Wine Centre of Australia **24**
South Australian Maritime Museum **1**
South Australian Museum **12**
Tandanya Aboriginal Cultural Institute **23**
The Migration Museum **11**

hourly (on the half-hour). Adult tickets are A$7.50 (US$6/UK£3) one-way, A$13 (US$10/UK£5) round-trip. Children's tickets cost A$2.50 (US$2/UK£1) each way.

By Taxi A taxi to the city from the airport will cost around A$19 (US$15/UK£7).

By Train The **Keswick Interstate Rail Passenger Terminal,** 2km (1¼ miles) west of the city center, is Adelaide's main railway station. The terminal has a small snack bar and a cafe.

Contact **Great Southern Railways** (✆ **13 21 47** in Australia, or 08/8213 4530; www.gsr.com.au) for information, timetables, fares, and bookings for all trains described below.

One of the great trains of Australia, the ***Indian Pacific*** ★ transports passengers from Sydney to Adelaide (trip time: 28 hr.) every Saturday and Wednesday at 2:55pm and from Perth to Adelaide (trip time: 36 hr.) on Wednesday and Sunday at 11:55am. One-way tickets from Sydney to Adelaide are around A$665 (US$532/UK£266) for adults and A$527 (US$422/UK£211) for children in first class; A$485 (US$388/UK£194) for adults and A$353 (US$282/UK£141) for children in an economy sleeper; and A$285 (US$228/UK£114) for adults and A$136 (US$109/UK£55) for children in coach. From Perth to Adelaide the one-way fare is A$1,353 (US$1,082/UK£541) for adults and A$926 (US$741/UK£372) for children in first class; A$960 (US$768/UK£384) for adults and A$576 (US$460/UK£230) for children in an economy sleeper; and A$395 (US$316/UK£157) for adults and A$186 (US$149/UK£75) for children in coach. Prices keep going up, so check before you leave home. Sydney-to-Perth prices come in at A$1,790 (US$1,432/UK£716) in first class for adults and A$1,293 (US$1,034/UK£517) for kids; A$1,320 (US$1,056/UK£528) for adults and A$859 (US$687/UK£344) for kids in an economy sleeper, and A$680 (US$544/UK£272) for adults and A$322 (US$258/UK£128) for kids in economy seats (you'd be crazy).

The other legendary Australian train is the ***Ghan,*** which runs from Adelaide to Alice Springs and on to Darwin twice a week on Sunday and Wednesday at 2:20pm. Trip time from Alice Springs to Adelaide is 20 hours. From Alice Springs to Adelaide and vice versa, the one-way fare is A$995 (US$796/UK£400) for adults and A$681 (US$544/UK£274) for children in first class; A$685 (US$548/UK£274) for adults and A$417 (US$334/UK£177) for children in an economy sleeper; and A$335 (US$268/UK£134) for adults and A$159 (US$127/UK£164) for children for an economy seat. From Adelaide to Darwin it costs A$1,920 (US$1,536/UK£768) for adults and A$1,496 (US$1,197/UK£1,000) for kids in first class; A$1,390 (US$1,112/UK£556) for adults and A$1,023 (US$818/UK£409) for kids in an economy sleeper; and A$690 (US$552/UK£276) for adults and A$454 (US$363/UK£183) for kids in an economy seat. It's a hard trip in an economy sleeper though, and all those old socks (it's the custom on trains for people to take off their shoes) make it smelly.

The *Overland* operates four weekly round-trips. It offers daylight service from Adelaide to Melbourne and overnight service from Melbourne to Adelaide (trip time: 12 hr.). From Melbourne to Adelaide, one-way ticket prices are A$139 (US$111/UK£56) for adults and A$98 (US$78/UK£39) for children in first class, and A$89 (US$71/UK£36) for adults and A$55 (US$44/UK£22) for children in an economy seat. The train leaves Adelaide every Monday, Wednesday, and Friday, and Melbourne on Tuesday, Thursday, and Saturday.

By Bus Intercity coaches serve the central bus station, 101 Franklin St. (✆ **08/8415 5533**), near Morphett Street in the city center. **Greyhound Australia** (✆ **13 14 99**

Tips World-Class Festivals in Adelaide

Adelaide is home to Australia's largest performing arts festival, the **Adelaide Festival** ★, which takes place over 3 weeks in March in even-numbered years. The festival includes literary and visual arts as well as dance, opera, classical music, jazz, cabaret, and comedy. The festival includes a Writers' Week and the **Adelaide Fringe Festival.**

In February or March, the 3-day **WOMADelaide Festival** of world music takes place. Crowds of 60,000 or more turn up to watch Australian and international artists.

For more information, visit **www.adelaidefestival.org.au** and **www.womadelaide.com.au**.

in Australia, or 07/4690 9950; www.greyhound.com.au) runs buses between Adelaide and all other major cities. The trip from Melbourne takes 11 hours and costs A$60 (US$48/UK£24); from Sydney, 25 hours and A$138 (US$110/UK£55); and from Alice Springs, 21 hours and A$258 (US$206/UK£103).

Adventurous types should consider traveling to Adelaide from Melbourne (or vice versa) on the **Wayward Bus,** operated by the Wayward Bus Touring Company, P.O. Box 7076, Adelaide, SA 5000 (© **1800/882 823** in Australia, or 08/8232 6646; www.waywardbus.com.au). The fare is A$365 (US$292/UK£146) with backpacker's accommodations and around A$512 (US$410/UK£205) with motel accommodations. You spend about 3 hours a day on the bus, and the driver acts as your guide. The fare includes a picnic or cafe lunch each day and entry to national parks. You can leave the trip and rejoin another later. Reservations are essential. Wayward Bus also runs 8-day overland trips traveling between Adelaide and Alice (or vice versa), via Uluru, Kata Tjuta (Olgas), Kings Canyon, Coober Pedy, Lake Eyre, William Creek, Wilpena Pound, the Flinders Ranges, and the Clare Valley wineries. It's a mix of camping, swags (thick sleeping bags), dugout cave, and hostel accommodations. It costs A$945 (US$756/UK£378). Check the website for more tours, including to Outback South Australia and Kangaroo Island.

Another bus company, the **Nullarbor Traveller** (P.O. Box 72, Glensside, SA 5065; © **08/8364 0407;** www.the-traveller.com.au), takes adventurous travelers from Adelaide to Perth in 9 days across the Nullarbor Plain. The tour includes a mixture of camping and pub accommodations and most meals. It costs A$1,295 (US$1,036/UK£518). A good area website is **www.nullarbornet.com.au**.

By Car To drive from Sydney to Adelaide on the Hume and Sturt highways takes roughly 20 hours; from Melbourne it takes around 10 hours on the Great Ocean Road and Princes Highway; from Perth it takes 32 hours on the Great Eastern and Princes highways; and from Alice Springs it takes 15 hours on the remote Stuart Highway. For more information on driving distances, consult **www.auinfo.com/distancecalc_process.asp**.

VISITOR INFORMATION Go to the **South Australia Visitor & Travel Centre,** 18 King William St. (© **1300/655 276** in Australia, or 08/8303 2033; fax 08/8303 2249), for maps, travel advice, and hotel and tour bookings. It's open weekdays from 8:30am to 5pm, weekends from 9am to 2pm. The info booth on Rundle Mall (© **08/8203 7611**) is open daily from 10am to 5pm.

CITY LAYOUT Adelaide is easy to navigate because of its gridlike pattern, planned down to each wide street and airy square by Colonel William Light in 1836. The city's official center is **Victoria Square,** where you'll find the Town Hall. Bisecting the city from south to north is the main thoroughfare, **King William Street.** Streets running perpendicular to King William Street change their names on either side; Franklin Street, for example, changes into Flinders Street. Of these cross streets, the most interesting are the restaurant strips of **Gouger Street** and **Rundle Street,** the latter running into the pedestrian-only shopping precinct of Rundle Mall. Another is **Hindley Street,** with inexpensive restaurants and nightlife. On the banks of the River Torrens just north of the city center, you'll find the Riverbank Precinct, the home of the Festival Centre, the Convention Centre, and the Skycity Adelaide Casino. Bordering the city center on the north and south are **North Terrace,** which is lined with galleries and museums and leads to the Botanic Gardens, and **South Terrace.**

Follow King William Street south and you'll be chasing the tram to the beachside suburb of **Glenelg;** follow it north, and it crosses the River Torrens and flows into sophisticated **North Adelaide,** an area crammed with Victorian and Edwardian architecture. The main avenues in North Adelaide, **O'Connell** and **Melbourne streets,** are lined with restaurants, cafes, and bistros that offer the tastes of a multicultural city.

Northwest of the city center is **Port Adelaide,** a seaport and the historic maritime heart of South Australia. It's home to some of the finest colonial buildings in the state, as well as good pubs and restaurants.

GETTING AROUND **By Bus** Adelaide's public bus network covers three zones, and fares are calculated according to the number of zones traveled. The city center is in Zone 1. The fare in Zone 1 is A$2.20 (US$1.75/UK90p) from 9am to 3pm on weekdays and A$3.80 (US$3/UK£1.50) at most other times. Kids travel for half price. You can buy tickets on board or at kiosks around the city. You can get timetable and destination information over the phone or in person from the **Passenger Transport Board Information Centre** (**© 08/8210 1000;** www.adelaidemetro.com.au), on the corner of Currie and King William streets. It's open Monday through Saturday from 8am to 6pm and Sunday from 10:30am to 5:30pm.

The free **CityLoop bus** (no. 99C) operates every 15 minutes (Mon–Thurs 8am–6pm; Fri 8am–9pm; Sat 8am–5pm) around the city center, along North Terrace, East Terrace, Grenfell Street, Pulteney Street, Wakefield Street, Grote Street, Morphett Street, Light Square, Hindley Street, and West Terrace. Another free bus, the **Bee Line** (no. 99B), runs along North Terrace, down King William Street to Victoria Square. Routes are well signposted. All free city buses are wheelchair accessible.

Bus nos. 181 and 182 run from the city to North Adelaide.

Value A Money-Saving Transit Pass

If you plan to get around the city on public transportation, it's a good idea to purchase a **Daytrip ticket,** which covers unlimited travel on buses, trams, and city trains within the metropolitan area for 1 day. The pass costs A$7.20 (US$5.80/UK£2.80) for adults and A$3.60 (US$2.90/UK£1.45) for children 5 to 15 and is available at most train stations, newsstands, and the **Passenger Transport Board Information Centre** (**© 08/8210 1000**).

The **Adelaide Explorer bus** (© **08/8293 2966;** www.adelaideexplorer.com.au) stops at 26 sights around town, including Glenelg, and costs A$30 (US$24/UK£12) for adults, A$19 (US$15/UK£7.50) for children aged 6 to 16, and A$70 (US$56/UK£28) for families of four. Buy tickets on the bus. The loop takes a leisurely 3 hours, with commentary, and you can get on and off when you want. The first bus departs from 38 King William St., on the corner of Rundle Mall (next to Haigh's Chocolates) at 9am. The company will pick you up from your hotel between 8 and 8:30am if you call ahead, and will drop you off at the airport (with your luggage) as part of the fare. Call or e-mail ahead. The last loop starts at 1:30pm, ending at 4:30pm.

By Tram The **Glenelg Tram** runs between Victoria Square and the beachside suburb of Glenelg. Tickets cost A$3.60 (US$2.90/UK£1.45) for adults and A$1.60 (US$1.30/UK65p) for children 5 to 14 from 9am to 3pm. The journey takes 29 minutes.

By Taxi & Car The major cab companies are **Yellow Cabs** (© **13 22 27** in South Australia), **Suburban** (© **08/8211 8888**), and **Amalgamated** (© **08/8223 3333**). **Access Cabs** (© **1300/360 940** in South Australia) offers wheelchair taxis.

Major car-rental companies are **Avis,** 136 N. Terrace (© **08/8410 5727**); **Budget,** 274 N. Terrace (© **08/8223 1400**); **Hertz,** 233 Morphett St. (© **08/8231 2856**); and **Thrifty,** 296 Hindley St. (© **08/8211 8788**).

The **Royal Automobile Association of South Australia (RAA),** 41 Hindmarsh Sq. (© **13 11 11** in South Australia, or 08/8202 4500; www.raa.net), has route maps and provides emergency breakdown services.

FAST FACTS: Adelaide

American Express The office, Shop 32, Rundle Mall (© **1300/139 060**), is open Monday to Friday 9am to 5pm, and Saturday 9am to noon.

Business Hours Generally, banks are open Monday through Thursday from 9:30am to 4pm and Friday from 9:30am to 5pm. Stores are generally open Monday through Thursday from 9am to 5:30pm, Friday from 9am to 9pm, Saturday from 9am to 5pm, and Sunday from 11am to 5pm.

Currency Exchange Banks and hotels, the casino, and the Myer department store in Rundle Mall cash traveler's checks. The **Thomas Cook** office is at Shop 4, Rundle Mall (© **08/8231 6977**). It's open Monday to Friday 9am to 5pm, and Saturday from 10am to 4pm.

Dentist Contact the **Australian Dental Association Emergency Information Service** (© **08/8272 8111**), open weeknights from 5 to 9pm, and Saturday and Sunday from 9am to 9pm. It will put you in touch with a dentist. You can also contact the office of **Dr. Brook,** 231 North Terrace (© **08/8223 6988**), during normal business hours.

Doctor Contact the **Royal Adelaide Hospital,** North Terrace (© **08/8222 4000**). **The Travellers' Medical & Vaccination Centre,** 29 Gilbert Place (© **08/8212 7522**), offers vaccinations and travel-related medicines.

Emergencies Dial © **000** to call an ambulance, the fire department, or the police in an emergency.

Hospitals The **Royal Adelaide Hospital,** North Terrace (✆ **08/8222 4000**), is on North Terrace in the city center.

Hot Lines The **Crisis Care Centre** (✆ 13 16 11 in Australia); the **Royal Automobile Association of South Australia,** or RAA (✆ 08/8202 4500); the **Disability Information and Resource Centre** (✆ 08/8223 7522).

Internet Access Zone Internet Café, 238 Rundle St. (✆ **08/8223 1947**), is open daily from 9:30am to 11pm. **Talking Cents,** 53 Hindley St. (✆ **08/8212 1266**), and **Café Boulevard,** 13 Hindley St. (✆ **08/8231 5734**).

Lost Property If you've lost something on the street, contact the nearest police station. For items left on public transport, contact the **Lost Property Office,** on the main concourse of the Adelaide Railway Station on North Terrace (✆ **08/8218 2552**); it's open Monday through Friday from 9am to 5pm.

Luggage Storage & Lockers There are luggage lockers at Adelaide Airport in the domestic terminal. At the **Central Bus Station** on Franklin Street (✆ **08/8415 5533**), luggage lockers cost A$2 (US$1.60/UK80p) for 24 hours.

Pharmacies (Chemist Shops) **Burden Chemists,** Shop 11, Southern Cross Arcade, King William Street (✆ **08/8231 4701**), is open Monday through Thursday from 8am to 6pm, Friday from 8am to 8pm, and Saturday from 9am to 1pm.

Post Office The **General Post Office (GPO),** 141 King William St., Adelaide, SA 5000 (✆ **08/8216 2222**), is open Monday through Friday from 8am to 6pm and Saturday from 8:30am to noon. General delivery mail *(poste restante)* can be collected Monday through Friday from 8am to 5pm and Saturday 8:30am to noon.

Restrooms Public restrooms are at the Central Market Arcade, between Grote and Gouger streets, in both Hindmarsh and Victoria squares, and at James Place (off Rundle Mall).

Safety Adelaide is a safe city, though it's wise to avoid walking along the River Torrens and through side streets near Hindley Street after dark.

WHERE TO STAY

The **South Australia Visitor & Travel Centre** (see "Visitor Information," above) can supply information on B&Bs and homestays around the state. Satellite or cable TV is rare in South Australian hotels, though some provide pay-per-view movies.

IN THE CITY CENTER

Very Expensive

Hilton Adelaide ★★ The Hilton is a luxurious establishment around the corner from a host of restaurants on Gouger Street. The lobby is polished marble with a cascading fountain and piano music tinkling throughout. Guest rooms are pleasant, with all you might expect from a classy establishment. There are 11 rooms equipped for travelers with disabilities. The Hilton has fabulous deals—A$210 (US$170/UK£85) for standard and A$235 (US$190/UK£95) for executive rooms—"subject to availability" (which means when it's not full). Each business room has a modem port and fax. I was surprised to find **Charlie's Bar**—full of photos of famous Charlies—virtually empty on a Saturday night. In a pinch I'd probably choose the Hyatt (see below) for the extensive views, but there's not much difference between them.

233 Victoria Sq., Adelaide, SA 5000. ✆ **1800/222 255** in Australia, or 08/8217 2000. Fax 08/8217 2001. www.hilton.com. 380 units. A$325–A$335 (US$260–US$270/UK£130–UK£135) double; A$440 (US$352/UK£220) executive floor; A$650 (US$520/UK£260) suite. Extra person A$45 (US$36/UK£18). Children under 12 stay free in parent's room. AE, DC, MC, V. Parking A$16 (US$13/UK£6.50). Tram stops in front of hotel. Bus: Bee Line to Victoria Sq. **Amenities:** 2 restaurants; bar; heated outdoor pool; tennis court; health club; Jacuzzi; sauna; concierge; salon; 24-hr. room service; massage; babysitting; laundry service; dry cleaning; nonsmoking rooms. *In room:* A/C, TV w/pay movies, dataport, minibar, coffeemaker, hair dryer, iron, safe.

Hyatt Regency Adelaide ★★ The 20-story Hyatt Regency is in the heart of the city and part of the complex that includes the Adelaide Festival Centre, the Casino, the Exhibition Hall, and the Convention Centre. The property overlooks the River Torrens and nearby parklands, and there are some wonderful views from the higher floors. The Hyatt doesn't scrimp, which shows in the attention to detail in the rooms. Guests staying in club-level Regency rooms get a good complimentary breakfast and free evening drinks and canapés. **Waves,** a cabaret-nightclub, offers a lively combination of video, disco, and live music; it's free for guests, though it can be dull and the drinks are expensive. Afternoon tea is served in the **Atrium Lounge,** which gets surprisingly full as the night wears on.

North Terrace, Adelaide, SA 5000. ✆ **13 12 34** in Australia, 800/233-1234 in the U.S. and Canada, or 08/8231 1234. Fax 08/8231 1120. www.hyatt.com. 367 units. A$250–A$300 (US$200–US$240/UK£100–UK£120) double; A $300–A$340 (US$240–US$272/UK£120–UK£136) Regency Club City View; A$320–A$360 (US$256–US$288/ UK£178–UK£144) Club River Park View; A$390 (US$312/UK£156) executive suite; A$840 (US$672/UK£336) deluxe suite. Extra person A$50 (US$40/UK£20). Children under 13 stay free in parent's room. Regency Club City View and Club River Park View rates include breakfast. Ask about packages and weekend discounts. AE, DC, MC, V. Parking A$18 (US$14/UK£7). Bus: CityLoop. **Amenities:** 3 restaurants; lounge; bar; nightclub; heated outdoor pool; health club and Jacuzzi; concierge; business center; 24-hr. room service; massage; babysitting; laundry service; dry cleaning. *In room:* A/C, TV w/pay movies, high-speed Internet access, minibar, hair dryer, iron.

Expensive

The Mercure Grosvenor Hotel *Value* This pleasant hotel is conveniently located in the center of Adelaide, opposite Skycity Casino and the Convention and Exhibition Centre. It's modern and the rooms are light-filled and come with all those gadgets you can't do without anymore, such as Wi-Fi. This hotel is a good example of the kind of discount you can get if you book over a hotel's website. Rooms here can cost as little as A$135 (US$108/UK£54) a night.

125 North Terrace, Adelaide 5000. ✆ **08/8407 8888.** Fax 08/8407 8866. www.mercuregrosvenorhotel.com.au. 250 units. A$229 (US$183/UK£93) double. Check website for good deals. AE, DC, MC, VBus: CityLoop. **Amenities:** Restaurant; bar; fitness center; sauna; concierge; 24-hr. room service. *In room:* A/C, TV w/pay movies, modem, fax, minibar, hair dryer, iron.

Moderate

Rockford Adelaide (The Townhouse) *Value* This contemporary boutique hotel is a 10- to 15-minute walk from the center of town, 5 minutes from the casino, and near the nightclub and red-light district. There are nice spa rooms, each with a large LCD

Tips Plan Ahead

If you plan to be in town during the Adelaide Festival, make sure you book accommodations *well* in advance. The town can be packed during Christmas and New Year's, so it's wise to book well in advance then, too.

TV. All rooms are spacious and comfortable, and modern and riverside rooms have balconies. Many of them were refurbished in 2007. There's an alfresco dining area, and you can eat some good seafood and chargrilled meats in the restaurant.

164 Hindley St., Adelaide, SA 5000. ✆ **1800/606 562** in Australia, or 08/8211 8255. Fax 08/8231 1179. www.rockford hotels.com.au. 68 units. A$140 (US$112/UK£66) standard double; A$180 (US$144/UK£72) business double; A$190 (US$152/UK£76) executive double; A$205 (US$164/UK£82) spa suite. Children under 12 stay free in parent's room. Off-season and weekend discounts available. Check for Internet specials. Ask about package deals. AE, DC, MC, V. Free parking. **Amenities:** Restaurant; bar; heated outdoor pool; golf course nearby; access to nearby health club; sauna; concierge; limited room service; laundry service; dry cleaning; nonsmoking rooms. *In room:* A/C, TV/DVD w/free movies, dataport, minibar, hair dryer, iron.

Saville City Suites Adelaide ★ You can't miss this conglomerate of russet-red bricks on the outskirts of the city center (about a 10-min. walk). Rooms are nice and spacious, if a bit formal, which is not surprising because the place is popular with business travelers. Great add-ons to all rooms are the kitchen and laundry.

255 Hindley St., Adelaide, SA 5000. ✆ **1800/882 601** in Australia, or 08/8217 2500. Fax 08/8217 2519. www.saville hotelsgroup.com. 142 units. A$152 (US$121/UK£62) studio for 2; A$178 (US$142/UK£71) 2-bedroom suite for up to 4. AE, DC, MC, V. Parking A$10 (US$8/UK£4). **Amenities:** Restaurant; free access to nearby City Gym; outdoor Jacuzzi; concierge; tour desk; car-rental desk; limited room service; babysitting; coin-op laundry; dry cleaning; nonsmoking rooms; rooms for those w/limited mobility. *In room:* A/C, TV w/pay movies, VCR (on request), dataport, kitchen, minibar, fridge, coffeemaker, hair dryer, iron.

Inexpensive

Adelaide City Park Motel ★ The spacious rooms in this high-end boutique motel have modern furnishings and nice bathrooms with showers. Some rooms have private balconies overlooking parkland. Family rooms sleep from four to six people: The largest has a double bed and two sets of bunks. The best double room is no. 45, which has two double beds and a large balcony.

471 Pulteney St., Adelaide, SA 5000. ✆ **1800 231 444** in Australia, or 08/8223 1444. Fax 08/8223 1133. www.city park.com.au. 18 units. A$88 (US$70/UK£35) double without bathroom; A$110 (US$110/UK£55) double with bathroom; A$130 (US$104/UK£52) double with balcony; A$110–A$130 (US$88–US$104/UK£44–UK£52) triple; A$120–A$180 (US$96–US$144/UK£48–UK£90) family. Extra person A$15 (US$12/UK£6). AE, DC, MC, V. Limited parking by arrangement. The tram to Glenelg is 5 min. walk away; 4 streets up is a bus stop for the free City Loop Bus. **Amenities:** Restaurant; bar; tour desk; car-rental desk; dry-cleaning service. *In room:* A/C, TV, fridge, coffeemaker, iron, microwave.

Moore's Brecknock Hotel Adelaide's original Irish pub, built in 1851, still attracts a lot of Irish patrons who come here for the great selection of beer and reasonably priced home-style cooking—it reputedly serves Adelaide's best hamburgers. It's also very popular with American guests who use the hotel accommodations upstairs as a base from which to discover Kangaroo Island and other parts of the state. The Brecknock, about 4 blocks from Victoria Square, is run by Kerry Moore and his Canadian wife, Tricia. Live bands play downstairs on Friday, Saturday, and Sunday, but the music finishes at 1am on Friday and Saturday and at 10pm on Sunday, so you shouldn't have too much trouble sleeping. Rooms are large, if a little spartan, and decorated in your granny's old-world style. Some rooms have a single bed as well as a double. Each has a sink, with the bathrooms down the hall.

Next door is **Nomads Backpackers** (✆ **08/8211 8985;** www.nomads-backpackers.com), which is associated with the hotel.

401 King William St., Adelaide, SA 5000. ✆ **08/8231 5467.** Fax 08/8410 1968. www.brecknockhotel.com.au. 10 units, none with bathroom. A$70 (US$56/UK£28) double; A$90 (US$72/UK£36) triple. Rates include continental breakfast. AE, DC, MC, V. Free parking. Tram: Glenelg route. **Amenities:** Restaurant; 3 bars; bike rental; tour desk; car-rental desk; coin-op laundry; dry cleaning; nonsmoking rooms. *In room:* A/C, fax, fridge, coffeemaker, iron, safe.

IN NORTH ADELAIDE

This suburb across the river is an interesting place with nice architecture and good restaurants. It's about a 10-minute bus ride from the city center.

North Adelaide Heritage Group ★★★ *Finds* It's worth coming all the way to Adelaide just for the experience of staying in one of these out-of-this-world apartments, cottages, or suites. Each of the 21 properties in North Adelaide and Eastwood are fabulous. I recommend particularly the former Friendly Meeting Chapel Hall, which was once the headquarters of the "Albert Lodge No. 6 of the Independent Order of Oddfellows, Manchester Unity Friendly Society, and the Court Huntsman's Pride No. 2478 of the Ancient Order of Foresters Friendly Society." The structure, a small, simple gabled hall of bluestone rubble trimmed with brick, resembles a small church. Built in 1878, it's stocked with period pieces and antiques and rounded off with a modern, fully stocked kitchen; a huge Jacuzzi; a queen-size bed; and a CD player and TV.

Another standout place is the George Lowe Esquire unit. The huge 19th-century apartment is decorated with antiques and has a huge four-poster bed, a lounge, and a full kitchen. Guests also have use of nice gardens. Owners Rodney and Regina Twiss have added little touches that make you feel at home, from magazines liberally piled everywhere to bacon and eggs in the fridge. The company also offers three apartments in the old North Adelaide Fire Station; the ground-floor apartment comes with a full-size, bright red, very old fire engine. All properties are within easy walking distance of the main attractions in the area, as well as tennis courts (around A$20/US$13/UK£650 an hour) and **Adelaide Golf Links** (✆ **08/8267 2171;** A$18/US$12/UK£6 weekdays, A$21/US$14/UK£7 weekends).

Office: 109 Glen Osmond Rd., Eastwood, SA 5063. ✆ **08/8272 1355.** Fax 08/8272 1355. www.adelaideheritage.com. 21 units. A$155–A$345 (US$124–US$276/UK£62–UK£138) double. Extra person A$60–A$85 (US$48–US$68/UK£24–UK£34). Child under 12 A$30 (US$24/UK£12). AE, DC, MC, V. Free parking. **Amenities:** Golf course nearby; tennis courts nearby; Jacuzzi; concierge; car-rental desk; free bus to city center; limited room service; massage; dry cleaning. *In room:* A/C, TV, kitchenette, fridge, coffeemaker, hair dryer, iron.

Princes Lodge Motel One of the best motels in Adelaide, the Princes Lodge looks more like a large private home than a simple brick roadside structure. Rooms are uninspiring standard motel-like and generally come with a double and a single bed. There are three family rooms; one has a double and three singles, and another has six beds in one room. The motel is within walking distance of the restaurant strip on O'Connell Street, on a bus route that follows King William Street, and a A$8 (US$6.40/UK£3.20) taxi ride from the city center.

73 Lefevre Terrace, North Adelaide, SA 5006. ✆ **08/8267 5566.** Fax 08/8239 0787. www.princeslodge.com.au. 21 units. A$71 (US$57/UK£28) double with separate bathroom; A$82 (US$66/UK£33) double with attached bathroom; A$92 (US$74/UK£38) queen-size-bed room with bathroom. Rates include continental breakfast. AE, DC, MC, V. Bus: 222 from Victoria Sq. **Amenities:** Golf course nearby; tour desk; car-rental desk; coin-op laundry. *In room:* A/C, TV, dataport, fridge, coffeemaker, hair dryer, iron.

IN GLENELG

I'd recommend, without hesitation, staying in Glenelg rather than in the city center. The journey to the city center by car or tram takes less than 30 minutes, and the airport is less than 10 minutes away. Add to this the sea, the lovely beach, the fun fair (amusement park), the great shops, the good pub, and the nice accommodations, and you have a perfect place to relax on your holiday.

Atlantic Tower Motor Inn If you're looking for relatively inexpensive accommodations near the beach, this is your place. You can't miss the tubular building, with its slowly revolving restaurant on the 12th floor. Rooms are simple but bright, and have nice park views through large windows. Each has a double and a single bed. Deluxe rooms are a bit nicer and come with bathrooms rather than just showers. Suites have two rooms and excellent views; the most expensive have Jacuzzis. The gently turning **Rock Lobster Cafe** upstairs is open for lunch on Thursday, Friday, and Sunday, and dinner every evening.

760 Anzac Hwy., Glenelg, SA 5045. © **08/8294 1011.** Fax 08/8376 0964. www.atlantictowermotorinn.com. 27 units, 20 with shower only. A$101 (US$80/UK£40) double; A$120 (US$96/UK£48) deluxe double; A$170 (US$136/UK£68) suite. Extra person A$15 (US$12/UK£6). Children under 15 stay free in parent's room. AE, DC, MC, V. Free parking. Tram: Glenelg route to stop 20. **Amenities:** Restaurant; tour desk; car-rental desk; room service; laundry service; dry cleaning; nonsmoking rooms. *In room:* A/C, TV, fax, minibar, hair dryer, iron.

Stamford Grand Adelaide ★★ A classic Adelaide photo is of trams awaiting passengers in front of the Stamford Grand. Located right on the beach, this classy hotel offers nice rooms with modern furnishings; many overlook the beach, the ocean, and the pier. **The Pier and Pines** is a popular bar bursting with youngish crowds most nights; for a mellower scene, there's Horizons piano bar, which offers quality live music, particularly on weekends.

Moseley Sq. (P.O. Box 600), Glenelg, SA 5045. © **1800/882 777** in Australia, or 08/8376 1222. Fax 08/8376 1111. 240 units. A$322 (US$257/UK£129) double; A$349–A$546 (US$279–US$437/UK£140–UK£219) suite. Children under 12 stay free in parent's room. AE, DC, MC, V. Parking A$10 (US$8/UK£4). Tram: Glenelg route. **Amenities:** 2 restaurants; 2 bars; indoor pool; health club and Jacuzzi; concierge; business center; 24-hr. room service. *In room:* A/C, TV w/pay movies, minibar, hair dryer, iron.

WHERE TO DINE

With more than 600 restaurants, pubs, and cafes, Adelaide boasts more dining spots per capita than anywhere else in Australia. Many cluster in areas such as Rundle Street, Gouger Street, and North Adelaide—where you'll find almost every style of cuisine you can imagine. For cheap noodles, laksas, sushi, and cakes, head to Adelaide's popular **Central Markets** (© **08/8203 7494**), behind the Hilton Adelaide between Gouger and Grote streets.

Glenelg has a host of nice cafes, including **Café Zest,** 2A Sussex St. (© **08/8295 3599**), which serves nice baguettes and bagels; and **Café Blu,** Ramada Pier Hotel, 16 Holdfast Promenade (© **08/8350 6688**), which has good pizzas.

As well as the restaurants featured below, other favorites include **Gaucho's Argentinian Restaurant,** 91 Gouger St. (© **08/8231 2299**), which carves up grilled meat on weekday lunchtimes Monday and daily from 5:30pm to late; **Shiki,** a top-rank Japanese restaurant in the Hyatt Regency Adelaide (© **08/8238 2382**), which is open Tuesday to Saturday from 6 to 10pm; and **Ned Kelly's Restaurant,** 26 O'Connell St., North Adelaide (© **08/8361 9994**), which has good steaks and Australian country music playing in the background. It's open for lunch Wednesdays to Sundays between noon and 2:30pm, and for dinner daily from 6 to 10pm.

Because of South Australia's healthy wine industry, you'll find that many of the more expensive restaurants have extensive wine lists—though with spicier foods, it's probably wiser to stick with beer or a fruity white in a pinch. Many Adelaide restaurants allow diners to bring their own wine (BYO), but most charge a steep corkage fee to open your bottle—A$6 (US$4.80/UK£2.40) or so is not uncommon.

Finds Something Different: Dining Tours

Adelaide's Top Food And Wine Tours (✆ 08/8263 0265; www.topfoodandwinetours.com.au) offers a range of food-based tours including both dawn and midmorning tours of the Central Market. Dawn Tours cost A$48 (US$38/UK£19) for adults and A$25 (US$20/UK£10) for kids, and start at 7:15am on Tuesday, Thursday, Friday, and Saturday.

IN THE CITY CENTER

Very Expensive

The Grange ★★ MODERN AUSTRALIAN The Grange is an open-plan restaurant specializing in Contemporary food by Adelaide's most influential chef, Cheong Liew. Liew offers an innovative fusion of Western and Asian ingredients, rounded off with an extensive wine list. The menu begins with a choice of two starters, one of them Liew's signature dish, "the four dances of the sea"—an antipasto of fish, octopus in garlic sauce, prawn sushi, raw cuttlefish, and black noodles. For the next course you could choose baby abalone, lobster baked with bourbon and lime, or Japanese quail with chestnuts and Chinese mushrooms.

In the Hilton Adelaide, 233 Victoria Sq. ✆ **08/8217 2000.** Reservations required. 3-course dinner A$81 (US$65/UK£38); 4-course dinner A$97 (US$78/UK£39). AE, DC, MC, V. Tues–Sat 7–10:30pm.

Moderate

Amalfi ITALIAN Come here for good cooking at reasonable prices in a lively atmosphere. The pizzas are the best in Adelaide—though a little expensive—and good veal and pasta dishes are always on the menu. Be sure to check out the daily specials, where you can pick a very good fish dish or two.

29 Frome St. (just off Rundle St.). ✆ **08/8223 1948.** Reservations recommended. Main courses A$14–A$17 (US$11–US$14/UK£5.50–UK£7). AE, DC, MC, V. Mon–Fri 11:30am–3pm and 5:30–11pm (until midnight Fri); Sat 5:30pm–midnight.

Jasmin Indian Restaurant ★★ *Finds* NORTH INDIAN This is a seriously good Indian restaurant. Prices have crept up as this place has gotten more popular, but this family-run Adelaide institution a block south of Rundle Mall is still a good value. Indian artifacts and signed cricket bats from visiting Indian teams decorate the walls. The atmosphere is comfortable yet busy, and the service is professional. The house special is very hot beef vindaloo, but all the old favorites, such as tandoori chicken, butter chicken (a big seller), lamb korma, and Malabari beef with coconut cream, ginger, and garlic are here, too. Mop it all up with nan bread, and cool your palate with a side dish of raita. The *suji halwa* (semolina pudding with nuts) is the best I've tasted.

31 Hindmarsh Sq. ✆ **08/8223 7837.** www.jasmine.com.au. Reservations recommended. Main courses A$22–A$24 (US$18–US$19/UK£9/UK£9.50). AE, DC, MC, V. Thurs–Fri noon–2:30pm; Tues–Sat 5:30–10:30pm.

Jolleys Boathouse Restaurant ★ MODERN AUSTRALIAN Jolleys is on the banks of the River Torrens, with views of boats, ducks, and black swans. Businesspeople and ladies who lunch rush for the three outside tables, but if you miss out, the bright and airy interior, with its cream-colored tablecloths and directors' chairs, isn't too much of a letdown. You might start with miso-crusted venison with grilled mushroom, mizuna salad, and Japanese mustard sauce. Moving on, you could tuck into the crisp-fried tea-smoked duck, with Chinese spinach, and blood plum and tamarind sauce. (Ignore the peaceful quacking out on the river if you can.)

Jolleys Lane. ✆ **08/8223 2891.** www.jolleysboathouse.com. Reservations recommended. Main courses A$25–A$38 (US$20–US$31/UK£10–UK£16). AE, DC, MC, V. Sun–Fri noon–2:30pm; Mon–Sat 6–8:30pm.

Matsuri ★ JAPANESE I like the atmosphere in this very good restaurant on the popular Gouger Street restaurant strip. Takaomi Kitamura, world-famous ice sculptor and sushi master, prepares the sushi and sashimi dishes, some of the best in Australia. Monday night is "sushi festival night," when sushi is half price. During happy hour Wednesday through Sunday, sushi is 30% off if you place your order before 7pm. (You can preorder over the phone and eat later.) Promised, too, is a 10% discount if you show this Frommer's guide. Other popular dishes include vegetarian and seafood tempura, *yose nobe* (a hot pot of vegetables, seafood, and chicken), and *chawan mushi* (a steamed custard dish). The service is friendly and considerate. The corkage fee is a steep A$4.50 (US$3.60/UK£1.80) a bottle.

167 Gouger St. ✆ **08/8231 3494.** Reservations recommended. Main courses A$8.60–A$28 (US$6.90–US$22/UK£3.50–UK£11). AE, DC, MC, V. Fri noon–2pm; Wed–Mon 5:30–10pm.

Mekong Thai THAI/MALAYSIAN/HALAL *Value* Though this place is not much to look at—with simple tables and chairs, some outside in a portico—it has a fiery reputation for good food among in-the-know locals. The food is spicy and authentic, and the portions are filling. It's also a vegetarian's paradise, with at least 16 meat-free mains on the ethnically varied menu. It's Adelaide's only fully halal (suitable for Muslims) restaurant.

68 Hindley St. ✆ **08/8231 2914.** Main courses A$11–A$13 (US$8.80–US$10/UK£4.40–UK£5). AE, DC, MC, V. Daily 5:15–10:30pm or later.

Rigoni's Bistro ITALIAN On a narrow lane west of King William Street, this traditional Italian trattoria is often packed at lunch and less frantic in the evening. It's big and bright, with high ceilings and russet quarry tiles. A long bar runs through the middle of the dining room; brass plates mark the stools of regular diners. The food is very traditional and quite good. The chalkboard menu often changes, but you are likely to find lasagna, veal in white wine, marinated fish, and various pasta dishes. It's a good place for a nice pasta lunch.

27 Leigh St. ✆ **08/8231 5160.** Reservations recommended. Main courses A$28–A$32 (US$22–US$26/UK£11–UK£13); pastas A$20–A$25 (US$16–US$20/UK£7.80–UK£10). AE, DC, MC, V. Mon–Fri noon–2:30pm; Mon–Sat 6:30–10pm.

IN NORTH ADELAIDE

The Manse ★★ FRENCH This restaurant gives some of the best restaurants in Sydney and Melbourne a run for their money. The place is a mix of stately elegance and contemporary cool, with blacks and whites predominating. The food is superb, particularly the duck and rabbit options: Try the rabbit cooked three ways (roasted loin, a small rabbit-and-mushroom pie, and braised rabbit leg in a prune and almanac sauce). The starter of roasted pork belly is a must. Book a table outside in the courtyard on a nice day. There's a minimum order of two courses per person on Friday and Saturday evenings.

142 Tynte St., North Adelaide. ✆ **08/8267 4636.** www.themanserestaurant.com.au. Reservations recommended. Main courses A$29–A$38 (US$23–US$31/UK£12–UK£16). AE, DC, MC, V. Fri noon–3pm (set menu); Mon–Sat 6:30–10pm. Bus: 182, 224, 226, 228, or 229.

SEEING THE SIGHTS

Adelaide is a laid-back city. It's not jampacked with tourist-oriented attractions like some of the larger state capitals, though The Migration Museum (see below) is easily one of the best museums in Australia. The best way to enjoy this pleasant city is to take things nice and easy. Walk beside the River Torrens, ride the tram to the beachside suburb of Glenelg, and spend the evenings sipping wine and sampling some of the country's best alfresco dining.

THE TOP ATTRACTIONS

Art Gallery of South Australia ★ Adelaide's premier public art gallery has a good range of local and overseas works and a fine Asian ceramics collection. Of particular interest are Charles Hall's *Proclamation of South Australia 1836;* Nicholas Chevalier's painting of the departure of explorers Burke and Wills from Melbourne; several works by Australian painters Sidney Nolan, Albert Tucker, and Arthur Boyd; and some excellent contemporary art. For an introduction, take a free guided tour. The bookshop has an extensive collection of art publications. Allow 1 to 2 hours.

North Terrace. ✆ **08/8207 7000.** Free admission. Daily 10am–5pm. Guided tours Mon–Fri 11am and 2pm; Sat–Sun 11am and 3pm. Closed Dec 25. Bus: City Loop.

The Migration Museum ★ *Finds* This tiny museum, dedicated to immigration and multiculturalism, is one of the most important and fascinating in Australia. With touching personal displays, it tells the story of the waves of immigrants who have helped shape this multicultural society, from the boatloads of convicts who came in 1788 to the ethnic groups who have trickled in over the past 2 centuries. Allow 1 hour.

82 Kintore Ave. ✆ **08/8207 7580.** Admission by donation. Mon–Fri 10am–5pm; Sat–Sun and public holidays 1–5pm. Closed Good Friday and Dec 25. Bus: Any to North Terrace.

The National Wine Centre of Australia ★ This architectural masterpiece concentrates on Australia's 53 wine regions. Interactive exhibits and displays allow you to blend your own virtual wine. The Tasting Gallery displays an extensive range of Australian wines, and wine-tasting packages allow you to sample some of the rarest vintages. A restaurant and bar overlook the Wine Centre, which has its own vineyard. You can fit in a trip here with a visit to the nearby Botanic Gardens.

Hackney Rd. (eastern end of N. Terrace). ✆ **08/8303 3355.** www.wineaustralia.com.au. Admission A$11 (US$8.80/UK£4.40) adults, A$6 (US$4.80/UK£2.40) children under 18 accompanied by an adult, A$29 (US$23/UK£12) families. Wine-tasting packages A$5–A$20 (US$4–US$16/UK£2–UK£8). Mon–Fri 9am–5:30pm. Closed Good Friday and Dec 25. Limited parking. Bus: CityLoop to Botanic Gardens.

South Australian Maritime Museum This Port Adelaide museum commemorates over 150 years of maritime history. Most of the exhibits are in the 1850s Bond Store, but the museum also incorporates an 1863 lighthouse and three vessels moored alongside Wharf No. 1, a short walk away. The fully rigged replica of the 16m (52-ft.) ketch *Active II* is very impressive. Allow 1½ hours. Port Adelaide is approximately 30 minutes from the city center by bus.

126 Lipson St., Port Adelaide. ✆ **08/8207 6255.** Admission A$8.50 (US$6.80/UK£3.40) adults, A$3.50 (US$2.80/UK£1.40) children, A$22 (US$18/UK£9) families. Daily 10am–5pm. Closed Dec 25. Bus: 151 or 153 from North Terrace opposite Parliament House to stop 40 (Port Adelaide). Train: Port Adelaide.

South Australian Museum ★ The star attraction of this interesting museum is the Australian Aboriginal Cultures Gallery. On display is an extensive collection of utensils, spears, tools, bush medicine, food samples, photographs, and the like. Also in the museum is a sorry-looking collection of stuffed native animals (sadly including a few extinct marsupials, such as the Tasmanian tiger); a good collection of Papua New Guinea artifacts; and excellent mineral and butterfly collections.

If you're interested in learning more about the exhibits, take a Behind-the-Scenes Tour. The tours take place after museum hours and cost A$12 (US$9.60/UK£4.80) for adults. Allow 2 hours to see the museum.

North Terrace, between State Library and Art Gallery of South Australia. ✆ **08/8207 7500.** www.samuseum.sa.gov.au. Free admission. Daily 10am–5pm. Closed Good Friday and Dec 25.

Tandanya Aboriginal Cultural Institute ★★ This place offers a great opportunity to experience Aboriginal life through Aboriginal eyes. Exhibits change regularly, but all give insight into Aboriginal art and cultural activities. At noon every day there's a didgeridoo performance. A shop sells Aboriginal art and books on Aboriginal culture, and a cafe on the premises serves several bush tucker (native food) items. Allow 1 hour.

253 Grenfell St. ✆ **08/8224 3200.** www.tandanya.com.au. Admission A$4 (US$3.20/UK£1.60) adults, A$3 (US$2.40/UK£1.20) children under 14, A$10 (US$8/UK£4) families. Daily 10am–5pm. Bus: City Loop.

THE FLORA & THE FAUNA

Adelaide Zoo *Kids* To be honest, if you've experienced the wonderful Melbourne Zoo, or even Taronga Zoo in Sydney, the Adelaide Zoo is probably not worth your while. But if this is your only chance to see a kangaroo in captivity, then plan a visit. Of course, other Australian animals live at the zoo, and the nicely landscaped gardens and lack of crowds make it a pleasant place for an entertaining stroll. The zoo houses the only pygmy blue-tongue lizard in captivity in Australia; the species was thought to be extinct since the 1940s, until a live specimen was discovered inside the belly of a dead snake. Allow 1 hour.

Frome Rd. ✆ **08/8267 3255.** Admission A$15 (US$12/UK£6) adults, A$9 (US$7.20/UK£3.60) children, A$48 (US$38/UK£19) family. Daily 9:30am–5pm. Bus: 272 or 273 from Currie St. to stop 2 (5 min.).

Botanic Gardens You'll feel as though you're at the heart of the city when you stroll through the huddles of office workers having picnic lunches on the lawns. Highlights include a broad avenue of Moreton Bay figs, duck ponds, giant water lilies, an Italianate garden, a palm house, and the Bicentennial Conservatory—a glass dome full of rainforest species. You might want to have lunch surrounded by bird song and lush vegetation in the **Botanic Gardens Restaurant** (✆ **08/8223 3526**), in the center of the park; it's open daily from 10am to 5pm.

North Terrace. ✆ **08/8222 9311.** www.environment.sa.gov.au/botanicgardens. Free admission. Mon–Fri 8am–sundown; Sat–Sun 9am–sundown.

FOR TRAIN BUFFS

National Railway Museum This former Port Adelaide railway yard houses Australia's largest and finest collection of locomotive engines and rolling stock. The 104 or so items on display include some 30 engines. Among the most impressive trains are the gigantic "Mountain" class engines, and "Tea and Sugar" trains that once ran between railway camps in remote parts of the desert. Entrance includes a train ride. Allow 1½ hours.

Lipton St., North Adelaide. ✆ **08/8341 1690.** Admission A$9 (US$7.20/UK£3.60) adults, A$3.50 (US$2.80/UK£1.40) children, A$20 (US$16/UK£8) families. Daily 10am–5pm. Bus: 151 or 153 from North Terrace, opposite Parliament House, to stop 40 (approximately 30 min.).

ORGANIZED TOURS

Grayline Day Tours (© **1300/858 687** in Australia; www.grayline.com) operates a city sightseeing tour for A$39 (US$31/UK£16) for adults and A$20 (US$16/UK£8) for children. It operates from 9:30am to noon Monday through Saturday. The bus can pick you up at your hotel. Other Grayline tours take in central Adelaide, with either Hahndorf or Cleland Wildlife Park included; the Flinders Ranges; and Kangaroo Island.

ENJOYING THE GREAT OUTDOORS

BIKING Adelaide's parks and riverbanks are very popular with cyclists. Rent your bicycle from **Linear Park Bikes,** Elder Park, King William Road (© **08/8223 6271**). The rate is A$15 to A$20 (US$12–US$16/UK£6–UK£8) for 24 hours, including helmet, lock, and baby seat (if needed). **Recreation SA** (© **08/8226 7301**) publishes a brochure showing Adelaide's bike routes. Pick one up at the **South Australia Visitor & Travel Centre** (see "Visitor Information," earlier in this chapter). **The Map Shop,** 6 Peel St. (© **08/8231 2033**), is also a good source for maps.

GOLF The **City of Adelaide Golf Course** (© **08/8267 2171**) is close to town and has two short 18-hole courses and a full-size championship course. Greens fees are A$14 to A$17 (US$11–US$14/UK£5.50–UK£7) weekdays and A$17 to A$19 (US$14–US$15/UK£7–UK£7.50) weekends, depending on the course. Club rental is available. Ask about cheaper prices after 4pm.

HIKING & JOGGING The banks of the River Torrens are a good place for a jog. The fit and adventurous might want to tackle the **Heysen Trail,** a spectacular 1,600km (992-mile) walk through bush, farmland, and rugged hill country that starts 80km (50 miles) south of Adelaide and goes to the Flinders Ranges by way of the Adelaide Hills and the Barossa Valley. For more information on the trail, visit the **South Australia Visitor & Travel Centre** (see "Visitor Information," earlier in this chapter).

SPECTATOR SPORTS

CRICKET The **Adelaide Oval** (© **08/8300 3800**), on the corner of War Memorial Drive and King William Street, is the venue for international matches during the summer season. The Institute Building, part of the State Library of S.A., displays the **Don Bradman Collection** (© **08/8207 7595**). The cricket legend died in Adelaide in 2001.

FOOTBALL Unlike New South Wales, where Rugby League is the most popular winter sport, in Adelaide you'll find plenty of Australian Rules fanatics. Games are usually played on Saturday at the **Adelaide Oval** (see above) or at **Football Park** (© **08/8268 2088**), Turner Drive, West Lakes. The home teams are the Adelaide Crows and the Port Adelaide Power. Games are played February through October, with the finals in September and October. Tickets must be purchased well in advance from **BASS** (© **13 12 46** in South Australia, or 08/8400 2205).

THE SHOPPING SCENE

Rundle Mall (between King William and Pulteney sts.) is Adelaide's main shopping street. This pedestrian-only thoroughfare is home to the big names in fashion.

Adelaide's Central Markets (© **08/8203 7494**), behind the Adelaide Hilton Hotel between Gouger and Grote streets, make up the largest produce market in the Southern Hemisphere. They're a good place to shop for vegetables, fruit, meat, fish, and the like, although the markets are worth popping into even if you're not looking for picnic fixings. The markets, held in a warehouselike structure, are open Tuesday

Finds Shopping for Opals

South Australia is home to the world's largest sources of white opals. (The more expensive black opals generally come from Lightning Ridge in New South Wales.) There are plenty of places to buy around town, but **Opal Field Gems,** 33 King William St. (© **08/8212 5300**), is one of the best. As a rule, you're not going to find any bargains, so just buy what you like (and can afford—good opals cost many thousands of dollars).

from 7am to 5:30pm, Thursday from 9am to 5:30pm, Friday from 7am to 9pm, and Saturday from 7am to 3pm.

The six-story **Myer Centre,** next door to the Myer department store, 22–38 Rundle Mall, has a Body Shop (on the ground floor), for beauty products; an Australian Geographic shop (on level 3), for top-quality Australiana; and Exotica (level 2), where you can find unusual futuristic gifts.

Just off Rundle Mall, at Shop no. 6 in the City Cross Arcade, is **L'Unique** (© **08/8231 0030**), a good crafts shop selling South Australian pottery, jewelry, woodcraft, hand-blown glass, and original paintings.

Elsewhere, the renowned **Jam Factory Craft and Design Centre,** in the Lions Art Centre, 19 Morphett St. (© **08/8410 0727**), sells an excellent range of locally made ceramics, glass, furniture, and metal items. You can also watch the craftspeople at work here.

Head to the **R.M. Williams** shop on Gawler Place (© **08/8232 3611**) for the best simple boots you're likely to find, as well as other Aussie fashion icons, including Akubra hats, moleskin pants, and Driza-bone coats.

ADELAIDE AFTER DARK

The ***Adelaide Advertiser*** lists all performances and exhibitions in its entertainment pages. The free tourist guide ***Today in Adelaide,*** available in most hotels, also has information. Tickets for theater and other entertainment events in Adelaide can be purchased from **BASS ticket outlets** (© **13 12 46** in South Australia, or 08/8400 2205) at the following locations: Festival Theatre, Adelaide Festival Centre, King William Road; Centre Pharmacy, 19 Central Market Arcade; Verandah Music, 182 Rundle St.; and on the fifth floor of the Myer department store, Rundle Mall.

THE PERFORMING ARTS

The major concert hall is the **Adelaide Festival Centre,** King William Road (© **08/8216 8600** for general inquiries, or 08/8400 2205 for box office). The Festival Centre encompasses three auditoriums: the 1,978-seat Festival Theatre, the 612-seat Playhouse, and the 350-seat Space Centre. This is the place in Adelaide to see opera, ballet, drama, orchestral concerts, the Adelaide Symphony Orchestra, plays, and experimental drama.

The complex also includes an outdoor amphitheater used for jazz, rock 'n' roll, and country-music concerts; an art gallery; a bistro; a piano bar; and the Silver Jubilee Organ, the world's largest transportable concert-hall organ (built in Austria to commemorate Queen Elizabeth II's Silver Jubilee).

The Adelaide Repertory Festival presents five productions a year, ranging from drama to comedy, at the **Arts Theatre,** 53 Angus St. (© **08/8221 5644**). Playwrights Alan Ayckbourne and Terrence Rattigan are among the many who have had plays performed here. The theater, which is a short walk from many hotels and restaurants, is also the home of the Metropolitan Musical Theatre Company, which presents two musical comedy productions a year. Tickets cost around A$16 (US$13/UK£7.50) for adults and A$11 (US$8.80/UK£4.40) for children.

Her Majesty's Theatre, 58 Grote St. (✆ **08/8216 8600**), is a 1,000-seat venue opposite Central Markets that presents drama, comedy, musicals, dance, opera, and recitals. Tickets generally cost A$30 to A$55 (US$24–US$44/UK£12–UK£22).

THE BAR & CLUB SCENE

Adelaide's nightlife ranges from twiddling your thumbs to nude lap dancers. For adult entertainment (clubs with the word *strip* in the name) head to **Hindley Street**—there are a few pubs there, but I wouldn't recommend them. For information on gay and lesbian options, pick up the ***Adelaide Gay Times.***

The popular **Universal Wine Bar,** 285 Rundle St. (✆ **08/8232 5000**), is the perfect place to start an evening, with great atmosphere and good wines by the glass.

Most pubs are open from 11am to midnight. For all-age pubs, locals will point you toward **The Austral,** 205 Rundle St. (✆ **08/8223 4660**); **The Exeter,** 246 Rundle St. (✆ **08/8223 2623**); **The Lion,** at the corner of Melbourne and Jerningham streets (✆ **08/8367 0222**); and the **British Hotel,** 58 Finniss St. (✆ **08/8267 2188**), in North Adelaide, where you can cook your own steak on the courtyard barbecue. Also popular with visitors and locals alike is the **Earl of Aberdeen,** 316 Pulteney St., at Carrington Street (✆ **08/8223 6433**), a colonial-style pub popular for after-work drinks. **The Port Dock,** 10 Todd St., Port Adelaide (✆ **08/8240 0187**), was licensed as a pub in 1864; it brews four of its own beers and pumps them directly to its three bars with old English beer engines.

TRYING YOUR LUCK AT THE CASINO

Right next to the Adelaide Hyatt, and dwarfed by the old railway station containing it, is the **Adelaide Casino** (now officially called "SkyCity" to make it sound trendier), North Terrace (✆ **1800/888 711** in Australia, or 08/8212 2811). The casino has two floors of gaming tables and slot machines, as well as four bars and several dining options, including a fast-food station and the excellent Pullman buffet restaurant. The casino is open Sunday through Thursday from 10am to 4am and Friday and Saturday from 10am to 6am.

2 Side Trips from Adelaide

THE BAROSSA: ON THE TRAIL OF THE GRAPE ★

More than a quarter of Australia's wines, and a disproportionate number of top labels, originate in the Barossa and Eden valleys—collectively known as the **Barossa.** Beginning just 45km (28 miles) northeast of Adelaide and easily accessible, the area has had an enormous influence on the city's culture. In fact, Adelaidians of all socioeconomic levels partake in more wine talk than the French. German settlers from Silesia, who came to escape religious persecution, first settled the area. They brought their culture, their food, and their vines. They built the Lutheran churches that dominate the Barossa's skyline. With the help of English aristocrats, the wine industry went from strength to strength. Today, there are over 50 wineries in an area that retains its German flavor.

The focal points of the area are **Angaston,** farthest from Adelaide; **Nuriootpa,** the center of the rural services industry; and **Tanunda,** the nearest town to the city. Each

> *Tips* **So Much Wine, So Little Time**
>
> If you have the choice of exploring the Barossa or the Hunter Valley in New South Wales (see chapter 5), I recommend the **Barossa,** which despite being a little more touristy has more to offer in history and architecture.
>
> Another famous wine-producing region is the **Coonawarra,** 381km (236 miles) southeast of Adelaide near the border with Victoria; it's particularly convenient if you're driving from Melbourne. The area is only 12km (7½ miles) long and 2km (1¼ miles) wide, but the scenic countryside is crammed with historic villages and 16 wineries. The **Clare Valley,** 135km (84 miles) north of Adelaide, is another pretty area; it produces some outstanding examples of cool-climate wine. Finally, the **McLaren Vale,** south of Adelaide, is home to some 42 wineries producing some of Australia's best aromatic white wines as well as Shiraz.

has interesting architecture, crafts and antiques shops, and specialty food outlets. If you are adventurous, you might want to rent a bike in Adelaide, take it on the train to **Gawler,** and cycle through the Barossa. Other options are exploring the area by hot-air balloon, motorcycle, or limousine.

ESSENTIALS

WHEN TO GO The best times to visit the Barossa and other South Australian wine regions are in the spring (Sept–Oct), when it's not too hot and there are plenty of flowering trees and shrubs, and in the fall (Apr–May), when the leaves turn red. The main wine harvest is in late summer and early autumn (Feb–Apr). The least crowded time is winter (June–Aug). Hotel prices can be more expensive on the weekend.

GETTING THERE If you have a car (by far the most flexible way to visit the Barossa), I recommend taking the scenic route from Adelaide. (The route doesn't have a specific name, but it's obvious on a map.) It takes about half an hour longer than the Main North Road through Gawler, but the trip is well worth it. Follow signs to Birdwood, Springton, Mount Pleasant, and Angaston.

Public buses run infrequently to the major centers from Adelaide. There are no buses between wineries.

ORGANIZED TOURS FROM ADELAIDE Various companies run limited sightseeing tours. **Adelaide Sightseeing** (**© 08/8413 6199;** www.adelaidesightseeing.com.au) offers a day trip from Adelaide, stopping off at three wineries. It costs A$105 (US$84/UK£42) for adults and A$55 (US$44/UK£22) for children, including lunch. Another option is the **Barossa Wine Train** (**© 08/8212 7888**), which departs from Adelaide Railway Station on Thursday, Saturday, and Sunday. A variety of day-tour and overnight packages are available including the Exclusive Barossa Wine Train Tour which includes two-way train fares, a coach tour, lunch, and wine-tasting at three wineries. It costs A$85 (US$68/UK£34) for adults and A$48 (US$38/UK£19) for kids aged 3 to 15. Another option is a vintage car from the **Mirror Image Vintage Touring Co.** (**© 08/8621 1400**). Chevrolets, stretch limos, or Caravelles rent for 1 hour to 2 days with a chauffeur-guide.

The Barossa

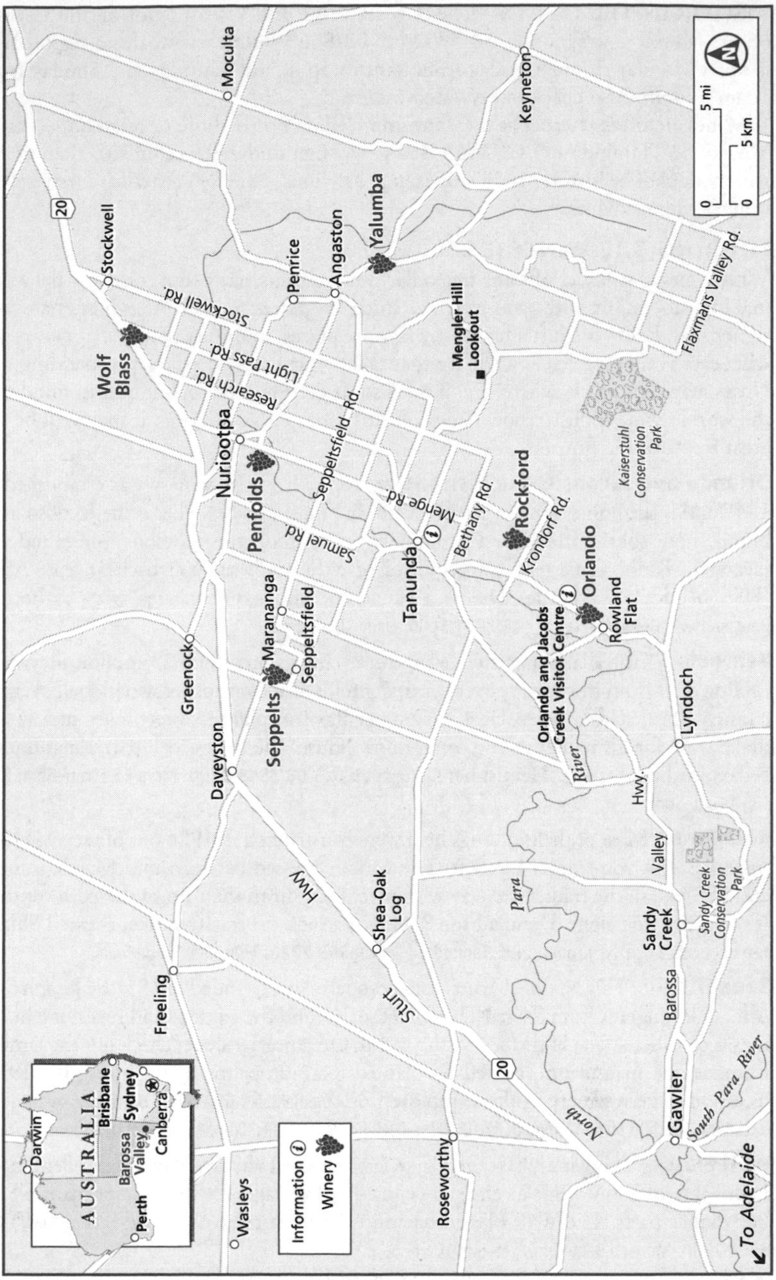

AUSTRALIA
Darwin
Brisbane
Barossa Valley
Sydney
Canberra
Perth
Information
Winery
Moculta
Keyneton
Stockwell
Penrice
Angaston
Yalumba
Wolf Blass
Stockwell Rd.
Light Pass Rd.
Research Rd.
Nuriootpa
Penfolds
Seppeltsfield Rd.
Mengler Hill Lookout
Flaxmans Valley Rd.
Kaiserstuhl Conservation Park
Rockford
Menge Rd.
Bethany Rd.
Krondorf Rd.
Samuel Rd.
Tanunda
Orlando
Orlando and Jacobs Creek Visitor Centre
Rowland Flat
Marananga
Seppeltsfield
Seppelts
Greenock
Daveyston
Lyndoch
River
Para
North
Hwy.
Valley
Barossa
Sandy Creek
Sandy Creek Conservation Park
Shea-Oak Log
Hwy
Stuart
Freeling
Wasleys
Roseworthy
Gawler
South Para River
To Adelaide
20
0
5 mi
5 km

VISITOR INFORMATION The **Barossa Wine and Visitor Information Centre,** 66–68 Murray St., Tanunda, SA 5352 (© **08/8563 0600;** www.barossa-region.org), is open Monday through Friday from 9am to 5pm, and Saturday and Sunday from 10am to 4pm. Also check out www.barossa.com.

Wines are often cheaper at the **Tanunda Cellars** bottle shop, or retail outlet, at 14 Murray St., Tanunda (© **08/8563 3544;** www.tanundacellars.com.au), than at the winery door. The historic 1858 stone shop also houses one of Australia's finest collections of vintage wines.

TOURING THE WINERIES

With some 50 wineries offering free cellar-door tastings, daily tours charting the winemaking process, or both, you won't be stuck for places to visit. All wineries are well signposted. Below are just a few of my favorite places, but don't be shy about stopping whenever you come across a winery that takes your fancy. ***A tip:*** Try a sparkling red. Noses may turn up elsewhere, and it takes some getting used to, but bear in mind that the world's wine industry now hangs on Australia's every offering; it may well be the great tipple of the future.

Orlando and Jacobs Creek Visitor Centre This large winery was established in 1847 and is the home of many award-winning brands. Its big seller is the Jacobs Creek brand, now sold worldwide. Premium wines include the Lawson Shiraz and the Jacaranda Ridge Cabernet; new vintages of either will set you back at least A$45 (US$36/UK£18) a bottle. There's a restaurant and a picnic area with barbecues. Barossa Hwy., Rowland Flat. © **08/8521 3000.** Daily 10am–5pm.

Penfolds Australia's biggest wine producer churns out some 23 million liters (5.8 million gal.) from this winery every year. Penfolds also owns other wineries all over the country. It all started when Dr. Christopher Rawson planted a few vines in 1844 to make wine for his patients. The winery now houses the largest oak barrel maturation cellars in the Southern Hemisphere. Nuriootpa. © **08/8568 9290.** Mon–Fri 10am–5pm; Sat–Sun 11am–5pm.

Rockford Most of the buildings here were constructed in 1984 out of recycled local materials, but you'd never know it. The wine is pressed between mid-March and the end of April, in the traditional way with machinery from the turn of the 20th century. It's a fascinating sight. Demand for Rockford wines, especially Basket Pressed Shiraz, far exceeds supply. Krondorf Rd., Tanunda. © **08/8563 2720.** Mon–Sat 11am–5pm.

Seppelts ★ This National Trust–listed property was founded in 1857 by Joseph Seppelt, an immigrant from Silesia. The wine tour around the gardens and bluestone buildings is considered one of the best in the world. On a nearby slope, check out the family's Romanesque mausoleum, skirted by planted roadside palms, built during the 1930s recession to keep winery workers employed. Seppeltsfield. © **08/8568 6200. Tour:** Adults A$10 (US$8/UK£4), children 5–16 free. Daily 10:30am–5pm. Tours daily 11:30am, 1:30pm, and 3:30pm.

Wolf Blass This winery's Germanic-style black-label vintages have an excellent international reputation, while its cheaper yellow-label vintages are the toast of many a Sydney dinner party. The Wolf Blass **museum** is worth a peek. Sturt Hwy., Nuriootpa. © **08/8568 7300.** Mon–Fri 9am–5pm; Sat–Sun 10am–5pm.

Yalumba This winery was built in 1849, making it the oldest family-owned winemaking business in Australia. It's also huge. Keep an eye out for the sad-looking Himalayan bear in the corner of the large tasting room; its sad look can be attributed

to a run-in with a hunting rifle, and it's been Yalumba's advertising symbol ever since. The winery's **Signature Red Cabernet-Shiraz** ★ is among the best you'll ever taste.
Eden Valley Rd., Angaston. ✆ **08/8561 3200.** www.yalumba.com.au. Mon–Fri 8:30am–5pm; Sat 10am–5pm; Sun noon–5pm.

WHERE TO STAY

There are plenty of standard motels and lots of interesting B&Bs throughout the Barossa, some with rooms for as little as A$60 (US$48/UK£24). Weekends often find lodgings sold out and prices higher than on weekdays. The **Barossa Wine and Visitor Information Centre** (see "Visitor Information," above) can provide information on additional accommodations choices and off-season deals.

Collingrove Homestead ★★★ *Finds* In my opinion, Collingrove is the best country-house experience not just in the Barossa but, dare I say it, in Australia. Built in 1856, it was originally the home of John Howard Angas, one of those involved in the initial settlement of South Australia. Additions were made as Angas's sheep business prospered. The hallway is festooned with spears, artillery shells, rifles, oil portraits, and the mounted heads of stags and tigers. English oak paneling and creaky floorboards add a certain nuance, and the cedar kitchen, library, glorious dining room, and various other places burst with antiques and knickknacks. What the quaint, individually decorated guest rooms lack in modern amenities (phones and TVs) they make up for in charm. One unit, room no. 5, does have a TV (with pay movies), as well as a minibar. The modern communal Jacuzzi is in the old stables, with flagstone floors and old horse harnesses; there's also a flagstone-floored tennis court.

Even if you don't stay here, you can indulge in **Devonshire tea** on the terrace daily for A$8 (US$6.40/UK£3.20) and can tour the property Monday through Friday from 1 to 4:30pm and Saturday and Sunday from 11am to 4:30pm. The Devonshire teas are served daily.

Eden Valley Rd., Angaston, SA 5353. ✆ **08/8564 2061.** Fax 08/8564 3600. www.collingrovehomestead.com.au. 6 units, 4 with bathroom. A$220 (US$176/UK£88) luxury double; A$250 (US$200/UK£100) deluxe double. Rates include full breakfast. AE, DC, MC, V. **Amenities:** Restaurant; tennis court; Jacuzzi; in-room massage; babysitting; nonsmoking rooms. *In room:* Hair dryer.

Marble Lodge ★★ Wake up and smell the roses—there are plenty in the beautiful gardens surrounding this romantic historic property (as well as a tennis court, and several deer and kangaroos). Away from the main house is a lodge made of local marble that holds two suites. The larger has two rooms and an open fireplace. The second is a large bed/sitting room, with an open fireplace. Both have access to the shared Jacuzzi (in 2007 this was temporarily closed because of the drought) and are tastefully furnished in antiques. There's always fresh fruit, homemade biscuits, and chocolates in the room, and it's a 5-minute walk to three local restaurants. A double room in the homestead, with shared bathroom, is sometimes available.

21 Dean St., Angaston, SA 5351. ✆ **08/8564 2478.** Fax 08/8564 2941. www.marblelodge.com.au. 2 units. A$250 (US$200/UK£100) double. Rates include breakfast. MC, V. **Amenities:** Tennis court; Jacuzzi; room service until 8pm; nonsmoking rooms; e-mail and fax facilities. *In room:* A/C, TV w/pay movies, fax, minibar, fridge, coffeemaker, hair dryer, iron.

Tanunda Caravan & Tourist Park This peaceful place is back from the road and abuts a nature lake and wildlife reserve. The cabins range from simple to quite luxurious, some being great for an extended family. Cottages are cozy and some come with a spa tub. Bike hire is also available.

Barossa Valley Way, Tanunda, SA 5355. ✆ **08/8563 2784.** www.tanundacaravantouristpark.com.au. A$49 (US$39/UK£20) double caravan without bathroom; A$59–A$75 (US$47–US$60/UK£24–UK£30) cabins; A$90–A$130 (US$72–US$104/UK£36–UK£52) cottages. AE, DC, MC, V. **Amenities:** Outdoor pool nearby; 2 tennis courts; coin-op laundry. *In room:* A/C, TV, kitchenette, coffeemaker, iron.

WHERE TO DINE

The Barossa prides itself on its cuisine as well as its wine, so you'll find plenty of places of note to eat, many of them serving traditional German food. A hot spot for lunch or dinner is **Vintner's Bar & Grill,** Nuriootpa Road, Angaston (✆ **08/8564 2488**); the wine list is six pages long! Try bay leaf risotto with prawns or roast veal rack with crisp polenta. Main courses cost A$22 to A$27 (US$18–US$22/UK£9–UK£11). It's open for lunch daily and Monday through Saturday for dinner. Another choice is **Salters,** Satram Winery, Nuriootpa Road, Angaston (✆ **08/8564 3344**); local produce is the specialty, with main courses such as slow-roasted baby pork, milk-fed lamb, and crisp-based pizzas. Main courses are A$20 to A$26 (US$16–US$21/UK£8–UK£11). It's open daily for lunch and from 6pm Wednesday to Saturday for dinner. Perhaps the best German-style bakery in the valley is the **Lyndoch Bakery,** on the Barossa Highway, Lyndoch (✆ **08/8524 4422**). In Angaston, you must stop off at **The Seasons of the Valley,** 6 Washington St. (✆ **08/8564 3688**). The restored 1840 homestead house has cottage gardens and a sunny veranda as well as delicious meals for A$15 to A$18 (US$12–US$14/UK£6–UK£7). It's open daily 10am to 5pm.

THE ADELAIDE HILLS

A 25-minute drive from Adelaide and visible even from the main shopping street, you'll find the tree-lined slopes and pretty valleys, orchards, vineyards, winding roads, and historic townships of the **Adelaide Hills.** You might want to walk part of the Heysen Trail (see "Enjoying the Great Outdoors" in the Adelaide section, earlier in this chapter), browse through the shops in Hahndorf, stop in Melba's Chocolate Factory in Woodside, or visit Cleland Wildlife Park or Warrawong Sanctuary. Otherwise, it's a nice outing just to hit the road and drive. Should you decide to stay overnight, the area offers lots of cozy B&Bs.

ESSENTIALS

GETTING THERE The Adelaide Hills are 25 minutes from Adelaide by car on Greenhill and Glen Osmond roads. **Adelaide Sightseeing** (✆ **08/8413 6199;** www.adelaidesightseeing.com.au) runs outings to the gorgeous town of Hahndorf (see below). An afternoon excursion to Hahndorf costs A$55 (US$44/UK£22) for adults and A$28 (US$22/UK£11) for children. The company also offers a range of trips to Kangaroo Island, the Flinders Ranges, the Coorong, Cleland Wildlife Park, and the Great Ocean Road.

VISITOR INFORMATION Visitor information and bookings are available through the **Adelaide Hills Tourist Information Centre,** 41 Main St., Hahndorf (✆ **08/8388 1185**). It's open Monday through Friday from 9am to 4pm. Maps are also available at the **South Australia Travel Centre** in Adelaide.

WOODSIDE: CHOCOLATE LOVERS UNITE!

Visitors come here for **Melba's Chocolate Factory,** Henry Street (✆ **08/8389 7868**), where chocoholics will find a huge range of handmade chocolates. Melba's is part of Heritage Park, a complex that includes a wood turner, a cheese maker, a ceramics studio, a

Adelaide Hills

leather maker, and a crafts shop. It's open Monday through Friday from 10am to 4pm, and Saturday, Sunday, and holidays from noon to 5pm.

MYLOR: GETTING BACK TO NATURE

Mylor is 25km (16 miles) southeast of Adelaide, and 10km (6 miles) south of Mount Lofty via the town of Crafters. Here you'll find the **Warrawong Sanctuary,** Stock Road, Mylor (P.O. Box 1135), Stirling, SA 5152 (✆ **08/8370 9197;** fax 08/8370 8332). Unlike the inhabitants of many other wildlife parks, the animals here are not kept in enclosed runs. Instead, park founder Dr. John Wamsley took a 14-hectare (35-acre) tract of farmland, replanted it with natural bush, fenced it off, and went around shooting the introduced rabbits, cats, dogs, and foxes that plague much of Australia. Then the good doctor reintroduced native animals such as kangaroos, various types of wallabies, bandicoots, beetongs, platypuses, possums, frogs, birds, and reptiles. They are all thriving, not only because he eliminated their unnatural predators but also because he re-created waterways, rainforests, and blackwater ponds. The animals roam free while you're guided through on a 1½-hour dawn or sunset walk (A$20/US$16/UK£8 adults, A$15/US$12/UK£6 children). There's a restaurant on the premises, and you can even stay overnight in large cabins with bathrooms, wall-to-wall carpeting, and air-conditioning. The cabins cost A$125 (US$100/UK£50) per person with both dawn and dusk tours, a two-course dinner, and breakfast.

Compared to Cleland Wildlife Park (see below), the Warrawong Sanctuary has fewer species—you won't find any koalas, for example—but it's more educational and you get the feeling that you're in the wild rather than in a zoo.

HAHNDORF: GERMAN HERITAGE, CRAFTS & MORE ★

This historic German-style village is one of South Australia's most popular tourist destinations. Lutherans fleeing religious persecution in eastern Prussia founded the town, which is 29km (18 miles) southeast of Adelaide, in 1839. They brought their wine-making skills, foods, and architectural inheritance, and put it all together here. Hahndorf still resembles a small German town in appearance and atmosphere, and is included on the World Heritage List as a Historical German Settlement. Walking around, you'll see **St. Paul's Lutheran Church,** erected in 1890. **The Wool Factory, L'Unique Fine Arts & Craft,** and **Bamfurlong Fine Crafts** are worth checking out and are within walking distance of Main Street.

Where to Stay

The Hahndorf Resort ★ This large resort has a variety of accommodations as well as approximately 80 trailer and tent sites. Lodgings include air-conditioned cabins, and motel-style rooms with queen-size beds (some have an extra single) and a shower. The chalets look as if they're straight out of Bavaria; each can accommodate two to five people in one or two bedrooms. Each has a full kitchen and an attached bathroom with shower. Some of them overlook a small lake. The larger spa chalets come with Jacuzzis. An on-site animal sanctuary has a few emus, kangaroos, and horses.

145A Main St., Hahndorf, SA 5245. © **08/8388 7921.** Fax 08/8388 7282. www.hahndorfresort.com.au. 60 units. A$68 (US$46/UK£23) cabin; A$99 (US$80/UK£40) motel room; A$125–A$159 (US$100–US$127/UK£50–UK£64) chalet. Extra adult A$12 (US$9.20/UK£4.60); extra child A$5.50 (US$4.40/UK£2.20). AE, DC, MC, V. **Amenities:** Restaurant; heated outdoor pool; 2 putting greens; half-size tennis court; small gym; bike rental; limited room service; coin-op laundry. *In room:* A/C, TV, kitchenette, minibar, coffeemaker, iron.

Where to Dine

If you want a treat, head to the **Bridgewater Mill,** Mt. Barker Road, Bridgewater (© **08/8339 3422;** www.bridgewatermill.com.au). In an impressive 1860s stone building with a terrace near a water wheel, this place serves some of the best-regarded food in the country. Try duck with braised cherries. Main courses cost A$33 (US$26/UK£13); a three-course menu, served Sunday only, is A$85 (US$68/UK£34). It's open for lunch Thursday to Monday.

OAKBANK: A DAY AT THE RACES

The **Easter Oakbank Racing Carnival** is part of the Australia-wide "picnic races" that take place in small towns throughout the nation. The Oakbank horse races attract crowds in excess of 70,000 a day over the long Easter weekend (and smaller crowds at other times). General admission is A$20 (US$16/UK£8) for adults. Children under 16 free. The **Oakbank Racing Club** (© **08/8212 6279**) is just off the main road; you can't miss it.

Where to Stay

Adelaide Hills Country Cottages ★★ These cottages have won several tourism awards. They are 1km (½ mile) apart and surrounded by 60 hectares (150 acres) of scenic countryside. The Apple Tree cottage, from around 1860, sleeps up to five, has a

Jacuzzi and antiques, and overlooks an orchard and a lake; the Gum Tree Cottage sleeps four and has wonderful country views; and the Lavender Fields Cottage sleeps up to four and overlooks a lily-fringed duck pond. All of the cottages have open fireplaces and full kitchens. This is a great place to relax and a good base for exploring the area. You'll get a couple of free drinks and a fruit basket upon arrival. Oakbank is 30 minutes from Adelaide, 7 minutes from Hahndorf, and less than 1 hour from the Barossa Valley.

P.O. Box 100, Oakbank, SA 5243. ✆ **08/8388 4193.** Fax 08/8388 4733. www.ahcc.com.au. 5 cottages. A$235–A$295 (US$188–US$236/UK£94–UK£118) cottage; A$205–A$265 (US$164–US$212/UK£82–UK£106) cottage for more than 1 night. Extra person A$70 (US$56/UK£28). Rates include provisions for breakfast. Weekly discounts available. AE, DC, MC, V. **Amenities:** Jacuzzi; tour desk; coin-op laundry; nonsmoking rooms. *In room:* A/C, TV/VCR, kitchen, coffeemaker, hair dryer, iron.

MOUNT LOFTY: VIEWS & 'ROOS

Visitors make the pilgrimage to the top of 690m (2,263-ft.) **Mount Lofty,** 16km (10 miles) southeast of Adelaide, for the panoramic views over Adelaide, the Adelaide plains, and the Mount Lofty Ranges. There are several nice bushwalks from the top.

Almost at the top of Mount Lofty, off Summit Road, is the **Cleland Wildlife Park** (✆ **08/8339 2444;** www.parks.sa.gov.au/cleland). Here you'll find all the usual Australian animals, including the largest male red kangaroo I've ever seen. Though the park is not as good as similar wildlife parks elsewhere in Australia, it does have a very good wetlands aviary. One of the drawbacks of Cleland is that it has some unimaginative enclosures, notably the one for the Tasmanian devils. The park is open daily from 9:30am to 5pm. Visitors can meet at the Tasmanian devil enclosure at 2pm and join the animal feed run by following a tractor around the park as it drops off food.

Admission to Cleland is A$14 (US$11/UK£5.50) for adults, A$8 (US$6.40/UK£3.20) for children 3 to 14, and A$36 (US$28/UK£14) for families. Koala holding is allowed during photo sessions from 2 to 4pm daily (but not on very hot summer days); on Sunday and public holidays there's an additional session from 10am to noon. The privilege will cost you A$12 (US$9.60/UK£4.80) per photo. A kiosk and restaurant are on the premises.

Public transport to either place is a bit of a hassle. To get to the Mount Lofty Lookout, take bus no. 163 Monday through Friday, or no. 165 Saturday and Sunday, from Currie Street in the city. Ask the driver to drop you off at Crafters. The trip takes 30 minutes. From there you'll need to take a short taxi ride to the top; prearrange pickup with **Tony's Taxi's** (✆ **08/8388 5988**).

To get to Cleland, take bus no. 822 from Currie Street to stop 19b. There are only two runs, at 10am and noon, Monday through Friday. Take the 10am bus and ask the bus driver for the exact return time. The trip to Cleland takes 40 minutes.

Where to Dine

While you're atop Mount Lofty, have lunch at **The Summit** restaurant (✆ **08/8339 2600;** www.mtloftysummit.com). Look out for the kangaroo filet with chile, lemon grass, and coconut sauce, and venison on rosemary polenta. Main courses cost A$25 to A$29 (US$20–US$23/UK£10–UK£12). It's open for lunch Monday and Tuesday, and for dinner Wednesday to Sunday. The **Summit Café** here also sells good sandwiches and cakes, fish and chips, Thai curry, and Devonshire tea.

3 Kangaroo Island ★★★

110km (68 miles) S of Adelaide

There is nowhere better than Kangaroo Island to see Australian marsupials in the wild. Spend a few days here with the right guide and you can walk along a beach past a colony of sea lions; spot hundreds of New Zealand fur seals playing; creep through the bush on the trail of wallabies or kangaroos; spot sea eagles, black swans, sacred ibis, pelicans, little penguins, the rare glossy black cockatoo, and other birds; come across goannas; pick out bunches of koalas hanging in the trees above your head; and, if you're lucky, see platypus, echidna, bandicoots, and pygmy possums—the list goes on.

The secrets to Kangaroo Island's success are its perfect conditions, the most important of which is the fact that there are no introduced foxes or rabbits to prey on the native inhabitants or their environment. The island was also never colonized by the dingo—Australia's "native" dog—which is believed to have been introduced from Asia some 4,000 years ago. About one-third of the island is unspoiled national park, and there are plenty of wildlife corridors to give the animals a chance to move about the island, lessening the problems of inbreeding.

While the animals are what most people come to see, no one goes away without also being impressed by the scenery. Kangaroo Island has low mallee scrubland, dense eucalyptus forests, rugged coastal scenery, gorgeous beaches, caves, lagoons, and blackwater swamps. The effect of 150 years of European colonization has taken its toll, though. In South Australia as a whole, some 27 mammal, 5 bird, 1 reptile, and 30 plant species have become extinct since the English seafarer Matthew Flinders arrived in 1802.

The island's history is a harsh one. Aborigines inhabited the island as early as 10,000 years ago but abandoned it for unexplained reasons. In the 19th century, pirates, mutineers, deserters from English, French, and American ships, and escaped convicts from the eastern colonies settled here. Sealers also arrived and devastated the seal and sea lion population—in just 1 year, 1803 to 1804, they killed more than 20,000 animals. Between 1802 and 1836, Aboriginal women from both the mainland and Tasmania were kidnapped, brought to Kangaroo Island, and forced to work catching and skinning seals, kangaroos, and wallabies, and lugging salt from the salt mines.

In 1836, Kangaroo Island became the first place in South Australia to be officially settled. The state's capital was Kingscote (which was abandoned a couple of years later in favor of Adelaide). In spite of its early settlement, Kangaroo Island had very few residents until after World War II, when returned soldiers set up farms here. Today, more than a million sheep are raised on the island. The island also acts as an official bee sanctuary to protect the genetic purity of the Ligurian bee, introduced in 1881, and it is believed to be the only place in the world where this strain of bee survives.

ISLAND ESSENTIALS

WHEN TO GO The best time to visit Kangaroo Island is between November and March (though you'll have difficulty finding accommodations over the Christmas school-holiday period). July and August tend to be rainy, and winter can be cold (though often milder than on the mainland around Adelaide). Many companies offer 1-day trips to Kangaroo Island from Adelaide, but I would advise you to tailor your holiday to spend at least 2 days here. Three or even 5 days would be better. There really is a lot to see, and you won't regret spending the extra time.

GETTING THERE **Regional Express** (✆ **13 17 13** in Australia, or 08/8553 2938; www.regionalexpress.com.au) serves Kangaroo Island from Adelaide. Flights leave from the General Aviation Terminal, Kel Barclay Avenue, Adelaide. The General Aviation Terminal is about a 20-minute walk (or shorter taxi ride!) from the main airport terminal. The flight from Adelaide to Kangaroo Island usually takes about 25 minutes.

If you prefer to go by sea, **Kangaroo Island SeaLink** (✆ **13 13 01** in Australia, or 08/8202 8688; www.sealink.com.au) operates two vehicle and passenger ferries three times daily at 9am, 10am, and 6pm (and on the hour from 9am–7pm in peak periods) from Cape Jervis on the tip of the Fleurieu Peninsula on the mainland to Penneshaw on Kangaroo Island. The trip takes 40 minutes and costs A$80 (US$64/UK£32) round-trip for adults, A$44 (US$35/UK£18) for children 3 to 14, and A$162 (US$129/UK£65) for cars. Connecting bus service from Adelaide to Cape Jervis costs an extra A$36 (US$29/UK£15) for adults, and A$18 (US$14/UK£7) for children round-trip. Off-peak prices may be cheaper; check when booking. Count on 3 hours for the whole trip from Adelaide if you take the connecting bus. Bookings are essential.

SeaLink also runs a range of island tours, including the 2-day, 1-night "K.I. coast to coast," which costs from A$389 (US$311/UK£156) per person sharing a double room. SeaLink also offers a wide range of accommodations, day tours, and adventure activities and offers Adelaide hotel pickups for selected tours.

VISITOR INFORMATION **Tourism Kangaroo Island,** Gateway Information Centre, Howard Drive (P.O. Box 336), Penneshaw, Kangaroo Island, SA 5222 (✆ **08/8553 1185;** fax 08/8553 1255; www.tourkangarooisland.com.au), has plenty of maps and information and can assist visitors with accommodations and tour information. For more information on the island's national parks, contact **National Parks and Wildlife South Australia,** known as NP&WSA, 39 Dauncey St. (P.O. Box 39), Kingscote, SA 5223 (✆ **08/8553 2381;** fax 08/8553 2531), open Monday through Friday from 9am to 5pm.

In addition, hotel and motel staff members generally can provide tourist brochures and sightseeing advice.

ISLAND LAYOUT Kangaroo Island is Australia's third-largest island, 156km (97 miles) long and 57km (35 miles) wide at its widest point. The distance across the narrowest point is only 2km (1¼ miles). Approximately 3,900 people live on the island. More than half live on the northeast coast in the three main towns: Kingscote (pop. 1,800), Penneshaw (pop. 250), and American River (pop. 200). The island's major attractions are farther from the mainland: Flinders Chase National Park is in the far

---

Value An Island Bargain

I'd advise buying an **NP&WSA Island Pass** if you'll be exploring the island on your own for 3 days or more and visiting the national park and attractions more than once. It costs A$44 (US$35/UK£18) for adults, A$27 (US$21/UK£11) for children, and A$120 (US$96/UK£48) for families, and includes guided tours of Seal Bay, Kelly Hill Caves, Cape Borda, and Cape Willoughby. The pass also includes access to Flinders Chase National Park. The pass doesn't cover penguin tours or camping fees. It's available at Tourism Kangaroo Island in Penneshaw and at the national parks office in Kingscote (see "Visitor Information," above).

Kangaroo Island

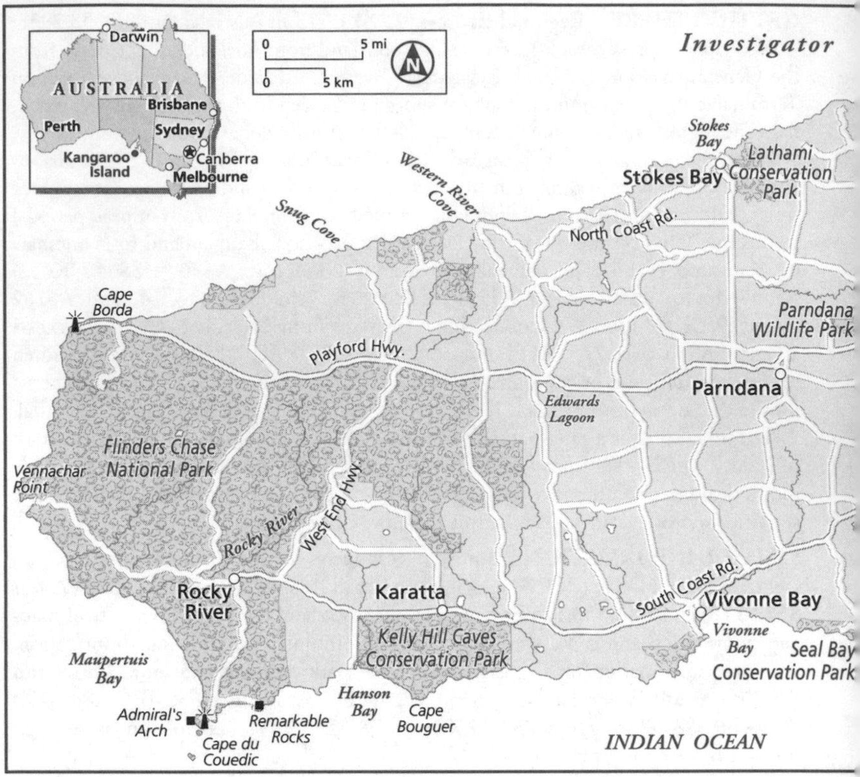

west, Lathami Conservation Park is on the north coast, and Seal Bay and Kelly's Caves are on the south coast.

GETTING AROUND Kangaroo Island is a big place, and apart from twice-daily SeaLink bus service, which connects Kingscote, Penneshaw, and American River, there is no public transport on the island. While you can get a lot out of the tours, I would heartily recommend you hire a car and spend at least 3 whole days here. **Airport Shuttle Service** (**© 1800/750 850**) meets all flights to Kangaroo Island and will take passengers to Kingscote, Emu Bay, and American River. Book the return trip from your accommodations to the airport in advance.

Major roads between Penneshaw, American River, Kingscote, and Parndana are paved, as are the road to Seal Bay and all major roads within Flinders Chase National Park. Most other roads are made of ironstone gravel, and can be very slippery if the driver approaches corners too quickly. All roads are accessible by two-wheel-drive vehicles; if you're in a rental car from the mainland, make sure your policy allows you to drive on Kangaroo Island's roads. Avoid driving at night—animals rarely fare best in a car collision.

Car-rental agencies on the island include **Budget** (**© 08/8553 3133** or 08/8553 1034; fax 08/8553 2888), **Hertz & Kangaroo Island Rental Cars** (**© 1800/088 296** in Australia, or 08/8553 2390; fax 08/8553 2878), and **Wheels over Kangaroo**

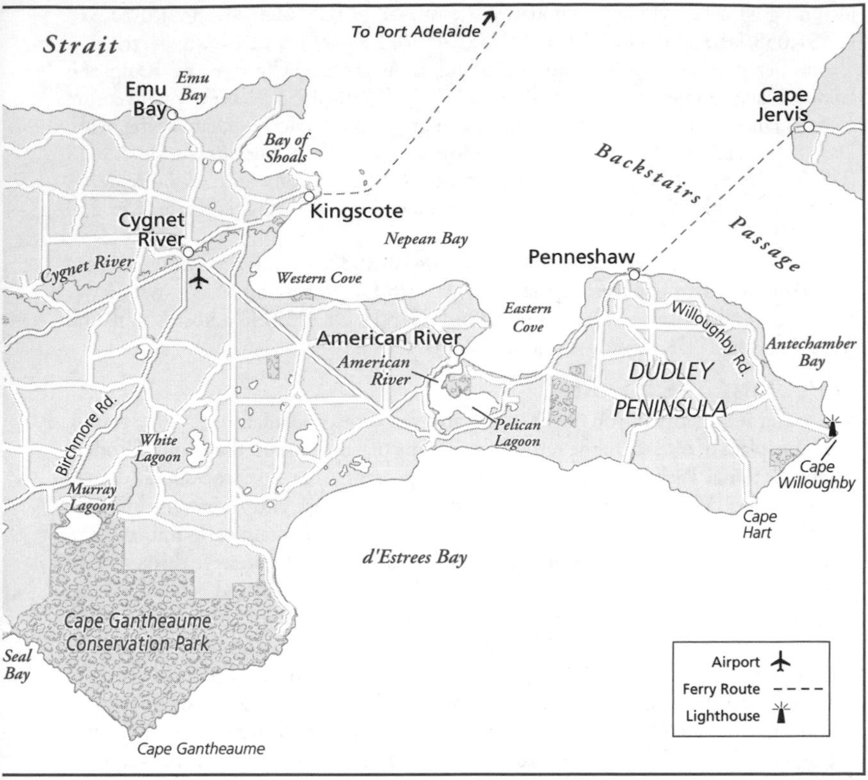

Island (© **1800/750 850** in Australia, or 08/8553 3030; woki@ozemail.com.au). You can pick up cars at the airport or ferry terminals.

ORGANIZED TOURS If you want to keep expenses down, you can't go wrong with one of the tours organized by **Kangaroo Island Ferry Connections** (© **08/8202 8688;** www.sealink.com.au). The most popular includes afternoon pickup from the main bus station in Adelaide, coach and ferry to the island, a penguin tour that evening, and dorm accommodations (you can pay a little extra to upgrade to a double room, or for more expensive hotels). The next day involves 10 hours of touring, taking in most of the main attractions. That evening you return to Adelaide. The tour costs A$302 (US$242/UK£121).

If you make your own way to the island you can join one of several day tours, departing Penneshaw or American River Thursday, Saturday, Sunday, Monday, and Wednesday, also stopping off at many of the main attractions. The tour costs A$119 (US$95/UK£48) for adults and A$86 (US$69/UK£35) for children 3 to 14 years old.

More expensive options include **Kangaroo Island Wilderness Tours** (© **08/8559 5033;** www.wildernesstours.com.au), which operates from the island with several small four-wheel-drive vehicles (maximum six people). Three different 1-day trips cost A$334 to A$365 (US$267–US$292/UK£134–UK£146) per person, including transfers, an excellent lunch with wine, and park entry fees. Two-, 3-, and 4-day trips, including all meals and accommodations, cost A$829 (US$663/UK£332), A$1,323 (US$1,058/UK£524), and A$1,818 (US$1,454/UK£727) per person, respectively.

Another excellent operator on the island is **Adventure Charters of Kangaroo Island,** Playford Highway, Cygnet River, SA 5223 (✆ **08/8553 9119;** www.adventurecharters.com.au), with the knowledgeable and gregarious Craig Wickham at the helm. Day trips cost A$340 (US$272/UK£136) a day with a big lunch, or A$648 (US$518/UK£260) for a 1-day safari including flights from and to Adelaide. A 2-day and 1-night safari including accommodations and flights costs A$1,230 (US$984/UK£492).

Another option is **Wayward Bus** (✆ **08/8410 8833;** www.waywardbus.com.au) from Adelaide. Two-day trips depart daily between December and March, with fewer departures at other times. They cost A$380 (US$304/UK£152) in a hostel bunk and A$410 (US$328/UK£164) twin/double shared room.

EXPLORING THE ISLAND

The island is bigger than you might think, and you can spend a fair bit of time getting from one place of interest to the next. Of the many places to see on the island, **Flinders Chase National Park** ★ is one of the most important. Your first stop should be the Flinders Chase Visitors Centre, where you can purchase park entry, view the interpretive display, dine at the licensed cafe, purchase souvenirs, and obtain parks information. After 30 years of lobbying, reluctant politicians finally agreed to preserve this region of the island in 1919. Today, it makes up around 17% of the island and is home to true wilderness, some beautiful coastal scenery, two old lighthouses, and plenty of animals. Birders have recorded at least 243 species here. Koalas are so common that they're almost falling out of the trees. Platypuses have been seen, but you'll probably need to make a special effort and sit next to a stream in the dark for a few hours for any chance of spotting one. The Platypus Waterholes walk is a 2-hour walk that's great for all ages. It begins at the Flinders Chase Visitors Centre and has a shorter option that's suitable for wheelchairs. This walk offers the best opportunity to see the elusive platypus. Kangaroos, wallabies, and brush-tailed possums, on the other hand, are so tame and numerous that the authorities were forced to erect a barrier around the Rocky River Campground to stop them from carrying away picnickers' sandwiches!

The most impressive coastal scenery is at **Cape du Couedic,** at the southern tip of the park. Millions of years of crashing ocean have created curious structures, like the hollowed-out limestone promontory called Admiral's Arch and the aptly named Remarkable Rocks, where you'll see huge boulders balancing on top of a massive granite dome. Admiral's Arch is home to a colony of some 4,000 New Zealand fur seals that play in the rock pools and rest on the rocks. During rough weather this place can be spectacular. A paved road leads from Rocky River Park Headquarters to Admiral's Arch and Remarkable Rocks, where there are a parking lot and a loop trail. There's a road, parking lot, and trail system around the Cape du Couedic heritage lighthouse district.

Tips Don't Feed the Animals, Please

Don't feed *any* native animals. Kangaroos and wallabies might beg, but they are lactose intolerant and can go blind or fall ill from being fed human food.

Culling Koalas—A National Dilemma

Koalas are cute. They're fluffy, they're sleepy, and they're awesomely cuddly. They also eat an awful lot. In the early 1920s, 18 koalas were introduced to Kangaroo Island. Over the years, without predators and disease, and with an abundant supply of eucalyptus trees, they have prospered. By 1996, there were an estimated 4,000 koalas, and their favorite trees were looking ragged. Some of the koalas were already suffering; some people even claimed the animals were starving to death.

The state government decided that the only option was to shoot Australia's ambassador to the world. The public outcry was enormous; Japan even threatened to advise its citizens to boycott Down Under. But what could be done? Some scientists maintained that the koalas could not be relocated to the mainland because there were few places left to put them. Conservationists blamed Kangaroo Island's farmers for depleting the island of more than 50% of its vegetation. The koala is endangered; the smaller northern variety is threatened with extinction in New South Wales; the larger subspecies in Victoria, which includes the Kangaroo Island koalas, is also under threat. A compromise was reached: The koalas are to be trapped and neutered, a few thousand per year, until their numbers stabilize. A few conscientious farmers will plant more trees. Other farmers will, no doubt, continue to see the koalas as pests.

You shouldn't miss out on the unforgettable experience of walking through a colony of Australian sea lions at Seal Bay. The **Seal Bay Conservation Park** (**© 08/8559 4207**) was created in 1972, and some 100,000 people visit it each year. Boardwalks through the dunes to the beach reduce the impact of so many feet. The colony consists of about 500 animals, but at any one time you might see up to 100 basking with their pups. The rangers who supervise the area lead guided trips throughout the day, every 15 to 30 minutes from 9am to 4:15pm. If you come here without a coach group, you must join a tour. Tours cost A$14 (US$11/UK£5.50) for adults and A$8 (US$6.40/UK£3.20) for children.

Lathami Conservation Park, just east of Stokes Bay, is a wonderful place to see wallabies in the wild. Just dip under the low canopy of casuarina pines and walk silently, keeping your eyes peeled. You're almost certain to spot them. If you're fortunate, you may even come across a rare glossy cockatoo—it's big and black and feeds mainly on casuarina nuts.

Another interesting spot, especially for birders, is **Murray Lagoon,** on the northern edge of Cape Gantheaume Conservation Park. It's the largest lagoon on the island and a habitat for thousands of water birds. Contact the NP&WSA (see "Visitor Information," above) for information on a ranger-guided Wetland Wade.

If you want to see little **penguins**—tiny animals that stand just 33 centimeters (13 in.) tall—forget the touristy show at Phillip Island near Melbourne. On Kangaroo Island, you can see them in a natural environment at both Kingscote and Penneshaw. The **NP&WSA** (**© 08/8553 2381**) conducts the tours. Call ahead to confirm times, which are subject to change. Nightly tours in Kingscote depart from the reception desk at the Ozone Seafront Hotel and cost A$7.50 (US$6/UK£3) for adults, A$6 (US$4.80/UK£2.40) for children. The Penneshaw Penguin Centre, adjacent to the beach and Lloyd Collins Reserve, has the largest penguin colony on the island. Tours depart twice per evening and cost A$6 (US$4.80/UK£2.40) for adults, A$4.50 (US$3.60/UK£3.30) for kids, free for children under 12.

For fabulous, though pricey, **fishing** for everything from King George whiting, trevally, and snapper to mullet and mackerel, contact **Kangaroo Island Fishing Charters** (✆ **08/8552 7000;** www.kifishchart.com.au). Prices for a day out start at A$125 (US$100/UK£50), including lunch; a half-day trip costs from A$90 (US$72/UK£36), and you keep what you catch. They also run coastal wilderness tours, looking for birds, seals and whales in season. **American River Fishing Charters** (✆ **0417/869 346** mobile) also runs trips.

Finally, Kangaroo Island is renowned for its fresh food, and across the island you'll see signs beckoning to you to have a taste of cheese, honey, wine, or the like. One place worth a stop is **Clifford's Honey Farm** (✆ **08/8553 8295**), which is open daily from 9am to 5pm. The farm is the home of the protected Ligurian honeybee, found nowhere else on earth but on the island. **Island Pure Sheep Dairy** (✆ **08/8553 9110**) is another worthwhile stop. Tours and tastings are conducted at milking time (1–5pm). It's a great chance to sample delicious sheep's milk, yogurts, and mouthwatering halloumi cheese. Ask at the tourist office for directions to both.

WHERE TO STAY

The island has a wide variety of places to choose from, from B&Bs to campgrounds. If you feel like sleeping in one of 40 cottages or coastal lodgings, contact **Kangaroo Island Remote and Coastal Farm Accommodation** (✆ **08/8553 1233;** fax 08/8553 1190). Prices range from A$65 to A$100 (US$52–US$80/UK£26–UK£40). The staff can also arrange lodgings in local farms, homes, and B&Bs for A$60 to A$110 (US$48–US$88/UK£24–UK£44) for a double with breakfast.

The NP&WSA (see "Visitor Information," above) also rents basic but comfortable lodgings, including relatively isolated **lighthouse cottages** ★★ (✆ **08/8559 7235;** kiparksaccom@saugov.sa.gov.au) at Cape Willoughby, Cape Borda, Rocky River, and Cape du Couedic. The price is A$95 and A$140 (US$76–US$112/UK£38–UK£56) per night.

If you're on a supertight budget, head to the **Penneshaw Youth Hostel,** 43 North Terrace, Penneshaw, Kangaroo Island, SA 5222 (✆ **08/8553 1284;** fax 08/8553 1295), with dorm beds for A$22 (US$18/UK£9) and doubles for A$72 (US$57/UK£29). It costs a few dollars less for YHA members.

Camping is allowed at designated sites around the island and in national parks for a minimal fee. There are many beach, river, and bush camping spots, including the Rocky River site in the Flinders Chase National Park. Call ✆ **08 8559 7235** to book. Camping costs A$8 to A$19 (US$6.40–US$15/UK£3.20–UK£7.50) per car and A$4 to A$5.50 (US$3.20–US$4.40/UK£1.60–UK£2.20) per occupant/person.

IN & NEAR KINGSCOTE

Ozone Seafront Hotel The best-known of Kangaroo Island's lodgings, the Ozone gets its name from the aroma of the sea—which virtually laps at its door. It's a nice, centrally located choice offering comfortable rooms with plenty of space; the majority of the more expensive ones have views of Nepean Bay. Family rooms have a double bed and two single beds. Prices are highest on Saturday night.

The Foreshore (P.O. Box 145), Kingscote, SA 5223. © **08/8553 2011.** Fax 08/8553 2249. www.ozonehotel.com. 37 units. A$220–A$286 (US$176–US$228/UK£88–UK£114) double; A$242–A$308 (US$193–US$246/UK£97–UK£123) Victorian double; A$297–A$374 (US$237–US$299/UK£119–UK£150) suite. Extra person A$13 (US$10/UK£5). AE, DC, MC, V. **Amenities:** 2 restaurants; 3 bars; heated outdoor pool; golf course nearby; Jacuzzi; sauna; tour desk; limited room service; babysitting; laundry service. *In room:* A/C, TV, fridge, coffeemaker, hair dryer, iron.

Wisteria Lodge ★ All rooms at the modern and definitely unglamorous-looking Wisteria Lodge are standard motel-type accommodations, with exposed brick walls and gray carpets. They have views over Nepean Bay. Deluxe rooms offer a Jacuzzi and queen-size beds. Packages include transport to the island, transfers, meals, and day tours. Reservations are essential for the restaurant. New management took over this hotel in 2007 and at the time of writing there was no website.

7 Cygnet Rd., Kingscote, SA 5223. © **08/8553 2707.** Reservations: Flag Inns © **800/624-3524** in the U.S. and Canada, 0800/892 407 in the U.K., 0800/803 524 in New Zealand, or 13 24 00 in Australia. Fax 08/8553 2200. 20 units. A$125 (US$100/UK£50) standard double; A$186 (US$149/UK£75) executive room; A$207 (US$166/UK£83) deluxe room. Extra adult A$20–A$22 (US$16–US$18/UK£8–UK£9); extra child 3–12 A$15–A$19 (US$12–US$15/UK£6–UK£7.50). Ask about packages. AE, DC, MC, V. **Amenities:** Restaurant; heated outdoor pool; half-size tennis court; Jacuzzi; children's center; tour desk; car-rental desk; business center; limited room service; laundry service; dry cleaning; nonsmoking rooms. *In room:* A/C, TV, minibar, fridge, coffeemaker, hair dryer.

IN AMERICAN RIVER

Popular with fishermen, American River is 37km (23 miles) from Kingscote. It lacks a beach but offers black swans on Pelican Lagoon. Wild wallabies abound, and egrets, magpies, and cockatoos offer early wake-up calls.

Casuarina Coastal Units These simple, country-style accommodations are not flashy, but they offer a cozy budget option. Each comes with a double bed, two singles, and an attached shower. The property has a playground and fish-cleaning facilities.

9 Ryberg Rd., American River, SA 5221. ©/fax **08/8553 7020.** www.casuarinaonki.com. 6 units. A$85 (US$68/UK£34) double; A$75 (US$60/UK£30) double for more than 1 night. MC, V. **Amenities:** Coin-op laundry. *In room:* TV.

Kangaroo Island Lodge ★ Though Kangaroo Island Lodge was built in 1801, it has been so overhauled that you would be hard-pressed to find anything rustic remaining. It's a nicely appointed property with pleasant, quiet motel-style rooms, a good pool, Jacuzzi, sauna, and a restaurant and bar (entrees average A$20/US$16/UK£8). Some units contain kitchens. The lodge looks over Pelican Lagoon (famous for its, well, pelicans), but it's a little too far away from it to make the water-view rooms too worthwhile.

Scenic Rd., American River, SA 5221. © **08/8553 7053.** Fax 08/8553 7030. www.kilodge.com.au. 38 units. A$295 (US$236/UK£118) double for a 2-night stay; A$363 (US$290/UK£145) double for a 3-night stay. Extra person A$24 (US$19/UK£9.50). AE, DC, MC, V. **Amenities:** Restaurant; heated outdoor pool; tennis court; game room; tour desk; car-rental desk; limited room service; coin-op laundry; nonsmoking rooms. *In room:* A/C, TV, fridge, hair dryer, iron.

Wanderers Rest This pleasant guesthouse sits on a hillside with panoramic views across the sea to the mainland. It has large, comfortably furnished rooms with balconies. All rooms come with king-size beds that convert to twins, and showers (no tubs). Breakfasts are hearty, packed lunches are available, and dinnertime can be a hoot, with guests sipping beer and wine around the dining-room table and tucking into King George whiting caught that day. Other meals include steak, lamb chops, local oysters, and a vegetarian stir-fry.

Bayview Rd. (P.O. Box 34), American River, SA 5221. ✆ **08/8553 7140.** Fax 08/8553 7282. www.wanderersrest.com.au. 9 units. A$195 (US$156/UK£78) double; A$250 (US$200/UK£100) triple. Rates include full breakfast. Ask about packages and ferry transport deals. AE, DC, MC, V. Limited parking. Children under 12 not accepted. **Amenities:** Restaurant; heated outdoor pool; game room; tour desk; car-rental desk. *In room:* A/C, TV, minibar, coffeemaker, hair dryer.

IN PARNDANA

Developed by soldier settlers after World War II, Parndana today is a rural service center 25 minutes by car from Seal Bay and Stokes Bay. It's just around the corner from Parndana Wildlife Park, which has more than 50 aviaries with collections of native and other birds, some of them rare and protected.

The Open House ★ The best thing about The Open House is breakfast time, when guests sit around a communal table and dive into delicious food before going off to explore. You can choose between either a room with a double or a queen-size bed, or a one-bedroom family room with a double bed and two singles, or a two-bedroom family room. Each has a ceiling fan and a private bathroom with shower. The owners are friendly and can offer good advice on what to do around the island.

70 Smith St., Parndana, SA 5221. ✆ **08/8559 6113.** Fax 08/8559 6088. www.theopenhouse.com.au. 4 units. A$230 (US$184/UK£92) for 2 in queen, double, or family room with breakfast. Extra person in family rooms cost A$115 (US$92/UK£46). MC, V. **Amenities:** Restaurant; nonsmoking rooms. *In room:* Hair dryer.

ON THE SOUTHWEST COAST

Hanson Bay Cabins ★ *Finds* On the southwest coast of the island on the South Coast Road, this property is a row of comfortable log cabins perched above a fabulous beach. Each cabin has a large picture window facing the ocean, a full kitchen, a bathroom, two bedrooms (including a double bed and three singles in all), and a wood stove. Bring your own food and supplies from Kingscote, American River, or Penneshaw. The ocean can get wild and dramatic around here, with strong offshore winds whipping up the sand and spray. The cottages are near most of the major attractions, so they make a good base. Salmon are often caught off the beach.

Hanson Bay Company, P.O. Box 614, Kingscote, SA 5225. ✆ **08/8853 2603.** Fax 08/8853 2673. www.hansonbay.com.au. 6 cabins. A$170 (US$136/UK£68) double. Extra adult A$30 (US$24/UK£12); extra child A$20 (US$16/UK£8). AE, DC, MC, V. **Amenities:** Bike rental; coin-op laundry; nonsmoking rooms. *In room:* Kitchen, fridge, coffeemaker, hair dryer, iron (on request).

WHERE TO DINE

Most accommodations on Kangaroo Island provide meals for guests (usually at an additional cost). In addition, most day tours around the island include lunch. You'll find a few cheap takeout booths scattered around the island at the most popular tourist spots. For lunch, you can get sandwiches at Roger's Deli on Dauncey Street, behind the Ozone Hotel, in Kingscote.

Dudley Wines Cellar Door and Cafe ★★ AUSTRALIAN This fabulous restaurant perches on a cliff top on the far eastern tip of the island, right next to Cape Willoughby Lighthouse (an attraction in itself) and about 30km (19 miles) from Penneshaw. One wall is all glass, and the veranda affords terrific ocean views. The restaurant serves as a way to sell the local wine, by the bottle or the glass, but there's some good food including a plastic yellow bucket full of ice and cooked prawns, cheese plates, dips, and a "Mediterranean Platter" of nibbles.

Cape Willoughby. ✆ **08/8553 1333.** Reservations required for lunch. Main courses A$15–A$20 (US$12–US$16/UK£6–UK£8). MC, V. Daily 10am–4pm for coffee and cakes; daily 12:30–2:30pm for lunch.

4 Outback South Australia

South Australia is the driest state in Australia. This becomes quite apparent once you leave behind the parklands of Adelaide and head into the interior. The Outback is as harsh as it is beautiful. Much of it consists of stony desert, salt pans, and sand hills, roamed by kangaroos and wild goats. After spring rains, though, the area can burst alive with wildflowers.

It was always difficult to travel through these parts, and even today only four main routes traverse it. One of them, the **Birdsville Track,** is famed in Outback history as the trail along which stockmen once drove their herds of cattle south from Queensland. Another, the **Strzelecki Track,** runs through remote sand-dune country to Innaminka and on to Coopers Creek. Both of these tracks cut through the "dog fence"—a 5,600km-long (3,472-mile) barrier designed to keep dingoes out of the pastoral lands to the south.

If you follow the **Stuart Highway** or the **Oodnadatta Track,** you'll pass the mining towns of Coober Pedy, Andamooka, and Mintabie, where people from all over the world have been turned loose in the maddening search for opal. Out here, too, are national parks, such as the daunting Simpson Desert Conservation Park, with its seemingly endless blood-red sand dunes and spinifex plains; and Lake Eyre National Park, with its dried-up salt pan that, during rare floods, is a temporary home to thousands of water birds.

THE FLINDERS RANGES NATIONAL PARK ★

460km (285 miles) N of Adelaide

The dramatic craggy peaks and ridges that make up the Flinders Ranges rise out of the South Australian desert. The colors of the rock vary from deep red to orange, with sedimentary lines visible as they run down the sides of cliffs. Much of the greenery around here is stunted arid-land vegetation. Growing shoots and saplings, which for decades were nibbled away before they grew up, have started to turn what was once bare land back into bush. This is the result of a devastating rabbit virus introduced in 1996, and the continued culling of hundreds of thousands of wild goats. The most remarkable attraction is **Wilpena Pound,** a natural circle of cliff faces that form a gigantic depression on top of a mountainous ledge. The wind whipping over the cliff edges can produce exhilarating white-knuckle turbulence if you fly over it in a light aircraft. Kangaroos and emus can sometimes be seen wandering around the park, but outside the park, kangaroos are heavily culled.

ESSENTIALS

GETTING THERE By car, take Highway 1 out of Adelaide to Port Augusta (3½ hr.), then head east on Route 47 via Quorn and Hawker (45 min.). It's another hour to Wilpena Pound, next to the tiny settlement of Wilpena. Alternatively, take the scenic

---

Tips An Outback Travel Warning

If you intend to drive through the Outback, take care. Distances between points of interest can be vast; water, gas, food, and accommodations are far apart. Always travel with a good map and plenty of advice. If you plan to travel off-road, a four-wheel-drive vehicle is a must.

---

route, which doesn't have a specific name, through the Clare Valley (around 5 hr.): From Adelaide, head to Gawler and then through the Clare Valley; follow signs to Gladstone, Melrose, Wilmington, and Quorn.

Premier Stateliner (© **08/8415 5500;** www.premierstateliner.com.au) runs five buses every day from Adelaide to Port Augusta for A$45 (US$36/UK£18) one-way (half price for kids). The company also runs buses to Wilpena Pound via Hawker and Quorn. **Heading Bush Adventures** (© **08/8356 5501;** www.headingbush.com) has great trips, including a 10-day tour to the Flinders Ranges, the Oodnadatta Track, Coober Pedy, the Simpson Desert, Uluru (Ayers Rock), the Olgas, Kings Canyon, and Aboriginal communities. This remarkable four-wheel-drive trip, which focuses on Aboriginal culture, costs A$1,495 (US$1,196/UK£598)—or A$1,420 (US$1,136/UK£568) with a YHA card—and includes meals and bush camping. It departs Adelaide every Monday and alternative Thursdays. There's a maximum of 10 passengers.

Another good operator is **Banksia Adventures** (© **08/8236 9141;** www.banksia-adventures.com.au), which has 1- to 4-day trips to the Flinders, either in hotels or camping. The 2-day trip, including a hotel, costs A$770 (US$616/UK£308) for adults and A$495 (US$396/UK£200) for kids. Camping is about 25% cheaper. This company also offers camping trips to salty Lake Eyre when it floods (it flooded in 2007), as well as the Great Aussie Pub Crawl. On this trip you fly by light plane from Adelaide and visit remote Outback pubs. You stay overnight at good hotels, including the Prairie Hotel in the Flinders and underground at Coober Pedy. The trip costs A$5,236 (US$4,189/UK£2,100) and is all-inclusive, with as much beer as you can drink (which you'd expect for the price).

Covering a huge slice of the Outback from Adelaide is another great operator, **South Australian Scenic Tours** (© **08/8289 3970;** www.oztourism.com.au/sascenic tours), which hits the dirt roads for 10-day trips up the Birdsville Track to remote townships and historic sites. You continue along the Strezelecki Track to Innamincka (where the explorers Burke and Wills came to a tragic end), cruise on Cooper Creek, and take in the Sturt Stony Desert and the Flinders Ranges. Expect to see plenty of wildlife, including kangaroos, emus, and possibly even the very rare yellow-footed rock wallaby. The trip costs A$2,167 (US$1,733/UK£866). A 3-day Flinders Ranges trip with this company costs A$682 (US$545/UK£273), and a 4-day Kangaroo Island tour is A$946 (US$757/UK£380).

Most operators will also make up personalized tours on request.

VISITOR INFORMATION Before setting off, contact the **Flinders Ranges and Outback of South Australia Regional Tourism Association (FROSATA),** P.O. Box 2083, Port Augusta, SA 5700 (© **1800/633 060** in Australia), for advice on roads and conditions. I strongly recommend a visit to the **Wadlata Outback Centre,** 41 Flinders Terrace, Port Augusta, SA 5700 (© **08/8642 4511**), an award-winning interactive museum and information center. The museum costs A$7 (US$5.60/UK£2.80) for adults and A$4.50 (US$3.60/UK£1.80) for children and is open Monday through Friday from 9am to 5:30pm, Saturday and Sunday from 10am to 4pm.

In Hawker, both the Mobil service station and the post office also act as information outlets.

GETTING AROUND If you decide to explore on your own using a rental car, I recommend renting one in Adelaide.

WHERE TO STAY

Andu Lodge ★ This fabulous backpackers' lodge is one of the best in Australia. In Quorn, in the central Flinders Ranges (42km/26 miles from Port Augusta), the upscale former hotel is air-conditioned in summer and heated in winter. It has nice clean rooms (dorms sleep six). There's also a nice TV room, a laundry, a computer for e-mailing, and a kitchen area. The hostel runs a range of trips with an emphasis on Aboriginal culture and ecotourism. Guests can also rent mountain bikes. Quorn (pop. 1,300) is where the old *Ghan* railway started and finished, and where part of the movie *Gallipoli* was filmed. The town has four friendly pubs, all serving meals for A$6.50 to A$7.50 (US$5.20–US$6/UK£2.60–UK£3). The lodge also offers 1-, 2-, and 3-day tours of the Flinders Ranges.

12 First St., Quorn, SA 5043. ✆ **1300 730 701** in Australia, or 08/8648 6020. Fax 08/8648 6030. steveandpaulaandu lodge@bigpond.com. 64 units. A$60 (US$48/UK£24) double; A$87 (US$70/UK£35) family room for up to 6; A$20 (US$16/UK£8) dorm bed. Breakfast included. MC, V. Free parking. **Amenities:** Shared lounge w/VCR; bike rental; tour desk; coin-op laundry; nonsmoking rooms. *In room:* TV in family rooms, no phone.

Prairie Hotel ★★ Finds If you are going to stay anywhere near the Flinders Ranges, stay here. The tiny, tin-roofed, stonewalled pub offers a memorable experience and is well worth the dusty 89km (55-mile) drive north alongside the Ranges from Hawker on the A83. A new addition to the pub contains nice rooms, each with a queen-size bed and a shower. The older-style rooms are smaller and quaint. Three units have Jacuzzis. The bar out front is a great place to meet the locals and other travelers (who all shake their heads in wonder that this magnificent place is still so undiscovered). Meals, prepared in a style the hotel likes to call "Flinders Feral Food," are very nearly the best of this kind I've had in Australia. Among the specialties are kangaroo tail soup to start and a mixed grill of emu sausages, camel steak, and kangaroo as a main course. The owner's brother runs remarkable scenic flights over Wilpena Pound and out to the salt lakes. From here you could head to the township of William Creek for a side trip to see the giant salt lake, Lake Eyre, and then onward west to Coober Pedy.

Corner of High St. and West Terrace, Parachilna, SA 5730. ✆ **08/8648 4844.** Fax 08/8648 4606. www.prairie hotel.com.au. 12 units. A$145–A$195 (US$116–US$156/UK£58–UK£78) double; A$260 (US$208/UK£54) double with Jacuzzi. Extra person A$35–A$45 (US$28–US$36/UK£14–UK£18). Rates include light breakfast. AE, DC, MC, V. **Amenities:** Restaurant; bar. *In room:* A/C, minibar, coffeemaker.

Wilpena Pound Resort The nearest place to the Wilpena Pound, this partly refurbished resort almost monopolizes the overnight tourist market around here. Standard rooms are adequate and offer respite from the summer heat. The self-contained units are rooms with a queen-size and a single bed, a stovetop, a microwave, a basin, and cooking utensils. The resort also operates a campground and some stand-alone cottages. You can borrow a hair dryer at the reception desk. There are some good walks around the area. Half-hour scenic flights over the Ranges cost A$95 (US$76/UK£38) per person for two people, or A$80 (US$64/UK£32) per person for 20 minutes. The resort also offers four-wheel-drive tours of the area.

Wilpena Pound, SA 5434. ✆ **1800/805 802** in Australia, or 08/8648 0004. Fax 08/8648 0028. www.wilpena pound.com.au. 60 units. A$130–A$179 (US$104–US$143/UK£52–UK£72) motel double; A$205 (US$164/UK£82) self-contained unit; A$180 (US$144/UK£72) cottages. Extra adult A$22 (US$18/UK£9); extra child 2–14 A$6.50 (US$5.20/UK£2.60). Campsite A$19 (US$15/UK£7.50); powered site A$26 (US$21/UK£11). AE, DC, MC, V. **Amenities:** Restaurant; bar; bistro; outdoor pool; game room; tour desk; laundry service; nonsmoking rooms; general store. *In room:* A/C, TV, fridge, coffeemaker.

WHERE TO DINE

The **Old Ghan Restaurant,** Leigh Creek Road, Hawker (✆ **08/8648 4176**), is open for lunch and dinner Wednesday through Sunday; the restaurant used to be a railway station on the *Ghan* railway line to Alice Springs before the line was shifted sideways due to flooding. The food is unexciting, but the homemade pies have a following. If you find yourself in Port Augusta, the area's main town, head to the **Standpipe Motor Inn** (✆ **08/8642 4033**) for excellent Indian food. The quiet rooms are nice enough; a double goes for A$80 (US$64/UK£32).

COOBER PEDY ★

854km (529 miles) NW of Adelaide; 689km (427 miles) S of Alice Springs

Tourists come to this Outback opal-mining town for one thing: the people. More than 3,500 people, from 44 nations, work mainly underground here. The majority suffer from opal fever, which keeps you digging on the trail of the elusive shimmering rocks. Though some residents are secretive and keep to themselves, many others are colorful characters ready to stop for a chat and spin a few yarns.

Historically, Coober Pedy was a rough place, and it still has a certain Wild West air about it. The first opal was found here in 1915, but it wasn't until 1917, when the Trans Continental Railway was completed, that people began seriously digging for opals. Since then, they have mainly lived underground—not surprising when you encounter the heat, the dust, and the flies for yourself.

The town got its name from the Aboriginal words *kupa piti,* commonly thought to mean "white man's burrow." Remnants of the holes left by early miners are everywhere, mostly in the form of bleached-white hills of waste called "mullock heaps." It's rather discouraged for tourists to wander around the tailing sites, because locals get fed up when visitors fall down the mine shafts.

As for the town, there isn't much to look at, except a couple of underground churches, some casual restaurants, a handful of opal stores, and the necessary service businesses. In the center of town you'll find lots of outdoor buildings; the hotels and youth hostel have aboveground entrances but rooms below ground. All are within stumbling distance of each other on the main street.

ESSENTIALS

GETTING THERE **Regional Express** (✆ **13 17 13** in Australia; www.regionalexpress.com.au) flies to Coober Pedy from Adelaide. The round-trip fare is about A$360 (US$288/UK£144). Check the website for discounted fares and specials. **Greyhound Australia** (✆ **13 14 99** in Australia, or 07/4690 9950; www.greyhound.com.au) runs buses from Adelaide to Coober Pedy for A$76 (US$61/UK£31) for adults and A$61 (US$49/UK£25) for children one-way. The trip takes about 12 hours. The bus from Alice Springs to Coober Pedy costs A$75 (US$60/UK£30) for adults and A$60 (US$48/UK£24) for children. Passengers bound for Uluru (Ayers Rock) transfer at Erldunda.

If you drive from Adelaide, it will take you about 9 hours to reach Coober Pedy along the Stuart Highway. It takes 7 hours to drive the 700km (434 miles) to Alice Springs.

VISITOR INFORMATION The **Coober Pedy Tourist Information Centre,** Hutchison Street, Coober Pedy (✆ **1800/637 076** in Australia, or 08/8672 5298), is open Monday through Friday from 8:30am to 5pm (closed holidays). A good website, **www.opalcapitaloftheworld.com.au**, gives a rundown of adventure operators in the area.

SEEING THE TOWN

Radeka's Downunder Motel (see "Where to Stay," below) runs half-day tours of the opal fields, including a visit to an underground mine. It costs A$30 (US$24/UK£12) for adults and A$15 (US$12/UK£6) for kids.

If you want to see parts of Australia that most Australians never see, join an honest-to-goodness **Mail Run** ★ for a 12-hour journey out into the bush. Tours leave Monday and Thursday from Coober Pedy's **Underground Books** (✆ **08/8672 5558**)—yep, it's a bookshop underground—and travel along 600km (372 miles) of dirt roads to Oodnadatta and William Creek cattle station, stopping at five stations along the route. It can get pretty hot and dusty outside (think endless horizons of flat lands), but it's relatively comfortable inside the air-conditioned four-wheel-drive, and you'll have the chance to see such wildlife as eagles, emus, and the ever-present kangaroos. Bring your own lunch or buy it along the way. Tours cost around A$165 (US$132/UK£66) for adults and A$85 (US$68/UK£34) for children under 12, though kids might find the long trip difficult. This up-close-and-personal look at life in the bush could easily be one of the most memorable experiences you have in Australia.

WHERE TO STAY

The Backpacker's Inn at Radeka's Downunder Motel ★ The other "underground" rooms in Coober Pedy are built into the side of a hill, but the centrally located hostel here is actually underground—some 6.5m (21 ft.) directly below the topside building. This makes for nice temperatures year-round. Odd-looking dorms have no doors and are scooped out of the rock. Most contain just four beds; two large dorms sleep up to 20 people. The twin rooms are simply furnished but pleasant. The motel rooms are quite comfortable and come with TVs, coffeemakers, and attached bathrooms with shower. Some have a kitchenette. Room no. 9 is huge, with a double and two sets of bunk beds. All motel rooms are dug out of the side of a hill. Radeka's also runs a good opal tour.

1 Oliver St., Coober Pedy, SA 5723. ✆ **08/8672 5223.** Fax 08/86725821. www.radekadownunder.com.au. 150 units, 10 motel rooms. A$22 (US$18/UK£9) dorm bed; A$55 (US$44/UK£22) dorm double; A$105 (US$84/UK£42) motel double; A$125 (US$100/UK£50) motel family suite. Extra person A$22 (US$18/UK£9). AE, MC, V. Free parking. **Amenities:** Bar; tour desk; coin-op laundry; kitchen/dining room; TV and video room; pool table.

The Desert Cave Hotel Though it's not the only underground hotel in the world (there's a wonderful one in White Cliffs, New South Wales), this is the only one with a pool and Jacuzzi. Nineteen units are underground. Personally, I find the place a little soulless. The bar's "pokie" (gambling) machines are noisy, and you can hear your neighbors in the next room. (Heaven help you if the TV is turned up loud.) The hotel can arrange transfers from the airport (A$9/US$7.20/UK£3.60). The tours from here go off to the Painted Desert (A$190/US$152/UK£76), and you can also join the Mail Run from here.

Hutchison St. (P.O. Box 223), Coober Pedy, SA 5723. ✆ **1800/088 521** in Australia, or 08/8672 5688. Fax 08/8672 5198. www.desertcave.com.au. 50 units. A$192 (US$153/UK£78) double; A$212 (US$169/UK£85) family room. Extra person A$20 (US$16/UK£8). Ask about packages. AE, DC, MC, V. Free parking. **Amenities:** Restaurant; bar; outdoor pool; golf nearby; health club w/Jacuzzi; sauna; tour desk; car-rental desk; limited room service; laundry service; dry cleaning; nonsmoking rooms. *In room:* TV, minibar, coffeemaker, hair dryer, iron.

WHERE TO DINE

The **Opal Inn** (✆ **08/8672 5054**) offers good-value counter meals of the typical pub-grub variety. Head to **Traces** (✆ **08/8672 5147**), the township's favorite Greek restaurant, for something a bit different.

Moments A Fabulous Four-Wheel-Drive Adventure

With a rented vehicle from Adelaide, the **Prairie Hotel** (p. 571) is a day's drive north through the Clare Valley wine region. Stop off along the way for a traditional Aussie lunch at **Bluey Blundstone's Café** ★ in Melrose (**© 08/8666 2173**). The next day it's a 3- to 4-hour drive to William Creek, an Outback town with a takeout restaurant, pub and hotel, satellite phone box, campground, and general store. **Explore the Outback Camel Safaris** (**© 08/8672 3968;** www.austcamel.com.au/explore) offers 4-day camel safaris across the desert from here (check the website for alternate ways to get to William Creek). Just 20km (12 miles) before you reach town is a turnoff to **Lake Eyre,** a giant salt lake that's more often than not as dry as a bone. **Wrightsair** (**© 0418/336 748** mobile) offers 1-hour flights over Lake Eyre for around A$180 (US$144/UK£72) per person. Camping beside the lake is a magical experience. The next day it's a 166km (103-mile) drive to Coober Pedy, and then a 9-hour drive back to Adelaide.

5 The Coorong

Few places in the world attract as much wildfowl as the **Coorong,** one of Australia's most precious sanctuaries. The Coorong area includes the mouth of the Murray River, huge Lake Alexandrina, smaller Lake Albert, and a long, thin sand spit called the Younghusband Peninsula. The **Coorong National Park** encompasses a small, but by far the most scenic, part of this area. The area is under environmental threat due to pollutants coming south in the Murray River from farmlands to the north. It still supports large colonies of native and visiting birds, such as the Australian pelican, black swan, royal spoonbill, greenshank, and extremely rare hooded plover.

If it were possible to count all the birds here, you'd probably run out of steam after some 45,000 ducks, 5,000 black swans, 2,000 Cape Barren geese, and 122,000 waders. This last figure is even more significant when you consider the total South Australian population of waders (200,000), and the overall Australian population (some 403,000).

Add to these figures the thousands of pelicans—with around 3,000 birds nesting here, it's the largest permanent breeding colony in Australia—and gulls, terns, and cormorants, and you'll realize why the Coorong and Lower Murray Lakes form one of the most important water-bird habitats in Australia.

The national park, which stands out starkly against the degraded farmland surrounding it, is also home to several species of marsupials, including wombats.

The best time to visit the Coorong is in December and January, when the lakes are full of migratory birds from overseas. However, plenty of birds can be spotted year-round. ***Note:*** Binoculars and patience are highly recommended.

ESSENTIALS

GETTING THERE The best way to visit the Coorong is by car. I highly recommend a guided tour of the area once you arrive at the main settlement of Goolwa, on the western fringe of the waterways, or at Meningie, on the eastern boundary. From Adelaide, follow the Princes Highway along the coast.

VISITOR INFORMATION The **Goolwa Tourist Information Centre,** BF Lawrie Lane, Goolwa (© **08/8555 1144**), has information on the area and can book accommodations. It's open from 9am to 5pm daily.

GETTING AROUND You either sightsee by car, with a tour operator from Adelaide, or by boat. **Coorong Cruises** (© **08/8555 2203;** www.coorongcruises.com.au) offers both a half-day and a day trip exploring the waterway. The day trip costs A$85 (US$68/UK£34) for adults and A$60 (US$48/UK£24) for children including lunch. The half-day cruise costs A$74 (US$59/UK£30) for adults and A$55 (US$44/UK£22) for kids and leaves at noon from the main wharf at Goolwa. Trips leave only on some days, so ring ahead.

WHERE TO STAY

Meningie, on Lake Albert, is the main town in the Coorong. You could stay at **Coorong Wilderness Lodge,** at Point Hack (© **08/8575 6001**), a stunning site on the sand dunes about 25km (16 miles) south of Meningie. Simple but good-enough rooms here cost A$65 (US$52/UK£26) a night. It's Aboriginal owned and you can try bush foods, and take a kayak out onto the lake.

Goolwa, another service town, has plenty of hotels, B&Bs, campgrounds, and trailer parks, as does the main road that runs parallel to the national park. One of the ones I prefer around here is the **Goolwa Camping and Tourist Park,** 40 Castle Rd., Goolwa, SA 5214 (© **08/8555 2144**). It has 70 trailer sites and a large area for tents. A two-berth van costs A$25 (US$20/UK£10) a night, and a six-berth van costs A$35 (US$28/UK£14) for the first two people; it's A$5 (US$4/UK£2) for an extra adult or A$3 (US$2.40/UK£1.20) for an extra child. Bring your own bedding.

Grahams Castle Resort This former conference center is a AAA-rated three-star backpackers' accommodations. Rooms are very basic, with two single beds, heating, and a shower shared between two rooms. It's very popular with budget groups, so it can get noisy.

Corner of Castle and Bradford sts., Goolwa, SA 5214. © **1800/243 303** in Australia, or 08/8555 3300. Fax 08/8555 3828. 22 units. A$15 (US$12/UK£6) per person. AE, DC, MC, V. **Amenities:** Restaurant; bar; heated outdoor pool; tennis court; tour desk. *In room:* No phone.

Poltalloch ★★ Smack in the middle of nowhere on the eastern edge of the Coorong, Poltalloch is a working farm property—with plenty of cows, ducks, chickens, and dogs wandering about—that seems more like a village. The whole place is classified as a heritage building by the National Trust of South Australia, and history is evident everywhere, from the cottages once used by farmhands to the giant wooden shearing shed and other outbuildings crammed with relics from the past.

You have a choice of five cottages on the property. The Shearer's Hut is a stone cottage that sleeps up to nine people; the Overseer's stone cottage sleeps up to eight people; the Boundary Rider's Cottage is built of timber, iron, and stone, and sleeps five; and the Station Hand's Cottage sleeps four. The Shearer's Quarters is mainly for large groups and sleeps 12. All of the units are modern and comfortable inside and have their own kitchen facilities and barbecues. I stayed in the Station Hand's Cottage, once the home of Aboriginal workers. I loved the mix of rural feeling and modern conveniences.

There's a private beach if you want to swim in the lake, and guests have the use of a dinghy, a canoe, and a Ping-Pong table. Breakfast provisions are available for A$15 (US$12/UK£6) per person. Coorong Nature Tours will pick you up from here for no extra charge. There's plenty of bird life all around.

Poltalloch, P.M.B. 3, Narrung via Tailem Bend, SA 5260. ✆ **08/8574 0043.** Fax 08/8574 0065. www.poltalloch.com.au. 5 units. A$140–A$160 (US$112–US$128/UK£56–UK£64) per cottage. Extra person A$35 (US$28/UK£14). MC, V. **Amenities:** Tennis court; use of watersports equipment; nonsmoking rooms. *In room:* A/C, TV, kitchen, fridge, coffeemaker, iron.

12

Melbourne

by Lee Mylne

It's rare to find anyone who lives in Melbourne who doesn't adore it. They are much more passionate about it than Sydneysiders are of their city, and it shows. I'm biased, of course, because I've chosen it for my home and here are just a few of the reasons why. Victoria's capital and Australia's largest city, Melbourne (pronounced *Mel-*bun) is a cultural melting pot. For a start, more people of Greek descent live here than in any other city except Athens. Chinese, Italian, Vietnamese, and Lebanese immigrants have all left their mark. Almost one-third of Melbournians were born overseas or have parents who were born overseas. With such a diverse population, and with trams rattling through the streets and stately European architecture surrounding you, you could forget you're in Australia.

Melbourne, which has a population of well over three million, is at the head of the pack when it comes to shopping, restaurants, fashion, music, nightlife, and cafe culture. It frequently beats out other state capitals in bids for major concerts, plays, exhibitions, and sporting events, such as the Formula One Grand Prix.

Melbourne's roots go back to the 1850s, when gold was found in the surrounding hills. British settlers took up residence and prided themselves on coming freely to their city, rather than having been forced here in convict chains. The city grew wealthy and remained a conservative bastion until World War II, when another wave of immigration, mainly from southern Europe, made it a more relaxed place.

So when Melbourne is described—as it often is—as one of the world's most "livable" cities, I'm happy to agree.

1 Orientation

ARRIVING

BY PLANE **Qantas** (✆ **13 13 13** in Australia; www.qantas.com.au) and discount airline **Virgin Blue** (✆ **13 67 89** in Australia; www.virginblue.com.au) both fly to Melbourne from all state capitals. Qantas's discount arm, **Jetstar** (✆ **13 15 38** in Australia, or 03/8341 4901; www.jetstar.com.au) flies to and from Darwin, Townsville, Hamilton Island, the Sunshine Coast and Gold Coast, and Hobart. Jetstar also flies between **Avalon Airport,** about a 50-minute drive outside Melbourne's city center, and Sydney, Brisbane, Perth, and Adelaide. With a rapidly expanding network more flights are likely to have been added before you arrive in Australia.

Melbourne Airport's international and domestic terminals (www.melair.com.au) are all under one roof at Tullamarine, 22km (14 miles) northwest of the city center (often referred to as Tullamarine Airport). A travelers' information desk is on the ground floor of the international terminal and is open from 6am until the last flight. The international terminal has snack bars, a restaurant, currency-exchange facilities, and duty-free shops. ATMs are available at both terminals. Showers are on the first floor of the international area. Baggage carts are free in the international baggage claim hall but cost A$3 (US$2.40/UK£1.20) in the parking lot, departure lounge, or domestic terminal. Baggage storage is available in the international terminal and costs from A$10 to A$20 (US$8–US$16/UK£4–UK£8) per day, depending on size. The storage desk is open from 5am to 12:30am daily, and you need photo ID. The **Hilton Melbourne Airport** (© **03/8336 2000**) and **Holiday Inn Melbourne Airport** (© **1300/724 944** in Australia) are both within 5 minutes' walk of the terminals.

Thrifty (© **1300/367 227** in Australia, or 03/9241 6100), **Budget** (© **13 27 27** in Australia, or 03/9938 6955), **Avis** (© **13 63 33** in Australia, or 03/9338 1800), **Hertz** (© **13 30 39** in Australia, or 03/9338 4044), and **Europcar** (© **1300/131 390** in Australia, or 03/9241 6800) have airport rental desks. The Tullamarine freeway to and from the airport joins with the CityLink, an electronic toll-way system. Drivers need a CityLink pass. A 24-hour pass costs A$11 (US$8.80/UK£4.40). Check with your car-rental company.

The distinctive red **Skybus** (© **03/9335 2811;** www.skybus.com.au) runs between the airport and Melbourne's Southern Cross Station in Spencer Street every 10 to 15 minutes throughout the day and every 30 to 60 minutes overnight 24 hours a day, every day. Buy tickets from Skybus desks outside the baggage claim areas or at the Travellers Information Desk in the international terminal. A free Skybus hotel shuttle will pick you up at your hotel to connect with the larger airport-bound bus at Southern Cross, but you must book this. It operates from 6am to 10pm weekdays and 7:30am to 6:30pm weekends. One-way tickets cost A$15 (US$12/UK£6) for adults and A$24 (US$19/UK£9.60) for a two-way journey. Kids cost A$5 (US$4/UK£2) each way. A family ticket for up to six people costs A$30 (US$24/UK£12) one-way or A$50 (US$40/UK£20) round-trip. The trip takes about 20 minutes from the airport to Southern Cross station, but allow longer for your return journey.

Sunbus (© **03/9689 6888;** www.sunbusaustralia.com.au) meets all flights and runs back to the airport from 167 Franklin St. and Southern Cross Station, and also operates a transfer service to Avalon Airport for Jetstar flights. One-way tickets from Melbourne airport cost A$21 (US$17/UK£8.40) for adults, A$15 (US$12/UK£6) children aged 4 to 14, and A$122 (US$98/UK£49) for a family of four. Round-trip fares are double. One-way fares from Avalon Airport are A$19 (US$15/UK£7.60) adults and A$9.50 (US$7.60/UK£3.80) children to Southern Cross station, more to other CBD locations and other suburbs.

A **taxi** to the city center takes about 30 minutes and costs around A$45 (US$36/UK£18).

BY TRAIN Interstate trains arrive at **Southern Cross Railway Station,** Spencer and Little Collins streets (5 blocks from Swanston St. in the city center). After a multimillion-dollar face-lift completed in 2006, the station was renamed Southern Cross, but you will still hear locals refer to it as Spencer Street Station. Taxis and buses connect with the city.

The **Sydney-Melbourne *XPT*** travels between Australia's two largest cities daily; trip time is 11 hours. The adult fare is A$75 (US$60/UK£30) for economy class or A$105 (US$84/UK£42) first class. A first-class sleep costs A$193 (US$154/UK£77). For more information, contact **Countrylink** (© **13 22 32** in Australia; www.countrylink.info).

The revamped ***Overland*** train, overhauled in 2007, provides daylight service between Melbourne and Adelaide (trip time: just under 11 hr.) three times a week.

Greater Melbourne

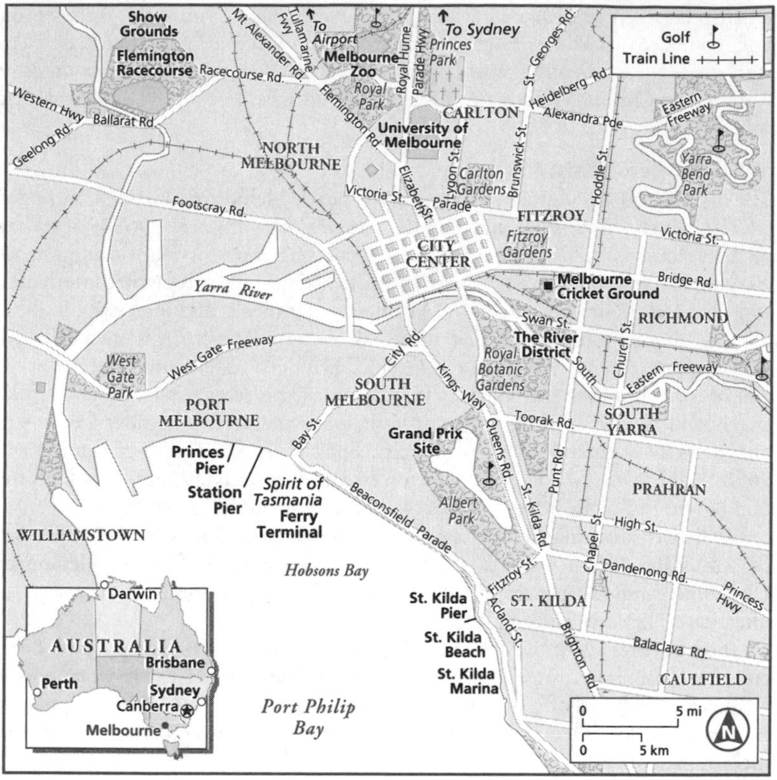

The adult one-way fare is A$139 (US$111/UK£56) in first class and A$89 (US$71/UK£36) in economy. For more information, contact **Great Southern Railways** (✆ **13 21 47** in Australia; www.gsr.com.au).

V/Line services also connect Melbourne with Adelaide. This trip is by train from Melbourne to Bendigo, and by bus from Bendigo to Adelaide. Total trip time is around 11 hours, and the fare is A$65 (US$52/UK£26) for adults and A$33 (US$26/UK£13) for children. The **Canberra Link** connects Melbourne with the nation's capital; it's a train journey from Melbourne to Bairnsdale, and bus from there to Canberra. The journey takes a little more than 10 hours and costs A$63 (US$50/UK£25) for adults, and A$33 (US$26/UK£13) for kids. For information and reservations, contact **V/Line** (✆ **13 61 96** in Australia; www.vline.com.au).

BY BUS Several bus companies connect Melbourne with other capitals and regional areas of Victoria. Among the biggest are **Greyhound Australia** (✆ **1300 4739 46863** in Australia, or 07/4690 9950; www.greyhound.com.au). Coaches serve Melbourne's **Transit Centre,** 58 Franklin St., 2 blocks north of the Southern Cross Railway Station in Spencer St. Trams and taxis serve the station; **V/Line buses** (✆ **13 61 96** in Australia; www.vline.com.au), which travel all over Victoria, depart from the Spencer Street Bus Terminal.

BY CAR You can drive from Sydney to Melbourne along the Hume Highway (a straight trip of about 9½ hr.), via Goulburn in NSW (good for supplies), and Wangaratta in Victoria (where you can detour into the Victorian Alps if you wish). Another route is along the coastal Princes Highway, for which you will need a minimum of 2 days, with stops. For information on all aspects of road travel in Victoria, contact the **Royal Automotive Club of Victoria** (© **13 13 29** in Australia, or 03/9790 2211; www.racv.com.au).

VISITOR INFORMATION

The first stop on any visitor's itinerary should be the **Melbourne Visitor Centre,** Federation Square, Swanston and Flinders streets (© **03/9658 9658;** www.thatsmelbourne.com.au). The center serves as a one-stop shop for tourism information, accommodations and tour bookings, event ticketing, public transport information, and ticket sales. Also here are an ATM, Internet terminals, and interactive multimedia providing information on Melbourne and Victoria. The center is open daily from 9am to 6pm (except Christmas and Good Friday). The Melbourne Greeter Service also operates from the Melbourne Visitor Centre. This service is available in 15 languages and connects visitors to enthusiastic local volunteers who offer free one-on-one, half-day orientation tours of the city. Book at least 3 days in advance (© **03/9658 9658**) if you can. The Melbourne Visitor Centre also operates staffed information booths in Bourke Street Mall, between Swanston and Elizabeth streets.

You'll find some information services at **Information Victoria,** 356 Collins St. (© **1300/366 356** in Australia). In the central city area, also look for **Melbourne's City Ambassadors**—people, usually volunteers, who give tourist information and directions. They'll be wearing bright red shirts and caps.

Good websites about the city include **CitySearch Melbourne, http://melbourne.citysearch.com.au**; as well as the official City of Melbourne site, **www.melbourne.vic.gov.au**; and the official tourism site for the city, **www.visitmelbourne.com**. Also worth a look are locally run sites, **www.onlymelbourne.com.au** and **www.thatsmelbourne.com.au**.

CITY LAYOUT

Melbourne is on the Yarra River and stretches inland from Port Philip Bay, which lies to its south. On a map, you'll see a distinct central oblong area surrounded by Flinders Street to the south, Latrobe Street to the north, Spring Street to the east, and Spencer Street to the west. Cutting north-to-south through its center are the two main shopping thoroughfares, Swanston Street and Elizabeth Street. Cross streets between these major thoroughfares include Bourke Street Mall, a pedestrian-only shopping promenade. If you continue south along Swanston Street and over the river, it turns into St. Kilda Road, which runs to the coast. Melbourne's various urban "villages," including South Yarra, Richmond, Carlton, and Fitzroy, surround the city center. The seaside suburb of St. Kilda is known for its diverse restaurants. If you've visited Sydney, you'll find Melbourne's city center smaller and far less congested with people and cars.

NEIGHBORHOODS IN BRIEF

At more than 6,110 sq. km (2,383 sq. miles), Melbourne is one of the biggest cities in the world by area. Below are the areas of most interest to visitors.

City Center Made up of a grid of streets north of the Yarra River, the city center is bordered by Flinders, Latrobe, Spring, and Spencer streets. There's good shopping and charming cafes, and in recent years an active nightlife has sprung up with the opening of a swath of funky bars and restaurants playing live and recorded music to suit all ages. The gateway to the city is the Flinders Street Station, with its dome and clock tower, flanked by the Federation Square precinct.

Chinatown This colorful section centers on Little Bourke Street between Swanston and Exhibition streets. The area marks Australia's oldest permanent Chinese settlement, dating from the 1850s, when a few boardinghouses catered to Chinese prospectors lured by gold rushes. Plenty of cheap restaurants crowd its alleyways. Tram: Any to the city.

Carlton North of the city center, Carlton is a rambling suburb famous for the Italian restaurants along Lygon Street with outdoor seating—though the quality of the food varies. It's the home of the University of Melbourne, so there's a healthy student scene. From Bourke Street Mall, count on a 15-minute walk to the restaurant strip. Tram: 1 or 22 from Swanston Street.

Fitzroy A ruggedly bohemian place, 2km (1¼ miles) north of the city center, Fitzroy is raw and funky, filled with students and artists and popular for people-watching. Fitzroy revolves around Brunswick Street, with its cheap restaurants, busy cafes, late-night bookshops, art galleries, and pubs. Around the corner, on Johnston Street, is a growing Spanish quarter with tapas bars, flamenco restaurants, and Spanish clubs. Tram: 11 from Collins Street.

Richmond One of Melbourne's earliest settlements is a multicultural quarter noted for its historic streets and back lanes. Victoria Street is reminiscent of Ho Chi Minh City, with Vietnamese sights, sounds, aromas, and restaurants everywhere. Bridge Road is a discount-fashion precinct. Tram: 48 or 75 from Flinders Street to Bridge Road; 70 from Batman Avenue at Princes Bridge to Swan Street; 109 from Bourke Street to Victoria Street.

Southgate & Southbank This flashy entertainment district on the banks of the Yarra River opposite Flinders Street Station (linked by pedestrian bridges) is home to the Crown Casino, Australia's largest gaming venue. Southbank has a myriad of restaurants, bars, cafes, nightclubs, cinemas, and designer shops. On the city side of the river is the Melbourne Aquarium. All are a 10-minute stroll from Flinders Street Station. Tram: 8 from Swanston Street.

Docklands Near the city center, at the rear of the Spencer Street station, this industrial area has become the biggest development in Melbourne. NewQuay on the waterfront has a diverse range of restaurants, shops, and cinemas. To celebrate the dominance of the Australian Rules Football, Melbournians recently constructed a 52,000-seat stadium, the Telstra Dome, to house their favorite game. Docklands is accessible by the free city circle tram or by river cruise boats.

St. Kilda Hip and bohemian in a shabby-chic sort of way, this bayside suburb (6km/3¾ miles south of the city center) has Melbourne's highest concentration of restaurants, ranging from glitzy to cheap, as well as some superb cake shops and delis. Historically it was Melbourne's red-light district. The Esplanade hugs a beach with a historic pier and is the scene of a lively arts-and-crafts market on Sundays. Acland Street houses many restaurants. Check out Luna Park, one of the world's oldest fun parks, built in 1912, and ride the wooden roller coaster. Tram: 10 or 12 from Collins Street; 15 or 16 from Swanston Street; 96 from Bourke Street.

South Yarra/Prahan This posh part of town abounds with boutiques, cinemas, nightclubs, and galleries. Chapel Street is famous for its upscale eateries and designer-fashion houses, while Commercial Road is popular with the gay and lesbian community. Off Chapel Street in Prahan is Greville Street, a bohemian enclave of retro boutiques and music outlets. Every Sunday from noon to 5pm the Greville Street Market offers arts, crafts, old clothes, and jewelry. Tram: 8 or 72 from Swanston Street.

South Melbourne One of the city's oldest working-class districts, South Melbourne is known for its historic buildings, old-fashioned pubs and hotels, and markets. Tram: 12 from Collins Street; 1 from Swanston Street.

The River District The muddy-looking Yarra River runs southeast past the Royal Botanic Gardens and near other attractions such as the Arts Centre, the National Gallery of Victoria, the Sidney Myer Music Bowl, and the Melbourne Cricket Ground, all described later in this chapter. Birrarung Marr is the first new major parkland in Melbourne in over 100 years. It is accessible by the free City Circle Tram.

Williamstown A lack of extensive development has left this outer waterfront suburb with a rich architectural heritage. It centers on Ferguson Street and Nelson Place—both reminiscent of old England. On the Strand overlooking the sea is a line of bistros and restaurants, and a World War II warship museum. Ferry: From Southgate, the World Trade Center, or St. Kilda Pier.

2 Getting Around

BY PUBLIC TRANSPORTATION

Trams, trains, and buses are operated by several private companies, including the National Bus Company, Yarra Trams, and Connex, to name a few. Generally, both tourists and locals travel around the city and inner suburbs by tram.

BY TRAM ★ Melbourne has the oldest tram network in the world. Trams are an essential part of the city, and a major cultural icon. Several hundred trams run over 325km (202 miles) of track. Instead of phasing out this non-smoggy method of transport, Melbourne is busily expanding the network.

The cheapest tram travel within the city center is with a **City Saver** ticket, which costs A$2.30 (US$1.85/UK90p) for adults, A$1.30 (US$1.05/UK50p) for children for a single journey. Or you can buy a **2-hour Metcard,** good for unlimited transport on buses or trams for up to 2 hours to all the attractions and suburbs listed in this book, for A$3.20 (US$2.55/UK£1.30) for adults and A$1.90 (US$1.50/UK75p) for children. If you plan to pack in the sightseeing, try the **Zone 1 Metcard Daily ticket,** which allows travel on all transport (trams and trains) within the city and close surrounding suburbs mentioned in this chapter from 5:30am to midnight (when transportation stops). It costs A$6.10 (US$4.90/UK£2.45) for adults and A$3.20 (US$2.55/UK£1.30) for children.

Buy single-trip and 2-hour tram tickets at ticket machines on trams, special ticket offices (such as at the tram terminal on Elizabeth St., near the corner of Flinders St.), at most newsdealers, and at Metcard vending machines at many railway stations. A Metcard needs to be validated by the Metcard Validator machine on the tram, on the station platform, or on the bus before each journey; the only exception to this is the

2-hour Metcard purchased from a vending machine on a tram, which is automatically validated for that journey only. Vending machines on trams only accept coins—but give change—whereas larger vending machines at train stations accept coins and paper money and give change up to A$10 (US$8/UK£4).

You can pick up a free route map from the Melbourne Visitor Centre, Federation Square, or the **Met Information Centre,** 103 Elizabeth St., at the corner of Collins Street (© **13 16 38** in Australia; www.metlinkmelbourne.com.au), which is open Monday through Friday from 8:30am to 4:30pm, and Saturday from 9am to 1pm.

The **City Circle Tram** is the best way to get around the center of Melbourne—and it's free. The burgundy-and-cream trams travel a circular route between all the major central attractions, and past shopping malls and arcades. The trams run, in both directions, every 12 minutes between 10am and 6pm, except Good Friday and December 25. The trams run along all the major thoroughfares including Flinders and Spencer streets. Burgundy signs mark City Circle Tram stops.

Normal trams stop at numbered green-and-gold tram-stop signs, sometimes in the middle of the road (so beware of oncoming traffic!). To get off the tram, press the red button near handrails or pull the cord above your head.

BY BUS The free **Melbourne City Tourist Shuttle** operates buses that pick up and drop off at 15 stops around the city, including the Melbourne Museum, Queen Victoria Market, Immigration Museum, Southbank Arts Precinct, the Shrine of Remembrance and Botanic Gardens, Chinatown, and Flinders Lane, among others. You can hop on and off during the day. The bus runs every 15 minutes from 10am until 4pm daily, taking in many of Melbourne's attractions.

BY BOAT

Melbourne River Cruises (© **03/8610 2600;** www.melbcruises.com.au) offers a range of boat trips up and down the Yarra River, taking about 1 hour 15 minutes. It's a really interesting way to get a feel for the city, and the tours include commentaries. Tours cost A$20 (US$16/UK£8) adults, A$11(US$8.80/UK£4.40) for kids, or A$50 (US$40/UK£20) for a family of four. Or you can combine both up- and downriver tours for A$34 (US$27/UK£14) adults, A$19 (US$15/UK£7.60) kids, or A$86 (US$69/UK£34) family. Call ahead to confirm cruise departure times, as they change, and pick up tickets from the blue Melbourne River Cruises kiosks at the Federation Square riverfront (opposite Flinders St. Station).

BY TAXI

Cabs are plentiful in the city, but it may be difficult to hail one in the city center late on Friday and Saturday night. Taxi companies include **Silver Top** (© **13 10 08** in Australia), **Embassy** (© **13 17 55** in Australia), and **Yellow Cabs** (© **13 22 27** in Australia). A large, illuminated rooftop light indicates that a cab is available for hire.

BY CAR

Driving in Melbourne can be challenging. Roads can be confusing, there are trams everywhere, and there is a rule about turning right from the left lane at major intersections in the downtown center (which leaves the left-hand lane free for trams and through traffic). Here, you must wait for the lights to turn amber before turning. Also, you must always stop behind a tram if it stops, because passengers usually step directly into the road. Add to this the general lack of parking and expensive hotel valet parking, and you'll know why it's better to get on a tram instead. For road rules, pick up a copy of the Victorian Road Traffic handbook from bookshops or from a **Vic Roads** office (✆ **13 11 71** in Australia for the nearest office).

Major car-rental companies, all with offices at Tullamarine Airport, include **Avis,** 8 Franklin St. (✆ 03/9663 6366); **Budget,** 398 Elizabeth St. (✆ 03/9203 4844); **Hertz,** 10 Dorcas St., South Melbourne (✆ 13 3039 in Australia, or 03/9698 2444); and **Thrifty,** 390 Elizabeth St. (✆ 1300 367 227 in Australia). Expect to pay at least A$40 (US$32/UK£16) a day for a small car.

FAST FACTS: Melbourne

American Express The main office is at 233 Collins St. (✆ **1300/139 060** in Australia, or 03/9633 6333). It's open Monday through Friday from 9am to 5pm, and Saturday from 10am to 1pm.

Business Hours In general, stores are open Monday through Wednesday and Saturday from 9am to 5:30pm, Thursday from 9am to 6pm, Friday from 9am to 9pm, and Sunday from 10am to 5pm. The larger department stores stay open on Thursday until 6pm and Friday until 9pm. Banks are open Monday through Thursday from 9:30am to 4pm, and Friday from 9:30am to 5pm.

Camera Repair **Vintech Camera Repairs,** Fifth Floor, 358 Lonsdale St. (✆ **03/9602 1820**), is well regarded.

Consulates The following English-speaking countries have consulates in Melbourne: United States, Level 6, 553 St. Kilda Rd. (✆ **03/9526 5900**); United Kingdom, Level 17, 90 Collins St. (✆ **03/9652 1600**); New Zealand, Level 3, 350 Collins St. (✆ **03/9642 1279**); Ireland, 295 Queen St. (✆ **03/9919 1802**); and Canada, Level 50, 101 Collins St. (✆ **03/9653 9674**).

Dentist Call the **Dental Emergency Service** (✆ **03/9341 1040**) for emergency referral to a local dentist.

Doctor The "casualty" department at the **Royal Melbourne Hospital,** Grattan Street, Parkville (✆ **03/9342 7000**), responds to emergencies. The **Traveller's Medical & Vaccination Centre,** Second Floor, 393 Little Bourke St. (✆ **03/9602 5788**), offers full vaccination and travel medical services.

Emergencies In an emergency, call ✆ **000** for police, ambulance, or the fire department.

Internet Access There are many Internet cafes along Elizabeth Street, between Flinders and Latrobe streets, and around Flinders Lane, and Little Bourke Street in Chinatown. Most are open from early until well into the night.

Lost Property Contact the nearest police station or visit the Melbourne Town Hall, Swanston Street (✆ **03/9658 9774**). If you lose something on a tram call ✆ **1800 800 166** between 6am and 10pm, or on a train call ✆ **03 9610 7512.**

Pharmacies (Chemist Shops) The **Mulqueeny Pharmacy** is on the corner of Swanston and Collins streets (✆ **03/9654 8569**). It's open Monday through Friday from 8am to 8pm, Saturday from 9am to 6pm, and Sunday 11am to 6pm.

Post Office The General Post Office (GPO) at 250 Elizabeth St. (✆ **13 13 18** in Australia) is open Monday through Friday 8:30am to 5:30pm, Saturday 9am to 4pm, and Sunday 10am to 4pm.

Safety St. Kilda might be coming up in the world, but walking there alone at night still isn't wise. Parks and gardens can also be risky at night, as can the area around the King Street nightclubs.

Taxes Sales tax, where it exists, is included in the price, as is the 10% Goods and Services Tax (GST). There is no hotel tax in Melbourne.

Telephones For directory assistance, call © **1223;** for international directory assistance, call © **1225.**

Weather Call © **1196** for recorded weather information.

3 Where to Stay

Getting a room is easy enough on weekends, when business travelers are back home. You need to book well in advance, however, during the city's hallmark events (say, the weekend before the Melbourne Cup, and during the Grand Prix and the Australian Open). Hostels in the St. Kilda area tend to fill up quickly in December and January.

You'll feel right in the heart of the action if you stay in the city center, which seems to buzz all day (and night). The city center has been rejuvenated in recent years, and you'll be certain to find plenty to do. Otherwise, the inner city suburbs are all exciting satellites, with good street life, restaurants, and pubs—and just a quick tram ride from the city center. Transportation from the airport to the suburbs is a little more expensive and complicated than to the city center, however.

If you arrive without booked accommodations, contact either of the **travelers' information desks** (© **03/9297 1805**) in the international airport terminal, open daily from 6am to the last flight. Or try the **Best of Victoria** booking service, Federation Square (© **1300 780 045** in Australia, or 03/9928 0000), open weekdays from 9am to 6pm and weekends from 9am to 5pm.

IN THE CITY CENTER

VERY EXPENSIVE

Adelphi Hotel It may be worth staying in this designer boutique hotel, a minute's walk from the city center, just for the experience of taking a dip in its top-floor 25m (82-ft.) lap pool, which juts out from the end of the building and overhangs the streets below. The pool has a glass bottom, so you can watch pedestrians below as you float. The rooms are similarly modern, with colorful leather seating and lots of burnished metal. Deluxe rooms differ from the so-called "Premier King" rooms in that they come with a bathtub. Executive rooms come with a separate lounge. Within the hotel is **Ezard,** a well-regarded restaurant offering contemporary Australian fare, and **Adelph*ish*,** which claims to offer the best breakfasts in Melbourne.

187 Flinders Lane, Melbourne, VIC 3000. © **1800/800 177** in Australia, or 03/9650 7555. Fax 03/9650 2710. www.adelphi.com.au. 34 units, most with shower only. A$560 (US$448/UK£224) Premier King Room; A$610 (US$488/UK£244) deluxe double; A$1,250 (US$1,000/UK£500) executive suite. Rates include breakfast. AE, DC, MC, V. Parking A$15 (US$12/UK£6). **Amenities:** 2 restaurants; cafe/bar; heated outdoor pool; exercise room; sauna; bike rental; concierge; tour desk; business center; babysitting; dry cleaning; nonsmoking rooms; executive rooms. *In room:* A/C, TV, DVD/CD, dataport, minibar, coffeemaker, hair dryer, iron.

Crown Towers ★★ One of Melbourne's grandest and most impressive hotels, Crown Towers is part of the Crown Casino complex, on the banks of the Yarra River.

Entry to the hotel is through a glittering lobby, paved in black marble. The complex has an enormous collection of gambling machines (called "pokies" in Australia), as well as gaming tables. Upstairs in the hotel, standard guest rooms are cozy. Superior guest rooms occupy floors 5 to 15, and those above the 10th floor have spectacular city views. Deluxe rooms, which run up to the 28th floor, are similar, and all have great views. Rooms above the 28th floor are part of Crown's Crystal Club, which offers club lounge services. From the 32nd floor upward are the luxury villas. The hotel is a 10-minute walk from the main shopping streets; trams stop right outside. **Crown Casino** offers 24-hour gambling. The 900-seat Showroom features live entertainment nightly, and a 14-screen cinema complex and three cabaret theaters provide additional activities. There are plenty of eateries and designer shops around here, too.

8 Whiteman St., Southbank, Melbourne, VIC 3006. ✆ **1800/811 653** in Australia, or 03/9292 6868. Fax 03/9292 6299. www.crowntowers.com.au. 482 units. A$335–A$455 (US$268–US$364/UK£134–UK£182) double; A$525–A$600 (US$420–US$480/UK£210–UK£240) double suite; A$1,200 (US$960/UK£480) 2-bedroom suite; from A$1,250 (US$1,000/UK£500) villas. Extra person A$55 (US$44/UK£22). Children under 13 stay free in parent's room. AE, DC, MC, V. Parking A$25 (US$20/UK£10). **Amenities:** 3 restaurants; Olympic-size indoor pool; health club; spa; concierge; tour desk; car-rental desk; business center; 24-hr. room service; babysitting; laundry service; dry cleaning; nonsmoking rooms; executive rooms. *In room:* A/C, TV w/pay movies, dataport, minibar, coffeemaker, hair dryer, iron.

Grand Hyatt Melbourne ★★ The Grand Hyatt is a glitzy, glamorous affair—the tower is infused with 24-carat gold—in the best part of town, a short walk from Swanston Street, Elizabeth Street, Chinatown, and public transport. Rooms are large and luxurious, and come with a nice-size marble bathroom and all the details you'd expect from a five-star establishment. The hotel's three diplomatic suites were refurbished in 2005 and feature floor-to-ceiling windows that overlook the Botanic Gardens and Yarra River. The suites' bathrooms boast sunken spa tubs, a sauna, and a rain shower. Prices vary with the view, but the best values are the Grand Club rooms, for which the rate includes evening cocktails, canapés, afternoon tea, and full breakfast in the Grand Club lounge. The hotel's gymnasium and fitness center is Australia's largest hotel gym, and there's also a day spa offering the usual treatments as well as treatments to combat jet lag. **Monsoon's** is a popular late-night disco in the hotel.

123 Collins St., Melbourne, VIC 3000. ✆ **13 12 34** in Australia, 800/492-8804 in the U.S. and Canada, or 03/9657 1234. Fax 03/9650 3491. www.melbourne.grand.hyatt.com. 548 units. A$280 (US$224/UK£112) Hyatt Guest double; A$350 (US$280/UK£140) Grand Club double; A$430 (US$344/UK£172) suites. Extra person A$55 (US$44/UK£22). Children under 12 stay free in parent's room. Ask about weekend rates and packages. AE, DC, MC, V. Parking A$5 (US$4/UK£2). **Amenities:** Restaurant; large indoor pool; outdoor lit tennis court; health club; concierge; tour desk; car-rental desk; business center; 24-hr. room service; in-room massage; babysitting; laundry service; dry cleaning; nonsmoking rooms; executive-level rooms. *In room:* A/C, TV w/pay movies, dataport, minibar, coffeemaker, hair dryer.

Hotel Lindrum ★★ *Finds* If you like your hotels stylish and contemporary, then the Hotel Lindrum is for you. It's quite typical of the new wave of modern hotels that emphasize trendy interior design and have features like broadband Internet access in the rooms and wireless access in the lobby. Standard rooms, if you can call them that, have a queen-size bed or two singles, lots of hardwood, soft lighting, and forest greens—and even a CD player. Superior rooms have king-size beds and lovely polished wood floorboards, and deluxe rooms have wonderful views across to the Botanic Gardens through large bay windows. The hotel boasts a smart restaurant, a billiard room, and a bar with an open fire.

26 Flinders St., Melbourne, VIC 3000. ✆ **03/9668 1111**. www.hotellindrum.com.au. 59 units. A$410 (US$328/UK£164) standard double; A$450 (US$360/UK£180) superior room; A$460 (US$368/UK£184) deluxe room; A$500

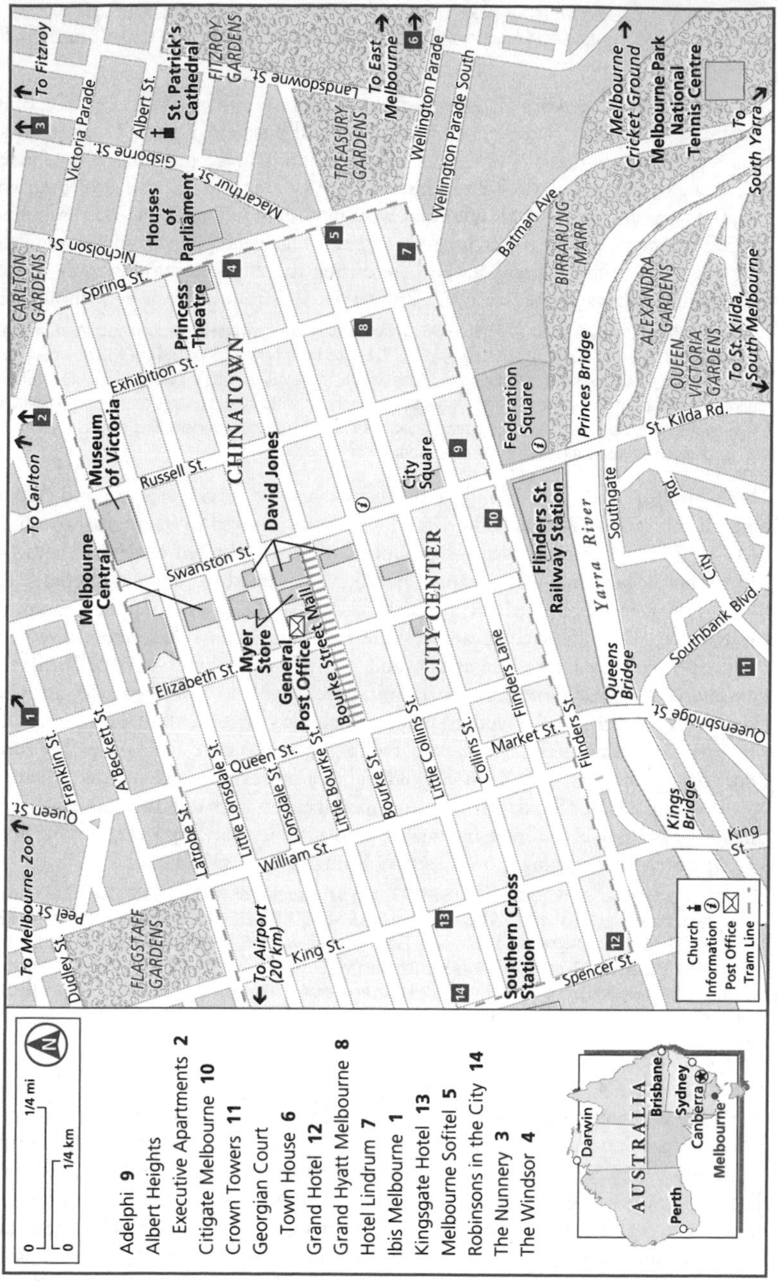
Adelphi 9
Albert Heights Executive Apartments 2
Citigate Melbourne 10
Crown Towers 11
Georgian Court Town House 6
Grand Hotel 12
Grand Hyatt Melbourne 8
Hotel Lindrum 7
Ibis Melbourne 1
Kingsgate Hotel 13
Melbourne Sofitel 5
Robinsons in the City 14
The Nunnery 3
The Windsor 4
0 1/4 mi
0 1/4 km
AUSTRALIA
Darwin
Brisbane
Sydney
Canberra
Melbourne
Perth
Church
Information
Post Office
Tram Line
To Melbourne Zoo
To Fitzroy
To Carlton
To East Melbourne
To Airport (20 km)
To St. Kilda, South Melbourne
To South Yarra
FLAGSTAFF GARDENS
CARLTON GARDENS
FITZROY GARDENS
TREASURY GARDENS
BIRRARUNG MARR
ALEXANDRA GARDENS
QUEEN VICTORIA GARDENS
CHINATOWN
CITY CENTER
Yarra River
Melbourne Central
Museum of Victoria
Princess Theatre
Houses of Parliament
St. Patrick's Cathedral
Myer Store
General Post Office
David Jones
City Square
Federation Square
Flinders St. Railway Station
Southern Cross Station
Melbourne Cricket Ground
Melbourne Park National Tennis Centre
Princes Bridge
Queens Bridge
Kings Bridge
Bourke Street Mall
Dudley St.
Peel St.
Queen St.
Franklin St.
A'Beckett St.
Latrobe St.
Little Lonsdale St.
Lonsdale St.
Little Bourke St.
Bourke St.
Little Collins St.
Collins St.
Flinders Lane
Flinders St.
Market St.
King St.
William St.
Spencer St.
Elizabeth St.
Swanston St.
Russell St.
Exhibition St.
Spring St.
Nicholson St.
Victoria Parade
Gisborne St.
Albert St.
Macarthur St.
Lansdowne St.
Wellington Parade
Wellington Parade South
Batman Ave.
St. Kilda Rd.
Southgate
City Rd.
Southbank Blvd.
Queensbridge St.

(US$400/UK£200) suite. AE, DC, MC, V. Parking A$15 (US$12/UK£6) off-site. **Amenities:** Restaurant; bar; laundry service; nonsmoking rooms; rooms for guests w/limited mobility. *In room:* A/C, TV w/free movies, dataport, coffeemaker, iron.

Sofitel Melbourne ★★ This beautiful luxury hotel, in the best area of Collins Street, is a short walk from the major shopping and business district. The hotel has a glass-topped atrium that allows natural light to flood in and a great bar with wonderful city views on the 35th floor. Breakfasts in **Café La** are fabulous, and also come with views. Rooms are large and pleasant and were renovated in late 2004 and throughout 2005. They come with a flatscreen TV, the latest high-tech gizmos, and comfortable king-size beds. Prince Edward stayed here during the 2006 Commonwealth Games. An executive lounge opened in 2007. The service is as impressive as everything else.

25 Collins St., Melbourne, VIC 3000. ✆ **03/9653 0000.** Fax 03/9650 4261. www.sofitelmelbourne.com.au. 363 units. A$350 (US$280/UK£140) double; A$430 (US$344/UK£172) suite. Extra person A$55 (US$44/UK£22). 1 child under 12 stays free in parent's room. Ask about weekend rates and packages. AE, DC, MC, V. Parking A$26 (US$21/UK£10). **Amenities:** Restaurant; bar; exercise room; concierge; tour desk; car-rental desk; business center; shopping arcade; 24-hr. room service; massage studio; babysitting; laundry service; dry cleaning; nonsmoking rooms. *In room:* A/C, TV/DVD, dataport, minibar, coffeemaker, hair dryer, iron.

The Windsor ★★ The Windsor is Australia's only surviving authentic "grand" hotel. It opened in 1883 (as "The Grand") and was restored to its original condition by Oberoi Hotels International. This upper-crust establishment oozes sophistication and has hosted such notables as Lauren Bacall, Muhammad Ali, and Omar Sharif. The lobby is luxuriously carpeted and the staff friendly and efficient. Standard rooms are comfortable, with high ceilings and tasteful furnishings. Each has a good-size bathroom. Deluxe rooms are twice as big, and many have striking views of Parliament House and the Melbourne Cathedral. Suites are huge and furnished with antiques. Guests can choose from 10 types of pillows, including an aromatherapy version filled with rose petals and herbs. The Grand Ballroom, with ornate ceilings, leather furniture, gorgeous carpets, and plenty of gold leaf, is a most impressive place to eat and is open to nonguests for Sunday brunch and special events such as Christmas and Valentine's Day. But you may also be inclined toward a traditional **"high tea,"** served in the **111 Spring Street** restaurant on weekdays from 3:30 to 5:30pm.

103 Spring St., Melbourne, VIC 3000. ✆ **1800/033 100** in Australia, or 03/9633 6000. Fax 03/9633 6001. www.thewindsor.com.au. 180 units. A$205–A$295 (US$164–US$236/UK£82–UK£118) double; A$405–A$1,350 (US$324–US$1,080/UK£162–UK£540) double suite. Extra person from A$55 (US$44/UK£22). AE, DC, MC, V. Valet parking A$30 (US$24/UK£12) per night. **Amenities:** Restaurant; 2 bars; health club; concierge; business center; 24-hr. room service; babysitting; laundry service; dry cleaning. *In room:* A/C, TV w/pay movies, minibar, coffeemaker, hair dryer, iron.

EXPENSIVE

Grand Hotel ★★ This majestic heritage-listed building is striking for its remarkable scale and imposing Italianate facade. Building started on the six-story site in 1887, and additions were still being made in 1958. It became a hotel in 1997 and is now managed by Sofitel. Suites have plush red Pullman carpets, a full kitchen with a dishwasher; the one-bedroom loft suites have European-style espresso machines, CD player, a second TV in the bedroom, and great views over the new Docklands area beyond—though rooms are whisper quiet. All rooms are similar but vary in size; some have balconies. Many of the suites are split-level, with bedrooms on the second floor.

33 Spencer St., Melbourne, VIC 3000. ✆ **1300/361 455** in Australia, or 03/9611 4567. Fax 03/9611 4655. www.grandhotelsofitel.com.au. 114 units. A$215–A$459 (US$172–US$367/UK£86–UK£184) studio suite; A$235–A$479

(US$188–US$383/UK£94–UK£192) 1-bedroom suite; A$364–A$590 (US$291–US$472/UK£146–UK£236) 2-bedroom suite; A$800 (US$640/UK£320) 3-bedroom suite. Extra person A$74 (US$59/UK£30). Children under 14 stay free in parent's room. Ask about weekend and seasonal packages. AE, DC, MC, V. Parking A$13 (US$10/UK£5.20). Tram: 48 or 75 from Flinders St. **Amenities:** Restaurant; bar; golf course nearby; exercise room; Jacuzzi; sauna; concierge; tour desk; car-rental desk; 24-hr. room service; in-room massage; babysitting; laundry service; dry cleaning; nonsmoking rooms. *In room:* A/C, TV w/pay movies, dataport, kitchen, minibar, fridge, coffeemaker, hair dryer, iron.

MODERATE

Citigate Melbourne ★ *Finds* Opened in 2003, this compact four-star hotel opposite Flinders Street Railway Station offers light and comfortable rooms. It's quiet and welcoming and is a short walk to the main shopping streets. It's a stroll away from Federation Square, the Crown Casino Entertainment Complex, and the Southbank district. You can get some wonderful packages.

270 Flinders St., Melbourne, VIC 3000. ✆ **1800/664 296** in Australia, or 03/9654 6888. Fax 03/9654 0368. www.mirvachotels.com.au. 180 units. A$149–A$189 (US$119–US$151/UK£60–UK£76) standard room; A$199–A$219 (US$159–US$175/UK£80–UK£88) with water views. Extra person A$40 (US$32/UK£16). Ask about packages. AE, DC, MC, V. Parking A$25 (US$20/UK£10). **Amenities:** Restaurant; bar; free access to nearby gymnasium; concierge; car-rental desk; tour desk; business center; 24-hr. room service; babysitting; dry cleaning; nonsmoking rooms. *In room:* A/C, TV w/pay movies, high-speed Internet, minibar, coffeemaker, hair dryer, iron, safe.

Ibis Melbourne ★ *Value* A good deal, the Ibis is next door to the bus station and a short walk from the central shopping areas. Rooms in the AAA-rated four-star hotel are spacious, immaculate, and bright, and have attached showers. Apartments have kitchenettes and tubs. Guests can make use of the swimming pool, sauna, and Jacuzzi up the road at the historic Melbourne City Baths.

15–21 Therry St., Melbourne, VIC 3000. ✆ **1300/656 565** in Australia, 800/221-4542 in the U.S. and Canada, 0800/44 44 22 in New Zealand, or 03/9639 2399. Fax 03/9662 9263. www.ibishotel.com. 250 units, some with shower only. A$109–A$129 (US$87–US$103/UK£44–UK£52) double; A$149 (US$119/UK£60) 1-bedroom apt. Extra person A$36 (US$29/UK£14). Children under 12 stay free in parent's room. Ask about packages. AE, DC, MC, V. Parking A$11 (US$8.80/UK£4.40). **Amenities:** Discount rates at nearby pool, sauna, and Jacuzzi. *In room:* A/C, TV, minibar, coffeemaker, iron.

Robinsons in the City ★ *Finds* Artfully created in what was once Melbourne's first commercial bakery, this lovely boutique hotel is tastefully elegant as well as being casual and comfortable, with lots of personal touches. Built around 1850, the building retains some original features, including the brick ovens that are now a feature of the breakfast room. There are nice touches such as bathrobes and lovely toiletries. All rooms have either queen- or king-size beds and each guest room has its own private bathroom just across the hallway. There's a guest lounge with an extensive library, wireless broadband Internet access, and a "butler's pantry" with a bar that operates on an honor system. New owner Paul Humphreys is passionate about Melbourne and has made a few subtle changes but the substance of this accommodations gem is the same.

405 Spencer St. (at Batman St.), Melbourne, VIC 3003. ✆ **03/9329 2552.** Fax 03/9329 3747. www.robinsonsinthecity.com.au. 6 units, some with shower only. A$165–A$295 (US$132–US$236/UK£66–UK£118) double. Rates include full "farmhouse" breakfast. Ask about discount rates. AE, DC, MC, V. Limited free off-street parking, which must be pre-booked. **Amenities:** Tour desk; guest laundry; dry cleaning. *In room:* A/C, TV, minibar, coffeemaker, hair dryer, iron.

INEXPENSIVE

Kingsgate Hotel A 10-minute walk from the city, this interesting hotel feels like a basic B&B, though a total refurbishment in 2002 gave it a better look. From the outside, it resembles a terrace building, but inside it's a maze of corridors and rooms. The staff is very friendly. The least expensive economy rooms are for backpackers only. They have two single beds and a hand basin; there's barely enough room to swing a backpack. Pricier executive rooms are light and spacious, with double beds or two twins as well as en-suite bathrooms. The 15 or so deluxe quad rooms have double beds and two singles. There is a 24-hour reception desk, free luggage-storage facilities, and free use of the safety deposit boxes. A cooked breakfast costs A$14 (US$11/UK£5.60) extra. Check the hotel's website for really good deals.

131 King St., Melbourne, VIC 3000. © **1300/734 171** in Australia, or 03/9629 4171. Fax 03/9629 7110. www.kingsgatehotel.com.au. 225 units, 104 with bathroom. A$89–A$139 (US$71–US$111/UK£36–UK£56) double; A$119–A$149 (US$95–US$119/UK£48–UK£60) triple; A$169 (US$135/UK£68) deluxe quad. AE, DC, MC, V. Parking A$7 (US$5.60/UK£2.80) at Crown Casino, a 5-min. walk away. **Amenities:** 2 restaurants; tour desk; guest laundry; same-day dry cleaning; executive-level rooms. *In room:* TV.

IN CARLTON

Albert Heights Serviced Apartments ✪ For good, moderately priced accommodations with cooking facilities (so you can cut down on meal costs), try the Albert Heights, a favorite of American travelers. It's in a nice area of Melbourne, about a 10-minute walk from the city center. There are parks at each end of the street. Each self-contained unit in the brick building is large and attractive. If you want your own space or are traveling with your family, you can use the sofa bed in the living room. "Superior" apartments come with a double bed; deluxe one-bedroom apartments with a queen-size bed; and deluxe two-bedroom apartments with a queen-size and two large singles. "Premier" apartments are newly refurbished and have a queen-size bed in the master bedroom, with a separate lounge room with a single divan and single trundle bed. Each unit comes with a full kitchen with a microwave (no conventional oven), dining area, and large bathroom. Check the website for major discounts.

83 Albert St., East Melbourne, VIC 3002. © **1800/800 117** in Australia, or 03/9419 0955. Fax 03/9419 9517. www.albertheights.com.au. 34 units. A$195 (US$156/UK£78) superior apt; A$215 (US$172/UK£86) premier apt; A$235 (US$188/UK£94) deluxe 1-bedroom apt; A$275 (US$220/UK£110) deluxe 2-bedroom apt. Extra adult A$20 (US$16/UK£8); extra child A$15 (US$12/UK£6). Ask about special deals. AE, DC, MC, V. Free parking. Tram: 42 or 109. **Amenities:** Jacuzzi; tour desk; car-rental desk; babysitting; laundry service; dry cleaning; nonsmoking rooms. *In room:* A/C, TV, dataport, kitchen, fridge, coffeemaker, hair dryer, iron, safe.

Georgian Court Guest House What greater recommendation can I give you than to say that my sister and her husband stayed here on a visit to Melbourne—and they absolutely loved it. The comfortable Georgian Court's appearance hasn't changed much since it was built in 1910, and is set in a beautiful tree-lined street. The sitting and dining rooms have high ceilings and offer old-world atmosphere. The guest rooms are simply furnished. Some have en-suite bathrooms; others have private bathrooms in the hallway. One room comes with a queen-size bed and a Jacuzzi. The Georgian Court is a 15-minute stroll through the Fitzroy and Treasury Gardens from the city center, and is also close to the fashion shops of Bridge Road.

21 George St., East Melbourne, VIC 3002. © **03/9419 6353.** Fax 03/9416 0895. www.georgiancourt.com.au. 31 units, 21 with bathroom. A$109 (US$87/UK£44) double without bathroom; A$129 (US$103/UK£52) double with bathroom; A$159 (US$127/UK£64) queen spa room. A$10–A$20 (US$8–US$16/UK£4–UK£8) surcharge during busy periods. Extra adult A$20 (US$16/UK£8); extra child under 14 A$12 (US$9.60/UK£4.80). Rates include buffet breakfast. AE, DC, MC, V. Free parking. Tram: 75 from Flinders St., or 48 from Spencer St. **Amenities:** Access to nearby health club; tour desk; car-rental desk; coin-op laundry; dry cleaning; nonsmoking rooms. *In room:* A/C, TV, fridge, coffeemaker, hair dryer, iron, safe.

IN FITZROY

The Nunnery Guesthouse ★★ *Value* This former convent offers pleasant accommodations a short tram ride from the city center. On the city's edge, The Nunnery is well-situated near the restaurant and nightlife of Brunswick and Lygon streets, in nearby Carlton. This informal, friendly place is well suited to couples and families. The Nunnery is split into three separate buildings, the Guesthouse, the Townhouse, and the Nunnery Budget Accommodation. Built in the 1860s, the Guesthouse has high ceilings, handmade light-fittings, polished floorboards, marble fireplaces, and a hand-turned staircase. The Townhouse was built in the early 1900s, and is comfy, stylish, and decorated with tasteful furnishings and artwork. Rooms in both buildings have wooden floors, rugs, and leafy views, and are lovely. All rooms share bathrooms. There are no elevators. The Budget Accommodation is in the former home of the Daughters of Charity, built in the 1880s. It features a grand staircase, stained-glass windows, and religious artwork. The rooms are simple (some come with a TV) but pleasant, and there's dorm accommodations, too. All rooms are nonsmoking.

112–120 Nicholson St., Fitzroy, Melbourne, VIC 3065. ✆ **1800/032 635** in Australia, or 03/9419 8637. Fax 03/9417 7736. www.nunnery.com.au. 30 units, none with bathroom. Guesthouse A$110 (US$88/UK£44) double, A$120 (US$96/UK£48) double family room, plus A$30 (US$24/UK£12) per extra person; Townhouse A$110–A$125 (US$88–US$100/UK£44–UK£50) double; Backpackers' section A$26–A$30 (US$21–US$24/UK£10–UK£12) bunk rooms, A$75–A$95 (US$60–US$76/UK£30–UK£38) double, A$95 (US$76/UK£38) triple. Rates include breakfast. MC, V. Free parking (reservation required). Tram: 96 to stop 13 (East Brunswick). **Amenities:** Tour desk; car-rental desk; coin-op laundry; kitchen; lounge. *In room:* TV.

IN ST. KILDA

Fountain Terrace ★★ *Finds* Built in 1880, Fountain Terrace has been lovingly restored to its former glory by Penny and Heikki Minkkinen. This boutique guesthouse has real character and is a wonderful alternative to traditional city hotels. It's on a tree-lined street just a few minutes' walk from the sea and to the many restaurants on Fitzroy and Acland streets. It's very classy inside with comfortable communal areas, including a sunny drawing room where breakfast is served at an antique refectory table. The rooms, which are named after famous Australian writers, artists, and pioneers, have all those classic old-fashioned hallmarks of a historic house, including nice prints on the walls and old fireplaces. Each one is a real individual, so it's well worth while checking out the pictures on their website. Guests also have free access to the St. Kilda Baths and gymnasium, a 5-minute walk away.

28 Mary St. (parallel to Fitzroy St.), St. Kilda West, Melbourne, VIC 3182. ✆ **03/9593 8123.** Fax 03/9593 8696. www.fountainterrace.com.au. 7 units. A$175–A$245 (US$140–US$196/UK£70–UK£98) double. Rates include breakfast. AE, DC, MC, V. Free parking. Tram: 96, 16, 112, or St. Kilda. **Amenities:** Nonsmoking rooms. *In room:* TV, coffeemaker, hair dryer.

Hotel Tolarno ★ The quirky Hotel Tolarno is in the middle of St. Kilda's cafe and restaurant strip, and a short stroll from the beach. Rich red carpets bedeck the corridors throughout the 1950s and 1960s retro-style building. In an earlier life, the building was owned by Melbourne artist Mirka Mora (after whom the hotel's new restaurant has been named), and the tradition continues today, with the walls hung with work by Melbourne artists. Rooms vary, but all are modern and nice. The most popular, the deluxe doubles, are in the front of the building and have balconies overlooking the main street. They are larger than the standard rooms. Superior doubles come with a microwave and two have Japanese baths. Suites come with a separate kitchen and lounge. Suites don't have balconies, though some have Jacuzzis.

42 Fitzroy St., St. Kilda, Melbourne, VIC 3182. ✆ **1800/620 363** in Australia, or 03/9537 0200. Fax 03/9534 7800. www.hoteltolarno.com.au. 31 units. A$130–A$240 (US$104–US$192/UK£52–UK£96) double; A$250 (US$200/UK£100) suite for up to 4; A$350 (US$280/UK£140) penthouse suite (sleeps 4). AE, DC, MC, V. Free on-street parking. Tram: 16 from Swanston St. or 96 from Flinders St. **Amenities:** Restaurant; bar; 4 lit tennis courts; bike rental; concierge; tour desk; car-rental desk; room service; massage; babysitting; nonsmoking rooms. *In room:* A/C, TV, dataport, kitchenette, fridge, coffeemaker, hair dryer, iron.

Olembia Guesthouse This sprawling Edwardian house, built in 1922, is set back from a busy street behind a leafy courtyard. It's popular with tourists, business travelers, and young families; everyone gets together for frequent video nights, wine-and-cheese parties, and barbecues. The rooms are simply furnished, with little more than a double bed or two singles, a desk, a hand basin, and a wardrobe. Dorm rooms have between three and six beds (there are mixed and girls-only dorms). Guests share six bathrooms. There's a comfortable sitting room. The Olembia is near St. Kilda beach and the restaurants lining Acland Street.

96 Barkly St., St. Kilda, Melbourne, VIC 3182. ✆ **03/9537 1412.** Fax 03/9537 1600. www.olembia.com.au. 23 units, none with bathroom. A$80 (US$64/UK£32) double; A$90 (US$72/UK£36) triple; A$26 (US$21/UK£10) dorm room. AE, MC, V. Free parking. Tram: 96 from Bourke St. or 16 from Swanston St. **Amenities:** Bike rental; tour desk; coin-op laundry; nonsmoking rooms. *In room:* No phone.

IN SOUTH YARRA & TOORAK

The Como Melbourne ★★★ Winner of many awards, The Como deservedly basks in its reputation for excellent service and terrific accommodations, which include studio rooms (some with shower only), open-plan suites (all with spa tubs, some with private offices and/or wet bars), one- or two-bedroom suites (all with kitchen, some with an office), and luxurious penthouse and executive suites (split-level, with oversize spa tubs). Most rooms are at least 40 sq. m (431 sq. ft.), and the bathrooms have a bath menu (and a rubber duck for you to take home). Some suites have a private Japanese garden, and the Como Suite has a grand piano. The hotel is right in the heart of South Yarra, Melbourne's renowned restaurant, shopping, and cafe district and is popular with the fashion and entertainment set. It is also adept at accommodating business travelers: All rooms have video-conferencing capability, and a complimentary limousine service carries you to the city center each weekday morning. The health club is painted in vibrant energizing colors and the pool has a wonderful retractable roof.

630 Chapel St., South Yarra, VIC 3141. ✆ **1800/033 400** in Australia, 800/552-6844 in the U.S. and Canada, 0800/389 7791 in the U.K., 0800/446 110 in New Zealand, or 03/9825 2222. Fax 03/9824 1263. www.mirvachotels.com.au. 107 units. A$295 (US$236/UK£118) studio; A$335 (US$268/UK£134) open-plan suite; A$375 (US$300/UK£150) 1-bedroom suite. Extra person A$30 (US$24/UK£12). Ask about weekend packages. AE, DC, MC, V. Parking A$15 (US$12/UK£6). **Amenities:** Restaurant; bar; indoor pool; health club; Jacuzzi; sauna; bike rental; game room; concierge; tour desk; car-rental desk; business center; salon; 24-hr. room service; massage; babysitting; laundry service; dry cleaning; nonsmoking rooms; currency exchange. *In room:* A/C, TV w/pay movies, dataport, kitchen, minibar, coffeemaker, hair dryer, iron, safe, CD stereos.

Cotterville ★ You will love the courtyard gardens as much as the art and music which surrounds you in this beautifully restored terrace house, and will likely go home fast friends with your hosts and their two schnauzers. Owners Howard Neil and Jeremy Vincent are extremely knowledgeable about the city's arts scene—Jeremy works at the Victorian Arts Centre and Howard is a former theater and television director. You can join them for "happy hour" drinks at 5pm and for an extra A$40 (US$32/UK£16) per person (and advance notice), Howard will whip up a three-course gourmet dinner.

Where to Stay & Dine in St. Kilda

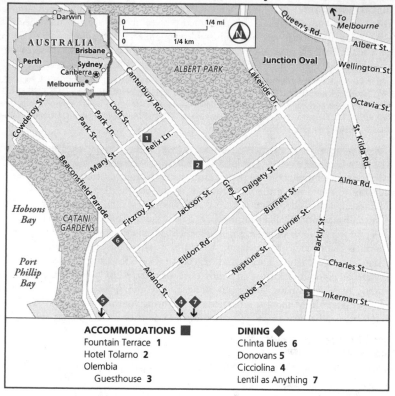

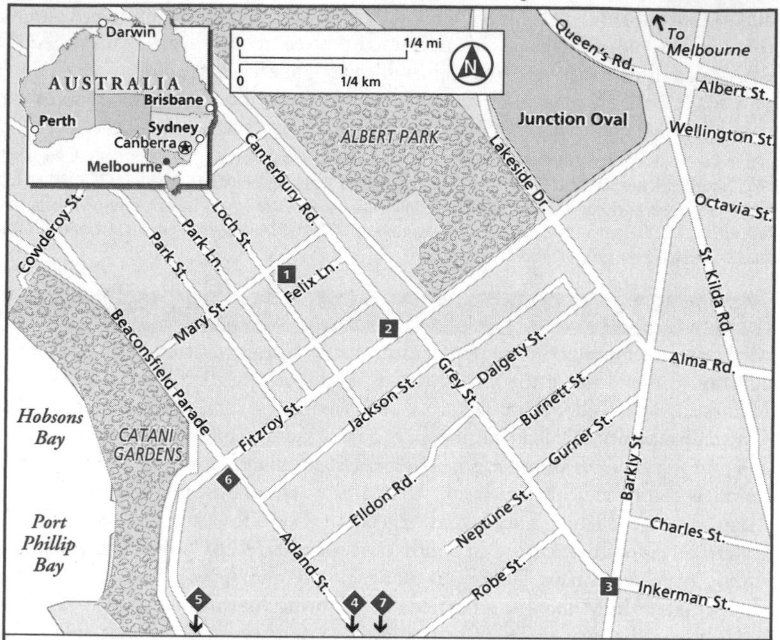

ACCOMMODATIONS ■
Fountain Terrace **1**
Hotel Tolarno **2**
Olembia Guesthouse **3**

DINING ◆
Chinta Blues **6**
Donovans **5**
Cicciolina **4**
Lentil as Anything **7**

204 Williams Rd., Toorak, Melbourne, VIC 3142. ✆ **1300/301 630** in Australia, 03/9826 9105, or mobile 0409 900807. www.cotterville.com. 2 units with shared bathroom. A$130 (US$104/UK£52) single; A$160 (US$128/UK£64) double. Weekly rates available. Rates include breakfast. MC, V. Free on-street parking. Train: Hawkesburn. **Amenities:** Coin-op laundry. *In room:* TV.

The Hatton ★ This striking Italianate mansion was built as a hotel in 1902. It's latest incarnation came 5 years ago, when it was meticulously restored and stylishly updated to become a sophisticated and contemporary boutique hotel. Many of the original features—rosettes, cornices, stained-glass windows, wide verandas, and high ceilings—have been retained, and the guest rooms have been fashioned from the original structure, making each an individual space. Clever combinations of old and new—antiques alongside modern art pieces specially commissioned—give it an unusual but welcoming atmosphere. A massive kauri pine counter dominates the front lounge, where you can read the papers or use the guests' computer for Internet access. 65 Park St., South Yarra, VIC 3141. ✆ **03/9868 4800.** Fax 03/9868 4899. www.hatton.com.au. 20 units. A$195–A$220 (US$156–US$176/UK£78–UK£88) standard double; A$300 (US$240/UK£120) suite. Extra person or crib A$30 (US$24/UK£12). Rates include continental breakfast. AE, DC, MC, V. Free off-street parking. Tram: No 8 from Swanston St. **Amenities:** Business center; in-room massage; dry cleaning and laundry service; nonsmoking rooms. *In room:* A/C, TV, dataport (and free wireless access), kitchenette, minibar, fridge, coffeemaker, hair dryer, iron, CD player.

Hotel Claremont The high ceilings and the mosaic tiles in the lobby welcome visitors into this old-world hotel. It's an attractive place, though sparsely furnished. The AAA-rated three-star rooms are comfortable enough; each comes with either a double or a single bed. There is no elevator in this three-story building with 72 stairs, so it could be a bad choice for travelers with disabilities. Internet access is available.

189 Toorak Rd., South Yarra, Melbourne, VIC 3141. ✆ **1300/301 630** in Australia, or 03/9826 8000. Fax 03/9827 8652. www.hotelclaremont.com. 80 units, none with bathroom. A$82 (US$66/UK£33) double; A$35 (US$28/UK£14) dorm (6 beds). Extra person A$20 (US$16/UK£8). Children stay free in parent's room. Rates include continental breakfast. AE, DC, MC, V. Free on-street parking; off-street parking A$12 (US$9.60/UK£4.80) per day. **Amenities:** Coin-op laundry; nonsmoking rooms. *In room:* TV.

4 Where to Dine

Melbourne's ethnically diverse population ensures a healthy selection of international cuisines. Chinatown, in the city center, is a fabulous hunting ground for Chinese, Malaysian, Thai, Indonesian, Japanese, and Vietnamese fare, often at bargain prices. Carlton has plenty of Italian cuisine, but the outdoor restaurants on Lygon Street aim at unsuspecting tourists and can be overpriced and disappointing; avoid them. Richmond is crammed with Greek and Vietnamese restaurants, and Fitzroy has cheap Asian, Turkish, Mediterranean, and vegetarian food. To see and be seen, head to Chapel Street or Toorak Road in South Yarra, or to St. Kilda, where you can join the throng of Melbournians dining out along Fitzroy and Acland streets. Most of the cheaper places in Melbourne are strictly BYO (bring your own wine or beer). Smoking is banned by law in cafes and restaurants, so don't even think about lighting up.

IN THE CITY CENTER

EXPENSIVE

Flower Drum ★★★ CANTONESE Praise pours in from all quarters for this upscale restaurant just off Little Bourke Street, Chinatown's main drag. Take a slow elevator up to the restaurant, which has widely spaced tables (perfect for politicians and businesspeople to clinch their deals). Take note of the specials—the chefs are extremely creative and use the best ingredients they find in the markets each day. The best idea is to put your menu selections in the hands of the waiter. The signature dish is Peking duck. King crab dumplings in soup is a great starter, and you can also order more unusual dishes, such as abalone. The atmosphere is clubby and a bit old-fashioned, but the service is beyond reproach. But be prepared to pay for the privilege.

17 Market Lane. ✆ **03/9662 3655.** Reservations required. Main courses A$30–A$45 (US$24–US$36/UK£12–UK£18). AE, DC, MC, V. Mon–Sat noon–2:30pm and 6–10pm; Sun 6–10:30pm.

Koko ★★ JAPANESE Though you'll find plenty of Japanese sushi and noodle bars around Chinatown, there's nothing quite like raw fish with a bit of panache. A visit to Crown Casino Entertainment Complex can be a memorable experience in itself, but stop off here and you'll wish you could remember these tastes forever. The restaurant has contemporary-traditional decor, with a goldfish pond in the center of the main dining room and wonderful views over the city. There are separate teppanyaki grills and screened tatami rooms where you sit on the matted floor. If you can manage grilled freshwater eel, go for it. Otherwise, there's a vast and changing seasonal menu which includes lots of seafood dishes or you can opt for a set menu to take the agony out of choosing. A large selection of different sakes helps digestion.

Where to Dine in Melbourne

Babka Bakery **6**
Bamboo House **7**
Becco **8**
Brunetti **1**
Café Segovia **18**
Chocolate Buddha **20**
Flower Drum **11**
Grossi Florentino **10**
Hopetoun Tearooms **17**
Il Bacaro **13**
Il Primo **3**
Il Solito Posto **15**
Irish Times **19**
Koko **22**
Le Restaurant **14**
Mario's **5**
Nudel Bar **9**
Shakahari **4**
Sheni's Curries **16**
Supper Inn **12**
Tjanabi @ Fed Square **12**
Vue du Monde **2**

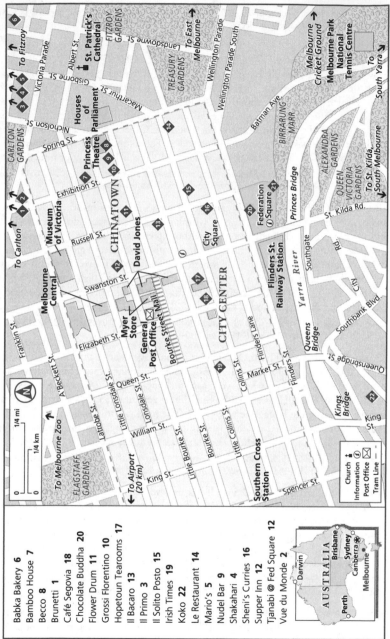

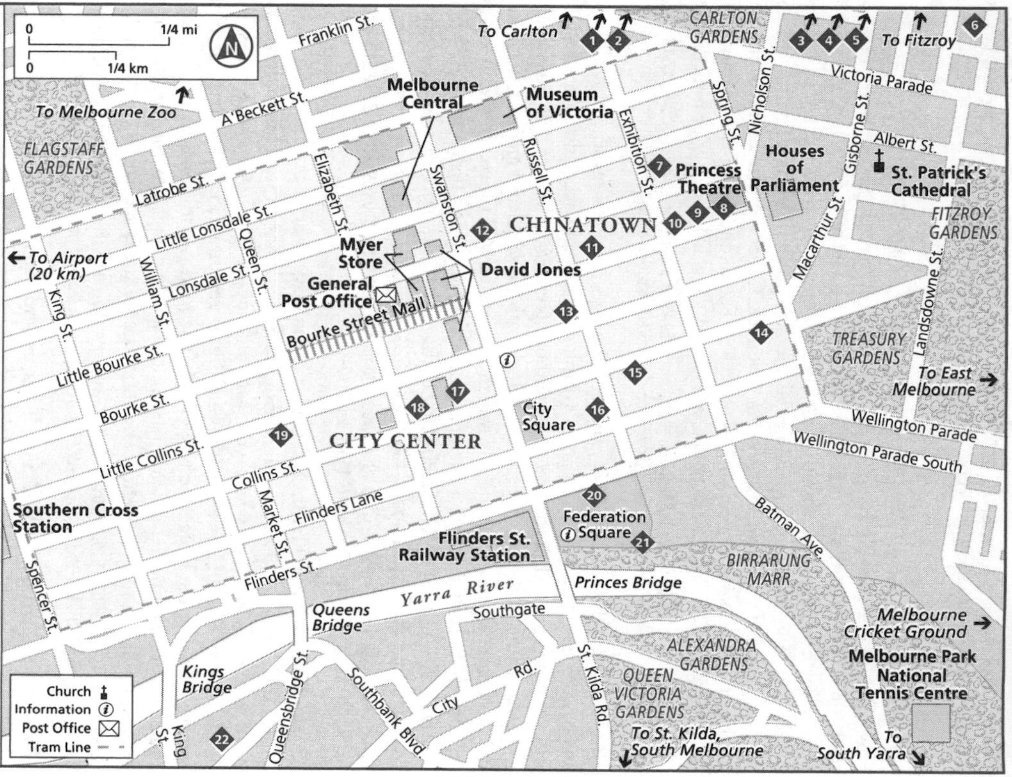

Level 3, Crown Towers, Southbank. ✆ **03/9292 6886.** Reservations required. Main courses A$30–A$48 (US$24–US$38/UK£12–UK£19). AE, DC, MC, V. Daily noon–2:30pm and 6–10:30pm.

MODERATE

Bamboo House ★ NORTHERN REGIONAL CHINESE/CANTONESE If Flower Drum (see above) is full or breaks your budget, try this place, esteemed by both the Chinese community and local business big shots. The service is a pleasure, and the food is worth writing home about. The waiters will help you construct a feast from the myriad Cantonese and northern Chinese dishes. It's worth ordering ahead to get a taste of the signature dish, Szechuan crispy fragrant duck. Other popular dishes include pan-fried beef dumplings and spring onion pancakes. The set menus for two to four people start at A$44 (US$35/UK£18) per person, for which you'll get eight or nine dishes.

47 Little Bourke St. ✆ **03/9662 1565.** Reservations recommended. Main courses A$22–A$30 (US$18–US$24/UK£9–UK£12). AE, DC, MC, V. Mon–Fri noon–3pm; Mon–Sat 5:30–11pm; Sun 5:30–10pm.

Becco ★ MODERN ITALIAN Tucked away in a lane, this favorite of Melbournians has not disappointed in 7 years of winning awards and accolades. Here you find stylish service and stylish customers, all without pretension. The cuisine mixes Italian favors with Australian flair. Try the roast duck with muscatel and grappa sauce, one of the tasty pasta dishes or the specials, which your waiter will fill you in on. If you prefer something lighter, there's a bar menu of equally tempting dishes from A$5.50 to A$16 (US$4.40–US$13/UK£2.20–UK£6.40). On the upstairs level is the ultracool late-night bar, **Bellavista Social Club** (p. 613).

11–25 Crossley St., near Bourke St. ✆ **03/9663 3000.** Main courses A$26–A$40 (US$21–US$32/UK£10–UK£16). AE, DC, MC, V. Mon–Sat noon–3pm and 6–11pm; Sun 5:30–10pm.

Grossi Florentino ★ ITALIAN Under the management of the Grossi family, this is probably the best Italian restaurant in Melbourne. It has a casual bistro downstairs, next to the Cellar Bar (where you can pick up a bowl of pasta for less than A$20/US$16/UK£8); upstairs is the fine-dining restaurant, with its chandeliers and murals reflecting the Florentine way of life. The food is traditional Italian, including the signature wet-roasted suckling lamb and suckling pig. On the menu, too, are risotto, seafood, and steak dishes. The chocolate soufflé is special.

80 Bourke St. ✆ **03/9662 1811.** Fax 03/9662 2518. www.grossiflorentino.com. Reservations recommended. Main courses A$35–A$65 (US$28–US$52/UK£14–UK£26). AE, DC, MC, V. Mon–Fri noon–3pm; Mon–Sat 6–11pm.

Il Bacaro ★ ITALIAN Walk into Il Bacaro and you'll feel as if you've been transported to Venice. Dominated by a horseshoe-shaped bar, it's jampacked with small tables and weaving waiters carrying dishes like organic baby chicken wrapped in prosciutto, filled with pumpkin and ricotta, served on an oyster mushroom ragu. The pasta dishes and the risotto of the day always go down well, as do the salad side dishes. It's often crowded at lunch with businesspeople digging into the excellent wine list.

168–170 Little Collins St. ✆ **03/9654 6778.** Reservations recommended. Main courses A$19–A$39 (US$15–US$31/UK£7.60–UK£16). AE, DC, MC, V. Mon–Sat noon–3pm and 6–11pm.

Il Solito Posto NORTHERN ITALIAN This below-ground restaurant consists of two parts. The casual bistro has a blackboard menu offering good pastas, soups, and salads. Then there's the sharper and more upmarket trattoria, with its a la carte menu offering the likes of steak, fish, and veal dishes. The coffee is excellent, too.

113 Collins St., basement (enter through George Parade). ✆ **03/9654 4466.** Reservations recommended. Main courses A$15–A$17 (US$12–US$14/UK£6–UK£7) in bistro, A$25–A$33 (US$20–US$26/UK£10–UK£13) in trattoria. AE, DC, MC, V. Mon–Fri 7:30am–1am; Sat 9am–1am. Closed late Dec to early Jan.

Nudel Bar NOODLES A favorite with city slickers, the Nudel Bar serves a variety of noodle dishes to diners at the crowded tables and bar. Examples include cold, spicy green-tea noodles and *mie goreng* (a noodle dish with peanuts and, here, often chicken). The signature dish is macaroni cheese and sticky rice pudding is a favorite for dessert.

76 Bourke St. ✆ **03/9662 9100.** Reservations recommended Fri–Sat night. Main courses A$13–A$20 (US$10–US$16/UK£5.20–UK£8). AE, DC, MC, V. Mon–Fri 11am–10:30pm; Sat 11am–11pm.

Tjanabi @ Fed Square INDIGENOUS AUSTRALIAN If you want to get a taste of what Aboriginal Australians have been eating for thousands of years, stop in at Aboriginal elder Carolyn Briggs' new Tjanabi (it means "to celebrate") restaurant at Federation Square. Native produce including plants, fruits, and berries, matched with quality Australian game (kangaroo, wild boar, barramundi) and fresh steaks from regional Victoria are on the menu—things like native pepper, lemon myrtle, roasted wattleseed, and saltbush leaves. There's a casual bistro outside, and a bar serving Victorian wines and boutique beers. The walls are adorned with contemporary Aboriginal artworks, in changing exhibitions. You can also book a 90-minute guided walking tour of indigenous Melbourne, which takes in the Ian Potter Centre: NGV Australia (p. 602), followed by dinner.

Federation Sq. ✆ **03/9662 2155.** www.tjanabi.com.au. Reservations recommended. Main courses A$9–A$20 (US$7.20–US$16/UK£3.60–UK£8) in the bistro, A$28–A$34 (US$22–US$27/UK£11–UK£14) in the restaurant. AE, DC, MC, V. Tues–Sun 11am–11pm. Closed Mon.

INEXPENSIVE

Café Segovia ★★ *Finds* CAFE This is one of my favorites. Café Segovia is always friendly, always busy, and in an atmospheric laneway. It has an intimate interior, and there's also seating outside in the arcade, but you'll have to come early at lunchtime to nab a chair. It serves typical cafe food, such as focaccias, cakes, and light meals (but the servings are generous). There's live music Thursday and Friday.

33 Block Place. ✆ **03/9650 2373.** Main courses A$16–A$27 (US$13–US$22/UK£6.40–UK£11). AE, DC, MC, V. Mon–Sat 8am–11pm; Sun 9am–5pm.

Chocolate Buddha *Finds* NOODLES This place offers mostly organic produce, including some organic wines. Based generally on Japanese-inspired noodle, ramen, and soba dishes to which the kitchen adds meat, chicken, or seafood, it's casual yet particularly satisfying dining. The food is creative, and the view across the square to the Yarra River and Southbank is a delight at dusk.

Federation Sq., corner of Flinders and Swanson sts. ✆ **03/9654 5688.** Main courses A$17–A$20 (US$14–US$16/UK£6.80–UK£8). AE, MC, V. Daily noon–10:30pm.

Hopetoun Tearooms ★ CAFE The first cup of coffee served in this Melbourne institution left the pot in 1892. It's very civilized, with green-and-white Regency wallpaper and marble tables. The cakes are very good. Scones, croissants, and grilled food are also available. A minimum charge of A$5 (US$4/UK£2) per person applies from noon to 2pm.

Shops 1 and 2, Block Arcade, 280–282 Collins St. ©/fax **03/9650 2777.** Main courses A$4.50–A$9.50 (US$3.60–US$7.60/UK£1.80–UK£3.80); sandwiches A$4.50–A$6.50 (US$3.60–US$5.20/UK£2.90–UK£4.15); focaccias A$7–A$8.50 (US$5.60–US$6.80/UK£2.80–UK£3.40). AE, DC, MC, V. Mon–Thurs 8:30am–5pm; Fri 8:30am–6pm; Sat 10am–3:30pm.

Sheni's Curries SRI LANKAN This tiny (it seats 30), basic, very busy place offers a range of excellent-value, authentic Sri Lankan curries. You can dine here or take your lunch special to go. Choose from three vegetable dishes and a selection of meat and seafood options. All meals come with rice, three types of chutney, and a pappadum. You can also buy extra items such as samosas and roti.

Shop 16, 161 Collins St. (corner of Flinders Lane and Russell St., opposite the entrance to the Grand Hyatt). © **03/9654 3535.** Lunch specials A$5.50–A$12 (US$4.40–US$9.60/UK£2.20–UK£4.80). No credit cards. Mon–Fri 11am–4pm.

Supper Inn CANTONESE Head here if you get the Chinese-food munchies late at night. It's a friendly place with a mixed crowd of locals and tourists chowing down on such dishes as steaming bowls of *congee* (rice-based porridge), barbecued suckling pig, mud crab, or stuffed scallops. Everything here is the "real thing!"

15 Celestial Ave. ©/fax **03/9663 4759.** Reservations recommended. Main courses A$11–A$22 (US$8.80–US$18/UK£4.40–UK£8.80). AE, DC, MC, V. Daily 5:30pm–2:30am.

CARLTON

Brunetti ★ TRATTORIA/PASTICCERIA Don't be daunted by the crowds around the cake counters—and there will be crowds. For a real Italian experience, get past the mouthwatering array of excellent cakes and head to the a la carte restaurant section. The lunch and dinner menu features authentic Italian cuisine, done very well. Or pop in for coffee and cake, or a gelato. If you can't get to Carlton, there's a cafe-style **Brunetti City Square** at Swanston Street and Flinders Lane in the city.

198–204 Faraday St., Carlton. © **03/9347 2801.** Main courses A$17–A$28 (US$14–US$22/UK£6.80–UK£11), with a minimum charge of A$18 (US$14/UK£7) per person. AE, DC, MC, V. Mon–Fri 7am–10pm; Sat 8am–10pm; Sun 8am–1pm. Tram: 1, 15, 21, or 22 traveling north on Swanston St.

Il Primo ★ SOUTHERN EUROPEAN This restaurant is tucked away in a pair of historic houses in the Italian sector of Carlton. The three cozy dining areas have antique bricks, wood-beamed ceilings, and tiled floors. It feels as though you're dining in a wine cellar, and indeed, there's a great wine list, including a range of unlabeled local wines at rock-bottom prices. The menu changes regularly, but you'll often see veal parmigiana, warm kangaroo salad, fish, garlic prawns, risotto, and pasta dishes. Live jazz brings in the customers every night from 10 or 11pm to closing time.

242 Lygon St., Carlton. © **03/9663 6100.** Reservations recommended. Main courses A$17–A$28 (US$14–US$22/UK£6.80–UK£11). AE, DC, MC, V. Tues–Fri 11:30am–late. Tram: 1, 15, 21, or 22 traveling north on Swanston St. (stop 12).

Shakahari VEGETARIAN Good vegetarian food isn't just a meal without meat; it's a creation in its own right. Shakahari assures you of a creative meal that's not at all bland. The large restaurant is quite low-key, but the service can be a bit inconsistent. The "Satay Legend"—skewered, lightly fried vegetables and tofu pieces with a mild but spicy peanut sauce—is a winner, as is the tagine of spiced turmeric couscous with a Moroccan herbal eggplant, zucchini, and tomato ratatouille. Also available are curries, croquettes, tempura avocado, and a fragrant laksa. Wine is available by the glass.

201–203 Faraday St., Carlton. © **03/9347 3848.** Main courses A$15–A$17 (US$12–US$14/UK£6–UK£6.80). AE, DC, MC, V. Mon–Sat noon–3:30pm; Sun–Thurs 6–9:30pm; Fri–Sat 6–10:30pm. Tram: 1, 15, 21, or 22 traveling north along Swanston St.

FITZROY

Mario's ITALIAN This place has ambience, groovy '60s decor, great coffee, and impeccable service. Offerings include a range of pastas and cakes. Breakfast is served all day. The art on the wall, all by local artists, is always interesting and for sale, too.

303 Brunswick St., Fitzroy. © **03/9417 3343.** Main courses A$11–A$18 (US$8.80–US$14/UK£4.40–UK£7.20). AE, DC, MC, V. Daily 7am–11pm.

ST. KILDA

Chinta Blues MALAYSIAN Head to this very popular eatery if you're looking for simple, satisfying food with a healthy touch of spice. The big sellers are laksa, *mie goreng,* chicken curry, *sambal* spinach, and a chicken dish called *ayam* blues. Lots of noodles, too. It's very busy, especially at lunch. They do take-away as well.

6 Acland St., St. Kilda. © **03/9534 9233.** Reservations recommended. Main courses A$13–A$25 (US$10–US$20/UK£5.20–UK£10). AE, MC, V. Daily noon–2:30pm; Sun–Thurs 6–10:30pm; Fri–Sat 6–11pm. Tram: 16 from Swanston St. or 96 from Bourke St.

Cicciolina ★★ CONTEMPORARY Telling you about Cicciolina is a hard decision. It's difficult enough to get a table at this wonderful place, which doesn't take bookings, without encouraging more people to line up. But I'd be depriving you of a terrific night out if I kept quiet. So let's just say that if you are looking for somewhere that's intimate, crowded, well-run, and has superb but simple food, you should look no further. You may have to wait for an hour or so for your seat (have a drink in the back bar, and they'll call you) but it will be worth it for delights such as yellowfin tuna carpaccio soused in lime-infused olive oil, beef carpaccio crusted with mustard and coriander seeds, or—my favorite—spaghettini tossed with spinach, chile, and oil.

130 Acland St., St. Kilda. © **03/9525 3333.** Main courses A$14–A$37 (US$11–US$30/UK£5.60–UK£15). AE, DC, MC, V. Daily noon–11pm (10pm on Sun). Tram: 16 from Swanston St., or 94 or 96 from Bourke St.

Donovans ★★ CONTEMPORARY A glass in hand while the sun goes down over St. Kilda beach, watched from the veranda at Donovans, is a perfect way to end the day. Gail and Kevin Donovan have transformed a 1920s bathing pavilion into a welcoming restaurant that's designed so you feel you're in their home (or at least their beach house). Lots of cushions, a log fire, coffee-table books, and the sound of jazz and breakers on the beach complete the picture. If that's not enough, the menu includes a mind-boggling array of dishes, many big enough for two. Chef Robert Castellani's trademarks include steamed mussels, linguine with seafood, and stuffed squid.

40 Jacka Blvd., St. Kilda. © **03/9534 8221.** Reservations recommended. Main courses A$19–A$48 (US$15–US$38/UK£7.60–UK£19). AE, DC, MC, V. Daily noon–10:30pm. Tram: 12 from Collins St., 16 from Swanston St., or 94 or 96 from Bourke St.

Tips The Staff of Life

The aroma of fresh bread attracts you to **Babka Bakery,** a Russian-style cafe-bakery which is nearly always packed. Come for breakfast or a light lunch of eggs on fresh sourdough, quiches, tarts, and brioches. Or perhaps try the homemade borscht. It's at 358 Brunswick St. in Fitzroy (© **03/9416 0091**).

Value **Pay What You Think**

With a novel approach that's not surprisingly become a hit, vegetarian restaurant **Lentil As Anything** has a menu without prices. Here, you can eat then pay whatever you feel the meal and service is worth. The food is organic, with lots of noodles and vegetables and things like tofu, curries, and stir-fries. Before you leave, you put your money in a box. There are four in Melbourne—at Abbotsford (**© 03/9419 6444**), St. Kilda (**© 03/9534 5833**), and Brunswick (**© 03/9388 0222**), where there is also **Lentil Africa** (**© 03/9387 4647**), run by a local African women's cooperative. They take cash only. Opening hours vary, so check the website, **www.lentilasanything.com**.

DOCKLANDS

Mecca Bah ★★ *Finds* *Kids* MIDDLE EASTERN Overlooking the Yarra River in the up-and-coming waterside precinct of Docklands, and a short trip from the city center, is this excellent Middle Eastern restaurant. You could go for a main course, such as a lamb or chicken tagine, but the best way to eat is to order several of the *meze* plates—little dishes of delicacies. Expect the likes of pastry filled with Middle Eastern cheeses, silverbeet rolls filled with chickpeas, rice, and herbs, or spicy lamb and pine nut *boureks* (meat-filled pastries)—whatever you choose, you'll be really impressed. There's also an interesting range of Turkish pizzas, too. The wine list is really good and not too expensive. Highly recommended. You could cruise up the river to get here with Melbourne River Cruises (see "Getting Around," earlier in this chapter).

55 Newquay Promenade, Docklands. **© 03/9642 1300.** www.meccabah.com. Reservations recommended. Main courses A$18–A$21 (US$14–US$17/UK£7.20–UK£8.40); meze plates A$6–A$12 (US$4.80–US$9.60/UK£2.40–UK£4.80). AE, DC, MC, V. Daily 11am–11pm. Tram: 30 or 48 from Latrobe or Swanston sts.

5 Seeing the Sights

Melbourne's attractions may not have quite the fame as some of Sydney's, but visitors come here to experience the contrasts of old-world architecture and the exciting feel of a truly multicultural city.

THE TOP ATTRACTIONS

City Museum at Old Treasury Designed by the architect J. J. Clarke (when he was only 19) and built in 1857, the Old Treasury Building is an imposing neoclassical sandstone structure that once housed precious metal from the Ballarat and Bendigo gold rushes. The gold was stored in eight thick-walled vaults underground and protected by iron bars. Today the building tells the story of Melbourne through several permanent exhibits and a variety of changing ones. "Making Melbourne" tells the city's history, while "Built on Gold" shows how Melbourne was built using the profits from the gold rushes. In the basement are the restored quarters of a caretaker who lived there from 1916 to 1928. Allow about 1 hour.

Old Treasury Building, Spring St. (top of Collins St.). **© 03/9651 2233.** Admission A$8.50 (US$6.80/UK£3.40) adults, A$5 (US$4/UK£2) children, A$18 (US$14/UK£7.20) families. Mon–Fri 9am–5pm; weekends and public holidays 10am–4pm. Closed Dec 25 and 26 and Good Friday. Tram: City Circle.

Melbourne Attractions

Birrarung Marr **21**
Cook's Cottage **9**
The Eureka Skydeck 88 **17**
Federation Square **13**
Fitzroy Gardens **8**
Gold Treasury Museum **11**
IMAX Theatre **4**
Latrobe's Cottage **23**
Melbourne Aquarium **16**
Melbourne Museum **5**
Melbourne Observation Deck **15**
Melbourne Zoo **2**
National Gallery of Victoria: the Ian Potter Centre-Australian Art **12**
National Gallery of Victoria, International **19**
Old Melbourne Gaol **3**
Queen Victoria Markets **1**
Royal Botanic Gardens **22**
Shrine of Remembrance **20**
St. Patrick's Cathedral **7**
St. Paul's Cathedral **14**
State Houses of Parliament **6**
Treasury Gardens **10**
Victorian Arts Centre **18**

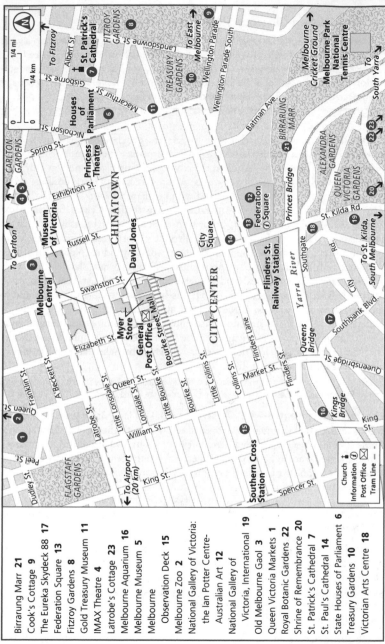

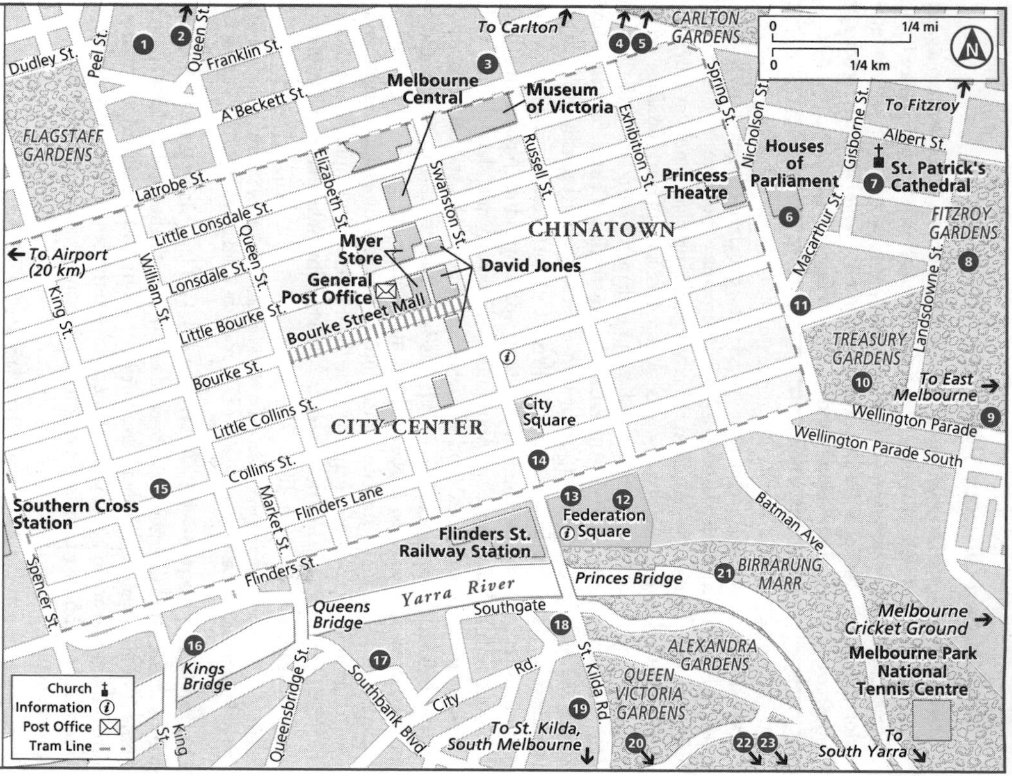

Tips Sorting Out Your Sightseeing

Much of Melbourne's appeal comes from soaking up the atmosphere on a walk around the city. If you have time to see only one major attraction, make it the atmospheric **Old Melbourne Gaol.** Other top-of-the-list sights include **Federation Square,** the **National Gallery of Victoria,** and the **Royal Botanic Gardens.** If you have time, head to **Phillip Island** to see the fairy penguins.

Federation Square ★★ You have to get into Federation Square, physically, to appreciate it. The controversial design—Melbournians either love it or hate it (I fall into the former category)—has given the city a gathering place, and you only have to visit at the weekends to see that it works. A conglomerate of attractions are centered on a large open piazza-style area cobbled with misshapen paving. Here you'll find the **The Ian Potter Centre: NGV Australia,** the **Australian Centre for the Moving Image (ACMI),** and a one-stop Visitor Centre (see "Visitor Information," earlier in this chapter). The three-level National Gallery of Victoria contains the largest collection of Australian art in the country, including works by Sidney Nolan, Russell Drysdale, and Tom Roberts, as well as Aboriginal and Torres Strait Islanders. The Gallery is a major focus for art festivals and special events. Many cafes and coffee shops operate throughout the precinct. The ACMI has two state-of-the-art cinemas and large areas where visitors can view movies, videos, and digital media. It's worth visiting "Fed Square" just to see the architecture, made up of strange geometrical designs, and the glassed atrium. Lots of events happen in the square's 450-seat amphitheater, including theatrical performances and free concerts. Other events take place on the plaza and along the banks of the Yarra River.

Flinders St. to the Yarra River (running north-south; to the left, facing Flinders St. Railway Station). www.federationsquare.com.au. Free admission; charges for some special events and exhibitions. Outdoor spaces open 24 hr. Tram: City Circle.

The Ian Potter Centre—NGV Australia ★ This fascinating gallery, featuring 20 rooms dedicated to Australian art, opened in 2002 in the heart of Federation Square. Some 20,000 objects are stored here, but only about 800 are on display at any one time. Aboriginal art and colonial art collections are the centerpieces of the gallery, but you will find modern paintings here, too. Temporary exhibitions include anything from ceramics to shoes.

Federation Sq. (runs north-south from Flinders St. to the Yarra River). ✆ **03/8660 2222.** www.ngv.vic.gov.au. Free admission. Tues–Sun 10am–5pm. Closed Mon (except public holidays), Good Friday, Dec 25, and until 1pm on Apr 25. Bus: City Explorer.

IMAX Theatre *Kids* This eight-story movie screen rivals the world's largest screen, at Sydney's Darling Harbour. Recent subjects have been exploration of Mars, the Nile River, the deep oceans, and fighter-pilot training.

Melbourne Museum Complex, Rathdowne St., Carlton. ✆ **03/9663 5454.** www.imaxmelbourne.com.au. Admission from A$18 (US$14/UK£7.20) adults, A$13 (US$10/UK£5.20) children 3–15, A$50 (US$40/UK£20) family of 4. Daily 10am–10pm. Closed Dec 25. Tram: City Circle.

Melbourne Aquarium *Overrated* The Melbourne Aquarium stretches over three levels and features a Barrier Reef–type exhibit, some interesting jellyfish displays, and an enormous walk-through tank with larger fish, sharks, and rays. However, if you've been to Sydney's aquarium, it may not measure up. Allow 30 minutes.

Corner of Queens Wharf Rd. and Kings St., opposite Crown Casino. ✆ **03/9620 0999.** www.melbourneaquarium.com.au. Admission A$24 (US$19/UK£9.60) adults, A$14 (US$11/UK£5.60) children 3–15, A$65 (US$52/UK£26) families of 5. Daily 9:30am–6pm. Tram: City Circle.

Melbourne Museum ★ *Kids* This museum opposite the 19th-century Royal Exhibition Buildings is Australia's largest and one of the most interesting. Some of the highlights include a real blue whale skeleton (you can't miss it), an indoor rainforest, and a truly brilliant insect and butterfly collection with lots of real-life exhibits, including cockroaches, ant colonies, and huge spiders. Apart from that there are interactive exhibits and science displays; Bunjikata, the award-winning Aboriginal and Torres Strait Islander Centre; and bits and pieces of social history, including a stuffed racehorse called Phar Lap. Check out the brightly colored Children's Museum, which will bring hours of enjoyment to the little ones. Allow 2 hours.

Melbourne Museum, 11 Nicholson St., Carlton. ✆ **13 11 02** in Victoria, or 03/8341 7777. Admission A$6 (US$4.80/UK£2.40) adults, free for children under 16. Daily 10am–5pm. Closed Good Friday and Dec 25. Tram: 86 or 96 to the Museum and Royal Exhibition Building tram stop at the corner of Nicholson and Gertrude sts., or the free City Circle Tram to Carlton Gardens.

Melbourne Zoo ★★ *Kids* Built in 1862, this is the oldest zoo in the world, and makes a great day out if you've got kids. There are some 3,000 animals here, including the ever-popular kangaroos, wallabies, echidnas, koalas, wombats, and platypuses. Rather than being locked in cages, most animals are in almost natural surroundings or well-tended gardens. Don't miss the butterfly house, with its thousands of colorful

---

Moments **The Air Up There**

Once Melbourne's highest lookout, the **Melbourne Observation Deck** now has hot competition in the bid to claim the city's best views. From May 2007, Melbourne has had a new vertigo-challenging experience. Unless you have an extreme fear of heights, head to the **Eureka Skydeck 88,** the highest public vantage point in the Southern Hemisphere. On the 88th floor of the Eureka Tower (Riverside Quay, Southbank; ✆ **03/9685 0188;** www.eurekatower.com.au), the viewing deck gives a 360-degree view of the city below from 285m (935 ft.) above ground. But there's more adrenaline-pumping action than just the view. A huge moving glass cube called The Edge is a 6-ton horizontal elevator, which moves from inside the walls of Skydeck 88, carrying 12 passengers out over the tower's east side. As the opaque glass cube reaches its full extension, the reinforced, 45 millimeter-thick (1¾-in.) glass becomes clear, giving passengers uninterrupted—and incredibly scary—views below, above, and to three sides. All this accompanied by recorded sounds of creaking chains and breaking glass—just to scare you more! Ticket prices are A$17 (US$14/UK£6.80) adults and A$9 (US$7.20/UK£3.60) children, plus an extra A$12 (US$9.60/UK£4.80) adults and A$8 (US$6.40/UK£3.20) children for the 4-minute-long ride on The Edge. Open daily 10am to 10pm. By contrast, the Melbourne Observation Deck on the 55th floor—that's 253m (830 ft.) above the street—of the Rialto Building, 525 Collins St. (✆ **03/9629 8222;** www.melbournedeck.com.au), now seems a bit tame. Admission A$15 (US$12/UK£6) adults, A$8 (US$6.40/UK£3.20) children 5 to 15, A$40 (US$32/UK£16) family of six. Daily 10am to 11pm.

---

occupants flying around; the free-flight aviary; the lowland gorilla exhibit; and the treetop orangutan exhibit. Allow at least 90 minutes if you just want to see the Australian natives, and around 4 hours for the whole zoo.

Elliott Ave., Parkville. ✆ **03/9285 9300.** www.zoo.org.au. Admission A$22 (US$18/UK£8.80) adults, A$11 (US$8.80/UK£4.40) children 4–15, A$52 (US$42/UK£21) families of 4. Daily 9am–5pm. Free guided tours daily from 10am–3pm; go to the Friends of the Zoo Office to arrange tours. Free parking. Tram: 55 going north on William St. to stop 25; 19 from Elizabeth St. to stop 16 (then a short walk to your left, following signposts). Train: Royal Park Station.

National Gallery of Victoria, International Opened to critical acclaim in late 2003, the NGV International is a showcase for Australia's finest collections of international art. There are four Gainsboroughs and four Constables here, as well as paintings by the likes of Bonnard, Delacroix, Van Dyck, El Greco, Monet, Manet, Magritte, and Rembrandt. Architecturally, the building is a masterpiece, with high ceilings, fabulous lighting, and great open spaces.

180 St. Kilda Rd. ✆ **03/8620 2222.** www.ngv.vic.gov.au. Free admission to general collection; fees for some temporary exhibitions. Wed–Mon 10am–5pm. Closed Tues, Good Friday, Dec 25, and until 1pm on Apr 25. Tram: 1, 3, 5, 6, 8, 16, 22, 25, 64, 67, or 72 from Swanston St. to Victorian Arts Centre stop (ask driver).

Old Melbourne Gaol ★★★ *Finds* I love this historic old prison, with its tiny cells and spooky collection of death masks and artifacts of 19th-century prison life. Some 135 hangings took place here, including that of notorious bushranger (and Australian folk hero) Ned Kelly, in 1880. The scaffold where he was hanged still stands, and his gun, as well as a suit of armor used by a member of his gang, is on display. The jail closed in 1929. Profiles of former prisoners give a fascinating perspective of what it was like to be locked up here. Each Saturday, free performances of "The Real Ned Kelly Story—Such a Life" are held at 12:30pm and 2pm (but be warned, when we attended a small girl burst into tears). Chilling night tours run every Monday, Wednesday, Friday, and Saturday, where you can experience the jail by candlelight with a "hangman," who will recount stories of the jail, its inmates, and his infamous art. Not for the fainthearted or children under 12. Tickets, available from Ticketek (✆ **13 28 49** or www.ticketek.com.au), cost A$25 (US$20/UK£10) for adults, A$17 (US$14/UK£6.80) for children under 15. Allow 1 hour or more.

Russell St. ✆ **03/9663 7228.** Admission A$13 (US$10/UK£5.20) adults, A$7.50 (US$6/UK£3) children, A$34 (US$27/UK£14) families. Daily 9:30am–5pm. Closed Good Friday and Dec 25. Tram: City Circle tram to corner of Russell and Latrobe sts.

Parliament House Victoria Now the home of the Victorian Parliament, this monument to Victorian (as in Queen Victoria) architecture at the top of a run of sandstone steps was built in 1856. During the Australian Federation (1900–27), it was used as the National Parliament. When the State Government is in session—generally on Tuesday afternoon and all day Wednesday and Thursday between March and July, and again between August and November (there's a break between sessions)—you can view the proceedings from the public gallery. However, you should ring ahead and check, as sitting times do vary. During non-sitting times, both the opulent Upper House and the less ornate Lower House chambers are open to the public. Allow 30 minutes.

Spring St. ✆ **03/9651 8568** or 03/9651 8569. www.parliament.vic.gov.au. Mon–Fri 9am–5pm. Free guided tours Mon–Fri 10 and 11am, noon, and 2, 3, and 3:45pm when Parliament is not in session. Reservations recommended.

Queen Victoria Market ★ This Melbourne institution covers several blocks. There are hundreds of indoor and outdoor stalls, where you can find anything from live rabbits to bargain clothes. The markets can get cramped, and there's a lot of junk to sort through, but you'll get a real taste of Melbourne and its ethnic mix. Look out for the interesting delicatessen section and cheap eateries. Allow at least an hour. The 2-hour **Foodies Tour** of the market explores its food and heritage. It departs Tuesday, Thursday, Friday, and Saturday at 10am and costs A$28 (US$22/UK£11) per person, including sampling. Well-known chefs give cooking classes, costing A$75 to A$80 (US$60–US$64/UK£30–UK£32) per session. Call ✆ **03/9320 5835** for reservations. **Night markets** are held every Wednesday from 5:30 to 10pm in summer (from late Nov to late Mar, except the last week of Dec).

Between Peel, Victoria, Elizabeth, and Therry sts. on the northern edge of the city center. ✆ **03/9320 5822.** www.qvm.com.au. Tues and Thurs 6am–2pm; Fri 6am–6pm; Sat 6am–3pm; Sun 9am–4pm. Closed Mon, Wed, and public holidays. Food stalls closed Sun. Tram: Any tram traveling north along William St. or Elizabeth St.

Rippon Lea Estate This grand Victorian house, 8km (5 miles) from the city center, is worth a visit to get a feel for old-money Melbourne. Socialite Sir Frederick Thomas Sargood built Rippon Lea House between 1868 and 1903; a pool and ballroom were added in the 1930s. Though the Romanesque architecture is interesting (note the stained glass and polychrome brickwork), the downside is that entry to the house is by guided tour only (I prefer to wander at my own pace). The real attraction is the 5.3 hectares (13 acres) of landscaped gardens, which include a conservatory, lake, and lookout tower. The tearoom is open on weekends, public holidays, and during school vacations, from 11am to 4pm. Allow 2 hours.

192 Hotham St., Elsternwick. ✆ **03/9523 6095.** Admission A$12 (US$9.60/UK£4.80) adults, A$6.50 (US$5.20/UK£2.60) children 5–16, A$30 (US$24/UK£12) families of 6. Daily 10am–5pm (house closes at 4:45pm). Daily guided tours of house every half-hour 10:30am–4pm; tour of estate 2pm. Closed Mon–Wed in winter (May to late Sept), Good Friday, and Dec 25. Tram: 67 to stop 40, then walk up Hotham St. Bus: 216/219 from Bourke and Queen sts. in the city to stop 4. Train: Sandringham Line from Flinders St. Station to Rippon Lea Station.

St. Patrick's Cathedral Though lacking the intricacy of design of St. Paul's (see below), Roman Catholic St. Patrick's is another interesting Gothic Revival construction with exceptional stained-glass windows. Built between 1858 and 1940 (consecrated in 1897), St. Patrick's was closely associated with immigrants from Ireland escaping the mid-19th-century potato famine. In the courtyard out front is a statue of the Irish patriot Daniel O'Connell.

Cathedral Place, East Melbourne. ✆ **03/9662 2233.** Mon–Fri 6:30am–6pm; Sat–Sun 7:15am–7:30pm. Free admission.

St. Paul's Cathedral Built from 1880 to 1892 from the designs of William Butterfield, a famous English Gothic Revival architect, St. Paul's Cathedral is noteworthy for its decorative interior and the English organ built by T.S. Lewis. Step in to see mosaics on the walls, Victorian tessellated tiles on the floors, woodcarvings, and stained-glass windows. The cathedral sports the second-highest spire (98m/321 ft.) in the Anglican Communion. A boys' choir sings at 5:10pm Tuesday through Friday during school times, and at Sunday services. Outside is a statue of Matthew Flinders, the first sailor to navigate the Australian mainland between 1801 and 1803.

Flinders and Swanston sts. ✆ **03/9650 3791.** Sun–Fri 8am–6pm; Sat 9am–5pm. Free guided tours at 11am and 2pm Mon–Fri. Services Sun 8, 9, and 10:30am; Evensong 6pm. Eucharist Mon–Fri 7:45am, 12:15pm, 5:10pm; Sat 12:15pm. Cathedral shop daily 10am–3:30pm.

PARKS & GARDENS

Birrarung Marr, along the Yarra River east of Federation Square on Batman Avenue (✆ **03/9658 9658;** www.melbourne.vic.gov.au/parks), is Melbourne's first new major parkland in more than 100 years. *Birrarung* means "river of mists" in the Woiwurrung language of the Wurundjeri people who originally inhabited the area; *marr* equates with the side of the river. Wide-open spaces and large, sculptured terraces were designed to host some of Melbourne's best events and festivals throughout the year, and the terraces give way to spectacular views of the city, Southbank, King's Domain, and the Yarra River.

The **Royal Botanic Gardens** ★★, 2km (1¼ miles) south of the city on Birdwood Avenue, off St. Kilda Road (✆ **03/9252 2300**), are the best gardens in Australia and well worth a few hours of wandering. More than 40 hectares (99 acres) are lush and blooming with more than 12,000 plant species from all over the world. Don't miss a visit to the oldest part of the garden, the Tennyson Lawn, with its 120-year-old English elm trees. Other special corners include a fern gully, camellia gardens, an herb garden, rainforests packed with fruit bats, and ponds full of ducks and black swans. Bring snacks and your picnic blanket to Shakespeare in the Park, a popular summer event from January to March. Tickets cost A$20 to A$35 (US$16–US$28/UK£8–UK£14). Call ✆ **03/8676 7511** for details. The gardens are open November through March daily from 7:30am to 8:30pm; April, September, and October daily from 7:30am to 6pm; and May through August daily from 7:30am to 5:30pm. Admission is free. To get there, catch the no. 8 tram, traveling south, and get off at stop 21. Allow 2 to 4 hours.

Nearby, in King's Domain, take a look at Victoria's first Government House, **Latrobe's Cottage** (✆ **03/9654 5528**). It was built in England and transported to Australia brick by brick in 1836. The cottage is open from 1 to 4pm on Sundays. Admission is by gold coin donation. You can also view it on a Government House tour (bookings essential, ✆ **03/9656 9841**) on Mondays and Wednesdays. On the other side of Birdwood Avenue is the **Shrine of Remembrance,** a memorial to the servicemen lost in Australia's wars. It's designed so that at 11am on Remembrance Day (Nov 11), a beam of sunlight hits the Stone of Remembrance in the Inner Shrine. Note the eternal flame in the forecourt. King's Domain is stop 12 on the no. 15 tram traveling south along St. Kilda Road.

In Fitzroy Gardens, off Wellington Parade, is **Cooks' Cottage** (✆ **03/9419 4677**), which was moved to Melbourne from Great Ayton, in Yorkshire, England, in 1934 to mark Victoria's centenary. The cottage was built by the parents of Captain Cook, and today it provides the opportunity to learn about his voyages of discovery around the world. Inside, it's spartan and cramped, not unlike a ship's cabin. Admission is A$4 (US$3.20/UK£1.60) for adults, A$2 (US$1.60/UK80p) for children 5 to 15, and A$11 (US$8.80/UK£4.40) for a family. It's open daily from 9am to 5pm (except Dec 25). Also east of the central business district are the **Treasury Gardens.** Look for the memorial to John F. Kennedy near the lake. To reach Treasury Gardens and Fitzroy Gardens, take tram no. 75 traveling east along Flinders Street. Get off at stop 14 for Treasury Gardens, stop 14A for Fitzroy Gardens.

6 Enjoying the Great Outdoors or Catching an Aussie Rules Football Match

OUTDOOR ACTIVITIES

BALLOONING **Balloon Sunrise** (✆ **1800 992 105** in Australia, or 03/9730 2422; fax 03/9730 2433; www.hotairballooning.com.au), offers flights over the city plus a champagne breakfast at the Grand Hyatt hotel afterward. Dawn flights cost A$345 (US$276/UK£138) for adults, and A$240 (US$192/UK£96) for children aged 6 to 12. Hotel pickup (but not drop-off) is included. Reservations are essential.

BIKING Extensive bicycle paths wind through the city and suburbs. For details on popular routes, pick up a copy of *Bike Rides Around Melbourne* by Julia Blunden (Open Spaces Publishing) which has 37 great rides with good directions and clear maps. *Bike Paths Victoria* also has some good maps of rides around Melbourne and Victoria. You can buy both books from **Bicycle Victoria,** Level 10, 446 Collins St., Melbourne (© **1800 639 634** in Australia, or 03/9636 8888; www.bv.com.au), and it is also worth checking our their website, which is a font of information. Bicycle Victoria also runs several major cycling tours throughout the state every year.

Real Melbourne Bike Tours (© **0417/339 203** mobile phone) can help you find your bearings and discover some of hidden Melbourne . . . the back streets and bluestone lanes, markets, cafes, arcades, and bike paths. Run by journalist Murray Johnson, the tours are fun and interesting. The cost is A$80 (US$64/UK£32), including bike hire, helmet, half-day guided tour, drinks, and snacks. Tours leave at 9am (or other times by arrangement) from Rentabike, Shop RE04 at Waterfront City, Docklands (take the free City Circle tram to New Quay and walk along the promenade to Waterfront City). Your ride takes in Docklands; the Crown entertainment promenade; Southbank; the MCG sports precinct; hidden inner-city shopping laneways; public gardens; bohemian Smith, Gertrude, and Brunswick streets' shops and cafes; Lygon Street; and the bustling Queen Victoria Market for a gourmet picnic lunch. Tours can be customised to suit your needs. Bookings are essential.

GOLF One of the best public golf courses in Australia is **Yarra Bend,** Yarra Bend Road, Fairfield (© **03/9481 3729**). Greens fees A$21 (US$17/UK£8.40) Monday to Friday, A$22 (US$18/UK£8.80) Saturday and Sunday; juniors pay A$10 (US$8/UK£4). Club rental is an extra A$25 (US$20/UK£10) for a full set and A$12 (US$9.60/UK£4.80) for a half-set.

The exclusive **Royal Melbourne Golf Club** (© **9598 6755;** www.royalmelbourne.com.au), in the suburb of Black Rock, 24km (15 miles) from the city center, is rated as one of the world's 10 best golf courses. If you have a letter of introduction from your golf club at home, a handicap of under 26 for men and 32 for women, and don't mind the A$360 (US$288/UK£144) greens fee for overseas visitors, you might be able to get a round.

For more information on golf in Victoria, contact the **Victorian Golf Association,** 15 Bardolph St., Burwood (© **03/9889 6731;** www.golfvic.org.au).

TENNIS The venue for the Australian Open, the **Melbourne Park National Tennis Centre,** on Batman Avenue (© **1300/836 647** in Australia, or 03/9286 1244), is a great place to play. When tournaments are not scheduled, its 22 outdoor courts (including the show courts) and seven indoor courts are open to the public. You can rent courts Monday through Friday from 7am to 11pm, Saturday and Sunday from 9am to 6pm. Charges range from A$26 to A$40 (US$21–US$32/UK£10–UK£16) per hour, depending on the court and time (outdoor courts are cheapest). Show courts 1, 2, and 3 are for rent at the same prices. Rackets are available for hire.

SPECTATOR SPORTS

CAR RACING The annual **Australian Formula One Grand Prix** takes place in March at Albert Park, about 3km (2 miles) from central Melbourne. Call Ticketek (© **13 28 49** in Australia) or check out the Grand Prix's website at www.grandprix.com.au for information on tickets, accommodations, and airfares.

CRICKET From October through March, cricket's the name of the game in Melbourne. The **Melbourne Cricket Ground (MCG),** Brunton Avenue, Yarra Park, Jolimont, is perhaps Australia's most hallowed cricket field. The facility (the main stadium for the 1956 Melbourne Olympic games) can accommodate 97,500 people. For the uninitiated, "one-day" games are the ones to look out for; "Test" games take several days to complete. Buy tickets at the gate or in advance from **Ticketmaster** (**© 13 61 00** in Australia; www.ticketmaster.com).

Tours of the MCG and its museum (**© 03/9657 8864;** www.mcg.org.au) start every half-hour daily from 10am to 3pm. Tours take about 75 minutes and cost A$15 (US$12/UK£6) for adults, A$11 (US$8.80/UK£4.40) for children, and A$40 (US$32/UK£16) for a family of four. The tour price includes admission to the Australian Gallery of Sport and the Olympic Museum, which are also at the MCG. They're open daily from 9:30am to 4:30pm. The Olympic Museum traces the development of the modern Olympics with individual display sections for each city. Tours leave from Gate 3 in the Olympic Stand on non-event days only. Also in the complex is a coffee shop that serves snacks and lunch.

FOOTBALL Melbourne's number-one sport is **Australian Rules Football**—or simply "the footy"—a skillful, fast, and sometimes violent game the likes of which you've never seen (unless you have ESPN). Melbourne is home to 10 of the 16 Australian Football League (AFL) teams, with the others coming from Adelaide, Perth, Sydney, and Brisbane. The season starts on the third weekend in March and ends with the Grand Final on the last Saturday in September. The most accessible fields are at the Melbourne Cricket Ground (take tram no. 75 along Wellington Parade), Telstra Dome (behind Southern Cross Station in Spencer St.), and the Optus Oval at Carlton (take tram no. 19 from Elizabeth St.). The cheapest tickets cost around A$20 (US$16/UK£8) per person, or A$40 (US$32/UK£16) for a family. For game information, call **AFL Headquarters** (**© 03/8663 3000;** www.afl.com.au). Buy tickets through **Ticketmaster** (**© 13 61 00** in Australia; www.ticketmaster.com.au).

HORSE RACING The **Melbourne Cup,** on the first Tuesday in November, has been contested by the best of Australia's thoroughbreds (and a few from overseas) since 1861. Melbourne society puts on a show, dressing up for the occasion, and the entire nation stops in its tracks to at least tune in on TV.

The city has four racetracks: **Flemington** (which holds the Melbourne Cup), 400 Epsom Rd., Flemington (**© 1300 727 575** in Australia, or 03/8378 0888; www.vrc.net.au); **Moonee Valley,** McPherson Street, Mooney Ponds (**© 03/9373 2222;** www.mvrc.net.au); **Caulfield,** Station Street, Caulfield (**© 03/9257 7200;** www.melbourneracingclub.net.au); and **Sandown,** Racecourse Drive, Springvale (**© 03/9518 1300**). If you're staying in the city center, Flemington and Moonee Valley are the easiest to get to. Take tram no. 57 from Flinders Street to reach the Flemington racetrack, and catch tram no. 59 from Elizabeth Street to Moonee Valley.

TENNIS The **Australian Open** ★, one of the four Grand Slam events, is played during the last 2 weeks of January every year at the Melbourne Park National Tennis Centre, Batman Avenue (**© 03/9286 1244**). Tickets go on sale in mid-October and are available through **Ticketek** (**© 13 28 49;** www.ticketek.com.au) and on the Open's website, www.australianopen.com. To get there, take a train from the Flinders Street Station at the bottom of Swanston Street to Richmond Station and catch the special Tennis Centre tram from there.

7 Shopping

Ask almost any Melbournian to help you plan your time in the city, and he or she will advise you to shop until you drop. All Australia regards Melbourne as a shopping capital—it has everything from fashion houses to major department stores and unusual souvenir shops. So even if you're also visiting Sydney, save your money until you get to Melbourne, and then indulge!

Start at the magnificent city arcades, such as the **Block Arcade** (between Collins and Little Collins sts.), which has more than 30 shops, including the historic Hopetoun Tearooms (p. 597), and the **Royal Arcade** (stretching from Little Collins St. to the Bourke St. Mall). Then hit the courts and lanes around **Swanston Street** and the huge **Melbourne Central shopping complex** between Latrobe and Lonsdale streets.

Next, fan out across the city, taking in **Chapel Street** in South Yarra, for its Australian fashions, and **The Jam Factory,** 500 Chapel St., South Yarra (© **03/9860 8500**), which is a series of buildings with a range of shops and food outlets, including a large branch of Borders bookshop, as well as 16 cinema screens. Get there on tram no. 8 or 72 from Swanston Street.

There's also **Toorak Road** in Toorak, for Gucci and other high-priced, high-fashion names; **Bridge Road** in Richmond, for budget fashions; **Lygon Street** in Carlton, for Italian fashion, footwear, and accessories; and **Brunswick Street** in Fitzroy, for a more alternative scene.

Serious shoppers might like to contact **Shopping Spree Tours** (© **03/9596 6600;** www.shoppingspree.com.au), a company that takes you to exclusive and alternative shopping venues, manufacturers, and importers you wouldn't be likely to find by yourself. Tours depart Monday through Saturday (except public holidays) at 8:30am and cost A$74 (US$59/UK£30) for adults and A$35 (US$28/UK£14) for children under 12. They will pick you up at one of six hotel locations in the city center.

MELBOURNE SHOPPING FROM A TO Z

ABORIGINAL CRAFTS

The Aboriginal Gallery of Dreamings This place stocks an extensive range of acrylic dot paintings and represents more than 120 artists. Boomerangs, didgeridoos, pottery, jewelry, bark paintings, prints, books, and music are also available. 73–77 Bourke St. Mall. © **03/9650 3277.**

Original & Authentic Aboriginal Art Stop here for original artworks, traditional bark paintings, and informative presentations. 90 Bourke St. © **03/9663 5133.** www.authaboriginalart.com.au.

CRAFTS

A good **arts-and-crafts market** is held on the Esplanade in St. Kilda on Sunday from 9am to 4pm. Take tram no. 16 from Swanston Street or no. 96 from Bourke Street.

The Australian Geographic Shop Head here for high-quality Australiana, including crafts, books, and various gadgets. Shop 253, Melbourne Central, 300 Lonsdale St. © **03/8616 6725;** and Galleria Shopping Plaza, Little Collins St. © **03/9670 5813.**

DEPARTMENT STORES

David Jones Like Myer (see below), its direct competition, David Jones—or DJ's, as it's affectionately known—spans 2 blocks, separated into men's and women's stores, and offers similar goods. Don't miss the food hall. 310 Bourke St. Mall. © **03/9643 2222.** www.davidjones.com.au.

Myer This is the grande dame of Melbourne's department stores, and is in hot competition with David Jones. It has household goods, perfume, jewelry, and fashions, as well as a food section. The clothes here are usually more modern and stylish than those at David Jones. 314 Bourke St. Mall. © **03/9661 1111.** www.myer.com.au.

FASHION

High-fashion boutiques line the eastern stretch of **Collins Street,** between the Grand Hyatt and the Hotel Sofitel, and **Chapel Street** in South Yarra. In addition, thousands of retail shops and factory outlets are around the city, many of them on **Bridge Road** near Punt Road and **Swan Street** near Church Street in Richmond. You'll find designer clothes, many just last season's fashions, at a fraction of the original price.

In the city, the hottest new fashion center is the QV building, which takes up a whole block, bordered by Swanston, Russell, Lonsdale, and Little Lonsdale streets. Despite its size, it has a nice feel to it. This is where you will find top Australian and international designers, tucked into QV's laneways. The premium fashion alley is Albert Coates Lane, where you'll find the likes of Christensen Copenhagen, Cactus Jam, and Wayne Cooper.

Collins Street features most international labels as well as shoe heaven **Miss Louise,** 123 Collins St. (© **03/9654 7730**). Nearby Flinders Lane has earned style status with the likes of **Christine,** 181 Flinders Lane (© **03/9654 2011**), where women have been known to faint over the accessories. Down the road is **Little Collins Street,** another fashion-rat run. Look for local labels **Bettina Liano** (© **03/9654 1912**), **Scanlan & Theodore** (© **03/9650 6195**), and **Verve** (© **03/9639 5886**). **Alice Euphemia,** 37 Swanston St. (© **03/9650 4300**), also stocks upcoming Australian and New Zealand designers.

Country Road Country Road is one of Australia's best-known names for men's and women's fashion. The cool, classic looks don't come cheap, but the quality is worth it. County Road also sells designer cooking equipment and housewares. 260 Collins St. and Melbourne Central on Lonsdale St., and other locations, including Toorak Rd., South Yarra. © **1800/801 911** in Australia, or 03/9650 5288. www.countryroad.com.au.

Ozmosis In addition to surfboards, boogie boards, and sunglasses, this store stocks a wide range of hip and happening beachwear at reasonable prices. All the big names in Australian surf wear are here, including Ripcurl, Quicksilver, and Billabong. 2 Melbourne Central, Lonsdale St. © **03/9662 3815.** www.ozmosis.com.au.

Saba Australian designer Joseph Saba has several in-vogue, very expensive boutiques for men and women in Melbourne, including one for women at 564 Chapel St., South Yarra. 234 Collins St. © **03/9654 3524.** www.saba.com.au.

Sam Bear Sam Bear is a good bet for Outback-style fashions: Driza-bone coats, Akubra bush hats, R.M. Williams boots and clothing, and Blundstone boots. It also sells a solid range of camping equipment. 225 Russell St. © **03/9663 2191.** www.sambear.com.au.

Vegan Wares Instead of leather, Vegan Wares uses microfiber to create tough, stylish shoes, bags, and belts. It's not just for vegetarians; carnivores enjoy it, too! 78 Smith St., Collingwood. © **03/9417 0230.** www.veganwares.com.

FOOD

Haigh's Chocolates Indulge in some 50 types of Australia's best chocolate, from milk to dark to fruit flavored. Try the Sparkling Shiraz truffle if you need a serious treat. 26 Collins St. ✆ **03/9650 2114;** and Shop 27, Block Arcade, 282 Collins St. ✆ 03/9654 7673. www.haighschocolates.com.

JEWELRY

Altman & Cherny Even if you're not in the market to buy, it's worth coming here to check out "Olympic Australis," the largest precious-gem opal in the world. It was found in Coober Pedy in South Australia in 1956 and is valued at A$2.5 million (US$2 million/UK£1 million). The store offers tax-free shopping for tourists armed with both a passport and an international airline ticket. 120 Exhibition St. ✆ **03/9650 9685.**

Dinosaur Designs Dinosaur Designs is taking the jewelry design world by storm with its range of artistic pieces made out of resin. The shop has modern housewares as well. None of it's cheap, but the odd item won't break the bank. 562 Chapel St., South Yarra. ✆ **03/9827 2600.** www.dinosaurdesigns.com.au.

e.g.etal Shop here for fresh, innovative jewelry by 50 or so of Australia's leading and emerging designers. 185 Little Collins St. ✆ **03/9663 4334.** 167 Flinders Lane. ✆ 03/9639 5111. www.egetal.com.au.

8 Melbourne After Dark

Melbourne can be an exciting place once the sun has set. The pubs and bars are far better than those in Sydney. Friday and Saturday nights will see most pubs (of both the trendy and the down-to-earth variety) packed to the rafters, and at lunchtime those that serve food are popular, too. To find out what's happening, check the Friday entertainment guide in *The Age,* Melbourne's daily broadsheet.

THE PERFORMING ARTS

Melbourne is the most dynamic performing-arts city in Australia. Its theaters offer the gamut, from offbeat independent productions to large-scale Broadway-style musicals. The city is also the home of the most prestigious festivals, with the annual **Melbourne Fringe Festival** (the first 3 weeks in Oct; **www.melbournefringe.com.au**) and the annual **Melbourne International Comedy Festival** (from the end of Mar to the end of Apr; **www.comedyfestival.com.au**), attracting top Australian and international talent.

Venues all over the city participate in the Melbourne International Comedy Festival, and the Fringe Festival sees the streets, pubs, theaters, and restaurants playing host to everyone from jugglers and fire-eaters to musicians and independent productions covering all art forms. Try to get tickets if you're in town during either festival, but keep in mind that hotels fill up fast at these times. Another good time to plan your visit is during the annual **Melbourne International Film Festival** (late July through mid-Aug; **www.melbournefilmfestival.com.au**), when new releases, shorts, and avant-garde movies play at venues around the city.

The official government entertainment information site, **www.melbourne.vic.gov.au/events**, shows "What's On" in the theater world for up to 2 months in advance, as well as what's happening in dance, film, comedy, music, exhibitions, sports, and tours.

The best place to buy tickets for everything from theater to major sporting events, and to obtain details on schedules, is **Ticketmaster** (✆ **13 61 00** in Australia; www.ticketmaster.com.au).

THE HEART OF MELBOURNE'S CULTURAL LIFE

The Arts Centre ★★ The spire atop the Theatres Building of The Arts Centre, on the banks of the Yarra River, crowns the city's leading performing arts complex. Beneath it, the State Theatre, the Playhouse, and the Fairfax Studio present performances that are the focal point of culture in Melbourne.

The **State Theatre,** seating 2,085 on three levels, can accommodate elaborate stagings of opera, ballet, musicals, and more. The **Playhouse** is a smaller venue that often books the Melbourne Theatre Company. The **Fairfax** is more intimate still, and is often used for experimental theater or cabaret. Adjacent to the Theatres Building is **Hamer Hall,** home of the Melbourne Symphony Orchestra and often host to visiting orchestras. Many international stars have graced this stage, which is known for its excellent acoustics.

Guided tours are run at noon and 2:30pm Monday to Saturday, and backstage tours on Sundays at 12:15pm. Tours cost A$11 (US$8.80/UK£4.40) adults and A$28 (US$22/UK£11) for a family, or A$14 (US$11/UK£5.60) per person on Sundays. Buy tickets from the concierge in the foyer of the Theatres Building.

100 St. Kilda Rd. ✆ **1300/136 166** for tickets (plus a A$7.15/US$5.70/UK£2.85 booking fee), or 03/9281 8000. Fax 03/9281 8282. www.theartscentre.net.au. Ticket prices vary depending on the event. Box Office open 9am–9pm Mon–Sat in the Theatres Building.

ADDITIONAL VENUES & THEATERS

Check *The Age* to see what productions are scheduled during your visit. Odds are that the leading shows will take place in one of the following venues:

The Comedy Club The Comedy Club is a Melbourne institution. Come here to see local and international comedy acts, musicals, and special shows. It offers a dinner and show Friday and Saturday for A$35 (US$28/UK£14). Discount ticket offers can bring the show-only price down to as low as A$7 (US$5.60/UK£2.80) sometimes, so ask what's on offer. Athenaeum Theatre, 188 Collins St. ✆ **03/9650 6668.**

Comedy Theatre The Comedy Theatre, with its ornate Spanish rococo interior, feels intimate even though it seats more than 1,000 people. Plays and musicals usually fill the bill, but dance companies and comedians also appear. 240 Exhibition St. (at Lonsdale St.) ✆ **03/9299 4951.**

The Forum Theatre The Forum books well-known bands and international comedians. Tables and chairs are in cabaret-style booths, from which you can order drinks and meals. 154 Flinders St. ✆ **03/9299 9700.**

Her Majesty's Theatre A fire destroyed the original theater here, but the current structure, revamped in 2002, retains the original facade and the Art Deco interior

---

Value Half-Price Tickets

Buy tickets for entertainment events, including opera, dance, and drama, on the day of the performance from the **Half-Tix Desk** (www.halftixmelbourne.com) in the Melbourne Town Hall on Swanston Street. The booth is open Monday from 10am to 2pm, Tuesday through Thursday 11am to 6pm, Friday 11am to 6:30pm, and Saturday 10am to 4pm (also selling for Sun shows). Tickets must be purchased in person and in cash. Available shows are displayed on the booth door and on the website.

---

added during a 1936 renovation. Musicals, such as *Chicago* and *Miss Saigon,* frequent the boards. 219 Exhibition St. All bookings through Ticketek © **1300/792 012.**

The Princess Theatre This huge facility hosts extravaganza productions. The theater opened its doors in 1886, and it still has a dramatic marble staircase and ornate plaster ceilings. 163 Spring St. © **03/9299 9800.**

The Regent Theatre Built in 1929, The Regent fell into disrepair, and its stage was dark for 25 years. Now, after a A$35-million (US$28-million/UK£14-million) renovation, it's been restored to its former glory. Tickets are available in the U.S. through ATS Tours (© **800/423-2880**). The theater offers a range of dining packages. 191 Collins St. © **03/9299 9500.**

Sidney Myer Music Bowl This huge outdoor entertainment center, run under the auspices of The Arts Centre, schedules opera, jazz, and ballet in the warmer months (and ice-skating in the winter). King's Domain, Alexandra Ave. Bookings through Ticketmaster © **1300/136 166.**

CINEMAS

Most of the city cinemas are within 2 blocks of the intersection of Bourke and Russell streets. Tickets usually cost around A$15 (US$12/UK£6) for adults. Among the independent cinemas, the one that stands out is the **Astor,** 1 Chapel St. (at Dandenong Rd.), East St. Kilda (© **03 9510 1414**). Housed in a superb Art Nouveau building, the Astor shows classic movies.

THE CLUB & MUSIC SCENE

Melbourne's nightclub scene used to center on King Street, and while that area is still popular with large disco-style venues, the city is now awash in unique, hidden bars and clubs. It's best just to follow the crowds—or in some cases that couple slipping down a side lane and disappearing into a dimly lit entrance. Otherwise, the following options are more enduring in their appeal.

Bellavista Social Club Owned by the team at Becco (see "Where to Dine," earlier in this chapter), BVSC is upstairs from the popular restaurant, in a converted diamond-cutting workshop. Ultramodern in a microsuede way, this place jumps with a late-night crowd of many splendid hues—arty young things mingling with the suits, all watching the goings-on in the laneway below on a large-screen hookup. Open Wednesday to Saturday, 6pm to 3am. 11–25 Crossley St. © **03/9663 3000.**

Bennetts Lane Jazz Club ★ Often exceptional and always varied, this venue is the best in Australia for jazz. The back-lane location may be a little hard to find, but inside it's everything you've always imagined a jazz club to be. The best international players seek it out. Open every night from 8:30pm (music starts at 9:30pm). 25 Bennetts Lane. © **03/9663 2856.** www.bennettslane.com. Cover A$12 (US$9.60/UK£4.80).

Cicciolina Back Bar This softly lit, alluring hideaway offers plush leather booths and a fine range of cocktails. Add an attentive staff, and you've got one of the best little bars in the greater St. Kilda region. Open Monday to Saturday 4:30pm to 1am, Sunday 3:30 to 11pm. 130 Acland St. (enter from arcade), St. Kilda. © **03/9525 3333.**

Double Happiness This tiny but hugely atmospheric bar is detail at its best. The retro-Asian theme would make Chairman Mao proud. Mix with the hip crowd from the business world, and try the "Gang of Four" cocktail (mango, vodka, Cointreau, and lemon). Open Monday to Thursday 5pm to 1am (3am on Thurs), Friday 4:30pm to 3am, Saturday 6pm to 3am, and Sunday 6pm to 1am. 21 Liverpool St. (off Bourke St.). ✆ **03/9650 4488.**

Hi-Fi Bar & Ballroom Featuring lots of live music—mostly of the hard rock and contemporary persuasion—and patronized by the younger set, this cavernous underground venue features many visiting acts. Ticket prices vary but can be anywhere between A$15 and A$55 (US$12–US$44/UK£6–UK£22). 125 Swanson St. ✆ **03/9654 7617.** www.thehifi.com.au.

KingPin Why not combine your love for bowling and drinking?! Experience the purple lounge, which really mixes it up, with cool DJs and great cocktails. In the Crown Casino complex, this venue is open until 2am, so happy days really are here again. Bowling costs A$10 (US$8/UK£4) for the first game and A$8 (US$6.40/UK£3.20) for extra games (until 4pm) and A$16 (US$13/UK£6.40) per game after 4pm on Friday and Saturday, or A$14 (US$11/UK£5.60) and A$10 (US$8/UK£4) after 4pm Sunday to Thursday. 8 Whiteman St., Southbank. ✆ **132 695** in Australia, or 03/8646 4100.

Melbourne Supper Club Upstairs from an ever-popular European cafe-restaurant, the Melbourne Supper Club is a perfect post-theater venue. Deep leather lounges and a giant circular window that looks onto the beautifully lit Parliament House buildings make this bar a place to idle, smoke a cigar, or dwell over a bottle of your favorite wine. 161 Spring St. ✆ **03/9654 6300.**

Misty Place Funk meets Barbarella in this ultrahip and arty venue, one of the quintessential Melbourne bars. Here, down a cobbled lane (and then upstairs), smooth cocktails mix with live combos or soulful DJs. 3–5 Hosier Lane. ✆ **03/9663 9202.**

Revolver Upstairs This venue usually pumps with techno music, although bands play on weekends with dancing later. 229 Chapel St., Prahan. ✆ **03/9521 5985.** www.revolverupstairs.com.au. Cover varies.

Tony Starr's Kitten Club Don't be put off by the name—this is one great place. A restaurant-bar on the lower level serves an array of excellent tapas and more exotic fare. But the action is at the upstairs Galaxy Space, where most nights you'll find entertainment—ranging from the peculiar to the animated to just plain bizarre. Don't forget to visit the Love Lounge, with its floor-to-ceiling red fabric, heart-shaped lounges, and secluded booths. The club is open for lunch and dinner until 1am. 267 Little Collins St. ✆ **03/9650 2448.** Cover Sat A$5 (US$4/UK£2).

WHERE TO SHARE A PINT

Pubs generally stay open from midmorning until at least midnight most nights. Many remain open until 2 or 3am on Friday and Saturday night, and you can always find a few open 24 hours.

Belgian Beer Café Bluestone Belgian beer culture in all its forms. Pretend that you're in Brussels in this atmospheric cafe. Full-bodied Belgian brews dominate. While downing your pint, try the traditional streamed mussels. In warmer weather, sitting in the parklike garden is a delight. 557 St. Kilda Rd. ✆ **03/9529 2899.**

Chaise Lounge Any semblance of barroom normality breaks down at this chic boudoir-style place featuring lipstick-colored walls, a bust of a Roman god, diamanté-strung curtains, lounges, and glitter balls. Basement, 105 Queen St. ✆ **03/9670 6120.**

Cookie The latest hot place to hang out is an unlikely combination of good-value Thai eatery, beer hall, and smart cocktail bar, complete with plastic doilies and murals. It's open from noon to 3am daily. 252 Swanston St. ✆ **03/9663 7660.**

Finds Pick a Card . . . for a Unique Pub-Crawl

All the rage in Melbourne is a pack of 52 playing cards called **Bar Secrets Melbourne (www.bar-secrets.com)**. The cards have pictures of and information (including maps) on the hippest and most unusual pubs and cocktail bars in town. Locals pick out a few at random, and the night's planned. The cards cost A$9.95 (US$7.95/UK£4) at bookshops and newsdealers in town. They are well worth seeking out. You will find yourself weaving up dark alleyways, climbing into lofts and down into basements, and always being faced with somewhere unique.

The Cricketer's Bar Locals come to this popular English-style pub to lift a glass surrounded by the relics of Australia's summer passion. Glass cases are packed full of cricket bats, pads, and stumps, and the plush green carpets and solid mahogany woodwork give the place a touch of class. Two large plasma-screen TVs screen the latest sporting action. In The Windsor Hotel, 103 Spring St. ✆ **03/9633 6000.**

The Croft Institute This laneway (at the end of an alley) bar is a small, lurid, bottle-green establishment, which is notably famous for its powerful cocktails and the city's largest private collection of laboratory apparatus. For the young only. 21–25 Croft Alley. ✆ **03/9671 4399.**

Jimmy Watson's Wine Bar While probably not the best spot for a pint, Jimmy's is somewhat of an institution. One of Melbourne's oldest wine bars, it's a cozy affair where all types of people chat while sampling a vast range of wines. In the attached dining area, excellent food is expertly teamed with the perfect wine. Come to talk or simply read the paper. 333 Lygon St., Carlton. ✆ **03/9347 3985.**

The Prince St. Kilda This pub is a legend among the locals. Though refurbished, it retains its original rough-at-the-edges appearance. Bands, some of them big names, play most nights. 29 Fitzroy St. (at Acland St.), St. Kilda. ✆ **03/9536 1177.**

Windsor Castle Up Chapel Street and through Prahan are Windsor and its best-kept secret, the Windsor Castle Hotel, home of the local stylemeisters. This is a perfect weekend meeting place for good pub food, which you can enjoy in the sunny courtyard or in the plush interior. You'll find DJs and barbecue on weekends. Look for the giant pink elephants outside. 89 Albert St. (at Upton St.), Windsor. ✆ **03/9525 0239.**

Young & Jackson After a major renovation, Melbourne's oldest and most famous pub is a newfound pleasure, whether for a drink or a meal in the stylish upstairs restaurant or bistro areas. Head upstairs to see the nude *Chloe,* a famous painting brought to Melbourne for the Great Exhibition in 1880. The pub, which was built in 1853 and started selling beer in 1861, has a few years on *Chloe,* which was painted in Paris in 1875. The painting has a special place in the hearts of customers and Melbournians. At the corner of Flinders and Swanston sts. ✆ **03/9650 3884.** www.youngandjacksons.com.au.

THE CASINO

Crown Casino Australia's largest casino is a plush affair that's open 24 hours. You'll find all the usual roulette and blackjack tables and so on, as well as an array of gaming machines. This is also a major venue for international headline acts, and there are around 25 restaurants and 11 bars on the premises, with more in the extended Southgate complex. Clarendon St., Southbank. ✆ **03/9292 6868.** www.crowncasino.com.au.

9 Side Trips from Melbourne

DANDENONG RANGES

40km (25 miles) E of Melbourne

Melbournians traditionally do a "day in the Dandenongs" from time to time, topping off their getaway with Devonshire tea, scones, and jam at one of the many cafes en route. Up in the cool, high country you'll find native bush, famous gardens, the Dandenong Ranges National Park, historic attractions such as the Puffing Billy—a vintage steam train—and plenty of restaurants and cozy B&Bs. The Dandenong Ranges National Park is one of the state's oldest, set aside in 1882 to protect its mountain ash forests and lush tree-fern gullies.

GETTING THERE To get to the area, take the Burwood Highway from Melbourne, then the Mount Dandenong Tourist Road, which starts at Upper Ferntree Gully and winds through the villages of Sassafras, Olinda, Mount Dandenong, and Kalorama to Montrose. If you take a turnoff to Sherbrook, or extend your journey into a loop taking in Seville, Woori Yallock, Emerald, and Belgrave, you'll see a fair slice of the local scenery. A really good tour operator is **A Tour With A Difference** (© **1300/36 27 36** in Australia, or 03/9754 1699; www.atwad.com.au). They pick up from Melbourne hotels in a 10-person bus and do lots of great things in the Dandenongs, including a ride on the Puffing Billy. The tour costs A$129 (US$103/UK£52) and includes morning tea, lunch, and all entry fees.

VISITOR INFORMATION The **Dandenong Ranges & Knox Visitor Information Centre,** 1211 Burwood Hwy., Upper Ferntree Gully, VIC 3156 (© **1800/645 505** in Australia, or 03/9758 7522; fax 03/9758 7533), is open daily (except Good Friday and Dec 25) from 9am to 5pm.

NATURE WALKS

Most people come here to get out of the city for a pleasant bushwalk, and in that way it's the equivalent of Sydney's Blue Mountains. Some of the better walks include the easy 2.5km (1½-mile) stroll from the **Sherbrook Picnic Ground** through the forest, and the **Thousand Steps** and the **Kokoda Track Memorial Walk,** a challenging rainforest track from the Fern Tree Gully Picnic Ground up to One Tree Hill. Along the way are plaques commemorating Australian troops who fought and died in Papua New Guinea in World War II.

FOR GARDENING BUFFS

National Rhododendron Gardens From September through November, thousands of rhododendrons and azaleas burst into bloom in these magnificent gardens. There are 42 hectares (104 acres) in all, with a 3km (1¾-mile) walking path leading past flowering exotics and native trees as well as vistas over the Yarra Valley. A tearoom is open every day in the spring and on weekends at other times. Visitors flock here in summer for the walks, and in autumn when the leaves are turning.

The Georgian Rd., Olinda. © **03/8627 4699.** www.parkweb.vic.gov.au. Admission Sept–Nov A$8 (US$6.40/UK£3.20) adults, A$3 (US$2.40/UK£1.20) children 10–16, A$18 (US$14/UK£7.20) families; Dec–Aug A$6 (US$4.80/UK£2.40) adults, A$3 (US$2.40/UK£1.20) children, A$15 (US$12/UK£6) families. Daily 10am–5pm. Closed Dec 25. Train to Croydon, then bus no. 688 to the gardens, or train to Belgrave and bus no. 694.

Tesselaar's Bulbs and Flowers Tens of thousands of flowers are on display here, putting on a flamboyantly colorful show in the spring (mid-Sept to mid-Oct). Expect to see a dazzling variety of tulips, daffodils, rhododendrons, azaleas, fuchsias, and ranunculuses. Bulbs are on sale at discount prices at other times.

357 Monbulk Rd., Silvan. © **03/9737 9811.** Admission during tulip festival (mid-Sept to mid-Oct) A$15 (US$12/UK£6) adults, free for children under 16 accompanied by an adult; free for everyone rest of the year. During tulip festival daily 10am–5pm; rest of year Mon–Fri 8am–4:30pm, Sat–Sun 1–5pm. Train to Lilydale, then bus no. 679.

William Ricketts Sanctuary *Moments* This wonderful garden, in a forest of mountain ash, features clay figures representing the Aboriginal Dreamtime. The sculptures were created over the lifetime of sculptor William Ricketts, who died in 1993 at the age of 94. The garden encompasses fern gullies and waterfalls spread out over 13 hectares (32 acres), with the sculptures occupying .8 hectare (2 acres).

Mt. Dandenong Tourist Rd., Mt. Dandenong. © **03/9751 1300.** www.parkweb.vic.gov.au. Admission A$6 (US$4.80/UK£2.40) adults, A$5 (US$4/UK£2) students, A$3 (US$2.40/UK£1.20) children 10–14, A$15 (US$12/UK£6) families of 4. Daily 10am–4:30pm. Closed Dec 25 and days of total fire ban. Train to Croydon, then bus no. 688.

FOR TRAIN BUFFS

Puffing Billy Railway *Kids* For almost a century, Puffing Billy steam railway has chugged over a 13km (8-mile) track from Belgrave to Emerald Lake. Passengers ride on open carriages and enjoy lovely views as the train passes through forests and fern gullies and over a National Trust–classified wooden trestle bridge. Trips take around an hour each way. Daily trips on a further stretch of track to Gembrook take an extra 45 minutes and cost A$29 (US$23/UK£12) for adults, A$15 (US$12/UK£6) for children. Timetables can be a bit complicated and changeable, so check the website to ensure you have the right information. Special fares including lunch aboard the train are also available, and on Friday and Saturday nights you can have dinner on board for A$71 (US$57/UK£28) or A$81 (US$65/UK£32), including entertainment.

Belgrave Station, Belgrave. © **03/9754 6800** (recorded information). www.puffingbilly.com.au. Admission A$19 (US$15/UK£7.60) adults, A$10 (US$8/UK£4) children 4–16, A$66 (US$53/UK£26) families. Mon–Fri 10:30am, 12:20 and 2:15pm; Sat–Sun 10 and 10:30am, 12:30 and 2:15pm. Closed Dec 25. Train from Flinders St. Station in Melbourne to Belgrave; Puffing Billy station is a short walk away.

WHERE TO DINE

Wild Oak CONTEMPORARY Young chef Ben Higgs has turned this former cafe into the best restaurant in the Dandenongs. The food includes the likes of Nasi Goreng, an Indonesian-style fried rice with toasted peanuts, sweet chile omelet and fresh tofu, or the signature slow-cooked confit duck leg served with duckling galantine, French-style beans and thyme-infused jus. There are daily specials, scotch filet steak, and tasty vegetarian selections. They open for breakfast at the weekend, and there's live jazz on Friday nights and Sunday lunchtimes. In winter, there's a log fire.

232 Ridge Rd., Olinda. © **03/9751 2033.** www.wildoak.com.au. Main courses A$18–A$34 (US$14–US$27/UK£7.20–UK£14). AE, DC, MC, V. Wed–Fri noon–4pm and 6–11pm; Sat–Sun 9am–11pm.

YARRA VALLEY ★

61km (38 miles) E of Melbourne

The Yarra Valley is a winegrowing region east of Melbourne. It's dotted with villages, historic houses, gardens, crafts shops, antiques centers, and restaurants, as well as dozens of wineries.

ESSENTIALS

GETTING THERE **McKenzie's Bus Lines** (© **03/9853 6264;** www.mckenzies.com.au) operates bus service from Lilydale Railway Station to Healesville. (Catch a train from Melbourne's Spencer St. Station to Lilydale; the trip takes about an hour.) Buses connect with trains frequently throughout the day (less often on weekends); check exact connection times.

If you're driving, pick up a map of the area from the Royal Automotive Club of Victoria (✆ **03/9790 3333**) in Melbourne. Maps are free if you're a member of an auto club in your home country, but remember to bring your membership card. Alternatively, you can pick up a map at the tourist office. Take the Maroondah Highway from Melbourne to Lilydale and on to Healesville. The trip takes around 1 hour and 15 minutes.

VISITOR INFORMATION Pick up details on attractions and lodging at the **Yarra Valley Visitor Information Centre,** Old Court House, Harker Street, Healesville (✆ **03/5962 2600;** fax 03/5962 2040; www.visityarravalley.com.au). It's open daily (except Dec 25) from 9am to 5pm.

EXPLORING THE VALLEY

There are three principal roads in the valley: Melba Highway, Maroondah Highway, and Myers Creek Road, which form a triangle. Within the triangle are three smaller roads, Healesville–Yarra Glen Road, Old Healesville Road, and Chum Creek Road, which all lead to wineries. Most people start their tour of the Yarra Valley from Lilydale and take in several cellar-door tastings at vineyards along the route.

Balloon Aloft (✆ **1800/028 568** in Australia; www.balloonaloft.com.au) offers dawn balloon rides over the wineries, followed by a champagne breakfast, for A$265 (US$212/UK£106) for adults and A$180 (US$144/UK£72) for children aged 8 to 12.

Healesville Sanctuary Forget about seeing animals in cages—this preserve is a great place to spot native animals in almost-natural surroundings. You can see wedge-tailed eagles, dingoes, koalas, wombats, reptiles, and more, all while strolling through the peppermint-scented gum forest, which rings with the chiming of bellbirds. Sir Colin McKenzie started the sanctuary in 1921 as a center to preserve endangered species and educate the public. Since early 2006, visitors have been able to visit the Wildlife Health Centre (an animal rescue hospital) where they can see veterinarians caring for (and even operating on) injured or orphaned wildlife. There's a gift shop, a cafe serving light meals, and picnic grounds.

Badger Creek Rd., Healesville. ✆ **03/5957 2800.** Fax 03/5957 2870. www.zoo.org.au. Admission A$22 (US$18/UK£8.80) adults, A$11 (US$8.80/UK£4.40) children ages 4–15, A$52 (US$42/UK£21) families of 4. Daily 9am–5pm. Train from Flinders St. Station to Lilydale, then bus no. 685.

WHERE TO STAY & DINE

Melba Lodge ★ These modern accommodations are in Yarra Glen, in the heart of the Yarra Valley wine region. Of the luxurious guest rooms, four have queen-size beds, and two have king-size beds and a Jacuzzi; all have private bathrooms. There's a comfortable lounge with an open fire, and a billiard room. If you prefer, there's also a self-contained cottage. The lodge is only a few minutes' walk from historic Yarra Glen, which has antiques shops and a crafts market. There are plenty of restaurants and wineries around, too. It's a short drive to Healesville Sanctuary.

939 Melba Hwy., Yarra Glen, VIC 3775. ✆ **03/9730 1511.** Fax 03/9730 1566. www.melbalodge.com.au. 8 units. A$140–A$175 (US$112–US$140/UK£56–UK£70) queen room; A$170–A$205 (US$136–US$164/UK£68–UK£82) king room, penthouse, or cottage. Extra person A$20 (US$16/UK£8). Ask about weekend or dinner packages. Rates include cooked breakfast. AE, DC, MC, V. **Amenities:** Bar; Jacuzzi; business center; massage; nonsmoking rooms. *In room:* A/C, TV.

Sanctuary House Motel Healesville This place is very handy for visiting the sanctuary and even better if you want to relax and sample some good Yarra Valley wine. Just 400m (1,312 ft.) from the Healesville Sanctuary, Sanctuary House sits in some 4 hectares (10 acres) of beautiful bushland. The rooms are typical motel-style. Also available are two units with kitchens and amenities to assist travelers with disabilities. A cedar cottage has two suites, each with a queen-size bed.

Badger Creek Rd. (P.O. Box 162), Healesville, VIC 3777. © **03/5962 5148.** Fax 03/5962 5392. www.sanctuaryhouse.com.au. 22 units, all with shower. A$80–A$170 (US$64–US$136/UK£32–UK£68) double; A$110–A$135 (US$88–US$108/UK£44–UK£54) family room (sleeps 5); A$120–A$160 (US$96–US$128/UK£48–UK£64) self-contained units (sleep 4–6); A$110–A$120 (US$88–US$96/UK£44–UK£48) cottage (sleeps 4). MC, V. Train from Flinders St. Station to Lilydale, then bus no. 685. **Amenities:** Restaurant; small outdoor heated pool; Jacuzzi; sauna; children's play area; game room; massage; babysitting; laundry service; nonsmoking rooms. *In room:* A/C, TV, kitchenette (self-contained units only), fridge, hair dryer, iron.

PHILLIP ISLAND: PENGUINS ON PARADE ★

139km (86 miles) S of Melbourne

Phillip Island's **penguin parade,** which happens every evening at dusk, is one of Australia's most popular animal attractions. There are other, less crowded places in Australia where watching homecoming penguins feels less staged (such as Kangaroo Island in South Australia) but at least the guides and boardwalks protect the little ones and their nesting holes from the throngs. Nevertheless, the commercialism of the Penguin Parade puts a lot of people off—busloads of tourists squashed into a sort of amphitheater hardly feels like being one with nature. Phillip Island also offers nice beaches, good bushwalking, fishing, and Seal Rocks. If you have the time, you could spend at least 2 days here.

ESSENTIALS

GETTING THERE Most visitors come to Phillip Island on a day trip from Melbourne and arrive in time for the Penguin Parade and dinner. Several tour companies run day trips. Among them are **Gray Line** (© **03/9663 4455;** www.grayline.com), which operates penguin trips daily departing Melbourne at 1:30pm and returning at around 11:30pm. Tours cost A$117 (US$94/UK£47) for adults and A$59 (US$47/UK£24) for children, and can be booked online in U.S. dollars before arrival.

If you're driving yourself, Phillip Island is an easy 2-hour trip from Melbourne along the South Gippsland Highway and then the Bass Highway. A bridge connects the highway to the mainland.

V/Line (© **13 61 96** in Australia) runs a bus from Melbourne to Cowes, but does not take you to any of the attractions on Phillip Island. Once on the island, you need to hire a car, take a tour, or hire a push bike to get around. The Penguin Parade is 15km (9½ miles) from the center of Cowes.

VISITOR INFORMATION The **Phillip Island Visitor Information Centre,** 895 Phillip Island Tourist Rd., Newhaven (© **1300/366 422** in Australia, or 03/5956 7447; www.visitphillipisland.com), is an attraction in itself, with interactive computer displays, dioramas giving visitors a glimpse into the penguins' world, and a small theater. It's open daily from 9am to 5pm (to 6pm in summer), and 1 to 5pm Good Friday and December 25.

EXPLORING THE AREA

Visitors approach the island from the east, passing through the town of **Newhaven.** Just a little past Newhaven is the Phillip Island Information Centre.

The main town on the island, **Cowes** (pop. 2,400), is on the north coast. A stroll along its Esplanade is worthwhile. The Penguin Parade is on the far southwest coast.

The trip to the west coast of Phillip Island's Summerland Peninsula ends in an interesting rock formation called **The Nobbies.** This strange-looking outcropping can be reached at low tide by a basalt causeway. You'll get some spectacular views of the coastline and two offshore islands from here. On the farthest of these islands is a population of up to **12,000 Australian fur seals,** the largest colony in Australia (bring your binoculars). This area is also home to thousands of nesting silver gulls.

On the north coast of the island, you can explore **Rhyll Inlet,** an intertidal mangrove wetland, where you can see wading birds such as spoonbills, oystercatchers, herons, egrets, cormorants, and the rare bar-tailed godwit and whimbrel.

Birders will also love **Swan Lake,** another breeding habitat for wetland birds.

Elsewhere, walking trails lead through heath and pink granite to **Cape Woolamai,** the island's highest point, where there are fabulous coastal views. From September through April, the cape is home to thousands of short-tailed shearwaters (also known as mutton birds).

PHILLIP ISLAND ATTRACTIONS

Koala Conservation Centre Koalas were introduced to Phillip Island in the 1880s, and at first they thrived in the predator-free environment. However, overpopulation, the introduction of foxes and dogs, and the clearing of land for farmland and roads have taken their toll. Though you can still see a few koalas in the wild, the best place to find them is at this sanctuary, set up for research and breeding purposes. Visitors can get quite close to them, especially on the elevated boardwalk, which lets you peek into their treetop homes. At around 4pm, the ordinarily sleepy koalas are on the move—but this is also the time when a lot of tour buses converge on the place, so it can get crowded.

Fiveways, Phillip Island Tourist Rd., Cowes. © **03/5952 1307.** Admission A$9.20 (US$7.35/UK£3.70) adults, A$4.60 (US$3.70/UK£1.85) children 4–15, A$23 (US$18/UK£9.20) families of 4. Daily 10am–5pm.

Phillip Island Penguin Reserve ★ *Kids* The Penguin Parade takes place every night at dusk, when hundreds of little penguins appear at the water's edge, gather in the shallows, and waddle up the beach toward their burrows in the dunes. They're the smallest of the world's 17 species of penguins, standing just 33 centimeters (13 in.) high, and they're the only penguins that breed on the Australian mainland. Flash photography is banned because it scares the little guys, as are smoking and touching the penguins. Wear a sweater or jacket, because it gets chilly after the sun goes down. A kiosk selling food opens an hour before the penguins turn up. Reservations for the Penguin Parade are essential during busy holiday periods such as Easter and summer.

For a better experience, there are more exclusive small group tours which allow you a better view of the penguins. **Penguins Plus** allows you to watch the parade from an exclusive boardwalk in the company of rangers, while the **Penguin Sky Box** is an adults-only elevated viewing tower staffed by a ranger. The **"Ultimate Penguin Tour"** for groups of only 10 people (no children under 16), takes you to a secluded beach away from the main viewing area to see penguins coming ashore. Another option is a ranger-guided tour, a few hours before the penguins appear, to see behind-the-scenes research.

Summerland Beach, Phillip Island Tourist Rd., Cowes. © **1300/366 422** in Australia, or 03/5951 2800. www.penguins.org.au. Admission A$17 (US$14/UK£6.80) adults, A$8.70 (US$6.95/UK£3.50) children 4–15, A$44 (US$34/UK£18) families of 4. Admission to visitor center only A$4 (US$3.20/UK£1.60) adults, A$2 (US$1.60/UK80p) children 4–15, A$11 (US$8.80/UK£4.40) family of 4. Penguins Plus A$29 (US$23/UK£12) adult, A$15 (US$12/UK£6) child, A$72 (US$58/UK£29) family; Penguin Sky Box A$40 (US$32/UK£16); Ultimate Penguin Tour A$60 (US$48/UK£24); ranger guided tour A$10 (US$8/UK£4) adult, A$5 (US$4/UK£2) child, A$25 (US$20/UK£10) family, in addition to visitor center entry. Visitor center summer daily 9am–6pm; winter daily 9am–5pm.

WHERE TO STAY

Abaleigh on Lovers Walk ★ The beach is right on the doorstep of these gorgeous town house suites. The studios are designed for couples, and a beachfront apartment sleeps up to six. All come with kitchens, log fires, Jacuzzis, double showers, and water views. The kitchen is stocked with breakfast items for your arrival, and the best place to enjoy it is either in the private courtyard or on the veranda. You also get free fishing gear, beach chairs and umbrellas, magazines and books, and fresh flowers. Lovers Walk, a romantic floodlit path along the foreshore, is a 5-minute walk from the center of Cowes, with its cafes, restaurants, and shops.

6 Roy Court., Cowes, Phillip Island, VIC 3922. ✆ **03/5952 5649.** Fax 03/5952 2549. www.abaleigh.com. 8 units. A$175–A$210 (US$140–US$168/UK£70–UK£84) double. Extra person A$50 (US$40/UK£20). Rates include breakfast. AE, MC, V. Children not accepted. **Amenities:** Golf course nearby; tour desk; laundry service; nonsmoking rooms. *In room:* A/C, TV/VCR, kitchen, coffeemaker, hair dryer, iron, CD player.

Glen Isla House ★★ This is one of the best places to stay in Phillip Island. Set in lovely heritage gardens, the house was built around 1870 and is one of the oldest homes on the island, offering old-world charm and elegance. It's beachside location is perfect for visiting the penguins. There are five guest rooms in the house, as well as the Anderson Suite Cottage, which features a king-size four-poster bed and a Jacuzzi, and the Gate Cottage, which has two bedrooms. No children under 12.

230 Church St., Cowes, Phillip Island, VIC 3922. ✆ **03/5952 1882.** Fax 03/5952 5028. www.glenisla.com. 7 units. A$265 (US$212/UK£106) double; A$395 (US$316/UK£158) double Anderson cottage; A$300 (US$240/UK£120) double Gate Cottage, extra person A$30 (US$24/UK£12). Rates include breakfast. AE, DC, MC, V. Secure off-street parking. **Amenities:** Restaurant; bar; massage. *In room:* A/C, TV (cottages only), DVD, fridge, coffeemaker, hair dryer, iron.

Holmwood Guesthouse ★ This charming 1934 guesthouse is set in lovely cottage gardens, just a short walk from the beach and center of Cowes. You can choose between three rooms, all with private bathrooms, in the main house or two stylish cottages built alongside, each with their own courtyard garden. Guesthouse rooms have a slightly old-fashioned feel (one is called the Jane Austen room), but the cottages are modern—one is seaside/nautical, the other Asian. There are also two self-contained two-bedroom town houses around the corner. Breakfasts are hearty, and you can stay in for dinner if you choose. The guest lounge has a fireplace and broadband access, as do the cottages.

37 Chapel St., Cowes, Phillip Island, VIC 3922. ✆ **03/5952 3082,** or 0421 444 810 mobile phone. Fax 03/5952 3083. www.holmwoodguesthouse.com.au. 7 units. A$190–A$200 (US$152–US$160/UK£76–UK£80) double B&B; A$225–A$250 (US$180–US$200/UK£90–UK£100) double cottage; A$240–A$265 (US$192–US$212/UK£96–UK£106) town house (sleeps 4), extra person A$25 (US$20/UK£10). A$55 (US$44/UK£22) extra adult, A$33 (US$26/UK£13) extra child under 12 in cottages and B&B. Rates include cooked breakfast. Ask about packages. 2-night minimum or longer for town houses on weekends or holiday periods. AE, DC, MC, V. Free off-street parking. **Amenities:** Restaurant; bar; bike rental; tour desk; business center; room service; laundry service; nonsmoking rooms. *In room:* A/C, TV, hair dryer, CD player.

AROUND PORT PHILLIP BAY

West of Melbourne, the Princes Highway (or Hwy. 1) heads toward Geelong via Werribee. South of Melbourne, the Nepean Highway travels along the coast to the Mornington Peninsula as far as Portsea. If you have time to stay the night, you can combine the two options, heading first down to the Mornington Peninsula (see below) and then taking the car and passenger ferry from Sorrento to Queenscliff (see below).

WERRIBEE

This small country town is 32km (20 miles) southwest of Melbourne, a 30-minute drive along the Princes Freeway. Trains run from Melbourne to Werribee station; a taxi from the station to the zoo costs around A$5 (US$4/UK£2).

The Mansion at Werribee Park ★★ This "palace in the paddock" is always on my list of places to take visitors. The 60-room Italianate mansion was built in 1877 and is surrounded by 132 hectares (326 acres) of magnificent formal gardens and bushland. You can tour the house, which has wonderful antique furniture, and each year from March to May the gardens are the venue for the **Helen Lempriere National Sculpture Awards** (www.lempriereaward.com.au), when around 25 works from Australia's leading sculptors are displayed in the gardens. There's a cafe, too. If you want to stay longer, there's a magnificent modern hotel attached to the back of the Mansion (www.mansionhotel.com.au).

K Rd., Werribee. ✆ **03/8734 5100.** www.werribeepark.com.au. Free admission to park and picnic grounds; admission to mansion A$13 (US$10/UK£5.20) adults, A$6.50 (US$5.20/UK£2.60) children 4–15, A$30 (US$24/UK£12) families. Daily 10am–4pm, until 5pm on weekends May–Oct. Closed Dec 25.

Werribee Open Range Zoo From inside your zebra-striped safari bus, you can almost touch the mainly African animals that wander almost freely over the plains—no cages here. This high-caliber open-air zoo also has a walk-through section featuring African cats, including cheetahs, and monkeys. The safari-bus tour takes 50 minutes.

K Rd., Werribee. ✆ **03/9731 9600.** www.zoo.org.au. Admission A$22 (US$18/UK£8.80) adults, A$11 (US$8.80/UK£4.40) children aged 4–15, A$52 (US$42/UK£21) families of 4. Daily 9am–5pm (entrance gate closes at 3:30pm). Safari tours hourly 10:30am–3:40pm.

THE MORNINGTON PENINSULA

The Mornington Peninsula, a scenic 40km (25-mile) stretch of windswept coastline and hinterland 80km (50 miles) south of Melbourne, is one of Melbourne's favorite day-trip and weekend-getaway destinations. The coast is lined with good beaches and thick bush. The **Cape Shanck Coastal Park** stretches along the peninsula's Bass Strait foreshore from Portsea to Cape Shanck. It's home to gray kangaroos, southern brown bandicoots, echidnas, native rats, mice, reptiles, bats, and many forest and ocean birds. The park has numerous interconnecting walking tracks providing access to some remote beaches. You can get more information on this and all the other Victorian National Parks by calling ✆ **13 19 63.**

The Mornington Peninsula is a popular wine-producing region. The peninsula's fertile soil, temperate climate, and rolling hills produce excellent wine, particularly pinot noir, Shiraz, and chardonnay. Many wineries offer cellar-door tastings, others have excellent restaurants.

Along the route to the south, stop at the **Morning Peninsula Regional Gallery,** Dunns Road, Mornington (✆ **03/5975 4395;** http://mprg.mornpen.vic.gov.au), to check out the work of well-known Australian artists (open Tues–Sun 10am–5pm), or visit the summit at **Arthurs Seat State Park** for glorious views of the coastline. At Sorrento, take time out to spot pelicans on the jetty, or visit the town's many galleries.

If you are traveling with kids, stop in at Australia's oldest maze, **Ashcombe Maze & Water Gardens,** Red Hill Road, Shoreham (✆ **03/5989 8387;** www.ashcombemaze.com.au). Mine loved it. As well as the big maze, there are extensive water and woodland gardens, and even a rose maze made out of 1,300 rose bushes. There's also a pleasant cafe with indoor and outdoor dining. The park is open daily from 10am to 5pm; admission is A$13 (US$10/UK£5.20) for adults, A$8 (US$6.40/UK£3.20) for children, and A$38 (US$30/UK£15) for a family of four.

GETTING THERE From Melbourne, take the Mornington Peninsula Freeway to Rosebud, and then the Point Nepean Road. If you want to cross Port Phillip Bay from Sorrento to Queenscliff, take the **Sea Road Ferry** (© **03/5258 3244;** www.searoad.com.au), which operates daily every hour on the hour between 7am and 6pm in both directions. The one-way fare is around A$49 (U$39/UK£20) for a car and driver, and about A$6 (US$4.80/UK£2.40) per extra passenger, but changes slightly depending on the season. Foot-passenger fares (one-way) are A$9 (US$7.20/UK£3.60) for adults, A$8 (US$6.40/UK£3.20) for students 16 and over, A$7 (US$5.60/UK£2.80) for children 5 to 15, and A$1 (US80¢/UK40p) for children under 5. The crossing takes 35 to 40 minutes.

VISITOR INFORMATION The **Peninsula Visitor Information Centre,** Point Nepean Road, Dromana (© **1800/804 009** in Australia, or 03/5987 3078; www.visitmorningtonpeninsula.org), has plenty of maps and information on the area and can also help book accommodations. It's open daily from 9am to 5pm, except December 25 and Good Friday.

Where to Stay & Dine

The Portsea Hotel The rooms in this typical Australian motel on the seafront are done up with country-style furnishings. The standard twin rooms are basic; all share bathrooms. Doubles have double beds and attached bathrooms with showers. Units with bathrooms also have TVs and refrigerators. The outdoor beer garden is very pleasant on a sunny day.

3746 Point Nepean Rd., Portsea, VIC 3944. © **03/5984 2213.** Fax 03/5984 4066. www.portseahotel.com.au. 26 units, 6 with bathroom. A$100–A$140 (US$80–US$112/UK£40–UK£56) double without bathroom; A$145–A$170 (US$116–US$136/UK£58–UK£68) double with bathroom; A$175–A$205 (US$140–US$164/UK£70–UK£82) bay-view suite. Extra adult A$40 (US$32/UK£16), extra child aged 5–12 A$25 (US$20/UK£10). More expensive prices are for weekends. Ask about golf and other packages. AE, DC, MC. V. **Amenities:** Restaurant; 3 bars; golf course nearby; tour desk; laundry service. *In room:* A/C, coffeemaker.

13

Victoria

by Lee Mylne

Most visitors to Victoria start out exploring Melbourne's cosmopolitan streets before taking a few day trips to the wineries or the gold fields around the historic city of Ballarat. Many experience only a fraction of what Victoria has to offer, but this wonderfully diverse region is worth a closer look.

Australia's southernmost mainland state has 35 national parks, encompassing every possible terrain, from rainforest and mountain ranges to sun-baked Outback desert and a coast where waves crash dramatically onto rugged sandstone outcroppings.

Melbourne (see chapter 12) may be the heart of this rugged state, but the Murray River, which separates Victoria from New South Wales, has been its lifeblood, providing irrigation for vast tracts of semidesert land. In recent years, as Australia's drought has worsened, the state of the once-mighty Murray has been a focus of concern which is likely to still be making headlines during your visit.

Visitors might head inland to the mountains (perhaps for skiing or bushwalking at Mount Hotham or Falls Creek), or seek out the wilderness of Snowy River National Park. Others head to the Outback, to Grampians National Park, and to Mildura through deserts and past pink lakes and red sand dunes.

Lots of options await, and because many of them are rural, prices for accommodations are very affordable. Whatever itinerary you choose, you're sure to find dramatic scenery—and friendly locals.

See "Side Trips from Melbourne," in chapter 12, for information on the Dandenong Ranges, Yarra Valley, Phillip Island, and the Mornington Peninsula.

1 Ballarat: Gold-Rush City ★★

113km (70 miles) W of Melbourne

Ballarat, Victoria's largest inland city (pop. 90,000), is all about gold. In 1851, two prospectors found gold nuggets scattered on the ground at a place known as, ironically, Poverty Point. Within a year, 20,000 people had drifted into the area, and Australia's El Dorado gold rush had begun.

In 1858, the second-largest chunk of gold discovered in Australia (the Welcome Nugget) was found, but by the early 1860s, most of the easily obtainable yellow metal was gone. Larger operators continued digging until 1918, and by then Ballarat had developed enough industry to survive without mining. Today, you can still see the gold rush's effects in the impressive buildings, built from the miners' fortunes, lining Ballarat's streets.

ESSENTIALS

GETTING THERE From Melbourne, Ballarat is a 1½-hour drive on the Great Western Highway. **V/Line** (✆ **13 61 96** in Victoria, or 03/9697 2076; www.vline.com.au)

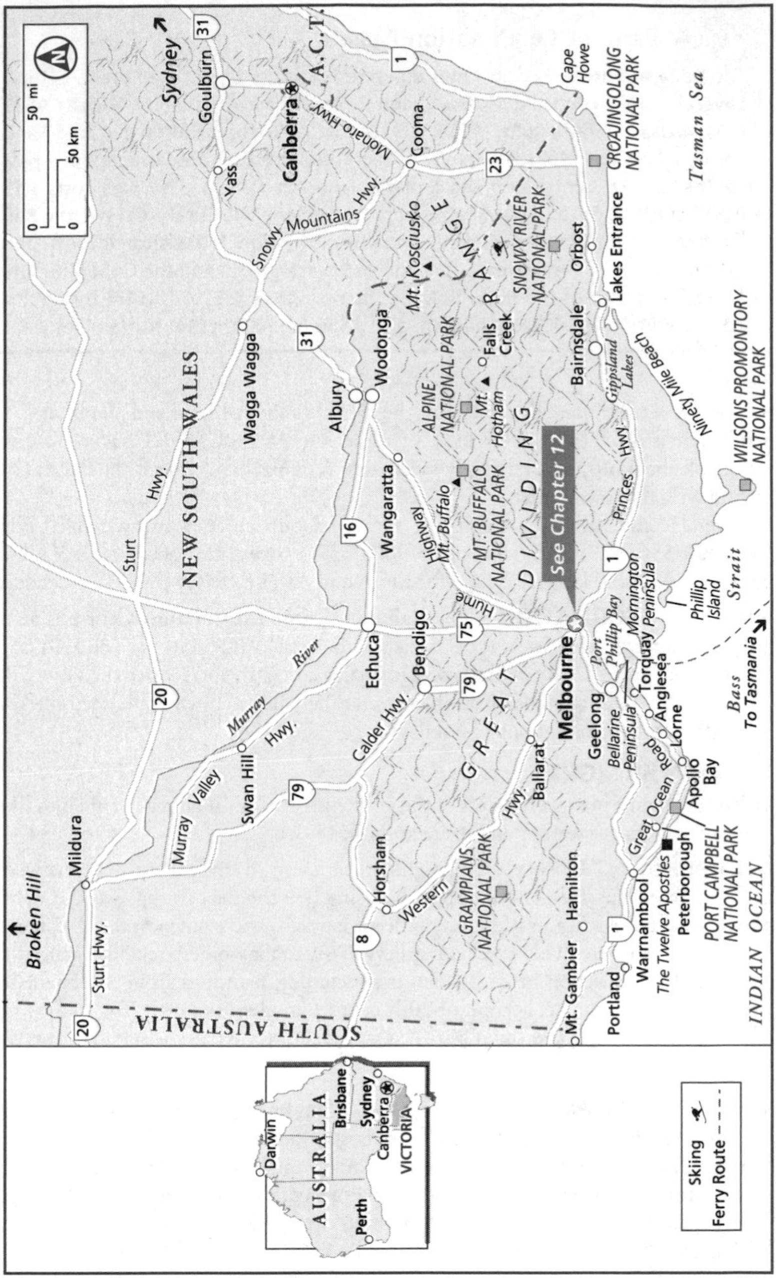

Sydney
Goulburn
31
Canberra
A.C.T.
1
Yass
Monaro Hwy.
Cooma
23
0 50 mi
0 50 km
Snowy Mountains Hwy.
Wagga Wagga
NEW SOUTH WALES
Sturt Hwy.
Broken Hill
Mildura
Sturt Hwy.
20
Murray Valley Hwy.
Swan Hill
Murray River
Echuca
16
Albury
Wodonga
Wangaratta
Hume Highway
Mt. Buffalo
MT. BUFFALO NATIONAL PARK
ALPINE NATIONAL PARK
Mt. Hotham
Falls Creek
Mt. Kosciusko
SNOWY RIVER NATIONAL PARK
GREAT DIVIDING RANGE
See Chapter 12
75
Bendigo
79
Calder Hwy.
Horsham
8
Western Hwy.
GRAMPIANS NATIONAL PARK
Ballarat
Melbourne
Geelong
Bellarine Peninsula
Port Phillip Bay
Mornington Peninsula
Torquay
Anglesea
Lorne
Great Ocean Road
Apollo Bay
PORT CAMPBELL NATIONAL PARK
Peterborough
The Twelve Apostles
Warrnambool
Hamilton
Mt. Gambier
Portland
SOUTH AUSTRALIA
INDIAN OCEAN
Bass Strait
To Tasmania
Phillip Island
WILSONS PROMONTORY NATIONAL PARK
Ninety Mile Beach
Gippsland Lakes
Princes Hwy.
Bairnsdale
Lakes Entrance
Orbost
CROAJINGOLONG NATIONAL PARK
Cape Howe
Tasman Sea
AUSTRALIA
Darwin
Perth
Brisbane
Sydney
Canberra
VICTORIA
Skiing
Ferry Route

Value Ballarat Combination Passes

The **Ballarat Eureka Pass** includes unlimited 3-day entry to The Eureka Centre, Sovereign Hill, The Gold Museum, and Ballarat Fine Art Gallery. It costs A$39 (US$31/UK£16) for adults, A$18 (US$14/UK£7.20) for children 5 to 15, and A$100 (US$80/UK£40) for a family of six. The **Art & Fact Pass** is an all-day pass to The Eureka Centre and the Ballarat Fine Art Gallery. The pass costs A$9 (US$7.20/UK£3.60) and is available from the gallery, The Eureka Centre, the Ballarat Visitor Information Centre, and the Sovereign Hill Visitor Information Centre. The **Gold Pass** covers admission to Sovereign Hill and the Gold Museum, as well as a tour of the Red Hill Mine. It costs A$34 (US$27/UK£14) for adults, A$16 (US$13/UK£6.40) for children, and A$86 (US$69/UK£34) for families.

runs trains between the cities every day; the trip takes about 1 hour and 30 minutes. The return fare is A$28 (US$22/UK£11) for adults and A$14 (US$11/UK£5.60) for children. Ask about off-peak and family-saver fares. A public bus connects the Ballarat train station with the town center.

Several companies offer day trips from Melbourne. They include **AAT Kings** (© **1300/556 100** in Australia, or 03/9663 3377; www.aatkings.com.au). A full-day tour costs A$118 (US$94/UK£47) for adults and A$59 (US$47/UK£24) for children.

VISITOR INFORMATION The **Ballarat Visitor Information Centre** is at The Eureka Centre, Rodier Street (at Eureka St.), Ballarat, VIC 3350 (© **1800/44 66 33** in Australia, or 03/5320 5758; www.visitballarat.com.au), and is open daily from 9am to 5pm. There is also an information center at the Ballarat Town Hall, open weekdays from 9am to 5pm except public holidays.

SEEING THE SIGHTS

Ballarat contains many reminders of the gold-rush era, but it all really comes to life in the colonial-era re-creation on Sovereign Hill.

Ballarat Fine Art Gallery The highlight of a visit to this gallery—especially after you've learned the story of the Eureka Uprising (see the next listing)—is the sight of the original Eureka flag, made from petticoat fabric by the women of the uprising and now enshrined here. This excellent gallery is Australia's oldest regional gallery and houses a fine collection of Australian art, including paintings from the Heidelberg School and a stunning collection of 20th-century modernists.

40 Lydiard St. N. © **03/5320 5858.** www.balgal.com. Admission A$5 (US$4/UK£2) adults, A$2.50 (US$2/UK£1) seniors, free for children under 16. Daily 9am–5pm. Closed Dec 25.

Blood on the Southern Cross ★ *Moments* This breathtaking sound-and-light show re-creates the Eureka Uprising, one of the most important events in Australia's history. You will be outdoors, so bring something warm to wear, because it can get chilly at night.

The story goes like this: After gold was discovered, the government introduced gold licenses, charging miners even if they came up empty-handed. The miners had to buy a license every month, and corrupt gold-field police (many of whom were former convicts) instituted a vicious campaign to extract the money. When license checks intensified in 1854, resentment flared. Prospectors began demanding political reforms, such as the right to vote, parliamentary elections, and secret ballots.

The situation exploded when the Eureka Hotel's owner murdered a miner but was set free by the government. The hotel was burned down in revenge, and more than 20,000 prospectors joined together, burned their licenses in a huge bonfire, and built a stockade over which they raised a flag.

Troops arrived at the "Eureka Stockade" the next month, but only 150 miners remained. The stockade was attacked at dawn, with 24 miners killed and 30 wounded. The uprising forced the government to act: The licenses were replaced with "miners rights" and cheaper fees, and the vote was introduced to Victoria. It's stirring stuff, and the reenactment does it justice. The show runs 90 minutes.

Sovereign Hill, Bradshaw St. ✆ **03/5333 5777.** www.sovereignhill.com.au. Reservations required. Admission A$41 (US$33/UK£16) adults, A$22 (US$18/UK£8.80) children 5–15, A$110 (US$88/UK£44) families of 4. Package with daytime entry to Sovereign Hill (see below) A$70 (US$56/UK£28) adults, A$35 (US$28/UK£14) children, A$187 (US$150/UK£75) families. Package with buffet dinner and stay at Sovereign Hill Lodge (see below) A$162 (US$130/UK£65) adults, A$69 (US$55/UK£28) children, A$427 (US$342/UK£171) families. Call ahead for information about other packages. 2 shows nightly (times vary seasonally).

The Eureka Centre You can't miss this building, with its huge sail, signifying the flag of the Southern Cross, above the original miners' stockade. Relive the action of the battle through multimedia displays.

Eureka St. ✆ **03/5333 1854.** www.eurekaballarat.com. Admission A$8 (US$6.40/UK£3.20) adults, A$4 (US$3.20/UK£1.60) children, A$22 (US$18/UK£8.80) families. Daily 9am–4:30pm (last entry at 4pm). Closed Dec 25.

The Gold Museum This surprisingly interesting museum houses a large collection of gold nuggets found at Ballarat, as well as alluvial deposits, gold ornaments, and coins. It also holds gallery displays relating to the history of gold mining in the area. One hour should be enough to take in the museum.

Bradshaw St. (opposite Sovereign Hill). ✆ **03/5337 1107.** Admission A$8 (US$6.40/UK£3.20) adults, A$4 (US$3.20/UK£1.60) children. See Gold Pass above. Daily 9:30am–5:20pm.

Sovereign Hill ★★ *Kids* Australia's best outdoor museum transports you back to the 1850s and the heady days of the gold rush. More than 40 stone-and-wood reproduction buildings, including shops and businesses on Main Street, sit on the 25-hectare (62-acre) former gold-mining site. There are also tent camps around the diggings on the lowest part of the site, which would have been the outskirts of town. There is a lot to see and do, so expect to spend at least 4 hours.

The township bustles with actors in period costumes going about their daily business. In addition to seeing how miners and their families lived, visitors can pan for real gold, ride in horse-drawn carriages, and watch potters, blacksmiths, and tanners make their wares. Don't miss the gold pour at the smelting works, or the redcoats as they parade through the streets.

On top of Sovereign Hill are the mine shafts and pithead equipment. The guided tour of a typical underground gold mine takes around 45 minutes. The **Voyage to Discovery** museum has artifacts from the gold rush, dioramas of mining scenes, and interactive computer displays. A restaurant, several cafes, coffee shops, and souvenir stores are around the site.

Bradshaw St. ✆ **03/5331 1944.** www.sovereignhill.com.au. Admission (including mine tour and Gold Museum) A$34 (US$27/UK£14) adults, A$16 (US$13/UK£6.40) children 5–15, A$86 (US$69/UK£34) families of 6. Daily 10am–5pm. Closed Dec 25. Bus: 9 from Curtis St. A free bus, "The Goldrush Special," meets the daily 9:08am (9:28am on Sun) train from Melbourne's Southern Cross railway station when it arrives at Ballarat Station and takes visitors direct to Sovereign Hill. Return service connects with the 4pm (4:10pm on Sat) train back to Melbourne. Passengers who show their V/Line tickets on arrival at Sovereign Hill receive a 10% discount off the entry price and as well as a free "Cobb & Co" coach ride.

WHERE TO STAY

The Ansonia ★ This boutique hotel in a restored Victorian building sports a glass atrium that runs the length of the property and is filled with plants and wicker chairs. Studio rooms are simply but comfortably furnished and have polished floorboards. The executive doubles are larger and a little plusher, and apartments have a separate lounge. The two family rooms can sleep four people in two bedrooms. There is a comfortable library and sitting room with an open fire and tea- and coffeemaking facilities, and plenty of flowers and art everywhere. Smoking is not allowed.

32 Lydiard St. S., Ballarat, VIC 3350. ✆ **03/5332 4678.** Fax 03/5332 4698. www.ballarat.com/ansonia.htm. 20 units. A$149 (US$119/UK£60) studio; A$169–A$189 (US$135–US$151/UK£68–UK£76) suite; A$249 (US$199/UK£100) apt; A$239 (US$191/UK£96) family room. Packages available. AE, DC, MC, V. Free parking. **Amenities:** Restaurant; tour desk; babysitting; laundry service; dry cleaning. *In room:* TV, dataport, hair dryer, iron.

Ballarat Heritage Homestay ★ *Finds* If you'd enjoy staying in a historic cottage, you might want to try Ballarat Heritage Homestay. Some of these Victorian and Edwardian cottages date from gold-rush days. All of them are different, but all have a historical feel. Two cottages have claw-foot tubs, and one has a Jacuzzi. Generally there's a queen-size and a double, and sometimes two singles in each cottage. All the cottages have two or three bedrooms, open fires, gas heating, a TV/VCR, and CD player.

185 Victoria St. (P.O. Box 1360), Ballarat Mail Centre, VIC 3354. ✆ **1800/813 369** in Australia, or 03/5332 8296. Fax 03/5331 3358. www.heritagehomestay.com. 5 cottages. All rates for 2 people: Cottages A$250 (US$200/UK£100) 1-night weekend stay (available for some cottages only); A$400–A$450 (US$320–US$360/UK£160–UK£180) 2-night weekend stay; A$180–A$200 (US$144–US$160/UK£72–UK£80) 1-night weekday stay. Extra adult A$30 (US$24/UK£12); extra child under 18 A$15 (US$12/UK£6). AE, DC, MC, V. **Amenities:** TV lounge. *In room:* Kitchen, hair dryer, iron.

Sovereign Hill Lodge The colonial-style wooden buildings adjacent to Sovereign Hill were built to resemble an 1850s government camp that was used to control (and tax) the mine fields. The residence building has rooms with queen-size beds and a set of single bunks, and the Offices building has heritage rooms with four-poster beds and Baltic pine furnishings, some with Jacuzzis. There are eight double rooms in the Superintendent's house; the Barracks houses dorm rooms that sleep up to eight people. There's a bar, 24-hour reception, and a game room. Guests get a 10% discount off entry to Sovereign Hill.

Magpie St., Ballarat, VIC 3350. ✆ **03/5333 3409.** Fax 03/5333 5861. www.sovereignhill.com.au. 37 units. A$130–A$146 (US$104–US$117/UK£52–UK£58) double; A$58 (US$46/UK£23) double for Barracks. Extra person A$14 (US$11/UK£5.60). Crib A$6.50 (US$5.20/UK£2.60). Ask about the many packages. AE, DC, MC, V. Free parking. **Amenities:** Restaurant; bar; babysitting; laundry service; nonsmoking rooms. *In room:* A/C, TV, fridge, coffeemaker, hair dryer, iron.

WHERE TO DINE

Oscar's CONTEMPORARY This cafe and bar inside one of Ballarat's historic old pubs is in the heart of the town, walking distance from shopping, the art gallery, and many other attractions. The former gold-rush era hotel was redeveloped in 2003, and now has an appealing open-plan restaurant, with a courtyard and bar. It's open for breakfast, lunch, and dinner and you can get snacks all day. Meals include Asian, pizzas, pasta, steaks, and gluten-free dishes.

18 Doveton St. South, Ballarat. ✆ **03/5331 1451.** Reservations recommended. Main courses A$16–A$26 (US$13–US$21/UK£6.40–UK£10). AE, DC, MC, V. Daily 7am–10pm.

2 The Great Ocean Road: One of the World's Most Scenic Drives ★★

Geelong: 75km (47 miles) SW of Melbourne; Torquay: 94km (58 miles) SW of Melbourne; Port Campbell National Park: 285km (177 miles) SW of Melbourne; Peterborough: 200km (124 miles) SW of Melbourne; Warrnambool: 263km (163 miles) SW of Melbourne

The Great Ocean Road—which hugs the coast from Torquay through Anglesea, Lorne, Apollo Bay, Port Campbell, and Peterborough, until it ends at Warrnambool—is one of Australia's most spectacular drives. The scenery along the 106km (66-mile) route includes huge cliffs, ocean vistas, beaches, rainforests, and some incredible rock formations. The most spectacular section is the 27km (17-mile) stretch between Princeton (the start of Port Campbell National Park) and Peterborough. The settlements along the highway are small, but they offer a number of accommodations choices.

The best way to travel along the Great Ocean Road is to drive yourself at a leisurely pace, stopping wherever your fancy takes you. The main attractions are in the coastal Port Campbell National Park, so don't be surprised if you're not overly impressed until you get there. If you are traveling on to Adelaide, you could stop off for 1 night along the Great Ocean Road and spend another night in the Coorong in South Australia (see section 5, "The Coorong," in chapter 11).

ESSENTIALS

ORGANIZED TOURS Even on an organized tour, when you are not doing the driving, I'd be reluctant to try this in 1 day unless absolutely pressed for time. All the tours which operate to the Great Ocean Road take around 12 hours (sometimes more), which makes for a big day out. The large coach operator **AAT Kings** (✆ **03/9663 3377** in Australia; www.aatkings.com.au) runs daily trips which cost A$129 (US$103/UK£52) for adults, and A$65 (US$52/UK£26) for children. **Gray Line Sightseeing Tours** (✆ **1300/858 687** in Australia, or 03/9663 4455; www.grayline.com) also has day trips for a similar price and duration; you can pay online in U.S. dollars. A better option would be Gray Line's 2-day Great Ocean Road tour, which overnights in Lorne. It costs A$349 (US$279/UK£140) adults double (single supplement is A$61/US$49/UK£25) and A$120 (US$96/UK£77) for children.

Wild-Life Tours (✆ **1300/661 730** in Australia, or 03/9741 6333; www.wildlifetours.com.au) offers several well-priced multiday backpacker-style tours that take in the Great Ocean Road tour from Melbourne. A 1-day tour costs A$90 (US$72/UK£36), and a 2-day tour which overnights at Hall's Gap and also takes in the Grampians (p. 643) costs A$183 (US$146/UK£73) including accommodations.

Autopia Tours (✆ **1800/000 507** in Australia, or 03/9419 8878; www.autopiatours.com.au) offers a 1-day tour from Melbourne taking in all the sights and including lunch and a bushwalk in the fabulous Otway National Park. It costs A$95 (US$76/UK£38). The company also does a more relaxed 3-day tour for A$375 (US$300/UK£150), including most meals and dorm accommodations in local hostels. Upgrades to double rooms are A$65 (US$52/UK£26) per person or single rooms A$150 (US$120/UK£60) per person.

VISITOR INFORMATION Most places along the route have their own information centers. If you're coming from Melbourne, stop at the **Geelong & Great Ocean Road Visitors Centre,** Stead Park, Princess Highway, Corio, VIC 3214 (✆ **1800/620 888** in Australia, or 03/5275 5797; www.greatoceanrd.org.au). You can book accommodations here, which you should do in advance, especially in summer. The really good website gives you plenty of tour options. There's also a visitor center at the **National Wool Museum,** 26 Moorabool St. (at Brougham St.), Geelong (© **1800/620 888** in Australia, or 03/5222 2900).

Along the route, the **Port Campbell Visitor Information Centre,** 26 Morris St., Port Campbell (© **03/5598 6089**), is a good place to pick up brochures. It has some interesting displays and an audiovisual show, and also acts as a hotel-booking service for the area. All these information centers are open from 9am to 5pm daily.

EXPLORING THE COASTAL ROAD

Along the route you might want to stop off at **Torquay,** a township dedicated to surfing. The main surf beach is much nicer than the one farther down the coast in Lorne. Check out **Surfworld Museum,** Surfcity Plaza, Beach Road, West Torquay (© **03/5261 4606;** www.surfworld.org.au), which has exhibits dealing with surfboard design and surfing history, and video of the world's best surfers. Admission is A$8.50 (US$6.80/UK£3.40) for adults, A$6 (US$4.80/UK£2.40) for children, and A$19 (US$15/UK£7.60) for families. It's open 9am to 5pm daily, except December 25. **Bells Beach,** just down the road, is world-famous in surfing circles for its perfect waves.

Lorne has some nice boutiques and is a good place to stop for lunch or stay the night. The stretch from Lorne to Apollo Bay is one of the most spectacular sections of the route; the road narrows and twists and turns along a cliff edge with the ocean on the other side. **Apollo Bay** is a pleasant town that was once a whaling station. It has good sandy beaches and is more low-key than Lorne.

Next you come to the **Angahook-Lorne State Park,** which protects most of the coastal section of the Otway Ranges from Aireys Inlet, south of Anglesea, to Kennett River. It has many well-marked rainforest walks and picnic areas at Shelly Beach, Elliot River, and Blanket Bay. There's plenty of wildlife around.

About 13km (8 miles) past Apollo Bay, just off the main road, you can stroll on the **Maits Rest Rainforest Boardwalk.** A little farther along the main road, an unpaved road leads north past Hopetoun Falls and Beauchamp Falls to the settlement of **Beech Forest.** Seven kilometers (4⅓ miles) farther along the main road, another unpaved road heads south for 15km (9⅓ miles) to a windswept headland and the **Cape Otway Lightstation** (© **03/5237 9240;** www.lightstation.com), one of several along the coast. Built by convicts in 1848, the 100m-tall (328-ft.) lighthouse is open to tourists. Admission is A$11 (US$8.80/UK£4.40) for adults and A$6 (US$4.80/UK£2.40) for children. It's open daily from 9am to 5pm. Free guided tours are run regularly.

Back on the main road, your route heads inland through an area known as **Horden Vale** before running to the sea at Glenaire—there's good surfing and camping at **Johanna,** 6km (3¾ miles) north of here. Then the Great Ocean Road heads north again to **Lavers Hill,** a former timber town. Five kilometers (3 miles) southwest of Lavers Hill is small **Melba Gully State Park,** where you can spot glowworms at night and walk along routes of rainforest ferns. Keep an eye out for one of the last giant gum trees that escaped the loggers—it's some 27m (88 ft.) in circumference and is estimated to be more than 300 years old.

The next place of note is Moonlight Head, which marks the start of the **Shipwreck Coast**—a 120km (74-mile) stretch running to Port Fairy that claimed more than 80 ships in only 40 years at the end of the 19th century and the beginning of the 20th.

Just past Princetown starts the biggest attraction of the trip, **Port Campbell National Park** ★★. With its sheer cliffs and coastal rock sculptures, it's one of the

Moments Great Ocean Walk

Getting out of your car and walking at least a part of Victoria's spectacular west coast is well worth the effort. The **Great Ocean Walk** stretches 91km (56 miles) from Apollo Bay to Glenample Homestead (near the Twelve Apostles), passing through National Parks and overlooking the Marine National Park and Sanctuary. The trail has been designed so walkers can "step on–step off" at a number of places, completing short walks of around 2 hours, or day or overnight hikes. If you are planning to stay overnight you must register with Parks Victoria (© **13 19 63**; www.greatoceanwalk.com.au), at least 2 weeks ahead. Camping fees are A$25 (US$20/UK£10) per tent site. The walk winds through beautiful and remote areas such as Station Beach and Moonlight Head, which until now have been difficult to access. It also reveals wet fern and rainforest gullies, which have huge specimens of the world's tallest flowering tree, the Mountain Ash; crosses coastal heathlands; and goes in and out of the sheltered coastal estuaries of the Aire and Gellibrand rivers. Check the website for detailed information on all aspects of the walk, including guided walks, assisted overnight walks with tour operators, camping and walking equipment hire, and food provision.

most immediately recognizable images of natural Australia. You can't miss the **Twelve Apostles,** a series of rock pillars (actually, there are eight left standing) in the foam just offshore. Other attractions are the **Blowhole,** which throws up huge sprays of water; the **Grotto,** a rock formation intricately carved by the waves; **London Bridge,** which looked quite like the real thing until the center crashed into the sea in 1990 (leaving a bunch of tourists stranded on the wrong end); and the **Loch Ard Gorge. Port Fairy,** a lovely fishing town once called Belfast by Irish immigrants who settled here to escape the potato famine, is also on the Shipwreck Coast.

Not far past the town of Peterborough, the Great Ocean Road heads inland to Warrnambool. It eventually joins the Princes Highway heading toward Adelaide.

WHERE TO STAY ALONG THE WAY

The **Great Ocean Road Accommodation Centre,** 136 Mountjoy Parade, Lorne, VIC 3232 (© **03/5289 4233;** www.gorac.com.au), rents cottages and units along the route.

IN LORNE

Lorne is a good option for a night's rest. Though the beach is nothing special, it's a great place to learn to surf. There are plenty of restaurants and lots of boutiques.

Cumberland Lorne Conference & Leisure Resort ★ *Value* This large resort, totally renovated in 2003, stands out between the sea and the foothills of the Otway Ranges. Still, I highly recommend it—it's a good deal, and quite luxurious. Every apartment has a queen-size bed and a sofa bed, a kitchen, a laundry, a Jacuzzi, a balcony, Internet access, free in-house movies, and a CD player. All units have large bathrooms with tub/shower combinations. More than half of the rooms have panoramic ocean views; the rest overlook gardens. Two-bedroom apartments have two extra single beds, and split-level penthouses have two Jacuzzis and two balconies.

150–178 Mountjoy Parade, Lorne, VIC 3232. © **1800/037 010** in Australia, or 03/5289 2400. Fax 03/5289 2256. www.cumberland.com.au. 99 units. Peak season (summer and Easter) A$315–A$375 (US$252–US$300/UK£126–UK£150) 1-bedroom apt, A$400–A$460 (US$320–US$368/UK£160–UK£184) 2-bedroom apt, A$525–A$545

(US$420–US$436/UK£210–UK£218) penthouse; off season A$250–A$315 (US$200–US$252/UK£100–UK£126) 1-bedroom apt, A$335–A$400 (US$268–US$320/UK£134–UK£160) 2-bedroom apt, A$430–A$460 (US$344–US$368/UK£172–UK£184) penthouse. Ask about packages. AE, DC, MC, V. Free undercover parking. **Amenities:** Restaurant; heated indoor pool and toddlers' pool; 2 lit tennis courts; exercise room; spa; Jacuzzi; sauna; watersports rental; bike rental; children's center; game room; concierge; tour desk; business center; room service (evening only); babysitting; dry cleaning; nonsmoking rooms. *In room:* A/C, TV w/pay movies, dataport, kitchenette, fridge, coffeemaker, hair dryer, iron, safe.

Great Ocean Road Cottages *Kids* This complex has it all, although with so many people (and quite a few children) around, it can be a little noisy in summer. The self-contained cottages, set away from each other in a quiet patch of bushland, lie about a 5-minute walk from the town center. Each cottage is a two-story wooden hut with a double bed, two twin beds, and a pullout mattress. There's also a bathroom and a full kitchen. Also on the property is **Great Ocean Road Backpackers,** which offers dorm-style accommodations. It has 30 dorm beds, three double rooms and one twin room, and two family rooms (each with a queen-size bed and two singles). Just down the road is **Waverley House,** a historic mansion that holds seven apartments. All of them are air-conditioned; they vary enormously in size and furnishings.

Great Ocean Rd. Cottages: 10 Erskine Ave. (P.O. Box 60), Lorne, VIC 3232. © **03/5289 1070.** Fax 03/5289 2508. www.greatoceanroadcottages.com. 10 cottages. A$150 (US$120/UK£60) double weekdays; A$170 (US$136/UK£68) double weekend. Extra adult A$25 (US$20/UK£10), extra child A$10 (US$8/UK£4). Weekly stays in high season (Dec 26–Jan 26). 2-night minimum on weekends. **Backpackers:** 10 Erskine Ave., Lorne, VIC 3232. © **03/5289 1809.** www.yha.com.au. A$20 (US$16/UK£8) dorms for YHA members and A$24 (US$19/UK£9.60) for nonmembers; A$50 (US$40/UK£20) doubles and twin room; A$75 (US$60/UK£30) family rooms. **Waverley House:** Waverley Ave. and Great Ocean Rd. (P.O. Box 60), Lorne, VIC 3232. © **03/5289 2044.** www.waverleyhouse.com. 7 apts. A$140 (US$112/UK£56) 1-bedroom apt (A$180/US$144/UK£72 daily high season); A$250 (US$200/UK£100) 2-bedroom apt (A$330/US$264/UK£132 daily high season; 3-night minimum). AE, DC, MC, V. **Amenities:** Jacuzzi; free use of bikes; free laundry; nonsmoking rooms. *In room:* TV/VCR, kitchenette, fridge, coffeemaker, hair dryer.

IN APOLLO BAY

Chris's Beacon Point Villas Perched high in the Otways, above the Great Ocean Road, these villas have wonderful views of the coast. Host Chris Talihmanidis is well known as a local restaurateur, with a passion for the food of southern Europe. There are two studios and six self-contained, stylishly furnished two-bedroom villas, all with the same panoramic views. Villas have a queen-size bed and a double or two singles, while studios sleep two in a king-size bed. Don't miss the chance to eat at Chris's award-winning **restaurant.**

280 Skenes Creek Rd., Apollo Bay, VIC 3233. © **03/5237 6411.** Fax 03/5237 6930. 8 units. A$160 (US$128/UK£64) double studio; A$220–A$290 (US$176–US$232/UK£88–UK£116) villa (sleeps 4). Rates include breakfast. AE, DC, MC, V. **Amenities:** Restaurant; bar; in-room massage (by appointment); babysitting; laundry; dry cleaning; nonsmoking rooms. *In room:* TV w/pay movies, VCR, kitchen, fridge, iron.

IN PORT CAMPBELL

Macka's Farm Lodge ★ *Finds* *Kids* This working farm is inland from the Twelve Apostles. The units all have kitchens, so you can cook your own feast. Otherwise, you can order meals by prior arrangement outside peak season, or visit one of the nearby restaurants. There are four self-contained lodges and a farmhouse. The lodges form the "homestead" complex and have wonderful views across the farm, bush, and to the ocean. Two of them sleep three people. The third lodge has three bedrooms, with a queen-size bed, a king-size bed (interchangeable to two singles), and a bedroom with singles and bunks. The fourth lodge has two bedrooms, each with a queen-size bed. The farmhouse has four bedrooms, three with queen-size beds, one with four singles.

All have a TV, DVD, and CD player—but you may not even turn them on, when there are lots of pigs, cows, ducks, and chickens running around to entertain the kids. Overall, it's a great farm experience.

RSD 2305 Princetown Rd., Princetown, VIC 3269. © **03/5598 8261.** Fax 03/5598 8201. www.mackasfarm.com.au. 3 units. A$165–A$360 (US$132–US$288/UK£66–UK£144), depending on the house and the season (check the website because there are dozens of different price categories). MC, V. From the Twelve Apostles, go 2km (1¼ miles), turn at the sign for Macka's Farm, and go 4km (2½ miles) inland. *In room:* Kitchen, fridge, hair dryer.

WHERE TO DINE

Marks Restaurant ★ CONTEMPORARY Seaside chic, friendly staff, and great food are a winning recipe for this favorite with locals and travelers. Marks is stylish, simple, and smart, with an emphasis on seafood. Dishes might include fried calamari salad, spicy octopus, chargrilled whole baby snapper, or heartier fare such as lamb shanks for those chilly coastal winter nights. There's a good wine list, or you can BYO.

124 Mount Joy Parade, Lorne. © **03/5289 2787.** Main courses A$18–A$25 (US$14–US$20/UK£7–UK£10). AE, MC, V. Daily 6pm–late. Closed Aug.

The Victoria Hotel ★ CONTEMPORARY Built in 1874, this historic bluestone pub in Port Fairy is a great place to recharge your batteries while driving the Great Ocean Road. By day, you can eat in the casual cafe overlooking the courtyard; by night it is transformed into an a la carte restaurant. As well as traditional pub favorites like fish and chips, you're likely to find the menu includes dishes such as lamb cutlets on a bed of olive, pine nut, and spinach risotto, homemade sweet potato and spinach gnocchi, or confit duck and wild mushroom pie with a baby beet root, pine nut, and rocket salad. Over summer (Dec–Mar) the restaurant becomes Simply Seafood, with a seasonal seafood. There's often live music in the courtyard on Friday or Saturday nights.

42 Bank St., Port Fairy. © **03/5568 2891.** Main courses A$15–A$21 (US$12–US$17/UK£6–UK£8.40) at lunch, A$20–A$30 (US$16–US$24/UK£8–UK£12) at dinner. AE, DC, MC, V. Tues–Sun noon–2pm and 6pm–late.

3 The Murray River ★

Mildura: 544km (337 miles) NW of Melbourne; Albury-Wodonga: 305km (189 miles) NE of Melbourne; Echuca: 210km (130 miles) N of Melbourne

The Murray River is Australia's version of the Mississippi. Though it's a rushing torrent of white water at its source in the Snowy Mountains, it becomes slow and muddy brown by the time it forms the meandering border between Victoria and New South Wales. The Darling River, which starts in Queensland, feeds the Murray; together they make Australia's longest river. Drought has made the fate of the Murray one of Australia's greatest environmental concerns in recent years, and by the time you get here, it may well be a trickle of its former self. That said, its importance is unlikely to diminish, one way or another.

Aborigines once used the Murray as a source of food and transportation, and later the water carried paddle steamers, laden with wool and crops from the land it helped irrigate. In 1842, the Murray was "discovered" by explorers Hamilton Hume and William Howell on the first overland trek from Sydney to Port Phillip, near Melbourne. As Hume later wrote, on their trek the explorers "suddenly arrived at the bank of a very fine river—at least 60m wide, apparently deep, the bank being 2.4m or 2.7m above the level, which is overflowed at the time of flood . . . In the solid wood of a healthy tree I carved my name." You can still see the carved initials on a tree standing by the riverbank in Albury, on the border between the two states.

ESSENTIALS

GETTING THERE Most visitors cross the river during an overland drive between cities. There are two ways to the Murray from Melbourne: the 2½-hour route down the Midland Highway to Echuca, and the Calder Highway to Mildura, a 6-hour drive. Traveling from Melbourne to Mildura is practical only if you're continuing to Broken Hill, which is 297km (184 miles) north of Mildura. Those in a hurry to get to and from Sydney can travel via the river-straddling twin towns of Albury-Wodonga on the Hume Highway (about a 12-hr. trip with short stops).

V/Line (✆ **13 61 96**) runs regular train service to Mildura, Echuca, and Albury-Wodonga.

VISITOR INFORMATION The **Echuca-Moama Visitor Information Centre,** 2 Heygarth St., Echuca, VIC 3564 (✆ **1800/804 446** in Australia, or 03/5480 7555; fax 03/5482 6413; www.echucamoama.com), has plenty of maps and information about accommodations and river cruises. It's open daily from 9am to 5pm (closed Dec 25). The **Mildura Visitor Information & Booking Centre,** 180–190 Deakin Ave., Mildura, VIC 3502 (✆ **1800/039 043** in Australia for bookings, or 1800/550 858 in Australia or 03/5018 8380; fax 03/5021 1836; www.visitmildura.com.au), offers similar services. It's open Monday through Friday from 9am to 5:30pm and weekends from 9am to 5pm (closed Dec 25). If you're passing through Albury-Wodonga, contact the **Gateway Visitor Information Centre,** Lincoln Causeway, Wodonga, VIC 3690 (✆ **1300/796 222** or 02/6051 3757; www.destinationalburywodonga.com.au). It's open daily from 9am to 5pm (closed Dec 25).

RIVER CRUISES

IN MILDURA Mildura is one of Australia's most important fruit-growing areas. There was a time, however, when this was semiarid red-dust country. The area bloomed because of a little ingenuity and, of course, the Murray. The original irrigation system consisted of two English water pumps and the manual labor of hundreds of immigrants, who were put to work clearing scrub and digging channels through the new fields. Today, the hungry land soaks up water and everyone prays for rain.

Several paddle steamers leave from Mildura wharf. One of the nicest boats is **PS *Melbourne*** (✆ **03/5023 2200;** fax 03/5021 3017; www.murrayriver.com.au), which was built in 1912 and is still powered by steam. It offers 2-hour trips leaving at 10:50am and 1:50pm daily (but check times in advance because they do change). The fare is A$19 (US$15/UK£7.60) for adults and A$7.50 (US$6/UK£3) for children, free for children under 5.

PS *Melbourne*'s sister ship, the ***Rothbury,*** was built in 1881; a conventional engine has replaced its steam engine. It offers a winery cruise every Thursday from 10:30am to 3:30pm, stopping at a winery for tastings and a barbecue lunch. The trip costs A$42 (US$34/UK£17) for adults and A$20 (US$16/UK£8) for children. The *Rothbury* has evening dinner cruises Thursday from 7 to 10pm for A$40 (US$32/UK£16) for adults and A$18 (US$14/UK£7.20) for children.

IN ECHUCA The paddle steamer ***Emmylou*** (✆ **03/5480 2237;** fax 03/5480 2927; www.emmylou.com.au) operates out of Echuca. A 2-day, 2-night cruise leaves Wednesday at 6pm and returns at noon on Friday (check sailings beforehand). The cruise includes (depending on river levels) a visit to the Barmah, an area famous for its wetlands and the largest red gum trees in the world, or a stop at Perricoota Station. The trip costs A$405 to A$460 (US$324–US$368/UK£162–UK£184) per person, including meals. Discounts are available for children and seniors. An overnight trip leaves on Saturday at 6pm and returns at 9:30am on Sunday. It costs A$195 to A$235 (US$156–US$188/UK£78–UK£94) per person, including breakfast and dinner. The *Emmylou* also offers short trips costing A$19 (US$15/UK£7.60) for adults and A$9 (US$7.20/UK£3.60) for kids aged 1 to 15 for 1 hour, and A$23 (US$18/UK£9.20) for adults and A$11 (US$8.80/UK£4.40) for kids for 1½ hours.

The **Port of Echuca** (© **03/5482 4248;** www.portofechuca.org.au) is definitely worth a look. The three-level red-gum wharf was built in 1865 and is still in use by paddle steamers. The Port owns PS *Adelaide,* the oldest operating wooden-hulled paddle steamer in the world (1866), PS *Pevensey* (1911), and PS *Alexander Arbuthnot* (1923). One-hour cruises, including a port tour, run daily at 10:15 and 11:30am, and 1:15, 2:30, and 3:45pm (though ring ahead to check, as they do change). They cost A$25 (US$20/UK£10) for adults, A$13 (US$10/UK£5.20) for children, and A$65 (US$52/UK£26) for a family. You can look around the wharf on a guided tour, priced at A$12 (US$9.60/UK£4.80) for adults and A$7.50 (US$6/UK£3) for children, and A$35 (US$28/UK£14) for a family. Outside the Port, the Echuca Port Precinct offers various things to do, including carriage rides and old penny arcade machines in Sharpes Magic Movies, in an old riverboat warehouse.

A TRIP INTO THE OUTBACK **Mungo National Park** ★ is a unique, arid region 110km (68 miles) northeast of Mildura, off the Sturt Highway. The park is famous for its red-sand dunes and shifting sands, and I recommend you see it. You can get there on your own, but it's best to have a four-wheel-drive vehicle. People come here to see the Walls of China, a moonscape of weathered red sand. The walls edge Lake Mungo, once a huge freshwater lake during the last Ice Age, now dry. A 60km (37-mile) driving tour starting at the visitor center at the park's entrance takes you across the lake bed to the Walls of China. Several short walks begin at the campsites at the park entrance. Contact the **National Parks & Wildlife Service NSW** (© **1300/361 967** in Australia; www.nationalparks.nsw.gov.au) for more information. Just outside the park, **Mungo Lodge** (© **03/5029 7297;** fax 03/5029 7296; www.mungolodge.com.au) offers affordable motel accommodations and a casual restaurant.

WHERE TO STAY

IN MILDURA

Quality Hotel Mildura Grand ★★★ This 19th-century hotel is right in the center of Mildura, overlooking the Murray River. Double rooms are comfortable, and many have been refurbished. Suites are bigger, and some have balconies and garden views. State suites are plush and come with a king-size bed. The Presidential suite (the most expensive) is Art Deco inspired, with a large marble bathroom and Jacuzzi. This place is famous for the multi-award-winning **Stefano's** ★ one of several dining spots run by celeb chef Stefano de Pieri. The hotel also operates the historic paddleboat *Avoca* (© **03/5022 1444**), on which you can cruise for Sunday luncheon for A$49 (US$39/UK£20) adults, A$15 (US$12/UK£6) children.

Seventh St., Mildura, VIC 3500. © **1800/034 228** in Australia, or 03/5023 0511. Fax 03/5022 1801. www.qualityhotelmilduragrand.com.au. 102 units. A$100–A$200 (US$80–US$160/UK£40–UK£80) double; A$230–A$400 (US$184–US$320/UK£92–UK£160) suite. Rates include breakfast. Extra person A$30 (US$24/UK£12). Children under 12 stay free in parent's room. Ask about packages. AE, DC, MC, V. **Amenities:** 5 restaurants; 4 bars; large heated outdoor pool; golf course nearby; gymnasium; Jacuzzi; sauna; 24-hr. concierge; tour desk; business center; shopping arcade; room service (7am–midnight); in-room massage; coin-op laundry and laundry service; same-day dry cleaning; nonsmoking rooms; executive rooms. *In room:* A/C, TV w/free movies, dataport, minibar, coffeemaker, hair dryer, iron.

Moments Ned Kelly Country

The bushranger Ned Kelly is an Australian icon. His story is a legend, and Kelly is a folk hero to many people. Opinion can be divided, but there's no question that his story still resonates 125 years after the events that made him famous. Now, the area of Victoria in which he lived is called "Kelly Country" and in 2005 to mark the anniversary of his death, the government created the **Ned Kelly Touring Route** (www.nedkellytouringroute.com.au), linking important sites in the story.

But first, here's the tale of Ned and his exploits, in brief. Ned was the eldest of eight children born to Irish parents in Victoria in 1854. When Ned was 12, his father died and the family moved to be near relatives at Greta, 240km (150 miles) northeast of Melbourne. Like many other poor families, the Kellys took up the government's offer of cheap land. As part of the deal, they had to clear the bushland, build a house, and plant crops. More often than not, the land parcels were too small and the soil too poor for them to make a living.

At 16, Ned Kelly was convicted of horse-rustling and sentenced to 3 years in jail. A few years later, his mother was imprisoned for allegedly attacking a police officer named Fitzpatrick, who was accused of attacking Ned's sister first. During the scuffle, Ned shot Fitzpatrick through the wrist. Ned escaped—with a bounty on his head.

On October 26, 1878, together with friends Joe Byrne and Steve Hart, Ned and his brother Dan came across police camped at Stringy Bark Creek. Ned believed the police intended to kill him and his brother, so he called on them to surrender. Three officers resisted, and in the fight that followed Ned Kelly shot them dead.

In the years that followed, the Kelly Gang avoided capture with the help of sympathetic locals. During this time, they robbed two banks, and during

IN ECHUCA

Echuca Gardens B&B and YHA This popular two-story log-cabin B&B offers evening gatherings around the piano, as well as a Jacuzzi in the front yard surrounded by murals and landscaped water gardens. Rooms are decorated in native flower themes, and all have balconies. It's a short stroll from the B&B to either the river or a state forest. The cottage next door sleeps 10 and can be rented for exclusive use. It has three bedrooms and is fully self-contained.

103 Mitchell St., Echuca, VIC 3564. ✆ **03/5480 6522,** or 0419 881 054 mobile. Fax 03/5482 6951. www.echucagardens.com. 3 B&B units. B&B room A$140–A$160 (US$112–US$128/UK£56–UK£64) double at weekends; A$100–A$130 (US$80–US$104/UK£40–UK£52) double weekdays. Rates include breakfast. Minimum 2-night stay at weekends, 3 nights in peak season (Dec 26–Jan 15). No children under 12 in the B&B. Cottage A$25–A$45 (US$20–US$36/UK£10–UK£18) adults, A$10–A$20 (US$8–US$16/UK£4–UK£8) children, depending on season. MC, V. **Amenities:** Jacuzzi; sauna; bike rental; tour desk; massage; coin-operated laundry; nonsmoking rooms. *In room:* A/C, TV, hair dryer.

each robbery Ned gave his hostages a letter, explaining to the government how he'd been persecuted by police.

In June 1880, police surrounded the Kelly Gang at the Glenrowan Hotel. Prepared for the fight, the four bushrangers put on homemade suits of armor. It was no use—Ned's body took 28 bullets, the others were all killed. Ned was hanged in Old Melbourne Gaol (see p. 604 in chapter 12) on November 11, 1880. He was 25 years old.

Historic **Beechworth,** one of Victoria's best-preserved gold-rush towns, is a good base for exploring this region. There are more than 30 buildings listed by the National Trust here, from pubs, churches, and government offices to miners' cottages and the jail where Ned Kelly was imprisoned. We stayed at **Kinross,** 34 Loch St., Beechworth (✆ **03/5728 2351;** fax 03/5728 3333; www.innhouse.com.au/kinross.html), a historic bungalow with five rooms for bed-and-breakfast guests. Rates are A$155 to A$180 (US$124–US$144/UK£62–UK£72) double. For a little luxury, check out **The Spa at Beechworth** (✆ **03/5728 3033;** www.thespaatbeechworth.com.au), a day spa located in the gorgeous Birches Building in Albert Road, which was once a lunatic asylum (they don't mince words in these parts).

You can also visit **Glenrowan,** a quiet little town surrounded by wineries and orchards. Here you'll find a 6m-high (20-ft.) outdoor statue of Ned Kelly clad in his homemade armor and helmet, with rifle in hand, as well as a couple of small museums full of Kelly memorabilia—and much more besides.

Other towns on the route include Avenel, Benalla, Mansfield, and Jerilderie in southern New South Wales. You can pick up a touring route brochure from the **Old Melbourne Gaol** before setting out, or from the **Beechworth Visitor Information Centre,** in the town hall, Ford Street (✆ **1300 366 321** in Australia, or 03/5728 8065). Other information centers will also have them.

BRIGHT

310km (193 miles) NE of Melbourne; 700km (435 miles) SW of Sydney; 74km (46 miles) E of Wangaratta

Set in a valley and surrounded by pine forests, Bright offers good access to the surrounding High Country and ski fields. The town is famous for the colors of its European trees in fall. There are nice walks around here, especially along the pretty Ovens River, while another option is to hire bicycles and take off through the countryside down a former railway track. Cycling at least part of the **Rail Trail** ★ (www.railtrail.com.au) will give you a nice feel for the area, with its surrounding mountains, farms, and river. The track stretches 94km (58 miles) from Bright to Wangaratta, but you can turn back whenever you want, of course. Rent bikes (and skis if you're off to the snowfields) in Bright.

VISITOR INFORMATION

Stop by the **Bright Visitors Centre,** 119 Gavan St., Bright (✆ **1800/500 117** in Australia, or 03/5755 2275; www.brightescapes.com.au), open 8:30am to 5pm daily.

GETTING THERE

V/Line trains (www.vline.com.au) run between Melbourne and Bright, via Wangaratta, daily. Return fares cost A$91 (US$73/UK£36), though if you travel in off-peak times it is considerably cheaper. The trip takes about 4 hours, and from Wangaratta, you take the bus to Bright. However, it's difficult to get around the area without your own transport.

WHERE TO STAY & DINE

The website **www.alpinelink.com.au** offers a comprehensive list of places to stay in Bright. The best place to eat in town in **Simone's of Bright,** 98 Gavan St. (**© 03/5755 2266**). It serves great Italian food in a refined atmosphere, with main courses around A$20 to A$30 (US$16–US$24/UK£8–UK£12). Otherwise, Bright has plenty of family-friendly cafes, restaurants, and pizza joints.

Alinga-Longa Holiday Units The large two-bedroom units here are spacious, clean, and comfortable. They are nothing special, but fine for a couple of days, especially if you're traveling with kids. The full kitchen means you never have to eat out; there's wireless Internet access and a barbecue area.

12 Gavan St. (Great Alpine Rd.), Bright, VIC 3741. **© 03/5755 1073.** www.alingalongaholidays.com.au. 6 units. A$90–A$120 (US$72–US$96/UK£36–UK£48) double. AE, DC, MC, V. **Amenities:** Small outdoor pool; free bikes and toboggans; playground; tour desk; laundry service. *In room:* A/C, TV/VCR, kitchen.

Villa Gusto This luxury Italian-style villa caters to only 18 guests. Built at the foot of Mt. Buffalo, with dramatic views, it is furnished with antiques and leather sofas, and is set in .8 hectare (2 acres) of Tuscan gardens. The central focus is the Great Room, with a log fire, and there is also an in-house cinema. The Grande Suite and three deluxe suites have Jacuzzis, and all have private terraces. There are also luxury touches like bathrobes, Bvlgari toiletries, and fine linens. A five-course Italian degustation menu is available from the restaurant for A$70 (US$56/UK£28) per person, but bookings are essential. The villa is about 6km (3¾ miles) from Bright.

630 Buckland Valley Rd., Buckland, VIC 3740. **© 03/5756 2000.** www.villagusto.com.au. 9 units. A$245 (US$196/UK£98) double standard room; A$285–A$325 (US$228–US$260/UK£114–UK£130) suite. Rates include breakfast. MC, V. No children under 10. **Amenities:** Restaurant (open Wed–Sun nights only). *In room:* A/C, TV, minibar, coffeemaker.

4 The High Country

Victoria's High Country consists of the hills and mountains of the Great Dividing Range, which runs from Queensland, through New South Wales, to just before Ballarat, where it drops away and reappears in the mountains of the Grampians, in the western part of Victoria. The range separates inland Australia from the greener coastal belt. The highest peak in the Victoria segment of the range is Mount Bogong which, at just 1,988m (6,521 ft.), is minuscule by world mountain standards.

The main attractions of the High Country are its natural features, which include moorland and mountainous alpine scenery. It's also popular for outdoor activities, including hiking, canoeing, white-water rafting, mountain-bike riding, and rock climbing. The High Country is also the home of the Victorian ski fields, based around Mount Buller, Mount Stirling, Falls Creek, Mount Buffalo, and Mount Hotham. If you plan to go walking here, make sure you have plenty of water and sunscreen, as well as a tent and a good-quality sleeping bag. As in any alpine region, temperatures can plummet dramatically. In summer, days can be very hot and nights very cold.

SNOWY RIVER NATIONAL PARK ★

390km (242 miles) NE of Melbourne

The Snowy River National Park, with its lovely river scenery and magnificent gorges, protects Victoria's largest forest wilderness areas. The Snowy River was once a torrent worthy of Banjo Paterson's famous poem, but since Snowy Mountain Hydro-Electric erected a series of dams, it's become a mere trickle of its former self.

GETTING THERE & GETTING AROUND There is no public transit in this area. The two main access roads are the Gelantipy Road from Buchan and the Bonang Freeway from the logging township of Orbost. MacKillop's Road (also known as Deddick River Rd.) runs across the park's northern border from Bonang to a little south of Wulgulmerang. The area around MacKillop's Bridge, along MacKillop's Road, has spectacular scenery and the park's best campgrounds, set beside some nice swimming holes and sandy river beaches. The Barry Way leads through the main township of Buchan, where you'll find some of Australia's best caves.

VISITOR INFORMATION The main place to get information on the Snowy River National Park and Alpine National Park is the **Buchan Caves Information Centre,** in the Buchan Caves complex. It's open daily from 9am to 4pm (closed Dec 25). Or call **Parks Victoria** (✆ **13 19 63** in Australia).

EXPLORING THE BUCHAN CAVES

The **Buchan Caves** ★ (✆ **13 19 63**) are in a scenic valley that is particularly beautiful in autumn, when all the European trees are losing their leaves. Tourists can visit the Royal and Fairy caves (which are quite similar), with their fabulous stalactites and stalagmites. There are several tours daily: from the end of Easter to September at 11am, 1pm, and 3pm; October to Easter at 10 and 11:15am, 1, 2:15, and 3:30pm. Entry to one cave costs A$13 (US$10/UK£5.20) for adults, A$6.50 (US$5.20/UK£2.60) for children 5 to 16, and A$32 (US$26/UK£13) for families of four.

To reach the caves from the Princes Highway, turn off at Nowa Nowa (it's well signposted). If you're coming south from Jindabyne in New South Wales (see chapter 5), follow the Barry Way, which runs alongside the Snowy River.

ALPINE NATIONAL PARK ★★

333km (206 miles) NE of Melbourne; 670km (415 miles) SW of Sydney

Victoria's largest national park, at 646,000 hectares (1.6 million acres), the Alpine National Park connects the High Country areas of New South Wales and the Australian Capital Territory. The park's scenery is spectacular, encompassing most of the state's highest mountains, wild rivers, impressive escarpments, forests, and high plains. Much of the park was devastated by horrific bushfires in December 2002, and it is slowly recovering. It's green, but evidence of the fire lingers; you'll still see blackened tree trunks. The flora is diverse; in all, some 1,100 plant species have been recorded within the park's boundaries, including 12 not found anywhere else. Walking here is particularly good in spring and summer, when a carpet of wildflowers covers the Bogong High Plains. Other impressive walking trails include the 5.7km (3½-mile) route through Bryce Gorge to The Bluff, a 200m-high (656-ft.) rocky escarpment with panoramic views. Of the numerous other walking trails in the park, the best known is the Alpine Walking Track, which bisects the park for 400km (248 miles) from Walhalla to the township of Tom Groggin, on the New South Wales border. There are plenty of access roads into the park, some of which close in winter.

Finds Walhalla: the Valley of the Gods

Tucked in a lush valley in the Victorian Alps, the village of **Walhalla** ★★ is home to only 11 people. A century ago, it was one of the world's richest gold mining towns and what remains of it is faithfully preserved, but without a suggestion of theme-park fakery. The gold ran out in 1914 and Walhalla was simply abandoned. Today, it has the fabulous **Star Hotel** (✆ **03/5165 6262;** fax 03/5165 6261; www.starhotel.com.au), rebuilt in 1999 just after electricity was connected to the town, and a surprising number of things to do. You can take an interesting guided tour of the old gold mine, ride a steam train through lovely bushland, explore the historic cemetery, potter in the small shops and museums, or take a walk along some of the many tracks. Star Hotel owner Michael Leaney will point you in all the right directions. Or you can just hole up in his comfortable, stylish hotel for the weekend. Walhalla is at the end of the Australian Alps Walking Track (which runs 650km/403 miles from Canberra) but the best option for visitors is the 2-day guided walk developed last year by the Star Hotel and nearby **Mt. Baw Baw Alpine Resort** (✆ **1300/651 136** in Australia; www.mountbawbaw.com.au). Walhalla is also a good stopover point to break the Sydney-Melbourne coastal drive. It is about 180km (112 miles) from Melbourne and is a popular day trip and weekend destination. Walhalla's Star Hotel has 12 air-conditioned guest rooms, all of a good size, some with verandas overlooking the street. There is also a restaurant and bar with wood fires for those chilly nights, cozy guest lounge with tea- and coffeemaking facilities, a small library (books and CDs), and guest computer. Next door, the GreyHorse Café sells snacks and drinks. Rates are A$279 (US$223/UK£112) double, including breakfast and dinner.

If you are a keen walker, you could lace up your boots and see the area by foot. **Ecotrek** (✆ **08/8383 4155;** www.ecotrek.com.au) offers an 8-day Bogong Alpine Traverse trek, including 4 nights camping and 3 nights in ski lodges. It is graded moderate/hard and you carry your own pack, but the pain is worth it for the incredible panoramic views of peaks, plains, and forested valleys. The trek costs A$1,695 (US$1,356/UK£678), including round-trip transport to Melbourne.

Horseback-riding treks are another option for seeing the area. **Stoney's High Country** ★★ (www.stoneys.com.au) acts as a one-stop shop for local tour operators offering trail rides. A 2-hour ride in the foothills costs around A$50 (US$40/UK£20); a day ride to higher elevations, A$180 (US$144/UK£72); a weekend ride, around A$400 (US$320/UK£160). Longer rides are also available—check the website for details and contact numbers of operators. Stoney's can also help you organize a custom ride on dates of your choice. Longer tours generally include camping, food, and just about everything else, though you should check whether you'll need a sleeping bag. Other horseback-riding operators include **Falls Creek Trail Rides** (✆ **0419/244 773** mobile phone) and **Bogong Horseback Adventures** (✆ **03/5754 4849;** www.bogonghorse.com.au).

Angling Expeditions (✆ **03/5754 1466;** www.anglingvic.com.au) is the best option for fly-fishing for trout in the alpine area during spring, summer, and fall. Trips last from 3 hours to all day and are suitable for everyone from beginners to experts. Overnight trips are also available.

GETTING THERE Routes from Melbourne include the Great Alpine Road (B500), the Kiewa Valley Highway (C531), and the Lincoln Road from Heyfield. The Bluff is accessible from Mansfield along the Maroondah Highway.

HITTING THE SLOPES: THE HIGH COUNTRY SKI RESORTS

Most of **Victoria's ski areas** are in, or on the edge of, the Alpine National Park (see above). Victoria's main snowfields are Mt. Buller, Mt. Hotham, and Falls Creek, all of which have a wide range of on-mountain accommodations. Closer to Melbourne, Mt. Baw Baw offers gentle slopes for beginners and snow-play, while Lake Mountain and Mt. Stirling are cross-country skiing destinations. The ski season in the Victorian High Country is June through October, with July and August the most popular months. Another popular ski resort area, Mount Buffalo, was dealt a major blow in late 2006 and early 2007 with the loss of its Cresta Lodge in summer bushfires and the subsequent closure of the historic **Mount Buffalo Chalet,** which at press time was facing an uncertain future. Updates will be posted on the resort website, **www.mtbuffalo chalet.com.au**.

MT. HOTHAM

373km (231 miles) NE of Melbourne

Hotham Snow Resort (1,750m/5,740 ft.) is the only resort in Australia with its own airport and summit-top village. Just 10km (6¼ miles) from the ski slopes of Mt. Hotham lies the alpine hamlet of Dinner Plain. There are 14 lifts (including those at Dinner Plain) servicing 320 hectares (791 acres) of terrain ranging from beginner to advanced. A shuttle bus service runs between Dinner Plain and Hotham Village. Ski lift tickets are available from **Hotham Skiing Company** (✆ **1800/468 426** in Australia, or 03/5759 4444; www.hotham.com.au). Full-day lift tickets cost A$90 (US$72/UK£36) for adults and A$45 (US$36/UK£18) for children aged 6 to 14, or A$149 (US$119/UK£60) adults and A$86 (US$69/UK£34) children with gear hire. The resort also offers some good cross-country skiing, including a route across the Bogong High Plains to Falls Creek. Resort entry costs A$28 (US$22/UK£11) per car for a day, payable at the entry gates or at the Mount Hotham Resort Management office (see "Visitor Information," below).

GETTING THERE From Melbourne, take the Hume Highway via Harrietville, or the Princes Highway via Omeo. The trip takes around 5½ hours (the Hume Hwy. is slightly quicker). **Qantaslink** (✆ **13 13 13** in Australia) flies to Mount Hotham Airport from Melbourne and Sydney during the snow season.

Trekset Snowball Express (✆ **1300/656 546;** www.snowballexpress.com.au) runs buses to Hotham daily from mid-June to mid-September. They depart Melbourne's Southern Cross Station in Spencer Street at 9am. The trip takes 6 hours and costs A$100 (US$80/UK£40) one-way or A$150 (US$120/UK£60) return for adults and A$70 (US$56/UK£28) one-way and A$95 (US$76/UK£38) return for children under 15, or A$395 (US$316/UK£158) return for a family of four. There are also coaches from Bright to Hotham. Bookings are essential.

VISITOR INFORMATION **Mount Hotham Alpine Resort Management,** Great Alpine Road, Mount Hotham (✆ **03/5759 3550**), is as close as you'll come to an information office. It has plenty of brochures. It's open daily from 8am to 5pm during ski season, and Monday through Friday from 9am to 5pm at other times. The general Mount Hotham website is **www.mthotham.com.au**.

WHERE TO STAY **Hotham Holidays** (✆ **1800/468 426** in Australia; www.hotham.com.au), has more than 180 properties for you to choose from, ranging from motel-style rooms to luxury chalets. They can book rooms and advise you on special deals, including flights. Another option is the **Mt. Hotham Accommodation Service** (✆ **1800/032 061** in Australia, or 03/5759 3636; www.mthothamaccommodation.com.au). During the ski season, most places will want you to book for a week. Prices are significantly lower in the non-ski season.

FALLS CREEK ★

375km (233 miles) NE of Melbourne

One of Victoria's best ski resorts, Falls Creek is on the edge of the Bogong High Plains overlooking the Kiewa Valley. This compact alpine village is the only one in Australia where you can ski from your lodge to the lifts and back again from the ski slopes. The nightlife is also very good in the ski season, with plenty of party options as well as a range of walk-in lodge restaurants.

The ski fields are in two parts, the Village Bowl and Sun Valley, with 17 lifts covering more than 90 trails. There are plenty of intermediate and advanced runs, as well as a sprinkling for beginners. You'll also find some of Australia's best cross-country skiing; Australia's major cross-country skiing event, the Kangaroo Hoppet, takes place here on the last Saturday in August every year. Entry to the resort costs A$28 (US$22/UK£11) per car per day or A$14 (US$11/UK£5.60) per car with a driver only. Full-day lift tickets cost A$90 (US$72/UK£36) for adults and A$45 (US$36/UK£18) for children, or A$145 (US$116/UK£58) per adult and A$85 (US$68/UK£34) per child for a combined lift and ski-rental ticket. Call **Falls Creek Ski Lifts** (✆ **03/5758 1000**) for details.

GETTING THERE **Pyles Coaches** (✆ **03/5754 4024;** www.pyles.com.au) runs buses to the ski resort from Melbourne every day during the ski season (end of June to end of Sept), departing Melbourne at 9am and Falls Creek at 3pm. The round-trip fare is A$133 (US$106/UK£53) for adults and A$100 (US$80/UK£40) for school-age children and includes the resort entrance fee. The company also runs shuttle buses to and from Albury (A$74/US$59/UK£30 round-trip for adults and A$63/US$50/UK£25 for kids), just over the border in New South Wales and accessible by train or air from Sydney; and between Mount Beauty and Falls Creek. Reservations are essential.

If you're driving from Melbourne, take the Hume Highway to Wangaratta, and then through Myrtleford and Mount Beauty to Falls Creek. The trip takes around 4½ hours. From Sydney, take the Hume Highway to Albury-Wodonga and follow the signs to Mount Beauty and the snowfields (about 8 hr.). If you're driving yourself to Falls Creek, you are legally obliged to carry a pair of snow chains. These can be hired for a small charge from either of Mt. Beauty's service stations and several ski rental stores. If you arrive in the ski season, a resort worker will direct you to a car park and bring you back in a little buggy to the resort entrance, from where you can take a caterpillar-tracked Oversnow taxi to your hotel. It costs A$17 (US$14/UK£6.80) one-way and A$31 (US$25/UK£12) return for adults and A$11 (US$8.80/UK£4.40) one-way and A$20 (US$16/UK£8) return for children 5 to 15. Or you could attempt the short but (probably) slippery walk yourself.

VISITOR INFORMATION The **Alpine Discovery Centre,** 31 Bogong High Plains Rd., Mt. Beauty (✆ **1800/808 277** in Australia, or 03/5754 1962; www.alpinediscoverycentre.com.au), has all the information you need about activities and also an accommodations service. Another good website is **www.fallscreek.com.au**, which has general information and lists ski ticket prices.

Where to Stay & Dine

Falls Creek is a year-round resort with a good range of accommodations. It tends to fill up fast during the ski season. As you might expect, room rates are much higher during the ski season. **Falls Creek Central Reservations** (✆ **1800/033 079** in Australia, or 03/5758 3733; www.fallscreek.com.au) or **Falls Creek Reservations Centre** (✆ **1800/453 525** in Australia) can tell you what deals are available and can book rooms.

If you fancy a self-contained apartment or free-standing chalet, try the **Frueauf Village** complex (✆ **1300/300 709** in Australia, or mobile phone 0412 881 305; www.fvfalls.com.au). These 28 properties were built in 2001 and 2002. The smallest unit, basically a nice studio, costs A$455 (US$364/UK£182) per couple for a 2-night stay in the earliest and latest part of the ski season and jumps to a whopping A$1,040 (US$832/UK£416) for 2 nights in the peak period.

Summit Ridge Alpine Lodge ★ Summit Ridge is an AAA-rated four-and-a-half-star property made from local rock and timber. All rooms are quite nice, if a little stark. Standard rooms come with a set of bunk beds and a couple of useless little desks. Queen suites have a queen-size bed and a couch, plus beautiful mountain views. The mezzanine suites are split-level with the bedroom upstairs; they have king-size beds and an attached bathroom with tub. There's a lounge and dining room on the ground floor and a library on the second. If the mist holds off, there are some fine valley views. The hosts pay a lot of attention to detail, and the homemade bread is worth waking early for. The restaurant excels in fine dining. The owner can take you on early-morning ski runs. The most expensive rates in the ranges below apply in August.

8 Schuss St., Falls Creek, VIC 3699. ✆ **03/5758 3800.** Fax 03/5758 3833. www.summitridge.com.au. A$280–A$460 (US$224–US$368/UK£112–UK£184) standard double; A$340–A$520 (US$272–US$416/UK£136–UK£208) queen double; A$360–A$540 (US$288–US$432/UK£144–UK£216) mezzanine suite. Children 5–14 25% off adult rate. Rates include breakfast and dinner. AE, DC, MC, V. Closed Oct to mid-June. Children under 5 not accepted. **Amenities:** Restaurant; bar; exercise room; Jacuzzi; sauna; in-room massage; babysitting; coin-op laundry. *In room:* TV, minibar, coffeemaker, hair dryer, iron (suites only).

5 The Northwest: Grampians National Park

260km (161 miles) NW of Melbourne

One of Victoria's most popular attractions, the rugged **Grampians National Park** rises some 1,000m (3,280 ft.) from the plains, appearing from the distance like some kind of monumental island. The park, which is an ecological meeting place of Victoria's western volcanic plains and the forested Great Dividing Range, contains one-third of all the wildflowers native to Victoria and most of the surviving Aboriginal rock art in southeastern Australia. Almost 200 species of birds, 35 species of mammals, 28 species of reptiles, 11 species of amphibians, and 6 species of freshwater fish have been discovered here. Kangaroos, koalas, emus, gliders, and echidnas are easy to spot.

In the summers of 2006 and 2007, parts of the Grampians were ravaged by bushfires. While all accommodations and tourist operations are operating, you may still see some of the effects on the landscape when you visit, including the fabulous process of nature regenerating the bush.

The main town in the Grampians is **Halls Gap,** which is in a valley between the southern tip of the Mount Difficult Range and the northern tip of the Mount William

Range. It's a good place to stock up on supplies. The Wonderland Range, with its stunning scenery, is close to Halls Gap, too. There are plenty of short strolls, and longer bushwalks are available.

A must-do stop is the **Brambuk Aboriginal Living Cultural Centre** ★ (✆ **03/5356 4452;** www.brambuk.com.au), adjacent to the park visitor center (see below). It offers an excellent introduction to the area's Aboriginal history and seven accessible rock-art sites. A 15-minute movie highlighting local Aboriginal history costs A$4.40 (US$3.50/UK£1.75) for adults and A$2.80 (US$2.25/UK£1.10) for children. Otherwise, entrance to the center is free. The center is open daily from 9am to 5pm.

ESSENTIALS

GETTING THERE By car, the park is accessible from the Western Highway at Ararat, Stawell (pronounced *Storl*), and Horsham. Alternatively, you can reach the southern entrance from the Glenelg Highway at Dunkeld. The western areas of the park are off the Henty Highway (A200).

V/Line (✆ **13 61 96** in Victoria; www.vline.com.au) has daily train and bus service to Halls Gap from Melbourne. (The train goes to Ballarat, and a bus continues to Halls Gap via Ararat and Stawell.) The trip takes around 4½ hours, and there is a half-hour wait at Ballarat.

GETTING AROUND Paved roads include the **Grampians Tourist Road,** which cuts through the park from Dunkeld to Halls Gap; the **Mount Victory Road,** from Halls Gap to Wartook; and the **Roses Gap Road,** which runs from Wartook across to Dadswells Bridge on the Western Highway. Many other roads in the park are unpaved, but most are passable with a two-wheel-drive car.

Autopia Tours (✆ **1800/000 507** in Australia, or 03/9419 8878; www.autopiatours.com.au) offers all-day tours of the park and surroundings from Melbourne, leaving every Wednesday, Friday, and Sunday (call ahead to check departure times and pickup points). The tour stops at Aboriginal rock-art sites, waterfalls, and lookouts. There's a bit of walking involved, so you need to be reasonably fit, and you certainly get the chance to spot native animals and ferret around among the native flora. The tour includes morning tea and National Park entry fees, and costs A$90 (US$72/UK£36).

VISITOR INFORMATION The **Halls Gap & Grampians National Park Visitor Centre** (✆ **1800/065 599** in Australia, or 03/5356 4616), 2.5km (1½ miles) south of Halls Gap, is open daily from 9am to 5pm. It has plenty of maps and brochures, and the rangers can advise you on walking trails and camping spots. Check out **www.visitgrampians.com.au**.

WHERE TO STAY

Boroka Downs ★★★ Sleep in five-star luxury, then wake up to breaking light over rolling farmland and kangaroos outside your glass floor-length windows. Boroka Downs has five private, contemporary Australian style self-contained residences, about 7km (4⅓ miles) from Hall's Gap. Each has stunning views: from your choice of the circular spa, the king-size bed, or the fireside. You'll be dazzled by the quality of the place, from the state-of-the-art sound system to the espresso coffee machine (fresh beans and grinder provided) and gourmet kitchen. Service here is "on demand," to ensure guests have their own desired level of privacy. There are lots of extras provided, such as backpacks and binoculars for walking, and bathrobes for lounging around.

Breakfast and supper packs can be provided for A$35 (US$28/UK£14) extra. It's private, elegant, and you probably won't want to leave. It's not suitable for children.

Birdswing Rd., Hall's Gap, VIC 3294. ✆ **03/5356 6243.** Fax 03/5356 6343. www.borokadowns.com.au. 5 units. A$545 (US$426/UK£213) double midweek; A$595 (US$476/UK£238) double weekends. Rates include breakfast pack for stays of up to 3 nights, and are reduced the more nights you stay. Ask about packages. AE, MC, V. **Amenities:** Tour desk; massage. *In room:* A/C, TV/VCR, DVD, kitchen, coffeemaker, iron, Jacuzzi.

Royal Mail Hotel & Bluestone Cottages ★ You have a choice of lodgings at this renovated historic hotel located between the Great Ocean Road and the Grampians National Park. There are motel-style rooms with either garden or mountain views, or eight private one- and two-bedroom bluestone cottages on a working sheep farm at Mt. Sturgeon, about 5km (3 miles) from the hotel, and frankly, these are my pick. Built by Chinese workers in the 1870s, they are a peaceful retreat, with huge comfortably worn brown-leather armchairs, an open fireplace, CD player, and patchwork quilts on the beds. Equally appealing are the rustic table and chairs outside, where you can watch the changing light on Mt. Sturgeon. The water tank against the back wall cunningly conceals your bathroom. There's a kitchen with microwave and a gas barbecue outside. A continental breakfast for your first morning is included, and can be picked up when you check in (at the Royal Mail). The drawback? There's no television, no phone, and no mobile phone reception. Mulberry House is a four-bedroom bluestone homestead just across the road from the hotel, with a gourmet kitchen, plasma-screen television, formal dining and sitting rooms, and library.

98 Parker St., Dunkeld, VIC 3294. ✆ **03/5577 2241.** Fax 03/5577 2577. www.royalmail.com.au. 33 units. A$130–A$200 (US$104–US$160/UK£52–UK£80) double with breakfast; A$210–A$250 (US$168–US$200/UK£84–UK£100) double 1-bedroom apt including breakfast; A$240–A$290 (US$192–US$232/UK£96–UK£116) 2-bedroom apt (sleeps 4) including breakfast; A$180–A280 (US$144–US$224/UK£72–UK£112) bluestone cottages. A$380 (US$304/UK£152) Mulberry House (sleeps 11). 2-night minimum for house and cottages. AE, DC, MC, V. **Amenities:** 2 restaurants; bar; swimming pool; free laundry. *In room:* A/C, TV (except cottages), fridge, coffeemaker, iron.

14

Canberra

by Marc Llewellyn

If you mention you're heading to Canberra (pronounced *Can*-bra, with very open vowels), most Australians will raise an eyebrow and say, "Why bother?" Even many Canberrans will admit that it's a great place to live but they wouldn't want to visit.

So what is it about Canberra (pop. 310,000) that draws so much lackluster comment? Simply put, Australians aren't used to having things so nice and ordered. You could compare Canberra to Washington, D.C., or any other town that was a planned community from the start. Some see its virtues as bland: The roads are wide and good, the buildings modern, and the suburbs are pleasant and leafy. Canberra is also the seat of government and home of thousands of civil servants—enough to make almost any freethinking, individualist Aussie shudder.

But to me, Canberra's differences are the things that make it special. The streets aren't clogged with traffic, and there are plenty of opportunities for safe biking—try that in almost any other city center and you'll be dusting the sides of cars and pushed onto the sidewalks. Canberra has plenty of open spaces, parklands, and monuments, and a lot to see and do—from museum- and gallery-hopping to ballooning with a champagne glass in hand or boating on Lake Burley Griffin. You can pack a lot into a few days.

Canberra was born after the Commonwealth of Australia was created in 1901. Melbourne and Sydney, even then jockeying for preeminence, bid to become the capital. In the end, Australian leaders decided to follow the example of their U.S. counterparts by creating a federal district; in 1908 they chose an undeveloped area between the two cities.

Designing the capital fell to Chicago landscape architect Walter Burley Griffin, a contemporary of Frank Lloyd Wright. The city he mapped out was called Canberra (a local Aboriginal word meaning "meeting place"), and by 1927, the first meeting of parliament took place.

Originally the land that became Canberra was predominantly grass plains. Over the years, millions of trees have been planted in and around the city, earning it the nickname "the bush capital." Massive bushfires in January 2003 destroyed much of the surrounding forest and more than 500 homes in the suburbs. A few years later, you would barely know it happened.

1 Orientation

ARRIVING

BY PLANE **Qantas** (© **13 13 13** in Australia; www.qantas.com.au) runs frequent daily service to Canberra from all state capitals. **Virgin Blue** (© **13 67 89** in Australia; www.virginblue.com.au) offers discount daily flights to Canberra from Melbourne, Brisbane, and Adelaide, but not Sydney. The Canberra Airport is about 10 minutes from the city center. It has car-rental desks, a currency exchange, a bar, a bistro, and a

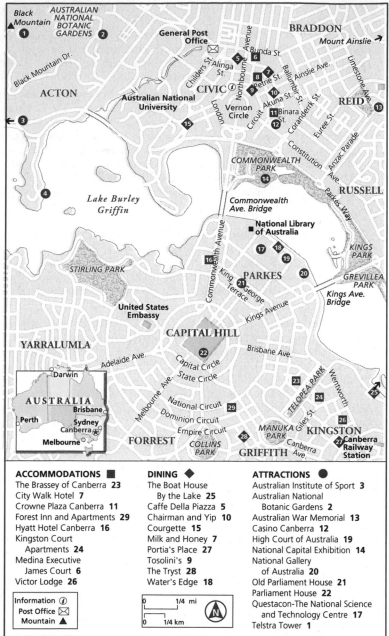

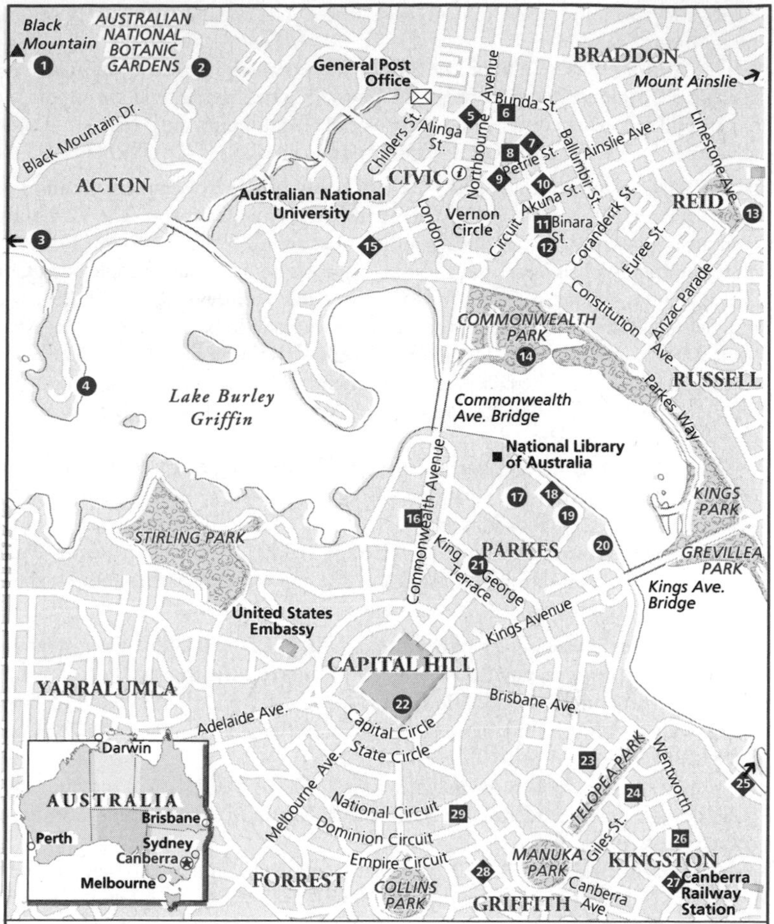

ACCOMMODATIONS ■

- The Brassey of Canberra **23**
- City Walk Hotel **7**
- Crowne Plaza Canberra **11**
- Forest Inn and Apartments **29**
- Hyatt Hotel Canberra **16**
- Kingston Court Apartments **24**
- Medina Executive James Court **6**
- Victor Lodge **26**

DINING ◆

- The Boat House By the Lake **25**
- Caffe Della Piazza **5**
- Chairman and Yip **10**
- Courgette **15**
- Milk and Honey **7**
- Portia's Place **27**
- Tosolini's **9**
- The Tryst **28**
- Water's Edge **18**

ATTRACTIONS ●

- Australian Institute of Sport **3**
- Australian National Botanic Gardens **2**
- Australian War Memorial **13**
- Casino Canberra **12**
- High Court of Australia **19**
- National Capital Exhibition **14**
- National Gallery of Australia **20**
- Old Parliament House **21**
- Parliament House **22**
- Questacon-The National Science and Technology Centre **17**
- Telstra Tower **1**

Information ⓘ
Post Office ✉
Mountain ▲

0 1/4 mi
0 1/4 km
N

mailbox for cards and letters (but no post office). The newsdealer sells stamps. There are no lockers or showers.

The **Airliner Bus** (✆ **02/6299 3722;** www.deanesbuslines.com.au/queanbeyan) operates a 20-minute shuttle between the central business district and the airport Monday to Friday, leaving every half-hour on weekdays and hourly on weekends. The one-way fare is A$7 (US$5.60/UK£2.80) and a round-trip costs A$12 (US$9.60/UK£4.80).

BY TRAIN **Countrylink** (✆ **13 22 32** in Australia; www.countrylink.info) runs three Canberra Xplorer trains daily between Sydney and Canberra. The 4¼-hour trip costs around A$70 (US$56/UK£28) in first class and A$50 (US$40/UK£20) in economy; children pay half price, and a round-trip costs double. Many people book Countrylink transport-hotel packages (call **Countrylink Holidays,** ✆ **13 28 29**), which can save you quite a bit. Depending on the accommodations in Canberra, prices range from A$90 to A$190 (US$72–US$152/UK£36–UK£76) a night for a couple, and if you book in advance (the company recommends 2 weeks), you can save up to 40% on the fare through a Rail Escape package. Countrylink has an office at Wynyard CityRail station in Sydney.

From Melbourne, the **Canberra Link,** run by **V/Line** (✆ **13 61 96** in Australia; www.vlinepassenger.com.au), involves a 5-hour bus trip and a 3½-hour train trip. It costs A$55 (US$44/UK£22) for adults and A$34 (US$27/UK£13) for children and students.

Canberra Railway Station (✆ **02/6239 6707**) is on Wentworth Avenue, Kingston, about 5km (3 miles) southeast of the city center. Coaches connect the railway station to the center.

BY BUS **Greyhound** (✆ **13 14 99** in Australia, or 07/4690 9950; www.greyhound.com.au) does 10 runs a day from Sydney to Canberra; the trip takes 4 to 4½ hours. Tickets cost around A$37 (US$30/UK£15) for adults, A$33 (US$27/UK£13) for students with an ISAC (International Student Activity Card), and A$29 (US$23/UK£12) for children 3 to 14.

From Melbourne, tickets to Canberra cost A$62 (US$50/UK£25) for adults, A$52 (US$42/UK£21) for students, and A$46 (US$37/UK£18) for children. Advance-purchase fares can be as much as 35% lower.

Murrays Australia (✆ **13 22 51** in Australia; www.murrays.com.au) runs from Sydney to Canberra five times a day for A$36 (US$29/UK£15) for adults and A$29 (US$23/UK£12) for children. Ask for YHA member discounts. Book over the Internet for further discounts. Several sightseeing companies in Sydney, including **AAT King's** and **Australia Pacific Tours,** offer day trips to Canberra.

Interstate buses arrive at **Jolimont Tourist Centre,** at the corner of Northbourne Avenue and Alinga Street, Canberra City.

BY CAR The ACT (Australian Capital Territory) is surrounded by New South Wales. Sydney is 306km (190 miles) northeast, and Melbourne is 651km (404 miles) southwest of Canberra. From Sydney, you can use an extension to the M5 motorway that links with the Eastern Distributor highway near Sydney Airport. Veer left before you reach the airport and follow signs heading toward Canberra, and veer left onto the M5. The drive takes between 3 and 3½ hours. From Melbourne, take the Hume Highway to Yass and switch to the Barton Highway; the trip will take about 8 hours.

VISITOR INFORMATION

The **Canberra Visitors' Centre,** 330 Northbourne Ave., Dickson (✆ **02/6205 0044**), dispenses information and books accommodations. The office is open Monday through Friday from 9am to 5:30pm, and Saturday and Sunday from 9am to 4pm. The official government website (**www.visitcanberra.com.au**) is worth checking out.

SPECIAL EVENTS A host of free events—from concerts to competitions—is part of the annual **Canberra National Multicultural Festival** the first 3 weeks of March. The fun includes Canberra Day (a local public holiday, the third Mon in Mar), a hot-air balloon fiesta, fireworks, food and wine promotions, music, and a large range of other activities that draw on Australia's ethnic mix. Visitors may find it a little more difficult to book accommodations during this time, but you should always be able to find something. There are many other major events, including the annual flower show **Floriade,** the **Subaru Rally of Canberra,** the **Canberra 400 V8 Supercars** meeting, and the **National Folk Festival.** Check dates at www.visitcanberra.com.au.

CITY LAYOUT

The first thing that strikes a visitor to Canberra is its parklike feel (amazing, because there was barely a tree on the original site). Half a dozen avenues radiate from **Capital Hill,** where Parliament House stands. Each of these broad, tree-shaded streets leads to a traffic circle, from which more streets emanate. Around each hub, the streets form a pattern of concentric circles—not the easiest layout for visitors trying to find their way.

Another of Canberra's most notable features is **Lake Burley Griffin,** created by damming the Molonglo River. The centerpiece of the lake is the **Captain Cook Memorial Jet,** a spire of water that reaches 147m (482 ft.) into the air. Wedged between Commonwealth Avenue and Kings Avenue is the suburb of **Parkes,** also known as the National Triangle. Here you'll find many of the city's most impressive attractions, such as the National Gallery of Australia, the High Court of Australia, and Questacon—the National Science and Technology Centre. Many embassies and consulates are in the suburb of **Yarralumla,** east of Capital Hill; most of the other suburbs are filled with pleasant homes and small retail areas.

Canberra's main shopping district is on the other side of the lake, centered on Northbourne Avenue, one of the city's main thoroughfares. Officially Canberra City, this area is more commonly known as **"Civic."** Northeast of Civic is **Mount Ainslie,** with the Australian War Memorial at its foot; from its summit there are spectacular views of the city and beyond. Another good lookout point is the top of the **Telstra Tower** on Black Mountain, west of Civic and reached by Black Mountain Drive.

2 Getting Around

BY CAR Advantage Car Rentals, 74 Northbourne Ave. (corner of Barry Dr.; & 1800/504 460 in Australia, or 02/6257 6888), has cars from A$35 (US$28/UK£14) per day, including 200km (124 miles) per day. Budget (& 02/6257 1305),

A Canberra Bus Tour

Canberra Day Tours (© 02/6298 3344; www.canberradaytours.com.au) offers a hop-on and hop-off day tour by bus including stops at Old Parliament House, the Australian War Memorial, Parliament House, the Embassy region, Telstra Tower, and Lake Burley Griffin. It costs A$35 (US$28/UK£14) for adults and A$15 (US$12/UK£6) for kids under 16. The first bus leaves at 9:30am from the Canberra Visitors' Centre.

Hertz (☎ 02/6249 6211), Thrifty (☎ 1300/367 227), Avis (☎ 02/6249 6088), and Delta Europcar (☎ 13 13 90) have desks at the airport.

If you rent your own wheels, you might follow one or more of the six tourist drives marked with signs; pick up details from the Canberra Visitors' Centre.

BY TAXI Canberra's only taxi company is **Canberra Cabs** (© **13 22 27** in Australia). Taxis are scarce and you may be asked to share a cab from the airport to the city with other passengers. For this you get a discounted fare.

BY BUS **ACTION** (© **13 17 10** in Australia, or 02/6207 7611; www.action.act.gov.au) coordinates Canberra's bus system. The central bus terminal is on Alinga Street, in Civic. Single tickets cost A$3 (US$2.40/UK£1.20) for adults and A$1.50 (US$1.20/UK60p) for children 5 to 15. Daily tickets cost A$6.60 (US$5.30/UK£2.70) for adults and A$3.30 (US$2.60/UK£1.30) for kids, and weekly tickets cost A$24 (US$19/UK£10) for adults and A$12 (US$9.60/UK£4.80) for kids. Purchase single tickets on the bus and daily and weekly tickets from most newsdealers and ACTION interchanges (transfer points).

For schedules, call ACTION Monday through Saturday from 7am to 9pm, and Sunday from 8am to 6pm. Pick up bus route maps at bus interchanges, newsdealers, and the Canberra Visitors' Centre.

BY BICYCLE Canberra is unique in Australia for its extensive system of cycle tracks—some 120km (74 miles) of them—which makes sightseeing on two wheels a pleasure. See "Outdoor Pursuits," later in this chapter, for details on bike rental.

FAST FACTS: Canberra

American Express The office at **Centrepoint,** Shop 1, 185 City Walk (at the corner of Petrie Plaza), Civic (© **02/6247 2333**), is open Monday through Friday from 9am to 5pm, and Saturday from 9am to noon.

Business Hours Banks are generally open Monday through Thursday from 9:30am to 4pm and Friday from 9:30am to 5pm. Stores and offices are open Monday through Friday from 9am to 5:30pm. Many shops, particularly in the large malls, are open on weekends and until 9pm Fridays.

Climate The best time to visit Canberra is in spring (Sept–Nov) or autumn (Mar–May). Summers are hot and winters are cool and crisp.

Currency Exchange Cash traveler's checks at banks; at **American Express** (above); or at **Travelex,** in the Harvey World Travel office at the Petrie Plaza entrance of the Canberra Centre (© **02/6257 2222**), open Monday through Friday from 9am to 5pm and Saturday from 9:30am to 12:30pm.

Doctor The **Capital Medical Centre,** 2 Mort St., Civic (© **02/6257 3766**), is open Monday through Friday from 8:30am to 4:30pm. A standard consultation costs around A$50 (US$40/UK£20). The **Travellers' Medical & Vaccination Centre,** Level 5, 8–10 Hobart Place, Civic (© **02/6257 7154**), offers vaccinations and travel medicines. Standard consultations cost A$50 (US$40/UK£20) and up.

Embassies & Consulates The **British High Commission** (consular section) is on the 10th floor of the SAP Building, corner of Bunda and Akuna streets, Canberra

City (✆ **02/6270 6666**); the **Canadian High Commission** is at Commonwealth Avenue, Yarralumla (✆ **02/6270 4000**); the **U.S. Embassy** is at Moonah Place, Yarralumla (✆ **02/6214 5600**); and the **New Zealand High Commission** is at Commonwealth Avenue, Yarralumla (✆ **02/6270 4211**).

Emergencies Call ✆ **000** for an ambulance, the police, or the fire department.

Eyeglasses For repairs, glasses, and contact lenses, try **OPSM Express,** Shop 5, Lower Ground Floor, Canberra Centre, Civic (✆ **02/6249 7344**). It's open 9am to 5:30pm Monday through Thursday, 9am to 9pm Friday, and 9am to 4pm Saturday.

Hospitals For medical attention, go to the Canberra Hospital, Yamba Drive, Garran (& 02/6244 2222), or call the Accident & Emergency Department (& 02/ 6244 2324).

Hot Lines **Rape Crisis Centre** (✆ 02/6247 2525); **Drug/Alcohol Crisis Line** (✆ 02/ 6205 4545; 24 hr.); **Lifeline Crisis Councelling** (✆ 13 11 14); **Salvation Army Councelling Service** (✆ 02/9331 6000); **Poison Information Centre** (✆ 02/6285 2852); **National Roads & Motorists Association** (✆ 13 21 32).

Internet Access The **National Library,** Parkes Place, Parkes (✆ **02/6262 1111**), has e-mail facilities available Monday through Thursday 9am to 5pm. Internet access is readily available around town at other libraries and in Internet cafes. The Canberra Visitors' Centre can provide you with a full list.

Pharmacies (Chemist Shops) The **Canberra Centre Pharmacy,** Civic (✆ **02/6249 8074**), is open during general shopping hours. A number of after-hours pharmacies are listed in the Canberra Yellow Pages.

Photographic Needs **Fletchers Fotographics,** Shop 2, 38 Akuna St., Civic (✆ **02/ 6247 8460**), is the best place to buy camera gear and film. It also repairs cameras and sells secondhand equipment.

Post Office The **Canberra GPO,** 53–73 Alinga St., Civic (✆ **02/6209 1680**), is open Monday through Friday from 8:30am to 5:30pm. The general delivery *(poste restante)* address is c/o Canberra GPO, ACT 2601.

Restrooms Found near the city bus exchange, City Hall, and London Circuit.

3 Where to Stay

Canberra has a good scattering of places to stay, and generally accommodations are much cheaper than in most other state capitals. Many people travel to Canberra during the week, so many hotels offer cheaper weekend rates. You should always ask about special deals. The rates given below are rack rates, or what the hotels hope they'll get on a good day—you can often get a room for less, especially booking directly through the hotel's website. The **Canberra Visitors' Centre** (✆ **02/6205 0044**) can provide information about other accommodations options.

VERY EXPENSIVE

Hyatt Hotel Canberra ★★ Visiting heads of state and pop stars make this their residence of choice in Canberra, and it's not hard to see why. It has a great location a 2-minute drive from the city center, in the shadow of Parliament House, and between Lake Burley Griffin and the Parliamentary Triangle. Originally the Hotel Canberra, it opened in 1924 and was based on the low-slung "prairie" design of the now-destroyed Imperial Hotel in Tokyo. For many years the Hyatt was an important part of Canberra's social and political life, with key decisions affecting all Australians being made over drinks in the bar. All staff members wear 1920s costumes to add to the atmosphere.

Some 39 rooms are in the original two-story section. The rooms have more historical appeal, but they are darker than their modern counterparts, which were added in the 1980s. Standard rooms have a king-size bed and marble bathrooms. They all come with the little luxuries you'd expect from a hotel of this class. A quick look at their website showed rooms for as cheap as A$238 (US$190/UK£95) a night.

Commonwealth Ave., Yarralumla, ACT 2600. ✆ **13 12 34** in Australia, 800/233-1234 in the U.S. and Canada, 0181/335 1220 in London, 0845/758 1666 elsewhere in the U.K., 0800/441 234 in New Zealand, or 02/6270 1234. Fax 02/6281 5998. http://canberra.park.hyatt.com/hyatt/hotels/index.jsp. 249 units. A$380 (US$304/UK£152) standard double; A$605 (US$484/UK£242) executive suite; A$1,200 (US$960/UK£480) diplomatic suite. Extra person A$28 (US$22/UK£11). Children under 18 stay free in parent's room. Ask about weekend packages and special rates. AE, DC, MC, V. Free parking. Bus: 31, 36, or 39. **Amenities:** Restaurant; cafe; indoor pool; lit tennis court; extensive health club and spa; bike rental; concierge; business center; 24-hr. room service; laundry service. *In room:* A/C, TV w/pay movies, minibar, hair dryer, iron, safe.

EXPENSIVE

Crowne Plaza Canberra ★★ This hotel is next door to the National Convention Centre and Casino Canberra. Its car-oriented approach makes it a little inconvenient for pedestrians, but the gardens (Glebe Park) at the back are good for early-morning strolls. Rooms face onto internal balconies that look down to the restaurants below. Standard rooms are user-friendly and comfortable; most come with one queen-size bed or two doubles. Park-view doubles overlook the gardens. Weekend rates drop dramatically, so it's worth checking the website.

1 Binara St., Canberra, ACT 2601. ✆ **1300/363 300** in Australia, or 02/6247 8999. Fax 02/6257 4903. www.crowneplaza.com. 295 units. A$300 (US$240/UK£120) standard double; A$315 (US$252/UK£126) park-view double; A$425–A$500 (US$340–US$400/UK£170–UK£200) suite. Extra person A$35 (US$28/UK£14). Weekend discounts available. Children under 15 stay free in parent's room. AE, DC, MC, V. Free parking. Bus: 30, 35, 38, or 80. **Amenities:** Restaurant; bar; medium-size indoor pool; health club; concierge; business center; 24-hr. room service; laundry service. *In room:* A/C, TV, minibar, hair dryer, iron, safe.

MODERATE

The Brassey of Canberra ★ Rooms in this 1927 heritage-listed building, formerly a boardinghouse for visiting government officials, are large, quiet, and somewhat plush. The garden bar and piano lounge are popular. Other good points include its proximity to Parliament House and other major attractions, and the hearty breakfasts. The hotel underwent extensive renovations a few years ago, which included the remodeling of many of the doubles into larger heritage rooms.

Belmore Gardens, Barton, ACT 2600. ✆ **1800/659 191** in Australia, or 02/6273 3766. Fax 02/6273 2791. www.brassey.net.au. 81 units. A$132 (US$105/UK£57) double; A$165 (US$132/UK£66) double family room; A$141 (US$113/UK£57) heritage double; A$187 (US$150/UK£75) heritage family room. Rates include full breakfast. Check for specials. AE, DC, MC, V. Free parking. Bus: 36 to National Press Club. **Amenities:** Restaurant; bar; coin-op laundry; dry cleaning. *In room:* A/C, TV, dataport, minibar, coffeemaker, hair dryer, iron.

Forrest Inn and Apartments *Kids* The Forrest Inn is far from fancy, but it's close to the Manuka shops and restaurants and Parliament House. The outside of this 1960s property looks tacky, but the interior has been refurbished. The motel-style rooms are small and colorless; the apartments are nicer and have full-size kitchens, so I recommend that you spend a little more money and go for these. Two-bedroom apartments are perfect for families, and even the one-bedroom apartments have a single bed in the living room. Internet prices are usually lower than the rack rates listed below.

30 National Circuit, Forrest, ACT 2603. ✆ **1800/676 372** in Australia, or 02/6295 3433. Fax 02/6295 2119. www.forrestinn.com.au. 102 units. A$110 (US$88/UK£44) motel room; A$150 (US$120/UK£60) 1-bedroom apt; A$175 (US$140/UK£70) 2-bedroom apt. AE, DC, MC, V. Free parking. Bus: 39 to Rydges Canberra Hotel. **Amenities:** Restaurant; limited room service (motel only); coin-op laundry. *In room:* A/C, TV, minibar, hair dryer, iron.

Kingston Court Apartments ★ About 1km (½ mile) from the Parliamentary Triangle and 6km (3¾ miles) from Civic, this government-rated four-and-a-half-star apartment complex is a good option if you're looking for the comforts of home. All the two-bedroom apartments are modern and spacious and come with a full kitchen, washer and dryer, and a balcony or a private courtyard.

4 Tench St., Kingston, ACT 2604. ✆ **1800/655 754** in Australia, or 02/6295 2244. Fax 02/6295 5300. www.kingstonterrace.com.au. 32 units. A$160 (US$128/UK£64) apt for 2. Extra adult A$20 (US$16/UK£8); extra child A$10 (US$8/UK£4). AE, DC, MC, V. Free parking. Bus: 38. **Amenities:** Small outdoor heated pool; half-size tennis court. *In room:* A/C, TV/VCR, dataport, kitchen, minibar, fridge, hair dryer, iron.

Medina Executive James Court ★★ I always heartily recommend staying at a Medina property in Australia. As with others scattered around the country, the Medina Executive James Court is modern, spankingly clean, centrally located, and has a fully equipped kitchen and laundry. There is a TV in the living room and another in the bedroom in both the one- and two-bedroom apartments, and all apartments come with a balcony. A sister property, the **Medina Classic,** at 11 Giles St., Kingston (✆ **02/6239 8100;** fax 02/6239 7226), is just 4km (2½ miles) from the city center in fashionable Kingston. It has both an indoor and outdoor pool and landscaped gardens, and also offers three-bedroom apartments. Internet rates for this property are A$186 (US$149/UK£75) for a one-bedroom apartment, A$227 (US$181/UK£90) for a two-bedroom apartment, and A$289 (US$231/UK£115) for a three-bedroom apartment.

74 Northbourne Ave., Canberra, ACT 2601. ✆ **1300 300 232** in Australia, or 02/6240 1234. Fax 02/6240 1235. www.medinaapartments.com.au. 150 units. A$201 (US$160/UK£80) 1-bedroom apt; A$267 (US$213/UK£56) 2-bedroom apt. A$30 (US$24/UK£12) extra person. AE, MC, V. Parking A$5 (US$4/UK£2). **Amenities:** Restaurant; bar; outdoor pool; health club/sauna; concierge; hair salon; 24-hr. room service; laundry service. *In room:* A/C, TV, kitchen, minibar, hair dryer, iron, safe, laundry.

INEXPENSIVE

City Walk Hotel You can hardly get closer to the city center than at this former YWCA-turned–budget hotel. Being near the Jolimont Tourist Centre bus interchange, it picks up a lot of business from backpackers and budget travelers arriving by bus. Twelve rooms are anything but basic though, coming with their own bathroom, fridge, tea- and coffee-making facilities, and TV. They are motel-like in style. Twelve more rooms are more basic and share bathrooms. There are also dorms. The hostel was completely refurbished in 2003. The communal facilities include a kitchen, laundry, and a lounge area with TV and VCR. On the premises is the popular **King O' Malley's Irish Pub,** which has live entertainment on Friday and Saturday evenings.

2 Mort St., Civic, ACT 2601. ✆ **1800/600 124** in Australia, or 02/6257 0124. Fax 02/6257 0116. www.citywalkhotel.com.au. 24 units, 12 with bathroom with shower only, plus dorm rooms sleeping between 6 and 10. A$26–A$28 (US$21–US$22/UK£10–UK£11) dorm room bed; A$65 (US$48/UK£24) double or twin without bathroom; A$90 (US$72/UK£36) double with bathroom; A$105 (US$84/UK£42) family room. MC, V. **Amenities:** Coin-op laundry; Internet cafe. *In room:* TV, fridge, coffeemaker, no phone.

Victor Lodge *Value* Backpackers and budget travelers frequent this friendly place, next to Kingston's shops and about a 10-minute drive from the city center. Rooms vary, from dorms with four or five beds to modern, simple doubles. Each has a wash basin. There are communal showers and toilets and a courtyard. The staff picks up guests from the train and bus stations daily and drops off guests in town every morning. It's a nice place, but you'll have to decide whether you want to put up with the short trek into the city.

Next door is the reasonable **Best Western** motel, at 27 Dawes St. (✆ **02/6295 2111;** http://motelmonaro.bestwestern.com.au). It charges A$129 (US$103/UK£52) for a double. Apparently, long-suffering parents often park their teenage kids at the lodge and live it up at the motel.

29 Dawes St., Kingston, ACT 2604. ✆ **02/6295 7777.** Fax 02/6295 2466. www.victorlodge.com.au. 29 units, none with bathroom. A$76 (US$61/UK£31) double; A$27 (US$17/UK£7.50) dorm bed. Rates include continental breakfast. MC, V. Free parking. Bus: 38 or 39. **Amenities:** Bike rental; tour desk; coin-op laundry; nonsmoking rooms; Internet facilities; dining room; TV room. *In room:* A/C, iron.

4 Where to Dine

EXPENSIVE

The Boat House by the Lake ★★ MODERN AUSTRALIAN On the shores of Lake Burley Griffin, The Boat House is a pleasant dining retreat with uninterrupted water views. The large dining room's floor-to-ceiling windows capture the view, and the outside terrace is a nice spot on a sunny day for lunch. To start, try Coffin Bay oysters, either natural with lemon, or topped with litchi, avocado, and chile salsa. Then go for Japanese peppered beef filet on garlic mashed potatoes with braised mushrooms, asparagus tempura, and wasabi hollandaise sauce. The wine list features local vintages.

Grevillea Park, Menindee Dr., Barton, ACT. ✆ **02/6273 5500.** www.boathousebythelake.com.au. Reservations required. Main courses A$32 (US$26/UK£16) lunch, A$35 (US$28/UK£14) dinner. AE, DC, MC, V. Mon–Fri noon–3pm; Mon–Sat 6–10:30pm.

The Chairman and Yip ★ ASIAN AUSTRALIAN This, they say, is one of Canberra's best restaurants. Upbeat and popular with political bigwigs, it has a reputation of being the place to see and be seen. The chairs are comfortable, the menus are tucked inside art magazines, and Mao-style pop art decorates the walls. One of my favorites is the prawns with homemade chile jam, served on vermicelli noodles with mango salsa. Abalone and lobster also find their way onto the menu. Panna cotta is the signature dessert, and chef William Suen keeps his regulars happy with his iconic Shanghai duck pancakes.

108 Bunda St., Civic. ✆ **02/6248 7109.** www.thechairmanandyip.com. Reservations required. Main courses A$27–A$40 (US$21–US$32/UK£10–UK£16). AE, DC, MC, V. Sun–Fri noon–3pm; daily 6–11pm.

Courgette ★★ *Finds* EUROPEAN/AUSTRALIAN This plush dining room features conical hanging lamps and candlelight, luxurious cream velour chairs, theatrical drapes, and thick blue carpets. There are two dining areas: an intimate place behind the bar, and a larger, brighter space with floor-to-ceiling windows overlooking a pebbled garden. The food is French-influenced and features standout dishes such as roasted rabbit with muscatel grapes, glazed pearl onions, bacon, Brussels sprouts, and butter puff pastry; or the caramelized suckling pig with cauliflower purée, cinnamon spiced apple, and aromatic jus. There are plenty of seafood options, too. A good

Ethnic Eating in Canberra

Canberra, like other Australian cities, has an interesting ethnic mix of people from all over the world. This is reflected in the cuisines on offer. Canberra's best ethnic eateries include **Ottoman Cuisine** (9 Broughton St., Barton; ✆ **02/6273 6111**) which features fabulous Turkish food costing around A$26 (US$21/UK£11) for a main course. Another highlight is **Rama's** (Shop 6, Pearce Shopping Centre, corner Mcfarland and Hodgson crescents, Pearce; ✆ **02/6286 1964**), which specializes in Fijian Indian food with mains averaging A$16 (US$13/UK£7.50). For Ethiopian food (such as hot curries, cauliflower fritters, and lamb and rosemary kabobs), try **Fekerte's** (74/2 Cape St., Dickson; ✆ **02/6262 5799**). Mains here cost around A$20 (US$16/UK£8). Japanese food addicts should head to tiny **Tasuke** (122 Alinga St., Civic; ✆ **02/6257 9711**). Try the udon noodles, the fish cakes, and the deep-fried oysters. Mains average around A$20 (US$16/UK£8).

choice is the seven-course degustation menu costing A$90 (US$72/UK£36) for food only and A$135 (US$108/UK£54) for food and wine. The wine list is very good, and all in all you should prepare for a refined dining experience.

54 Marcus Clarke St., Civic. ✆ **02/6247 4042.** www.courgette.com.au . Reservations required. Main courses A$32–A$36 (US$25–US$28/UK£13–UK£14). AE, DC, MC, V. Mon–Fri noon–3pm; Mon–Sat 6–11pm.

Waters Edge ★★ CONTEMPORARY Minimalist decor, vaulted ceilings, crisp linen, and white leather chairs offset the striking architecture at Waters Edge. Sweeping views across Lake Burley Griffin to the Australian War Memorial offer diners an outlook befitting of the national capital's most highly awarded restaurant. In keeping with the prime location, outstanding food, and carefully designed wine list, the polished service is non-intrusive but knowledgeable. Waters Edge has received several high-profile awards including Canberra's Restaurant of the Year 2006. Try the finely sliced cuttlefish on a bed of refried beans and cauliflower surrounded by crisply fried sweetbreads on a rich meat jus with a vinegar reduction.

Commonwealth Place, Parkes. ✆ **02/6273 5066.** www.outincanberra.com.au/watersedge. Reservations required. Main courses A$26–A$38 (US$21–US$31/UK£11–UK£16). AE, DC, MC, V. Tues–Fri noon–2:30pm; Tues–Sun 6:30–11pm.

MODERATE

Milk and Honey ★ CONTEMPORARY/CAFE There's a happy buzz of students and workers in this youthful joint. It offers everything from light snacks, smoothies, and milkshakes to full meals. The food is reasonably priced and contemporary, and the decor is 1970s retro. There's also a great choice of alcoholic drinks from the bar, including cocktails, and a big range of freshly squeezed fruit juices. Milk and Honey also does pasta well, and its generous risotto stacked with seafood is recommended, too.

Centre Cinema Building, 29 Garema Place, Civic. ✆ **02/6247 7722.** Reservations recommended. Main courses A$14–A$25 (US$11–US$20/UK£5.50–UK£10). AE, DC, MC, V. Mon–Fri 7:30–10pm; Sat 8am–10pm; Sun 9am–3pm.

Tosolini's ★ CAFE/MODERN AUSTRALIAN Because it's next to the busy central bus terminal and close to the major shopping areas, Tosolini's really pulls in the passing crowd. You can sit out on the sidewalk terrace and watch the world go by. Battered flathead and pan-fried broadbill (both are local fish) are tasty, but Tosolini's really made its name with its pastas and focaccias. Try the popular *spaghettini con granchio:*

succulent pieces of blue swimmer crab, fresh tomato, rocket leaves, chile, garlic, and extra virgin olive oil served on a bed of spaghettini. The tiramisu is a delight.

Corner of London Circuit at East Row, Civic. ✆ **02/6247 4317.** www.tosolinis.com.au. Main courses A$15–A$18 (US$12–US$14/UK£6–UK£7). AE, DC, MC, V. Sun–Mon 7:30am–5pm; Tues–Sat 7:30am–10:30pm.

The Tryst ★★ *Finds* MODERN AUSTRALIAN The personal touches and service shine here, and the food is consistently delicious. The restaurant is tastefully decorated in upscale cafe style, with the kitchen staff on show as they rustle up some of the capital's best tucker. It's relaxed, feeling more communal than intimate on busy nights. My favorite dish is Atlantic salmon served with beurre blanc sauce and potatoes; other popular choices include eye filet steak and pumpkin risotto. If you have room left for dessert, don't miss out on sticky date pudding served with hot butterscotch sauce, pralines, and ice cream—it's as good as it sounds. The long list of daily specials that complement the extensive menu could keep you busy for weeks.

Bougainville St., Manuka. ✆ **02/6239 4422.** Reservations recommended. Main courses A$15–A$23 (US$12–US$18/UK£6–UK£9). AE, DC, MC, V. Daily noon–2:30pm; Mon–Sat 6–10pm.

INEXPENSIVE

Caffe Della Piazza ★ ITALIAN/CAFE Good eating isn't hard to find in Canberra, and this place is up there with the best. It has won several awards for its Italian-inspired cooking, including the catering industries' award for the best restaurant in the state. The restaurant offers both indoor and outdoor dining in pleasant surroundings, and is a good place to pop in for a light meal and a coffee or something more substantial. Pastas cost around A$12 (US$9.60/UK£4.80), and the best seller is chicken breast strips in macchiato sauce. Reserve early for Friday or Saturday evenings.

19 Garema Place, Civic. ✆ **02/6248 9711.** Reservations recommended. Main courses A$7.50–A$19 (US$6–US$15/UK£3–UK£8). AE, DC, MC, V. Daily 10:30am–midnight.

Portia's Place CANTONESE/MALAYSIAN/PEKING A small restaurant serving excellent traditional cookery, Portia's Place often fills up early and does a roaring lunchtime trade. The best things on the menu are lamb ribs in *shang tung* sauce, King Island filet steak in pepper sauce, flaming pork (brought to your table wrapped in foil and, yes, flaming), and Queensland trout stir-fried with snow peas.

11 Kennedy St., Kingston. ✆ **02/6239 7970.** Main courses A$9.80–A$19 (US$7.80–US$15/UK£4–UK£7.50). AE, DC, MC, V. Daily noon–2:30pm; Sun–Wed 5–10pm; Thurs–Sat 5–10:30pm.

5 Seeing the Sights

Australian War Memorial ★★ This monument to Australian troops who gave their lives for their country is truly moving and well worth a visit. Artifacts and displays tell the story of Australia's conflicts abroad. You won't soon forget the exhibition on Gallipoli, the bloody World War I battle in which so many Anzac (Australian and New Zealand Army Corps) servicemen were slaughtered. The Hall of Memory is the focus of the memorial, where the body of the Unknown Soldier lies entombed. (His remains were brought back from a World War I battlefield in 1993.) The memorial also holds one of the largest collections of Australian art in the world, including works by Tom Roberts, Arthur Streeton, and Grace Cossington-Smith. Recently added exhibits include a film showing the surrender of Singapore, projected onto the actual table on which the surrender was signed, and a simulated ride aboard an original Lancaster bomber. ANZAC Hall and Bradbury Aircraft Hall house significant aircraft and large pieces of war memorabilia.

At the head of Anzac Parade on Limestone Ave. ✆ **02/6243 4211.** Free admission. Daily 10am–5pm (when the Last Post is played). Closed Dec 25. Guided tours at 10, 10:30, and 11am, and 1:30 and 2pm. Bus: 33 or 40.

Black Mountain Tower The tower, which rises 195m (640 ft.) above the summit of Black Mountain, has both open-air and enclosed viewing galleries that provide magnificent 360-degree views over Canberra and the surrounding countryside. It was formally known as Telstra Tower, and most people still know it as such. Up top is **Alto Restaurant** (✆ **02/6247 5518**) with a revolving floor that does a full circuit in just under 90 minutes. The decor is modern and bright, and the food has French flourish. To start try the sautéed duck liver served on an onion purée with streaky bacon, and a leaf and hazelnut salad. Follow it up with the Wagyu rib-eye steak with slow-cooked red onions and béarnaise sauce. Alto is open for dinner Tuesday to Sunday, and for lunch Wednesday to Sunday. There's no bus service to the tower.

Black Mountain Dr. ✆ **02/6219 6111.** Admission A$4 (US$3.20/UK£1.60) adults, A$2 (US$1.60/UK80p) children. Daily 9am–10pm.

Canberra Deep Space Communication Complex ★ This information center, which stands beside huge tracking dishes, is a must for anyone interested in space. There are plenty of models, audiovisual recordings, and displays, including a space suit, space food, and archival film footage of the Apollo moon landings. The complex is still active, tracking and recording results from the Mars Pathfinder, *Voyager 1* and *2*, and the Cassini, Soho, Galileo, and Ulysses space exploration projects, as well as providing a link with NASA spacecraft. This is a great stop on the way back from the **Tidbinbilla Nature Reserve** (p. 659). There's no public bus service, but several tour companies offer programs that include the complex.

Tidbinbilla, 39km (24 miles) southwest of Civic. ✆ **02/6201 7880.** www.cdscc.nasa.gov. Free admission. Summer daily 9am–8pm; rest of year daily 9am–5pm.

High Court of Australia The High Court, an impressive concrete-and-glass building that overlooks Lake Burley Griffin and stands next to the National Gallery of Australia, was opened by Elizabeth II in 1980. It is home to the highest court in Australia's judicial system and contains three courtrooms, a video display, and a huge seven-story-high public hall. When the court is in session, visitors can observe the proceedings from the public gallery. Check ahead for session details.

Overlooking Lake Burley Griffin, Parkes Place. ✆ **02/6270 6811.** www.hcourt.gov.au. Free admission. Mon–Fri 9:45am–4:30pm. Closed public holidays. Bus: 34.

National Capital Exhibition If you want to find out more about Canberra's beginnings—and get a memorable view of Lake Burley Griffin, the Captain Cook Memorial Water Jet, and the Carillon in the bargain—then head here. The displays are well done, and a film provides an overview of the city's design.

On the lakeshore at Regatta Point in Commonwealth Park. ✆ **02/6257 1068.** Free admission. Daily 9am–6pm (until 5pm in winter).

National Gallery of Australia Linked to the High Court by a pedestrian bridge, the National Gallery showcases both Australian and international art. The permanent collection and traveling exhibitions are on display in 11 separate galleries. You'll find paintings by big names such as Claude Monet and Jackson Pollock, and Australian painters Arthur Boyd, Sidney Nolan, Arthur Streeton, Charles Condor, Tom Roberts, and Albert Tucker. The exhibition of Tiwi islander burial poles in the foyer is also interesting (the Tiwi Islands include Melville and Bathurst islands off Darwin), and there's a large collection of Aboriginal bark paintings from central Australia. Free guided tours start daily at 11am and 2pm. On Sunday and Thursday at 11am, a free tour focuses on Aboriginal art. A sculpture garden surrounding the gallery has 24 sculptures and is always open to the public.

Parkes Place. ✆ **02/6240 6502.** www.nga.gov.au. Free admission (except for major touring exhibitions). Daily 10am–5pm. Closed Dec 25. Bus: 36 or 39 from Old Parliament House, or 34 from Parkes Place in front of the High Court.

National Museum of Australia ★ The first official all-encompassing museum dedicated to the nation of Australia opened in 2001 to rave reviews. Using state-of-the-art technology and hands-on exhibits, the museum concentrates on three main themes: Australian society and its history since 1788; the interaction of people with the Australian environment; and Aboriginal and Torres Strait Islander cultures and histories. It relies more on images and sound than on historical objects to tell the stories of Australia. Allow a couple of hours if it grabs you, and 30 minutes to rush around baffled if it doesn't.

Acton Peninsula (about 5km/3 miles from the city center). ✆ **1800/026 132** or 02/6208 5000. www.nma.gov.au. Free admission (fees for special exhibitions). Daily 9am–5pm. Bus: 34.

National Zoo and Aquarium This private zoo would not be that impressive if it didn't have a few things going for it. For a start, it's privately owned—so having 28 endangered species in your back garden is quite a feat when you think about it. It also has Australia's largest collection of big cats, including a couple of ligers—or are they tigons? If you're an animal lover with deep pockets and you're looking for the thrill of a lifetime, then a Zoo Venture Tour is just the thing. The zoo offers participants the chance to hand-feed a Bengal tiger through the fence, stroke a dingo, pass grapes to a sun bear, and have a brown bear lick honey from your hands.

Scrivener Dam, Lady Denman Dr., Yarralumla. ✆ **02/6287 8483.** www.zooquarium.com.au. Admission A$24 (US$19/UK£10) adults, A$13 (US$10/UK£5) kids 4–15, A$70 (US$56/UK£28) families. Daily 9am–5pm. Bus: 81.

Old Parliament House The seat of government from 1927 to 1988, the Old Parliament House is now home to exhibitions from the National Museum and the Australian Archives. The National Portrait Gallery is also here, and outside on the lawn is the Aboriginal Tent Embassy, which was set up in 1972 in a bid to persuade the authorities to recognize the land ownership claims of Aboriginal and Torres Strait Islander people. The red, black, and yellow Aboriginal flag first came to prominence here. Interestingly, the Australian Heritage Commission now recognizes the campsite as a place of special cultural significance. There's a nice cafe, too.

On King George Terrace, midway between the new Parliament House (see below) and the lake. ✆ **02/6270 8222.** www.oph.gov.au. Admission A$2 (US$1.60/UK80p) adults, A$1 (US80¢/UK£40p) children, A$5 (US$4/UK£2) families. Daily 9am–5pm. Bus: 31, 36, or 39.

Parliament House Conceived by American architect Walter Burley Griffin in 1912, but not built until 1988, Canberra's focal point was designed to blend organically into its setting at the top of Capital Hill; only a national flag supported by a giant four-footed flagpole rises above the peak of the hill. In good weather, picnickers crowd the grass that covers the roof, where the view is spectacular. Inside are more than 3,000 works of Australian arts and crafts, and extensive areas of the building are open to the general public. Just inside the main entrance, look for a mosaic by Michael Tjakamarra

Nelson, *Meeting Place,* which represents a gathering of Aboriginal tribes. There's also a 20m-long (66-ft.) tapestry by Arthur Boyd in the Great Hall on the first floor and one of the four known versions of the Magna Carta in the Great Hall beneath the flagpole. Free 50-minute guided tours run throughout the day.

Parliament is usually in session Monday through Thursday between mid-February and late June and from mid-August to mid-December. Both the Lower House—the House of Representatives (where the prime minister sits)—and the Upper House (the Senate) have public viewing galleries. The best time to see the action is during Question Time, which starts at 2pm in the Lower House. If you turn up early, you might get a seat; otherwise, make reservations for gallery tickets through the **sergeant-at-arms** (✆ **02/6277 4889**) at least a day in advance. Free 45-minute tours of the building start every 30 minutes beginning at 9am.

Capital Hill. ✆ **02/6277 5399.** Free admission. Daily 9am–5pm. Closed Dec 25. Bus: 39.

Questacon—The National Science and Technology Centre *Kids* Questacon offers some 200 hands-on exhibits that can keep you and your inner child occupied for hours. Exhibits cluster in six galleries, each representing a different aspect of science. The artificial earthquake is a big attraction. The center is great for kids, but skip it if you've already visited the Powerhouse Museum (p. 166) in Sydney.

King Edward Terrace, Parkes. ✆ **02/6270 2800.** Admission A$16 (US$12/UK£6) adults, A$9 (US$7/UK£3.50) children, A$46 (US$37/UK£18) families. Daily 10am–5pm. Closed Dec 25. Bus: 34.

Tidbinbilla Nature Reserve *Moments* A huge bushfire in January 2003 destroyed much of this once-glorious nature reserve and killed all but one of its resident koalas. Things recover quickly in Australia though, and many of the animals are back. Expect to see kangaroos and wallabies in their natural environment. In the new wetlands section, visitors "walk on water" on elevated boardwalks and viewing platforms, which afford looks at pelicans, blue-billed ducks, and other water fowl. Bushbird feeding time is 2:30pm daily. For the more adventurous, trails run to the mountaintops. Unlike other wildlife parks around the country, this one has plenty of space, so sometimes you'll have to look hard to spot the animals. A printed guide is available from the visitor center. Call the visitor center for information on free weekend talks and walks.

There's no public bus service, but several tour companies offer programs that include the reserve. **Go Bush Tours** (✆ **02/6231 3023**) runs tours to the reserve as well as the neighboring Canberra Deep Space Communication Complex for A$120 (US$96/UK£48), including morning tea and lunch. By the way, for the same price you can go on a tour of Namadgi National Park, where you are assured of seeing large mobs of eastern gray kangaroos.

Tidbinbilla. Paddys River Rd., RMB 141 via Tharwa, ✆ **02/6205 1233.** www.environment.act.gov.au. Admission A$10 (US$8/UK£4) per vehicle. Daily 9am–6pm (8pm in summer). Visitor center Mon–Fri 9am–4:30pm; Sat–Sun 9am–5:30pm. Take Tourist Rte. 5 (following large brown signs with orange number) from central Canberra.

BOTANIC GARDENS & A NEARBY NATIONAL PARK

The **Australian National Botanic Gardens** ★, Clunies Ross Street, Black Mountain, Acton (✆ **02/6250 9540**), are home to the best collection of Australian native plants anywhere. The gardens, on 51 hectares (126 acres) on the lower slopes of Black Mountain, feature a Eucalyptus Lawn containing more than 600 species of eucalyptus, a rainforest area, a Tasmanian alpine garden, and self-guided walking trails. Free guided tours depart from the visitor center at 11am on weekdays and 11am and 2pm on weekends.

The gardens are open daily from 9am to 5pm (to 8pm in summer). The visitor center is open daily from 9:30am to 4:30pm. There's no bus service to the gardens.

The **Namadgi National Park** ★ covers almost half of the Australian Capital Territory. Parts of the park, which has rolling plateaus, trout-fishing streams, and dense forest, are just 30km (19 miles) from Canberra. Marked hiking trails run throughout the park. Spring is the best time to visit for the display of bush flowers. In the past, sections of the park were cleared for sheep grazing, but these days the pastures are popular with hundreds of gray kangaroos. (They're easiest to spot in the early morning and late afternoon.) At Yankee Hat, off the Nass/Boboyan Road, is an Aboriginal rock-art site. The **Namadgi Visitors Centre** (✆ **02/6207 2900**), on the Nass/Boboyan Road, 3km (1¾ miles) south of the township of Tharwa, has maps and information on walking trails. The January 2003 fires burned much of the park, but the forests regenerate rapidly, and animals are back in abundance. **Go Bush Tours** (✆ **02/6231 3023**) runs a day tour for A$120 (US$96/UK£48) per person including lunch.

6 Outdoor Pursuits

BIKING With 120km (74 miles) of bike paths, Canberra is made for exploring on two wheels. Rent a bike from **Mr. Spoke's Bike Hire,** Barrine Drive, near the ferry terminal, Acton (✆ **02/6257 1188**). Bikes for adults cost A$12 (US$9.60/UK£4.70) for an hour, A$20 (US$16/UK£8) for a half-day, and A$30 (US$24/UK£12) for a day.

BOATING **Burley Griffin Boat Hire,** Barrine Drive, near the ferry terminal, Acton (✆ **02/6249 6861**), rents paddle boats for A$20 (US$16/UK£8) per hour and canoes for A$14 (US$11/UK£5.60) per hour. It's open daily. **Row 'n' Ride,** near the MacDermott Place Boat Ramp, Belconnen (✆ **02/6254 7838**), is open on weekends and school and public holidays and offers canoes from A$9 (US$7.20/UK£3.60) per hour, kayaks for A$10 (US$8/UK£4) per hour, and mountain bikes for A$9 (US$7.20/UK£3.60) per hour.

SWIMMING The indoor heated pool at the **Australian Institute of Sport** (✆ **02/6214 1281**), Leverrier Crescent, Bruce, a short drive northwest of Civic, is open to the public at certain times during the day (call ahead to check schedules). Adults pay A$4 (US$3.20/UK£1.60) to swim, and children pay A$2 (US$1.60/UK80p). You must wear swimming caps, which you can buy there for A$2.50 (US$2/UK£1). It costs A$6 (US$4.80/UK£2.40) to use the pool, Jacuzzi, and sauna.

TENNIS The **National Tennis and Squash Centre,** Federal Highway, Lyneham (✆ **02/6247 0929**), has squash courts available for A$14 to A$18 (US$11–US$14/UK£5.50–UK£7) per hour, depending on when you want to play. Tennis courts can be booked for A$11 to A$17 (US$8.80–US$14/UK£4.40–UK£7). The Australian Institute of Sport (see above) also rents courts.

7 Canberra After Dark

The **"Times Out"** section in Thursday's *Canberra Times* has entertainment listings.

Of the pubs in town, the best in the city center are the British-style **Wig & Pen,** on the corner of Limestone and Alinga streets (✆ **02/6248 0171**); the popular **Moosehead's Pub,** 105 London Circuit, in the south of the city (✆ **02/6257 6496**); the **Phoenix,** 21 E. Row (✆ **02/6247 1606**), which has live music upstairs (cover charge); and **P. J. O'Reileys** (✆ **02/6230 4752**), on the corner of West Row and Alinga Street, an authentic-style Irish pub. **King O'Malleys** (✆ **02/6257 0111**), Mort Street, is another popular Irish pub in the city.

If you're looking to roll some dice, the **Casino Canberra,** in Glebe Park, 21 Binara St., Civic (✆ **1800/806 833** in Australia, or 02/6257 7074), is a small, older-style casino offering all the usual casino games daily from noon to 6am. Dress regulations prohibit leisurewear, running shoes, and denim, but overall it's a casual place to lose some money.

15

Tasmania

by Marc Llewellyn

The name "Tasmania" suggests an unspoiled place, with vast stretches of wilderness roamed by strange creatures like the Tasmanian devil. Many mainland residents still half-jokingly refer to their "country cousins" on the island as rednecks. In truth, most Tasmanians are hospitable and friendly people, lacking the harsh edge that big cities can foster. Most also care passionately for the environment, decrying the belief that anything that moves deserves a bullet and anything that stands still needs chopping down. Despite this, forests are still being clear-felled, noxious chemicals are being sprayed to inhibit undergrowth in plantations, and there are reports of native animals being killed in the process. Tasmania's "clean-green" image is being badly damaged in the process. The possible extinction of Tasmanian devils due to a spreading facial tumor disease, reports of introduced foxes, and a proposed pulp mill that will pump vast quantities of effluent into Bass Straight, does little to help. Tasmania has even been described as an "extinction hotspot" by scientists in a 2006 study.

Visitors to Tasmania are surprised by its size, though compared to the scale of the rest of Australia, the distances are more manageable. Dense rainforests, mountain peaks, alpine meadows, great lakes, eucalyptus stands, and fertile farmland are all easily accessible, but you should be prepared for several hours of concentrated driving between the main attractions. Among Tasmania's chief attractions is its natural environment. More than 20% of the island has been declared a World Heritage area, and nearly a third of the island is protected within 14 national parks.

Tasmania's other main draw is its history. Remains of the Aboriginal people who lived here for thousands of years are evident in rock paintings, engraving, stories, and the aura of spirituality that still holds in places where modern civilization has not yet reached.

Europeans arrived in Tasmania (or Van Diemen's Land, as it was once known) in 1642, when the seafarer Abel Tasman set anchor off its southwest coast. It wasn't identified as an island until 1798. Tasmania made its mark as a dumping ground for convicts, who were more often than not transported for petty crimes in their homeland. The brutal system of control, still evident in the ruins at Port Arthur and elsewhere, spilled over into persecution of the native population. The last full-blooded Tasmanian Aborigine died in 1876, 15 years after the last convict transportation. Most had already died of disease and maltreatment at the hands of the settlers.

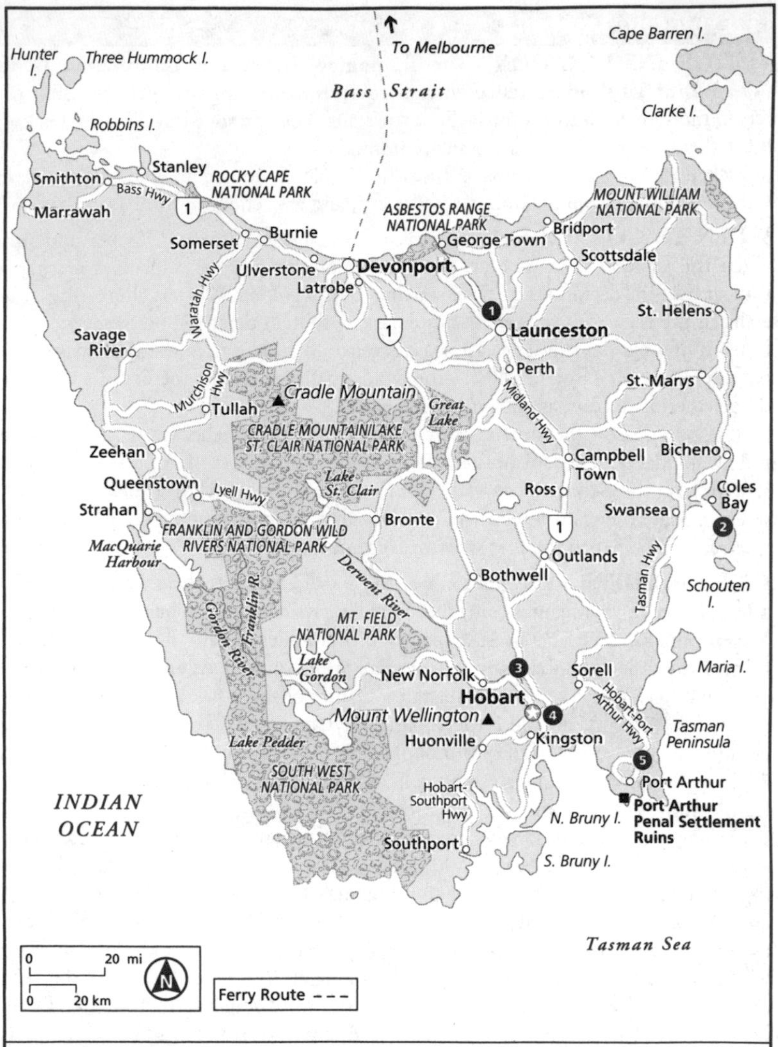

Bonorong Park Wildlife Centre **3**
Cataract Gorge **1**
Freycinet National Park **2**
Royal Tasmanian Botanical Gardens **4**
Tasmanian Devil Park Wildlife Rescue Centre **5**

1 Exploring Tasmania

VISITOR INFORMATION The **Tasmanian Travel and Information Centre** (© **1300/655 145** in Australia; www.discovertasmania.com.au) operates visitor centers in more than 30 towns throughout the state. It can arrange travel passes, ferry and bus tickets, car rentals, cruises, and accommodations.

Pick up a copy of *Travelways,* Tourism Tasmania's tourist tabloid, for details on transportation, accommodations, restaurants, and attractions around Tasmania.

WHEN TO GO The best time to visit Tasmania is between October and April, when the weather is at its best. By May, nights are getting cold, days are getting shorter, and the deciduous trees are starting to turn golden. Winters (June–Aug), especially in the high country, can be quite harsh—though that's the best time to curl up in front of a blazing fire. The east coast is generally milder than the west coast, which is buffeted by the "Roaring 40s"—the winds that blow across the ocean and the 40-degree meridian, from as far away as Argentina.

The busy season for tourism runs December through February, as well as during public holiday and school holiday periods. Unlike the rest of Australia, Tasmanian schools have three terms. Term dates are from the second week in February to the last week in May; the third week in June to the first week in September; and the fourth week in September to the first week in December.

GETTING THERE The quickest way to get to Tasmania is by air. **Qantas** (© **13 13 13** in Australia; www.qantas.com) flies from the mainland to Hobart and Launceston. **Virgin Blue** (© **13 67 89** in Australia; www.virginblue.com.au) offers discounted trips from Melbourne to Hobart and Launceston, with connections from other capitals, if you book early from the website. **Jetstar,** a Qantas offshoot (© **13 15 38** in Australia; www.jetstar.com.au), also flies to Hobart and Launceston. Two-way fares cost from around A$240 (US$192/UK£96) if booked on the Net. **Regional Express** (© **13 17 13** in Australia; www.regionalexpress.com.au) flies from Melbourne to Devonport and Burnie in the state's north.

Two high-speed ferry services connect Melbourne and Tasmania. The *Spirit of Tasmania I* and *II* can each carry 1,400 passengers as well as cars. They make the crossing from Melbourne's Station Pier to Tasmania's Devonport (on the north coast) in around 10 hours. The ferries leave both Melbourne and Devonport at 9pm and arrive at around 7am. From roughly December 20 to April 27, there's also day service on weekends, leaving both ports at 9am and arriving at 7pm. Prices are based on "shoulder" and "peak" times: The shoulder seasons run from roughly August 31 to December 6, and from January 27 to April 27. A one-way seat costs A$114 to A$168 (US$91–US$134/UK£46–UK£67) for adults depending on season, and A$102 to A$131 (US$82–US$105/UK£41–UK£53) for children. Three- to four-berth cabins cost from A$212 to A$272 (US$170–US$218/UK£85–UK£109) for adults and A$118 to A$146 (US$94–US$117/UK£47–UK£58) for kids depending on the season and if you have a porthole. Twin cabins cost A$236 to A$302 (US$189–US$242/UK£95–UK£121) for adults and A$128 to A$162 (US$102–US$130/UK£51–UK£65) for children. Deluxe cabins cost A$326 to A$418 (US$261–US$334/UK£131–UK£167) for adults and kids. Transporting a standard-size car costs A$79 to A$121 (US$63–US$97/UK£32–UK£48), depending on size, year-round.

Make reservations for any of the ferries through **TT-Line** (© **1800/634 906** in Australia, or 03/9206 6211; www.spiritoftasmania.com.au). Special offers are regularly

Tips **Tasmania's Tricky Roads**

Driving in Tasmania can be dangerous; there are more accidents involving tourists on Tasmania's roads than anywhere else in Australia. Many roads are narrow, and bends can be tight, especially in the mountainous inland regions, where you may also come across black ice early in the morning or at anytime in winter. Marsupials are also common around dusk, and swerving to avoid them has caused countless crashes.

available. **Tasmanian Redline Coaches** (© **03/6336 1446**) connect with each ferry and transfer passengers to Launceston and Hobart.

GETTING AROUND The regional airline **Tasair** (© **03/6248 5088;** www.tasair.com.au) flies to some settlements in Tasmania. **Par Avion** (© **03/6248 5390;** www.paravion.com.au) concentrates on the southwest World Heritage areas of the state and also operates wonderful sightseeing tours. A 2½-hour southwest wilderness flight, for example, costs A$170 (US$136/UK£68).

Tasmanian Redline Coaches (© **1300/360 000** in Australia, or 03/6336 1446; www.tasredline.com.au) and **Tassielink** (© **1300/300 520** in Australia, or 03/6230 8900; www.tigerline.com.au) operate coach service statewide and offer a series of coach tours to major places of interest. **Hobart Coaches** (© **1800/030 620** in Australia, or 03/6234 4077) runs trips around the Hobart area.

The cheapest way to get around by coach is to buy a travel pass. The **Tassielink Explorer Pass,** which covers all Tassielink routes, comes in four categories: A 7-day pass good for travel within 10 days is A$180 (US$144/UK£72); a 10-day pass for travel in 15 days is A$225 (US$180/UK£95); a 14-day pass for travel in 20 days is A$260 (US$208/UK£104); a 21-day pass for travel in 30 days is A$299 (US$239/UK£120). Kids' passes are half price.

Driving a car from Devonport on the north coast to Hobart on the south coast takes less than 4 hours. From Hobart to Strahan on the west coast also takes around 4 hours, while the journey from Launceston to Hobart takes about 2 hours. The **Royal Automobile Club of Tasmania,** Murray and Patrick streets, Hobart (© **13 27 22** in Australia), can supply maps.

TOUR OPERATORS Dozens of operators run organized hiking, horse trekking, sailing, caving, fishing, bushwalking, diving, cycling, rafting, climbing, kayaking, and canoeing trips. For a full listing, see the "Outdoor Adventure" section of *Travelways,* the Tasmanian tourist board's publication (see "Visitor Information," above).

One of the best operators is **Tasmania Adventure Tours** (© **1300/654 604** in Australia, or 08/8132 8230; www.adventuretours.com.au). It offers a 3-day East Coast Explorer tour from Devonport, taking in Launceston, Freycinet National Park, and Port Arthur, before finishing in Hobart. The tour costs A$425 to A$575 (US$340–US$460/UK£170–UK£230) depending on accommodations. A 6-day Taste of Tasmania Tour starts in Devonport, takes in Mount Field National Park, Lake St. Clair, Strahan, Cradle Mountain, Freycinet, and Port Arthur, and ends up in Hobart. This tour costs A$795 to A$1,105 (US$636–US$884/UK£318–UK£442). Other tours are available. Call for departure days.

Value National Park Entry Fees

A **Tassie Holiday Pass** costs A$56 (US$45/UK£22) and allows entry for a car and passengers to Tasmania's national parks for 2 months. Pedestrians, cyclists, motorcyclists, and coach passengers pay A$28 (US$22/UK£11) for 2 months. Occasional users can buy a 24-hour pass for A$22 (US$18/UK£9) per car; walkers, cyclists, motorcyclists, and coach passengers pay A$11 (US$9/UK£4.50) per day. Passes are available at all major parks and Tasmanian Visitor Information Centres. For more information, contact the **Parks and Wildlife Service** (**© 03/6233 2621**; www.parks.tas.gov.au).

Peregrine Adventures (**© 03/9662 2800;** www.peregrine.net.au) runs rafting tours of the Franklin River, which carves its way through some of the most beautiful, rugged, and inaccessible wilderness in the world. Another good operator is the **Roaring 40's Ocean Kayaking Company** (**© 1800/653 712** in Australia; www.roaring40skayaking.com.au); both offer paddling expeditions lasting from 1 to 11 days. **Tasmanian Expeditions** in Launceston (**© 1800/030 230** in Australia, or 03/6267 5000; www.tasmanianexpeditions.com.au), runs a whole range of cycling, trekking, and rafting trips around the country, some starting or finishing in Hobart.

Check out **www.tastravel.com.au**, an online travel agency, for more general information, and bookings for tours, hire cars, camper vans, and more.

SUGGESTED ITINERARIES Planning my first trip to Tasmania, I'd pack my walking boots, raincoat, and shorts, and head first to either **Launceston** or **Hobart,** the island's two main cities. I'd take in **Freycinet National Park** for its wonderful scenery and abundant wildlife, stop at **Port Arthur** for its beautiful setting and disturbing convict past, and head to the central highlands for a stomp around **Cradle Mountain.** If I had more time, I'd drive to **Strahan** on the far west coast to discover the southwest wilderness, take some time to go trout fishing in the central lakes, and head to the quaint coastal towns of the north.

2 Hobart

198km (123 miles) S of Launceston

Tasmania's capital (pop. 126,000), second in age only to Sydney, is an appealing place worth visiting for a couple of days. Hobart's main features are its wonderful harbor and the colonial cottages that line the narrow lanes of Battery Point. As in Sydney, Hobart's harbor is the city's focal point, attracting yachts from all over the world. Down by the waterfront, picturesque Salamanca Place bursts with galleries, pubs, cafes, and an excellent market on Saturdays. Europeans settled in Hobart in 1804, a year after Tasmania's first colony was set up at Risdon (10km/6¼ miles up the Derwent River). Hobart, the southernmost Australian state capital, is closer to the Antarctic coast than it is to Perth in Western Australia; navigators, whalers, and explorers have long regarded it as the gateway to the south.

ESSENTIALS

GETTING THERE The trip from the airport to the city center takes about 20 minutes and costs about A$25 (US$20/UK£10) by taxi. The **Airporter Shuttle Bus**

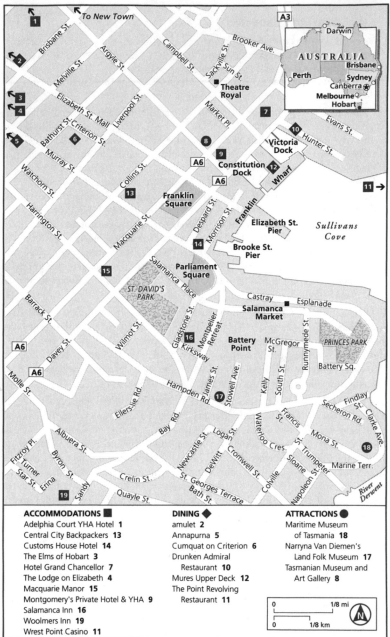

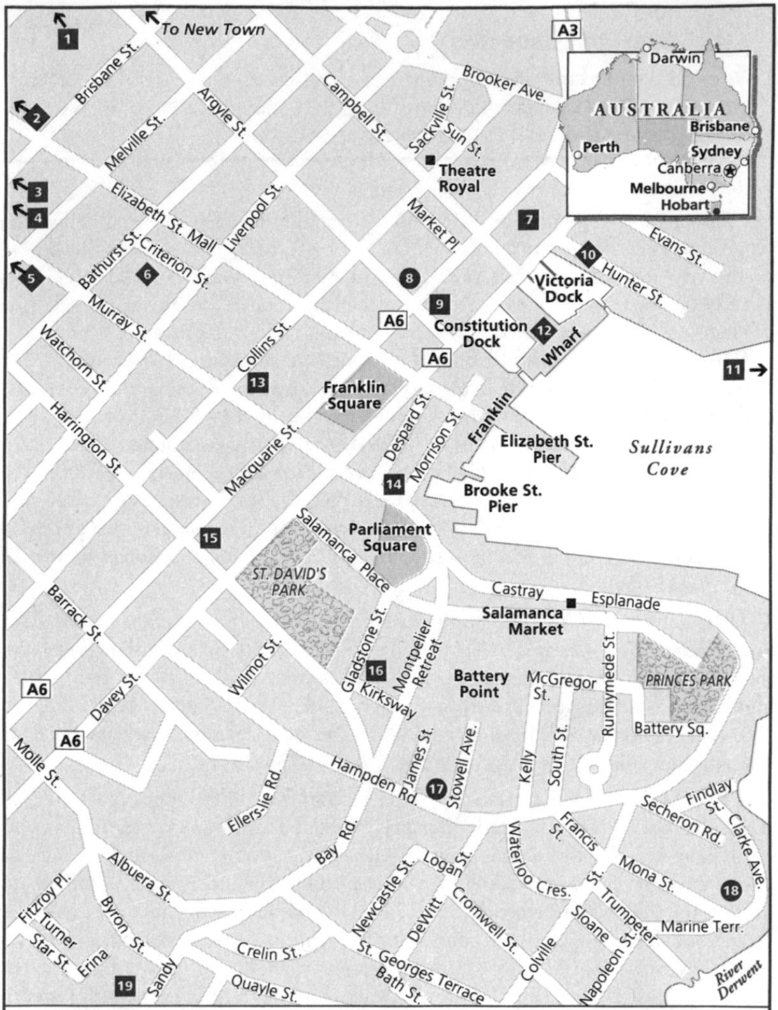

ACCOMMODATIONS ■

Adelphia Court YHA Hotel **1**
Central City Backpackers **13**
Customs House Hotel **14**
The Elms of Hobart **3**
Hotel Grand Chancellor **7**
The Lodge on Elizabeth **4**
Macquarie Manor **15**
Montgomery's Private Hotel & YHA **9**
Salamanca Inn **16**
Woolmers Inn **19**
Wrest Point Casino **11**

DINING ◆

amulet **2**
Annapurna **5**
Cumquat on Criterion **6**
Drunken Admiral Restaurant **10**
Mures Upper Deck **12**
The Point Revolving Restaurant **11**

ATTRACTIONS ●

Maritime Museum of Tasmania **18**
Narryna Van Diemen's Land Folk Museum **17**
Tasmanian Museum and Art Gallery **8**

0 1/8 mi
0 1/8 km
N

Tips **Staying Connected**

It's relatively hard to find public Web access in Hobart, but you can try **Drifters Internet Café,** in Salamanca Galleria, Shop 9/33 Salamanca Place (✆ **03/6224 6286**). The cafe charges A$5 (US$4/UK£2) per half-hour.

(✆ **0419/382 240** mobile, or 0419/383 462 mobile) meets planes and delivers passengers to hotels in the city and farther afield for A$12 (US$9.60/UK£4.80) one-way to the city center for adults (A$20/US$16/UK£8 both ways) and A$6 (US$4.80/ UK£2.40) one-way for kids. If you are departing Hobart on an early flight (6am, 6:30am, or 7:25am) you need to make a booking by 8pm the previous evening.

Car- and camper-rental offices at the airport include **Hertz** (✆ 03/6237 1155), **Advance** (✆ 1800/030 118 in Australia; www.advancecars.com.au), **Avis** (✆ 03/ 6248 5424), **Budget** (✆ 1300/362 848 in Australia, or 03/6248 5333), and **Thrifty** (✆ 1800/030 730 in Australia, or 03/6234 1341). Cars cost around A$55 (US$44/ UK£22) for 1 day, A$50 (US$40/UK£20) per day for 2 days, A$45 (US$36/UK£18) per day for 4 days, and A$40 (US$32/UK£16) per day for a week or more. You might find even better bargains in town with lower-priced rental companies such as **Lo-Cost Auto Rent** (✆ 1800/030 023 in Australia, or 03/6231 0550) and **Range Rent-a-Bug** (✆ 03/6231 0300).

VISITOR INFORMATION Information is available from the **Tasmanian Travel and Information Centre,** 20 Davey St. (✆ **03/6230 8233;** tasbookings@tasvisinfo.com.au). It's open Monday through Friday from 8:30am to 5:15pm, Saturday and public holidays from 9am to 4pm, and Sunday from 9am to 1pm (9am–4pm Dec–Apr). You can pick up information on the state's national parks at the **Lands Information Bureau,** 134 Macquarie St. (✆ **03/6233 8011**).

CITY LAYOUT Hobart straddles the Derwent River on the south coast of Tasmania. **Salamanca Place** and nearby **Battery Point** abut Sullivan's Cove, home to hundreds of yachts. The row of sandstone warehouses that dominate Salamanca Place date to the city's heyday as a whaling base in the 1830s. Behind Princes Wharf, Battery Point is the city's historic district, which in colonial times was the home of sailors, fishermen, whalers, coopers, merchants, shipwrights, and master mariners. The open ocean is about 50km (31 miles) down the river, though the Derwent empties into Storm Bay, just 20km (12 miles) downstream. The central business district is on the west side of the water, with the main thoroughfares—**Campbell, Argyle, Elizabeth, Murray,** and **Harrington streets**—sloping down to the busy harbor. The Tasman Bridge and regular passenger ferries cross the Derwent River. Set back from and overlooking the city is 1,270m-tall (4,166-ft.) **Mount Wellington.**

GETTING AROUND Central Hobart is very small, and most of the attractions are in easy walking distance. **Metro Tasmania** (✆ **03/6233 4232** or 13 22 01; www.metrotas.com.au) operates public buses throughout the city and suburban areas. Single tickets cost A$1.90 to A$4.30 (US$1.50–US$3.40/UK£.75–UK£1.70) depending on how far you're going. **Day Rover** tickets are good between 9am and 4:30pm and after 6pm during the week and all day on weekends; they cost A$4.60 (US$3.70/UK£1.85). A family day ticket costs A$13 (US$10/UK£5). Purchase tickets from bus drivers. If you plan on busing about, stop at the Metro Shop, in the General Post Office building on the corner of Elizabeth and Macquarie streets, and pick up a timetable, brochures, and sightseeing information.

SPECIAL EVENTS The **Sydney-to-Hobart Yacht Race,** starting in Sydney on December 26, fills the Constitution Dock Marina and harbor area close to overflowing with spectators and partygoers when the ships turn up in Tasmania. The race takes anywhere from 2 to 4 days, and the sailors and fans stay on to celebrate New Year's Eve. Food and wine lovers indulge themselves after the race during the 2-month-long **Hobart Summer Festival,** which starts on December 28.

EXPLORING THE CITY & ENVIRONS

Simply strolling around the harbor and popping into the shops at Salamanca Place can keep you nicely occupied.

Also take a look around Battery Point, an area chock-full of colonial stone cottages. The area got its name from a battery of guns set up on the promontory in 1818 to defend the town against potential invaders (particularly the French). Today, there are plenty of tearooms, antiques shops, restaurants, and atmospheric pubs interspersed between grand dwellings. One of the houses worth looking into is **Narryna Van Diemen's Land Folk Museum,** 103 Hampden Rd. (© **03/6234 2791**), which depicts the life of upper-class pioneers. It's open Tuesday through Friday from 10:30am to 5pm and Saturday and Sunday from 2 to 5pm (closed July). Admission is A$5 (US$4/UK£2) for adults and A$2 (US$1.60/UK80p) for children. Also in this area is the **Maritime Museum of Tasmania** ★, 16 Argyle St. (© **03/6234 1427**), one of the best museums of its type in Australia. It's open daily from 10am to 5pm, and admission is A$7 (US$5.60/UK£2.80) for adults, A$3 (US$2.40/UK£1.20) for children 4 to 16, and A$16 (US$13/UK£6.50) for a family. It arranges a gallery and port tour for A$12 (US$9.60/UK£4.80) for adults, free for kids.

Hobart Historic Tours (© **03/6230 8233** or 03/6278 3338; www.hobarthistorictours.com.au) runs a fascinating 2-hour walking tour of Hobart daily between October 1 and April 30. It departs at 10am from outside the Tasmanian Travel and Information Centre (above). A Historic Pub Tour, departing at 5pm in the same months, takes you to three waterfront pubs and will enthrall you with stories of alcohol-sodden shenanigans. You even get to meet some shady actor-characters. The tour price includes two tastings. Both tours cost A$25 (US$20/UK£10) for adults and A$13 (US$10/UK£5) for kids aged 8 to 16. Kids under 8 are free. The company also runs a Battery Point Walk looking at the small artisans cottages and grand houses. It departs at 3:30pm daily and costs A$23 (US$18/UK£9).

Tassielink (© **1300/300 520** in Australia, or 03/6230 8900; www.tassielink.com.au) offers half-day sightseeing tours of Hobart and Mount Wellington by coach. The tours leave at 2pm Tuesday and Thursday afternoons and 9am on Sunday morning from the Hobart Bus terminal, 64 Brisbane St. They cost A$55 (US$44/UK£22) for adults and A$33 (US$26/UK£13) for kids.

For magnificent views over Hobart and across a fair-size chunk of Tasmania, drive to the **Pinnacle** on top of Mount Wellington, about 40 minutes from the city center. Take a warm coat; the wind in this alpine area can bite. An extensive network of walking trails offers good hiking. Pick up a copy of *Mt. Wellington Day Walk Map and Notes* from the **Department of Environment Tasmap Centre,** at the Lands Building, 134 Macquarie St. (© **03/6233 3382**).

THE TOP ATTRACTIONS

Bonorong Park Wildlife Centre *Kids* I don't think I've ever seen so many wallabies in one place—they were hopping all over. There are lots of other native animals around here, too, including snakes, koalas, Tasmanian devils, and wombats. The Bush Tucker shed serves lunch, billy teas (basically tea brewed in a metal pot with a gum leaf thrown in), and damper (Australian-style campfire bread). Koala cuddling isn't allowed in Tasmania, but if you're around at feeding time, it's possible to stroke one—they're not as shy as you might think. Feeding times are 12:30 and 3pm daily. The park is on the side of a steep hill, so travelers in wheelchairs are likely to fare badly. Allow 1 hour.

Briggs Rd., Brighton. ✆ **03/6268 1184.** Admission A$11 (US$8.80/UK£4.40) adults, A$6 (US$4.80/UK£2.40) children under 15. Daily 9am–5pm. Closed Dec 25. Bus to Glenorchy from the central bus terminal in Hobart (about 10 min.), then take bus 125 or 126 to the park. Drive north on Rte. 1 to Brighton; it's about 25 min. north of Hobart and is well signposted.

Cadbury Chocolate Factory ★ Eat chocolates until they make you sick on this Willy Wonka–type trip. Book well ahead, because chocolate tours are very popular. Keep in mind you'll need to climb lots of stairs inside the factory, where you'll see chocolate being made. You can visit the factory on a ferry tour (details below).

Claremont, 16km (10 miles) north of Hobart. ✆ **1800/627 367** in Australia, or 03/6249 0333. Tours A$13 (US$10/UK£5.20) adults, A$6.50 (US$5.20/UK£2.60) children. Tours Mon–Fri 9, 9:30, 10, 10:30, and 11am, noon, 1, and 1:30pm.

Cascade Brewery Tours Cascade Premium is one of the best beers in the country, in my opinion. To see how this heady amber nectar is produced, head to Australia's oldest brewery and tag along on a 2-hour tour, which includes a stroll through the grand old Woodstock Gardens behind the factory. The tour involves lots of stairs.

Cascade Rd., South Hobart. ✆ **03/6224 1117.** Tours (which include tastings) A$18 (US$14/UK£7.20) adults, A$7 (US$5.60/UK£2.80) children 5–12, A$42 (US$34/UK£17) families. Tours Mon–Fri 9, 9:30, 10, 10:30, and 11am, noon, 1, and 1:30pm. Closed public holidays. Reservations required. Bus: 44, 46, or 49 (stop 18).

Female Factory Historic Site and Island Produce Fudge Factory ★ *Finds* This is an interesting stopover if you're visiting the Cascade Brewery or Mount Wellington. You get not only a trip around the successful fudge-making factory, but a guided tour around the remains of the women's prison next door. The tales told here will make the hairs on your neck stand on end—like the fact that 17 out of every 20 children born within the walls of the institution died soon after birth, and that women who died were tossed into an unmarked mass grave. All the proceeds of the tour go toward preserving the prison. Allow 1½ hours.

16 Degraves St., South Hobart. ✆ **03/6223 1559.** Fax 03/6223 1556. www.femalefactory.com.au. Tours A$10 (US$8/UK£4) adults, A$5 (US$4/UK£2) children, A$25 (US$20/UK£10) family. Tours Easter Tuesday to Dec 24 Mon–Fri 9:30am (closed weekends and public holidays); Dec 26 to Easter Monday daily 9:30am, Mon–Fri 2pm. Bus: 43, 44, 46, or 49 from GPO to South Hobart and Cascade Rd. (stop 14).

Royal Tasmanian Botanical Gardens ★ Established in 1818, these gardens are known for English-style plant and tree layouts—including a great conifer collection—a superb Japanese garden (better than some I've seen in Kyoto, Japan), and seasonal blooming plants. A busy road nearby can disturbs the peaceful atmosphere. A restaurant provides lunch and teas. To walk here from the city center, partly along a pleasant country lane known as Soldier's Walk, takes around 40 minutes—but it's badly signposted. (When you come to a shelter and plaque with a missing YOU-ARE-HERE marker, turn right—the gardens are walled and there's an obvious entrance gate.)

On the Queens Domain near Government House. © **03/6234 6299.** Free admission. Daily 8am–6:30pm (until 5pm in winter). Bus: 17.

Tasmanian Museum and Art Gallery ★ Come here to find out more about Tasmania's Aboriginal heritage, its history since settlement, and the island's wildlife. Traveling art exhibitions are mounted from time to time, but always on display are the paintings of the colonial era. The art gallery has a particularly impressive collection of paintings by Tom Roberts and by several convict artists. The pride of the collection is *The Conciliation* by Benjamin Duttereau, the second-most historically significant painting in Australia, after Tom Roberts' *Shearing of the Rams,* which you can see in the National Gallery of Victoria in Melbourne. Allow 1 to 2 hours.

40 Macquarie St. © **03/6211 4177.** Free admission. Daily 10am–5pm.

CRUISE TOURS

Captain Fells Ferries (© **03/6223 5893;** www.captainfellshistoricferries.com.au) offers morning tea, lunch, afternoon, and dinner cruises. A dinner cruise onboard a historic ferry, for example, costs A$40 (US$32/UK£16) for adults, A$110 (US$88/UK£44) for a family, while lunch cruises cost A$35 (US$28/UK£14) for adults and A$85 (US$68/UK£34) for a family. A 90-minute Discovery Cruise departs at 10:30am and 2:30pm and costs A$20 (US$16/UK£8) for adults and A$50 (US$40/UK£20) for a family.

The company also runs **Cadbury Factory Tours,** which include a double-decker bus transfer, a tour of the factory, a harbor cruise, and a two-course lunch for A$55 (US$44/UK£22) for adults and A$140 (US$112/UK£56) for a family; these leave in the morning on most weekdays (check with company for departure days and times). Cruises depart from Franklin Wharf behind the wooden cruise-sales booths beside Elizabeth Street Wharf at the bottom of Elizabeth Street.

Derwent River Cruises, Brook Street, Pier (© **03/6233 1914;** www.derwentrivercruises.com.au), offers a 75-minute cruise of the harbor daily at 10am (summer only), and 11:30am and 2pm. It costs A$25 (US$20/UK£10) for adults, A$12 (US$9.60/UK£4.80) for children, and A$66 (US$53/UK£27) for a family. It also offers a 2-hour Storm Bay Cruise which includes cliff views, tales of whales and history, and a view of Iron Pot lighthouse, the oldest lighthouse in Australia. It costs A$35 (US$28/UK£14) for adults, A$18 (US$14/UK£7) for kids, and A$90 (US$72/UK£36) for a family. It leaves at 3:30pm between October 1 and May 31. The company also runs a cruise to Port Arthur.

THE SHOPPING SCENE

If you are in Hobart on a Saturday, don't miss the **Salamanca Market** ★★, in Salamanca Place—it's one of the best markets in Australia. Some 200 stalls offer everything from fruit and vegetables to crafts made from pottery, glass, and native woods. The market is open from 8:30am to 3pm.

Salamanca Place has plenty of crafts and souvenir shops that are worth exploring, though the prices reflect the fashionable area. The best bookshop in town is a beauty; it sells a large range of new and secondhand books, many relating to Tasmania. Find the **Hobart Bookshop** at 22 Salamanca Sq. (© **03/6223 1803**). For great chocolate and the best licorice, head to **Darrell Lea,** shop 36 in the Cat & Fiddle Arcade, between Collins and Liverpool streets. There are plenty of other interesting shops here, too.

Store hours are Monday through Thursday from 9am to 6pm, Friday from 9am to 9pm, and Saturday from 9am to noon (though some are open all day).

WHERE TO STAY

Hobart has some of the best hotels, guesthouses, and B&Bs in Australia. For something different, you can stay with a Tasmanian family in town or at a farm in the country, or arrange accommodations in one of the many boutique B&Bs throughout Tasmania. Contact **Heritage Tasmania Pty Ltd.,** P.O. Box 780, Sandy Bay, TAS 7005 (✆ **03/6233 5511;** fax 03/6233 5510). Nightly B&B rates range from about A$60 (US$48/UK£24) to around A$160 (US$128/UK£64) for a double.

There are 11 YHA **hostels** in Tasmania. In Hobart, the best is Montgomery's Private Hotel & YHA Backpackers, 9 Argyle St., Hobart (✆ **03/6231 2660**), which has double rooms from A$70 to A$94 (US$56–US$75/UK£28–UK£38) and family rooms from A$70 to A$134 (US$56–US$107/UK£28–UK£54). There are also hostels in Launceston (✆ **03/6343 3119**), which has family rooms from A$100 to A$115 (US$80–US$92/UK£40–UK£46); Devonport (✆ **03/6424 5696**); Coles Bay (✆ **03/6257 0115**); Port Arthur (✆ **03/6250 2311**), which has doubles for A$44 (US$35/UK£18) and family rooms for A$57 (US$46/UK£23); and Stanley (✆ **03/6458 1266**). The state YHA office is at 28 Critereon St., Hobart (✆ **03/6234 9617;** www.yha.com.au).

VERY EXPENSIVE

Hotel Grand Chancellor ★ If you prefer standard hotel accommodations to a stately old homestead, book a room at this imposing property overlooking the yachts and fishing boats in Victoria Dock. Standard rooms are large and comfortable, with large polished granite bathrooms. More than 50% of the rooms have water views. Eight rooms are equipped for travelers with disabilities. The lobby is an impressive marble-and-granite construction complete with a large curved window to catch the action on the docks. There's also a first-class restaurant specializing in innovative Tasmanian cuisine. Check the website for reduced rates (such as a Harbour View room for as little as A$154/US$123/UK£62).

1 Davey St., Hobart, TAS 7000. ✆ **1800 753 379** in Australia, or 03/6235 4535. Fax 03/6223 8175. www.ghihotels.com/hgc. 240 units. A$260 (US$208/UK£104) double; A$365 (US$292/UK£146) executive suite. Extra person A$30 (US$24/UK£12). Check the website for good deals. Children under 15 stay free in parent's room. AE, DC, MC, V. Free parking. **Amenities:** Restaurant; lounge w/good views; heated indoor pool; health club; concierge; business center; salon; 24-hr. room service; massage; babysitting; laundry service; rooms for those w/limited mobility. *In room:* A/C, TV w/pay movies, dataport, minibar, hair dryer, iron.

Wrest Point Casino ★★ A pricey face-lift in 1998 transformed this Hobart icon, built in 1973, and launched Australia's annual A$2-billion (US$1.7-billion/UK£800-million) casino industry. Beside the Derwent River, 3km (almost 2 miles) from the city center, the complex looks out across the harbor and the city and up to Mount Wellington. All rooms feature Tasmanian oak furniture and plush carpets, and more expensive units have exceptional views. While it may not be as convenient to the city center as the Hotel Grand Chancellor (though it's certainly walkable), the views make it a class above. Adjacent to the casino is the 61-room **Wrest Point Motor Inn,** which has nice rooms costing between A$120 and A$131 (US$96–US$104/UK£48–UK£52). Taxis from Wrest Point to the city cost around A$7 (US$5.60/UK£2.80), and the bus operates to and from the city every 15 minutes.

410 Sandy Bay Rd., Sandy Bay, TAS 7005. ✆ **1800 703 006** in Australia, or 03/6211 1750. Fax 03/6225 3744. www.wrestpoint.com.au. 197 units. A$242–A$264 (US$193–US$211/UK£97–UK£49) double; A$330 (US$264/UK£132) suite with Jacuzzi. Extra adult A$33 (US$26/UK£13). AE, DC, MC, V. Free parking. Bus: Busy Bee route 54 or 55 from Franklin Sq., Macquarie St., to stop 15. **Amenities:** 3 restaurants; 3 bars; nightclub; large indoor pool; 9-hole putting course; 2 lit tennis courts; health club; playground; concierge; business center; 24-hr. room service; massage; babysitting; laundry service; harbor boardwalk w/indoor and outdoor entertainment; boutique casino. *In room:* A/C, TV w/pay movies, dataport, minibar, hair dryer, iron, safe.

EXPENSIVE

The Elms of Hobart This lovely National Trust–classified mansion is too far from the city (2km/1¼ miles) to walk to, and I think Macquarie Manor is nicer. However, it's just .5km (⅓ mile) from a wide range of restaurants along the popular North Hobart food strip. Each room has heritage appeal and is furnished with antiques. The delightful Honeymoon Suite can be booked by non-honeymooners of course, and it costs around A$220 (US$176/UK£88) per night. The property has a "grog" room, where guests can help themselves to beer and wine on an honor system, and a quaint front living room. Two outstanding features are the Tasmanian oak staircase and paneling. Rooms at the front face the road and can be noisy.

452 Elizabeth St., North Hobart, TAS 7000. ✆ **03/6231 3277.** Fax 03/6231 3276. www.theelmsofhobart.com. 6 units. A$145–A$185 (US$116–US$148/UK£58–UK£74) double. Rates include full breakfast. AE, DC, MC, V. Free parking. Bus: Any up Elizabeth St. from the city. Children under 11 not accepted. **Amenities:** Lounge; tour desk; nonsmoking rooms. *In room:* TV, dataport, coffeemaker, hair dryer.

The Lodge on Elizabeth ★ The Lodge on Elizabeth is in the second-oldest building in Tasmania, some parts of which date to 1810. Originally a gentleman's residence, it later became the first private boys' school in Tasmania. It's well situated just a 12-minute walk from Salamanca Place and is surrounded by restaurants. All rooms are decorated with antiques; many are quite romantic, with four-poster beds. Standard rooms have just a shower, whereas deluxe rooms come with more antiques and a large granite bathroom with a Jacuzzi. Complimentary drinks are served in the communal living room in the evening. The Convict's Cottage is a cute self-contained spa cottage, just for two, in the grounds.

249 Elizabeth St., Hobart, TAS 7000. ✆ **03/6231 3830.** Fax 03/6234 2566. www.thelodge.com.au. 13 units. A$120 (US$96/UK£48) small double with bathroom; A$140 (US$112/UK£56) large double with bathroom; A$160 (US$128/UK£65) convict cottage with spa. Extra person A$30 (US$24/UK£12). Rates include breakfast. AE, DC, MC, V. **Amenities:** Tour desk; car-rental desk; coin-op laundry; dry cleaning; nonsmoking rooms. *In room:* TV, dataport, fridge, coffeemaker, hair dryer, iron.

Macquarie Manor ★★ As soon as you walk into this classic colonial-style manor you'll know you want to stay. Macquarie Manor was built in 1875 as a doctor's surgery and residence. Extra rooms were added in 1950. Thick carpets and double-glazed windows keep the place very quiet, even though it's on the main road, 2 blocks from the central bus terminal. Rooms, which vary enormously, are comfortable and elegantly furnished. One room is suitable for people with disabilities. The staff is very friendly and will be happy to escort you around the premises in search of your favorite room. Check out the delightful dining room and the drawing room complete with old couches and a grand piano. Parking is just to the left down the side of the main building. Smoking is not permitted.

172 Macquarie St., Hobart, TAS 7000. ✆ **1800/243 044** in Australia, or 03/6224 4999. Fax 03/6224 4333. www.macmanor.com.au. 18 units, most with shower only. A$190 (US$152/UK£76) double; A$250 (US$200/UK£100) Heritage suite; A$275 (US$220/UK£110) Macquarie suite. Extra adult A$40 (US$32/UK£16); extra child A$20 (US$16/UK£8). Rates

include full breakfast. AE, DC, MC, V. Free parking. **Amenities:** Tour desk; dry cleaning; nonsmoking rooms. *In room:* TV, minibar, coffeemaker, hair dryer, iron.

Salamanca Inn Conveniently located on the edge of the central business district and toward the waterfront near Battery Point, Salamanca Inn features modern and pleasant apartments. The place features queen-size beds, leather couches, Tasmanian oak furniture, galley-style kitchens, and spacious living areas. The more expensive suites are a bit plusher.

10 Gladstone St., Hobart, TAS 7000. ✆ **03/6223 3300.** Fax 03/6223 7167. www.salamancainn.com.au. 68 units. A$198 (US$158/UK£78) 1-bedroom apt; A$220 (US$176/UK£88) 2-bedroom suite; A$260 (US$208/UK£104) 2-bedroom deluxe suite. Extra adult A$25 (US$20/UK£10), extra child 3–14 A$15 (US$12/UK£6). Ask about weekend and long-stay packages. AE, DC, MC, V. Free parking. Bus: 54B. **Amenities:** Restaurant; bar; indoor pool; Jacuzzi; tour desk; business center; room service; babysitting; laundry service; dry cleaning. *In room:* TV, free in-house movies, dataport, kitchenette, minibar, fridge, coffeemaker, hair dryer, iron.

MODERATE

Customs House Hotel You won't find a better value than the rooms above this historic sandstone pub overlooking the waterfront. Built in 1846, the property offers nice, colonial-style rooms, seven of which look across at the water. Some of the other rooms look across Parliament House and its gardens, and the rest are toward the back of the hotel with no views to speak of. Downstairs, a public bar overlooks the water, and at the back of the building is a popular restaurant known for its seafood, steaks, and stir-fries. Live music is on hand downstairs between Wednesday and Saturday nights (it finishes at 1am on Fri and Sat nights, so book rooms on the second or third floors, as those on the first floor can be noisy). All waterfront rooms are nice and quiet.

1 Murray St., Hobart, TAS 7000. ✆ **03/6234 6645.** Fax 03/6223 8750. www.customshousehotel.com. 22 units. A$130 (US$104/UK£52) waterfront doubles; A$115 (US$92/UK£46) doubles. Rates include hot breakfast. AE, DC, MC, V. **Amenities:** Restaurant; 2 bars; dry cleaning. *In room:* A/C, TV, tea- and coffeemaker.

Woolmers Inn Situated 2km (1¼ miles) south of the city, Woolmers Inn offers cozy one- or two-bedroom units with fully equipped kitchens. One unit is suitable for travelers with disabilities. Sandy Bay is Hobart's main suburb; it's halfway between the casino and the city (within walking distance of Salamanca Place) and features a "golden mile" of boutique shopping.

123–127 Sandy Bay Rd., Hobart, TAS 7000. ✆ **1800/030 780** in Australia, or 03/6223 7355. Fax 03/6223 1981. www.woolmersinn.com. 36 units. A$160 (US$128/UK£64) 1-bedroom apt; A$190 (US$152/UK£76) 2-bedroom apt. Rates 10% higher from mid-Dec to end of Jan, and cheaper in winter. AE, DC, MC, V. Free parking. Bus: Sandy Bay route (no number) from Elizabeth St. Mall on Elizabeth St. **Amenities:** Tour desk; babysitting; coin-op laundry; dry cleaning. *In room:* TV/VCR, kitchen, fridge, coffeemaker, hair dryer, iron.

INEXPENSIVE

Central City Backpackers This place is typical of backpacker-type accommodations—cheap and cheerful, a little frayed around the edges, but right in the heart of things. The central shopping district is outside the door; it's only a short walk to the harbor and a 2-minute walk to the central bus terminal.

138 Collins St., Hobart, TAS 7000. ✆ **1800/811 507** in Australia, or 03/6224 2404. Fax 03/6224 2316. www.centralbackpackers.com.au. 80 units. A$62 (US$50/UK£25) double; A$22–A$26 (US$18–US$21/UK£9–UK£11) dorm bed. No credit cards. **Amenities:** Bar (summer only); tour desk; coin-op laundry; Internet access; pool table; kitchen; dining room. *In room:* No phone.

Montgomery's Private Hotel & YHA Backpackers One of two Hobart YHAs (the other, Adelphi Court YHA, ✆ **03/6228 4829,** is in North Hobart), Montgomery's is right in the heart of the city. As with most hostels it has a common room with TV, and communal cooking facilities. It's friendly and convenient.

9 Argyle St., Hobart, TAS 7000. ✆ **03/6231 2660.** Fax 03/6231 4817. www.yha.com.au. 7 dorms, 5 double/twin rooms with shared bathroom, 10 double/twin rooms with own bathroom, 5 family rooms sharing bathrooms, 2 family rooms with own bathrooms. A$70 (US$56/UK£28) double without bathroom; A$94 (US$75/UK£38) double with bathroom; A$70–A$110 (US$56–US$88/UK£28–UK£44) family room without bathroom; A$94–A$134 (US$75–US$107/UK38–UK£54) family room with bathroom; A$20–A$23 (US$16–US$18/UK£8–UK£9) dorm bed. Non-YHA members pay A$3.50 (US$2.80/UK£1.40) per person per night extra. MC, V. Free parking. **Amenities:** TV room; tour-booking desk. *In room:* No phone.

WHERE TO DINE

Tasmania is known for its fresh seafood, including oysters, crab, crayfish, salmon, and trout. Once cheap, in recent years prices have crept up to match or even surpass those on the mainland. Generally, the food is of good quality.

EXPENSIVE

amulet ★ CONTEMPORARY North Hobart has got a reputation for happening restaurants and the eatery of the moment is amulet, a top-nosh restaurant which prides itself on seasonal produce and local ingredients. Inside it's light and lovely during the day and moody at night. It's a wonderful place for both breakfast and a weekend brunch—the extensive menus are truly inspiring. As for dinner, try the eggplant *cordon bleu* stuffed with smoked soy on hummus and pine nuts, or the spice-crusted lamb on pumpkin mash with sour cherry sauce.

333 Elizabeth St., North Hobart. ✆ **03/6234 8113.** www.northhobart.com/amulet. Reservations recommended. Main courses A$26–A$28 (US$21–US$22/UK£10–UK£11). AE, MC, V. Daily 10am–3pm and 6–10pm.

Mures Upper Deck ★ SEAFOOD This bustling waterfront restaurant offers great views of bobbing yachts as well as fine seafood caught on the owner's fishing boats. I recommend starting with a bowl of the signature Mures Smokey Chowder or local oysters. Main courses could include grilled Atlantic salmon with an asparagus and smoked salmon terrine; or a blue eye (a fish) pan-fried in a spice mix of cumin, fennel, and black pepper. Ribs, steaks, fettuccine, fish and chips, and beer-battered prawns and scallops are also available. A real treat is the seafood platter, costing A$50 (US$40/UK£20). The best summer dessert is the restaurant's summer pudding, which almost bursts with berries. The complex also includes **Lower Deck,** a self-service family restaurant where you can dine well for under A$20 (US$16/UK£8).

Between Victoria and Constitution Docks, Hobart. ✆ **03/6231 2121.** www.mures.com.au. Reservations recommended. Main courses A$26–A$33 (US$21–US$26/UK£11–UK£13). AE, DC, MC, V. Daily noon–10pm.

The Point Revolving Restaurant ★ TASMANIAN/AUSTRALIAN This revolving restaurant on the 17th floor of the Wrest Point Hotel Casino is known for its spectacular harbor and mountain views. Criticism of its consistency has led to a complete review of its cuisine, and now it seems to be ticking away very nicely. The food has gone up in price with the quality. Expect a few game dishes, such as venison and rabbit, as well as duck, steak, and fish. If it's on the menu when you get there try the Highland venison with sauerkraut and a potato-and-apple gratin. The service is friendly and relaxed and a small but rich lunch menu—and a children's menu featuring steak, chicken, and fish (and tempting desserts)—make it worth a visit for the daytime views. This place is packed on weekends.

In the Wrest Point Hotel Casino, 410 Sandy Bay Rd. © **03/6225 0112.** www.wrestpoint.com.au. Reservations recommended. Main courses A$47 (US$38/UK£19). Signature Menu, 2-courses with wine A$85 (US$68/UK£34), 3-courses with wine A$95 (US$76/UK£38). AE, DC, MC, V. Daily noon–2pm and 6:30–9:30pm.

MODERATE

Annapurna ★ INDIAN This is a fabulous Indian restaurant, with rich red walls and richer food. All your usual Indian restaurant fare is on the menu plus some more unusual dishes, such as the Calcutta chicken, a Goan prawn curry, and a goat curry. Top of the lot is the *masala dosa,* a south Indian crepe filled with curried potato. There are plenty of vegetarian options. I can't wait to return; my mouth is already watering.

305 Elizabeth St., North Hobart. © **03/6236 9500.** www.northhobart.com/annapurna. Reservations recommended. Main courses A$12–A$17 (US$9.50–US$14/UK£4.80–UK£7). AE, MC, V. Mon–Fri noon–3pm; daily 5:30–10pm.

Drunken Admiral Restaurant ★ SEAFOOD The Drunken Admiral, opposite the Hotel Grand Chancellor on the waterfront, is an extremely popular spot with tourists and can get raucous on busy evenings. The main attraction to start the meal is its famous seafood chowder, swimming with anything that was on sale at the docks that morning. The large Yachties Seafood Grill (for A$28/US$22/UK£11) is a full plate of squid, scallops, fish, mussels, and prawns, but there are plenty of simpler fish dishes on the menu, too. I recommend the Tassie mussels steamed in white wine, tomatoes, and shallots with a hunk of bread.

17–19 Hunter St. © **03/6234 1903.** Reservations required. Main courses A$20–A$28 (US$16–US$22/UK£8–UK£11). AE, DC, MC, V. Daily 6–10:30pm.

INEXPENSIVE

Cumquat on Criterion ★ *Value* ASIAN/AUSTRALIAN This cafe is an excellent breakfast venue, offering everything from egg on toast to porridge with brown sugar. On the menu for lunch and dinner you could find Thai beef curry, laksa, a daily risotto, and chermoula-marinated fish. The desserts can be great. Vegetarians, vegans, and those on a gluten-free diet are very well catered to, as are carnivores.

10 Criterion St. © **03/6234 5858.** Reservations recommended. Main courses A$7.50–A$15 (US$6–US$12/UK£3–UK£6). No credit cards. Mon–Fri 8am–6pm.

HOBART AFTER DARK

Built in 1837, the 747-seat **Theatre Royal,** 29 Campbell St. (© **03/6233 2299**), is the oldest live theater in the country. It's known for its excellent acoustics and its classical Victorian decor. Ticket prices vary depending on the performance, but A$25 (US$20/UK£10) is average.

Opened in 1829 as a tavern and a brothel frequented by whalers, **Knopwood's Retreat,** 39 Salamanca Place (© **03/6223 5808**), is still a raucous place to be on Friday and Saturday evenings, when crowds cram the historic interior and spill out onto the streets. Light lunches are popular throughout the week, and occasionally you'll find jazz or blues on the menu.

My favorite drinking hole in Hobart is **Irish Murphy's,** 21 Salamanca Place (© **03/6223 1119**), an atmospheric pub with stone walls and lots of dark wood. Local bands play Friday and Saturday evenings.

If you want to tempt Lady Luck, head to the **Wrest Point Casino,** in the Wrest Point Hotel, 410 Sandy Bay Rd. (© **03/6225 0112**), Australia's first legal gambling club. Smart, casual attire required (collared shirts for men).

A SIDE TRIP TO MOUNT FIELD NATIONAL PARK ★

80km (50 miles) NW of Hobart

Mount Field National Park is one of the prettiest in Tasmania. It was proclaimed a national park in 1916 to protect a plateau dominated by dolerite-capped mountains and dramatic glaciated valleys. Mount Field West is the highest point at 1,417m (4,647 ft.), and in the central and western regions of the park in particular, there are examples of lakes and tarns formed in the Ice Age of 30,000 years ago. The most mountainous regions support alpine moorlands of cushion plants, pineapple and sword grass, waratahs, and giant pandani. You can get a good look at these changing environments on a 16km (10-mile) drive from the park entrance to Lake Dobson along an unpaved and often badly rutted road, which is not suitable for conventional vehicles in winter or after heavy rain.

Bennett's and rufous wallabies are common, as are wombats, barred bandicoots, Tasmanian devils, and quolls. Platypuses inhabit the lakes. Birds common to the park include black cockatoos, olive whistlers, green rosellas, honeyeaters, currawongs, wedge-tailed eagles, and lyrebirds, which were introduced from Victoria in the 1930s. Also here are rare native hens, yellow wattlebirds, and dusky robins.

There are many walking trails in the park, including one to Tasmania's most photographed waterfalls, the spectacular 45m (148-ft.) **Russell Falls,** near the park's entrance. The walk to the falls along a paved, wheelchair-accessible track takes 15 minutes and passes ferns and forests, with some of Tasmania's tallest trees, mighty swamp gums up to 85m (279 ft.) high.

GETTING THERE **Tassielink** (✆ **1300/300 520** in Australia, or 03/6272 6611; www.tigerline.com.au) offers daily transfer service from December through March for A$35 (US$28/UK£14) one-way. A day tour with the same company, leaving Monday, Wednesday, and Friday, costs A$109 (US$87/UK£44) for adults and A$63 (US$50/UK£25) for kids. All fares are from Hobart. By car, take the Lyall Highway from Hobart to the Gordon River and follow the signs after the township of Westerway.

VISITOR INFORMATION

The park's visitor center (✆ **03 6288 1149**) on Lake Dobson Road has a cafe and has information on walks. It's open daily from 8:30am to 5pm between November and April and 9am to 4pm in winter.

WHERE TO STAY

Russell Falls Holiday Cottages These cottages are right at the entrance to the park, in a rural setting with rolling fields. Each is spacious and comfortable, with gas heat and an attached toilet and shower, as well as a lounge and dining room.

Lake Dobson Rd., National Park, TAS 7140. ✆ **03/6288 1198.** Fax 03/6288 1341. 4 units. A$140 (US$112/UK£56) double. Extra adult A$20 (US$16/UK£8); extra child under 15 A$10 (US$8/UK£4). MC, V. *In room:* TV, kitchen, fridge, iron.

3 Port Arthur: Discovering Tasmania's Convict Heritage ★

102km (63 miles) SE of Hobart

Port Arthur, on the Tasman Peninsula, is one of Australia's prettiest harbors. It houses the remains of Tasmania's largest penal colony—essentially Australia's version of Devil's Island. It's the state's number-one tourist destination, and you really should plan to spend at least a whole day in this incredibly picturesque, yet haunting, place.

From 1830 to 1877, Port Arthur was one of the harshest institutions of its type anywhere in the world. It was built to house the settlement's most notorious prisoners, many of whom had escaped into the bush from lesser institutions. Nearly 13,000 convicts found their way here, and nearly 2,000 died while incarcerated. A strip of land called Eaglehawk Neck connects Port Arthur to the rest of Tasmania. Guards and dogs kept watch over this narrow path, while the authorities circulated rumors that the waters around the peninsula were shark-infested. Only a few convicts ever managed to escape, and most of them either perished in the bush or were tracked down and hanged. Look out for the blowhole and other coastal formations, including Tasman's Arch, Devil's Kitchen, and the Tessellated Pavement, as you pass through Eaglehawk Neck.

ESSENTIALS

GETTING THERE Port Arthur is a 1½-hour drive from Hobart on the Lyell and Arthur highways. **Tassielink** (© **1300/300 520** in Australia, or 03/6230 8900) runs trips from Hobart to the former penal settlement on Tuesday, Wednesday (in summer only), Thursday, Friday, and Sunday. Tours cost A$90 (US$72/UK£36) for adults and A$54 (US$43/UK£22) for children 4 to 16. The trip includes a guided tour of the Port Arthur site.

Derwent River Cruises, Brook Street, Pier (© **03/6233 1914;** www.derwentrivercruises.com.au), runs an exceptional tour to Port Arthur. Travel the sea route of convicts transported from Hobart to Port Arthur. The all-day journey includes a 2½-hour cruise along the coastline to Port Arthur, entrance to the site and another 20-minute cruise, and a return by bus to Hobart. It costs A$149 (US$119/UK£69) for adults, A$110 (US$88/UK£44) for kids, and A$434 (US$347/UK£174) for a family. The cruise runs on Wednesdays, Fridays, and Sundays from October 1 to May 31.

EXPLORING THE SITE

The **Port Arthur Historic Site** ★★ (© **03/6251 2310;** www.portarthur.org.au) is large and scattered, with some 30 19th-century buildings. (Most of the main ones were damaged during bushfires in 1877, shortly after the property ceased to be a penal institution.) You can tour the remains of the church, guard tower, model prison, and several other buildings. It's best to tour the area with a guide, who can describe what the buildings were used for. Don't miss the fascinating museum in the old lunatic asylum, which has a scale model of the prison complex, as well as leg irons and chains.

The site is open daily from 9am to 5pm; admission is A$25 (US$20/UK£10) for adults, A$11 (US$8.80/UK£4.40) for children 4 to 12, and A$55 (US$44/UK£22) for a family. The admission price is good for 2 consecutive days and includes a walking tour and a boat cruise around the harbor, which leaves eight times daily in summer. There is also a separate cruise to the **Isle of the Dead** off the coast of Port Arthur twice a day; some 1,769 convicts and 180 free settlers were buried here, mostly in mass graves with no headstones. The cruise costs an extra A$10 (US$8/UK£4) for adults, A$6.50 (US$5.20/UK£2.60) for kids, and A$29 (US$23/UK£12) for a family.

The main feature of the visitor center is a fabulous **Interpretive Gallery,** which takes visitors through the process of sentencing in England to transportation to Van Diemen's Land. The gallery contains a courtroom, a section of a transport ship's hull, a blacksmith's shop, a lunatic asylum, and more. Allow between 3 and 4 hours to explore the site and the gallery.

Allow at least 1½ hours to enjoy the scenic drive from Hobart to Port Arthur. The drive along the Tasman and Arthur Highways forms part of the Convict Trail Touring

Finds Something Spooky

Lantern-lit **Ghost Tours of Port Arthur** ★ leave nightly at 6:30, 8:30, and 9:30pm (only 8:30pm during winter months) and cost A$17 (US$14/UK£7) for adults and A$10 (US$8/UK£4) for children. A family ticket (two adults and up to six children) costs A$45 (US$36/UK£18). Reservations are essential; call ✆ **1800/659 101** in Australia.

Route and takes in breathtaking seascapes, rolling farmlands and villages, vineyards, and artists' studios.

EN ROUTE TO PORT ARTHUR

On the way to Port Arthur you might want to stop off at the historic village of Richmond and at the Tasmanian Devil Park Wildlife Rescue Centre.

Richmond is just 26km (16 miles) northeast of Hobart and is the site of the country's oldest bridge (1823), the best-preserved convict jail in Australia (1825), and several old churches, including St. John's Church (1836), the oldest Catholic church in the country. Richmond also has tearooms, crafts shops, galleries, and antiques stores.

Eighty kilometers (50 miles) from Hobart is the **Tasmanian Devil Conservation Park,** Port Arthur Highway, Taranna (✆ **03/6250 3230;** www.tasmaniandevilpark.com), which houses orphaned or injured native animals, including Tasmanian devils, quolls, kangaroos, eagles, and owls. The park is open daily from 9am to 5pm. Admission is A$12 (US$9.60/UK£4.80) for adults, A$6 (US$4.80/UK£2.40) for children, and A$30 (US$24/UK£12) for a family. Tasmanian devils are fed daily at 10am, 11am, and 5pm. The center is breeding devils with genes that could make them resistant to the facial tumor disease that's devastating the population. If you want to help save the Tassie devil then go to the park's website.

WHERE TO STAY & DINE

Comfort Inn Port Arthur If you decide to stop over rather than drive all the way back to Hobart (remember, marsupials get killed all the time on the roads at night—and they can do a lot of damage to a rental car), this AAA-rated three-and-one-half-star motor inn is a good choice. The rooms overlook the historic site. The spa rooms are the most attractive, and are a better choice than the standard options. A range of packages are available, including a room with dinner, breakfast, and the ghost tour; or a room, 2 days' entrance to the Port Arthur site, the ghost tour, and breakfast. It's worth checking the website for all package details as they change.

Port Arthur Historic Site, Arthur Hwy., Port Arthur, TAS 7182. ✆ **1800/030 747** in Australia, or 03/6250 2101. Fax 03/6250 2417. www.portarthur-inn.com.au. 35 units. A$68–A$89 (US$54–US$71/UK£27–UK£36) double (most expensive are spa suites). Extra person A$25 (US$20/UK£10). Children under 12 stay free in parent's room. AE, DC, MC, V. Free parking. Bus: Hobart Coaches (✆ **1800/030 620** in Australia, or 03/6234 4077) from Hobart (weekdays). **Amenities:** Restaurant; playground; coin-op laundry. *In room:* TV, coffeemaker, iron.

4 Freycinet National Park ★★

206km (128 miles) NE of Hobart; 214km (133 miles) SW of Launceston

If you only have time to visit one place in Tasmania, make sure it's **Freycinet National Park.** The Freycinet Peninsula hangs down off the eastern coast of Tasmania. It's a place of craggy pink-granite peaks, spectacular white beaches, wetlands, heathland, coastal dunes, and dry eucalyptus forests. This is the place to come to spot sea eagles, wallabies, seals, pods of dolphins, and humpback and southern right whales during their migration to and from the warmer waters of northern New South Wales from May through August. The township of **Coles Bay** is the main staging post, and there are many **bushwalks** in the area. The **Moulting Lagoon Game Reserve**—an important breeding ground for black swans and wild ducks—is signposted along the highway into Coles Bay from Bicheno. Some 10,000 black swans inhabit the lake, so it's unusual not to see them. Six kilometers (3¾ miles) outside town and inside the national park is the **Cape Tourville Lighthouse,** which allows extensive views north and south along the coast and across several of the small islands in the Tasman Ocean.

Spectacular **Wineglass Bay** ★★, named one of the world's top 10 beaches by *Outside* magazine, is a lovely spot for a walk.

ESSENTIALS

GETTING THERE There are no direct public buses from Hobart. **Tasmanian Redline Coaches** (✆ **1300 360 000** in Australia, or 03/6336 1446) run from 112 George St., Launceston, to Bicheno at 2pm Monday through Thursday, and at 3:45pm on Friday, and take less than 3 hours. **Tassielink** (✆ **1300/300 520** in Australia, or 03/6272 6611; www.tigerline.com.au) runs buses from Launceston to Bicheno on Monday, Wednesday, Friday, and Sunday at 8:30am. From Bicheno, catch a local bus run by **Bicheno Coach Services** (✆ **03/6257 0293,** or 0419 570 293 mobile) for the 35-minute trip to the park. Buses leave at 9am daily and 3pm Sunday through Friday from the Freycinet Bakery and Cafe. Buses also meet every coach from Launceston, but you need to book in advance. **Tassielink** (✆ **1300/300 520** in Australia, or 03/6230 8900) offers a day trip to Freycinet with an optional walking trip to Wineglass Bay from both Hobart and Launceston on Friday and Sunday year-round. It costs A$85 (US$68/UK£34) for adults and A$51 (US$41/UK£21) for children. It's worth it if you are traveling for a limited time.

From Hobart it's about a 3-hour drive to the park.

VISITOR INFORMATION The **Visitor Information Centre** (✆ **03/6375 1333;** fax 03/6375 1533) on the Tasman Highway at Bicheno can arrange tour bookings. Otherwise, the **Tasmanian Travel and Information Centre** in Hobart (✆ **03/6230 8383**) can supply you with maps and details. Daily entry to the park costs A$10 (US$8/UK£4) per vehicle.

EXPLORING THE PARK

If you have time to do only one walk, head out from Freycinet Lodge on a 30-minute uphill hike past beautiful pink-granite outcrops to **Wineglass Bay Lookout** for breathtaking views. You can then head down to Wineglass Bay itself and back up again. The walk takes around 2½ hours. A longer route takes you along the length of **Hazards Beach,** where you'll find plenty of shell middens—seashell refuse heaps—left behind by the Aborigines who once lived here. This walk takes 6 hours.

Tasmanian Expeditions (✆ **1300/666 851** in Australia, or 03/6339 3999; www.tas-ex.com) offers a 3-day trip from Launceston and back that includes 2 nights in cabins at Coles Bay. The trip includes guided walks to Wineglass Bay and Mount Amor. It costs A$690 (US$552/UK£276) and departs year-round on Wednesday. The company also offers 6- and 12-night walking, rafting, and cycling trips, as well as walking trips all over Tasmania.

Not to be missed is a trip aboard Freycinet Sea Charter's vessel ***Kahala*** (© **03/6257 0355**; www.freycinetseacharters.com), which offers whale-watching between June and September, bay and game fishing, dolphin-watching, diving, scenic and marine wildlife cruises, and sunset cruises. Half-day cruises cost A$110 (US$88/UK£44) per person with a minimum of four adults onboard.

WHERE TO STAY & DINE

Camping is available in the park for A$10 (US$8/UK£4) per tent, though water is scarce. For inquiries, call the **Parks and Wildlife Service** (© **03/6257 0107**).

Freycinet Lodge ★★ I can't praise this ecofriendly lodge enough. They offer comfortable one- and two-room cabins spread unobtrusively through the bush, connected by raised walking tracks. Each has a balcony, and the more expensive ones have a huge Jacuzzi. (The deluxe cabins are recently refurbished, and some have water views.) Twenty cabins have their own kitchens. The main part of the lodge houses a lounge room and an excellent restaurant that sweeps out onto a veranda overlooking the green waters of Great Oyster Bay. The lodge is right next to the white sands of Hazards Beach, and from here it's an easy stroll to the start of the Wineglass Bay walk.

Freycinet National Park, Coles Bay, TAS 7215. © **1800 420 155** or 03/6225 7000. Fax 03/6257 0278. www.puretasmania.com.au. 60 units. A$190 (US$152/UK£76) standard cabin; A$225 (US$180/UK£90) cabin with Jacuzzi; A$255 (US$204/UK£102) deluxe cabin with Jacuzzi. Extra adult A$54 (US$41/UK£21). Children under 14 stay free in parent's room. Check the website for good-deal packages. AE, DC, MC, V. **Amenities:** 2 restaurants; bar; outdoor tennis court; bike rental; activities desk; coin-op laundry; nonsmoking rooms; Internet kiosk. *In room:* Fridge, coffeemaker, hair dryer.

HOBART TO LAUNCESTON: THE "HERITAGE HIGHWAY"

By the 1820s several garrison towns had been built between Launceston and Hobart, and by the middle of the 19th century convict labor had produced what was considered to be the finest highway of its time in Australia. Today, many of the towns along the route harbor magnificent examples of Georgian and Victorian architecture. It takes about 2 hours to drive between Launceston and Hobart on the "Heritage Highway" (known as the A1, or the Midland Hwy.), but you need 2 days to fully explore.

ROSS ★

121km (75 miles) N of Hobart; 78km (48 miles) S of Launceston

One of Tasmania's best-preserved historic villages, picturesque Ross was established as a garrison town in 1812 on a strategically important crossing point on the Macquarie River. **Ross Bridge,** the third oldest in Australia, was built in 1836 to replace an earlier span made of logs. The bridge is decorated with Celtic symbols, animals, and faces of notable people of the time. It is lit up at night, and there are good views of it from a dirt track that runs along the river's north bank.

The town's **main crossroads** is the site of four historic buildings, humorously known as "temptation" (represented by the Man-o'-Ross Hotel), "salvation" (the Catholic church), "recreation" (the town hall), and "damnation" (the old jail). The **Ross Female Factory,** built in the early 1840s, consists of ruins, a few interpretive signs, and a model of the original site and buildings inside the original Overseer's Cottage. Entry is free. Women convicts were imprisoned here from 1847 to 1854.

The **Tasmanian Wool Centre** and tourist information center, on Church Street (© **03/6381 5466**), holds an exhibition detailing the growth of the region and the wool industry since settlement. It's open daily from 9am to 5pm (until 6pm Jan–Mar). Entry is by donation.

Where to Stay & Dine

Colonial Cottages of Ross ★ These delightful historic cottages sit on the edge of the village in a rural setting complete with a small apple orchard. Apple Dumpling Cottage (ca. 1880) is a two-bedroom wooden structure, sleeping four, with impressive sandstone fireplaces. The spacious Church Mouse Cottage (ca. 1840), set in an old Sunday school, sleeps just two. Captain Samuel's Cottage (ca. 1830), accommodates six people in three bedrooms, with two double and two single beds. Hudson Cottage (ca. 1850) sleeps four. All cottages have modern bathrooms and kitchen facilities.

12 Church St., Ross, TAS 7209. ✆ **03/6381 5354.** Fax 03/6381 5408. www.cottagesofthecolony.com.au. 4 units. A$138–A$156 (US$110–US$125/UK£55–UK£63) for 2. Extra person A$25–A$33 (US$20–US$27/UK£10–UK£14). MC, V. *In room:* TV, kitchen.

The Ross Village Bakery and Inn This coaching inn, built in 1832, offers homey rooms done in old English style. One room has a double bed, another a double and two singles. The third is a double, which opens onto a fourth room that has two singles (suitable as a family room). A separate lounge has a TV and free tea, coffee, sherry, and cakes. The bakery on the premises, an excellent place for lunch, serves filled baked potatoes and some of the best pies in Australia, baked in a wood-fired oven from 1860.

15 Church St., Ross, TAS 7209. ✆ **03/6381 5246.** Fax 03/6381 5360. www.rossbakery.com.au. 4 units. A$120 (US$96/UK£48) per room. AE, MC, V. **Amenities:** Bakery; TV lounge. *In room:* Hair dryer.

5 Launceston ★

198km (123 miles) N of Hobart

Tasmania's second-largest city is Australia's third oldest, after Sydney and Hobart. Situated at the head of the Tamar River, 50km (31 miles) inland from the state's north coast, and surrounded by delightful undulating farmland, Launceston is a pleasant city crammed with elegant Victorian and Georgian architecture and plenty of remnants of convict days. Unfortunately, shortsighted local and state governments are gradually overseeing the chipping away of its great architectural heritage in favor of the usual parking garages and ugly concrete monoliths. However, Launceston (pop. 104,000) is still one of Australia's most beautiful cities and has plenty of delightful parks and churches. It's also the gateway to the wineries of the Tamar Valley, the highlands and alpine lakes of the north, and the stunning beaches to the east.

ESSENTIALS

GETTING THERE **Qantas** (✆ **13 13 13** in Australia), **Virgin Blue** (✆ **13 67 89** in Australia), and **Jetstar** (✆ **13 15 38** in Australia) carry passengers from Sydney and Melbourne to Launceston. The **Airport Shuttle** (✆ **03/6343 6677**) provides transportation between city hotels and the airport from 8:45am to 5pm daily for A$11 (US$8/UK£4) each way, kids 4 to 16 A$5 (US$4/UK£2).

Tasmanian Redline Coaches (✆ **1300 360 000** in Australia; www.tasredline.com.au) departs Hobart for Launceston several times daily (trip time: around 2 hr., 40 min.). The one-way fare is around A$30 (US$24/UK£12). Launceston is 1½ hours from Devonport if you plan to take a ferry from Melbourne across Bass Strait to Devonport. The bus ride from Devonport to Launceston costs around A$20 (US$16/UK£8).

The drive from Hobart to Launceston takes just over 2 hours on Highway 1.

VISITOR INFORMATION The **Gateway Tasmania Travel Centre,** at the corner of St. John and Paterson streets (✆ **03/6336 3133;** fax 03/6336 3118), is open Monday

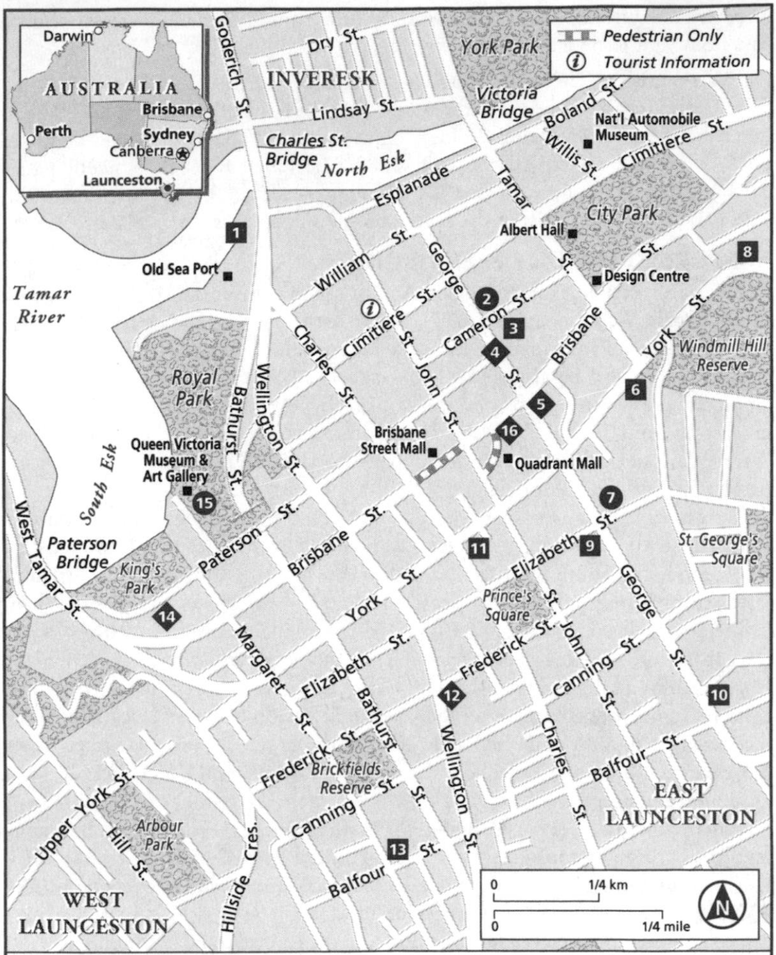

ACCOMMODATIONS ■

Alice's Cottages & Spa Hideaways **13**
Colonial on Elizabeth Boutique Hotel **9**
Hillview House **10**
Hotel Grand Chancellor Launceston **3**
Hotel Tasmania **11**
Peppers Seaport Hotel **1**
Waratah on York **8**
York Mansions **6**

DINING ◆

Croplines Coffee Bar **16**
Fee & Me Restaurant **12**
Konditorei Cafe Manfred **5**
Lucks **4**
Stillwater River Café **14**

ATTRACTIONS ●

Aquarius Roman Baths **7**
The Old Umbrella Shop **2**
The Queen Victoria Museum & Art Gallery **15**

through Friday from 9am to 5pm, Saturday from 9am to 3pm, and Sunday and holidays from 9am to noon.

CITY LAYOUT The main pedestrian shopping mall, Brisbane Street, along with St. John and Charles streets on either side, forms the heart of the central area. The Victorian-Italianate Town Hall is 2 blocks north on Civic Square, and opposite the red-brick Post Office building dating from 1889. The Tamar River slips quietly past the city's northern edge and is crossed at two points by Charles Bridge and Tamar Street. City Park, to the northeast of the central business district, is a nice place for a stroll.

EXPLORING THE CITY & ENVIRONS

Launceston is easy to explore on foot. A must for any visitor is a stroll with **Launceston Historic Walks** ★ (✆ **03/6331 3679;** harris.m@bigpond.com), which leaves from the Gateway Tasmania Travel Centre Monday through Friday at 9:45am. (Weekend walks can also be arranged.) The 1-hour walk gives a fascinating insight into Launceston's history and costs A$15 (US$12/UK£6). **Tassielink** (✆ **1300/300 520** in Australia, or 03/6230 8900) operates a half-day coach tour of the city on Monday, Wednesday, and Friday at 9:30am. It costs A$51 (US$41/UK£21) for adults and A$31 (US$25/UK£13) for children.

A must-see is **Cataract Gorge** ★, the result of violent earthquakes that rattled Tasmania some 40 million years ago. It's a wonderfully scenic area just 10 minutes from Launceston. The South Esk River flows through the gorge and collects in a small lake traversed by a striking yellow suspension bridge and the longest single-span chairlift in the world. The chairlift (✆ **03/6331 5915**) is open daily from 9am to 4:30pm (except June 23–Aug 11, when it operates Sat–Sun only), and costs A$8.50 (US$6.80/UK£3.40) for adults and A$6 (US$4.80/UK£2.40) for children under 16. Outdoor concerts sometimes take place on the lake bank. The hike to the Duck Reach Power Station takes about 45 minutes. Take good footwear and a raincoat. Other walks in the area are shorter and easier. The **Gorge Restaurant** (✆ **03/6331 3330**) and the kiosk next door serve meals with glorious views from the outdoor tables.

Tamar River Cruises (✆ **03/6334 9900**) offers lunch, afternoon, and evening buffet dinner cruises up the Tamar River from Home Point Wharf in Launceston.

Mountain biking is popular in this area. Contact **Tasmanian Expeditions** (✆ **1800/030 230** in Australia, or 03/6334 3477) for information on its 4- to 7-day trips along the east coast in summer. You can rent bicycles from the Launceston City Youth Hostel at 36 Thistle St. (✆ **03/6344 9779**) for around A$15 (US$12/UK£6) per day for a touring bike or A$20 (US$16/UK£8) per day for a mountain bike. (You can also rent bushwalking equipment, including boots, tents, sleeping bags, and stoves.)

The **Trevallyn State Recreation Area,** on the outskirts of Launceston off Reatta Road, is a man-made lake surrounded by a beautiful wildlife reserve with several walking tracks. There are barbecue facilities, picnic areas, and a beach.

OTHER ATTRACTIONS

Aquarius Roman Baths Adorned with gold, Italian marble, and works of art, this remarkable Romanesque structure is worth visiting just for the architectural experience. Indulge in warm-, hot-, and cold-water baths; visit the steam room; or get a massage or a beauty makeover.

127 George St. ✆ **03/6331 2255.** www.romanbath.com.au. Entry to baths A$24 (US$19/UK£10). 30-min. massage and entry to baths A$65 (US$52/UK£26). Other packages available. Mon–Fri 8:30am–9pm; Sat–Sun 9am–6pm.

The Old Umbrella Shop Built in the 1860s, this unique shop is the last genuine period store in Tasmania and has been operated by the same family since the turn of the 20th century. Umbrellas spanning the last 100 years are on display, and modern "brollies" and souvenirs are for sale. Allow 15 minutes.

60 George St. ✆ **03/6331 9248.** Free admission. Mon–Fri 9am–5pm; Sat 9am–noon.

The Queen Victoria Museum & Art Gallery Opened in honor of Queen Victoria's Golden Jubilee in 1891, this museum houses a large collection of stuffed wildlife, including the extinct Tasmanian tiger, or thylacine. There are also temporary exhibits and historical items on display. Allow 1 hour.

2 Wellington St. ✆ **03/6323 3777.** Free admission. Daily 10am–5pm. Closed Dec 25.

WHERE TO STAY

VERY EXPENSIVE

Peppers Seaport Hotel ★★ One of Australia's most respected boutique-hotel operators, Peppers Retreats & Resorts, opened this hotel on the Tamar riverfront in 2004. The hotel is part of a major redevelopment of the Seaport Dock area—just 5 minutes by car from downtown—which also includes new restaurants, entertainment venues, and shopping facilities. The hotel is built on the site of an old dry dock and has been designed in the shape of a ship. The decor is luxurious and contemporary nautical in style, using soft, light colors, natural timbers, and chromes. Rooms are spacious and most have balconies either looking out over the river, or over the town center to the mountains beyond. Each has a good kitchenette and an extra fold-out sofa bed.

28 Seaport Blvd., Launceston, TAS 7250. ✆ **03 6345 3333.** Fax 03/6345 3300. www.peppers.com.au. 60 units. A$125 (US$100/UK£50) river-view double; A$120 (US$96/UK£48) city-view double; A$146–A$224 (US$116–US$195/UK£58–UK£98) suite. AE, DC, MC, V. Car: From the Mall on Brisbane St., turn right onto St. John St., turn right onto York St. Proceed 3 blocks and turn right onto Bathurst St. Proceed 1.5km (1 mile) and on the left is the Seaport Precinct. **Amenities:** Restaurant; bar; tour desk. *In room:* A/C, TV, kitchenette, minibar, coffeemaker, hair dryer, iron, in-room laundry.

EXPENSIVE

Alice's Cottages & Spa Hideaways ★★★ I highly recommend these delightful cottages: **Alice's Place,** which sleeps two, was made entirely from bits and pieces of razed historic buildings; **Ivy Cottage** is a restored Georgian house (ca. 1831). Both places are furnished with antiques and fascinating period bric-a-brac. Kitchens are fully equipped, and both units have large Jacuzzis; they share a garden. Guests come and go as they please, and stay here on their own. (Check in at the reception area, 129 Balfour St.) Also available are **Alice's Hideaways,** five other cottages in a colonial Australian theme, some of which sleep four; and four cute cottages collectively known as **The Shambles.** A recent addition is **Aphrodites Delux Spa,** a large, regal setup with a formal dining room.

129 Balfour St., Launceston, TAS 7250. ✆ **03/6334 2231.** Fax 03/6334 2696. www.cottagesofthecolony.com.au. 11 units. Alice's Place A$197 (US$157/UK£79) for 2; Ivy Cottage A$197 (US$157/UK£79) for 2; Alice's Hideaways: Bonnie Doon, Captain Stirlings, Camelot, and French Boudoir A$197 (US$157/UK£78); Shambles cottages A$160 (US$128/UK£80); Aphrodites A$230 (US$184/UK£92), 2-night minimum. Extra person A$55 (US$44/UK£22). Rates include breakfast ingredients left in your fridge. AE, DC, MC, V. Free parking. *In room:* A/C, TV, kitchen.

Hotel Grand Chancellor Launceston ★★ This centrally located European-influenced "grand" hotel is only a short stroll from the main shopping precinct, public gardens, and other city features. The rooms are large and elegant and the restaurant is good, too. Standard rooms have two double beds or a king-size bed. There's a piano bar and a brasserie, too. Smoking is not permitted.

29 Cameron St., Launceston, TAS 7250. ✆ **1800/555 811** in Australia, or 03/6334 3434. Fax 03/6331 7347. 158 units. A$220 (US$176/UK£88) double; A$245 (US$196/UK£99) room with Jacuzzi; A$290–A$500 (US$232–US$400/UK£116–UK£200) suite. Children stay free in parent's room. Ask about packages. AE, DC, MC, V. Free parking. **Amenities:** Restaurant; bar; concierge; car-rental desk; business center; 24-hr. room service; massage by arrangement; babysitting; coin-op laundry; laundry service; nonsmoking rooms. *In room:* A/C, TV, dataport, minibar, coffeemaker, hair dryer, iron.

York Mansions ★★★ If you feel that where you stay is as important to your visit as what you see, then you must stay here. Within the walls of the National Trust–classified York Mansions, built in 1840, are five spacious apartments, each with a distinct character. The Duke of York apartment is fashioned after a gentleman's drawing room, complete with rich leather sofa, antiques, and an extensive collection of historical books. The light and airy Duchess of York unit has two bedrooms, hand-painted silk panels, and a Jacuzzi. Each apartment has its own kitchen, dining room, living room, bedrooms, bathroom, and laundry. A CD player and large-screen TV add modern touches. The ingredients for a hearty breakfast can be found in the refrigerator. There's also a delightful cottage garden.

9–11 York St., Launceston, TAS 7250. ✆ **03/6334 2933.** Fax 03/6334 2870. www.yorkmansions.com.au. 5 units. A$216–A$242 (US$173–US$194/UK£87–UK£97) double. Extra person A$55 (US$44/UK£22). Rates include breakfast provisions. AE, DC, MC, V. Free parking. **Amenities:** Tour desk; laundry service; nonsmoking rooms. *In room:* TV/VCR, dataport, kitchen, minibar, coffeemaker, hair dryer, iron.

MODERATE

Colonial on Elizabeth Boutique Hotel ★ Those who desire tried-and-true above-standard motel lodging will feel at home at the recently refurbished Colonial, a place that combines old-world ambience with modern facilities. The large rooms have attractive furnishings. They're fairly standard and attract a large corporate clientele. Beautiful gardens surround this property.

31 Elizabeth St., Launceston, TAS 7250. ✆ **1800 060 955** in Australia, or 03/6331 6588. Fax 03/6334 2765. www.colonialinn.com.au. 63 units. A$148 (US$118/UK£60) double; A$165–A$245 (US$132–US$196/UK£66–UK£99) suite. Extra person A$15 (US$12/UK£6). Lower weekend rates. Children under 3 stay free in parent's room. AE, DC, MC, V. Free parking. **Amenities:** Restaurant; lounge; tour desk; limited room service; laundry service. *In room:* A/C, TV, minibar, coffeemaker, hair dryer, iron.

Waratah on York ★★ The Waratah on York is a carefully renovated Victorian mansion, built in 1862 for Alexander Webster, an ironmonger by trade and mayor of Launceston in the 1860s and 1870s. The current owners have spent considerable time and energy restoring the property to its former glory. Some of the original features—pressed brass ceiling roses and a staircase with a cast-iron balustrade—remain, while others have been faithfully re-created. Six rooms come with a Jacuzzi, one with a balcony, and another with a sunroom. All have high ceilings and ornate (but nonfunctional) fireplaces. The executive rooms have four-poster beds and sweeping views of the Tamar River.

12 York St., Launceston, TAS 7250. ✆ **03/6331 2081.** Fax 03/6331 9200. www.waratahonyork.com.au. 9 units. A$192 (US$154/UK£77) standard double; A$218 (US$174/UK£87) double with Jacuzzi; A$256 (US$205/UK£103) executive suite with Jacuzzi. Rates include continental breakfast. AE, DC, MC, V. Free parking. **Amenities:** Bar; lounge w/fireplace; tour desk; business facilities; massage; laundry service; same-day dry cleaning; nonsmoking rooms. *In room:* TV, minibar, coffeemaker, hair dryer, iron.

INEXPENSIVE

Hillview House The rooms at this restored farmhouse are cozy and quite comfortable. Each comes with a double bed and a shower. The family room has an extra single bed; it's the nicest unit and has the best views. The hotel overlooks the city, and the large veranda and colonial dining room have extensive views over the city and the Tamar River.

193 George St., Launceston, TAS 7250. ✆ **03/6331 7388.** Fax 03/6331 7388. www.hillviewhouse.net.au. 9 units. A$110–A$115 (US$88–US$92/UK£44–UK£46) double; A$115–A$125 (US$92–US$100/UK£46–UK£50) family room for 3. Rates include full breakfast. MC, V. Free parking. **Amenities:** Laundry service. *In room:* TV.

Hotel Tasmania In the heart of town, this budget hotel offers simple rooms with modern furnishings and attached showers. Downstairs there's a saloon-style bar with a cowboy theme, which schedules live music Wednesday, Friday, and Saturday. The popular **Saloon nightclub** also kicks off late on Wednesday, and it's free for students before 11pm.

191 Charles St., Launceston, TAS 7250. ✆ **03/6331 7355.** Fax 03/6331 2414. www.saloon.com.au. 25 units. A$80 (US$64/UK£32) double. Extra person A$19 (US$15/UK£7.50). Rates include continental breakfast. AE, MC, V. Free street parking. **Amenities:** Restaurant; bar. *In room:* TV, fridge, coffeemaker.

WHERE TO DINE

Most places to eat in Launceston don't have a fixed closing time; rather, they close when the last customer has eaten.

EXPENSIVE

Fee & Me Restaurant ★★ MODERN AUSTRALIAN Perhaps the best restaurant in Launceston, Fee & Me is in a grand old mansion. The menu is structured so that diners choose a selection from five categories, each one moving from light to rich. An extensive wine list complements selections for each course. A five-course meal could go something like this: Tasmanian smoked salmon with salad, capers, and a soft poached egg; followed by chile oysters with coconut sauce and vermicelli noodles; then ricotta and goat cheese gnocchi with creamed tomato and red capsicum; followed by Asian-style duck on bok choy with citrus sauce; topped off with coffee and chicory soufflé. The dishes change frequently, so you never know what you might find.

Corner of Charles and Frederick sts. ✆ **03/6331 3195.** Reservations recommended. A$42 (US$34/UK£17) for 3 courses; A$48 (US$38/UK£19) for 4 courses; A$50 (US$40/UK£20) for 5 courses. AE, DC, MC, V. Mon–Sat 7–10:30pm.

Lucks ★★ BISTRO The food here is good bistro-style; and the interior matches, with classic bentwood chairs, banquette seating on one side of the room, and a white interior broken with ornate aqua and gold wallpaper and a huge 1960s poster advertising a French cabaret show behind the bar. Try the spaghetti *vongole* (clams), the ox filet with roasted marrow and beef jus, or the roast venison. A couple of fish dishes are usually on the menu.

70 George St. ✆ **03/6334 8596.** www.lucks.com.au. Reservations recommended for dinner and lunch. Main courses A$22–A$34 (US$18–US$27/UK£9–UK£14). AE, DC, MC, V. Daily breakfast 7–10am (8–11am Sat–Sun), noon–3pm, and 6–10pm.

Stillwater River Café ★★ MODERN AUSTRALIAN This fabulous eatery in located inside an old mill beside the Tamar River. Come here for a good breakfast (the eggs Benedict cost A$12/US$9.60/UK£4.80), a casual lunch at one of the tables outside overlooking the river, or an atmospheric dinner. The dinner menu is fascinating with all sorts of delicacies on the menu including abalone and even sea urchin. Try the seared scallops or the Vietnamese sugar-cooked pork belly. The wine cellar brings up a good selection of Tasmanian wines. It's a good idea to go for the six-course tasting menu, which comes in at a respectable A$98 (US$78/UK£39), or A$139 (US$111/UK£56) including matching wines.

Ritchies Mill (bottom of Paterson St.). ✆ **03/6331 4153.** www.stillwater.net.au. Reservations recommended. Lunch A$19–A$24 (US$15–US$19/UK£7.50–UK£10); dinner A$66 (US$53/UK£27) 2 courses, A$91 (US$73/UK£37) 3 courses. AE, MC, V. Daily 8am–10pm.

INEXPENSIVE

Konditorei Cafe Manfred PATISSERIE This German patisserie had to move to larger premises to keep up with demand for its sensational cakes and breads. It also added an a la carte restaurant serving up the likes of pastas and steaks. Light meals include croissants, salads, and cakes. You can eat inside or outside.

106 George St. ✆ **03/6334 2490.** Light meals A$4–A$5 (US$3.20–US$4/UK£1.60–UK£2); main courses A$15 (US$7.20–US$14/UK£3.60–UK£7). AE, DC, MC, V. Mon–Fri 9am–5:30pm; Sat 8:30am–4pm.

A CAFE

Croplines Coffee Bar ★ *Finds* CAFE If you crave good coffee, bypass every other place in Launceston and head here. It's a bit hard to find, and you may have to ask for directions, but basically it's behind the old Brisbane Arcade. The owners are dedicated to coffee, grinding their beans on the premises daily. If coffee's not your cup of tea, then try the hot chocolate—it's the best I've tasted.

Brisbane Court, off Brisbane St. ✆ **03/6331 4023.** Coffees and teas A$1.80–A$2.60 (US$1.45–US$2.10/UK75p–UK£1.05). Cakes under A$3 (US$2.40/UK£1.20). AE, MC, V. Daily 8am–5:30pm.

6 Cradle Mountain & Lake St. Clair National Park ★★

85km (53 miles) S of Devonport; 175km (109 miles) NW of Hobart

The national park and World Heritage area that encompasses both Cradle Mountain and Lake St. Clair is one of the most spectacular regions in Australia and, after Hobart and Port Arthur, the most visited place in Tasmania. The 1,545m (5,068-ft.) mountain dominates the north part of the island, and the long, deep lake is to its south. Between them lie steep slopes, button grass plains, majestic alpine forests, dozens of lakes filled with trout, and several rivers. **Mount Ossa,** in the center of the park, is Tasmania's highest point at 1,617m (5,304 ft.). The **Overland Track** (see "Hiking the Overland Track," below), links Cradle Mountain with Lake St. Clair and is the best known of Australia's walking trails. Another option in the area is a visit to the **Walls of Jerusalem National Park,** a high alpine area with spectacular granite walls, small lakes, and old-growth forest.

ESSENTIALS

GETTING THERE **Tassielink** (✆ **1300/300 520** in Australia, or 03/6272 6611; www.tigerline.com.au) runs buses to Cradle Mountain from Hobart, Launceston, Devonport, and Strahan. Its special summer Overland Track service leaves from either Launceston or Hobart and drops off passengers at the beginning of the walk (Cradle Mountain), then picks them up at Lake St. Clair before returning back to either Launceston or Hobart. It costs A$90 (US$72/UK£36) starting from Launceston and returning to Hobart; A$119 (US$95/UK£48) starting at and returning to Hobart; and A$110 (US$88/UK£44) starting at and returning to Launceston. Check the website for departure times, which change.

Maxwells Cradle Mountain–Lake St. Clair Charter Bus and Taxi Service (✆/fax **03/6492 1431**) runs buses from Devonport and Launceston to Cradle Mountain. The fare starts at A$35 (US$28/UK£14). The buses also travel to other areas nearby, such as the Walls of Jerusalem, as well as Lake St. Clair. Buses also run from the Cradle Mountain campground to the start of the Overland Track.

Motorists enter the park off the Lyall Highway from Hobart, via Deloraine or Poatina from Launceston, and via Sheffield or Wilmot from Devonport. Both Cradle Mountain and Lake St. Clair are well signposted.

Finds **Hiking the Overland Track**

The best-known hiking trail in Australia is the **Overland Track** ★★, an 85km (53-mile) route between Cradle Mountain and Lake St. Clair. The trek takes 5 to 10 days and goes through high alpine plateaus, button grass plains, heathland, and rainforests, and passes glacial lakes, ice-carved crags, and waterfalls. The trek gives you a good look at the beauty of Tasmania's pristine wilderness, and although the first day is quite tough, you soon get into the rhythm. After climbing to Pelion Gap, the track descends southward toward the towering myrtle forests on the shores of Lake St. Clair. There are many rewarding side trips, including the 1-day ascent of Mount Ossa (1,617m/5,304 ft.), Tasmania's highest peak.

Several companies offer guided walks of the Overland Track October through April. For those who wish to do it solo, simple public huts (on a first-come, first-served basis) and camping areas are available. Every summer up to 200 people a day start the trek. Most trekking companies employ at least two guides who carry tents and cooking gear, while you carry your sleeping bag, lunch, and personal belongings. Wet-weather gear is essential, because heavy downpours can be frequent. Make sure your boots are well broken in, to avoid blisters.

Tasmanian Expeditions (© **1800/030 230** in Australia, or 03/6334 3477; www.tas-ex.com) offers 3-day walking tours around Cradle Mountain, staying at Waldheim Cabins. The tours depart from Launceston and cost A$660 (US$528/UK£265), all-inclusive. Trips leave every Sunday all year round and Sunday and Wednesday between October and May. The company also offers a full 8-day trek on the Overland Track from Launceston. The price is A$1,790 (US$1,432/UK£716), all-inclusive; renting wet-weather gear costs extra. These trips depart every Saturday between November and April, with extra trips from late December to the end of January. Another trip, a 6-day Cradle Mountain and Walls of Jerusalem National Park trip, includes 3 nights of wilderness camping and 3 nights in a cabin. It costs A$1,290 (US$1,032/UK£516) and leaves every Sunday between October and mid-May. Many people have reported that this trek was the highlight of their trip to Australia.

I also recommend **Cradle Mountain Huts,** P.O. Box 1879, Launceston, TAS 7250 (© **03/6331 2006**; fax 03/6331 5525; www.cradlehuts.com.au). Six-day walks cost A$2,450 (US$1,960/UK£998); rates are all-inclusive and include transfers to and from Launceston. Children under 12 are not permitted. The huts are fully equipped, heated, and quite comfortable, with showers, a main living area, and a full kitchen. You get a good three-course meal every night. The treks leave daily between Christmas and early February, and around five times a week between November and April.

VISITOR INFORMATION The park headquarters, **Cradle Mountain Visitor Centre** (© **03/6492 1133;** fax 03/6492 1120; www.parks.tas.gov.au), on the northern edge of the park outside Cradle Mountain Lodge, offers the best information on walks and treks. It's open daily 8am to 5pm (6pm in summer).

EXPLORING THE PARK

Cradle Mountain Lodge (see "Where to Stay & Dine," below) runs a daily program of guided walks, abseiling (rappelling), rock-climbing, and trout-fishing excursions for lodge guests. The park has plenty of trails that can be attempted by people equipped with directions from the staff at the park headquarters (see "Visitor Information," above). Be warned, though, that the weather changes quickly in the high country; so go prepared with wet-weather gear and always tell someone where you are headed. Of the shorter walks, the stroll to Pencil Pines and the 5km (3-mile) walk to Dove Lake are the most pleasant. Between June and October it's sometimes possible to cross-country ski in the park.

WHERE TO STAY & DINE

Cradle Mountain Lodge ★★ If you like luxury with your rainforests, then this award-winning lodge is the place for you. Cradle Mountain Lodge is marvelous. Just minutes from your bed are giant buttresses of 1,500-year-old trees, moss forests, mountain ridges, limpid pools and lakes, and hordes of scampering marsupials. The cabins are comfortable, the food excellent, the staff friendly, and the open fireplaces well worth cuddling up in front of for a couple of days. Each modern wood cabin has a potbellied stove as well as an electric heater for chilly evenings, a shower, and a small kitchen. There are no telephones or TVs in the rooms—but who needs them? Spa cabins come with carpets, a Jacuzzi, and a balcony offering a variety of views. Some have a separate bedroom. Two cabins have limited facilities for travelers with disabilities. Guests have the use of the casual, comfortable main lodge where almost every room has a log fire.

G.P.O. Box 478, Sydney, NSW 2001. ✆ **13 24 69** in Australia, or 03/6492 1303. P&O Resorts: ✆ **800/225-9849** in the U.S. and Canada, 020/7805-3875 in the U.K., 1800/737 678 in Australia, or 02/9364 8900. Fax 02/9299 2477. www.cradlemountainlodge.com.au. 96 units. A$274 (US$219/UK£110) Pencil Pine cabin double; A$342 (US$274/UK£137) spa cabin double; A$418 (US$334/UK£117) spa suite. Extra person A$58 (US$46/UK£23). Children under 3 stay free in parent's room. Ask about winter packages. AE, DC, MC, V. Free parking. **Amenities:** Cafe; 2 bars; laundry service. *In room:* Kitchenette, no phone.

Waldheim Cabins For a real wilderness experience, head to these cabins run by the Parks and Wildlife Service, located 5km (3 miles) from Cradle Mountain Lodge. Nestled between button grass plains and temperate rainforest, they are simple and affordable and offer good access to plenty of walking tracks. Each heated cabin has single bunk beds, basic cooking utensils, crockery, cutlery, and a gas stove. Each accommodates four or eight people; if your party is smaller, you won't have to share with strangers. Two outbuildings with sanitary facilities (composting toilets and showers) serve all the cabins. Generated power is provided for lighting between 6 and 11pm only. Stores and fuel can be bought at Cradle Mountain Lodge. Bring your own bed linen and toiletries. Guests can pick up keys from the National Park Visitor Centre, just inside the national park, daily between 8am and 5:30pm.

Cradle Mountain Visitor Centre, P.O. Box 20, Sheffield, TAS 7306. ✆ **03/6492 1110.** Fax 03/6492 1120. www.parks.tas.gov.au. 8 cabins. Cabin A$70 (US$56/UK£28) for 2 adults; A$25 (US$20/UK£10) for each additional adult; A$9.90 (US$7.90/UK£4) for each additional child 6–16. Children under 6 stay free in parent's room. Linen A$5.50 (US$4.40/UK£2.20) per person. MC, V. *In room:* No phone.

LAKE ST. CLAIR ★

Australia's deepest natural freshwater lake is a narrow, 15km-long (9⅓-mile) waterway, enclosed within the Cradle Mountain–Lake St. Clair National Park. On the lake's southern edge is **Cynthia Bay,** site of an informative ranger station where you must register if you're attempting the Overland Track from this end, as well as a restaurant, cabin accommodations, and a backpackers' hostel operated by **Lakeside St. Clair**

(✆ **03/6289 1137**). National park rangers run several tours between Boxing Day and the end of February, including spotlighting tours and guided walks around the area. Call ✆ **03/6289 1172** for details.

7 The West Coast

296km (184 miles) NW of Hobart; 245km (152 miles) SW of Devonport

Tasmania's west coast is wild and mountainous, with a scattering of mining and logging towns and plenty of wilderness. The pristine Franklin and Gordon rivers tumble through World Heritage areas once contested by loggers, politicians, and environmentalists, whereas the bare, poisoned hills that make up the eerily beautiful "moonscape" of Queenstown show the results of mining and industrial activity. **Strahan** ★ (pronounced *Strawn*), the only town of any size in the area, is the starting point for cruises up the Gordon River and into the rainforest.

ESSENTIALS

GETTING THERE **Tassielink** (✆ **1300/300 520** in Australia, or 03/6272 6611; www.tigerline.com.au) runs coaches between Strahan and Launceston, Devonport, and Cradle Mountain every Tuesday, Thursday, and Saturday; it serves Hobart on Friday and Sunday. Operating days tend to change, so check the website. The trip from Launceston takes over 8 hours. The drive from Hobart to Strahan takes about 4½ hours without stops. From Devonport, allow 3½ hours. Although the roads are good, they twist and turn and are particularly hazardous at night, when marsupial animals come out to feed. The cheapest way to travel between these places is by bus with a **Tassielink Explorer Pass.**

VISITOR INFORMATION **Strahan Visitors Centre,** on The Esplanade (✆ **03/6471 7622;** fax 03/6471 7533), is open daily from 10am to 6pm in autumn and winter and to 8pm in spring and summer. It has good information on local activities. A good website for the area is www.westcoasttourism.com.au.

CRUISING THE RIVERS & OTHER ADVENTURES

Gordon River Cruises (✆ **1800 420 155** in Australia, or 03/625 7000) offers a half-day trip daily at 9am, an afternoon cruise at 2pm in the first 3 weeks of January, and a full-day trip from October to the end of May. Cruises take passengers across Macquarie Harbour and up the Gordon River past historic **Sarah Island,** where convicts—working in horrendous conditions—once logged valuable Huon pine. During a stop at **Heritage Landing,** you can get a taste of the rainforest on a half-hour walk. The full-day cruise in the high season (Oct–May) includes lunch and a guided tour through the convict ruins on Sarah Island. Cruises depart from the Main Wharf on The Esplanade, in the town center. The full-day cruises, including a meal, cost A$80

Moments **Dune Buggy Rides**

What's more fun than scooting across the sand in a dune buggy? **Four-Wheelers** (✆ **03/6471 7622,** or 0419/508 175 mobile) offers 40-minute rides across the **Henty Sand Dunes** ★, about 10 minutes north of Strahan. Trips cost A$50 (US$40/UK£20), and A$30 (US$24/UK£12) for a passenger. Longer trips are offered outside the summer months.

Tasmanian Devil Disaster

Made famous as the angry, spinning creature in the Warner Brothers cartoons, the Tassie devil is in real trouble. Back in 1996 mysterious red, fleshy lumps appeared on the faces of the animals in northern Tasmania. This cancer, possibly caused by a virus, makes it hard for them to eat, and can even suffocate them as it spreads to the throat. Most quickly weaken and die of starvation within a few weeks. In some areas the population of adult devils has been reduced by 90%, and the disease is spreading rapidly across the state. It's estimated that around half the state's 150,000 Tasmanian devils have been killed by the disease, and some scientists believe it may wipe out the wild population entirely. Healthy specimens are being captured and relocated to try and preserve the species from extinction. For more information on the epidemic and efforts to save Taz, visit **www.tassiedevil.com.au**.

(US$64/UK£32) for an internal seat, A$105 (US$84/UK£42) for a window recliner, and A$175 (US$140/UK£70) for a seat upstairs with the captain.

World Heritage Cruises (✆ **03/6471 7174;** www.worldheritagecruises.com.au) offers daily "Heritage Cruises" year-round, leaving Strahan Wharf at 9am and returning at 3pm, or 2pm returning at 8pm. The company's MV *Wanderer III* stops at Sarah Island, Heritage Landing, and the salmon and trout farm at Liberty Point. Meals and drinks are available on board. The cruises cost A$65 (US$52/UK£26) for adults, A$25 (US$20/UK£10) for children 5 to 14 (free for children under 5), and A$165 (US$132/UK£66) for a family of five. It also offers a Morning Express cruise starting at 9am and returning at 1:30pm. (It doesn't stop at Sarah Island.) This cruise costs A$60 (US$48/UK£24) for adults, A$22 (US$18/UK£9) for children, and A$145 (US$116/UK£58) for a family.

West Coast Yacht Charters (✆ **03/6471 7422**) runs 2-day, 2-night sailing cruises for A$390 (US$312/UK£156) for adults and A$185 (US$148/UK£74) for children, all-inclusive. The company also offers other cruises.

Although cruises are the main attraction in the area, you can also enjoy jet-boat rides, sightseeing in a seaplane that lands on the Gordon River, helicopter flights, and four-wheel-drive tours.

WHERE TO STAY & DINE

Franklin Manor ★ Built in 1886 as the home of the harbor master, this superior B&B offers standard rooms with queen-size beds, deluxe rooms with king-size ones, and a very plush executive deluxe room. Also on the premises are four delightful cottages, which allow you to really get away from it all. The main lounge is comfortable and warmed by a log fire; the simple Huon-pine bar in the foyer and the wine cellar operate on the honor system. The specialties at the manor's restaurant include salmon, duck, seafood, beef, and venison.

The Esplanade, Strahan, TAS 7468. ✆ **03/6471 7311.** Fax 03/6471 7267. www.franklinmanor.com.au. 18 units, including 4 cottages. A$180 (US$144/UK£72) standard double; A$220 (US$176/UK£88) deluxe double or cottage; A$260 (US$208/UK£104) executive deluxe. Rates include breakfast. AE, DC, MC, V. Ask about winter discounts. Free parking. **Amenities:** Bar; tour desk; car-rental desk; business center; limited room service; massage; babysitting; laundry service. *In room:* TV, coffeemaker, iron.

Gordon Gateway Chalets These modern self-contained units are on a hill with good views of the harbor and Strahan township. Each has cooking facilities, so you can save on meal costs. The two-bedroom suites have bathtubs, the studios just showers. Breakfast is provided on request. Guests have the use of a barbecue area. One unit has facilities for travelers with disabilities.

Grining St., Strahan, TAS 7468. ✆ **1300 134 425** in Australia, or 03/6471 7165. Fax 03/6471 7588. www.gordongateway.com.au. 19 units. A$135 (US$108/UK£54) studio; A$260 (US$208/UK£104) suite. Winter discounts available. MC, V. **Amenities:** Playground; tour desk; massage; babysitting; coin-op laundry; nonsmoking rooms. *In room:* TV, kitchenette, fridge, coffeemaker, hair dryer, iron, safe.

Ormiston House ★★ Ormiston House is a gem. Built in 1899 for the family that gave it its name, under the present owners it has become a sort of shrine to their predecessors. Each room is styled to represent one of the original family members. Each is intricately furnished and wallpapered in busy designs and comes with a good-size bathroom. There's a morning room and a restaurant serving good food. The owners are friendly and have plenty of time for their guests. The website has good deals.

The Esplanade, Strahan, TAS 7468. ✆ **03/6471 7077.** Fax 03/6471 7007. www.ormistonhouse.com.au. 5 units. A$200–A$260 (US$160–US$208/UK£80–UK£104) double. Extra person A$62 (US$49/UK£25). Rates include breakfast. AE, DC, MC, V. **Amenities:** Bar; lounge; concierge; tour desk; laundry service; nonsmoking rooms. *In room:* A/C, TV, coffeemaker, hair dryer, iron.

STANLEY

140km (87 miles) W of Devonport; 430km (267 miles) NW of Hobart

Among the least-known areas of Tasmania, the coastline west of Devonport can throw up some surprises. Not least of them is "The Nut," a kind of miniature Ayers Rock rising from the sea and towering above the township of Stanley. The Nut is the remains of a volcanic plug that forced its way through a crack in the earth's crust some 12 million years ago. You can walk to the top or, if you're brave, take a chairlift for A$8 (US$6.40/UK£3.20) for adults, A$5 (US$4/UK£2) for children. A warning, though: Don't attempt to ride the chairlift back down if you're afraid of heights—the descent is incredibly steep, and there's no getting off! A small buggy on top will take you on a tour of The Nut for A$8 (US$6.40/UK£3.20), free for children under 10.

WHERE TO STAY

The Old Cable Station ★ Darryl Stafford, an ex-logger, and his wife, Heather, have turned the former exchange building for the telephone line from the mainland into a cozy B&B. The rooms are comfortable; two have TVs, but you'll probably spend all your time in the lounge chatting around the fire anyway. Darryl is as Aussie as you can get and will keep you entranced for hours with his stories. Seal cruises and wildlife-viewing packages are offered. The restaurant serves home-cooked dinners daily.

West Beach Rd., Stanley, TAS 7331. ✆ **03/6458 1312.** Fax 03/6458 2009. www.users.bigpond.com/staffordseals. 4 units. A$100 (US$80/UK£40) double; A$135–A$145 (US$108–US$116/UK£54–UK£58) suite with Jacuzzi. Rates include continental breakfast. MC, V. **Amenities:** Restaurant; lounge; tour desk; laundry service. *In room:* Kitchen, fridge, coffeemaker, hair dryer.

WHERE TO DINE

Hursey Seafoods SEAFOOD Plenty of people rate this little place as having the best seafood in Australia. Downstairs is a casual cafe, where you choose what you want from fish tanks; upstairs is a more formal restaurant. An unusual specialty is mutton bird (shearwater), an oily seabird that you either like seeing flying around or like seeing on your plate. You can't have it both ways.

2 Alexander Terrace, Stanley. ✆ **03/6458 1103.** Main courses A$10 (US$8/UK£4) in cafe, A$18 (US$14/UK£7) in restaurant. MC, V. Takeout/cafe daily 9am–6pm; restaurant daily 6–10pm.

Appendix: Australia in Depth

by Marc Llewellyn

The "land Down Under" is a modern nation coming to terms with its identity. The umbilical cord with Mother England has been cut, and the nation is still trying to find its position within Asia.

One thing Australia realized early on was the importance of tourism to its economy. Millions visit every year. You'll find Australians helpful and friendly, and services, tours, and food and drink to rival any in the world. Factor in the landscape, the native Australian culture, the sunshine, the animals, and some of the world's best cities, and you've got a fascinating, accessible destination of amazing diversity and variety.

1 Australia's Natural World

THE LAND OF THE NEVER-NEVER

People who have never visited Australia wonder why such a huge country has a population of just 21 million people. The truth is, Australia can barely support that many. About 90% of those 21 million people live on only 2.6% of the continent. Climatic and physical land conditions ensure that the only relatively decent rainfall occurs along a thin strip of land around Australia's coast. Even then, Australia is in the grip of the worst drought in a century. The vast majority of Australia is harsh Outback, characterized by saltbush plains, arid brown crags, shifting sand deserts, and salt lake country. People survive where they can in this arid land because of one thing—the Great Artesian Basin. This saucer-shaped geological formation comprises about one-fifth of Australia's landmass, stretching over much of inland New South Wales, Queensland, South Australia, and the Northern Territory. Beneath it are massive underground water supplies stored during Jurassic and Cretaceous times (some 66 million–208 million years ago), when the area was much like the Amazon basin is today. Bore holes bring water to the surface and allow sheep, cattle, and humans a respite from the dryness.

The Queensland coast is blessed with one of the greatest natural attractions in the world. The **Great Barrier Reef** stretches some 2,000km (1,240 miles) from off Gladstone in Queensland, to the Gulf of Papua, near New Guinea. It's relatively new, not more than 8,000 years old, although many fear that rising seawater, caused by global warming, will cause its demise. As it is, the non-native Crown of Thorns starfish and a bleaching process believed to be the result of excessive nutrients flowing into the sea from Australia's farming land are already causing significant damage. The Reef is covered in chapter 7.

AUSTRALIA'S FAUNA

NATIVE ANIMALS Australia's isolation from the rest of the world over millions of years has led to the evolution of forms of life found nowhere else. Probably the strangest of all is the **platypus.** This *monotreme,* or egg-laying marsupial, has webbed feet, a ducklike bill, and a tail like a beaver's. It lays eggs, and the young suckle from their mother. When a specimen was first brought back to Europe, skeptical scientists insisted it was a fake—a concoction of several different animals sewn together. You will probably never see this shy, nocturnal creature in the wild, although there are a few at Sydney's Taronga Zoo.

Another strange one is the **koala.** This fluffy marsupial, whose nearest relative is the wombat, eats virtually indigestible gum (eucalyptus) leaves and sleeps about 20 hours a day. There's just one koala species, although those found in Victoria are much larger than their brethren in more northern climes. Australia is also famous for **kangaroos.** There are 45 kinds of kangaroos and wallabies, ranging in scale from small rat-size kangaroos to the man-size red kangaroos.

The animal you're most likely to come across in your trip is the **possum,** named by Capt. James Cook after the North American "opossum," which he thought they resembled. (In fact they are from an entirely different family of the animal kingdom.) The brush-tailed possum is commonly found in suburban gardens, including those in Sydney. Then there's the **wombat.** There are four species of this bulky burrower in Australia, but the common wombat is most frequently found. You might come across the smaller hairy-nosed wombat in South Australia and Western Australia.

The **dingo,** thought by many to be a native of Australia, was in fact introduced—probably by Aborigines, or traders from the north. They vary in color from yellow to a russet red, and are heavily persecuted by farmers. Commonly seen **birds** include the fairy penguin along the coast, black swans, parrots and cockatoos, and honeyeaters. **Tasmanian devils** can be found in (you guessed it) the island/state of Tasmania, though a virulent disease has swept through the animals and decimated the wild population.

DANGEROUS NATIVES **Snakes** are common throughout Australia, but you will rarely see one. The most dangerous land snake is the taipan, which hides in the grasslands in northern Australia—one bite contains enough venom to kill up to 200 sheep. If by the remotest chance you are bitten, immediately demobilize the limb, wrapping it tightly (but not tight enough to restrict the blood flow) with a cloth or bandage, and head to the nearest hospital where antivenin should be available.

There are two types of **crocodile** in Australia: the relatively harmless freshwater croc, which grows to 3m (10 ft.); and the dangerous estuarine (or saltwater) crocodile, which reaches 5 to 7m (16–23 ft.). Freshwater crocs eat fish; estuarine crocs aren't so picky. *Never* swim in or stand on the bank of any river, swamp, or pool in northern Australia unless you know *for certain* it's croc-free.

Spiders are common all over Australia, with the funnel web spider and the red-back spider being the most aggressive. Funnel webs live in holes in the ground (they spin their webs around a hole's entrance) and stand on their back legs when they're about to attack. Red-backs have a habit of resting under toilet seats and in car trunks, generally outside the main cities. Caution is a good policy.

If you go bushwalking, check your body carefully. **Ticks** are common, especially in eastern Australia, and can cause severe itching and fever. If you find one on you, dab it with methylated spirits or another noxious chemical. Wait awhile and pull it out gently with tweezers, taking care not to leave the head behind.

Fish to avoid are stingrays, porcupine fish, stonefish, lionfish, and puffer fish. Never touch an **octopus** if it has blue rings on it, or a cone shell, and be wary of the painful and sometimes deadly tentacles of the box **jellyfish** along the northern Queensland coast in summer. If you brush past one of these creatures, pour vinegar over the affected site immediately—authorities leave bottles of vinegar on the beach for this purpose. Vinegar deactivates the stinging cells that haven't already affected you, but doesn't affect the ones that already have.

In Sydney, you might come across "stingers" or "blue bottles" as they are also called. These long-tentacled blue jellyfish can inflict a nasty stinging burn that can last for hours. Sometimes you'll see warning signs on patrolled beaches. The best remedy if you are severely stung is to wash the affected area with fresh water and have a very hot bath or shower.

2 The People Down Under

It's generally thought that more races of people live in Australia at the present time than anywhere else in the world, including North America. Heavy immigration has led to people from some 165 nations making the country their home. In general, relations between the different ethnic groups have been peaceful. Today Australia is an example of a multicultural society, despite an increasingly vocal minority that believes Australia has come too far in welcoming people from races other than their own.

THE ABORIGINES When Capt. James Cook landed at Botany Bay in 1770 determined to claim the land for the British Empire, at least 300,000 Aborigines were already on the continent. Whether you believe a version of history that suggests the Aboriginal people were descendants of migrants from Indonesia to the north, or the Aboriginal belief that they have occupied Australia since the beginning of time, there is scientific evidence that people were walking the continent at least 60,000 years ago.

At the time of the white "invasion" of their lands, there were at least 600 different, largely nomadic tribal communities, each linked to their ancestral land by **"sacred sites"** (certain features of the land, such as hills or rock formations). They were hunter-gatherers, spending about 20 hours a week harvesting the resources of the land, rivers, and the ocean. The rest of the time was taken up by a complex social and belief system, as well as by life's practicalities, such as making utensils, weapons, and musical instruments such as didgeridoos and clapsticks.

The basis of Aboriginal spirituality rests in the **Dreamtime** stories, in which spirits created everything—land, stars, mountains, the moon, the sun, the oceans, water holes, animals, and humans. Much Aboriginal art is related to their land and the sacred sites that are home to the Dreamtime spirits. Some Aboriginal groups believe these spirits came in giant human form, while others believed they were animals or huge snakes. According to Aboriginal custom, individuals can draw on the power of the Dreamtime spirits by reenacting various stories and practicing certain ceremonies.

Aboriginal groups had encountered people from other lands before the British arrived. Dutch records from 1451 show that the Macassans, from islands now belonging to Indonesia, had a long relationship trading Dutch glass, smoking pipes, and alcohol, for edible sea slugs from Australia's northern coastal waters, which they sold to the Chinese in the Canton markets. Dutch, Portuguese, French, and Chinese vessels also encountered

Australia—in fact, the Dutch fashion for pointy beards caught on through northern Australia long before the British First Fleet arrived in 1778.

When the British came, bringing their **diseases** with them, coastal communities were virtually wiped out by smallpox. Even as late as the 1950s, large numbers of Aborigines in remote regions of South Australia and the Northern Territory succumbed to deadly outbreaks of influenza and measles.

Although relationships between the settlers and Aborigines were initially peaceful, conflicts over land and food led to skirmishes in which Aborigines were massacred and settlers and convicts attacked—Governor Phillip was speared in the back by an Aborigine in 1790.

Within a few years, some 10,000 Aborigines and 1,000 Europeans had been killed in Queensland alone, while in Tasmania, a campaign to rid the island entirely of local Aborigines was ultimately successful, with the last full-blooded Tasmanian Aborigine dying in 1876. By the start of the 20th century, the Aboriginal people were considered a dying race. Most of those who remained lived in government-owned reserves or church-controlled missions.

Massacres of Aborigines continued to go largely or wholly unpunished into the 1920s, by which time it became official government policy to remove light-skinned Aboriginal children from their families and to sterilize young Aboriginal women. Many children of the "stolen generation" were brought up in white foster homes or church refuges and never reunited with their biological families—many children with living parents were told that their parents were dead.

Today, there are some 283,000 Aborigines living in Australia, and in general a great divide still exists between them and the rest of the population. Aboriginal life expectancy is 20 years lower than that of other Australians, with overall death rates between two and four times higher. Aborigines make up the highest percentage of the country's prison population, and many Aborigines die while incarcerated.

A landmark in Aboriginal affairs occurred in 1992 when the High Court determined that Australia was not an empty land *(terra nullius)* as it had been seen officially since the British invasion. The **"Mabo" decision** resulted in the **1993 Native Title Act,** which allowed Aboriginal groups, and the ethnically distinct people living in the Torres Strait islands off northern Queensland, to claim government-owned land if they could prove continual association with it since 1788. The later **"Wik" decision** determined that Aborigines could make claims on government land leased to agriculturists. The federal government, led by the right-leaning Prime Minister John Howard, curtailed these rights following pressure from farming and mining interests.

Issues currently facing the Aboriginal population include harsh mandatory sentencing laws (enacted in Western Australia and the Northern Territory state governments in 1996 and 1997, respectively), which came to international attention in 2000. The Aboriginal community believes such laws specifically target them. When a 15-year-old Aboriginal boy allegedly committed suicide less than a week before he was due to be released from a Northern Territory prison in early 2000, and a 21-year-old Aboriginal youth was imprisoned for a year for stealing A$23 (US$18/UK£9.20) worth of fruit cordial and cookies, Aboriginal people protested, activists of all colors demonstrated, and even the United Nations weighed in.

Added to this was the simmering issue of the federal government's decision not to apologize to the Aboriginal people for the "stolen generation." In March 2000, a government-sponsored report stated there was never a "stolen generation," while independent researchers believed the report underestimated how many people were personally affected.

Before the Sydney 2000 Olympic games, a popular movement involving people of all colors and classes called for reconciliation and an apology to the Aboriginal people. In Sydney, an estimated 250,000 people marched across the Sydney Harbour Bridge. The Liberal (read "conservative") Government refused to bow to public pressure. Despite threats of boycotts and rallies during the Olympics, the Games passed without major disturbance, and a worldwide audience watched as Aboriginal runner Cathy Freeman lit the Olympic cauldron.

THE REST OF AUSTRALIA "White" Australia was always used to distinguish the Anglo-Saxon population from that of the Aboriginal population, and until 1974 there existed a "White Australia Policy"—a result of conflict between European settlers and Chinese immigrants in the gold fields in the 1850s. This policy severely restricted the immigration of people who lacked European ancestry. These days, though, a walk through any of the major cities would show that things have changed dramatically. About 100,000 people immigrate to Australia each year. Of these, the latest figures state that approximately 18% were from New Zealand, and 10% were born in the U.K. or Ireland. More than 28% hail from Asia, 6% from South Africa, and 2% from the U.S. and Canada.

Waves of immigration have brought in millions of people since the end of World War II. Results from the census in 2001 show that more than 4.1 million Australian residents were born overseas, or 22% of the population. Of those born overseas, 43% were born in one of four countries—the United Kingdom (6% of all Australian residents), New Zealand (2%), Italy (1%), and Vietnam (1%). New waves of immigration have come from countries such as Iraq and Somalia. So what's the typical Australian like? Well, he's hardly Crocodile Dundee.

3 Australian History 101

IN THE BEGINNING In the beginning there was the **Dreamtime**—at least according to the Aborigines of Australia. Between then and now, perhaps, the supercontinent referred to as **Pangaea** split into two huge continents called **Laurasia** and **Gondwanaland.** Over millions of years, continental drift carried the landmasses apart. Laurasia broke up and formed North America, Europe, and

Dateline

- **60,000** B.C. Aborigines living in Arnhemland in the far north fashion stone tools.
- **24,500** B.C. The world's oldest known ritual cremation takes place at Lake Mungo.
- A.D. **1606** Dutch explorer Willem Jansz lands on the far north coast of Van Diemen's Land (Tasmania).
- **1622** First English ship to reach Australia wrecks on the west coast.
- **1642** Abel Tasman charts the Tasmanian coast.
- **1770** Capt. James Cook lands at Botany Bay.
- **1787** Capt. Arthur Phillip's First Fleet leaves England with convicts aboard.
- **1788** Captain Phillip raises British flag at Port Jackson (Sydney Harbour).
- **1788–1868** Convicts are transported from England to the colony of Australia.
- **1793** The first free settlers arrive.
- **1830** Governor Arthur lines up 5,000 settlers across Van Diemen's Land to walk the length of the island to capture and rid it of all Aborigines.
- **1850** Gold discovered in Bathurst, New South Wales.
- **1852** Gold rush begins in Ballarat, Victoria.

most of Asia. Meanwhile, Gondwanaland divided into South America, Africa, India, Australia and New Guinea, and Antarctica. **Giant marsupials** evolved to roam the continent of Australia: Among them were a plant-eating animal that looked like a wombat the size of a rhinoceros; a giant squashed-face kangaroo standing 3m (10 ft.) high; and a flightless bird the same size as an emu, but four times heavier. The last of these giant marsupials are believed to have died out some 40,000 years ago, possibly helped toward extinction by Aborigines.

EARLY EXPLORERS The existence of Australia had been in the minds of Europeans since the Greek astronomer Ptolemy drew a map of the world in about A.D. 150 showing a large landmass in the south, which he believed had to be there to balance out the land in the Northern Hemisphere. He called it *Terra Australia Incognita*—the unknown southland.

Evidence suggests Portuguese ships reached Australia as early as 1536 and even charted part of its coastline. In 1606 William Jansz was sent by the Dutch East India Company to open up a new route to the Spice Islands, and to find New Guinea, which was supposed to be rich in gold. He landed on the north coast of Queensland and fought with local Aborigines. Between 1616 and 1640, many more Dutch ships made contact with Australia as they hugged the west coast of what they called "New Holland," after sailing with the *westerlies* (west winds) from the Cape of Good Hope.

In 1642, the Dutch East India Company, through the governor general of the Indies, Anthony Van Diemen, sent Abel Tasman to search out and map the great south land. During two voyages, he charted the northern Australian coastline and discovered Tasmania, which he named Van Diemen's Land.

THE ARRIVAL OF THE BRITISH In 1697, English pirate William Dampier published a book about his adventures. The text mentions Shark Beach on the northwest coast of Australia as the place his pirate ship made its repairs after robbing ships on the Pacific Ocean. Sent to further explore by England's King William III, Dampier returned and found little to recommend.

Capt. James Cook turned up in 1770 and charted the east coast in his ship HMS *Endeavour*. He claimed the land for Britain and named it New South Wales, probably as a favor to Thomas Pennant, a Welsh patriot and botanist who was a friend of the *Endeavour*'s botanist, Joseph Banks. On April 29, Cook landed at Botany Bay, which he named after the discovery of scores of plants hitherto unknown to science. Turning northward, Cook passed an entrance to a possible

- **1853** The last convict arrives in Van Diemen's Land and to celebrate, the colony is renamed Tasmania after Abel Tasman.
- **1860** The white population of Australia reaches more than one million.
- **1875** Silver found at Broken Hill, New South Wales.
- **1889** Australian troops fight in the Boer War in South Africa.
- **1895** Banjo Paterson's "The Man from Snowy River" published.
- **1901** The six states join together to become the Commonwealth of Australia.
- **1902** Women gain the right to vote.
- **1911** Australian (non-Aboriginal) population reaches 4.4 million.
- **1915** Australian and New Zealand troops massacred at Gallipoli.
- **1931** The first airmail letters are delivered to England by Charles Kingsford Smith and Charles Ulm.
- **1931** The Arnhemland Aboriginal Reserve is proclaimed.
- **1932** Sydney Harbour Bridge opens.
- **1942** Darwin bombed; Japanese mini-submarines found in Sydney Harbour.

continues

harbor, which appeared to offer safe anchorage, and named it Port Jackson after the secretary to the admiralty, George Jackson. Back in Britain, King George III viewed Australia as a potential colony and repository of Britain's overflowing prison population, which could no longer be transported to the United States of America following the War of Independence.

The First Fleet left England in May 1787, made up of 11 store and transport ships (none of them were bigger than the passenger ferries that ply modern-day Sydney Harbour from Circular Quay to Manly) led by Arthur Phillip. Aboard were 1,480 people, including 759 convicts. Phillip's flagship, *The Supply,* reached Botany Bay in January 1788, but Phillip decided the soil was poor and the surroundings too swampy. On January 26, now celebrated as Australia Day, he settled for Port Jackson (Sydney Harbour) instead.

SETTLING DOWN The convicts were immediately put to work clearing land, planting crops, and constructing buildings. The early food harvests were failures, and by early 1790, the fledgling colony was facing starvation.

Phillip decided to give some convicts pardons for good behavior and service, and even grant small land parcels to those who were really industrious. In 1795, coal was discovered; in 1810 Governor Macquarie began extensive city building projects; and in 1813 the explorers Blaxland, Wentworth, and Lawson forged a passage over the Blue Mountains to the fertile plains beyond.

When gold was discovered in Victoria in 1852, and in Western Australia 12 years later, hundreds of thousands of immigrants from Europe, America, and China flooded into the country in search of their fortunes. By 1860, more than a million non-Aboriginal people were living in Australia.

The last 10,000 convicts were transported to Western Australia between 1850 and 1868, bringing the total shipped to Australia to 168,000.

FEDERATION & THE GREAT WARS On January 1, 1901, the six states that made up Australia proclaimed themselves to be part of one nation, and the Commonwealth of Australia was formed. In the same ceremony, the first governor general was sworn in as the representative of the queen, who remained head of state. In 1914, Australia joined the Mother Country in war. In April the following year, the Australian and New Zealand Army Corps (Anzac) formed a beachhead on the peninsula of Gallipoli in Turkey. The Turkish troops had been warned, and 8 months of fighting ended with 8,587 Australian dead and more than 19,000 wounded.

- **1953** British nuclear tests at Emu in South Australia lead to a radioactive cloud that kills and injures many Aborigines.
- **1956** Olympics held in Melbourne.
- **1957** British atomic tests conducted at Maralinga, South Australia. Aborigines again affected by radiation.
- **1962** Commonwealth government gives Aborigines the right to vote.
- **1967** Aborigines granted Australian citizenship and are counted in census.
- **1968** Australia's population passes 12 million following heavy immigration.
- **1971** The black, red, and yellow Aboriginal flag flown for the first time.
- **1973** Sydney Opera House completed.
- **1976** The Aboriginal Land Rights (Northern Territory) Act gives some land back to native people.
- **1983** Ayers Rock given back to local Aborigines, who rename it Uluru.
- **1983** Australia wins the Americas Cup, ending 112 years of American domination of the event.
- **1986** Queen Elizabeth II severs the Australian Constitution from Great Britain's.

Australians fought in World War II in North Africa, Greece, and the Middle East. In March 1942, Japanese aircraft bombed Broome in Western Australia and Darwin in the Northern Territory. In May 1942, Japanese midget submarines entered Sydney Harbour and torpedoed a ferry before being destroyed. Later that year, Australian volunteers fought an incredibly brave retreat through the jungles of Papua New Guinea on the Kokoda Track against superior Japanese forces. Australian troops fought alongside Americans in subsequent wars in Korea and Vietnam and sent military support to the Persian Gulf conflicts.

RECENT TIMES Following World War II, mass immigration to Australia, primarily from Europe, boosted the population. In 1974 the left-of-center Whitlam government put an end to the White Australia policy that had largely restricted black and Asian immigration since 1901. In 1986 the official umbilical cord to Britain was cut when the Australian Constitution was separated from that of its motherland. Australia had begun the march to complete independence.

In 1992 the High Court handed down the "Mabo" decision that ruled that Aborigines had a right to claim government-owned land if they could prove a continued connection with it. The following year, huge crowds filled Sydney's Circular Quay to hear that the city had won the 2000 Olympic games.

The games put medal-winning Australian athletes Cathy Freeman and swimmer Ian Thorpe in the spotlight, and spurred a new wave of interest and tourism in the land Down Under.

Australia's reputation was tarnished on Boxing Day 2005, when thousands of people, many draped in Australian flags, congregated at the Sydney beachside suburb of Cronulla to protest against the bashing of local Lifesavers, and reported long-term intimidation by gangs of Australian-Lebanese. Alcohol, and a core group of troublemakers, ensured that anyone of "Middle Eastern appearance" was attacked. The gangs responded over several nights, rampaging through the streets, burning Australian flags, smashing windows, and attacking anyone of Anglo-Saxon appearance.

4 Australia in Literature

Australian literature has come a long way since the days when the bush poets A. B. "Banjo" Paterson and Henry Lawson penned their odes to a way of life now largely lost. The best known of these is Paterson's epic "The Man from Snowy

- **1988** Aborigines demonstrate as Australia celebrates its Bicentennial with a reenactment of the First Fleet's entry into Sydney Harbour.
- **1991** Australia's population reaches 17 million.
- **1994** High Court "Mabo" decision overturns the principle of *terra nullius,* which suggested Australia was unoccupied at time of white settlement.
- **1995** Australians protest as France explodes nuclear weapons in the South Pacific.
- **1996** High Court hands down *Wik* decision, which allows Aborigines the right to claim some Commonwealth land.
- **2000** Sydney Olympics held.
- **2003** Bushfires ravage much of NSW and Victoria. Hundreds of homes are burned in the capital city, Canberra. The country faces a severe drought.
- **2005** Australia commits extra troops to Iraq—to protect Japanese railway workers (many Australian soldiers captured by the Japanese in World War II died while working on the Burma Railway between Thailand and Burma/Myanmar).
- **2006** Australia mourns the loss of native son Steve "Crocodile Hunter" Irwin, the wildlife expert and conservationist.

River" which first hit the bestseller list in 1895 and was made into a film. But the literary scene has always been lively, and Australia has a wealth of classics, many of them with the Outback at their heart.

Miles Franklin wrote *My Brilliant Career* (HarperCollins, 2001), the story of a young woman faced with the dilemma of choosing between marriage and a career, in 1901 (made into a film starring Judy Davis); Colleen McCullough's *Thorn Birds* (Avon, 1996) is a romantic epic about forbidden love between a Catholic priest and a young woman (made into a famous television miniseries); *We of the Never Never* (Avon, 1984) by Mrs. Aeneas Gunn, tells the story of a young woman who leaves the comfort of her Melbourne home to live on a cattle station in the Northern Territory; and *Walkabout* (Sundance, 1984) by James V. Marshall explores the relationship between an Aborigine and two lost children in the bush. It was later made into a powerful film by Peter Weir.

If you can find it, *The Long Farewell* (Penguin Books, 1983) by Don Charlwood presents firsthand diary accounts of long journeys from Europe to Australia in the last century. A good historical account of the early days is Geoffrey Blainey's *The Tyranny of Distance* (Pan Macmillan, 1977), first published in 1966. Robert Hughes's *The Fatal Shore: The Epic of Australia's Founding* (Vintage Books, 1988) is a best-selling nonfiction study of the country's early days (and later adapted into the award-wininng play, *Our Country's Good*).

For a contemporary, if somewhat dark, take on the settlement and development of Sydney, delve into John Birmingham's *Leviathan* (Random House, 1999). From an Aboriginal perspective, *Follow the Rabbit-Proof Fence* (University of Queensland Press, 1997) by Doris Pilkington tells the true story of three young girls from the "stolen generation" who ran away from a mission school to return to their families (a movie version was released in 2002).

Modern novelists include David Malouf, Elizabeth Jolley, Helen Garner, Sue Woolfe, and Peter Carey, whose *True History of the Kelly Gang* (Vintage Books, 2001), a fictionalized autobiography of the outlaw Ned Kelly, won the Booker Prize in 2001. West Australian Tim Winton evokes his part of the continent in stunning prose; his latest novel, *Dirt Music* (Scribner, 2002), is no exception.

Outsiders who have tackled Australia include Jan Morris and Bill Bryson. Morris's *Sydney* (Viking) was published in 1992, and Bryson's *In a Sunburned Country* (Broadway Books, 2001), while not always a favorite with Australians, may appeal to American readers.

Index

See also Accommodations and Restaurant indexes, below.

General Index

ACCOMMODATIONS

Restaurants

FROMMER'S® COMPLETE TRAVEL GUIDES

Alaska
Amalfi Coast
American Southwest
Amsterdam
Argentina & Chile
Arizona
Atlanta
Australia
Austria
Bahamas
Barcelona
Beijing
Belgium, Holland & Luxembourg
Belize
Bermuda
Boston
Brazil
British Columbia & the Canadian Rockies
Brussels & Bruges
Budapest & the Best of Hungary
Buenos Aires
Calgary
California
Canada
Cancún, Cozumel & the Yucatán
Cape Cod, Nantucket & Martha's Vineyard
Caribbean
Caribbean Ports of Call
Carolinas & Georgia
Chicago
China
Colorado
Costa Rica
Croatia
Cuba
Denmark
Denver, Boulder & Colorado Springs
Edinburgh & Glasgow
England
Europe
Europe by Rail
Florence, Tuscany & Umbria
Florida
France
Germany
Greece
Greek Islands
Hawaii
Hong Kong
Honolulu, Waikiki & Oahu
India
Ireland
Israel
Italy
Jamaica
Japan
Kauai
Las Vegas
London
Los Angeles
Los Cabos & Baja
Madrid
Maine Coast
Maryland & Delaware
Maui
Mexico
Montana & Wyoming
Montréal & Québec City
Moscow & St. Petersburg
Munich & the Bavarian Alps
Nashville & Memphis
New England
Newfoundland & Labrador
New Mexico
New Orleans
New York City
New York State
New Zealand
Northern Italy
Norway
Nova Scotia, New Brunswick & Prince Edward Island
Oregon
Paris
Peru
Philadelphia & the Amish Country
Portugal
Prague &
Republi
Provence &
Puerto Rico
Rome
San Antonio &
San Diego
San Francisco
Santa Fe, Taos &
Scandinavia
Scotland
Seattle
Seville, Granada & th
Andalusia
Shanghai
Sicily
Singapore & Malaysia
South Africa
South America
South Florida
South Pacific
Southeast Asia
Spain
Sweden
Switzerland
Tahiti & French Polynesia
Texas
Thailand
Tokyo
Toronto
Turkey
USA
Utah
Vancouver & Victoria
Vermont, New Hampshire & Maine
Vienna & the Danube Valley
Vietnam
Virgin Islands
Virginia
Walt Disney World® & Orlando
Washington, D.C.
Washington State

FROMMER'S® DAY BY DAY GUIDES

Amsterdam
Chicago
Florence & Tuscany
London
New York City
Paris
Rome
San Francisco
Venice

PAULINE FROMMER'S GUIDES! SEE MORE. SPEND LESS.

Hawaii
Italy
New York City

FROMMER'S® PORTABLE GUIDES

Acapulco, Ixtapa & Zihuatanejo
Amsterdam
Aruba
Australia's Great Barrier Reef
Bahamas
Big Island of Hawaii
Boston
California Wine Country
Cancún
Cayman Islands
Charleston
Chicago
Dominican Republic
Dublin
Florence
Las Vegas
Las Vegas for Non-Gamblers
London
Maui
Nantucket & Martha's Vineyard
New Orleans
New York City
Paris
Portland
Puerto Rico
Puerto Vallarta, Manzanillo & Guadalajara
Rio de Janeiro
San Diego
San Francisco
Savannah
St. Martin, Sint Maarten, Anguila & St. Bart's
Turks & Caicos
Vancouver
Venice
Virgin Islands
Washington, D.C.
Whistler

...ES

...uises & Ports of Call

European Cruises & Ports of Call

...ES

... of the American West

...d Teton

Yosemite and Sequoia & Kings Canyon

Zion & Bryce Canyon

San Francisco

...onal Parks

...ew York City

San Francisco

Toronto

Walt Disney World® & Orlando

Washington, D.C.

...RN TO SHOP GUIDES

...ijing

London

New York

Paris

San Francisco

... IRREVERENT GUIDES

London

Los Angeles

Manhattan

Paris

Rome

San Francisco

Walt Disney World®

Washington, D.C.

...OMMER'S® BEST-LOVED DRIVING TOURS

...ustria

Britain

California

France

Germany

Ireland

Italy

New England

Northern Italy

Scotland

Spain

Tuscany & Umbria

THE UNOFFICIAL GUIDES®

Adventure Travel in Alaska

Beyond Disney

California with Kids

Central Italy

Chicago

Cruises

Disneyland®

England

Florida

Florida with Kids

Hawaii

Ireland

Las Vegas

London

Maui

Mexico's Best Beach Resorts

Mini Mickey

New Orleans

New York City

Paris

San Francisco

South Florida including Miami & the Keys

Walt Disney World®

Walt Disney World® for Grown-ups

Walt Disney World® with Kids

Washington, D.C.

SPECIAL-INTEREST TITLES

Athens Past & Present

Best Places to Raise Your Family

Cities Ranked & Rated

500 Places to Take Your Kids Before They Grow Up

Frommer's Best Day Trips from London

Frommer's Best RV & Tent Campgrounds in the U.S.A.

Frommer's Exploring America by RV

Frommer's NYC Free & Dirt Cheap

Frommer's Road Atlas Europe

Frommer's Road Atlas Ireland

Great Escapes From NYC Without Wheels

Retirement Places Rated

FROMMER'S® PHRASEFINDER DICTIONARY GUIDES

French

Italian

Spanish